Child Development

FIFTH EDITION

LAURA E. BERK

ILLINOIS STATE UNIVERSITY

ALLYN AND BACON

BOSTON   LONDON

TORONTO   SYDNEY

TOKYO   SINGAPORE

In loving memory of my parents, Sofie and Philip Eisenberg

Executive Editor: *Carolyn O. Merrill*
Senior Development Editor: *Sue Gleason*
Editorial Assistants: *Jill Jeffrey, Lara Zeises*
Vice-President/Director of Marketing: *Joyce Nilsen*
Cover Administrator: *Linda Knowles*
Composition and Prepress Buyer: *Linda Cox*
Manufacturing Buyer: *Megan Cochran*
Production Manager: *Elaine Ober*
Editorial-Production Service: *Thomas E. Dorsaneo/Publishing Consultants*
Text Design: *Seventeenth Street Studios*
Electronic Paging: *Omegatype Typography, Inc.*
Cover and chapter opening illustrations: *Lance Hidy, Newburyport, MA*

Copyright © 2000, 1997, 1994, 1991, 1989 by Allyn & Bacon
A Pearson Education Company
160 Gould Street
Needham Heights, Massachusetts, 02494
Internet: www.abacon.com

Library of Congress Cataloging-in-Publication Data
Berk, Laura E.
    Child development / Laura E. Berk. — 5th ed.
        p.   cm.
    Includes bibliographical references (p.   ) and index.
    ISBN 0-205-28634-8
    1. Child development.   I. Title.
HQ767.9.B464   2000
305.231—dc21   99-21227
                                                 CIP

Printed in the United States of America
10 9 8 7 6 5 4 3 2 1 VHP 03 02 01 00 99

ABOUT THE AUTHOR

Laura E. Berk is a distinguished professor of psychology at Illinois State University, where she teaches child development to both undergraduate and graduate students. She received her bachelor's degree in psychology from the University of California, Berkeley, and her master's and doctoral degrees in early childhood development and education from the University of Chicago. She has been a visiting scholar at Cornell University, UCLA, Stanford University, and the University of South Australia. Berk has published widely on the effects of school environments on children's development and, more recently, on the development of private speech. Her research has been funded by the U.S. Office of Education and the National Institute of Child Health and Human Development. It has appeared in many prominent journals, including *Child Development, Developmental Psychology, Merrill-Palmer Quarterly, Journal of Abnormal Child Psychology,* and *Development and Psychopathology.* Her empirical studies have attracted the attention of the general public, leading to contributions to *Psychology Today* and *Scientific American.* Berk has served as a research editor for *Young Children* and is a consulting editor for *Early Childhood Research Quarterly.* She is author of the chapter on the extracurriculum for the *Handbook of Research on Curriculum* (American Educational Research Association) and of the chapter on development for *The Many Faces of Psychological Research in the Twenty-First Century* (American Psychological Association). Her books include *Private Speech: From Social Interaction to Self-Regulation, Scaffolding Children's Learning: Vygotsky and Early Childhood Education,* and *Landscapes of Development: An Anthology of Readings.* In addition to *Child Development,* she is author of the best-selling texts *Infants, Children, and Adolescents* and *Development Through the Lifespan,* published by Allyn and Bacon.

Laura Berk with sons Peter and David

BRIEF CONTENTS

Variations

From Research to Practice

Cultural Influences

Social Issues

Part III
Cognitive and Language
Development 220

CHAPTER 6
COGNITIVE DEVELOPMENT: PIAGETIAN AND VYGOTSKIAN PERSPECTIVES 221

CHAPTER 7
COGNITIVE DEVELOPMENT: AN INFORMATION-PROCESSING PERSPECTIVE 271

CHAPTER 8
INTELLIGENCE 315

Part IV
Personality and Social
Development 396

CHAPTER 10
EMOTIONAL DEVELOPMENT 397

CONTENTS

Part V
Contexts for Development 556

M Y DECISION TO WRITE *Child Development* was inspired by a wealth of professional and personal experiences. First and foremost were the interests and needs of hundreds of students of child development with whom I have worked in nearly three decades of college teaching. I aimed for a text that is intellectually stimulating, that provides depth as well as breadth of coverage, that portrays the complexities of child development with clarity and excitement, and that is relevant and useful in building a bridge from theory and research to children's everyday lives. Instructor and student enthusiasm for the book not only has been among my greatest sources of pride and satisfaction, but also has inspired me to rethink and improve each edition.

The decade since *Child Development* first appeared has been a period of unprecedented expansion and change in theory and research. This fifth edition ushers in a new millenium with a wealth of new content that reflects four contemporary trends in the field:

- *Diverse pathways of change are highlighted.* Investigators have reached broad consensus that variations in biological makeup, everyday tasks, and the people who support children in mastery of those tasks lead to wide individual differences in children's skills. This edition pays more attention to variability in development and to recent theories—including ecological, sociocultural, and dynamic systems—that attempt to explain it. A new Variations feature grants special attention to this emphasis in contemporary research.

- *The interconnected roles of biology and environment are given greater emphasis.* Accumulating evidence on development of the brain, motor skills, cognitive competencies, temperament, and developmental problems underscores the way biological factors emerge in, are modified by, and share power with experience. The interconnection between biology and environment is revisited throughout the text narrative.

- *The link between theory, research, and applications—a theme of this book since its inception—is strengthened.* As researchers intensify their efforts to generate findings that can be applied to real-life situations, I have placed greater weight on social policy issues and sound theory- and research-based applications.

- *Inclusion of interdisciplinary research is expanded.* The move toward viewing the child's thoughts, feelings, and behavior as an integrated whole, affected by a wide array of influences in biology, social context, and culture, has motivated developmental researchers to strengthen their links with other fields of psychology and other disciplines. Topics and findings included in this edition increasingly reflect the contributions of educational psychology, social psychology, health psychology, clinical psychology, neuropsychology, biology, pediatrics, sociology, anthropology, and other fields.

TEXT PHILOSOPHY

The basic approach of this book has been shaped by my own professional and personal history as a teacher, researcher, and parent. It consists of seven philosophical ingredients that I regard as essential for students to emerge from a course with a thorough understanding of child development. Each theme is woven into every chapter:

- **1. AN UNDERSTANDING OF THE DIVERSE ARRAY OF THEORIES IN THE FIELD AND THE STRENGTHS AND SHORTCOMINGS OF EACH.** The first chapter begins by emphasizing that only knowledge of multiple theories can do justice to the richness of child development. In each topical domain, I present a variety of theoretical perspectives, indicate how each highlights previously overlooked contributions to development, and discuss research that has been used to evaluate them. If one or two theories have emerged as especially prominent in a particular area, I indicate why, in terms of the theory's broad explanatory power. Consideration of contrasting theories also serves as the context for an evenhanded analysis of many controversial issues throughout the text.

■ **2. AN APPRECIATION OF BASIC RESEARCH STRATEGIES TO INVESTIGATE CHILD DEVELOPMENT.** To evaluate theories, students need a firm grounding in basic research design and methodology. I devote an entire chapter to a description and critique of research strategies. Throughout the book, numerous studies are discussed in sufficient detail for students to use what they have learned to critically assess the findings, conclusions, and implications of research.

■ **3. KNOWLEDGE OF BOTH THE SEQUENCE OF CHILD DEVELOPMENT AND THE PROCESSES THAT UNDERLIE IT.** Students are provided with a description of the organized sequence of development, along with a discussion of processes of change. An understanding of process—how complex combinations of biological and environmental events produce development—has been the focus of most recent research. Accordingly, the text reflects this emphasis. But new information about the timetable of change has also emerged. In many ways, children have proven to be far more competent than they were believed to be in the past. Current evidence on the timing and sequence of development, along with its implications for process, is presented throughout the book.

■ **4. AN APPRECIATION OF THE IMPACT OF CONTEXT AND CULTURE ON CHILD DEVELOPMENT.** A wealth of research indicates that children live in rich physical and social contexts that affect all aspects of development. In each chapter, the student travels to distant parts of the world as I review a growing body of cross-cultural evidence. The text narrative also discusses many findings on socioeconomically and ethnically diverse children within the United States. Besides highlighting the role of immediate settings, such as family, neighborhood, and school, I make a concerted effort to underscore the impact of larger social structures—societal values, laws, and government programs—on children's well-being.

■ **5. AN UNDERSTANDING OF THE JOINT CONTRIBUTIONS OF BIOLOGY AND ENVIRONMENT TO DEVELOPMENT.** The field recognizes more powerfully than ever before the joint roles of hereditary/constitutional and environmental factors—that these contributions to development combine in complex ways and cannot be separated in a simple manner. Numerous examples of how biological dispositions can be maintained as well as transformed by social contexts are presented throughout the book.

■ **6. A SENSE OF THE INTERDEPENDENCY OF ALL ASPECTS OF DEVELOP- MENT—PHYSICAL, COGNITIVE, EMOTIONAL, AND SOCIAL.** Every chapter takes an integrated approach to understanding children. I show how physical, cognitive, emotional, and social development are interwoven. Within the text narrative and in a special series of Connections questions at the end of major sections, students are referred to other parts of the book to deepen their grasp of relationships between various aspects of change.

■ **7. AN APPRECIATION OF THE INTERRELATEDNESS OF THEORY, RESEARCH, AND APPLICATIONS.** Throughout this book, I emphasize that theories of child development and the research stimulated by them provide the foundation for sound, effective practices with children. The link between theory, research, and applications is reinforced by an organizational format in which theory and research are presented first, followed by implications for practice. In addition, a current focus in the field—harnessing child development knowledge to shape social policies that support children's needs—is reflected in every chapter. The text addresses the current condition of children in the United States and around the world and shows how theory and research have sparked successful interventions.

TEXT ORGANIZATION

I have organized this text topically, in a manner best suited to a comprehensive discussion of theory, research, and applications and an uninterrupted view of development within each domain. The book retains the same basic structure that received praise from users in its previous editions. It is divided into 5 parts and 15 chapters.

■ **PART I. THEORY AND RESEARCH IN CHILD DEVELOPMENT.** This section provides an overview of the history of the field, twentieth-century theories, and research strategies. **Chapter 1** stresses the importance of theories as organizing frameworks for understanding child development and traces changes in views of childhood from medieval to modern times. The study of child development is depicted as an interdisciplinary endeavor that aims to both understand children and improve their life conditions. **Chapter 2** is devoted to strategies for conducting scientifically sound research. Commonly used research methods and both general and developmental research designs are explained and critiqued. The chapter concludes with a consideration of ethics in research on children.

■ **PART II. FOUNDATIONS OF DEVELOPMENT.** A trio of chapters introduces students to the foundations of development. **Chapter 3** combines a discussion of genetic mechanisms and prenatal and perinatal environmental influences into a single, integrated discussion of these earliest determinants of development. A concluding section takes up the various ways in which researchers conceive of the relationship between heredity and environment, as a prelude to revisiting the nature–nurture controversy in later chapters. **Chapter 4** is devoted to an overview of the rapidly expanding literature on infant capacities. Research on newborn reflexes, states, and learning is reviewed, followed by a consideration of early motor and perceptual development. The chapter closes with the question of whether infancy is a sensitive period in which certain experiences must occur to ensure healthy development. **Chapter 5** addresses physical growth, including development of the brain, and emphasizes the close connection between physical and psychological development. A variety of hereditary and environmental influences on physical growth are considered. A special section focuses on puberty and its diverse consequences for adolescent health and well-being.

■ **PART III. COGNITIVE AND LANGUAGE DEVELOPMENT.** Four chapters examine the diverse theories and wealth of research on cognitive and language development. **Chapter 6** is devoted to Piaget's cognitive-developmental theory and Vygotsky's sociocultural theory. Students receive a thorough grounding in Piagetian theory as a prerequisite to studying language, emotional, and social-cognitive development in later chapters. With its strong emphasis on the social context of cognition, Vygotsky's theory has risen to the forefront of the field and therefore shares the title of Chapter 6. The chapter also introduces the nativist, modular view of the mind. **Chapter 7** offers an introduction to information processing. General and developmental models are reviewed, along with research on each major facet of the information-processing system. The chapter also discusses recent applications of information processing to children's academic learning and concludes with an analysis of the strengths and weaknesses of the information-processing perspective. **Chapter 8,** on intelligence, provides an overview of the intelligence-testing movement and addresses a wide variety of controversial issues and research findings, including ethnic and socioeconomic differences in IQ, heritability of intelligence, cultural bias in the tests, and early intervention for economically disadvantaged children. The concluding section considers the development of creativity. **Chapter 9** provides a comprehensive introduction to language development, including behaviorist, nativist, and interactionist theories. The main body of the chapter is organized around the four components of language: phonology, semantics, grammar, and pragmatics. The chapter also answers such questions as, Can nonhuman primates acquire language? Is there a sensitive period for language learning? How does bilingualism affect children's development?

■ **PART IV. PERSONALITY AND SOCIAL DEVELOPMENT.** Coverage of personality and social development is divided into four chapters: **Chapter 10,** on emotional development, provides an overview of theory and research on children's expression and understanding of emotion, the origins of temperament and its implications for cognitive and social development, and infant–caregiver attachment. The influence of quality of caregiving, infant temperament, parents' internal working models, maternal employment and child care, and social and cultural contexts on the attachment bond are among the issues considered. **Chapter 11,** offering an overview of the development of social cognition, is divided into three sections: children's understanding of self, other people, and relationships between people. Among the topics included are young children's theory of mind; self-concept and self-esteem; achievement-related attributions; identity; perspective taking; friendship; and social problem solving. **Chapter 12** addresses moral development. The main body of the chapter is devoted to a review of sociobiological, psychoanalytic, social learning, and cognitive-developmental theories and related research. Child-rearing practices that foster conscience development; cross-cultural research on moral reasoning; the controversial issue of whether males and females differ in moral understanding; children's ability to distinguish the moral, social-conventional, and personal domains; and the development of self-control and aggression are among the features of this chapter. **Chapter 13** focuses on sex-related differences and gender roles. Biological and environmental influences on gender stereotyping and gender-role adoption, diverse theories and research on the development of gender identity, and sex-related differences in mental abilities and personality traits are discussed. The chapter also includes an applied section on developing non-gender-stereotyped children.

■ **PART V CONTEXTS FOR DEVELOPMENT.** A final pair of chapters examines four influential contexts for development—family, peers, media, and schooling. **Chapter 14** considers the family from an evolutionary and a social systems perspective. The bidirectional nature of parent–child interaction, the importance of links between the family and community for children's well-being, and styles of child rearing are highlighted. The central portion of this chapter discusses the impact of family lifestyles and transitions on children's development. It includes expanded treatment of family diversity—such as smaller families, one-child families, gay and lesbian families, never-married single-parent families, and adoptive families—and sections on divorce, remarriage, maternal employment, and child care. The chapter concludes with a discussion of child maltreatment. In **Chapter 15,** the social systems perspective is extended to extrafamilial contexts for development. In the section on peer relations, research on the development of peer sociability, peer acceptance, peer groups, and peers as socialization agents is discussed. The middle portion of the chapter addresses the impact of television and computers on cognitive and social development. A concluding section on schooling considers such topics as class and student body size, educational philosophies, school transitions, teacher–pupil interaction, grouping practices, mainstreaming and full inclusion, and cross-national research on academic achievement.

NEW COVERAGE IN THE FIFTH EDITION

In this edition I continue to represent a rapidly transforming contemporary literature with theory and research from over 1,700 new citations. To make room for new coverage, I have condensed and reorganized some topics and eliminated others that are no longer as crucial in view of new evidence. The following is a sampling of major content changes, organized by chapter (a more complete description of changes can be found in the Annotated Instructor's Manual that accompanies the text):

■ **Chapter 1:** Revised section on basic issues on which major theories take a stand; new From Research to Practice box on social change and the popular literature on parenting; new section on development as a dynamic system.

■ **Chapter 2:** New section on methods for studying culture; new Variations box on case studies of prodigies; new example of longitudinal-sequential research; all research strategies richly illustrated with real studies.

■ **Chapter 3:** New Social Issues box on the Human Genome Project; expanded attention to fetal sensory and behavioral capacities; new Variations box on fetal activity as a predictor of infant temperament; updated research on teratogens; new research on the role of paid employment leave in safeguarding the well-being of mothers and newborn babies.

■ **Chapter 4:** Expanded attention to dynamic systems theory of motor development and related research; new section on infant perception of balance and self-movement; new Variations box on development of infants with severe visual impairments.

■ **Chapter 5:** New section on gross motor development in childhood and adolescence; updated research on brain lateralization; expanded discussion of obesity, including cross-cultural research highlighting the role of Western high-fat diets; new Variations box on coming out among homosexual youths; new evidence on prevention of and intervention in adolescent parenthood.

■ **Chapter 6:** Updated evidence on representation in infancy, including categorization and analogical problem solving; new research on the development of drawing, including cultural variations; enhanced discussion of categorization in early childhood, including contributions of language, general knowledge, and adult teaching; new Variations box on parent–child interaction and cognitive development of deaf children; expanded discussion of Vygotsky and education, including the impact of culture on cooperative learning and a new section on the classroom as a community of learners.

■ **Chapter 7:** Revised section on developmental models of information processing, including Case's neo-Piagetian theory, connectionism, and Siegler's model of strategy choice; new From Research to Practice box on speech–gesture mismatches in children's problem solving and consequent educational implications; new section on cognitive inhibition; enhanced discussion of the development of autobiographical memory; expanded treatment of information processing and academic learning, including reading, mathematics, and scientific reasoning.

■ **Chapter 8:** Enhanced discussion of genetic and nonshared environmental influences on IQ; new section challenging the assumption that genetic racial differences determine ethnic differences in psychological traits; expanded attention to dynamic testing; new From Research to Practice box on authentic assessment; new evidence on academic achievement of immigrant ethnic minority adolescents; new evidence on early intervention and intellectual development.

■ **Chapter 9:** New evidence on the capacity of apes to acquire language; new Variations box on language development in children with Williams syndrome, with implications for nativist theory; updated findings on the role of language learning in brain lateralization; new evidence on how child-directed speech and adult–child conversations promote language development; recent research on strategies for acquiring vocabulary and grammar; revised Social Issues box on bilingual education.

■ **Chapter 10:** Updated and expanded sections on the development of emotional self-regulation and empathy; new Cultural Influences box on father–infant relationships among the Aka hunter–gatherers of Central Africa; updated discussion of the impact of infant–mother attachment security on later development; revised section on maternal employment and infant child care, including findings of the NICHD Study of Early Child Care.

■ **Chapter 11:** Expanded attention to development of the I-self and me-self; new section on the role of language in early self-development, addressing the categorical and remembered selves; updated discussion of the young child's theory of mind; new Variations box on "mindblindness" and infantile autism; expanded attention to development of self-concept and self-esteem, including the role of social comparison; revised and updated section on development of achievement-related attributions; expanded discussion of person perception, with a new section on children's understanding of ethnicity and social class.

PREFACE FOR INSTRUCTORS

- **Chapter 12:** New evidence on children's active, positive contribution to the process of moral internalization; enhanced discussion of the importance of a warm, cooperative parent–child relationship for conscience development; revised section on culture and moral reasoning, addressing both universals and variations; expanded discussion of children's capacity to distinguish moral imperatives, social conventions, and matters of personal choice; revised consideration of the development of aggression, including the distinction between overt and relational aggression; new Variations box on two routes to adolescent delinquency.

- **Chapter 13:** Current findings on children with congenital adrenal hyperplasia; new evidence on sex-related differences in parental autonomy-granting in middle childhood; updated evidence on boys' and girls' styles of social influence; revised and expanded section on development of gender identity in adolescence; new Variations box on sex-related differences in spatial skills and their implications for mathematical reasoning; new section on sex-related differences in adolescent depression; updated findings on sex-related differences in overt and relational aggression.

- **Chapter 14:** New From Research to Practice box on the transition to parenthood; new findings on ethnic variations in child-rearing practices; enhanced discussion of identity development in transracially and transculturally adopted children; new section on children's development in never-married, single-parent families; new Variations box on grandparents rearing grandchildren: the skipped-generation family.

- **Chapter 15:** New findings on characteristics of rejected-aggressive and rejected-withdrawn children; new Variations box on peer victimization; updated research on the impact of television and computers on children's social and cognitive development, with enhanced attention to videogames and the Internet; expanded section on Vygotsky-inspired directions in education; new evidence on factors affecting adjustment to kindergarten; updated research on educational self-fulfilling prophecies; new Social Issues box on school desegregation and life chances of African-American adolescents; revised section on elementary school grouping practices, including multigrade classrooms; discussion of both mainstreaming and full inclusion; new section on parent–school partnerships.

INSTRUCTOR'S SUPPLEMENTS

A variety of teaching tools are available to assist instructors in organizing lectures, planning demonstrations and examinations, and ensuring student comprehension.

■ **ANNOTATED INSTRUCTOR'S MANUAL (AIM)** This convenient teaching tool provides Learning Objectives, Test Bank Item numbers, references to Lecture Extensions and Learning Activities, answers to "Ask Yourself . . ." and "Connections" questions, and other instructors' annotations keyed to reduced versions of actual text pages. It also offers a chapter summary, list of new material, and Chapter-at-a-Glance grid for each chapter.

■ **INSTRUCTOR'S RESOURCE MANUAL (IRM)** Prepared by Gabrielle Principe of North Carolina State University, Betty Nylund Barr, and myself, this thoroughly revised IRM contains additional material to enrich your class presentations. For each chapter, the IRM provides a Brief Chapter Summary, detailed Lecture Outline, Lecture Extensions, Learning Activities, Suggested Readings, and Media Materials.

■ **TEST BANK** Prepared by Gabrielle Principe of North Carolina State University and Naomi Tyler of Vanderbilt University, the test bank contains over 2,000 multiple-choice questions, each of which is cross-referenced to a Learning Objective, page-referenced to chapter content, and classified by type (factual, applied, or conceptual); essay questions; and premade tests.

■ **COMPUTERIZED TEST BANK** This computerized version of the test bank is available in Windows and Macintosh formats using Test Manager, the best-selling test-generation software.

■ **TRANSPARENCIES** Over 200 full-color transparencies taken from the text and other sources are referenced in the margins of the Annotated Instructor's Manual for the most appropriate use in your classroom presentations.

■ **SEASONS OF LIFE VIDEO SERIES** Illustrating the text's interdisciplinary focus, this five-video series explores a multitude of biological, psychological, and social influences on development. Nearly 75 psychologists, biologists, sociologists, and anthropologists present theory, methods, and research. Your publisher's representative can provide you with details on class enrollment restrictions.

■ **FILMS FOR THE HUMANITIES AND SCIENCES: CHILD DEVELOPMENT VIDEOTAPE** Complementing the text's linkage of theory and research to application, this revised videotape features high-interest segments on topics such as genetic counseling, fetal alcohol syndrome, the child's theory of mind, and teen depression.

■ **"CHILD DEVELOPMENT IN ACTION" OBSERVATION PROGRAM** In conjunction with the Illinois State University Television Production Studio, I have revised and expanded this real-life videotape, containing hundreds of observation segments that illustrate the many theories, concepts, and milestones of child development. An Observation Guide helps students use the video in conjunction with the textbook, deepening their understanding of the material and applying what they have learned to everyday life. The videotape and Observation Guide are free to instructors who adopt the text and are available to students at a discount when packaged with the text.

■ **WEBSITE** http://www.abacon.com/berk Designed for students and faculty of Child Development and Human Development or Lifespan classes, this comprehensive website encourages online and interactive learning and also offers current links and information about development. It includes an Online Study Guide, a Teaching Aids section, and a variety of additional features.

ACKNOWLEDGMENTS

The dedicated contributions of many individuals helped make this book a reality and contributed to refinements and improvements in each edition. An impressive cast of reviewers provided many helpful suggestions, constructive criticisms, and encouragement and enthusiasm for the organization and content of the book. I am grateful to each one of them.

■ **REVIEWERS OF THE FIRST THROUGH FOURTH EDITIONS**

Daniel Ashmead
Vanderbilt University

Dana W. Birnbaum
University of Main
at Orono

Kathryn N. Black
Purdue University

Cathryn L. Booth
University of Washington

J. Paul Boudreau
University of Prince
Edward Island

Sam Boyd
University of Central
Arkansas

Celia A. Brownell
University of Pittsburgh

Toni A. Campbell
San Jose State University

Beth Casey
Boston College

John Condry
Cornell University

Rhoda Cummings
University of Nevada, Reno

James L. Dannemiller
University of Wisconsin,
Madison

Darlene DeSantis
West Chester University

Rebecca Eder
Bryn Mawr College

Claire Etaugh
Bradley University

Bill Fabricius
Arizona State University

Beverly Fagot
University of Oregon

John C. Gibbs
Ohio State University

Peter Gordon
University of Pittsburgh

Katherine Green
Millersville University

Kenneth Hill
Saint Mary's University,
Halifax

Alice S. Honig
Syracuse University

Elizabeth J. Hrncir
University of Virginia

Mareile Koenig
George Washington
University Hospital

Claire Kopp
University of California,
Los Angeles

Beth Kurtz-Costes
University of North
Carolina, Chapel Hill

Gary W. Ladd
University of
Illinois at Urbana–
Champaign

Daniel Lapsley
Ball State University

Frank Laycock
Oberlin College

Mary D. Leinbach
University of Oregon

Robert S. Marvin
University of Virginia

Tom McBride
Princeton University

Carolyn J. Mebert
University of New
Hampshire

Gary B. Melton
University of Nebraska,
Lincoln

Mary Evelyn Moore
Illinois State University

Lois Muir
University of Wisconsin,
La Crosse

Bonnie K. Nastasi
State University of New
York at Albany

Larry Nucci
University of Illinois
at Chicago

Carol Pandey
Pierce College, Los Angeles

Thomas S. Parish
Kansas State University

B. Kay Pasley
Colorado State University

Ellen F. Potter
University of South
Carolina at Columbia

Kimberly K. Powlishta
Northern Illinois
University

Kathleen Preston
Humboldt State University

Bud Protinsky
Virginia Polytechnic
Institute and State
University

Daniel Reschly
Iowa State University

Rosemary Rosser
University of Arizona

Jane Rysberg
California State University,
Chico

Phil Schoggen
Cornell University

Maria E. Sera
University of Iowa

Beth Shapiro
Emory University

Robert Siegler
Carnegie Mellon University

Gregory J. Smith
Dickinson College

Robert J. Sternberg
Yale University

Harold Stevenson
University of Michigan

Ross A. Thompson
University of Nebraska,
Lincoln

Barbara A. Tinsley
University of Illinois
at Urbana-Champaign

Kim F. Townley
University of Kentucky

Janet Valadez
Pan American University

Amye R. Warren
University of Tennessee
at Chattanooga

■ REVIEWERS OF THE FIFTH EDITION

Margarita Azmitia
University of California,
Santa Cruz

James L. Dannemiller
University of Wisconsin,
Madison

Zoe Ann Davidson
Alabama A&M University

James Garbarino
Cornell University

John C. Gibbs
Ohio State University

Janis Jacobs
Pennsylvana State
University

Claire Kopp
Claremont Graduate School

Elise Lehman
George Mason University

John P. Murray
Kansas State University

Larry Nucci
University of Illinois
at Chicago

Peter Ornstein
University of North
Carolina

Randall Osbourne
Indiana University East

Alan Russell
Flinders University

Robert J. Sternberg
Yale University

Ross A. Thompson
University of Nebraska,
Lincoln

In addition, I thank the following individuals for responding to a survey that provided
vital feedback for the new edition.

Lynne Baker-Ward
North Carolina State
University

Ann C. Barbour
University of Texas
at San Antonio

James Barnard
University of South Florida

John D. Bonvillian
University of Virginia

Lyn Boultor
Catawba College

Maria A. Crisafi
Barnard College

Julie Earles
Furman University

Nancy Eldred
San Jose University

Nancy Eldred
San Jose University

Janis Jacobs
Pennsylvania State
University

Sandra Machida
California State
University, Chico

Mary Ann McLaughlin
Clarion University

Gary Montgomery
University of Texas–
Pan American

Tina Moreau
Queens College

Ruth Reese
Arizona State University

Jane Rysberg
California State University,
Chico

K. Saudino
Boston University

John M. Spores
Purdue University

Roger Van Horn
Central Michigan
University

Joan H. Witham
Southwest Texas State
University

I have been fortunate to work with an outstanding editorial team at Allyn and Bacon. Sean Wakely was my editor for nearly four years, guiding *Child Development* through most of this revision. Although Sean has moved on to a new position, his creative energy and keen knowledge of instructors' and students' needs continue to inspire my work, and I wish him much success in the future. Carolyn Merrill, Executive Editor, took over midstream with competence and ease. Her outstanding management skills, enthusiasm, originality, and vision have contributed greatly to this project, and I look forward to working with her in the years to come.

I would like to express a heartfelt thank you to Joyce Nilsen, Director of Marketing, for the wonderful work she has done in marketing my texts. Joyce has made sure that accurate and clear information about the texts and their ancillaries reached Allyn and Bacon's sales force and that the needs of prospective and current adopters were met. It has been a privilege and pleasure to have her in command of marketing activities for *Child Development.*

Sue Gleason, Senior Development Editor, worked closely with me as I revised each chapter, making sure that every line and paragraph would be clear, every thought and concept precisely expressed and well developed. Sue's astute advice and prompt and patient responses to my concerns and queries have enhanced every aspect of this edition. I thank her, also, for overseeing the preparation of an excellent set of text supplements.

Elaine Ober, Production Manager, assembled an outstanding production team. Tom Dorsaneo coordinated the complex production tasks that resulted in a beautiful fifth edition. His competence, courtesy, diplomatic problem solving, and interest in the subject matter as an involved grandfather of an energetic preschooler have made working with him a great delight. Betty Barr's meticulous, caring copy editing ensured accuracy and precision on every page. I thank Annie Reid for her fine work in planning the photo program and Sarah Evertson for obtaining the exceptional photos that so aptly illustrate the text narrative. Lance Hidy has captured the radiance of childhood in a set of beautiful cover and chapter-opening images. Jill Jeffrey and Lara Zeises, Editorial Assistants, graciously arranged for manuscript reviews and attended to a wide variety of pressing details.

A final word of gratitude goes to my family, whose love, patience, and understanding have enabled me to be wife, mother, teacher, researcher, and text author at the same time. My sons, David and Peter, grew up with my child development texts, passing from childhood to adolescence and then to young adulthood as successive editions were written. David has a special connection with the books' subject matter as an elementary school teacher; Peter embarked on the study of law as I prepared this edition. Both continue to enrich my understanding through reflections on events and progress in their own lives. My husband, Ken, willingly made room for this time-consuming endeavor in our life together and communicated his belief in its importance in a great many unspoken, caring ways.

Laura E. Berk

y 29 years of teaching child development have brought me in contact with thousands of students like you—students with diverse college majors, future goals, interests, and needs. Some are affiliated with my own department, psychology, but many come from other child-related fields—education, sociology, anthropology, family studies, and biology, to name just a few. Each semester, my students' aspirations have proven to be as varied as their fields of study. Many look toward careers in applied work with children—teaching, caregiving, nursing, counseling, social work, school psychology, and program administration. Some plan to teach child development, and a few want to do research. Most hope someday to have children, whereas others are already parents who come with a desire to better understand and rear their own youngsters. And almost all arrive with a deep curiosity about how they themselves developed from tiny infants into the complex human beings they are today.

My goal in preparing this fifth edition of *Child Development* is to provide a textbook that meets the instructional goals of your course as well as your own personal needs. I aimed for a text that is intellectually stimulating, that provides depth as well as breadth of coverage, and that portrays the complexities of child development in a way that will capture your interest while helping you learn.

To achieve these objectives, I have grounded this book in a carefully selected body of classic and current theory and research. In addition, the text highlights the joint contribution of biology and environment to development, explains how the research process helps solve real-world problems, highlights commonalities and differences between ethnic groups and cultures, and pays special attention to policy issues that are crucial for safeguarding children's well-being in today's world. I have also used a clear, engaging writing style and provided a pedagogical program that will assist you in mastering information, integrating the various aspects of development, critically examining controversial issues, and applying what you have learned.

PEDAGOGICAL FEATURES

Maintaining a highly accessible writing style—one that is lucid and engaging without being simplistic—continues to be one of this text's goals. I will frequently converse with you and encourage you to relate what you read to your own life. In doing so, I hope to make the study of child development involving and pleasurable.

■ **CHAPTER INTRODUCTIONS AND END-OF-CHAPTER SUMMARIES.** To provide a helpful preview of what you are about to read, I include an outline and overview of chapter content in each chapter introduction. Especially comprehensive end-of-chapter summaries, organized according to the major divisions of each chapter and highlighting important terms, will remind you of key points in the text discussion. Review questions are included in the summaries to encourage active study.

■ **BRIEF REVIEWS.** Interim summaries of text content appear at the end of most major sections in each chapter. They enhance retention by encouraging you to reflect on information you have just read before moving on to a new section.

■ **ASK YOURSELF . . . .** Active engagement with the subject matter is also supported by critical-thinking questions, **new to this edition,** which can be found in the margins at the end of major sections. The focus of these questions is divided between theory and applications. Many describe problematic situations faced by parents, teachers, and children and ask you to resolve them in light of what you have learned. In this way, the questions inspire deeper mastery of child development and new insights.

■ **CONNECTIONS.** Also **new to this edition,** this feature appears within "Ask Yourself . . . ." By stretching your ability to integrate what you have learned across chapters, these questions will help you see the "whole child" and think more deeply about development. This integrative effort is not limited to the Connections questions; it also occurs within the text narrative.

■ **BOXES.** Four types of boxes accentuate the philosophical themes of this book:

▨ *Variations* boxes, a feature on developmental variations from the norm, **new to this edition,** emphasize one of this text's key themes—diverse pathways of change. These boxes illustrate how studying children with problems or exceptional abilities highlights important contributions to the development of all children. Topics covered include resilient children, child prodigies, cognitive development in

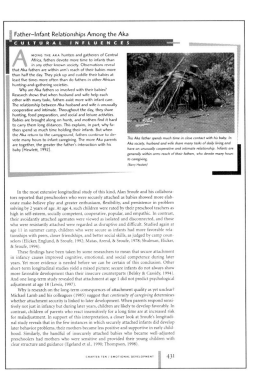

Father–Infant Relationships Among the Aka

CULTURAL INFLUENCES

A MONG THE AKA hunters and gatherers of Central Africa, fathers devote more time to infants than in any other known society. Observations reveal that Aka fathers are within arm's reach of their babies more than half the day. They pick up and cuddle their babies at least five times more often than do fathers in other African hunting-and-gathering societies.

Why are Aka fathers so involved with their babies? Research shows that when husband and wife help each other with many tasks, fathers assist more with infant care. The relationship between Aka husband and wife is unusually cooperative and intimate. Throughout the day, they share hunting, food preparation, and social and leisure activities. Babies are brought along on hunts, and mothers find it hard to carry them long distances. This explains, in part, why fathers spend so much time holding their infants. But when the Aka return to the campground, fathers continue to devote many hours to infant caregiving. The more Aka parents are together, the greater the father's interaction with his baby (Hewlett, 1992).

This Aka father spends much time in close contact with his baby. In Aka society, husband and wife share many tasks of daily living and have an unusually cooperative and intimate relationship. Infants are generally within arm's reach of their fathers, who devote many hours to caregiving.
(Barry Hewlett)

In the most extensive longitudinal study of this kind, Alan Sroufe and his collaborators reported that preschoolers who were securely attached as babies showed more elaborate make-believe play and greater enthusiasm, flexibility, and persistence in problem solving by 2 years of age. At age 4, such children were rated by their preschool teachers as high in self-esteem, socially competent, cooperative, popular, and empathic. In contrast, their avoidantly attached agemates were viewed as isolated and disconnected, and those who were resistantly attached were regarded as disruptive and difficult. Studied again at age 11 in summer camp, children who were secure as infants had more favorable relationships with peers, closer friendships, and better social skills, as judged by camp counselors (Elicker, Englund, & Sroufe, 1992; Matas, Arend, & Sroufe, 1978; Shulman, Elicker, & Sroufe, 1994).

These findings have been taken by some researchers to mean that secure attachment in infancy causes improved cognitive, emotional, and social competence during later years. Yet more evidence is needed before we can be certain of this conclusion. Other short-term longitudinal studies yield a mixed picture; secure infants do not always show more favorable development than their insecure counterparts (Belsky & Cassidy, 1994). And one long-term study revealed that attachment at age 1 did not predict psychological adjustment at age 18 (Lewis, 1997).

Why is research on the long-term consequences of attachment quality as yet unclear? Michael Lamb and his colleagues (1985) suggest that *continuity of caregiving* determines whether attachment security is linked to later development. When parents respond sensitively not just in infancy but during later years, children are likely to develop favorably. In contrast, children of parents who react insensitively for a long time are at increased risk for maladjustment. In support of this interpretation, a closer look at Sroufe's longitudinal study reveals that in the few instances in which securely attached infants did develop later behavior problems, their mothers became less positive and supportive in early childhood. Similarly, the handful of insecurely attached babies who became well-adjusted preschoolers had mothers who were sensitive and provided their young children with clear structure and guidance (Egeland et al., 1990; Thompson, 1998).

CHAPTER TEN / EMOTIONAL DEVELOPMENT   431

children with hearing and visual impairments, language development in children with Williams syndrome, "mindblindness" and infantile autism, and peer victimization.

- *Cultural Influences* boxes highlight the impact of context and culture on all aspects of development. They include such topics as Father–Infant Relationships among the Aka, a hunter–gatherer people of Central Africa, addressing the importance of a warm marital bond for infant–father attachment; and the impact of ethnic and political violence on children, emphasizing the importance of parental and community supports in safeguarding children's development.

- *Social Issues* boxes discuss the condition of children in the United States and around the world and stress the need for sensitive social policies to ensure their well-being. They include the U.N. Convention on the Rights of the Child, the first legally binding human rights treaty to recognize the civil, political, economic, social, and cultural rights of children; and regulating children's television, addressing societal obstacles to controlling harmful TV and providing strategies parents can use to protect their children.

Bilingual Education

SOCIAL ISSUES

V INCENTE, A 7-YEAR-OLD boy who recently immigrated from Mexico to the United States, attends a bilingual education classroom in a large American city. His teacher, Serena, is fluent in both Spanish and English. At the beginning of the year, Serena instructed Vincente and his classmates in their native tongue. As the children mixed with English-speaking youngsters at school and in the community, they quickly picked up English phrases, such as "My name is . . . ," "I wanna," and "Show me."

Serena reinforced her pupils' first efforts to speak English, helping them feel confident about communicating in a second language. Gradually, she introduced more English into classroom learning experiences. At the same time, she continued to strengthen the children's native language and culture.

Vincente is enrolled in one of many bilingual education programs serving the growing number of American children with limited proficiency in English. Yet the question of how Vincente and his classmates should be taught continues to be hotly debated.

On one side of the controversy are those who believe that Vincente should be instructed only in English. According to this view, time spent communicating in the child's native tongue subtracts from English language achievement, which is vital for forging national unity and easing communication in education, business, and everyday life.

On the other side are educators like Serena, who are committed to truly bilingual education—developing Vincente's native language while fostering his mastery of English. Supporters of this view believe that providing instruction in the native tongue lets minority children know that their heritage is respected (McGroarty, 1992). In addition, by avoiding abrupt submersion in an English-speaking environment, bilingual education prevents *semilingualism,* or inadequate proficiency in both languages. When minority children experience a gradual decline of the first language as a result of being taught the second, they end up limited in both languages for a period of time, a circumstance that leads to serious academic difficulties. Semilingualism is one factor believed to contribute to the high rates of school failure and dropout among low-income Hispanic youngsters, who make up nearly 50 percent of the American language minority population.

At present, public opinion sides with the first of these two viewpoints. Many states have passed laws declaring

These Pueblo children attend a bilingual education program in which they receive instruction in their native language and in English. In classrooms where both the first and the second language are integrated into the curriculum, ethnic minority children are more involved in learning, participate more actively in class discussions, and acquire the second language more easily.
(Robert E. Daemmrich/Tony Stone Images)

English to be their official language, creating conditions in which schools have no obligation to teach minority pupils in languages other than English. In 1998, California voters passed a law that eliminated bilingual education in favor of a one-year, English-only immersion course for non-English-speaking pupils, a move expected to spread to other states. Yet research underscores the value of instruction in the child's native tongue. In classrooms where both languages are integrated into the curriculum, minority children are more involved in learning, participate more actively in class discussions, and acquire the second language more easily. In contrast, when teachers speak only a language their pupils can barely understand, children display frustration, boredom, withdrawal, and academic failure (Crawford, 1995, 1997).

English-only supporters often point to Canada, which recognizes the linguistic rights of its French-speaking minority but where friction between English- and French-speaking groups is intense. Nevertheless, both English and French are official languages, and most Canadian children become fluent in both—ideal conditions for building greater ethnic harmony (Piatt, 1993).

CHAPTER NINE / LANGUAGE DEVELOPMENT   393

legally binding human rights treaty to recognize the civil, political, economic, social, and cultural rights of children; and regulating children's television, addressing societal obstacles to controlling harmful TV and providing strategies parents can use to protect their children.

Long-Term Impact of Early Hearing Loss on Development: The Case of Otitis Media

FROM RESEARCH TO PRACTICE

D URING HIS FIRST year in day care, 18-month-old Alex caught five colds, had the flu on two occasions, and experienced repeated *otitis media* (middle ear infection). Alex is not unusual. By age 3, over 70 percent of children have had respiratory illnesses resulting in at least one bout of otitis media; 33 percent have had three or more bouts. Some episodes are painful, but as many as half are accompanied by few or no symptom. Parents learn of them only on routine visits to the doctor. Although antibiotics eliminate the bacteria responsible for otitis media, they do not reduce fluid buildup in the middle ear, which causes mild to moderate hearing loss that can last for weeks or months (Feagans & Proctor, 1994).

The incidence of otitis media is greatest between 6 months and 3 years, when children are first acquiring language. Frequent infection predict delayed language progress and social isolation in early childhood and poorer academic performance after school entry (Feagans & Proctor, 1994; Teele et al., 1990; Vernon-Feagans, Manlove, & Volling, 1996).

How might otitis media disrupt language and academic progress? Difficulties in hearing speech sounds, particularly in noisy settings, may be responsible. Early and recurrent episodes of infection are consistently associated with impaired speech perception and production (Feagans Proctor, 1994; Gravel & Wallace, 1992). Furthermore, children with many bouts are less attentive to the speech of others and less persistent at tasks (Feagans et al., 1987; Roberts, Burchinal, & Campbell, 1994). Their distractibility may be due to repeated instances in which they could not make out what people around them were saying. When children have trouble paying attention, they may reduce the quality of others' interactions with them. In one study, mothers of preschoolers with frequent illnesses were less effective in teaching their child a task (Chase et al., 1995).

Current evidence argues strongly in favor of early prevention of otitis media, especially since the illness is so widespread. Crowded living conditions and exposure to cigarette smoke and other pollutants are linked to the disease—factors that probably account for its high incidence among low-income children. In addition, enrollment of millions of infants and young children in child care creates opportunities for close contact, greatly increasing the number of otitis media episodes among these children (Froom & Culpepper, 1991).

Negative developmental outcomes of early otitis media can be prevented in the following ways:

- *Preventive doses of xylitol,* a sweetener derived from birch bark. A recent Finnish study revealed that children in child-care centers given a daily dose of xylitol in gum or syrup form show a 30- to 40-percent drop in otitis media

High-quality child-care centers reduce or eliminate language delays, social isolation, and later academic difficulties associated with frequent bouts of otitis media. These toddlers profit from verbally stimulating caregivers and a small group size, which ensures a relatively quiet environment where spoken language can be heard easily.
(Stuart Cohen/The Image Works)

compared with controls receiving gum or syrup without the sweetener. Xylitol appears to have natural, bacteria-fighting ingredients (Uhari, Kontiokari, & Niemelä, 1998). However, dosage must be carefully monitored, since too much xylitol can cause abdominal pain and diarrhea.

- *Frequent screening of infants and preschoolers for the disease,* followed by prompt medical intervention. (Plastic tubes that drain the middle ear are often used to treat chronic otitis media, although their effectiveness remains controversial.)

- *Regular cleaning and arrangement of child-care setting to control infection.* Because infants and young children often put toys in their mouths, these objects should be rinsed frequently with a disinfectant solution. Spacious, well-ventilated rooms and small group sizes also limit the spread of disease.

- *Verbally stimulating adult–child interaction.* Developmental problems associated with otitis media can be reduced or eliminated in high-quality child-care centers. When caregivers are verbally stimulating and keep noise to a minimum, children have more opportunities to hear spoken language (Feagans, Kipp, & Blood, 1994; Roberts, Burchinal, & Campbell, 1994).

spectrum (Brown, 1990; Burr, Morrone, & Fiorentini, 1996). By 4 to 5 months, they regard a particular color as the same, even under very different lighting conditions (Dannemiller, 1989). Once color sensitivity is well established, habituation–dishabituation research reveals that babies organize different hues into categories—red, blue, yellow, and green—just as adults do. Four-month-olds, for example, perceive two blues as more alike

155

CHAPTER FOUR / INFANCY: EARLY LEARNING, MOTOR SKILLS, AND PERCEPTUAL CAPACITIES

- *From Research to Practice* boxes integrate theory, research, and applications. They include speech–gesture mismatches in problem solving and implications for children's readiness to learn, children's understanding of death, and maternal depression and child development.

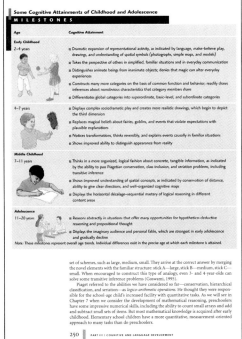

Some Cognitive Attainments of Childhood and Adolescence

MILESTONES

Age	Cognitive Attainment
Early Childhood 2–4 years	▪ Dramatic expansion of representational activity, as indicated by language, make-believe play, drawings, and understanding of spatial symbols (photographs, simple maps, and models) ▪ Takes the perspective of others in simplified, familiar situations and in everyday communication ▪ Distinguishes animate beings from inanimate objects; denies that magic can alter everyday experiences ▪ Constructs many more categories on the basis of common function and behavior; readily draws inferences about nonobvious characteristics that category members share ▪ Differentiates global categories into superordinate, basic-level, and subordinate categories
4–7 years	▪ Displays complex sociodramatic play and creates more realistic drawings, which begin to depict the third dimension ▪ Replaces magical beliefs about fairies, goblins, and events that violate expectations with plausible explanations ▪ Notices transformation, thinks reversibly, and explains events causally in familiar situations ▪ Shows improved ability to distinguish appearance from reality
Middle Childhood 7–11 years	▪ Thinks in a more organized, logical fashion about concrete, tangible information, as indicated by the ability to pass Piagetian conservation, class inclusion, and seriation problems, including transitive inference ▪ Shows improved understanding of spatial concepts, as indicated by conservation of distance, ability to give clear directions, and well-organized cognitive maps ▪ Displays the horizontal décalage—sequential mastery of logical reasoning in different content areas
Adolescence 11–20 years	▪ Reasons abstractly in situations that offer many opportunities for hypothetico-deductive reasoning and propositional thought ▪ Displays the imaginary audience and personal fable, which are strongest in early adolescence and gradually decline

Note: These milestones represent overall age trends. Individual differences exist in the precise age at which each milestone is attained.

set of schemes, such as large, medium, small. They arrive at the correct answer by merging the novel elements with the familiar structure: stick A—large, stick B—medium, stick C—small. When encouraged to construct this type of analogy, even 3- and 4-year-olds can solve some transitive inference problems (Goswami, 1995).

Piaget referred to the abilities we have considered so far—conservation, hierarchical classification, and seriation—as *logico-arithmetic operations.* He thought they were responsible for the school-age child's increased facility with quantitative tasks. As we will see in Chapter 7 when we consider the development of mathematical reasoning, preschoolers have some impressive numerical skills, including the ability to count small arrays and add and subtract small sets of items. But most mathematical knowledge is acquired after early childhood. Elementary school children have a more quantitative, measurement-oriented approach to many tasks than do preschoolers.

250   PART III / COGNITIVE AND LANGUAGE DEVELOPMENT

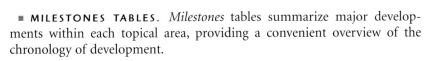

- **MILESTONES TABLES.** *Milestones* tables summarize major developments within each topical area, providing a convenient overview of the chronology of development.

■ **ADDITIONAL TABLES, ILLUSTRATIONS, AND PHOTOGRAPHS.** Additional tables are liberally included to help readers grasp essential points in the text discussion, extend information on a topic, and consider applications. The many full-color illustrations throughout the book depict important theories, methods, and research findings. In this edition, the photo program has been carefully selected to portray the text discussion and to represent the diversity of children in the United States and around the world.

■ **MARGINAL GLOSSARY, END-OF-CHAPTER TERM LIST, AND END-OF-BOOK GLOSSARY.** Mastery of terms that make up the central vocabulary of the field is promoted through a marginal glossary, an end-of-chapter term list, and an end-of-book glossary. Important terms and concepts also appear in boldface type in the text narrative and in the end-of-chapter summaries.

STUDY AIDS

Beyond the study aids found in the textbook, Allyn and Bacon offers a number of supplements for students. The website is open to all visitors to the Internet.

■ **STUDY GUIDE.** Prepared by Leslie M. Bach, Jessica L. Friedberg, and myself, this helpful guide offers Chapter Summaries, Learning Objectives, Study Questions organized according to major headings in the text, "Ask Yourself . . . " and "Connections" questions that also appear in the text margin, crossword puzzles for mastering important terms, and multiple-choice self-tests.

■ **PRACTICE TESTS.** Twenty multiple-choice items per chapter plus an answer key with justifications are drawn from the test bank to assist you in preparing for course exams.

I hope that learning about child development will be as rewarding for you as I have found it over the years. I would like to know what you think about both the field of child development and this book. I welcome your comments; please feel free to send them to me at Department of Psychology, Box 4620, Illinois State University, Normal, IL 61790, or care of the publisher, who will forward them to me.

Laura E. Berk

Child Development

History, Theory, and Applied Directions

NOT LONG AGO, I left my Midwestern home to live for a year near the small city in northern California where I spent my childhood. One morning, I visited the neighborhood where I grew up—a place I had not been to since I was 12 years old. I stood at the entrance to my old schoolyard. Buildings and grounds that had looked large to me as a child now seemed strangely small from my grown-up vantage point. I peered through the window of my first-grade classroom. The desks were no longer arranged in rows but grouped in intimate clusters around the room. A computer rested on a table against the far wall, near where I once sat. I walked my old route home from school, the distance shrunken by my larger stride. I stopped in front of my best friend Kathryn's house, where we once drew sidewalk pictures, crossed the street to play kick ball, produced plays in the garage for neighborhood audiences, and traded marbles and stamps in the backyard. In place of the small shop where I had purchased penny candy stood a neighborhood child-care center, filled with the voices and vigorous activity of toddlers and preschoolers.

As I walked, I reflected on early experiences that contributed to who I am and what I am like today—weekends helping my father in his downtown clothing shop; the year my mother studied to become a high school teacher; moments of companionship and rivalry with my sister and brother; Sunday trips to museums and the seashore; and overnight visits to my grandmother's house, where I became someone extra special.

As I passed the homes of my childhood friends, I thought of what I knew about their present lives: My close friend Kathryn, star pupil and president of our sixth-grade class—today a successful corporate lawyer and mother of two children. Shy, withdrawn Phil, cruelly teased because of his cleft lip—now owner of a thriving chain of hardware stores and member of the city council. Julio, immigrant from Mexico who joined our class in third grade—today director of an elementary school bilingual education program and single parent of an adopted Mexican boy. And finally, my next-door neighbor Rick, who had picked fights at recess, struggled with reading, repeated fourth grade, dropped out of high school, and (so I heard) moved from one job to another over the following 10 years.

As you begin this course in child development, perhaps you, too, have wondered about some of the same questions that crossed my mind during that nostalgic neighborhood walk:

■ Is the infant's and young child's understanding of the world much the same as the adult's, or is it different in basic respects?

■ What determines the features that humans have in common and those that make each of us unique—in physical characteristics, mental capabilities, interests, and behaviors?

- How did Julio, transplanted to a foreign culture at 8 years of age, master its language and customs and succeed in its society, yet remain strongly identified with his ethnic community?

- In what ways are children's home, school, and neighborhood experiences the same today as they were in generations past, and in what ways are they different?

- How does cultural change—employed mothers, child care, divorce, smaller families, and new technologies—affect children's characteristics and skills?

- Why do some of us, like Kathryn and Rick, retain the same styles of responding that characterized us as children, whereas others, like Phil, change in essential ways?

These are central questions addressed by **child development,** a field devoted to understanding all aspects of human growth and change from conception through adolescence. Child development is part of a larger discipline known as **developmental psychology,** or, in its interdisciplinary sense, **human development,** which includes all changes we experience throughout the lifespan. Great diversity characterizes the interests and concerns of the thousands of investigators who study child development. But all have a single goal in common: to describe and identify those factors that influence the dramatic changes in young people during the first two decades of life.

Child Development as a Scientific, Applied, and Interdisciplinary Field

Look again at the questions just listed, and you will see that they are not just of scientific interest. Each is of *applied,* or practical, importance as well. In fact, scientific curiosity is just one factor that has led child development to become the exciting field of study it is today. Research about development has also been stimulated by social pressures to better the lives of children. For example, the beginning of public education in the early part of the twentieth century led to a demand for knowledge about what and how to teach children of different ages. The interest of pediatricians in improving children's health required an understanding of physical growth and nutrition. The social service profession's desire to treat children's anxieties and behavior problems required information about personality and social development. And parents have continually asked for advice about child-rearing practices and experiences that would promote the well-being of their child.

Our large storehouse of information about child development is *interdisciplinary.* It has grown through the combined efforts of people from many fields of study. Because of the need for solutions to everyday problems concerning children, scientists from psychology, sociology, anthropology, and biology joined forces in research with professionals from a variety of applied fields, including education, family studies, medicine, public health, and social service, to name just a few. Today, the field of child development is a melting pot of contributions. Its body of knowledge is not just scientifically important but relevant and useful.

Domains of Development as Interwoven

To make the vast, interdisciplinary study of human change more orderly and convenient, development is often divided into three broad *domains,* or aspects:

- *Physical development*—changes in body size, proportions, appearance, and the functioning of various body systems; brain development; perceptual and motor capacities; and physical health.

- *Cognitive development*—development of a wide variety of thought processes and intellectual abilities, including attention, memory, academic and everyday knowledge,

child development A field of study devoted to understanding all aspects of human growth and change from conception through adolescence.

developmental psychology A branch of psychology devoted to understanding all changes that human beings experience throughout the lifespan.

human development An interdisciplinary field of study devoted to understanding all changes that human beings experience throughout the lifespan.

problem solving, imagination, creativity, and the uniquely human capacity to represent the world through language.

■ *Emotional and social development*—development of emotional communication, self-understanding, ability to manage one's own feelings, knowledge about other people, interpersonal skills, friendships, intimate relationships, and moral reasoning and behavior.

Turn to the Contents of this book on page iv and review its part divisions and chapter titles. Notice that we will largely consider the domains of development in the order just listed. Yet we must keep in mind that they are not really distinct; instead, they combine in an integrated, holistic fashion to yield the living, growing child. Furthermore, each domain continually influences and is influenced by the others. For example, in Chapter 4, we will see that new motor capacities, such as reaching, sitting, crawling, and walking (physical), contribute greatly to infants' understanding of their surroundings (cognition). When babies think and act more competently, adults begin to stimulate them more with games, language, and expressions of delight at the child's new achievements (emotional and social). These enriched experiences return to promote all aspects of development.

Although each chapter focuses on a major topic within a domain, you will encounter instances of the interwoven nature of all domains on almost every page of this text. In addition, look for the special Connections questions alongside the Brief Reviews, which will help you explore the entire book to form a coherent, unified picture of child development.

Domains of development—physical, cognitive, emotional, and social—are interwoven. As this 1-year-old takes his first steps, his triumphant smile of accomplishment evokes expressions of delight and encouragement from his parents. An upright posture opens the door to new realms of exploration and social participation.
(Laura Dwight)

Periods of Development

An additional dilemma arises in discussing development: how to divide the flow of time into phases that are sensible and manageable. Usually, researchers segment child development into the following five periods, since each brings with it new capacities and social expectations that serve as important transitions in major theories:

1. *The prenatal period: from conception to birth.* This 9-month period is the most rapid phase of change, during which a one-celled organism is transformed into a human baby with remarkable capacities for adjusting to life in the surrounding world.

2. *Infancy and toddlerhood: from birth to 2 years.* This period brings dramatic changes in the body and brain that support the emergence of a wide array of motor, perceptual, and intellectual capacities; the beginnings of language; and first intimate ties to others. Infancy spans the first year; toddlerhood spans the second, during which children take their first independent steps, marking a shift from dependence to greater autonomy.

3. *Early childhood: from 2 to 6 years.* During this period, the body becomes longer and leaner, motor skills are refined, and children become more self-controlled and self-sufficient. Make-believe play blossoms and supports every aspect of psychological development. Thought and language expand at an astounding pace, a sense of morality becomes evident, and children establish ties with peers.

4. *Middle childhood: from 6 to 11 years.* These are the school years, a phase in which children learn about the wider world and master new responsibilities that increasingly resemble those they will perform as adults. Improved athletic abilities, participation in organized games with rules, more logical thought processes, mastery of basic literacy skills, and advances in understanding the self, morality, and friendship are hallmarks of this phase.

5. *Adolescence: from 11 to 20 years.* This period is the bridge between childhood and adulthood. Puberty leads to an adult-size body and sexual maturity. Thought becomes abstract and idealistic, and school achievement becomes more serious as young people prepare for the world of work. Defining personal values and goals and establishing autonomy from the family are major concerns of this phase.

With this introduction in mind, let's turn to some basic issues that have captivated, puzzled, and divided child development theorists. Then our discussion will trace the emergence of the field and survey major theories. (We will return to each contemporary theory in greater detail in later chapters of this book.)

Basic Issues

Before scientific study of the child, questions about children were answered by turning to common sense, opinion, and belief. Systematic research on children did not begin until the late nineteenth and early twentieth centuries. Gradually it led to the construction of theories of child development to which professionals and parents could turn for understanding and guidance.

Although a great many definitions exist, for our purposes a **theory** is an orderly, integrated set of statements that describes, explains, and predicts behavior. For example, a good theory of infant–caregiver attachment would (1) *describe* the behaviors that lead up to babies' strong desire to seek the affection and comfort of a familiar adult around 6 to 8 months of age, (2) *explain* why infants have such a strong desire, and (3) *predict* what might happen if babies do not develop this close emotional bond.

Theories are vital tools in child development (and any other scientific endeavor) for two reasons. First, they provide organizing frameworks for our observations of children. In other words, they *guide and give meaning to what we see.* Second, theories that are verified by research often serve as a sound basis for practical action. Once a theory helps us *understand* development, we are in a much better position to *know what to do* in our efforts to improve the welfare and treatment of children.

As we will see later, theories are influenced by cultural values and belief systems of their times. But theories differ in one important way from mere opinion and belief: A theory's continued existence depends on *scientific verification* (Scarr, 1985). This means that the theory must be tested using a fair set of research procedures agreed on by the scientific community. (We will consider research strategies in Chapter 2.)

In the field of child development, there are many theories with very different ideas about what children are like and how they develop. The study of child development provides no ultimate truth, since investigators do not always agree on the meaning of what they see. In addition, children are complex beings; they grow physically, mentally, emotionally, and socially. As yet, no single theory has been able to explain all these aspects. Finally, the existence of many theories helps advance knowledge, since researchers are continually trying to support, contradict, and integrate these different points of view.

Although there are many theories, we can easily organize them, since almost all take a stand on four basic issues about child development: (1) Is the course of development continuous or discontinuous? (2) Is there one general course of development that characterizes all children, or are there many possible courses? (3) Are genetic or environmental factors more important in determining development? (4) Do individual children establish stable, lifelong patterns of behavior early in development, or are they open to change?

To help you remember these controversial issues, they are briefly summarized in Table 1.1. Let's take a close look at each in the following sections.

CONTINUOUS OR DISCONTINUOUS DEVELOPMENT?

Recently, the mother of a 20-month-old boy named Angelo reported to me with amazement that her young son pushed a toy car swiftly across the living room floor while mak-

theory An orderly, integrated set of statements that describes, explains, and predicts behavior.

TABLE 1.1

Basic Issues in Child Development

Issue	Questions About Development
Continuous or discontinuous development?	Is child development a matter of cumulative adding on of skills and behaviors, or does it involve qualitative, stagewise changes? Do *both* continuous and discontinuous changes characterize development?
One course of development or many?	Is there one course of development that characterizes all children, or are there many possible courses, depending on the contexts—unique combinations of personal and environmental circumstances—that children experience? Does development have *both* universal features and features unique to the individual and his or her context?
Nature or nurture?	Are genetic or environmental factors more important determinants of development? If *both* nature and nurture play major roles, how do they work together to influence the individual's traits and capacities?
The individual—stable or open to change	To what extent do heredity and early experiences establish lifelong patterns of behavior? Can later experiences overcome early negative effects? How does the impact of early versus later experiences vary across domains of development and across individuals?

ing a motorlike sound, "Brmmmm, brmmmm," for the first time. When he hit a nearby wall with a bang, Angelo let go of the car, exclaimed, "C'ash," and laughed heartily.

"How come Angelo can pretend, but he couldn't a few months ago?" queried his mother. "And I wonder what 'Brrmmmm, brmmmm' and 'Crash!' mean to Angelo? Is his understanding of motorlike sounds and collision similar to mine?"

Angelo's mother has raised a puzzling issue about development: How can we best describe the differences in capacities and behavior between small infants, young children, adolescents, and adults? As Figure 1.1 illustrates, major theories recognize two possibilities.

On the one hand, babies and preschoolers may respond to the world in much the same way as do adults. The difference between the immature and mature being may simply be one of amount or complexity of behavior. For example, little Angelo's thinking might be just as logical and well organized as our own. Perhaps (as his mother reports) he can sort objects into simple categories, recognize whether there are more of one kind than another, and remember where he left his favorite toy at day care the week before. Angelo's only limitation may be that he cannot perform these skills with as much information and precision

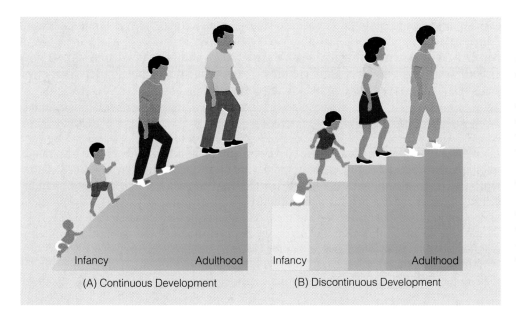

Infancy — Adulthood

(A) Continuous Development

Infancy — Adulthood

(B) Discontinuous Development

FIGURE 1.1

Is development continuous or discontinuous? (a) Some theorists believe that development is a smooth, continuous process. Children gradually add more of the same types of skills. (b) Other theorists think that development takes place in discontinuous stages. Children change rapidly as they step up to a new level of development and then change very little for a while. With each new step, the child interprets and responds to the world in a qualitatively different way.

as we can. If this is true, then Angelo's development must be **continuous**—a process that consists of gradually adding more of the same types of skills that were there to begin with.

On the other hand, Angelo may have ways of thinking, feeling, and behaving that must be understood on their own terms—ones quite different from our own. If so, then development is a **discontinuous** process in which new ways of understanding and responding to the world emerge at particular time periods. From this perspective, Angelo is not yet able to organize objects or remember and interpret experiences as adults do. Instead, he will move through a series of developmental steps, each of which has unique features, until he reaches the highest level of human functioning.

Theories that accept the discontinuous perspective include a special developmental concept: the concept of **stage.** Stages are qualitative changes in thinking, feeling, and behaving that characterize particular time periods of development. In stage theories, development is much like climbing a staircase, with each step corresponding to a more mature, reorganized way of functioning than the one that came before. The stage concept also assumes that children undergo periods of rapid transformation as they step up from one stage to the next, followed by plateaus during which they stand solidly within a stage. In other words, change is fairly sudden rather than gradual and ongoing.

Does development actually take place in a neat, orderly sequence of stages? For now, let's note that this is an ambitious assumption that has not gone unchallenged. We will review some very influential stage theories later in this chapter.

ONE COURSE OF DEVELOPMENT OR MANY?

Stages are always assumed to be universal across children and cultures; that is, because children have similar brains and bodies and live in stimulating environments, stage theorists assume that children everywhere follow the same sequence of development. For example, in the domain of cognition, a stage theorist might try to identify the common biological and environmental factors that lead children to represent their world through language and make-believe play in early childhood; think more logically and systematically in middle childhood; and reason abstractly in adolescence.

At the same time, the field of child development is becoming increasingly aware that different children grow up in distinct **contexts;** that is, children experience unique combinations of personal and environmental circumstances. For example, a shy child who fears social encounters develops in very different contexts from those of a sociable agemate who readily seeks out adults and peers. Children in non-Western village societies encounter experiences in their families and communities that differ sharply from those of children in large Western cities. These unique circumstances can result in markedly different cognitive capacities, social skills, and feelings about the self and other people (Rubin & Coplan, 1998).

As we will see later, contemporary theorists regard the contexts that shape development as many-layered and complex. These include immediate settings (such as home, child-care center, school, and neighborhood) as well as conditions more remote from children's everyday lives (such as community resources, societal values and priorities, and historical time period). Finally, a special interest in culture has made child development researchers more conscious of diversity in development than ever before.

NATURE OR NURTURE?

In addition to describing the course of development, each theory takes a stand on a major question about its underlying causes: Are genetic or environmental factors more important? This is the age-old **nature–nurture controversy.** By *nature*, we mean inborn biological givens—the hereditary information children receive from their parents at the moment of conception that signals the body to grow and affects all their characteristics and skills. By *nurture*, we mean the complex forces of the physical and social world that influence children's biological makeup and psychological experiences before and after birth.

Although all theories grant at least some role to both nature and nurture, they vary in the emphasis placed on each. For example, consider the following questions: Is the older

continuous development Development as a cumulative process of adding on more of the same types of skills that were there to begin with.

discontinuous development Development as taking place in stages, in which new and different ways of interpreting and responding to the world emerge at particular time periods.

stage A qualitative change in thinking, feeling, and behaving that characterizes a particular time period of development.

contexts Unique combinations of personal and environmental circumstances that can result in markedly different paths of development.

nature–nurture controversy Disagreement among theorists about whether genetic or environmental factors are more important determinants of development and behavior.

child's ability to think in more complex ways largely the result of an inborn timetable of growth, or is it primarily influenced by stimulation from parents and teachers? Do young children acquire language rapidly because they are genetically predisposed to do so, or because parents tutor them from an early age? And what accounts for the vast individual differences among children—in height, weight, physical coordination, intelligence, personality, and social skills? Is nature or nurture more responsible?

THE INDIVIDUAL: STABLE OR OPEN TO CHANGE?

The position a theory takes on nature versus nurture affects its explanation of individual differences. Some theorists emphasize *stability*—that children who are high or low in a characteristic (such as verbal ability, anxiety, or sociability) will remain so at later ages. These theorists typically stress the importance of *heredity*. If they regard environment as crucial, they generally point to *early experiences* as establishing lifelong patterns of behavior. Powerful negative events in the first few years, they argue, cannot be fully overcome by later, more positive ones (Bowlby, 1980; Sroufe, Egeland, & Kreutzer, 1990). Other theorists take a more optimistic view. They believe that *change* is possible and likely if new experiences support it (Chess & Thomas, 1984; Sampson & Laub, 1993; Werner & Smith, 1992).

Throughout this chapter and the remainder of this book, we will see that investigators disagree, often sharply, on the issue of **stability versus change.** And the answers they provide are of great applied significance. If you believe that development is largely due to nature, then providing experiences aimed at inducing change would be of little value. If, on the other hand, you are convinced of the supreme importance of early experience, then you would intervene as soon as possible, offering children high-quality stimulation and support to ensure that they realize their potential. Finally, if you think that environment is profoundly influential throughout development, you would extend high-quality early experiences into later years. In addition, you would offer assistance any time children or adolescents run into difficulty, believing that they can recover from early negative events with the help of new opportunities and favorable life circumstances.

Will this 2-year-old boy's frequent tantrums extend into a lifelong pattern of difficult behavior? Theorists emphasizing stability—that the boy will remain difficult to manage—typically stress the importance of heredity. Others regard stability as due to early experiences—in this case, the way the mother handles her young child's emotional outbursts. Still others believe that change is possible at later ages if new experiences support it.
(Laura Dwight)

A BALANCED POINT OF VIEW

So far, we have discussed the basic issues of child development in terms of extremes—solutions on one side or the other. As we trace the unfolding of the field in the rest of this chapter, you will see that the positions of many theories have softened. Modern ones, especially, recognize the merits of both sides. Some theorists believe that both continuous and discontinuous changes characterize development and alternate with one another. And some acknowledge that development can have both universal features and features unique to the individual and his or her contexts. Furthermore, investigators have moved away from asking which is more important, heredity or environment. Instead, they want to know precisely how nature and nurture work together to influence the child's traits and capacities.

Finally, as we will see in later parts of this book, the relative impact of early and later experiences varies substantially from one domain of development to another and even (as the Variations box on page 10 indicates) across individuals! In each chapter, you will find a Variations box that highlights researchers' growing concern with documenting and explaining individual variability in developmental paths and progress (Cicchetti & Toth, 1998b). These boxes illustrate how studying children with developmental problems or exceptional abilities can help us identify important influences on development that are not always apparent when we focus only on well-functioning children.

In sum, because of the complex network of factors contributing to human change and the challenges involved in isolating the effects of each, many theoretical points of view have gathered research support. Although debate continues, this circumstance has also sparked more balanced visions of child development.

stability versus change Disagreement among theorists about whether stable individual differences emerge early and persist due to heredity and early experience, or whether change is possible and likely if new experiences support it.

Resilient Children

OHN AND HIS BEST friend, Gary, grew up in a run-down, crime-ridden inner-city neighborhood. By age 10, each had experienced years of family conflict followed by parental divorce. Reared for the rest of childhood and adolescence in mother-headed households, John and Gary rarely saw their fathers. Both achieved poorly, dropped out of high school, and were in and out of trouble with the police.

Then John and Gary's paths of development diverged. By age 30, John had fathered two children with women he never married, had spent time in prison, was unemployed, and drank alcohol heavily. In contrast, Gary had returned to finish high school, had studied auto mechanics at a community college, and became manager of a gas station and repair shop. Married with two children, he had saved his earnings and bought a home. He was happy, healthy, and well adapted to life.

A wealth of evidence shows that environmental risks—poverty, negative family interactions, and parental divorce, job loss, mental illness, and drug abuse—predispose children to future problems (Masten & Coatsworth, 1998). On the basis of these findings, we would have expected both John and Gary to develop serious psychological difficulties. Why did Gary "beat the odds" and come through unscathed?

New evidence on **resiliency**—the ability to adapt effectively in the face of adversity—is receiving increasing attention because investigators want to find ways to protect young people from the damaging effects of stressful life conditions (Cicchetti & Garmezy, 1993). This interest was inspired by several long-term studies on the relationship of life stressors in childhood to competence and adjustment in adolescence and adulthood (Garmezy, 1993; Rutter, 1985, 1987; Werner & Smith, 1992). In each study, some children were shielded from negative outcomes, whereas others had lasting problems. Three broad factors seemed to offer protection from the damaging effects of stressful life events.

PERSONAL CHARACTERISTICS OF CHILDREN. A child's biologically endowed characteristics can reduce exposure to risk or lead to experiences that compensate for early stressful events. Temperament is particularly powerful. Children with calm, easy-going, sociable dispositions who are willing to take initiative have a special capacity to adapt to change and elicit positive responses from others. Children who are emotionally reactive and irritable often strain the patience of people around them (Gribble et al., 1993; Milgram & Palti, 1993; Smith & Prior, 1995; Wyman et al., 1992). For example, both John and Gary moved several times during their childhoods. Each time, John became anxious and angry, picking arguments with his parents, siblings, and peers. In contrast, Gary was sad to leave his home but soon looked forward to making new friends and exploring new parts of the neighborhood. Intellectual ability is another protective factor. It increases the chances of rewarding experiences in school that may offset the impact of a stressful home life (Masten et al., 1999).

A WARM PARENTAL RELATIONSHIP. A close relationship with at least one parent who provides affection and as-

This child's special relationship with her grandfather provides the social support she needs to cope with stress and solve problems constructively. A warm tie with a person outside the immediate family can promote resilience.
(Alan Hicks/Tony Stone Images)

sistance and introduces order and organization into the child's life fosters resilience. But note that this factor (as well as the next one) is not independent of children's personal characteristics. Children who are relaxed, socially responsive, and able to deal with change are easier to rear and more likely to enjoy positive relationships with parents and other people. At the same time, some children may develop more attractive dispositions as a result of parental warmth and attention (Luthar & Zigler, 1991; Smith & Prior, 1995).

SOCIAL SUPPORT OUTSIDE THE IMMEDIATE FAMILY. A person outside the immediate family—perhaps a grandparent, teacher, or close friend—who forms a special relationship with the child can promote resilience. Gary may have overcome the effects of a stressful home life because of the support he received in adolescence from his grandfather, who listened to Gary's concerns and helped him solve problems constructively. In addition, Gary's grandfather had a stable marriage and work life and handled stressors skillfully. Consequently, he served as a model of effective coping (Zimmerman & Arunkumar, 1994).

Research on resiliency highlights the complex connections between heredity and environment. Armed with positive characteristics, which may stem from innate endowment, favorable rearing experiences, or both, children take action to reduce stressful situations. Nevertheless, when many risks pile up, they become increasingly difficult to overcome (Sameroff et al., 1993). Therefore, effective interventions need to reduce risks and enhance relationships at home, in school, and in the community that inoculate children against the negative effects of risk. This means attending to both the person and the environment—building capacity as well as reducing problems.

Historical Foundations

odern theories of child development are the result of centuries of change in Western cultural values, philosophical thinking about children, and scientific progress. To understand the field as it exists today, we must return to its beginnings—to influences that long preceded scientific child study. We will see that many early ideas about children linger as important forces in current theory and research.

MEDIEVAL TIMES

In medieval Europe (the sixth through the fifteenth centuries), little importance was placed on childhood as a separate phase of the life cycle. The idea accepted by many theories today, that the child's nature is unique and different from that of youths and adults, was much less common then. Instead, once children emerged from infancy, they were regarded as miniature, already-formed adults, a view called **preformationism.** This attitude is reflected in the art, everyday entertainment, and language of the times. Look carefully at medieval paintings, and you will see that children are depicted in dress and expression as immature adults. Before the sixteenth century, toys and games were not designed to amuse children but were for all people. And age, so central to modern personal identity, was unimportant in medieval custom and usage. People did not refer to it in conversation, and it was not even recorded in family and civil records until the fifteenth and sixteenth centuries (Ariès, 1962).

Nevertheless, faint glimmerings of the idea that children are unique emerged during medieval times. Some laws recognized that children needed protection from adults who might mistreat them, and medical works provided special instructions for children's care. But even though in a practical sense there was some awareness of the vulnerability of children, as yet there were no theories about the uniqueness of childhood or separate developmental periods (Borstelmann, 1983; Sommerville, 1982).

THE REFORMATION

In the sixteenth century, a revised image of childhood sprang from the religious movement that gave birth to Protestantism—in particular, from the Puritan belief in original sin. According to Puritan doctrine, children were born evil and stubborn and had to be civilized toward a destiny of virtue and salvation (Ariès, 1962; Shahar, 1990).

Harsh, restrictive child-rearing practices were recommended as the most efficient means for taming the depraved child. Children were dressed in stiff, uncomfortable clothing that held them in adultlike postures, and disobedient pupils were routinely beaten by their schoolmasters (Stone, 1977). Although these attitudes represented the prevailing child-rearing philosophy of the time, they probably were not typical of everyday practices in Puritan families. Recent historical evidence suggests that love and affection for their children made many Puritan parents reluctant to use extremely repressive discipline (Moran & Vinovskis, 1986).

As the Puritans emigrated from England to the United States, they brought with them the belief that child rearing was one of their most important obligations. Although they continued to regard the child's soul as tainted by original sin, they tried to promote reason in their sons and daughters so they would be able to separate right from wrong. The Puritans were the first to develop special reading materials for children that instructed them in religious and moral ideals. As they trained their children in self-reliance and self-control, Puritan parents gradually adopted a moderate balance between discipline and indulgence, severity and permissiveness (Pollock, 1987).

PHILOSOPHIES OF THE ENLIGHTENMENT

The seventeenth-century Enlightenment brought new philosophies of reason and emphasized ideals of human dignity and respect. Conceptions of childhood appeared that were more humane than those of centuries past.

In this medieval painting, young children are depicted as miniature adults. Their dress and expressions resemble those of their elders. Through the fifteenth century, little emphasis was placed on childhood as a unique phase of the life cycle.
(Eric Lessing/Art Resources)

resiliency The ability to adapt effectively in the face of adverse life circumstances.

preformationism Medieval view of the child as a miniature adult.

■ **JOHN LOCKE.** The writings of John Locke (1632–1704), a leading British philosopher, viewed the child as a **tabula rasa.** Translated from Latin, this means "blank slate." According to this idea, children were not basically evil. They were, to begin with, nothing at all, and their characters could be shaped by all kinds of experiences while growing up. Locke (1690/1892) described parents as rational tutors who could mold the child in any way they wished through careful instruction, effective example, and rewards for good behavior. In addition, Locke was ahead of his time in recommending to parents child-rearing practices that were eventually supported by twentieth-century research. For example, he suggested that parents reward children not with money or sweets but with praise and approval. Locke also opposed physical punishment: "The child repeatedly beaten in school cannot look upon books and teachers without experiencing fear and anger." Locke's philosophy led to a change from harshness toward children to kindness and compassion.

Look carefully at Locke's ideas, and you will see that he took a firm stand on basic issues discussed earlier in this chapter. Locke regarded development as *continuous;* adult-like behaviors are gradually built up through the warm, consistent teachings of parents. Furthermore, Locke's view of the child as tabula rasa led him to champion *nurture*—the power of the environment to determine whether children become good or bad, bright or dull, kind or selfish. And his faith in nurture suggests the possibility of *many courses of development* and of *change at later ages* due to new experiences.

Finally, Locke's philosophy characterizes children as passive—as doing little to shape their own destiny, which is written on blank slates by others. This vision has been discarded. Instead, all contemporary perspectives view children as active, purposeful beings who make sense of their world and contribute substantially to their own development.

■ **JEAN-JACQUES ROUSSEAU.** In the eighteenth century, a new theory of childhood was introduced by French philosopher of the Enlightenment Jean Jacques Rousseau (1712–1778). Children, Rousseau (1762/1955) thought, were not blank slates and empty containers to be filled by adult instruction. Instead, they were **noble savages,** naturally endowed with a sense of right and wrong and with an innate plan for orderly, healthy growth. Unlike Locke, Rousseau thought children's built-in moral sense and unique ways of thinking and feeling would only be harmed by adult training. His was a child-centered philosophy in which adults should be receptive to the child's needs at each of four stages of development: infancy, childhood, late childhood, and adolescence.

Rousseau's philosophy includes two vitally important concepts that are found in modern theories. The first is the concept of *stage,* which we discussed earlier in this chapter. The second is the concept of **maturation,** which refers to a genetically determined, naturally unfolding course of growth. If you accept the notion that children mature through a sequence of stages, then they cannot be preformed, miniature adults. Instead, they are unique and different from adults, and their development is determined by their own inner nature. Unlike Locke, Rousseau saw children as determining their own destinies. And he took a very different stand on basic developmental issues. He saw development as a *discontinuous, stagewise process* that follows a *single, unified course* mapped out by *nature*.

DARWIN: FOREFATHER OF SCIENTIFIC CHILD STUDY

A century after Rousseau, another ancestor of modern child study—this time of its scientific foundations—emerged. In the mid-nineteenth century, Charles Darwin (1809–1882), a British naturalist, joined an expedition to distant parts of the world, where he made careful observations of fossils and animal and plant life. Darwin (1859/1936) noticed the infinite variation among species. He also saw that within a species, no two individuals are exactly alike. From these observations, he constructed his ground-breaking theory of evolution.

The theory emphasized two related principles: *natural selection* and *survival of the fittest.* Darwin explained that certain species were selected by nature to survive in particular parts of the world because they had physical characteristics and behaviors that fit with, or were adapted to, their surroundings. Other species died off because they were not well suited to their environments. Individuals within a species who best met the survival requirements of the environment lived long enough to reproduce and pass their more favorable characteristics to future generations. These evolutionary concepts found their

tabula rasa Locke's view of the child as a blank slate whose character is shaped by experience.

noble savage Rousseau's view of the child as naturally endowed with a sense of right and wrong and with an innate plan for orderly, healthy growth.

maturation A genetically determined, naturally unfolding course of growth.

way into important developmental theories and have had a major impact on child development research (Cairns, 1998).

During his explorations, Darwin discovered that the early prenatal growth of many species was strikingly similar. This suggested that all species, including human beings, were descended from a few common ancestors. Other scientists concluded from Darwin's observation that the development of the human child, from conception to maturity, followed the same general plan as the evolution of the human species. Although this belief eventually proved to be inaccurate, efforts to chart parallels between child growth and human evolution prompted researchers to make careful observations of all aspects of children's behavior. Out of these first attempts to document an idea about development, the science of child study was born.

SCIENTIFIC BEGINNINGS

Scientific child study evolved quickly during the late nineteenth and early twentieth centuries. Rudimentary observations of single children were soon followed by improved methods and theoretical ideas. Each advance contributed to the firm foundation on which the field rests today.

■ **THE BABY BIOGRAPHIES.** Imagine yourself as a forerunner in the field of child development, confronted with studying children for the first time. How might you go about this challenging task? Scientists of the late nineteenth and early twentieth centuries did what most of us would probably do in their place. They selected a child of their own or of a close relative. Then, beginning in early infancy, they jotted down day-by-day descriptions and impressions of the youngster's behavior. Dozens of these baby biographies were published by the early twentieth century. In the following excerpt from one of them, the author reflects on the birth of her young niece, whose growth she followed during the first year of life:

> Its first act is a cry, not of wrath, . . . nor a shout of joy, . . . but a snuffling, and then a long, thin tearless á—á, with the timbre of a Scotch bagpipe, purely automatic, but of discomfort. With this monotonous and dismal cry, with its red, shriveled, parboiled skin . . . , it is not strange that, if the mother . . . has not come to love her child before birth, there is a brief interval occasionally dangerous to the child before the maternal instinct is fully aroused.
>
> It cannot be denied that this unflattering description is fair enough, and our baby was no handsomer than the rest of her kind. . . . Yet she did not lack admirers. I have never noticed that women (even those who are not mothers) mind a few little aesthetic defects, . . . with so many counterbalancing charms in the little warm, soft, living thing. (Shinn, 1900, pp. 20–21)

Can you tell from this passage why baby biographies have sometimes been upheld as examples of how *not* to study children? These first investigators tended to be emotionally invested in the infants they observed, and they seldom began with a clear idea of what they wanted to find out about the child. Not surprisingly, many of their records were eventually discarded as biased. But we must keep in mind that the baby biographers were like explorers first setting foot on alien soil. When a field is new, we cannot expect its theories and methods to be well formulated.

Nevertheless, the baby biographies were a step in the right direction. In fact, two theorists of the nineteenth century, Darwin (1877) and German biologist William Preyer (1882/1888), contributed to these early records of children's behavior. Preyer, especially, set high standards for making observations. He recorded what he saw immediately, as completely as possible, and at regular intervals. And he checked the accuracy of his own notes against those of a second observer (Cairns, 1998). These are the same standards that modern researchers use when observing children. As a result of the biographers' pioneering efforts, in succeeding decades the child became a common subject of scientific research.

■ **THE NORMATIVE PERIOD OF CHILD STUDY.** G. Stanley Hall (1844–1924), one of the most influential American psychologists of the early twentieth century, is generally regarded as the founder of the child study movement (Dixon & Lerner, 1999). Inspired by Darwin's work, Hall and his well-known student Arnold Gesell (1880–1961) developed theories based on evolutionary ideas. These early leaders regarded child development as a genetically determined series of events that unfolds automatically, much like a blooming flower (Gesell, 1933; Hall, 1904).

Hall and Gesell are remembered less for their one-sided theories than for their intensive efforts to describe all aspects of child development. Aware of the limitations of the baby biographies, Hall set out to collect a sound body of facts about children. This launched the **normative approach** to child study. In a normative investigation, measures of behavior are taken on large numbers of children. Then age-related averages are computed to represent the typical child's development. Using this approach, Hall constructed elaborate questionnaires asking children of different ages almost everything they could tell about themselves—interests, fears, imaginary playmates, dreams, friendships, favorite toys, and more (White, 1992).

In the same fashion, Gesell collected detailed normative information on the motor achievements, social behaviors, and personality characteristics of infants and children. He hoped to relieve parents' anxieties by informing them of what to expect at each age. If, as he believed, the timetable of development is the product of millions of years of evolution, then children are naturally knowledgeable about their needs. His child-rearing advice, in the tradition of Rousseau, recommended sensitivity and responsiveness to children's cues (Thelen & Adolph, 1992). Gesell's books were widely read. Along with Benjamin Spock's famous *Baby and Child Care,* they became a central part of a rapidly expanding child development literature for parents (see the From Research to Practice box on the following page).

Although Hall and Gesell's work offered a large body of descriptive facts about children of different ages, it offered little information on *process*—the how and why of development. Yet the child's development had to be described before it could be understood, and the normative approach provided the foundation for the more effective explanations of development that came later.

■ **THE MENTAL TESTING MOVEMENT.** While Hall and Gesell were developing their theories and methods in the United States, French psychologist Alfred Binet (1857–1911) was also taking a normative approach to child development, but for a different reason. In the early 1900s, Binet and his colleague Theodore Simon were asked to find a way to identify retarded children in the Paris school system who needed to be placed in special classes. The first successful intelligence test, which they constructed for this purpose, grew out of practical educational concerns.

Previous attempts to create a useful intelligence test had met with little success. But Binet's effort was unique in that he began with a well-developed theory. In contrast to earlier views, which reduced intelligence to simple elements of reaction time and sensitivity to physical stimuli, Binet captured the complexity of children's thinking (Siegler, 1992). He defined intelligence as good judgment, planning, and critical reflection. Then he selected test questions that directly measured these abilities, creating a series of age-graded items that permitted him to compare the intellectual progress of different children.

In 1916, at Stanford University, Binet's test was translated into English and adapted for use with American children. It became known as the *Stanford-Binet Intelligence Scale.* Besides providing a score that could successfully predict school achievement, the Binet test sparked tremendous interest in individual differences in development. The mental testing movement was in motion. Comparisons of the intelligence test scores of children who vary in sex, ethnicity, birth order, family background, and other characteristics became a major focus of research. Intelligence tests also rose quickly to the forefront of the controversy over nature versus nurture that continues today.

■ **JAMES MARK BALDWIN: EARLY DEVELOPMENTAL THEORIST.** A final important figure, overlooked in the history of child development for decades but now recognized as having had a major influence, is American psychologist James Mark Baldwin (1861–1934). A theorist rather than an observer of children, Baldwin's (1897) rich interpretations of development are experiencing a revival today. He believed that children's understanding of their physical and social worlds develops through a sequence of stages, beginning

normative approach An approach in which age-related averages are computed to represent the typical child's development.

Social Change and the Popular Literature on Parenting

ALMOST ALL PARENTS—especially new ones—feel a need for sound advice on how to rear their children. To meet this need, experts have long been communicating with the general public through a wide variety of popular books and magazines. Parenting advice has evolved over the years to reflect both new child development theories and social realities.

Prior to the 1970s, publications emphasized the central role of the mother in healthy child development. The succeeding decade brought fewer references to the primacy of the mother until, in the mid-1980s, an about-face was evident. Fathers were encouraged to share in the full range of child-rearing responsibilities, since research revealed that their role is unique and important to all aspects of development. Around this time, information about nonparental child care appeared. Experts reassured employed mothers that their babies did not require their continuous presence and offered advice on how to select good day care (Young, 1990).

In the 1990s, the themes of the popular parenting literature changed again. A spate of books expressed concern over the consequences of social change for parents' and children's well-being. On the basis of extensive interviews with employees at a Midwestern company, Arlie Hochschild (1997), in *The Time Bind*, asserts that parents are overly consumed by their jobs, putting in 10- to 11-hour days. Regardless of whether they were clerical workers or executives, the majority of working parents complained that they were frequently short of time; they had too little left for home and child rearing.

Sylvia Hewlett and Cornel West's (1998) *The War Against Parents* extends the theme of parental overload. The authors argue that although most parents want to put children at the center of their lives, good parenting is receiving less and less support in American society. Too many parents earn low wages, must work longer hours to make ends meet, and are under siege by the media, which readily blames them for troubled children. In a similar vein, Stephanie Coontz (1997), in *The Way We Really Are: Coming to Terms with America's Changing Families*, chronicles a wide range of parental stressors, including high rates of poverty, out-of-wedlock births to young mothers, divorce, and employed parents without access to affordable, high-quality child care.

American culture, William Damon (1995) adds in *Greater Expectations*, has fostered an overly permissive, child-centered philosophy, leading too many of today's children to be indulged through excessive adult praise and unconditional acceptance. The outcome, he believes, is a false sense of self-esteem—one that is fragile because it is not based on commitment, responsibility, and real accomplishment. Damon points to a study of parents' and teachers' reports of American children's behavior, gathered in 1976 and again in 1989, that showed declines for all ages and both sexes. Over the 13-year period, children were viewed as more likely to "do poorly on schoolwork," "hang around with peers who get into trouble," and "destroy things belonging to others." Fewer were involved in worthwhile activities that truly engaged them (Achenbach & Howell, 1993). A recent survey of 4,500 American adults, 2,500 of whom were parents, echoes this trend. Most respondents viewed today's youngsters as

Parents often turn to books and magazines for expert advice on how to rear their children. The information they find reflects cultural beliefs and social realities of their times.
(M. Steinbacher/Photo Edit)

problematic—too out-of-control and undirected (Farkas & Johnson, 1997).

In terms of solutions, what do experts writing for parents recommend? Most affirm the importance of greater adult involvement in children's lives and reasonable expectations for mature behavior. But increasingly, popular advice has underscored that parents cannot do the job alone; they need the help of a caring community and society.

- Hochschild (1997) appeals to employers to require working parents to leave earlier, for the sake of children.

- In place of a disconnected social system that presents children with contradictory, confusing messages, Damon (1995) advocates that parents, schools, and communities work together to create a unified set of values—one in which children must meet standards for both personal achievement and helping others.

- Hewlett and West (1998) call for an assault on American policies that fail to provide parents with essential resources for rearing children effectively: "Unlike new parents in other rich nations, American moms and dads are expected to do a stellar job without the benefits of a living wage, medical coverage, decent child care, or [paid] parenting leave." (See the discussion of child development and social policy at the end of this chapter.)

In a review of the history of twentieth-century expert advice to American parents, Julia Grant (1998) describes wide variation in "correct methods" over time. She concludes, "As we can readily see, experts cannot solve the problems that beset American [parents] and their families. . . . Practices and discourse about children should become the concern of all citizens" (p. 250).

As you study child development, read one or more popular books on parenting and evaluate the advice on the basis of what you have learned. How is the growing consensus of experts that, in Hillary Rodham Clinton's (1996) words, "It takes a village to rear a child" consistent with the focus of current theories on contexts for development, described later in this chapter?

with the simplest behavior patterns of the newborn infant and concluding with the adult's capacity to think abstractly and reflectively (Cairns, 1992, 1998). Yet in describing the process of change, Baldwin differed from other leaders of his time in emphasizing diverse contributions to development.

Baldwin regarded neither the child nor the environment as in control of development. Instead, nature and nurture were granted equal importance. Children, he argued, actively revise their ways of thinking about the world, but they also learn through habit or by copying others' behaviors. As development proceeds, the child and his social surroundings influence each other, forming an inseparable, interwoven network. In other words, children are affected by those around them, but they also influence others' reactions toward them.

Consider these ideas, and you will see why Baldwin (1895) argued that heredity and environment should not be viewed as distinct, opposing forces. Instead, he claimed, most human characteristics are "due to both causes working together" (p. 77). As we turn now to an overview of modern theories of child development, you will find Baldwin's ideas represented in several, especially the more recent ones.

ASK YOURSELF . . .

◆ Suppose we could arrange a debate between John Locke, Jean Jacques Rousseau, and James Baldwin on the nature–nurture controversy. Summarize the argument each historical figure is likely to present.

◆ CONNECTIONS
Although the baby biographies had flaws, they foreshadowed important research strategies—specifically, naturalistic observation and the longitudinal design. Describe the link between these first efforts to study the child and contemporary research techniques. (See Chapter 2, pages 45 and 58.)

Reread the example on page 8, which indicates that shy and sociable children experience very different contexts for development. Explain how those contexts can affect all domains of functioning—physical, cognitive, emotional and social? What can be done to help shy children develop more adaptively? (See Chapter 10, pages 417 and 420.)

BRIEF REVIEW

The modern field of child development has roots dating far back into the past. In medieval times, children were regarded as preformed, miniature adults. By the sixteenth century, childhood came to be recognized as a distinct phase of the life cycle. The Puritan belief in original sin fostered a harsh, authoritarian approach to child rearing. During the seventeenth century Enlightenment, Locke's "blank slate" and Rousseau's "inherently good" child promoted more humane treatment of children. Darwin's evolutionary ideas inspired maturational theories and the first attempts to study the child directly, in the form of baby biographies and Hall and Gesell's normative investigations. Out of the normative approach arose Binet's first successful intelligence test and a concern with individual differences among children. Baldwin's balanced view of the process of development survives in modern theories.

Mid-Twentieth-Century Theories

In the mid-twentieth century, the field of child development expanded into a legitimate discipline. Specialized societies were founded, and research journals were launched. As child development attracted increasing interest, a variety of mid-twentieth-century theories emerged, each of which continues to have followers today. In these theories, the European concern with the child's inner thoughts and feelings contrasts sharply with the focus of American academic psychology on scientific precision and concrete, observable behavior.

THE PSYCHOANALYTIC PERSPECTIVE

By the 1930s and 1940s, many parents whose children suffered from serious emotional stress and behavior problems sought help from psychiatrists and social workers. The earlier normative movement had answered the question, What are children like? But to treat children's difficulties, child guidance professionals had to address the question, How and why did children become the way they are? They turned for help to the **psychoanalytic perspective** on personality development because of its emphasis on the unique developmental history of each child.

According to the psychoanalytic approach, children move through a series of stages in which they confront conflicts between biological drives and social expectations. The way these conflicts are resolved determines the individual's ability to learn, to get along with

TABLE 1.2

Freud's Psychosexual Stages

Psychosexual Stage	Period of Development	Description
Oral	Birth–1 year	The new ego directs the baby's sucking activities toward breast or bottle. If oral needs are not met appropriately, the individual may develop such habits as thumb sucking, fingernail biting, and pencil chewing in childhood and overeating and smoking in later life.
Anal	1–3 years	Young toddlers and preschoolers enjoy holding and releasing urine and feces. Toilet training becomes a major issue between parent and child. If parents insist that children be trained before they are ready or make too few demands, conflicts about anal control may appear in the form of extreme orderliness and cleanliness or messiness and disorder.
Phallic	3–6 years	Id impulses transfer to the genitals, and the child finds pleasure in genital stimulation. Freud's *Oedipus conflict* for boys and *Electra conflict* for girls take place. Young children feel a sexual desire for the opposite-sex parent. To avoid punishment, they give up this desire and, instead, adopt the same-sex parent's characteristics and values. As a result, the superego is formed, and children feel guilty each time they violate its standards. The relations between id, ego, and superego established at this time determine the individual's basic personality orientation.
Latency	6–11 years	Sexual instincts die down, and the superego develops further. The child acquires new social values from adults outside the family and from play with same-sex peers.
Genital	Adolescence	Puberty causes the sexual impulses of the phallic stage to reappear. If development has been successful during earlier stages, it leads to marriage, mature sexuality, and the birth and rearing of children.

others, and to cope with anxiety. Although many individuals contributed to the psychoanalytic perspective, two have been especially influential: Sigmund Freud, founder of the psychoanalytic movement, and Erik Erikson.

■ **FREUD'S THEORY.** Freud (1856–1939), a Viennese physician, saw patients in his practice with a variety of nervous symptoms—such as hallucinations, fears, and paralyses—that appeared to have no physical basis. Seeking a cure for these troubled adults, Freud found that their symptoms could be relieved by having patients talk freely about painful events of their childhood. On the basis of adult remembrances, he examined the unconscious motivations of his patients and constructed his **psychosexual theory** of development. It emphasized that how parents manage their child's sexual and aggressive drives in the first few years is crucial for healthy personality development.

THREE PARTS OF THE PERSONALITY. In Freud's theory, three parts of the personality—id, ego, and superego—become integrated during a sequence of five stages of development summarized in Table 1.2. The *id*, the largest portion of the mind, is the source of basic biological needs and desires. The *ego*—the conscious, rational part of personality—emerges in early infancy to redirect the id's impulses so they are discharged on appropriate objects at acceptable times and places. For example, aided by the ego, the hungry baby of a few months of age stops crying when he sees his mother unfasten her clothing for breast-feeding or warm a bottle. And the more competent preschooler goes into the kitchen and gets a snack on her own.

Between 3 and 6 years of age, the *superego*, or conscience, develops from interactions with parents, who eventually insist that children conform to the values of society. Now the ego faces the increasingly complex task of reconciling the demands of the id, the external world, and conscience (Freud, 1923/1974). For example, when the ego is tempted to gratify an id impulse by hitting a playmate to get an attractive toy, the superego may warn that such behavior is wrong. The ego must decide which of the two forces (id or superego) will win this inner struggle or work out a reasonable compromise, such as asking for a turn with the toy. According to Freud, the relations established between the id, ego, and superego during the preschool years determine the individual's basic personality.

PSYCHOSEXUAL DEVELOPMENT. Freud believed that over the course of childhood, sexual impulses shift their focus from the oral to the anal to the genital regions of the body. In

psychoanalytic perspective An approach to personality development introduced by Sigmund Freud that assumes children move through a series of stages in which they confront conflicts between biological drives and social expectations. The way these conflicts are resolved determines psychological adjustment.

psychosexual theory Freud's theory, which emphasizes that how parents manage their child's sexual and aggressive drives during the first few years is crucial for healthy personality development.

Erik Erikson expanded Freud's theory, emphasizing the psychosocial outcomes of development. At each psychosexual stage, a major psychological conflict is resolved. If the outcome is positive, individuals acquire attitudes and skills that permit them to contribute constructively to society. (Olive Pierce/Black Star)

each stage of development, parents walk a fine line between permitting too much or too little gratification of their child's basic needs. If parents strike an appropriate balance, then children grow into well-adjusted adults with the capacity for mature sexual behavior, investment in family life, and rearing of the next generation.

Freud's psychosexual theory highlighted the importance of family relationships for children's development. It was the first theory to stress the role of early experience. But Freud's perspective was eventually criticized for several reasons. First, the theory overemphasized the influence of sexual feelings in development. Second, because it was based on the problems of sexually repressed, well-to-do adults, it did not apply in cultures differing from nineteenth-century Victorian society. Finally, Freud's ideas were called into question because he did not study children directly.

■ **ERIKSON'S THEORY.** Several of Freud's followers took what was useful from his theory and stretched and rearranged it in ways that improved on his vision. The most important of these neo-Freudians for the field of child development is Erik Erikson (1902–1994).

Although Erikson (1950) accepted Freud's basic psychosexual framework, he expanded the picture of development at each stage. In his **psychosocial theory,** Erikson emphasized that the ego does not just mediate between id impulses and superego demands. It is also a positive force in development. At each stage, it acquires attitudes and skills that make the individual an active, contributing member of society. A basic psychosocial conflict, which is resolved along a continuum from positive to negative, determines healthy or maladaptive outcomes at each stage. As Table 1.3 shows, Erikson's first five stages parallel Freud's stages, but Erikson added three adult stages to Freud's model. He was one of the first to recognize the lifespan nature of development.

Finally, unlike Freud, Erikson pointed out that normal development must be understood in relation to each culture's life situation. For example, among the Yurok Indians (a tribe of fishermen and acorn gatherers on the northwest coast of the United States), babies are deprived of breast-feeding for the first 10 days after birth and are instead fed a thin soup from a small shell. At age 6 months, infants are abruptly weaned—an event enforced, if necessary, by having the mother leave for a few days. These experiences, from our cultural vantage point, might seem cruel. But Erikson explained that the Yurok live in a world in which salmon fill the river just once a year, a circumstance that requires the development of considerable self-restraint for survival. In this way, he showed that child rearing can be understood only by making reference to the competencies valued and needed by the child's society.

■ **CONTRIBUTIONS AND LIMITATIONS OF THE PSYCHOANALYTIC PERSPECTIVE.** A special strength of the psychoanalytic perspective is its emphasis on the individual's unique life history as worthy of study and understanding (Emde, 1992). Consistent with this view, psychoanalytic theorists accept the *clinical method,* which synthesizes information from a variety of sources into a detailed picture of the personality functioning of an individual child. (We will discuss the clinical method further in Chapter 2.) Psychoanalytic theory has also inspired a wealth of research on many aspects of emotional and social development, including infant–caregiver attachment, aggression, sibling relationships, child-rearing practices, morality, gender roles, and adolescent identity.

Despite its extensive contributions, the psychoanalytic perspective is no longer in the mainstream of child development research (Cairns, 1998; Miller, 1993). Psychoanalytic theorists may have become isolated from the rest of the field because they were so strongly committed to the clinical approach that they failed to consider other methods. In addition, many psychoanalytic ideas, such as Freud's Oedipus conflict and the psychosexual stages, are so vague and subject to interpretation that they are difficult or impossible to test empirically.

BEHAVIORISM AND SOCIAL LEARNING THEORY

As psychoanalytic theory gained in prominence, child study was also influenced by a very different perspective: **behaviorism,** a tradition with philosophical roots in Locke's image

psychosocial theory Erikson's theory, which expands Freud's theory by emphasizing that the ego is a positive force in development, ensuring that individuals acquire attitudes and skills that help them become active, contributing members of their society. Recognizes the lifespan nature of development and the impact of culture.

behaviorism An approach that views directly observable events—stimuli and responses—as the appropriate focus of study and the development of behavior as taking place through classical and operant conditioning.

Erikson's Psychosocial Stages

Psychosocial Stage	Period of Development	Description	Corresponding Psychosexual Stage
Basic trust versus mistrust	Birth–1 year	From warm, responsive care, infants gain a sense of trust, or confidence, that the world is good. Mistrust occurs when infants have to wait too long for comfort and are handled harshly.	Oral
Autonomy versus shame and doubt	1–3 years	Using new mental and motor skills, children want to choose and decide for themselves. Autonomy is fostered when parents permit reasonable free choice and do not force or shame the child.	Anal
Initiative versus guilt	3–6 years	Through make-believe play, children experiment with the kind of person they can become. Initiative—a sense of ambition and responsibility—develops when parents support their child's new sense of purpose and direction. The danger is that parents will demand too much self-control, which leads to overcontrol, or too much guilt.	Phallic
Industry versus inferiority	6–11 years	At school, children develop the capacity to work and cooperate with others. Inferiority develops when negative experiences at home, at school, or with peers lead to feelings of incompetence and inferiority.	Latency
Identity versus identity confusion	Adolescence	The adolescent tries to answer the questions, Who am I, and What is my place in society? Self-chosen values and vocational goals lead to a lasting personal identity. The negative outcome is confusion about future adult roles.	Genital
Intimacy versus isolation	Young adulthood	Young people work on establishing intimate ties. Because of earlier disappointments, some individuals cannot form close relationships and remain isolated from others.	
Generativity versus stagnation	Middle adulthood	Generativity means giving to the next generation through child rearing, caring for other people, or productive work. The person who fails in these ways feels an absence of meaningful accomplishment.	
Ego integrity versus despair	Old age	In this final stage, individuals reflect on the kind of person they have been. Integrity results from feeling that life was worth living as it happened. Old people who are dissatisfied with their lives fear death.	

of the tabula rasa. American behaviorism began with the work of psychologist John Watson (1878–1958) in the early part of the twentieth century. Watson wanted to create an objective science of psychology. Unlike psychoanalytic theorists, he believed in studying directly observable events—stimuli and responses—rather than the unseen workings of the mind (Horowitz, 1992).

■ **TRADITIONAL BEHAVIORISM.** Watson was inspired by studies of animal learning carried out by famous Russian physiologist Ivan Pavlov. Pavlov knew that dogs release saliva as an innate reflex when they are given food. But he noticed that his dogs were salivating before they tasted any food—when they saw the trainer who usually fed them. The dogs, Pavlov reasoned, must have learned to associate a neutral stimulus (the trainer) with another stimulus (food) that produces a reflexive response (salivation). As a result of this association, the neutral stimulus could bring about the response. Anxious to test this idea, Pavlov successfully taught dogs to salivate at the sound of a bell by pairing it with the presentation of food. He had discovered *classical conditioning*.

Watson wanted to find out if classical conditioning could be applied to children's behavior. In a historic experiment, he taught Albert, an 11-month-old infant, to fear a neutral stimulus—a soft white rat—by presenting it several times with a sharp, loud sound, which naturally scared the baby. Little Albert, who at first had reached out eagerly to touch the furry rat, began to cry and turn his head away when he caught sight of it (Watson & Raynor, 1920). In fact, Albert's fear was so intense that researchers eventually questioned the ethics of studies like this one (an issue we will take up in Chapter 2). On the basis of findings like these, Watson concluded that environment is the supreme force in child development. Adults could mold children's behavior in any way they wished, he thought, by carefully controlling stimulus–response associations. And development is a continuous process, consisting of a gradual increase with age in the number and strength of these associations.

After Watson, American behaviorism developed along several lines. The first was Clark Hull's *drive reduction theory*. According to this view, people continually act to satisfy physiological needs and reduce states of tension. As *primary drives* of hunger, thirst, and sex are met, a wide variety of stimuli associated with them become *secondary,* or *learned, drives*. For example, a Hullian theorist believes that infants prefer the closeness and attention of adults who have given them food and relieved their discomfort. To ensure adults' affection, children will acquire all sorts of responses that adults desire of them—politeness, honesty, patience, persistence, obedience, and more.

Another form of behaviorism was B. F. Skinner's (1904–1990) *operant conditioning theory*. Skinner rejected Hull's idea that primary drive reduction is the only way to get children to learn. According to Skinner, a child's behavior can be increased by following it with a wide variety of *reinforcers* besides food and drink, such as praise, a friendly smile, or a new toy. A behavior can also be decreased through *punishment*, such as withdrawal of privileges, parental disapproval, or being sent to be alone in one's room. As a result of Skinner's work, operant conditioning became a broadly applied learning principle in child psychology. We will consider these conditioning principles more fully when we explore the infant's learning capacities in Chapter 4.

■ **SOCIAL LEARNING THEORY.** Psychologists quickly became interested in whether behaviorism might offer a more direct and effective explanation of the development of children's social behavior than the less precise concepts of psychoanalytic theory. This concern sparked the emergence of **social learning theory.** Social learning theorists accepted the principles of conditioning and reinforcement. They also built on these principles, offering expanded views of how children and adults acquire new responses. By the 1950s, social learning theory had become a major force in child development research.

Several kinds of social learning theory emerged. The most influential was devised by Albert Bandura and his colleagues. Bandura (1977) demonstrated that *modeling,* otherwise known as *imitation* or *observational learning,* is the basis for a wide variety of children's behaviors. He recognized that children acquire many favorable and unfavorable responses simply by watching and listening to people around them. The baby who claps her hands after her mother does so, the child who angrily hits a playmate in the same way that he has been punished at home, and the teenager who wears the same clothes and hairstyle as her friends at school are all displaying observational learning.

Bandura's work continues to influence much research on children's social development. However, like changes in the field of child development as a whole, today his theory stresses the importance of *cognition,* or thinking. Bandura has shown that children's ability to listen, remember, and abstract general rules from complex sets of observed behavior affects their imitation and learning. In fact, the most recent revision of Bandura's (1986, 1989, 1992) theory places such strong emphasis on how children think about themselves and other people that he calls it a *social–cognitive* rather than a social learning approach.

According to this view, children gradually become more selective in what they imitate. From watching others engage in self-praise and self-blame and through feedback about the worth of their own actions, children develop *personal standards* for behavior and a *sense of self-efficacy*—beliefs about their own abilities and characteristics—that guide responses in particular situations (Bandura, 1997). For example, imagine a parent who often remarks, "I'm glad I kept working on that task, even though it was hard," who explains the value of persistence to her child, and who encourages it by saying, "I know you can do a good job on that homework!" As a result, the child starts to view himself as hard working and high achieving and, from the many people available in the environment, selects models with these characteristics to copy.

social learning theory An approach that emphasizes the role of modeling, or observational learning, in the development of behavior.

■ **CONTRIBUTIONS AND LIMITATIONS OF BEHAVIORISM AND SOCIAL LEARN-ING THEORY.** Like psychoanalytic theory, behaviorism and social learning theory have had a major impact on applied work with children. Yet the techniques used are decidedly different. **Applied behavior analysis** refers to procedures that combine conditioning and modeling to eliminate undesirable behaviors and increase socially acceptable responses. It has been used to relieve a wide range of serious developmental problems, such as persistent aggression, language delays, and extreme fears (Pierce & Epling, 1995; Wolpe & Plaud, 1997). But it is also effective in dealing with more common difficulties of childhood. For example, in one study, preschoolers' anxious reactions during dental treatment were reduced by reinforcing them with small toys for answering questions about a story read to them while the dentist worked. Because the children could not listen to the story and kick and cry at the same time, their disruptive behaviors subsided (Stark et al., 1989).

Nevertheless, modeling and reinforcement do not provide a complete account of development (Horowitz, 1987). We will see in later sections that many theorists believe that behaviorism and social learning theory offer too narrow a view of important environmental influences. These extend beyond immediate reinforcements and modeled behaviors to the richness of children's physical and social worlds. Finally, in emphasizing cognition and granting children an active role in their own learning, Bandura is unique among theorists whose work grew out of the behaviorist tradition. Behaviorism and social learning theory have been criticized for underestimating children's contributions to their own development.

Through careful observations of and clinical interviews with children, Jean Piaget developed his comprehensive theory of cognitive development. His work has inspired more research on children than any other theory.

(Yves de Braine/Black Star)

PIAGET'S COGNITIVE–DEVELOPMENTAL THEORY

If one individual has influenced the contemporary field of child development more than any other, it is Swiss cognitive theorist Jean Piaget (1896–1980). American investigators had been aware of Piaget's work since 1930. However, they did not grant it much attention until 1960, mainly because Piaget's ideas and methods of studying children were very much at odds with behaviorism, which dominated American psychology during the middle of the twentieth century (Beilin, 1992). Piaget did not believe that knowledge was imposed on a passive, reinforced child. According to his **cognitive–developmental theory,** children actively construct knowledge as they manipulate and explore their world, and their cognitive development takes place in stages.

■ **PIAGET'S STAGES.** Piaget's view of development was greatly influenced by his early training in biology. Central to his theory is the biological concept of *adaptation* (Piaget, 1971). Just as the structures of the body are adapted to fit with the environment, so the structures of the mind develop during childhood to better fit with, or represent, the external world. In infancy and early childhood, children's understanding is very different from adults'. For example, Piaget believed that young babies do not realize that an object hidden from view—a favorite toy or even the mother—continues to exist. He also concluded that preschoolers' thinking is full of faulty logic. For example, children younger than age 7 commonly say that the amount of milk or lemonade changes when it is poured into a differently shaped container. According to Piaget, children eventually revise these incorrect ideas in their ongoing efforts to achieve an *equilibrium,* or balance, between internal structures and information they encounter in their everyday worlds (Beilin, 1992; Kuhn, 1992).

In Piaget's theory, as the brain matures and children's experiences expand, they move through four broad stages of development, each of which is characterized by qualitatively distinct ways of thinking. Table 1.4 on page 22 provides a brief description of Piaget's stages. In the *sensorimotor stage,* cognitive development begins with the baby's use of the senses and movements to explore the world. These action patterns evolve into the symbolic but illogical thinking of the preschooler in the *preoperational stage.* Then cognition is transformed into the more organized reasoning of the school-age child in the *concrete operational stage.* Finally, in the *formal operational stage,* thought becomes the complex, abstract reasoning system of the adolescent and adult.

applied behavior analysis Procedures that combine conditioning and modeling to eliminate undesirable behaviors and increase socially acceptable responses.

cognitive-developmental theory An approach introduced by Piaget that views the child as actively constructing knowledge and cognitive development as taking place in stages.

TABLE 1.4

Piaget's Stages of Cognitive Development

Stage	Period of Development	Description
Sensorimotor	Birth–2 years	Infants "think" by acting on the world with their eyes, ears, and hands. As a result, they invent ways of solving sensorimotor problems, such as pulling a lever to hear the sound of a music box, finding hidden toys, and putting objects in and taking them out of containers.
Preoperational	2–7 years	Preschool children use symbols to represent their earlier sensorimotor discoveries. Language and make-believe play develop. However, thinking lacks the logical qualities of the two remaining stages.
Concrete operational	7–11 years	Children's reasoning becomes logical. School-age children understand that a certain amount of lemonade or play dough remains the same even after its appearance changes. They also organize objects into hierarchies of classes and subclasses. However, thinking falls short of adult intelligence. It is not yet abstract.
Formal operational	11 years on	The capacity for abstraction permits adolescents to reason with symbols that do not refer to objects in the real world, as in advanced mathematics. They can also think of all possible outcomes in a scientific problem, not just the most obvious ones.

■ **PIAGET'S METHODS OF STUDY.** Piaget devised special methods for investigating how children think. In the early part of his career, he carefully observed his three infant children and also presented them with everyday problems, such as an attractive object that could be grasped, mouthed, kicked, or searched for when hidden from view. From their reactions, Piaget derived his ideas about cognitive changes during the first 2 years.

In studying childhood and adolescent thought, Piaget took advantage of children's ability to describe their thinking. He adapted the clinical method of psychoanalysis, conducting open-ended *clinical interviews* in which a child's initial response to a task served as the basis for the next question he would ask. We will look at an example of a Piagetian clinical interview, as well as the strengths and limitations of this technique, in Chapter 2.

■ **CONTRIBUTIONS AND LIMITATIONS OF PIAGET'S THEORY.** Piaget's cognitive–developmental perspective convinced the field that children are active learners whose minds consist of rich structures of knowledge. Besides investigating children's understanding of the physical world, Piaget explored their reasoning about the social world. As we will see in Chapters 11 and 12, Piaget's stages of cognitive development have sparked a wealth of research on children's conceptions of themselves, other people, and human relationships. Practically speaking, Piaget's theory encouraged the development of educational philosophies and programs that emphasize discovery learning and direct contact with the environment.

Despite Piaget's overwhelming contribution to child development and education, in recent years his theory has been challenged. Research indicates that Piaget underestimated the competencies of infants and preschoolers. We will see in Chapter 6 that when young children are given tasks scaled down in difficulty, their understanding appears closer to that of the older child and adult than Piaget believed. This discovery has led many researchers to conclude that the maturity of children's thinking may depend on their familiarity with the task and the kind of knowledge sampled. Finally, many studies show that children's performance on Piagetian problems can be improved with training. This finding raises questions about his assumption that discovery learning rather than adult teaching is the best way to foster development.

Today, the field of child development is divided over its loyalty to Piaget's ideas. Those who continue to find merit in Piaget's approach accept a modified view of his cognitive stages—one in which changes in children's thinking are not sudden and abrupt but take place much more gradually than Piaget believed (Case, 1992, 1998; Fischer & Pipp, 1984). Others have given up the idea of cognitive stages in favor of a continuous approach to development—information processing, which we will take up in the next section.

hree perspectives dominated child development research in the middle of the twentieth century. Child guidance professionals turned to Freud's psychoanalytic approach, and Erikson's expansion of it, for help in understanding personality development and children's emotional difficulties. Behaviorism and social learning theory rely on conditioning and modeling to explain the appearance of new responses and to treat behavior problems. Piaget's stage theory of cognitive development revolutionized the field with its view of children as active beings who take responsibility for their own learning.

ASK YOURSELF . . .

◆ *Explain how behaviorism is consistent with Locke's image of the tabula rasa. Why is Bandura's social–cognitive approach a departure from that image?*

◆ *A 4-year-old becomes frightened of the dark and refuses to go to sleep at night. How would a psychoanalyst and a behaviorist differ in their views of how this problem developed?*

◆ **CONNECTIONS**
What biological concept is emphasized in Piaget's cognitive–developmental approach? From which nineteenth-century theory did Piaget borrow this idea? (See Chapter 6, pages 222–223, for more information about the biological basis of Piagetian concepts.)

Recent Theoretical Perspectives

ew ways of understanding children are constantly emerging—questioning, building on, and enhancing the discoveries of earlier theories. Today, a burst of fresh approaches and research emphases, including information processing, ethology, Vygotsky's sociocultural theory, ecological systems theory, and the dynamic systems perspective, is broadening our understanding of child development.

INFORMATION PROCESSING

During the 1970s, child development researchers became disenchanted with behaviorism as a complete account of children's learning and disappointed in their efforts to completely verify Piaget's ideas. They turned to new trends in the field of cognitive psychology for ways to understand the development of children's thinking. Today, a leading perspective is **information processing,** a general approach that emerged with the design of digital computers that use mathematically specified steps to solve problems. These systems suggested to psychologists that the human mind might also be viewed as a symbol-manipulating system through which information flows (Klahr & MacWhinney, 1998). From presentation to the senses at *input* and behavioral responses at *output,* information is actively coded, transformed, and organized.

Information processing researchers often use flowcharts to map the precise steps individuals use to solve problems and complete tasks, much like the plans devised by programmers to get computers to perform a series of "mental operations." Let's look at an example to clarify the usefulness of this approach. Figure 1.2 shows the steps that Andrea, an academically successful 8-year-old, used to complete a two-digit subtraction problem. It also shows the faulty procedure of Jody, who arrived at the wrong answer. The flowchart approach ensures that models of child and adult thinking will be very clear. For example, by comparing the two procedures shown in Figure 1.2, we know exactly what is necessary for effective problem solving and precisely where Jody went wrong in searching for a solution. As a result, we can pinpoint Jody's difficulties and design an intervention to improve her reasoning.

A wide variety of information-processing models exist. Some (like the one in Figure 1.2 on page 24) are fairly narrow in that they track children's mastery of one or a few tasks. Others describe the human cognitive system as a whole (Atkinson & Shiffrin, 1968; Lockhart & Craik, 1990). Although these general models focus on adult information processing, they are used as guides for asking questions about broad age changes in children's thinking. For example, does a child's ability to search the environment for information needed to solve a problem become more organized and planful with age? How much new information can preschoolers hold in memory compared with older children and adults? To what extent does children's current knowledge influence their ability to learn more?

The information-processing approach is also being used to clarify the processing of social information—for example, how children come to view themselves and others in gender-linked terms (Liben & Signorella, 1993; Ruble & Martin, 1998). If we can identify how rigid gender stereotypes arise in childhood, then we are in a good position to design

information processing An approach that views the human mind as a symbol-manipulating system through which information flows and that regards cognitive development as a continuous process.

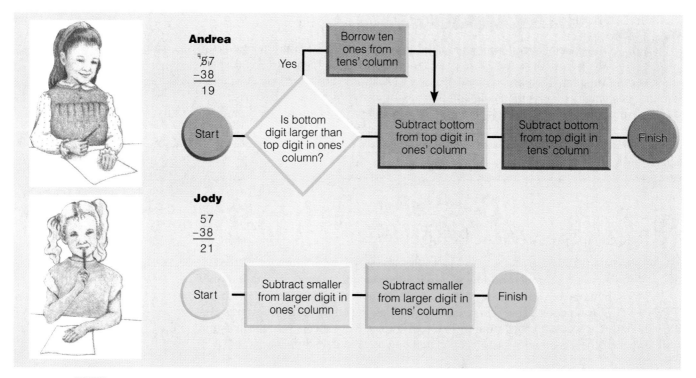

Andrea

$$^4\!\!\!\not{5}7$$
$$-38$$
$$\overline{19}$$

Start — Is bottom digit larger than top digit in ones' column? — Yes — Borrow ten ones from tens' column → Subtract bottom from top digit in ones' column — Subtract bottom from top digit in tens' column — **Finish**

Jody

$$57$$
$$-38$$
$$\overline{21}$$

Start — Subtract smaller from larger digit in ones' column — Subtract smaller from larger digit in tens' column — **Finish**

FIGURE 1.2

Information-processing flow-charts showing the steps that two 8-year-olds used to solve a math problem. In this two-digit subtraction problem with a borrowing operation, Andrea's procedure is correct, whereas Jody's results in a wrong answer.

interventions that promote more flexible conceptions of male and female role possibilities at an early age.

Like Piaget's cognitive–developmental theory, the information-processing approach regards children as active, sense-making beings who modify their own thinking as the brain matures and they confront new environmental demands (Klahr & MacWhinney, 1998). But unlike Piaget's theory, there are no stages of development. Rather, the thought processes studied—perception, attention, memory, planning strategies, categorization of information, and comprehension of written and spoken prose—are assumed to be similar at all ages but present to a lesser extent in children. Consequently, the view of development is one of continuous increase rather than abrupt, stagewise change.

A great strength of the information-processing approach is its commitment to careful, rigorous research methods to investigate cognition. Because it has provided precise accounts of how children of different ages engage in many aspects of thinking, its findings have important implications for education (Geary, 1994; Siegler, 1998). But information processing has fallen short in some respects. Aspects of cognition that are not linear and logical, such as imagination and creativity, are all but ignored by this approach (Greeno, 1989). In addition, information-processing research has largely been conducted in artificial laboratory situations. Consequently, critics complain that it isolates children's thinking from important features of real-life learning situations. Recently, information-processing investigators have addressed this concern by focusing on more realistic materials and tasks. Today they can be found studying children's conversations, stories, memory for everyday events, and strategies for performing academic tasks.

A major advantage of having many theories is that they encourage one another to attend to previously neglected dimensions of children's lives. A unique feature of the final four perspectives we will discuss is the emphasis they place on *contexts for development*—the way children's biological makeup combines with diverse environmental circumstances to affect pathways of change. The first of these views, ethology, emphasizes that human capacities have been shaped by a long evolutionary history in which our brains and bodies adapted to their surroundings.

ETHOLOGY

ethology An approach concerned with the adaptive, or survival, value of behavior and its evolutionary history.

Ethology is concerned with the adaptive, or survival, value of behavior and its evolutionary history (Dewsbury, 1992; Hinde, 1989). It was first applied to research on children in the 1960s but has become even more influential today. The origins of ethology can be traced to the work of Darwin. Two European zoologists, Konrad Lorenz and Niko Tinbergen, laid its modern foundations.

Watching the behaviors of diverse animal species in their natural habitats, Lorenz and Tinbergen observed behavior patterns that promote survival. The best known of these is *imprinting*, the early following behavior of certain baby birds that ensures that the young will stay close to the mother and be fed and protected from danger. Imprinting takes place during an early, restricted time period of development. If the mother goose is not present during this time, but an object resembling her in important features is, young goslings may imprint on it instead (Lorenz, 1952).

Observations of imprinting led to a major concept that has been widely applied in child development: the *critical period*. It refers to a limited time span during which the child is biologically prepared to acquire certain adaptive behaviors but needs the support of an appropriately stimulating environment. Many researchers have conducted studies to find out whether complex cognitive and social behaviors must be learned during certain time periods. For example, if children are deprived of adequate food or physical and social stimulation during their early years, will their intelligence be impaired? If language is not mastered during early childhood, is the child's capacity to acquire it reduced?

As we address these and other similar questions in later chapters, we will discover that the term *sensitive period* offers a better account of human development than does the strict notion of a critical period (Bornstein, 1989). A **sensitive period** is a time that is optimal for certain capacities to emerge and in which the individual is especially responsive to environmental influences. However, its boundaries are less well defined than are those of a critical period. Development may occur later, but it is harder to induce at that time.

Inspired by observations of imprinting, British psychoanalyst John Bowlby (1969) applied ethological theory to the understanding of the human infant–caregiver relationship. He argued that attachment behaviors of babies, such as smiling, babbling, grasping, and crying, are built-in social signals that encourage the parent to approach, care for, and interact with the baby. By keeping the mother near, these behaviors help ensure that the infant will be fed, protected from danger, and provided with stimulation and affection necessary for healthy growth.

The development of attachment in human infants is a lengthy process involving changes in psychological structures that lead the baby to form a deep affectional tie with the caregiver (Bretherton, 1992). As we will see in Chapter 10, it is far more complex than imprinting in baby birds. But for now, note how the ethological view of attachment, which emphasizes the role of innate infant signals, differs sharply from the behaviorist drive reduction explanation we mentioned earlier—that the baby's desire for closeness to the mother is a learned response based on feeding.

Observations by ethologists have shown that many aspects of children's social behavior, including emotional expressions, aggression, cooperation, and social play, resemble those of our primate relatives. Today, efforts are also under way to apply an evolutionary perspective to children's cognition (Bjorklund, 1997; Siegler, 1996). Researchers are returning to the central question posed by Piaget: How must children think to adapt to the environments in which they find themselves? We will explore some new answers in later chapters.

Although ethology emphasizes the genetic and biological roots of development, learning is also considered important because it lends flexibility and greater adaptiveness to behavior. The interests of ethologists are broad. They want to understand the entire organism–environment system (Hinde, 1989; Miller, 1993). The next contextual perspective we will discuss, Vygotsky's sociocultural theory, serves as an excellent complement to ethology, since it highlights the social and cultural dimensions of children's experiences.

Konrad Lorenz was one of the founders of ethology and a keen observer of animal behavior. He developed the concept of imprinting. Here, young geese who were separated from their mother and placed in the company of Lorenz during an early, critical period show that they have imprinted on him. They follow him about as he swims through the water, a response that promotes survival.

(Nina Leen/Life Magazine © Time Warner)

sensitive period A time that is optimal for certain capacities to emerge and in which the individual is especially responsive to environmental influences.

According to Lev Semenovich Vygotsky, many cognitive processes and skills are socially transferred from more knowledgeable members of society to children. Vygotsky's sociocultural theory helps us understand the wide variation in cognitive competencies from culture to culture. Vygotsky is pictured here with his daughter.

(Courtesy of James V. Wertsch, Washington University)

sociocultural theory Vygotsky's theory, in which children acquire the ways of thinking and behaving that make up a community's culture through cooperative dialogues with more knowledgeable members of that society.

ecological systems theory Bronfenbrenner's approach, which views the child as developing within a complex system of relationships affected by multiple levels of the environment, from immediate settings of family and school to broad cultural values and programs.

microsystem In ecological systems theory, the activities and interaction patterns in the child's immediate surroundings.

VYGOTSKY'S SOCIOCULTURAL THEORY

The field of child development has recently seen a dramatic increase in studies addressing the cultural context of children's lives. Investigations that make comparisons across cultures, and among ethnic groups within cultures, provide insight into whether developmental pathways apply to all children or are limited to particular environmental conditions. As a result, cross-cultural and multicultural research helps untangle the contributions of biological and environmental factors to the timing, order of appearance, and diversity of children's behaviors (Greenfield, 1994).

In the past, cross-cultural studies focused on broad cultural differences in development—for example, whether children in one culture are more advanced in motor development or do better on intellectual tasks than children in another. However, this approach can lead us to conclude incorrectly that one culture is superior in enhancing development, whereas another is deficient. In addition, it does not help us understand the precise experiences that contribute to cultural differences in children's behavior.

Today, more research is examining the relationship of *culturally specific practices* to child development. The contributions of Russian psychologist Lev Semenovich Vygotsky (1896–1934) have played a major role in this trend. Vygotsky's (1934/1987) perspective is called **sociocultural theory.** It focuses on how *culture*—the values, beliefs, customs, and skills of a social group—is transmitted to the next generation. According to Vygotsky, *social interaction*—in particular, cooperative dialogues between children and more knowledgeable members of society—is necessary for children to acquire the ways of thinking and behaving that make up a community's culture (Wertsch & Tulviste, 1992). Vygotsky believed that as adults and more expert peers help children master culturally meaningful activities, the communication between them becomes part of children's thinking. As children internalize the essential features of these dialogues, they use the language within them to guide their own thought and actions and acquire new skills. The young child instructing herself while working a puzzle or tying her shoes has started to produce the same kind of guiding comments that an adult previously used to help her master important tasks (Berk, 1994a).

Vygotsky's theory has been especially influential in the study of children's cognition. But Vygotsky's approach to cognitive development is different from Piaget's. Recall that Piaget did not regard direct teaching by adults as important for cognitive development. Instead, he emphasized children's active, independent efforts to make sense of their world. Vygotsky agreed with Piaget that children are active, constructive beings. But unlike Piaget, he viewed cognitive development as a *socially mediated process*—as dependent on the support that adults and more mature peers provide as children try new tasks. Finally, Vygotsky did not regard all children as moving through the same sequence of stages. Instead, as soon as children acquire language, their enhanced ability to communicate with others leads to continuous changes in thought and behavior that can vary greatly from culture to culture.

A major finding of cross-cultural and multicultural research is that cultures select different tasks for children's learning. In line with Vygotsky's theory, social interaction surrounding these tasks leads to knowledge and skills essential for success in a particular culture (Rogoff & Chavajay, 1995). For example, among the Zinacanteco Indians of southern Mexico, girls become expert weavers of complex garments at an early age through the informal guidance of adult experts (Childs & Greenfield, 1982). In Brazil, child candy sellers with little or no schooling develop sophisticated mathematical abilities as the result of buying candy from wholesalers, pricing it in collaboration with adults and experienced peers, and bargaining with customers on city streets (Saxe, 1988). And as the research reported in the Cultural Influences box on page 28 indicates, adults begin to encourage culturally valued skills in children at a very early age.

Vygotsky's theory, and the research stimulated by it, reveals that children in every culture develop unique strengths that are not present in other cultures. A cultural perspective reminds us that the majority of child development specialists reside in the United States, and their research includes only a small minority of humankind. We cannot assume that the developmental sequences observed in our own children are "natural" or that the experiences fostering them are "ideal" without looking around the world.

This Zinacanteco Indian girl is learning to weave an intricate garment through the informal guidance of adult experts. Her weaving skills illustrate the impact of cultural and social experience on cognitive development.
(Robert Frerck/Odyssey Chicago)

At the same time, Vygotsky's emphasis on culture and social experience led him to neglect the biological side of development. Although he recognized the importance of biology, he said little about the role of heredity and brain growth in cognitive change. Furthermore, Vygotsky's focus on social transmission of knowledge meant that he placed less emphasis than did other theorists on children's capacity to shape their own development. Contemporary followers of Vygotsky grant the individual and society more balanced roles (Rogoff, 1998; Wertsch & Tulviste, 1992).

ECOLOGICAL SYSTEMS THEORY

Urie Bronfenbrenner, an American psychologist, is responsible for an approach that has risen to the forefront of the field over the past 2 decades because it offers the most differentiated and complete account of contextual influences on children's development. **Ecological systems theory** views the child as developing within a complex *system* of relationships affected by multiple levels of the surrounding environment. Since the child's biological dispositions join with environmental forces to mold development, Bronfenbrenner recently characterized his perspective as a *bioecological model* (Bronfenbrenner & Morris, 1998).

Before Bronfenbrenner's (1979, 1989, 1993) theory, most researchers viewed the environment fairly narrowly—as limited to events and conditions immediately surrounding the child. As Figure 1.3 on page 29 shows, Bronfenbrenner expanded this view by envisioning the environment as a series of nested structures that includes but extends beyond home, school, and neighborhood settings in which children spend their everyday lives. Each layer of the environment is viewed as having a powerful impact on children's development.

■ **THE MICROSYSTEM.** The innermost level of the environment is the **microsystem,** which refers to activities and interaction patterns in the child's immediate surroundings. Bronfenbrenner emphasizes that to understand child development at this level, we must keep in mind that all relationships are *bidirectional.* That is, adults affect children's behavior, but children's biologically and socially influenced characteristics—their physical attributes, personalities, and capacities—also affect the behavior of adults. For example, a friendly, attentive child is likely to evoke positive and patient reactions from parents, whereas a distractible youngster is more likely to be responded to with restriction and punishment (Danforth, Barkley, & Stokes, 1990). As these reciprocal interactions become

Urie Bronfenbrenner is the originator of ecological systems theory. He views the child as developing within a complex system of relationships affected by multiple levels of the surrounding environment, from immediate settings to broad cultural values, laws, and customs.
(Courtesy of Urie Bronfenbrenner, Cornell University)

!Kung Infancy: Acquiring Culture

NTERACTION BETWEEN CAREGIVERS and infants takes different forms in different cultures. Through it, adults begin to transmit their society's values and skills to the next generation, channeling the course of future development.

Focusing on a culture very different from our own, researchers studied how caregivers respond to infants' play with objects among the !Kung, a hunting-and-gathering society living in the desert regions of Botswana, Africa (Bakeman et al., 1990). Daily foraging missions take small numbers of adults several miles from the campground, but most obtain enough food to contribute to group survival by working only 3 out of every 7 days. A mobile way of life also prevents the !Kung from collecting many possessions that require extensive care and maintenance. Adults have many free hours to relax around the campfire, and they spend it in intense social contact with one another and with children (Draper & Cashdan, 1988).

In this culture of intimate social bonds and minimal property, objects are valued as things to be shared, not as personal possessions. This message is conveyed to !Kung children at a very early age. Between 6 and 12 months, grandmothers start to train babies in the importance of exchanging objects by guiding them in handing beads to relatives. The child's first words generally include *i* ("Here, take this") and *na* ("Give it to me").

In !Kung society, no toys are made for infants. Instead, natural objects, such as twigs, grass, stones, and nutshells, are always available, along with cooking implements. However, adults do not encourage babies to play with these objects. In fact, adults are unlikely to interact with infants while they are exploring objects independently. But when a baby offers an object to another person, adults become highly responsive, encouraging and vocalizing much more than at other times. Thus, the !Kung cultural emphasis on the interpersonal rather than physical aspects of existence is reflected in how adults interact with the very youngest members of their community.

When you next have a chance, observe the conditions under which parents in your own society respond to infants' involvement with objects. How is parental responsiveness linked to cultural values? How does it compare with findings on the !Kung?

!Kung children grow up in a hunting-and-gathering society in which possessions are a burden rather than an asset. From an early age, children experience warm social contact with adults and are taught the importance of sharing.
(Irven DeVore/Anthro-Photo)

well established and occur often over time, they have an enduring impact on development (Bronfenbrenner, 1995).

But whether parent–child (or other two-person) relationships enhance or undermine development is affected by *third parties.* If other individuals in the setting are supportive, the quality of relationships is enhanced. For example, when parents encourage one another in their child-rearing roles, each engages in more effective parenting (Cowan, Powell, & Cowan, 1998). In contrast, marital conflict is associated with inconsistent discipline and hostile reactions toward children. In response, children typically become hostile, and their adjustment suffers (Davies & Cummings, 1994).

■ **THE MESOSYSTEM.** For children to develop at their best, child-rearing supports must also exist in the larger environment. The second level of Bronfenbrenner's model is the **mesosystem.** It encompasses connections between microsystems, such as home, school, neighborhood, and child-care center, that foster children's development. For example, a child's academic progress depends not just on activities that take place in classrooms. It is also promoted by parental involvement in school life and the extent to which academic learning is carried over into the home (Grolnick & Slowiaczek, 1994). Similarly, parent–child interaction is likely to be affected by the child's relationships with nonparental caregivers, and vice versa. Parent–child and caregiver–child relationships are each likely to support development when there are links, in the form of visits and exchange of information, between home and child-care setting.

mesosystem In ecological systems theory, connections between children's immediate settings.

FIGURE 1.3

Values
Community
health services
Laws
Immediate
family
Extended
family
Day care
center
Workplace
Friends and neighbors
Neighborhood
play area
Chronosystem
(dynamic change
in environments)
Time
Mesosystem
Individual
Microsystem
Exosystem
Macrosystem
Customs

Structure of the environment in ecological systems theory. The *microsystem* concerns relations between the developing person and the immediate environment; the *mesosystem*, connections between immediate settings; the *exosystem*, social settings that affect but do not contain the child; and the *macrosystem*, the values, laws, customs, and resources of the culture that affect activities and interaction at all inner layers. The *chronosystem* is not a specific context. Instead, it refers to the dynamic, ever-changing nature of child's environment.

■ **THE EXOSYSTEM.** The **exosystem** refers to social settings that do not contain children but nevertheless affect their experiences in immediate settings. These can be formal organizations, such as the parents' workplace or health and welfare services in the community. For example, flexible work schedules, paid maternity and paternity leave, and sick leave for parents whose children are ill are ways that work settings can help parents rear children and, indirectly, enhance development. Exosystem supports can also be informal, such as parents' social networks—friends and extended-family members who provide advice, companionship, and even financial assistance. Research confirms the negative impact of a breakdown in exosystem activities. Families who are socially isolated because they have few personal or community-based ties or who are affected by unemployment show increased rates of conflict and child abuse (Emery & Laumann-Billings, 1998).

■ **THE MACROSYSTEM.** The outermost level of Bronfenbrenner's model, the **macrosystem,** is not a specific context. Instead, it consists of the values, laws, customs, and resources of a particular culture. The priority that the macrosystem gives to children's needs affects the support children receive at inner levels of the environment. For example, in countries that require high-quality standards for child care and workplace benefits for employed parents, children are more likely to have favorable experiences in their immediate settings. As we will see in greater detail later in this chapter and in other parts of this book, although many other industrialized nations have such programs in place, they are not yet widely available in the United States (Children's Defense Fund, 1998; Kamerman, 1993).

■ **AN EVER-CHANGING SYSTEM.** According to Bronfenbrenner, the environment is not a static force that affects children in a uniform way. Instead, it is ever-changing. Important life events, such as the birth of a sibling, entering school, moving to a new neighborhood, or parents' divorce, modify existing relationships between children and their environments, producing new conditions that affect development. In addition, the timing of environmental change affects its impact. The arrival of a new sibling has very

exosystem In ecological systems theory, social settings that do not contain children but that affect their experiences in immediate settings. Examples are parents' workplace and health and welfare services in the community.

macrosystem In ecological systems theory, the values, laws, customs, and resources of a culture that influence experiences and interactions at inner levels of the environment.

different consequences for a homebound toddler than for a school-age child with many satisfying relationships and activities beyond the family.

Bronfenbrenner refers to the temporal dimension of his model as the **chronosystem** (the prefix *chrono-* means time). Changes in life events can be imposed on the child, as in the examples just given. But they can also arise from within the child, since as children get older they select, modify, and create many of their own settings and experiences. How they do so depends on their physical, intellectual, and personality characteristics and the environmental opportunities available to them. Therefore, in ecological systems theory, development is neither controlled by environmental circumstances nor driven by inner dispositions. Instead, children are both products and producers of their environments, both of which form a network of interdependent effects. Notice how our discussion of resilient children on page 10 illustrates this idea. We will see many more examples in later chapters of this book.

NEW THEORETICAL DIRECTIONS: DEVELOPMENT AS A DYNAMIC SYSTEM

Today, researchers recognize both consistency and variability in child development. But instead of merely describing consistencies, they want to do a better job of explaining variation.

A new wave of theorists has adopted a **dynamic systems perspective** on development (Fischer & Bidell, 1998; Thelen & Smith, 1998). According to this view, the child's mind, body, and physical and social worlds form an *integrated system* that guides mastery of new skills. The system is *dynamic,* or constantly in motion. A change in any part of it—from brain maturation to physical and social surroundings—disrupts the current organism–environment relationship. When this happens, the child actively reorganizes his or her behavior so that the various components of the system work together again, but in a more complex and effective way (van Geert, 1997).

Researchers adopting a dynamic systems perspective try to find out just how children attain new levels of functioning by studying their behavior while they are in transition. For example, when presented with an attractive toy, how does a 3-month-old baby who shows many, varied nonreaching movements discover how to reach for it? On hearing a new word, how does a 2-year-old figure out the category of objects or events to which it refers?

Dynamic systems theorists acknowledge that a common human genetic heritage and basic regularities in children's physical and social worlds yield certain universal, broad outlines of development. But biological makeup, everyday tasks, the people who support children in mastery of those tasks, and the quality of children's experiences vary greatly, leading to wide individual differences in specific skills. Even when children master the same skills, such as walking, talking, or adding and subtracting, they often do so in unique ways. And because children build competencies by engaging in real activities in real contexts, different skills vary in maturity within the same child. From this perspective, development cannot be characterized as a single line of stagewise or continuous change. Instead, it is more like a web of fibers branching out in many directions, each of which may undergo continuous and stagewise transformations (see Figure 1.4) (Fischer & Bidell, 1998).

The dynamic systems view has been inspired by similar ideas in other scientific disciplines, especially biology and physics (Thelen & Smith, 1994, 1998). In addition, it draws on information-processing and contextual theories—ethology, sociocultural theory, and ecological systems theory. At present, dynamic systems research is in its early stages. The perspective has largely been applied to children's motor and cognitive skills, but some investigators think that it might help explain emotional and social development as well (Fogel, 1993; Lewis, 1995). As the field of child development enters the twenty-first century, researchers are analyzing development in all its complexity, in search of an all-encompassing approach to understanding change.

These children are about the same age, but they vary widely in competencies and the precise ways they developed specific skills. The dynamic systems perspective aims to explain this variation.

(B. Daemmrich/The Image Works)

chronosystem In ecological systems theory, temporal changes in children's environments, which produce new conditions that affect development. These changes can be imposed externally or arise from within the organism, since children select, modify, and create many of their own settings and experiences.

dynamic systems perspective A view that regards the child's mind, body, and physical and social worlds as a dynamic, integrated system. A change in any part of the system leads the child to reorganize his or her behavior so that the system operates in a more complex and effective way.

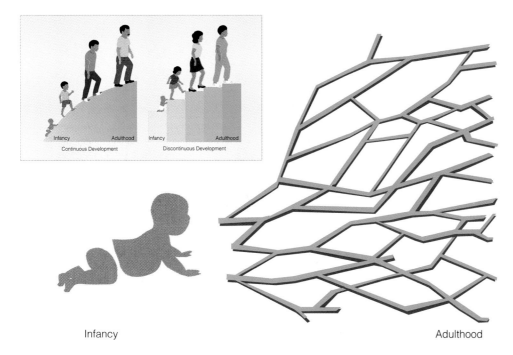

Infancy   Adulthood

FIGURE 1.4

The dynamic systems view of development. Rather than envisioning a single line of stagewise or continuous change (see inset of Figure 1.1), dynamic systems theorists conceive of development as a web of fibers branching out in many directions. Each strand in the web represents a potential area of skill within the major domains of development—physical, cognitive, emotional, and social. The differing directions of the strands signify possible variations in developmental paths and outcomes as the child masters skills necessary for participation in diverse contexts. The interconnection of the strands portrays stagelike changes—periods of major transformation in which various skills work together as a functioning whole. As the web expands, skills become more numerous, complex, and effective.

BRIEF REVIEW

New child development theories are constantly emerging, questioning and building on earlier discoveries. Using computerlike models of mental activity, information processing has brought exactness and precision to the study of children's thinking. Ethology highlights the adaptive, or survival, value of children's behavior and its evolutionary history. Ecological systems theory stresses that adult–child interaction is a two-way street affected by a range of environmental influences, from immediate settings of home and school to broad cultural values and programs. Vygotsky's sociocultural theory takes a closer look at social relationships that foster development. Through cooperative dialogues with more mature members of society, children acquire unique, culturally adaptive competencies. To account for variation in development, researchers have begun to characterize development as a dynamic system.

ASK YOURSELF . . .

◆ *Return to the Variations box on page 10. Does the story of John and Gary illustrate bidirectional relationships within the microsystem, as described in Bronfenbrenner's model? Explain.*

◆ *Explain how each of the following perspectives regards children as active, purposeful beings who contribute substantially to their own development: Bandura's social–cognitive theory, Piaget's cognitive–developmental theory, information processing, ethology, Vygotsky's sociocultural theory, ecological systems theory, and the dynamic systems perspective.*

◆ CONNECTIONS
How might an information-processing flowchart be helpful to a researcher who wants to develop an intervention program to help children solve everyday social problems, such as how to enter an ongoing play activity or resolve a dispute over a toy? (See Chapter 11, pages 472–474.)

Comparing Child Development Theories

In the preceding sections, we reviewed theoretical perspectives that are major forces in modern child development research. They differ in many respects. First, they focus on different domains of development. Some, such as psychoanalytic theory and ethology, emphasize children's emotional and social development. Others, such as Piaget's cognitive–developmental theory, information processing, and Vygotsky's sociocultural theory, stress important changes in children's thinking. The remaining approaches—behaviorism, social learning theory, ecological systems theory, and the dynamic systems perspective—discuss factors assumed to affect many aspects of children's functioning.

Second, every theory contains a point of view about child development. As we conclude our review of theoretical perspectives, take a moment to identify the stand each theory takes on the four controversial issues presented at the beginning of this chapter. Then check your analysis of theories against Table 1.5 on page 32. If you had difficulty

TABLE 1.5

Stance of Major Theories on Four Basic Issues in Child Development

Theory	Continuous or Discontinuous Development?	One Course of Development or Many?	Nature or Nurture as More Important?	The Individual as Stable or Open to Change?
Psychoanalytic perspective	*Discontinuous:* Stages of psychosexual and psychosocial development are emphasized.	*One course:* Stages are assumed to be universal.	*Both nature and nurture:* Innate impulses are channeled and controlled through child-rearing experiences.	*Stable:* Early experiences set the course of later development.
Behaviorism and social learning theory	*Continuous:* Development involves an increase in learned behaviors.	*Many possible courses:* Behaviors reinforced and modeled may vary from child to child.	*Emphasis on nurture:* Development is the result of conditioning and modeling.	*Open to change:* Both early and later experiences are important.
Piaget's cognitive–developmental theory	*Discontinuous:* Stages of cognitive development are emphasized.	*One course:* Stages are assumed to be universal.	*Both nature and nurture:* Development occurs as the brain matures and children exercise their innate drive to discover reality in a generally stimulating environment.	*Open to change:* Both early and later experiences are important.
Information processing	*Continuous:* Children gradually improve in perception, attention, memory, and problem-solving skills.	*One course:* Changes addressed are typically common to most or all children.	*Both nature and nurture:* Children are active, sense-making beings who modify their thinking as the brain matures and they confront new environmental demands.	*Open to change:* Both early and later experiences are important.
Ethology	*Both continuous and discontinuous:* Children gradually develop a wider range of adaptive behaviors. Sensitive periods, in which qualitatively distinct capacities emerge fairly suddenly, are emphasized.	*One course:* Species-wide adaptive behaviors and sensitive periods determine behavior.	*Both nature and nurture:* Biologically based, evolved behavior patterns are stressed, but an appropriately stimulating environment is necessary to elicit them.	*Stable:* Biologically based behavior patterns combine with early experiences to set the course of later development.
Vygotsky's sociocultural theory	*Continuous:* Through interaction with more expert members of society, children gradually acquire culturally adaptive skills.	*Many possible courses:* Socially mediated changes in thought and behavior vary from culture to culture.	*Both nature and nurture:* Maturation and dialogues with more knowledgeable members of society jointly contribute to development.	*Open to change:* Both early and later experiences are important.
Ecological systems theory	*Not specified*	*Many possible courses:* Children's biological dispositions join with environmental forces at multiple levels to mold development in unique ways.	*Both nature and nurture:* Children's characteristics and the reactions of others affect each other in a bidirectional fashion.	*Open to change:* Both early and later experiences are important.
Dynamic systems perspective	*Both continuous and discontinuous:* Change in the system is always ongoing. Stagelike transformations occur as various parts of the system join together to work as a functioning whole.	*Many possible courses:* Biological makeup, everyday tasks, and social experiences vary, yielding wide individual differences in specific skills.	*Both nature and nurture:* The child's mind, body, and physical and social surroundings form an integrated system that guides mastery of new skills.	*Open to change:* Both early and later experiences are important.

classifying any of them, return to the relevant section of this chapter and reread the description of that theory.

Finally, we have seen that theories have strengths and weaknesses. This may remind you of an important point made earlier in this chapter—that no theory provides a complete account of development. Perhaps you found that you were attracted to some theories, but you had doubts about others. As you read more about child development research in later chapters of this book, you may find it useful to keep a notebook in which you test your own theoretical likes and dislikes against the evidence. Don't be surprised if you revise your ideas many times, just as theorists have done throughout this century. By the end of the course, you will have built your own personal perspective on child development. It might turn out to be a blend of several theories, since each viewpoint we have discussed has contributed in important ways to what we know about children. And like researchers in the field of child development, you will still have some unanswered questions. I hope they will motivate you to continue your quest to understand children in the years to come.

New Applied Directions: Child Development and Social Policy

n recent years, the field of child development has become increasingly concerned with applying its vast knowledge base to solving pressing social problems faced by children and adolescents. At the dawn of a new millennium, we know much more than ever before about family, school, and community contexts that foster the development of physically healthy, cognitively competent, and socially mature children. Although many American children fare well, the condition of a substantial minority is much less than satisfactory. Consider the following **childhood social indicators,** or periodic measures of children's health, living conditions, achievement, and psychological well-being.

■ **Poverty.** Over the past 3 decades, the poverty rate among American children has climbed from 14 percent to nearly 20 percent, a circumstance that threatens all aspects of development. Approximately 11.5 million young people under age 18 are affected. Nearly half of these are in desperate straits, with family incomes of less than half the *poverty line* (earnings judged by the federal government to be

In the United States, nearly 22 percent of children live in poverty, a circumstance that threatens all aspects of development. Poverty is as high as 60 percent among preschool children in mother–only households.

(Jeff Greenberg/Photo Researchers, Inc.)

childhood social indicators
Periodic measures of children's health, living conditions, achievement, and psychological well-being that lend insight into their overall status in a community, state, or nation.

necessary for bare subsistence). Today, children are the poorest of any American age group. Poverty is as high as 60 percent among preschool children in mother-only households. And it is three to four times higher and far more likely to persist for most of childhood among ethnic-minority than cultural-majority children. Today, 32 percent of Hispanic-American, 40 percent of African-American, and 32 percent of Native-American children are poor (Children's Defense Fund, 1999; U.S. Bureau of the Census, 1998).

▪ **Health care.** Approximately 15 percent of American children have no health insurance, making them the largest segment of the uninsured population. As employer-based health insurance became less available to families in the 1990s, the number of uninsured children increased. Among industrialized nations, only the United States and South Africa fail to guarantee every citizen basic health care services (Children's Defense Fund, 1998; Oberg, 1988). In addition, as many as 29 percent of American preschoolers are not fully immunized, a rate that rises to 40 percent for poverty-stricken children (U.S. Department of Health and Human Services, 1998b). This leaves several million children vulnerable to such infectious illnesses as measles, tetanus, and polio.

▪ **Low birth weight and infant death.** Approximately 7 percent of American infants—about 250,000 babies—are born underweight annually. Low birth weight is a powerful predictor of serious health difficulties and early death. Nearly 8 out of every 1,000 American babies do not survive their first year, a figure that compares dismally to that of other industrialized nations (Bellamy, 1998).

▪ **Teenage parenthood.** Each year, about 350,000 babies are born to American teenagers, who are neither psychologically nor economically prepared to raise a child (Coley & Chase-Lansdale, 1998). The rates of adolescent pregnancy and childbearing in the United States are the highest of any industrialized nation. Teenage parenthood is strongly linked to poverty and risks the development of both adolescent and child.

▪ **Divorce.** Family breakdown is common in the lives of American children. One out of every 65 youngsters experiences parental divorce annually, a rate exceeding that of any other nation in the world (U.S. Bureau of the Census, 1998). In Chapter 14, we will see that marital dissolution is linked to temporary— and occasionally long-term—declines in family income and highly stressful living conditions.

▪ **Mental illness.** When environments undermine development during the early years, many children reach middle childhood and adolescence with serious mental health problems. Approximately 7.7 million American youngsters suffer from emotional and behavioral difficulties severe enough to warrant treatment. Yet only 20 to 30 percent of mentally ill children and adolescents have access to the treatment services they need (Children's Defense Fund, 1998).

▪ **Child abuse and neglect.** In 1997, juvenile authorities in the United States received 3 million reports of child abuse and neglect. The figure greatly underestimates the true number, since many cases go unreported (U.S. Department of Health and Human Services, 1999).

▪ **Child care.** Sixty-four percent of American children under age 6 have mothers in the labor force (U.S. Bureau of the Census, 1998). Yet unlike other Western nations, the United States has been slow to move toward a national system of high-quality child care to serve its single-parent and dual-earner families. According to recent surveys, much child care in the United States is substandard (Cost, Quality, and Outcomes Study Team, 1995). Low-income parents, who cannot afford the high

social policy Any planned set of actions directed at solving a social problem or attaining a social goal.

public policy Laws and government programs designed to improve current conditions.

cost of child care, often have no choice but to place their children in poor-quality settings (Raikes, 1998).

■ **School achievement.** Many students are graduating from American high schools without the educational preparation they need to contribute fully to society. From 30 to 60 percent of 17-year-olds have difficulty with moderately complex reasoning in reading, writing, mathematics, and science (Campbell, Voelkl, & Donahue, 1997). Non-college-bound youths generally lack vocational skills for well-paid jobs. And about 13 percent of adolescents leave high school without a diploma. Those who do not return to finish their education are at risk for lifelong poverty (Children's Defense Fund, 1999).

The dire condition of many American youngsters is particularly disturbing, since the United States is among the wealthiest of nations and has the broadest knowledge base for intervening effectively in children's lives. Yet, as Table 1.6 reveals, it does not rank among the top countries on any key measure of children's health and well-being. Let's consider why this is so.

THE POLICY-MAKING PROCESS

Social policy is any planned set of actions directed at solving a social problem or attaining a social goal. Policies can be proposed and implemented by small groups or large formal organizations; by private or public institutions, such as schools, businesses, and social service agencies; and by governing bodies, such as the U.S. Congress, state legislatures, the courts, and city councils.

When widespread social problems arise, nations attempt to solve them by developing a special type of social policy called **public policy**—laws and government programs designed to improve current conditions. Return for a moment to Bronfenbrenner's ecological systems theory on page 27, and notice how the concept of the macrosystem suggests that sound public policies are essential for protecting children's well-being. When governing bodies authorize programs to meet children's health, safety, and educational needs, they serve as broad societal plans for action.

Why have attempts to help children been more difficult to realize in the United States than in other industrialized nations? To answer this question, we must understand the

TABLE 1.6

How Does the United States Compare to Other Nations on Indicators of Child Health and Well-Being?

Indicator	U.S. Rank	Some Countries the United States Trails
Childhood poverty[a]	8th (among 8 industrialized nations considered)	Australia, Canada, Germany, Great Britain, Norway, Sweden, Switzerland
Infant deaths in the first year of life	22nd (worldwide)	Hong Kong, Ireland, Singapore, Spain
Low-birth-weight newborns	20th (worldwide)	Bulgaria, Egypt, Greece, Iran, Jordan, Kuwait, Paraguay, Romania, Saudi Arabia
Teenage pregnancy rate	11th (among 11 industrialized nations considered)	Australia, Canada, Czech Republic, France, New Zealand, Sweden
Percentage of young children immunized against measles	43rd (worldwide)	Chile, Czechoslovakia, Jordan, Poland, Romania
Expenditures on education as percentage of gross national product[b]	14th (among 16 industrialized nations considered)	Canada, France, Great Britain, the Netherlands, Sweden

[a]The U.S. child poverty rate of nearly 20 percent is more than twice that of any of these nations. For example, the rate is 9 percent in Australia, 9.3 percent in Canada, 4.6 percent in France, and 1.6 percent in Sweden.

[b]Gross national product is the value of all goods and services produced by a nation during a specified time period. It serves as an overall measure of a nation's wealth.

Sources: Bellamy, 1998; Central Intelligence Agency, 1999; Children's Defense Fund, 1998; Harris, 1996; Sivard, 1996.

complex forces that combine to foster effective public policies. Among the most important are cultural values, special interests, economic conditions, and child development research.

■ **CULTURAL VALUES.** The political culture of a nation—dominant beliefs about the relationship that should exist between citizen and government—has a major impact on the policy-making process. When you next have a chance, ask several residents of your community the following question: "Who should be responsible for rearing young children?" Many Americans respond in ways like these: "If parents decide to have a baby, then they should be ready to care for it." "Most people are not happy about others intruding into family matters." These statements reflect a widespread opinion in the United States—that the care and rearing of children during the early years is the duty of parents, and only parents (Rickel & Becker, 1997; Scarr, 1996; Shweder & Haidt, 1993).

This autonomous view of the family has a long history—one in which independence, self-reliance, and the privacy of family life emerged as central American values. It is one reason, among others, that the American public has been slow to accept the idea of government-supported health insurance and child care (Hayghe, 1990). It has also contributed to the large number of American families that remain poor, despite the fact that their members are gainfully employed (Chase-Lansdale & Vinovskis, 1995).

Consider our discussion so far, and you will see that it reflects a broad dimension on which cultures differ: the extent to which individualism versus collectivism is emphasized. In **collectivist societies,** people define themselves as part of a group and stress group over individual goals. In **individualistic societies,** people think of themselves as separate entities and are largely concerned with their own personal needs (Triandis, 1995). Although individualism tends to increase as cultures become more complex, cross-national differences remain. The United States is more individualistic than most other industrialized nations. Consequently, its citizens are less approving of generous government provision of family services.

■ **SPECIAL INTERESTS.** Of course, not all people hold the same political beliefs. In complex societies, distinct subcultures exist, based on such factors as geographic region, ethnicity, income, education, and age, that stand alongside a nation's dominant values. The diversity of American society has led *special interest groups* to play an especially strong role in policy making.

In this jockeying for public influence, the needs of children can easily remain unrecognized. Instead of making immediate contributions to the welfare of a nation, children are a costly drain on economic resources that people with quite different interests want for their own pressing needs. In addition, children are not capable of organizing and speaking out to protect their own unique concerns, as adult citizens do. Because they must rely on the goodwill of others for becoming an important government priority, children are constantly in danger of becoming a "forgotten constituency" in the United States.

■ **ECONOMIC CONDITIONS.** Besides dominant values and the demands of special interests, the current state of a nation's economy affects what it does to improve the welfare of children and families. Scarce public resources are commonplace in less developed countries of the world, which depend on economic aid from richer nations like the United States to feed, educate, and provide health care for many citizens. But even in large industrialized nations, the government does not always have enough resources to solve pressing social problems. In times of economic difficulty, governments are less likely to initiate new social programs, and they may cut back or even eliminate those that exist.

Following a 15-year phase in which its federal deficit skyrocketed and funding of many child-related services declined, the United States has recently entered a period of greater economic prosperity. Still, it restricts most support to the very poorest children

collectivist societies Societies in which people define themselves as part of a group and stress group over individual goals.

individualistic societies Societies in which people think of themselves as separate entities and are largely concerned with their own personal needs.

and families, leaving many economically stressed parents and children without the help they need. In this respect, the United States differs from European nations, which provide all families with benefits, in the form of child allowances (a standard yearly payment for each child in a family), universal health care, paid parental leave for childbirth and child illness, and free or inexpensive child care (McLoyd, 1998a).

■ **CHILD DEVELOPMENT RESEARCH.** For a policy to be most effective in meeting children's needs, research should guide it at every step along the way—during design, implementation, and evaluation of the program. The recent trend toward greater involvement of child development researchers in the policy process was stimulated by events of the 1960s and 1970s, a time of greater receptiveness to government-sponsored social services. Investigators quickly realized that they could have an impact on policy formation (Zigler & Finn-Stevenson, 1999).

For example, in 1965, research on the importance of early experiences for children's intellectual development played a major role in the founding of Project Head Start, the nation's largest preschool intervention program for low-income families. As we will see in Chapter 8, two decades of research on the long-term benefits of intervening with education and family services in the first few years of life helped Head Start survive when its funding was threatened and contributed to the increase in support it has received in recent years (Zigler & Styfco, 1994). In another instance, findings on the severe impact of malnutrition on early brain development stimulated passage by Congress of the Special Supplemental Food Program for Women, Infants, and Children. Since the early 1970s, this program has supplied food packages to many poverty-stricken pregnant women and young children (see Chapter 3).

Policy-relevant research, investigators soon realized, has the added benefit of expanding our knowledge base of child development. As researchers started to examine the impact of children's services, they became more aware of the power of settings remote from children's daily lives to affect their well-being. As a result, researchers broadened their focus of study to include wider social contexts, such as school, workplace, community, mass media, and government. They also began to address the impact of societal change on children—poverty, divorce, family violence, teenage parenthood, and child care. All these efforts have, in turn, helped forge new policy directions.

Still, as we mentioned earlier, a large gap exists between what we know about children and the application of that knowledge. For several reasons, scientific research does not invariably affect policy making:

■ *The impact of research depends on its interactions with other components of the policy process.* In the case of both Head Start and the Special Supplemental Food Program, if public sentiments had not been so receptive to helping poor children at the time these policies were proposed, compelling findings on the importance of early education and nutrition might have been less influential.

■ *Research that sheds light on policy often takes many years to conduct.* Arriving at an appropriate solution generally requires large numbers of studies that yield consensus on an issue. Consequently, besides focusing on current concerns, researchers must anticipate future policy issues and work on them in advance.

■ *Child development researchers have had to learn how to communicate effectively with policy makers and the general public.* Today, researchers are doing a better job than ever before of disseminating their findings in easily understandable ways, through television documentaries, newspaper stories, and magazine articles as well as direct reports to government officials (Huston, 1994). As a result, they are helping create a sense of immediacy about children's condition that is necessary to spur a society into action.

In 1973, Marion Wright Edelman founded the Children's Defense Fund, a private, non-profit organization that provides a strong, effective voice for American children, who cannot vote, lobby, or speak for themselves. Edelman continues to serve as president of the Children's Defense Fund today.

(Westenberger/Liaiso, Agency)

ASK YOURSELF . . .

◆ Check your local newspaper, television listings, and one or two national news magazines to see how often articles appear on the condition of children and families. Why is it important for researchers to communicate with the general public about children's needs?

◆ CONNECTIONS
What kinds of public policies might help reduce the high infant mortality, teenage pregnancy and parenthood, and child abuse and neglect rates in the United States? Why is poverty linked to each of these threats to children's well-being? (See Chapter 3, page 116; Chapter 5, page 214, and Chapter 14, page 593.)

PROGRESS IN MEETING THE NEEDS OF AMERICAN CHILDREN

Public policies aimed at fostering children's development can be justified on two important grounds. The first is humanitarian—children's basic rights as human beings (Huston, 1991). In 1989, the United Nations' General Assembly drew up the Convention on the Rights of the Child, an international treaty written in the form of a legal agreement among nations. It commits each participating country to work toward guaranteeing children environments that foster their development and protect them from harm. (To find out more about the Convention, refer to the Social Issues box on the following page.) Second, child-oriented policies can be justified on the basis that children are the parents, workers, and citizens of tomorrow. Investing in them can yield valuable returns to a nation's quality of life. In contrast, failure to invest in children can result in "economic inefficiency, loss of productivity, shortages in needed skills, high health care costs, growing prison costs, and a nation that will be less safe, less caring, and less free" (Hernandez, 1994, p. 20).

To be sure, a wide variety of government-sponsored child and family programs do exist in the United States, and we will see many examples in later chapters. But they are largely crisis oriented, aimed at handling the most severe family difficulties rather than preventing problems before they happen. Furthermore, funding for these efforts has waxed and waned and been seriously threatened at various times. In most cases, only a minority of needy children and adolescents are helped (Harris, 1996; McLoyd, 1998a).

Nevertheless, policy initiatives are under way that promise to improve the status of American children. For example, extra federal dollars have been allocated to upgrade the quality of child care and to cover costs for low-income employed parents (although the amount granted is still far short of the need). A recent federal law increases the ease with which payroll deductions can be made when a noncustodial parent fails to make child support payments after divorce. Furthermore, public health insurance coverage for low-income pregnant women and their children has recently expanded. And beginning in 1994, all medically uninsured children were guaranteed free vaccinations. (Still, as Table 1.6 shows, the U.S. immunization rate falls behind that of many other nations.) (Children's Defense Fund, 1998).

Child-related professional organizations are also taking a strong leadership role. In the absence of federal guidelines for high-quality child care, the National Association for the Education of Young Children (NAEYC, a 100,000-member organization of early childhood educators) established a voluntary accreditation system for preschools and child-care centers. It grants special professional recognition to programs that meet its rigorous standards of quality. Efforts like these are serving as inspiring models for the nation as a whole.

Finally, child development specialists are joining with concerned citizens to become advocates for children's causes. One of the most vigorous of the resulting interest groups is the Children's Defense Fund, a private nonprofit organization founded by Marion Wright Edelman in 1973. It engages in research, public education, legal action, drafting of legislation, congressional testimony, and community organizing. Each year, it publishes *The State of America's Children*, which provides a comprehensive analysis of the current condition of children, government-sponsored programs serving them, and proposals for improving child and family programs.[1]

By forging more effective partnerships with government and the general public, the field of child development is playing a significant role in spurring the policy process forward. As these efforts continue, there is every reason to expect increased attention to the needs of children and families in the years to come.

---

[1]To obtain a copy of The State of America's Children, contact The Children's Defense Fund, 122 C Street, N.W., Washington, DC 20001. Telephone (800) 424-9602. Website: www.childrensdefense.org

The U.N. Convention on the Rights of the Child

THE U.N. CONVENTION on the Rights of the Child is the first legally binding human rights treaty to recognize the civil, political, economic, social, and cultural rights of children. Many nations helped draft it, making it a rich blend of views that affirm children's rights to protection from harm, to environments that support their development, and to participation and self-determination in their community (Murphy-Berman & Weisz, 1996).

When a nation's legislature ratifies the Convention, it agrees to meet or work toward meeting an extensive list of obligations to children. Each reflects the Convention's basic themes—that children's best interests be primary in any actions concerning them, that they be accorded rights in a manner consistent with their capacities, and that their dignity be respected. (See Table 1.7 below for examples.)

To accomplish its goals, the Convention established an international committee of experts to monitor participating nations' progress toward guaranteeing children's rights. Within 2 years of ratifying the Convention and every 5 years thereafter, each country must submit a report to the committee on the measures it has taken. It must also make that report widely available to its citizens. In this way, the Convention tries to create a constructive dialogue aimed at improving children's condition.

Since its initiation in 1989, the Convention has been ratified by more than 180 nations. Although the United States played a crucial role in drawing up the document, it is one of the very few countries that has not yet ratified it. American individualism has stood in the way. Opponents maintain that the Convention's provisions will shift the burden of child rearing from the family to the state (Levesque, 1996; Limber & Wilcox, 1996). Supporters counter that this belief is unfounded, since the Convention stresses parents' responsibilities while also recognizing that society must actively support children and families.

The U.N. Convention on the Rights of the Child is a human rights treaty aimed at guaranteeing children everywhere protection from harm, development-enhancing environments, and participation and self-determination in their community. Since its initiation in 1989, it has been ratified by over 180 nations, each of which promises to meet or work toward meeting an extensive list of obligations to children. (Shelley Rotner/Omni-Photo Communications, Inc.)

Yet another frequently voiced reservation is that the Convention will do little to change the lives of American children and families. But many experts disagree, arguing that an international consensus on children's rights can energize change—and has already done so in many parts of the world (Limber & Flekkøy, 1995). At present, the United States is in compliance with many aspects of the Convention but falls far short of its total expectations. Even in the absence of ratification, the Convention offers lawmakers and child advocates a valuable guide for devising policies that ensure children safety, personhood, and favorable environments for development.

TABLE 1.7

A Sampling of Children's Rights in the U.N. Convention on the Rights of the Child

Category of Rights	Examples
Protection from harm	• Protection from all forms of abuse and neglect
	• Protection from participation in armed conflict
Survival and development	• The highest attainable standard of health
	• A standard of living adequate for physical, mental, spiritual, moral, and social development
	• A happy, understanding, and loving family environment
	• Free and compulsory education that develops physical abilities, the intellect, personality, and respect for one's cultural identity, one's homeland, other civilizations, and the environment
	• Rest, leisure, and age-appropriate play and recreational activities; participation in cultural activities and the arts
Community participation and self-determination	• Freedom to seek, receive, and impart information and ideas of all kinds, subject to respect for the rights of others, public health, and morals
	• Expression of personal opinions in all matters affecting the child
	• Protection against interference with privacy, family, home, and correspondence
	• Freedom of thought, conscience, and religion, subject to appropriate parental guidance and national law and in a manner consistent with the child's developing capacities

CHILD DEVELOPMENT AS A SCIENTIFIC, APPLIED, AND INTERDISCIPLINARY FIELD

What is child development, and what factors stimulated expansion of the field?

◆ **Child development** is the study of human growth and change from conception through adolescence. It is part of a larger discipline known as **developmental psychology** or **human development,** which includes all changes that take place throughout the lifespan. Research on child development has been stimulated by both scientific curiosity and social pressures to better the lives of children. Our knowledge is interdisciplinary; it has grown through the combined efforts of people from many fields of study.

DOMAINS OF DEVELOPMENT AS INTERWOVEN

Cite three broad domains of development.

◆ To make the vast, interdisciplinary study of human change more orderly and convenient, development is often divided into three broad domains: physical development, cognitive development, and emotional and social development. These domains are not really distinct; instead, they combine in an integrated, holistic fashion.

PERIODS OF DEVELOPMENT

How can we divide child development into sensible, manageable periods?

◆ Usually, researchers segment child development into five periods, each of which brings with it new capacities and social expectations that serve as important transitions in major theories: (1) the prenatal period; (2) infancy and toddlerhood; (3) early childhood; (4) middle childhood; and (5) adolescence.

BASIC ISSUES

Identify three basic issues on which child development theories take a stand.

◆ Child development **theories** can be organized according to the stand they take on four controversial issues: (1) Is development a **continuous** process, or does it follow a series of **discontinuous stages?** (2) Is there one general course of development that characterizes all children, or are there many possible courses depending on the **contexts** in which children grow up? (3) Is development primarily determined by **nature** or **nurture?** (4) Do individual children establish **stable,** lifelong patterns of behavior early in development, or are they open to **change?**

◆ Some theories, especially the more recent ones, take an intermediate stand on these issues. Contemporary researchers realize that answers may vary across domains of development and even, as research on **resiliency** illustrates, across individuals.

HISTORICAL FOUNDATIONS

Describe major historical influences on theories of child development.

◆ Modern theories of child development have roots extending far into the past. In medieval times, children were regarded as miniature adults, a view called **preformationism.** By the sixteenth and seventeenth centuries, childhood came to be recognized as a distinct phase of the life cycle. However, the Puritan conception of original sin led to a harsh philosophy of child rearing.

◆ The Enlightenment brought new ideas favoring more humane treatment of children. Locke's **tabula rasa** provided the philosophical basis for twentieth-century behaviorism, and Rousseau's **noble savage** foreshadowed the concepts of stage and **maturation.** A century later, Darwin's theory of evolution stimulated the beginnings of scientific child study.

◆ Efforts to observe children directly began in the late nineteenth and early twentieth centuries with baby biographies. Soon after, Hall and Gesell introduced the **normative approach,** which produced a large body of descriptive facts about children. Binet and Simon constructed the first successful intelligence test, which initiated the mental testing movement. Baldwin's theory was ahead of its time in granting nature and nurture equal importance and regarding children and their social surroundings as mutually influential.

MID-TWENTIETH-CENTURY THEORIES

What theories influenced the study of child development in the mid-twentieth century?

◆ In the 1930s and 1940s, child guidance professionals turned to the **psychoanalytic perspective** for help in understanding children with emotional problems. In Freud's **psychosexual theory,** children move through five stages, during which three parts of the personality—id, ego, and superego—become integrated. Erikson's **psychosocial theory** builds on Freud's theory by emphasizing the ego as a positive force in development, the development of culturally relevant attitudes and skills, and the lifespan nature of development.

◆ Academic psychology also influenced child study. From **behaviorism** and **social learning theory** came the principles of conditioning and modeling and practical procedures of **applied behavior analysis** with children.

◆ In contrast to behaviorism, Piaget's **cognitive-developmental theory** emphasizes that children actively construct knowledge as they manipulate and explore their world. According to Piaget, children move through four broad stages, beginning with the baby's sensorimotor action patterns and ending with the elaborate, abstract reasoning system of the adolescent and adult. Piaget's theory has stimulated a wealth of research on children's thinking and encouraged educational programs that emphasize discovery learning.

RECENT THEORETICAL PERSPECTIVES

Describe recent theoretical perspectives on child development.

- **Information processing** views the mind as a complex, symbol-manipulating system, operating much like a computer. This approach helps researchers achieve a clear understanding of what children of different ages do when faced with tasks or problems. Information processing has led to the design of instructional procedures that help children overcome cognitive limitations and approach tasks in more advanced ways.

- Four modern theories place special emphasis on contexts for development. **Ethology** stresses the evolutionary origins and adaptive value of behavior and inspired the **sensitive period** concept.

- Vygotsky's **sociocultural theory** has enhanced our understanding of cultural influences, especially in the area of cognitive development. Through cooperative dialogues with more mature members of society, children acquire culturally relevant knowledge and skills.

- In **ecological systems theory,** nested layers of the environment—**microsystem, mesosystem, exosystem,** and **macrosystem**—are seen as major influences on children's well-being. The **chronosystem** represents the dynamic, ever-changing nature of children and their experiences.

- Inspired by ideas in other sciences and recent perspectives in child development, a new wave of theorists has adopted a **dynamic systems perspective.** They want to account for wide variation in development.

COMPARING CHILD DEVELOPMENT THEORIES

Identify the stand taken by each major theory on the basic issues of child development.

- Theoretical perspectives that are major forces in child development research vary in their focus on different domains of development,

in their view of the nature of development, and in their strengths and weaknesses. (For a full summary, see Table 1.5 on page 32.)

NEW APPLIED DIRECTIONS: CHILD DEVELOPMENT AND SOCIAL POLICY

Explain the importance of social policies for safeguarding children's well-being, and cite factors that affect the policy-making process, noting the role of child development research.

- The field of child development has become increasingly concerned with applying its vast knowledge base to solving pressing social problems. **Childhood social indicators** reveal that many children in the United States are growing up under conditions that threaten their well-being.

- A special type of **social policy** called **public policy**—laws and government programs designed to improve current conditions—is essential for protecting children's development. Dominant cultural values, especially **individualism** versus **collectivism**; competing claims of special interest groups; the state of a nation's economy; and child development research combine to influence the policy-making process. Policy-relevant research not only helps forge new policy directions but expands our understanding of child development.

- Although many government-sponsored child and family policies are in effect in the United States, they are largely crisis oriented and do not reach all individuals in need. A variety of new public policies are under way. In addition, child development researchers are joining with concerned citizens to become advocates for children's causes. These efforts offer hope of improving the well-being of children and families in the years to come.

IMPORTANT TERMS AND CONCEPTS

applied behavior analysis (p. 21)
behaviorism (p. 18)
child development (p. 4)
childhood social indicators (p. 33)
chronosystem (p. 30)
cognitive–developmental theory (p. 21)
collectivist society (p. 36)
contexts (p. 8)
continuous development (p. 8)
developmental psychology (p. 4)
discontinuous development (p. 8)
dynamic systems perspective (p. 30)
ecological systems theory (p. 27)

ethology (p. 24)
exosystem (p. 29)
human development (p. 4)
individualistic society (p. 36)
information processing (p. 23)
macrosystem (p. 29)
maturation (p. 12)
mesosystem (p. 28)
microsystem (p. 27)
nature–nurture controversy (p. 8)
noble savage (p. 12)
normative approach (p. 14)
preformationism (p. 11)

psychoanalytic perspective (p. 17)
psychosexual theory (p. 17)
psychosocial theory (p. 18)
public policy (p. 34)
resiliency (p. 11)
sensitive period (p. 25)
social learning theory (p. 20)
social policy (p. 34)
sociocultural theory (p. 26)
stability versus change (p. 9)
stage (p. 8)
tabula rasa (p. 12)
theory (p. 6)

Research Strategies

ONE AFTERNOON, MY COLLEAGUE Ron crossed the street between his academic department and our laboratory school, the expression on his face reflecting a deep sense of apprehension. After weeks of planning, Ron had looked forward to launching his study on the development of children's peer relations. Thinking back to his own elementary school years, he recalled the anguish experienced by several of his classmates, who were repeatedly ridiculed, taunted, and shunned by their peers. Ron wanted to find ways to help rejected children, many of whom go on to lead unhappy and troubled lives. In view of the importance of his research, Ron was puzzled by the request he had received to appear before the school's research committee.

Ron was joined at the committee meeting by teachers and administrators charged with evaluating research proposals on the basis of their ethical integrity. A third-grade teacher spoke up:

"Ron, I see the value of your work, but frankly, I'm very concerned about your asking my pupils whom they like most and whom they like least. I've got a couple of kids who are soundly disliked and real troublemakers, and I'm doing my best to keep the lid on the situation. There's also an immigrant West Indian child who's new to my classroom, and right now she's being ostracized because of the way she dresses and speaks. If you come in and start sensitizing my class to whom they like and dislike, the children are going to share these opinions. Unfortunately, I think your study is likely to promote conflict and negative interaction in my classroom!"

Imagine the jolt Ron must have felt to hear someone suggest that the research he had been so carefully planning might have to be abandoned. Anyone who has undertaken the time-consuming process of preparing for such a study could commiserate with Ron's dismay. This chapter takes a close look at the research process—the many challenges investigators face as they plan and implement studies of children. Ron had already traveled a long and arduous path before he arrived at the door of the laboratory school, prepared to collect his data. First, he spent many weeks developing a researchable idea, based on theory and prior knowledge about children's peer relations. Next, he had to decide on an appropriate research strategy, which involves two main tasks. First, he had to choose from a wide variety of *research methods*, the specific activities of participants, such as taking tests, answering questionnaires, responding to interviews, or being observed. Second, he had to select a *research design*, an overall plan for his study that would permit the best possible test of his research idea. Finally, Ron scrutinized his procedures for any possible harm they might cause to the participants involved.

Still, as Ron approached a committee charged with protecting the welfare of young research participants, he faced an ethical dilemma. Research, whether on animals or humans, must meet certain standards that protect participants from stressful treatment. Because of children's immaturity and vulnerability, extra precautions must be taken to ensure that their rights are not violated in the course of a research study. In the final section of this chapter, we will see how Ron resolved the committee's earnest challenge to the ethical integrity of his research.

From Theory to Hypothesis

n Chapter 1, we saw how theories structure the research process by identifying important research concerns and, occasionally, preferred methods for collecting data. We also discussed how theories guide the application of findings to real-life circumstances and practices with children. In fact, research usually begins with a prediction about behavior drawn directly from a theory, or what we call a **hypothesis.** Think back to the various child development theories presented in Chapter 1. Many hypotheses can be drawn from any one of them that, once tested, would reflect on accuracy of the theory.

Sometimes research pits a hypothesis taken from one theory against a hypothesis taken from another. For example, a theorist emphasizing the role of maturation in development would predict that adult encouragement will have little effect on the age at which children utter their first words, learn to count, or tie their shoes. A sociocultural theorist, in contrast, would speculate that these skills can be promoted through adult teaching.

At other times, research tests predictions drawn from a single theory. For example, ecological systems theory suggests that providing isolated divorced mothers with social supports will lead them to be more patient with their children. An ethologist might hypothesize that an infant's cry will stimulate strong physiological arousal in adults who hear it, motivating them to soothe and protect a suffering baby.

Occasionally, little or no theory exists on a topic of interest. In these instances, rather than making a specific prediction, the investigator may start with a *research question,* such as, Are children reaching puberty earlier and growing taller than they did a generation ago? Once formulated, hypotheses and research questions offer investigators vital guidance as they settle on research methods and a research design.

At this point, you may be wondering, Why learn about research strategies? Why not leave these matters to research specialists and concentrate on what is already known about the child and how this knowledge can be applied? There are two reasons. First, each of us must be wise and critical consumers of knowledge, not naive sponges who soak up facts about children. Knowing the strengths and weaknesses of various research strategies becomes important in separating dependable information from misleading results. Second, individuals who work directly with children are sometimes in a position to test hypotheses or research questions, either on their own or with an experienced investigator. At other times, they may have to provide information on how well their goals for children are being realized to justify continued financial support for their programs and activities. Under these circumstances, an understanding of the research process becomes essential practical knowledge.

Common Methods Used to Study Children

ow does a researcher choose a basic approach to gathering information about children? Common methods in the field of child development include systematic observation, self-reports, psychophysiological measures, and clinical or case studies of a single child. In addition, researchers interested in culture and development may draw on the observational and self-report approaches just mentioned. At other times, they may construct ethnographies, which capture the life circumstances of a particular group of children. As you read about these methods, you may find it helpful to refer to Table 2.1, which summarizes the strengths and limitations of each.

SYSTEMATIC OBSERVATION

hypothesis A prediction about behavior drawn from a theory.

To find out how children actually behave, a researcher may choose *systematic observation.* Observations of the behavior of children, and of the adults who are important

TABLE 2.1

Strengths and Limitations of Common Research Methods

Method	Description	Strengths	Limitations
Systematic Observation			
Naturalistic observation	Observation of behavior in natural contexts	Observations reflect participants' everyday lives.	Conditions under which participants are observed cannot be controlled; observer influence and bias can reduce accuracy of observations.
Structured observation	Observation of behavior in a laboratory	Conditions of observation are the same for all children. Investigators can study behaviors rarely seen in everyday life.	Observations may not be typical of the way participants behave in everyday life; observer influence and observer bias can reduce accuracy of observations.
Self-Reports			
Clinical interview	Flexible interviewing procedure in which the investigator obtains a complete account of the participant's thoughts	Comes as close as possible to the way participants think in everyday life; great breadth and depth of information can be obtained in a short time.	Participants may not report information accurately; flexible procedure makes comparing individuals' responses difficult.
Structured interviews, tests, and questionnaires	Self-report instruments in which each participant is asked the same question in the same way	Standardized method of asking questions permits comparisons of participants' responses and efficient data collection and scoring.	Do not yield the same depth of information as a clinical interview; responses are still subject to inaccurate reporting.
Psychophysiological Methods	Methods that measure the relationship between physiological processes and behavior	Reveals which central nervous system structures contribute to development and individual differences in certain competencies. Helps identify the perceptions, thoughts, and emotions of infants and young children, who cannot report them clearly.	Cannot reveal with certainty how an individual processes stimuli. Many factors besides those of interest to the researcher can influence a physiological response.
Clinical Method (Case Study)	A full picture of a single individual's psychological functioning, obtained by combining interviews, observations, test scores, and sometimes psychological assessments	Provides rich, descriptive insights into processes of development.	May be biased by researcher's theoretical preferences; findings cannot be applied to individuals other than the participant.
Ethnography	Understanding a culture or distinct social group through participant observation; by making extensive field notes, the researcher tries to capture the culture's unique values and social processes	Provides a more complete and accurate description than can be derived from a single observational visit, interview, or questionnaire.	May be biased by researcher's cultural values and theoretical preferences; findings cannot be applied to individuals and settings other than the ones studied.

in their lives, can be made in different ways. One approach is to go into the field, or the natural environment, and record the behavior of interest, a method called **naturalistic observation.**

A study of preschoolers' responses to their peers' distress provides a good example of this technique (Farver & Branstetter, 1994). Observing 3- and 4-year-olds in child-care centers, the researchers recorded each instance of crying and the reactions of nearby children—whether they ignored, watched curiously, commented on the child's unhappiness, scolded or teased, or shared, helped, or expressed sympathy. Caregiver behaviors, such as explaining why a child was crying, mediating conflict, or offering comfort, were noted to see if adult sensitivity was related to children's caring responses. A strong relationship

naturalistic observation A method in which the researcher goes into the natural environment to observe the behavior of interest.

In naturalistic observation, the researcher goes into the field and records the behavior of interest. This researcher might be recording children's attention, activity preferences, or reactions to peers' emotional expressions or social contacts. Although she can see directly the everyday behaviors of interest, not all children have the same opportunity to display a particular behavior in everyday life.

(Michael Newman/Photo Edit)

structured observation A method in which the researcher sets up a situation that evokes the behavior of interest and observes it in a laboratory.

specimen record An observational procedure in which the researcher records a description of the participant's entire stream of behavior for a specified time period.

event sampling An observational procedure in which the researcher records all instances of a particular behavior during a specified time period.

time sampling An observational procedure in which the researcher records whether or not certain behaviors occur during a sample of short time intervals.

emerged. The great strength of naturalistic observation in studies like this one is that investigators can see directly the everyday behaviors they hope to explain (Miller, 1998).

Naturalistic observation also has a major limitation: Not all children have the same opportunity to display a particular behavior in everyday life. In the study just mentioned, some children might have witnessed a child crying more often than had others or been exposed to more cues for positive social responses from caregivers. For this reason, they might have displayed more compassion.

Researchers commonly deal with this difficulty by making **structured observations** in a laboratory. In this approach, the investigator sets up a situation that evokes the behavior of interest so that every participant has an equal opportunity to display the response. In one study, children's comforting behavior was observed by playing a tape recording of a baby crying in the next room. Using an intercom, children could either talk to the baby or flip a button so they did not have to listen. Children's facial reactions, the length of time they talked, and the extent to which they spoke in a comforting manner were recorded (Eisenberg et al., 1993).

Structured observation permits greater control over the research situation than does naturalistic observation. In addition, the method is especially useful for studying behaviors that investigators rarely have an opportunity to see in everyday life. For example, in a recent study, researchers wanted to find out how the presence of distracting toys influences children's attention to and learning from educational television (Landau, Lorch, & Milich, 1992). They were particularly interested in inattentive, hyperactive boys, who have great difficulty concentrating. Television viewing, under these conditions, is hard to measure in children's homes. So the researchers furnished a laboratory like a living room, where they could control both TV programming and the presence of distracters. As expected, when toys were available, hyperactive 6- to 12-year-olds found them irresistible; they spent only half as much time watching the TV as did their nonhyperactive counterparts (see Figure 2.1). Yet surprisingly, recall of televised information in the presence of toys was similar for hyperactive and nonhyperactive boys. The inattentive, overactive participants appeared to learn effectively from TV, even when their attention was frequently diverted. These findings suggest that television may be an especially effective medium of instruction for hyperactive children, who typically do poorly in school. Of course, the great disadvantage of structured observations in studies like this one is that children may not behave in the laboratory as they do in their natural environments.

■ **PROCEDURES FOR COLLECTING SYSTEMATIC OBSERVATIONS.** The procedures used to collect systematic observations vary, depending on the research problem posed. Some investigators choose the **specimen record,** a description of the entire stream of behavior—everything said and done over a certain time period. In one of my own studies, I wanted to find out how sensitive, responsive, and verbally stimulating caregivers were when they interacted with children in child-care centers (Berk, 1985). In this case, everything each caregiver said and did—even the amount of time she spent away from the children, taking coffee breaks and talking on the phone—was important.

In other studies, information on only one or a few kinds of behavior is needed, so it is not necessary to capture the entire behavior stream. In these instances, researchers may select more efficient observation procedures. One common approach is **event sampling,** in which the observer records all instances of a behavior of interest during a specified time period, ignoring other behaviors. In the study of preschoolers' responses to their peers' distress reported earlier, the researchers used event sampling by recording each instance in which a child cried at day care.

Another way to observe efficiently is **time sampling.** In this procedure, the researcher records whether or not certain behaviors occur during a sample of short time intervals. First, a checklist of the behaviors of interest is prepared. Then the observation period is divided into a series of brief time segments. For example, a half-hour observation period might be divided into 120 fifteen-second intervals. The observer collects data by alternately watching the child for an interval and then checking off behaviors during the next interval, repeating this process until the entire observation period is complete. Recently, one of my students and I used time sampling to find out whether two preschools differed in the opportunities they offered for make-believe play. Our team of observers checked

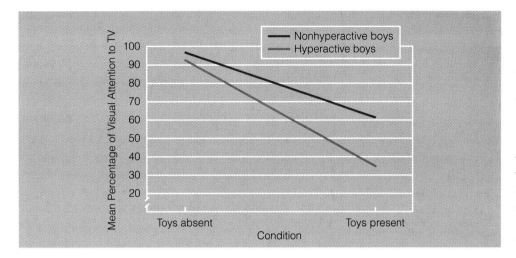

FIGURE 2.1

Results of a study that used structured observations. The researchers wanted to know how the presence of distracting toys influenced hyperactive and non-hyperactive boys' attention to and learning from educational television. When toys were absent, attention to TV by both groups was high. When toys were present, hyperactive boys spent only half as much time attending to TV as did their nonhyperactive counterparts.

(From S. Landau, E. P. Lorch, & R. Milich, 1992, Visual attention to and comprehension of television in attention-deficit hyperactivity disordered and normal boys, *Child Development, 63,* p. 933. © The Society for Research in Child Development, Inc. Reprinted by permission.)

off the type of play each child displayed during 80 thirty-second intervals distributed over 4 days, to yield a representative picture of children's play activities (Krafft & Berk, 1998).

■ **LIMITATIONS OF SYSTEMATIC OBSERVATION.** A major problem in collecting systematic observations is the influence of the observer on the behavior being studied. The presence of a watchful, unfamiliar individual may cause children and adults to react in unnatural ways. For children under age 7 or 8, **observer influence** is generally limited to the first session or two that the unknown adult is present in the setting. Young children cannot stop "being themselves" for very long, and they quickly get used to the observer's presence. Older children and adults often engage in more positive, socially desirable behavior when they know that they are being observed. In these instances, researchers can take their responses as an indication of the best behavior they can display under the circumstances.

There are ways that researchers can minimize observer influence. Adaptation periods, in which observers visit the research setting so participants have a chance to get used to their presence, are helpful. Another approach is to ask individuals who are part of the child's natural environment to do the observing. For example, in several studies, parents have been trained to record their children's behavior. Besides reducing the impact of an unfamiliar observer, this method permits information to be gathered on behaviors that would require observers to remain in the natural setting for a very long time to see them. In one such study, researchers wanted to know what kinds of TV programs children watch with their parents and which ones they watch alone. To find out, they asked parents to keep detailed diaries of the viewing behaviors of all family members for several 1-week periods (St. Peters et al., 1991).

In addition to observer influence, **observer bias** is a serious danger in observational research. When observers are aware of the purposes of a study, they may see and record what is expected rather than participants' actual behaviors. To guard against this problem, it is wise to have people who have no knowledge of the investigator's hypotheses—or who at least have little personal investment in them—collect the observations.

Finally, although systematic observation provides invaluable information on how children and adults actually behave, it generally tells us little about the thinking and reasoning that underlie their behavior. For this kind of information, researchers must turn to another type of method—self-report techniques.

SELF-REPORTS: INTERVIEWS AND QUESTIONNAIRES

Self-reports are instruments that ask research participants to provide information on their perceptions, thoughts, abilities, feelings, attitudes, beliefs, and past experiences. They range from relatively unstructured clinical interviews, the method used by Piaget to study children's thinking, to highly structured interviews, questionnaires, and tests.

■ **CLINICAL INTERVIEWS.** Let's look at an example of a **clinical interview** in which Piaget questioned a 5-year-old child about his understanding of dreams:

observer influence The tendency of participants to react to the presence of an observer and behave in unnatural ways.

observer bias The tendency of observers who are aware of the purposes of a study to see and record what is expected rather than participants' actual behaviors.

clinical interview A method in which the researcher uses flexible, open-ended questions to probe for the participant's point of view.

Where does the dream come from?—I think you sleep so well that you dream.—*Does it come from us or from outside?*—From outside.—*What do we dream with?*—I don't know.—*With the hands? . . . With nothing?*—Yes, with nothing.—*When you are in bed and you dream, where is the dream?*—In my bed, under the blanket. I don't really know. If it was in my stomach, the bones would be in the way and I shouldn't see it.—*Is the dream there when you sleep?*—Yes it is in the bed beside me . . . —*You see the dream when you are in the room, but if I were in the room, too, should I see it?*—No, grownups don't ever dream.—*Can two people ever have the same dream?*—No, never.—*When the dream is in the room, is it near you?*—Yes, there! (pointing to 30 cm in front of his eyes). (Piaget, 1926/1930, pp. 97–98)

Using the clinical interview, this researcher asks a mother to describe her child's development. The method permits large amounts of information to be gathered in a relatively short period of time. However, a major drawback of this method is that participants do not always report information accurately.

(Tony Freeman/Photo Edit)

Notice how Piaget used a flexible, conversational style to encourage the child to expand his ideas. Although a researcher interviewing more than one child would typically ask the same first question to ensure a common task, individualized prompts are used to obtain a fuller picture of each child's reasoning (Ginsburg, 1997).

The clinical interview has two major strengths. First, it permits people to display their thoughts in terms that are as close as possible to the way they think in everyday life. Second, the clinical interview can provide a large amount of information in a fairly brief period of time. For example, in an hour-long session, we can obtain a wide range of child-rearing information from a parent—much more than we could capture by observing parent–child interaction for the same amount of time.

■ **LIMITATIONS OF CLINICAL INTERVIEWS.** A major limitation of the clinical interview has to do with the accuracy with which people report their thoughts, feelings, and experiences. Some participants, wanting to please the interviewer, may make up answers that do not represent their actual thinking. And because the clinical interview depends on verbal ability and expressiveness, it may not accurately assess individuals who have difficulty putting their thoughts into words. Skillful interviewers minimize these problems by wording questions carefully. They also watch for cues indicating that the participant may not have clearly understood a question or may need extra time to feel comfortable in the situation.

Interviews on certain topics are particularly vulnerable to distortion. In a few instances, researchers have been able to compare parents' and children's descriptions of events with information gathered years earlier, at the same time the events occurred. Reports of psychological states and family processes obtained on the two occasions showed little or no agreement (Henry et al., 1994). Parents often recall their child's development in glowing terms, reporting faster progress, fewer childhood problems, and child-rearing practices more in line with current expert advice than with records of behavior (Yarrow, Campbell, & Burton, 1970). Interviews that focus on current rather than past information and on specific characteristics rather than global judgments show a better match with observations and other sources of information. Even so, parents are far from perfect in describing their practices and their children's personalities, preferences, and cognitive abilities (Kochanska, Kuczynski, & Radke-Yarrow, 1989; Miller & Davis, 1992).

Finally, we mentioned in Chapter 1 that the clinical interview has been criticized because of its flexibility. When questions are phrased differently for each participant, responses may be due to the manner of interviewing rather than real differences in the way people think about a certain topic. A second self-report method, the structured interview, reduces this problem.

■ **STRUCTURED INTERVIEWS, TESTS, AND QUESTIONNAIRES.** In a **structured interview,** each individual is asked the same set of questions in the same way. As a result, this approach eliminates the possibility that an interviewer might press and prompt some participants more than others, thereby distorting the results. In addition, compared with clinical interviews, structured interviews are much more efficient. Answers are briefer, and

structured interview A method in which the researcher asks each participant the same questions in the same way.

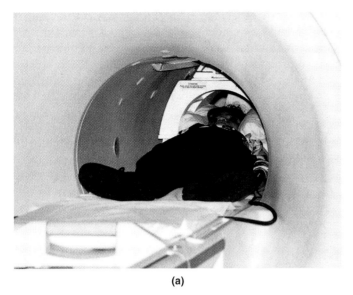

(a)

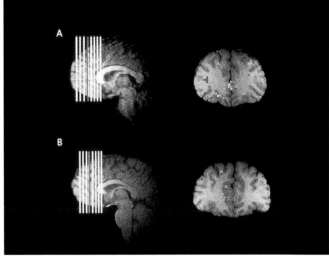

(b)

researchers can obtain written responses from an entire class of children or group of parents at the same time. Also, when structured interviews use multiple choice, yes/no, and true/false formats, as is done on many tests and questionnaires, the answers can be tabulated by machine. However, keep in mind that these procedures do not yield the same depth of information as a clinical interview. And they can still be affected by the problem of inaccurate reporting.

PSYCHOPHYSIOLOGICAL METHODS

Researchers' desire to uncover the biological bases of children's perceptual, cognitive, and emotional responses has led to the use of **psychophysiological methods,** which measure the relationship between physiological processes and behavior. Investigators who rely on these methods want to find out which central nervous system structures contribute to development and individual differences. Another benefit of psychophysiological methods is that they help identify the perceptions, thoughts, and emotions of infants and young children, who cannot report their psychological experiences clearly.

■ **PSYCHOPHYSIOLOGICAL PROCEDURES.** Involuntary activities of the autonomic nervous system[1]—changes in heart rate, blood pressure, respiration, pupil dilation, and electrical conductance of the skin—are among the most commonly used physiological measures because of their sensitivity to psychological state. For example, heart rate can be used to infer whether an infant is staring blankly at a stimulus (heart rate is stable), attending to and processing information (heart rate slows during concentration), or experiencing distress (heart rate rises) (Izard et al., 1991; Porges, 1991). Heart rate variations are also linked to particular emotional expressions, such as interest, anger, and sadness (Fox & Fitzgerald, 1990). And as Chapter 10 will reveal, distinct patterns of autonomic activity are related to aspects of temperament, such as shyness and sociability (Kagan, 1992, 1998).

Autonomic indicators of cognitive and emotional reactions have been enriched by measures of brain functioning. In an *electroencephalogram (EEG)*, researchers tape electrodes to the scalp to record the electrical activity of the brain. EEG waves are linked to different states of arousal, from deep sleep to alert wakefulness, permitting researchers to see how these states change with age. EEG patterns also vary with infants' and children's emotional states—whether they are upbeat and happy or sad and distressed (Jones et al.,

In functional magnetic resonance imaging (fMRI), the child looks up at a stimulus, and changes in blood flow within brain tissue are detected magnetically (a). The result is a computerized image of activated areas (b), permitting study of age-related changes in brain organization and the brain functioning of children with serious learning and emotional problems.
(B. J. Casey/UPMC)

psychophysiological methods
Methods that measure the relationship between physiological processes and behavior. Among the most common are measures of autonomic nervous system activity (such as heart rate and respiration) and measures of brain functioning (such as the electroencephalogram [EEG], event-related potentials [ERPs], and functional magnetic resonance imaging [fMRI]).

[1]The autonomic nervous system regulates involuntary actions of the body. It is divided into two parts: the *sympathetic nervous system,* which mobilizes energy to deal with threatening situations (as when your heart rate rises in response to a fear-arousing event); and the *parasympathetic nervous system,* which acts to conserve energy (as when your heart rate slows as you focus on an interesting stimulus).

1997). At times, investigators study *event-related potentials (ERPs)*, or EEG waves that accompany particular events. For example, a unique wave pattern appears when infants over 4 months of age are re-exposed to a stimulus they saw earlier. This reaction seems to reflect babies' active efforts to search their memories (Nelson, 1993).

Functional brain-imaging techniques, which yield three-dimensional pictures of brain activity, provide the most precise information on which brain regions are specialized for certain functions, such as language or emotion. *Functional magnetic resonance imaging (fMRI)* is the most promising of these methods, since it does not depend on X-ray photography, which requires injection of radioactive substances. Instead, when a child is shown a stimulus, changes in blood flow within the brain are detected magnetically, producing a computerized image of active areas. Currently, fMRI is being used to study age-related changes in brain organization and the brain functioning of children with serious learning and emotional problems (Giedd et al., 1996; Lyoo et al., 1996; Schifter et al., 1994).

■ **LIMITATIONS OF PSYCHOPHYSIOLOGICAL METHODS.** Despite their virtues, psychophysiological methods have limitations. First, interpreting physiological responses involves a high degree of inference. Even though a stimulus produces a consistent pattern of autonomic or brain activity, investigators cannot be certain that an infant or child has consciously processed it in a particular way.

Second, many factors besides those of interest can influence a physiological response. A researcher who takes a change in heart rate, respiration, or brain activity as an indicator of information processing must make sure that it was not due to hunger, boredom, or fatigue. In addition, the child's fearful reaction to the laboratory equipment can affect the validity of physiological measures. fMRI, for example, requires confinement to a small space and operation of noisy equipment. Preparing children by taking them through a simulated fMRI procedure prior to actual fMRI scanning greatly reduces their fear (Rosenberg et al., 1997; Tyc et al., 1995). Without such efforts to minimize extraneous influences, detection of correspondences between physiological and psychological reactions is difficult or impossible.

THE CLINICAL, OR CASE STUDY, METHOD

In Chapter 1, we discussed the **clinical method** (sometimes called the **case study** approach) as an outgrowth of the psychoanalytic perspective, which stresses the importance of understanding the individual. Recall that the clinical method brings together a wide range of information on a single child, including interviews, observations, and test scores. Today, psychophysiological measures are sometimes included as well (Haynes, 1991). The aim is to obtain as complete a picture as possible of a child's psychological functioning and the experiences that led up to it.

Although clinical studies are usually carried out on children with developmental problems, they sometimes focus on exceptional, well-adjusted youngsters. For example, the method has been used to find out what contributes to the accomplishments of *prodigies*—extremely gifted children who attain the competence of an adult in a particular field before age 10. Consider Adam, a boy who read, wrote, and composed musical pieces before he was out of diapers. By age 4, Adam was deeply involved in mastering human symbol systems—BASIC for the computer, French, German, Russian, Sanskrit, Greek, ancient hieroglyphs, music, and mathematics. Adam's parents provided a home exceedingly rich in stimulation and raised him with affection, firmness, and humor. They searched for schools in which he could develop his talents while forming rewarding social relationships (Feldman & Goldsmith, 1991).

Because prodigious children are few in number and vary widely in their special abilities, it is risky to study all of them in the same way. Consequently, the clinical method is well suited to investigating such children. To explore the possibility of common themes in development, researchers can examine other similar cases as they accumulate (Gardner, 1998b). For example, could Adam have realized his abilities without parents who sensitively nurtured his talents? For some reflections on this question, refer to the Variations box on the following page.

clinical, or case study, method
A method in which the researcher attempts to understand the unique individual child by combining interview data, observations, test scores, and sometimes psychophysiological assessments.

Case Studies of Prodigies

WHAT FACTORS IN the backgrounds of prodigies distinguish them from other children and enable them to realize their extraordinary abilities? Case studies of prodigious children shed light on this question. Together, they suggest that a unique biological disposition to excel in a particular field combines with intense motivation and highly supportive early child rearing to permit full expression of the child's special capacity.

Adam, the linguistically gifted child described on page 50, was more than unusually curious. He made "omnivorous intellectual demands" on his parents (Feldman & Goldsmith, 1991, p. 101). Like other prodigies, Adam figured out a great deal about his domain of interest independently. But as soon as his parents recognized his gift, it became their highest priority. They were available to him nearly all the time, exposing him to rich, varied stimulation; discussing abstract concepts with him; posing interesting questions; and encouraging him to play with ideas. For example, on a walk in the woods, 3-year-old Adam stopped to investigate some decomposing plants. His father engaged him in speculation about how long the matter had been decaying, what chemical reactions were taking place, and how long the entire process would take. By age 8, as Adam's interests centered on music, he composed a symphony. Immediately, his parents sought teachers who could advance his already astounding level of musical accomplishment. And without being rigid or domineering, they communicated to Adam their expectation that he work hard and strive to do his very best.

Adam's story resembles that of Yani, a Chinese child whose paintings at age 3 were remarkable. Driven to paint, she produced more than 4,000 pictures in 3 years, fully mastering the impressionistic style of Chinese brush painting (Goldsmith & Feldman, 1989). Yani's father, an artist, spent much time encouraging (and possibly teaching) her. Like Adam's parents, he arranged his life around her needs. He shielded Yani from traditional Chinese drawing instruction, which is based on copying, because he believed it would dampen her imagination. Instead, she spent many hours a day in her father's art studio, painting alongside him. Eventually, Yani's father gave up painting so that his own style would not constrain his daughter's creativity.

Adam and Yani's childhoods parallel the early experiences of well-known prodigies—for example, Midori, who by age 11 ranked as a world-class violinist; Tara Lipinski, who won the figure-skating Olympic gold medal at age 16; and Michael Kearney, who performed astounding feats in mathematics by age 3 and graduated from college at age 10. All of them were blessed with phenomenal biological endowment; a burning desire to achieve; parents willing to devote all their energies to their child's pursuits; a loving, harmonious family life; outstanding teachers; and a culture that values their field of expertise.

As these and other cases suggest, prodigious children seem to be characterized by "a coincidence of factors, all of which converge to yield a level of performance that sometimes seems to border on the unbelievable" (Gardner, 1998b, p. 446). Although each child's development may begin as a

Tara Lipinski won the figure-skating Olympic gold medal at age 16. Her childhood parallels that of other well-known prodigies—a combination of phenomenal biological endowment; a burning desire to achieve; a mother willing to devote all her energies to Tara's development; a loving, harmonious family life; outstanding teachers; and a culture that values Tara's expertise.

(David Kelley/Archive Photos)

sped-up version of the norm, precocious capacity appears to join with other personal and environmental factors to yield a unique, highly beneficial configuration (Gardner, 1997).

Can prodigious development occur when any of the ingredients just mentioned is missing? Several case studies suggest that the quality of early child rearing is vital. When parents are overly demanding and care only about the child's gifts rather than about the child herself, prodigious children can end up disengaged, depressed, and resentful. At the same time, parental directiveness seems to vary with the child's area of talent. Parental management of the child's learning is greatest in performance domains, such as music and athletics; somewhat less in academic fields, such as linguistics and mathematics; and even less in the visual arts (Winner, 1996). Still, more research, using a variety of methods, is needed to confirm the conditions necessary for prodigies in diverse fields to realize their potential.

This Western ethnographer is spending months living in the village of Phudu-huru on the edge of the Kalahari Desert in Botswana, Africa, getting to know members of the !Kung Bakwa clan. The researcher's goal is to uncover the cultural meanings of children and adults' behaviors by becoming as familiar as possible with their way of life. Here, she asks about various native crafts and their uses.

(Jason Laure)

ethnography A method by which the researcher attempts to understand the unique values and social processes of a culture or a distinct social group by living with its members and taking field notes for a period of months or years.

The clinical method yields case narratives that are rich in descriptive detail and that offer valuable insights into the multiplicity of factors that affect development. Nevertheless, like all other methods, it has drawbacks. Information is often collected unsystematically and subjectively, permitting too much leeway for researchers' theoretical preferences to bias their observations and interpretations. In addition, investigators cannot assume that clinical findings apply to anyone other than the particular child studied. Even when patterns emerge across several cases, it is wise to try to confirm them with other research strategies.

METHODS FOR STUDYING CULTURE

A growing interest in the impact of culture (see Chapter 1, page 26) has led researchers to adjust the methods we have just considered as well as tap procedures specially devised for cross-cultural and multicultural research. Which approach investigators choose depends on their research goals (Triandis, 1995, 1998).

Sometimes researchers are interested in characteristics believed to be universal but that vary in degree from one society to the next. These investigators might ask, How strong are gender stereotypes in different nations? Do parents make greater maturity demands of children in some cultures than in others? How much, and in what ways, do adults in diverse cultures talk to babies? In each instance, several cultural groups will be compared, and all participants must be questioned or observed with equivalent measures. Therefore, researchers draw on the self-report and observational procedures we have already considered, adapting them through translation so they can be understood in each cultural context. For example, to study cultural variation in parenting attitudes, the same questionnaire, asking for ratings on such items as "If my child gets into trouble, I expect him or her to handle the problem mostly by himself or herself," is given to all participants (Chen et al., 1998).

At other times, researchers are far less certain that they can draw on their own cultural perspective to interpret another culture's practices. They want to uncover the *cultural meanings* of children's and adults' behaviors by becoming as familiar as possible with their way of life (Shweder et al., 1998). To achieve this goal, researchers rely on a method borrowed from the field of anthropology—**ethnography.** Like the clinical method, ethnographic research is largely a descriptive, qualitative technique. But instead of aiming to understand a single individual, it is directed at understanding a culture or a distinct social group (Jessor, 1996; Shweder, 1996).

The ethnographic method achieves its goals through *participant observation.* Typically, the researcher lives with the cultural community for a period of months or years, participating in all aspects of its daily life. Extensive field notes, which consist of a mix of observations and self-reports from members of the culture and careful interpretations by the investigator, are gathered. Later, these notes are put together into a description of the community that tries to capture its unique values and social processes.

The ethnographic approach assumes that by entering into close contact with a social group, researchers can understand the beliefs and behavior of its members more accurately, in a way not possible with an observational visit, interview, or questionnaire. Ethnographies of children from diverse cultures currently exist, and many more are being compiled. In some, investigators focus on many aspects of children's experience, as one team of researchers did in describing what it is like to grow up in a small American town (Peshkin, 1978). In other instances, the research is limited to one or a few settings, such as home, school, or neighborhood life (LeVine et al., 1994; Peshkin, 1997; Valdés, 1998). Because the ethnographic method is committed to trying to understand others' viewpoints, it often overturns widely held stereotypes, as the Cultural Influences box on the following page reveals.

Researchers interested in cultural comparisons may supplement traditional self-report and observational methods with ethnography if they suspect that unique meanings underlie cultural variations (Triandis, 1998; Weisner, 1996). For example, recent evidence indicates that Chinese parents are more strict and demanding of their children than are Caucasian-American parents. As we will see in Chapter 14, an ethnographic look reveals that parental control in Chinese families does not carry the negative, authoritarian

School Matters in Mexican-American Homes: An Ethnographic Study

FOR MANY YEARS, the poor school achievement of low-income minority children was attributed to "cultural deficits"—home environments that place little value on education. An ethnographic study of Mexican-American families challenges this assumption. Concha Delgado-Gaitan (1992, 1994) spent many months getting to know the residents of a Mexican-American community in a small California city. There she collected extensive field notes on six families in which parents had recently immigrated to the United States. Each had a second-grade child. While in the homes, Delgado-Gaitan carefully examined children's experiences related to education.

HOME ENVIRONMENTS. Although the Mexican-American parents had little schooling themselves, they regarded education as a great privilege and supported their children's learning in many ways. Their homes were cramped, one-bedroom apartments, occasionally shared with relatives. Still, parents did their best to create a stable environment that encouraged children to think positively about school. They offered material rewards for good grades (such as a new book or dinner at a favorite restaurant), set regular bedtime hours, and, where possible, provided a special place for doing schoolwork. And they frequently spoke to their children about their own educational limitations and the importance of taking advantage of the opportunity to study.

SOCIAL SUPPORT. During the week, many parent–child conversations revolved around homework. All parents did their best to help with assignments and foster behaviors valued in school. But how well they succeeded depended on social networks through which they could obtain information about educational matters. Some parents relied on relatives who had more experience in dealing with the school system. Others sought out individuals at church or at work as advisers.

When social support was available, perplexing school problems were quickly resolved. For example, one parent, Mrs. Matias, received repeated reports from her son Jorge's teacher about his unruly behavior. Finally, a note arrived threatening suspension if Jorge did not improve. Mrs. Matias consulted one of her co-workers, who suggested that she ask for permission to leave during the lunch hour to talk with Jorge's teacher. After a conference revealed that Jorge needed to stay away from certain boys who were provoking him, his fighting subsided.

LINKS BETWEEN HOME AND SCHOOL. Despite sincere efforts, lack of familiarity with school tasks hampered Mexican-American parents' ability to help their children. Mrs. Serna insisted that her poorly achieving daughter Norma do her homework at regularly scheduled times, and she checked to make sure that Norma completed her assignments. But when she tried to assist Norma, Mrs. Serna frequently misinterpreted the instructions. And she did not understand the school environment well enough to contact teachers for information about how to support her child. As a result, Norma's progress remained below average.

Discontinuity between Mexican cultural values and the requirements of the school was often at the heart of chil-

This Mexican-American mother tries to support her daughter's academic development by helping with homework and providing a quiet place to study. Ethnographic research reveals that the success of the mother's efforts depends on access to resources and information from the school.

(Myrleen Ferguson Cate/PhotoEdit)

dren's academic difficulties. At home, respect for elders was emphasized. Mexican-American children learned not to express verbal opinions (especially contrary opinions) to adults. Instead, they listened and followed directions. Yet in their classrooms, they were expected to ask questions and engage in verbal argument—behaviors in conflict with their parents' teachings (Delgado-Gaitan, 1994).

Although the Mexican-American families had limited income and material resources, these deficits did not detract from their desire to create a home environment conducive to learning. As they became increasingly aware of cultural differences between home and school, the parents formed a community organization whose major purpose was sharing knowledge about how to help their children succeed in the classroom. For example, parents began to accept their children's questions as necessary for academic progress. Gradually, the organization became a source of empowerment, opening lines of communication with teachers.

Delgado-Gaitan's ethnographic research shows that education of ethnic minority children can be promoted through informal social ties and community organizing. In this Mexican-American community, parents joined together as catalysts for cultural change, establishing vital links between home and school.

meaning attached to it in the United States. Instead, it signifies deep concern and caring for the child (Chao, 1994).

Ethnographers strive to minimize their influence on the culture being studied by becoming part of it. Nevertheless, at times their presence does alter the situation. And as with clinical research, investigators' cultural values and theoretical commitments sometimes lead them to observe selectively or misinterpret what they see. In addition, the findings of ethnographic studies cannot be assumed to generalize beyond the people and settings in which the research was originally conducted (Hammersley, 1992).

ASK YOURSELF . . .

◆ A researcher wants to study the thoughts and feelings of children who have experienced their parents' divorce. Which method is best suited to investigating this question? Explain.

◆ A researcher is interested in how Pueblo Indian adolescents experience daily life in a New Mexico high school where the large majority of students are Caucasian Americans. Which method should he use, and why?

◆ CONNECTIONS
Recall from Chapter 1 (page 5) that domains of development—physical, cognitive, emotional, and social—are not really distinct; they combine to form the living, growing child. Of the methods discussed in the preceding sections, which ones are best suited to uncovering the interconnections between domains?

BRIEF REVIEW

Researchers use naturalistic observation to gather information on children's everyday behaviors. When it is necessary to control the conditions of observation, researchers often make structured observations in a laboratory. The flexible, conversational style of the clinical interview provides a wealth of information on the reasoning behind behavior. However, participants may not report their thoughts accurately, and comparing their responses is difficult. The structured interview is a more efficient method that questions each person in the same way, but it does not yield the same depth of information as a clinical interview. Psychophysiological methods are used to uncover the biological bases of children's behavior. However, they require a high degree of inference about the meaning of physiological responses. Clinical studies of individual children provide rich insights into processes of development, but the information obtained is often unsystematic and subjective.

Methods for studying culture depend on the purpose of the investigation. When researchers want to compare cultures on characteristics assumed to be universal but that vary in degree, they use traditional observational and self-report procedures. Ethnographic research is appropriate when researchers cannot rely on their own perspective to grasp the meanings of another culture's practices. Like clinical studies, ethnographies can be affected by researchers' theoretical biases, and the findings may not generalize beyond the people studied.

Reliability and Validity:
Keys to Scientifically Sound Research

Once investigators choose their research methods, they must take special steps to ensure that their procedures provide trustworthy information about the topic of interest. To be acceptable to the scientific community, self-reports, observations, and physiological measures must be both *reliable* and *valid*—two keys to scientifically sound research.

RELIABILITY

reliability The consistency, or repeatability, of measures of behavior.

validity The extent to which methods in a research study accurately measure what the investigator set out to measure.

correlational design A research design in which the investigator gathers information without altering participants' experiences and examines relationships between variables. Does not permit inferences about cause and effect.

Suppose you go into a classroom and record the number of times a child behaves in a helpful and cooperative fashion toward others, but your research partner, in simultaneously observing the same child, comes up with very different judgments. Or you ask a group of children some questions about their interests, but a week later when you question them again, their answers are very different. **Reliability** refers to the consistency, or repeatability, of measures of behavior. To be reliable, observations of peoples' actions cannot be unique to a single observer. Instead, observers must agree on what they see. And an interview, test, or questionnaire, when given again within a short period of time (before participants can reasonably be expected to change their opinions or develop more sophisticated responses) must yield similar results on both occasions.

Researchers determine the reliability of data in different ways. In observational research, observers are asked to record the same behavior sequences, and agreement between them is assessed. Reliability of self-report and psychophysiological data can be demonstrated by finding out how similar children's responses are when the same measures are given on another occasion. In the case of self-reports, researchers can also compare children's answers on different forms of the same test. If necessary, reliability can be estimated from a single testing session by comparing children's answers on different halves of the test.

Because clinical and ethnographic studies do not yield quantitative scores that can be matched with those of another observer or test form, the reliability of these methods must be assessed with other procedures. After examining the qualitative records, one or more judges can see if they agree with the researcher that the patterns and themes identified are grounded in evidence and plausible (Fredericks & Miller, 1997).

VALIDITY

For research methods to have high **validity,** they must accurately measure characteristics that the researcher set out to measure. Think, for a moment, about this idea, and you will see that reliability is absolutely essential for valid research. Methods that are implemented carelessly, unevenly, and inconsistently cannot possibly represent what an investigator originally intended to study.

But reliability by itself is not sufficient to ensure that a method will reflect the investigator's goals. Researchers must go further to guarantee validity, and they generally do so in several ways. They may carefully examine the content of observations and self-reports to make sure the behaviors of interest are included. For example, a test intended to measure fifth-grade children's knowledge of mathematics would not be valid if it contained addition problems but no subtraction, multiplication, or division problems (Miller, 1998). Another approach to validity is to see how effective a method is in predicting behavior in other situations that we would reasonably expect it to predict. If scores on a math test are valid, they should be related to how well children do on their math assignments in school or even to how quickly and accurately they can make change in a game of Monopoly.

As we turn now to research designs, you will discover that the concept of validity can also be applied more broadly, to the overall accuracy of research findings and conclusions. If, during any phase of carrying out a study—selecting participants, choosing research settings and tasks, and implementing procedures—the researcher permits factors unrelated to the hypothesis to influence behavior, then the validity of the results is in doubt, and they cannot be considered a fair test of the investigator's theory.

General Research Designs

n deciding which research design to use, investigators choose a way of setting up a study that permits them to test their hypotheses with the greatest certainty possible. Two main types of designs are used in all research on human behavior: correlational and experimental.

CORRELATIONAL DESIGN

In a **correlational design,** researchers gather information on already existing groups of individuals, generally in natural life circumstances, and no effort is made to alter their experiences in any way. Suppose we want to answer such questions as, Does parents' provision of an organized, predictable schedule and stimulating activities at home make a difference in children's school performance? Does attending a child-care center promote children's friendliness with peers? Do mothers' styles of interacting with their children have any bearing on the children's intelligence? In these and many other instances, the conditions of interest are very difficult to arrange and control.

Is warm, attentive parenting related to children's development? A correlational design can be used to answer this question, but it does not permit researchers to determine the precise cause of their findings.
(Myrleen Ferguson Cate/PhotoEdit)

The correlational design offers a way of looking at relationships between participants' experiences or characteristics and their behavior or development. But correlational studies have one major limitation: We cannot infer cause and effect. For example, if we find in a correlational study that maternal interaction does relate to children's intelligence, we would not know whether mothers' behavior actually *causes* intellectual differences among children. In fact, the opposite is certainly possible. The behaviors of highly intelligent children may be so attractive that they cause mothers to interact more favorably. Or a third variable, such as the amount of noise and distraction in the home, may be causing both maternal interaction and children's intelligence to change together in the same direction.

In correlational studies, and in other types of research designs, investigators often examine relationships among variables by using a **correlation coefficient,** which is a number that describes how two measures, or variables, are associated with one another. Although other statistical approaches to examining relationships are also available, we will encounter the correlation coefficient in discussing research findings throughout this book. So let's look at what it is and how it is interpreted. A correlation coefficient can range in value from +1.00 to –1.00. The *magnitude, or size, of the number* shows the *strength of the relationship.* A zero correlation indicates no relationship; but the closer the value is to +1.00 or –1.00, the stronger the relationship that exists. For instance, a correlation of –.78 is high, –.52 is moderate, and –.18 is low. Note, however, that correlations of +.52 and –.52 are equally strong. The *sign of the number* (+ or –) refers to the *direction of the relationship.* A positive sign (+) means that as one variable increases, the other also increases. A negative sign (–) indicates that as one variable increases, the other decreases.

Let's take some examples to illustrate how a correlation coefficient works. In one study, a researcher found that a measure of maternal language stimulation at 13 months was positively correlated with the size of children's vocabularies at 20 months, at +.50 (Tamis-LeMonda & Bornstein, 1994). This is a moderate correlation, which indicates that the more mothers spoke to their infants, the more advanced their children tended to be in spoken language during the second year of life. In another study, a researcher reported that the extent to which mothers ignored their 10-month-olds' bids for attention was negatively correlated with children's willingness to comply with parental demands 1 year later—at –.46 for boys and –.36 for girls (Martin, 1981). These moderate correlations reveal that the more mothers ignored their babies, the less cooperative their children were during the second year of life.

Both of these investigations found a relationship between maternal behavior in the first year and children's behavior in the second year. Although the researchers suspected that maternal behavior affected children's responses, in neither study could they really be sure about cause and effect. However, finding a relationship in a correlational study suggests that tracking down its cause—with a more powerful experimental strategy, if possible—would be worthwhile.

EXPERIMENTAL DESIGN

Unlike correlational studies, an **experimental design** permits inferences about cause and effect. In an experiment, the events and behaviors of interest are divided into two types: independent and dependent variables. The **independent variable** is the one anticipated by the investigator, on the basis of a hypothesis or research question, to cause changes in another variable. The **dependent variable** is the one the investigator expects to be influenced by the independent variable. Inferences about cause-and-effect relationships are possible because the researcher directly *controls* or *manipulates* changes in the independent variable. This is done by exposing participants to two or more treatment conditions and comparing their performance on measures of the dependent variable.

In one **laboratory experiment,** researchers explored the impact of adults' angry interactions on children's adjustment (El-Sheikh, Cummings, & Reiter, 1996). They hypothesized that the way angry encounters end (independent variable) affects children's emotional reactions (dependent variable). Four- and 5-year-olds were brought one at a time to a laboratory, accompanied by their mothers. One group of children was exposed

correlation coefficient A number, ranging from +1.00 to –1.00, that describes the strength and direction of the relationship between two variables.

experimental design A research design in which the investigator randomly assigns participants to two or more treatment conditions. Permits inferences about cause and effect.

independent variable The variable manipulated by the researcher in an experiment by randomly assigning participants to treatment conditions.

dependent variable The variable the researcher expects to be influenced by the independent variable in an experiment.

laboratory experiment An experiment conducted in the laboratory, permitting the maximum possible control over treatment conditions.

to an unresolved-anger treatment, in which two adult actors entered the room and argued but did not work out their disagreements. The other group witnessed a resolved-anger treatment, in which the adults ended their disputes by apologizing and compromising. As Figure 2.2 shows, during a follow-up adult conflict, more children in the resolved-anger treatment showed a decline in distress behaviors such as anxious facial expressions, freezing in place, and seeking closeness to their mothers. The experiment revealed that anger resolution can reduce the stressful impact of adult conflict on children.

In experimental studies, investigators must take special precautions to control for characteristics of participants that could reduce the accuracy of their findings. For example, in the study just described, if a greater number of children from homes high in parental conflict happened to end up in the unresolved-anger treatment, we could not tell whether the independent variable or children's background characteristics produced the results. **Random assignment** of participants to treatment conditions offers protection against this problem. By using an evenhanded procedure, such as drawing numbers out of a hat or flipping a coin, the experimenter increases the chances that children's characteristics will be equally distributed across treatment groups.

Sometimes researchers combine random assignment with another technique called **matching.** In this procedure, participants are measured ahead of time on the factor in question—in our example, parental conflict. Then children from homes high and low in parental conflict are assigned in equal numbers to each treatment condition. In this way, the experimental groups are deliberately matched, or made equivalent, on characteristics that are likely to distort the results.

MODIFIED EXPERIMENTAL DESIGNS

Most experiments are conducted in laboratories, where researchers can achieve the maximum possible control over treatment conditions. But, as we have already indicated, findings obtained in laboratories may not always apply to everyday situations. The ideal solution to this problem is to do experiments in the field as a complement to laboratory investigations. In **field experiments,** researchers capitalize on rare opportunities to randomly assign people to treatment conditions in natural settings. In the experiment we just considered, we can conclude that the emotional climate established by adults affects children's behavior in the laboratory. But does it also do so in daily life?

Another study helps answer this question (Yarrow, Scott, & Waxler, 1973). This time, the research was carried out in a child-care center. A caregiver deliberately interacted differently with two groups of preschoolers. In one condition (the *nurturant treatment*), she modeled many instances of warmth and helpfulness. In the second condition (the *control*, since it involved no treatment), she behaved as usual, with no special emphasis on concern for others. Two weeks later, the researchers created several situations that called for helpfulness. For example, a visiting mother asked each child to watch her baby for a few moments, but the baby's toys had fallen out of the playpen. The investigators recorded whether or not each child returned the toys to the baby. They found that children exposed to the nurturant treatment behaved in a much more helpful way than did those in the control condition.

Often researchers cannot randomly assign participants and manipulate conditions in the real world, as these investigators were able to do. Sometimes researchers can compromise by conducting **natural experiments.** Treatments that already exist, such as different family environments, schools, child-care centers, and preschool programs, are compared. These studies differ from correlational research only in that groups of people are carefully chosen to ensure that their characteristics are as much alike as possible. In this way, investigators rule out as best they can alternative explanations for treatment effects.

In one such study, researchers wanted to know the extent to which witnessing spouse abuse (a husband physically hurting his wife) affects children's psychological adjustment (Sternberg et al., 1993). They conducted their investigation in Israel, where domestic violence is not as closely associated with other stressors (such as parental drug and alcohol abuse, divorce, and poverty) as it is in the United States. Consequently, they could control

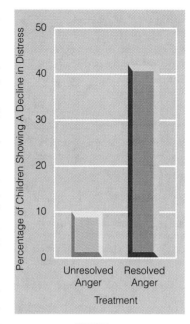

FIGURE 2.2

Does the way adults end their angry encounters affect children's emotional reactions? A laboratory experiment showed that when adults resolve their disputes by apologizing and compromising, children are more likely to decline in distress than when adults leave their arguments unresolved.

(Adapted from El-Sheikh, Cummings, & Reiter, 1996.)

random assignment An evenhanded procedure for assigning participants to treatment groups, such as drawing numbers out of a hat or flipping a coin. Increases the chances that participants' characteristics will be equally distributed across treatment conditions in an experiment.

matching A procedure in which participants are measured ahead of time on the factor in question, enabling researchers to assign participants with similar characteristics in equal numbers to each treatment condition in an experiment. Ensures that groups will be equivalent on factors likely to distort the results.

field experiment A research design in which participants are randomly assigned to treatment conditions in natural settings.

natural experiment A research design in which the investigator studies already existing treatments in natural settings by carefully selecting groups of participants with similar characteristics.

FIGURE 2.3

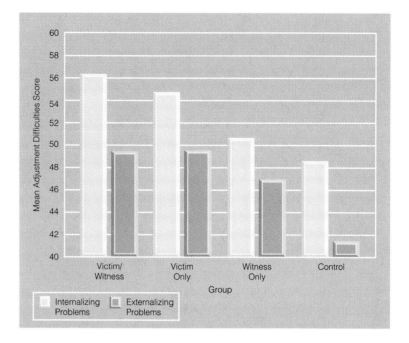

Relationship of domestic violence to 8- to 12-year-olds' self-reports of two types of adjustment difficulties: internalizing problems (feeling sad, unwanted, and less healthy than peers) and externalizing problems (behaving in ways likely to get children in trouble with parents and teachers, such as aggressing or committing delinquent acts). Both victims and witnesses of violence reported more problems than did controls from nonviolent homes. However, children who experienced abuse reacted more strongly than did those who merely observed it.

(Adapted from Sternberg et al., 1993.)

these factors more easily. As Figure 2.3 reveals, four groups of 8- to 12-year-olds were compared: children who were both victims and witnesses of abuse, victims only, witnesses only, and controls from nonviolent homes. Findings showed that children experiencing abuse reported more unhappiness and troubled behavior than did children witnessing abuse. Child witnesses, in turn, reported more adjustment difficulties than did controls. In sum, either type of exposure to domestic violence appeared harmful, although child victims reacted more strongly than did witnesses. Despite careful efforts of investigators to equate existing groups, however, natural experiments cannot achieve the precision and rigor of true experimental research.

To help you compare the correlational and experimental designs we have discussed, Table 2.2 summarizes their strengths and limitations. Now let's take a close look at designs for studying development.

Designs for Studying Development

cientists interested in child development require information about the way research participants change over time. To answer questions about development, they must extend correlational and experimental approaches to include measurements at different ages. Longitudinal and cross-sectional designs are special *developmental* research strategies. In each, age comparisons form the basis of the research plan.

THE LONGITUDINAL DESIGN

In a **longitudinal design,** a group of participants is studied repeatedly at different ages, and changes are noted as the participants mature. The time span may be relatively short (a few months to several years) or very long (a decade or even a lifetime).

■ **ADVANTAGES OF THE LONGITUDINAL DESIGN.** The longitudinal approach has two major strengths. First, since it tracks the performance of each person over time, researchers can identify common patterns of development as well as individual differences in the paths children follow to maturity. Second, longitudinal studies permit investigators to examine relationships between early and later events and behaviors. Let's take an example to illustrate these ideas.

A group of researchers wondered whether children who display extreme personality styles—either angry and explosive or shy and withdrawn—retain the same dispositions

longitudinal design A research design in which one group of participants is studied repeatedly at different ages.

TABLE 2.2

Strengths and Limitations of General Research Designs

Design	Description	Strengths	Limitations
Correlational design	The investigator obtains information on already existing groups, without altering participants' experiences.	Permits study of relationships between variables.	Does not permit inferences about cause-and-effect relationships.
Laboratory experiment	Under controlled laboratory conditions, the investigator manipulates an independent variable and looks at its effect on a dependent variable; requires random assignment of participants to treatment conditions.	Permits inferences about cause-and-effect relationships.	Findings may not generalize to the real world.
Field experiment	The investigator randomly assigns participants to treatment conditions in natural settings.	Permits generalization of experimental findings to the real world.	Control over treatment is generally weaker than in a laboratory experiment.
Natural experiment	The investigator compares already existing treatments in the real world, carefully selecting them to ensure that groups of participants are as much alike in characteristics as possible.	Permits study of naturally occurring variables not subject to experimenter manipulation.	Obtained differences may be due to variables other than the treatment.

when they become adults. In addition, they wanted to know what kinds of experiences promote stability or change in personality and what consequences explosiveness and shyness have for long-term adjustment. To answer these questions, the researchers delved into the archives of the Guidance Study, a well-known longitudinal investigation initiated in 1928 at the University of California, Berkeley, and continued over several decades (Caspi, Elder, & Bem, 1987, 1988).

Results revealed that the two personality styles were only moderately stable. Between ages 8 and 30, a good number of individuals remained the same, whereas others changed substantially. When stability did occur, it appeared to be due to a "snowballing effect," in which children evoked responses from adults and peers that acted to maintain their dispositions (Caspi, 1998). In other words, explosive youngsters were likely to be treated with anger and hostility (to which they reacted with even greater unruliness), whereas shy children were apt to be ignored.

Persistence of extreme personality styles affected many areas of adult adjustment, but these outcomes were different for males and females. For men, the results of early explosiveness were most apparent in their work lives, in the form of conflicts with supervisors, frequent job changes, and unemployment. Since few women in this sample of an earlier generation worked after marriage, their family lives were most affected. Explosive girls grew up to be hotheaded wives and mothers who were especially prone to divorce. Sex-related differences in the long-term consequences of shyness were even greater. Men who had been withdrawn in childhood were delayed in marrying, becoming fathers, and developing careers. Because a withdrawn, unassertive style was socially acceptable for females, women who had shy personalities showed no special adjustment problems.

■ **PROBLEMS IN CONDUCTING LONGITUDINAL RESEARCH.** Despite their strengths, longitudinal investigations confront researchers with a number of problems. There are practical difficulties, such as obtaining enough financial support and waiting the many years it takes for meaningful results in a long-term study. In addition, many factors can create serious difficulties for the validity of the findings.

Biased sampling is a common problem in longitudinal research. People who willingly participate in research that requires them to be continually observed and tested over many years are likely to have unique characteristics—at the very least, a special appreciation for

biased sampling Failure to select participants who are representative of the population of interest in a study.

the scientific value of research. As a result, we cannot easily generalize from them to the rest of the population. Furthermore, due to **selective attrition,** longitudinal samples generally become more biased as the investigation proceeds. Participants may move away or drop out for other reasons, and the ones who remain are likely to differ in important ways from the ones who do not continue.

The very experience of being repeatedly observed, interviewed, and tested can also threaten the validity of a longitudinal study. Children and adults may gradually be alerted to their own thoughts, feelings, and actions, think about them, and revise them in ways that have little to do with age-related change. In addition, with repeated testing, participants may become "test-wise." Their performance may improve as a result of **practice effects**—better test-taking skills and increased familiarity with the test, not because of factors commonly associated with development.

But the most widely discussed threat to the validity of longitudinal findings is cultural–historical change, or what are commonly called **cohort effects.** Longitudinal studies examine the development of *cohorts*—children born in the same time period who are influenced by a particular set of cultural and historical conditions. Results based on one cohort may not apply to children growing up at other times. For example, children's intelligence test performance has risen since the middle of the twentieth century and is still rising (Flynn, 1996, 1999). Gains in nutrition, the stimulating quality of schooling and daily life, and parental attitudes toward fostering children's mental development may be involved. And a longitudinal study of child and adolescent social development would probably result in quite different findings if it were carried out in the 1990s, around the time of World War II, or during the Great Depression of the 1930s. (See the Social Issues box on the following page.)

In the examples just given, cohort effects consist of broad, pervasive social changes affecting an entire generation. But even in contemporary longitudinal studies, cohort effects can operate through specific experiences that profoundly affect development. Consider a city that decides to consolidate several small high schools into a large high school. Compared with students in small schools, adolescents entering the large school are less likely to participate in extracurricular activities or to view their school's climate as warm and open and more likely to leave school before graduation (Berk, 1992b; Mahoney & Cairns, 1997).

Finally, changes occurring within the field of child development may create problems for longitudinal research covering an extended time period. Theories and methods are constantly changing, and those that first inspired a longitudinal study may become outdated. For this reason, as well as the others just mentioned, many recent longitudinal studies are short term, spanning only a few months or years in a child's life. Although short-term longitudinal research does not yield the same breadth of information as long-term studies, researchers are spared at least some of the formidable obstacles that threaten investigations lasting from childhood to maturity.

THE CROSS-SECTIONAL DESIGN

The length of time it takes for many behaviors to change, even in limited longitudinal studies, has led researchers to turn to a more convenient strategy for studying development. In the **cross-sectional design,** groups of people differing in age are studied at the same point in time.

A study in which children in grades 3, 6, 9, and 12 filled out a questionnaire asking about their sibling relationships provides a good illustration (Buhrmester & Furman, 1990). Findings revealed that sibling interaction was characterized by greater equality and less power assertion with age. Also, feelings of sibling companionship declined during adolescence. The researchers thought that these age-related changes were due to several factors. As later-born children become more competent and independent, they no longer need and are probably less willing to accept direction from older siblings. In addition, as adolescents move from psychological dependence on the family to greater involvement with peers, they may have less time and emotional need to invest in their siblings. These intriguing ideas about the development of sibling relationships, as we will see in Chapter 14, have been confirmed in subsequent research.

selective attrition Selective loss of participants during an investigation, resulting in a biased sample.

practice effects Changes in participants' natural responses as a result of repeated testing.

cohort effects The effects of cultural-historical change on the accuracy of findings: Children born in one period of time are influenced by particular cultural and historical conditions.

cross-sectional design A research design in which groups of participants of different ages are studied at the same point in time.

Impact of Historical Times on Development: The Great Depression and World War II

ECONOMIC DISASTER, WARS, and periods of rapid social change can profoundly affect people's lives. Yet their impact depends on when they strike during the life course. Glen Elder (1974) capitalized on the extent to which families experienced economic hardship during the Great Depression of the 1930s to study its influence on development. He delved into the vast archives of two major longitudinal studies: (1) the Oakland Growth Study, an investigation of individuals born in the early 1920s who were adolescents when the Depression took its toll; and (2) the Guidance Study, whose participants were born in the late 1920s and were young children when their families faced severe economic losses.

In both cohorts, relationships changed when economic deprivation struck. As unemployed fathers lost status, mothers were granted greater control over family affairs. This reversal of traditional gender roles often sparked conflict. Fathers sometimes became explosive and punitive toward their children. At other times, they withdrew from family interaction into passivity and depression. Mothers often became frantic with worry over the well-being of their husbands and children, and many entered the labor force to make ends meet (Elder, Liker, & Cross, 1984).

OUTCOMES FOR ADOLESCENTS. Although unusual burdens were placed on them as family lives changed, the Oakland Growth Study cohort—especially the boys—weathered economic hardship quite well. As adolescents, they were too old to be wholly dependent on their highly stressed parents, and their energies were often channeled into productive activities. Boys spent less time at home as they searched for part-time jobs, and many turned toward adults and peers outside the family for emotional support. Girls took over the responsibility of household chores and caring for younger siblings. Their greater involvement in family affairs led them to be exposed to more parental conflict and unhappiness. Consequently, adjustment of adolescent girls in economically deprived homes was somewhat less favorable than that of adolescent boys (Elder, Van Nguyen, & Caspi, 1985).

These changes in adolescents' lives had major consequences for their future aspirations. Girls' interests focused on home and family even more than was typical for that time period, and they were less likely to think about college and careers. Boys learned that economic resources could not be taken for granted, and they tended to make a very early commitment to an occupational choice.

The impact of the Depression continued to be apparent as adolescents entered adulthood. Girls from economically deprived homes remained committed to domestic life, and many married at an early age. Men had a strong desire for economic security, and they changed jobs less often than did those from nondeprived backgrounds. The chance to become a parent was especially important to men whose lives had been disrupted by the Depression. Perhaps because they believed that a rewarding career could not be guaranteed, these men viewed children as the most enduring benefit of their adult lives.

The Great Depression of the 1930s left this farm family without a steady income. The adolescent girl (in the back row on the far right) may have been more negatively affected by economic hardship than her brother (second from left). And overall, younger children probably suffered more than older children.

(Culver Pictures)

OUTCOMES FOR CHILDREN. Unlike the Oakland Growth Study cohort, the Guidance Study participants were within the years of intense family dependency when the Depression struck. For young boys (who, as we will see in later chapters, are especially prone to adjustment problems in the face of family stress), the impact of economic strain was severe. They showed emotional difficulties and poor attitudes toward school and work that persisted through the teenage years (Elder & Caspi, 1988; Elder, Caspi, & Van Nguyen, 1986).

But as the Guidance Study sample became adolescents, another major historical event occurred: in 1939, the United States entered World War II. As a result, thousands of men left their communities for military bases, establishing conditions that favored dramatic life changes. Some heavy combat veterans came away with symptoms of emotional trauma that persisted for decades (Elder & Clipp, 1988). Yet for most young soldiers, war mobilization broke the hold of family hardship and vanishing opportunity. It broadened their range of knowledge and experience. It also granted time out from civilian responsibilities, giving many soldiers a chance to consider where their lives were and where they were going. And the GI Bill of Rights enabled them to expand their education and acquire new skills after the war. By middle adulthood, the Guidance Study war veterans had reversed the early negative impact of the Great Depression. They were more successful educationally and occupationally than their counterparts who had not entered the service (Elder & Hareven, 1993).

Clearly, cultural-historical change does not have a uniform impact on development. Outcomes can vary considerably, depending on the pattern of historical events and the age at which they take place.

Notice how in cross-sectional studies, researchers do not have to worry about many difficulties that plague the longitudinal design. When participants are measured only once, investigators do not need to be concerned about selective attrition, practice effects, or changes in the field of child development that might make the findings obsolete by the time the study is complete.

■ **PROBLEMS IN CONDUCTING CROSS-SECTIONAL RESEARCH.** The cross-sectional design is a very efficient strategy for describing age-related trends. But when researchers choose it, they are shortchanged in the kind of information they can obtain about development. Evidence about change at the level at which it actually occurs—the individual—is not available. For example, in the cross-sectional study of sibling relationships just discussed, comparisons are limited to age-group averages. We cannot tell if important individual differences exist in the development of sibling relationships. Indeed, recent longitudinal findings reveal that children vary considerably in the changing quality of their sibling relationships, some becoming more supportive and intimate and others becoming increasingly distant with age (Dunn, Slomkowski, & Beardsall, 1994).

Cross-sectional studies—especially those that cover a wide age span—have another problem. Like longitudinal research, their validity can be threatened by cohort effects. For example, comparisons of 5-year-old cohorts and 15-year-old cohorts—groups of children born and reared in different years—may not really represent age-related changes. Instead, they may reflect unique experiences associated with the different time periods in which the age groups were growing up.

IMPROVING DEVELOPMENTAL DESIGNS

Researchers have devised ways of building on the strengths and minimizing the weaknesses of longitudinal and cross-sectional approaches. Several modified developmental designs have resulted.

■ **COMBINING LONGITUDINAL AND CROSS-SECTIONAL APPROACHES.** Researchers merge longitudinal and cross-sectional strategies in the **longitudinal-sequential design.** It is called sequential because it is composed of a sequence of samples, each of which is followed longitudinally for a given period of time. For example, suppose we select three samples—sixth, seventh, and eighth graders—and follow them for two years. That is, we observe each sample this year and next year, as follows: Sample 1 from grades 6 to 7; Sample 2 from grades 7 to 8; and Sample 3 from grades 8 to 9.

The design has three advantages. First, it permits us to find out whether cohort effects are operating by comparing children of the same age (or grade in school) who were born in different years. Using our example, we can compare children from different samples at grades 7 and 8. If they do not differ, then we can rule out cohort effects. Second, we can make both longitudinal and cross-sectional comparisons. If outcomes are similar in both, then we can be especially confident about our findings. Third, the design is efficient. In our example, we can find out about change over a 4-year period by following each cohort for just 2 years.

A recent study of adolescents' gender-stereotyped beliefs included the longitudinal-sequential features just described (Alfieri, Ruble, & Higgins, 1996). The researchers focused on the development of stereotype flexibility—that is, young people's willingness to say that "masculine" traits (such as strong) and "feminine" traits (such as gentle) characterize *both* males and females. As Figure 2.4 shows, a sharp longitudinal decline in stereotype flexibility occurred for Samples 2 and 3, whose scores were similar when measured at the same grade (grade 8). But Sample 1, on reaching seventh grade, scored much lower than seventh graders in Sample 2! The reason, the researchers discovered, was that Sample 1 remained in the same school from sixth to seventh grade, whereas Samples 2 and 3 had made the transition from elementary to junior high school. Entry into junior high sparked a temporary rise in gender-stereotype flexibility, perhaps because of exposure to a wide range of older peers, some of whom challenged previously held stereotypes. Over time, stereotype flexibility decreases as adolescents experience pressures to conform to traditional gender roles—a topic we will take up in Chapter 13.

longitudinal-sequential design
A research design with both longitudinal and cross-sectional components in which groups of participants born in different years are followed over time.

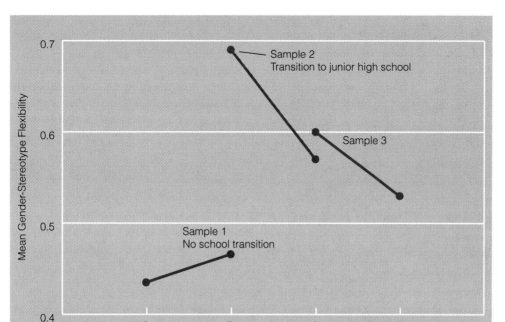

FIGURE 2.4

A longitudinal-sequential study of the development of gender-stereotyped beliefs during adolescence. Three samples were followed longitudinally from one school year to the next. To test for cohort effects, the researchers compared Sample 1 with Sample 2 at grade 7 and Sample 2 with Sample 3 at grade 8. The scores of Samples 1 and 2 did not match! The reason, the investigators discovered from additional evidence, was that a cohort effect—transition to junior high school—prompts a temporary rise in gender-stereotype flexibility. Because the scores of Samples 2 and 3 were similar at grade 8, the researchers were confident that gender-stereotype flexibility declines sharply in the years following transition to junior high school.

(Adapted from Alfieri, Ruble, & Higgins, 1996.)

Notice how the developmental trend shown in Figure 2.4—high gender-stereotype flexibility at grade 7 that drops off steeply—characterizes only adolescents who enter a self-contained junior high school. Researchers have become increasingly interested in identifying such cohort effects because they help explain diversity in development (Magnusson & Stattin, 1998).

■ **EXAMINING MICROCOSMS OF DEVELOPMENT.** Look back at the examples of developmental research we have discussed. In all instances, observations of children are fairly widely spaced. When we observe once a year or every few years, we can describe development, but we have little opportunity to capture the processes that produce change. A modification of the longitudinal approach, called the **microgenetic design,** is becoming more popular because it offers unique insights into how development takes place (Kuhn, 1995; Siegler & Crowley, 1991, 1992).

In microgenetic studies, researchers track change while it occurs, observing frequently from the time it begins until it stabilizes. Since it is not practical to use this approach over a long developmental period, investigators usually present children with a novel task or a task from their everyday environment and follow their mastery over a series of sessions. Within this "microcosm" of development, they see how change occurs.

In one microgenetic study, researchers watched how parents helped their fifth graders master challenging long-division problems. Children who progressed the fastest had parents who sensitively adjusted the help they offered to the child's moment-by-moment performance on the task. If the child failed to solve a problem, the parent provided more direct guidance on the next try. If the child succeeded, the parent gave less direct support, permitting the child to assume greater responsibility for the task (Pratt, Green, & MacVicar, 1992). In this investigation, the researchers focused on parental teaching techniques. In other microgenetic studies, they have examined the strategies children use to acquire new knowledge in reading, mathematics, and science (Kuhn et al., 1995; Siegler & Munakata, 1993).

As these examples illustrate, the microgenetic design is especially useful for studying cognitive development. In Chapter 4, we will see that it has also been used to test a dynamic systems approach to infant motor development. (Return to Chapter 1, page 30, if you need to review this theoretical perspective.)

Nevertheless, microgenetic studies are very difficult to carry out. Researchers must pore over hours of videotaped records, analyzing each participant's behavior. In addition, the time required for children to change is hard to anticipate. It depends on a careful

microgenetic design A research design in which change is tracked from the time it begins until it stabilizes, as participants master an everyday or novel task.

What strategies does this child use to solve puzzles, and how does she become proficient at puzzle solving? In the microgenetic design, researchers track change while it occurs, observing frequently from the time it begins until it stabilizes.

(Alex Bartel/The Picture Cube, Inc.)

match between the child's capabilities and the demands of the task (Siegler & Crowley, 1991). Finally, as in other longitudinal research, practice effects can distort the findings of microgenetic studies (Pressley, 1992). To find out whether this has occurred, researchers can compare microgenetic with cross-sectional observations. If new behaviors that emerge microgenetically reflect typical development, they should match the behaviors displayed by more advanced participants in cross-sectional studies, who are observed only once (Kuhn, 1995). In sum, when researchers find ways to surmount the challenges of microgenetic research, they reap the benefits of seeing development as it takes place.

■ COMBINING EXPERIMENTAL AND DEVELOPMENTAL DE-SIGNS. Perhaps you noticed that all the examples of longitudinal and cross-sectional research we have considered provide only correlational, and not causal, inferences about development. Yet ideally, causal information is desirable, both for testing theories and for coming up with ways to improve children's lives. If a developmental design indicates that children's experiences and behavior are related, in some instances we can explore the causal link between them by experimentally manipulating the experience in a later study. If, as a result, development is enhanced, we would have strong evidence for a causal association between experience and behavior. Today, research that combines an experimental strategy with either a longitudinal or cross-sectional approach appears with increasing frequency in the research literature. These designs are vital in helping investigators move beyond correlated variables to a causal account of developmental change. For a summary of the strengths and limitations of developmental research designs, refer to Table 2.3.

ASK YOURSELF . . .

◆ A researcher compares children who went to summer leadership camps with children who attended athletic camps. She finds that those who attended leadership camps are friendlier. Should the investigator tell parents that sending children to leadership camp promotes sociability? Why or why not?

◆ A researcher wants to find out if children enrolled in child-care centers in the first few years of life do as well in school as those who are not in child care. Which developmental design, longitudinal or cross-sectional, is appropriate for answering this question? What precautions should the researcher take to help ensure that child care is responsible for any differences between the groups? Explain.

◆ CONNECTIONS
Which research designs are best suited for detecting diversity in development? Which theories discussed in Chapter 1 are likely to be especially committed to those designs? Explain. (See Chapter 1, pages 26–32.)

BRIEF REVIEW

A variety of research designs are commonly used to study children. In correlational research, information is gathered on existing groups of individuals. Investigators can examine relationships between variables, but they cannot infer cause and effect. Because the experimental design involves random assignment of participants to treatment groups, researchers can find out if an independent variable causes change in a dependent variable. Field and natural experiments permit generalization to everyday life, but they sacrifice rigorous experimental control.

Longitudinal and cross-sectional designs are uniquely suited for studying development. Longitudinal research provides information on common patterns as well as individual differences in development and the relationship between early and later events and behaviors. The cross-sectional approach is more efficient, but comparisons are limited to age-group averages. The longitudinal-sequential design permits researchers to reap the benefits of both longitudinal and cross-sectional strategies and to identify cohort effects. A special longitudinal approach, the microgenetic design, offers unique insights into the processes of development. Experimental approaches can be combined with longitudinal or cross-sectional designs to examine causal influences on development.

Ethics in Research on Children

Research into human behavior creates ethical issues because, unfortunately, the quest for scientific knowledge can sometimes exploit people. When children take part in research, the ethical concerns are especially complex. Children are more vulnerable than adults to physical and psychological harm. In addition, immaturity makes it difficult or impossible for children to evaluate for themselves what

TABLE 2.3

Strengths and Limitations of Developmental Research Designs

Design	Description	Strengths	Limitations
Longitudinal design	The investigator studies the same group of participants repeatedly at different ages.	Permits study of common patterns and individual differences in development and relationships between early and later events and behaviors.	Age-related changes may be distorted because of biased sampling, selective attrition, practice effects, and cohort effects. In long-term studies, theoretical and methodological changes in the field can make findings obsolete.
Cross-sectional design	The investigator studies groups of participants differing in age at the same point in time.	More efficient than the longitudinal design. Not plagued by such problems as selective attrition, practice effects, or theoretical and methodological changes in the field.	Does not permit study of individual developmental trends. Age differences may be distorted because of cohort effects.
Longitudinal–sequential design	The investigator studies two or more groups of participants born in different years at the same point in time.	Permits both longitudinal and cross-sectional comparisons. Reveals existence of cohort effects. Permits tracking of age-related changes more efficiently than the longitudinal design.	May have the same problems as longitudinal and cross-sectional strategies, but the design itself helps identify difficulties.
Microgenetic design	The investigator tracks change from the time it begins until it stabilizes, as participants master an everyday or novel task.	Offers unique insights into the processes of development.	Requires intensive study of participants' moment-by-moment behaviors; the time required for participants to change is difficult to anticipate; practice effects may distort developmental trends.

participation in research will mean. For these reasons, special ethical guidelines for research on children have been developed by the federal government, by funding agencies, and by research-oriented associations such as the American Psychological Association (1992) and the Society for Research in Child Development (1993).

Table 2.4 on page 66 presents a summary of children's basic research rights drawn from these guidelines. Once you have examined them, think back to the ethical controversy faced by my colleague Ron, described at the beginning of this chapter. Then take a close look at the following research situations, each of which poses an additional ethical dilemma. What precautions do you think should be taken to protect the rights of children in each instance? Is any one of these studies so threatening to children's well-being that it should not be carried out?

■ To study children's willingness to separate from their caregivers, an investigator decides to ask mothers of 1- and 2-year-olds to leave their youngsters alone for a brief time period in an unfamiliar playroom. The researcher knows that under these circumstances, some children become very upset.

■ In a study of moral development, a researcher wants to assess children's ability to resist temptation by videotaping their behavior without their knowledge. Seven-year-olds are promised an attractive prize for solving some very difficult puzzles. They are also told not to look at a classmate's correct solutions, which are deliberately placed at the back of the room. If the researcher has to tell children ahead of time that cheating is being studied or that their behavior is being closely monitored, she will destroy the purpose of her study.

Did you find it difficult to decide on the best course of action in these examples? Virtually every organization that has worked on developing ethical principles for research has concluded that the conflicts raised by studies like these cannot be resolved with simple right-or-wrong answers. The ultimate responsibility for the ethical integrity of research lies with the investigator.

TABLE 2.4

Children's Research Rights

Research Right	Description
Protection from harm	Children have the right to be protected from physical or psychological harm in research. If in doubt about the harmful effects of research, investigators should seek the opinion of others. When harm seems possible, investigators should find other means for obtaining the desired information or abandon the research.
Informed consent	All research participants, including children, have the right to have explained to them, in language appropriate to their level of understanding, all aspects of the research that may affect their willingness to participate. When children are participants, informed consent of parents as well as others who act on the child's behalf (such as school officials) should be obtained, preferably in writing. Children, and the adults responsible for them, have the right to discontinue participation in the research at any time.
Privacy	Children have the right to concealment of their identity on all information collected in the course of research. They also have this right with respect to written reports and any informal discussions about the research.
Knowledge of results	Children have the right to be informed of the results of research in language that is appropriate to their level of understanding.
Beneficial treatments	If experimental treatments believed to be beneficial are under investigation, children in control groups have the right to alternative beneficial treatments if they are available.

Sources: American Psychological Association, 1992; Society for Research in Child Development, 1993.

risks–versus–benefits ratio A comparison of the costs of a research study to participants in terms of inconvenience and possible psychological or physical injury against its value for advancing knowledge and improving conditions of life. Used in assessing the ethics of research.

protection from harm The right of research participants to be protected from physical or psychological harm.

informed consent The right of research participants, including children, to have explained to them, in language they can understand, all aspects of a study that may affect their willingness to participate.

However, researchers are advised or, in the case of federally funded research, required to seek advice from others. Special committees, like the one that evaluated Ron's research, exist in colleges, universities, and other institutions for this purpose. These review boards evaluate research studies on the basis of a **risks-versus-benefits ratio.** This involves weighing the costs of the research to participants in terms of inconvenience and possible psychological or physical injury against the study's value for advancing knowledge and improving conditions of life.

Ron's procedures, the school's research committee claimed, might not offer children sufficient **protection from harm.** If there are any risks to the safety and welfare of participants that the research does not justify, then priority should always be given to the research participants. Vulnerability to harm, as the From Research to Practice box on the following page reveals, varies with children's age and characteristics. Occasionally, further inquiry can help resolve perplexing ethical dilemmas about whether children might suffer. In Ron's case, he provided the research committee with findings showing that asking elementary school pupils to identify disliked peers does not lead them to interact less frequently or more negatively with those children (Bell-Dolan, Foster, & Sikora, 1989). At the same time, Ron agreed to take special precautions when requesting such information. He promised to ask all the children to keep their comments confidential. Also, he arranged to conduct the study at a time when classmates have limited opportunity to interact with one another—just before a school vacation. With these safeguards in place, the committee felt comfortable with Ron's research, and they approved it.

The ethical principle of **informed consent** requires special interpretation when the research participants are children. Investigators must take into account the competence of youngsters of different ages to make choices about their own participation. Parental consent is meant to protect the safety of children whose ability to make these decisions is not yet fully mature. Besides obtaining parental consent, researchers should seek agreement of other individuals who act on children's behalf, such as institutional officials when research is conducted in schools, child-care centers, or hospitals. This is especially important when studies include special groups whose parents may not represent their best interests (refer again to the From Research to Practice box).

For children 7 years and older, their own informed consent should be obtained in addition to parental consent. Around age 7, changes in children's thinking permit them to better understand simple scientific principles and the needs of others. Researchers should respect and enhance these new capacities by providing school-age children with a full explanation of research activities in language they can understand (Fisher, 1993).

Finally, young children rely on a basic faith in adults to feel secure in unfamiliar situations. For this reason, some types of research may be particularly disturbing to them.

Children's Research Risks: Developmental and Individual Differences

RESEARCHERS INTERESTED IN children's behavior face formidable challenges in defining their ethical responsibilities. Compared with adults, children are less capable of benefiting from research experiences. Furthermore, the risks they are likely to encounter are psychological rather than physical (as in medical research) and therefore difficult to anticipate and sometimes even detect (Thompson, 1992). Consider, for example, 7-year-old Henry, who did not want to answer a researcher's questions about how he feels about his younger brother, who has physical disabilities. Since Henry's parents told him they had granted permission for his participation, he did not feel free to say no to the researcher. Or take 11-year-old Isabelle, who tried to solve a problem unsuccessfully. Despite the researcher's assurances that the task was set up to be impossible, Isabelle returned to her classroom concerned about her own competence.

How can we make sure that children are subjected to the least research risk possible? One valuable resource is our expanding knowledge of age-related capacities and individual differences. A close look reveals that research risks vary with development in complex ways. Some risks decrease with age, others increase, and still others occur at many or all ages (Thompson, 1990b). And because of their personal characteristics and life circumstances, some children are more vulnerable to harm than others.

Research plans for younger children typically receive the most scrutiny, since their limited cognitive competencies restrict their ability to make reasoned decisions and resist violations of their rights. In addition, as Henry's predicament illustrates, young children's limited social power in the context of parental and school support for an investigation can make it difficult for them to refuse participation. In a study that examined 5- to 12-year-olds' understanding of research procedures, few children comprehended why they were asked to engage in the research activities. And although the majority understood that they could end their participation at any time, some believed there would be negative consequences for doing so (the experimenter might be upset) or that they could stop only on a temporary basis (for example, to go to the bathroom). The youngest children, especially, did not know how to go about terminating their involvement (Abramovitch et al., 1991). However, if the researcher explicitly says that she would not mind if the child stops, children understand their right much better and are more likely to exercise it (Abramovitch et al., 1995).

Whereas young children have special difficulties understanding the research process, older children are more susceptible to procedures that threaten the way they think of themselves. In Chapter 11, we will see that compared with preschoolers, school-age children have a more coherent, differentiated understanding of their own strengths and weaknesses. As children become increasingly sensitive to the evaluations of others, giving false feedback or inducing failure (as happened to Isabelle) is more stressful. In adolescence, when views of the self are well established and questioning of authority is common, young people are probably better at sizing up and rejecting researchers' deceptive evaluations (Thompson, 1992).

At times, children's backgrounds, prior experiences, and other characteristics introduce special vulnerabilities. For ex-

This investigator is inviting a 6-year-old boy to participate in a research study as his mother looks on. Although the boy seems eager to comply, the researcher must explain that he can end his participation at any time. She must also tell him how he can terminate his involvement if his initial pleasurable response changes. Even after explanation, some children believe that there will be negative consequences, such as parental or researcher disapproval, if they do not continue.

(Will Faller)

ample, parents of maltreated children are not always good advocates for the interests of their children. The consent of an additional adult invested in the child's welfare—perhaps a relative, teacher, or therapist—may be necessary to protect the child's rights. And because abuse is associated with deep psychological wounds, such children are at greater risk than their agemates when research procedures induce anxiety or threaten their self-image. In certain cases, such as adolescent substance abusers or delinquents, parents may be so eager to get their children into contact with professionals that they would agree to any research without much forethought (Osher & Telesford, 1996). And even after a thorough explanation, their children may continue to believe that if they do not say yes, they will be punished by legal or school authorities. In these instances, researchers should take extra steps to assess each young person's understanding and motivation to make sure that the decision to participate is not influenced by real or imagined external pressures (Grisso, 1992).

Finding ways to reconcile the risks–benefits conflicts we have considered is vital, since research on children is of great value to society. In view of the complexity of children's research risks, convergent judgments of researchers, institutional review boards, child development experts, parents, and others responsible for children's welfare are likely to work best in safeguarding their interests. As each study is evaluated, participants' age and unique characteristics should be central to the discussion. Because of pressures they sometimes feel, children and adolescents need explanations of their right to dissent from participation. And their decision should be the final word in most investigations, even though this standard is not mandatory in current guidelines (Thompson, 1992).

All ethical guidelines advise that special precautions be taken in the use of deception and concealment, as occurs when researchers observe children from behind one-way mirrors, give them false feedback about their performance, or do not tell them the truth regarding what the research is about. When these kinds of procedures are used with adults, **debriefing,** in which the experimenter provides a full account and justification of the activities, occurs after the research session is over. Debriefing should also take place with children, but it often does not work as well. Despite explanations, children may come away from the research situation with their belief in the honesty of adults undermined. Ethical standards permit deception in research with children if investigators satisfy institutional committees that such practices are necessary. Nevertheless, since deception may have serious emotional consequences for some youngsters, many child development specialists believe that its use is always unethical and that investigators should come up with other research strategies when children are involved (Cooke, 1982).

debriefing Providing a full account and justification of research activities to participants in a study in which deception was used.

SUMMARY

FROM THEORY TO HYPOTHESIS

Describe the role of theories, hypotheses, and research questions in the research process.

- Research usually begins with a **hypothesis,** or prediction about behavior drawn from a theory. When little or no theory exists on a topic of interest, it starts with a research question. On the basis of the hypothesis or question, the investigator selects research methods (specific activities of participants) and a research design (overall plan for the study).

COMMON METHODS USED TO STUDY CHILDREN

Describe research methods commonly used to study children.

- **Naturalistic observations,** gathered in children's everyday environments, permit researchers to see directly the everyday behaviors they hope to explain. In contrast, **structured observations** take place in laboratories, where every participant has an equal opportunity to display the behaviors of interest.
- Depending on the researcher's purpose, observations can preserve participants' entire behavior stream, as in the **specimen record,** or they can be limited to one or a few behaviors, as in **event sampling** and **time sampling. Observer influence** and **observer bias** can reduce the accuracy of observational findings.
- Self-report methods can be flexible and open-ended like the **clinical interview,** which permits participants to express their thoughts in ways similar to their thinking in everyday life. Alternatively, **structured interviews,** tests, and questionnaires, which permit efficient administration and scoring, can be given. Both approaches depend on people's ability and willingness to engage in accurate reporting.
- **Psychophysiological methods** measure the relation between physiological processes and behavior. They help researchers uncover the biological bases of children's perceptual, cognitive, and emotional responses.
- Investigators rely on the **clinical,** or **case study, method** to obtain an in-depth understanding of a single child. In this approach, inter-

views, observations, test scores, and sometimes psychophysiological assessments are synthesized into a complete description of the participant's development and unique psychological functioning.
- A growing interest in the impact of culture has prompted child development researchers to adapt observational and self-report methods to permit direct comparisons of cultures. To uncover the cultural meanings of children's and adults' behaviors, they rely on a method borrowed from the field of anthropology—**ethnography.** It uses participant observation to understand the unique values and social processes of a culture or distinct social group.

RELIABILITY AND VALIDITY: KEYS TO SCIENTIFICALLY SOUND RESEARCH

Explain how reliability and validity apply to research methods and to the overall accuracy of research findings and conclusions.

- To be acceptable to the scientific community, research methods must be both reliable and valid. **Reliability** refers to the consistency, or repeatability, of observational, self-report, and psychophysiological measures. In the case of clinical and ethnographic research, reliability involves assessing whether the patterns and themes identified by the researcher are grounded in evidence and plausible.
- A method has high **validity** if, after examining its content and relationships with other measures of behavior, the researcher finds that it reflects what it was intended to measure. The concept of validity can also be applied more broadly, to the overall accuracy of research findings and conclusions. In designing a study, investigators must take special precautions to make sure that factors unrelated to the hypothesis do not influence participants' behavior.

GENERAL RESEARCH DESIGNS

Distinguish correlational and experimental research designs, noting their strengths and limitations.

- Two main types of designs are used in all research on human behavior. The **correlational design** examines relationships between variables as they happen to occur, without any intervention. The **correlation coefficient** is often used to measure the association between variables. Correlational studies do not permit inferences about cause and effect. However, their use is justified when it is difficult or impossible to control the variables of interest.

♦ An **experimental design** permits inferences about cause and effect. Researchers manipulate an **independent variable** by exposing groups of participants to two or more treatment conditions. Then they determine what effect this has on a **dependent variable. Random assignment** and **matching** ensure that characteristics of participants do not reduce the accuracy of experimental findings.

♦ **Laboratory experiments** usually achieve high degrees of control, but their findings may not apply to everyday life. To overcome this problem, researchers sometimes conduct **field experiments,** in which they manipulate treatment conditions in the real world. When this is impossible, investigators may compromise and conduct **natural experiments,** in which already existing treatments, consisting of groups of people whose characteristics are as much alike as possible, are compared. This approach, however, is less precise and rigorous than a true experimental design.

DESIGNS FOR STUDYING DEVELOPMENT

Describe designs for studying development, noting their strengths and limitations.

♦ Longitudinal and cross-sectional designs are uniquely suited for studying development. The **longitudinal design** permits study of common patterns as well as individual differences in development and the relationship between early and later events and behaviors.

♦ Researchers face a variety of problems in conducting longitudinal research, including **biased sampling, selective attrition, practice effects,** and changes in accepted theories and methods during long-term studies. But the most widely discussed threat to the validity of longitudinal findings is **cohort effects**—difficulty generalizing to children growing up during different time periods.

♦ The **cross-sectional design,** in which groups of participants differing in age are studied at the same time, offers an efficient approach to studying development. Although not plagued by such problems as selective attrition, practice effects, or theoretical and methodological changes in the field, it is limited to comparisons of age-group averages. Like longitudinal research, cross-sectional studies can be threatened by cohort effects, especially when they cover a wide age span.

♦ Modified developmental designs overcome some of the limitations of longitudinal and cross-sectional research. By combining the two approaches in the **longitudinal-sequential design,** researchers can test for cohort effects, make longitudinal and cross-sectional comparisons, and gather information about development efficiently. In the **microgenetic design,** researchers track change as it occurs. In doing so, they obtain unique insights into the processes of development. Drawbacks of the microgenetic design include the difficulty of anticipating the time required for participants to change and practice effects. When experimental procedures are combined with developmental designs, researchers can examine causal influences on development.

ETHICS IN RESEARCH ON CHILDREN

What special ethical issues arise in doing research on children?

♦ Because of their immaturity, children are especially vulnerable to harm and often cannot evaluate the risks and benefits of research. Ethical guidelines and special committees that weigh research in terms of a **risks-versus-benefits** ratio help ensure that children's rights are safeguarded and that they are afforded **protection from harm.** In addition to parental consent and agreement of other individuals who act on children's behalf, researchers should seek the **informed consent** of children age 7 and older for research participation. The use of deception in research with children is especially risky, since **debriefing** can undermine their basic faith in the trustworthiness of adults.

IMPORTANT TERMS AND CONCEPTS

Biological Foundations, Prenatal Development, and Birth

"IT'S A GIRL," ANNOUNCES the doctor, who holds up the squalling lit-tle creature, while her new parents gaze with amazement at their miracu-lous creation.

"A girl! We've named her Sarah!" exclaims the proud father to eager rela-tives waiting by the telephone for word about their new family member.

As we join these parents in thinking about how this wondrous being came into existence and imagining her future, we are struck by many questions. How could this well-formed baby, equipped with everything necessary for life outside the womb, have developed from the union of two tiny cells? What en-sures that Sarah will, in due time, roll over, reach for objects, walk, talk, make friends, imagine, and create—just like every other normal child born before her? Why is she a girl and not a boy, dark-haired rather than blond, calm and cuddly instead of wiry and energetic? What difference will it make that Sarah is given a name and place in one family, community, nation, and culture rather than another?

We begin our discussion of these questions by considering genetic foun-dations. Because nature has prepared us for survival, all human beings have features in common. Yet a brief period of time spent in the company of any child and his or her family reveals that each human being is unique. Take a moment to jot down the most obvious similarities in physical characteris-tics and behavior for several children and parents whom you know well. Did you find that one child shows combined features of both parents, another resembles just one parent, whereas still a third is not like either parent? These directly observable characteristics are called **phenotypes.** They depend in part on the individual's **genotype**—the complex blend of genetic infor-mation that determines our species and influences all our unique characteris-tics. But phenotypes, as our discussion will show, are also affected by a long history of environmental influences—ones that begin even before the mo-ment of conception.

Next, we trace development during the most rapid phase of growth, the prenatal period, in which complex transactions between heredity and envi-ronment begin to shape the course of development. We consider environ-mental supports that are necessary for normal prenatal growth, as well as damaging influences that threaten the child's health and survival. Then we turn to the drama of birth and to developmental risks for infants born un-derweight or prematurely, before the prenatal phase is complete.

Finally, we take a look ahead. This earliest period introduces us to the op-eration of the two basic determinants of development: heredity and environ-ment. We will consider how researchers think about and study the relationship between nature and nurture as they continue to influence the individual's emerging characteristics from infancy through adolescence.

FIGURE **3.1**

A karyotype, or photograph, of human chromosomes. The 46 chromosomes shown here were isolated from a body cell, stained, greatly magnified, and arranged in pairs according to decreasing size of the upper arm of each chromosome. Note the twenty-third pair, XY. The cell donor is a male. In a female, the twenty-third pair would be XX.

(CNRI/Science Photo Library/Photo Researchers.)

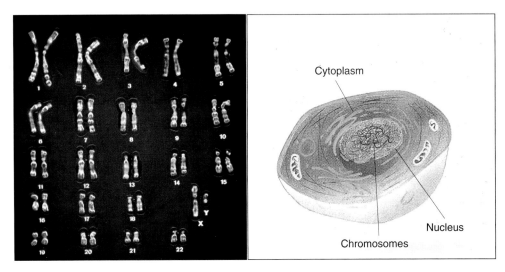

Genetic Foundations

ach of us is made up of trillions of separate units called cells. Inside every cell is a control center, or *nucleus*. When cells are chemically stained and viewed through a powerful microscope, rodlike structures called **chromosomes** are visible in the nucleus. Chromosomes store and transmit genetic information. Their number varies from species to species—48 for chimpanzees, 64 for horses, 40 for mice, and 46 for human beings.

Chromosomes come in matching pairs (an exception is the XY pair in males, which we will discuss shortly). Each member of a pair corresponds to the other in size, shape, and the traits genes regulate. One is inherited from the mother and one from the father. Therefore, in humans, we speak of *23 pairs* of chromosomes residing in each human cell (see Figure 3.1).

THE GENETIC CODE

Chromosomes are made up of a chemical substance called **deoxyribonucleic acid,** or **DNA.** As Figure 3.2 shows, DNA is a long, double-stranded molecule that looks like a twisted ladder. Notice that each rung of the ladder consists of a specific pair of chemical substances called *bases*, joined together between the two sides. Although the bases always pair up in the same way across the ladder rungs—A with T, and C with G—they can occur in any order along its sides. It is this sequence of base pairs that provides genetic instructions. A **gene** is a segment of DNA along the length of the chromosome. Genes can be of different lengths—perhaps 100 to several thousand ladder rungs long. Altogether, about 50,000 to 100,000 genes lie along the human chromosomes (Schuler et al., 1996).

Genes accomplish their task by sending instructions for making a rich assortment of proteins to the *cytoplasm,* the area surrounding the nucleus of the cell. Proteins, which trigger chemical reactions throughout the body, are the biological foundation on which our characteristics and capacities are built.

A unique feature of DNA is that it can duplicate itself. This special ability makes it possible for a single cell, formed at conception, to develop into a complex human being composed of a great many cells. The process of cell duplication is called **mitosis.** In mitosis, the DNA ladder splits down the middle, opening somewhat like a zipper (refer again to Figure 3.2). Then, each base is free to pair up with a new mate from cytoplasm of the cell. Notice how this process creates two identical DNA ladders, each containing one new side and one old side of the previous ladder. At the level of chromosomes, during mitosis each chromosome copies itself. As a result, each new body cell contains the same number of chromosomes and the identical genetic information.

phenotype The individual's physical and behavioral characteristics, which are determined by both genetic and environmental factors (see page 71).

genotype The genetic makeup of an individual (see page 71).

chromosomes Rodlike structures in the cell nucleus that store and transmit genetic information.

deoxyribonucleic acid (DNA) Long, double-stranded molecules that make up chromosomes.

gene A segment of a DNA molecule that contains instructions for production of various proteins that contribute to growth and functioning of the body.

mitosis The process of cell duplication, in which each new cell receives an exact copy of the original chromosomes.

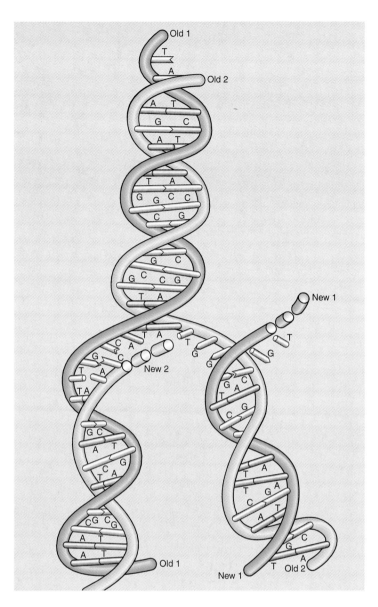

DNA's ladderlike structure. This figure shows that the pairings of bases across the rungs of the ladder are very specific: adenine (A) always appears with thymine (T), and cytosine (C) always appears with guanine (G). Here, the DNA ladder duplicates by splitting down the middle of its ladder rungs. Each free base picks up a new complementary partner from the area surrounding the cell nucleus.

THE SEX CELLS

New individuals are created when two special cells called **gametes,** or sex cells—the sperm and ovum—combine. Gametes are unique in that they contain only 23 chromosomes, half as many as a regular body cell. They are formed through a cell division process called **meiosis,** which halves the number of chromosomes normally present in body cells.

Meiosis takes place according to the steps in Figure 3.3 on page 74. First, chromosomes pair up within the original cell, and each one copies itself. Then, a special event called **crossing over** occurs. In crossing over, chromosomes next to each other break at one or more points along their length and exchange segments, so that genes from one are replaced by genes from another. This shuffling of genes creates new hereditary combinations. Next, the paired chromosomes separate into different cells, but chance determines which member of each pair will gather with others and end up in the same gamete. Finally, in the last phase of meiosis, each chromosome leaves its duplicate and becomes part of a sex cell containing 23 chromosomes instead of the usual 46.

In the male, four sperm are produced each time meiosis is complete. Also, the cells from which sperm arise are produced continuously throughout life. For this reason, a healthy man can father a child at any age after sexual maturity. In the female, gamete production is much more limited, since meiosis produces just one ovum. In addition, the female is born with all her ova already present in her ovaries, and she can bear children for

gametes Human sperm and ova, which contain half as many chromosomes as a regular body cell.

meiosis The process of cell division through which gametes are formed and in which the number of chromosomes in each cell is halved.

crossing over Exchange of genes between chromosomes next to each other during meiosis.

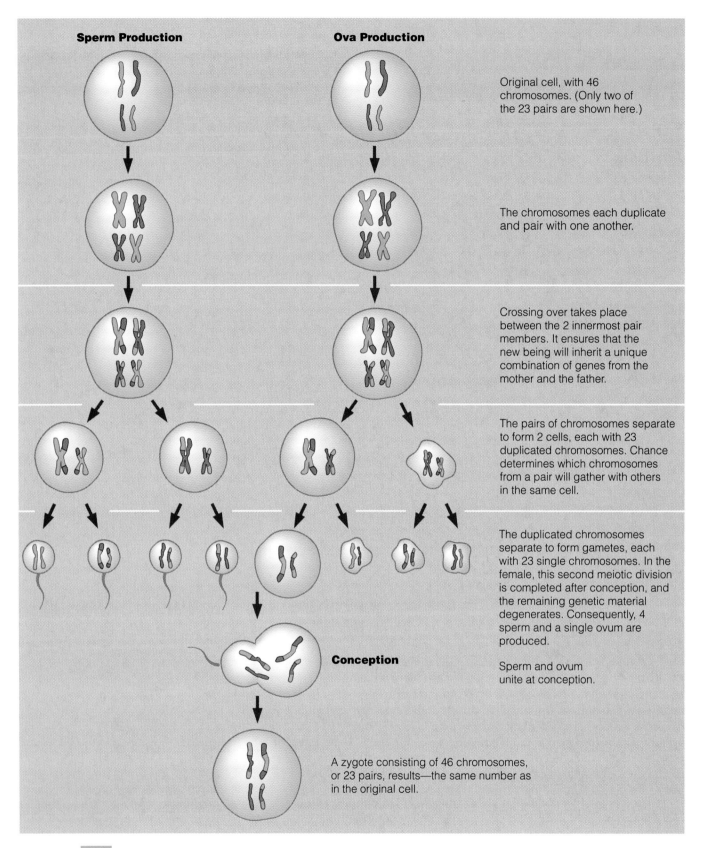

Sperm Production

Ova Production

Original cell, with 46 chromosomes. (Only two of the 23 pairs are shown here.)

The chromosomes each duplicate and pair with one another.

Crossing over takes place between the 2 innermost pair members. It ensures that the new being will inherit a unique combination of genes from the mother and the father.

The pairs of chromosomes separate to form 2 cells, each with 23 duplicated chromosomes. Chance determines which chromosomes from a pair will gather with others in the same cell.

The duplicated chromosomes separate to form gametes, each with 23 single chromosomes. In the female, this second meiotic division is completed after conception, and the remaining genetic material degenerates. Consequently, 4 sperm and a single ovum are produced.

Sperm and ovum unite at conception.

Conception

A zygote consisting of 46 chromosomes, or 23 pairs, results—the same number as in the original cell.

FIGURE 3.3

The cell division process of meiosis leading to gamete formation. (Here, original cells are depicted with 2 rather than the full complement of 23 pairs.) Meiosis creates gametes with only half the usual number of chromosomes. When sperm and ovum unite at conception, the first cell of the new individual (the zygote) has the correct, full number of chromosomes.

only three to four decades. Still, there are plenty of female sex cells. About 1 to 2 million are present at birth, 40,000 remain at adolescence, and approximately 350 to 450 will mature during a woman's childbearing years (Moore & Persaud, 1998).

Look again at the steps of meiosis in Figure 3.3, and notice how they ensure that a constant quantity of genetic material (46 chromosomes in each cell) is transmitted from one generation to the next. When sperm and ovum unite at fertilization, the cell that results, called a **zygote,** will again have 46 chromosomes.

Can you also see how meiosis leads to variability among offspring? Crossing over and random sorting of each member of a chromosome pair into separate sex cells mean that the chances of offspring of the same two parents being genetically the same is extremely slim—about 1 in 700 trillion (Gould & Keeton, 1996). Therefore, meiosis helps us understand why siblings differ from each other even though they also have features in common, since their genotypes come from a common pool of parental genes. The genetic variability produced by meiosis is important in an evolutionary sense. It increases the chances that at least some members of a species will be able to cope with ever-changing environments and survive.

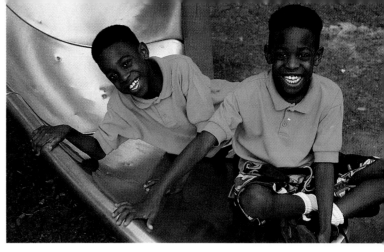

These identical, or monozygotic, twins were created when a duplicating zygote separated into two clusters of cells, and two individuals with the same genetic makeup developed. Identical twins look alike, and as we will see later in this chapter, tend to resemble each other in a variety of psychological characteristics.
(Reg Parker/FPG International)

MULTIPLE OFFSPRING

Only under one circumstance do offspring *not* display the genetic variability we have just discussed. Sometimes a zygote that has started to duplicate separates into two clusters of cells that develop into two individuals. These are called **identical,** or **monozygotic, twins** because they have the same genetic makeup. The frequency of identical twins is the same around the world—about 3 out of every 1,000 births (Tong, Caddy, & Short, 1997). Animal research has uncovered a variety of environmental influences that prompt this type of twinning, including temperature changes, variation in oxygen levels, and late fertilization of the ovum.

There is another way that twins can be created. **Fraternal,** or **dizygotic, twins,** the most common type of multiple birth, result when two ova are released from a woman's ovaries at the same time and both are fertilized. The resulting twins are genetically no more alike than ordinary siblings. As Table 3.1 indicates, both hereditary and environmental factors seem to be involved in fraternal twinning.

TABLE **3.1**

Maternal Factors Linked to Fraternal Twinning

Factor	Description
Ethnicity	About 8 per 1,000 births among whites, 12 to 16 per 1,000 among blacks, and 4 per 1,000 among Asians[a]
Age	Rises with maternal age, peaking at 35 years, and then rapidly falls
Nutrition	Occurs less often among women with poor diets; occurs more often among women who are tall and overweight or of normal weight as opposed to slight body build
Number of births	Chances increase with each additional birth
Fertility drugs and in vitro fertilization	Treatment of infertility with hormones and through in vitro fertilization (see page 84) increases the likelihood of multiple fraternal births, from twins to quintuplets

[a]Worldwide rates, with the effects of fertility drugs removed.
Source: Collins, 1994; Mange & Mange, 1994.

zygote The union of sperm and ovum at conception.

identical, or monozygotic, twins Twins that result when a zygote that has started to duplicate separates into two clusters of cells that develop into two individuals with the same genetic makeup.

fraternal, or dizygotic, twins Twins that result from the release and fertilization of two ova. They are genetically no more alike than ordinary siblings.

TABLE 3.2

Examples of Dominant and Recessive Characteristics

Dominant	Recessive
Dark hair	Blond hair
Normal hair	Pattern baldness
Curly hair	Straight hair
Nonred hair	Red hair
Facial dimples	No dimples
Normal hearing	Some forms of deafness
Normal vision	Nearsightedness
Farsightedness	Normal vision
Normal vision	Congenital eye cataracts
Normally pigmented skin	Albinism
Double-jointedness	Normal joints
Type A blood	Type O blood
Type B blood	Type O blood
Rh-positive blood	Rh-negative blood

Note: Many normal characteristics that were previously thought to be due to dominant–recessive inheritance, such as eye color, are now regarded as due to multiple genes. For the characteristics listed here, there still seems to be fairly common agreement that the simple dominant–recessive relationship holds.
Source: McKusick, 1995.

autosomes The 22 matching chromosome pairs in each human cell.

sex chromosomes The twenty-third pair of chromosomes, which determines the sex of the child. In females, this pair is called *XX;* in males, it is called *XY.*

allele Each of two or more forms of a gene located at the same place on the chromosomes.

homozygous Having two identical alleles at the same place on a pair of chromosomes.

heterozygous Having two different alleles at the same place on a pair of chromosomes.

dominant–recessive inheritance A pattern of inheritance in which, under heterozygous conditions, the influence of only one allele is apparent.

carrier A heterozygous individual who can pass a recessive trait to his or her offspring.

BOY OR GIRL?

Using special microscopic techniques, the 23 pairs of chromosomes in each human cell can be distinguished from one another. Twenty-two of them are matching pairs, called **autosomes.** They are numbered by geneticists from longest (1) to shortest (22) (refer back to Figure 3.1). The twenty-third pair consists of **sex chromosomes.** In females, this pair is called XX; in males, it is called XY. The X is a relatively long chromosome, whereas the Y is short and carries less genetic material. When gametes form in males, the X and Y chromosomes separate into different sperm cells. In females, all gametes carry an X chromosome. The sex of the new organism is determined by whether an X-bearing or a Y-bearing sperm fertilizes the ovum. In fact, scientists have isolated a gene on the Y chromosome that triggers male sexual development by switching on the production of male sex hormones. When that gene is absent, the fetus that develops is female (Goodfellow & Lovell, 1993).

PATTERNS OF GENETIC INHERITANCE

Two or more forms of each gene occur at the same place on the chromosomes, one inherited from the mother and one from the father. Each different form of a gene is called an **allele.** If the alleles from both parents are alike, the child is said to be **homozygous** and will display the inherited trait. If the alleles are different, then the child is **heterozygous,** and relationships between the alleles determine the trait that will appear.

■ **DOMINANT–RECESSIVE RELATIONSHIPS.** In many heterozygous pairings, only one allele affects the child's characteristics. It is called *dominant;* the second allele, which has no effect, is called *recessive.* Hair color is an example of **dominant–recessive inheritance.** The allele for dark hair is dominant (we can represent it with a capital *D*), whereas the one for blond hair is recessive (symbolized by a lowercase *b*). Children who inherit either a homozygous pair of dominant alleles (*DD*) or a heterozygous pair (*Db*) will be dark-haired, even though their genetic makeup is different. Blond hair can result only from having two recessive alleles (*bb*). Still, heterozygous individuals with just one recessive allele (*Db*) can pass that trait to their children. Therefore, they are called **carriers** of the trait.

Some human characteristics and disorders that follow the rules of dominant–recessive inheritance are listed in Table 3.2 above and Table 3.3 on pages 78–79. As you can see, many disabilities and diseases are the product of recessive alleles. One of the most frequently occurring recessive disorders is *phenylketonuria,* or *PKU.* It affects the way the body breaks down proteins contained in many foods, such as cow's milk, bread, eggs, and fish. Infants born with two recessive alleles lack an enzyme that converts one of the basic amino acids that make up proteins (phenylalanine) into a by-product essential for body functioning (tyrosine). Without this enzyme, phenylalanine quickly builds to toxic levels that damage the central nervous system. Around 3 to 5 months, infants with untreated PKU start to lose interest in their surroundings. By 1 year, they are permanently retarded.

Despite its potentially damaging effects, PKU provides an excellent illustration of the fact that inheriting unfavorable genes does not always mean that the child's condition is untreatable. All U.S. states and Canadian provinces require that each newborn be given a blood test for PKU. If the disease is found, doctors place the baby on a diet low in phenylalanine. Children who receive this treatment show delayed development of higher-order cognitive skills, such as planning and problem solving, in infancy and early childhood because even small amounts of phenylalanine interfere with brain functioning (Diamond et al., 1997). But as long as dietary treatment begins early and continues, children with PKU

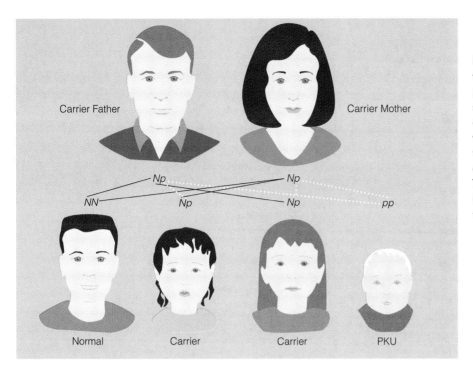

FIGURE 3.4

Carrier Father

Carrier Mother

Np   Np

NN   Np   Np   pp

Normal   Carrier   Carrier   PKU

Dominant–recessive mode of inheritance as illustrated by PKU. When both parents are heterozygous carriers of the recessive allele, we can predict that 25 percent of their offspring will be normal, 50 percent will be carriers, and 25 percent will inherit the disorder. Notice that the PKU-affected child, in contrast to his siblings, has light hair. The recessive gene for PKU is *pleiotropic* (affects more than one trait). It also leads to fair coloring.

usually attain an average level of intelligence and have a normal lifespan (Mazzocco et al., 1994).

In dominant–recessive inheritance, if we know the genetic makeup of the parents, we can predict the percentage of children in a family who are likely to display a trait or be carriers of it. Figure 3.4 shows one example for PKU. Notice that for a child to inherit the condition, both parents must be carriers of a recessive allele (p). As the figure also illustrates, it is possible for a single gene to affect more than one trait—a genetic principle known as **pleiotropism.** Due to their inability to convert phenylalanine into tyrosine (which is responsible for pigmentation), children with PKU usually have light hair and blue eyes. Furthermore, children vary in the degree to which phenylalanine accumulates in their tissues and in the extent to which they respond to treatment. This is due to the action of **modifier genes,** which can enhance or dilute the effects of alleles controlling particular traits.

As Table 3.3 suggests, only rarely are serious diseases due to dominant alleles. Think about why this is so. Children who inherit the dominant allele would always develop the disorder. They would seldom live long enough to reproduce, and the harmful allele would be eliminated from the family's heredity in a single generation. Some dominant disorders, however, do persist. One of them is *Huntington disease,* a condition in which the central nervous system degenerates. Why has this disease endured in some families? Its symptoms usually do not appear until age 35 or later, after the person has passed the dominant gene on to his or her children.

■ **CODOMINANCE.** In some heterozygous circumstances, the dominant–recessive relationship does not hold completely. Instead, we see **codominance,** a pattern of inheritance in which both alleles influence the person's characteristics.

The *sickle cell trait,* a heterozygous condition present in many black Africans, provides an example. *Sickle cell anemia* (see Table 3.3) occurs in full form when a child inherits two recessive alleles. They cause the usually round red blood cells to become sickle shaped, a response that is especially great under low oxygen conditions. The sickled cells clog the blood vessels and block the flow of blood. Individuals who have the disorder suffer severe attacks involving intense pain, swelling, and tissue damage. They generally die in the first 20 years of life; few live past age 40. Heterozygous individuals are protected from the disease under most circumstances. However, when they experience oxygen deprivation—for example, at high altitudes or after intense physical exercise—the single recessive allele asserts itself, and a temporary, mild form of the illness occurs.

pleiotropism The influence of a single gene on more than one characteristic.

modifier genes Genes that can enhance or dilute the effects of alleles controlling particular traits.

codominance A pattern of inheritance in which both alleles, in a heterozygous combination, are expressed.

Examples of Dominant and Recessive Diseases

Disease	Description	Mode of Inheritance	Incidence	Treatment	Prenatal Diagnosis	Carrier Identification*
Autosomal Diseases						
Cooley's anemia	Pale appearance, retarded physical growth, and lethargic behavior begin in infancy.	Recessive	1 in 500 births to parents of Mediterranean descent	Frequent blood transfusions; death from complications usually occurs by adolescence.	Yes	Yes
Cystic fibrosis	Lungs, liver, and pancreas secrete large amounts of thick mucus, leading to breathing and digestive difficulties.	Recessive	1 in 2,000 to 2,500 Caucasian births; 1 in 16,000 African–American births	Bronchial drainage, prompt treatment of respiratory infections, dietary management. Advances in medical care allow survival with good life quality into adulthood.	Yes	Yes
Phenylketonuria (PKU)	Inability to metabolize the amino acid phenylalanine, contained in many proteins, causes severe central nervous system damage in the first year of life.	Recessive	1 in 8,000 births	Placing the child on a special diet results in average intelligence and normal lifespan. Subtle difficulties with planning and problem solving are often present.	Yes	Yes
Sickle cell anemia	Abnormal sickling of red blood cells causes oxygen deprivation, pain, swelling, and tissue damage. Anemia and susceptibility to infections, especially pneumonia, occur.	Recessive	1 in 500 African–American births	Blood transfusions, painkillers, prompt treatment of infections. No known cure; 50 percent die by age 20.	Yes	Yes
Tay–Sachs disease	Central nervous system degeneration, with onset at about 6 months, leads to poor muscle tone, blindness, deafness, and convulsions.	Recessive	1 in 3,600 births to Jews of European descent	None. Death by 3 to 4 years of age.	Yes	Yes

The sickle cell allele is prevalent among black Africans for a special reason. Carriers of it are more resistant to malaria than are individuals with two alleles for normal red blood cells. In Africa, where malaria is common, these carriers survived and reproduced more frequently than others, leading the gene to be maintained in the black population. In regions of the world where the risk of malaria is low, the frequency of the gene is steadily declining. For example, only 10 percent of African Americans carry it, compared with 20 percent of black Africans (Mange & Mange, 1994).

■ **X-LINKED INHERITANCE.** Males and females have an equal chance of inheriting recessive disorders carried on the autosomes, such as PKU and sickle cell anemia. But when a harmful allele is carried on the X chromosome, **X-linked inheritance** applies. Males are more likely to be affected because their sex chromosomes do not match. In females, any recessive allele on one X chromosome has a good chance of being suppressed by a dominant allele on the other X. But the Y chromosome is only about one-third as long and therefore lacks many corresponding alleles to override those on the X.

Red–green color blindness (a condition in which individuals cannot tell the difference between shades of red and green) is one example of an X-linked recessive trait. It affects

X-linked inheritance A pattern of inheritance in which a recessive gene is carried on the X chromosome. Males are more likely to be affected.

TABLE 3.3

(continued)

Disease	Description	Mode of Inheritance	Incidence	Treatment	Prenatal Diagnosis	Carrier Identification*
Huntington disease	Central nervous system degeneration leads to muscle coordination difficulties, mental deterioration, and personality changes. Symptoms usually do not appear until age 35 or later.	Dominant	1 in 18,000 to 25,000 American births	None. Death occurs 10 to 20 years after symptom onset.	Yes	Not applicable
Marfan syndrome	Tall, slender build; thin, elongated arms and legs. Heart defects and eye abnormalities, especially of the lens. Excessive lengthening of the body results in a variety of skeletal defects.	Dominant	1 in 20,000 births	Correction of heart and eye defects sometimes possible. Death from heart failure in young adulthood common.	Yes	Not applicable
X-Linked Diseases						
Duchenne muscular dystrophy	Degenerative muscle disease. Abnormal gait, loss of ability to walk between 7 and 13 years of age.	Recessive	1 in 3,000 to 5,000 male births	None. Death from respiratory infection or weakening of the heart muscle usually occurs in adolescence.	Yes	Yes
Hemophilia	Blood fails to clot normally. Can lead to severe internal bleeding and tissue damage.	Recessive	1 in 4,000 to 7,000 male births	Blood transfusions. Safety precautions to prevent injury.	Yes	Yes
Diabetes insipidus	A form of diabetes present at birth caused by insufficient production of the hormone vasopressin. Results in excessive thirst and urination. Dehydration can cause central nervous system damage.	Recessive	1 in 2,500 male births	Hormone replacement.	Yes	Yes

ᵃCarrier status detectable in prospective parents through blood test or genetic analyses.

Sources: Behrman, Kliegman, & Arvin, 1996; Child, 1997; Gilfillan et al., 1992; Knoers et al., 1993; McKusick, 1995; Simpson & Harding, 1993.

males twice as often as females (Mange & Mange, 1994). Refer again to Table 3.3 and review the diseases that are X-linked. A well-known example is *hemophilia,* a disorder in which the blood fails to clot normally. Figure 3.5 on page 80 shows its greater likelihood of inheritance by male children whose mothers carry the abnormal allele.

Besides X-linked disorders, many sex-related differences reveal the male to be at a disadvantage. Rates of miscarriage and infant and childhood deaths are greater for males. Learning disabilities, behavior disorders, and mental retardation are also more common among boys (Halpern, 1997). It is possible that these sex differences can be traced to the genetic code. The female, with two X chromosomes, benefits from a greater variety of genes. Nature, however, seems to have adjusted for the male's disadvantage. Worldwide, about 106 boys are born for every 100 girls, and judging from miscarriage and abortion statistics, an even greater number of males are conceived (Pyeritz, 1998).

Nevertheless, in recent decades, the proportion of male births has declined in many industrialized countries, including Canada, Denmark, Germany, Finland, the Netherlands, Norway, and the United States (Davis, Gottlieb, & Stampnitzky, 1998). Increased occupational and community exposure to pesticides is believed to have prompted a re-

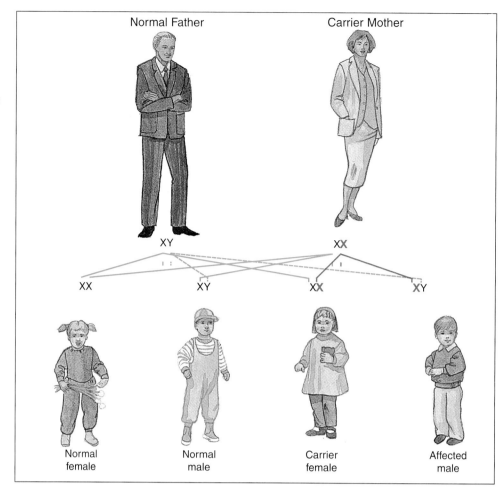

FIGURE 3.5

X-linked inheritance. In the example shown here, the allele on the father's X chromosome is normal. The mother has one normal and one abnormal allele on her X chromosomes. By looking at the possible combinations of the parents' alleles, we can predict that 50 percent of male children will have the disorder and 50 percent of female children will be carriers of it.

Normal Father   Carrier Mother

XY   XX

XX   XY   XX   XY

Normal female   Normal male   Carrier female   Affected male

duction in sperm counts, with greater damage to Y-bearing sperm, and a rise in birth defects and infant deaths, particularly among males.

■ **GENETIC IMPRINTING.** More than 1,000 human characteristics follow the rules of dominant–recessive and codominant inheritance (McKusick, 1995). In these cases, regardless of which parent contributes a gene to the new individual, the gene responds in the same way. Geneticists, however, have identified some exceptions governed by a recently discovered mode of inheritance. In **genetic imprinting,** alleles are *imprinted,* or chemically *marked,* in such a way that one pair member (either the mother's or the father's) is activated, regardless of its makeup. The imprint is often temporary; it may be erased in the next generation, and it may not occur in all individuals (Cassidy, 1995).

Imprinting helps us understand the confusion in inheritance of some disorders. For example, children are more likely to develop diabetes if their father, rather than their mother, suffers from it. And people with asthma or hay fever tend to have mothers, not fathers, with the illness. Scientists do not yet know what causes this parent-specific genetic transmission. At times, it reveals itself in heartbreaking ways. Imprinting is involved in several childhood cancers and in *Praeder-Willi syndrome,* a disorder with symptoms of mental retardation and severe obesity. It may also explain why Huntington disease, when inherited from the father, tends to emerge at an earlier age and progress more rapidly (Day, 1993).

In these examples, genetic imprinting affects traits carried on the autosomes. It can also operate on the sex chromosomes, as *fragile X syndrome* reveals. In this disorder, an abnormal repetition of a sequence of DNA bases occurs in a special spot on the X chromosome, damaging a particular gene (Ryynänen et al., 1995; Turk, 1995). Fragile X syndrome is the most common inherited cause of mild to moderate mental retardation. It has also been linked to 2 to 3 percent of cases of infantile autism, a serious emotional dis-

genetic imprinting A pattern of inheritance in which alleles are imprinted, or chemically marked, in such a way that one pair member is activated, regardless of its makeup.

order of early childhood involving bizarre, self-stimulating behavior and delayed or absent language and communication (Bailey et al., 1993; Hagerman, 1996). Research reveals that the defective gene at the fragile site is expressed only when it is passed from mother to child (Rose, 1995; Thapar et al., 1994).

■ **MUTATION.** How are harmful genes created in the first place? The answer is **mutation,** a sudden but permanent change in a segment of DNA. A mutation may affect only one or two genes, or it may involve many genes, as is the case for the chromosomal disorders we will discuss shortly. Some mutations occur spontaneously, simply by chance. Others are caused by a wide variety of hazardous environmental agents.

For many years, ionizing radiation has been known to cause mutations. Women who receive repeated doses of radiation before conception are more likely to miscarry or give birth to children with hereditary defects (Zhang, Cai, & Lee, 1992). Genetic abnormalities are also higher when fathers are exposed to radiation in their occupations. In one instance, men who worked at a reprocessing plant for nuclear fuel in England fathered an unusually high number of children who developed cancer. Exposure to radiation at the plant is believed to have damaged chromosomes in sperm, causing cancer in the children years later (Gardner et al., 1990). Does this mean that routine chest and dental X-rays are dangerous to future generations? Research indicates that infrequent and mild exposure to radiation does not cause genetic damage. Instead, high doses over a long period of time appear to be required.

Although only 3 percent of pregnancies result in the birth of a baby with a hereditary abnormality, these children account for about 40 percent of childhood deaths and 5 to 10 percent of childhood hospital admissions (Shiloh, 1996). As these figures reveal, progress in preventing and treating genetic diseases still lags far behind that of nongenetic diseases, although (as we will see shortly) great strides are currently being made.

■ **POLYGENIC INHERITANCE.** So far, we have discussed patterns of inheritance in which people either display a particular trait or do not. These cut-and-dried individual differences are much easier to trace to their genetic origins than are characteristics that vary continuously among people. Many traits of interest to child development specialists, such as height, weight, intelligence, and personality, are of this type. People are not just tall or short, bright or dull, outgoing or shy. Instead, they show gradations between these extremes. Continuous traits like these are due to **polygenic inheritance,** in which many genes determine the characteristic in question. Polygenic inheritance is complex, and much about it is still unknown. In the final section of this chapter, we will pay special attention to this form of genetic transmission by examining ways that researchers infer the influence of heredity on human attributes when knowledge of precise patterns of inheritance is unavailable.

CHROMOSOMAL ABNORMALITIES

Besides inheriting harmful recessive alleles, abnormalities of the chromosomes are a major cause of serious developmental problems. Most chromosomal defects are the result of mistakes during meiosis, when the ovum and sperm are formed. A chromosome pair does not separate properly, or part of a chromosome breaks off. Since these errors involve far more DNA than problems due to single genes, they usually produce disorders with many physical and mental symptoms.

■ **DOWN SYNDROME.** The most common chromosomal abnormality, occurring in 1 out of every 800 live births, is *Down syndrome.* In 95 percent of cases, it results from a failure of the twenty-first pair of chromosomes to separate during meiosis, so the new individual inherits three of these chromosomes rather than the normal two. For this reason, Down syndrome is sometimes called *trisomy 21.* In other, less frequent forms, an extra broken piece of a twenty-first chromosome is present. Or an error occurs during the early stages of mitosis, causing some but not all body cells to have the defective chromosomal makeup (called a *mosaic* pattern). In these instances, since less genetic material is involved, symptoms of the disorder are less extreme (Hodapp, 1996).

mutation A sudden but permanent change in a segment of DNA.

polygenic inheritance A pattern of inheritance involving many genes that applies to characteristics that vary continuously among people.

The facial features and short, stocky build of the boy on the left are typical of Down syndrome. Although his intellectual development is impaired, he is doing well because he is growing up in a stimulating home where his special needs are met and he is loved and accepted.

(Stephen Frisch/Stock Boston)

TABLE 3.4

Risk of Giving Birth to a Down Syndrome Child by Maternal Age

Maternal Age	Risk
20	1 in 1,900 births
25	1 in 1,200
30	1 in 900
33	1 in 600
36	1 in 280
39	1 in 130
42	1 in 65
45	1 in 30
48	1 in 15

Note: The risk of giving birth to a Down syndrome baby after age 35 has increased slightly over the past 20 years, due to improved medical interventions during pregnancy and consequent greater likelihood of a Down syndrome fetus surviving to be liveborn. *Sources:* Adapted from Halliday et al., 1995; Meyers et al., 1997.

Children with Down syndrome have distinct physical features—a short, stocky build, a flattened face, a protruding tongue, almond-shaped eyes, and an unusual crease running across the palm of the hand. In addition, infants with Down syndrome are often born with eye cataracts and heart and intestinal defects. Because of medical advances, fewer Down syndrome children die early than was the case in the past. Three decades ago, most died by early adulthood. Today, many survive into their sixties and beyond (Carr, 1995).

The behavioral consequences of Down syndrome include mental retardation, speech difficulties, limited vocabulary, and slow motor development. These problems become more evident with age, since Down syndrome children show a gradual slowing in development when compared with normal children (Dykens, Hodapp, & Evans, 1994).

Down syndrome babies are more difficult to care for than are normal infants. Their facial deformities often lead to breathing and feeding difficulties. In addition, they smile less readily, show poor eye-to-eye contact, and explore objects less persistently. Therefore, caregivers need to be more assertive in getting these infants to become engaged in their surroundings. When parents make this effort, their children show better developmental progress (Harris, Kasari, & Sigman, 1996). Early intervention programs also foster the development of Down syndrome youngsters, although emotional, social, and motor skills improve more than intellectual performance (Van Dyke et al., 1990). These findings indicate that even though Down syndrome is a genetic disorder, environmental factors affect how well these children fare in the long run.

As Table 3.4 shows, the risk of a Down syndrome baby rises dramatically with maternal age. Why is this so? Geneticists believe that the ova, present in the woman's body since her own prenatal period, weaken over time because of the aging process or increased exposure to harmful environmental agents. As a result, chromosomes do not separate properly as they complete the process of meiosis at conception. A second possibility is that with age, mothers are less likely to miscarry defective conceptions (Antonarakis, 1992). The mother's gamete, however, is not always the cause of a Down syndrome child. In about 20 percent of cases, the extra genetic material originates with the father. However, Down syndrome and other chromosomal abnormalities are not related to advanced paternal age. In these instances, the mutation occurs for other unknown reasons (Phillips & Elias, 1993).

■ **ABNORMALITIES OF THE SEX CHROMOSOMES.** Disorders of the autosomes other than Down syndrome usually disrupt development so severely that miscarriage occurs. When such babies are born, they rarely survive beyond early childhood. In contrast, abnormalities of the sex chromosomes usually lead to fewer problems. In fact, sex chromosome disorders often are not recognized until adolescence when, in some of the deviations, puberty is delayed. The most common problems involve the presence of an extra chromosome (either X or Y) or the absence of one X chromosome in females (see Table 3.5).

A variety of myths about individuals with sex chromosome disorders exist. For example, many people think that males with *XYY syndrome* are more aggressive and antisocial than XY males. This is not necessarily true. Also, it is widely believed that children with sex chromosome disorders suffer from mental retardation. Yet most do not. The intelligence of boys with XYY syndrome is similar to that of normal children (Netley, 1986; Stewart, 1982). And the intellectual problems of children with *triple X, Klinefelter, and Turner syndromes* are very specific. Verbal difficulties (for example, with reading and vocabulary) are common among girls with triple X syndrome and boys with Klinefelter syndrome, each of whom inherits an extra X chromosome (Netley, 1986; Rovet et al., 1996). In contrast, Turner syndrome girls, who are missing an X, have trouble with spatial relationships. Their handwriting is poor, and they have difficulty telling right from left, following travel directions, and noticing changes in facial expressions (Money, 1993; Romans et al., 1997; Temple & Carney, 1995). These findings tell us that adding to or subtracting from the usual number of X chromosomes results in particular intellectual deficits. At present, geneticists do not know the reason why.

TABLE 3.5

Sex Chromosomal Disorders

Disorder	Description	Incidence	Treatment
XYY syndrome	Inheritance of an extra Y chromosome. Typical characteristics are above-average height, large teeth, and sometimes severe acne. Intelligence, development of male sexual characteristics, and fertility are normal.	1 in 1,000 male births	No special treatment necessary.
Triple X syndrome (XXX)	Inheritance of an extra X chromosome. Impaired verbal intelligence. Affected girls are no different in appearance or sexual development from normal agemates, except for a greater tendency toward tallness.	1 in 500 to 1,250 female births	Special education to treat verbal ability problems.
Klinefelter syndrome (XXY)	Inheritance of an extra X chromosome. Impaired verbal intelligence. Afflicted boys are unusually tall, have a body fat distribution resembling females, and show incomplete development of sex characteristics at puberty. They are usually sterile.	1 in 500 to 1,000 male births	Hormone therapy at puberty to stimulate development of sex characteristics. Special education to treat verbal ability problems.
Turner syndrome (XO)	All or part of the second X chromosome is missing. Impaired spatial intelligence. Ovaries usually do not develop prenatally. Incomplete development of sex characteristics at puberty. Other features include short stature and webbed neck.	1 in 8,000 female births	Hormone therapy in childhood to stimulate physical growth and at puberty to promote development of sex characteristics. Special education to treat spatial ability problems.

Sources: Moore & Persaud, 1998; Money, 1993; Netley, 1986; Pennington et al., 1982; Ratcliffe, Pan, & McKie, 1992; Schiavi et al., 1984.

Reproductive Choices

n the past, many couples with genetic disorders in their families chose not to bear a child at all rather than risk having an abnormal baby. Today, genetic counseling and prenatal diagnosis help people make informed decisions about conceiving or carrying a pregnancy to term.

GENETIC COUNSELING

Genetic counseling is a communication process designed to help couples assess their chances of giving birth to a baby with a hereditary disorder and choose the best course of action in view of risks and family goals (Shiloh, 1996). Individuals likely to seek counseling are those who have had difficulties bearing children, such as repeated miscarriages, or who know that genetic problems exist in their families. In addition, women who delay childbearing past age 35 are candidates for genetic counseling. After this time, the overall rate of chromosomal abnormalities rises sharply, from 1 in every 190 to as many as 1 in every 10 pregnancies at age 48 (Meyers et al., 1997).

If a family history of mental retardation, physical defects, or inherited diseases exists, the genetic counselor interviews the couple and prepares a *pedigree,* a picture of the family tree in which affected relatives are identified. The pedigree is used to estimate the likelihood that parents will have an abnormal child, using the same genetic principles discussed earlier in this chapter. In the case of many disorders, blood tests or genetic analyses can reveal whether the parent is a carrier of the harmful gene. Turn back to pages 78–79, and you will see that carrier detection is possible for all of the recessive diseases listed in Table 3.3. A carrier test has been developed for fragile X syndrome as well (Ryynänen et al., 1995).

genetic counseling Counseling that helps couples assess the likelihood of giving birth to a baby with a hereditary disorder and choose the best course of action in view of risks and family goals.

The Pros and Cons of Reproductive Technologies

OME COUPLES DECIDE not to risk pregnancy because of a history of genetic disease. And many others—in fact, one-sixth of all couples who try to conceive—discover that they are sterile. Today, increasing numbers of individuals are turning to alternative methods of conception—technologies that, although fulfilling the wish of parenthood, have become the subject of heated debate.

DONOR INSEMINATION AND IN VITRO FERTILIZATION. For several decades, *donor insemination*—injection of sperm from an anonymous man into a woman—has been used to overcome male reproductive difficulties. In recent years, it has also permitted women without a heterosexual partner to bear children. In the United States alone, 30 thousand children are conceived through donor insemination each year (Nachtigall et al., 1997).

In vitro fertilization is another reproductive technology that has become increasingly common. Since the first "test tube" baby was born in England in 1978, many thousands of infants have been created as a result of this technique. With in vitro fertilization, hormones are given to a woman, stimulating ripening of several ova. These are removed surgically and placed in a dish of nutrients, to which sperm are added. Once an ovum is fertilized and begins to duplicate into several cells, it is injected into the mother's uterus, where, hopefully, it will implant and develop.

In vitro fertilization is usually used to treat women whose fallopian tubes are permanently damaged, and it is successful for 20 percent of those who try it. These results have been encouraging enough that the technique has been expanded. By mixing and matching gametes, pregnancies can be brought about when either or both partners have a reproductive problem. Fertilized ova and sperm can even be frozen and stored in embryo banks for use at some future time, thereby guaranteeing healthy zygotes should age or illness lead to fertility problems. For example, a childless widow conceived after in vitro fertilization with sperm donated by her husband before he received radiation treatment for testicular cancer, which left him sterile (Ahaja et al., 1997).

Children conceived through these methods may be genetically unrelated to one or both of their parents. In addition most parents who have used in vitro fertilization do not tell

their children about their origins, although health professionals now encourage them to do so (Cook et al., 1995). Does lack of genetic ties or secrecy surrounding these techniques interfere with parent–child relationships? Apparently not. Research reveals that parenting is somewhat warmer and more emotionally involved for young children conceived through in vitro fertilization or donor insemination than for children who were easily conceived. A strong desire for parenthood among couples who have experienced reproductive problems seems to enhance family functioning (Golombok et al., 1995; van Balen, 1996). Consistent with this interpretation, children of in vitro fertilization score just as well as, and sometimes better than, other children in cognitive social skills (McMahon et al., 1995).

Clearly donor insemination and in vitro fertilization have many benefits. Nevertheless, serious questions have arisen about their use. Many U.S. states have no legal guidelines for these procedures. As a result, donors are not always screened for genetic or sexually transmitted diseases. In addition, few American doctors keep records of donor characteristics. Yet the resulting children may someday want to know their genetic background or need to for medical reasons (Nachtigall, 1993).

SURROGATE MOTHERHOOD. A more controversial form of medically assisted conception is *surrogate motherhood*. Typically in this procedure, sperm from a man whose wife is infertile are used to inseminate a woman, who is paid a fee for her childbearing services. In return, the surrogate agrees to turn the baby over to the man (who is the natural father). The child is then adopted by his wife.

Although most of these arrangements proceed smoothly, those that end up in court highlight serious risks for all concerned. In one case, both parties rejected the infant with severe disabilities that resulted from the pregnancy. In several others, the surrogate mother changed her mind and wanted to keep the baby. These children came into the world in the midst of family conflict that threatened to last for years to come.

Since surrogacy favors the wealthy as contractors for infants and the less economically advantaged as surrogates, it may promote exploitation of financially needy women (Sureau, 1997). In addition, most surrogates already have children of their own, who may be deeply affected by the pregnancy. Knowledge that their mother would give away a

---

When all the relevant information is in, the genetic counselor helps people consider appropriate options. These include "taking a chance" and conceiving, adopting a child, or choosing from among a variety of reproductive technologies. The Social Issues box above describes these medical interventions into conception along with the host of legal and ethical dilemmas that have arisen in their application.

PRENATAL DIAGNOSIS AND FETAL MEDICINE

prenatal diagnostic methods
Medical procedures that permit detection of developmental problems before birth.

If couples who might bear an abnormal child decide to conceive, several **prenatal diagnostic methods**—medical procedures that permit detection of problems before birth—are available (see Table 3.6 on page 86). Women of advanced maternal age are prime candidates for *amniocentesis* or *chorionic villus sampling* (see Figure 3.6 on page 87). Except for *ultra-*

Fourteen years after menopause, 63-year-old Arceli Keh gave birth to a baby using a donor ovum that was fertilized in vitro with her 61-year-old husband's sperm and injected into her uterus. Will baby Cynthia's parents live to see her reach adulthood? Post-menopausal childbearing is highly controversial.

(National Enquirer)

baby for profit may cause these youngsters to worry about the security of their own family circumstances.

NEW REPRODUCTIVE FRONTIERS. Reproductive technologies are evolving faster than societies can weigh the ethics of these procedures. Doctors have used donor ova from younger women in combination with in vitro fertilization to help post-menopausal women become pregnant. Most recipients are in their 40s, but a 62-year-old has given birth in Italy and a 63-year-old in the United States (Beck, 1994; Kalb, 1997). Even though candidates for post-menopausal-assisted childbirth are selected on the basis of good health, serious questions arise about bringing children into the world whose parents may not live to see them reach adulthood. Based on U.S. life expectancy data, 1 in 3 moth-

ers and 1 in 2 fathers having a baby at age 55 will die before their child enters college (Bowman & Saunders, 1994).

Currently, experts are debating other reproductive options. At donor banks, customers can select ova or sperm on the basis of physical characteristics and even the IQ of potential donors. Some worry that this practice is a dangerous step toward selective breeding of the human species. Another potentially worrisome ethical concern stems from researchers who have delivered baby mice using the transplanted ovaries of aborted fetuses (Hashimoto, Noguchi, & Nakatsuji, 1992). If the same procedure were eventually applied to human beings, it would create babies whose genetic mothers had never been born.

Finally, scientists have successfully cloned (made multiple copies of) fertilized ova in sheep, cattle, and monkeys, and they are working on effective ways to do so in humans (Haworth & Strosnider, 1997). By providing extra ova for injection, cloning might improve the success rate of in vitro fertilization. But it also opens the possibility of mass producing genetically identical people. Consequently, no federal grants are available for research on human cloning.

Although new reproductive technologies permit many barren couples to rear healthy newborn babies, laws are needed to regulate them. In Australia, New Zealand, and Sweden, individuals conceived with donated gametes have a right to information about their genetic origins (Daniels & Lewis, 1996). Pressure from those working in the field of assisted reproduction may soon lead to a similar policy in the United States.

In the case of surrogate motherhood, the ethical problems are so complex that 18 U.S. states have sharply restricted the practice, and Australia, Canada, and many European nations have banned it, arguing that the status of a baby should not be a matter of commercial arrangement and that a part of the body should not be rented or sold (McGee, 1997). England, France, and Italy have prohibited in vitro fertilization for women past menopause (Beck, 1994). At present, nothing is known about the psychological consequences of being a product of these procedures. Research on how such children grow up, including what they know and how they feel about their origins, is important for weighing the pros and cons of these techniques.

sound and *maternal blood analysis*, prenatal diagnosis should not be used routinely, since other methods have some chance of injuring the developing organism (Steele et al., 1996).

Improvements in prenatal diagnosis have led to new advances in fetal medicine. Today, some medical problems are being treated before birth. For example, by inserting a needle into the uterus, doctors can administer drugs to the fetus. Surgery has been performed to repair such problems as heart and lung malformations, urinary tract obstructions, and neural defects. Recently, a fetus with a hereditary immune deficiency received a bone marrow transplant from his father that succeeded in creating a normally functioning immune system (Flake et al., 1996).

Nevertheless, these practices remain controversial. Although some babies are saved, the techniques frequently result in complications, the most common being premature labor and miscarriage (Quinn & Adzick, 1997). Yet when parents are told that their

TABLE 3.6

Prenatal Diagnostic Methods

Method	Description
Amniocentesis	The most widely used technique. A hollow needle is inserted through the abdominal wall to obtain a sample of fluid in the uterus. Cells are examined for genetic defects. Can be performed by 11 to 14 weeks after conception; 1 to 2 more weeks are required for test results. Small risk of miscarriage.
Chorionic villus sampling	A procedure that can be used if results are desired or needed very early in pregnancy. A thin tube is inserted into the uterus through the vagina or a hollow needle is inserted through the abdominal wall. A small plug of tissue is removed from the end of one or more chorionic villi, the hairlike projections on the membrane surrounding the developing organism. Cells are examined for genetic defects. Can be performed at 6 to 8 weeks after conception, and results are available within 24 hours. Entails a slightly greater risk of miscarriage than does amniocentesis. Also associated with a small risk of limb deformities, which increases the earlier the procedure is performed.
Fetoscopy	A small tube with a light source at one end is inserted into the uterus to inspect the fetus for defects of the limbs and face. Also allows a sample of fetal blood to be obtained, permitting diagnosis of such disorders as hemophilia and sickle cell anemia as well as neural defects (see below). Usually performed between 15 and 18 weeks after conception, although can be done as early as 5 weeks. Entails some risk of miscarriage, which increases the earlier the procedure is performed.
Ultrasound	High-frequency sound waves are beamed at the uterus; their reflection is translated into a picture on a videoscreen that reveals the size, shape, and placement of the fetus. By itself, permits assessment of fetal age, detection of multiple pregnancies, and identification of gross physical defects. Also used to guide amniocentesis, chorionic villi biopsy, and fetoscopy. When used five or more times, may increase the chances of low birth weight.
Maternal blood analysis	By the second month of pregnancy, some of the developing organism's cells enter the maternal bloodstream. An elevated level of alphafetoprotein may indicate kidney disease, abnormal closure of the esophagus, or neural tube defects, such as anencephaly (absence of most of the brain) and spina bifida (bulging of the spinal cord from the spinal column). Isolated cells can be examined for genetic defects, such as Down syndrome.
Preimplantation genetic diagnosis	After in vitro fertilization and duplication of the zygote into a cluster of about eight cells, one cell is removed and examined for hereditary defects. Only if that cell is free of detectable genetic disorders is the fertilized ovum implanted in the woman's uterus.

Sources: Canick & Saller, 1993; Eiben et al., 1997; Lissens & Sermon, 1997; Moore & Persaud, 1998; Newnham et al., 1993; Quintero, Puder, & Cotton, 1993; Shurtleff & Lemire, 1995; Steele et al., 1996; Wapner, 1997.

unborn child has a serious defect, they may be willing to try almost any option, even if there is only a slim chance of success. Currently, the medical profession is struggling with how to help parents make informed decisions about fetal surgery. One suggestion is that the advice of an independent counselor be provided—a doctor or nurse who understands the risks but is not involved in doing research on or performing the procedure.

Advances in *genetic engineering* also offer new hope for correcting hereditary defects. Genetic repair of the prenatal organism is one goal of today's genetic engineers. As part of the Human Genome Project, researchers are mapping human chromosomes, finding the precise location of genes for specific traits and devising new, gene-based treatments. To find out about the project's progress, refer to the From Research to Practice box on pages 88–89.

If prenatal diagnosis shows that the fetus has a condition that cannot be corrected, parents are faced with whether or not to have an abortion. The decision to terminate a desired pregnancy is painful for all who have to make it. Parents must deal with the emotional shock of the news and decide what to do within a short period of time. If they choose abortion, they face the grief that comes with having lost a wanted child, worries about future pregnancies, and possible guilt about the abortion itself. Fortunately, 95 per-

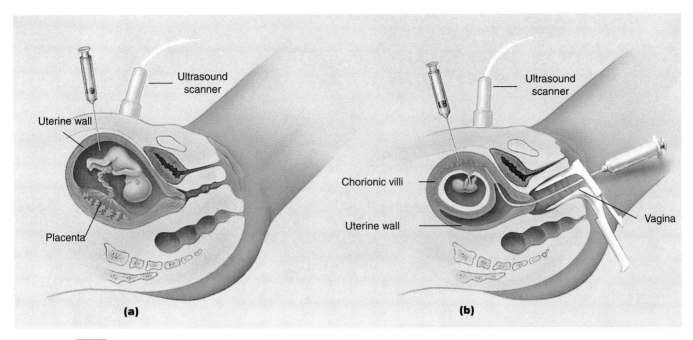

(a) **(b)**

FIGURE 3.6

Amniocentesis and chorionic villus sampling. Today, many defects and diseases can be detected before birth using these procedures. (a) In amniocentesis, a hollow needle is inserted through the abdominal wall into the uterus. Fluid is withdrawn and fetal cells are cultured, a process that takes 1 to 2 weeks. (b) Chorionic villus sampling can be performed much earlier in pregnancy, at 6 to 8 weeks after conception, and results are available within 24 hours. Two approaches to obtaining a sample of chorionic villi are shown: inserting a thin tube through the vagina into the uterus or a needle through the abdominal wall. In both amniocentesis and chorionic villus sampling, an ultrasound scanner is used for guidance.

(From K. L. Moore & T. V. N. Persaud, 1998, *Before We Are Born*, 5th ed., Philadelphia: Saunders, p. 115. Adapted by permission of the publisher and author.)

cent of fetuses examined through prenatal diagnosis are normal (Jones, 1997). Because such tests are possible, many individuals whose age or family history would have caused them to avoid pregnancy entirely can now have healthy children.

BRIEF REVIEW

ach individual is made up of trillions of cells. Inside each cell nucleus are chromosomes, which contain a molecule called DNA. Genes are segments of DNA that determine our species and unique characteristics. Gametes, or sex cells, are formed through a process of cell division called meiosis, which halves the usual number of chromosomes in human cells. Then, when sperm and ovum unite to form the zygote, each new being has the correct number of chromosomes. A different combination of sex chromosomes establishes whether a child will be a boy or a girl. Two types of twins—identical and fraternal—are possible. Identical twins have the same genetic makeup, whereas fraternal twins are genetically no more alike than ordinary siblings.

Four patterns of inheritance—dominant–recessive, codominant, X-linked, and genetic imprinting—underlie many traits and disorders. Continuous characteristics, such as height and intelligence, result from the enormous complexities of polygenic inheritance, which involves many genes. Chromosomal abnormalities occur when meiosis is disrupted during gamete formation. Disorders of the autosomes are usually more severe than those of the sex chromosomes.

Genetic counseling helps people with a family history of reproductive problems or hereditary defects make informed decisions about bearing a child. Prenatal diagnostic methods permit early detection of fetal problems. Advances in fetal medicine and genetic engineering offer new hope for treating disorders before birth.

ASK YOURSELF . . .

◆ *Gilbert and Jan are planning to have children. Gilbert's genetic makeup is homozygous for dark hair; Jan's is homozygous for blond hair. What proportion of their children are likely to be dark haired? Explain.*

◆ *Ashley and Harold both carry the defective gene for fragile X syndrome. Explain why Ashley's child inherited the disorder but Harold's did not.*

◆ CONNECTIONS
Families of children with a genetic disorder, such as Down syndrome, face increased stresses. What factors, within and beyond the home, can help them cope well? (Return to Chapter 1, pages 27–30, to review ecological systems theory; also see the discussion of family functioning in Chapter 14, pages 559–562.)

The Human Genome Project

BEGUN IN 1990, the Human Genome Project is an ambitious, international research project aimed at deciphering the chemical makeup of human genetic material (genome) and identifying all 50,000 to 100,000 human genes. Its main goals are to provide powerful new approaches for understanding human evolution and the development of genetic disorders, so they can be prevented and treated. An additional goal is to examine the ethical, legal, and social implications of new genetic technologies and to educate the public about them.

The research is an enormous undertaking. The human genome contains 3 billion chemical building blocks, or base pairs—enough to fill a thousand 1000-page telephone books if each is represented by a single letter. Given the size of the project, researchers have had to develop methods for DNA analysis that can process large amounts of information relatively quickly and accurately. Even with these procedures, scientists will have worked for over a decade before they attain their goal, at a cost of billions of dollars.

MAPPING AND SEQUENCING DNA. The Human Genome Project yields three main research tools, which enable scientists to identify specific genes (Lander, 1996). Each tool is a major phase of the research:

1. *Genetic map.* A genetic map consists of thousands of *markers,* or short, distinctive pieces of DNA, spaced along the chromosomes. Just as finding a landmark in your city is easier if you can narrow its location between two nearby points, so researchers first try to limit their search for a particular gene to a small segment of a chromosome. Genetic mapping begins with collection of blood or tissue samples from families in which a trait or disorder is common. After extracting DNA from these samples, researchers look for sequences of bases shared among affected family members, which mark the location of the gene.

2. *Physical map.* To further pinpoint the gene, researchers create a physical map, made up of overlapping DNA fragments that span the marked regions of a chromosome. Using various methods, the chromosome is snipped into pieces. These are cloned, stored in the order in which they originally occurred along the chromosome, and used for further studies aimed at finding the specific gene. The fragments can then be analyzed to discover the base-by-base sequence of DNA.

3. *Sequence map.* The most challenging task is the creation of a sequence map of all 3 billion DNA bases of the human genome. Now that the genetic and physical maps are largely complete, the sequence map is being constructed, which allows scientists to find specific genes. Sequencing is expected to be accomplished by the year 2005.

To make all the information available to researchers worldwide, computer methods for easy storage, retrieval, and analysis of data are being devised. Also, since valuable information about human genes and their functions can be obtained by comparing them with corresponding genes in other species, mapping of six other organisms—the mouse, the rat, the fruit fly, the roundworm, yeast, and the common intestinal bacterium E. coli—is either under way or complete.

APPLICATIONS. The detailed genetic, physical, and sequence maps produced by the Human Genome Project are vital for understanding both disorders due to single genes and those that result from a complex interplay of multiple genes and environmental factors, such as heart disease, many forms of cancer, and mental illnesses, including depression and alcoholism. As of 1999, more than 38,000 human genes had been mapped or identified, including those for hundreds of inherited disorders, such as cystic fibrosis, Huntington disease, Duchenne muscular dystrophy, and some forms of cancer (Human Genome Program, 1999).

Prenatal Development

The sperm and ovum that unite to form the new individual are uniquely suited for the task of reproduction. The ovum is a tiny sphere, measuring $\frac{1}{175}$ of an inch in diameter, that is barely visible to the naked eye as a dot the size of a period at the end of this sentence. But in its microscopic world, it is a giant—the largest cell in the human body. The ovum's size makes it a perfect target for the much smaller sperm, which measure only $\frac{1}{500}$ of an inch.

CONCEPTION

About once every 28 days, in the middle of a woman's menstrual cycle, an ovum bursts from one of her *ovaries,* two walnut-sized organs located deep inside her abdomen (see Figure 3.7 on page 90). Surrounded by thousands of nurse cells that will feed and protect it along its path, the ovum is drawn into one of two *fallopian tubes*—long, thin structures

Discovery of disease-associated genes is leading to rapid advances in genetic counseling and prenatal diagnosis as additional tests for detecting abnormal genes become available. The Human Genome Project is also providing the basis for a new, molecular medicine. Gene-based treatments are being developed for hereditary disorders, cancer, and AIDS. Among these experimental procedures is *gene splicing*—delivering DNA carrying a functional gene to the patient's cells, thereby correcting a genetic abnormality.

Although inserting a gene into its proper place in a patient's genome is an immense challenge, one successful experiment reveals its potential. Four-year-old Ashanthi and 9-year-old Cynthia, each born with an inherited defect of the immune system, had experienced one life-threatening infection after another until researchers found a way to inject a normal, disease-fighting gene into their white blood cells. Because the body constantly replaces these cells, the procedure is not a cure; it must be repeated regularly. But today, Ashanthi and Cynthia are leading healthy, active lives (Bodmer & McKie, 1997).

A technician examines a DNA fingerprinting, or visual image of the sequence of bases in a particular region of a chromosome. Sequence mapping of all human DNA bases in the Human Genome Project permits meaningful interpretation of sequence variations between people, which can reveal who is healthy and who is susceptible to or stricken by certain diseases.

(Peter Menzel/Stock Boston)

ETHICAL, LEGAL, AND SOCIAL CONCERNS. As the Human Genome Project transforms biological research and medical practice, it has sparked concerns about how its tools will be applied. That abnormal DNA findings on one family member may have implications for others raises questions about whether those individuals should be told and, if so, how to ensure that they receive appropriate genetic counseling (Plomen & Rutter, 1998). Another major controversy involves testing children and adults who are at risk for genetic diseases but who do not yet show symptoms. Delay between the availability of diagnostic tests and effective intervention means that affected people must live with the anxiety of a future illness they cannot prevent. And some have encountered discrimination because of their heredity;

they have lost their health insurance and even their jobs. As a result, guidelines for responsible use of genetic technologies are being drawn up, and ethical principles have been devised to ensure the privacy of genetic information and protection against genetic discrimination (Marshall, 1996).

The Human Genome Project is making invaluable contributions to our knowledge of the hereditary basis of human biology and disease—information that offers great promise for improving human health. As its maps and sequences become broadly available to the scientific community, investigators continue to debate the best ways to protect the public interest while reaping the project's monumental rewards.

that lead to the hollow, soft-lined uterus. While the ovum is traveling, the spot on the ovary from which it was released, now called the *corpus luteum*, begins to secrete hormones that prepare the lining of the uterus to receive a fertilized ovum. If pregnancy does not occur, the corpus luteum shrinks, and the lining of the uterus is discarded 2 weeks later with menstruation.

The male produces sperm in vast numbers—an average of 300 million a day. In the final process of maturation, each sperm develops a tail that permits it to swim long distances, upstream in the female reproductive tract and into the fallopian tube, where fertilization usually takes place. The journey is difficult, and many sperm die. Of the approximately 360 million sperm released during sexual intercourse, only 300 to 500 reach the ovum, if one happens to be present. Sperm live for up to 6 days and can lie in wait for the ovum, which survives for only 1 day after being released into the fallopian tube. However, most conceptions result from intercourse during a 3-day period—on the day of or the 2 days preceding ovulation (Wilcox, Weinberg, & Baird, 1995).

With conception, the story of prenatal development begins to unfold. The vast changes that take place during the 38 weeks of pregnancy are usually divided into three

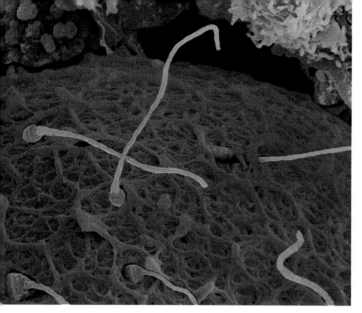

In this photo taken with the aid of a powerful microscope, sperm have completed their journey up the female reproductive tract and are beginning to penetrate the surface of the enormous-looking ovum, the largest cell in the human body. When one of the sperm is successful at fertilizing the ovum, the resulting zygote will begin to duplicate.

(Jack Burns/Ace/Phototake)

phases: (1) the period of the zygote, (2) the period of the embryo, and (3) the period of the fetus. As we look at what happens in each, you may find it useful to refer to the Milestones table on the following page.

THE PERIOD OF THE ZYGOTE

The period of the zygote lasts about 2 weeks, from fertilization until the tiny mass of cells drifts down and out of the fallopian tube and attaches itself to the wall of the uterus. The zygote's first cell duplication is long and drawn out; it is not complete until about 30 hours after conception. Gradually, new cells are added at a faster rate. By the fourth day, 60 to 70 cells exist that form a hollow, fluid-filled ball called a *blastocyst* (refer again to Figure 3.7). The cells on the inside, called the *embryonic disk*, will become the new organism; the outer ring will provide protective covering.

■ **IMPLANTATION**. Sometime between the seventh and ninth day, implantation occurs: the blastocyst burrows deep into the uterine lining. Surrounded by the woman's nourishing blood, now it starts to grow in earnest. At first, the protective outer layer multiplies fastest. A membrane, called the **amnion,** forms that encloses the developing organism in *amniotic fluid*. It helps keep the temperature of the prenatal world constant and provides a cushion against any jolts caused by the mother's movement. A *yolk sac* also appears. It produces blood cells until the developing liver, spleen, and bone marrow are mature enough to take over this function (Moore & Persaud, 1998).

The events of these first 2 weeks are delicate and uncertain. As many as 30 percent of zygotes do not make it through this phase. In some, the sperm and ovum do not join

FIGURE

Journey of the ovum to the uterus. Once every 28 days, an ovum matures, is released from one of the woman's ovaries, and is drawn into the fallopian tube. After fertilization, it begins to duplicate, at first slowly and then more rapidly. By the fourth day, it forms a hollow, fluid-filled ball called a blastocyst. The inner cells, or the embryonic disk, will become the new organism; the outer cells will provide protective covering. At the end of the first week, the blastocyst begins to implant in the uterine lining.

(Adapted from K. L. Moore & T. V. N. Persaud, 1998, *Before We Are Born*, 5th ed., Philadelphia: Saunders, p. 44. Reprinted by permission of the publisher and author.)

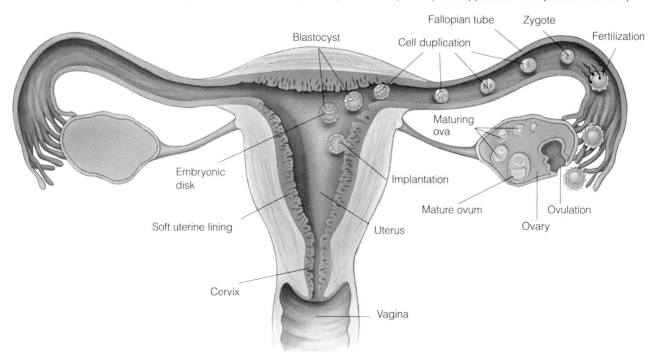

Prenatal Development

Trimester	Period	Weeks	Length and Weight	Major Events
First	Zygote	1		The one-celled zygote multiplies and forms a blastocyst.
		2		The blastocyst burrows into the uterine lining. Structures that feed and protect the developing organism begin to form—amnion, chorion, yolk sac, placenta, and umbilical cord.
	Embryo	3–4	¼ inch	A primitive brain and spinal cord appear. Heart, muscles, backbone, ribs, and digestive tract begin to develop.
		5–8	1 inch; ⅐ ounce	Many external body structures (for example, face, arms, legs, toes, fingers) and internal organs form. The sense of touch begins to develop, and the embryo can move.
	Fetus	9–12	3 inches; less than 1 ounce	Rapid increase in size begins. Nervous system, organs, and muscles become organized and connected, and new behavioral capacities (kicking, thumb sucking, mouth opening, and rehearsal of breathing) appear. External genitals are well formed, and the fetus's sex is evident.
Second		13–24	12 inches; 1.8 pounds	The fetus continues to enlarge rapidly. In the middle of this period, fetal movements can be felt by the mother. Vernix and lanugo keep the fetus's skin from chapping in the amniotic fluid. All of the neurons that will ever be produced in the brain are present by 24 weeks. Eyes are sensitive to light, and the fetus reacts to sound.
Third		25–38	20 inches; 7.5 pounds	The fetus has a chance of survival if born around this time. Size continues to increase. Lungs gradually mature. Rapid brain development causes sensory and behavioral capacities to expand. In the middle of this period, a layer of fat is added under the skin. Antibodies are transmitted from mother to fetus to protect against disease. Most fetuses rotate into an upside-down position in preparation for birth.

Sources: Moore & Persaud, 1998; Nilsson & Hamberger, 1990.

properly. In others, for some unknown reason, cell duplication never begins. By preventing implantation in these cases, nature eliminates most prenatal abnormalities in the very earliest stages of development (Sadler, 1995).

■ **THE PLACENTA AND UMBILICAL CORD.** By the end of the second week, another protective membrane, called the **chorion,** surrounds the amnion. From the chorion, tiny hairlike *villi* begin to emerge.[1] As these villi burrow into the uterine wall and develop into blood vessels, a special organ called the **placenta** starts to develop. By bringing the embryo's and mother's blood close together, the placenta will permit food and oxygen to reach the organism and waste products to be carried away. A membrane forms that allows these substances to be exchanged but prevents the mother's and embryo's blood from mixing directly.

amnion The inner membrane that forms a protective covering around the prenatal organism and encloses it in amniotic fluid, which helps keep temperature constant and provides a cushion against jolts caused by the mother's movement.

chorion The outer membrane that forms a protective covering around the prenatal organism. It sends out tiny hairlike villi, from which the placenta begins to emerge.

placenta The organ that separates the mother's bloodstream from the embryo's or fetus's bloodstream but permits exchange of nutrients and waste products.

[1]Recall from Table 3.6 on page 86 that chorionic villus sampling, in which tissue from the ends of the villi are removed and examined for genetic abnormalities, is the prenatal diagnostic method that can be performed earliest, by 6 to 8 weeks after conception.

During the period of the zygote, the fertilized ovum begins to duplicate at an increasingly rapid rate, forming a hollow ball of cells, or blastocyst, by the fourth day of fertilization. Here the blastocyst, magnified thousands of times, burrows into the uterine lining between the seventh and ninth day.

(© Lennart Nilsson, A Child Is Born/Bonniers)

The placenta is connected to the developing organism by the **umbilical cord.** In the period of the zygote, it first appears as a primitive body stalk, but during the course of pregnancy, it grows to a length of 1 to 3 feet. The umbilical cord contains one large vein that delivers blood loaded with nutrients and two arteries that remove waste products. The force of blood flowing through the cord keeps it firm, much like a garden hose, so it seldom tangles while the embryo, like a space-walking astronaut, floats freely in its fluid-filled chamber (Moore & Persaud, 1998).

By the end of the period of the zygote, the developing organism has found food and shelter in the uterus. Already it is a very complex being. These dramatic beginnings take place before all but the most sensitive woman knows she is pregnant.

THE PERIOD OF THE EMBRYO

The period of the **embryo** lasts from implantation through the eighth week of pregnancy. During these brief 6 weeks, the most rapid prenatal changes take place as the groundwork for all body structures and internal organs is laid down. Because all parts of the body are forming, the embryo is especially vulnerable to interference with healthy development. But the fact that embryonic growth takes place over a fairly short time span helps limit opportunities for serious harm to occur.

■ **LAST HALF OF THE FIRST MONTH.** In the first week of this period, the embryonic disk forms three layers of cells: (1) the *ectoderm*, which will become the nervous system and skin; (2) the *mesoderm*, from which will develop the muscles, skeleton, circulatory system, and other internal organs; and (3) the *endoderm*, which will become the digestive system, lungs, urinary tract, and glands. These three layers give rise to all parts of the body.

At first, the nervous system develops fastest. The ectoderm folds over to form a *neural tube*, or primitive spinal cord. At 3½ weeks, the top swells to form a brain. Production of *neurons* (nerve cells that store and transmit information) begins deep inside the neural tube. Once formed, neurons travel along tiny threads to their permanent locations, where they will form the major parts of the brain (Casaer, 1993).

This curled embryo is about 4 weeks old. In actual size, it is only ¼-inch long, but many body structures have begun to form. The primitive tail will disappear by the end of the embryonic period.

(© Lennart Nilsson, A Child Is Born/Bonniers)

By 7 weeks, the embryo's posture is more upright. Body structures—eyes, nose, arms, legs, and internal organs—are more distinct. An embryo of this age responds to touch. It can also move, although at less than an inch long and an ounce in weight, it is still too tiny to be felt by the mother.

(© Lennart Nilsson, A Child Is Born/Bonniers)

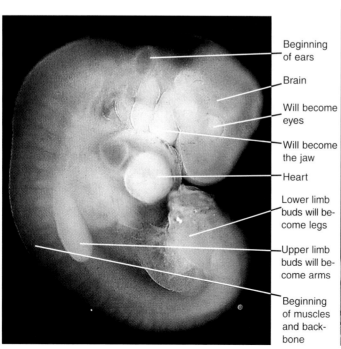

Beginning of ears

Brain

Will become eyes

Will become the jaw

Heart

Lower limb buds will become legs

Upper limb buds will become arms

Beginning of muscles and backbone

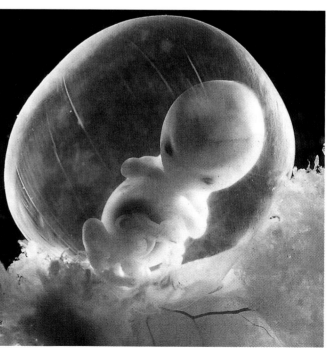

While the nervous system is developing, the heart begins to pump blood around the embryo's circulatory system, and muscles, backbone, ribs, and digestive tract start to appear. At the end of the first month, the curled embryo consists of millions of organized groups of cells with specific functions, although it is only one-fourth inch long.

■ **THE SECOND MONTH.** In the second month, growth continues rapidly. The eyes, ears, nose, jaw, and neck form. Tiny buds become arms, legs, fingers, and toes. Internal organs are more distinct: the intestines grow, the heart develops separate chambers, and the liver and spleen take over production of blood cells so that the yolk sac is no longer needed. Changing body proportions cause the embryo's posture to become more upright. Now 1 inch long and one-seventh of an ounce in weight, the embryo can already sense its world. It responds to touch, particularly in the mouth area and on the soles of the feet. And it can move, although its tiny flutters are still too light to be felt by the mother (Nilsson & Hamberger, 1990).

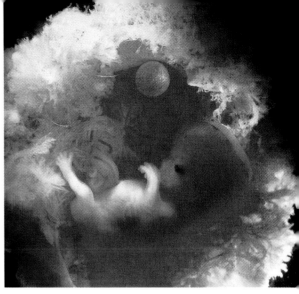

THE PERIOD OF THE FETUS

Lasting from the ninth week until the end of pregnancy, the period of the **fetus** is the "growth and finishing" phase. During this longest prenatal period, the organism begins to increase rapidly in size. The rate of body growth is extraordinary, especially from the ninth to the twentieth week (Moore & Persaud, 1998).

■ **THE THIRD MONTH.** In the third month, the organs, muscles, and nervous system start to become organized and connected. The brain signals, and in response, the fetus kicks, bends its arms, forms a fist, curls its toes, opens its mouth, and even sucks its thumb. The tiny lungs begin to expand and contract in an early rehearsal of breathing movements. By the twelfth week, the external genitals are well formed, and the sex of the fetus can be detected with ultrasound. Other finishing touches appear, such as fingernails, toenails, tooth buds, and eyelids that open and close. The heartbeat is now stronger and can be heard through a stethoscope.

Prenatal development is often divided into *trimesters,* or three equal periods of time. At the end of the third month, the first trimester is complete. Two more must pass before the fetus is fully prepared to survive outside the womb.

■ **THE SECOND TRIMESTER.** By the middle of the second trimester, between 17 and 20 weeks, the new being has grown large enough that its movements can be felt by the mother. If we could look inside the uterus at this time, we would find the fetus completely covered with a white, cheeselike substance called **vernix.** It protects the skin from chapping during the long months spent in the amniotic fluid. A white, downy hair covering called **lanugo** also appears over the entire body, helping the vernix stick to the skin.

At the end of the second trimester, many organs are quite well developed. And a major milestone is reached in brain development, in that nearly all the neurons are now in place. Few will be produced after this time. However, *glial cells,* which support and feed the neurons, continue to increase at a rapid rate throughout the remaining months of pregnancy, as well as after birth (Nowakowski, 1987).

Brain growth means new behavioral capacities. The 20-week-old fetus can be stimulated as well as irritated by sounds. And if a doctor has reason to look inside the uterus with fetoscopy (see Table 3.6), fetuses try to shield their eyes from the light with their hands, indicating that the sense of sight has begun to emerge (Nilsson & Hamberger, 1990). Still, a fetus born at this time cannot survive. Its lungs are too immature, and the brain has not yet developed to the point at which it can control breathing movements and body temperature.

■ **THE THIRD TRIMESTER.** During the final trimester, a fetus born early has a chance for survival. The point at which the baby can first survive is called the **age of viability.** It occurs sometime between 22 and 26 weeks (Moore & Persaud, 1998). If born between

---

During the period of the fetus, the organism increases rapidly in size, and body structures are completed. At 11 weeks, the brain and muscles are better connected. The fetus can kick, bend its arms, open and close its hands and mouth, and suck its thumb. Notice the yolk sac, which shrinks as pregnancy advances. The internal organs have taken over its function of producing blood cells.

(© Lennart Nilsson, A Child is Born/ Bonniers)

umbilical cord The long cord connecting the prenatal organism to the placenta that delivers nutrients and removes waste products.

embryo The prenatal organism from 2 to 8 weeks after conception, during which time the foundations of all body structures and internal organs are laid down.

fetus The prenatal organism from the beginning of the third month to the end of pregnancy, during which time completion of body structures and dramatic growth in size take place.

vernix A white, cheeselike substance covering the fetus and preventing the skin from chapping due to constant exposure to the amniotic fluid.

lanugo A white, downy hair that covers the entire body of the fetus, helping the vernix stick to the skin.

age of viability The age at which the fetus can first survive if born early. Occurs sometime between 22 and 26 weeks.

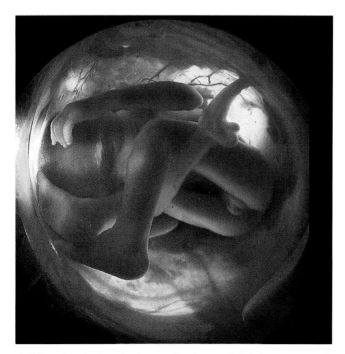

At 22 weeks, this fetus is almost a foot long and slightly over a pound in weight. Its movements can be clearly felt by the mother and by other family members who place a hand on her abdomen. If born at this time, a baby has a slim chance of surviving.
(© Lennart Nilsson, A Child Is Born/Bonniers)

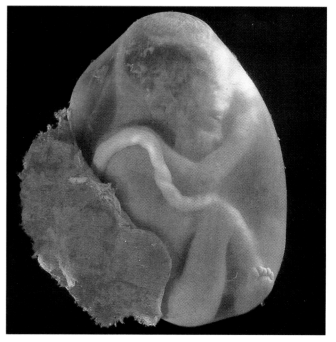

This 36-week-old fetus fills the uterus. To support its need for nourishment, the umbilical cord and placenta have grown very large. Notice the vernix (cheeselike substance), which protects the skin from chapping. The fetus has accumulated a layer of fat to assist with temperature regulation after birth. In another 2 weeks, it will be full term.
(© Lennart Nilsson, A Child Is Born/Bonniers)

the seventh and eighth months, a baby would still have trouble breathing, and oxygen assistance would be necessary. Although the respiratory center of the brain is now mature, tiny air sacs in the lungs are not yet ready to inflate and exchange carbon dioxide for oxygen.

The brain continues to make great strides during the last 3 months. The *cerebral cortex*, the seat of human intelligence, enlarges (see Figure 3.8). As neurological organization improves, the fetus spends more time awake. At 20 weeks, heart rate variability reveals no periods of alertness. But by 28 weeks, fetuses are awake about 11 percent of the time, a figure that rises to 16 percent just before birth (DiPietro et al., 1996a). And from the vigor of its movements and its daily cycles of activity and rest, the fetus takes on the beginnings of a personality (see the Variations box on page 96).

The third trimester also brings greater responsiveness to external stimulation. Around 24 weeks, fetuses can first feel pain, so after this time painkillers should be used in any surgical procedures (Royal College of Obstetricians and Gynecologists, 1997). By 25 weeks, fetuses react to nearby sounds with body movements (DiPietro et al., 1996a; Kisilevsky & Low, 1998). And in the last weeks of pregnancy, they learn to prefer the tone and rhythm of their mother's voice. In one clever study, mothers were asked to read aloud Dr. Seuss's lively book *The Cat in the Hat* to their unborn babies for the last 6 weeks of pregnancy. After birth, their infants were given a chance to suck on nipples that turned on recordings of the mother reading this book or different rhyming stories. The infants sucked hardest to hear *The Cat in the Hat*, the sound they had come to know while still in the womb (DeCasper & Spence, 1986).

During the final 3 months, the fetus gains more than 5 pounds and grows 7 inches. As it fills the uterus, it gradually moves less often. In addition, brain maturation, which permits the organism to inhibit behavior, may contribute to a decline in physical activity (DiPietro et al., 1996a).

In the eighth month, a layer of fat is added under the skin to assist with temperature regulation. The fetus also receives antibodies from the mother's blood that protect against illnesses, since the newborn's own immune system will not work well until several months

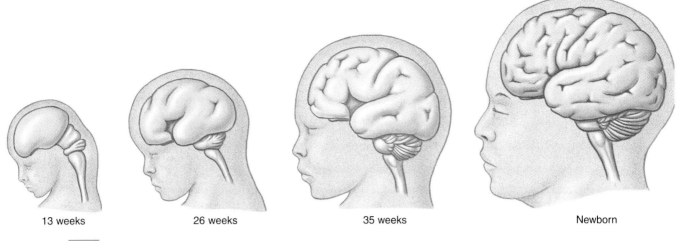

| 13 weeks | 26 weeks | 35 weeks | Newborn |

FIGURE 3.8

Growth of the brain during the prenatal period, shown one-half actual size. The *cerebral cortex*, the outer layer of gray matter, is responsible for higher brain functions, including sensation, voluntary movement, and thought. At 13 weeks, its surface is smooth. By 26 weeks (beginning of the third trimester), grooves and convolutions start to appear. These permit a dramatic increase in surface area without extensive increase in head size. As a result, maximum prenatal brain growth takes place while still permitting the full-term baby's head to pass through the birth canal. As cortical folds become more apparent (35 weeks), fetal sensory and behavioral capacities expand. The fetus spends more time awake, responds to external stimulation, and moves more vigorously (although less often as it fills the uterus). It also learns to prefer familiar sounds, such as the tone and rhythm of the mother's voice.

(Adapted from Moore, Persaud, & Shiota, 1994.)

after birth. In the last weeks, most fetuses assume an upside-down position, partly because of the shape of the uterus and because of gravity: the head is heavier than the feet. Growth starts to slow, and birth is about to take place.

Prenatal Environmental Influences

lthough the prenatal environment is far more constant than the world outside the womb, many factors can affect the embryo and fetus. In the following sections, we will see that there is much that parents—and society as a whole—can do to create a safe environment for development before birth.

TERATOGENS

The term **teratogen** refers to any environmental agent that causes damage during the prenatal period. It comes from the Greek word *teras*, meaning "malformation" or "monstrosity." This label was selected because scientists first learned about harmful prenatal influences from cases in which babies had been profoundly damaged.

Yet the harm done by teratogens is not always simple and straightforward. It depends on the following factors:

- *Dose.* We will see as we discuss particular teratogens that larger doses over longer time periods usually have more negative effects.

- *Heredity.* The genetic makeup of the mother and the developing organism plays an important role. Some individuals are better able to withstand harmful environments.

- *Other negative influences.* The presence of several negative factors at once, such as poor nutrition, lack of medical care, and additional teratogens, can worsen the impact of a single harmful agent.

- *Age.* The effects of teratogens vary with the age of the organism at time of exposure.

teratogen Any environmental agent that causes damage during the prenatal period.

Temperament in the Womb

A s YOLANDA, IN her seventh month of pregnancy, rested one afternoon, she felt several bursts of fetal activity, interspersed with quiet periods. "Hey, little one," she whispered, looking down at her large abdomen as it bulged after a foot kick, "you're on the move again. You always do this when I try to take a nap!" Then Yolanda wondered, "Can the fetus's behavior tell us anything about what he or she will be like after birth?"

Yolanda's question is at the heart of current efforts to determine whether individual differences in temperament have genetic origins. The earlier in development that predictors of temperamental traits can be identified, the greater the likelihood that heredity contributes to those traits.

Until recently, limited access to the fetus made it hard to study the relationship between fetal measures and temperament after birth. Today, sophisticated equipment for monitoring fetal responses permits researchers to address this issue.

In the most extensive study to date, 31 volunteer women, whose newborns were delivered healthy and full term, were monitored periodically during the prenatal period, from 20 weeks to just before birth (DiPietro et al., 1996b). During each session, the mothers lay quietly while a variety of fetal measures, including heart rate and activity level, were recorded. Then, at 3 and 6 months after birth, the mothers

were asked to rate various aspects of their baby's temperament, including fussiness, adaptability to new persons and situations, activity level, and regularity of eating and sleeping.

Findings revealed that pattern of fetal activity in the last few weeks of pregnancy was the best predictor of infant temperament. Fetuses (like Yolanda's) who cycled between quiet and active periods tended to become calm babies with predictable sleep–waking schedules. In contrast, fetuses who were highly active for long stretches were more likely to become difficult, unpredictable babies—fussy, especially when confronted with new people and situations; irregular in eating and sleeping; constantly wriggling and squirming; and waking often during the night (see Figure 3.9).

We must keep in mind that these links between prenatal measures and infant characteristics are only modest. In Chapter 10, we will see that sensitive care can modify a difficult baby's temperamental style. Furthermore, researchers have yet to determine whether fetal activity predicts *actual* infant behavior or just *maternal judgments* of that behavior.

But if the relationships just described hold up, then parents whose fetuses are very active can prepare for extra caregiving challenges. Recognizing that their baby-to-be may have a fussy, difficult disposition, they can take extra steps to provide a sympathetic environment as soon as the baby is born.

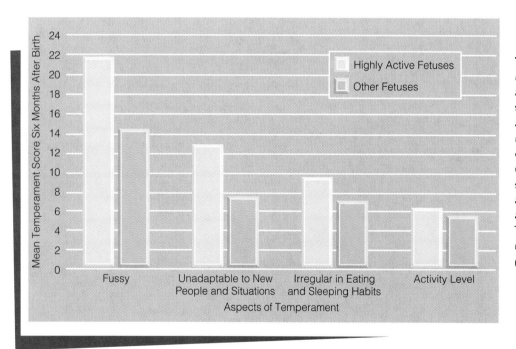

FIGURE 3.9

Temperament scores 6 months after birth of highly active fetuses versus other fetuses. Fetuses who were very active in the last weeks of pregnancy developed into 6-month-old babies who were fussier, more unadaptable to new people and situations, more irregular in eating and sleeping habits, and more active, as judged by their mothers. They also woke more often at night (not shown in the graph). (Adapted from DiPietro et al., 1996b.)

We can best understand this last idea if we think of prenatal development in terms of the *sensitive period* concept introduced in Chapter 1. Recall that a sensitive period is a limited time span in which a part of the body or a behavior is biologically prepared to develop rapidly. During that time, it is especially vulnerable to its surroundings. If the environment is harmful, then damage occurs that would not have otherwise happened, and recovery is difficult and sometimes impossible.

Figure 3.10 summarizes sensitive periods during prenatal development. Look carefully at it, and you will see that some parts of the body, such as the brain and eye, have long sensitive periods that extend throughout the prenatal phase. Other sensitive periods, such as those for the limbs and palate, are much shorter. Figure 3.10 also indicates that we can make some general statements about the timing of harmful influences. During the period of the zygote, before implantation, teratogens rarely have any impact. If they do, the tiny mass of cells is usually so completely damaged that it dies. The embryonic period is the time when serious defects are most likely to occur, since the foundations for all body parts are being laid down. During the fetal period, damage caused by teratogens is usually minor. However, some organs, such as the brain, eye, and genitals, can still be strongly affected.

The effects of teratogens are not limited to immediate physical damage. Although deformities of the body are easy to notice, important psychological consequences are harder to identify. Some may not show up until later in development. Others may occur as an indirect effect of physical damage. For example, a defect resulting from drugs the mother took during pregnancy can change reactions of others to the child as well as the child's ability to move about the environment. Over time, parent–child interaction, peer relations, and opportunities to explore may suffer. These experiences, in turn, can have far-reaching consequences for cognitive, emotional, and social development (Friedman, 1996).

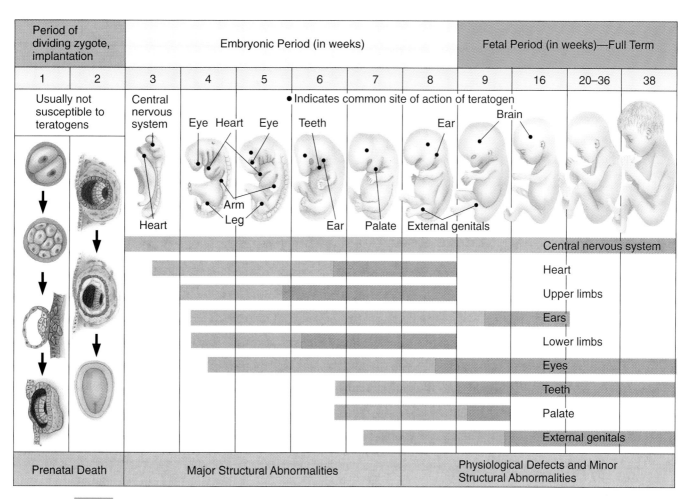

FIGURE 3.10

Sensitive periods in prenatal development. Each organ or structure has a sensitive period, during which its development may be disturbed. Gray horizontal lines indicate highly sensitive periods. Pink horizontal lines indicate periods that are somewhat less sensitive to teratogens, although damage can occur.

(From K. L. Moore & T. V. N. Persaud, 1998, *Before We Are Born,* 5th ed., Philadelphia: Saunders, p. 166. Adapted by permission of the publisher and author.)

Notice how an important idea about development discussed in Chapter 1 is at work here—that of *bidirectional* influences between child and environment. Now let's look at what scientists have discovered about a variety of teratogens.

■ **PRESCRIPTION AND NONPRESCRIPTION DRUGS.** Just about any drug a woman takes can enter the embryonic or fetal bloodstream. In the early 1960s, the world learned a tragic lesson about drugs and prenatal development. At that time, a sedative called thalidomide was widely available in Europe, Canada, and South America. Although the embryos of test animals were not harmed by it, in humans it had drastic effects. When taken by mothers between the fourth and sixth week after conception, thalidomide produced gross deformities of the embryo's developing arms and legs and, less frequently, damage to the ears, heart, kidneys, and genitals. About 7,000 infants around the world were affected (Moore & Persaud, 1998). As children exposed to thalidomide grew older, many scored below average in intelligence. Perhaps the drug damaged the central nervous system directly. Or the child-rearing conditions of these severely deformed youngsters may have impaired their intellectual development (Vorhees & Mollnow, 1987).

Despite the bitter lesson of thalidomide, many pregnant women continue to take over-the-counter drugs without consulting their doctors. Aspirin is one of the most common. Several studies suggest that regular use of aspirin is linked to low birth weight, infant death around the time of birth, poorer motor development, and lower intelligence test scores in early childhood (Barr et al., 1990; Streissguth et al., 1987). Other research, however, has failed to confirm these findings (see, for example, Hauth et al., 1995).

Another frequently consumed drug is caffeine, contained in coffee, tea, cocoa, and cola. Heavy caffeine intake (more than 3 cups of coffee per day) is associated with low birth weight, miscarriage, and newborn withdrawal symptoms, such as irritability and vomiting (Dlugosz & Bracken, 1992; Eskenazi, 1993). Some researchers report *dose-related* effects: the more caffeine consumed, the greater the likelihood of negative outcomes (Fortier, Marcoux, & Beaulac-Baillargeon, 1993; Infante-Rivard et al., 1993).

Because children's lives are involved, we must take findings like these quite seriously. At the same time, we cannot yet be sure that these drugs actually cause the problems mentioned. Often mothers take more than one kind of drug. If the prenatal organism is injured, it is hard to tell which drug might be responsible or if other factors correlated with drug taking are really at fault. Until we have more information, the safest course of action for pregnant women is to cut down on or avoid these drugs entirely.

■ **ILLEGAL DRUGS.** The use of highly addictive mood-altering drugs, such as cocaine and heroin, is widespread, especially in poverty-stricken inner-city areas, where these drugs provide a temporary escape from a daily life of hopelessness. The number of "cocaine babies" born in the United States has reached crisis levels in recent years. About 100,000 to 375,000 infants are affected annually, a figure that is rising (Barton, Harrigan, & Tse, 1995; Landry & Whitney, 1996).

Babies born to users of cocaine, heroin, or methadone (a less addictive drug used to wean people away from heroin) are at risk for a wide variety of problems, including prematurity, low birth weight, physical defects, breathing difficulties, and death around the time of birth (Burkett et al., 1994; Handler et al., 1994; Kandall et al., 1993; Miller, Boudreaux, & Regan, 1995; Ostrea, Ostrea, & Simpson, 1997). In addition, these infants arrive drug addicted. They are feverish and irritable and have trouble sleeping. Their cries are abnormally shrill and piercing—a common symptom among stressed newborns that we will discuss in Chapter 4 (Delaney-Black et al., 1996; Friedman, 1996; Martin et al., 1996). When mothers with many problems of their own must take care of these babies, who are difficult to calm down, cuddle, and feed, behavior problems are likely to persist.

Throughout the first year, heroin- and methadone-exposed infants are less attentive to the environment, and their motor development is slow. After infancy, some children get better, whereas others remain jittery and inattentive. The kind of parenting these youngsters receive may explain why there are long-term problems for some but not for others (Cosden, Peerson, & Elliott, 1997).

Unlike findings on heroin and methadone, growing evidence on cocaine suggests that many prenatally exposed babies have lasting difficulties. Cocaine constricts the blood vessels, causing oxygen delivered to the developing organism to fall dramatically for 15 minutes following a high dose. It also alters the chemical balance in the fetus's brain (Vogel, 1997). These effects may contribute to inattention and behavior problems in infancy and childhood and to a specific set of cocaine-linked physical defects, including eye, bone, genital, urinary tract, kidney, and heart deformities as well as brain hemorrhages and seizures (Block, Moore, & Scharre, 1997; Mayes et al., 1996; Moroney & Allen, 1994).

Babies born to mothers who smoke crack (a cheap form of cocaine that delivers high doses quickly through the lungs) seem to be worst off in terms of low birth weight and damage to the central nervous system. Visual, motor, and language problems are present during the preschool years (Bender et al., 1995; Richardson et al., 1996). Fathers may contribute to these outcomes. Research suggests that cocaine can attach itself to sperm, "hitchhike" its way into the zygote, and cause birth defects (Yazigi, Odem, & Polakoski, 1991).

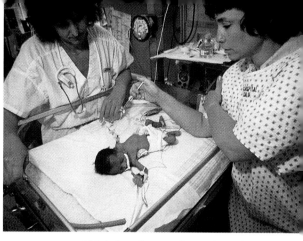

This baby, whose mother took crack during pregnancy, was born many weeks premature. He breathes with the aid of a respirator. His central nervous system may be seriously damaged. Researchers do not yet know if these outcomes are actually caused by crack or by the many other high-risk behaviors of drug users.

(Chuck Nacke/Woodfin Camp & Associates)

Still, it is difficult to isolate the precise damage caused by cocaine, since users often take several drugs and engage in other high-risk behaviors (Inciardi, Surratt, & Saum, 1997). For example, the majority of cocaine users smoke cigarettes and drink alcohol. The joint impact of these substances combined with a stressful daily life may be responsible for negative outcomes and lead the development of many cocaine-exposed infants to worsen over time (Alessandri, Bendersky, & Lewis, 1998).

Another illegal drug, marijuana, is used more widely than cocaine and heroin. Studies examining its relationship to low birth weight and prematurity reveal mixed findings (Fried, 1993). Several researchers have linked prenatal marijuana exposure to newborn startles, an abnormally high-pitched cry, and reduced visual attention to the environment (Dahl et al., 1995; Lester & Dreher, 1989). These outcomes certainly put newborn babies at risk for future problems, even though long-term effects have not been established.

■ **TOBACCO**. Although smoking has declined in Western nations, an estimated one-fourth to one-third of adults are regular cigarette users. The rate of tobacco use is especially high among women younger than 25 years of age—30 to 40 percent (Birenbaum-Carmeli, 1995; U.S. Bureau of the Census, 1998). The most well-known effect of smoking during pregnancy is low birth weight. But the likelihood of other serious consequences, such as prematurity, impaired breathing during sleep, miscarriage, infant death, and cancer later in childhood, is also increased. The more cigarettes a mother smokes, the greater the chances that her baby will be affected. If a pregnant woman decides to stop smoking at any time, even during the last trimester, she can help her baby. She immediately reduces the likelihood that her infant will be born underweight and suffer from future problems (Ahlsten, Cnattingius, & Lindmark, 1993; Groff et al., 1997; Kahn et al., 1994).

Even when a baby of a smoking mother appears to be born in good physical condition, slight behavioral abnormalities may threaten the child's development. Newborns of smoking mothers are less attentive to sounds and display more muscle tension (Fried & Makin, 1987). An unresponsive, restless baby may not evoke the kind of interaction from adults that promotes healthy psychological development. Some long-term studies report that prenatally exposed children have shorter attention spans and poorer mental test scores in early childhood, even after many other factors have been controlled (Fergusson, Horwood, & Lynskey, 1993; Fried & Watkinson, 1990). But other researchers have not been able to confirm these findings, so long-term effects remain uncertain (Barr et al., 1990; Streissguth et al., 1989).

Exactly how can smoking harm the fetus? Nicotine, the addictive substance in tobacco, causes the placenta to grow abnormally. As a result, transfer of nutrients is reduced, and the fetus gains weight poorly. Also, smoking raises the concentration of carbon monoxide in the bloodstreams of both mother and fetus. Carbon monoxide displaces oxygen from red blood cells. It damages the central nervous system and reduces birth weight in the fetuses of laboratory animals. Similar effects may occur in humans (Cotton, 1994; Friedman, 1996).

Finally, from one-third to one-half of nonsmoking pregnant women are "passive smokers" because their husbands, relatives, and co-workers use cigarettes. Passive smoking is also related to low birth weight, infant death, and possible long-term impairments

The mother of the severely retarded boy above drank heavily during pregnancy. His widely spaced eyes, thin upper lip, and short eyelid openings are typical of fetal alcohol syndrome. The adolescent girl below also has these physical symptoms. The brain damage caused by alcohol before she was born is permanent. It has made learning in school and adapting to everyday challenges extremely difficult.

(George Steinmetz)

fetal alcohol syndrome (FAS)
A set of defects that results when pregnant women consume large amounts of alcohol during most or all of pregnancy. Includes mental retardation; impaired motor coordination, attention, memory, and language; overactivity; slow physical growth; and facial abnormalities.

fetal alcohol effects (FAE)
The condition of children who display some but not all of the defects of fetal alcohol syndrome. Usually their mothers drank alcohol in smaller quantities during pregnancy.

in attention and learning (Fortier, Marcoux, & Brisson, 1994; Makin, Fried, & Watkinson, 1991). Clearly, expectant mothers should do what they can to avoid smoke-filled environments, and family members, friends, and employers need to assist them in this effort.

■ **ALCOHOL.** In a moving story, Michael Dorris (1989), a Dartmouth University anthropology professor, described what it was like to rear his adopted son Adam, whose biological mother drank heavily throughout pregnancy and died of alcohol poisoning shortly after his birth. A Sioux Indian, Adam was 3 years old when he came into Dorris's life. He was short and underweight and had a vocabulary of only 20 words.

Although he ate well, Adam grew slowly and remained painfully thin. He was prone to infection and had repeated brain seizures. His vocabulary did not expand like that of normal preschoolers. When he was 7, special testing revealed that Adam's intelligence was below average. At age 12, he could not add, subtract, or identify the town in which he lived.

Fetal alcohol syndrome (FAS) is the scientific name for Adam's condition. Mental retardation; impaired motor coordination, attention, memory, and language; and overactivity are typical of children with the disorder. Distinct physical symptoms also accompany it. These include slow physical growth and a particular pattern of facial abnormalities: widely spaced eyes; short eyelid openings; a small, upturned nose; and a thin upper lip. The small heads of these children indicate that the brain has been prevented from reaching full development. Other defects—of the eyes, ears, nose, throat, heart, genitals, urinary tract, or immune system—may also be present. In all babies with FAS, the mother drank heavily through most or all of her pregnancy (Streissguth, 1997).

Even when provided with enriched diets, FAS babies fail to catch up in physical size during infancy or childhood. Mental impairment is also permanent: In his teens and twenties, Adam's intelligence remained below average, and he had trouble concentrating and keeping a routine job. He also suffered from poor judgment. For example, he would buy something and not wait for change, or he would wander off in the middle of a task.

Sometimes children display only some of the physical abnormalities associated with FAS. In these cases, the child is said to suffer from **fetal alcohol effects (FAE).** Usually, mothers of these children drank alcohol in smaller quantities. The defects of FAE children vary with the timing and length of alcohol exposure during pregnancy. And many children of alcohol-abusing mothers escape the physical features of FAS but nevertheless display an FAS-like pattern of cognitive impairments (Mattson et al., 1998).

The more alcohol consumed by a woman during pregnancy, the poorer her child's motor coordination, information processing, reasoning, and intelligence and achievement test scores during the preschool and school years (Aronson, Hagberg, & Gillberg, 1997; Hunt et al., 1995; Streissguth et al., 1994). In adolescence, prenatal alcohol exposure is associated with disrupted school experiences, trouble with the law, inappropriate sexual behavior, alcohol and drug abuse, and lasting mental health problems (Streissguth, Bookstein, & Barr, 1996).

How does alcohol produce its devastating consequences? Researchers believe it does so in two ways. First, alcohol interferes with cell duplication and migration in the primitive neural tube. Psychophysiological measures, including fMRI and EEGs, reveal structural damage and abnormalities in brain functioning, including electrical and chemical activity involved in transferring messages from one part of the brain to another (Mattson & Riley, 1995; Swayze et al., 1997). Second, large quantities of oxygen are required to metabolize alcohol. When pregnant women drink heavily, they draw oxygen away from the embryo or fetus that is vital for cell growth in the brain and other parts of the body (Jenkins & Culbertson, 1996).

Like heroin and cocaine, alcohol abuse is higher in poverty-stricken sectors of the population (Streissguth, 1997). On the reservation where Adam was born, many children show symptoms of prenatal alcohol exposure. Unfortunately, when girls with FAS and FAE later become pregnant, the poor judgment caused by the syndrome often prevents them from understanding why they should avoid alcohol themselves. Thus, the tragedy is likely to be repeated in the next generation.

At this point you may be wondering, How much alcohol is safe during pregnancy? Is it all right to have a drink or two, either daily or occasionally? One study found that as little as 2 ounces of alcohol a day, taken very early in pregnancy, was associated with FAS-like facial features (Astley et al., 1992). Recall that other factors—both genetic and environmental—can make some fetuses more vulnerable to teratogens. A precise dividing line between safe and dangerous drinking levels cannot be established. Therefore, it is best for pregnant women to avoid alcohol entirely.

■ **HORMONES**. Earlier in this chapter, we saw that the Y chromosome causes male sex hormones (called *androgens*) to be secreted prenatally, leading to formation of male reproductive organs. In the absence of male hormones, female structures develop. Hormones are released as part of a delicately balanced system. If their quantity or timing is off, then defects of the genitals and other organs can occur.

Between 1945 and 1970, a synthetic hormone called *diethylstilbestrol* (DES) was widely used in the United States to prevent miscarriages in women with a history of pregnancy problems. As the daughters of these mothers reached adolescence and young adulthood, they showed an unusually high rate of cancer of the vagina and malformations of the uterus. When they tried to have children, their pregnancies more often resulted in prematurity, low birth weight, and miscarriage than did those of non-DES-exposed women. Young men whose mothers took DES prenatally were also affected. They showed an increased risk of genital abnormalities and cancer of the testes (Giusti, Iwamoto, & Hatch, 1995; Palmlund, 1996). Because of these findings, pregnant women are no longer treated with DES. But many children whose mothers took it are now of childbearing age, and they need to be carefully monitored by their doctors.

■ **RADIATION**. Earlier in this chapter, we saw that ionizing radiation can cause mutation, damaging the DNA in ova and sperm. When mothers are exposed to radiation during pregnancy, additional harm can come to the embryo or fetus. Defects due to radiation were tragically apparent in the children born to pregnant Japanese women who survived the atomic bombing of Hiroshima and Nagasaki near the end of World War II. Miscarriage, slow physical growth, an underdeveloped brain, and malformations of the skeleton and eyes were common (Michel, 1989). Even when an exposed child appears normal at birth, the possibility of later problems cannot be ruled out. For example, research suggests that even low-level radiation, as the result of industrial leakage or medical X-rays, can increase the risk of childhood cancer (Smith, 1992).

■ **ENVIRONMENTAL POLLUTION**. An astounding number of potentially dangerous chemicals are released into the environment in industrialized nations. In the United States, over 100,000 are in common use, and many new ones are introduced each year (Samuels & Samuels, 1996). Although many chemicals cause serious birth defects in laboratory animals, the impact on the human embryo and fetus is known for only a small number of them.

MERCURY AND LEAD. Among metallic elements, mercury and lead are established teratogens. In the 1950s, an industrial plant released waste containing high levels of mercury into a bay providing food and water for the town of Minimata, Japan. Many children born at the time were mentally retarded and showed other serious symptoms, including abnormal speech, difficulty in chewing and swallowing, and uncoordinated movements. Autopsies of those who died revealed widespread brain damage (Vorhees & Mollnow, 1987).

Pregnant women can absorb lead from car exhaust, lead-based paint flaking off the walls in old houses and apartment buildings, and other materials used in industrial occupations. High levels of lead exposure are consistently linked to prematurity, low birth weight, brain damage, and a wide variety of physical defects (Dye-White, 1986). Even a very low level of prenatal lead exposure seems to be dangerous. Affected babies show slightly poorer mental development during the first 2 years (Bellinger et al., 1987).

POLYCHLORINATED BIPHENYLS (PCBs). For many years, polychlorinated biphenyls (PCBs) were used to insulate electrical equipment. In 1977, they were banned by the U.S. government after research showed that, like mercury, they found their way into waterways and entered the food supply. In Taiwan, prenatal exposure to very high levels of PCBs in rice oil resulted in low birth weight, discolored skin, deformities of the gums and nails, brain-wave abnormalities, and delayed cognitive development (Chen & Hsu, 1994; Chen et al., 1994).

Steady, low-level PCB exposure may also be harmful. In one study, newborn babies of women who frequently ate PCB-contaminated fish, compared with newborns whose mothers ate little or no fish, had a variety of problems, including slightly reduced birth weight, smaller heads (suggesting brain damage), and less interest in their surroundings (Jacobson et al., 1984). When studied again at 7 months of age, PCB-exposed infants did more poorly on memory tests (Jacobson et al., 1985). A follow-up at 4 years of age showed persisting memory difficulties and lower verbal intelligence test scores (Jacobson, Jacobson, & Humphrey, 1990; Jacobson et al., 1992).

■ **MATERNAL DISEASE.** Five percent of women catch an infectious disease of some sort while pregnant. Most of these illnesses, such as the common cold and various strains of the flu, seem to have no impact on the embryo or fetus. However, as Table 3.7 indicates, a few diseases can cause extensive damage.

VIRUSES. *Rubella* (3-day German measles) is a well-known teratogen. In the mid-1960s, a worldwide epidemic of rubella led to the birth of over 20,000 American babies with serious defects. Consistent with the sensitive period concept, the greatest damage occurs when rubella strikes during the embryonic period. Over 50 percent of infants whose mothers become ill during that time show heart defects; eye cataracts; deafness; genital, urinary, and intestinal abnormalities; and mental retardation. Infection during the fetal period is less harmful, but low birth weight, hearing loss, and bone defects may still occur (Eberhart-Phillips, Frederick, & Baron, 1993).

Since 1966, infants and young children have been routinely vaccinated against rubella, so the number of prenatal cases today is much less than it was a generation ago. Still, 10 to 20 percent of American women of childbearing age lack the rubella antibody, so new outbreaks of the disease are still possible (Lee et al., 1992).

The *human immunodeficiency virus (HIV),* which leads to *acquired immune deficiency syndrome (AIDS),* a disease that destroys the immune system, is infecting increasing numbers of newborn babies. The percentage of AIDS victims who are women has risen dramatically over the past decade—from 6 to 13 percent in the United States and to more than

TABLE 3.7

Effects of Some Infectious Diseases During Pregnancy

+ = established finding, o = no present evidence, ? = possible effect that is not clearly established.

Disease	Miscarriage	Physical Malformations	Mental Retardation	Low Birth Weight and Prematurity
Viral				
Acquired immune deficiency syndrome (AIDS)	o	?	+	?
Chicken pox	o	+	+	+
Cytomegalovirus	+	+	+	+
Herpes simplex 2 (genital herpes)	+	+	+	+
Mumps	+	?	o	o
Rubella (German measles)	+	+	+	+
Bacterial				
Syphilis	+	+	+	?
Tuberculosis	+	?	+	+
Parasitic				
Malaria	+	o	o	+
Toxoplasmosis	+	+	+	+

Sources: Chatkupt et al., 1989; Cohen, 1993; Nelson, 1996; Peckham & Logan, 1993; Qazi et al., 1988; Samson, 1988; Sever, 1983; Vorhees, 1986.

50 percent in Africa. When they become pregnant, about 20 to 30 percent of the time they pass the deadly virus to the developing organism (Grant, 1995; Nourse & Butler, 1998).

In older children and adults, AIDS symptoms take years to emerge. In contrast, the disease proceeds rapidly in infants. By 6 months, weight loss, diarrhea, and repeated respiratory illnesses are common. The virus also causes brain damage, as indicated by seizures, a gradual loss in brain weight, and delayed mental and motor development. Most prenatal AIDS babies survive for only 5 to 8 months after the appearance of these symptoms (Parks, 1996). The antiviral drug zidovudine (ZDV) reduces prenatal AIDS transmission by 60 to 70 percent, but it can also cause birth defects (Dattel, 1997).

As Table 3.7 reveals, the developing organism is especially sensitive to the family of herpes viruses, for which there is no vaccine or treatment. Among these, *cytomegalovirus* (the most frequent prenatal infection, transmitted through respiratory or sexual contact) and *herpes simplex 2* (which is sexually transmitted) are especially dangerous. In both, the virus invades the mother's genital tract. Babies can be infected either during pregnancy or at birth.

BACTERIAL AND PARASITIC DISEASES. Table 3.7 also includes several bacterial and parasitic diseases. Among the most common is *toxoplasmosis,* caused by a parasite found in many animals. Pregnant women may become infected from eating raw or undercooked meat or from contact with the feces of infected cats. About 40 percent of women who have the disease transmit it to the developing organism. If it strikes during the first trimester, it is likely to cause eye and brain damage. Later infection is linked to mild visual and cognitive impairments (Peckham & Logan, 1993). Expectant mothers can avoid toxoplasmosis by making sure that the meat they eat is well cooked, having pet cats checked for the disease, and turning over the care of litter boxes to other family members.

OTHER MATERNAL FACTORS

Besides teratogens, maternal exercise, nutrition, and emotional well-being affect the embryo and fetus. In addition, many prospective parents wonder about the impact of a woman's age on the course of pregnancy. We examine each of these influences in the following sections.

■ EXERCISE. In healthy, physically fit women, regular moderate exercise, such as walking, swimming, biking, and aerobics, is related to increased birth weight (Hatch et al., 1993). However, very frequent, vigorous exercise (working up a sweat four or more times a week) predicts the opposite outcome—lower birth weight than in healthy, non-exercising controls (Bell, Palma, & Lumley, 1995).

During the last trimester, when the abdomen grows very large, mothers have difficulty moving freely and often must cut back on exercise. In most cases, a mother who has remained fit during the earlier months is likely to experience fewer of the physical discomforts that arise at this time, such as back pain, upward pressure on the chest, and difficulty breathing.

Pregnant women with health problems, such as circulatory difficulties or a history of miscarriage, should consult their doctors before beginning or continuing a physical fitness routine (Samuels & Samuels, 1996). For these mothers, exercise (especially the wrong kind) can endanger the pregnancy.

■ NUTRITION. Children grow more rapidly during the prenatal period than at any other phase of development. During this time, they depend totally on the mother for nutrients to support their growth. A healthy diet that results in a weight gain of 25 to 30 pounds helps ensure the health of mother and baby.

CONSEQUENCES OF PRENATAL MALNUTRITION. During World War II, a severe famine occurred in the Netherlands, giving scientists a rare opportunity to study the impact of nutrition on prenatal development. Findings revealed that the sensitive period concept operates with nutrition, just as it does with the teratogens discussed earlier in this chapter. Women affected by the famine during the first trimester were more likely to have miscarriages or to give birth to babies with physical defects. When women were past the first trimester, fetuses usually survived, but many were born underweight and had small heads (Stein et al., 1975).

We now know that prenatal malnutrition can cause serious damage to the central nervous system. Autopsies of malnourished babies who died at or shortly after birth reveal fewer brain cells and a brain weight as much as 36 percent below average. The poorer the mother's diet, the greater the loss in brain weight, especially if malnutrition occurred during the last trimester. During that time, the brain is growing rapidly in size, and a maternal diet high in all the basic nutrients is necessary for it to reach its full potential (Morgane et al., 1993). An inadequate diet during pregnancy can also distort the structure of other organs, including the pancreas, liver, and blood vessels, thereby increasing the risk of heart disease and diabetes in adulthood (Barker et al., 1993).

Prenatally malnourished babies enter the world with serious problems. They frequently catch respiratory illnesses, since poor nutrition suppresses development of the immune system (Chandra, 1991). In addition, these infants are irritable and unresponsive to stimulation around them. Like drug-addicted newborns, they have a high-pitched cry that is particularly distressing to their caregivers. The effects of poor nutrition quickly combine with an impoverished, stressful home life. With age, low intelligence test scores and serious learning problems become more apparent (Lozoff, 1989).

PREVENTION AND TREATMENT. Many studies show that providing pregnant women with adequate food has a substantial impact on the health of their newborn babies. Yet the growth demands of the prenatal period require more than just increasing the quantity of a typical diet. Finding ways to optimize maternal nutrition through vitamin–mineral enrichment as early as possible is also crucial.

For example, the power of folic acid to prevent abnormalities of the neural tube, such as anencephaly and spina bifida (see Table 3.6 on page 86), has captured the attention of medical and public health experts. In a British study of nearly 2,000 women in seven countries who had previously given birth to a baby with a neural tube defect, half were randomly selected to receive a folic acid supplement around the time of conception and half a mixture of other vitamins or no supplement. As Figure 3.11 reveals, the folic acid group showed 72 percent fewer neural tube defects (MCR Vitamin Study Research Group, 1991). In addition, adequate folate intake during the last 10 weeks of pregnancy cuts the risk of premature delivery and low birth weight in half (Scholl, Heidiger, & Belsky, 1996). Because of these findings, the U.S. Public Health Service recommends that all women of childbearing age consume at least 0.4 but not more than 1 milligram of folic acid per day, and bread, flour, rice, pasta, and other grain products are being fortified with it (McBride, 1997).

Other vitamins and minerals also have established benefits. Enriching women's diets with calcium helps prevent maternal high blood pressure and premature births (Repke, 1992). Adequate magnesium and zinc reduce the risk of many prenatal and birth complications (Facchinetti et al., 1992; Jameson, 1993; Spätling & Spätling, 1988). Fortifying table salt with iodine virtually eradicates cretinism—a common cause of mental retardation and stunted growth in many parts of the world (Dunn, 1993). And taking a multivitamin supplement beginning in the first few weeks of pregnancy protects against cleft lip and palate (Tolarova, 1986).

At the same time, excessive vitamin-mineral intake can be harmful. For example, overdoses of vitamins A and D (by taking even two or three multivitamin pills) can result in birth defects. Too much folic acid can prevent detection of a serious vitamin B_{12} deficiency (Rosa, 1993; Rothman et al., 1995). Furthermore, a supplement program should complement, not replace, programs designed to improve maternal diets during pregnancy. For women who do not get enough food or an adequate variety of foods, multivitamin tablets are a necessary, but not sufficient, intervention.

When poor nutrition is allowed to continue through most or all of pregnancy, infants usually require more than dietary improvement. Their tired, restless behavior leads mothers to be less sensitive and stimulating, and in response, babies become even more passive and withdrawn. Successful interventions must break this cycle of apathetic mother–baby interaction. Some do so by teaching parents how to interact effectively with their infants, whereas others focus on stimulating infants to promote active engagement with their

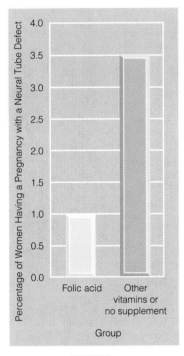

FIGURE 3.11

Percentage of pregnancies with a neural tube defect in folic-acid-supplemented women versus other-vitamins or no-supplement controls. Folic acid taken around the time of conception dramatically reduced the incidence of neural tube defects—a finding confirmed by other large-scale studies. Note, however, that folic acid did not eliminate all neural tube defects. These abnormalities, like many others, have multiple origins in the embryo's genetic disposition and factors in the environment.

(Adapted from MCR Vitamin Study Research Group, 1991.)

physical and social surroundings (Grantham-McGregor et al., 1994; Zeskind & Ramey, 1978, 1981).

Although prenatal malnutrition is highest in poverty-stricken regions of the world, it is not limited to developing countries. Each year, 80,000 to 120,000 American infants are born seriously undernourished. The federal government provides food packages to impoverished pregnant women through its Special Supplemental Food Program for Women, Infants, and Children. Unfortunately, because of funding shortages the program serves only 70 percent of those who are eligible (Children's Defense Fund, 1998).

■ EMOTIONAL STRESS. When women experience severe emotional stress during pregnancy, their babies are at risk for a wide variety of difficulties. Intense anxiety is associated with a higher rate of miscarriage, prematurity, low birth weight, and newborn respiratory illness. It is also related to certain physical defects, such as cleft lip and palate and pyloric stenosis (tightening of the infant's stomach outlet, which must be treated surgically) (Hoffman & Hatch, 1996; Omer & Everly, 1988).

To understand how the developing organism is affected, think back to the way your own body felt the last time you were under considerable stress. When we experience fear and anxiety, stimulant hormones are released into our bloodstream. These cause us to be "poised for action." Large amounts of blood are sent to parts of the body involved in the defensive response—the brain, the heart, and muscles in the arms, legs, and trunk. Blood flow to other organs, including the uterus, is reduced. As a result, the fetus is deprived of a full supply of oxygen and nutrients. Stress hormones also cross the placenta, leading the fetus's heart rate and activity level to rise dramatically. In addition, stress weakens the immune system, making pregnant women more susceptible to infectious disease (Cohen & Williamson, 1991). Finally, women who experience long-term anxiety are more likely to smoke, drink, eat poorly, and engage in other behaviors that harm the embryo or fetus.

But women under severe emotional stress do not always give birth to babies with problems. Prenatal complications are greatly reduced when mothers have husbands, other family members, and friends who offer support (McLean et al., 1993; Nuckolls, Cassel, & Kaplan, 1972). The link between social support and positive pregnancy outcomes is particularly strong for low-income women (Hoffman & Hatch, 1996). These results suggest that finding ways to provide supportive social ties to isolated expectant mothers can help prevent pregnancy problems.

■ MATERNAL AGE AND PREVIOUS BIRTHS. First births to women in their 30s have increased greatly over the past quarter-century in the United States and other industrialized nations (see Figure 3.12 on page 106). Many more couples are putting off childbearing until their careers are well established and they know they can support a child. Earlier we indicated that women who delay having children face a greater risk of giving birth to babies with chromosomal defects. Are other pregnancy problems more common among older mothers?

For many years, scientists thought that aging and repeated use of the mother's reproductive organs increased the likelihood of a wide variety of complications. Recently, these ideas have been questioned. When women without serious health difficulties are considered, even those in their forties do not experience more prenatal problems than those in their twenties (Ales, Druzin, & Santini, 1990; Dildy et al., 1996). And a large study of over 50,000 pregnancies showed no relationship between number of previous births and pregnancy complications (Heinonen, Slone, & Shapiro, 1977).

In the case of teenage mothers, does physical immaturity cause prenatal problems? Again, research shows that it does not. A teenager's body is large enough and strong enough to support pregnancy. In fact, as we will see in Chapter 5, young adolescent girls grow taller and heavier and their hips broaden (in preparation for childbearing) *before* their menstrual periods begin. Nature tries to ensure that once a girl can conceive, she is physically ready to carry and give birth to a baby. Infants of teenagers are born with a higher rate of problems for quite different reasons. Many adolescents do not have access to medical care or are afraid to seek it. In addition, most pregnant teenagers come from low-income backgrounds where stress, poor nutrition, and health problems are common (Coley & Chase-Lansdale, 1998).

FIGURE 3.12

First births to American women of different ages in 1970 and 1996. The birthrate decreased over this time period for women 20 to 24 years of age, whereas it increased for women 25 years and older. For women in their thirties, the birthrate more than doubled.

(Adapted from U.S. Department of Health and Human Services, 1998b; Ventura, 1989.)

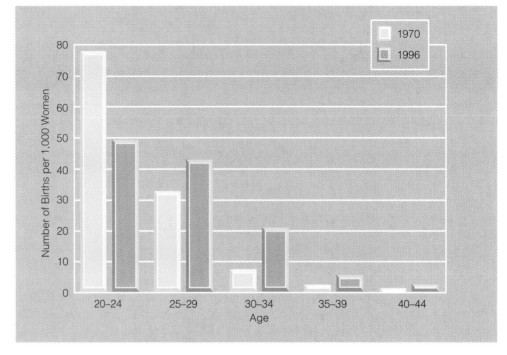

BRIEF REVIEW

The vast changes that take place during pregnancy are usually divided into three periods. In the period of the zygote, the tiny, one-celled fertilized ovum begins to duplicate and implants itself in the uterine lining. In the period of the embryo, the foundations for all body tissues and organs are rapidly laid down. The longest prenatal phase, the period of the fetus, is devoted to growth in size and completion of body systems.

Teratogens—cigarettes, alcohol, certain drugs, radiation, environmental pollutants, and diseases—can seriously harm the embryo and fetus. The effects of teratogens depend on amount and length of exposure, the genetic makeup of mother and baby, the presence of other harmful environmental agents, and the age of the organism at time of exposure. Teratogens operate according to the sensitive period concept. In general, greatest damage occurs during the embryonic phase, when body structures are formed. Poor maternal nutrition and severe emotional stress can also endanger the developing organism. As long as they are in good health, teenagers, women in their thirties and forties, and women who have given birth to several children have a high likelihood of problem-free pregnancies.

Childbirth

It is not surprising that childbirth is often referred to as labor. It is the hardest physical work a woman may ever do. A complex series of hormonal changes initiates the process, which naturally divides into three stages (see Figure 3.13):

1. *Dilation and effacement of the cervix.* This is the longest stage of labor, lasting, on the average, 12 to 14 hours in a first birth and 4 to 6 hours in later births. Contractions of the uterus gradually become more frequent and powerful, causing the cervix, or uterine opening, to widen and thin to nothing. As a result, a clear channel from the uterus into the vagina, or birth canal, is formed.

2. *Delivery of the baby.* Once the cervix is fully open, the baby is ready to be born. This second stage is much shorter than the first, lasting about 50 minutes in a first birth and 20 minutes in later births. Strong contractions of the uterus

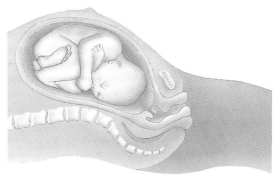

(a) Dilation and Effacement of the Cervix

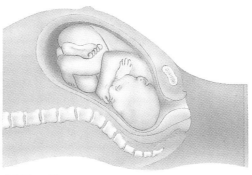

(b) Transition

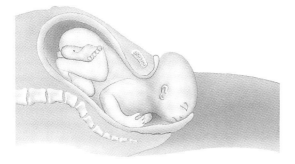

(c) Pushing

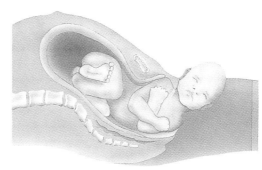

(d) Birth of the Baby

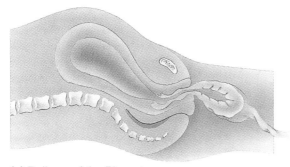

(e) Delivery of the Placenta

FIGURE 3.13

The three stages of labor. Stage 1: (a) Contractions of the uterus cause dilation and effacement of the cervix. (b) Transition is reached when the frequency and strength of the contractions are at their peak and the cervix opens completely. Stage 2: (c) The mother pushes with each contraction, forcing the baby down the birth canal, and the head appears. (d) Near the end of Stage 2, the shoulders emerge and are followed quickly by the rest of the baby's body. Stage 3: (e) With a few final pushes, the placenta is delivered.

continue, but the mother also feels a natural urge to squeeze and push with her abdominal muscles. As she does so with each contraction, she forces the baby down and out.

3. *Birth of the placenta.* Labor comes to an end with a few final contractions and pushes. These cause the placenta to separate from the wall of the uterus and be delivered, in about 5 to 10 minutes.

THE BABY'S ADAPTATION TO LABOR AND DELIVERY

Consider, for a moment, what childbirth must be like for the baby. After being squeezed and pushed for many hours, the infant is forced to leave the warm, protective uterus for a cold, brightly lit external world. The strong contractions expose the head to a great deal of pressure, and they squeeze the placenta and umbilical cord repeatedly. Each time, the baby's supply of oxygen is temporarily reduced.

At first glance, these events may strike you as a dangerous ordeal. Fortunately, healthy babies are well equipped to withstand the trauma of childbirth. The force of the contractions causes the infant to produce high levels of stress hormones. Recall that during pregnancy, maternal stress can endanger the baby. In contrast, during childbirth, the infant's production of stress hormones is adaptive. It helps the baby withstand oxygen deprivation by sending a rich supply of blood to the brain and heart. In addition, it prepares the

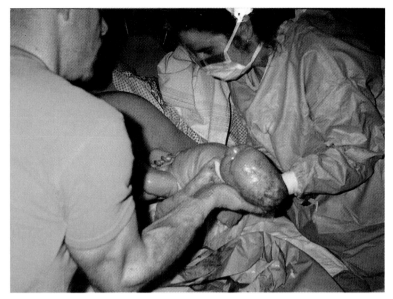

This newborn baby is held by his mother's birthing coach (on the left) and midwife (on the right) just after delivery. The umbilical cord has not yet been cut. Notice how the infant's head is molded from being squeezed through the birth canal for many hours. It is also very large in relation to its body. As the infant takes his first few breaths, his body turns from blue to pink. He is wide awake and ready to get to know his surroundings.

(Dakoda Brandon Dorsaneo)

baby to breathe by causing the lungs to absorb excess liquid and expanding the bronchial tubes (passages leading to the lungs). Finally, stress hormones arouse infants into alertness so they are born wide awake, ready to interact with the surrounding world (Emory & Toomey, 1988; Lagercrantz & Slotkin, 1986).

THE NEWBORN BABY'S APPEARANCE

Parents are often surprised at the odd-looking newborn, who is a far cry from the storybook image many created in their minds before birth. The average newborn is 20 inches long and 7½ pounds in weight; boys tend to be slightly longer and heavier than girls. Body proportions contribute to the baby's strange appearance. The head is very large in relation to the trunk and legs, which are short and bowed. The combination of a big head (with its well-developed brain) and a small body means that human infants learn quickly in the first few months of life. But unlike most mammals, they cannot get around on their own until much later.

Even though newborn babies may not match the idealized expectations of their parents, some features do make them attractive. Their round faces, chubby cheeks, large foreheads, and big eyes make adults feel like picking them up and cuddling them (Berman, 1980; Lorenz, 1943). These characteristics, as we will see in later chapters, are among the many ways nature helps get the parent–infant relationship off to a good start.

ASSESSING THE NEWBORN'S PHYSICAL CONDITION: THE APGAR SCALE

Infants who have difficulty making the transition to life outside the uterus require special assistance at once. To quickly assess the baby's physical condition, doctors and nurses use the **Apgar Scale.** As Table 3.8 shows, a rating of 0, 1, or 2 on each of five characteristics is made at 1 and 5 minutes after birth. An Apgar score of 7 or better indicates that the infant is in good physical condition. If the score is between 4 and 6, the baby requires special help in establishing breathing and other vital signs. If the score is 3 or below, the infant is in serious danger, and emergency medical attention is needed. Two Apgar ratings are given, since some babies have trouble adjusting at first but are doing well after a few minutes (Apgar, 1953).

TABLE 3.8

The Apgar Scale

	Score		
Sign[a]	**0**	**1**	**2**
Heart rate	No heartbeat	Under 100 beats per minute	100 to 140 beats per minute
Respiratory effort	No breathing for 60 seconds	Irregular, shallow breathing	Strong breathing and crying
Reflex irritability (sneezing, coughing, and grimacing)	No response	Weak reflexive response	Strong reflexive response
Muscle tone	Completely limp	Weak movements of arms and legs	Strong movements of arms and legs
Color[b]	Blue body, arms, and legs	Body pink with blue arms and legs	Body, arms, and legs completely pink

[a]To remember these signs, you may find it helpful to use a technique in which the original labels are reordered and renamed as follows: color = Appearance, heart rate = Pulse, reflex irritability = Grimace, muscle tone = Activity, and respiratory effort = Respiration. Together, the first letters of the new labels spell Apgar.

[b]Color is the least reliable of the Apgar signs. Vernix, the white, cheesy substance that covers the skin, often interferes with the doctor's rating, and the skin tone of nonwhite babies makes it difficult to apply the "pink" criterion. However, newborns of all races can be rated for a pinkish glow that results from the flow of oxygen through body tissues, since skin color is generally lighter at birth than the baby's inherited pigmentation.

Source: Apgar, 1953.

Approaches to Childbirth

C hildbirth practices, like other aspects of family life, are molded by the society of which mother and baby are a part. In many village and tribal cultures, expectant mothers are well acquainted with the childbirth process. For example, the Jarara of South America and the Pukapukans of the Pacific Islands treat birth as a vital part of daily life. The Jarara mother gives birth in a passageway or shelter in full view of the entire community, including small children. The Pukapukan girl is so familiar with the events of labor and delivery that she can frequently be seen playing at it. Using a coconut to represent the baby, she stuffs it inside her dress, imitates the mother's pushing, and lets the nut fall at the proper moment. In most nonindustrialized cultures, women are assisted during the birth process, often by being held from behind. Among the Mayans of the Yucatán, the mother leans against the body and arms of a woman called the "head helper," who supports her weight and breathes with her during each contraction (Jordan, 1993; Mead & Newton, 1967).

In large Western nations, childbirth customs have changed dramatically over the centuries. Before the late 1800s, birth usually took place at home and was a family-centered event. The industrial revolution brought greater crowding to cities, along with new health problems. As a result, childbirth began to move from home to hospital, where the health of mothers and babies could be protected. Once doctors assumed responsibility for childbirth, women's knowledge about it declined, and relatives and friends were no longer welcome to participate (Borst, 1995).

By the 1950s and 1960s, women started to question the medical procedures that came to be used routinely during labor and delivery. Many felt that frequent use of strong drugs and delivery instruments had robbed them of a precious experience and were often not necessary or safe for the baby. Gradually, a natural childbirth movement arose in Europe and spread to the United States. Its purpose was to make hospital birth as comfortable and rewarding for mothers as possible. Today, most hospitals carry this theme further by offering birth centers that are family centered in approach and homelike in appearance. Freestanding birth centers, which operate independently of hospitals and offer less in the way of backup medical care, also exist. And a small but growing number of American women are rejecting institutional birth entirely and choosing to have their babies at home.

NATURAL, OR PREPARED, CHILDBIRTH

Natural, or **prepared, childbirth** tries to overcome the idea that birth is a painful ordeal that requires extensive medical intervention. Although many natural childbirth programs exist, most draw on methods developed by Grantly Dick-Read (1959) in England and Ferdinand Lamaze (1958) in France. These physicians emphasized that cultural attitudes had taught women to fear the birth experience. An anxious, frightened woman in labor tenses muscles throughout her body, turning the mild pain that sometimes accompanies strong contractions into a great deal of pain.

A typical natural childbirth program consists of three parts:

- *Classes.* Expectant mothers and fathers attend a series of classes in which they learn about the anatomy and physiology of labor and delivery. Natural childbirth is based on the idea that knowledge about the birth process reduces a mother's fear.

- *Relaxation and breathing techniques.* Expectant mothers are taught relaxation and breathing exercises aimed at counteracting any pain they might feel during uterine contractions. They also practice creating pleasant visual images in their minds instead of thinking about pain.

- *Labor coach.* While the mother masters breathing and visualization techniques, the father or another supportive companion learns to be a "labor coach." The coach assists the mother by reminding her to relax and breathe, massaging her back, supporting her body during labor and delivery, and offering words of encouragement and affection.

Among the !Kung of Botswana, Africa, a mother gives birth in a sitting position, and she is surrounded by women who encourage and help her.
(Shostak/Anthro-Photo)

Apgar Scale A rating system used to assess the newborn baby's physical condition immediately after birth.

natural, or prepared, childbirth An approach designed to reduce pain and medical intervention and to make childbirth a rewarding experience for parents.

FIGURE 3.14

Sitting position often used for delivery in a birth center or at home. It facilitates pushing during the second stage of labor; increases blood flow to the placenta, which grants the baby a richer supply of oxygen; and permits the mother to see the delivery.

About to give birth at home, this mother discusses the progress of her labor with the midwife while her husband and their older child look on. Mothers who choose home birth want to make the experience an important part of family life, avoid unnecessary medical procedures, and exercise greater control over their own care and that of their babies.

(Susan Ames)

■ POSITIONS FOR DELIVERY. When natural childbirth is combined with delivery in a birth center or at home, mothers often give birth in the upright, sitting position shown in Figure 3.14 rather than lying flat on their backs with their feet in stirrups (the traditional hospital delivery room practice). When mothers are upright, labor is shortened because pushing is easier and more effective. The baby benefits from a richer supply of oxygen because blood flow to the placenta is increased (Davidson et al., 1993). And since the mother can see the delivery, she can track the effectiveness of each contraction in pushing the baby out of the birth canal. This helps her work with the doctor or midwife to ensure that the baby's head and shoulders emerge slowly, which reduces the chances of tearing the vaginal opening (Samuels & Samuels, 1996).

■ CONSEQUENCES OF NATURAL CHILDBIRTH. Studies comparing mothers who experience natural childbirth with those who do not reveal many benefits. Because mothers feel more in control of labor and delivery, their attitudes toward the childbirth experience are more positive (Green, Coupland, & Kitzinger, 1990; Mackey, 1995). They also feel less pain. As a result, they require less medication—usually very little or none at all (Hetherington, 1990).

Research suggests that social support may be an important part of the success of natural childbirth techniques. In Guatemalan and American hospitals that routinely isolated patients during childbirth, some mothers were randomly assigned a companion who stayed with them throughout labor, talking to them, holding their hands, and rubbing their backs to promote relaxation. These mothers had fewer birth complications, and their labors were several hours shorter than those of women who did not have companionship. Guatemalan mothers who received social support were more likely to respond to their babies in the first hour after delivery by talking, smiling, and gently stroking (Kennell et al., 1991; Sosa et al., 1980).

Social support is particularly helpful in reducing stress during a first childbirth, when mothers are more anxious than in later births (Keinan, 1997). In addition, mothers are best off if they can choose the most competent individual to coach during labor and delivery. Some fathers are reluctant to become involved or are overwhelmed by the medical situation or their empathy for the mother's pain. In these instances, the supportive role can be filled by another relative or friend or by a professional labor companion (DiMatteo & Kahn, 1997).

Finally, natural childbirth may make Western birth customs more acceptable to women from parts of the world where assistance from family and community members is the norm. One Ethiopian immigrant to Israel, used to her culture's practice of surrounding a laboring mother with a personal circle of support, commented on her first hospital birth experience, "The worst thing . . . is the attitude. When I came to the hospital with contractions, they examined me but left me alone. When labor started I stayed alone. In Ethiopia my family was always around" (Granot et al., 1996).

HOME DELIVERY

Home birth has always been popular in certain industrialized nations, such as England, the Netherlands, and Sweden. The number of American women choosing to have their babies at home has increased since 1970, although it remains small, at about 1 percent. These mothers want birth to be an important part of family life. In addition, most want to avoid unnecessary medical procedures and exercise greater control over their own care and that of their babies than hospitals typically permit (Bastian, 1993). Although some home births are attended by doctors, many more are handled by certified nurse-midwives, who have degrees in nursing and additional training in childbirth management.

Is it just as safe to give birth at home as in a hospital? For healthy women who are assisted by a well-trained doctor or midwife, it seems so, since complications rarely occur (Olsen, 1997; Remez, 1997). However, when attendants are not carefully trained and prepared to handle emergencies, the rate of infant death is high (Mehlmadrona & Madrona, 1997). For mothers at risk for any kind of complication, the appropriate place for labor and delivery is the hospital, where life-saving treatment is available should it be needed.

LABOR AND DELIVERY MEDICATION

Although natural childbirth techniques lessen or eliminate the need for pain-relieving drugs, some form of medication is still used in 80 to 95 percent of births in the United States (Glosten, 1998). *Analgesics* are drugs that relieve pain. When given during labor, the dose is usually mild and intended to help a mother relax. *Anesthetics* are a stronger type of painkiller that blocks sensation. During childbirth, they are generally injected into the spinal column to numb the lower half of the body.

In complicated deliveries, pain-relieving drugs are essential because they permit life-saving medical interventions to be carried out. But when used routinely, they can cause problems. Anesthesia weakens uterine contractions during the first stage of labor and interferes with the mother's ability to feel contractions and push during the second stage. As a result, labor is prolonged—on the average, by an hour or two compared with an unmedicated birth (Alexander et al., 1998). In addition, the chances are greater that the baby will have to be pulled from the birth canal with *forceps* (a metal device placed around the infant's head) or a *vacuum extractor* (a plastic suction cup that fits over the top of the head). Both of these instruments involve some risk of injury to the baby (King, 1997). Because anesthesia increases the likelihood that labor will not progress normally, it is linked to *cesarian section,* a surgical delivery in which the doctor makes an incision in the mother's abdomen and lifts the baby out of the uterus (Masten et al., 1994; Young, 1997).

Labor and delivery medication rapidly crosses the placenta. When given in large doses, it produces a depressed state in the newborn baby that may last for several days. The infant is sleepy and withdrawn, sucks poorly during feedings, and is likely to be irritable and hard to console when awake (Brazelton, Nugent, & Lester, 1987; Emory, Schlackman, & Fiano, 1996).

Does the use of medication during childbirth have a lasting impact on infant physical and mental development? Some researchers claim so (Brackbill, McManus, & Woodward, 1985), but their findings have been challenged, and contrary results exist (Golub, 1996). Anesthesia may be related to other risk factors that could account for long-term consequences in some studies, and more research is needed to sort out these effects. In the meantime, the negative impact of these drugs on the early parent–infant relationship supports the current trend to limit their use.

Birth Complications

In the preceding sections, we saw that some babies—in particular, those whose mothers are in poor health, do not receive good medical care, or have a history of pregnancy problems—are especially likely to experience birth complications. Inadequate oxygen, a pregnancy that ends too early, and a baby who is born underweight are serious difficulties that we have mentioned many times. Let's look more closely at the impact of each on development.

OXYGEN DEPRIVATION

A small number of infants experience *anoxia,* or inadequate oxygen supply, during the birth process. Sometimes the problem results from a failure to start breathing immediately after delivery. Although newborns can survive periods without oxygen longer than adults, there is risk of brain damage if breathing is delayed for more than 3 minutes (Stechler & Halton, 1982).

At other times, anoxia occurs during labor. Squeezing of the umbilical cord is a common cause, a condition that is especially likely when infants are in **breech position**—turned in such a way that the buttocks or feet would emerge first. Because of this danger, breech babies are often delivered by cesarean section. Another cause of oxygen deprivation is *placenta abruptio,* or premature separation of the placenta, a life-threatening event that requires immediate delivery. Although the reasons for placenta abruptio are not well understood, teratogens that cause abnormal development of the placenta, such as cigarette smoking, are strongly related to it (Handler et al., 1994).

Incompatibility between mother and baby in a blood protein called the **Rh factor** can also lead to anoxia. When the mother is Rh negative (lacks the protein) and the father is Rh positive (has the protein), the baby may inherit the father's Rh-positive blood type. (Recall from Table 3.2 on page 76 that Rh-positive blood is dominant and Rh-negative blood is recessive, so the chances are good that a baby will be Rh positive.) During the third trimester and at the time of birth, some maternal and fetal blood cells usually cross the placenta in small enough amounts to be quite safe. But if even a little of the baby's Rh-positive blood passes into the mother's Rh-negative bloodstream, she begins to form antibodies to the foreign Rh protein. If these enter the baby's system, they destroy red blood cells, reducing the supply of oxygen. Mental retardation, damage to the heart muscle, and infant death can occur. Since it takes time for the mother to produce antibodies, first-born children are rarely affected. The danger increases with each additional pregnancy. Fortunately, the harmful effects of Rh incompatibility can be prevented in most cases. After the birth of each Rh-positive baby, Rh-negative mothers are routinely given a vaccine called RhoGam, which prevents the buildup of antibodies.

Children deprived of oxygen during labor and delivery remain behind their agemates in intellectual and motor progress in early childhood (Raz, Shah, & Sander, 1996). But by the school years, most catch up in development (Corah et al., 1965). When serious problems emerge and persist—for example, learning disabilities, epilepsy, or *cerebral palsy* (a general term for motor and mental impairments that result from brain damage before, during, or just after birth)—the anoxia was probably extreme. Perhaps it was caused by prenatal insult to the baby's respiratory system. Or it may have happened because the infant's lungs were not yet mature enough to breathe.

For example, babies born more than 6 weeks early commonly have a disorder called *respiratory distress syndrome* (otherwise known as *hyaline membrane disease*). Their tiny lungs are so poorly developed that the air sacs collapse, causing serious breathing difficulties. Today, mechanical ventilators keep many such infants alive. In spite of these measures, some babies suffer permanent brain damage from lack of oxygen, and in other cases their delicate lungs are harmed by the treatment itself (Vohr & Garcia-Coll, 1988). Respiratory distress syndrome is only one of many risks for babies born too soon, as we will see in the following section.

PRETERM AND LOW-BIRTH-WEIGHT INFANTS

Babies born 3 weeks or more before the end of a full 38-week pregnancy or who weigh less than 5½ pounds (2,500 grams) have, for many years, been referred to as "premature." A wealth of research indicates that premature babies are at risk for many problems. Birth weight is the best available predictor of infant survival and healthy development. Many newborns who weigh less than 3½ pounds (1,500 grams) experience brain hemorrhages and other severe biological traumas, an effect that becomes stronger as birth weight decreases (Fletcher et al., 1997; Novy, McGregor, & Iams, 1995). Frequent illness, inattention, overactivity, language delays, low intelligence test scores, and deficits in motor coordination and school learning are some of the problems that extend into the childhood years (Hack et al., 1994, 1995; Mayes & Bornstein, 1997).

About 1 in 14 infants in the United States is born underweight. Although the problem can strike unexpectedly, it is highest among poverty-stricken pregnant women, especially ethnic minorities (Children's Defense Fund, 1998). These mothers, as we indicated earlier in this chapter, are more likely to be undernourished and to be exposed to other harmful environmental influences. In addition, they often do not receive the prenatal care necessary to protect their vulnerable babies.

breech position A position of the baby in the uterus that would cause the buttocks or feet to be delivered first.

Rh factor A protein that, when present in the fetus's blood but not in the mother's, can cause the mother to build up antibodies if the fetus's blood enters the mother's bloodstream. If these antibodies return to the fetus's system, they destroy red blood cells, reducing the oxygen supply to organs and tissues.

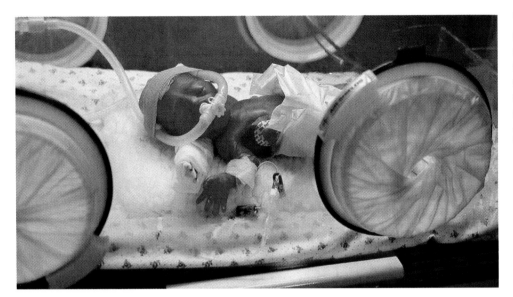

Prematurity is also common when mothers are carrying twins. Twins are usually born about 3 weeks early, and because of restricted space inside the uterus, they gain less weight after the twentieth week of pregnancy than do singletons.

■ **PRETERM VERSUS SMALL FOR DATE.** Although low-birth-weight infants face many obstacles to healthy development, individual differences exist in how well they do. More than half go on to lead normal lives—even some who weighed only a couple of pounds at birth (Vohr & Garcia-Coll, 1988). To better understand why some of these babies do better than others, researchers have divided them into two groups. The first is called **preterm.** These infants are born several weeks or more before their due date. Although small in size, their weight may still be appropriate for the amount of time they spent in the uterus. The second group is called **small for date.** These babies are below their expected weight when length of pregnancy is taken into account. Some small-for-date infants are actually full term. Others are preterm infants who are especially underweight.

Of the two types of babies, small-for-date infants usually have more serious problems. During the first year, they are more likely to die, catch infections, and show evidence of brain damage. By middle childhood, they have lower intelligence test scores, are less attentive, and achieve more poorly in school (Copper et al., 1993; Schothorst & van Engeland, 1996). Small-for-date infants probably experienced inadequate nutrition before birth. Perhaps their mothers did not eat properly, the placenta did not function normally, or the babies themselves had defects that prevented them from growing as they should.

■ **CHARACTERISTICS OF PRETERM INFANTS: CONSEQUENCES FOR CAREGIVING.** Imagine a scrawny, thin-skinned infant whose body is only a little larger than the size of your hand. You try to play with the baby by stroking and talking softly, but he is sleepy and unresponsive. When you feed him, he sucks poorly. He is usually irritable during the short, unpredictable periods in which he is awake.

Unfortunately, the appearance and behavior of preterm babies can lead parents to be less sensitive and responsive in caring for them. Compared with full-term infants, preterm babies—especially those who are very ill at birth—are less often held close, touched, and talked to gently. At times, mothers of these infants are overly intrusive, engaging in interfering pokes and verbal commands in an effort to obtain a higher level of response from a baby who is a passive, unrewarding social partner (Barratt, Roach, & Leavitt, 1996; Patteson & Barnard, 1990).

Some parents may step up these intrusive acts when faced with continuing ungratifying infant behavior. This may explain why preterm babies as a group are at risk for child abuse. When these infants are born to isolated, poverty-stricken mothers who have difficulty managing their own lives, the likelihood of unfavorable outcomes is increased. In contrast, parents with stable life circumstances and social supports can usually overcome

preterm Infants born several weeks or more before their due date.

small for date Infants whose birth weight is below normal when length of pregnancy is taken into account. May be full term or preterm.

These fraternal twins, who were born several weeks preterm, are celebrating their second birthday. Sensitive, stimulating care has helped them catch up, physically and mentally. Interventions that teach parents in low-stress households how to care for low-birth-weight babies are highly successful in fostering development. When infants are born into poverty, long-term, intensive intervention is necessary.

(Michael Newman/Photo Edit)

the stresses of caring for a preterm infant. In these cases, even sick preterm babies have a good chance of catching up in development by middle childhood (Liaw & Brooks-Gunn, 1993).

These findings suggest that how well preterm infants develop has a great deal to do with the kind of relationship established between parent and child, to which both partners contribute. If a good relationship between mother and baby can help prevent the negative effects of early birth, then interventions directed at supporting this relationship should help these infants recover.

■ **INTERVENTIONS FOR PRETERM INFANTS.** Hospital intensive care nurseries care for preterm babies in isolettes—plexiglass-enclosed beds in which air is filtered to protect against infection and in which temperature is carefully controlled, since these infants cannot yet regulate their own body temperature effectively. When a preterm infant is fed through a stomach tube, breathes with the aid of a respirator, and receives medication through an intravenous needle, the isolette can be very isolating indeed! Physical needs that otherwise would lead to close contact and other forms of stimulation from an adult are met mechanically.

At one time, doctors believed that stimulating such a fragile baby could be harmful. Now we know that certain kinds of stimulation in proper doses can help preterm infants develop.

SPECIAL INFANT STIMULATION. In some intensive care nurseries, preterm infants can be seen rocking in suspended hammocks or lying on waterbeds—interventions designed to replace the gentle motion they would have received while being carried in the mother's uterus. Other forms of stimulation have also been used—for example, an attractive mobile or a tape recording of a heartbeat, soft music, or the mother's voice. Many studies show that these experiences have important short-term benefits. They promote faster weight gain, more predictable sleep patterns, and greater alertness during the weeks after birth (Beckwith & Sigman, 1995).

Touch is an especially important form of stimulation for preterm newborns. In studies of baby animals, touching the skin releases certain brain chemicals that support physical growth. These effects are believed to occur in humans as well (Field, 1998). When preterm infants were massaged several times each day in the hospital, they gained weight faster and, at the end of the first year, were advanced in mental and motor development over preterm infants not given this stimulation (Field et al., 1986).

In developing countries where hospitalization is not always possible, skin-to-skin "kangaroo baby care," in which the preterm infant is tucked between the mother's breasts and peers over the top of her clothing, is encouraged. The technique is used often in Europe as a supplement to hospital intensive care. It fosters oxygenation of the baby's body, temperature regulation, improved feeding, and infant survival (Anderson, 1991; Hamelin & Ramachandran, 1993).

Some very small or sick babies are too weak to handle much stimulation. The noise, bright lights, and constant medical monitoring of the intensive care nursery are already overwhelming for them. And much like full-term infants, preterm infants differ in how excited and irritable they get when exposed to sights and sounds (Korner, 1996). Consequently, amount and kind of stimulation must be carefully adjusted to fit the individual baby's needs.

TRAINING PARENTS IN INFANT CAREGIVING SKILLS. When effective stimulation helps preterm infants develop, parents are likely to feel good about their infant's growth and interact with the baby more effectively. Interventions that support the parenting side of this relationship generally teach parents about the infant's characteristics and promote caregiving skills.

For parents with the economic and personal resources to care for a low-birth-weight infant, just a few sessions of coaching in recognizing and responding to the baby's needs is helpful. Infants of mothers randomly selected to receive this training in the months after hospital discharge, compared with infants of mothers who were not, gained steadily in mental test performance over the childhood years until their scores equaled those of full-term youngsters (Achenbach et al., 1990). Warm parenting that helps preterm infants sustain attention (for example, gently commenting on and showing the baby interesting features of a toy) predicts favorable early cognitive and language development. Very low-birth-weight babies seem to profit, especially, from parent attention-maintaining strategies (Landry et al., 1996; Smith et al., 1996).

When preterm infants live in stressed, low-income households, long-term, intensive intervention is required to reduce developmental problems. In a recent study, preterm babies born into poverty received a comprehensive intervention that combined medical follow-up, weekly parent training through home visits, and enrollment in cognitively stimulating day care from 1 to 3 years of age. As Figure 3.15 shows, compared with controls receiving only medical follow-up, more than four times as many intervention children were within normal range at age 3 in intelligence, psychological adjustment, and physical growth (Bradley et al., 1994).

Yet by age 5, the intervention children had lost ground. And by age 8, group differences were no longer present for children who had been very low-birth-weight (Brooks-Gunn et al., 1994; McCarton et al., 1997). To sustain developmental gains in these very vulnerable children, they seem to need high-quality intervention well beyond age 3—even into the school years.

Finally, the high rate of low birth weight and infant death in the United States—one of the worst in the industrialized world—could be greatly reduced by improving the health and social conditions described in the Cultural Influences box on page 116. Fortunately, today we can save many preterm infants. But an even better course of action would be to prevent this serious threat to infant survival and development before it happens.

UNDERSTANDING BIRTH COMPLICATIONS

In the preceding sections, we discussed a variety of birth complications that threaten children's well-being. Now let's try to put the evidence together. Are there any general principles that might help us understand how infants who survive a traumatic birth are likely to develop? A landmark longitudinal study carried out in Hawaii provides answers to this question.

In 1955, Emmy Werner and Ruth Smith began to track the development of nearly 700 infants on the island of Kauai who experienced either mild, moderate, or severe birth complications. Each was matched, on the basis of social class and ethnicity, with a healthy newborn (Werner & Smith, 1982). Findings revealed that the likelihood of long-term

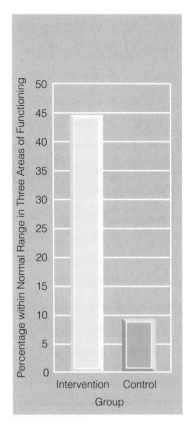

FIGURE 3.15

Percentage of preterm infants assigned to an intensive intervention or a control group who were developing normally at age 3. Children who experienced the intervention, consisting of medical follow-up, parent training, and cognitively stimulating day care, were more than four times more likely than medical-follow-up-only controls to be within normal range in intelligence, psychological adjustment, and physical growth. Without continued intervention, however, these gains are not sustained. (Adapted from Bradley et al., 1994.)

CULTURAL INFLUENCES

NFANT MORTALITY IS an index used around the world to assess the overall health of a nation's children. It refers to the number of deaths in the first year of life per 1,000 live births. Although the United States has the most up-to-date health care technology in the world, it has made less progress than many other countries in reducing infant deaths. Over the past three decades, it slipped down in the international rankings, from seventh in the 1950s to twentieth in the mid-1990s. Members of America's poor ethnic minorities, African-American babies especially, are at greatest risk. Black infants are more than twice as likely as white infants to die in the first year of life. Their infant mortality rate is about the same as in developing nations with poor economies, such as Trinidad and Tobago (Bellamy, 1998; Children's Defense Fund, 1999).

Neonatal mortality, the rate of death within the first month of life, accounts for 67 percent of the high infant death rate in the United States. Two factors are largely responsible for neonatal mortality. The first is serious physical defects, most of which cannot be prevented. The percentage of babies born with physical defects is about the same in all ethnic and income groups. The second leading cause of neonatal mortality is low birth weight, which is largely preventable. Black babies are more than four times as likely as white infants to die because they are born early and underweight. On an international scale, the number of underweight babies born in the United States is alarmingly high. It is greater than that of 22 other countries (Bellamy, 1998).

Experts agree that widespread poverty and weak health care programs for mothers and young children are largely responsible for these trends. High-quality prenatal care beginning early in pregnancy is consistently related to birth weight and infant survival. Yet 18 percent of pregnant women in the United States wait until after the first trimester to seek prenatal care, and 4 percent delay until the end of pregnancy or never get any at all (Children's Defense Fund, 1999).

Financial problems are a major barrier to early prenatal care. Most American women who delay going to the doctor do not receive health insurance as a fringe benefit of their

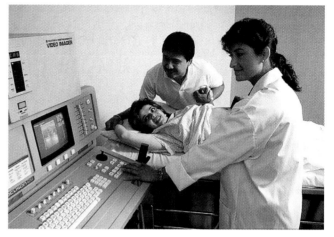

During a routine check-up, a nurse uses an ultrasound scanner to check the growth of the fetus while mother and father watch with eager anticipation. Early prenatal care is vital to ensure the health of mothers and newborn babies. Yet many low-income women in the United States do not have access to affordable health care.
(David Joel/Tony Stone Worldwide)

jobs. Others have no insurance because they are unemployed. Although the very poorest of these mothers are eligible for government-sponsored health services, many women who have low incomes and need benefits do not qualify. Unfortunately, expectant women who wait to see a doctor usually lead highly stressful lives and engage in harmful behaviors, such as smoking and drug abuse (Melnikow & Alemagno, 1993). These women, who have no medical attention for most or all of their pregnancies, are among those who need it most!

Each country in Figure 3.16 that outranks the United States in infant survival provides all its citizens with government-sponsored health care benefits. And each takes extra steps to make sure that pregnant mothers and babies have access to good nutrition, high-quality medical care, and social and economic supports that promote effective parenting.

---

difficulties increased if birth trauma was severe. But among mildly to moderately stressed children, the best predictor of how well they did in later years was the quality of their home environments. Children growing up in stable families did almost as well on measures of intelligence and psychological adjustment as did those with no birth problems. Those exposed to poverty, family disorganization, and mentally ill parents often developed serious learning difficulties, behavior problems, and emotional disturbance during childhood and adolescence.

The Kauai study tells us that as long as birth injuries are not overwhelming, a supportive home environment can restore children's growth. But the most intriguing cases in this study were the handful of exceptions to this rule. A few children with fairly serious birth complications and troubled family environments grew into competent adults who fared as well as controls in career attainment and psychological adjustment. Werner

infant mortality The number of deaths in the first year of life per 1,000 live births.

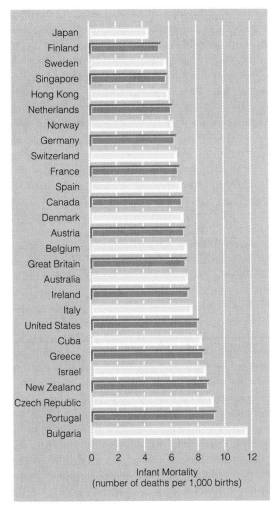

FIGURE 3.16

Infant mortality in 27 nations. Despite its advanced health care technology, the United States ranks poorly. It is twentieth in the world, with a death rate of nearly 8 infants per 1,000 births. (Adapted from Central Intelligence Agency, 1998.)

For example, all European nations guarantee women a certain number of prenatal visits at very low or no cost. Some even offer special incentives, such as a monetary allowance, for taking advantage of health benefits! After a baby is born, a health professional routinely visits the home to provide counseling about infant care and to arrange continuing medical services. Home assistance is especially extensive in the Netherlands. For a token fee, each mother is granted a specially trained maternity helper, who assists with infant care, shopping, housekeeping, meal preparation, and the care of other children during the days after delivery (Buekens et al., 1993; Kamerman, 1993).

Paid employment leave is another vital societal intervention for new parents. It is widely available in Western Europe, where it typically ranges from 2 to 12 months. In Sweden, a couple has the right to 15 months of paid leave to share between them. Even less-developed nations provide this benefit. For example, in the People's Republic of China, a new mother is granted 3 months' leave at regular pay (Hyde, 1995). Yet in the United States, the federal government mandates only 12 weeks of *unpaid* leave.

When a family is stressed by a baby's arrival, short employment leaves of 6 weeks or less (the norm in the United States) are linked to maternal anxiety and depression and negative interactions with the baby. Longer leaves of 12 weeks or more predict favorable maternal mental health and sensitive, responsive caregiving (Clark et al., 1997; Hyde et al., 1995). Single women and their babies are most hurt by the absence of a national paid leave policy. These mothers are usually the sole source of support for their families and can least afford to take time from their jobs.

In countries with low rates of infant mortality and low birth weight, expectant mothers need not wonder how they will get health care and other resources to support their baby's development. The powerful impact of universal, high-quality medical and social services on maternal and infant well-being provides strong justification for implementing such programs in the United States.

and Smith found that these children relied on factors outside the family and within themselves to overcome stress. Some had especially attractive personalities that caused them to receive positive responses from relatives, neighbors, and peers. In other instances, a grandparent, aunt, uncle, or baby-sitter established a warm relationship with the child and provided the needed emotional support (Werner, 1989, 1993; Werner & Smith, 1992).

Do these outcomes remind you of the characteristics of resilient children, discussed in Chapter 1? The Kauai study and other similar investigations reveal that the impact of early biological risks often wanes as children's personal characteristics and social experiences contribute increasingly to their functioning (Laucht, Esser, & Schmidt, 1997; Thompson et al., 1997). In sum, when the overall balance of life events tips toward the favorable side, children with serious birth problems can develop successfully. When negative factors outweigh positive ones, even a sturdy newborn baby can become a lifelong casualty.

ASK YOURSELF . . .

◆ *How do long-term outcomes reported for anoxic and preterm newborns fit with findings of the Kauai Study?*

◆ **CONNECTIONS**
List prenatal environmental influences discussed earlier in this chapter that increase the chances of anoxia and preterm birth. What does your list imply about effective ways to prevent these birth complications? (See pages 95–105.)

Why might very low-birth-weight and ill newborns face special challenges in forming a secure infant–caregiver attachment? (See Chapter 10, page 427.)

BRIEF REVIEW

The hard work of labor takes place in three stages: dilation and effacement of the cervix, birth of the baby, and delivery of the placenta. Stress hormones help the infant withstand the trauma of childbirth. The Apgar Scale provides a quick rating of the baby's physical condition immediately after birth. Natural, or prepared, childbirth improves mothers' attitudes toward labor and delivery and reduces the need for medication. Home births are safe for healthy women, provided attendants are well trained. Pain-relieving drugs can cross the placenta, producing a depressed state in the newborn baby. However, long-term effects of medication have not been established.

Birth complications can threaten children's development. Oxygen deprivation, when extreme, causes lasting brain damage. Preterm and low-birth-weight infants are at risk for many problems. Providing these babies with special stimulation and teaching parents how to care for and interact with them helps restore favorable growth. Preterm infants living in stressed, low-income households require long-term, intensive intervention to reduce developmental difficulties. When newborns with serious complications grow up in positive social environments, they have a good chance of catching up in development.

Heredity, Environment, and Behavior: A Look Ahead

Throughout this chapter, we have discussed a wide variety of genetic and early environmental influences, each of which has the power to alter the course of development. When we consider them together, it may seem surprising that any newborn babies arrive intact, but the vast majority do. Over 90 percent of pregnancies in the United States result in normal infants. Born healthy and vigorous, these developing members of the human species soon show wide variation in traits and abilities. Some are outgoing and sociable, whereas others are shy and reserved. By school age, one child loves to read, another is attracted to mathematics, while still a third excels at music or athletics. **Behavioral genetics** is a field devoted to discovering the origins of this great diversity in human characteristics. We have already seen that researchers are only beginning to understand the genetic and environmental events preceding birth that affect the child's potential. How, then, do they unravel the roots of the many characteristics emerging after birth that are the focus of the remaining chapters in this book?

All behavioral geneticists agree that both heredity and environment are involved in every aspect of development. There is no real controversy on this point because an environment is always needed for genetic information to be expressed (Plomin, 1994c). But for polygenic traits (due to many genes) such as intelligence and personality, scientists are a long way from knowing the precise hereditary influences involved. They must study the impact of genes on these characteristics indirectly, and the nature–nurture controversy remains unresolved because researchers do not agree on how heredity and environment influence these complex traits.

Some believe that it is useful and possible to answer the question of *how much* each factor contributes to differences among children. A second group regards the question of which factor is more important as neither useful nor answerable. These investigators believe that heredity and environment do not make separate contributions to behavior. Instead, they are always related, and the real question we need to explore is *how* they work together. Let's consider each of these two positions in turn.

behavioral genetics A field of study devoted to uncovering the hereditary and environmental origins of individual differences in human traits and abilities.

THE QUESTION, "HOW MUCH?"

Behavioral geneticists use two methods—heritability estimates and concordance rates—to infer the role of heredity in complex human characteristics. Let's look closely at the information these procedures yield, along with their limitations.

■ HERITABILITY. **Heritability estimates** measure the extent to which individual differences in complex traits in a specific population are due to genetic factors. Researchers have obtained heritabilities for intelligence and a variety of personality characteristics. We will take a brief, introductory look at their findings here, returning to them in later chapters devoted to these topics. Heritability estimates are obtained from **kinship studies,** which compare the characteristics of family members. The most common type of kinship study compares identical twins, who share all their genes, with fraternal twins, who share only some. If people who are genetically more alike are also more similar in intelligence and personality, then the researcher assumes that heredity plays an important role.

Identical twins Bob and Bob were separated by adoption shortly after birth and not reunited until adulthood. The two Bobs discovered they were alike in many ways. Both hold bachelor's degrees in engineering, are married to teachers named Brenda, wear glasses, have mustaches, smoke pipes, and are volunteer firemen. The study of identical twins reared apart reveals that heredity contributes to many psychological characteristics. Nevertheless, not all separated twins match up as well as this pair, and generalizing from twin evidence to the population is controversial.

(T. K. Wanstall/The Image Works)

Kinship studies of intelligence provide some of the most controversial findings in the field of child development. Some experts claim a strong role for heredity, whereas others believe that genetic factors are barely involved. Currently, most researchers support a moderate role for heredity. When many twin studies are examined, correlations between the scores of identical twins are consistently higher than those of fraternal twins. In a summary of more than 13,000 twin pairs, the correlation for intelligence was .86 for identical twins and .55 for fraternal twins (Scarr, 1997).

Researchers use a complex statistical procedure to compare these correlations, arriving at a heritability estimate ranging from 0 to 1.00. The value for intelligence is about .50 in Western industrialized nations, which indicates that half the variation in intelligence can be explained by individual differences in genetic makeup (Plomin, 1994c). The fact that the intelligence of adopted children is more strongly related to the scores of their biological parents than to those of their adoptive parents offers further support for the role of heredity (Horn, 1983; Scarr & Weinberg, 1983).

Heritability research also reveals that genetic factors are important in personality. In fact, for personality traits that have been studied a great deal, such as sociability, emotional expressiveness, and activity level, heritability estimates are at about the same moderate level as that reported for intelligence (Braungart et al., 1992; Loehlin, 1992).

■ CONCORDANCE. A second measure that has been used to infer the contribution of heredity to complex characteristics is the **concordance rate.** It refers to the percentage of instances in which both twins show a trait when it is present in one twin. Researchers typically use concordance to study emotional and behavior disorders, which can be judged as either present or absent.

A concordance rate ranges from 0 to 100 percent. A score of 0 indicates that if one twin has the trait, the other twin never has it. A score of 100 means that if one twin has the trait, the other one always has it. When a concordance rate is much higher for identical twins than for fraternal twins, then heredity is believed to play a major role. As Figure 3.17 (page 120) reveals, twin studies of schizophrenia[2] and severe depression show this pattern of findings. Look carefully at the figure, and you will see that the evidence for heredity is less convincing for delinquency and criminality. In that case, the difference between the concordance rates for identical and fraternal twins is not great enough to support a strong genetic role (Plomin, 1994a). Once again, adoption studies lend support to these results. Biological relatives of schizophrenic and depressed adoptees are more likely to share the same disorder than are adoptive relatives (Loehlin, Willerman, & Horn, 1988).

heritability estimate A statistic that measures the extent to which individual differences in complex traits in a specific population are due to genetic factors.

kinship studies Studies comparing the characteristics of family members to determine the importance of heredity in complex human characteristics.

concordance rate The percentage of instances in which both twins show a trait when it is present in one twin.

[2]Schizophrenia is a disorder involving serious difficulty distinguishing fantasy from reality, frequent delusions and hallucinations, and irrational and inappropriate behaviors.

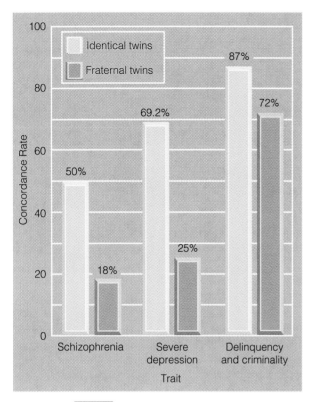

FIGURE 3.17

Concordance rates for schizophrenia, severe depression, and delinquency and criminality.
Heredity plays some role in schizophrenia and is even more influential in severe depression, since the concordance rate is much higher for identical than for fraternal twins. Heredity contributes much less to delinquency and criminality, since the difference in concordance rates for identical and fraternal twins is relatively small.

(From Gottesman, 1991; Gottesman, Carey, & Hanson, 1983; McGuffin & Sargeant, 1991.)

Taken together, concordance and adoption research suggests that the tendency for schizophrenia and depression to run in families is partly due to genetic factors. However, we also know that environment is involved, since the concordance rate for identical twins would have to be 100 percent for heredity to be the only influence operating. Already we have seen that environmental stresses, such as poverty, family conflict, and a disorganized home life, are often associated with emotional and behavior disorders. We will encounter many more examples of this relationship in later chapters.

■ **LIMITATIONS OF HERITABILITY AND CONCORDANCE.** Although heritability estimates and concordance rates provide evidence that genetic factors contribute to complex human characteristics, questions have been raised about their accuracy. First, we must keep in mind that each value refers only to the particular population studied and its unique range of genetic and environmental influences. If the range of either factor changes, then heritability estimates will change. To take an extreme example, imagine a country in which children's home, school, and neighborhood experiences are very similar. Under these conditions, individual differences in behavior would be largely due to heredity, and heritability estimates would be close to 1.00. Conversely, the more environments vary, the greater their opportunity to account for individual differences, and the lower heritability estimates are likely to be (Plomin, 1994c).

Second, the accuracy of heritability estimates and concordance rates depends on the extent to which the twin pairs on which they are computed reflect genetic and environmental variation in the population. Yet consider these findings: Identical twins reared together under highly similar conditions have more strongly correlated intelligence test scores than do those reared apart. When the former are used in research, the importance of heredity is overestimated (Hoffman, 1994). To overcome this difficulty, investigators try to find twins who have been reared apart in adoptive families. But few separated twin pairs are available, and when they are, social service agencies often place them in advantaged homes that are alike in many ways (Eisenberg, 1998). Because the environments of most twin pairs do not represent the broad range of environments found in the general population, it is often difficult to generalize heritability and concordance findings to the population as a whole.

Heritability estimates are controversial measures because they can easily be misapplied. For example, high heritabilities have been used to suggest that ethnic differences in intelligence, such as the poorer performance of black children in relation to white children, have a genetic basis (Jensen, 1969, 1985). Yet this line of reasoning is widely regarded as incorrect. Heritabilities computed on mostly white twin samples do not tell us what is responsible for test score differences between ethnic groups. We have already seen that large economic and cultural differences are involved. In Chapter 8, we will discuss research indicating that when black children are adopted into economically advantaged homes at an early age, their scores are well above average and substantially higher than those of children growing up in impoverished families.

Perhaps the most serious criticism of heritability estimates and concordance rates has to do with their usefulness. Although they are interesting statistics that tell us heredity is undoubtedly involved in complex traits such as intelligence and personality, they give us no precise information on how these traits develop or how children might respond when exposed to family, school, and peer experiences aimed at helping them develop as far as possible (Bronfenbrenner & Ceci, 1994). Indeed, research shows that the heritability of intelligence is higher in advantaged homes and communities, which permit children to actualize their genetic endowment. In disadvantaged environments, children are prevented from realizing their potential. Consequently, enhancing their experiences through interventions (such as parent education and high-quality preschool or child care) has a greater impact on development (Bronfenbrenner & Morris, 1998; Scarr, 1998).

In response to these criticisms, investigators who conduct heritability research argue that their studies are a first step. As more evidence accumulates to show that heredity underlies important human characteristics, then scientists can begin to ask better questions—about the specific genes involved, the way they affect development, and how their impact is modified by environmental factors.

THE QUESTION, "HOW?"

According to a second perspective, heredity and environment cannot be divided into separate influences. Instead, behavior is the result of a dynamic interplay between these two forces. How do heredity and environment work together to affect development? Several important concepts shed light on this question.

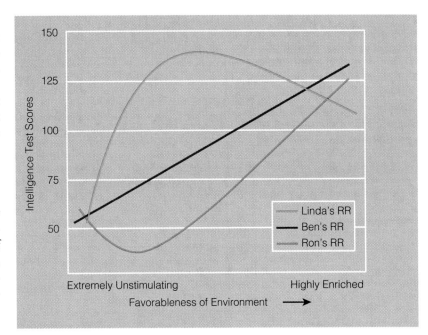

FIGURE 3.18

Intellectual ranges of reaction (RR) for three children in environments that vary from extremely unstimulating to highly enriched. Each child, due to his or her genetic makeup, responds differently as quality of the environment changes. Ben's intelligence increases steadily, Linda's rises sharply and then falls off, and Ron's begins to increase only after the environment becomes modestly stimulating.

(Adapted from Wahlsten, 1994.)

■ **REACTION RANGE.** The first of these ideas is **range of reaction** (Gottesman, 1963). It emphasizes that each person responds to the environment in a unique way because of his or her genetic makeup. Let's explore this idea in Figure 3.18. Reaction range can apply to any characteristic; here it is illustrated for intelligence. Notice that when environments vary from extremely unstimulating to highly enriched, Ben's intelligence increases steadily, Linda's rises sharply and then falls off, and Ron's begins to increase only after the environment becomes modestly stimulating.

Reaction range highlights two important points about the relationship between heredity and environment. First, it shows that because each of us has a unique genetic makeup, we respond quite differently to the same environment. Look carefully at Figure 3.18, and notice how a poor environment results in similarly low scores for all three children. But Linda is by far the best-performing child when environments provide an intermediate level of stimulation. And when environments are highly enriched, Ben does best, followed by Ron, both of whom now exceed Linda. Second, sometimes different genetic–environmental combinations can make two children look the same! For example, if Linda is reared in a minimally stimulating environment, her score will be about 100—average for children in general. Ben and Ron can also obtain this score, but to do so they must grow up in a fairly enriched home.

The concept of range of reaction tells us that children differ in their range of possible responses to the environment. And it illustrates the meaning of the statement "Heredity and environment interact," since it shows that unique blends of heredity and environment lead to both similarities and differences in behavior (Wahlsten, 1994).

■ **CANALIZATION.** The concept of canalization provides another way of understanding how heredity and environment combine. **Canalization** is the tendency of heredity to restrict the development of some characteristics to just one or a few outcomes. A behavior that is strongly canalized follows a genetically set growth plan, and only strong environmental forces can change it (Waddington, 1957). For example, infant perceptual and motor development seems to be strongly canalized, since all normal human babies eventually roll over, reach for objects, sit up, crawl, and walk. It takes extreme conditions to modify these behaviors or cause them not to appear. In contrast, intelligence and personality are less strongly canalized, since they vary much more with changes in the environment. When we look at the kinds of behaviors that are constrained by heredity, we can see that canalization is highly adaptive. Through it, nature ensures that children will develop certain species-typical skills under a wide range of rearing conditions, thereby promoting survival.

Recently, scientists have expanded the notion of canalization to include environmental influences. We now know that environments can also limit development (Gottlieb, 1996). For example, when children experience harmful environments early in life, there

range of reaction Each person's unique, genetically determined response to a range of environmental conditions.

canalization The tendency of heredity to restrict the development of some characteristics to just one or a few outcomes.

This mother is an accomplished musician who exposes her son to a stimulating musical environment. In addition, the boy may have inherited his mother's talent for music. When heredity and environment are correlated, they jointly foster the same capacities, and the influence of one cannot be separated from the influence of the other.
(D. Smith/Monkmeyer Press)

may be little that later experiences can do to change characteristics (such as intelligence) that were quite flexible to begin with. We have already seen that this is the case for babies who were prenatally exposed to high levels of alcohol or radiation or who experienced anoxia before or during birth. And later in this book, we will find that it is also true for children who spend many years living in extremely deprived homes and institutions (Turkheimer & Gottesman, 1991).

Using the concept of canalization, we learn that genes restrict the development of some characteristics more than others. And over time, even very flexible behaviors can become fixed and canalized, depending on the environments to which children are exposed.

■ GENETIC–ENVIRONMENTAL CORRELATION. Nature and nurture work together in still another way. Several investigators point out that a major problem in trying to separate heredity and environment is that they are often correlated (Plomin, 1994b; Scarr & McCartney, 1983). According to the concept of **genetic–environmental correlation,** our genes influence the environments to which we are exposed. In support of this idea, a recent study showed that the greater the genetic similarity between pairs of adolescents, the more alike they were on many aspects of child rearing, including parental discipline, affection, conflict, and monitoring of the young person's activities (Plomin et al., 1994).

These findings indicate that heredity plays a role in molding children's experiences. The way this happens changes with development.

PASSIVE AND EVOCATIVE CORRELATION. At younger ages, two types of genetic–environmental correlation are common. The first is called *passive* correlation because the child has no control over it. Early on, parents provide environments that are influenced by their own heredity. For example, parents who are good athletes are likely to emphasize outdoor activities and enroll their children in swimming and gymnastics lessons. Besides getting exposed to an "athletic environment," the children may have inherited their parents' athletic ability. As a result, they are likely to become good athletes for both genetic and environmental reasons.

The second type of genetic–environmental correlation is *evocative.* Children evoke responses from others that are influenced by the child's heredity, and these responses strengthen the child's original style of responding. For example, an active, friendly baby is likely to receive more social stimulation from those around her than is a passive, quiet infant. And a cooperative, attentive preschooler will probably receive more patient and sensitive interactions from parents than will an inattentive, distractible child.

genetic–environmental correlation The idea that heredity influences the environments to which individuals are exposed.

niche-picking A type of genetic–environmental correlation in which individuals actively choose environments that complement their heredity.

ACTIVE CORRELATION. At older ages, *active* genetic–environmental correlation becomes common. As children extend their experiences beyond the immediate family to school, neighborhood, and community and are given the freedom to make more of their own choices, they play an increasingly active role in seeking out environments that fit with their genetic tendencies. The well-coordinated, muscular child spends more time at after-school sports, the musically talented youngster joins the school orchestra and practices his violin, and the intellectually curious child is a familiar patron at her local library.

This tendency to actively choose environments that complement our heredity is called **niche-picking** (Scarr & McCartney, 1983). Infants and young children cannot do much niche-picking, since adults select environments for them. In contrast, older children and adolescents are much more in charge of their own environments. The niche-picking idea explains why pairs of identical twins reared apart during childhood and later reunited may find, to their great surprise, that they have similar hobbies, food preferences, friendship choices, and vocations—a trend that is especially marked when twins' environmental opportunities are similar (Bouchard et al., 1990; Plomin, 1994b). Niche-picking also helps us understand some curious longitudinal findings indicating that identical twins become somewhat more alike and fraternal twins less alike in intelligence from infancy to adolescence (Loehlin, Horn, & Willerman, 1997). The influence of heredity and environment is not constant but changes over time. With age, genetic factors may become more important in influencing the environments we experience and choose for ourselves.

A major reason child development researchers are interested in the nature–nurture issue is that they want to improve environments in order to help children develop as far as possible. The concepts of range of reaction, canalization, and genetic–environmental correlation remind us that development is best understood as a series of complex exchanges between nature and nurture. When a characteristic is strongly influenced by heredity, it can still be modified. However, children cannot be changed in any way we might desire. The success of any attempt to improve development depends on the characteristics we want to change, the genetic makeup of the child, and the type and timing of our intervention.

ASK YOURSELF . . .

♦ *Bianca's parents are both accomplished musicians. Bianca began taking piano lessons when she was 4 years old and was accompanying her school choir by age 10. When she reached adolescence, she asked her parents if she could attend a special music high school. Explain how genetic and environmental factors work together to promote Bianca's talent.*

♦ **CONNECTIONS**
After reading a news article about the heritability of complex traits, Ross concluded that there wasn't much he could do to influence his children's intellectual and personality development. Explain the limitations of heritability estimates to Ross. Cite evidence indicating that parents play vital roles in children's development. (See Chapter 8, pages 343–344; Chapter 10, pages 420–421, 426–428; and Chapter 14, pages 563–566.)

SUMMARY

GENETIC FOUNDATIONS

What are genes, and how are they transmitted from one generation to the next?

♦ Each individual's **phenotype,** or directly observable characteristics, is a product of both **genotype** and environment. **Chromosomes,** rodlike structures within the cell nucleus, contain our hereditary endowment. Along their length are **genes,** segments of **DNA** that make us distinctly human and influence our development and characteristics.

♦ **Gametes,** or sex cells, are produced through the process of cell division known as **meiosis. Crossing over** and independent assortment of chromosomes ensure that each gamete receives a unique set of genes from each parent. Once sperm and ovum unite, the resulting **zygote** starts to develop into a complex human being through cell duplication, or **mitosis.**

♦ **Identical,** or **monozygotic, twins** develop when a zygote divides in two during the early stages of cell duplication. **Fraternal,** or **dizygotic, twins** result when two ova are released from the mother's ovaries and both are fertilized. If the fertilizing sperm carries an X chromosome, the child will be a girl; if it contains a Y chromosome, a boy will be born.

Describe various patterns of genetic inheritance.

♦ **Dominant–recessive** and **codominant** relationships are patterns of inheritance that apply to traits controlled by single genes. In dominant–recessive inheritance, **heterozygous** individuals with one recessive **allele** are **carriers** of the recessive trait. **Pleiotropism,** the ability of a single gene to affect more than one trait, and **modifier genes,** which alter the expression of other genes, affect many characteristics.

♦ When recessive disorders are **X-linked** (carried on the X chromosome), males are more likely to be affected. **Genetic imprinting** is a recently discovered pattern of inheritance in which one parent's allele is activated, regardless of its makeup.

♦ Unfavorable genes arise from **mutations,** which can occur spontaneously or be induced by hazardous environmental agents.

♦ Human traits that vary continuously, such as intelligence and personality, are **polygenic,** or influenced by many genes. Since the genetic principles involved are unknown, scientists must study the influence of heredity on these characteristics indirectly.

Describe major chromosomal abnormalities, and explain how they occur.

◆ Most chromosomal abnormalities are due to errors in meiosis. The most common chromosomal disorder is Down syndrome, which results in physical defects and mental retardation.

◆ Disorders of the **sex chromosomes** are generally milder than defects of the **autosomes.** Contrary to popular belief, males with XYY syndrome are not necessarily more aggressive than XY males. Studies of children with triple X, Klinefelter, and Turner syndromes reveal that adding to or subtracting from the usual number of X chromosomes leads to specific intellectual problems.

REPRODUCTIVE CHOICES

What procedures are available to assist prospective parents in having healthy children?

◆ **Genetic counseling** helps couples at risk for giving birth to children with hereditary defects decide whether or not to conceive. **Prenatal diagnostic methods** make early detection of abnormalities possible. In some cases, treatment can be initiated before birth. Although donor insemination, in vitro fertilization, surrogate motherhood, and post-menopausal-assisted childbirth permit many barren couples to become parents, reproductive technologies raise serious legal and ethical concerns.

PRENATAL DEVELOPMENT

List the three phases of prenatal development, and describe the major milestones of each.

◆ Prenatal development is usually divided into three phases. The period of the zygote lasts about 2 weeks, from fertilization until the blastocyst becomes deeply implanted in the uterine lining. During this time, structures that will support prenatal growth begin to form. The embryonic disk is surrounded by the **amnion,** which is filled with amniotic fluid. From the **chorion,** villi emerge that burrow into the uterine wall, and the **placenta** starts to develop. The developing organism is connected to the placenta by the **umbilical cord.**

◆ The period of the **embryo** lasts from implantation through the eighth week of pregnancy, during which the foundations for all body structures are laid down. In the first week of this period, the neural tube forms, and the nervous system starts to develop. Other organs follow and grow rapidly. At the end of this phase, the embryo responds to touch and can move.

◆ The period of the **fetus,** lasting until the end of pregnancy, involves a dramatic increase in body size and completion of physical structures. By the middle of the second trimester, the mother can feel movement. The fetus becomes covered with **vernix,** which protects the skin from chapping due to constant exposure to the amniotic fluid. White, downy hair called **lanugo** helps the vernix stick to the skin. At the end of the second trimester, the production of neurons in the brain is complete.

◆ The **age of viability** occurs at the beginning of the final trimester, sometime between 22 and 26 weeks. The brain continues to develop rapidly, and new sensory and behavioral capacities

emerge. Gradually, the lungs mature, the fetus fills the uterus, and birth is near.

PRENATAL ENVIRONMENTAL INFLUENCES

Cite factors that influence the impact of teratogens on the developing organism, noting agents that are known or suspected of being teratogens.

◆ **Teratogens** are environmental agents that cause damage during the prenatal period. Their effects conform to the sensitive period concept. The organism is especially vulnerable during the embryonic period, when body structures are rapidly emerging.

◆ The impact of teratogens differs from one case to the next, due to amount and length of exposure, the genetic makeup of mother and fetus, the presence or absence of other harmful agents, and the age of the organism at time of exposure. The effects of teratogens are not limited to immediate physical damage. Serious psychological consequences may appear later in development. Drugs, tobacco, alcohol, hormones, radiation, environmental pollution, and certain infectious diseases are teratogens that can endanger the prenatal organism.

Describe the impact of additional maternal factors on prenatal development.

◆ Other maternal factors can either support or complicate prenatal development. In healthy, physically fit women, regular moderate exercise contributes to an expectant woman's general health and the baby's birth weight. However, very frequent, vigorous exercise results in lower birth weight. When the mother's diet is inadequate, low birth weight and brain damage are major concerns. Vitamin–mineral supplementation beginning early in pregnancy can improve maternal health and prevent certain prenatal and birth complications. Severe emotional stress is associated with many pregnancy complications, although its impact can be reduced by providing mothers with social support.

◆ Aside from the risk of chromosomal abnormalities, older women in good health do not experience more prenatal problems than do younger women. Poor health and environmental risks associated with poverty are the strongest predictors of pregnancy complications in teenagers and older women.

CHILDBIRTH

Describe the three stages of childbirth, the baby's adaptation to labor and delivery, and the newborn baby's appearance.

◆ Childbirth takes place in three stages, beginning with contractions that open the cervix so the baby can be pushed through the birth canal and ending with delivery of the placenta. During labor, infants produce high levels of stress hormones, which help them withstand oxygen deprivation and arouse them into alertness at birth.

◆ Newborn babies' large heads and small bodies are odd-looking, but their attractive facial features make adults feel like picking them up and cuddling them. The **Apgar Scale** is used to assess the newborn baby's physical condition at birth.

APPROACHES TO CHILDBIRTH

Describe natural childbirth and home delivery, and explain the benefits and risks of using pain-relieving drugs during labor and delivery.

◆ **Natural,** or **prepared, childbirth** involves classes in which prospective parents learn about labor and delivery, instruction of the mother in relaxation and breathing techniques, and a companion who serves as a coach during childbirth. The method helps reduce stress and pain during labor and delivery.

◆ As long as mothers are healthy and assisted by a well-trained doctor or midwife, it is just as safe to give birth at home as in a hospital.

◆ Analgesics and anesthetics are necessary in complicated deliveries. When given in large doses, these pain-relieving drugs produce a depressed state in the newborn that affects the early parent–infant relationship. They also increase the likelihood of an instrument delivery.

BIRTH COMPLICATIONS

What risks are associated with oxygen deprivation and preterm and low birth weight, and what factors can help infants who survive a traumatic birth develop?

◆ Anoxia can result when breathing fails to start immediately after delivery, the umbilical cord is squeezed because the baby is in **breech position,** or **Rh** incompatibility leads to destruction of the baby's red blood cells. Oxygen deprivation is a serious birth complication that can damage the brain and other organs. As long as anoxia is not extreme, most affected children catch up in development by the school years.

◆ **Preterm** and low-birth-weight babies are especially likely to be born to poverty-stricken, ethnic minority mothers. **Small-for-date** infants usually have longer-lasting difficulties than do preterm babies. Some interventions for low-birth-weight infants provide special stimulation in the intensive care nursery. Others teach parents how to care for and interact with these fragile babies. When preterm infants live in stressed, low-income households, long-term, intensive intervention is necessary to reduce developmental problems. A major cause of **infant mortality** is low birth weight.

◆ When infants experience birth trauma, a supportive home environment can help restore their growth. Even children with fairly serious birth complications can recover with the help of favorable life events.

HEREDITY, ENVIRONMENT, AND BEHAVIOR: A LOOK AHEAD

Explain the various ways heredity and environment may combine to influence complex traits.

◆ **Behavioral genetics** is a field devoted to discovering the hereditary and environmental origins of complex characteristics, such as intelligence and personality. Some researchers believe it is useful and possible to determine "how much" each factor contributes to individual differences. These investigators compute **heritability estimates** and **concordance rates** from **kinship studies.** Although these measures show that genetic factors contribute to such traits as intelligence and personality, questions have been raised about their accuracy and usefulness.

◆ Other researchers believe the important question is "how" heredity and environment work together. The concepts of **range of reaction, canalization,** and **genetic–environmental correlation** remind us that development is best understood as a series of complex exchanges between nature and nurture.

IMPORTANT TERMS AND CONCEPTS

age of viability (p. 93)
allele (p. 76)
amnion (p. 91)
Apgar Scale (p. 109)
autosomes (p. 76)
behavioral genetics (p. 118)
breech position (p. 112)
canalization (p. 121)
carrier (p. 76)
chorion (p. 91)
chromosomes (p. 72)
codominance (p. 77)
concordance rate (p. 119)
crossing over (p. 73)
deoxyribonucleic acid (DNA) (p. 72)
dominant–recessive inheritance (p. 76)
embryo (p. 93)
fetal alcohol effects (FAE) (p. 100)
fetal alcohol syndrome (FAS) (p. 100)

fetus (p. 93)
fraternal, or dizygotic, twins (p. 75)
gametes (p. 73)
gene (p. 72)
genetic counseling (p. 83)
genetic–environmental correlation (p. 122)
genetic imprinting (p. 80)
genotype (p. 72)
heritability estimate (p. 119)
heterozygous (p. 76)
homozygous (p. 76)
identical, or monozygotic, twins (p. 75)
infant mortality (p. 116)
kinship studies (p. 119)
lanugo (p. 93)
meiosis (p. 73)
mitosis (p. 72)
modifier genes (p. 77)
mutation (p. 81)

natural, or prepared, childbirth (p. 109)
niche-picking (p. 122)
phenotype (p. 72)
placenta (p. 91)
pleiotropism (p. 77)
polygenic inheritance (p. 81)
prenatal diagnostic methods (p. 84)
preterm (p. 113)
range of reaction (p. 121)
Rh factor (p. 112)
sex chromosomes (p. 76)
small for date (p. 113)
teratogen (p. 95)
umbilical cord (p. 93)
vernix (p. 93)
X-linked inheritance (p. 78)
zygote (p. 75)

Infancy:
Early Learning,
Motor Skills, and
Perceptual Capacities

INFANCY IS THE PERIOD of development that begins at birth and ends at around 18 months to 2 years of age. Although it comprises only 2 percent of the lifespan, it is one of the most remarkable and busiest times of development. The newborn baby, or *neonate,*[1] enters the world with surprisingly sophisticated perceptual and motor abilities, a set of skills for interacting with people, and a capacity to learn that is put to use immediately after birth. By the end of infancy, the small child is a self-assertive, purposeful being who walks on her own, has developed refined manual skills, and is prepared to acquire the most unique of human abilities—language.

Our view of the infant has changed drastically over this century. At one time, the newborn baby was considered a passive, incompetent being whose world was, in the words of turn-of-the-century psychologist William James, "a blooming, buzzing confusion." Recently developed methods and equipment permitting researchers to test the young baby's capacities have shown this image to be wrong. Witness the following diary notes by a modern child development researcher about her own baby:

> At 3.5 weeks, you lift your head when I put you on your tummy, showing off your strength with shaky half-push-ups. In your crib, you stare at your mobile, your face serious and still, utterly absorbed. When you are bored, I carry you to a new place, sing to you. At the sound of my voice, your face perks up, and you turn toward me with rapt attention. When you are unhappy, I hold you close to my heart so you can feel its rhythmic sound. Your cry has become a language I can understand. Your tiny fingers grasp whatever comes near—the folds of my clothing, my fingers in your palm—and you hold on tightly. I marvel at your determination to master your world!

These observations clearly reflect the widely accepted view that infants, from the outset, are skilled, capable beings who display many complex human abilities.

Development during infancy proceeds at an astonishing pace. Excited relatives who visit just after the birth and return a few months later often remark that the baby does not seem like the same individual! Although researchers agree that infants are competent beings, fervent debates continue over questions like these: Which capacities are present from the very beginning? Which must wait to mature with the passage of time? And which are acquired through constant interaction with the physical and social worlds?

In this chapter, we explore the infant's remarkable capabilities—early reflexes, ability to learn, motor skills, and perceptual capacities. Throughout our discussion, we will return to these controversial themes. We will also see how

[1]The term *neonate* refers to an infant from birth through the first month of life.

a burst of new findings adds to our practical understanding of experiences necessary to support the dramatic changes of the first 2 years.

The Organized Newborn

he newborn baby, as we saw in Chapter 3, is a homely looking creature. The head, misshapen from being squeezed through the narrow birth canal, is overly large in relation to the potbellied trunk and bowlegged lower body. In addition, the baby's skin is usually wrinkled and "parboiled" in appearance. At first glance, many parents assume that this odd little being can do nothing but eat and sleep. Yet a few hours spent in the company of a neonate reveals that the tiny being is not a creature at all! Newborns display a wide variety of typically human capacities that are crucial for survival and that evoke the care and attention they receive from adults. In relating to the physical world and building their first social relationships, babies are active from the very start.

NEWBORN REFLEXES

A **reflex** is an inborn, automatic response to a particular form of stimulation. Reflexes are the neonate's most obvious organized patterns of behavior. Infants come into the world with dozens of them. A father, changing his newborn baby's diaper, accidentally bumps the side of the table. The infant reacts by flinging her arms wide and bringing them back toward her body. A mother softly strokes her infant's cheek, and the baby turns his head in her direction. Holding the infant upright with feet touching a flat surface, she watches the baby make little stepping movements. Table 4.1 lists the major newborn reflexes. See if you can identify the ones described here and in the diary excerpt at the beginning of this chapter. Then let's consider the meaning and purpose of these curious behaviors.

■ **ADAPTIVE VALUE OF REFLEXES.** Some newborn reflexes have survival value. The rooting reflex helps a breast-fed baby find the mother's nipple. Once found, imagine what it would be like if we had to teach the infant the complex lip and tongue movements involved in sucking. If sucking were not automatic, our species would be unlikely to survive for a single generation! The swimming reflex helps a baby who is accidentally dropped into water stay afloat, increasing the chances of retrieval by the caregiver.

Other reflexes probably helped babies survive during our evolutionary past. For example, the Moro or "embracing" reflex is believed to have helped infants cling to their mothers when babies were carried about all day. If the baby happened to lose support, the reflex caused the infant to embrace and, along with the powerful grasp reflex (so strong

In the Moro reflex, loss of support or a sudden loud sound causes this baby to arch her back, extend her arms outward, and then bring them in toward her body.
(Mimi Forsyth/Monkmeyer Press)

TABLE 4.1

Some Newborn Reflexes

Reflex	Stimulation	Response	Age of Disappearance	Function
Eye blink	Shine bright light at eyes or clap hand near head	Infant quickly closes eyelids	Permanent	Protects infant from strong stimulation
Withdrawal	Prick sole of foot with pin	Foot withdraws, with flexion of knee and hip	Weakens after 10 days	Protects infant from un-pleasant tactile stimulation
Rooting	Stroke cheek near corner of mouth	Head turns toward source of stimulation	3 weeks (becomes voluntary head turning at this time)	Helps infant find the nipple
Sucking	Place finger in infant's mouth	Infant sucks finger rhythmically	Permanent	Permits feeding
Swimming	Place infant face down in pool of water	Baby paddles and kicks in swimming motion	4–6 months	Helps infant survive if dropped into water
Moro	Hold infant horizontally on back and let head drop slightly, or produce a sudden loud sound against surface supporting infant	Infant makes an "embracing" motion by arching back, extending legs, throwing arms outward, and then bringing arms in toward the body	6 months	In human evolutionary past, may have helped infant cling to mother
Palmar grasp	Place finger in infant's hand and press against palm	Spontaneous grasp of finger	3–4 months	Prepares infant for voluntary grasping
Tonic neck	Turn baby's head to one side while lying awake on back	Infant lies in a "fencing position." One arm is extended in front of eyes on side to which head is turned, other arm is flexed	4 months	May prepare infant for voluntary reaching
Stepping	Hold infant under arms and permit bare feet to touch a flat surface	Infant lifts one foot after another in stepping response	2 months	Prepares infant for voluntary walking
Babinski	Stroke sole of foot from toe toward heel	Toes fan out and curl as foot twists in	8–12 months	Unknown

Sources: Knobloch & Pasamanick, 1974; Prechtl & Beintema, 1965.

during the first week that it can support the baby's entire weight), regain its hold on the mother's body (Kessen, 1967; Prechtl, 1958).

Finally, several reflexes help parents and infants establish gratifying interaction as soon as possible. A baby who searches for and successfully finds the nipple, sucks easily during feedings, and grasps when her hand is touched encourages parents to respond lovingly and feel competent as caregivers. Reflexes can also help parents comfort the baby, since they permit infants to control distress and amount of stimulation. As any new mother who remembers to bring a pacifier on an outing with her young baby knows, sucking readily reduces the mass uncoordinated activity of a fussy neonate.

■ **REFLEXES AND THE DEVELOPMENT OF MOTOR SKILLS.** Most newborn reflexes disappear during the first 6 months, due to a gradual increase in voluntary control over behavior as the cerebral cortex matures (Touwen, 1984). Do reflexes simply wane before voluntary behavior appears? Or are they an integral and essential prelude to organizing the voluntary skills that come after them?

That babies adapt their reflex actions to changes in stimulation immediately after birth suggests that many reflexes form the basis for complex, purposeful behaviors. For example, different finger movements appear in the palmar grasp reflex, depending on how the palm of the hand is stimulated (Touwen, 1978).

A few reflexes appear to be related to voluntary behavior in subtle ways. For example, the tonic neck reflex may prepare the infant for voluntary reaching. When babies lie on

reflex An inborn, automatic response to a particular form of stimulation.

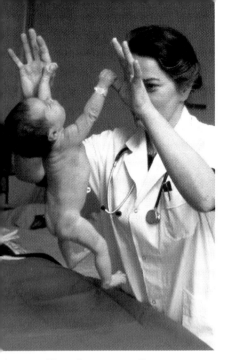

The palmar grasp reflex is so strong during the first week after birth that many infants can use it to support their entire weight.

(J. da Cunha/Petit Format/Photo Researchers, Inc.)

When held upright under the arms, newborn babies show reflexive stepping movements.

(Innervisions)

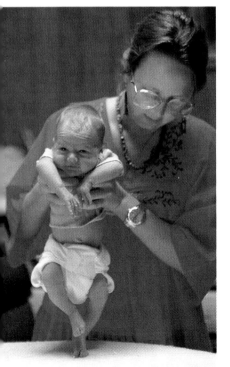

their backs in this "fencing position," they naturally gaze at the hand in front of their eyes. The reflex may encourage them to combine vision with arm movements and, eventually, to reach for objects (Knobloch & Pasamanick, 1974).

Other reflexes, such as the palmar grasp, swimming, and stepping, drop out early in the first year, but the motor functions involved seem to be renewed later. In a series of studies, Philip Zelazo showed that babies given daily stimulation of the stepping reflex during the first few months displayed more spontaneous stepping movements and walked several weeks earlier than did those who did not receive this practice (Zelazo et al., 1993; Zelazo, Zelazo, & Kolb, 1972).

How does early reflexive stimulation contribute to motor control? Zelazo (1983) believes that exercising the stepping reflex promotes development of areas of the cerebral cortex that govern voluntary walking. But research by Esther Thelen (1983) provides a different explanation. She showed that babies who gained the most weight during the first month of life had the weakest stepping reflex. Also, when she dipped the lower part of the infant's body in water (which lightens the load on the baby's muscles), the reflex strengthened (Thelen, Fisher, & Ridley-Johnson, 1984).

According to Thelen, the stepping reflex drops out because early infant weight gain is not matched by an increase in muscle strength, which permits babies to lift their increasingly heavy legs. But the infant permitted to exercise the stepping reflex builds leg strength early, in the same way that exercise causes an athlete to gain muscle power. Stronger leg muscles, in turn, enable infants to retain the reflex and to stand and walk earlier. Regardless of which position is correct, the work of both Zelazo and Thelen reveals that even though reflexive stepping subsides in many infants, the mechanism responsible for it is used by the brain at a later age.

Do these findings suggest that parents should deliberately exercise newborn stepping and other responses? There is no special reason to do so, since reflexive practice does not produce a child who is a better walker! In the case of the swimming reflex, it is risky to try to build on it. Although young babies placed in a swimming pool will paddle and kick, they open their mouths and swallow large amounts of water. Consuming too much water lowers the concentration of salt in the baby's blood, which can cause swelling of the brain and seizures (Micheli, 1985). Despite the presence of this remarkable reflex, swimming lessons are best postponed until at least 3 years of age.

■ THE IMPORTANCE OF ASSESSING NEWBORN REFLEXES. Pediatricians test infant reflexes carefully, especially if a newborn has experienced birth trauma, since reflexes provide one way of assessing the health of the baby's nervous system. In brain-damaged infants, reflexes may be weak or absent or, in some cases, exaggerated and overly rigid. Brain damage may also be indicated when reflexes persist past the point in development when they should normally disappear. However, individual differences in reflexive responses exist that are not cause for concern. Newborn reflexes must be combined with other observations of the baby to accurately distinguish normal from abnormal central nervous system functioning (Touwen, 1984).

NEWBORN STATES

Throughout the day and night, newborn infants move in and out of six different **states of arousal,** or degrees of sleep and wakefulness, described in Table 4.2. During the first month, these states alternate frequently. Quiet alertness is the most fleeting. It usually moves relatively quickly toward fussing and crying. Much to the relief of their fatigued parents, newborns spend the greatest amount of time asleep—about 16 to 18 hours a day.

Between birth and 2 years, the organization of sleep and wakefulness changes substantially. The decline in total sleep time is not great; the average 2-year-old still needs 12 to 13 hours. Instead, short periods of sleep and wakefulness are gradually put together. Although by the end of the prenatal period and after birth, babies sleep more at night than during the day, this pattern increases steadily with age (Borghese, Minard, & Thoman, 1995; Whitney & Thoman, 1994). By 4 months, the nightly sleep period of many babies reared in Western nations is 8 hours, resembling that of the parents; by 6 months, it is 10

TABLE 4.2

Infant States of Arousal

State	Description	Daily Duration in Newborns
Regular sleep	The infant is at full rest and shows little or no body activity. The eyelids are closed, no eye movements occur, the face is relaxed, and breathing is slow and regular.	8–9 hours
Irregular sleep	Gentle limb movements, occasional stirring, and facial grimacing occur. Although the eyelids are closed, occasional rapid eye movements can be seen beneath them. Breathing is irregular.	8–9 hours
Drowsiness	The infant is either falling asleep or waking up. Body is less active than in irregular sleep but more active than in regular sleep. Eyes open and close; when open, they have a glazed look. Breathing is even but somewhat faster than in regular sleep.	Varies
Quiet alertness	The infant's body is relatively inactive. The eyes are open and attentive. Breathing is even.	2–3 hours
Waking activity	The infant shows frequent bursts of uncoordinated motor activity. Breathing is very irregular. The face may be relaxed or tense and wrinkled.	2–3 hours
Crying	Waking activity sometimes evolves into crying, which is accompanied by diffuse, vigorous motor activity.	1–2 hours

Source: Wolff, 1966.

to 12 hours. And over time, infants remain awake for longer daytime periods and need fewer naps—by the second year, only one or two (Blum & Carey, 1996).

These changes in arousal patterns are largely due to brain maturation, but they are affected by the social environment as well. In the United States and other Western nations, many parents try to get their babies to sleep through the night as soon as possible— usually by offering an evening feeding before putting them down in a separate, quiet room. In this way, they push young infants to the limits of their neurological capacities. Not until the middle of the first year is the secretion of *melatonin*, a hormone within the brain that promotes drowsiness, much greater at night than during the day (Sadeh, 1997).

As the Cultural Influences box on page 132 shows, the practice of isolating infants to promote sleep is rare elsewhere in the world. In non-Western societies, babies typically remain in constant contact with their mothers throughout the day and night, sleeping and waking to nurse at will. For babies experiencing this type of care, the average nightly sleep period remains constant at 3 hours from 1 to 8 months of age. Only at the end of the first year do they move in the direction of an adultlike sleep–waking schedule (McKenna et al., 1994; Super & Harkness, 1982).

Although arousal states become more patterned and regular for all infants, striking individual differences in daily rhythms exist that affect parents' attitudes toward and interactions with the baby (Thoman & Whitney, 1990). A few infants sleep for long periods at an early age, increasing the rest their parents get and the energy they have for sensitive, responsive care. Babies who cry a great deal require that parents try harder to soothe them. If these efforts are not successful, parents' positive feelings for the infant and sense of competence may suffer. Babies who spend more time in the alert state are likely to receive more social stimulation. And since this state provides opportunities to explore the environment, infants who favor it may have a slight advantage in cognitive development (Moss et al., 1988).

Of the states listed in Table 4.2, the two extremes—sleep and crying—have been of greatest interest to researchers. Each tells us something about normal and abnormal early development.

states of arousal Different degrees of sleep and wakefulness.

rapid-eye-movement (REM) sleep An "irregular" sleep state in which brain wave activity is similar to that of the waking state; eyes dart beneath the lids; heart rate, blood pressure, and breathing are uneven; and slight body movements occur.

■ SLEEP. A mother and father I know watched one day while their newborn baby slept and wondered why his eyelids and body twitched and his rate of breathing varied, speeding up at some points and slowing down at others. "Is this how babies are supposed to sleep?" they asked, somewhat worried. Indeed it is.

Sleep is made up of at least two states. Irregular, or **rapid-eye-movement (REM) sleep,** is the one these new parents happened to observe. The expression "sleeping like a baby"

Cultural Variation in Infant Sleeping Arrangements

CULTURAL INFLUENCES

W HILE AWAITING THE birth of a new baby, American middle-class parents typically furnish a special room as the infant's sleeping quarters. At first, young babies may be placed in a bassinet or cradle in the parents' bedroom for reasons of convenience, but most are moved by 3 to 6 months of age. Many adults in the United States regard this nighttime separation of baby from parent as perfectly natural. Throughout the twentieth century, child-rearing advice from experts strongly encouraged it. For example, the most recent edition of Dr. Spock's *Baby and Child Care* recommends that babies be moved out of their parents' room early in the first year, explaining, "Otherwise, there is a chance that they may become dependent on this arrangement" (Spock & Parker, 1998, p. 102).

Yet parent–infant "cosleeping" is common around the globe, in industrialized and nonindustrialized countries alike. Japanese children usually lie next to their mothers throughout infancy and early childhood and continue to sleep with a parent or other family member until adolescence (Takahashi, 1990). Cosleeping is also frequent in some American subcultures. African-American children are more likely than Caucasian-American children to fall asleep with parents and to remain with them for part or all of the night (Lozoff et al., 1995). Appalachian children of eastern Kentucky typically sleep with their parents for the first 2 years of life (Abbott, 1992). Among the Maya of rural Guatemala, mother–infant cosleeping is interrupted only by the birth of a new baby, at which time the older child is moved beside the father or to another bed in the same room (Morelli et al., 1992).

Available household space plays a minor role in infant sleeping arrangements. Dominant child-rearing beliefs are much more important. In one study, researchers interviewed Caucasian-American mothers and Guatemalan Mayan mothers about their sleeping practices. American mothers frequently mentioned the importance of early independence training, preventing bad habits, and protecting their own privacy. In contrast, Mayan mothers explained that cosleeping helps build a close parent–child bond, which is necessary for children to learn the ways of people around them. When told that American infants sleep by themselves, Mayan mothers reacted with shock and disbelief, stating that it would be painful for them to leave their babies alone at night (Morelli et al., 1992).

Infant sleeping practices affect other aspects of family life. Sleep problems are not an issue for Mayan parents. Babies doze off in the midst of ongoing social activities and are carried to bed by their mothers. In the United States, getting young children ready for bed often requires an elab-

This Cambodian father and child sleep together—a practice common in their culture and around the globe. When children fall asleep with their parents, sleep problems are rare during the early years. And many parents who practice cosleeping believe that it helps build a close parent–child bond.

(Stephen L. Raymer/National Geographic Image Collection)

orate ritual that takes a good part of the evening. Many infants and preschoolers insist on taking security objects to bed with them—a blanket or teddy bear that recaptures the soft, tactile comfort of physical closeness to the mother. In societies in which caregivers are continuously available to babies, children seldom develop these object attachments (Wolf & Lozoff, 1989). Perhaps bedtime struggles, so common in American homes but rare elsewhere in the world, are related to the stress young children feel when they are required to fall asleep without assistance (Kawasaki et al., 1994). The few Caucasian-American parents who permit cosleeping tend to regard their child's sleep behavior as very problematic—a sign of ambivalence about the practice (Lozoff, Askew, & Wolf, 1996).

Infant sleeping arrangements, like other parenting practices, are meant to foster culturally valued characteristics in the young. Caucasian-American parents view babies as dependent beings who must be urged toward independence, and so they usually require them to sleep alone. In contrast, Japanese, Mayan, and Appalachian parents regard young infants as separate beings who need to establish an interdependent relationship with the community to survive.

---

non-rapid-eye-movement (NREM) sleep A "regular" sleep state in which the body is quiet and heart rate, breathing, and brain wave activity are slow and regular.

was probably not meant to describe this state! During REM sleep, the brain and parts of the body are highly active. Electrical brain-wave activity, measured with an EEG, is remarkably similar to that of the waking state. The eyes dart beneath the lids; heart rate, blood pressure, and breathing are uneven; and slight body movements occur. In contrast, during regular, or **non-rapid-eye-movement (NREM) sleep,** the body is quiet, and heart rate, breathing, and brain-wave activity are slow and regular.

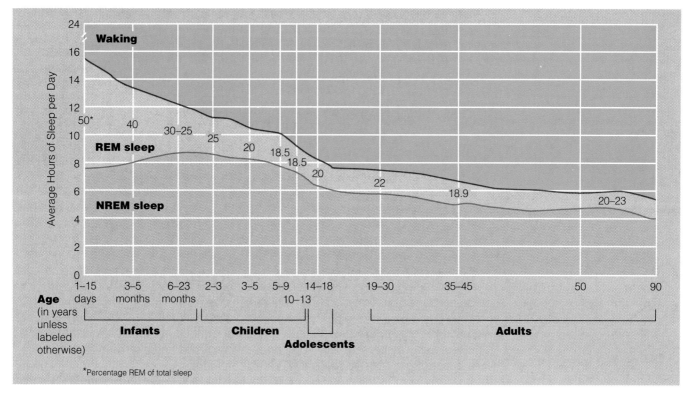

FIGURE 4.1

Changes in REM sleep, NREM sleep, and the waking state from birth through adulthood. REM sleep declines steadily over the first few years of life. Between 3 and 5 years, it consumes about the same percentage of sleep time as it does in adulthood. In contrast, NREM sleep changes very little over infancy and childhood. It gradually declines in adolescence and adulthood as total sleep time drops off.

(Adapted from H. P. Roffwarg, J. N. Muzio, & W. C. Dement, 1966, "Ontogenetic Development of the Human Sleep–Dream Cycle," *Science*, 152, p. 608. Copyright © 1966 by the AAAS. Revised from original publication by the authors in 1969 on the basis of additional data. Reprinted by permission.)

Like children and adults, newborns alternate between REM and NREM sleep. However, as Figure 4.1 shows, they spend far more time in the REM state than they ever will again throughout their lives. REM sleep accounts for 50 percent of the newborn baby's sleep time. It declines steadily to 20 percent between 3 and 5 years of age, which is about the same percentage it consumes in adulthood.

Why do young infants spend so much time in REM sleep? In older children and adults, the REM state is associated with dreaming. Babies probably do not dream, at least not in the same way we do. According to **autostimulation theory,** young infants are believed to have a special need for the EEG activity of REM sleep because they spend little time in an alert state, when they can get input from the environment. REM sleep seems to be a way in which the brain stimulates itself (Roffwarg, Muzio, & Dement, 1966). Sleep researchers regard this stimulation as vital for growth of the central nervous system. In support of this idea, the percentage of REM sleep is especially great in fetuses and in preterm babies, who are even less able to take advantage of external stimulation than are full-term newborns (DiPietro et al., 1996a; Sahni et al., 1995). And the more time a fetus or young infant spends awake, the less time spent in REM sleep, although time devoted to NREM sleep remains unchanged (Thoman, Davis, & Denenberg, 1987).

Whereas the brain-wave activity of REM sleep safeguards the central nervous system, rapid eye movements protect the health of the eye. During the waking state, eye movements cause the vitreous humor (fluid within the eye) to circulate, thereby delivering oxygen to parts of the eye that do not have their own blood supply. During sleep, when the eyes and vitreous humor are still, visual structures are at risk for anoxia. As the brain cycles through REM-sleep periods, rapid eye movements stir up the vitreous humor, ensuring that the eye is fully oxygenated (Blumberg & Lucas, 1996).

autostimulation theory The theory that REM sleep provides stimulation necessary for central nervous system development in young infants.

Because the normal sleep behavior of the newborn baby is organized and patterned, observations of sleep states can help identify central nervous system abnormalities. In infants who are brain damaged or who have experienced birth trauma, disturbed sleep cycles are often present, generally in the form of disorganized transitions between REM and NREM sleep that cannot be identified as a particular state. Babies with poor sleep organization are likely to be behaviorally disorganized and, therefore, to have difficulty learning while awake and eliciting caregiver interactions that enhance their development (Groome et al., 1997; Halpern, MacLean, & Baumeister, 1995).

■ **CRYING.** Crying is the first way that babies communicate, letting parents know they need food, comfort, and stimulation. During the weeks after birth, all infants seem to have some fussy periods during which they are difficult to console. But most of the time, the nature of the cry helps guide parents toward its cause. The baby's cry is a complex auditory stimulus that varies in intensity, from a whimper to a message of all-out distress (Gustafson & Harris, 1990). As early as the first few weeks of life, individual infants can be identified by the unique vocal "signature" of their cries. Recognition of their own baby's cry helps parents locate their infant from a distance and is especially advantageous once babies move on their own (Gustafson, Green, & Cleland, 1994).

Events that cause young infants to cry usually have to do with physical needs. Hunger is the most common cause, but babies may also cry in response to temperature change when undressed, a sudden loud sound, or a painful stimulus. An infant's state often makes a difference in whether the baby will cry in response to a sight or sound. Infants who, when quietly alert, regard a colorful object or the sound of a toy horn with interest and pleasure may react to the same events with a burst of tears when in a state of mild discomfort and diffuse activity (Tennes et al., 1972).

ADULT RESPONSIVENESS TO INFANT CRIES. The next time you hear a baby cry, notice your own mental and physical reaction. A crying baby stimulates strong feelings of arousal and discomfort in just about anyone—men and women, parents and nonparents alike (Boukydis & Burgess, 1982; Murray, 1985). The powerful effect of the cry is probably innately programmed in all humans to make sure that babies receive the care and protection they need to survive.

Although parents do not always interpret the baby's cry correctly, experience quickly improves their accuracy. As babies get older, parents respond to more subtle cues in the cry—not just intensity but whimpering and calling sounds—to detect anxiety in their infant (Thompson & Leger, 1999). They combine these cues with events leading up to the cry to figure out what is wrong. If the baby has not eaten for several hours, she is likely to be hungry. If a period of wakefulness and stimulation preceded the cry, the infant may be tired. A wet diaper, indigestion, or just a desire to be held and cuddled may be the cause. A sharp, piercing, sustained cry usually means the baby is in pain. When caregivers hear this sound, they rush to the infant, anxious and worried. Very intense cries are rated as more unpleasant and produce greater physiological arousal in adults, as measured by heart rate and skin conductance (Crowe & Zeskind, 1992). These are adaptive reactions that help ensure that an infant in danger will quickly get help.

SOOTHING A CRYING INFANT. Even when parents are fairly certain about the cause of the cry, the baby may not always calm down. Fortunately, as Table 4.3 indicates, there are many ways to soothe a crying young baby when feeding and diaper changing do not work. The technique that Western parents usually try first, lifting the baby to the shoulder, is also the one that works the best.

Another common soothing method is swaddling—wrapping the baby's body snuggly in a blanket. And various methods listed in Table 4.3 can be combined. Among the Quechua, who live in the cold, high-altitude desert regions of Peru, young babies are dressed in several layers of clothing and blankets. Then a cloth

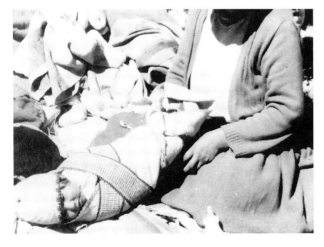

This Quechua mother dresses her infant in several layers of clothing and blankets and winds a cloth belt tightly around the body, over which will be placed additional blankets. The resulting sealed, warm pouch placed on the mother's back reduces crying and promotes sleep, conserving energy for early growth in the harsh Peruvian highlands.

(Edward Tronick)

Ways to Soothe a Crying Newborn

Method	Explanation
Lift the baby to the shoulder and rock or walk.	This provides a combination of physical contact, upright posture, and motion. It is the most effective soothing technique.
Swaddle the baby.	Restricting movement and increasing warmth often soothe a young infant.
Offer a pacifier.	Sucking helps babies control their own level of arousal.
Talk softly or play rhythmic sounds.	Continuous, monotonous, rhythmic sounds, such as a clock ticking, a fan whirring, or peaceful music, are more effective than intermittent sounds.
Take the baby for a short car ride or walk in a baby carriage; swing the baby in a cradle.	Gentle, rhythmic motion of any kind helps lull the baby to sleep.
Massage the baby's body.	Stroke the baby's torso and limbs with continuous, gentle motions. This technique is used in some non-Western cultures to relax the baby's muscles.
Combine several of the methods listed above.	Stimulating several of the baby's senses at once is often more effective than stimulating only one.
If these methods do not work, permit the baby to cry for a short period of time.	Occasionally, a baby responds well to just being put down and will, after a few minutes, fall asleep.

Sources: Campos, 1989; Heinl, 1983; Lester, 1985; Reisman, 1987.

belt is tightly wound around the body, over which are placed additional blankets that cover the head and face and serve as a carrying cloth. The result—a nearly sealed, warm pouch placed on the mother's back that moves rhythmically as she walks—reduces crying and promotes sleep, thereby conserving energy for early growth in the harsh Peruvian highlands (Tronick, Thomas, & Daltabuit, 1994).

HOW QUICKLY TO RESPOND TO A CRYING BABY. Will reacting promptly and consistently to infant cries give babies a sense of confidence that their needs will be met and, over time, reduce fussing and complaining? Or will it strengthen crying behavior and produce a miniature tyrant? Answers to this question are contradictory.

According to *ethological theory,* parental responsiveness is adaptive in that it ensures the infant's basic needs will be met and provides protection from danger (see Chapter 1, pages 24–25). At the same time, it brings the baby into close contact with the caregiver, who can respond sensitively to a wide range of infant behaviors and, in the process, encourage the infant to communicate through means other than crying. In support of this view, two studies showed that mothers who delayed or failed to respond to their young baby's cries had infants who cried more at the end of the first year and less often used alternative ways of expressing their desires, such as gestures and vocalizations (Bell & Ainsworth, 1972; Hubbard & Van IJzendoorn, 1991).

Behaviorists, however, have challenged the ethological view, arguing that consistently responding to a crying infant reinforces the crying response and results in a whiny, demanding child (Gewirtz & Boyd, 1977). A study carried out in Israel provides support for this position. Infants of Bedouin (nomadic) tribespeople, who believe that babies should never be left to fuss and cry, were compared with home-reared babies as well as with infants raised together in children's houses on Israeli kibbutzim.[2] Bedouin babies (whose mothers rush to them at the first whimper) fussed and cried the most during the first year, followed by infants living in homes, where there is greater opportunity to respond promptly to a crying baby than on a kibbutz, where infants are cared for in groups (Landau, 1982).

[2] A *kibbutz* (plural: *kibbutzim*) is an Israeli cooperative agricultural settlement in which children are reared communally, freeing both parents for full participation in the economic life of the society.

These contrasting theories and findings reveal that there is no easy formula for how parents should respond to their infant's cries. The conditions that prompt infant crying are complex, and parents must make reasoned choices about what to do on the basis of culturally accepted practices, the suspected reason for the cry, its intensity, and the context in which it occurs—for example, in the privacy of the parents' own home or while having dinner at a restaurant.

As Figure 4.2 shows, infant crying is greatest during the first 3 months of life, and through most of the first year it peaks in the evenings. Researchers believe that normal difficulties in readjusting the sleep–waking cycle as the central nervous system matures, not parental attention, are responsible for these trends. They appear in many cultures with vastly different infant care practices. They are also evident in preterm infants as they reach the age since conception of their full-term counterparts (Barr et al., 1991, 1996). Fortunately, crying declines for most babies, and over time it occurs more often for psychological (demands for attention, expressions of frustration) than physical reasons. Both ethological and behaviorist investigators would probably agree that one way parents can lessen older babies' need to cry is to encourage more mature ways of communicating.

ABNORMAL CRYING. Like reflexes and sleep patterns, the infant's cry offers a clue to central nervous system distress. The cries of brain-damaged babies and those who have experienced prenatal and birth complications are often shrill and piercing (Huntington, Hans, & Zeskind, 1990; Lester, 1987). An extreme example are infants with *cri du chat (cry-of-the-cat) syndrome,* a chromosomal disorder involving severe mental retardation, heart disease, and a catlike cry. Even neonates with a fairly common problem—*colic,* or persistent crying—tend to have high-pitched, harsh, and turbulent-sounding cries (Zeskind & Barr, 1997). Although the cause of colic is unknown, some researchers believe it is due to disturbed brain regulation of sleep–waking cycles (Papousek & Papousek, 1996).

The abnormal cries of at-risk infants prompt a rise in parental heart rate—a physiological response to threat. In contrast, the cries of healthy babies induce a decrease in parental heart rate, which is associated with orienting and attention (Bryan & Newman, 1988). Most parents try to respond to a sick baby's call for help with extra care and sensitivity. But sometimes the cry is so unpleasant and the infant so difficult to soothe that parents become frustrated, resentful, and angry. Preterm and ill babies are more likely to be abused by their parents, who frequently mention a high-pitched, grating cry as one factor that caused them to lose control and harm the baby (Frodi, 1985).

FIGURE 4.2

Crying patterns during the first year of life. A sample of 400 mothers answered questions about how much time their infants spent crying. (a) Crying was greatest during the first 3 months but declined with age. The largest drop occurred after 3 months. (b) During the first 9 months, crying peaked in the evening.

(Adapted from St James-Roberts & Halil, 1991.)

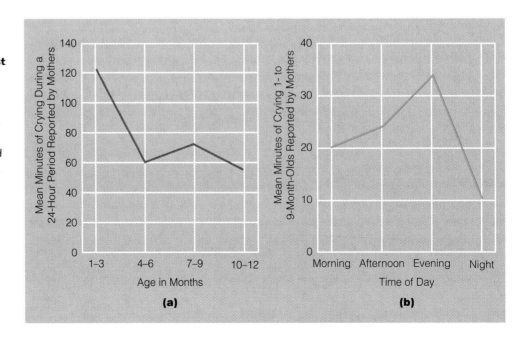

NEONATAL BEHAVIORAL ASSESSMENT

A variety of instruments permit doctors, nurses, and researchers to assess the overall behavioral status of the infant during the newborn period. The most widely used of these tests is T. Berry Brazelton's **Neonatal Behavioral Assessment Scale (NBAS)** (Brazelton & Nugent, 1995). Within it, an examiner looks at the baby's reflexes, state changes, and a variety of other behaviors elicited by routine caregiving, such as cuddling, consoling, and exposure to visual and auditory events. A major goal is to evaluate the infant's ability to initiate caregiver support and to adjust his or her own responses so as not to become overwhelmed by internal or external stimulation. According to Brazelton, the NBAS brings out the most complex, organized functioning of which newborns are capable.

Similar to women in the Zambian culture, this Inuit mother of Northern Canada carries her baby about all day, providing close physical contact and a rich variety of stimulation.
(Eastcott/Momatiak/Woodfin Camp & Associates)

When neonatal assessment is combined with information from a physical examination, it permits all but a few cases of severe central nervous system impairment to be diagnosed in the first few weeks of life (Gorski & VandenBerg, 1996). The NBAS and other, similar instruments have also helped investigators describe the effects of pregnancy and birth complications on infant behavior (Richardson et al., 1996).

The NBAS has been given to many infants around the world. As a result, researchers have learned a great deal about individual and cultural differences in newborn behavior and how a baby's reactions can be maintained or changed by child-rearing practices. For example, NBAS scores of Asian and Native-American babies reveal that they are less irritable than Caucasian infants. Mothers in these cultures often encourage their babies' calm dispositions through swaddling, close physical contact, and nursing at the first signs of discomfort (Chisholm, 1989; Freedman & Freedman, 1969; Murett-Wagstaff & Moore, 1989). In contrast, the poor NBAS scores of undernourished infants born in Zambia, Africa, are quickly changed by the way their mothers care for them. The Zambian mother carries her baby about on her hip all day, providing a rich variety of sensory stimulation. By 1 week of age, a once unresponsive newborn has been transformed into an alert, contented baby (Brazelton, Koslowski, & Tronick, 1976).

Can you tell from these examples why a single NBAS score is not a good predictor of later development? Since newborn behavior and parenting styles combine to shape development, *changes in NBAS scores* over the first week or two of life (rather than a single score) provide the best estimate of the baby's ability to recover from the stress of birth. NBAS "recovery curves" predict intelligence with moderate success well into the preschool years (Brazelton, Nugent, & Lester, 1987).

The NBAS has also been used to help parents get to know their infants. In some hospitals, the examination is given in the presence of parents to teach them about their newborn baby's capacities. Parents of both preterm and full-term newborns have been found to interact more confidently and effectively with their babies (Eiden & Reifman, 1996; Tedder, 1991). Although lasting effects on development have not been demonstrated, NBAS-based interventions are clearly useful in helping the parent–infant relationship get off to a good start.

LEARNING CAPACITIES

Learning refers to changes in behavior as the result of experience. Babies come into the world with built-in learning capacities that permit them to profit from experience immediately. Infants are capable of two basic forms of learning, which were introduced in Chapter 1: classical and operant conditioning. In addition, they learn through a natural preference they have for novel stimulation. Finally, newborn babies have a remarkable ability to imitate the facial expressions and gestures of adults.

Neonatal Behavioral Assessment Scale (NBAS) A test developed to assess the behavioral status of the infant during the newborn period.

■ **CLASSICAL CONDITIONING.** Newborn reflexes make **classical conditioning** possible in the young infant. In this form of learning, a new stimulus is paired with a stimulus that leads to a reflexive response. Once the baby's nervous system makes the connection between the two stimuli, then the new stimulus by itself produces the behavior.

Recall from Chapter 1 that Russian physiologist Ivan Pavlov first demonstrated classical conditioning in his famous research with dogs (see page 19). Classical conditioning is of great value to human infants, as well as other animals, because it helps them recognize which events usually occur together in the everyday world. As a result, they can anticipate what is about to happen next, and the environment becomes more orderly and predictable (Rovee-Collier, 1987). Let's take a closer look at the steps of classical conditioning.

Imagine a mother who gently strokes her infant's forehead each time she settles down to nurse the baby. Soon the mother notices that every time the baby's forehead is stroked, he makes active sucking movements. The infant has been classically conditioned. Here is how it happened (see Figure 4.3):

1. Before learning takes place, an **unconditioned stimulus (UCS)** must consistently produce a reflexive, or **unconditioned, response (UCR).** In our example, the stimulus of sweet breast milk (UCS) resulted in sucking (UCR).

2. To produce learning, a *neutral stimulus* that does not lead to the reflex is presented at about the same time as the UCS. Ideally, the neutral stimulus should occur just before the UCS. The mother stroked the baby's forehead as each nursing period began. Therefore, the stroking (neutral stimulus) was paired with the taste of milk (UCS).

3. If learning has occurred, the neutral stimulus by itself produces the reflexive response. The neutral stimulus is then called a **conditioned stimulus (CS),** and the response it elicits is called a **conditioned response (CR).** We know that the baby has been classically conditioned because stroking his forehead outside the feeding situation (CS) results in sucking (CR).

If the CS is presented alone enough times, without being paired with the UCS, the CR will no longer occur. In other words, if the mother strokes the infant's forehead again and again without feeding him, the baby will gradually stop sucking in response to stroking. This is referred to as **extinction.** In a classical conditioning experiment, the occurrence of responses to the CS during the extinction phase shows that learning has taken place.

Young babies can be classically conditioned most easily when the association between two stimuli has survival value. They learn quickly in the feeding situation, since learning which stimuli regularly accompany feeding improves the infant's ability to get food and survive (Blass, Ganchrow, & Steiner, 1984). In fact, babies are so sensitive to stimulus cues surrounding feeding that even the passage of time between meals can serve as an effective CS. Most newborns are fed about every 3 to 4 hours. As the end of this time period approaches (CS), mouthing, sucking, and salivation (CR) increase in frequency and intensity (Rovee-Collier, 1987).

Some responses are very difficult to classically condition in young infants. Fear is one of them. Until infants have the motor skills to escape unpleasant events, they do not have a biological need to form these associations. But between 8 and 12 months, the conditioning of fear is easily accomplished, as seen in the famous example of little Albert, conditioned by John Watson to withdraw and cry at the sight of a furry white rat. Return to Chapter 1, page 19, to review this well-known experiment. Then test your knowledge of classical conditioning by identifying the UCS, UCR, CS, and CR in Watson's study. In Chapter 10, we will discuss the development of fear, as well as other emotional reactions, in detail.

■ **OPERANT CONDITIONING.** In classical conditioning, babies build expectations about stimulus events in the environment, but their behavior does not influence the stimuli that occur. **Operant conditioning** is quite different. In this form of learning, infants act (or operate) on the environment, and stimuli that follow their behavior change the probability that the behavior will occur again. A stimulus that increases the occurrence of

classical conditioning A form of learning that involves associating a neutral stimulus with a stimulus that leads to a reflexive response.

unconditioned stimulus (UCS) In classical conditioning, a stimulus that leads to a reflexive response.

unconditioned response UCR) In classical conditioning, a reflexive response that is produced by an unconditioned stimulus (UCS).

conditioned stimulus (CS) In classical conditioning, a neutral stimulus that through pairing with an unconditioned stimulus (UCS) leads to a new, conditioned response (CR).

conditioned response (CR) In classical conditioning, an originally reflexive response that is produced by a conditioned stimulus (CS).

extinction In classical conditioning, decline of the conditioned response (CR), as a result of presenting the conditioned stimulus (CS) enough times without the unconditioned stimulus (UCS).

operant conditioning A form of learning in which a spontaneous behavior is followed by a stimulus that changes the probability that the behavior will occur again.

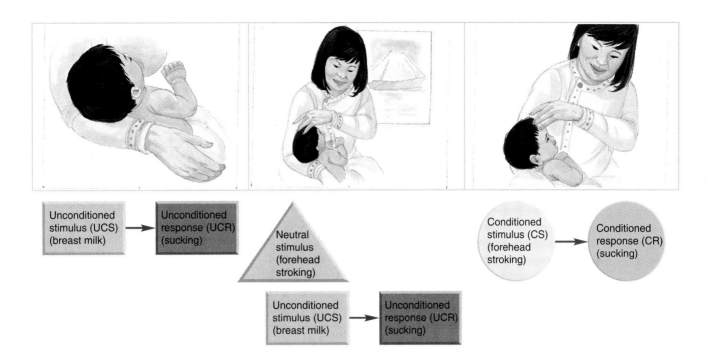

Unconditioned stimulus (UCS) (breast milk) → Unconditioned response (UCR) (sucking)

Neutral stimulus (forehead stroking)

Unconditioned stimulus (UCS) (breast milk) → Unconditioned response (UCR) (sucking)

Conditioned stimulus (CS) (forehead stroking) → Conditioned response (CR) (sucking)

FIGURE 4.3

The steps of classical conditioning. The example here shows how a mother classically conditioned her baby to make sucking movements by stroking his forehead at the beginning of feedings.

a response is called a **reinforcer.** Removing a desirable stimulus or introducing an unpleasant one to decrease the occurrence of a response is called **punishment.**

Operant conditioning of newborn babies has been demonstrated in many studies. Because the young infant can control only a few behaviors, successful operant conditioning is limited to head-turning and sucking responses. For example, newborns quickly learn to turn their heads to the side when this response is followed by a sugar water reinforcer, and they vary their sucking rate according to the sweetness of the liquid they receive (Lipsitt, 1990).

Stimulus variety and change are just as reinforcing to young infants as food. Researchers have created special laboratory conditions in which the baby's rate of sucking on a nipple produces a variety of interesting sights and sounds. Newborns will suck faster to see visual designs or to hear music and human voices (Floccia, Christophe, & Bertoncini, 1997; Rovee-Collier, 1987).

Even preterm babies seek reinforcing stimulation. In one study, they increased their contact with a soft teddy bear that "breathed" quietly at a rate reflecting the infant's respiration, whereas they decreased their contact with a nonbreathing bear (Thoman & Ingersoll, 1993). The infants seemed biologically motivated to snuggle up to the breathing bear because its rhythmic stimulation increased time spent in quiet sleep, thereby helping a vulnerable baby conserve energy and gain weight. As these findings suggest, operant conditioning has become a powerful tool for finding out what stimuli babies can perceive and which ones they prefer.

As infants get older, operant conditioning expands to include a wider range of stimuli and responses. For example, Carolyn Rovee-Collier places special mobiles over the cribs of 2- to 6-month-olds. When the baby's foot is attached to the mobile with a long cord, it takes only a few minutes for the infant to start kicking vigorously (Rovee-Collier & Hayne, 1987; Shields & Rovee-Collier, 1992). As we will see shortly, this technique has yielded important information about infant memory. And as Chapter 6 will reveal, it has also been used to study babies' ability to group similar stimuli into categories.

Operant conditioning soon modifies parents' and infants' reactions to each other. As the baby gazes into the adult's eyes, the adult looks and smiles back, and then the infant looks and smiles again. The behavior of each partner reinforces the other, and both continue their pleasurable interaction. In Chapter 10 we will see that this kind of contingent responsiveness plays an important role in the development of infant–caregiver attachment.

reinforcer In operant conditioning, a stimulus that increases the occurrence of a response.

punishment In operant conditioning, removing a desirable stimulus or presenting an unpleasant one to decrease the occurrence of a response.

The Mysterious Tragedy of Sudden Infant Death Syndrome

BEFORE THEY WENT to bed, Millie and Stuart looked in on 3-month-old Sasha. She was sleeping soundly, her breathing no longer as labored as it had been 2 days before, when she caught her first cold. There had been reasons to worry about Sasha at birth. She was born 3 weeks early, and it took more than a minute before she started breathing. "Sasha's muscle tone seems a little weak," Millie remembered the doctor saying. "She just needs to get busy and gain a little weight, and then she'll be well on her way."

Millie awoke with a start the next morning and looked at the clock. It was 7:30, and Sasha had missed her night waking and early morning feeding. Wondering if she were all right, Millie tiptoed into the room. Sasha lay still, curled up under her blanket. She had died silently during her sleep.

Sasha was a victim of **sudden infant death syndrome (SIDS),** the unexpected death, usually during the night, of an infant under 1 year of age that remains unexplained after thorough investigation. In industrialized nations, SIDS is the leading cause of infant mortality between 1 week and 12 months of age. It accounts for over one-third of these deaths in the United States (Cadoff, 1995). Millie and Stuart's grief was especially hard to bear because no one could give them a definite answer about why Sasha died. They felt guilty and under attack by relatives, and their 5-year-old daughter Jill reacted with sorrow that lasted for months.

Although the precise cause of SIDS is not known, infants who die of it usually show physical problems from the very beginning. Early medical records of SIDS babies reveal higher rates of prematurity and limp muscle tone. Abnormal heart rate, cry patterns, and respiration as well as disturbances in sleep–waking activity are also associated with the disorder (Corwin et al., 1995; Malloy & Hoffman, 1995). At the time of death, over half of SIDS babies have a mild respiratory infection. This seems to increase the chances of respiratory failure in an already vulnerable baby (Cotton, 1990).

One hypothesis about the cause of SIDS is that problems in brain functioning prevent these infants from learning how to respond when their survival is threatened—for example, when respiration is suddenly interrupted (Lipsitt, 1990). Between 2 and 4 months of age, when SIDS is most likely to occur, reflexes decline and are replaced by voluntary, learned responses. Respiratory and muscular weaknesses of SIDS babies may stop them from acquiring behaviors that replace defensive reflexes. As a result, when breathing diffi-

culties occur during sleep, infants do not wake up, shift the position of their bodies, or cry out for help. Instead, they simply give in to oxygen deprivation and death.

In an effort to reduce the occurrence of SIDS, researchers are studying environmental factors related to it. Although babies of poverty-stricken, ethnic minority mothers are at greater risk, these findings may be due to mistaking other causes of infant death for SIDS. When SIDS diagnoses are "certain" rather than "questionable," family background closely resembles that of the general population (Taylor & Sanderson, 1995). In contrast, maternal cigarette smoking, both during and after pregnancy, as well as smoking by other caregivers is strongly predictive of the disorder. Babies exposed to cigarette smoke are 2 to 3 times more likely to die of SIDS than are non-exposed infants (Anderson & Cook, 1997).

Other consistent findings are that SIDS babies are more likely to sleep on their stomachs or sides than their backs and often are wrapped very warmly in clothing and blankets (Fleming et al., 1996; Irgens et al., 1995). Why are these factors associated with SIDS? Scientists think that smoke and excessive body warmth (which can result from putting babies down on their stomachs) place a strain on the respiratory control system in the brain. In an at-risk baby, the respiratory center may stop functioning. In other cases, healthy babies sleeping face down in soft bedding may die from continually breathing their own exhaled breath (Kemp & Thach, 1993).

Research confirms that quitting smoking, changing an infant's sleeping position, and removing a few bedclothes can reduce the incidence of SIDS. For example, if women refrained from smoking while pregnant, an estimated 30 percent of SIDS would be prevented. Public education campaigns that discourage parents from putting babies down on their stomachs have led to dramatic reductions in SIDS in many countries, including Australia, Denmark, Great Britain, New Zealand, Sweden, and the United States (American Academy of Family Physicians, 1997; McKenna, 1996).

When SIDS does occur, surviving family members require a great deal of help to overcome a sudden and unexpected infant death. Parent support groups exist in many communities. As Millie commented 6 months after Sasha's death, "It's the worst crisis we've ever been through. What's helped us most are the comforting words of others who've experienced the same tragedy."

---

sudden infant death syndrome (SIDS) The unexpected death, usually during the night, of an infant under 1 year of age that remains unexplained after thorough investigation.

Recall from Chapter 1 that classical and operant conditioning originated with behaviorism, an approach that views the child as a relatively passive responder to environmental stimuli. If you look carefully at the findings just described, you will see that young babies are active learners; they use any means they can to explore and control their surroundings, in an effort to meet their needs for rest, nutrition, stimulation, and social contact (Rovee-Collier, 1996). In fact, when infants' environments are so disorganized that their behavior does not lead to predictable, satisfying outcomes, serious developmental problems, ranging from intellectual retardation to apathy and depression, can result (Cicchetti & Aber, 1986; Seligman, 1975). In addition, as the Social Issues box above re-

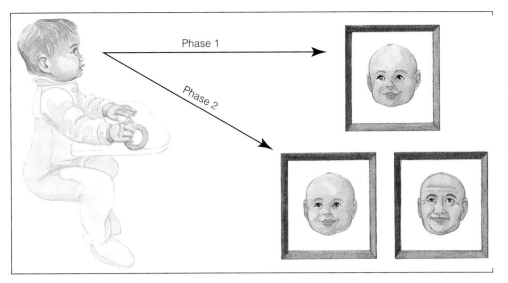

FIGURE 4.4

Example of how the habituation–dishabituation sequence can be used to study infant perception and memory. In Phase 1, infants are shown (habituated to) a photo of a baby. In Phase 2, infants are again shown the baby photo, but this time it appears alongside a photo of a bald-headed man. Infants dishabituated to (spent more time looking at) the photo of the man, indicating that they remembered the baby and perceived the man's face as different from it. (Adapted from Fagan & Singer, 1979.)

veals, deficits in brain functioning may prevent some babies from actively learning certain lifesaving responses; and the absence of such responses may lead to sudden infant death syndrome (SIDS), a major cause of infant mortality.

■ **HABITUATION AND DISHABITUATION**. Take a moment to walk through the rooms of the library, your home, or wherever you happen to be reading this book. What did you notice? Probably those things that are new and different caught your attention first, such as a recently purchased picture on the wall or a piece of furniture that has been moved.

At birth, the human brain is set up to be attracted to novelty. **Habituation** refers to a gradual reduction in the strength of a response due to repetitive stimulation. Looking, heart rate, and respiration may all decline, indicating a loss of interest. Once this has occurred, a new stimulus—some kind of change in the environment—causes responsiveness to return to a high level. This recovery is called **dishabituation.** Habituation and dishabituation enable us to focus our attention on those aspects of the environment we know least about. As a result, learning is more efficient.

CLUES TO EARLY ATTENTION, PERCEPTION, AND MEMORY. By studying the stimuli that infants of different ages habituate and dishabituate to, researchers can tell much about their understanding of the world. Let's look at an example. In one study, habituation and dishabituation were used to find out whether 5- and 6-month-olds could discriminate two similar photos—one of a baby and the other of a bald man (see Figure 4.4). In Phase 1 (habituation), infants were shown the baby photo for a short time. Next, in Phase 2 (dishabituation), the baby photo was paired with a photo of a bald man. Because infants spent more time looking at the bald-headed man than the baby, the researchers concluded that infants both remembered the baby face and perceived the man as new and different from it (Fagan & Singer, 1979).

As these findings reveal, the habituation–dishabituation sequence provides a marvelous window into infant attention, perception, and memory. It is evident as early as the third trimester of pregnancy and has even been used to study the fetus's sensitivity to external stimuli—for example, by measuring changes in fetal heart rate to repeated presentations of various sounds (Hepper, 1997; Sandman et al., 1997).

Habituation–dishabituation research reveals that young babies discriminate and remember a wide variety of distinct sights, sounds, and smells. Preterm and newborn babies require a long time to habituate and dishabituate to novel visual stimuli—about 3 or 4 minutes. But by 4 or 5 months, infants require as little as 5 to 10 seconds to take in a complex new visual stimulus and recognize that it is different from a previous one, indicating that their processing of information is becoming more efficient (Slater et al., 1996).

Yet a fascinating exception to this trend exists. Two-month-olds actually take longer to habituate to novel visual forms than do newborns and older infants (Hood et al., 1996;

habituation A gradual reduction in the strength of a response due to repetitive stimulation.

dishabituation Increase in responsiveness after stimulation changes.

Slater et al., 1996). Later we will see that 2 months is a time of dramatic gains in visual perception. Perhaps when young babies are first able to perceive certain information, they require more time to take it in (Johnson, 1996).

Another reason that young babies' habituation times are so long is that they sometimes have difficulty disengaging their attention from very bright, patterned stimuli, even when they try to do so (Posner et al., 1997). Just as important as attending to a stimulus is the ability to shift attention from one stimulus to another. By 4 months, infants' attention becomes more flexible—a change believed to be due to maturation of brain structures controlling eye movements (Hood et al., 1996).

LIMITATIONS OF HABITUATION–DISHABITUATION RESEARCH. Habituation–dishabituation evidence reveals that infants gradually make finer distinctions among visual stimuli and remember them longer—at 3 months for about 24 hours, by the end of the first year for several days (Fagan, 1973; Martin, 1975). However, these findings tell us only how long babies retain a new stimulus in the laboratory. They underestimate infants' ability to remember real-world events they can actively control.

Recall Rovee-Collier's operant conditioning research, in which infants learned to make a mobile move by kicking. In a series of studies, she showed that 2-month-olds remember how to activate the mobile for 2 days after training; 3-month-olds remember for 1 week, and 6-month-olds for 2 weeks (Hartshorn & Rovee-Collier, 1997). These impressive performances can be improved further by giving babies a reminder (the experimenter briefly rotates the mobile for the baby). Under these conditions, 2-month-olds remember for as long as 2 weeks and 3-month-olds for 6 weeks!

Rovee-Collier's findings also highlight a curious feature of infant memory. During the first 6 months, it is highly *context dependent*. That is, if babies are not tested in the same situation in which they were trained with the mobile (in a crib with the identical patterned bumper and in the same room), their retention is severely disrupted (Hayne & Rovee-Collier, 1995; Rovee-Collier & Shyi, 1992). Once infants begin to move about on their own, they construct relations between contexts—for example, where the crib is in relation to the bathtub, the rocking chair, and the high chair. As different places are associated with one another, memories of events that took place in them also become linked. Consequently, infants can recognize a familiar event out of context; changing the place where they originally learned a response no longer impairs memory.

HABITUATION–DISHABITUATION AND LATER MENTAL DEVELOPMENT. Although habituation and dishabituation to visual stimuli do not provide a full picture of early memory, at present they are the best available infant predictors of later mental development. Correlations between the speed of these responses and 3- to 18-year-old IQ consistently range from the .30s to the .60s (McCall & Carriger, 1993; Sigman, Cohen, & Beckwith, 1997). The habituation–dishabituation sequence seems to be an especially effective early index of intelligence because it assesses quickness of thinking, a characteristic of bright individuals. It also taps basic cognitive processes—attention, memory, and response to novelty—that underlie intelligent behavior at all ages (Colombo, 1995; Rose & Feldman, 1997). In Chapter 8, we will describe an infant intelligence test made up entirely of habituation–dishabituation items.

So far, our discussion has considered only one type of memory—*recognition*. It is the simplest form of remembering because all babies have to do is indicate (by looking or kicking) whether a new stimulus is identical or similar to one previously experienced. *Recall* is a second, more challenging form of memory, since it involves remembering something that is not present. Can infants engage in recall? By the end of the first year, they can, since they find hidden objects and imitate the actions of others hours or days after they first observed the behavior. Recall undergoes much more extended and elaborate development than recognition. We will take it up in more detail in Chapter 7.

■ NEWBORN IMITATION. For many years, researchers believed that imitation—learning by copying the behavior of another person—was beyond the capacity of very young infants. They were not expected to imitate until several months after birth. Then a growing number of studies began to report that newborns come into the world with the ability to imitate the behavior of their caregivers.

142

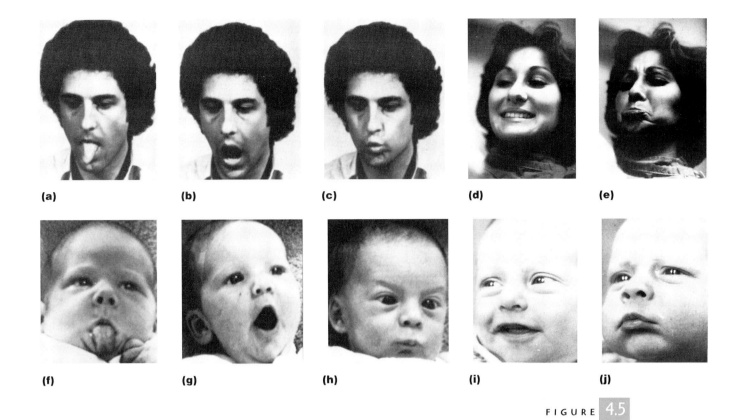

(a)   (b)   (c)   (d)   (e)

(f)   (g)   (h)   (i)   (j)

FIGURE 4.5

Photographs from two of the first studies of newborn imitation. Those on the left show 2- to 3-week-old infants imitating tongue protrusion (a), mouth opening (b), and lip protrusion (c). Those on the right show 2-day-old infants imitating happy (d) and sad (e) adult facial expressions.

(From A. N. Meltzoff & M. K. Moore, 1977, "Imitation of Facial and Manual Gestures by Human Neonates," *Science*, 198, p. 75; and T. M. Field et al., 1982, "Discrimination and Imitation of Facial Expressions by Neonates," *Science*, 218, p. 180. Copyright © 1977 and 1982, respectively, by the AAAS. Reprinted by permission.)

Figure 4.5 shows examples of responses obtained in two of the first studies of newborn imitation (Field et al., 1982; Meltzoff & Moore, 1977). As you can see, babies from 2 days to several weeks old imitated a wide variety of adult facial expressions. Since then, the neonate's capacity to imitate has been demonstrated in many ethnic groups and cultures (Meltzoff & Kuhl, 1994).

Explanations of the response are more controversial. Imitation is more difficult to induce in babies 2 to 3 months old than just after birth. Some investigators regard the capacity as little more than an automatic response to particular stimuli that recedes with age, much like a reflex. But Andrew Meltzoff (1990) points out that newborns model diverse facial expressions and head movements, and they do so even after short delays—when the adult is no longer demonstrating the behavior. These observations suggest that the capacity is flexible and voluntary. Furthermore, imitation does not recede as reflexes do. Babies several months old often do not imitate an adult's behavior right away because they try to play social games of the sort they are used to in face-to-face interaction—smiling, cooing, and waving their arms. When an adult model displays a gesture repeatedly, older babies soon get down to business and imitate (Meltzoff & Moore, 1992).

According to Meltzoff (1996), neonates imitate in much the same way we do—by actively matching body movements they "see" with ones they "feel" themselves make. Later in this chapter, we will encounter evidence that young infants are surprisingly adept at coordinating information across sensory systems. These findings provide additional support for Meltzoff's view of newborn imitation as a flexible, voluntary capacity.

As we will see in Chapter 6, infants' capacity to imitate changes greatly over the first 2 years. But however limited it is at birth, imitation provides the baby with a powerful means of learning. Using imitation, newborns begin to explore their social world, getting to know people by sharing behavioral states with them. In the process, babies notice similarities between their own actions and those of others, and they start to find out about themselves (see Chapter 11). Furthermore, by capitalizing on imitation, adults can get infants to express desirable behaviors, and once they do, adults can encourage these further. Finally, caregivers take great pleasure in a baby who imitates their facial gestures and actions. Newborn imitation clearly seems to be one of those capacities that helps get the infant's relationship with parents off to a good start.

imitation Learning by copying the behavior of another person. Also called modeling or observational learning.

ASK YOURSELF . . .

◆ *How do the capacities of newborn babies contribute to their first social relationships? Provide as many examples as you can.*

◆ *Jackie, who had a difficult birth, observes her 2-day-old daughter, Kelly, being given the NBAS. Kelly scores poorly on many items. Jackie wonders if this means that Kelly will not develop normally. On the basis of research evidence, how would you respond to Jackie's concern?*

◆ CONNECTIONS
Recall that fear is difficult to classically condition in young babies. When do expressions of fear typically emerge in infancy, and why is later development of this emotion adaptive? (See Chapter 10, page 403.)

BRIEF REVIEW

The newborn baby has a wide variety of capacities for relating to the surrounding world. Reflexes are the neonate's most obvious organized patterns of behavior. Some, like sucking, have survival value, whereas others, like stepping, form the basis for motor skills that will develop later. Reflexes also permit early, gratifying interaction between infants and their caregivers.

Infants move in and out of six states of arousal that become more organized and predictable with age. Sleep is the dominant state. Compared with children and adults, infants spend far more time in REM sleep, which stimulates the developing brain. A crying baby evokes strong feelings of discomfort in nearby adults. Over time, crying declines as the central nervous system matures and infants acquire alternative ways of communicating their desires. Neonatal behavioral assessment permits doctors, nurses, and researchers to assess the organized functioning of newborn babies.

Infants are marvelously equipped to learn immediately after birth. Through classical conditioning, babies acquire stimulus associations that have survival value. Operant conditioning enables them to control events in the surrounding world. Habituation and dishabituation reveal that infants are naturally attracted to novel stimuli and that their recognition memory improves steadily with age. Finally, newborns' amazing ability to imitate the facial expressions and gestures of adults helps them get to know their social world.

Motor Development in Infancy

Virtually all parents eagerly await their infant's mastery of new motor skills. Baby books are filled with proud notations as soon as children hold up their heads, reach for objects, sit by themselves, crawl, and walk alone. Parents' enthusiasm for these achievements makes perfect sense. They are, indeed, milestones of development. With each new motor skill, babies master their bodies and the environment in a new way. For example, sitting alone grants infants an entirely different perspective on the world than does lying on their backs and stomachs. Voluntary reaching permits babies to find out about objects by acting on them. And when infants can move on their own, their opportunities for exploration are multiplied.

Babies' motor achievements have a powerful effect on their social relationships. For example, once infants can crawl, parents start to restrict their activities by saying no and expressing mild anger and impatience—strategies that were unnecessary when the baby, placed on a blanket, would stay there! Walking often brings first "testing of wills" (Biringen et al., 1995). Despite her parents' warnings, one newly walking 12-month-old continued to pull items from shelves that were "off limits." "I said not to do that!" her mother remarked as she repeatedly took the infant by the hand and redirected her activities.

At the same time, parents' expressions of affection and playful activities increase as their independently moving baby seeks them out for greetings, hugs, and a gleeful game of hide-and-seek around the living room sofa (Campos, Kermoian, & Zumbahlen, 1992). Certain motor skills, such as pointing to and showing toys, permit infants to communicate more effectively. Finally, babies' expressions of delight—laughing, smiling, and babbling—as they work on new motor competencies trigger pleasurable reactions in others, which encourage infants' efforts further (Mayes & Zigler, 1992). Motor skills, emotional and social competencies, cognition, and language develop together and support one another.

THE SEQUENCE OF MOTOR DEVELOPMENT

Gross motor development refers to control over actions that help infants get around in the environment, such as crawling, standing, and walking. In contrast, *fine motor development* has to do with smaller movements, such as reaching and grasping. The Milestones table

Gross and Fine Motor Development in the First Two Years

MILESTONES

Motor Skill	Average Age Achieved	Age Range in Which 90 Percent of Infants Achieve the Skill
When held upright, holds head erect and steady	6 weeks	3 weeks–4 months
When prone, lifts self by arms	2 months	3 weeks–4 months
Rolls from side to back	2 months	3 weeks–5 months
Grasps cube	3 months, 3 weeks	2–7 months
Rolls from back to side	4½ months	2–7 months
Sits alone	7 months	5–9 months
Crawls	7 months	5–11 months
Pulls to stand	8 months	5–12 months
Plays pat-a-cake	9 months, 3 weeks	7–15 months
Stands alone	11 months	9–16 months
Walks alone	11 months, 3 weeks	9–17 months
Builds tower of two cubes	13 months, 3 weeks	10–19 months
Scribbles vigorously	14 months	10–21 months
Walks up stairs with help	16 months	12–23 months
Jumps in place	23 months, 2 weeks	17–30 months
Walks on tiptoe	25 months	16–30 months

Note: These milestones represent overall age trends. Individual differences exist in the precise age at which each milestone is attained.
Sources: Bayley, 1969, 1993.

above shows the average ages at which a variety of gross and fine motor skills are achieved during infancy and toddlerhood.

Notice that the table also presents the age ranges during which the majority of infants accomplish each skill. These indicate that although the sequence of motor development is fairly uniform across children, large individual differences exist in the rate at which motor development proceeds. Also, a baby who is a late reacher is not necessarily going to be a late crawler or walker. We would be concerned about a child's development only if many motor skills were seriously delayed.

Look at the table once more, and you will see that there is organization and direction to the infant's motor achievements. First, motor control of the head comes before control of the arms and trunk, and control of the arms and trunk is achieved before control of the legs. This head-to-tail sequence is called the **cephalocaudal trend.** Second, motor development proceeds from the center of the body outward, in that head, trunk, and arm control is mastered before coordination of the hands and fingers. This is the **proximodistal trend.** Physical growth follows these same trends during the prenatal period, infancy, and childhood (see Chapter 5). This physical–motor correspondence suggests a genetic contribution to the pattern of motor development.

However, we must be careful not to think of motor skills as isolated, unrelated accomplishments that follow a fixed, maturational timetable. Earlier in this century, researchers made this mistake. Today we know that each new motor skill is a product of earlier motor attainments and a contributor to new ones (Thelen, 1995). Furthermore, children acquire motor skills in highly individual ways. For example, most babies crawl before they pull to a stand and walk. Yet one infant I know, who disliked being placed on her tummy but enjoyed sitting and being held upright, pulled to a stand and walked before she crawled!

Many influences—both internal and external to the child—join together to support the vast transformations in motor competencies of the first 2 years. The dynamic systems

cephalocaudal trend An organized pattern of physical growth and motor control that proceeds from head to tail.

proximodistal trend An organized pattern of physical growth and motor control that proceeds from the center of the body outward.

This baby pushes up with arms and legs in unison and then lifts one foot. Now he must combine these accomplishments with other motor skills into a more complex system that permits forward motion. To do so, he will experiment with muscle patterns, observe the consequences of his movements, and revise them, perfecting the crawling motion in his own individual way. A strong desire to explore and control the environment motivates his efforts.

(Elizabeth Crews)

perspective, a new theoretical approach introduced in Chapter 1 (see page 30), helps us understand how motor development takes place.

MOTOR SKILLS AS DYNAMIC SYSTEMS

According to **dynamic systems theory of motor development,** mastery of motor skills involves acquiring increasingly complex *systems of action.* When motor skills work as a *system,* separate abilities blend together, each cooperating with others to produce more effective ways of exploring and controlling the environment. For example, during infancy, control of the head and upper chest are combined into sitting with support. Kicking, rocking on all fours, and reaching are gradually put together into crawling. Then crawling, standing, and stepping are united into walking alone (Hofsten, 1989; Pick, 1989; Thelen, 1989).

Each new skill is a joint product of the following factors: (1) central nervous system development; (2) movement possibilities of the body; (3) the task the child has in mind; and (4) environmental supports for the skill. Change in any one of these elements leads to loss of stability in the system, and the child starts to explore and select new, more effective motor patterns.

The factors that induce change vary with age. In the early weeks of life, brain and body growth are especially important as infants achieve postural control over the head, shoulders, and upper torso. Later, the tasks the baby wants to accomplish (getting a toy or crossing the room) and environmental supports (parental encouragement, objects in the infants' everyday setting) play a greater role. The broader physical world also has a profound impact on motor skills. For example, if children were reared in the moon's reduced gravity, they would find it more efficient to jump than to walk or run!

When a skill is first acquired, it is tentative and uncertain. Infants must refine it so it becomes smooth and accurate. For example, one baby who was just starting to crawl often collapsed on her tummy and ended up moving backward instead of forward. Gradually, she figured out how to propel herself along by alternately pulling with her arms and pushing with her feet. During this phase of highly variable and unstable behavior, she experimented with muscle patterns, observed the consequences of her movements, and gradually perfected the new motion (Adolph, Vereijken, & Denny, 1998). Her efforts fostered the growth of new synaptic connections in the brain that govern motor activity.

Look carefully at dynamic systems theory, and you will see why motor development cannot be a genetically predetermined process. Since it is motivated by exploration and the desire to master new tasks, it can only be mapped out by heredity at a very general level. Instead of behaviors being *hardwired* into the nervous system, they are *softly assembled* (Hopkins & Butterworth, 1997; Thelen & Smith, 1998). This means that each skill is acquired by revising and combining earlier accomplishments into a more complex system that permits the child to reach a desired goal. Consequently, different paths to the same motor skill exist.

dynamic systems theory of motor development A theory that views new motor skills as reorganizations of previously mastered skills that lead to more effective ways of exploring and controlling the environment. Motor development is jointly influenced by central nervous system maturation, movement possibilities of the body, environmental supports for the skill, and the task the child has in mind.

■ **DYNAMIC MOTOR SYSTEMS IN ACTION.** To study infants' mastery of motor milestones, researchers have conducted *microgenetic studies* (see Chapter 2, page 63), following babies from their first attempts at a skill until it becomes smooth and effortless. Using this research strategy, Esther Thelen (1994) illustrated how infants acquire motor skills by modifying what the body can already do to fit a new task. She placed 3-month-old babies under the special mobile attached to the baby's foot with a long cord, described earlier in this chapter. To produce the dazzling sight of the dancing mobile, infants quickly learned to kick with one foot or two feet in alternation.

Then Thelen changed the movement environment; she linked the babies' legs together with a soft piece of elastic attached to ankle cuffs (see Figure 4.6). Although this permitted single- or alternate-leg kicking, it made kicking both legs in unison much more effective for activating the mobile. When the elastic was in place, infants gradually discovered the new motion. They began with a few tentative simultaneous kicks and, seeing the effects, replaced earlier movements with this new form. When the elastic was removed, infants quickly gave up the simultaneous pattern in favor of their previous behavior. They readily experimented, revising their motor behavior appropriately to fit changing conditions of the task.

The way previously learned acts are reorganized into more effective motor systems is especially apparent in the area of fine motor skills. As we will see when we discuss the development of voluntary reaching, the various components—grasping, looking, and moving the arms—at first emerge independently. Then, as babies become increasingly aware of a world of objects to explore, they combine these skills into successful reaching. Common to all infants is an effort to adapt current skills to get an object. As Thelen (1995) explains, the desire to accomplish a task motivates behavior. Then the new behavior permits the child to accomplish new tasks, and motor development changes again. In sum, motor development results from infants' active problem-solving efforts.

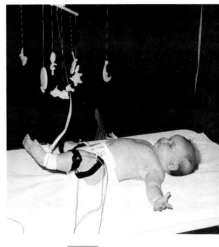

FIGURE 4.6

A three-month-old infant in the mobile experiment, with legs linked together by an elastic ankle cuff. Consistent with dynamic systems theory, the baby revised previously learned motor acts into a more effective motor system for activating the mobile. In response to the cuff, he replaced single- and alternate-leg kicking with simultaneous kicks.

(Courtesy of Esther Thelen, Indiana University.)

■ **CULTURAL VARIATIONS IN MOTOR DEVELOPMENT.** Cross-cultural research demonstrates how early movement opportunities and a stimulating environment contribute to motor development. Several decades ago, Wayne Dennis (1960) observed infants in Iranian orphanages who were deprived of the tantalizing surroundings that motivate infants in most homes to acquire motor skills. The Iranian babies spent their days lying on their backs in cribs, without toys to play with. As a result, most did not move about on their own until after 2 years of age. When they finally did move, the constant experience of lying on their backs led them to scoot in a sitting position rather than crawl on their hands and knees. Since babies who scoot come up against objects such as furniture with their feet, not their hands, they are far less likely to pull themselves to a standing position in preparation for walking. As a result, walking was delayed. Indeed, only 15 percent of the Iranian orphans walked alone by 3 to 4 years of age.

Cultural variations in infant-rearing practices also affect motor development. Take a quick survey of several parents you know, asking these questions: Can babies profit from training? Should sitting, crawling, and walking be deliberately encouraged? Answers vary widely from culture to culture. Japanese mothers, for example, believe such efforts are unnecessary and unimportant. Among the Zinacanteco Indians of southern Mexico, rapid motor progress is actively discouraged. Babies who walk before they know enough to keep away from cooking fires and weaving looms are viewed as dangerous to themselves and disruptive to others (Greenfield, 1992).

In contrast, among the Kipsigis of Kenya and the West Indians of Jamaica, babies hold their heads up, sit alone, and walk considerably earlier than do North American infants. Kipsigi parents deliberately teach these motor skills. In the first few months, babies are seated in holes dug in the ground, and rolled blankets are used to keep them upright. Walking is promoted by frequently bouncing babies on their feet (Super, 1981). Unlike the Kipsigis, the West Indians of Jamaica do not train their infants in specific skills. Instead, beginning in the first few weeks of life, babies experience a highly stimulating, formal handling routine (see Figure 4.7 on page 148). Asked why they use this routine, West Indian mothers refer to the traditions of their culture and the need to help babies grow up strong, healthy, and physically attractive (Hopkins & Westra, 1988).

Putting together the evidence we have discussed so far, we must conclude that early motor skills, like other aspects of development, are due to complex transactions between nature and nurture. As dynamic systems theory suggests, heredity establishes the broad outlines of change, but experience contributes to the precise sequence of motor milestones and the rate at which they are reached.

FINE MOTOR DEVELOPMENT: VOLUNTARY REACHING, GRASPING, AND MANIPULATION OF OBJECTS

Of all motor skills, voluntary reaching is believed to play the greatest role in infant cognitive development, since it opens up a whole new way of exploring the environment (Bushnell & Boudreau, 1993). By grasping things, turning them over, and seeing what happens when they are released, infants learn a great deal about the sights, sounds, and feel of objects.

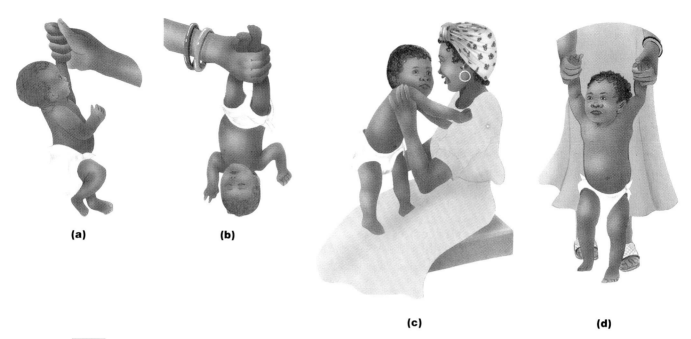

The development of reaching and grasping, shown in Figure 4.8, provides an excellent example of how motor skills start out as gross, diffuse activity and move toward mastery of fine movements. When supported in an upright position, newborns make poorly coordinated swipes or swings, called **prereaching,** toward an object dangled in front of them. Because they cannot control their arms and hands, they are rarely successful in contacting the object. Like newborn reflexes, prereaching eventually drops out, around 7 weeks of age.

■ **DEVELOPMENT OF VOLUNTARY REACHING, GRASPING, AND MANIPULATION OF OBJECTS.** At about 3 months, voluntary reaching appears and gradually improves in accuracy (Bushnell, 1985; Hofsten, 1984). Infants of this age reach just as effectively for a glowing object in the dark as for an object in the light. This indicates that early reaching does not require visual guidance of the arms and hands. Instead, it is controlled by *proprioception,* our sense of movement and location in space, arising from stimuli within the body (Clifton et al., 1994). From the start, vision is freed from the basic act of reaching so it can focus on more complex adjustments.

Improvements in reaching are largely a matter of controlling arm and hand movements. By 5 months, infants reduce their reaching behavior when an object is moved beyond their reach (Yonas & Hartman, 1993). Around 7 months, the two arms become more independent. As a result, infants more often reach for a small object with one arm, rather than extending both (Fagard & Pezé, 1997). At 9 months, they can redirect an arm to obtain a moving object that changes direction (Ashmead et al., 1993).

Individual differences in movement styles affect how reaching is perfected (Thelen, Corbetta, & Spencer, 1996). Babies with large, forceful arm movements must make them less vigorous to reach for a toy successfully. Those with quiet, gentle actions must use more muscle power to lift and extend their arms (Thelen et al., 1993). Each infant builds the act of reaching uniquely by exploring the match between current movements and those demanded by the task.

prereaching The poorly coordinated, primitive reaching movements of newborn babies.

ulnar grasp The clumsy grasp of the young infant, in which the fingers close against the palm.

pincer grasp The well-coordinated grasp emerging at the end of the first year, in which thumb and forefinger are used opposably.

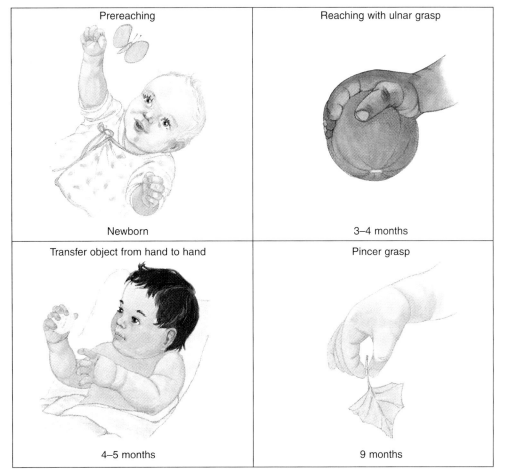

Prereaching	Reaching with ulnar grasp
Newborn	3–4 months
Transfer object from hand to hand	Pincer grasp
4–5 months	9 months

FIGURE 4.8

Some milestones of voluntary reaching, including the average age at which each skill is attained.

(Ages from Bayley, 1969; Rochat & Goubet, 1995.)

This 3-month-old baby looks at patterns hung over his crib that match his level of visual development. Research shows that a moderate amount of stimulation, tailored to the young baby's needs, results in earlier development of reaching. Either very little or excessive stimulation yields slower motor progress.

(Julie O'Neil/The Picture Cube)

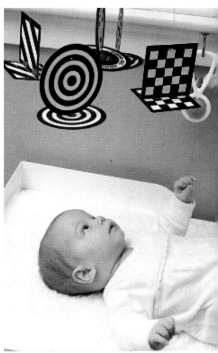

Once infants can reach, they start to modify their grasp. When the grasp reflex of the newborn period weakens at 3 to 4 months, it is replaced by the **ulnar grasp,** a clumsy motion in which the fingers close against the palm. Around 4 to 5 months, when infants begin to master sitting, they no longer need their arms to maintain body balance. This frees both hands to become coordinated in exploring objects. Babies of this age can hold an object in one hand while the other scans it with the tips of the fingers, and they frequently transfer objects from hand to hand (Rochat, 1992; Rochat & Goubet, 1995). By the latter part of the first year, infants use the thumb and index finger opposably in a well-coordinated **pincer grasp.** Then the ability to manipulate objects greatly expands. The 1-year-old can pick up raisins and blades of grass, turn knobs, and open and close small boxes.

Between 8 and 11 months, reaching and grasping are well practiced. As a result, attention is released from coordinating the motor skill itself to events that occur before and after obtaining the object. As we will see in Chapter 6, around this time infants can first solve simple problems involving reaching, such as searching for and finding a hidden toy.

■ **EARLY EXPERIENCE AND VOLUNTARY REACHING.** Like other motor milestones, voluntary reaching is affected by early experience. In a well-known study, Burton White and Richard Held (1966) found that institutionalized babies provided with a moderate amount of visual stimulation—at first, simple designs and later, a mobile hung over their crib—reached for objects 6 weeks earlier than did infants given nothing to look at. A third group of babies provided with massive stimulation—patterned crib bumpers and mobiles at an early age—also reached sooner than unstimulated babies. But this heavy dose of enrichment took its toll. These infants looked away and cried a great deal, and they were not as advanced in reaching as the moderately stimulated group. White and Held's findings remind us that more stimulation is not necessarily better. Trying to push infants beyond their current readiness to handle stimulation can undermine the development of important motor skills.

ASK YOURSELF . . .

- *Cite an example showing that motor development is not hard-wired but softly assembled.*

- *Rosanne read in a magazine that motor development could be accelerated through exercise and visual stimulation. She hung mobiles and pictures all over her newborn baby's crib, and she massages and manipulates his body daily. Is Rosanne doing the right thing? Why or why not?*

- CONNECTIONS
  Recall from Chapter 1 (see page 30) that dynamic systems theorists are interested in explaining variations in development. Describe variations highlighted by dynamic systems research on motor development. Cite factors that promote such variation.

Touch is a major means through which babies investigate their world. This 6-month-old infant explores objects by running her lips and tongue over the surface and then removing the object to take a good look at it. In the next few months, mouthing will give way to increasingly elaborate touching with the hands. (Caitlin Merrill)

BRIEF REVIEW

The overall sequence of motor development follows the cephalocaudal and proximodistal trends. However, motor development is not programmed into the brain from the start. According to dynamic systems theory, it is energized by the baby's exploration and desire to master new tasks and jointly influenced by central nervous system development, movement possibilities of the body, and environmental supports for the skill. Microgenetic studies reveal how previously learned acts are reorganized into new motor attainments. Cross-cultural research underscores the contribution of movement opportunities, a stimulating environment, and infant-rearing practices to motor progress.

Voluntary reaching plays a vital role in infant cognitive development. It begins with the uncoordinated prereaching of the newborn baby and gradually evolves into flexible control of arm and hand movements and a refined pincer grasp by the end of the first year. Once reaching and grasping are well practiced, infants integrate these behaviors into increasingly elaborate motor systems.

Perceptual Development in Infancy

Think back to White and Held's study, described at the end of the previous section. It illustrates the close link between perception and action in discovering new skills. To reach for objects, maintain balance, or move across various surfaces, infants must continually coordinate their motor behavior with perceptual information (Bertenthal, 1996). Acting and perceiving are not separate aspects of experience. Instead, motor activity provides infants with a vital means for exploring and learning about the world, and improved perception brings about more effective motor activity. The union of perceptual and motor information is basic to our nervous systems, and each domain supports development of the other (Bertenthal & Clifton, 1998).

What can young infants perceive with their senses, and how does perception change with age? Researchers have sought answers to these questions for two reasons:

- *Infant perception is relevant to the age-old nature–nurture controversy.* Are infants born with an adultlike perception of the world, or must they acquire it through experience? As we will see shortly, newborns have an impressive array of perceptual capacities. Nevertheless, since improvements occur as the result of both maturation and experience, an appropriate resolution to the nature–nurture debate seems, once again, to lie somewhere between the two extremes.

- *Infant perception sheds light on other areas of development.* For example, because touch, vision, and hearing permit us to interact with others, they are a basic part of emotional and social development. Through hearing, language is learned. And perception provides the foundation for cognitive development, since knowledge about the world is first gathered through the senses.

Studying infant perception is especially challenging because babies cannot describe their experiences. Fortunately, investigators can make use of a variety of nonverbal responses that vary with stimulation, such as looking, sucking, head turning, facial expressions, and startle reactions. Psychophysiological measures, such as changes in respiration and heart rate, are also used. And as we noted earlier, researchers sometimes take advantage of operant conditioning and the habituation–dishabituation sequence to find out whether infants can make certain discriminations. We will see many examples of these methods as we explore the baby's sensitivity to touch, taste, smell, sound, and visual stimulation.

TOUCH

Touch is a fundamental means of interaction between parents and young babies. Within the first few days of life, mothers can recognize their own newborn by stroking the infant's cheek or hand, and fathers can do the same by stroking the infant's hand (Kaitz et al., 1993a, 1993b). In our discussion of preterm infants in Chapter 3, we indicated that touch helps stimulate early physical growth. As we will see in Chapter 10, it is important for emotional development as well. Therefore it is not surprising that sensitivity to touch is well developed at birth. Return to the reflexes listed in Table 4.1 on page 129. They reveal that the newborn baby responds to touch, especially around the mouth, on the palms of the hands, and on the soles of the feet. During the prenatal period, these areas, along with the genitals, are the first to become sensitive to touch (Humphrey, 1978).

Reactions to temperature change are also present at birth. When young infants are undressed, they often express discomfort by crying and becoming more active. Newborn babies are more sensitive to stimuli that are colder than body temperature than to those that are warmer (Humphrey, 1978).

At birth, infants are quite sensitive to pain. If male newborns are circumcised, anesthesia is sometimes not used because of the risk of giving pain-relieving drugs to a very young infant. Babies typically respond with a high-pitched, stressful cry and a dramatic rise in heart rate and blood pressure. A few infants show dangerous stress reactions, including breath holding and gagging (Lander et al., 1997; Williamson, 1997). Recent research establishing the safety of certain local anesthetics for newborns promises to ease the pain of these procedures. Offering a nipple that delivers a sugar solution is also helpful; it quickly reduces crying and discomfort in young babies, preterm and full-term alike (Smith & Blass, 1996). Although many doctors are convinced that neonates cannot remember pain, a severely painful experience persists long enough to affect later behavior. As Figure 4.9 shows, compared with their anesthetized counterparts, newborns not given local anesthesia during circumcision show a more intense pain response to routine vaccination at 4 to 6 months of age (Taddio et al., 1997).

Sensitivity to touch enhances babies' responsiveness to the environment. In one study, the soft caresses of an experimenter led babies to smile and become increasingly attentive to the adult's face (Stack & Muir, 1992). As soon as infants can reach and grasp, touch becomes a major means through which they investigate their world. Watch babies at play, and you will see that they frequently mouth novel objects, running their lips and tongue over the surface, after which they remove the object to take a good look at it. Exploratory mouthing peaks in the middle of the first year as hand–mouth contact becomes more accurate (Lew & Butterworth, 1997). Then it declines in favor of more elaborate touching with the hands, in which infants turn, poke, and feel the surface of things while looking at them intently (Ruff et al., 1992). In Chapter 6, we will see that Piaget regarded this hands-on manipulation of objects, in which touch and vision combine, as essential for early cognitive development.

TASTE AND SMELL

All infants come into the world with the ability to communicate their taste preferences to caregivers. Facial expressions reveal that newborns can distinguish several basic tastes. Much like adults, they relax their facial muscles in response to sweetness, purse their lips when the taste is sour, and show a distinct archlike mouth opening when it is bitter (Rosenstein & Oster, 1988; Steiner, 1979). These reactions are important for survival, since (as we will see in Chapter 5) the food that is ideally suited to support the infant's early growth is the sweet-tasting milk of the mother's breast.

Salty taste develops differently from sweet, sour, or bitter. At birth, infants are either indifferent to or reject salt solutions in comparison to water. But by 4 months, they prefer the salty taste, a change that may prepare them to accept solid foods (Beauchamp et al., 1994). Furthermore, after brief exposures to tastes that evoke either a neutral reaction or an innate aversion, young babies readily learn to like those tastes. For example, feeding infants a salty cereal leads them to accept a wide range of salty foods (Harris & Booth, 1987). And infants allergic to cow's-milk formula who are given a soy or other vegetable-based substitute (typically very strong and bitter-tasting) soon prefer it to regular formula (Harris, 1993). Clearly, neonates can form conditioned preferences for tastes they previously disliked when those tastes are paired with relief of hunger (Harris, 1997).

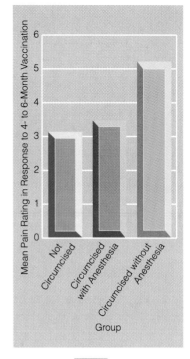

FIGURE 4.9

Pain response to a 4- to 6-month routine vaccination of newborns not circumsized, circumsized with a local anesthetic, and circumcized without anesthetic (but given a placebo, or substance with no medication). Pain ratings were made by an observer who had no knowledge of the infants' circumcision or medication status. Infants who had been circumsized without anesthetic were rated as having a more intense pain response. (Adapted from Taddio et al., 1997.)

Like taste, certain odor preferences are innate. For example, the smell of bananas or chocolate causes a relaxed, pleasant facial expression, whereas the odor of rotten eggs makes the infant frown (Steiner, 1979). Newborns can also identify the location of an odor and, if it is unpleasant, defend themselves. When a whiff of ammonia is presented to one side of the baby's nostrils, infants less than 6 days old quickly turn their heads in the other direction (Reiser, Yonas, & Wikner, 1976).

In many mammals, the sense of smell plays an important role in eating and in protecting the young from predators by helping mothers and babies identify each other. Although smell is less well developed in humans than in other mammals, traces of its survival value are still present. Mothers can identify their own baby by smell shortly after birth. Infants' recognition of smells associated with their mother begins to develop before birth. Three-day-old neonates given a choice between two gauze pads—one moistened with their own mother's amniotic fluid and the other with amniotic fluid from another mother—spend more time oriented toward the familiar fluid (Marlier, Schaal, & Soussignan, 1998a, 1998b).

By 4 days of age, breast-fed babies prefer the smell of their own mother's breast to that of an unfamiliar lactating mother (Cernoch & Porter, 1985). Bottle-fed babies remain attracted to the odor of their mother's amniotic fluid, preferring it to the odor of their familiar formula. At the same time, they orient to the smell of any lactating (milk-producing) woman over the smells of formula or a nonlactating woman (Makin & Porter, 1989; Marlier & Schaal, 1997; Porter et al., 1992). Newborn infants' dual attraction to the odors of their mother and the lactating breast probably helps them locate an appropriate food source and, in the process, distinguish their caregiver from other people.

In sum, young babies are quite adept at making taste and odor discriminations. Unfortunately, little is known about how these two senses develop as the result of further brain maturation and experience.

BALANCE AND SELF-MOVEMENT

To take in and make sense of their surroundings, infants must be able to balance the body, adjusting their movements so they remain in a steady position relative to the surface on which they are sitting or standing. Making these postural changes is so important that three sources of sensory information specify a need to adapt body position: (1) *proprioceptive stimulation,* arising from sensations in the skin, joints, and muscles; (2) *vestibular stimulation,* arising from the semicircular canals of the inner ear; and (3) *optical flow stimulation,* arising from movements in the visual field.

Research largely focuses on **optical flow,** since it can be manipulated easily. Consider how you use optical flow information. You sense that you are in motion when the entire visual field moves, and you make postural adjustments in accord with its direction and speed. For example, on a train ride, scenery flowing past you signals that you are moving. Your perceived direction (forward) is opposite the direction of optical flow, so you compensate by swaying backward to remain upright. The faster the scenery flies by, the stronger your sway.

To examine infants' sense of balance and self-movement, researchers create conditions in the laboratory like those just described. Their findings reveal that even neonates adapt their head movements to optical flow (Jouen & Lepecq, 1989). As motor control improves, postural adjustments become more precise. In a series of studies, researchers placed 5- to 13-month-olds in a seat with pressure-sensitive receptors in the "moving room" shown in Figure 4.10. When the front and side walls of the room oscillated forward and backward, all infants displayed appropriate body movements. Between 5 and 9 months, as infants perfected sitting without support, their back-and-forth sway became more finely tuned to the optical-flow changes produced by oscillating walls of the moving room (Bertenthal, Rose, & Bai, 1997; Rose & Bertenthal, 1995).

Clearly, newborn babies have a built-in sense of balance that is refined with experience and motor control. Like adults', infants' postural adjustments to self-movement take place unconsciously; an inner control system responds automatically to stimulation that threatens to upset a steady body position. This frees babies' attention for other pursuits, including motor skills and the auditory and visual attainments we are about to consider

optical flow Movements in the visual field signaling that the body is in motion, leading to postural adjustments so the body remains upright.

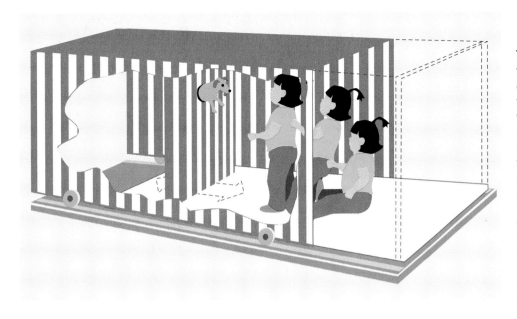

FIGURE 4.10

The "moving room" used to test infants' sensitivity to balance and self-movement. The front and side walls are mounted on wheels that roll on a track. This permits systematic variation of *optical flow* by moving the walls back and forth at different speeds. To make sure the infant faces forward, a box containing a mechanical dog who "comes alive" is located on the front wall. The figure shows a child falling backward as the room moves toward her. This postural compensation occurs if the child perceives the optical flow as a forward sway of her body. To test 5- to 13-month-olds, a seat with pressure-sensitive receptors is used that measures backward and forward body sway.

(From B. I. Bertenthal, J. L. Rose, & D. L. Bai, 1997, "Perception–Action Coupling in the Development of Visual Control of Posture," *Journal of Experimental Psychology: Human Perception and Performance, 23,* p. 1632. Copyright © 1997 by the American Psychological Association. Reprinted by permission.)

(Bertenthal, 1996; Bertenthal & Clifton, 1998). Balance is probably an innate capacity because it is fundamental to everything babies learn through exploration—listening, looking, and acting on their world.

HEARING

Newborn infants can hear a wide variety of sounds, but they are more responsive to some than to others. For example, they prefer complex sounds, such as noises and voices, to pure tones (Bench et al., 1976). In the first few days, infants can already tell the difference between a few sound patterns, such as a series of tones arranged in ascending and descending order, utterances with two versus three syllables, and the stress patterns of words, such as *ma*-ma versus ma-*ma* (Bijeljac-Babic, Bertoncini, & Mehler, 1993; Sansavini, Bertoncini, & Giovanelli, 1997).

Over the first year, infants organize sounds into increasingly elaborate patterns. For example, between 4 and 7 months, they have a sense of musical and speech phrasing. They prefer Mozart minuets and sentences with pauses between natural phrases to those with awkward breaks (Hirsh-Pasek et al., 1987; Krumhansl & Jusczyk, 1990). And around 12 months, if two melodies differing only slightly are played, infants can tell that they are not the same (Morrongiello, 1986).

Responsiveness to sound provides support for the young baby's visual and tactile exploration of the environment. Infants as young as 3 days old turn their eyes and head in the general direction of a sound. By 4 months, they can reach fairly accurately toward a sounding object in the dark (Clifton et al., 1994). The ability to identify the precise location of a sound improves greatly over the first 6 months (Litovsky & Ashmead, 1997). By this time, infants start to make judgments about how far away a sound is. They are less likely to try to retrieve a sounding object in the dark if it is beyond their reach (Clifton, Perris, & Bullinger, 1991).

Neonates are particularly sensitive to sounds within the frequency range of the human voice, and they come into the world prepared to respond to the sounds of any human language. Young infants can make fine-grained distinctions among a wide variety of speech sounds—"ba" and "ga," "ma" and "na," and the short vowel sounds "a" and "i," to name just a few. In fact, there are only a few speech discriminations that young infants cannot detect, and their ability to perceive sounds not found in their language environment is more precise than an adult's (Jusczyk, 1995). As we will see in Chapter 9, by the middle of the first year, infants start to "screen out" sounds not used in their own language as they listen closely to the speech of those around them (Kuhl et al., 1992; Polka & Werker, 1994). These capacities reveal that the human baby is marvelously equipped for the awesome task of acquiring language.

(a) Newborn View

(b) Adult View

FIGURE 4.11

Newborn and adult view of the human face. The newborn baby's limited focusing ability and poor visual acuity lead the parent's face, even when viewed from close up, to look much like the fuzzy image in (a) rather than the clear image in (b). (Laura Berk)

visual acuity Fineness of visual discrimination.

Listen carefully to yourself the next time you talk to a young baby. You are likely to speak in a high-pitched, expressive voice and use a rising tone at the ends of phrases and sentences. Adults probably communicate this way because they notice that infants are more attentive when they do so. Indeed, newborns prefer human speech with these characteristics (Aslin, Jusczyk, & Pisoni, 1998). They will also suck more on a nipple to hear a recording of their mother's voice than that of an unfamiliar woman, and to hear their mother's native tongue as opposed to a foreign language (Moon, Cooper, & Fifer, 1993; Spence & DeCasper, 1987). These preferences probably developed from hearing the muffled sounds of the mother's voice before birth.

Infants' special responsiveness to speech probably encourages parents to talk to the baby. As they do so, both readiness for language and the emotional bond between caregiver and child are strengthened. By 3 months of age, infants pick up information about the feelings of others through hearing. They can distinguish happy- from sad-sounding adult voices (Walker-Andrews & Grolnick, 1983). As we will see, it will take somewhat more time before babies can discriminate these emotions visually.

Clearly, infants' acute sensitivity to sound supports many competencies. Therefore, it is not surprising that even mild hearing impairments that go untreated in the early years can endanger development. To find out more about this topic, see the From Research to Practice box on the following page. Before we turn to vision, consult the Milestones table on page 156 for a summary of the perceptual capacities we have just considered.

VISION

Humans depend on vision more than any other sense for active exploration of the environment. Yet vision is the least mature of the newborn baby's senses. Visual structures in both the eye and the brain continue to develop after birth. For example, the muscles controlling the *lens,* the part of the eye that permits us to adjust our focus to varying distances, are weak. Also, cells in the *retina,* the membrane lining the inside of the eye that captures light and transforms it into messages that are sent to the brain, are not as mature or densely packed as they will be in several months (Banks & Bennett, 1988). Furthermore, the optic nerve and other pathways that relay these messages, along with cells in the visual cortex that receive them, will not be adultlike for several years (Hickey & Peduzzi, 1987).

■ **ACUITY AND COLOR PERCEPTION.** Because of the immaturity of visual structures, newborn babies cannot focus their eyes very well. In addition, their **visual acuity,** or fineness of discrimination, is limited. When you have your vision tested, the doctor estimates how finely you perceive stimuli in comparison to an adult with normal vision. Applying this same index to newborn babies, researchers have found that they see objects at a distance of 20 feet about as clearly as adults do at 600 feet (Courage & Adams, 1990; Held, 1993). Furthermore, unlike adults (who see nearby objects most clearly), newborn babies see *equally unclearly* across a wide range of distances. As a result, no visual cues are available to help them notice that a near or far object can be sharpened by refocusing the lens (Banks, 1980). Images such as a parent's face, even from close up, look much like the blur shown in Figure 4.11.

Newborn infants cannot yet see well, but they actively explore their environment with the limited visual abilities they do have. They scan the visual field for interesting sights and try to track moving objects. However, their eye movements are slow and inaccurate (Aslin, 1993).

The visual system matures rapidly over the first few months of life. By 3 months, infants can focus on objects just as well as adults can. Visual acuity improves steadily throughout infancy. By 6 months, it is about 20/100. At 2 years, it reaches a near-adult level (Courage & Adams, 1990). Scanning and tracking undergo rapid gains as eye movements increasingly come under voluntary control (Johnson, 1995). By 1 month, babies can follow a slowly moving object with a smooth eye movement, a capacity that continues to improve during the first half-year (Hainline, 1993).

Color perception is also refined in the early months. Newborns are sensitive to color, since they prefer to look at colored rather than gray stimuli, but they do not show a definite ability to distinguish particular hues. Pathways in the brain that process color information mature rapidly, since 2-month-olds can discriminate colors across the entire

Long-Term Impact of Early Hearing Loss on Development: The Case of Otitis Media

URING HIS FIRST year in day care, 18-month-old Alex caught five colds, had the flu on two occasions, and experienced repeated *otitis media* (middle ear infection). Alex is not unusual. By age 3, over 70 percent of children have had respiratory illnesses resulting in at least one bout of otitis media; 33 percent have had three or more bouts. Some episodes are painful, but as many as half are accompanied by few or no symptoms. Parents learn of them only on routine visits to the doctor. Although antibiotics eliminate the bacteria responsible for otitis media, they do not reduce fluid buildup in the middle ear, which causes mild to moderate hearing loss that can last for weeks or months (Feagans & Proctor, 1994).

The incidence of otitis media is greatest between 6 months and 3 years, when children are first acquiring language. Frequent infections predict delayed language progress and social isolation in early childhood and poorer academic performance after school entry (Feagans & Proctor, 1994; Teele et al., 1990; Vernon-Feagans, Manlove, & Volling, 1996).

How might otitis media disrupt language and academic progress? Difficulties in hearing speech sounds, particularly in noisy settings, may be responsible. Early and recurrent episodes of infection are consistently associated with impaired speech perception and production (Feagans & Proctor, 1994; Gravel & Wallace, 1992). Furthermore, children with many bouts are less attentive to the speech of others and less persistent at tasks (Feagans et al., 1987; Roberts, Burchinal, & Campbell, 1994). Their distractibility may be due to repeated instances in which they could not make out what people around them were saying. When children have trouble paying attention, they may reduce the quality of others' interactions with them. In one study, mothers of preschoolers with frequent illnesses were less effective in teaching their child a task (Chase et al., 1995).

Current evidence argues strongly in favor of early prevention of otitis media, especially since the illness is so widespread. Crowded living conditions and exposure to cigarette smoke and other pollutants are linked to the disease—factors that probably account for its high incidence among low-income children. In addition, enrollment of millions of infants and young children in child care creates opportunities for close contact, greatly increasing the number of otitis media episodes among these children (Froom & Culpepper, 1991).

Negative developmental outcomes of early otitis media can be prevented in the following ways:

- *Preventive doses of xylitol, a sweetener derived from birch bark.* A recent Finnish study revealed that children in child-care centers given a daily dose of xylitol in gum or syrup form show a 30- to 40-percent drop in otitis media

High-quality child-care centers reduce or eliminate language delays, social isolation, and later academic difficulties associated with frequent bouts of otitis media. These toddlers profit from verbally stimulating caregivers and a small group size, which ensures a relatively quiet environment where spoken language can be heard easily.
(Stuart Cohen/The Image Works)

compared with controls receiving gum or syrup without the sweetener. Xylitol appears to have natural, bacteria-fighting ingredients (Uhari, Kontiokari, & Niemelä, 1998). However, dosage must be carefully monitored, since too much xylitol can cause abdominal pain and diarrhea.

- *Frequent screening of infants and preschoolers for the disease, followed by prompt medical intervention.* (Plastic tubes that drain the inner ear are often used to treat chronic otitis media, although their effectiveness remains controversial.)

- *Regular cleaning and arrangement of child-care settings to control infection.* Because infants and young children often put toys in their mouths, these objects should be rinsed frequently with a disinfectant solution. Spacious, well-ventilated rooms and small group sizes also limit the spread of disease.

- *Verbally stimulating adult–child interaction.* Developmental problems associated with otitis media are reduced or eliminated in high-quality child-care centers. When caregivers are verbally stimulating and keep noise to a minimum, children have more opportunities to hear spoken language (Feagans, Kipp, & Blood, 1994; Roberts, Burchinal, & Campbell, 1994).

spectrum (Brown, 1990; Burr, Morrone, & Fiorentini, 1996). By 4 to 5 months, they regard a particular color as the same, even under very different lighting conditions (Dannemiller, 1989). Once color sensitivity is well established, habituation–dishabituation research reveals that babies organize different hues into categories—red, blue, yellow, and green—just as adults do. Four-month-olds, for example, perceive two blues as more alike

Development of Touch, Taste, Smell, Balance/Self-Movement, and Hearing

Age	Touch	Taste and Smell	Balance/Self-Movement	Hearing
Birth	■ Is responsive to touch, temperature change, and pain	■ Can distinguish sweet, sour, and bitter tastes; prefers sweetness ■ Distinguishes odors; prefers those of sweet-tasting foods ■ Prefers smell of own mother and smell of the lactating breast	■ Adapts head movements to optical flow	■ Prefers complex sounds to pure tones ■ Can distinguish some sound patterns ■ Recognizes differences between almost all speech sounds ■ Turns in the general direction of a sound
1–6 months		■ Prefers salt solution to plain water ■ Taste preferences can be easily changed through experience	■ As motor control improves, postural adjustments to self-movement become more precise	■ Organizes sounds into more complex patterns, such as musical and speech phrases ■ Can identify the location of a sound more precisely ■ By the end of this period, begins to screen out speech sounds not used in own language ■ Picks up others' emotions through tone of voice

Note: These milestones represent overall age trends. Individual differences exist in the precise age at which each milestone is attained.

than a blue and a green (Bornstein, Kessen, & Weiskopf, 1976; Catherwood, Crassini, & Freiberg, 1989). This grouping of colors is probably an innate property of the visual system, since young infants could not have learned through language that a certain range of hues is called by the same name.

As babies see more clearly, explore the visual field more adeptly, and use color and brightness cues, they work on sorting out features of the environment and their arrangement in space. We can best understand how they do so by examining the development of three additional aspects of vision: depth, pattern, and object perception.

■ **DEPTH PERCEPTION.** Depth perception is the ability to judge the distance of objects from one another and from ourselves. It is important for understanding the layout of the environment and for guiding motor activity. To reach for objects, babies must have some sense of depth. Later, when infants crawl, depth perception helps prevent them from bumping into furniture and falling down staircases.

Although we live in a three-dimensional world, the surface of the retina that captures visual images is two-dimensional. A variety of visual cues help us translate this two-dimensional representation into a three-dimensional view of reality. Research on depth perception focuses on two main questions: Do very young infants perceive depth? How does sensitivity to various cues for depth develop during the first year of life?

The earliest studies of depth perception used a well-known apparatus called the **visual cliff** (see Figure 4.12). Devised by Eleanor Gibson and Richard Walk (1960), it consists of a glass-covered table with a platform at the center. On one side of the platform (the shallow side) is a checkerboard pattern just under the surface of the glass. On the other side (the deep side), the checkerboard is several feet beneath the glass. The researchers placed crawling infants on the platform and asked their mothers to entice them across both the deep and shallow sides by calling to them and holding out a toy. Although the babies readily crossed the shallow side, all but a few reacted with fear to the deep side. The researchers concluded that around the time infants crawl, most distinguish deep and shallow surfaces and avoid drop-offs that look dangerous.

Gibson and Walk's research shows that crawling and avoidance of drop-offs are linked, but it does not tell us how they are related or when depth perception first appears. To better understand the development of depth perception, investigators have turned to babies' ability to detect particular depth cues, using methods that do not require that they crawl.

KINETIC DEPTH CUES. How do we know when an object is near rather than far away? Try these exercises to find out. Look toward the far wall while moving your head from side to side. Notice that objects close to your eye move past your field of vision more quickly than those far away. Next, pick up a small object (such as your cup) and move it toward and away from your face. Did its image grow larger as it approached and smaller as it receded?

Motion provides us with a great deal of information about depth, and **kinetic depth cues** are the first to which infants are sensitive. Babies 3 to 4 weeks of age blink their eyes defensively to a surface looming toward their face that looks as if it is going to hit (Nánez, 1987; Nánez & Yonas, 1994). As they are carried about and as people and things turn and move before their eyes, infants learn more about depth. For example, complex habituation–dishabituation studies reveal that by 3 to 4 months, infants use motion to detect that objects are not flat shapes but are instead three-dimensional (Arterberry, Craton, & Yonas, 1993).

BINOCULAR DEPTH CUES. Motion is not the only important depth cue. Because our eyes are separated, each receives a slightly different view of the visual field. In children and adults, the brain blends these two images but also registers the difference between them, providing us with **binocular** (meaning two eyes) **depth cues.** Researchers have used ingenious methods to find out if infants are sensitive to binocular cues. One approach is similar to a 3-D movie. The experimenter projects two overlapping images before the baby, who wears special goggles to ensure that each eye receives one of the images. If babies use binocular cues, they see and visually track an organized form rather than random dots. Results reveal that binocular sensitivity emerges between 2 and 3 months and improves rapidly over the first half-year (Birch, 1993). Infants soon make use of binocular cues in their reaching, adjusting arm and hand movements to match the distance of objects from the eye.

PICTORIAL DEPTH CUES. We also use the same set of depth cues that artists rely on to make a painting look three-dimensional. These are called **pictorial depth cues.** Examples are receding lines that create the illusion of perspective, changes in texture (nearby textures are more detailed than those far away), and overlapping objects (an object partially hidden by another object is perceived to be more distant).

Albert Yonas and his colleagues have explored infants' sensitivity to pictorial cues by covering one eye (so the baby cannot rely on binocular vision), presenting stimuli with

visual cliff An apparatus used to study depth perception in infants. Consists of a glass-covered table and a central platform, from which babies are encouraged to crawl. Patterns placed beneath the glass create the appearance of a shallow and deep side.

kinetic depth cues Depth cues created by movements of the body or of objects in the environment.

binocular depth cues Depth cues that rely on each eye receiving a slightly different view of the visual field; the brain blends the two images, creating three-dimensionality.

pictorial depth cues Depth cues such as those that artists use to make a painting look three-dimensional, including receding lines, texture changes, and overlapping objects.

FIGURE 4.13

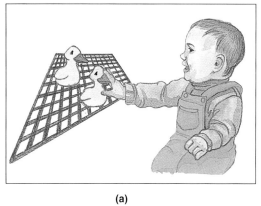
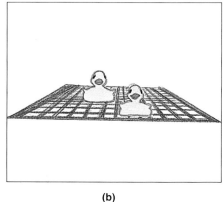

(a)   (b)

Test of an infant's ability to perceive depth from pictorial cues. (a) A side view of an apparatus in which two toy ducks are placed on a background in which lines and texture create the illusion of depth. A baby reaching for the lower, or closer appearing, duck responds to pictorial cues. (b) This view shows how the experimental display looks to a baby who is sensitive to pictorial cues.

(Adapted from Yonas et al., 1986.)

certain cues, and seeing which ones infants reach for. For example, Figure 4.13 shows two ducks placed on a vertical background in which lines and texture create the illusion of depth. If infants use pictorial cues, they should grasp the lower of the two toys. Experiments like this show that 7-month-olds are sensitive to a variety of pictorial cues, but 5-month-olds are not (Arterberry, Yonas, & Bensen, 1989; Yonas et al., 1986). Pictorial depth perception is last to develop, emerging around the middle of the first year.

EXPLAINING SENSITIVITY TO DEPTH CUES. Why does perception of depth cues emerge in the order just described? According to researchers, kinetic sensitivity develops first (and may even be present at birth) because it provides the most dependable information about the location of objects and events (Kellman, 1993). Using motion-carried information, even neonates can protect themselves from harmful situations. For example, their capacity to avoid looming stimuli is adaptive, since their worlds are full of moving objects—blankets, objects, and their own hands—that might damage the delicate eye if allowed to contact it.

Proper alignment of the two eyes is essential for detection of binocular cues. Without early corrective surgery, infants with *strabismus* (a condition in which one eye does not focus with the other because of muscle weakness) show permanent deficits in binocular sensitivity, reduced visual acuity in the weak eye, and distorted perception of the spatial layout of the environment (Birch, 1993).

Motor development may also contribute to depth cue sensitivity. For example, control of the head during the early weeks of life may help babies notice kinetic cues. And around 5 to 6 months, the ability to turn, poke, and feel the surface of objects may promote perception of pictorial cues as infants pick up information about size, texture, and shape (Bushnell & Boudreau, 1993). Indeed, as we will see next, research shows that one aspect of motor progress—the baby's ability to move about independently—plays a vital role in the refinement of depth perception.

Crawling promotes three-dimensional understanding, such as wariness of dropoffs and memory for object locations. As this baby moves about, he takes note of how to get from place to place, where objects are in relation to himself and to other objects, and what they look like from different points of view.

(Bob Daemmrich/The Image Works)

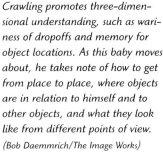

■ **INDEPENDENT MOVEMENT AND DEPTH PERCEPTION.** A mother I know described her newly crawling baby daughter as a "fearless daredevil." "If I put April down in the middle of our bed, she crawls right over the edge," the mother exclaimed. "The same thing's happened by the stairs."

Will April become more wary of the side of the bed and the staircase as she becomes a more experienced crawler? Research suggests that she will. In one study, infants with more crawling experience (regardless of when they started to crawl) were far more likely to refuse to cross the deep side of the visual cliff (Bertenthal, Campos, & Barrett, 1984). Avoidance of heights, the investigators concluded, is "made possible by independent locomotion" (Bertenthal & Campos, 1987, p. 563).

Independent movement is related to other aspects of three-dimensional understanding as well. For example, crawling infants are better at remembering object locations and finding hidden objects than are their noncrawling agemates, and the more crawling experience they have, the better their performance on these tasks (Bai & Bertenthal, 1992; Campos & Bertenthal, 1989). Why does crawling make such a difference? Compare your own experience of the environment when you are driven from one place to another as opposed to when you walk or drive yourself. When you move on your own, you are much more aware of landmarks and routes of travel, and you take more careful note of what things look like from different points of view. The same is true for infants.

In fact, crawling is so important in structuring babies' experience of the world that it seems to promote a new level of brain organization (Fox, Calkins, & Bell, 1994). During the weeks in which babies master crawling, EEG activity becomes synchronized across various regions of the cerebral cortex. Researchers speculate that crawling leads to strengthening of certain neural connections, especially those involved in vision, motor planning, and understanding of space (Bell & Fox, 1996). Finally, as the Variations box on page 160 reveals, the link between independent movement and spatial knowledge is evident in a population with a very different perceptual experience: infants with severe visual impairments.

Two checkerboards differing in complexity

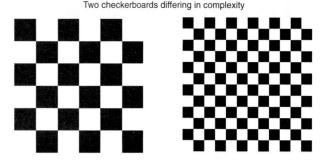

Appearance of checkerboards to very young infants

■ **PATTERN PERCEPTION**. Are young babies sensitive to the pattern, or form, of things they see, and do they prefer some patterns to others? Early research revealed that even newborns prefer to look at patterned rather than plain stimuli—for example, a drawing of the human face or one with scrambled facial features to a black-and-white oval (Fantz, 1961).

Since then, many studies have shown that as infants get older, they prefer more complex patterns. For example, when shown black-and-white checkerboards, 3-week-old infants look longest at ones with a few large squares, whereas 8- and 14-week-olds prefer those with many squares (Brennan, Ames, & Moore, 1966). Infant preferences for many other patterned stimuli have been tested—curved versus straight lines, connected versus disconnected elements, and whether the pattern is organized around a central focus (as in a bull's eye), to name just a few.

CONTRAST SENSITIVITY. For many years, investigators did not understand why babies of different ages find certain patterns more attractive than others. Then a general principle was discovered that accounts for early pattern preferences: **contrast sensitivity** (Banks & Ginsburg, 1985). *Contrast* refers to the difference in the amount of light between adjacent regions in a pattern. If babies *are sensitive to* (can detect) the contrast in two or more patterns, they prefer the one with more contrast.

To understand this idea, look at the two checkerboards in the top row of Figure 4.14. To the mature viewer, the one with many small squares has more contrasting elements. Now look at the bottom row, which shows how these checkerboards appear to infants in the first few weeks of life. Because of their poor vision, very young babies cannot resolve the small features in more complex patterns. To them, the large, bold checkerboard has more contrast, so they prefer to look at it. By 2 months of age, detection of fine-grained detail has improved considerably. As a result, infants become sensitive to the contrast in complex patterns and start to spend much more time looking at them (Dodwell, Humphrey, & Muir, 1987).

COMBINING PATTERN ELEMENTS. In the early weeks of life, infants respond to the separate parts of a pattern. For example, when shown a triangle or a drawing of the human face, very young babies look at the outskirts of the stimulus and stare at single high-contrast features—one corner of the triangle or the hairline and chin of the face (see Figure 4.15 on page 161). At about 2 months, when scanning ability and contrast sensitivity have improved, infants inspect the entire border of a geometric shape. And they explore the

FIGURE 4.14

The way two checkerboards differing in complexity look to infants in the first few weeks of life. Because of their poor vision, very young infants cannot resolve the fine detail in the more complex checkerboard. It appears blurred, like a gray field. The large, bold checkerboard appears to have more contrast, so babies prefer to look at it.

(Adapted from M. S. Banks & P. Salapatek, 1983, "Infant Visual Perception," in M. M. Haith & J. J. Campos [Eds.], *Handbook of Child Psychology: Vol. 2. Infancy and Developmental Psychobiology* [4th ed.], New York: Wiley, p. 504. Copyright © 1983 by John Wiley & Sons. Reprinted by permission.)

contrast sensitivity Ability to detect contrast—differences in light levels between adjacent spatial regions.

Development of Infants with Severe Visual Impairments

RESEARCH ON INFANTS who can see very little or nothing at all dramatically illustrates the interdependence of vision, social interaction, motor exploration, and understanding of the world. In a recent longitudinal study, infants with a visual acuity of 20/800 or worse (they had only dim light perception or were blind) were followed through the preschool years. Compared with agemates who have less severe visual impairments, they showed serious delays in all aspects of development—motor, cognitive, language, and personal/social. Their motor and cognitive functioning suffered the most; with age, performance in both domains became increasingly distant from that of other children (Hatton et al., 1997).

What explains these profound developmental delays? Minimal or absent vision seems to alter the child's experiences in at least two crucial, interrelated ways:

IMPACT ON THE CAREGIVER–INFANT RELATIONSHIP. Compared with sighted babies, infants who see very poorly are less likely to elicit stimulating caregiver interaction. They cannot make eye contact, imitate or otherwise respond contingently to the parent's communications, or pick up nonverbal social cues. Their emotional expressions are muted; for example, their smile is fleeting and unpredictable. Consequently, the infant may receive little adult attention, play, and other stimulation vital for all aspects of development (Tröster & Brambring, 1992).

When a visually impaired child does not learn how to participate in dialogues during infancy, capacity to interact with teachers and peers is compromised in early childhood. In an observational study of blind children enrolled in preschools with sighted agemates, the blind children seldom initiated contact with their peers and teachers. When they did interact, they had trouble interpreting the meaning of others' reactions and responding appropriately (Preisler, 1991, 1993).

IMPACT ON MOTOR EXPLORATION AND SPATIAL UNDERSTANDING. Infants with severe visual impairments attain gross and fine motor milestones many months later than do their sighted counterparts (Fraiberg, 1977; Tröster & Brambring, 1993). For example, on the average, blind infants do not reach for and engage in extensive manipulation of objects until 12 months, crawl until 13 months, and walk until 19 months (compare these averages with the norms given in the Milestones table on page 145). Why is this so?

Infants with severe visual impairments must rely entirely on sound to identify the location of objects. But sound does not function as a precise clue to object location until much later than vision—around the middle of the first year (see page 153). And because infants who cannot see have difficulty engaging their caregivers, adults may not provide them with rich, early exposure to sounding objects. As a result, the baby comes to understand relatively late that there is a world of tantalizing objects out there to explore.

Until "reaching on sound" is achieved, infants with severe visual impairments are not motivated to move on their own (Fraiberg, 1977; Tröster & Brambring, 1993). Even after they do move, their postural control is poor due to many months of inactivity and lack of access to visual cues that assist with balance (see page 152). Furthermore, because of

This 20-month-old, who has no vision, reacts with glee as her father guides her exploration of a novel object through touch and sound. Adults who encourage and reinforce children's efforts to make contact with their physical and social surroundings prevent developmental delays typically associated with severely impaired vision. (Byron/Monkmeyer Press)

their own uncertainty and parental fear of injury and resulting restriction, blind infants are typically tentative in their movements. These factors delay motor development further.

Motor and cognitive development are inextricably linked for infants with little or no vision, even more than for their sighted counterparts. These babies build an understanding of the location and arrangement of objects in space only after reaching and crawling (Bigelow, 1992; Tröster & Brambring, 1993). Inability to imitate the motor actions of others presents additional challenges as visually impaired children get older, contributing to their increasingly divergent motor and cognitive progress relative to peers with better vision (Hatton et al., 1997).

INTERVENTIONS. Although many infants and preschoolers with severe visual impairments are substantially delayed in development, considerable variation exists. Once language emerges and the child can rely on verbal communication for learning, some children with limited or no vision show impressive rebounds, eventually acquiring a unique capacity for abstract thinking and social and practical skills that permit them to lead productive, independent lives (Warren, 1994).

Parents, teachers, and professional caregivers can help infants with minimal vision overcome early developmental delays. Especially important is stimulating, responsive interaction. Until a close emotional bond with an adult is forged, visually impaired babies cannot establish vital links with their environments.

Techniques that help infants focus attention and become aware of their physical and social surroundings include heightened sensory input through combining sound and touch (holding, touching, or bringing the baby's hands to the adult's face while talking or singing), many repetitions, and consistently reinforcing the infant's efforts to make contact. Manipulative play with objects that make sounds is also vital (Fraiberg, 1977; Rogow, 1988). These experiences facilitate "reaching on sound," which motivates independent movement. Finally, rich language stimulation can compensate for visual loss by granting young children a ready means of finding out about objects, events, and behaviors they cannot see.

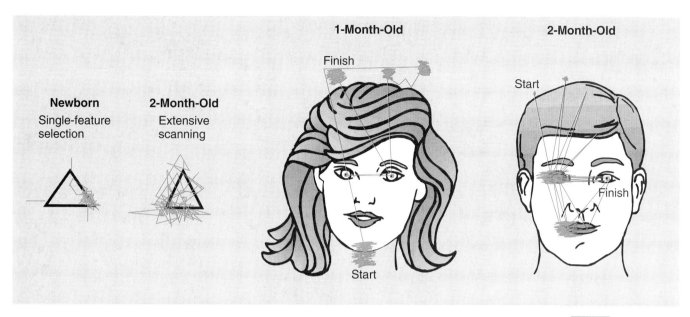

FIGURE 4.15

Visual scanning of simple and complex patterns by young infants. When scanning a simple triangle, newborns focus only on a single feature, whereas 2-month-olds scan the entire border. When patterns are complex, such as a human face, 1-month-olds limit their scanning to single features on the outskirts of the stimulus, whereas 2-month-olds examine internal features.

(From P. Salapatek, 1975, "Pattern Perception in Early Infancy," in L. B. Cohen & P. Salapatek (Eds.), *Infant Perception: From Sensation to Cognition,* New York: Academic Press, p. 201. Reprinted by permission.)

internal features of complex stimuli like the human face, pausing briefly to look at each salient part (Bronson, 1991).

Once babies can take in all aspects of a pattern, at 2 to 3 months they start to combine pattern elements, integrating them into a unified whole. By 4 months, they are so good at detecting pattern organization that they even perceive subjective boundaries that are not really present. For example, look at Figure 4.16. Four-month-olds perceive a square in the center of this pattern, just as you do (Ghim, 1990).

Older infants carry this responsiveness to subjective form even further. Nine-month-olds can detect the organized, meaningful pattern in a series of moving lights that resemble a person walking, in that they look much longer at this display than they do at upside-down or disorganized versions. Although 3- to 5-month-olds can tell the difference between these patterns, they do not show a preference for one with both an upright orientation and a humanlike movement pattern (Bertenthal et al., 1985; Bertenthal et al., 1987).

By the end of the first year, infants extract meaningful patterns on the basis of very little information. For example, 12-month-olds can figure out an object's shape from a succession of partial views as it passes behind a small opening (Arterberry, 1993). They can also recognize a shape by watching a moving light trace its outline. In two studies, babies of this age preferred to look at a geometric shape that was different from the one they had just seen outlined by a blinking light (Rose, 1988; Skouteris, McKenzie, & Day, 1992). Finally, 12-month-olds can even detect objects represented by incomplete figures—ones missing as much as two-thirds of their contour (see Figure 4.17 on page 162) (Rose, Jankowski, & Senior, 1997). These findings suggest that by 1 year of age, a global representation is sufficient for babies to perceive the similarity between two forms.

EXPLAINING CHANGES IN PATTERN PERCEPTION. Researchers believe that maturation of the visual system combined with exposure to a wide variety of stimuli underlie younger infants' increasing ability to detect more fine-grained pattern elements and integrated forms (Banks & Shannon, 1993; Proffitt & Bertenthal, 1990). As we saw earlier, visual acuity, scanning, and contrast sensitivity improve greatly during the first few months, supporting exploration of complex stimuli (Pipp & Haith, 1984). Also, studies of the visual cortex in animals, along with indirect research on humans, reveal that brain cells respond to specific pattern stimuli, such as vertical, horizontal, and curved lines. The sensitivity and organization of these receptors improve as babies search for regularities in their rich, patterned external world (Braddick, 1993).

Besides gains in basic sensory processes, infants' expanding knowledge of their surroundings affects perception of complex patterns, especially in the second half of the first year. As we will see in Chapter 6, by 5 to 6 months of age, babies categorize their world,

FIGURE 4.16

Subjective boundaries in a visual pattern. Do you perceive a square in the middle of this figure? By 4 months of age, infants do, too.

(Adapted from Ghim, 1990.)

FIGURE 4.17

Contour-deleted versions of a figure of a bicycle, used to test whether infants can extract meaningful patterns on the basis of very little visual information. After 12-month-olds habituated to 33-percent (a), 50-percent (b), or 66-percent (c) contour deletions, the intact figure (d) was paired with a novel figure. Infants recognized the corresponding intact figure, since they dishabituated to (looked longer at) the novel form.

(Adapted from Rose, Jankowski, & Senior, 1997.)

(a) 33% Contour Deletion

(b) 50% Contour Deletion

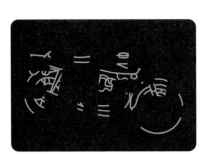

(c) 66% Contour Deletion

(d) Intact Figure

extracting common properties of similar stimuli. Consider, for example, older infants' preference for a pattern of moving lights that corresponds to a person walking. From many occasions of observing people move, they build an image of the human gait as distinct from other stimuli. As evidence for this influence, when 5-month-olds are shown moving light displays of a person walking in different ways (forward, backward, and while marching), they extract the general pattern and show improved performance on the light display task (Pinto & Davis, 1991).

In sum, over time, infants' knowledge of familiar actions, objects, and events increasingly governs pattern sensitivity (Bertenthal, 1993). As we turn now to perception of the human face, we will see additional examples of this idea.

■ **PERCEPTION OF THE HUMAN FACE.** Do babies have an innate tendency to orient toward human faces? Some researchers think so, since newborns will track a facelike pattern moving across their visual field farther than they will track other stimuli (Morton & Johnson, 1991). This behavior is believed to be a built-in, adaptive capacity to orient toward members of one's own species, just as many other newborn creatures do.

But all agree that infants younger than 2 months cannot discriminate a static image of the human face from other equally complex patterns, such as one with scrambled facial features, largely because (as we noted earlier) 1-month-olds do not inspect the internal features of a stimulus.[3] At 2 to 3 months, when infants explore an entire stimulus, they do prefer a facial pattern over other, similar configurations. For example, in one study, 3-month-olds, but not 6-week-olds, looked longer at a face than at the same pattern with its contrast reversed (that is, a negative of a face). They showed no similar preference when an abstract pattern was paired with its negative (Dannemiller & Stephens, 1988). Infants' recognition of faces does not seem to be a built-in capacity. Instead, it follows the same developmental course as other aspects of visual perception.

The baby's tendency to search for structure in a patterned stimulus is quickly applied to face perception. By 3 months of age, infants make fine distinctions among the features of different faces. For example, they can tell the difference between the photos of two strangers, even when the faces are moderately similar. Around this time, babies also rec-

---

[3]Perhaps you are wondering how neonates can display the remarkable imitative capacities described earlier in this chapter if they do not scan the internal features of a face. Recall that facial expressions in newborn imitation research were not static poses but live demonstrations. Their dynamic quality probably caused infants to notice them.

(a)   (b)

FIGURE 4.18

Testing newborns for size constancy. (a) First, infants were habituated to a small black-and-white cube at varying distances from the eye. In this way, the researchers hoped to desensitize babies to changes in the cube's retinal image size and direct their attention to its actual size. (b) Next, the small cube and a new, large cube were presented together, but at different distances so they cast the same size retinal image. All babies dishabituated to (looked much longer at) the novel large cube, indicating that they distinguish objects on the basis of actual size, not retinal image size. (Adapted from Slater, Mattock, & Brown, 1990.)

ognize their mother's face in a photo, since they look longer at it than at the face of a stranger (Morton, 1993). Between 7 and 10 months, infants start to react to emotional expressions as organized wholes. They treat positive faces (happy and surprised) as different from negative ones (sad and fearful), even when these expressions are demonstrated in slightly varying ways by different models (Ludemann, 1991).

Extensive face-to-face interaction between infants and their caregivers undoubtedly contributes to the refinement of face perception. As we will see in Chapter 10, babies' developing sensitivity to the human face supports their earliest social relationships and helps regulate exploration of the environment in adaptive ways.

■ **OBJECT PERCEPTION.** Research on pattern perception involves only two-dimensional stimuli, but our environment is made up of stable, three-dimensional objects. Do infants perceive a world of independently existing objects, much like we do?

SIZE AND SHAPE CONSTANCY. As we move around the environment and look at objects, the images they cast on our retina are constantly changing in size and shape. To perceive objects as stable and unchanging, we must translate these varying retinal images into a single representation.

Size constancy—perception of an object's size as stable, despite changes in its retinal image size—is evident in the first week of life. To test for it, researchers capitalized on the habituation–dishabituation response using the procedure described and illustrated in Figure 4.18 (Slater, 1997). Perception of an object's shape as stable, despite changes in the shape projected on the retina, is called **shape constancy.** Habituation–dishabituation research reveals that it, too, is present within the first week of life, long before babies can actively rotate objects with their hands and view them from different angles (Slater, 1996).

In sum, both shape and size constancy appear to be innate perceptual capacities that assist babies in detecting a coherent world of objects. Gains in the accuracy of size-constancy detection occur as sensitivity to binocular depth cues improves during the first few months (Kellman, 1996). Nevertheless, both size and shape constancy provide only a partial picture of young infants' object perception.

PERCEPTION OF OBJECTS AS DISTINCT, BOUNDED WHOLES. As adults, we distinguish a single object from its surroundings by looking for a regular shape and uniform texture and color. Observations by Piaget (1936/1952b) first suggested that young infants do not use these same cues. Piaget dangled a small, attractive object in front of his 6-month-old son

size constancy Perception of an object's size as stable, despite changes in the size of its retinal image.

shape constancy Perception of an object's shape as stable, despite changes in the shape of its retinal image.

FIGURE **4.19**

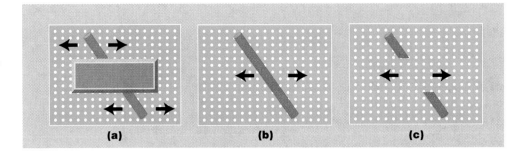

(a)   **(b)**   **(c)**

Example of a display used to test infants' ability to perceive object unity. (a) Infants are habituated to a rod moving back-and-forth behind a box against a textured background. Next, they are shown (b) a complete rod or (c) a broken rod with a gap corresponding to the location of the box. Each of these stimuli is moved back and forth against a textured background, in the same way as the habituation stimulus. Infants 2 months of age and older typically dishabituate to (look longer at) the broken rod than the complete rod. This suggests that they perceive the rod behind the box in the first display as a single unit. (Adapted from Johnson, 1997.)

Laurent, who eagerly grabbed it. But as soon as it was placed on top of a bigger object, such as a book or pillow, Laurent no longer reached for it. Instead, he reached for the larger, supporting object. Laurent's behavior suggests that he did not perceive the boundary between two objects created by their different sizes, shapes, and textures. Rather, he treated two objects close together as a single unit.

Recent research supports Piaget's informal observations and also reveals that it is the movement of objects relative to one another and to their background that gradually enables infants to construct a visual world of separate objects. In one series of studies, 3- to 5-month-olds viewed two objects. Sometimes the objects touched each other; at other times they were separated. Also, sometimes the objects were stationary; at other times they moved independently or together. When objects touched and either stood still or moved in the same direction, infants reached for them as a whole. When they were separated or moved in opposite directions, infants behaved as if the objects were distinct, and they reached for only one of them (Hofsten & Spelke, 1985; Spelke, Hofsten, & Kestenbaum, 1989).

These findings indicate that at first, motion and spatial arrangement determine infants' identification of objects (Kellman, 1996; Spelke & Hermer, 1996). Indeed, young babies are fascinated by moving objects. They almost always prefer to look at a moving stimulus instead of an identical stationary one. As infants track moving objects, they pick up information that permits them to identify a stationary object's boundaries, such as distinct shape, color, and texture and consistent distance of all the object's parts from the eye.

For example, as Figure 4.19 reveals, after 2 months of age, babies realize that a moving rod whose center is hidden behind a box is a complete rod rather than two rod pieces. Motion, a textured background, and alignment of the top and bottom of the rod are necessary for young infants to infer object unity; they cannot do so without all of these cues (Johnson & Aslin, 1995, 1996). When an object (such as a rod) moves behind another object and across a distinct background, its various features remain in the same relationship to one another, helping infants distinguish the object from other surfaces in the visual field. During the second half-year, as infants become familiar with many types of objects, they rely more on stationary cues to identify them as separate units (Johnson, 1997; Spelke, Gutheil, & Van de Walle, 1995).

The Milestones table on the following page provides an overview of the vast changes that take place in visual perception during the first year. Up to this point, we have considered the sensory systems one by one. Now let's examine their coordination.

INTERMODAL PERCEPTION

When we take in information from the environment, we often use **intermodal perception.** That is, we combine information from more than one *modality,* or sensory system. For example, we know that the shape of an object is the same whether we see it or touch it, that lip movements are closely coordinated with the sound of a voice, and that dropping a rigid object on a hard surface will cause a sharp, banging sound. Recent evidence reveals that from the start, babies perceive the world in an intermodal fashion (Meltzoff, 1990; Spelke, 1987).

Recall that newborns turn in the general direction of a sound, and they reach for objects in a primitive way. These behaviors suggest that infants expect sight, sound, and

intermodal perception Perception that combines information from more than one modality, or sensory system.

Visual Development in Infancy

Age	Acuity, Color Perception, Focusing, and Exploration	Depth Perception	Pattern Perception	Object Perception
Birth–1 month	■ Visual acuity is 20/600 ■ Scans the visual field and tracks moving objects	■ Responds to kinetic depth cues	■ Prefers large, bold patterns ■ Scans the outskirts of a pattern	■ Displays size and shape constancy
2–3 months	■ Has adultlike focusing ability ■ Perceives colors across the entire spectrum	■ Responds to binocular depth cues	■ Prefers patterns with fine details ■ Scans internal pattern features ■ Begins to perceive overall pattern structure ■ Perceives human facial pattern ■ Recognizes mother's face in a photo	■ Uses motion and spatial layout to identify objects
4–5 months	■ Organizes colors into categories like those of adults	■ Sensitivity to binocular depth cues improves	■ Detects subjective boundaries in patterns	■ Uses kinetic cues to perceive objects as three-dimensional ■ Uses stationary cues (shape, texture, color) to identify objects
6–8 months	■ Visual acuity improves to 20/100 ■ Tracks moving objects with smooth, efficient eye movements	■ Responds to pictorial depth cues ■ Avoids the deep side of the visual cliff		
9–12 months	■ Visual acuity continues to improve		■ Can extract pattern information in the absence of a full image (from a moving light or partial picture) ■ Perceives patterns (such as human walking movements and facial expressions of emotion) as meaningful wholes	

Note: These milestones represent overall age trends. Individual differences exist in the precise age at which each milestone is attained.

touch to go together. In one study, 1-month-old babies were given a pacifier with either a smooth surface or a surface with nubs on it. After exploring it in their mouths, the infants were shown two pacifiers—one smooth and one nubbed. They preferred to look at the shape they had sucked, indicating that they could match touch and visual stimulation without much experience seeing and feeling objects (Meltzoff & Borton, 1979).

Other research reveals that by 4 months, vision and hearing are well coordinated. Lorraine Bahrick (1983) showed infants of this age two films side by side, one with two blocks banging and the other with two sponges being squashed together. At the same time, the soundtrack for only one of the films (either a sharp banging noise or a soft squashing sound) could be heard. Infants looked at the film that went with the soundtrack, indicating that they detected a common rhythm in what they saw and heard. In similar studies, 3- and 4-month-olds related the shape and tempo of an adult's moving lips to the corresponding sounds in speech (Pickens et al., 1994; Walton & Bower, 1993). And 7-month-olds united emotional expressions across modalities, matching a happy- or angry-sounding voice with the appropriate face of a speaking person (Pickens et al., 1994; Soken & Pick, 1992).

Of course, many intermodal associations, such as the way a train sounds or a teddy bear feels, must be based on experience. But what is so remarkable about intermodal perception is how quickly infants acquire these associations. Most of the time, they need just one exposure to a new situation (Spelke, 1987). In addition, when researchers try to teach intermodal matches by pairing sights and sounds that do not naturally go together, babies will not learn them (Bahrick, 1988, 1992). Intermodal perception is yet another capacity that helps infants build an orderly, predictable perceptual world.

UNDERSTANDING PERCEPTUAL DEVELOPMENT

Now that we have reviewed the development of infant perceptual capacities, how can we put together this diverse array of amazing achievements? Do any general principles account for perceptual development? Eleanor and James Gibson's **differentiation theory** provides widely accepted answers.

According to the Gibsons, infants actively search for **invariant features** of the environment—those that remain stable—in a constantly changing perceptual world. For example, in pattern perception, at first babies are confronted with a confusing mass of stimulation. But very quickly, they search for features that stand out along the border of a stimulus. Then they explore its internal features, noticing stable relationships between those features. As a result, they detect patterns, such as squares and faces. The development of intermodal perception also reflects this principle. Babies seem to seek out invariant relationships, such as a similar tempo in an object's motion and sound, that unite information across different modalities.

The Gibsons use the word *differentiation* (meaning analyze or break down) to describe their theory because over time, the baby detects finer and finer invariant features among stimuli. In addition to pattern perception, differentiation applies to depth and object perception. Recall how in each, sensitivity to motion precedes awareness of detailed stationary cues. So one way of understanding perceptual development is to think of it as a built-in tendency to search for order and stability in the surrounding world, a capacity that becomes increasingly fine-tuned with age (Gibson, 1970; Gibson, 1979).

Acting on the environment plays a major role in perceptual differentiation. According to the Gibsons, perception is guided by discovery of **affordances**—the action possibilities a situation offers an organism with certain motor capabilities (Gibson, 1988). As adults, we know when we can execute particular actions—when an object can be touched or a surface is appropriate for sitting or walking. Infants discover these affordances as they act on their world. For example, when they move from crawling to walking, they first realize that a steeply sloping surface *affords the possibility of falling*, since they hesitate to go down it. Experience in trying to remain upright but frequently tumbling over on various surfaces seems to make new walkers more aware of the consequences of their actions in different situations. As a result, they differentiate surfaces in new ways and act more competently when confronted with them (Adolph, 1997; Adolph, Eppler, & Gibson,

differentiation theory The view that perceptual development involves the detection of increasingly fine-grained, invariant features in the environment.

invariant features Features that remain stable in a constantly changing perceptual world.

affordances The action possibilities a situation offers an organism with certain motor capabilities. Discovery of affordances is believed to guide perceptual development.

Perception is guided by the discovery of affordances. The crawling infant on the left plunges headlong down a steeply sloping surface. He has not yet learned that it affords the possibility of falling. The newly walking toddler on the right approaches the slope more cautiously. Experience in trying to remain upright but frequently tumbling over has made him more aware of the consequences of his actions in this situation. He perceives the incline differently than he did at a younger age.

(Courtesy of Karen Adolph, Emory University)

1993). Can you think of other links between motor milestones and perceptual development described in this chapter?

At this point, it is only fair to note that some researchers believe babies do not just make sense of their world by detecting invariant features and discovering affordances. Instead, they *impose meaning* on what they perceive, constructing categories of objects and events in the surrounding environment. We have seen the glimmerings of this cognitive point of view in this chapter. For example, older babies *interpret* a happy voice and face as a source of pleasure and affection and a pattern of blinking lights as a moving human being. We will save our discussion of infant cognition for later chapters, acknowledging for now that the cognitive perspective also has merit in understanding the achievements of infancy. In fact, many researchers combine these two positions, regarding infant development as proceeding from a perceptual to a cognitive emphasis over the first year of life (Haith & Benson, 1998; Mandler, 1998).

BRIEF REVIEW

Recent research has greatly expanded our understanding of infant perceptual development. Sensitivity to touch, taste, smell, and sound are well developed in the newborn baby. Newborns also have a built-in sense of balance that is refined with experience and motor control, as their postural adjustments to optical flow reveal. During the first year, infants organize sounds into more complex patterns and become sensitive to the sounds of their own language.

Of all the senses, vision is least mature at birth. Visual acuity, scanning, tracking, and color perception improve during the early months. Depth perception develops as infants detect kinetic, binocular, and pictorial cues. Experience in independent movement influences avoidance of heights as well as other aspects of three-dimensional understanding. The principle of contrast sensitivity accounts for young babies' pattern preferences. As vision improves in the first few months, infants perceive the parts of a pattern as an organized whole. By the end of the first year, they extract meaningful patterns on the basis of partial information.

Size and shape constancy are present at birth. At first, infants distinguish objects by attending to their motion and spatial arrangement; only later do they respond to stationary cues. Young babies have a remarkable ability to combine information across sensory modalities. The Gibsons' differentiation theory provides an overall account of perceptual development.

ASK YOURSELF . . .

◆ *Can differentiation theory of perceptual development account for infants' changing responsiveness to sound, described on page 153? Explain, citing examples of babies' discovery of invariant features.*

◆ *Diane hung bright wallpaper with detailed pictures of animals in Jana's room before she was born. During her first 2 months, Jana hardly noticed the wallpaper. Then, around 2 months, she showed keen interest. What new visual abilities probably account for this change?*

◆ CONNECTIONS
How do gains in visual perception foster early emotional development? (See Chapter 10, pages 402 and 408.)

Early Deprivation and Enrichment: Is Infancy a Sensitive Period of Development?

Throughout this chapter, we have discussed how a variety of early experiences affect the development of perceptual and motor skills. In view of the findings already reported, it is not surprising that many investigations have found that stimulating physical surroundings and warm caregiving that is responsive to infants' self-initiated efforts promote active exploration of the environment and earlier achievement of developmental milestones (see, for example, Bendersky & Lewis, 1994; Bradley et al., 1989).

The powerful effect of early experience is dramatically apparent in the development of infants who lack the rich, varied stimulation of normal homes. Babies reared in severely deprived family situations or institutions show delays in early motor milestones, typically display stereotyped movements and immature play, and are overly fearful of new situations that present attractive opportunities for exploration. Although these children eventually catch up in motor functioning, their mental development generally remains substantially behind throughout childhood and adolescence (Dennis & Najarian, 1957; Fujinaga et al., 1990).

Although these findings indicate that early experience has a profound impact on development, they do not tell us for sure whether infancy is a *sensitive period*. That is, if babies do not experience appropriate stimulation of their senses in the first year or two of life, will there be lasting deficits from which they cannot fully recover? This question is highly controversial. Recall from Chapter 1 (see page 8) that some theorists argue that early experience leaves a lasting imprint on the child's competence. Others believe that experience operates much like a tape recording that can be made and erased. According to this view, the child's previous adaptations, and the events that led up to them, can be overcome by the quality of the current environment.

For ethical reasons, we cannot deliberately deprive some infants of normal rearing experiences and wait to observe the long-term consequences. However, several natural experiments in which children were victims of deprived early environments but were later exposed to stimulating, sensitive care provide the best available test of whether infancy is a sensitive period. A unique feature of these studies is that they allow us to examine the long-term effects of early deprivation without the contaminating influence of later deprivation. If the sensitive period hypothesis is correct, then the impact of deprivation during infancy should persist, even when children are moved into enriched settings.

In an early study of this kind, Wayne Dennis (1973) followed the development of children who were placed in a Lebanese orphanage shortly after birth. Through most of the first year, they lay in their cribs and received practically no individual attention from caregivers. Extreme retardation in motor and language development resulted. Many did not sit up until 1 year of age or walk until well into the preschool years. Their IQs between 1 and 6 years were severely depressed, averaging only 53. In 1957, adoption was legalized in Lebanon, and children of a variety of ages left the orphanage for normal homes. By comparing those adopted early (before 2 years of age) with those adopted later, Dennis tested the sensitive period hypothesis. Findings showed that children adopted before age 2 achieved an average IQ of 100 within 2 years. In contrast, the IQs of those adopted later were only in the high 70s, even after 6 to 8 years with their adoptive families. Dennis concluded that environmental improvement by age 2 is necessary for recovery of deprived infants.

A similar, more recent study reveals that the earlier infants are removed from deprived conditions, the greater their catch-up in development. Michael Rutter and his colleagues (1998) followed the progress of a large sample of children transferred between birth and 2 years from barren, neglectful Romanian orphanages and homes to adoptive families in Great Britain. On arrival,

These Romanian institutionalized babies, orphaned shortly after birth, spend their days confined to a crib, with little adult contact and stimulation. The longer they remain in a barren environment, the more they will withdraw and wither. Complete catch up in physical and cognitive development depends on early placement in a caring adoptive home. (B. Bisson/Sygma)

FIGURE 4.20

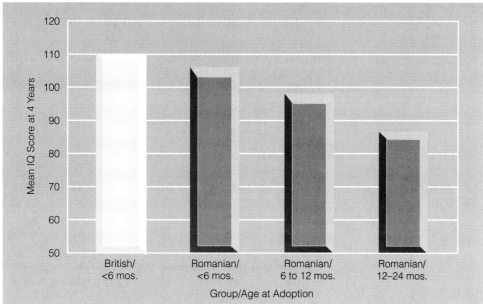

IQs of Romanian 4-year-olds who varied in age of entry into British adoptive families, compared with British 4-year-olds adopted before age 6 months. Romanian children adopted in the first 6 months of life scored as well as their British counterparts, suggesting that they had fully recovered from extreme early deprivation. Romanian children adopted after 6 months of age did not score as well. The older they were, the lower their scores. (Adapted from Rutter et al., 1998.)

most were malnourished, prone to infection, and impaired in all domains of psychological development. By age 4, physical catch-up for almost all the children was dramatic. Although cognitive catch-up was also impressive, it was not as great for those adopted after 6 months of age. These children scored lower in IQ than did Romanian and British children adopted in the first 6 months of life (see Figure 4.20). That Romanian children adopted before age 6 months were similar to British adoptees in preschool IQ suggests complete recovery from severe early deprivation.

Other research suggests that less extreme early deprivation can also have lasting consequences. Alan Sroufe, Byron Egeland, and Terri Kreutzer (1990) charted the experiences and competencies of a group of low-income children from infancy through middle childhood. Then they looked to see if early measures—attachment of infants to their mothers, exploration and problem solving at age 2, and quality of the home environment during the third year—added anything to later assessments in predicting cognitive, emotional, and social competence in childhood. Each of the early measures remained important. In addition, among children exposed to stresses during the preschool years, those with the greatest capacity for rebound in middle childhood had a history of positive adaptation during infancy.

Unfortunately, most infants reared in underprivileged environments continue to be affected by disadvantaged conditions during their childhood years. As we will see in later chapters, interventions that try to break this pattern by training caregivers to engage in warm, stimulating interaction and providing children with environmental enrichment starting in infancy and extending through early childhood have lasting cognitive and social benefits. One of the most important outcomes of these programs is that passive, apathetic babies become active, alert beings with the capacity to evoke positive interactions from caregivers and initiate stimulating play for themselves.

Finally, it is important to keep in mind that besides impoverished environments, ones that overwhelm children with expectations beyond their current capacities also undermine development. In recent years, expensive early learning centers have sprung up around the United States in which infants are trained with letter and number flash cards and slightly older toddlers are given a full curriculum of reading, math, art, music, gym, and more. There is no evidence that these programs yield smarter, better, "super babies." Instead, trying to prime infants with stimulation for which they are not ready can cause them to withdraw, threatening their spontaneous interest and pleasure in learning (Roe et al., 1990). In addition, when such programs promise but do not produce young geniuses, they are likely to lead to disappointed parents who view their children as failures at a very tender age (White, 1990). Thus, they rob infants of a psychologically healthy start on the road to maturity, and they deprive parents of relaxed, pleasurable participation in their children's early growth.

ASK YOURSELF . . .

◆ *What evidence presented earlier in this chapter indicates that overstimulating young infants can delay their development?*

◆ CONNECTIONS . . . *Does research on early brain growth support the view that infancy is a sensitive period? Explain. (See Chapter 5, pages 190–191.)*

Drawing on research findings, explain why the prenatal period is a sensitive period. (See Chapter 3, pages 95–97.)

THE ORGANIZED NEWBORN

Explain the functions of newborn reflexes, and describe changing states of arousal during infancy, emphasizing the two most extreme states: sleep and crying.

*   Infants begin life with remarkable skills for relating to their physical and social worlds. **Reflexes** are the newborn baby's most obvious organized patterns of behavior. Some have survival value, whereas others provide the foundation for voluntary motor skills that will develop later. Several reflexes help parents and infants establish gratifying interaction as soon as possible.
*   The neonate has a sleep–waking cycle that becomes more organized and patterned with age. Although newborns alternate frequently between various **states of arousal,** they spend most of their time asleep. Sleep consists of at least two states: **rapid-eye-movement (REM)** and **non-rapid-eye-movement (NREM) sleep.**
*   REM sleep time is greater during the prenatal and newborn periods than at any later age. According to **autostimulation theory,** the EEG activity of REM sleep provides young infants with stimulation essential for central nervous system development. Rapid eye movements ensure that structures of the eye remain oxygenated during sleep. Individual and cultural differences in sleep–waking patterns are evident in early infancy. Disturbed REM–NREM cycles are a sign of central nervous system abnormalities.
*   A crying baby stimulates strong feelings of discomfort in nearby adults. The intensity of the cry and the events that led up to it help parents figure out what is wrong. Once feeding and diaper changing have been tried, lifting the baby to the shoulder is the most effective soothing technique. Ethological and behaviorist theories disagree on how promptly caregivers should respond to infant cries. A shrill, piercing cry is an indicator of central nervous system distress.

Why is neonatal behavioral assessment useful?

*   The most widely used instrument for assessing the organized functioning of newborn infants is Brazelton's **Neonatal Behavioral Assessment Scale (NBAS).** The NBAS is useful in detecting early central nervous system impairment. It has also helped researchers understand individual and cultural differences in newborn behavior. Sometimes it is used to teach parents about their baby's capacities.

Describe infant learning capacities, the conditions under which they occur, and the unique value of each.

*   In **classical conditioning,** a neutral stimulus is paired with an **unconditioned stimulus (UCS)** that produces a reflexive, or **unconditioned, response (UCR).** Once learning has occurred, the neutral stimulus, now called the **conditioned stimulus (CS),** elicits the response, which is called the **conditioned response (CR).** Young infants can be classically conditioned when the pairing of a UCS with a CS has survival value.
*   **Operant conditioning** of infants has been demonstrated in many studies. In addition to food, interesting sights and sounds serve as effective **reinforcers,** increasing the occurrence of a preceding behavior. **Punishment** involves removing a desirable stimulus or pre-

venting an unpleasant one to decrease the occurrence of a response. With age, operant conditioning expands to include a wider range of stimuli and responses.

*   **Habituation** and **dishabituation** reveal that at birth, babies are attracted to novelty. Their ability to discriminate and remember a wide variety of stimuli improves over the first year. Older infants also habituate and dishabituate more rapidly. However, the habituation–dishabituation sequence underestimates how long infants can remember real-world events they can actively control and overlooks the context-dependent nature of young infants' memories. Nevertheless, habituation and dishabituation are the best available infant predictors of later mental development.
*   Newborn infants have a remarkable ability to **imitate** the facial expressions and gestures of adults. Although some researchers regard newborn imitation as little more than an automatic response to particular stimuli, others believe it is a flexible, voluntary capacity.

MOTOR DEVELOPMENT IN INFANCY

Describe the general course of gross and fine motor development during the first 2 years, including the dynamic systems view of factors that influence motor progress.

*   Infants' rapidly emerging motor skills support other domains of development. Like physical development, motor development follows the **cephalocaudal** and **proximodistal trends.** According to **dynamic systems theory,** new motor skills are a matter of combining existing skills into increasingly complex systems of action. Each new skill develops as a joint product of central nervous system maturation, movement possibilities of the body, environmental supports for the skill, and the task the child has in mind.
*   Experience profoundly affects motor development, as shown by research on infants raised in deprived institutions. Variations in encouragement and stimulation of infant motor skills account for cross-cultural differences in motor development.
*   During the first year, infants gradually perfect their reaching and grasping. The poorly coordinated **prereaching** of the newborn period eventually drops out. As control of arm and hand movements improves, voluntary reaching gradually becomes more accurate and efficient. Once infants master sitting, they use both hands cooperatively to explore objects. By the end of the first year, the clumsy **ulnar grasp** is transformed into a refined **pincer grasp.**

PERCEPTUAL DEVELOPMENT IN INFANCY

Describe the newborn baby's senses of touch, taste, smell, and hearing, noting changes during infancy.

*   The study of infant perception sheds light on the nature–nurture controversy and helps us understand many aspects of psychological development. The senses of touch, taste, smell, and hearing are well developed at birth.
*   Newborns are highly sensitive to touch, temperature change, and pain. They have an innate preference for a sweet taste and certain odors; a preference for salty tastes emerges later and probably sup-

ports acceptance of solid foods. The taste preferences of young infants can be readily modified.

♦ As responsiveness to **optical flow** reveals, newborn babies have a built-in sense of balance and self-movement that is fundamental to everything they learn through exploration. Postural adjustments take place automatically and improve with experience and motor control.

♦ Over the first year, babies organize sounds into more complex patterns. Newborns are especially responsive to high-pitched expressive voices, prefer the sound of their mother's voice, and can distinguish almost all sounds in human languages.

Describe the development of vision in infancy, placing special emphasis on depth, pattern, and object perception.

♦ Vision is the least mature of the newborn baby's senses. As the eye and visual centers in the brain mature during the first few months, focusing ability, **visual acuity,** scanning, tracking, and color perception improve rapidly.

♦ Depth perception helps infants understand the layout of the environment and guides motor activity. Responsiveness to **kinetic depth cues** appears by the end of the first month, followed by sensitivity to **binocular depth cues** between 2 and 3 months. Perception of **pictorial depth cues** emerges last, between 6 and 7 months of age. Experience in moving about independently enhances babies' three-dimensional understanding, including avoidance of edges and drop-offs, such as the deep side of the **visual cliff.**

♦ **Contrast sensitivity** accounts for infants' early pattern preferences. At first, babies look at the border of a stimulus and at single features. Around 2 months, they explore the internal features of a pattern, and soon they combine pattern elements into a unified whole and start to discriminate increasingly complex, meaningful patterns. By the end of the first year, they can detect patterns on the basis of very little information, including subjective forms traced by moving lights and contour-deleted figures.

♦ Perception of the human face follows the same sequence of development as sensitivity to other patterned stimuli. By 3 months, infants make fine distinctions between the features of different faces. Between 7 and 10 months, they react to emotional expressions as organized, meaningful wholes.

♦ At birth, **size** and **shape constancy** assist infants in building a coherent world of three-dimensional objects. Young infants depend on motion and spatial arrangement to identify objects. During the second half-year, they rely more on stationary cues, such as distinct shape, color, and texture and consistent distance of all the object's parts from the eye.

Describe infants' capacity for intermodal perception, and explain differentiation theory of perceptual development.

♦ Infants have a remarkable, built-in capacity to engage in **intermodal perception.** Although many intermodal associations are learned, babies acquire them quickly, often after just one exposure to a new situation.

♦ **Differentiation theory** is the most widely accepted account of perceptual development. Over time, infants detect increasingly fine-grained, **invariant features** in a constantly changing perceptual world. Perception is guided by discovery of **affordances**—the action possibilities a situation offers the individual.

EARLY DEPRIVATION AND ENRICHMENT: IS INFANCY A SENSITIVE PERIOD OF DEVELOPMENT?

Explain how research on early deprivation and enrichment sheds light on the question of whether infancy is a sensitive period of development.

♦ Theorists disagree on whether infancy is a sensitive period in which warm caregiving and appropriate stimulation of the senses have a lasting impact on development. Research indicates that early experience combines with current conditions to affect the child's development. Recovery from a deprived early environment can occur if rearing conditions improve; the earlier conditions improve the better the child's chances for complete recovery.

IMPORTANT TERMS AND CONCEPTS

affordances (p. 166)
autostimulation theory (p. 133)
binocular depth cues (p. 157)
cephalocaudal trend (p. 145)
classical conditioning (p. 138)
conditioned response (CR) (p. 138)
conditioned stimulus (CS) (p. 138)
contrast sensitivity (p. 159)
differentiation theory (p. 166)
dishabituation (p. 141)
dynamic systems theory (p. 146)
extinction (p. 138)
habituation (p. 141)
imitation (p. 143)

intermodal perception (p. 164)
invariant features (p. 166)
kinetic depth cues (p. 157)
Neonatal Behavioral Assessment Scale (NBAS) (p. 137)
non-rapid-eye-movement (NREM) sleep (p. 132)
operant conditioning (p. 138)
optical flow (p. 152)
pictorial depth cues (p. 157)
pincer grasp (p. 148)
prereaching (p. 148)
proximodistal trend (p. 145)
punishment (p. 139)

rapid-eye-movement (REM) sleep (p. 131)
reflex (p. 129)
reinforcer (p. 139)
shape constancy (p. 163)
size constancy (p. 163)
states of arousal (p. 131)
sudden infant death syndrome (SIDS) (p. 140)
ulnar grasp (p. 148)
unconditioned response (UCR) (p. 138)
unconditioned stimulus (UCS) (p. 138)
visual acuity (p. 154)
visual cliff (p. 157)

Physical Growth

AS TIME PASSES DURING the first two decades of life, the human body changes continuously and dramatically, until it reaches the mature adult state. Think, for a moment, about the vast physical differences between a newborn baby and a full-grown young adult. From birth to maturity, the average individual's height multiplies more than threefold, and weight increases as much as fifteen- to twentyfold. The top-heavy, chubby infant, whose head represents a quarter of the body's total length, gradually becomes the better proportioned child and eventually the taller, broader, more muscular adolescent, whose head takes up only a seventh of the body's total length.

As we examine these changes closely, you will quickly see that the story of physical growth is not just a matter of becoming taller and larger. Instead, it involves a complex series of changes in body size, proportion, and composition. This chapter traces the course of human growth, along with biological and environmental factors that regulate and control it. We also consider how the brain develops and how it depends on precise interaction between the environment and maturing nerve cells.

Throughout our discussion, we will encounter many examples of the close link between physical and psychological development. But just how the child's transforming body is related to cognitive, emotional, and social changes has puzzled philosophers and scientists for centuries. And more than any other phase of growth, they have pondered this question with respect to *puberty*, the flood of biological events leading to an adult-sized body and sexual maturity at adolescence. When you next have a chance, ask several new parents what they expect their sons and daughters to be like as teenagers. You will probably get answers like these: "Rebellious and uncontrollable." "Full of rages and tempers" (Maggs, Schulenberg, & Hurrelmann, 1997).

This view, widespread in contemporary American society, dates back to the writings of eighteenth-century philosopher Jean-Jacques Rousseau, to whom you were introduced in Chapter 1. Rousseau believed that a natural outgrowth of the biological upheaval of puberty was heightened emotionality, conflict, and defiance of adults. Although Rousseau's impressions were not based on scientific evidence, they were nevertheless picked up and extended by twentieth-century theorists. The most influential was G. Stanley Hall, who described adolescence as a cascade of instinctual passions, a phase of growth so turbulent that it resembled the period in which human beings evolved from savages into civilized beings.

Were Rousseau and Hall correct in this image of adolescence as a biologically determined, inevitable period of storm and stress? Or do social and cultural factors combine with biological change to shape psychological development? In the course of our discussion, we will see what modern research has to say about this issue.

The Course of Physical Growth

ompared with other animals, primates (including humans) experience a prolonged period of physical growth. For example, among mice and rats, the time between birth and puberty is only a matter of weeks; it takes no more than 2 percent of the lifespan. In chimpanzees, who are closest to humans in the evolutionary hierarchy, growth is extended to about 7 years, or one-sixth of the lifespan. Physical immaturity is even more exaggerated in humans, who devote about one-fifth of their total years to growing.

Evolutionary reasons for this long period of physical growth are not hard to find. Because physical immaturity ensures that children remain dependent on adults, it provides added time for them to acquire the knowledge and skills necessary for life in a complex social world. In the words of anthropologist Weston LaBarre (1954), "Biologically, it takes more time to become human. Obviously, too, it is the human brain and human learning that gain particular advantages from this biological slow-down" (p. 153).

CHANGES IN BODY SIZE

To parents, the most obvious signs of physical growth are changes in the overall size of the child's body. During infancy, these changes are rapid—faster than they will be at any time after birth. By the end of the first year, the infant's height is 50 percent greater than it was at birth; by 2 years, it is 75 percent greater. Weight shows similar dramatic gains. By 5 months, birth weight has doubled, at 1 year it has tripled, and at 2 years it has quadrupled. In fact, if children kept growing at the rate they do during the early months of life, by age 10 they would be 10 feet tall and weigh over 200 pounds! Fortunately, growth slows in early and middle childhood. Children add about 2 to 3 inches in height and 5 pounds in weight each year. Then, puberty brings a sharp acceleration in rate of growth. On the average, adolescents add nearly 10 inches in height and about 40 pounds in weight to reach a mature body size.

Two types of growth curves are used to track these changes in height and weight. The first, shown in Figure 5.1, is a **distance curve,** which plots the average height

FIGURE 5.1

Height and weight distance curves for North American boys and girls, drawn from longitudinal measurements of approximately 175 individuals. (From R. M. Malina, 1975, *Growth and Development: The First Twenty Years in Man,* p. 19. Minneapolis: Burgess Publishing Company. Copyright © 1975 by Burgess Publishing Company. Adapted by permission.)

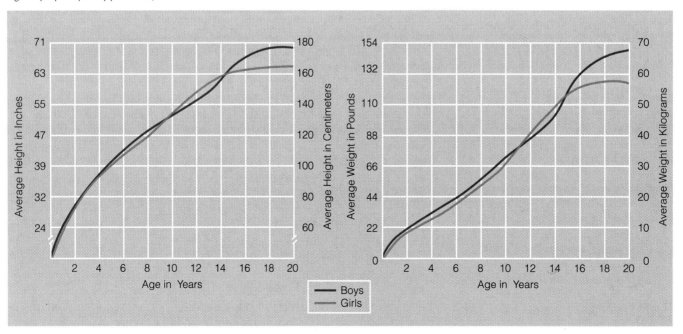

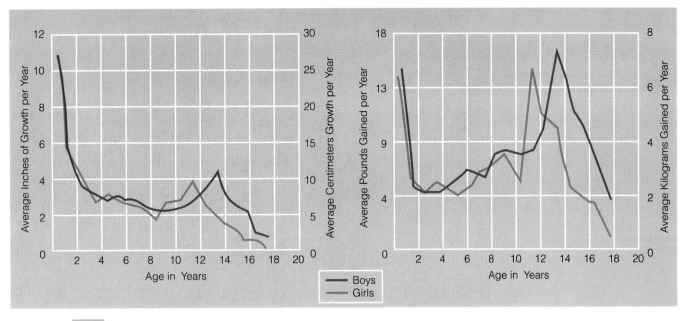

FIGURE 5.2

Height and weight velocity curves for North American boys and girls, drawn from longitudinal measurements on approximately 175 individuals.

(From R. M. Malina, 1975, *Growth and Development: The First Twenty Years in Man,* p. 20. Minneapolis: Burgess Publishing Company. Copyright © 1975 by Burgess Publishing Company. Adapted by permission.)

and weight of a sample of children at each age. It is called a distance curve because it indicates typical yearly progress toward mature body size. The group averages are referred to as *growth norms* and serve as useful standards to which individual children can be compared. Other information about growth can also be obtained from these curves. Notice how during infancy and childhood the two sexes are similar, with the typical girl just slightly shorter and lighter than the typical boy. Around age 11, the girl becomes taller and heavier for a time because her pubertal growth spurt takes place 2 years earlier than the boy's. But this advantage is short-lived. At age 14, she is surpassed by the typical boy, whose growth spurt has started, whereas hers is almost finished. Growth in height is complete for most North American and European girls by age 16, for boys by age 17½ (Tanner, 1990).

A second type of growth curve is the **velocity curve,** depicted in Figure 5.2. It plots the average amount of growth at each yearly interval. As a result, it reveals the exact timing of growth spurts. Note the rapid but decelerating growth in infancy; a slower, constant rate of growth during early and middle childhood; and a sharp increase in growth in early adolescence followed by a swift decrease as the body approaches its adult size.

Since these overall growth trends are derived from group averages, they are deceiving in one respect. Researchers who have carefully tracked height changes of individual children report that rather than steady gains, little growth spurts occur. In one investigation, infants followed over the first 21 months of life went for periods of 7 to 63 days with no growth and then added as much as a half-inch in a 24-hour period. Almost always, parents described their babies as irritable, restless, and very hungry on the day before the spurt (Lampl, 1993; Lampl, Veldhuis, & Johnson, 1992). A study of Scottish children, who were followed between ages 3 and 10, revealed similar but more widely spaced spurts in height. Girls tended to forge ahead at ages 4½, 6½, 8½, and 10, boys slightly later, at 4½, 7, 9, and 10½. Between these spurts were lulls in which growth was slower (Butler, McKie, & Ratcliffe, 1990).

CHANGES IN BODY PROPORTIONS

As the child's overall size increases, different parts of the body grow at different rates. Recall from Chapter 3 that during the prenatal period, the head develops first from the

distance curve A growth curve that plots the average height and weight of a sample of children at each age. Shows typical yearly progress toward mature body size.

velocity curve A growth curve that plots the average amount of growth at each yearly interval for a sample of children. Clarifies the timing of growth spurts.

Sex-related differences in pubertal growth are obvious among these fifth graders. Although all the children are 10 or 11 years old, the girls are taller and more mature looking. The growth spurt takes place, on the average, 2 years earlier for girls than boys. *(Bob Daemmrich/Stock Boston)*

primitive embryonic disk, followed by the lower part of the body. During infancy, the head and chest continue to have a growth advantage, but the trunk and legs gradually pick up speed. Do you recognize the familiar *cephalocaudal trend* we discussed in Chapter 4? You can see it depicted in Figure 5.3. Notice that the ratio of leg length to total height is less than 1:4 in the early prenatal period, increases to 1:3 at birth, and is 1:2 by adulthood. Physical growth during infancy and childhood also follows the *proximodistal trend*. It begins at the center of the body and moves outward, with the head, chest, and trunk growing first, followed by the arms and legs, and finally the hands and feet.

Exceptions to these basic growth trends occur during puberty, when growth proceeds in the reverse direction. At first, the hands, legs, and feet accelerate, and then the torso, which accounts for most of the adolescent height gain (Wheeler, 1991). This pattern of development explains why young adolescents stop growing out of their shoes and pants before they stop growing out of their jackets. It also helps us understand why early adolescents often appear awkward and out of proportion—long legged with giant feet and hands.

FIGURE 5.3

Changes in body proportions from the early prenatal period to adulthood. This figure illustrates the cephalocaudal trend of physical growth. The head gradually becomes smaller, and the legs longer, in proportion to the rest of the body.

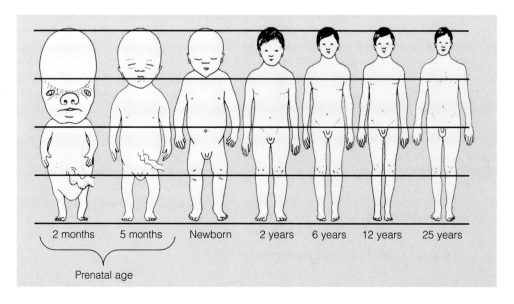

2 months   5 months   Newborn   2 years   6 years   12 years   25 years

Prenatal age

Although body proportions of girls and boys are similar in infancy and childhood, major differences that are typical of young adults appear during adolescence. The most obvious are the broadening of the shoulders relative to the hips in boys and the broadening of the hips relative to the shoulders and waist in girls. These differences are caused by the action of sex hormones on skeletal growth. Of course, boys also end up much larger than girls, and their legs are longer in relation to the rest of the body. The major reason is that boys benefit from 2 extra years of preadolescent growth, when the legs are growing the fastest (Tanner, 1990).

Body proportions and muscle–fat makeup change dramatically between 1 and 5 years. The top-heavy, chubby infant gradually becomes the longer-legged, slender young child.
(Bob Daemmrich/Stock Boston)

CHANGES IN BODY COMPOSITION

Major changes in the body's muscle–fat makeup take place with age. Body fat (most of which lies just beneath the skin) begins to increase in the last few weeks of prenatal life and continues to do so after birth, reaching a peak at about 9 months of age. This very early rise in "baby fat" helps the small infant keep a constant body temperature. Then, beginning in the second year, children become more slender, a trend that continues into middle childhood. At birth, girls have slightly more body fat than boys, a difference that becomes greater over the course of childhood. Around age 8, girls start to add more fat than do boys on their arms, legs, and trunk, and they do so throughout puberty. In contrast, the arm and leg fat of adolescent boys decreases (Tanner & Whitehouse, 1975).

Muscle grows according to a different pattern than fat, accumulating very slowly throughout infancy and childhood. Then it rises dramatically at adolescence. Although both sexes gain in muscle at puberty, the increase is much greater for boys, who develop larger skeletal muscles, hearts, and lung capacity. Also, the number of red blood cells, and therefore the ability to carry oxygen from the lungs to the muscles, increases in boys but not in girls (Beunen & Malina, 1996). Altogether, boys gain far more muscle strength than do girls, a difference that contributes to sex differences in motor development during the teenage years.

CHANGES IN GROSS MOTOR SKILLS

Visit a playground on a pleasant weekend afternoon and jot down preschool and school-age children's various physical activities. You will see that changes in body size, proportions, and muscle strength support an explosion of new gross motor skills.

As children's bodies become more streamlined and less top-heavy, their center of gravity shifts downward, toward the trunk. As a result, balance improves greatly, paving the way for new motor skills involving large muscles of the body. By age 2, preschoolers' gaits become smooth and rhythmic—secure enough that soon they leave the ground, at first by running and jumping and then, between 3 and 6 years, by hopping, galloping, and skipping. Eventually, upper and lower body skills combine into more effective actions (Getchell & Roberton, 1989). For example, at ages 2 and 3, children throw a ball rigidly, using only the arms. By ages 4 and 5, they involve the shoulders, torso, trunk, and legs (Roberton, 1984). They rotate the body and step forward as they throw, so the ball travels faster and farther.

Over the school years, improved balance, strength, agility, and flexibility support refinements in running, jumping, hopping, and ball skills. Children burst into sprints as they race across the playground, jump quickly over rotating ropes, engage in intricate patterns of hopscotch, kick and dribble soccer balls, and swing bats at balls pitched by their classmates. Increased body size and muscle at adolescence bring continued motor gains. Athletic options expand to include track and field, football, wrestling, weight lifting, floor hockey, archery, tennis, and golf, to name just a few. The Milestones table on page 178 summarizes gross motor achievements in early and middle childhood.

Gross Motor Development in Early and Middle Childhood

M I L E S T O N E S

Age	Gross Motor Skills
2–3 years	■ Walks more rhythmically; hurried walk changes to run. ■ Jumps, hops, throws, and catches with rigid upper body. ■ Pushes riding toy with feet; little steering.
3–4 years	■ Walks up stairs, alternating feet, and downstairs, leading with one foot. ■ Jumps and hops, flexing upper body. ■ Throws and catches with slight involvement of upper body; still catches by trapping ball against chest. ■ Pedals and steers tricycle.
4–5 years	■ Walks downstairs, alternating feet; runs more smoothly. ■ Gallops and skips with one foot. ■ Throws ball with increased body rotation and transfer of weight on feet; catches ball with hands. ■ Rides tricycle rapidly, steers smoothly.
5–6 years	■ Increases running speed to 12 feet per second. ■ Gallops more smoothly; engages in true skipping and sideways stepping. ■ Displays mature, whole-body throwing and catching pattern; increases throwing speed. ■ Rides bicycle with training wheels.
7–12 years	■ Increases running speed to more than 18 feet per second. ■ Displays continuous, fluid skipping and sideways stepping. ■ Increases vertical jump from 4 to 12 inches and broad jump from 3 to over 5 feet; accurately jumps and hops from square to square. ■ Increases throwing and kicking accuracy, distance, and speed. ■ Involves the whole body in batting a ball; batting increases in speed and accuracy. ■ Dribbling changes from awkward slapping of the ball to continuous, relaxed, even stroking.

Note: These milestones represent overall age trends. Individual differences exist in the precise age at which each milestone is attained.
Sources: Cratty, 1986; Furuno et al., 1987; Malina & Bouchard, 1991; Newborg, Stock, & Wnek, 1984; Roberton, 1984.

skeletal age An estimate of physical maturity based on development of the bones of the body.

epiphyses Growth centers in the bones where new cartilage cells are produced and gradually harden.

The same principle that governs motor development during the first 2 years continues to operate in childhood and adolescence. Children integrate previously acquired skills into more complex, *dynamic systems of action*. (Return to Chapter 4, page 146, to review this concept.) Then they revise each skill as their bodies become larger and stronger, their central nervous systems become better developed, their interests and goals become clearer, and their environments present new challenges. Sex-related differences in motor skills, present as early as the preschool years, illustrate these multiple influences. Although size and strength contribute to boys' superior athletic performance in adolescence, physical growth cannot fully account for boys' childhood advantage (Beunen & Malina, 1996). As the From Research to Practice box on page 180 reveals, the social environment plays a prominent role.

SKELETAL GROWTH

Children of the same age differ in *rate* of physical growth. As a result, researchers have devised methods for measuring progress toward physical maturity. These techniques are useful for studying the causes and consequences of individual differences in physical growth. They also provide rough estimates of children's chronological age in areas of the world where birth dates are not recorded.

■ **SKELETAL AGE.** The best way of estimating a child's physical maturity is to use **skeletal age,** a measure of development of the bones of the body. The embryonic skeleton is first formed out of soft, pliable tissue called *cartilage.* Then, beginning in the sixth week of pregnancy, cartilage cells harden into bone, a gradual process that continues throughout childhood and adolescence.

Once bones have taken on their basic shape, special growth centers called **epiphyses** appear just before birth and increase throughout childhood. In the long bones of the body, epiphyses emerge at the two extreme ends of each bone (see Figure 5.4). As growth continues, the epiphyses get thinner and disappear. Once this occurs, no more growth in bone length is possible. As Figure 5.5 shows, skeletal age can be estimated by X-raying the bones and seeing how many epiphyses there are and the extent to which they are fused. These X-rays are compared with norms for bone maturity based on large representative samples of children (Malina & Bouchard, 1991).

When the skeletal ages of infants and children are examined, African-American children tend to be slightly ahead of Caucasian-American children at all ages. In addition, girls are considerably ahead of boys. At birth, the difference between the sexes amounts to about 4 to 6 weeks, a gap that widens over infancy and childhood and is responsible for the fact that girls reach their full body size several years before boys. Girls are advanced in development of other organs as well. Their greater physical maturity may

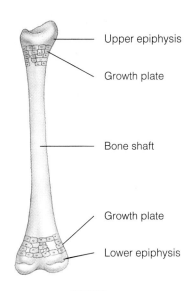

FIGURE 5.4

Diagram of a long bone showing upper and lower epiphyses. Cartilage cells are produced at the growth plates and gradually harden into bone.

(From J. M. Tanner, 1990, *Foetus into Man* (2nd ed.), Cambridge, MA: Harvard University Press, p. 32. Copyright © 1990 by J. M. Tanner. All rights reserved. Reprinted by permission of the publisher and author.)

FIGURE 5.5

X-rays of a girl's hand, showing skeletal maturity at three ages. Notice how, at age 2½, wide gaps exist between the wrist bones and at the ends of the finger and arm bones. By age 6½, these have filled in considerably. At age 14½ (when this girl reached her adult size), the wrist and long bones are completely fused.

(From J. M. Tanner, R. H. Whitehouse, N. Cameron, W. A. Marshall, M. J. R. Healy, & H. Goldstein, 1983, *Assessment of Skeletal Maturity and Prediction of Adult Height [TW2 Method]*, 2nd ed., Academic Press [London, Ltd.], p. 86. Reprinted by permission.)

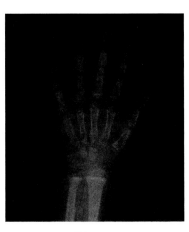

2½ years

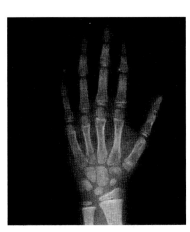

6½ years

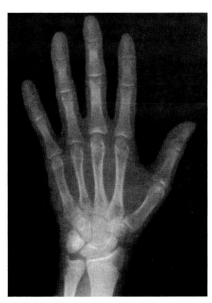

14½ years

Sex-Related Differences in Gross Motor Development

FROM RESEARCH TO PRACTICE

SEX-RELATED DIFFERENCES in gross motor development are present as early as the preschool years, increase during middle childhood, and are large at adolescence. What underlies this expanding gender gap, and how can we ensure that both boys and girls are granted opportunities that optimize skill and enjoyment of athletics?

EARLY AND MIDDLE CHILDHOOD. In early childhood, boys are slightly advanced over girls in abilities that emphasize force and power. By age 5, they can broad jump a little farther, run a little faster, and throw a ball much farther (about 5 feet beyond the distance covered by girls). Girls have an edge in certain gross motor capacities that require a combination of good balance and foot movement, such as hopping and skipping. During middle childhood, these differences intensify. For example, a ball thrown by a 12-year-old boy travels, on the average, 43 feet farther than one thrown by a 12-year-old girl. Boys are also more adept at batting, kicking, dribbling, and catching (Cratty, 1986; Fischman, Moore, & Steele, 1992; Roberton, 1984).

Girls are ahead of boys in overall physical maturity, which may be partly responsible for their better balance and precision of movement. Boys' slightly greater muscle mass and (in the case of throwing) longer forearms probably contribute to their skill advantages. But sex-related differences in physical growth during childhood are not large enough to explain boys' superiority in so many gross motor capacities. Instead, adult encouragement and example are powerfully influential. From an early age, footballs, baseballs, and bats are purchased for boys; jump ropes, hula hoops, and skates for girls. And despite improved media attention to women's athletics, most players in public sports events continue to be men (Coakley, 1990; Greendorfer, Lewko, & Rosengren, 1996).

A study of more than 800 elementary school pupils found that parents hold higher expectations for boys' athletic performance, and children absorb these social messages at an early age. Kindergartners through third graders of both sexes viewed sports in a gender-stereotyped fashion—as much more important for boys. Boys were also more likely to indicate that it was important to their parents that they participate in athletics. These attitudes affected children's self-confidence and behavior. Girls saw themselves as having

Parental encouragement of girls' athletic skills and belief in their ability to excel promotes self-confidence, effort, and involvement in sports activities. As this 9-year-old becomes accomplished at handling a bat and ball, she will also learn much about competition, assertiveness, problem solving, and teamwork.
(Elizabeth Crews)

less talent at sports, and by sixth grade they devoted less time to athletics than did their male classmates (Eccles & Harold, 1991; Eccles, Jacobs, & Harold, 1990).

ADOLESCENCE. Not until puberty do sharp sex-related differences in physical size and muscle strength account for large differences in athletic ability. During adolescence, girls' gains in gross motor performance are slow and gradual, leveling off by age 14. In contrast, boys show a dramatic spurt in strength, speed, and endurance that continues through the end of the teenage years. Consequently, the gender gap widens over time. By midadolescence, very few girls perform as well as the average boy in such skills as running speed, broad jump, and throwing distance. And practically no boys score as low as the average girl (Malina & Bouchard, 1991).

That the sexes are no longer evenly matched physically may heighten differential encouragement during the teenage years. Although competence at sports is strongly related to peer admiration among adolescent boys, it is far

---

contribute to the fact that they are more resistant to harmful environmental influences. As we pointed out in Chapter 3, girls experience fewer developmental problems than do boys, and infant and childhood mortality for girls is also lower (Tanner, 1990).

■ **GROWTH OF THE SKULL.** Pediatricians routinely measure children's head circumference between birth and 2 years of age. Skull growth is especially rapid during the first 2 years because of large increases in brain size. At birth, the bones of the skull are separated by six gaps, or "soft spots," called **fontanels** (see Figure 5.7 on page 182). The gaps permit the bones to overlap as the large head of the baby passes through the mother's narrow birth canal. You can easily feel the largest gap, the anterior fontanel, at the top of

fontanels Six soft spots that separate the bones of the skull at birth.

less important to girls. In 1972, the federal government required schools receiving public funds to provide equal opportunities for males and females in all educational programs, including athletics. As Figure 5.6 shows, high school girls' sports participation quadrupled during the following decade and has continued to increase, although it still falls far short of boys'.

The sex differences just described also characterize physical activity rates of American adolescents. Overall, 73 percent of high school boys but only 54 percent of girls report regular vigorous physical activity (at least 20 minutes, 3 days a week). The number of boys engaging in regular exercise increases from ninth to twelfth grade. In contrast, about 15 percent of girls who were physically active in ninth grade are no longer exercising regularly by grade 12 (U.S. Department of Health and Human Services, 1998c). A sharp drop in girls' enrollment in physical education over the high school years contributes to this trend.

INTERVENTIONS. Sports do not just improve motor performance. They influence cognitive and social development as well. Interschool and intramural athletics provide important lessons in competition, assertiveness, problem solving, and teamwork—experiences less available to girls (Newcombe & Boyle, 1995). And regular physical activity has many health benefits, including enhanced functioning of the immune system, cardiovascular fitness, and psychological well-being.

Clearly, steps need to be taken to raise girls' confidence that they can do well at athletics. Educating parents about the minimal differences in school-age boys' and girls' physical capacities and sensitizing them to unfair biases against girls' athletic ability may prove helpful. In addition, greater emphasis on skill training, along with increased attention to the athletic achievements of girls, is likely to improve their participation and performance. Finally, required daily physical education in school, aimed at helping children and adolescents find pleasure in sports and exercise, is particularly beneficial for girls, many of whom have not developed other routes to regular exercise and sports involvement.

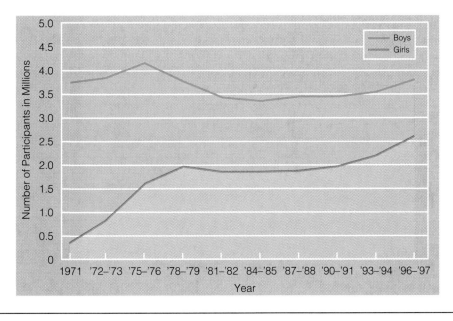

FIGURE 5.6

High school sports participation trends in the United States, 1971–1997. A legal mandate for equality of opportunity in school athletic participation led girls' involvement in sports to increase dramatically from the early 1970s to 1980. Since then, girls' participation has continued to rise gradually, although it still falls far short of boys'.
(From National Federation of State High School Associations, 1997.)

a baby's skull. It is slightly more than an inch across. It gradually shrinks and is filled in during the second year. The other fontanels are smaller and close more quickly. As the skull bones come in contact with one another, they form *sutures*, or seams. These permit the skull to expand easily as the brain grows. The sutures disappear completely after puberty, when skull growth is complete.

HORMONAL INFLUENCES ON PHYSICAL GROWTH

The vast physical changes of childhood and adolescence are controlled by the endocrine glands of the body. These glands manufacture *hormones*, chemical substances secreted by

FIGURE 5.7

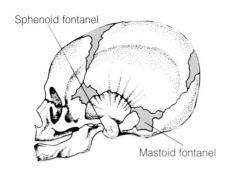
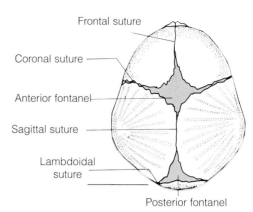

The skull at birth, showing the fontanels and sutures. The fontanels gradually close during the first 2 years, forming sutures that permit the skull to expand easily as the brain grows.

(From P. M. Hill & P. Humphrey, 1982, *Human Growth and Development Throughout Life, A Nursing Perspective,* Delmar Publishers, Inc., p. 42. Copyright 1982. Reprinted by permission.)

specialized cells in one part of the body that pass to and influence cells in another. Because receptors in our cells respond to some hormones and not others, the action of each hormone is unique.

The most important hormones for human growth are released by the **pituitary gland,** located at the base of the brain near the **hypothalamus,** a structure that initiates and regulates pituitary secretions (see Figure 5.8). Once pituitary hormones enter the bloodstream, they act directly on body tissues to induce growth, or they stimulate the release of other hormones from endocrine glands located elsewhere in the body. The hypothalamus contains special receptors that detect hormone levels in the bloodstream. Through a highly sensitive feedback loop, it instructs the pituitary gland to increase or decrease the amount of each hormone. In this way, growth is carefully controlled. You may find it useful to refer to Figure 5.9 as we review major hormonal influences.

Growth hormone (GH) is the only pituitary secretion produced continuously throughout life. It affects the development of all body tissues except the central nervous system and the genitals. GH acts directly on body tissues but also accomplishes its task with the help of an intermediary. It stimulates the liver and epiphyses of the skeleton to release another hormone called *somatomedin,* which triggers cell duplication in the bones. Although GH does not seem to affect prenatal growth, it is necessary for physical development from birth on. Children who lack it reach an average mature height of only 4 feet, 4 inches. When treated with injections of GH, such children grow faster than expected (a phenomenon called *catch-up growth,* discussed later in this chapter) and then grow at a normal rate (Tanner, 1990). Reaching their genetically expected height, however, depends on starting treatment early, before the epiphyses of the skeleton are very mature.

FIGURE 5.8

Cross section of the human brain, showing the location of the hypothalamus and pituitary gland. Also shown are three additional structures—the cerebellum, the reticular formation, and the corpus callosum—that we will discuss in a later section.

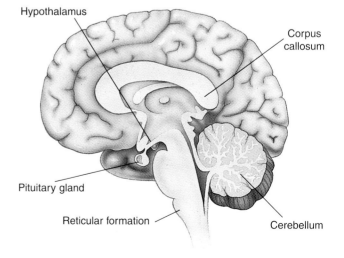

pituitary gland A gland located near the base of the brain that releases hormones affecting physical growth.

hypothalamus A structure located at the base of the brain that initiates and regulates pituitary secretions.

growth hormone (GH) A pituitary hormone that affects the development of all body tissues except the central nervous system and the genitals.

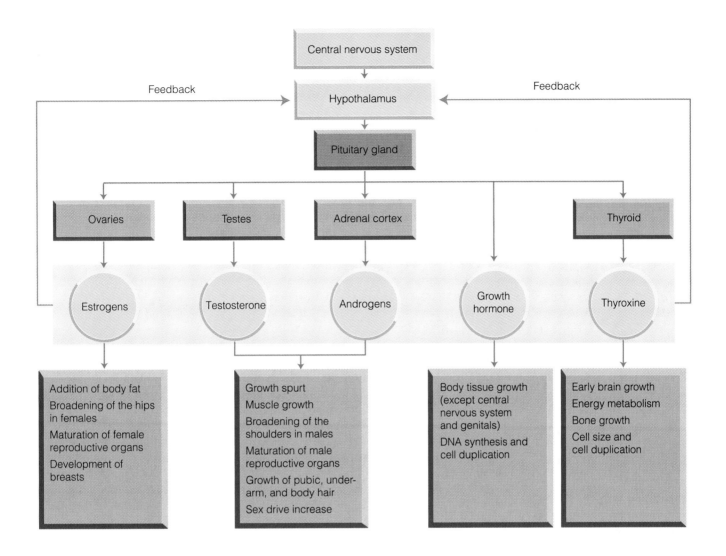

FIGURE 5.9

Hormonal influences on postnatal growth. The hypothalamus stimulates the pituitary gland to release hormones that either induce growth directly or stimulate other endocrine glands to release growth-inducing hormones (red lines). A highly sensitive feedback loop exists in which the hypothalamus detects hormone levels in the bloodstream and instructs the pituitary gland to increase or decrease the amount of each hormone accordingly (blue lines).

Together, the hypothalamus and pituitary gland also prompt the thyroid gland (located in the neck) to release **thyroxine,** which is necessary for normal development of the nerve cells of the brain and for GH to have its full impact on body size. Infants born with a deficiency of thyroxine must receive it at once, or they will be mentally retarded. At later ages, children with too little thyroxine grow at a below-average rate. However, the central nervous system is no longer affected, since the most rapid period of brain development is complete. With prompt treatment, such children catch up in body growth and eventually reach normal size (Tanner, 1990).

Sexual maturation is controlled by pituitary secretions that stimulate the release of sex hormones. Although **estrogens** are thought of as female hormones and **androgens** as male hormones, both types are present in each sex, but in different amounts. The boy's testes release large quantities of the androgen *testosterone*, which leads to muscle growth, body and facial hair, and other male sex characteristics. Testosterone also contributes to gains in body size. The testes secrete small amounts of estrogen as well—the reason that 50 percent of adolescent boys experience temporary breast enlargement (Larson, 1996).

thyroxine A hormone released by the thyroid gland that is necessary for central nervous system development and body growth.

estrogens Hormones produced chiefly by the ovaries that cause the breasts, uterus, and vagina to mature and the body to take on feminine proportions during puberty.

androgens Hormones produced chiefly by the testes, and in smaller quantities by the adrenal glands, that influence the pubertal growth spurt, the appearance of body hair, and male sex characteristics.

Body size is sometimes the result of evolutionary adaptations to a particular climate. These nomadic boys of Niger in west-central Africa, who live in a hot, tropical region of the world, have long, lean physiques, which permit the body to cool easily.
(Victor Englebert/Photo Researchers, Inc.)

Estrogens released by the girl's ovaries cause the breasts, uterus, and vagina to mature and the body to take on feminine proportions. In addition, estrogens contribute to regulation of the menstrual cycle. Girls' changing bodies are also affected by the release of androgens from the adrenal glands, located on top of each kidney. *Adrenal androgens* influence the girl's height spurt and stimulate growth of underarm and pubic hair. They have little impact on boys, whose physical characteristics are influenced mainly by androgen secretions from the testes.

WORLDWIDE VARIATIONS IN BODY SIZE

Observe a group of same-age children, and you will see that they differ greatly in physical growth. Diversity in body size is especially apparent when we travel to different nations. Measurements of 8-year-olds living in many parts of the world reveal a 9-inch gap between the smallest and largest youngsters. The shortest children tend to be found in South America, Asia, the Pacific Islands, and parts of Africa and include such ethnic groups as Colombian, Burmese, Thai, Vietnamese, Ethiopian, and Bantu. The tallest children reside in Australia, northern and central Europe, and the United States and consist of Czech, Dutch, Latvian, Norwegian, Swiss, and American black and white children (Meredith, 1978).

Ethnic variations in rate of growth are also common. For example, African-American and Asian children tend to mature faster than North American Caucasian children, who are slightly advanced over European children (Berkey et al., 1994; Eveleth & Tanner, 1990). These findings remind us that growth norms must be interpreted cautiously, especially in countries like the United States, where many ethnic groups are represented.

What accounts for these vast differences in body size and rate of growth? As we will soon see in greater detail, both heredity and environment are involved. Body size is sometimes the result of evolutionary adaptations to a particular climate. For example, long, lean physiques are typical in hot, tropical regions and short, stocky ones in cold, Arctic areas. At the same time, children who grow tallest usually reside in developed countries, where food is plentiful and infectious diseases are largely controlled. In contrast, small children tend to live in less developed regions, where poverty, hunger, and disease are common (Tanner, 1990).

SECULAR TRENDS

Over the past century, **secular trends in physical growth**—changes in body size and rate of growth from one generation to the next—have taken place in industrialized nations. Most children today are taller and heavier than their parents and grandparents were as children. These trends have been found in nearly all European nations, in Japan, and among black and white children in the United States. The difference appears early in life and becomes greater over childhood and early adolescence. Then, as mature body size is reached, it declines. This pattern suggests that the larger size of modern children is mostly due to a faster rate of physical maturation. This speeding up of physical growth is especially apparent in age of first menstruation in girls. As Figure 5.10 shows, it declined steadily from 1860 to 1970, by about 3 to 4 months per decade.

Biologists believe that improved nutrition and health are largely responsible for these secular gains. As evidence for these influences, orphaned babies from developing countries who are adopted by American parents often show faster physical growth and reach greater mature stature than do infants remaining in

FIGURE 5.10

Secular trend in age of first menstruation (menarche) from 1860 to 1970 in industrialized nations. Data for Norway, which extend to 1980, suggest that secular change has recently leveled off.

(From J. M. Tanner, 1990, *Foetus into Man* (2nd ed.), Cambridge, MA: Harvard University Press, p. 160. Copyright © 1990 by J. M. Tanner. All rights reserved. Reprinted by permission of the publisher and author.)

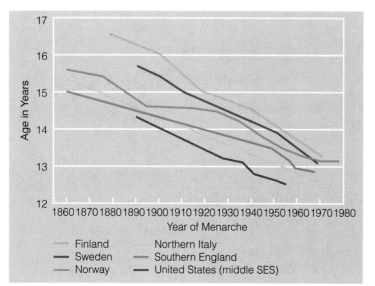

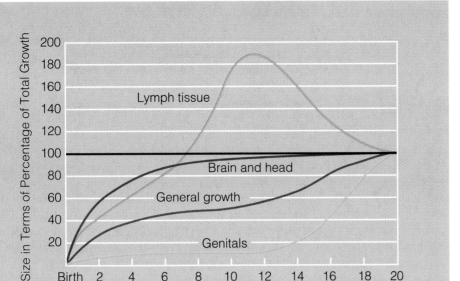

FIGURE

Growth of three different organ systems and tissues contrasted with the body's general growth.
Growth is plotted in terms of percentage of change from birth to 20 years. Notice how the lymph tissue rises to twice its adult level by the end of childhood. Then it declines.

(Reprinted by permission of the publisher from J. M. Tanner, 1990, *Foetus into Man*, 2nd ed., Cambridge, MA: Harvard University Press, p. 16. Copyright © 1990 by J. M. Tanner. All rights reserved.)

the land of origin. Also, secular trends are not as large for low-income children, who have poorer diets and are more likely to suffer from growth-stunting illnesses. And in regions of the world where poverty, famine, and disease are widespread, either no secular change or a secular decrease in body size has occurred (Barnes-Josiah & Augustin, 1995; Proos, 1993).

Of course, humans cannot keep growing larger and maturing earlier indefinitely, since we cannot exceed the genetic limitations of our species. Secular gains have slowed or stopped entirely in some developed countries, such as Canada, Great Britain, Japan, Norway, Sweden, and the United States (McAnarney et al., 1992; Roche, 1979). Consequently, modern children reared under good nutritional and social conditions are likely to resemble their parents in physical growth more than at any time during the previous 130 years.

ASYNCHRONIES IN PHYSICAL GROWTH

From what you have learned so far, can you come up with a single overall description of physical growth? If you found yourself answering no to this question, you are correct. Figure 5.11 shows that physical growth is an *asynchronous* process. Different body systems have their own unique, carefully timed patterns of maturation.

Notice the **general growth curve,** which describes changes in overall body size as measured by height and weight. It takes its name from the fact that outer dimensions of the body, as well as a variety of internal organs, follow the same pattern—rapid growth during infancy, slower gains in early and middle childhood, and rapid growth again during adolescence.

Figure 5.11 also depicts some important exceptions to this trend. The genitals develop slowly from birth to age 4, change little throughout middle childhood, and then grow rapidly during adolescence. In contrast, the lymph tissue (small clusters of glands found throughout the body) grows at an astounding pace in infancy and childhood, but its growth declines in adolescence. The lymph system fights infection and assists in the absorption of nutrients, thereby supporting children's health and survival (Malina & Bouchard, 1991).

Another growth trend is illustrated in Figure 5.11. During the first few years, the brain grows faster than any other body structure, exceeding even the lymph tissue. Let's take a closer look at brain development.

secular trends in physical growth Changes in body size and rate of growth from one generation to the next.

general growth curve Curve that represents changes in overall body size—rapid growth during infancy, slower gains in early and middle childhood, and rapid growth once more during adolescence.

Compared with other mammals, human beings experience a prolonged period of physical growth in which changes in body size take place rapidly in infancy, slowly during childhood, and rapidly again at adolescence. Physical development during infancy and childhood follows the cephalocaudal and proximodistal trends. Changes in body proportions and muscle–fat makeup that contribute to sex differences in athletic skill occur at adolescence. Skeletal age is the best indicator of progress toward physical maturity: At birth, girls are advanced over boys, a gap that widens with age. Girls' pubertal growth spurt takes place, on the average, 2 years earlier than boys'. Body growth is controlled by a complex set of hormonal secretions released by the pituitary gland and regulated by the hypothalamus.

Worldwide variations in body size and rate of maturation are influenced by both heredity and environment. Over the past century, secular trends in physical growth have occurred. Children in industrialized nations are growing larger and reaching maturity earlier than they did in previous generations. Physical growth is an asynchronous process. Different body systems follow unique, carefully timed patterns of maturation.

ASK YOURSELF . . .

◆ Explain why boys' childhood advantage over girls in throwing, batting, kicking, dribbling, and catching cannot be accounted for, except in small measure, by sex-related differences in physical growth.

◆ When Joey was born, the doctor found that his anterior fontanel had started to close prematurely. Joey had surgery to open the fontanel when he was 3 months old. From what you know about the function of the fontanels, why was early surgery necessary?

◆ CONNECTIONS
What do secular trends in physical growth and cohort effects, discussed on page 60 of Chapter 2, have in common? Why would a researcher engaged in a longitudinal or cross-sectional study of physical growth need to be concerned about cohort effects?

Development of the Brain

The human brain is the most elaborate and effective living structure on earth today. Despite its complexity, the brain reaches its adult size earlier than any other organ. To best understand brain growth, we need to look at it from two vantage points: (1) the microscopic level of individual brain cells, and (2) the larger level of the cerebral cortex, the most complex brain structure and the one responsible for the highly developed intelligence of our species.

DEVELOPMENT OF NEURONS

The human brain has 100 to 200 billion **neurons,** or nerve cells, that store and transmit information, many of which have thousands of direct connections with other neurons. Neurons differ from other body cells in that they are not tightly packed together. There are tiny gaps, or **synapses,** between them where fibers from different neurons come close together but do not touch. Neurons release chemicals that cross the synapse, thereby sending messages to one another.

The basic story of brain growth concerns how neurons develop and form this elaborate communication system. Each neuron passes through three developmental steps: (1) cell production, (2) cell migration, and (3) cell differentiation. Recall from Chapter 3 that neurons are produced in the primitive neural tube of the embryo. From there, they migrate to form the major parts of the brain, traveling along threads produced by a special network of guiding cells. By the end of the second trimester of pregnancy, production of neurons is largely complete.

Once neurons are in place, they begin to differentiate, establishing their unique functions by extending their fibers to form synaptic connections with neighboring cells. Because developing neurons require space for these connective structures, a surprising aspect of brain growth is that many surrounding neurons die when synapses are formed. Consequently, the peak period of development in any brain area is also marked by the greatest rate of **programmed cell death** (Huttenlocher, 1994). Fortunately, during embryonic growth, the neural tube produces an excess of neurons—far more than the brain will ever need.

As neurons form connections, a new factor becomes important in their survival: *stimulation.* Neurons that are stimulated by input from the surrounding environment continue to establish new synapses, forming increasingly elaborate systems of communication that lead to more complex cortical functions. Neurons seldom stimulated soon lose

neurons Nerve cells that store and transmit information in the brain.

synapses The gap between neurons, across which chemical messages are sent.

programmed cell death Death of many surrounding neurons during the peak period of development in any brain area to make room for growth of neural fibers that form synaptic connections.

their synapses, a process called **synaptic pruning.** Initially, stimulation leads to an overabundance of synapses, many of which serve identical functions, thereby helping to ensure that the child will acquire certain abilities. Synaptic pruning returns neurons not needed at the moment to an uncommitted state so they can support the development of future skills (Huttenlocher, 1994; Johnson, 1998). Notice how, for this process to go forward, appropriate stimulation of the child's brain is vital during periods in which the formation of synapses is at its peak (Greenough et al., 1993).

Perhaps you are wondering, If no more neurons are produced after the prenatal period, what causes the dramatic increase in skull size we mentioned earlier in this chapter? Growth of neural fibers results in some increase in brain weight, but not as much as a second type of cell in the brain. About half the brain's volume is made up of **glial cells,** which do not carry messages. Instead, their most important function is **myelinization,** a process in which neural fibers are coated with an insulating fatty sheath (called *myelin*) that improves the efficiency of message transfer. Glial cells multiply at a dramatic pace from the fourth month of pregnancy through the second year of life, after which their rate of production slows down (Casaer, 1993). Myelinization is responsible for the rapid gain in overall size of the brain. At birth, the brain is nearly 30 percent of its adult weight; by age 2, it is 70 percent, and at 6 years, 90 percent (Thatcher et al., 1996).

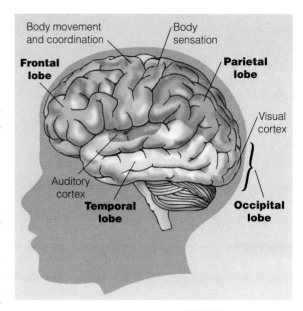

FIGURE 5.12

The left side of the human brain, showing the cerebral cortex. The cortex is divided into different lobes, each of which contains a variety of regions with specific functions. Some major ones are labeled here.

DEVELOPMENT OF THE CEREBRAL CORTEX

The **cerebral cortex** surrounds the rest of the brain, much like a half-shelled walnut. It is the largest structure of the human brain (accounting for 85 percent of brain weight and containing the greatest number of neurons and synapses) and the one responsible for the unique intelligence of our species. The cerebral cortex is also the last brain structure to stop growing. For this reason, it is believed to be much more sensitive to environmental influences than any other part of the brain.

■ **REGIONS OF THE CORTEX.** As Figure 5.12 shows, different regions of the cerebral cortex have specific functions, such as receiving information from the senses, instructing the body to move, and thinking. To study the development of these regions, researchers examine age-related changes in brain activity, using such procedures as the EEG, ERP, or fMRI (see Chapter 2, pages 49–50). In addition, they analyze the chemical makeup and myelinization of the brains of young children who have died.

Findings reveal that the order in which areas of the cortex develop corresponds to the sequence in which various capacities emerge during infancy and childhood. For example, a burst of synaptic growth and myelinization in the auditory and visual cortexes (refer to Figure 5.12) occurs around 3 to 4 months, continuing until the end of the first year—a period of dramatic gains in auditory and visual perception (see Chapter 4) (Johnson, 1998). Among areas responsible for body movement, neurons that control the head, arms, and chest form elaborate connections ahead of those that control the trunk and legs. (Do you recognize a familiar developmental trend?) Language areas of the cortex develop quickly from late infancy into the preschool years, when young children acquire language (Thatcher, 1991).

One of the last regions of the cortex to develop synaptic connections and myelinate are the *frontal lobes,* which are responsible for thought—in particular, consciousness, inhibition of impulses, and regulation of behavior through planning. From age 2 onward, this area functions more effectively, and it continues its growth for years, well into the second and third decades of life (Fischer & Rose, 1994, 1995; Johnson, 1998).

■ **LATERALIZATION OF THE CORTEX.** Figure 5.12 shows only one *hemisphere,* or side, of the cortex. The brain has two hemispheres—left and right. Although they look

synaptic pruning Loss of connective fibers by seldom-stimulated neurons, thereby returning them to an uncommitted state so they can support the development of future skills.

glial cells Cells responsible for myelinization of neural fibers.

myelinization A process in which neural fibers are coated with an insulating fatty sheath (called myelin) that improves the efficiency of message transfer.

cerebral cortex The largest structure of the human brain; accounts for the highly developed intelligence of the human species.

alike, the hemispheres do not have precisely the same functions. Some tasks are done mostly by one and some by the other. For example, each hemisphere receives sensory information from and controls only one side of the body—the one opposite to it.[1] For most of us, the left hemisphere is largely responsible for verbal abilities (such as spoken and written language) and positive emotion (for example, joy), whereas the right hemisphere handles spatial abilities (judging distances, reading maps, and recognizing geometric shapes) and negative emotion (such as distress). This pattern may be reversed in left-handed people, but more often, the cortex of left-handers is less clearly specialized than that of right-handers.

Specialization of the two hemispheres is called **lateralization.** Why are behaviors and abilities lateralized as just described? According to one view, the left hemisphere is better at processing information in a sequential, analytic (piece-by-piece) way, which is a good approach for dealing with communicative information—both verbal (lan-guage) and emotional (a joyful smile). In contrast, the right hemisphere is specialized for processing information in a holistic, integrative manner, ideal for making sense of spatial information and regulating negative emotion (Banish, 1998; Banish & Heller, 1998). A lateralized brain is certainly adaptive. It permits a wider array of functions to be carried out effectively than if both sides processed information exactly the same way.

BRAIN PLASTICITY. Few topics in child development have stimulated more interest than the question of when brain lateralization occurs. Researchers are interested in this issue because they want to know more about **brain plasticity.** A highly *plastic* cortex is still adaptable because many areas are not yet committed to specific functions. If a part of the brain is damaged, other parts can take over tasks that would have been handled by the damaged region. But once the hemispheres lateralize, damage to a particular region means that the abilities controlled by it will be lost forever.

Researchers used to think that lateralization of the cortex did not begin until after 2 years of age (Lenneberg, 1967). Today we know that hemispheric specialization is already under way at birth. For example, the majority of neonates favor the right side of the body in their reflexive responses (Grattan et al., 1992). And like adults, most infants show greater electrical activity in the left hemisphere while listening to speech sounds and displaying positive emotion. In contrast, the right hemisphere reacts more strongly to non-speech sounds as well as stimuli (such as a sour-tasting fluid) that cause infants to display negative emotion (Davidson, 1994; Fox & Davidson, 1986).

Specialization of brain regions begins early in life but is far from complete, as the development of brain-injured children reveals. Research on preterm babies with brain hemorrhages offers dramatic evidence for early plasticity. Although hemorrhaging damaged the brain, it was a poor predictor of mental and motor development at 2 years of age (Sostek et al., 1987). Similarly, in a large sample of preschool children with a wide variety of brain injuries sustained early in the first year of life, language and spatial deficits were milder than those observed in brain-injured adults. And by age 5, cognitive impairments had largely disappeared (Stiles et al., 1999). As brain-injured children gained perceptual, cognitive, and motor experiences, other stimulated cortical structures compensated for the damaged areas, regardless of the site of injury.

Another illustration of how early experience molds brain organization comes from studies of deaf adults who had been deprived of any spoken language since birth but, instead, learned to communicate visually and manually through signing. Electrical activity of brain regions revealed that compared with their hearing counterparts, these individuals depended more on the right hemisphere for language processing (Mills, Coffey-Corina, & Neville, 1994). Furthermore, 20-month-olds advanced in vocabulary development show greater left-hemispheric specialization for language than do their more slowly developing agemates, who rely on both hemispheres. Apparently, the very process of acquiring spoken language promotes lateralization (Mills, Coffey-Corina, & Neville, 1993, 1997).

lateralization *Specialization of functions of the two hemispheres of the cortex.*

brain plasticity *The ability of other parts of the brain to take over functions of damaged regions.*

[1]The eyes are an exception. Messages from the right half of each retina go to the left hemisphere; messages from the left half of each retina go to the right hemisphere. Therefore, visual information from *both* eyes is received by *both* hemispheres.

In sum, during the first few years, the brain is more plastic than at any later time in life, perhaps because many of its synapses have not yet been established. Although the cortex is programmed from the start for hemispheric specialization, the rate and success of this genetic program are greatly influenced by experience (Stiles, 1998). Around age 8 to 10, lateralization is largely complete. Neuroimaging studies reveal adultlike patterns of cortical activity in response to stimulation. And older children have only a limited capacity to recover functions following brain injury (Chugani, 1994; Johnson, 1998).

LATERALIZATION AND HANDEDNESS. A growing literature on the development of handedness is also providing new insights into the joint contributions of nature and nurture to brain lateralization. A strong hand preference reflects the greater capacity of one side of the brain—often referred to as the individual's **dominant cerebral hemisphere**—to carry out skilled motor action. Other abilities located on the dominant side may be superior as well. In support of this idea, for right-handed people, who make up 90 percent of the population in Western nations, language is housed with hand control in the left hemisphere. For the remaining 10 percent who are left-handed, language is often shared between the hemispheres rather than located in only one. This indicates that the brains of left-handers tend to be less strongly lateralized than those of right-handers (Dean & Anderson, 1997). Consistent with this idea, many left-handed individuals are also ambidextrous. That is, although they prefer their left hand, they sometimes use their right hand skillfully as well (McManus et al., 1988).

Is handedness hereditary? Although researchers disagree on this issue, certain findings argue against a genetic explanation. Twins—whether identical or fraternal—are more likely than ordinary siblings to display opposite handedness, yet we would expect identical twins to be more alike if heredity played a powerful role. Furthermore, the hand preference of each twin is related to positioning in the uterus (twins usually lie in opposite orientations) (Derom et al., 1996). According to one theory, cerebral dominance can be traced to prenatal events. The way most fetuses lie—turned toward the left—may promote greater postural control by the right side of the body (Previc, 1991).

A second idea is that practice heavily affects hand preference. In support of this view, strength of hand preference varies from one activity to the next. It is strongest for complex skills requiring considerable training, such as eating with utensils, writing, and various athletic skills. Although most societies discourage left-handedness and provide a strongly right-hand–biased environment, wide cultural variation in the percentage of left-handers exists. For example, in Tanzania, Africa, children are physically restrained and punished for favoring the left hand. Less than 1 percent of the Tanzanian population is left-handed (Provins, 1997).

Hand preference shows up early in development—by 5 or 6 months of age (McCormick & Maurer, 1988). However, it is not stable until around 2 years, and some intriguing research suggests why. Handedness seems to undergo dips and recoveries that coincide with bursts in language competence. When language forges ahead at a quick pace, it places extra demands on the left hemisphere, resulting in a temporary loss in motor dominance that returns as each new skill—at first babbling, then first words, and finally combining words—becomes well established (Ramsay, 1985; Ramsay & McCune, 1984). Then, in early and middle childhood, hand preference increases, indicating that specialization of brain regions strengthens during this time (Brito et al., 1992).

What about left-handed children, whose hand preference suggests an unusual organization of brain functions? Do these youngsters develop normally? Perhaps you have heard that left- or mixed-handedness is more frequent among severely retarded and mentally ill people than it is in the general population. Although this is true, you also know that when two variables are correlated, this does not mean that one causes the other. Atypical lateralization is probably not responsible for the problems of these individuals. Instead,

Twins typically lie in the uterus in opposite orientations during the prenatal period, which may explain why they are more often opposite-handed than are ordinary siblings. Although left-handedness is associated with developmental problems, the large majority of left-handed children are completely normal.
(Laura Dwight)

dominant cerebral hemisphere The hemisphere of the brain responsible for skilled motor action. The left hemisphere is dominant in right-handed individuals. In left-handed individuals, the right hemisphere may be dominant, or motor and language skills may be shared between the hemispheres.

they may have suffered early brain damage to the left hemisphere, which caused their disabilities and, at the same time, led to a shift in handedness. In support of this idea, left-handedness is associated with prenatal and birth difficulties that can result in brain damage, including prolonged labor, prematurity, Rh incompatibility, and breech delivery (O'Callaghan et al., 1993; Powls et al., 1996). In cases of mixed-handedness, individuals with severe mental disabilities may have been less able to profit from early experiences that foster lateralization of motor, language, and other skills (Provins, 1997).

Keep in mind, however, that only a small number of left-handers show developmental problems of any kind. In fact, unusual lateralization may have certain advantages. Left- and mixed-handed youngsters are more likely than their right-handed agemates to develop outstanding verbal and mathematical talents (Flannery & Liederman, 1995). More even distribution of cognitive functions across both hemispheres may be responsible for this trend.

OTHER ADVANCES IN BRAIN DEVELOPMENT

Besides the cortex, other areas of the brain make strides during infancy and childhood. As we look at these changes, you will see that they have one feature in common: All involve establishing links between different parts of the brain, increasing the coordinated functioning of the central nervous system. (To see where the structures we are about to discuss are located, turn back to Figure 5.8 on page 182.)

At the rear and base of the brain is the **cerebellum,** a structure that aids in balance and control of body movement. Fibers linking the cerebellum to the cerebral cortex begin to myelinate after birth, but they do not complete this process until about age 4 (Tanner, 1990). This change undoubtedly contributes to dramatic gains in motor control, so that by the end of the preschool years, children can play a game of hopscotch, pump a playground swing, and throw a ball with a well-organized set of movements.

The **reticular formation,** a structure in the brain stem that maintains alertness and consciousness, myelinates throughout early childhood, continuing its growth into adolescence. Neurons in the reticular formation send out fibers to other areas of the brain. Many go to the frontal lobes of the cerebral cortex (McGuinness & Pribram, 1980). Development of the reticular formation contributes to gains in sustained, controlled attention, which we will discuss in Chapter 7.

A final brain structure that undergoes major changes during early childhood is the **corpus callosum.** It is a large bundle of nerve fibers that connects the two hemispheres so that they can communicate with one another. Myelinization of the corpus callosum does not begin until the end of the first year of life. By 4 to 5 years, its development is fairly advanced (Banish, 1997). About this time, children become more proficient at tasks that require transfer of information between the cerebral hemispheres, such as comparing two textured stimuli when each is presented to a different hand (Galin et al., 1979). The corpus callosum continues to mature at a slower rate during middle childhood. More information on how it develops is likely to enhance our understanding of abilities that require collaboration between many parts of the brain, such as abstract thinking and creativity.

BRAIN GROWTH SPURTS AND SENSITIVE PERIODS OF DEVELOPMENT

Earlier we suggested that stimulation of the brain may be vital during periods in which it is growing most rapidly—when formation of synapses is at a peak. The existence of sensitive periods in postnatal development of the cortex has been amply demonstrated in studies of animals exposed to extreme forms of sensory deprivation. For example, there seems to be a time when rich and varied visual experiences must occur for the visual centers of the brain to develop normally. If a month-old kitten is deprived of light for as brief a time as 3 or 4 days, these areas of the brain start to degenerate. If the kitten is kept in the dark for as long as 2 months, the damage is permanent (Hubel & Wiesel, 1970). Severe stimulus deprivation also affects overall brain growth. When animals reared as pets

cerebellum A brain structure that aids in balance and control of body movements.

reticular formation A structure in the brain stem that maintains alertness and consciousness.

corpus callosum The large bundle of fibers that connects the two hemispheres of the brain.

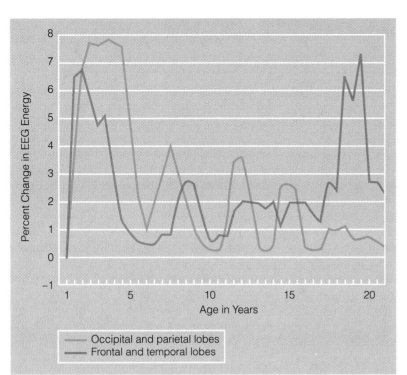

FIGURE 5.13

Brain growth spurts, based on findings of a Swedish cross-sectional study in which EEGs were measured in individuals 1 to 21 years of age. EEG energy peaks indicate periods of rapid growth. These occurred around 1½ to 2, 7½ to 9, 12, 15, and 18 to 20 years of age in all lobes of the cortex (frontal, temporal, occipital, and parietal). The spurts coincide with peaks in children's intelligence test performance and major gains in cognitive competence.

(From K. W. Fischer & S. P. Rose, 1995, Concurrent Cycles in the Dynamic Development of Brain and Behavior. *Newsletter of the Society for Research in Child Development*, p. 16. Reprinted by permission of the authors.)

are compared with animals reared in isolation, the brains of the pets are heavier and thicker (Greenough & Black, 1992; Greenough, Black, & Wallace, 1987).

Because we cannot ethically expose children to such experiments, researchers interested in identifying sensitive periods for human brain development must rely on less direct evidence. Several investigators have identified intermittent brain growth spurts from infancy through adolescence, based on gains in brain weight and skull size as well as changes in electrical activity of the cortex, as measured by the EEG (Epstein, 1980; Hudspeth & Pribram, 1992; Thatcher, 1991, 1994). These spurts coincide with peaks in children's intelligence test performance and major cognitive changes. For example, Figure 5.13 shows the findings of a Swedish study, in which EEGs were measured during a quiet, alert state in individuals ranging from 1 to 21 years of age. The first EEG energy spurt occurred around age 1½ to 2, a period in which representation and language flourish. The next three spurts, at ages 7½ to 9, 12, and 15, probably reflect the emergence and refinement of abstract thinking. Another spurt, around age 18 to 20, may signal the capacity for mature, reflective thought (Fischer & Rose, 1995; Kitchener et al., 1993).

New connections between brain growth spurts and mental and motor development are continually being discovered. For example, several surges in EEG activity in the frontal lobes, which gradually spread to other cortical regions, occur during the first year of life: at 3 to 4 months, when infants typically engage in voluntary reaching; around 8 months, when they begin to crawl and search for hidden objects; and around 12 months, when they walk and display more advanced object-search behaviors (Bell & Fox, 1994, 1996; Fischer & Bidell, 1998). That these early spurts begin in the frontal lobes suggests that this region plays a central role in organizing the cortex as a whole.

Massive production of synapses may underlie brain growth spurts in the first 2 years. Development of more complex and efficient neural networks, due to synaptic pruning, myelinization, and longer-distance connections between the frontal lobes and other cortical regions, may account for the later ones. Researchers are convinced that what "wires" a child's brain during each of these periods is experience. Yet exactly how brain and behavioral development might best be supported by stimulation during each growth spurt is still a question for future research. Once we have such information, it will have major implications for child-rearing and educational practices.

BRIEF REVIEW

The human brain grows faster early in development than any other organ of the body. Neurons develop in a three-step sequence—production, migration, and differentiation—that leads to an overabundance of synapses, myelinization, and synaptic pruning. Although the cerebral cortex has already begun to lateralize at birth, it retains considerable plasticity during the early years. Brain organization is a product of both a genetic program and experience. Hand preference is strongly influenced by practice. It emerges in infancy and strengthens over early childhood, a sign of increasing brain lateralization. Left-handedness is sometimes associated with developmental disabilities; however, the majority of left-handed children show no problems of any kind.

The cerebellum, the reticular formation, and the corpus callosum undergo considerable development during early childhood, contributing to connections between different parts of the brain. Research supports the existence of intermittent brain growth spurts from infancy through adolescence. Each may be a sensitive period during which appropriate stimulation is required for optimal development of human intelligence.

ASK YOURSELF . . .

◆ Explain why overproduction of synapses and synaptic pruning are adaptive processes that foster optimal development.

◆ We are used to thinking of brain growth as following a strict genetic program, but research shows that this is not so. List examples that reveal the effects of experience on brain growth and organization.

◆ CONNECTIONS
Are findings on early brain plasticity consistent with the modular view of the mind, introduced in Chapter 6 (see page 234)? Explain.

Factors Affecting Physical Growth

Physical growth, like other aspects of development, results from the continuous and complex interplay between heredity and environment. In the following sections, we take a closer look at this familiar theme. We will see that, in addition to genetic makeup, nutrition, relative freedom from disease, and emotional well-being affect the body's development.

HEREDITY

Since identical twins are much more alike in body size than are fraternal twins, we know that heredity is an important factor in physical growth. However, this resemblance depends on when twins are measured. At birth, the differences in lengths and weights of identical twins are actually greater than those of fraternal twins. The reason is that identical twins share the same placenta, and one baby usually gets more nourishment. As long as negative environmental factors are not severe, the smaller baby recovers and swings back to her genetically determined path of growth within a few months. This tendency is called **catch-up growth,** and it persists throughout childhood and adolescence. Physical growth is a strongly canalized process (see Chapter 3, page 121).

Genes influence growth by controlling the body's production of and sensitivity to hormones. Sometimes mutations disrupt this process, leading to deviations in physical size. For example, return to Tables 3.2 on page 76 and 3.3 on pages 78–79 to review the impact of hereditary defects on physical growth. Occasionally, a mutation becomes widespread in a population. Consider the Efe of Zaire, an African people who normally grow to an adult height of less than 5 feet. During early childhood, the growth of Efe children tapers off to a greater extent than that of other preschoolers. By age 5, the average Efe child is shorter than over 97 percent of 5-year-olds in the United States. For genetic reasons, growth hormone (GH) has less effect on Efe youngsters than on other children (Bailey, 1990).

When environmental conditions are adequate, height and rate of physical growth (as measured by skeletal age and timing of first menstruation) are strongly influenced by heredity. For example, identical twins generally begin menstruating within a month or two of each other, whereas fraternal twins differ by about 12 months (Malina & Bouchard, 1991; Tanner, 1990). Body weight is also affected by heredity, since the weights of adopted children correlate more strongly with those of their biological than adoptive parents (Stunkard et al., 1986). Nevertheless, reaching genetic potential in any aspect of physical growth depends on environmental support, and good nutrition is essential.

catch-up growth Physical growth that returns to its genetically determined path after being delayed by environmental factors.

192   PART II / FOUNDATIONS OF DEVELOPMENT

Breast-feeding is especially important in developing countries, where infants are at risk for malnutrition and early death due to widespread poverty. This baby of Rajasthan, India, is likely to grow normally during the first year because his mother decided to breast-feed.
(Jane Schreirman/Photo Researchers)

NUTRITION

Many substances are required for normal growth and daily functioning of the human body. Proteins, fats, and carbohydrates are the three basic components of the diet. Proteins are vital for growth, maintenance, and repair of body tissues; carbohydrates supply the primary fuel to meet the body's energy needs; and fats contribute to energy reserves and insulate the body against heat loss. We also need minerals, such as calcium for bone tissue and iron to support the oxygen-carrying power of red blood cells. Vitamins are critical as well, such as A for sight and D for skeletal growth. As extensive as it is, the current U.S. government-recommended list of essential nutrients is probably not exhaustive. Some substances are believed to be important but are not yet established as essential.

■ **AGE-RELATED NUTRITIONAL NEEDS.** Nutrition is important at any time of development, but it is especially crucial during infancy because the baby's brain and body are growing so rapidly. Pound for pound, a young baby's energy needs are twice as great as those of an adult. This is because 25 percent of the infant's total caloric intake is devoted to growth, and extra calories are needed to keep rapidly developing organs of the body functioning properly (Pipes, 1996).

BREAST- VERSUS BOTTLE-FEEDING. Babies not only need enough food, they need the right kind of food. In early infancy, breast-feeding is especially suited to their needs, and bottled formulas try to imitate it. Table 5.1 summarizes the major nutritional and health advantages of breast milk.

Because of these benefits, breast-fed babies in poverty-stricken regions of the world are much less likely to be malnourished and 6 to 14 times more likely to survive the first year of life. Breast-feeding exclusively for the first 6 months would save the lives of one million infants annually. And breast-feeding for just a few weeks would offer some protection against respiratory and intestinal infections that are devastating to young children in developing countries. Furthermore, because a mother is less likely to get pregnant while she is nursing, breast-feeding helps increase spacing between siblings, a major factor in

TABLE 5.1

Nutritional and Health Advantages of Breast-Feeding

Advantage	Description
Correct balance of fat and protein	Compared to the milk of other mammals, human milk is higher in fat and lower in protein. This balance, as well as the unique proteins and fats contained in human milk, is ideal for a rapidly myelinating nervous system.
Nutritional completeness	A mother who breast-feeds need not add other foods to her infant's diet until the baby is 6 months old. The milks of all mammals are low in iron, but the iron contained in breast milk is much more easily absorbed by the baby's system. Consequently, bottle-fed infants need iron-fortified formula.
Protection against disease	Through breast-feeding, antibodies and other infection-fighting agents are transferred from mother to child. As a result, breast-fed babies have far fewer respiratory and intestinal illnesses and allergic reactions than do bottle-fed infants. Components of human milk that protect against disease can be added to formula, but breast-feeding provides superior immunity.
Protection against faulty jaw development and tooth decay	Breast-feeding helps avoid malocclusion, a condition in which the upper and lower jaws do not meet properly. It also protects against tooth decay due to sweet liquid remaining in the mouths of infants who fall asleep while sucking on a bottle.
Digestibility	Since breast-fed babies have a different kind of bacteria growing in their intestines than do bottle-fed infants, they rarely become constipated or have diarrhea.
Smoother transition to solid foods	Breast-fed infants accept new solid foods more easily than do bottle-fed infants, perhaps because of their greater experience with a variety of flavors, which pass from the maternal diet into the mother's milk.

Sources: Bruerd & Jones, 1996; Pickering et al., 1998; Räihä & Axelsson, 1995; Sullivan & Birch, 1994.

reducing infant and childhood deaths in developing countries (Grant, 1995). (Note, however, that breast-feeding is not a reliable method of birth control.)

Yet many mothers in the developing world do not know about the benefits of breast-feeding. Consequently, they give their babies low-grade nutrients, such as rice water, highly diluted cow's and goat's milk, or commercial formula. These foods often lead to illness because they are contaminated due to poor sanitation. The United Nations has encouraged all hospitals and maternity units in developing countries to promote breast-feeding—a campaign that has been highly successful. For example, of over 70 countries that previously allowed free or subsidized formula to be distributed to new mothers, all but one banned the practice (Grant, 1995).

Partly as a result of the natural childbirth movement, over the past two decades, breast-feeding has become more common in industrialized nations, especially among well-educated women. Today, nearly two-thirds of American mothers breast-feed (National Center for Health Statistics, 1998). However, breast-feeding is not for everyone. Some mothers simply do not like it, or they are embarrassed by it. A few others, for physiological reasons, are unable to produce enough milk. Occasionally, medical reasons prevent a mother from nursing. If she is taking certain drugs, they can be transmitted to the baby through the milk. If she has a serious viral or bacterial disease, such as AIDS or tuberculosis, she runs the risk of infecting her baby (Kuhn & Stein, 1997). As we will see in Chapter 10, emotional well-being is affected by the warmth and sensitivity of caregiving, not by the type of milk offered. Breast- and bottle-fed youngsters show no differences in psychological development (Fergusson, Horwood, & Shannon, 1987).

NUTRITION IN CHILDHOOD AND ADOLESCENCE. By 6 months of age, infants require the nutritional diversity of solid foods, and around 1 year, their diets should include all the basic food groups. At about age 2, there is often a dramatic change in the quantity and variety of foods that children will eat. Many become picky eaters. This decline in appetite is normal. It occurs because growth has slowed. And preschoolers' wariness of new foods may be adaptive. By sticking to familiar foods, young children are less likely to swallow dangerous substances when adults are not around to protect them (Birch & Fisher, 1995). Parents need not worry about variations in amount eaten from meal to meal. Over the course of a day, preschoolers' food intake is fairly constant. They compensate for a meal in which they ate little with a later one in which they eat more (Birch et al., 1991).

The wide variety of foods eaten in cultures around the world indicates that the social environment has a powerful impact on young children's food preferences. For example, Mexican preschoolers enthusiastically eat chili peppers, whereas American children quickly reject them. What accounts for this difference? Children tend to imitate the food choices of people they admire—peers as well as adults. In Mexico, children often see family members delighting in the taste of peppery foods (Birch, Zimmerman, & Hind, 1980). Repeated exposure to a new food (without any direct pressure to eat it) also increases children's acceptance (Sullivan & Birch, 1990, 1994).

Once puberty arrives, rapid body growth leads to a dramatic rise in food intake. This increase in nutritional requirements comes at a time when the eating habits of many young people are the poorest. Of all age groups, adolescents are the most likely to consume empty calories. As a result, about 75 percent of North American teenagers suffer from iron deficiency, the most common nutritional problem of childhood and adolescence. A tired, listless youngster may be suffering from anemia rather than unhappiness and should have a medical checkup. Most teenagers also do not get enough calcium, and they tend to be deficient in riboflavin (vitamin B_2) and magnesium, both of which support metabolism (Adams, 1997; Malina, 1990). Adolescents' poor diets do not have serious consequences if they are merely a temporary response to peer influences and a busy schedule, but they can be harmful if they extend a lifelong pattern of poor nutrition.

■ MALNUTRITION. In developing countries where food resources are limited, malnutrition is widespread. Recent evidence indicates that 40 to 60 percent of the world's children do not get enough to eat (Bellamy, 1998; Bread for the World Institute, 1994). Among the 4 to 7 percent who are severely affected, malnutrition leads to two dietary diseases: marasmus and kwashiorkor.

Marasmus is a wasted condition of the body that usually appears in the first year of life. It is caused by a diet that is low in all essential nutrients. The disease often occurs when a baby's mother cannot produce enough breast milk and bottle-feeding is also inadequate. Her starving baby becomes painfully thin and is in danger of dying.

Unlike marasmus, **kwashiorkor** is not the result of general starvation. It is due to an unbalanced diet that is very low in protein. Kwashiorkor usually strikes after weaning, between 1 and 3 years of age. It is common in areas of the world where children get just enough calories from starchy foods, but protein resources are scarce. The child's body responds by breaking down its own protein reserves. Soon the child's belly enlarges, the feet swell, the hair begins to fall out, and a rash appears on the skin. A once bright-eyed, curious youngster becomes irritable and listless.

Children who manage to survive these extreme forms of malnutrition grow to be smaller in all body dimensions (Galler, Ramsey, & Solimano, 1985a). In addition, the brain is seriously affected. One long-term study of marasmic children revealed that an improved diet led to some catch-up growth in height, but the children failed to catch up in head size (Stoch et al., 1982). The malnutrition probably interfered with myelinization, causing a permanent loss in brain weight. By middle childhood, these youngsters score low on intelligence tests, show poor fine motor coordination, and have difficulty paying attention in school (Galler et al., 1984, 1990; Galler, Ramsey, & Solimano, 1985b).

Recall from our discussion of prenatal malnutrition in Chapter 3 that the passivity and irritability of malnourished children make the impact of poor diet even worse. These behaviors appear even when protein-calorie deprivation is only mild to moderate or the child is growing normally but has *iron-deficiency anemia,* a condition that interferes with many central nervous system processes. Withdrawal and listlessness reduce the child's ability to pay attention, explore, and evoke sensitive caregiving from parents, whose lives are already disrupted by poverty and stressful living conditions (Lozoff et al., 1998; Wachs, 1993). For this reason, interventions for malnourished children must improve the family situation as well as the child's nutrition.

Even better are efforts at prevention—providing food and medical care before the effects of malnutrition run their course. Research in Guatemalan rural villages, where dietary deficiencies are common, underscores the importance of early nutritional intervention. Children receiving food supplements prenatally and during the first 2 years of life scored higher on a variety of mental tests in adolescence than did children given supplements only after their second birthday (Pollitt et al., 1993). Other longitudinal findings from Egypt, Kenya, and Mexico reveal that quality of food (protein, vitamin, and mineral content) is far more important than quantity of food in contributing to the favorable cognitive outcomes just described (Sigman, 1995; Watkins & Pollitt, 1998).

Like prenatal malnutrition, malnutrition after birth is not confined to developing countries. Recent surveys indicate that over 12 percent of children in the United States go to bed hungry (Children's Defense Fund, 1998; Wachs, 1995). Although few of these children have marasmus or kwashiorkor, their physical growth and ability to learn in school are still affected. Malnutrition is clearly a national and international crisis—one of the most serious problems confronting the human species today.

■ OBESITY. Nearly 25 percent of American children suffer from **obesity,** a greater-than-20-percent increase over average body weight, based on the child's age, sex, and physical build (U.S. Department of Health and Human Services, 1997). Overweight and obesity are growing problems in affluent nations like the United States. Obesity is also rising in developing nations, as greater urbanization is accompanied by a shift toward sedentary lifestyles and diets high in refined foods, meats, and eggs (Popkin & Doak, 1998). And as the Social Issues box on page 196 reveals, growth stunting due to early malnutrition leaves many children in developing countries vulnerable to later excessive weight gain.

Over 80 percent of affected youngsters remain overweight as adults (Serdula et al., 1993). Besides serious emotional and social difficulties, obese children are at risk for lifelong health problems. High blood pressure and cholesterol levels, along with respiratory abnormalities, begin to appear in the early school years. As obesity continues, it becomes a powerful predictor of heart disease, adult-onset diabetes, certain forms of cancer, and early death (Figueroa-Colon et al., 1997; Unger, Kreeger, & Christoffel, 1990).

The swollen abdomen and listless behavior of this Honduran child are classic symptoms of kwashiorkor, a nutritional illness that results from a diet very low in protein.

(Bob Daemmrich/The Image Works)

marasmus A disease usually appearing in the first year of life that is caused by a diet low in all essential nutrients. Leads to a wasted condition of the body.

kwashiorkor A disease usually appearing between 1 and 3 years of age that is caused by a diet low in protein. Symptoms include an enlarged belly, swollen feet, hair loss, skin rash, and irritable, listless behavior.

obesity A greater-than-20-percent increase over average body weight, based on the child's age, sex, and physical build.

Growth Stunting Due to Early Malnutrition: Risk Factor for Childhood Obesity

SOCIAL ISSUES

N RESEARCH ON overweight children in four developing nations, a disheartening link between early growth stunting due to malnutrition and childhood obesity has emerged. Nationwide surveys in Brazil, China, Russia, and South Africa yielded information on height for age (a measure of poor diet and stunting) and weight for height (a measure of obesity) for thousands of children (Popkin, Richards, & Montiero, 1996). The proportion of children who were stunted (very short for their age) ranged from 15 percent in Brazil to 22 percent in China and 30 percent in South Africa. In Russia, stunting is a new problem. It has emerged only in the last 8 years, after poverty rose while government-sponsored maternal and child nutrition programs deteriorated. About 9 percent of Russian children are growth stunted.

As Figure 5.14 shows, in each country except Brazil, the rate of overweight was far greater among stunted than nonstunted children. Short, growth-retarded children were twice as likely as their peers to be fat in South Africa, three times as likely in China, and seven times as likely in Russia. Family income seemed to account for the lack of association between stunting and fatness in Brazil; many overweight Brazilian children come from financially better-off homes. But in the other three countries, income had no impact on the stunting–overweight relationship.

What explains excessive weight gain among growth-stunted children? Researchers believe that two physiological changes are involved:

- To protect itself, a malnourished body establishes a low basal metabolism rate, stretching its energy resources as far as possible—a change that may endure after nutrition improves.

- Early malnutrition may cause brain structures responsible for appetite control to be reset at a higher level. Consequently, stunted children are likely to overeat when food—especially high-fat products—become more widely available as developing nations gain economically and modernize (Barker, 1994; Popkin, 1994).

The growth stunting–obesity link is evident among certain low-income ethnic minorities in the United States, including Mexican-American and Hmong (Laotian) groups

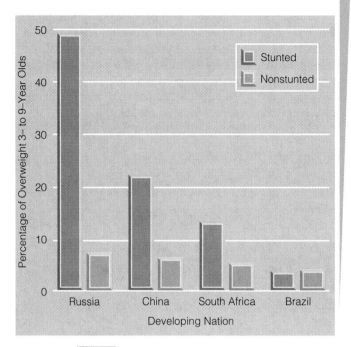

FIGURE 5.14

Relationship of growth stunting to overweight among 3- to 9-year-olds in four developing nations. Children identified as growth stunted were below the second percentile in height for their age, based on World Health Organization standards. Children identified as overweight were above the ninety-eighth percentile in weight for their height. Stunted children were twice as likely as their peers to be fat in South Africa, three times as likely in China, and seven times as likely in Russia. Family income seems to account for the lack of association between stunting and overweight in Brazil.

(Adapted from Popkin, Richards, & Montiero, 1996.)

(Himes et al., 1992; Valdez et al., 1994). As economic conditions improve worldwide, a high-quality diet from the earliest ages may be vital for shielding children everywhere from an epidemic of obesity.

CAUSES OF OBESITY. Childhood obesity is a complex physical disorder with multiple causes. Not all children are equally at risk for becoming overweight. Fat children tend to have fat parents, and concordance for obesity is greater in identical than fraternal twins. These findings suggest that heredity has some effect. But similarity among family members is not strong enough to imply that genetics accounts for any more than a tendency to gain weight (Bouchard, 1994; Dietz, Bandini, & Gortmaker, 1990).

One indication that environment is powerfully important is the consistent relation between family economic status and overweight. Low-income youngsters in industrialized nations are not just at greater risk for malnutrition. They are also more likely to be obese (Stunkard & Sørenson, 1993). Among the factors responsible are lack of knowledge about healthy diet; a tendency to buy high-fat, low-cost foods; and family stress, which prompts overeating in some individuals. And 6 percent of American low-income and ethnic minority children are growth stunted due to early malnutrition and are therefore at increased risk for obesity (consult the Social Issues box on page 196).

Only a slight relationship exists between very rapid weight gain in infancy and fatness in childhood. When early overweight persists, parental food choices and feeding practices seem to play important roles. In a recent study, fatter preschoolers were more likely to prefer and eat larger quantities of high-fat foods, perhaps because these foods were a prominent part of the diets offered by their parents, who also tended to be overweight (Fisher & Birch, 1995). Some parents anxiously overfeed their infants and young children, interpreting almost all their discomforts as a desire for food. Others are overly controlling, constantly monitoring what their children eat. In either case, they fail to help children learn to regulate their own energy intake appropriately. Furthermore, parents of obese children often use food to reinforce other behaviors—a practice that leads children to attach great value to the treat and other similar foods (Birch & Fisher, 1995). In families in which these practices are common, high-calorie treats gradually come to symbolize warmth, comfort, and relief of tension.

Because of these feeding experiences, obese children soon develop maladaptive eating habits (Johnson & Birch, 1994). They are more responsive to external stimuli associated with food—taste, sight, smell, and time of day—and less responsive to internal hunger cues than are normal-weight individuals. This difference is present in middle childhood and may develop even earlier (Ballard et al., 1980; Constanzo & Woody, 1979). Overweight individuals also eat faster and chew their food less thoroughly, a behavior pattern that appears in overweight children as early as 18 months of age (Drabman et al., 1979).

Fat children are also less physically active than their normal-weight peers. This inactivity is both cause and consequence of their overweight condition. Recent evidence indicates that the rise in childhood obesity in the United States over the past 40 years is in part due to television viewing. Next to already existing obesity, time spent in front of the TV set is the best predictor of future obesity among school-age children. The rate of obesity increases by 2 percent for each additional hour of TV watched per day (Gortmaker, Dietz, & Cheung, 1990). Television greatly reduces the time devoted to physical exercise. At the same time, TV ads encourage children to eat fattening, unhealthy snacks—soft drinks, sweets, and salty chips and popcorn (Carruth, Goldberg, & Skinner, 1991).

Finally, the broader food environment affects the incidence of obesity. When a group of 13 Tarahumara Indians living in a traditional way in northern Mexico were fed a Western high-fat diet for just 5 weeks, weight gain averaged 8.4 pounds and blood cholesterol rose dramatically (McMurphy et al., 1991). The Pima Indians of Arizona, who recently changed from a traditional diet of unprocessed plant foods to an affluent, high-fat diet, have one of the highest rates of obesity in the world. Compared with descendants of their ancestors living in the remote Sierra Madre region of Mexico, the Arizona Pima have body weights 50 percent higher and blood cholesterol levels 13 to 27 percent higher. Half the population has diabetes (8 times the national average), with many disabled by the disease as early as their twenties and thirties—blind, confined to a wheelchair, and on kidney dialysis (Gladwell, 1998; Ravussin et al., 1994). Although the Pima are believed to have a genetic susceptibility to overweight, it emerges only under Western dietary conditions, with tragic health consequences.

PSYCHOLOGICAL CONSEQUENCES OF OBESITY. Unfortunately, physical attractiveness is a powerful predictor of social acceptance in Western societies. Both children and adults rate obese youngsters as less likable than children with a wide range of physical disabilities (Brenner & Hinsdale, 1978; Lerner & Schroeder, 1971). By middle childhood, obese children have a low sense of self-esteem, report feeling more depressed, and display more behavior problems than do their peers. A vicious cycle emerges in which unhappiness and overeating contribute to one another, and the child remains overweight (Braet, Mervielde, & Vandereycken, 1997; Pierce & Wardle, 1997).

The psychological consequences of obesity combine with continuing discrimination to result in reduced life chances. By young adulthood, overweight individuals have completed fewer years of schooling, have lower incomes, and marry less often than do

This Pima Indian medicine man of Arizona is very obese. By the time his two daughters reach adolescence, they are likely to follow in his footsteps. Because of a high-fat diet, the Pima residing in the Southwestern United States have one of the highest rates of obesity in the world. In contrast, the Pima living in the remote Sierra Madre region of Mexico are average weight.

(Stephanie Trimble)

individuals with other chronic health problems. These outcomes are particularly strong for females (Gortmaker et al., 1993).

TREATING OBESITY. Childhood obesity is difficult to treat because it is a family disorder. A recent study found that the most effective intervention was family based and focused on changing behaviors. Both parent and child revised eating patterns, exercised daily, and reinforced each other with praise and points for progress, which they exchanged for special activities and times together. Follow-ups after 5 and 10 years showed that children maintained their weight loss more effectively than did adults—a finding that underscores the importance of intervening at an early age. Furthermore, weight loss was greater when treatments focused on both dietary and lifestyle changes, including regular vigorous exercise (Epstein et al., 1990, 1994).

Getting obese children to exercise, however, is challenging, since they find being sedentary so pleasurable. Positively reinforcing them for spending less time inactive is a successful technique. In two studies, researchers offered rewards (such a tickets to the zoo or a baseball game) for reducing sedentary time. Children receiving this treatment showed greater liking for and involvement in physical activity and lost more weight than did children reinforced for being physically active or punished (by loss of privileges) for inactivity (Epstein, Saelens, & O'Brien, 1995; Epstein et al., 1997). Rewarding children for giving up sedentary pursuits seems to increase their sense of personal control over exercise behavior—a factor linked to sustained physical activity.

INFECTIOUS DISEASE

Among well-nourished youngsters, ordinary childhood illnesses have no effect on physical growth. But when children are poorly fed, disease interacts with malnutrition in a vicious spiral, and the consequences can be severe.

■ **INFECTIOUS DISEASE AND MALNUTRITION.** In developing nations where a large proportion of the population lives in poverty, illnesses such as measles and chicken pox (which typically do not appear until after age 3 in industrialized nations) occur in infancy and take the form of severe illnesses. In these countries, many children do not receive a program of immunizations. In addition, poor diet depresses the body's immune system, making children far more susceptible to disease (Eveleth & Tanner, 1990).

Disease, in turn, is a major cause of malnutrition and, through it, affects physical growth. Illness reduces appetite, and it limits the body's ability to absorb foods. These outcomes are especially severe among children with intestinal infections. In developing countries, diarrhea is widespread and increases in early childhood due to unsafe water and contaminated foods, leading to several million childhood deaths each year (Grant, 1995). Research in poverty-stricken Guatemalan villages showed that 7-year-olds who had been relatively free of diarrhea since birth were significantly heavier than their frequently ill peers (Martorell, 1980).

Most growth retardation and deaths due to diarrhea can be prevented with nearly cost-free **oral rehydration therapy (ORT),** in which sick children are given a glucose, salt, and water solution that quickly replaces fluids the body loses. Since 1990, public health workers have taught nearly half of families in the developing world how to administer ORT. As a result, the lives of more than 1 million children are being saved annually (Bellamy, 1998).

■ **IMMUNIZATION.** In industrialized nations, childhood diseases have declined dramatically during the past half-century, largely due to widespread immunization of infants and young children. Although the majority of preschoolers in the United States are immunized, a sizable minority do not receive full protection until 5 or 6 years of age, when it is required for school entry (Children's Defense Fund, 1999).

To remedy this problem, in 1994 all medically uninsured American children were guaranteed free immunizations. As a result, immunization rates in the United States improved, but they continue to lag behind those of Canada and other Western European nations. For example, 29 percent of American preschoolers are not fully immunized, a rate that rises to 40 percent for poverty-stricken children (U.S. Department of Health and Human Services, 1998b). In contrast, fewer than 10 percent of preschoolers lack immu-

To inform parents about the importance of immunization, the U.S. Department of Health and Human Services distributes this poster free of charge.

nizations in Denmark and Norway, less than 7 percent in the Netherlands and Sweden (Bellamy, 1998; de Winter, Balleduz, & de Mare, 1997).

How is it that these countries have managed to achieve high rates of immunization, whereas the United States' record is so poor? In earlier chapters, we noted that many children in the United States do not have access to the medical care they need. Inability to pay for vaccines, however, is only one cause of lower immunization rates in the United States. Misconceptions about safe medical practices also contribute. American parents often report that they delay taking their child in for a vaccination because they believe the child might have an adverse reaction (Abbotts & Osborn, 1993; Shalala, 1993). Public education programs directed at increasing parental knowledge about the importance and safety of timely immunizations are badly needed.

Widespread, government-sponsored immunization of infants and young children is a cost-effective means of supporting healthy growth by dramatically reducing the incidence of childhood diseases. Although this boy finds a routine inoculation painful, it will offer him lifelong protection. (Russell D. Curtis/Photo Researchers, Inc.)

EMOTIONAL WELL-BEING

We are not used to thinking of love and stimulation as necessary for healthy physical growth, but they are just as vital as food. Two serious growth disorders result from lack of affection and attention.

Nonorganic failure to thrive is usually present by 18 months of age. Infants who have it show all the signs of marasmus, described earlier in this chapter. However, no organic (or biological) cause for the baby's wasted appearance can be found. Enough food is offered, and the infant does not have a serious illness. The behavior of babies with failure to thrive provides a strong clue to its diagnosis. In addition to apathy and withdrawal, these infants keep their eyes on nearby adults, anxiously watching their every move. They rarely smile when the mother comes near or cuddle when picked up (Black et al., 1994; Leonard, Rhymes, & Solnit, 1986).

Family circumstances surrounding failure to thrive help explain these typical reactions. During feeding, diaper changing, and play, mothers of these infants seem cold and distant, at other times controlling, impatient, and hostile (Hagekull, Bohlin, & Rydell, 1997). In response, babies try to protect themselves by keeping track of the threatening adult's whereabouts and, when she approaches, avoiding her gaze. Often an unhappy marriage and parental psychological disturbance contribute to these serious caregiving problems (Drotar, Pallotta, & Eckerle, 1994; Duniz et al., 1996). Sometimes the baby is irritable and displays abnormal feeding behaviors, such as poor sucking or vomiting—circumstances that stress the parent–child relationship further (Ramsay, Gisel, & Boutry, 1993). When treated early, through intensive family therapy or placement in a caring foster home, failure-to-thrive infants show quick catch-up growth. But if the problem is not corrected in infancy, some children remain small and display lasting cognitive and emotional difficulties (Heffner & Kelley, 1994).

Deprivation dwarfism appears later than failure to thrive, usually between 2 and 15 years. Its most striking features are substantially below-average stature, decreased GH secretion, and immature skeletal age. Children with the disorder do not look malnourished; their weight is usually appropriate for their height. Researchers believe that severe emotional deprivation affects communication between the hypothalamus and pituitary gland, resulting in stunted growth. When such children are removed from their emotionally inadequate environments, their GH levels quickly return to normal, and they grow rapidly. But if treatment is delayed until later in development, the dwarfism can be permanent (Oates, Peacock, & Forrest, 1985).

Caregiving problems associated with these growth disorders are often grounded in poverty and family disorganization, which place parents under severe stress. With their own emotional resources depleted, parents have little energy available to meet the psychological needs of their children. However, failure to thrive and deprivation dwarfism do not occur just among the poor. They sometimes appear in economically advantaged families when marital conflict or other pressures cause parents to behave insensitively and destructively toward their children.

oral rehydration therapy (ORT) A treatment for diarrhea, in which sick children are given a glucose, salt, and water solution that quickly replaces fluids the body loses.

nonorganic failure to thrive A growth disorder usually present by 18 months of age that is caused by lack of affection and stimulation.

deprivation dwarfism A growth disorder observed between 2 and 15 years of age. Characterized by substantially below-average stature, weight that is usually appropriate for height, immature skeletal age, and decreased GH secretion. Caused by severe emotional deprivation.

ASK YOURSELF . . .

◆ *Explain why the United Nations engages in vigorous public education campaigns to promote breast-feeding in developing nations.*

◆ **CONNECTIONS**
Select one of the following growth problems of childhood: malnutrition, obesity, or non-organic failure to thrive. Use ecological systems theory to show how bidirectional influences between caregiver and child combine with factors in the surrounding environment to compromise children's development. (See Chapter 1, pages 27–30.)

Are infants with nonorganic failure to thrive likely to develop a secure attachment with the familiar caregiver? Explain. (See Chapter 10, pages 426–427.)

eredity, nutrition, resistance to disease, and emotional well-being all contribute to early physical growth. Studies of twins show that height and weight are affected by genetic makeup. Breast-feeding offers the ideal nutrition between birth and 6 months and protects many poverty-stricken infants against malnutrition, disease, and early death. However, breast- and bottle-fed babies do not differ in psychological development. Although preschoolers' appetites decline and they resist new foods, good nutrition remains important throughout childhood and adolescence. Greater nutritional needs at puberty come at a time when the eating habits of many young people are the poorest.

Malnutrition is a serious global problem. When marasmus and kwashiorkor are allowed to persist, physical size, brain growth, and ability to learn are permanently affected. In affluent nations like the United States, childhood obesity is a widespread health problem. Although heredity contributes to obesity, parental food choices and feeding practices, physical activity, and the broader food environment determine whether a genetic susceptibility becomes manifest. Infectious disease can interact with malnutrition to seriously undermine children's growth, an effect that is common in developing countries. Weak immunization rates in the United States leave many poverty-stricken youngsters at risk for preventable childhood illnesses. Nonorganic failure to thrive and deprivation dwarfism remind us of the close connection between sensitive, loving care and how children grow.

Puberty: The Physical Transition to Adulthood

uring **puberty,** young people become physically mature and capable of producing offspring. Accompanying rapid changes in body size and proportions discussed earlier in this chapter are changes in physical features related to sexual functioning. Some, called **primary sexual characteristics,** involve the reproductive organs (ovaries, uterus, and vagina in females; penis, scrotum, and testes in males). Others, called **secondary sexual characteristics,** are visible on the outside of the body and serve as additional signs of sexual maturity (for example, breast development in females, appearance of underarm and pubic hair in both sexes).

Clearly, puberty is the period of greatest sexual differentiation since prenatal life. As we will see in the following sections, its impact on psychological development and social relationships is pervasive. Let's begin with physical changes. As you can see in the Milestones table on page 201, these develop in a fairly standard sequence, although the age at which each begins and is completed varies greatly.

SEXUAL MATURATION IN GIRLS

Menarche (from the Greek word *arche,* meaning "beginning") is the scientific name for first menstruation. Because most people view it as the major sign that puberty has arrived in girls, you may be surprised to learn that menarche actually occurs late in the sequence of pubertal events. Female puberty usually begins with the budding of the breasts and the growth spurt. (For about 15 percent of girls, pubic hair is present before breast development.) Menarche typically happens around 12½ years for North American girls, 13 for Europeans. But the age range is wide, extending from 10½ to 15½ years. Following menarche, underarm hair appears, and pubic hair and breast development are completed. Most girls take about 3 to 4 years to complete this sequence. Some mature more rapidly, in as little as a year and a half. Others take longer, perhaps as much as 5 years (Tanner, 1990; Wheeler, 1991).

All girls experience menarche after the peak of the height spurt, once they have nearly reached their mature body size. This sequence has clear adaptive value. Nature delays menstruation until the girl's body is large enough for successful childbearing. As an extra measure of security, for 12 to 18 months following menarche, the menstrual cycle often takes place without an ovum being released from the ovaries. However, this temporary

puberty Biological changes during adolescence that lead to an adult-sized body and sexual maturity.

primary sexual characteristics Physical features that involve the reproductive organs (ovaries, uterus, and vagina in females; penis, scrotum, and testes in males).

secondary sexual characteristics Features visible on the outside of the body that serve as signs of sexual maturity but do not involve the reproductive organs (for example, breast development in females, appearance of underarm and pubic hair in both sexes).

menarche First menstruation.

Pubertal Development in North American Boys and Girls

MILESTONES

Girls	Average Age Attained	Age Range	Boys	Average Age Attained	Age Range
Breasts begin to "bud."	10	(8–13)	Testes begin to enlarge.	11.5	(9.5–13.5)
Height spurt begins.	10	(8–13)	Pubic hair appears.	12	(10–15)
Pubic hair appears.	10.5	(8–14)	Penis begins to enlarge.	12	(10.5–14.5)
Peak of strength spurt.	11.6	(9.5–14)	Height spurt begins.	12.5	(10.5–16)
Peak of height spurt.	11.7	(10–13.5)	Spermarche (first ejaculation) occurs.	13	(12–16)
Menarche (first menstruation) occurs.	12.5	(10.5–15.5)	Peak of height spurt.	14	(12.5–15.5)
Adult stature reached; underarm hair appears.	13	(10–16)	Facial and body hair begin to grow.	14	(12.5–15.5)
			Voice begins to deepen.	14	(12.5–15.5)
Breast growth completed.	14	(10–16)	Penis growth completed.	14.5	(12.5–16)
Pubic hair growth completed.	14.5	(14–15)	Peak of strength spurt.	15.3	(13–17)
			Adult stature reached.	15.5	(13.5–17.5)
			Pubic hair growth completed.	15.5	(14–17)

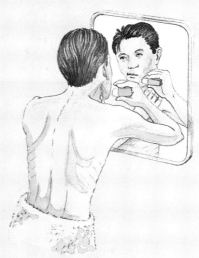

Note: These milestones represent overall age trends. Individual differences exist in the precise age at which each milestone is attained.
Sources: Malina & Bouchard, 1991; Tanner, 1990.

period of sterility does not apply to all girls, and it cannot be counted on for protection against pregnancy (Tanner, 1990).

SEXUAL MATURATION IN BOYS

The first sign of puberty in boys is the enlargement of the testes (glands that manufacture sperm), accompanied by changes in the texture and color of the scrotum. Pubic hair emerges a short time later, about the same time the penis begins to enlarge (Graber, Petersen, & Brooks-Gunn, 1996).

Refer again to the Milestones table above, and you will see that the growth spurt occurs much later in the sequence of pubertal events for boys than for girls. When it reaches its peak (at about age 14), enlargement of the testes and penis is nearly complete, and underarm hair appears soon after. Facial and body hair also emerge just after the peak in body growth, but it increases slowly, continuing to develop for several years after puberty. Another landmark of male physical maturity is the deepening of the voice as the larynx enlarges and the vocal cords lengthen. (Girls' voices also deepen slightly.) Voice change usually takes place at the peak of the male growth spurt and is often not complete until puberty is over. When it first occurs, many boys have difficulty with voice control. Occasionally, their newly acquired baritone breaks into a high-pitched sound (Katchadourian, 1977).

While the penis is growing, the prostate gland and seminal vesicles (which together produce semen, the fluid in which sperm are bathed) enlarge. Then, around age 13, **spermarche,** or first ejaculation, occurs (Jorgensen & Keiding, 1991). For a while, the semen contains few living sperm. So, like girls, many boys have an initial period of reduced fertility. Spermarche may be as psychologically significant for boys as menarche is for girls, an issue we will take up shortly.

INDIVIDUAL AND GROUP DIFFERENCES IN PUBERTAL GROWTH

Heredity is partly responsible for the timing of puberty, since identical twins generally reach menarche within a month or two of each other, whereas fraternal twins differ by about 12 months (Tanner, 1990). Nutrition and exercise also contribute. In females, a sharp rise in body weight and fat may trigger sexual maturation. Girls who begin serious athletic training at young ages or who eat very little (both of which reduce the percentage of body fat) often show delayed menarche. In contrast, overweight girls typically start menstruating early (Post & Kemper, 1993; Rees, 1993).

Variations in pubertal growth also exist between regions of the world and income groups. Heredity probably plays little role, since adolescents with very different genetic origins living under similarly advantaged conditions resemble one another in pubertal timing. For example, in Japan, the United States, and Western Europe, menarche occurs at approximately the same age—between 12½ and 13½ years (Eveleth & Tanner, 1990). Instead, physical health is largely responsible. In poverty-stricken regions where malnutrition and infectious disease are widespread, menarche is greatly delayed. In many parts of Africa, it does not occur until age 14 to 17. And within countries, girls from higher-income families consistently reach menarche 6 to 18 months earlier than do those living in economically disadvantaged homes.

The Psychological Impact of Pubertal Events

Think back to your late elementary school and junior high school days. Were you early, late, or about on time in physical maturation with respect to your peers? How did your feelings about yourself and your relationships with others change? Were your reactions similar to Rousseau's and Hall's image of biologically determined storm and stress, described at the beginning of this chapter?

IS PUBERTY AN INEVITABLE PERIOD OF STORM AND STRESS?

Recent research on large numbers of teenagers suggests that Rousseau's and Hall's conclusions are greatly exaggerated. A number of problems, such as eating disorders, depression, suicide (see Chapter 11), and lawbreaking (see Chapter 12), occur more often in adolescence than earlier. But the overall rate of serious psychological disturbance rises only slightly from childhood to adolescence, when it is the same as in the adult population—about 20 percent (Costello & Angold, 1995). Although some teenagers encounter serious difficulties, emotional turbulence is not a routine feature of this phase of development.

The first researcher to point out the wide variability in adolescent adjustment and the contribution of social and cultural factors to it was anthropologist Margaret Mead. In 1926, she traveled to the Pacific islands of Samoa and returned with a startling conclusion: Samoan adolescence was free of all the characteristics that made it hazardous for young people and dreaded by adults in complex societies. Because of the culture's relaxed social relationships and openness toward sexuality, adolescence, Mead (1928) reported, "is perhaps the pleasantest time the Samoan girl (or boy) will ever know" (p. 308).

Mead offered an alternative view in which the social environment was judged to be entirely responsible for the range of teenage experiences, from erratic and agitated to calm

spermarche First ejaculation of seminal fluid.

and stress free. Yet this conclusion is just as extreme as the biological perspective it was supposed to replace! Later researchers, who looked more closely at Samoan society, found that adolescence was not as smooth and untroubled as Mead made it out to be (Freeman, 1983).

Still, Mead's work had an enormous impact. Today we know that adolescence is neither biologically nor socially determined, but rather a product of the two. In line with Mead's observations, young people growing up in nonindustrialized societies generally experience a shorter and smoother transition to adulthood. But adolescence is not absent (Weisfield, 1997). A study of 186 tribal and village cultures revealed that almost all had an intervening phase, however brief, between childhood and full assumption of adult roles (Schlegel & Barry, 1991).

In industrialized nations, successful participation in economic life requires many years of education. Young people face extra years of dependence on parents and postponement of sexual gratification while they prepare for a productive work life. As a result, adolescence is greatly extended, and teenagers confront a wider array of psychological challenges. A large body of research reveals that puberty is linked to important changes in self-image, mood, and interaction with parents and peers. In the following sections, we will see many examples of how biological and social forces combine to affect teenagers' adjustment.

REACTIONS TO PUBERTAL CHANGES

How do girls and boys react to the massive physical changes of puberty? Most research aimed at answering this question has focused on girls' feelings about menarche.

■ **GIRLS' REACTIONS TO MENARCHE.** Research of a generation or two ago indicated that menarche was often traumatic. Today, girls commonly react with "surprise," undoubtedly due to the sudden nature of the event. Otherwise, they typically report a mixture of positive and negative emotions—"excited and pleased" as well as "scared and upset" (Brooks-Gunn, 1988b). Yet wide individual differences exist that depend on prior knowledge and support from family members. Both are influenced by cultural attitudes toward puberty and sexuality.

For girls who have no advance information about sexuality, menarche can be shocking and disturbing. In the 1950s, up to 50 percent were given no prior warning (Shainess, 1961). Today, no more than 10 to 15 percent are uninformed (Brooks-Gunn, 1988b). This shift is probably due to modern parents' greater willingness to discuss sexual matters with their children. Almost all girls get some information from their mothers. And girls whose fathers are told about pubertal changes adjust especially well. Perhaps a father's involvement reflects a family atmosphere that is highly understanding and accepting of physical and sexual matters (Brooks-Gunn & Ruble, 1980, 1983).

■ **BOYS' REACTIONS TO SPERMARCHE.** Like girls' reactions to menarche, boys' responses to spermarche reflect mixed feelings. Virtually all boys know about ejaculation ahead of time, but few get any information from parents. Usually they obtain it from reading material (Gaddis & Brooks-Gunn, 1985). Despite advance information, many boys say that their first ejaculation occurred earlier than they expected and that they were unprepared for it. As with girls, the better prepared boys feel, the more positively they react (Stein & Reiser, 1994).

In addition, although at first girls keep menarche secret from their peers, within 6 months almost all tell a friend that they are menstruating. In contrast, far fewer boys ever tell anyone about spermarche (Brooks-Gunn et al., 1986; Downs & Fuller, 1991). Overall, boys seem to get much less social support for the physical changes of puberty than do girls. This suggests that boys might benefit, especially, from opportunities to ask questions and discuss feelings with a sympathetic parent or health professional.

■ **CULTURAL INFLUENCES.** The experience of puberty is affected by the larger cultural context in which boys and girls live. Many tribal and village societies celebrate puberty with a *rite of passage*—a community-wide initiation ceremony that marks an important change in privilege and responsibility. Consequently, these young people know that pubertal changes are honored and valued in their culture (see the Cultural Influences

Adolescent Initiation Ceremonies

A N ADOLESCENT INITIATION **ceremony** is a ritualized announcement to the community that a young person is ready to make the transition from childhood into adolescence or full adulthood. These special rites of passage reach their fullest expression in small tribal and village societies. Besides celebration, they often include such features as separation from parents and members of the other sex; instruction in cultural customs and work roles; and fertility rituals that incorporate the young person into the sexual and childbearing world of adults. According to anthropologists, each of these ceremonial features is a cultural expression of the adaptive value of biological puberty.

SEPARATION. The beginning of an initiation ceremony is usually marked by separation from parents and members of the other sex, and sometimes by seclusion from the entire settlement. Among the !Kung hunters and gatherers of Botswana, Africa, a girl menstruating for the first time is carried to a special shelter by an old woman, who cares for her until the menstrual flow stops. Some Native American boys must begin a lonely pilgrimage to seek their vision. The Tiwi, an Aboriginal group of northern Australia, greet male puberty by arranging to have a group of strange men take boys to a special campsite in the bush. Initiates are expected to shed their childish ways abruptly in favor of adultlike reverence and self-restraint (Spindler, 1970).

A same-sex nonparent usually oversees the initiation, since puberty is accompanied by a rise in conflict and psychological distancing between parent and child (see pages 204–206), which reduces parents' power to teach the adolescent (Eibl-Eibesfeldt, 1989). Gender segregation fosters the young person's assumption of adult gender roles, which are sharply divided in most tribal and village societies (Weisfield, 1986).

In this adolescent initiation ceremony, N'Jembe women of Gabon in west-central Africa celebrate the arrival of puberty in two young girls (located just behind the leader, wearing elaborate headdresses) with a special ritual.

(Sylvain Grandadam/Photo Researchers, Inc.)

Boys are typically initiated in large peer groups, a custom that promotes social solidarity. When agemates undergo challenging and painful experiences together, they bond with one another, an outcome that enhances cooperation in hunting, defending the group, and other adult tasks (Schlegel & Barry, 1991). Girls, in contrast, are generally initiated singly. In adulthood, they will spend more time with their family and in small groups. Consequently, large-group unity is deemed less important (Schlegel, 1995).

box above). In contrast, Western societies grant little formal recognition to movement from childhood to adolescence or from adolescence to adulthood. Certain religious ceremonies, such as confirmation and the Jewish bar or bat mitzvah, do resemble a rite of passage. But not all young people take part in these rituals, and they usually do not lead to any meaningful change in social status.

Instead, Western adolescents are confronted with many ages at which they are granted partial adult status—for example, an age for starting employment, for driving, for leaving high school, for voting, and for drinking. In some contexts (on the highway and at their place of work), they may be treated like adults. In others (at school and at home), they may still be regarded as children. The absence of a widely accepted marker of physical and social maturity makes the process of becoming an adult especially confusing.

PUBERTAL CHANGE, EMOTION, AND SOCIAL BEHAVIOR

In the preceding sections, we considered adolescents' reactions to their sexually maturing bodies. Puberty can also affect the young person's emotional state and social behavior. A common belief is that pubertal change has something to do with adolescent moodiness and the desire for greater physical and psychological separation from parents.

adolescent initiation ceremony A ritual, or rite of passage, announcing to the community that a young person is ready to make the transition from childhood into adolescence or full adulthood.

■ ADOLESCENT MOODINESS. Recently, researchers have explored the role of sex hormones in adolescents' emotional reactions. Indeed, higher hormone levels are related to

INSTRUCTION. During initiation rights, years of childhood teachings are supplemented with information on ceremonial matters, courtship, sexual techniques, duties to one's spouse and in-laws, and subsistence skills. Elders often convey tribal secrets and stress cultural values. Among the Mano of Liberia, older men take young boys off into the forest, where they are taught secret folklore along with farming and other skills they will need to earn a living. They return with a new name, signifying their adult identity, and an even stronger allegiance to their culture. !Kung women teach the newly menstruating girl not to shame her husband or touch his hunting gear and about birth and infant care (Fried & Fried, 1980).

INCORPORATION INTO ADULT SOCIETY. The training period culminates in a formal celebration, which usually grants young people permission to engage in sex and to marry. Most of the time, the appearance of initiates is changed so that all members of the community can identify them and treat them differently. Sometimes physical markers of increased status involve temporary body decorations, such as painting and jewelry. At other times, the changes are permanent, consisting of new types of clothing or scars engraved on some part of the body—usually the face, back, chest, or penis.

Many ceremonies include an ordeal, typically more severe for males than for females. A boy might need to kill game or endure cold and hunger, a girl might grind grain or remain secluded for several days. These rites stress responsibility, wisdom, and bravery. They also subject adolescents with a rebellious streak to the authority of their elders (Weisfield, 1997).

Male genital operations (usually circumcision) occur in about one-third of cultures with puberty rites and are typically followed by sexual activity. Female surgery (removal of part or all of the clitoris and sometimes the labia) takes place in only 8 percent of initiation ceremonies, for the purpose of ensuring the girl's continued virginity and therefore her value as a bride (Weisfield, 1990).[1]

CULTURAL VARIATIONS. In the simplest societies, adolescent initiation ceremonies for girls are more common than those for boys. In small bands of hunters and gatherers, females are in short supply. The loss of any woman of child-bearing age can threaten the survival of the group. In these cultures, female rites typically last for several weeks and are especially elaborate, designed to provide the girl with both social recognition and magical protection. As cultures move from simple foraging to farming communities, rituals for boys increase in frequency. Initiation rites in farming villages typically recognize young people of both sexes for their distinct reproductive and economic roles. In more complex cultures, adolescent initiation ceremonies recede in importance and disappear (Schlegel & Barry, 1980).

---

[1]*Female genital mutilation*, widespread in Africa, Indonesia, Malaysia, and the Middle East, as a means of guaranteeing chastity and therefore a good marriage partner, is usually inflicted on girls in infancy or early childhood, before they know enough to resist (Weisfield, 1997). Although illegal in many countries, the practice is difficult for governments to control. Today, there are millions of genitally mutilated girls and women in the developing world. International organizations are sending social scientists and health professionals into villages to work within each culture's belief system to bring an end to this violation of human rights (Bashir, 1997).

---

greater moodiness, in the form of anger and irritability for males and anger and depression for females, between 9 and 14 years of age (Brooks-Gunn & Warren, 1989; Nottelmann et al., 1990). But these links are not strong and are less consistent for boys than girls (Buchanan, Eccles, & Becker, 1992). We cannot really be sure that a rise in pubertal hormones causes adolescent moodiness.

What else might contribute to the common observation that adolescents are moody? In several studies, the mood fluctuations of children, adolescents, and adults were tracked over a week by having them carry electronic pagers. At random intervals, they were beeped and asked to write down what they were doing, whom they were with, and how they felt.

As expected, adolescents reported somewhat lower moods than did school-age children and adults (Csikszentmihalyi & Larson, 1984; Larson & Lampman-Petraitis, 1989). But young people whose moods were especially negative were experiencing a greater number of negative life events, such as difficulties in getting along with parents, disciplinary actions at school, and breaking up with a boyfriend or girlfriend. Negative events increased steadily from childhood to adolescence, and teenagers also seemed to react to them with greater emotion than did children (Larson & Ham, 1993).

Furthermore, compared with the moods of adults, adolescents' feelings were less stable. They often varied from cheerful to sad and back again. But teenagers also moved from one situation to another more often, and their mood swings were strongly related to these changes. High points of their days were times spent with friends and in self-chosen leisure and hobby activities. Low points tended to occur in adult-structured settings—class, job, school halls, school library, and church. Taken together, these findings suggest that situational factors may act in concert with hormonal influences to affect teenagers' moodiness—an explanation consistent with the balanced view of biological and social forces described earlier in this chapter.

■ **PARENT–CHILD RELATIONSHIPS.** Parents are quick to notice that as children enter adolescence, their bedroom doors start to close, they often resist spending time with the family, and they become more argumentative. Many studies show that puberty is related to a rise in parent–child conflict. Bickering and standoffs increase as adolescents move toward the peak of pubertal growth and, for girls, just after menarche occurs. During this time, both parents and teenagers report feeling less close to one another (Holmbeck, 1996; Holmbeck & Hill, 1991).

Why should a youngster's more adultlike appearance and sexual maturity trigger these petty disputes between parent and child? Researchers believe that the association may have some adaptive value. Among nonhuman primates, the young typically leave the family group around the time of puberty. The same is true in many nonindustrialized cultures (Caine, 1986; Schlegel & Barry, 1991). Departure of young people from the family discourages sexual relations between close blood relatives. But because children in industrialized societies usually remain economically dependent on parents long after they reach puberty, they cannot leave the family. Consequently, a modern substitute for physical departure seems to have emerged—increased psychological distancing between parents and children (Steinberg, 1987).

In later chapters, we will see that adolescents' new powers of reasoning may also contribute to a rise in family tensions. In addition, the need for families to redefine relationships as children become physically mature and demand to be treated in adultlike ways can induce a temporary period of conflict. The greater the gap between parents' and adolescents' views of teenagers' readiness to take on developmental tasks (such as handling their own money, getting involved in a sexual relationship, or choosing a philosophy of life), the more quarreling there tends to be (Deković, Noom, & Meeus, 1997).

The conflict that does take place is generally mild; it diminishes by age 14 or 15. With age, teenagers spend less and less time with parents—not because parental ties are disrupted—but because they have more opportunities at school and in the community (Larson et al., 1996). Only a small minority of families experience a serious break in parent–child relationships. In reality, parents and adolescents display both conflict and affection toward one another. This also makes sense from an evolutionary perspective. Although separation from parents is adaptive, both generations benefit from warm, protective family bonds that last for many years to come (Steinberg, 1990).

EARLY VERSUS LATE MATURATION

In addition to dramatic physical change, the timing of puberty has a major impact on psychological adjustment. As we will see in the following sections, having physical characteristics that help gain social acceptance can be very comforting to adolescent boys and girls.

■ **EFFECTS OF PUBERTAL TIMING.** Many studies indicate that maturational timing acts in opposite directions for boys and girls. Early maturing boys appeared advantaged in many aspects of emotional and social functioning. Both adults and peers viewed them as relaxed, independent, self-confident, and physically attractive. Popular with agemates, they held many leadership positions in school and tended to be athletic stars. In contrast, late maturing boys were not well liked. Peers and adults viewed them as anxious, overly talkative, and attention seeking in behavior (Brooks-Gunn, 1988a; Clausen, 1975; Jones, 1965; Jones & Bayley, 1950).

Among girls, the impact of early versus late maturation was just the reverse. Early maturing girls had social difficulties. They were below average in popularity; appeared withdrawn, lacking in self-confidence, and psychologically stressed; and held few positions of leadership (Ge, Conger, & Elder, 1996; Jones & Mussen, 1958). In addition, they were more involved in deviant behavior (getting drunk, staying out late, participating in early sexual activity) and achieved less well in school (Caspi et al., 1993; Stattin & Magnusson, 1990). In contrast, their late maturing counterparts were well adjusted—regarded as physically attractive, lively, sociable, and leaders at school.

Two factors seem to account for these trends: (1) how closely the adolescent's body matches cultural ideals of physical attractiveness, and (2) how well young people "fit in" physically with their agemates.

■ **THE ROLE OF PHYSICAL ATTRACTIVENESS.** Flip through the pages of your favorite popular magazine, and look at the figures of men and women in the ads. You will see convincing evidence for our society's view of an attractive female as thin and long legged and a good-looking male as tall, broad shouldered, and muscular. The female image is a girlish shape that favors the late developer. The male image is consistent with that of the early maturing boy.

As their bodies change, adolescents become preoccupied with their physical selves. Girls are especially likely to analyze all their body features—whether their eyebrows are too thick or too thin, their breasts and hips too large or too small, and their arms and legs sufficiently shapely (Wertheim et al., 1997). In addition, teenagers get a great deal of feedback from others—both directly, through remarks about their appearance, and indirectly, through the tendency of children and adults to treat physically attractive people more positively. The conclusions young people draw about their appearance strongly affect their satisfaction with their bodies and, ultimately, their self-esteem and psychological well-being (Mendelson, White, & Mendelson, 1996; Usmiani & Daniluk, 1997).

In several studies, early maturing girls reported a less positive **body image**—conception of and attitude toward their physical appearance—than did their on-time and late maturing agemates. Among boys, the opposite occurred: Early maturation was linked to a positive body image, whereas late maturation predicted dissatisfaction with the physical self (Alsaker, 1995). The difference in body image between early and late maturing boys was short lived; it disappeared as the late maturers reached puberty. Early maturing girls' less favorable body image not only persisted but became more extreme. In sum, the adoption of society's "beauty is best" stereotype seems to be a factor in pubertal timing effects, particularly for girls.

■ **THE IMPORTANCE OF FITTING IN WITH PEERS.** A second way of explaining differences in adjustment between early and late maturers is in terms of their physical status in relation to agemates. From this perspective, early maturing girls and late maturing boys have difficulty because they fall at the far extremes in physical development. Support for the importance of fitting in socially comes from evidence that adolescents feel most comfortable with peers who match their own level of biological maturity (Brooks-Gunn et al., 1986; Stattin & Magnusson, 1990).

Since few agemates of the same pubertal status are available, early maturing adolescents of both sexes seek out older companions—a tendency that can lead to some unfavorable consequences. Older peers often encourage early maturing youngsters into activities they find difficult to resist and are not yet ready to handle emotionally, including sexual activity, drug and alcohol use, and minor delinquent acts. Perhaps because of involvements like these, the academic performance of early maturers tends to suffer (Caspi et al., 1993; Stattin & Magnusson, 1990).

Interestingly, school contexts can modify these maturational timing effects. In one study, early maturing sixth-grade girls felt better about themselves when they attended kindergarten through sixth-grade (K–6) rather than kindergarten through eighth-grade (K–8) schools, where they could mix with older adolescents. In the K–6 settings, they were relieved of pressures to adopt behaviors for which they were not ready (Blyth, Simmons, & Zakin, 1985). Similarly, a New Zealand study found that delinquency among early maturing girls was greatly reduced in all-girl schools, which limit opportunities to associate with norm-violating peers (most of whom are older boys) (Caspi et al., 1993).

When early maturing girls seek out older companions, they may become involved in unfavorable activities, such as alcohol use, sexual activity, and delinquency. In all-girl schools, however, delinquency among early maturers is greatly reduced, since there are few opportunities to associate with norm–violating boys. (Windsor School)

body image Conception of and attitude toward one's physical appearance.

■ **LONG-TERM CONSEQUENCES.** Do the effects of early and late maturation persist into adulthood? Long-term follow-ups reveal some striking turnabouts in overall well-being. Many early maturing boys and late maturing girls, who had been the focus of admiration in adolescence, became rigid, inflexible, conforming, and somewhat discontented adults. In contrast, late maturing boys and early maturing girls, who were stress-ridden as teenagers, often developed into adults who were independent, flexible, cognitively competent, and satisfied with the direction of their lives (Livson & Peshkin, 1980; Macfarlane, 1971). How can we explain these remarkable reversals? Perhaps the confidence-inducing adolescence of early maturing boys and late maturing girls does not promote the coping skills needed to solve life's later problems. In contrast, the painful experiences associated with off-time pubertal growth may, in time, contribute to sharpened awareness, clarified goals, and greater stability.

Finally, it is important to note that these long-term outcomes may not hold completely in all cultures. In a Swedish study, achievement difficulties of early maturing girls persisted into young adulthood. They were twice as likely as their on-time and later maturing counterparts to leave high school after completing the minimum years of compulsory education (Stattin & Magnusson, 1990). In countries with highly selective college entrance systems, perhaps early maturers have more difficulty recovering from declines in school performance. Clearly, the effects of maturational timing involve a complex blend of biological, immediate social setting, and cultural factors.

ASK YOURSELF . . .

◆ *Sasha remembers menarche as a traumatic experience. When she discovered she was bleeding, she thought she had a deadly illness. What is the likely cause of Sasha's negative reaction?*

◆ *How might adolescent moodiness contribute to the psychological distancing between parents and children that accompanies puberty? (Hint: Think about bidirectional influences in parent–child relationships.)*

◆ **CONNECTIONS**
At puberty, many boys and girls display a rise in gender-stereotyped beliefs and behaviors. Why is this so? (See Chapter 13, page 541.)

BRIEF REVIEW

Puberty is the time of greatest sexual differentiation since the prenatal period. Although changes in primary and secondary sexual characteristics take place in a fairly regular sequence, wide individual, regional, and income-group differences in pubertal timing exist. In contrast to early biologically oriented theories, modern researchers recognize that adolescent adjustment is a product of both biological and social forces.

Puberty has important psychological and social consequences. Typically, girls' reactions to menarche and boys' reactions to spermarche are mixed, although prior knowledge and social support affect their responses. Adolescent moodiness is related to both sex hormones and changes in the social environment. Puberty prompts increased conflict and psychological distancing between parent and child. Expectations of the culture and peer group lead early maturing boys and late maturing girls to be advantaged in emotional and social adjustment. In contrast, late maturing boys and early maturing girls have adjustment difficulties.

Puberty and Adolescent Health

The arrival of puberty is accompanied by new health concerns related to adolescents' striving to meet physical and psychological needs. As the body takes on mature proportions, eating disturbances appear in many young people who worry about falling short of their idealized image of attractiveness and fitness. Homosexual teenagers face formidable challenges in forging an open, positive sexual identity. And sexual activity brings with it the risk of sexually transmitted disease and early pregnancy and childbearing.

As our discussion will reveal, the adolescent's own behavior, or lifestyle, plays a much larger role in health than it did at earlier ages (Bearison, 1998). Yet none of the health concerns we are about to discuss can be traced to a single cause within the individual. Instead, biological, psychological, family, and cultural factors jointly contribute to adolescent well-being.

Girls who reach puberty early, who are very dissatisfied with their body image, and who grow up in homes where a cultural concern with weight and thinness is especially strong are at risk for eating problems. The two most serious eating disorders with adolescent onset are anorexia nervosa and bulimia.

■ ANOREXIA NERVOSA. **Anorexia nervosa** is a tragic eating disturbance in which young people starve themselves because of a compulsive fear of getting fat. About 1 in every 500 teenage girls in the United States is affected, with a peak age of onset between ages 14 and 18. Occasionally, boys are diagnosed, although little is known about their development (Seligmann, 1994). Caucasian-American girls are at greater risk than African-American girls, who are more satisfied with their size and shape (Abood & Chandler, 1997). Hispanics and Asian Americans, who report as much dissatisfaction with their body image as do their Caucasian agemates, are at considerable risk as well (Robinson et al., 1996). The unhealthy behaviors involved in anorexia nervosa occur equally often among teenagers from economically advantaged and disadvantaged families (Rogers et al., 1997).

Anorexics have an extremely distorted body image. Even after they have become severely underweight, they conclude that they are fat. Most lose weight by going on a self-imposed diet so strict that they struggle to avoid eating in response to hunger. To enhance weight loss, they exercise strenuously.

The physical consequences of this attempt to reach "perfect" slimness are severe. Anorexics lose between 25 and 50 percent of their body weight and appear painfully thin. Because a normal menstrual cycle requires a body fat content of about 15 percent, either menarche does not occur or menstrual periods stop. Malnutrition causes additional physical symptoms—pale skin; brittle, discolored nails; fine dark hairs all over the body; and extreme sensitivity to cold. If allowed to continue, anorexia nervosa can result in shrinking of the heart muscle, kidney failure, permanent loss of bone mass, and brain damage. About 6 percent of those with the disorder die of it (Neumärker, 1997).

Forces within the person, family, and culture give rise to anorexia nervosa. We have already seen that the societal image of "thin is beautiful" contributes to the poorer body image of early maturing girls, who are at greatest risk for anorexia (Graber et al., 1994). But although almost all adolescent girls go on diets at one time or another, anorexics persist in weight loss to an extreme. Many are perfectionists with high standards for their own behavior and performance. Typically, these girls are excellent students who are responsible and well behaved—ideal daughters in many respects.

Yet interactions between parents and anorexic daughters reveal problems related to adolescent autonomy that may trigger the compulsive dieting. Often their mothers have high expectations for achievement and social acceptance, are overprotective and controlling, and have eating problems themselves (Pike & Rodin, 1991). Although the daughter tries to meet these demands, inside she is angry at not being recognized as an individual in her own right. Instead of rebelling openly, the anorexic girl indirectly tells her parents, "I am a separate person from you, and I can do what I want with my own body!" At the same time, this youngster, who has been so used to having parents make decisions for her, responds to the challenges of adolescence with depression and lack of self-confidence. Starving herself is also a way of avoiding new expectations by returning to a much younger, preadolescent image (Maloney & Kranz, 1991).

Because anorexic girls typically deny that any problem exists, treating the disorder is difficult. Hospitalization is often necessary to prevent life-threatening malnutrition. Family therapy, in which efforts are made to change parent–child interaction and expectations, is the most successful treatment. As a supplementary approach, applied behavior analysis—in which hospitalized anorexics are reinforced for gaining weight with praise, social contact, and opportunities for exercise—is helpful. Still, only 50 percent of anorexics fully recover (Fichter & Quadflieg, 1996).

■ BULIMIA. One-fifth of anorexics develop **bulimia,** a less severe disorder in which young people (again, mainly girls, but gay adolescent boys are also vulnerable) engage in

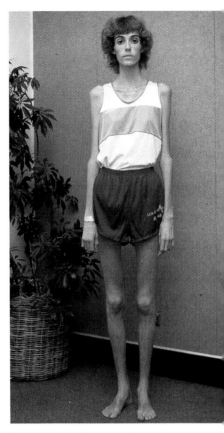

This anorexic girl's strict, self-imposed diet and obsession with strenuous physical exercise has led her to become painfully thin. Even so, her body image is so distorted that she probably regards herself as fat. (Wm. Thompson/The Picture Cube)

anorexia nervosa An eating disorder in which individuals (usually females) starve themselves because of a compulsive fear of getting fat.

bulimia An eating disorder in which individuals (mainly females) engage in binge eating followed by deliberate vomiting, purging with laxatives, and strict dieting.

binge eating followed by deliberate vomiting, purging with laxatives, and strict dieting (Heffernan, 1994). Bulimia is much more common than anorexia nervosa. About 1 to 3 percent of teenage girls are affected; only 5 percent have previously been anorexic (Fairburn & Beglin, 1990).

Although bulimics share with anorexics a pathological fear of getting fat and a family background with high expectations, they may have experienced their parents as disengaged and emotionally unavailable rather than controlling. One conjecture is that bulimics turn to food to compensate for a feeling of emptiness resulting from lack of parental involvement (Attie & Brooks-Gunn, 1996; Johnson & Connors, 1987).

Typically, bulimics are not just impulsive eaters; they also lack self-control in other areas of their lives. Although they tend to be good students and liked by peers, many engage in petty shoplifting and alcohol abuse. Bulimics also differ from anorexics in that they are aware of their abnormal eating habits, feel depressed and guilty about them, and usually are desperate for help. As a result, bulimia is usually easier to treat through individual and family therapy, support groups, and nutrition education (Harris, 1991; Thakwray et al., 1993).

SEXUALITY

Virtually all theorists agree that adolescence is an especially important time for the development of sexuality. With the arrival of puberty, hormonal changes—in particular, the production of androgens in young people of both sexes—lead to an increase in sex drive (Halpern, Udry, & Suchindran, 1997; Udry, 1990). In response, adolescents become very concerned about how to manage sexuality in social relationships, and new cognitive capacities affect their efforts to do so. Yet, like the eating behaviors we have just discussed, adolescent sexuality is heavily influenced by the young person's social context.

■ **THE IMPACT OF CULTURE.** Think, for a moment, about when you first learned the "facts of life" and how you found out about them. In your family, was sex discussed openly or treated with secrecy? Cross-cultural research reveals that exposure to sex, education about it, and efforts to restrict the sexual curiosity of children and adolescents vary widely around the world. At one extreme are a number of Middle Eastern peoples, who are known to kill girls who dishonor their families by losing their virginity before marriage. At the other extreme are several Asian and Pacific Island groups with very permissive sexual attitudes and practices. For example, among the Trobriand Islanders of Melanesia, older companions provide children with explicit instruction in sexual practices. Bachelor houses are maintained, where adolescents are expected to engage in sexual experimentation with a variety of partners (Benedict, 1934b; Ford & Beach, 1951).

Despite the publicity granted to the image of a sexually free and sophisticated modern adolescent, sexual attitudes in the United States are relatively restrictive. Typically, American parents give children little information about sex, discourage them from engaging in sex play, and rarely talk about sex in their presence. When young people become interested in sex, they seek information from friends, books, magazines, movies, and television. On prime-time television shows, which adolescents watch the most, sex between partners with little commitment to each other occurs often and is spontaneous and passionate. Characters are rarely shown taking steps to avoid pregnancy or sexually transmitted disease (Ward, 1995).

Consider the contradictory and confusing messages delivered by these two sets of sources. On the one hand, adults emphasize that sex at a young age and outside of marriage is wrong. On the other hand, adolescents encounter much in the broader social environment that extols the excitement and romanticism of sex. These mixed messages leave many American teenagers bewildered, poorly informed about sexual facts, and with little sound advice on how to conduct their sex lives responsibly.

■ **ADOLESCENT SEXUAL ATTITUDES AND BEHAVIOR.** Although differences between subcultural groups exist, over the past 30 years the sexual attitudes of both adolescents and adults have become more liberal. Compared to a generation ago, more people believe that sexual intercourse before marriage is all right, as long as two people are emotionally committed to each other (Michael et al., 1994). Recently, a slight swing back in

Adolescence is an especially important time for the development of sexuality. American teenagers receive contradictory and confusing messages from the social environment about the appropriateness of sex. Although the rate of premarital sex has risen among adolescents, most engage in low levels of sexuality and have only a single partner.

(Richard Hutchings/PhotoEdit)

TABLE 5.2

Teenage Sexual Activity Rates by Sex, Ethnic Group, and Grade

Sex	Ethnic Group			Grade				
	White	Black	Hispanic	9	10	11	12	Total
Male	43.3	80.3	57.7	41.8	41.7	49.3	60.1	48.9
Female	44.0	65.6	45.7	34.0	43.5	50.3	61.9	47.7
Total	43.6	72.7	52.2	38.0	42.5	49.7	60.9	48.5

Note: Data reflect the percentage of high school students who report ever having had sexual intercourse.

Source: U.S. Department of Health and Human Services, 1998c.

the direction of conservative sexual beliefs has occurred, largely due to the risk of sexually transmitted disease, especially AIDS (Glassman, 1996).

Trends in the sexual activity of adolescents are quite consistent with their attitudes. The rate of premarital sex among young people rose over several decades but recently declined. For example, among unmarried 15- to 19-year-olds, females claiming to have had sexual intercourse grew from 28 percent in 1971 to 55 percent in 1990 and then dropped to 49 percent in 1997 (U.S. Department of Health and Human Services, 1998c). Nevertheless, as Table 5.2 reveals, a substantial minority of boys and girls are sexually active quite early, by ninth grade. Males tend to have their first intercourse earlier than do females, and sexual activity is especially high among black adolescents—particularly boys.

Yet timing of first intercourse provides only a limited picture of adolescent sexual behavior. Most teenagers engage in relatively low levels of sexual activity. The typical 15- to 19-year-old sexually active male—white, black, or Hispanic—has relations with only one girl at a time and spends half the year with no partner at all (Sonenstein, Pleck, & Ku, 1991). Contrary to popular belief, a runaway sexual revolution does not characterize American young people. In fact, the rate of teenage sexual activity in the United States is about the same as in Western European nations (Creatsas et al., 1995).

■ **CHARACTERISTICS OF SEXUALLY ACTIVE ADOLESCENTS**. Early and frequent teenage sexual activity is linked to a wide range of personal, familial, peer, and educational variables. These include early physical maturation, parental divorce, large family size, sexually active friends and older siblings, poor school performance, lower educational aspirations, and tendency to engage in norm-violating acts, including alcohol and drug use and delinquency (Braverman & Strasburger, 1994; Cooper & Orcutt, 1997).

Since many of these factors are associated with growing up in a low-income family, it is not surprising that early sexual activity is more common among young people from economically disadvantaged homes. In fact, the high rate of premarital intercourse among black teenagers can largely be accounted for by widespread poverty in the black population (Sullivan, 1993).

■ **CONTRACEPTIVE USE**. Although adolescent contraceptive use has increased in recent years, one-third to one-half of sexually active American teenagers are at risk for unplanned pregnancy because they do not use birth control at all or delay using it for months after they have become sexually active (Moore et al., 1998). Why do so many teenagers fail to take precautions? In Chapter 6, we will see that compared with school-age children, adolescents can consider many more possibilities when faced with a problem. But at first, they fail to apply this reasoning to everyday situations. In several studies, teenagers were asked to explain why they did not use contraception (Stevens-Simon et al., 1996; Zabin, Stark & Emerson, 1991). Here are some typical answers: "I was waiting until I had a steady boyfriend." "I thought I could not get pregnant." "I wasn't planning to have sex."

One reason for responses like these is that advances in perspective taking—the capacity to imagine what others may be thinking and feeling (see Chapters 6 and 11)—lead teenagers, for a time, to be extremely concerned about others' opinions of them. Another reason for lack of planning before sex is that intense self-reflection leads many adolescents to believe they are unique and invulnerable to danger. Recent evidence indicates that teenagers and adults differ very little on questionnaires asking about consequences of engaging in risky behaviors; both report similar levels of vulnerability (Beyth-Marom et al., 1993). Still, in the midst of everyday social pressures, adolescents often seem to conclude that pregnancy happens to others, not to themselves (Beyth-Marom & Fischhoff, 1997).

Although adolescent cognition may have something to do with teenagers' reluctance to use contraception, the social environment also contributes to it. Teenagers who talk openly with their parents about sex are not less sexually active, but they are more likely to use birth control (Brooks-Gunn, 1988b). Unfortunately, many adolescents say they are too scared or embarrassed to ask parents questions about sex or contraception. And too many leave sex education classes with incomplete or factually incorrect knowledge. Some do not know where to get birth control counseling and devices. When they do, they often worry that a doctor or family planning clinic might not keep their visit confidential (Alan Guttmacher Institute, 1994; Winn, Roker, & Coleman, 1995).

■ **SEXUAL ORIENTATION.** Up to this point, our discussion has focused only on heterosexual behavior. About 3 to 6 percent of young people discover they are lesbian or gay (see the Variations box on the following page). An as yet unknown but significant number are bisexual (Michael et al., 1994; Patterson, 1995). Adolescence is an equally crucial time for the sexual development of these individuals, and societal attitudes, once again, loom large in how well they fare.

Although the extent to which homosexuality is due to genetic versus environmental forces remains highly controversial, new evidence indicates that heredity makes an important contribution. Identical twins of both sexes are much more likely than fraternal twins to share a homosexual orientation; the same is true for biological as opposed to adoptive relatives (Bailey & Pillard, 1991; Bailey et al., 1993). Furthermore, male homosexuality tends to be more common on the maternal than paternal side of families. This suggests that it might be X-linked (see Chapter 3). Indeed, one gene-mapping study found that among 40 pairs of homosexual brothers, 33 (83 percent) had an identical segment of DNA on the X chromosome. One or several genes in that region might predispose males to become homosexual (Hamer et al., 1993).

How might heredity lead to homosexuality? According to some researchers, certain genes affect prenatal sex hormone levels, which modify brain structures in ways that induce homosexual feelings and behavior (Bailey et al., 1995; LeVay, 1993). Keep in mind, however, that both genetic and environmental factors can alter prenatal hormones. Girls exposed prenatally to abnormal levels of androgens or estrogens—because of either a genetic defect or drugs given to the mother to prevent miscarriage—are more likely to become homosexual or bisexual (Meyer-Bahlburg et al., 1995). Furthermore, homosexual men tend to have a later birth order and a higher-than-average number of older brothers (Blanchard et al., 1995; Blanchard & Bogaert, 1996). One controversial speculation is that mothers with several male children sometimes produce antibodies to androgens, which reduce the prenatal impact of male sex hormones on the brains of later-born boys.

Family factors are also linked to homosexuality. Looking back on their childhoods, both male and female homosexuals tend to view their same-sex parent as cold, rejecting, or distant (Bell, Weinberg, & Hammersmith, 1981; McConaghy & Silove, 1992). This does not mean that parents cause their youngsters to become homosexual. Rather, for some children, an early genetic bias away from traditional gender-role behavior may prompt negative reactions from same-sex parents and peers. A strong desire for affection from people of their own sex may join with biology to strengthen their homosexual orientation (Green, 1987). Once again, however, homosexuality does not always develop in this way, since some homosexuals are very comfortable with their gender role and have warm relationships with their parents. Homosexuality probably results from a variety of biological and environmental combinations that are not yet well understood (Horton, 1995).

SEXUALLY TRANSMITTED DISEASE

Sexually active adolescents, both homosexual and heterosexual, are at risk for sexually transmitted disease (STD). Adolescents have the highest incidence of STD of any age

Homosexuality: Coming Out to Oneself and Others

ULTURES VARY AS much in their acceptance of homosexuality as they do in their approval of premarital sex. In the United States, homosexuals are stigmatized, as shown by the degrading language often used to describe them. This makes forming a sexual identity a much greater challenge for gay and lesbian youths than for their heterosexual counterparts, who appreciate from an early age that people like themselves fall in love with members of the other sex (Rotheram-Borus & Fernandez, 1995).

Wide variations in homosexual identity formation exist, depending on personal, family, and community factors. Yet interviews with homosexual adolescents and adults reveal that many (but not all) move through a three-phase sequence in coming out to themselves and others:

FEELING DIFFERENT. Gay men and lesbians often say that they felt different from other children when they were young. Typically, this first sense of their biologically determined sexual orientation appears between ages 6 and 12 and results from play interests more like those of the other gender (Mondimore, 1996). Boys may find that they are less interested in sports, drawn to quieter activities, and more emotionally sensitive than other boys; girls that they are more athletic and active than other girls.

In Chapter 13, we will see that children who do not conform to traditional gender roles (especially boys) are often ridiculed—an early experience of many homosexuals. In addition, when children hear derogatory labels for homosexuality, they absorb a bias against their own sexual orientation at an early age.

CONFUSION. With the arrival of puberty, feeling different begins to include feeling sexually different. In one study of 200 ethnically diverse gay, lesbian, and bisexual youths, awareness of a same-sex attraction occurred, on the average, between ages 11 and 12 (Herdt & Boxer, 1993). Realizing that homosexuality has personal relevance generally sparks confusion, largely because most young people had assumed they were heterosexual like everyone else.

A few adolescents resolve their discomfort by crystallizing a gay or lesbian identity quickly, with a flash of insight into their sense of being different. Most experience an inner struggle and deep sense of isolation—outcomes intensified by lack of role models and social support. Some throw themselves into activities they have come to associate with heterosexuality. Boys may go out for athletic teams; girls may drop the softball team in favor of dance. And they may try heterosexual dating. Others are so bewildered, uncomfortable, guilt-ridden, and lonely that they escape into alcohol and drug abuse and suicidal thinking (Mondimore, 1996).

ACCEPTANCE. The majority of gay and lesbian teenagers reach a point of accepting their homosexuality. Then they face another crossroad: whether to tell others. The most difficult disclosure is to parents, but many fear rejection

This gay couple enjoys an evening at a high school prom. As long as friends and family members react with acceptance, coming out strengthens the young person's view of homosexuality as a valid, meaningful, and fulfilling identity.

(Donnie Binder/Impact Visuals)

by peers as well (Cohen & Savin-Williams, 1996). Powerful stigma against their sexual orientation at home and school lead some to decide that no disclosure is possible. As a result, they self-define but otherwise "pass" as heterosexual. In one interview study of gay adolescents, 85 percent said they tried concealment for a time (Newman & Muzzonigro, 1993).

Many homosexuals eventually acknowledge their sexual orientation publicly, usually by telling trusted friends first, then family members and acquaintances. When people whose love and acceptance is strongly desired react positively, coming out strengthens the young person's view of homosexuality as a valid, meaningful, and fulfilling identity. Contact with other gays and lesbians is important for reaching this phase, and changes in society permit many adolescents in urban areas to attain it earlier than they did a decade or two ago (Anderson, 1994; Edwards, 1996). Gay and lesbian communities exist in large cities, along with specialized interest groups, social clubs, religious groups, newspapers, and periodicals. Small towns and rural areas remain difficult places to meet other homosexuals and to find a supportive environment. Teenagers in these locales have a special need for caring adults and peers who can help them find self and social acceptance.

Gay and lesbian adolescents who succeed in coming out to themselves and others integrate their sexual orientation into a broader sense of identity, a process we will address in Chapter 11. As a result, they no longer need to focus so heavily on their homosexual self, and energy is freed for other aspects of psychological growth.

group. Despite a recent decline in STD in the United States, one out of six sexually active teenagers—3 million young people—contract an STD each year, a rate 50 to 100 times higher than that of other industrialized nations (U.S. Centers for Disease Control, 1998). If left untreated, sterility and life-threatening complications can result. Teenagers in greatest danger of STD are the same ones who tend to engage in irresponsible sexual behavior—poverty-stricken young people who feel a sense of inferiority and hopelessness about their lives (Holmbeck, Waters, & Brookman, 1990).

By far the most serious STD is AIDS. Although not many adolescents have AIDS, over one-fifth of cases in the United States occur between ages 20 and 29. Nearly all of these originate in adolescence, since AIDS symptoms typically take 8 to 10 years to emerge in a person infected with HIV. Drug-abusing and homosexual teenagers account for most cases, but heterosexual spread is increasing, especially among females. It is at least twice as easy for a male to infect a female with any STD, including AIDS, as it is for a female to infect a male (U.S. Centers for Disease Control, 1998).

As the result of school courses and media campaigns, over 90 percent of high school students are aware of basic facts about AIDS. But some hold false beliefs that put them at risk—for example, that birth control pills provide some protection or that it is possible to tell whether people have AIDS by looking at them (DiClemente, 1993). To prevent this deadly disease, almost all parents favor AIDS education in the public schools, and most states now require it.

ADOLESCENT PREGNANCY AND PARENTHOOD

Over 900,000 American teenage girls—20 percent of those who have had sexual intercourse—become pregnant annually, 30,000 under age 15. Despite a steady decline since 1991, the adolescent pregnancy rate in the United States is the highest in the industrialized world—twice that of Great Britain, Canada, France, and Australia, three times that of Sweden, and more than nine times that of the Netherlands (see Figure 5.15). The United States differs from these nations in three important ways: (1) effective sex education reaches fewer teenagers; (2) convenient, low-cost contraceptive services for adolescents are scarce; and (3) many more families live in poverty, which encourages young people to take risks without considering the future implications of their behavior.

About 40 percent of teenage pregnancies end in abortion, 14 percent in miscarriage (Alan Guttmacher Institute, 1998). Because the United States has one of the highest adolescent abortion rates of any developed country, the total number of teenage births is actually lower than it was 30 years ago (Ventura et al., 1997). But teenage parenthood is a much greater problem today because modern adolescents are far less likely to marry before childbirth. In 1960, only 15 percent of teenage births were to unmarried females, whereas today, 75 percent are (Coley & Chase-Lansdale, 1998).

Increased social acceptance of a young single mother raising a child, along with the belief of many teenage girls that a baby might fill a void in their lives, has meant that only a small number give their infants up for adoption. Each year, about 320,000 unmarried adolescent girls take on the responsibilities of parenthood before they are psychologically mature.

Teenage pregnancy imposes lasting hardships on both adolescent and newborn baby. The chances are reduced that these girls will finish high school, marry, and enter a satisfying, well-paid vocation. Because of stressful life conditions, children of teenagers are at risk for poor parenting.

(Stephen Fiorella/Liason International)

■ **CORRELATES AND CONSEQUENCES OF ADOLESCENT PARENTHOOD.** Becoming a parent is challenging and stressful for any person, but it is especially difficult for adolescents. Teenage parents have not yet established a clear sense of direction for their own lives. And most face stressful life circumstances that are compounded after the baby is born.

As we have seen, adolescent sexual activity is linked to economic disadvantage. Teenage parents are many times more likely to be poor than are agemates who postpone childbearing. Their life experiences often include poor school performance; alcohol and drug use; adult models of unmarried parenthood, limited education, and unemployment; and residence in neighborhoods where other adolescents also display these risks. A high percent-

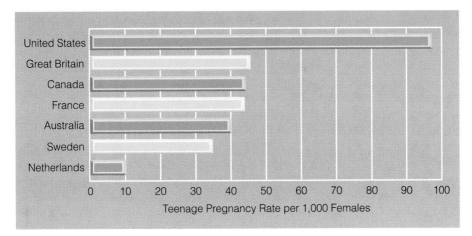

FIGURE 5.15

Teenage pregnancy rate in seven industrialized nations.

(Adapted from Alan Guttmacher Institute, 1998.)

age of out-of-wedlock births are to members of low-income minorities, especially Hispanic, African-American, and Native-American teenagers (see Figure 5.16). Many of these young people seem to turn to early parenthood as a way to move into adulthood when educational and career avenues are unavailable (Luker, 1996; Fagot et al., 1998).

Think about these characteristics of teenage parents, and you will quickly see why early childbirth imposes lasting hardships on two generations—adolescent and newborn baby. The lives of pregnant teenagers are often troubled in many ways, and after the baby is born, their circumstances tend to worsen in at least three respects:

- *Educational attainment.* Giving birth before age 18 reduces the likelihood of finishing high school. Only 50 percent of adolescent mothers graduate with either a regular diploma or general equivalency diploma (GED), compared with 96 percent of girls who wait to become parents (Hotz, McElroy, & Sanders, 1997).

- *Marital patterns.* Teenage motherhood reduces the chances of marriage. When these mothers do marry, they are more likely to divorce than are their peers who delay childbearing (Moore et al., 1993). Consequently, teenage mothers spend more of their parenting years as single parents. Often they have additional out-of-wedlock births in quick succession.

- *Economic circumstances.* Because of low educational attainment, marital instability, and poverty, many teenage mothers are on welfare. If they are employed, their limited education restricts them to unsatisfying, low-paid jobs (Moore et al., 1993). Adolescent fathers work more hours than their nonparent agemates in the years following their child's birth. Perhaps for this reason, they obtain less education and are also economically disadvantaged (Brien & Willis, 1997).

In Chapter 3, we saw that poverty-stricken pregnant women are more likely to have inadequate diets and to expose their unborn babies to harmful environmental influences, such as illegal drugs. And many do not receive early prenatal care. These conditions are widespread among pregnant teenagers. As a result, adolescent mothers often experience prenatal and birth complications, and their infants are likely to be born underweight and premature (Scholl, Heidiger, & Belsky, 1996).

Children of teenagers are also at risk for poor parenting. Compared to adult mothers, adolescent mothers know less about child development, have unrealistically high expectations, perceive their infants as more difficult, and interact less effectively with them (Brooks-Gunn & Chase-Lansdale, 1995). As they get older, many children of adolescent mothers score low on intelligence tests, achieve poorly in school, and engage in disruptive social behavior. Too often, the cycle of adolescent pregnancy is repeated in the next generation (Furstenberg, Hughes, & Brooks-Gunn, 1992; Moore, Morrison, & Greene, 1997).

FIGURE 5.16

Births per 1,000 females ages 15 to 19 by ethnic group.
Poverty, weak academic skills, and resulting narrowing of life options are key reasons birth rates are much higher among Hispanic, African-American, and Native-American teenagers than among whites and Asian Americans.

(From Donovan, 1998.)

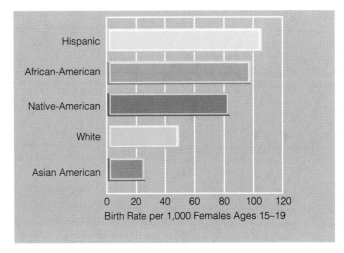

Still, how well adolescent parents and their children fare varies a great deal. If the teenage mother finishes high school, avoids additional births, and finds a stable marriage partner, long-term disruptions in her own and her child's development are less severe. The small minority of young mothers who fail in all three of these areas face a life of continuing misfortune (Furstenberg, Brooks-Gunn, & Morgan, 1987).

■ **PREVENTION STRATEGIES.** Preventing teenage pregnancy and childbearing requires strategies addressing the many factors that underlie early sexual activity and lack of contraceptive use. Informing adolescents about sex and contraception is crucial. Too often, sex education courses are given late in high school (after sexual activity has begun), last no more than a few sessions, and are limited to a catalogue of facts about anatomy and reproduction. Sex education that goes beyond this bare minimum does not encourage early sex, as some opponents claim. It does improve awareness of sexual facts—knowledge that is necessary for responsible sexual behavior (Katchadourian, 1990).

Knowledge, however, is not sufficient to convince adolescents of the importance of postponing sexual activity and practicing contraception. Sex education must help them build a bridge between what they know and what they do (Frost & Forrest, 1995). Today, more effective sex education programs have emerged with the following key elements:

■ Teaching skills for handling sexual situations through creative discussion and role-playing techniques, which permit teenagers to confront sexual situations similar to those they will encounter in everyday life

■ Promoting the value of abstinence to teenagers not yet sexually active

■ Providing information about and ready access to contraceptives

The most controversial aspect of adolescent pregnancy prevention is increasing the availability of contraceptives. Many Americans argue that placing birth control pills or condoms in the hands of teenagers is equivalent to saying that early sex is okay. Yet sex education programs that focus only on abstinence and neglect contraception have little impact on the sexual practices of most adolescents (Kirby et al., 1994). And in Western Europe, where school-based health clinics offering contraceptive services are common, teenage sexual activity is no higher than it is in the United States, but pregnancy, childbirth, and abortion rates are much lower (Zabin & Hayward, 1993).

Efforts to prevent adolescent pregnancy and parenthood must go beyond sex education and contraception to build social competence. In one study, researchers randomly assigned at-risk high school students to either a year-long community service class, called Teen Outreach, or to regular classroom experiences in health or social studies. In Teen Outreach, adolescents participated in at least 20 hours per week of volunteer work tailored to their interests. They returned to school for discussions that focused on enhancing their community service skills and ability to cope with everyday challenges. At the end of the school year, pregnancy, school failure, and school suspension were substantially lower in the group enrolled in Teen Outreach, which fostered social skills, connectedness to the community, and self-respect (Allen et al., 1997).

Finally, teenagers who look forward to a promising future are far less likely to engage in early and irresponsible sex. Society can provide young people with good reasons to postpone early childbearing by expanding their educational and vocational opportunities. We will take up these issues in Chapter 15.

■ **INTERVENING WITH ADOLESCENT PARENTS.** The most difficult and costly way to deal with adolescent parenthood is to wait until after it has happened. Young single mothers need health care for themselves and their children, encouragement to stay in school, job training, instruction in parenting and life-management skills, and high-quality, affordable child care. School programs that provide these services reduce the incidence of low-birthweight babies, increase mothers' educational success, and decrease their likelihood of rapid additional childbearing (Seitz & Apfel, 1993, 1994; Seitz, Apfel, & Rosenbaum, 1991).

Adolescent mothers also benefit from family relationships that are sensitive to their developmental needs. Very young mothers who continue to live in the same household as their own mother (the child's grandmother) engage in more positive parent–child inter-

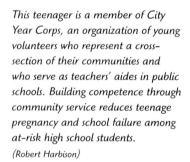

This teenager is a member of City Year Corps, an organization of young volunteers who represent a cross-section of their communities and who serve as teachers' aides in public schools. Building competence through community service reduces teenage pregnancy and school failure among at-risk high school students.

(Robert Harbison)

action. Older teenage mothers, however, benefit from establishing their own residence with the help of relatives—an arrangement that grants the adolescent a balance of autonomy and support. Independent living combined with high levels of grandparent assistance is associated with more effective parenting, warmer family ties, and children who are developing more favorably (Chase-Lansdale, Brooks-Gunn, & Zamsky, 1994; East & Felice, 1996). These findings raise questions about a new U.S. welfare policy that requires teenage mothers to live at home to receive benefits.

Programs focusing on fathers are attempting to increase their emotional and financial commitment to the baby (Coley & Chase-Lansdale, 1998). Although almost half of young fathers visit their children during the first few years after birth, contact usually diminishes. By school age, fewer than one-fourth are still involved (Lerman, 1993). But new laws that encourage mothers to help establish paternity and that enforce child support payments may lead to a turnabout in paternal responsibility and interaction. Teenage mothers who receive financial and child-care assistance from the child's father are less distressed and interact more favorably with their infants (Caldwell & Antonucci, 1997). And children of teenagers with warm ties to their fathers show better long-term adjustment (Furstenberg & Harris, 1993).

A CONCLUDING NOTE

Because some of the most rapid and complex physical and psychological changes are sparked by puberty, teenagers are vulnerable to certain problems. Yet the unhealthy behaviors of the adolescent years are not an irrational response to inner turmoil, as theorists once believed. Instead, every level of the ecological system contributes to teenagers' behavior.

Furthermore, adolescent risks are interconnected; teenagers with one problem frequently display others (Dryfoos, 1990; Lerner, Ostrom, & Freel, 1997). This co-occurrence will become even clearer when we take up delinquency, depression, suicide, substance abuse, and school underachievement and failure. In designing more powerful interventions, researchers face the challenge of how to deal with simultaneous risks and the multiple contexts in which each is embedded. Think back to the successful intervention efforts discussed in the preceding sections, and notice how they employ several strategies, target multiple behaviors, and involve several contexts.

Finally, adolescence is not just a time of risk; it is also a time of tremendous opportunity. Teenagers gain a better understanding of how the world works, greater control over their own social contexts, broader access to social support, and increased ability to avoid or alter risky behaviors. Yet families, schools, communities, and nations must create conditions that permit adolescents to exercise their expanding capacity for positive health practices (Maggs, Schulenberg, & Hurrelmann, 1997). This is a theme we will revisit when we address other aspects of adolescent development in later chapters.

ASK YOURSELF . . .

◆ *Fourteen-year-old Lindsay says she's pretty certain she couldn't get pregnant from having sex with her boyfriend, since he told her he'd never do anything to "mess her up." What factors might account for Lindsay's unrealistic reasoning?*

◆ *Explain how cultural forces are involved in each of the following health concerns: adolescent eating disorders; homosexual adolescents' self-acceptance; and teenage pregnancy and childbearing. What implications does your analysis have for the accuracy of the "storm and stress" view of adolescence?*

◆ CONNECTIONS
Cite commonalities in the life circumstances of adolescents who engage in early and unprotected sex, who commit delinquent acts, and who abuse alcohol and drugs. Explain why these risk behaviors often co-occur. (See Chapter 12, page 511, and Chapter 15, page 614.)

SUMMARY

THE COURSE OF PHYSICAL GROWTH

Describe the course of physical growth, including changes in body size, proportions, and composition and their relation to gains in gross motor skills during childhood and adolescence.

◆ Compared with other animal species, humans experience a prolonged period of physical growth. **Distance** and **velocity curves** show the overall pattern of change: Gains in height and weight are rapid during infancy, slower during early and middle childhood, and rapid again during puberty.

◆ In childhood, physical growth follows cephalocaudal and proximodistal trends. During puberty, growth actually proceeds in the reverse direction, and sex-related differences in body proportions appear. Body fat is laid down quickly during the first 9 months, then rapidly again at adolescence for girls. In contrast, muscle development is slow and gradual until puberty, when it rises dramatically, especially for boys.

◆ In early childhood, body growth causes the child's center of gravity to shift toward the trunk, and balance improves, paving the way for an explosion of gross motor milestones. During the school years, improved balance, strength, agility, and flexibility support refinements in running, jumping, hopping, and ball skills. Increased body size and muscle strength lead to continued motor gains in adolescence. Children continue to integrate previously acquired motor skills into more complex, dynamic systems of action.

Describe skeletal growth and hormonal influences on physical growth.

- **Skeletal age,** a measure based on the number of **epiphyses** and the extent to which they are fused, is the best way to estimate the child's overall physical maturity. Girls are advanced over boys, a gap that widens over infancy and childhood. At birth, infants have six **fontanels,** which permit skull bones to expand as the brain grows rapidly in the first few years.
- Physical growth is controlled by hormones released by the **pituitary gland,** located at the base of the brain near the **hypothalamus,** which initiates and regulates pituitary secretions. **Growth hormone (GH)** affects the development of almost all body tissues. **Thyroxine,** released by the thyroid gland, influences brain growth and body size. Sexual maturation is controlled by the sex hormones—**estrogens** and **androgens.**

Discuss factors that contribute to worldwide variations, secular trends, and asynchronies in physical growth.

- Worldwide variations in body size are the combined result of heredity and environment. **Secular trends in physical growth** have occurred in industrialized nations. Because of improved health and nutrition, many children are growing larger and reaching physical maturity earlier than did their ancestors.
- Physical growth is an asynchronous process. The **general growth curve** refers to change in overall body size. Other systems of the body, such as the genitals, the lymph tissue, and the brain, have their own unique timetables of maturation.

DEVELOPMENT OF THE BRAIN

Cite major milestones in brain development, at the level of individual brain cells and at the level of the cerebral cortex.

- During the first few years, the human brain grows faster than any other organ. Once **neurons** are in place, they form **synapses** at a rapid rate. During the peak period of development in any brain area, **programmed cell death** makes room for growth of neural fibers that form synaptic connections. Stimulation determines which neurons will continue to establish new synapses and which will lose their connective fibers through **synaptic pruning. Glial cells,** which are responsible for **myelinization,** multiply dramatically through the second year and result in large gains in brain weight.
- **Lateralization** refers to specialization of the hemispheres of the **cerebral cortex.** Although some specialization exists at birth, in the first few years of life there is high **brain plasticity.** Both heredity and early experience contribute to brain organization.
- Hand preference reflects the individual's **dominant cerebral hemisphere.** It first appears in infancy and gradually increases, indicating that lateralization strengthens during early and middle childhood. New environmental theories, including the way fetuses lie in the uterus and the strong role of practice, have been proposed to explain handedness. Although left-handedness is more frequent among children with developmental problems, the great majority of left-handers show no abnormalities of any kind.

Describe changes in other brain structures, and discuss evidence on brain growth spurts as sensitive periods of development.

- During infancy and early childhood, connections are established between different brain structures. Fibers linking the **cerebellum** to the cerebral cortex myelinate, enhancing children's balance and motor control. The **reticular formation,** responsible for alertness and consciousness, and the **corpus callosum,** which connects the two cerebral hemispheres, also develop rapidly.
- Changes in the electrical activity of the cortex, along with gains in brain weight and skull size, indicate that brain growth spurts occur intermittently from infancy into adolescence. These coincide with major cognitive changes and peaks in intelligence test performance and may be sensitive periods in which appropriate stimulation is necessary for full development.

FACTORS AFFECTING PHYSICAL GROWTH

How do heredity, nutrition, infectious disease, and affection and stimulation contribute to physical growth?

- Twin and adoption studies reveal that heredity contributes to children's height, weight, and rate of physical maturation. As long as negative factors are not severe, children and adolescents who lag behind in body size show **catch-up growth** under improved environmental conditions.
- Good nutrition is crucial for children to reach their full growth potential. Breast-feeding is especially suited to infants' growth needs and is crucial for protecting the health of babies in the developing world. As growth slows in early childhood, appetite declines. It rises sharply during puberty.
- The importance of nutrition is tragically evident in the dietary diseases of **marasmus** and **kwashiorkor,** which affect large numbers of children in developing countries. In industrialized nations, **obesity** is a nutritional problem with severe health and psychological consequences. Low-income status, maladaptive parental feeding practices, physical inactivity, Western high-fat diets, and early growth stunting due to malnutrition contribute to obesity.
- Infectious disease can combine with poor nutrition to undermine healthy physical development. In developing countries, diarrhea is widespread and claims millions of young lives. Teaching families how to administer **oral rehydration therapy (ORT)** can prevent most of these deaths.
- **Nonorganic failure to thrive** and **deprivation dwarfism** illustrate the importance of affection and stimulation for normal human growth.

PUBERTY: THE PHYSICAL TRANSITION TO ADULTHOOD

Describe sexual maturation in girls and boys, noting genetic and environmental influences on pubertal timing.

- Accompanying rapid changes in body size and proportions at **puberty** are changes in **primary** and **secondary sexual characteristics. Menarche** (first menstruation) occurs relatively late in the girl's sequence of pubertal events, after the peak in the height spurt. In the following year, growth of the breasts and pubic hair are completed, and underarm hair appears. As the boy's body and sex organs enlarge and pubic and underarm hair emerges, **spermarche** (first ejaculation) and deepening of the voice take place, followed by growth of facial and body hair.
- Besides genetic influences evident in twin comparisons, nutrition and overall physical health contribute to the timing of puberty. Menarche is delayed in poverty-stricken regions of the world and among girls from economically disadvantaged homes.

THE PSYCHOLOGICAL IMPACT OF PUBERTAL EVENTS

What factors influence adolescents' reactions to the physical changes of puberty?

◆ Recent research shows that puberty is not a biologically determined, inevitable period of storm and stress. Emotional turbulence is not a routine feature of adolescence. Adjustment varies widely and is a product of both biological and social forces.

◆ Girls generally react to menarche with surprise and mixed emotions, but whether their feelings are more positive or negative depends on advance information and support from family members. Boys usually know ahead of time about spermarche and also respond with mixed feelings. They receive less social support for the physical changes of puberty than do girls.

◆ Tribal and village societies often celebrate puberty with an **adolescent initiation ceremony.** The absence of a widely accepted marker for physical and social maturity in contemporary society makes the process of becoming an adult especially confusing.

◆ Besides higher hormone levels, situational changes are associated with adolescent moodiness. Puberty is accompanied by an increase in mild conflict and psychological distancing between parent and child.

Describe the impact of pubertal timing on adolescent adjustment, noting sex-related differences.

◆ Timing of puberty influences psychological adjustment. Early maturing boys and late maturing girls, whose appearance closely matches cultural standards of physical attractiveness, have a more positive **body image,** feel more self-confident, and hold more positions of leadership. In contrast, early maturing girls and late maturing boys, who fit in least well physically with peers, experience emotional and social difficulties.

PUBERTY AND ADOLESCENT HEALTH

What factors contribute to eating disorders at adolescence?

◆ Girls who reach puberty early, who are dissatisfied with their body images, and who grow up in homes in which thinness is important are at risk for eating disorders. **Anorexia nervosa** tends to appear in girls who have perfectionist personalities and overprotective and controlling parents. The impulsive eating and purging of **bulimia** is

associated with disengaged parenting and lack of self-control in other areas of life.

Discuss individual, social, and cultural influences on adolescent sexual attitudes and behavior.

◆ The hormonal changes of puberty lead to an increase in sex drive, but social factors affect how teenagers manage their sexuality. Compared with most cultures, the United States is fairly restrictive in its attitude toward adolescent sex. Sexual attitudes of adolescents and adults have become more liberal, with a slight swing back in recent years, largely due to the risk of sexually transmitted disease.

◆ One-third to one-half of sexually active American teenagers do not practice contraception regularly. Adolescent cognitive processes and a lack of social support for responsible sexual behavior underlie this trend.

Discuss factors involved in the development of homosexuality.

◆ About 3 to 6 percent of young people discover they are lesbian or gay. Although heredity makes an important contribution, homosexuality probably results from a variety of biological and environmental combinations that are not yet well understood. Lesbian and gay teenagers face special problems in establishing a positive sexual identity.

Discuss factors related to sexually transmitted disease, pregnancy, and parenthood in adolescence, noting prevention and intervention strategies.

◆ Sexually active teenagers are at risk for contracting sexually transmitted diseases (STDs). The most serious is AIDS. Drug-abusing and homosexual young people account for most cases, but heterosexual spread is increasing, especially for females.

◆ Adolescent pregnancy, abortion, and parenthood are higher in the United States than in other industrialized nations. Teenage parenthood is associated with dropping out of school, reduced chances of marriage, greater likelihood of divorce, and poverty—circumstances that risk the well-being of both adolescent and newborn child.

◆ Improved sex education, access to contraceptives, programs that build social competence, and expanded educational and vocational opportunities help prevent early pregnancy. Adolescent mothers benefit from family support that is sensitive to their developmental needs. When teenage fathers stay involved, their children develop more favorably.

IMPORTANT TERMS AND CONCEPTS

adolescent initiation ceremony (p. 204)
androgens (p. 183)
anorexia nervosa (p. 209)
body image (p. 207)
brain plasticity (p. 188)
bulimia (p. 209)
catch-up growth (p. 192)
cerebellum (p. 190)
cerebral cortex (p. 187)
corpus callosum (p. 190)
deprivation dwarfism (p. 199)
distance curve (p. 175)
dominant cerebral hemisphere (p. 189)
epiphyses (p. 178)

estrogens (p. 183)
fontanels (p. 180)
general growth curve (p. 185)
glial cells (p. 187)
growth hormone (GH) (p. 182)
hypothalamus (p. 182)
kwashiorkor (p. 195)
lateralization (p. 188)
marasmus (p. 195)
menarche (p. 200)
myelinization (p. 187)
neurons (p. 186)
nonorganic failure to thrive (p. 199)
obesity (p. 195)

oral rehydration therapy (ORT) (p. 199)
pituitary gland (p. 182)
primary sexual characteristics (p. 200)
programmed cell death (p. 186)
puberty (p. 200)
reticular formation (p. 190)
secondary sexual characteristics (p. 200)
secular trends in physical growth (p. 185)
skeletal age (p. 178)
spermarche (p. 202)
synapses (p. 186)
synaptic pruning (p. 187)
thyroxine (p. 183)
velocity curve (p. 175)

Cognitive Development: Piagetian and Vygotskian Perspectives

COGNITION REFERS TO THE inner processes and products of the mind that lead to "knowing." It includes all mental activity—remembering, symbolizing, categorizing, problem solving, creating, fantasizing, and even dreaming. Indeed, we could easily expand this list, since mental processes make their way into virtually everything human beings do.

Among the great contributions of the Swiss theorist Jean Piaget was his view of human cognition as an integrated set of reasoning abilities that develop together and can be applied to any task. Piaget's *cognitive-developmental* stage theory stands as one of the three dominant twentieth-century positions on cognitive development (see Chapter 1). The other two are Lev Semenovich Vygotsky's *sociocultural theory,* which we consider alongside Piaget's perspective, and *information processing,* which we examine in Chapter 7.

The theories of Piaget and Vygotsky form a natural counterpoint. Both men were born in 1896, although they lived and worked in widely separated parts of the world—Piaget in Switzerland, Vygotsky in Russia. In their earliest investigations, each addressed the same puzzling issue—the role of language in cognitive development—in similarly titled volumes. Do children first master ideas and then translate them into words? Or does the capacity for language open new cognitive doors, enabling children to think in more advanced ways?

In *The Language and Thought of the Child,* Piaget (1923/1926) claimed that major cognitive advances take place as children act directly on the physical world, discover the shortcomings of their current ways of thinking, and revise them to create a better fit with external reality. Language, Piaget argued, was relatively unimportant in sparking change in the young child's thinking.

A few years later, the bold young Vygotsky (1934/1986) challenged this conclusion. In *Thought and Language,* he claimed that human mental activity is the result of social, not independent, learning. According to Vygotsky, as children master challenging everyday tasks, they engage in cooperative dialogues with adults and more expert peers, who assist them in their efforts. During these interactions, cognitive processes that are adaptive in a particular culture are socially transferred to children. Vygotsky viewed language as crucial for cognitive change, since it is the primary means through which humans exchange social meanings. Indeed, he regarded language acquisition as the most significant attainment in children's development.

On the basis of this brief description, do you find it difficult to decide between Piaget's and Vygotsky's perspectives? Before we can evaluate the work of these two giants of cognitive development, we must become thoroughly acquainted with each theory and the research it has stimulated.

As we do so, we will encounter additional controversies about the nature of the child's mind. Among the most widely debated are these:

According to Piaget, at first schemes are motor action patterns. As this toddler experiments with water by filling and pouring from a variety of containers, he discovers that his actions have predictable effects on objects and that objects influence one another in regular ways.

(Lynne Weinstein/Woodfin Camp & Associates)

- Is cognitive development a matter of **domain-general changes**—similar transformations across all types of knowledge, as Piaget claimed? Or does it involve a variety of **domain-specific changes**—the perfection of separate, specialized abilities, each adapted to handling certain types of information?

- Does a **constructivist approach** like Piaget's, in which children *discover virtually all knowledge about the world through their own activity,* provide an accurate account of cognitive development? Or is a **nativist approach** more effective—the idea that children *are born with substantial innate knowledge,* which guides their interpretations of reality and gets cognitive development off to a speedy, efficient start?

Piaget's Cognitive-Developmental Theory

Piaget conceived of human cognition as a network of psychological structures created by an active organism constantly striving to make sense of experience. This view was revolutionary when it first reached the United States in the middle of the twentieth century. It represented a dramatic break with the then-dominant perspective of behaviorism, which steered clear of any constructs of mind and regarded the child as passively shaped by external forces (Beilin, 1992). By the 1960s, American researchers embraced Piaget's ideas with enthusiasm. His vision of the child as an intrinsically motivated learner, the variety of tasks he devised to assess cognitive development, and the relevance of his theory for education made it especially attractive.

Piaget received his early training in biology and philosophy. As a young boy, he spent his afternoons at the Museum of Natural History in Neufchâtel, where he became interested in how the shell structures of mollusks, which populate the lakes of Switzerland, are uniquely adapted to the animal's habitat. During his teenage years, his godfather introduced him to epistemology, the branch of philosophy concerned with the foundations of knowledge. Shortly after completing his Ph.D. in zoology, Piaget began to construct a biological account of the origins of knowledge (Piaget, 1952a). As a result, his theory of cognitive development has a distinctly biological flavor.

According to Piaget, just as the body has physical structures that enable it to adapt to the environment, so the mind builds psychological structures—organized ways of making sense of experience—that permit it to adapt to the external world. In the development of these structures, children are intensely active. They select and interpret experience in terms of their current structures, and they also modify those structures so that they take into account more subtle aspects of reality.

Piaget believed that children move through four stages of development—sensorimotor, preoperational, concrete operational, and formal operational—during which the exploratory behaviors of infants are transformed into the abstract, logical intelligence of adolescence and adulthood. Each stage groups together similar changes in many schemes that occur during the same time period. As a result, Piaget's stage sequence has two important characteristics. First, it is *invariant,* meaning that the stages always follow a fixed order, and no stages can be skipped. Second, the stages are *universal;* they are assumed to describe the cognitive development of children everywhere (Piaget, Inhelder, & Szeminska, 1948/1960).

Although Piaget regarded the order of development as genetically determined, he emphasized that many factors—both hereditary and environmental—affect the speed with which individual children move through the stages (Piaget, 1926/1928). To appreciate his view of how development occurs, we must examine a set of important concepts. These convey Piaget's ideas about *what changes with development* and *how cognitive change takes place.*

WHAT CHANGES WITH DEVELOPMENT

According to Piaget, specific psychological structures, or **schemes,** change with age. At first, schemes are motor action patterns. For example, watch a 6-month-old baby grasp and release objects, and you will see that the "dropping scheme" is fairly rigid; the infant

domain-general changes Similar transformations across all types of knowledge, resulting in the perfection of general reasoning abilities.

domain-specific changes Distinct transformations within each type of knowledge, resulting in the perfection of separate, specialized abilities.

constructivist approach An approach to cognitive development in which children discover virtually all knowledge about the world through their own activity. Consistent with Piaget's cognitive-developmental theory.

nativist approach An approach to cognitive development in which children are born with substantial innate knowledge, which guides their interpretations of reality and gets cognitive development off to a speedy, efficient start.

scheme In Piaget's theory, a specific structure, or organized way of making sense of experience, that changes with age.

simply lets go of a rattle or teething ring in her hand. By 18 months, the "dropping scheme" has become much more deliberate and creative. Given an opportunity, a baby of this age is likely to toss all sorts of objects down the basement stairs, throwing some up in the air, bouncing others off walls, releasing some gently and others forcefully. Soon schemes will move from an action-based level to a mental level. Instead of just acting on objects, the child shows evidence of thinking before she acts. This change, as we will see later, marks the transition from sensorimotor to preoperational thought.

HOW COGNITIVE CHANGE TAKES PLACE

In Piaget's theory, two processes account for changes in schemes: *adaptation* and *organization.*

■ **ADAPTATION**. The next time you have a chance, notice how infants and children tirelessly repeat actions that lead to interesting effects. **Adaptation** involves building schemes through direct interaction with the environment. It consists of two complementary activities: assimilation and accommodation. During **assimilation,** we use our current schemes to interpret the external world. For example, the infant who repeatedly drops objects is assimilating them to his sensorimotor dropping scheme. And the preschooler who sees her first camel at the zoo and calls out, "Horse!" has sifted through her schemes until she finds one that resembles the strange-looking creature. In **accommodation,** we adjust old schemes or create new ones after noticing that our current thinking does not capture the environment completely. The baby who begins to drop objects in different ways is modifying his dropping scheme to take account of the varied properties of objects. And the preschooler who calls a camel a "lumpy horse" has noticed that certain characteristics of camels are not like horses and has revised her "horse scheme" accordingly.

So far, we have referred to assimilation and accommodation as separate activities, but Piaget regarded them as always working together. In every interchange with the environment, we interpret information using our existing structures, and we also refine them to achieve a better fit with experience. But the balance between assimilation and accommodation varies over time. When children are not changing very much, they assimilate more than they accommodate. Piaget called this a state of cognitive *equilibrium,* implying a steady, comfortable condition. During times of rapid cognitive change, however, children are in a state of *disequilibrium,* or cognitive discomfort. They realize that new information does not match their current schemes, so they shift away from assimilation toward accommodation. Once they have modified their schemes, they move back toward assimilation, exercising their newly changed structures until they are ready to be modified again.

Piaget used the term **equilibration** to sum up this back-and-forth movement between equilibrium and disequilibrium throughout development. Each time equilibration occurs, more effective schemes are produced. They take in a wider range of aspects of the environment, and less and less throws them out of balance (Piaget, 1985). Because the times of greatest accommodation are the earliest ones, the sensorimotor stage is Piaget's most complex period of development.

■ **ORGANIZATION**. Schemes also change through a second process called **organization.** It takes place internally, apart from direct contact with the environment. Once children form new structures, they start to rearrange them, linking them with other schemes to create a strongly interconnected cognitive system. For example, eventually the baby will relate "dropping" to "throwing" and to his developing understanding of "nearness" and "farness." According to Piaget, schemes reach a true state of equilibrium when they become part of a broad network of structures that can be jointly applied to the surrounding world (Piaget, 1936/1952b).

In the following sections we will first describe development as Piaget saw it, noting research that supports his observations. Then, for each stage, we will consider evidence inspired by Piaget's theory that has enlarged our understanding of children's cognitive competencies as well as challenged some of Piaget's ideas, prompting alternative conceptions of development. Before we begin, return to Table 1.4 on page 22 for an overview of Piaget's stages.

adaptation In Piaget's theory, the process of building schemes through direct interaction with the environment. Consists of two complementary activities: *assimilation* and *accommodation.*

assimilation That part of adaptation in which an individual interprets the external world in terms of current schemes.

accommodation That part of adaptation in which an individual adjusts old schemes and creates new ones to produce a better fit with the environment.

equilibration In Piaget's theory, back-and-forth movement between cognitive equilibrium and disequilibrium throughout development, which leads to more effective schemes.

organization In Piaget's theory, the internal rearrangement and linking together of schemes so they form a strongly interconnected cognitive system.

The Sensorimotor Stage (Birth to 2 Years)

The difference between the newborn baby and the 2-year-old child is so vast that the **sensorimotor stage** is divided into six substages. Piaget's observations of his own three children served as the basis for this description of development. Although this is a very small sample, Piaget watched carefully and also presented his son and two daughters with everyday problems (such as hidden objects) that helped reveal their understanding of the world.

According to Piaget, at birth infants know so little that they cannot purposefully explore their surroundings. The **circular reaction** provides them with a special means of adapting their first schemes. It involves stumbling onto a new experience caused by the baby's own motor activity. The reaction is "circular" because the infant tries to repeat the event again and again. As a result, a sensorimotor response that first occurred by chance becomes strengthened into a new scheme. For example, imagine a 2-month-old who accidentally makes a smacking noise when finishing a feeding. The baby finds the sound intriguing, so she tries to repeat it until, after a few days, she becomes quite expert at smacking her lips.

During the first 2 years, the circular reaction changes in several ways. At first, it centers on the infant's own body. Later, it turns outward, toward manipulation of objects. Finally, it becomes experimental and creative, aimed at producing novel effects in the environment. Piaget considered these revisions in the circular reaction so important that he named the sensorimotor substages after them.

Two additional means for solidifying schemes and creating new ones—*play* and *imitation*—first appear during the sensorimotor stage. Piaget viewed play as the purest form of assimilation—practicing already acquired schemes just for the pleasure of doing so. (Later we will see that other theorists, including Vygotsky, regard this definition as too narrow.) In contrast, imitation emphasizes accommodation, since it involves copying behaviors that are not yet in the child's repertoire. According to Piaget, what infants and children play at and imitate reflects their advancing cognitive capacities.

THE SENSORIMOTOR SUBSTAGES

As we examine Piaget's six sensorimotor substages, you may find it helpful to refer to Table 6.1, which provides a summary of each.

■ **SUBSTAGE 1: REFLEXIVE SCHEMES (BIRTH TO 1 MONTH).** Piaget regarded newborn reflexes as the building blocks of sensorimotor intelligence. At first, babies suck, grasp, and look in much the same way, no matter what experiences they encounter. In one amusing example, a mother reported to me that her 2-week-old daughter lay on the bed next to her sleeping father. Suddenly, he awoke with a start. The baby had latched on and begun to suck on his back!

■ **SUBSTAGE 2: PRIMARY CIRCULAR REACTIONS—THE FIRST LEARNED ADAPTATIONS (1 TO 4 MONTHS).** Infants start to gain voluntary control over their actions by repeating chance behaviors that lead to satisfying results. Consequently, they develop some simple motor habits, such as sucking their fists or thumbs and opening and closing their hands. Babies of this substage also begin to vary their behavior in response to environmental demands. For example, they open their mouths differently for a nipple than for a spoon. Young infants also begin to anticipate events. A hungry 3-month-old is likely to stop crying as soon as his mother enters the room and moves toward the crib—an event signaling that feeding time is near.

Piaget called the first circular reactions *primary,* and he regarded them as quite limited. Notice how, in the examples just given, infants' adaptations are oriented toward their own bodies and motivated by basic needs. According to Piaget, babies of this age are not yet very concerned with the effects of their actions on the external world.

In Substage 2, babies begin to exercise schemes playfully, smiling gleefully as they repeat a newly developed action. Piaget believed that first efforts at imitation also appear at

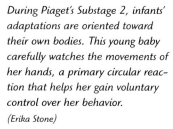

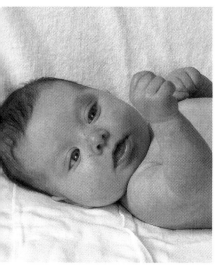

During Piaget's Substage 2, infants' adaptations are oriented toward their own bodies. This young baby carefully watches the movements of her hands, a primary circular reaction that helps her gain voluntary control over her behavior.

(Erika Stone)

TABLE 6.1

Summary of Cognitive Development During the Sensorimotor Stage

Sensorimotor Substage	Typical Adaptive Behaviors
1. Reflexive schemes (birth to 1 month)	Newborn reflexes (see Chapter 4, page 129)
2. Primary circular reactions (1–4 months)	Simple motor habits centered around the infant's own body; limited anticipation of events
3. Secondary circular reactions (4–8 months)	Actions aimed at repeating interesting effects in the surrounding world; imitation of familiar behaviors
4. Coordination of secondary circular reactions (8–12 months)	Intentional, or goal-directed, behavior; beginning appreciation of physical causality; improved anticipation of events; imitation of behaviors slightly different from those the infant usually performs; ability to find a hidden object in the first location in which it is hidden (object permanence)
5. Tertiary circular reactions (12–18 months)	Exploration of the properties of objects by acting on them in novel ways; imitation of unfamiliar behaviors; ability to search in several locations for a hidden object (AB search)
6. Mental representation (18 months–2 years)	Internal representation of absent objects and past events, as indicated by sudden solutions to sensorimotor problems; ability to find an object that has been moved while out of sight (invisible displacement); deferred imitation; make-believe play

this time, but they are limited to copying someone else's imitation of the baby's own actions. However, recall from Chapter 4 that neonates can imitate, so imitation seems to be one area in which Piaget misjudged the young baby's competence.

■ **SUBSTAGE 3: SECONDARY CIRCULAR REACTIONS—MAKING INTERESTING SIGHTS LAST (4 TO 8 MONTHS).** Between 4 and 8 months, infants sit up and become skilled at reaching for, grasping, and manipulating objects (see Chapter 4). These motor achievements play a major role in turning their attention outward toward the environment. Using the *secondary* circular reaction, they try to repeat interesting effects in the surrounding world that are caused by their own actions. For example, Piaget (1936/1952b) tried dangling several dolls in front of his 4-month-old son, Laurent. After accidentally knocking them and producing a fascinating swinging motion, Laurent gradually built the sensorimotor scheme of "hitting."

Improved control over their own behavior permits infants of this substage to imitate the behaviors of others more effectively. However, they cannot adapt flexibly and quickly enough to imitate behaviors not in their current repertoire (Kaye & Marcus, 1981). Therefore, although 4- to 8-month-olds enjoy watching an adult demonstrate a game of pat-a-cake or peekaboo, they are not yet able to participate.

■ **SUBSTAGE 4: COORDINATION OF SECONDARY CIRCULAR REACTIONS (8 TO 12 MONTHS).** Now infants start to organize schemes. They combine secondary circular reactions into new, more complex action sequences. As a result, two landmark cognitive changes take place.

First, babies can engage in **intentional,** or **goal-directed, behavior.** Before this substage, actions that led to new schemes had a random, hit-or-miss quality to them—*accidentally* bringing the thumb to the mouth or *happening* to hit the doll. But by 8 months, infants have had enough practice with a variety of schemes that they coordinate them deliberately to solve sensorimotor problems. The clearest example is provided by Piaget's object-hiding tasks, in which he shows the baby an attractive toy and then hides it behind his hand or under a cover. Infants of this substage can find the object. In doing so, they coordinate two schemes: "pushing" aside the obstacle and "grasping" the toy. Piaget regarded these *means–end action sequences* as the first sign that babies appreciate **physical causality** (the causal action one object exerts on another through contact) and as the foundation for all later problem solving.

The fact that infants can retrieve hidden objects reveals that they have begun to attain a second cognitive milestone: **object permanence,** the understanding that objects continue to exist when they are out of sight. But awareness of object permanence is not yet

sensorimotor stage Piaget's first stage, during which infants "think" with their eyes, ears, hands, and other sensorimotor equipment. Spans the first 2 years of life.

circular reaction In Piaget's theory, a means of building schemes in which infants try to repeat a chance event caused by their own motor activity.

intentional, or goal-directed, behavior A sequence of actions in which schemes are deliberately combined to solve a problem.

physical causality The causal action one object exerts on another through contact.

object permanence The understanding that objects continue to exist when they are out of sight.

As this 15-month-old masters the nuances of object permanence, she delights in hiding-and-finding games, such as peekaboo. Her flexible imitative abilities permit her to participate more actively in the game than she could at a younger age.

(Tony Freeman/PhotoEdit)

complete. If an object is moved from one hiding place (A) to another (B), babies will search for it only in the first hiding place (A). Because 8- to 12-month-olds make this **AB search error,** Piaget concluded that they do not have a clear image of the object as persisting when hidden from view.

Substage 4 brings several additional advances. First, infants are better at anticipating events, so they sometimes use their new capacity for intentional behavior to try to change those events. For example, a baby of this age might crawl after his mother when she puts on her coat, whimpering to keep her from leaving. Second, babies can imitate behaviors slightly different from those they usually perform. After watching someone else, they try to stir with a spoon, push a toy car, or drop raisins in a cup. Once again, they draw on their capacity for intentional behavior, purposefully modifying schemes to fit an observed action (Piaget, 1945/1951).

■ **SUBSTAGE 5: TERTIARY CIRCULAR REACTIONS—DISCOVERING NEW MEANS THROUGH ACTIVE EXPERIMENTATION (12 TO 18 MONTHS).** At this substage, the circular reaction—now called *tertiary*—becomes experimental and creative. Toddlers repeat behaviors with variation, provoking new outcomes. Recall the example on page 223 of the child dropping objects over the basement steps, trying this, then that, and then another action. Because they approach the world in this deliberately exploratory way, 12- to 18-month-olds are far better sensorimotor problem solvers than they were before. For example, they can figure out how to fit a shape through a hole in a container by turning and twisting it until it falls through, and they can use a stick to obtain a toy that is out of reach.

According to Piaget, this new capacity to experiment leads to a more advanced understanding of object permanence. Older infants look in not just one but several locations to find a hidden toy; they no longer make the AB search error. Their more flexible action patterns also permit them to imitate many more behaviors, such as stacking blocks, scribbling on paper, and making funny faces.

■ **SUBSTAGE 6: MENTAL REPRESENTATION—INVENTING NEW MEANS THROUGH MENTAL COMBINATIONS (18 MONTHS TO 2 YEARS).** Substage 5 is the last truly *sensorimotor* stage, since Substage 6 brings with it the ability to create **mental representations** of reality—internal images of absent objects and past events. As a result, children can solve problems symbolically instead of by trial-and-error behavior. One sign of this new capacity is that children arrive at solutions to sensorimotor problems suddenly, suggesting that they experiment with actions inside their heads. Faced with her doll carriage stuck against the wall, Piaget's daughter Lucienne paused for a moment, as if to "think," and then immediately went to the other side to push it in the reverse direction. Had she been in Substage 5, she would have pushed, pulled, and bumped it in a random fashion until it was free to move again.

AB search error The error made by 8- to 12-month-olds after an object is moved from hiding place A to hiding place B. Infants in Piaget's Substage 4 search for it only in the first hiding place (A).

mental representation An internal image of an absent object or a past event.

With the capacity to represent, toddlers arrive at a more advanced understanding of object permanence—that objects can move or be moved when out of sight. Try the following object-hiding task with an 18- to 24-month-old as well as a younger child: Put a small toy inside a box and the box under a cover. Then, while the box is out of sight, dump the toy out and show the toddler the empty box. The Substage 6 child finds the hidden toy in this **invisible displacement task** easily. Younger infants are baffled by this situation.

Representation also brings with it the capacity for **deferred imitation**—the ability to remember and copy the behavior of models who are not immediately present. A famous example is Piaget's daughter Jacqueline's imitation of another child's temper tantrum:

> Jacqueline had a visit from a little boy . . . who, in the course of the afternoon, got into a terrible temper. He screamed as he tried to get out of a playpen and pushed it backwards, stamping his feet. Jacqueline stood watching him in amazement. . . . The next day, she herself screamed in her playpen and tried to move it, stamping her foot lightly several times in succession. (Piaget, 1936/1952b, p. 63)

Finally, the emergence of representation leads to a major change in the nature of play. At the end of the sensorimotor period, children engage in **make-believe play,** in which they act out familiar activities, such as pretending to eat, go to sleep, or drive a car. As the sensorimotor period draws to a close, mental symbols quickly become major instruments of thinking.

RECENT RESEARCH ON SENSORIMOTOR DEVELOPMENT

Many researchers have tried to confirm Piaget's observations of sensorimotor development. Their findings show that infants display a wide array of cognitive capacities, in partial and sometimes full-blown form, much sooner than Piaget believed. Think back to the challenge posed by studies of newborn imitation, mentioned in our discussion of Substage 2 (see page 224). You have already read about other evidence as well. Recall the operant-conditioning research reviewed in Chapter 4, in which newborns sucked vigorously on a nipple to gain access to a variety of interesting sights and sounds. This behavior, which closely resembles Piaget's secondary circular reaction, shows that babies try to explore and control the external world before 4 to 8 months. In fact, they do so as soon as they are born.

Piaget may have underestimated infant capacities because he did not have the sophisticated experimental techniques for studying early cognitive development that are available today. As we consider recent research on sensorimotor development, we will see that operant conditioning and the habituation–dishabituation sequence have been used ingeniously to find out what the young baby knows.

■ **REASONING ABOUT THE PHYSICAL WORLD.** Piaget concluded that not until 8 to 12 months of age do infants appreciate important regularities of their physical world—that objects continue to exist when out of sight and act on one another in predictable ways. Yet as the following findings reveal, even very young babies are knowledgeable about object characteristics.

OBJECT PERMANENCE. Before 8 months, do infants really believe that an object spirited out of sight no longer exists? Apparently not. In a series of studies in which babies did not have to engage in active search, Renée Baillargeon (1987; Baillargeon & DeVos, 1991) found evidence for at least some understanding of object permanence as early as 3½ months of age!

To discern infants' grasp of this and other aspects of physical reasoning, researchers often use a **violation-of-expectation method,** in which they habituate babies to a physical event and then determine whether they dishabituate to (look longer at) a possible event (a variation of the first event that conforms to physical laws) or an impossible event (a variation that violates physical laws). Dishabituation to the impossible event suggests surprise at a deviation from expected object actions and, therefore, an understanding of that aspect of physical reality. One of Baillargeon's object-permanence studies, using this method, is described in Figure 6.1 on page 228.

invisible displacement task A type of object-hiding task in which the object is moved from one place to another while out of sight.

deferred imitation The ability to remember and copy the behavior of models who are not immediately present.

make-believe play A type of play in which children pretend, acting out everyday and imaginary activities.

violation-of-expectation method A method for studying physical reasoning in which researchers habituate babies to a physical event and then determine whether they dishabituate to (look longer at) a possible event (a variation of the first event that conforms to physical laws) or an impossible event (a variation that violates physical laws). Dishabituation to the impossible event suggests surprise at a deviation from expected object actions and, therefore, an understanding of that aspect of physical reality.

FIGURE 6.1

Habituation Events

Short-carrot event

Tall-carrot event

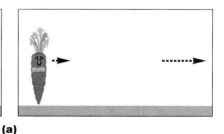

(a)

Testing infants for understanding of object permanence using the violation-of-expectation method. (a) First, infants were habituated to two events: a short carrot and a tall carrot moving behind a yellow screen, on alternative trials. Next the researchers presented two test events. The color of the screen was changed to help infants notice its window. (b) In the *possible event,* the carrot shorter than the window's lower edge moved behind the blue screen and reappeared on the other side. (c) In the *impossible event,* the carrot taller than the window's lower edge moved behind the screen, did not appear in the window, but then emerged intact on the other side. Infants as young as 3½ months dishabituated to (looked longer at) the impossible event, suggesting that they understood object permanence.

(Adapted from R. Baillargeon & J. DeVos, 1991, "Object Permanence in Young Infants: Further Evidence," *Child Development,* 62, p. 1230. © The Society for Research in Child Development. Reprinted by permission.)

Test Events

Possible event

Impossible event

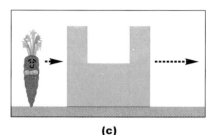

(b) (c)

If 3-month-olds grasp the idea of object permanence, then what explains Piaget's finding that much older infants (who are quite capable of voluntary reaching) do not try to search for hidden objects? One idea is that just as Piaget's theory suggests, they cannot yet coordinate the separate means–end schemes—pushing aside the obstacle and grasping the object—necessary to retrieve a hidden toy. In other words, what they *know* about object permanence is not yet *evident* in their searching behavior (Baillargeon et al., 1990). In support of this idea, when researchers simplify the search part of the task by reducing it to one action—permitting babies to reach directly for an object in the dark after hearing a sound signaling its location—even 6½-month-olds easily retrieve the object (Goubet & Clifton, 1998).

SEARCHING FOR OBJECTS HIDDEN IN MORE THAN ONE LOCATION. Once 8- to 12-month-olds actively search for hidden objects, they make the AB search error. For some years, researchers thought that babies had trouble remembering an object's new location after it was hidden in more than one place. But recent findings reveal that poor memory cannot fully account for infants' unsuccessful performance.

Between 5 and 12 months, babies increasingly *look* at the correct location yet *reach* incorrectly (Hofstadter & Reznick, 1996). And in violation-of-expectation procedures, in which an experimenter hides a toy at A, moves it to B, and then retrieves it either from B (possible event) or from A (impossible event), 8- to 12-month-olds look longer at the impossible event. This indicates that they remember where the object was last hidden (at B) and expect it to be there (Ahmed & Ruffman, 1998).

Perhaps babies search at A (where they first found the object) instead of B (its most recent location) because they have trouble inhibiting a previously rewarded response (Diamond, Cruttenden, & Neiderman, 1994). Once again, before 12 months, infants have difficulty translating what they know about an object moving from one place to another into a successful search strategy. This ability to integrate knowledge with action coincides with rapid development of the frontal lobes of the cerebral cortex at the end of the first year (Bell & Fox, 1992; Diamond, 1991; Nelson, 1995).

OTHER ASPECTS OF PHYSICAL REASONING. The violation-of-expectation method reveals that young babies are aware of many object properties and the rules governing their behavior. For example, 3- to 4-month-olds are sensitive to object substance and physical limits on object motion. They realize that one solid object cannot move through another solid object. By 5 to 6 months, infants also appreciate that an object much larger than an opening cannot pass through that opening. Furthermore, in the first half-year, babies are sensitive to the effects of gravity. They look intently when a moving object stops in midair without support (Sitskoorn & Smitsman, 1995; Spelke et al., 1992).

In the next few months, infants apply these understandings to a wider range of circumstances. For example, with respect to gravity, 7-month-olds (but not 5-month-olds) are aware that an object on a sloping surface will roll down, not up (Kim & Spelke, 1992). And as Figure 6.2 shows, 6½-month-olds (but not 5½-month-olds) realize that an object placed on top of another object will fall unless a large portion of its bottom surface contacts the lower object (Baillargeon, 1994a; Baillargeon, Needham, & DeVos, 1992).

A beginning grasp of physical causality is also present quite early. When a moving object (such as a rolling ball) collides with a stationary object, infants as young as 2½ months expect the stationary object to be displaced. By 5½ to 6½ months, they figure out that a larger moving object can cause the stationary object to travel farther (Baillargeon, 1994b; Kotovsky & Baillargeon, 1998). Around 7 months, infants realize that an object hitting a second object will launch it on a continuous path of motion immediately (not after a delay). Soon infants extend their understanding of physical causality to more complex collision conditions. For example, after watching a blue ball disappear behind a screen and a red ball appear on the other side, 10-month-olds infer that the first object launched the second while out of their sight (Oakes, 1994; Oakes & Cohen, 1995).

In sum, infants have a rich appreciation of the regularities of their physical world. Basic understandings—that objects continue to exist when masked by other objects, cannot move through the space occupied by other objects, fall without support, and move along continuous paths—are present within the first few months (long before infants can engage in Piagetian means–end action sequences) and are gradually refined over the first year.

■ **MENTAL REPRESENTATION.** In Piaget's theory, infants lead purely sensorimotor lives; they cannot represent experience until about 18 months of age. Yet new studies of deferred imitation, categorization, and problem solving reveal that the transition to mental representation takes place much earlier.

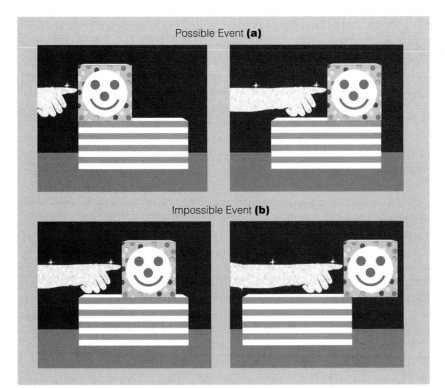

Possible Event **(a)**

Impossible Event **(b)**

FIGURE 6.2

Testing infants' understanding of object support using the violation-of-expectation method. First, infants were habituated to an event in which a hand pushed an attractive box partway across a long platform (not shown). Next, the researchers presented two test events in which the hand pushed the box across a shorter platform. (a) In the *possible event,* the hand pushed the box until its leading edge reached the end of the platform, so it remained fully supported. (b) In the *impossible event,* the hand pushed the box until only 15 percent of its bottom surface remained on the platform. Results indicated that 5½-month-olds looked equally at the two test events. In contrast, 6½-month-olds dishabituated to the impossible event, suggesting that they expect the object to fall unless a large portion of its bottom surface lies on the platform.

(From R. Baillargeon, A. Needham, & J. DeVos, 1992, "The Development of Young Infants' Intuitions About Support," *Early Development and Parenting,* 1, p. 71. Reprinted by permission.)

DEFERRED IMITATION. Piaget studied imitation by noting when his own three children demonstrated it in their everyday behavior. Under these conditions, a great deal has to be known about the infant's daily life to be sure that deferred imitation has occurred. Also, some babies might be capable of deferred imitation but have few opportunities to display it.

Andrew Meltzoff and Keith Moore (1994) brought 6-week-old babies into the laboratory and deliberately tried to induce deferred imitation of facial expressions. Infants who watched an adult open her mouth or stick out her tongue imitated the facial gesture when exposed to the same adult 24 hours later. These findings show that deferred imitation, a form of representation, is present by the second month of life. Perhaps young babies use it as a way to identify and communicate with people they have seen before.

As motor capacities improve, infants start to copy adults' actions on objects. In one study, 6- to 18-month-olds were shown a puppet wearing a mitten with a jingle bell inside it. An experimenter removed the mitten, shook it, and replaced it on the puppet's right hand. As long as these novel behaviors were repeated many times, even 6-month-olds were more likely to reproduce them after a 24-hour delay than were infants exposed to the puppet without the modeled actions (Barr, Dowden, & Hayne, 1996). By 14 months, infants use deferred imitation skillfully to enrich their range of sensorimotor schemes. They retain highly unusual modeled behaviors for several months and copy the actions of peers as well as adults. They also imitate across a change in context—for example, enact in the home a behavior learned at child care and generalize actions to functionally similar objects varying in size and color (Barnat, Klein, & Meltzoff, 1996; Hanna & Meltzoff, 1993; Meltzoff, 1994).

Around 18 months, toddlers imitate not only an adult's behavior, but the actions he or she *tries* to produce, even if these are not fully realized (Meltzoff, 1995). On one occasion, a mother attempted to pour some raisins into a small bag but missed, spilling them onto the counter. A moment later, her 18-month-old son climbed on a stool and began dropping the raisins into the bag, indicating that he had begun to infer others' intentions and perspectives. By age 2, children mimic entire social roles—such as mommy, daddy, or baby—during make-believe play.

BEGINNINGS OF CATEGORIZATION. Young babies' ability to categorize objects and events is also incompatible with a strictly sensorimotor approach to experience in which mental representation is absent. Recall the operant conditioning research in which infants kicked to move a mobile attached to their foot by a long cord (see Chapter 4, page 230). By creatively varying the mobile stimuli, Carolyn Rovee-Collier and her colleagues showed that categorization is present in the early months of life.

In one series of studies, 3-month-olds kicked a mobile made of a uniform set of stimuli—small blocks, all with the letter *A* on them. After a delay, kicking returned to a high level only if the babies were given a mobile whose elements were labeled with the same form (the letter *A*). If the form was changed (from *A*'s to *2*'s), infants no longer kicked vigorously. While learning to make the mobile move, the babies had mentally grouped together its features, associating the kicking response with the category "*A*" and, at later testing, distinguishing it from the category "*2*" (Bhatt, Rovee-Collier, & Weiner, 1994; Hayne, Rovee-Collier, & Perris, 1987).

Habituation–dishabituation research has also been used to study early categorization. For example, infants can be shown a series of pictures belonging to one category (such as hot dog, piece of bread, slice of salami). Then the experimenter observes whether they look longer at, or dishabituate to, a picture that is not a member of the category (chair) than one that is (apple). Findings of such studies reveal that 7- to 12-month-olds structure objects into an impressive array of adultlike categories—food items, birds, animals, vehicles, kitchen utensils, plants, spatial location ("above" and "below"), and more (Mandler & McDonough, 1993, 1996, 1998; Oakes, Coppage, & Dingel, 1997; Quinn & Eimas, 1996; Younger, 1985, 1993). Besides organizing the physical world, infants of this age also categorize their social worlds. They sort people and their voices into male and female (Francis & McCroy, 1983; Poulin-Dubois et al., 1994), have begun to distinguish emotional expressions, and can separate the natural movements of people from other motions (see Chapter 4, pages 161 and 163).

This 3-month-old infant discovered that by kicking, she could shake a mobile made of small blocks with the letter A on them. After a delay, the baby continued to kick vigorously only if the mobile she saw was labeled with the same form (the letter A). She did not kick when given a mobile with a different form (the number 2). The infant's behavior shows that she groups similar stimuli into categories and can distinguish the category "A" from the category "2."
(Courtesy of Carolyn Rovee-Collier/Rutgers University)

At first, infants rely on physical features to discriminate categories—for example, legs for animals and wheels for vehicles. The earliest categories are *perceptual*—based on similar overall appearance or prominent object part (Rakison & Butterworth, 1998). But by the end of the first year, categories are becoming *conceptual*—based on common function and behavior. In fact, older infants can make categorical distinctions when the perceptual contrast between two categories—animals and vehicles—is made as minimal as possible (for an illustration, see Figure 6.3).

In the second year, children become active categorizers during play. Given an array of objects, 12-month-olds touch those that belong together, without grouping them. At about 16 months, toddlers can group objects into a single category. And around 18 months, they can sort objects exhaustively into two classes (Gopnik & Meltzoff, 1987a).

Compared to looking in the habituation–dishabituation sequence, touching, sorting, and other play behaviors are much better at revealing the *meaning* infants attach to categories, since babies are applying those meanings in their everyday activities. For example, after having watched an experimenter give a toy dog a drink from a cup, 14-month-olds shown a rabbit and a motorcycle usually offer the drink only to the rabbit. Even after the experimenter models a categorically inappropriate behavior (giving a drink to the motorcycle), infants are likely to persist in selecting the rabbit (Mandler & McDonough, 1998). Their behavior reveals a clear understanding that particular actions are more appropriate for some categories of items (animals) than for others (vehicles).

PROBLEM SOLVING. Findings on infants' capacity to remember, imitate, and categorize suggest that they might be able to use their representational skills to solve problems more effectively than Piaget's substages suggest. Consider a means–end action sequence usually not evident until after 8 months: pulling a cloth to retrieve a toy placed out of reach on the end of the cloth. When 6½-month-olds were given a hint, in which an adult pulled back a cloth to reveal a hidden toy, most succeeded at the means–end problem (Kolstad & Aguiar, 1995). Notice that the hint was not a direct demonstration of the solution, only a similar action. In imitating the behavior, infants had to transfer and adapt it to the problem at hand.

By 10 to 12 months, infants can engage in **analogical problem solving,** in which they extract a solution strategy from one problem-solving context and apply it in other appropriate contexts. In one study, babies were presented with three means–end problems with similar goals but differing in all aspects of their superficial features, depicted in Figure 6.4 on page 232. In each, they had to remove or reach over a barrier (empty box), grasp the relevant string (the one attached to the object), and pull it toward them to obtain the toy. On the first problem, the parent demonstrated the solution and encouraged the child to imitate. Problem-solving efficiency—touching relevant rather than irrelevant items in the situation and readily obtaining the toy—increased over the three problems, suggesting that the babies had formed a flexible, generalizable representation of the solution (Chen, Sanchez, & Campbell, 1997).

With age, children become better at reasoning by analogy, generalizing across increasingly dissimilar situations (Goswami, 1996). But even in the first year, infants have some ability to move beyond trial-and-error experimentation, mentally represent a problem solution, and apply it in new contexts.

When we combine the diverse capacities just considered with other milestones that we will discuss in later chapters—for example, that events taking place before 10 to 11 months can be recalled up to a year and a half later (see Chapter 7) and that at the end of the first year, infants communicate with symbolic gestures (see Chapter 9)—it is clear that mental representation is not the culmination of sensorimotor development. Instead, sensorimotor and symbolic schemes develop concurrently during the first 2 years.

EVALUATION OF THE SENSORIMOTOR STAGE

The Milestones table on page 233 summarizes the remarkable cognitive attainments of infancy. Compare this table with the description of Piaget's sensorimotor substages on page 225. You will see that on the one hand, infants anticipate events, actively search for hidden objects, flexibly vary their sensorimotor schemes, and engage in make-believe play within Piaget's time frame. Yet on the other hand, many other capacities—including sec-

FIGURE 6.3

Categorical distinction made by 9- to 11-month olds. After infants were given an opportunity to examine (by looking or touching) the objects in one category, they were shown a new object from each of the categories. They dishabituated to (spent more time looking at and touching) the object from the contrasting category, indicating that they distinguished the birds from the airplanes, despite their perceptual similarity.

(Adapted from Mandler & McDonough, 1993.)

analogical problem solving
Extracting a solution strategy from one problem-solving context and applying it in other contexts with similar goals but different features.

FIGURE 6.4

Analogical problem solving by 10- to 12-month-olds. After the parent demonstrated the solution to problem (a), infants solved (b) and (c) with increasing efficiency, even though those problems differed in all aspects of their superficial features.

(From Z. Chen, R. P. Sanchez, & T. Campbell, 1997, "From Beyond to Within Their Grasp: The Rudiments of Analogical Problem Solving in 10- to 13-month-olds. *Developmental Psychology, 33,* p. 792. Copyright © 1997 by the American Psychological Association. Reprinted by permission of the publisher and author.)

(a) (b) (c)

ondary circular reactions, understanding of object permanence and physical causality, deferred imitation, categorization, and analogical problem solving—emerge much earlier than Piaget expected.

Notice, also, that the cognitive attainments of infancy do not develop in the neat, stepwise fashion predicted by Piaget's substages. For example, deferred imitation and analogical problem solving are present long before children pass invisible displacement tasks, probably because invisible displacement requires a more complex form of representation. To understand that an object can be moved while out of sight, infants must go beyond *recall of a past event* to *infer a novel unseen event* (Rast & Meltzoff, 1995). Yet Piaget assumed that all representational capacities emerge in synchrony in Substage 6. These findings, and others like them, are among an accumulating body of evidence that questions Piaget's stagewise view of development.

Discrepancies between Piaget's observations and those of recent research also raise controversial questions about how early development takes place. Consistent with Piaget's ideas, motor activity facilitates the construction of some forms of knowledge. For example, in Chapter 4, we indicated that crawling babies are better than are their noncrawling peers at perceiving depth on the visual cliff and finding hidden objects. Yet we have also seen that infants comprehend a great deal before they are capable of the motor behaviors Piaget assumed led to those understandings. How can we account for babies' amazing cognitive accomplishments? At present, there are many speculations. Let's explore two prominent ideas.

■ **A PERCEPTUAL VIEW.** Some researchers believe that important schemes develop through perceptual means—by looking and listening—rather than just through acting on the world. At the same time, they preserve Piaget's belief that the baby *constructs* new understandings.

For example, Renée Baillargeon (1994b, 1995, 1998) argues that infants come to understand physical phenomena by first making all-or-none distinctions, to which they add as they are exposed to relevant information. For example, 3-month-olds realize that an object will fall when released in midair and stop falling when it contacts a surface because they have watched adults drop toys in baskets and clothes in hampers many times. But not until the middle of the first year, when infants sit independently and can put objects on

Some Cognitive Attainments of Infancy

Age	Typical Adaptive Behaviors	Physical Reasoning	Imitation	Categorization
Birth–1 month	■ Newborn reflexes ■ Exploration using limited motor skills, such as head turning and sucking	■ Size and shape constancy (see Chapter 4)	■ Imitation of adult facial expressions and gestures (see Chapter 4)	
1–4 months	■ Exploration using more advanced motor skills, such as kicking, reaching, and grasping ■ Limited anticipation of events	■ Awareness of object permanence ■ Awareness of object solidity and certain effects of gravity and object collision (physical causality) ■ Use of motion and spatial layout to identify objects as separate units (see Chapter 4)	■ Deferred imitation of adult facial expressions	■ Categorization of perceptually similar stimuli
4–8 months	■ Exploration using improved reaching and grasping, swiping, banging, and throwing	■ Improved understanding of the effects of gravity and object collision (physical causality) ■ Use of shape, texture, and color to identify objects as separate units (see Chapter 4)	■ Deferred imitation of adults' actions on objects over a short time interval (24 hours), but limited to behaviors the infant has observed many times	■ Beginning categorization of objects by function and behavior
8–12 months	■ Intentional, or goal-directed, behavior ■ Improved anticipation of events ■ Means-end problem solving by analogy to other similar problems	■ Ability to retrieve an object from the first location in which it is hidden ■ Understanding of more complex object collision conditions	■ Imitation of behaviors slightly different from ones the infant usually performs ■ Deferred imitation of adults' actions on objects over a short time interval (24 hours), after observing behaviors only a few times	■ Categorization of many objects by function and behavior ■ Categorization of social stimuli (for example, emotional expressions, human versus nonhuman movement patterns)
12–18 months	■ Exploration of objects by acting on them in novel ways ■ Flexible solutions to sensorimotor problems	■ Ability to search in several locations for a hidden object (AB search)	■ Imitation of adults' and peers' novel behaviors ■ Deferred imitation of behaviors over longer time intervals ■ Deferred imitation across a change in context (for example, from child care to home and to similar objects)	■ Active object sorting: touching objects that go together followed by grouping objects into a single category
18 months–2 years	■ Sudden solutions to sensorimotor problems, suggesting mental representation ■ Beginnings of make-believe play	■ Ability to find an object that has been moved while out of sight	■ Imitation of actions an adult tries to produce, even if these are not fully realized ■ Imitation of entire social roles in make-believe play	■ Active object sorting: grouping objects into two categories

Note. These milestones represent overall age trends. Individual differences exist in the precise age at which each milestone is attained.

Did this toddler figure out that one container can rest on top of another through rich, constructive interaction with objects, as Piaget assumed? Or did he begin life with innate knowledge that enables him to grasp the regularities of his physical world with very little hands-on exploration? The future is likely to bring compromises between these clashing viewpoints.

(Elizabeth Crews)

surfaces themselves, do they have a chance to see that an object will tumble over unless much of its bottom surface is supported. Lisa Oakes and Leslie Cohen (1995) believe that an appreciation of physical causality develops similarly. As object perception improves (see Chapter 4) and infants have many opportunities to watch objects contacting one another, they detect increasingly fine-grained rules of object collision.

Likewise, Jean Mandler (1992a, 1992b, 1998) proposes that babies form their first categories through a natural process of perceptual analysis, in which they detect commonalities in the features and movements of objects and translate these into simplified images of experience. At first, categories are based on objects' perceptual similarities; for example, dogs go together and rabbits go together. But gradually, as infants gain experience with the functions of objects, they engage in higher-order analysis of perceptual information. For example, they might notice that both rabbits and horses move on their own, drink and eat, and are often petted by people. Consequently, they realize that even though rabbits and horses are *perceptually distinct,* they are *conceptually alike* because both display similar behaviors and evoke similar reactions from others.

■ **A NATIVIST VIEW.** Other researchers take a nativist (meaning inborn) view. They are convinced that infants' remarkable cognitive skills are based on innate knowledge. Development is a matter of these built-in, core understandings becoming more elaborate as they come in contact with new information.

Elizabeth Spelke (1994) believes that infants know from the start that objects move as connected wholes on continuous paths, do not change shape or pass through one another as they move, and cannot act on one another until they come in contact. Later-emerging schemes are direct extensions of these innate structures, which channel infants' attention to relevant features of the environment. This gets their physical reasoning "off the ground" quickly (Spelke & Newport, 1998).

A growing number of researchers believe that innate knowledge guides other aspects of development—for example, mastery of number concepts (Chapter 7), language (Chapter 9), and social understanding (Chapters 11 and 12) (Carey & Spelke, 1994; Chomsky, 1988; Wellman & Gelman, 1992). These investigators view the mind as a collection of separate *modules,* or genetically prewired, special-purpose neural systems in the brain, which trigger new understandings with exposure to stimulation. Consequently, this perspective is called the **modular view of the mind.**

Think about this alternative to Piaget's theory. Since so much is laid down in advance, the child is a far less active participant in constructing schemes than Piaget assumed. Critics complain that in emphasizing innate knowledge, the modular view sidesteps vital questions about development. As infants and children explore their surroundings, they display many new skills. How these arise from built-in structures is not clear (Fischer & Bidell, 1998; Haith & Benson, 1998). Furthermore, the more predetermined we assume the child's mind to be, the less individual variability in thinking we would expect. Yet later in this chapter and throughout this book, we will see many examples of wide individual differences in cognitive development.

Finally, according to the modular approach, we should be able to identify brain regions that govern specific types of knowledge at an early age. Yet research supports substantial brain plasticity in the early years and growth spurts across many areas of the cortex at once rather than in separate regions (see Chapter 5, page 191). At present, neurological support for a separate brain/mind module is strongest for language. In Chapter 9, we will take up a nativist view of language development.

■ **A COMPROMISE POSITION.** How can we make sense of these clashing viewpoints? The future is likely to bring compromises between them. Clearly, infants must have some built-in mental equipment for making sense of experience, since young babies are not knowledge free. But this initial equipment might best be viewed as a set of biases, or learning procedures. Each grants infants a means for constructing and flexibly adapting certain types of knowledge, some of which are acquired more easily than others (Elman et al., 1996; Haith & Benson, 1998; Karmiloff-Smith, 1992a). Cognitive skills emerge gradually over the first 2 years as infants apply these procedures to an expanding array of relevant experiences.

modular view of the mind A domain-specific, nativist view that regards the mind as a collection of separate modules—genetically prewired, independent, special purpose neural systems, each of triggers new understandings with exposure to stimulation.

Finally, in the sensorimotor stage (and in later stages), Piaget largely focused on full-blown attainments, such as the ability to find hidden objects and representational competencies clearly evident at the end of the second year. For this reason, change seems more abrupt in his theory than it actually is (Siegler & Ellis, 1996). Think back to the research we have reviewed, and note how it identifies many partial attainments that lead up to Piagetian milestones. For example, violation-of-expectation studies reveal some appreciation of object permanence in early infancy, but not a complete understanding, since babies cannot yet apply that knowledge in reaching for hidden toys (Munakata et al., 1997). And although deferred imitation is present in young infants, it is not very enduring and flexible until 18 months of age. In sum, by combining Piaget's findings with the wealth of new evidence his theory has inspired, we obtain a more precise and enlarged picture of infant cognitive development.

BRIEF REVIEW

According to Piaget, children actively build psychological structures, or schemes, as they manipulate and explore their world. Two processes, adaptation (which combines assimilation and accommodation) and organization, account for the development of schemes. Equilibration, an ever-changing balance between assimilation and accommodation, yields more effective schemes.

The vast changes of the sensorimotor stage are divided into six substages. The circular reaction, a special means that infants use to adapt schemes, changes from being oriented toward the infant's own body, to being directed outward toward objects, to producing novel effects in the surrounding world. During the last three substages, infants make strides in intentional behavior and understanding object permanence. By Substage 6, they represent reality and show the beginnings of make-believe play.

Recent research reveals that secondary circular reactions, understanding of object permanence and physical causality, and diverse representational capacities—deferred imitation, categorization, and analogical problem solving—are present much earlier than Piaget believed. These findings challenge Piaget's claim that infants construct all aspects of their world through motor activity and that early cognitive development is best characterized as a purely sensorimotor stage. Modern researchers regard infants as having more built-in equipment for making sense of experience than did Piaget, but they differ on whether they think that infants have built-in biases, or learning procedures, for constructing schemes or substantial innate knowledge.

ASK YOURSELF . . .

♦ While sitting in her high-chair, 7-month-old Mimi dropped her rattle, which fell out of sight on her lap. Mimi looked around but did not try to retrieve it. Does Mimi know that the rattle still exists? Why doesn't she search for it?

♦ At 14 months, Tony pushed his toy bunny through the slats of his crib onto a nearby table. To retrieve it, he tried jerking, turning, and throwing the bunny. What kind of circular reaction is Tony demonstrating? If Tony's parents showed him how to get the bunny, could he use that procedure to retrieve a different toy in another context? Explain, using research findings.

♦ CONNECTIONS
Cite evidence that supports a nativist, modular account of language development. What questions have been raised about this explanation? (See Chapter 9, pages 359–364.) Do those questions resemble reservations about the modular view raised earlier in this chapter?

The Preoperational Stage (2 to 7 Years)

As children move from the sensorimotor to the **preoperational stage,** the most obvious change is an extraordinary increase in representational, or symbolic, activity. We have seen that infants have some capacity to represent their world. This capacity blossoms between the ages of 2 and 7.

LANGUAGE AND THOUGHT

As we will see in Chapter 9, around the end of the second and beginning of the third year, children make tremendous strides in language. Piaget acknowledged that language is our most flexible means of mental representation. By detaching thought from action, it permits cognition to be far more efficient than it was during the sensorimotor stage. When we think in words, we overcome the limits of our momentary perceptions. We can deal with the past, present, and future at once, creating larger, interconnected images of reality (Miller, 1993).

preoperational stage Piaget's second stage, in which rapid development of representation takes place. However, thought is not yet logical. Spans the years from 2 to 7.

Despite the power of language, Piaget did not believe that it plays a major role in children's cognitive development. Instead, he believed that sensorimotor activity leads to internal images of experience, which children then label with words (Piaget, 1936/1952b). Some evidence is certainly consistent with this idea. For example, children's first words have a strong sensorimotor basis. They usually refer to objects that move or can be acted on or to familiar actions (see Chapter 9). Also, certain early words are linked to nonverbal cognitive achievements. For example, disappearance terms, such as "all gone," emerge at about the same time as mastery of advanced object-permanence problems. And success and failure expressions—"There!" and "Uh-oh"—appear when children solve sensorimotor problems suddenly, in Piaget's Substage 6 (Gopnik & Meltzoff, 1987b). Finally, a sharp vocabulary spurt between 18 months and 2 years coincides with gains in categorization, as children's sorting behavior reveals (Fenson et al., 1994; Reznick & Goldfield, 1992).

Still, Piaget's theory does not tell us exactly how sensorimotor schemes are transformed into images, and then into categories, to which words are eventually attached (Mandler, 1998). And as we have already suggested in the introduction to this chapter, Piaget may have misjudged the power of language to spur children's cognition forward. For example, we will see later that whereas language development is supported by early categories, conversations with adults and children's expanding vocabularies enhance conceptual skills.

MAKE-BELIEVE PLAY

Make-believe play provides another excellent example of the development of representation during the preoperational stage. Like language, it increases dramatically during early childhood. Piaget believed that through pretending, children practice and strengthen newly acquired representational schemes. Drawing on Piaget's ideas, several investigators have traced changes in make-believe play during the preschool years.

■ **DEVELOPMENT OF MAKE-BELIEVE PLAY.** Compare an 18-month-old's pretending with that of a 2- to 3-year-old. You are likely to see examples of three important changes, each of which reflects the preschool child's growing symbolic mastery:

1. *Over time, play becomes increasingly detached from the real-life conditions associated with it.* In early pretending, children use only realistic objects—for example, a toy telephone to talk into or a cup to drink from. Around age 2, they use less realistic toys, such as a block for a telephone receiver, more frequently. Soon after, children use body parts to stand for objects—for example, a finger for a toothbrush. Sometime during the third year, children can imagine objects and events without any support from the real world. This indicates that their representations are becoming more flexible, since a play symbol no longer has to resemble the object for which it stands (Corrigan, 1987; O'Reilly, 1995).

2. *The way the "child as self" participates in play changes with age.* When make-believe first appears, it is directed toward the self—that is, children pretend to feed or wash only themselves. A short time later, children direct pretend actions toward other objects, as when the child feeds a doll. And early in the third year, they use objects as active agents, and the child becomes a detached participant who makes a doll feed itself or a parent doll feed a baby doll. Make-believe gradually becomes less self-centered, as children realize that agents and recipients of pretend actions can be independent of themselves (Corrigan, 1987; McCune, 1993).

3. *Make-believe gradually includes more complex scheme combinations.* For example, an 18-month-old can pretend to drink from a cup but does not yet combine pouring and drinking. Later, children combine pretend schemes with those of peers in **sociodramatic play,** the make-believe with others that is under way by age 2½ (Haight & Miller, 1993; Howes & Matheson, 1992). By age 4 to 5, children build on one another's play themes, create and coordinate several roles in an elaborate plot, and have a sophisticated understanding of story lines (Göncü, 1993).

sociodramatic play The make-believe play with others that is under way by age 2½.

The appearance of complex sociodramatic play signals a major change in representation. Children do not just represent their world; they display *awareness* that make-believe is a representational activity, an understanding that increases steadily from 4 to 8 years of age (Jarrold et al., 1994; Lillard, 1998). Listen closely to preschoolers as they jointly create an imaginary scene. You will hear them assign roles and negotiate make-believe plans: "*You pretend to be* the astronaut, *I'll act like* I'm operating the control tower!" "Wait, *I gotta set up* the spaceship." In communicating about pretend, children think about and manipulate their own and others' fanciful representations. This indicates that they have begun to reason about people's mental activities, a topic to which we will return in later chapters.

These 4-year-olds coordinate several make-believe roles with the assistance of a very cooperative family pet. Their enjoyment of sociodramatic play contributes to cognitive, emotional, and social development. (Tom McCarthy/Stock South)

■ **ADVANTAGES OF MAKE-BELIEVE PLAY.** Piaget captured an important aspect of make-believe when he underscored its role in exercising representational schemes. He also noted its emotionally integrative function, a feature emphasized in psychoanalytic theory. Young children often revisit anxiety-provoking events, such as a trip to the doctor's office or discipline by a parent, but with roles reversed so the child is in command and compensates for the unpleasant experience (Erikson, 1950; Piaget, 1945/1951). In addition, Piaget recognized that by pretending, children become familiar with social role possibilities. In cultures around the world, young children act out family scenes and highly visible occupations—police officer, doctor, and nurse in Western nations; rabbit hunter and potter among the Hopi Indians; and hut builder and spear maker among the Baka of West Africa (Garvey, 1990; Roopnarine et al., 1998). In this way, make-believe provides children with important insights into the link between self and wider society.

Nevertheless, today Piaget's view of make-believe as mere practice of representational schemes is regarded as too limited. Research indicates that play not only reflects but contributes to children's cognitive and social skills (Nicolopoulou, 1993; Singer & Singer, 1990). Sociodramatic play has been studied most thoroughly. In contrast to social nonpretend activities (such as jointly solving a puzzle or playing a board game), during social pretend, preschoolers' interactions last longer, show more involvement, draw larger numbers of children into the activity, and are more cooperative (Creasey, Jarvis, & Berk, 1998).

When we consider these findings, it is not surprising that preschoolers who spend more time at sociodramatic play are advanced in general intellectual development and seen as more socially competent by their teachers (Burns & Brainerd, 1979; Connolly & Doyle, 1984). And many studies reveal that make-believe strengthens a wide variety of mental abilities, including memory, logical reasoning, language and literacy, imagination, creativity, and the ability to reflect on one's own thinking and take another's perspective (Dias & Harris, 1990; Ervin-Tripp, 1991; Kavanaugh & Engel, 1998; Newman, 1990).

What about children who spend much time in solitary make-believe creating *imaginary companions*—invisible characters with whom they form a special relationship, converse, and act out play scenes over an extended time period, usually several months? In the past, imaginary companions were viewed as a sign of maladjustment, but recent research challenges this assumption. Preschoolers who have them display more complex pretend play, are advanced in mental representation, and are actually more (not less) sociable with peers (Taylor, Cartright, & Carlson, 1993).

These findings offer strong justification for play as a central part of preschool and child-care programs and the daily life of the young child. Later we will return to the origins and consequences of make-believe from an alternative perspective—Vygotsky's.

DRAWINGS

Children's drawings are an additional early mode of symbolic expression. When given crayon and paper, even young toddlers scribble in imitation of others, but their scrawls seem like little more than random tangles of lines.

■ **FROM SCRIBBLES TO PICTURES.** As the young child's ability to mentally represent the world expands, marks on the page take on definite meaning. Gains in planning skills, spatial understanding (a move from a focus on separate objects to a broader visual perspective), and fine motor control also contribute to children's artful creations (Golomb, 1992). Typically, preschoolers' drawings progress through the following three-stage sequence:

1. *Scribbles.* Western children begin to draw during the second year. At first, action rather than the resulting scribble contains the intended representation. For example, one 18-month-old took her crayon and hopped it around the page, explaining as she made a series of dots, "Rabbit goes hop-hop" (Winner, 1986).

2. *First representational shapes and forms.* Around age 2, children realize that pictures can depict pretend objects—a basic feature of artistic expression (Kavanaugh & Harris, 1994). Over the next year, children's scribbles start to become pictures. Often this happens after they make a gesture with the crayon, notice that they have drawn a recognizable shape, and then decide to label it. In one case, a 2-year-old made some random marks on a page and then, realizing the resemblance between his scribbles and noodles, named the creation "chicken pie and noodles" (Winner, 1986).

   A major milestone in drawing occurs when children begin to use lines to represent the boundaries of objects. This permits them to draw their first picture of a person by age 3 or 4. Look at the tadpole image—a circular shape with lines attached—on the left in Figure 6.5. It is a universal one in which fine motor and cognitive limitations lead the preschooler to reduce the figure to the simplest form that still looks like a human being. Gradually, preschoolers add features, such as eyes, nose, mouth, hair, fingers, and feet.

3. *More realistic drawings.* Unlike many adults, young children do not demand that a drawing be realistic. But as cognitive and fine motor skills improve, they learn to desire greater realism. As a result, they create more complex drawings, like the one shown on the right in Figure 6.5, made by a 6-year-old child. Within these, more conventional figures, in which the body is differentiated from the arms and legs, appear. (Look closely at the human and animal figures in the 6-year-old's drawing.) Over time, children improve the proportions of the head, trunk, and extremities and add more details.

   Still, children of this age are not very particular about mirroring reality. Their drawings contain perceptual distortions, which help make their pictures look fanciful and inventive. Only at the end of the preschool years do children start to represent the third dimension in their drawings (Braine et al., 1993). Use of depth cues, such as overlapping objects, smaller distant than near objects, diagonal placement, and converging lines, increase during the elementary school years (Cox & Littleton, 1995; Nicholls & Kennedy, 1992).

FIGURE 6.5

Example of young children's drawings. The universal tadpolelike form that children use to draw their first picture of a person is shown on the left. The tadpole soon becomes an anchor for greater detail as arms, fingers, toes, and facial features sprout from the basic shape. By the end of the preschool years, children produce more complex, differentiated pictures like the one on the right, drawn by a 6-year-old child. Notice the beginning representation of perspective in the converging lines of the railroad tracks.

(Tadpole drawings from H. Gardner, 1980, *Artful Scribbles: The Significance of Children's Drawings,* New York: Basic Books, p. 64. Reprinted by permission of Basic Books, a division of HarperCollins Publishers, Inc. Six-year-old's picture from E. Winner, August 1986, "Where Pelicans Kiss Seals," *Psychology Today,* 20[8], p. 35. Reprinted by permission of the author.)

■ **CULTURAL VARIATIONS.** Children's drawings are greatly influenced by the art of their society. Children in cultures with little interest in art produce simpler forms. In cultures that emphasize artistic expression, children's drawings reflect the conventions of their culture and are more sophisticated. For example, the women of Walbiri, an Aboriginal group in Australia, draw symbols in sand to illustrate stories for preschoolers. When their children draw, these symbols are often mixed with more realistic images. In one instance, a child drew a chair with a semicircle on it to represent a seated person (Wales, 1990).

Preschools and elementary schools provide many opportunities to draw and write, see pictures, and grasp the notion that artistic forms have meanings that are shared by others (Cox, 1993). The Jimi Valley is a remote region of Papua New Guinea with no indigenous pictorial art. Many children do not go to school and therefore have little chance to develop drawing skills. When a Western researcher asked nonschooled Jimi 10- to 15-year-olds to draw a human figure for the first time, most produced nonrepresentational scribbles and shapes or simple "stick" or "contour" images (see Figure 6.6). Compared to the Western tadpole image, Jimi figures emphasize the body, hands, and feet over the head and face—a different view of what is salient in the human form (Martlew & Connolly, 1996).

No Jimi child enrolled in school produced nonrepresentational scribbles and shapes. Most drew Jimi-style contour images with greater detail or well-proportioned human figures with differentiated heads and bodies. That older Jimi children with no schooling often produce nonrepresentational forms suggests that this is a universal beginning stage in drawing. Once children realize that lines on the page must evoke human features, they find solutions to figure drawing that vary somewhat from culture to culture but, overall, follow the three-stage sequence described earlier.

When young children experiment with crayons and paint, they not only develop fine motor skills but acquire the artistic traditions of their culture. This Australian Aboriginal 4-year-old creates a dot painting. To Westerners, it looks abstract. To the child, it expresses a "dreamtime" story about the life and land of his ancestors. If asked about the painting, he might respond, "Here are the boulders on the creek line, the hills with kangaroos and emus, and the campsites."
(Laura Berk)

SPATIAL SYMBOLS

Closely related to drawings are spatial symbols. When we understand that photographs, models, or maps correspond to circumstances in everyday life, we can use them to acquire information about objects and places we have not experienced.

When do children realize that a spatial symbol stands for a specific state of affairs in the real world? In one study, 2½- and 3-year-olds watched as an adult hid a small doll (little Snoopy) in a scale model of a room. Then they were asked to find a larger doll (big Snoopy) hidden in the room that the model represented. Not until age 3 could most children find big Snoopy (DeLoache, 1987; Uttal et al., 1998). Younger preschoolers did not realize that the model could be two things at once: a toy room and *a symbol of another room.*

FIGURE 6.6

Drawings produced by nonschooled 10- to 15-year-old children of the Jimi Valley of Papua New Guinea when asked to draw a human figure for the first time. Many produced nonrepresentational scribbles and shapes (a), "stick" figures (b), or "contour" figures (c). Compared to the Western tadpole form, the Jimi "stick" and "contour" figures emphasize the hands and feet over the head and face. Otherwise, the drawings of these older children, who had little opportunity to develop drawing skills, resemble those of young preschoolers.

(From M. Martlew & K. J. Connolly, 1996, "Human Figure Drawings by Schooled and Unschooled Children in Papua New Guinea," *Child Development*, 67, pp. 2750–2751. © The Society for Research in Child Development, Inc. Adapted by permission.)

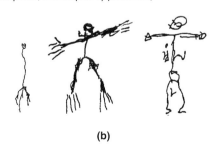
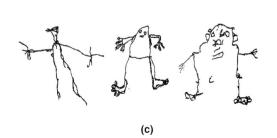

(a)   (b)   (c)

An ingenious variation of the search task confirmed 2½-year-olds' difficulty. An adult hid a large doll in a large room and led children to believe that a special shrinking machine had reduced the room to a scale model. This removed the symbolic aspect of the problem, since the model became a transformation rather than a representation of the room. As a result, very young children found the doll easily (DeLoache, Miller, & Rosengren, 1997).

How do children grasp the meaning of spatial symbols during the third year? Insight into one type of symbol–real world relation seems to help preschoolers understand others. For example, they understand photographs very early, by age 2, since a photo's primary purpose is to stand for something. It is not an interesting object in its own right. Using a photograph to show where big Snoopy is hidden helps 2½-year-olds do better on the model task (DeLoache, 1991). And 3-year-olds who pass the model task readily transfer their understanding to a new spatial medium—using a simple map to locate big Snoopy (Marzolf & DeLoache, 1994).

Granting young children many opportunities to learn about the functions of diverse symbols—picture books, photographs, models, maps, drawings, and make-believe—enhances their understanding that one object can stand for another (DeLoache, 1995). As a result, the door is opened to new realms of knowledge.

LIMITATIONS OF PREOPERATIONAL THOUGHT

Aside from the development of representation, Piaget described preschool children in terms of what they *cannot*, rather than *can*, understand (Beilin, 1992). He compared them to older, more capable children in the concrete operational stage, as the term "*pre*operational" suggests. According to Piaget, young children are not capable of **operations**—mental representations of actions that obey logical rules. Instead, their thinking is rigid, limited to one aspect of a situation at a time, and strongly influenced by the way things appear at the moment.

■ **EGOCENTRISM AND ANIMISM.** For Piaget, the most serious deficiency of preoperational thinking, the one that underlies all others, is **egocentrism.** He believed that when children first begin to mentally represent the world, they are unaware of any symbolic viewpoints other than their own, and they believe that everyone else perceives, thinks, and feels the same way they do (Piaget, 1950).

Piaget's most convincing demonstration of egocentrism involves his *three-mountains problem,* described in Figure 6.7 (Piaget & Inhelder, 1948/1956). Egocentrism, Piaget pointed out, is responsible for preoperational children's **animistic thinking**—the belief that inanimate objects have lifelike qualities, such as thoughts, wishes, feelings, and intentions, just like themselves (Piaget, 1926/1930). The 3-year-old who charmingly explains that the sun is angry at the clouds and has chased them away is demonstrating this kind of reasoning. According to Piaget, because young children egocentrically assign human purposes to physical events, magical thinking is especially common during the preschool years.

Piaget argued that egocentrism leads to the rigidity and illogical nature of preoperational thought. Young children's thinking proceeds so strongly from their own point of view that they do not *accommodate,* or revise their schemes, in response to feedback from the physical and social world. Egocentric thought is not reflective thought, which critically examines itself. But to fully appreciate these shortcomings of the preoperational stage, let's consider some additional tasks that Piaget presented to children.

■ **INABILITY TO CONSERVE.** Piaget's famous conservation tasks reveal a variety of deficiencies of preoperational thinking. **Conservation** refers to the idea that certain physical characteristics of objects remain the same, even when their outward appearance changes. A typical example is the conservation-of-liquid problem. The child is presented with two identical tall glasses of water and asked if they contain equal amounts. Once the child agrees, the water in one glass is poured into a short, wide container, changing the appearance of the water but not its amount. Then the child is asked whether the amount of water is still the same or whether it has changed. Preoperational children think the quantity of water is no longer the same. They explain, "There is less now because the water is

operations In Piaget's theory, mental representations of actions that obey logical rules.

egocentrism The inability to distinguish the symbolic viewpoints of others from one's own.

animistic thinking The belief that inanimate objects have lifelike qualities, such as thoughts, wishes, feelings, and intentions.

conservation The understanding that certain physical characteristics of objects remain the same, even when their outward appearance changes.

Piaget's three-mountains problem. A child is permitted to walk around a display of three mountains. Each is distinguished by its color and by its summit. One has a red cross, another a small house, and the third a snow-capped peak. Then the child stands on one side, and a doll is placed at various locations around the display. The child must choose a photograph that shows what the display looks like from the doll's perspective. Before age 6 or 7, most children select the photo that shows the mountains from their own point of view.

way down here" (that is, its level is so low in the short, wide container) or "There is more water now because it is all spread out." In Figure 6.8 on page 242, you will find other conservation tasks that you can try with children.

Preoperational children's inability to conserve highlights several related aspects of their thinking. First, their understanding is *centered,* or characterized by **centration.** In other words, they focus on one aspect of a situation and neglect other important features. In the case of conservation of liquid, the child centers on the height of the water in the two containers, failing to realize that all changes in height are compensated by changes in width. Second, their thinking is **perception bound.** They are easily distracted by the concrete, perceptual appearance of objects. It *looks like* there is less water in the short, wide container, so there *must be* less water. Third, children focus on **states rather than transformations.** In the conservation-of-liquid problem, they treat the initial and final *states* of the water as completely unrelated events, ignoring the *dynamic transformation* (pouring of water) between them.

The most important illogical feature of preoperational thought is *irreversibility.* Children of this stage cannot mentally go through a series of steps and then reverse direction, returning to the starting point. **Reversibility** is part of every logical operation. In the case of conservation of liquid, the preoperational child fails to see how the same amount is ensured by imagining it being poured back into its original container.

■ **TRANSDUCTIVE REASONING.** Reversible thinking is flexible and well organized. Because preoperational children are not capable of it, Piaget concluded that their causal reasoning often consists of disconnected facts and contradictions. He called young children's incorrect explanations **transductive reasoning,** which means reasoning from particular to particular. In other words, preschoolers simply link together two events that occur close in time and space in a cause-and-effect fashion. Sometimes this leads to some fantastic connections, as in the following interview Piaget conducted with a young child about why the clouds move:

> *You have already seen the clouds moving along? What makes them move?*—When we move along, they move along too.—*Can you make them move?*—Everybody can, when they walk.—*When I walk and you are still, do they move?*—Yes.—*And at night, when everyone is asleep, do they move?*—Yes.—*But you tell me that they move when somebody walks.*—They always move. The cats, when they walk, and then the dogs, they make the clouds move along. *(Piaget, 1926/1929, p. 62)*

■ **LACK OF HIERARCHICAL CLASSIFICATION.** Because preoperational children are not yet capable of logical operations, they cannot organize objects into classes and subclasses on the basis of similarities and differences between the groups. Piaget illustrated

centration The tendency to focus on one aspect of a situation to the neglect of other important features.

perception bound Being easily distracted by the concrete, perceptual appearance of objects.

states rather than transformations The tendency to treat the initial and final states in a problem as completely unrelated.

reversibility The ability to mentally go through a series of steps and then reverse direction, returning to the starting point. In Piaget's theory, part of every logical operation.

transductive reasoning Reasoning from particular to particular, instead of from general to particular or particular to general.

FIGURE 6.8

Some Piagetian conservation tasks. Children at the preoperational stage cannot yet conserve. These tasks are mastered gradually over the concrete operational stage. Children in Western nations typically acquire conservation of number, length, mass, and liquid sometime between 6 and 7 years and weight between 8 and 10 years.

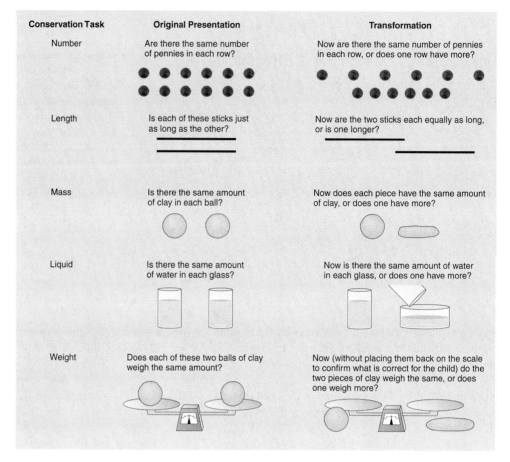

Conservation Task	Original Presentation	Transformation
Number	Are there the same number of pennies in each row?	Now are there the same number of pennies in each row, or does one row have more?
Length	Is each of these sticks just as long as the other?	Now are the two sticks each equally as long, or is one longer?
Mass	Is there the same amount of clay in each ball?	Now does each piece have the same amount of clay, or does one have more?
Liquid	Is there the same amount of water in each glass?	Now is there the same amount of water in each glass, or does one have more?
Weight	Does each of these two balls of clay weigh the same amount?	Now (without placing them back on the scale to confirm what is correct for the child) do the two pieces of clay weigh the same, or does one weigh more?

this difficulty with **hierarchical classification** in his well-known *class inclusion problem,* described in Figure 6.9. Preoperational children center on the overriding perceptual feature of yellow instead of thinking reversibly by moving from the whole class (flowers) to the parts (yellow and blue) and back again.

RECENT RESEARCH ON PREOPERATIONAL THOUGHT

Over the past two decades, Piaget's account of a cognitively deficient preschool child has been seriously challenged. If researchers give his tasks in just the way he originally designed them, they indeed find that preschoolers perform poorly. But a close look at Piagetian problems reveals that many contain unfamiliar elements or too many pieces of information for young children to handle at once. As a result, preschoolers' responses often do not reflect their true abilities. Piaget also missed many naturally occurring instances of preschoolers' effective reasoning. Let's look at some examples to illustrate these points.

■ **EGOCENTRISM.** Are young children really so egocentric that they believe a person standing in a different location in a room sees the same thing they see? When researchers change the nature of Piaget's three-mountains problem to include familiar objects and use methods other than picture selection (which is difficult even for 10-year-olds), 4-year-olds show clear awareness of others' vantage points (Borke, 1975; Newcombe & Huttenlocher, 1992).

Nonegocentric responses also appear in young children's conversations. For example, preschoolers adapt their speech to fit the needs of their listeners. Four-year-olds use shorter, simpler expressions when talking to 2-year-olds than to agemates or adults (Gelman & Shatz, 1978). Also, in describing objects, children do not use such words as "big" and "little" in a rigid, egocentric fashion. Instead, they *adjust* their descriptions, taking

hierarchical classification The organization of objects into classes and subclasses on the basis of similarities and differences between the groups.

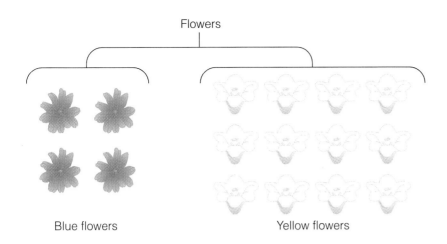

Flowers

Blue flowers

Yellow flowers

FIGURE 6.9

A Piagetian class inclusion problem.
Children are shown 16 flowers, 4 of which are blue and 12 of which are yellow. Asked whether there are more yellow flowers or more flowers, the preoperational child responds, "More yellow flowers," failing to realize that both yellow and blue flowers are included in the category "flowers."

account of context. By age 3, children judge a 2-inch shoe as small when seen by itself (because it is much smaller than most shoes) but as big when asked about its appropriateness for a very tiny 5-inch doll (Ebeling & Gelman, 1994).

In later chapters, we will encounter a wealth of evidence indicating that young children have a much greater appreciation of other people's mental states than is implied by Piaget's notion of egocentrism. For example, by 18 months, they begin to understand that another's emotional reactions may differ from their own (see Chapter 10). Between 2 and 3 years, this realization extends to others' intentions and desires. And 4-year-olds are adept at tricking others in a deliberate effort to alter their beliefs (see Chapter 11). At the same time, preschoolers' understanding of others' mental life is far from complete. In Chapter 7, we will see that 3- and 4-year-olds tend to fuse action with thought; to them, a person standing still is not thinking. And preschoolers often have trouble discerning what other people are thinking about, even when given obvious situational cues.

In sum, many findings challenge Piaget's description of young children as strongly egocentric. As we revisit the topic of perspective taking in the cognitive, emotional, and social domains, we will see that understanding others' viewpoints develops gradually throughout childhood and adolescence.

■ **ANIMISTIC AND MAGICAL THINKING.** Piaget also overestimated preschoolers' animistic beliefs because he asked children about objects with which they have little direct experience, such as the clouds, sun, and moon. Recall that at the end of the first year, infants form categories that distinguish living from nonliving things with which they are familiar, such as animals (dogs, rabbits) and vehicles (motorcycles, cars).

Consequently, it is not surprising that young preschoolers rarely think that very familiar inanimate objects, like rocks and crayons, are alive. Three-year-olds do make errors when questioned about certain vehicles, such as trains and airplanes. But these objects *appear* to be self-moving, a characteristic of almost all living things. And they also have some lifelike features—for example, headlights that look like eyes and animate-like movement patterns (Massey & Gelman, 1988; Poulin-Dubois & Héroux, 1994; Richards & Siegler, 1986). Children's responses result from incomplete knowledge about objects, not from a rigid belief that inanimate objects are alive.

The same is true for other fantastic beliefs of the preschool years. Most 3- and 4-year-olds believe in the supernatural powers of fairies, goblins, and other enchanted creatures that appear in storybooks, movies, and holiday legends. But they deny that magic can alter their everyday experiences—for example, turn a picture into a real object or a living being (Subbotsky, 1994). Instead, they think that magic accounts for events that violate their expectations and that they cannot otherwise explain.

Between 4 and 8 years, as familiarity with physical events increases and scientific explanations are taught in school, magical thinking declines. Children figure out who is really behind the activities of Santa Claus and the tooth fairy! They also realize that the antics of magicians are due to trickery, not special powers (Phelps & Woolley, 1994;

Young Children's Understanding of Death

IVE-YEAR-OLD Miriam arrived at preschool the day after her dog Pepper died. Instead of running to play with the other children, she stayed close by her teacher Leslie's side. Leslie noticed Miriam's discomfort and asked, "What's wrong?"

"Daddy said Pepper had a sick tummy. He fell asleep and died." For a moment, Miriam looked hopeful, "When I get home, Pepper might be up."

Leslie answered directly, "No, Pepper won't get up again. He's not asleep. He's dead, and that means he can't sleep, eat, run, or play anymore."

Miriam wandered off. Later, she returned to Leslie and confessed, "I chased Pepper too hard," tears streaming from her eyes.

Leslie put her arm around Miriam. "Pepper didn't die because you chased him. He was very old and very sick," she explained.

Over the next few days, Miriam asked many more questions: "When I go to sleep, will I die?" "Can a tummy ache make you die?" "Does Pepper feel better now?" "Will Mommy and Daddy die?"

DEVELOPMENT OF THE DEATH CONCEPT. A realistic understanding of death is based on three ideas:

1. *Permanence:* Once a living thing dies, it cannot be brought back to life.

2. *Universality:* All living things eventually die.

3. *Nonfunctionality:* All living functions, including thought, feeling, movement, and body processes, cease at death.

Without clear explanations, young children rely on egocentric and magical thinking to make sense of death. They may believe, as Miriam did, that they are responsible for a

By examining this dead mouse, these boys are likely to develop a more accurate understanding of death—that once a living thing dies, it cannot be brought back to life, that death happens to all living things, and that all living functions (both physical and mental) cease at death.

(A. Carey/The Image Works)

Rosengren & Hickling, 1994). How quickly children give up certain fantastic ideas varies with religion and culture. For example, Jewish preschool and school-age children express greater disbelief in Santa Claus and the tooth fairy than do their Christian agemates. Having been taught at home about the unreality of Santa, they seem to generalize this attitude to other mythical figures (Woolley, 1997).

The importance of knowledge, experience, and culture can be seen in preschoolers' grasp of other natural concepts. Refer to the From Research to Practice box above to find out about young children's developing understanding of death.

■ **ILLOGICAL CHARACTERISTICS OF THOUGHT.** Many studies have reexamined the illogical characteristics that Piaget saw in the preoperational stage. Results show that when preschoolers are given tasks that are simplified and made relevant to their everyday lives, they do better than Piaget might have expected.

For example, when a conservation of number task is scaled down to include only three items instead of six or seven, 3-year-olds perform well (Gelman, 1972). And when preschoolers are asked carefully worded questions about what happens to familiar substances

relative or pet's death. And they can easily arrive at incorrect conclusions—in Miriam's case, that sleeping or having a stomachache can cause someone to die.

Preschoolers grasp the three components of the death concept in the order just given, with most children mastering them by age 7. *Permanence* is the first and most easily understood idea. When Leslie explained that Pepper would not get up again, Miriam accepted this fact quickly, perhaps because she had seen it in other, less emotionally charged situations, such as the dead butterflies and beetles that she picked up and inspected while playing outside (Furman, 1990). Appreciation of *universality* comes slightly later. At first, children think that certain people do not die, especially those with whom they have close emotional ties or who are like themselves—other children. Finally, *nonfunctionality* is the most difficult component of death for children to grasp. Many preschoolers view dead things as retaining living capacities. When they first comprehend nonfunctionality, they do so in terms of its most visible aspects, such as heartbeat and breathing. Only later do they understand that thinking, feeling, and dreaming cease (Lazar & Torney-Purta, 1991; Speece & Brent, 1992, 1996).

CULTURAL INFLUENCES. Although a mature appreciation of death is usually reached by the end of early childhood, ethnic variations suggest that religious teachings affect children's understanding. A comparison of four ethnic groups in Israel revealed that Druze and Moslem children's death concepts lagged behind those of Christian and Jewish children (Florian & Kravetz, 1985). The Druze emphasis on reincarnation and the greater religiosity of both the Druze and Moslem groups may underlie these findings. Religious teachings seem to have an especially strong impact on children's grasp of the permanence of death. For example, children of Southern Baptist families, who believe in an afterlife, are less likely to endorse permanence than are children from North-ern Unitarian families, who focus on the here and now—peace and justice in today's world (Candy-Gibbs, Sharp, & Petrun, 1985).

In another study, Israeli Jewish children had a more advanced understanding of the permanence of death than did American children (Schonfeld & Smilansky, 1989). Variations in death-related experiences are probably responsible, since at the time of the research, Israel was at war. Some Israeli children had relatives who died in battle, and conversations about death at home and in classrooms were common.

ENHANCING CHILDREN'S UNDERSTANDING. Preschoolers' incompletely formed ideas about death are important to keep in mind when the death of a pet or relative occurs. Simple, direct explanations help children understand. Although parents often worry that discussing death with children will fuel their fears, this is not so. Instead, children who have a good grasp of the facts of death have an easier time accepting it (Essa & Murray, 1994). When preschoolers ask very difficult questions—"Will I die?" "Will you die?"—parents can be truthful as well as comforting by taking advantage of children's sense of time. They can say something like "Not for many, many years. First I'm going to enjoy you as a grown-up and be a grandparent."

Discussions with children about death should also be culturally sensitive. Rather than presenting scientific evidence as counteracting religious beliefs, parents and teachers can assist children in blending the two sources of knowledge. As children get older, their grasp of permanence, universality, and nonfunctionality is often integrated with spiritual and philosophical views, which offer solace during times of bereavement (Cuddy-Casey & Orvaschel, 1997). Open, honest, and respectful communication with children contributes not only to their cognitive appreciation of the death concept but also to their emotional well-being.

(such as sugar) after they are dissolved in water, they give very accurate explanations. Most 3- to 5-year-olds know that the substance is conserved—that it continues to exist, can be tasted, and makes the liquid heavier, even though it is invisible in the water. And the majority of 5-year-olds reconcile the apparent contradiction between invisibility and continued existence by indicating that particles too tiny to be seen are in the water (Au, 1994; Au, Sidle, & Rollins, 1993; Rosen & Rozin, 1993).

Preschoolers' ability to notice and reason about transformations is evident on other problems. For example, they can engage in impressive analogical reasoning about physical transformations. Presented with the problem, *playdough is to cut-up playdough as apple is to ?*, even 3-year-olds choose the correct answer from a set of alternatives, several of which share physical features with the right choice (the same object or the same physical change, but not both) (see Figure 6.10 on page 246) (Goswami, 1996; Goswami & Brown, 1989).

By age 4, children think reversibly about physical transformations. In one study, children were shown "picture stories" of familiar experiences. In some, an object went from its basic state to a changed condition. For example, a cup became a wet cup. In others, it returned from its changed condition to its basic state. That is, a wet cup became

FIGURE 6.10

Analogical problem about physical transformations. Preschoolers were told they would be playing a picture-matching game. Then the researchers showed each child the first three pictures of a four-picture sequence—in this example, playdough, cut-up playdough, and apple—and asked the child to complete the sequence by choosing from five alternatives. Several wrong answers shared features with the right choice—for example, correct physical change but wrong object (E), correct object but wrong physical change (F). Children as young as 3 years of age could combine the correct physical change with the correct object and solve the problem.

(Adapted from Goswami & Brown, 1989.)

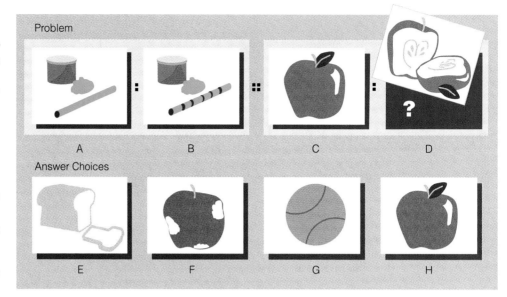

Problem

A   B   C   D

Answer Choices

E   F   G   H

a (dry) cup. Children were asked to pick an item from three choices (in this case, water, drying-up cloth, or feather) that caused the object to change. Most 3-year-olds had difficulty: they picked water for both transformations. But 4-year-olds selected the appropriate intermediate objects and reasoned effectively in either direction (Das Gupta & Bryant, 1989).

Indeed, a close look at 3- and 4-year-olds' conversations reveals that they use causal terms, such as "if–then" and "because," with the same degree of accuracy as adults do (McCabe & Peterson, 1988). Transductive reasoning occurs only when children grapple with unfamiliar topics. Consistent with this idea, recall that preschoolers are reluctant to resort to magical explanations unless they are faced with an extraordinary event. This supports the conclusion that they have a good understanding of causal principles that govern their everyday experiences. In sum, although young children cannot yet consider the complex interplay of forces that adolescents and adults can, they often analyze events accurately in terms of basic cause-and-effect relations.

■ **CATEGORIZATION.** Even though preschoolers have difficulty with Piagetian class inclusion tasks, their everyday knowledge is organized into nested categories at an early age. Earlier we saw that even young infants categorize, grouping together objects with similar physical features. By the second half of the first year, children have begun to form global categories consisting of objects that do not necessarily look alike but that are the same kind of thing (turn back to page 230 to review).

Between 1 and 2½ years, many more such categories are added, such as bathroom objects, toys, and dinosaurs (Gelman & Coley, 1990; Mandler, 1998; Mandler, Bauer, & McDonough, 1991). Consider these object groupings, and you will see that they provide yet another challenge to Piaget's assumption that young children's thinking is always perception bound (Keil, 1989). To the contrary, 2- to 5-year-olds readily draw inferences about nonobvious characteristics that category members share. For example, after being told that a bird has warm blood and a stegosaurus (dinosaur) has cold blood, preschoolers infer that a pterodactyl (labeled a dinosaur) has cold blood, even though it closely resembles a bird.

Over the early preschool years, these global categories differentiate. Children form many *basic-level categories*—ones at an intermediate level of generality, such as "chairs," "tables," "dressers," and "beds." By the third year, preschoolers easily move back and forth between basic-level and *superordinate categories,* such as "furniture" (Blewitt, 1994). Soon after, they break down basic-level categories into *subcategories,* such as "rocking chairs" and "desk chairs." Gradually, children clarify the features that distinguish subcategories and perfect their understanding of hierarchical relations (Johnson, Scott, & Mervis, 1997).

How do preschoolers become such skilled categorizers? Children's rapidly growing vocabularies probably contribute to categorical discriminations, since 1- and 2-year-olds who comprehend more object names score higher on object-sorting tasks (Gershoff-Stowe et al., 1997). Perhaps the process of acquiring names for things helps children detect more refined categories in the world of objects. In support of this idea, Korean children learn a language that emphasizes verbs rather than nouns, and object names are often omitted from sentences. They develop object-grouping skills later than do their English-speaking counterparts (Gopnik & Choi, 1990).

Children's expanding general knowledge also enhances categorization. As they learn more about their world, preschoolers devise theories about underlying characteristics that category members share. For example, they realize that animals have internal organs and an inborn potential for certain physical features and behaviors that are crucial for determining their identity (Gelman & Wellman, 1991; Hirshfeld, 1995). In one study, researchers made up two categories of animals: One had horns, armor, and a spiky tail; the other had wings, large ears, long toes, and a monkey-like tail (see Figure 6.11). Four-year-olds who were given a theory that explained the coexistence of the surface features—animals in the first category "like to fight," those in the second category "like to hide in trees"—easily classified new examples of animals. Those for whom animal features were simply pointed out or who were given a separate function for each feature could not remember the categories (Krascum & Andrews, 1998).

Finally, adults label categories and explain the basis of category membership to young children, and picture-book reading seems to be an especially rich context for doing so. While looking at books with their preschoolers, parents make such categorical statements as "Penguins live at the South Pole, swim, and catch fish" and "Fish breathe by taking water into their mouths." Parents rarely point out relations on the basis of perceptual similarity alone (Callanan, 1991; Gelman et al., 1998). The information they provide helps guide children's inferences about the structure of categories.

In sum, young children's category systems are not yet very complex, and concrete operational reasoning facilitates their development (Ricco, 1989). But the capacity to classify hierarchically is present in early childhood.

■ **APPEARANCE VERSUS REALITY.** So far, we have seen that young children show some remarkably advanced reasoning when presented with familiar situations and simplified problems. Yet in certain situations, preschoolers are easily tricked by the outward appearance of things.

John Flavell and his colleagues took a close look at the ability to distinguish appearance from reality. They presented children with objects that were disguised in various ways and asked what the items were, "really and truly." At age 3, children could separate the way an object appeared to feel from the way it truly felt. For example, they understood that even though an ice cube did not feel cold to their gloved finger, it "really and truly" was cold (Flavell, Green, & Flavell, 1989). In this task, the real and apparent object states were present at the same time, and children could easily compare them.

Preschoolers have more difficulty with problems involving sights and sounds, but not because (as Piaget suggested) they always confuse appearance and reality. Instead, these tasks require them to recall the real image of an object in the face of a second, contradictory representation. When asked whether a white piece of paper placed behind a blue filter is "really and truly blue" or whether a can that sounds like a baby crying when turned over is "really and truly a baby," preschoolers often respond "Yes!" Not until age 6 to 7 do children do well on these problems (Flavell, 1993; Flavell, Green, & Flavell, 1987).

How do children go about mastering distinctions between appearance and reality? Make-believe play may be important. Children can tell the difference between pretend play and real experiences long before they answer many appearance–reality tasks correctly (Golomb & Galasso, 1995; Woolley & Wellman, 1990). In addition, presenting an appearance–reality task in the context of tricking someone else into thinking an object (a sponge) has another

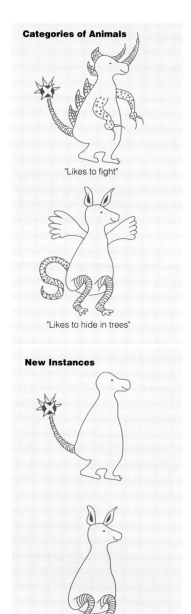

Categories of Animals

"Likes to fight"

"Likes to hide in trees"

New Instances

FIGURE 6.11

Categories of imaginary animals shown to preschoolers. When given a theory about the coexistence of the animals' surface features—"likes to fight" and "likes to hide in trees"—4-year-olds easily classified new examples of animals with only one or two features. Without the theory, preschoolers could not remember the categories. Theories about underlying characteristics support the formation of many new categories in early childhood.

(From R. M. Krascum & S. Andrews, 1998, "The Effects of Theories on Children's Acquisition of Family-Resemblance Categories," *Child Development*, 69, p. 336. © The Society for Research in Child Development, Inc. Reprinted by permission.)

identity (a "rock," since it looks like a rock) helps 3-year-olds perform better on standard, non-trick appearance–reality tasks (Rice et al., 1997). Experiencing the contrast between everyday and playful, "trick" circumstances seems to help young children realize that people can perceive objects in ways that do not correspond to reality.

■ **EVALUATION OF THE PREOPERATIONAL STAGE.** How can we make sense of the contradictions between Piaget's conclusions and the findings of recent research? The evidence as a whole indicates that Piaget was partly wrong and partly right about young children's cognitive capacities. When given simplified tasks based on familiar experiences, preschoolers show the beginnings of logical operations long before the concrete operational stage. But their reasoning is not as well developed as that of school-age children, since they fail Piaget's three-mountains, conservation, and class inclusion tasks and have difficulty separating appearance from reality.

The fact that preschoolers have some logical understanding suggests that the attainment of operations takes place gradually. Over time, children rely on increasingly effective mental as opposed to perceptual approaches to solving problems. For example, research shows that children who cannot use counting to compare two sets of items do not conserve number (Sophian, 1995). Once preschoolers acquire this counting strategy, they apply it to conservation-of-number tasks with only a few items. As counting improves, they extend the strategy to problems with more items. By age 6, they have formed a mental understanding that number remains the same after a transformation as long as nothing is added or taken away. Consequently, they no longer need to use counting to verify their answer (Klahr & MacWhinney, 1998; Siegler & Robinson, 1982). This sequence indicates that young children pass through several phases of understanding, although (as Piaget indicated) they do not fully grasp conservation until the school years.

Evidence that preschool children can be trained to perform well on Piagetian problems, such as conservation and class inclusion, also supports the idea that operational thought is not absent at one point in time and present at another. It makes sense that children who possess part of a capacity will benefit from training, unlike those with little or no understanding. A variety of training methods are effective, including having children interact with more capable peers, explain an adult's correct reasoning, listen to an adult point out contradictions in the child's logic (language-based techniques), and measure a transformed quantity (for example, determine how many ladles of liquid are in two differently shaped glasses) (Beilin, 1978; Roazzi & Bryant, 1997; Siegler, 1995).

The idea that logical operations develop gradually poses yet another challenge to Piaget's stage concept, which assumes sudden and abrupt change toward logical reasoning around 6 or 7 years of age. Although the minds of young children still have a great deal of developing to do, research shows that they are considerably more logical than Piaget thought they were.

ASK YOURSELF . . .

◆ *At home, 4-year-old Will understands very well that his tricycle isn't alive and can't move by itself. Yet when Will went fishing with his family and his father asked, "Why do you think the river is flowing along?" Will responded, "Because it's alive and wants to." What explains this contradiction in Will's reasoning?*

◆ CONNECTIONS
Do children separate appearance from reality in the emotional domain—that is, realize that an emotion a person expresses may not be the one he or she truly feels—at about the same time they solve the appearance–reality tasks discussed in this chapter? (See Chapter 10, page 410.)

BRIEF REVIEW

During Piaget's preoperational stage, mental representation flourishes, as indicated by growth in language, make-believe play, drawings, and understanding of spatial symbols, such as photographs, models, and simple maps. Aside from representation, Piaget's theory emphasizes the young child's cognitive limitations. Egocentrism is assumed to underlie a variety of illogical features of preoperational thought, including animism, inability to pass conservation tasks, transductive reasoning, and lack of hierarchical classification.

Recent research reveals that when tasks are simplified and made relevant to children's everyday experiences, preschoolers reason logically. They give nonegocentric responses (can take another's perspective), know that familiar inanimate objects are not alive, conserve substances, reason about transformations, and classify objects hierarchically and on the basis of nonobvious features. These findings indicate that operational thought is not absent during early childhood, and they challenge Piaget's notion of stage.

The Concrete Operational Stage (7 to 11 Years)

iaget viewed the **concrete operational stage,** which spans the years from 7 to 11, as a major turning point in cognitive development. When children attain it, their thought more closely resembles that of adults than that of the sensorimotor and preoperational child (Piaget & Inhelder, 1967/1969). According to Piaget, concrete operational reasoning is far more logical, flexible, and organized than cognition was during the preschool period. The Milestones table on page 250 summarizes major cognitive changes from early to middle childhood, along with the attainments of adolescence that will follow.

OPERATIONAL THOUGHT

Concrete operations are evident in the school-age child's performance on a wide variety of Piagetian tasks. Let's look closely at these diverse accomplishments.

■ **CONSERVATION.** The ability to pass *conservation tasks* provides clear evidence of *operations.* In conservation of liquid, for example, children state that the amount of liquid has not changed, and they are likely to explain in ways like this: "The water's shorter but it's also wider. If you pour it back, you'll see that it's the same amount." Notice how in this response, the child coordinates several aspects of the task rather than centering on only one, as a preschooler would do. In other words, school-age children are capable of *decentration;* they recognize that a change in one aspect of the water (its height) is compensated for by a change in another aspect (its width). This explanation also illustrates *reversibility*— the capacity to imagine the water being returned to the original container as proof of conservation.

■ **HIERARCHICAL CLASSIFICATION.** Perhaps because they are more aware of classification hierarchies and can focus on superordinate and subordinate categories at the same time, by the end of middle childhood children pass Piaget's *class inclusion problem* (Achenbach & Weisz, 1975; Hodges & French, 1988). Around this time, they also group objects into hierarchies more effectively than they did at earlier ages. You can see this in children's play activities. Collections of all kinds of objects—stamps, coins, baseball cards, rocks, bottle caps, and more—become common during the school years. At age 10, one boy I know spent hours sorting and resorting his large box of baseball cards. At times he grouped them by league and team membership, at other times by playing position and batting average. He could separate the players into a variety of classes and subclasses and flexibly rearrange them. This understanding is beyond preschoolers, who usually insist that a set of objects can be sorted in only one way.

■ **SERIATION.** The ability to order items along a quantitative dimension, such as length or weight, is called **seriation.** To test for it, Piaget asked children to arrange sticks of different lengths from shortest to longest. Older preschoolers can form the series, but they do so haphazardly. They put the sticks in a row but make many errors and take a long time to correct them. In contrast, 6- to 7-year-olds are guided by an orderly plan. They create the series efficiently by beginning with the smallest stick, then moving to the next smallest, and so on, until the ordering is complete.

The concrete operational child's improved grasp of quantitative arrangements is also evident in a more challenging seriation problem—one that requires children to seriate mentally. This ability is called **transitive inference.** In a well-known transitive inference problem, Piaget showed children pairings of differently colored sticks. From observing that stick A is longer than stick B and stick B is longer than stick C, children must make the mental inference that A is longer than C. Not until age 9 or 10 do children perform well on this task (Chapman & Lindenberger, 1988; Piaget, 1967).

How might children master transitive inference? Graeme Halford (1992, 1993) argues that they do so by drawing on their capacity for analogical problem solving. For example, children can solve the task just described by relating the three sticks to a familiar, ordered

concrete operational stage
Piaget's third stage, during which thought is logical, flexible, and organized in its application to concrete information. However, the capacity for abstract thinking is not yet present. Spans the years from 7 to 11.

seriation The ability to arrange items along a quantitative dimension, such as length or weight.

transitive inference The ability to seriate—or arrange items along a quantitative dimension—mentally.

Some Cognitive Attainments of Childhood and Adolescence

Age	Cognitive Attainment
Early Childhood	
2–4 years 	■ Dramatic expansion of representational activity, as indicated by language, make-believe play, drawings, and understanding of spatial symbols (photographs, simple maps, and models) ■ Takes the perspective of others in simplified, familiar situations and in everyday communication ■ Distinguishes animate beings from inanimate objects; denies that magic can alter everyday experiences ■ Constructs many more categories on the basis of common function and behavior; readily draws inferences about nonobvious characteristics that category members share ■ Differentiates global categories into superordinate, basic-level, and subordinate categories
4–7 years 	■ Displays complex sociodramatic play and creates more realistic drawings, which begin to depict the third dimension ■ Replaces magical beliefs about fairies, goblins, and events that violate expectations with plausible explanations ■ Notices transformations, thinks reversibly, and explains events causally in familiar situations ■ Shows improved ability to distinguish appearance from reality
Middle Childhood	
7–11 years 	■ Thinks in a more organized, logical fashion about concrete, tangible information, as indicated by the ability to pass Piagetian conservation, class inclusion, and seriation problems, including transitive inference ■ Shows improved understanding of spatial concepts, as indicated by conservation of distance, ability to give clear directions, and well-organized cognitive maps ■ Displays the horizontal décalage—sequential mastery of logical reasoning in different content areas
Adolescence	
11–20 years	■ Reasons abstractly in situations that offer many opportunities for hypothetico-deductive reasoning and propositional thought ■ Displays the imaginary audience and personal fable, which are strongest in early adolescence and gradually decline

Note: These milestones represent overall age trends. Individual differences exist in the precise age at which each milestone is attained.

set of schemes, such as large, medium, small. They arrive at the correct answer by merging the novel elements with the familiar structure: stick A—large, stick B—medium, stick C—small. When encouraged to construct this type of analogy, even 3- and 4-year-olds can solve some transitive inference problems (Goswami, 1995).

Piaget referred to the abilities we have considered so far—conservation, hierarchical classification, and seriation—as *logico-arithmetic operations*. He thought they were responsible for the school-age child's increased facility with quantitative tasks. As we will see in Chapter 7 when we consider the development of mathematical reasoning, preschoolers have some impressive numerical skills, including the ability to count small arrays and add and subtract small sets of items. But most mathematical knowledge is acquired after early childhood. Elementary school children have a more quantitative, measurement-oriented approach to many tasks than do preschoolers.

■ **SPATIAL OPERATIONS.** In addition to logico-arithmetic operations, the concrete operational child also masters a variety of *spatial operations.* These deal with distance, directions, and spatial relationships between objects.

DISTANCE. Comprehension of distance improves during middle childhood, as a special conservation task reveals. To give this problem, make two small trees out of modeling clay and place them apart on a table. Next, put a block or thick piece of cardboard between the trees. Then ask the child whether the trees are nearer together, farther apart, or still the same distance apart.

Preschoolers say the distance has become smaller. They do not understand that a filled space has the same value as an empty space (Piaget, Inhelder, & Szeminska, 1948/1960). By the early school years, children grasp this idea easily. Four-year-olds can conserve distance when questioned about a very familiar scene or when a path is marked between two objects, which helps them represent the distance. However, their understanding is not as solid and complete as that of the school-age child (Fabricius & Wellman, 1993; Miller & Baillargeon, 1990).

DIRECTIONS. School-age children's more advanced understanding of space can also be seen in their ability to give directions. Stand facing a 5- or 6-year-old, and ask the child to name an object on your left and one on your right. Children of this age answer incorrectly; they apply their own frame of reference to that of others. Between 7 and 8 years, children start to perform *mental rotations,* in which they align the self's frame to match that of a person in a different orientation. As a result, they can identify left and right for positions they do not occupy (Roberts & Aman, 1993).

Around 8 to 10 years, children can give clear, well-organized directions for how to get from one place to another. Aided by their capacity for operational thinking, they use a "mental walk" strategy in which they imagine another person's movements along a route (Gauvain & Rogoff, 1989a). Six-year-olds give more organized directions after they walk the route themselves or are specially prompted. Otherwise, they focus on the end point without describing exactly how to get there (Plumert et al., 1994).

COGNITIVE MAPS. Children's drawings of familiar environments, such as their neighborhood or school, also undergo important changes from early to middle childhood (Piaget & Inhelder, 1948/1956). These mental representations of large-scale spaces are called **cognitive maps.** They require considerable perspective-taking skill, since the entire space cannot be seen at once. Instead, children must infer the overall layout by relating the separate parts to one another.

Preschoolers' maps display *landmarks,* but their placement is fragmented and disorganized. In the early school years, children start to arrange landmarks along an *organized route of travel,* such as the path they usually walk from home to school—an attainment that resembles their improved direction giving. However, they have not yet mastered the relationship of routes to one another. By the end of middle childhood, children form an *overall configuration of a large-scale space* in which landmarks and routes are interrelated (Newcombe, 1982; Siegel, 1981).

Once again, however, the ability to represent spatial layouts does not emerge suddenly. Even 3-year-olds can use a simple map to navigate their way through an unfamiliar space (Uttal & Wellman, 1989). However, preschoolers have difficulty interpreting a map when landmarks are represented by shapes rather than pictures of objects (Liben & Yekel, 1996). Nor can they create an organized map of their own. "Map literacy" improves greatly during middle childhood (Liben & Downs, 1989).

An improved ability to categorize underlies children's interest in collecting objects during middle childhood. These fourth graders can sort this shell collection into an elaborate structure of classes and subclasses. (Brian Smith)

LIMITATIONS OF CONCRETE OPERATIONAL THOUGHT

Because of their improved ability to conserve, classify, seriate, and deal with spatial concepts, school-age children are far more capable problem solvers than they were during the

cognitive maps Mental representations of large-scale spaces.

In tribal and village societies, conservation is often delayed. This boy, who is growing up in Belize, Central America, gathers firewood for his family. His everyday activities may not promote the kind of reasoning required to pass Piagetian conservation tasks. Compared to his age-mates in Western industrialized nations, he may have fewer opportunities to see the same quantity arranged in different ways.

(Jeff Lawrence/Stock Boston)

preschool years. But concrete operational thinking suffers from one important limitation. Children think in an organized, logical fashion only when dealing with concrete information they can directly perceive. Their mental operations work poorly when applied to abstract ideas—ones not apparent in the real world.

Children's solutions to transitive inference problems provide a good illustration. When shown pairs of sticks of unequal length, 9-year-olds readily figure out that if stick A is longer than stick B and stick B is longer than stick C, then stick A is longer than stick C. But they have great difficulty with an entirely hypothetical version of this task, such as "Susan is taller than Sally and Sally is taller than Mary. Who is the tallest?" Not until age 11 or 12 can children solve this problem easily.

The fact that logical thought is at first tied to immediate situations helps account for a special feature of concrete operational reasoning. Perhaps you have already noticed that school-age children do not master all of Piaget's concrete operational tasks at once. Instead, they do so in a step-by-step fashion. For example, they usually grasp the conservation problems in Figure 6.8 on page 242 in a certain order: first number; then length, mass, and liquid; and finally weight. Piaget used the term **horizontal décalage** (meaning development within a stage) to describe this gradual mastery of logical concepts.

The horizontal décalage is another indication of the concrete operational child's difficulty with abstractions. School-age children do not come up with general logical principles and then apply them to all relevant situations. Instead, they seem to work out the logic of each problem they encounter separately.

RECENT RESEARCH ON CONCRETE OPERATIONAL THOUGHT

According to Piaget, brain maturation combined with experience in a rich and varied external world should lead children everywhere to reach the concrete operational stage. He did not believe that operational thinking depends on particular kinds of experiences. Yet recent evidence indicates that specific cultural practices have a great deal to do with mastery of Piagetian tasks (Rogoff & Chavajay, 1995).

In tribal and village societies, conservation is often delayed. For example, among the Hausa of Nigeria, who live in small agricultural settlements and rarely send their children to school, even the most basic conservation tasks—number, length, and liquid—are not understood until age 11 or later (Fahrmeier, 1978). This suggests that for children to master conservation and other Piagetian concepts, they must take part in everyday activities that promote this way of thinking (Light & Perret-Clermont, 1989). Many children in Western nations, for example, have learned to think of fairness in terms of equal distribution—a value emphasized by their culture. They have many opportunities to divide materials, such as crayons, Halloween treats, and lemonade, equally among their friends. Because they often see the same quantity arranged in different ways, they grasp conservation early. In societies where equal sharing of goods is not common, conservation may not appear at the expected age.

The very experience of going to school seems to promote mastery of Piagetian tasks. When children of the same age are tested, those who have been in school longer do better on transitive inference problems (Artman & Cahan, 1993). The opportunities schooling affords for seriating objects, learning about order relations, and remembering the parts of a complex problem are probably responsible.

Yet certain nonschool, informal experiences can also foster operational thought. In one study, Brazilian 6- to 9-year-old street vendors, who seldom attend school, were given two class inclusion problems: (1) the traditional Piagetian task, and (2) an informal version in which the researcher became a customer and questioned the child. As Figure 6.12 shows, street-vendor children did much better on the informal problem, which captured their interest and motivation. Brazilian children from middle-class homes were more suc-

horizontal décalage Development within a Piagetian stage. Gradual mastery of logical concepts during the concrete operational stage is an example.

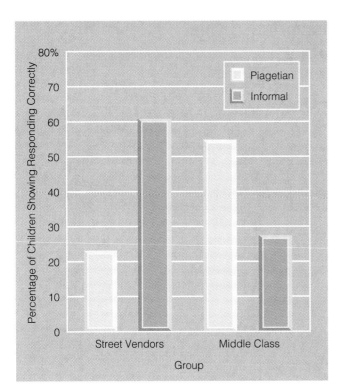

FIGURE 6.12

Comparison of Brazilian street vendors with Brazilian middle-class children on the traditional Piagetian class inclusion task and an informal, street-vending version. For the informal task, the researcher asked the child for the price of two different kinds of chewing gum (mint and strawberry). After setting aside four units of mint and two units of strawberry, the investigator continued, "For you to get more money, is it better to sell me the mint chewing gum or [all] the chewing gum? Why?" Street vendors performed better on the informal version, whereas middle-class children did better on the Piagetian task.

(Adapted from Ceci & Roazzi, 1994.)

cessful on the Piagetian task than on a version in which they were asked to role-play street vendors—an activity unfamiliar to them (Ceci & Roazzi, 1994).

Besides specific experiences, the phrasing of questions and the objects to which they refer can profoundly affect Piagetian task performance. In one study, researchers asked college students misleading questions about conservation of weight. Sometimes the question referred to the student's body ("When do you weigh more, when you are walking or running?") and sometimes it referred to an external object ("When did the modeling clay weigh more, when it was a ball or when it was in the shape of a sausage?"). Misleading questions led to many nonconserving responses, especially when they referred to the student's body. Interestingly, students who were asked to explain their answers and who had heard of Piaget were less likely to be tricked by the misleading questions (Winer, Craig, & Weinbaum, 1992).

These findings reveal that concrete operations are not always used, even by adults! Instead, people seem to have at least two modes of thinking that are evoked in different situations: one that is person-centered and intuitive, and one that is object-centered and logically consistent. Taken together, the research just reviewed is troublesome for Piaget's theory, since it indicates that concrete operational reasoning may not emerge universally in middle childhood and, once present, override less mature ways of thinking (Light & Perrett-Clermont, 1989; Robert, 1989). Instead, it appears to be heavily influenced by training, context, and cultural conditions.

BRIEF REVIEW

During the concrete operational stage, thought is more logical, flexible, and organized than it was during the preschool years. The ability to conserve indicates that children can decenter and reverse their thinking. School-age children also have an improved grasp of classification, seriation, and spatial concepts. However, they master logical problems one by one, in a horizontal décalage; they cannot yet think abstractly.

Research indicates that concrete operational reasoning is often delayed in non-Western societies and it is strongly subject to situational conditions. These findings indicate that it may not emerge spontaneously and universally in middle childhood, as Piaget believed.

ASK YOURSELF . . .

◆ *Mastery of conservation problems provides one illustration of Piaget's horizontal décalage. Review the preceding sections. Then list additional examples showing that operational reasoning develops gradually in middle childhood.*

◆ CONNECTIONS
Gains in perspective-taking skill are vital for self- and social understanding. Explain how the development of perspective taking in middle childhood contributes to self-concept and moral reasoning. (See Chapter 11, page 448, and Chapter 12, pages 495–496.)

How do school-age children's flexible classification skills affect their gender-stereotyped thinking? (See Chapter 13, page 543.)

The Formal Operational Stage (11 Years and Older)

A ccording to Piaget, the capacity for abstract thinking begins around age 11. At the **formal operational stage,** the adolescent reasons much like a scientist searching for solutions in the laboratory. Concrete operational children can only "operate on reality," but formal operational adolescents can "operate on operations." In other words, concrete things and events are no longer required as objects of thought (Inhelder & Piaget, 1955/1958). Instead, adolescents can come up with new, more general logical rules through internal reflection.

HYPOTHETICO-DEDUCTIVE REASONING

At adolescence, young people first become capable of **hypothetico-deductive reasoning.** When faced with a problem, they start with a *general theory* of all possible factors that might affect an outcome and *deduce* from it specific *hypotheses* (or predictions) about what might happen. Then they test these hypotheses in an orderly fashion to see which ones work in the real world. Notice how this form of problem solving begins with possibility and proceeds to reality. In contrast, concrete operational children start with reality—with the most obvious predictions about a situation. When these are not confirmed, they cannot think of alternatives and fail to solve the problem.

Adolescents' performance on Piaget's famous *pendulum problem* illustrates this new hypothetico-deductive approach. Suppose we present several school-age children and adolescents with strings of different lengths, objects of different weights to attach to the strings, and a bar from which to hang the strings. Then we ask each of them to figure out what influences the speed with which a pendulum swings through its arc.

Formal operational adolescents come up with four hypotheses: (1) the length of the string, (2) the weight of the object hung on it, (3) how high the object is raised before it is released, and (4) how forcefully the object is pushed. Then, by varying one factor at a time while holding all others constant, they try out each of these possibilities. Eventually they discover that only string length makes a difference.

In contrast, concrete operational children's experimentation is unsystematic. They cannot separate the effects of each variable. For example, they may test for the effect of string length without holding weight constant by comparing a short, light pendulum with a long, heavy one. Also, they fail to notice variables that are not immediately suggested by the concrete materials of the task—the height and the forcefulness with which the pendulum is released.

PROPOSITIONAL THOUGHT

A second important characteristic of the formal operational stage is **propositional thought.** Adolescents can evaluate the logic of propositions (verbal statements) without referring to real-world circumstances. In contrast, children can evaluate the logic of statements only by considering them against concrete evidence in the real world.

In one study of propositional reasoning, an experimenter showed children and adolescents a pile of poker chips and indicated that some statements would be made about them. Each participant was asked to tell whether each statement was true, false, or uncertain. In one condition, the experimenter hid a chip in her hand and then asked the subject to evaluate the following propositions:

"*Either* the chip in my hand is green *or* it is not green."

"The chip in my hand is green *and* it is not green."

In another condition, the experimenter held either a red or a green chip in full view and made the same statements.

School-age children focused on the concrete properties of the poker chips rather than on the logic of the statements. As a result, they replied that they were uncertain to both statements when the chip was hidden from view. When it was visible, they judged both statements to be true if the chip was green and false if it was red. In contrast, adolescents analyzed the logic of the statements as propositions. They understood that the "either–or" statement is always true and the "and" statement is always false, regardless of the poker chip's color (Osherson & Markman, 1975).

Although Piaget believed that language does not play a central role in children's cognitive development, he acknowledged that it is more important during adolescence. Abstract thought requires language-based systems of representation that do not stand for real things, such as those that exist in higher mathematics. Junior high and high school students use these systems in algebra and geometry. Formal operational thought also involves verbal reasoning about abstract concepts. Adolescents demonstrate their capacity to think in this way when they ponder the relations between time, space, and matter in physics and wonder about justice and freedom in philosophy and social studies.

In Piaget's formal operational stage, adolescents engage in propositional thought. As these students discuss problems in a precalculus class, they show that they can reason with symbols that do not necessarily represent objects in the real world.
(Will Hart)

CONSEQUENCES OF ABSTRACT THOUGHT

Adolescents' capacity to think abstractly, combined with the physical changes they are undergoing, means that they start to think more about themselves. Piaget believed that the arrival of this stage is accompanied by a new form of egocentrism: the inability to distinguish the abstract perspectives of self and others (Inhelder & Piaget, 1955/1958). As teenagers imagine what others must be thinking, two distorted images of the relation between self and other appear.

The first is called the **imaginary audience.** Young teenagers regard themselves as always on stage. They are convinced that they are the focus of everyone else's attention and concern (Elkind & Bowen, 1979). As a result, they become extremely self-conscious, often going to great lengths to avoid embarrassment. The imaginary audience helps us understand the long hours adolescents spend in the bathroom, inspecting every detail of their appearance as they envision the response of the rest of the world. It also accounts for their sensitivity to public criticism. To teenagers, who believe that everyone around them is monitoring their performance, a critical remark from a parent or teacher can be mortifying.

A second cognitive distortion is the **personal fable.** Because teenagers are so sure that others are observing and thinking about them, they develop an inflated opinion of their own importance. They start to feel that they are special and unique. Many adolescents view themselves as reaching great heights of glory as well as sinking to unusual depths of despair—experiences that others could not possibly understand (Elkind, 1994). As one teenager wrote in her diary, "My parents' lives are so ordinary, so stuck in a rut. Mine will be different. I'll realize my hopes and ambitions." The personal fable may also contribute to adolescent risk taking. Teenagers who have sex without contraceptives or weave in and out of traffic at 80 miles an hour seem, at least for the moment, to be convinced of their uniqueness and invulnerability.

Consistent with Piaget's theory, the imaginary audience and personal fable are strongest during the transition from concrete to formal operations. They gradually decline as abstract thinking becomes better established (Enright, Lapsley, & Shukla, 1979; Lapsley et al., 1988). Yet these distorted visions of the self may not represent a return to egocentrism. Instead, they may be an outgrowth of advances in perspective taking, which cause young teenagers to be very concerned with what others think (Lapsley et al., 1986).

Recent evidence indicates that the capacity to "step in another person's shoes" and look back at the self, a perspective-taking milestone of late childhood and early adolescence, contributes to the imaginary audience and personal fable (Vartanian & Powlishta, 1996). Adolescents also have emotional reasons for clinging to the idea that others are preoccupied with their appearance and behavior. Doing so helps them maintain a hold

imaginary audience Adolescents' belief that they are the focus of everyone else's attention and concern.

personal fable Adolescents' belief that they are special and unique. Leads them to conclude that others cannot possibly understand their thoughts and feelings. May promote a sense of invulnerability to danger.

on important relationships as they struggle to separate from parents and establish an independent sense of self (Lapsley, 1993; Vartanian, 1997).

RECENT RESEARCH ON FORMAL OPERATIONAL THOUGHT

Many researchers have conducted follow-up studies of formal operational thought, asking questions similar to those we discussed with respect to earlier stages: Is there evidence that abstract reasoning appears earlier than Piaget expected? Do all individuals reach formal operations during the teenage years?

■ ARE YOUNG CHILDREN CAPABLE OF ABSTRACT REASONING?
School-age children show the glimmerings of abstract reasoning, but they are not as competent as adolescents and adults. For example, in simplified situations—ones involving no more than two possible causal variables—6-year-olds understand that hypotheses must be confirmed by appropriate evidence. They also realize that once supported, a hypothesis shapes predictions about what might happen in the future (Ruffman et al., 1993). But unlike adolescents, children cannot sort out evidence that bears on three or more variables at once.

School-age children's capacity for propositional thought is also limited. For example, they have great difficulty reasoning from premises that contradict reality or their own beliefs. Consider the following set of statements: "If dogs are bigger than elephants and elephants are bigger than mice, then dogs are bigger than mice." Children younger than 10 judge this reasoning to be false, since all the relations specified do not occur in real life (Moshman & Franks, 1986). They fail to grasp the **logical necessity** of propositional reasoning—that the validity of conclusions drawn from premises rests on the rules of logic, not on real-world confirmation.

As Piaget's theory indicates, around age 11, young people in Western nations begin to analyze the logic of propositions irrespective of their content. Propositional thought improves over the adolescent years (Markovits & Bouffard-Bouchard, 1992; Markovits & Vachon, 1989, 1990).

■ DO ALL INDIVIDUALS REACH THE FORMAL OPERATIONAL STAGE?
Try giving one or two of Piaget's formal operational tasks to your friends, and see how well they do. You are likely to find that even well-educated adults have difficulty with abstract thinking! About 40 to 60 percent of college students fail Piaget's formal operational problems (Keating, 1979).

Why is it that so many college students, and adults in general, are not fully formal operational? The reason is that people are most likely to think abstractly in situations in which they have had extensive experience. This is supported by the finding that adolescents and adults can be trained to a high level of performance on formal operational tasks (Kuhn, Ho, & Adams, 1979). Other evidence indicates that taking college courses leads to improvements in formal reasoning related to course content. For example, math and science prompt gains in propositional thought, social science in methodological and statistical reasoning (Lehman & Nisbett, 1990). Consider these findings carefully, and you will see that formal operational thought, like the concrete reasoning that preceded it, does not emerge in all contexts at once. Rather, it is often specific to situation and task (Keating, 1990).

Furthermore, in many tribal and village societies, formal operational tasks are not mastered at all (Cole, 1990; Gellatly, 1987). For example, when asked to engage in propositional thought, people in nonliterate cultures often refuse. In response to a hypothetical proposition, "In the far North, where there is snow, all bears are white. Novaya Zemlya is in the Far North and there is always snow there. What color are the bears there?" a Central Asian peasant explains that he must see the event to discern its logical implications. The peasant insists on first-hand knowledge, whereas the interviewer states that truth can be based on ideas alone. Yet the peasant uses propositions to defend his

If asked, these nonliterate Mongolian nomads would probably refuse to engage in propositional thought, explaining that an event must be seen to discern its logical implications. Because of lack of opportunity to solve hypothetical problems, formal operational reasoning is not evident in all societies.

(Noburu Komine/Photo Researchers, Inc.)

point of view: "*If* a man . . . had seen a white bear and had told about it, *[then]* he could be believed, *but* I've never seen one and *hence* I can't say" (Luria, 1976, pp. 108–109). Although he rarely displays it in everyday life, clearly the peasant is capable of formal operational thought!

Piaget acknowledged that because of lack of opportunity to solve hypothetical problems, formal operations might not be evident in some societies. Still, cross-cultural research raises questions similar to those discussed earlier. Is the highest stage really an outgrowth of children's independent efforts to make sense of their world? Or is it a culturally transmitted way of thinking that is specific to literate societies and taught in school? These findings, along with others, have prompted many investigators to doubt important aspects of Piaget's theory.

Larger Questions About Piaget's Theory

iaget awakened psychologists and educators to a view of children as active knowledge seekers who undergo complex cognitive changes from infancy through adolescence. Yet research reveals that his theory has a variety of shortcomings.

ISSUES OF CLARITY AND ACCURACY

Some of Piaget's ideas are not clearly spelled out. Think, for a moment, about Piaget's explanation of cognitive change—in particular, equilibration and its attendant processes of adaptation and organization. Because Piaget focused on broad transformations in thinking, exactly what the child does to equilibrate seems vague and imprecise (Miller, 1993; Siegler & Ellis, 1996). As an example of this problem, recall our description of organization—that the structures of each stage form a coherent whole. Piaget is not very explicit about how the diverse achievements of each stage—for example, conservation, hierarchical classification, seriation, and spatial concepts during concrete operations—are bound together by a single, underlying form of thought.

Throughout this chapter, we have noted that several of Piaget's ideas are now regarded as either incorrect or only partially correct. For example, Piaget's belief that infants and young children must act on the environment to revise their cognitive structures is too narrow a notion of how learning takes place. We have also seen that cognitive development is not always self-generating. Left to their own devices, children may not notice those aspects of a situation that are needed for an improved understanding. Furthermore, many efforts to verify Piaget's timetable of development have not been fully successful (Flavell, 1992). Overall, infants and young children appear more competent and adolescents and adults less competent than Piaget assumed.

ARE THERE STAGES OF COGNITIVE DEVELOPMENT?

This brings us to the most controversial question about Piaget's theory: Does cognitive development take place in stages? Throughout this chapter, we have seen that many cognitive changes proceed slowly and gradually. Few abilities are absent during one period and then suddenly present in another. Also, there seem to be few periods of cognitive equilibrium. Instead, children are constantly modifying structures and acquiring new skills. Today, virtually all experts agree that children's cognition is not as broadly stagelike as Piaget believed (Bjorklund, 1995; Flavell, 1992). At the same time, contemporary researchers disagree on how general or specific cognitive development actually is.

Some theorists regard development as domain general, but they reject the existence of any stagewise change. They believe that thought processes are similar at all ages—just present to a greater or lesser extent—and that uneven performance across tasks can largely be accounted for by variations in children's knowledge and experience. These assumptions form the basis of a major competing approach to Piaget's theory—*information processing,* which we take up in Chapter 7.

logical necessity A basic property of propositional thought, which specifies that the validity of conclusions drawn from premises rests on the rules of logic, not on real-world confirmation. A grasp of logical necessity permits individuals to reason from premises that contradict reality or their own beliefs.

Other researchers think the stage notion is still valid, but it must be modified. They point to strong evidence for certain stagelike changes, such as the flourishing of representation around age 2 and the move toward abstraction in adolescence. Yet they recognize many smaller developments that lead up to these dramatic transformations. In Chapter 7, we will consider a *neo-Piagetian perspective,* which combines Piaget's stage approach with information-processing ideas (Case, 1992, 1996, 1998; Fischer & Farrar, 1987; Halford, 1993). According to this view, Piaget's strict definition of stage needs to be modified into a less tightly knit concept, one in which a related set of competencies develops over an extended time period, depending on brain development and experience. These investigators point to findings indicating that as long as the complexity of tasks in different domains is carefully controlled, children and adolescents approach physical and social reasoning problems in similar, stage-consistent ways (Case et al., 1992; Marini & Case, 1989, 1994)

Still other theorists deny not only Piaget's stages but his belief that the human mind is made up of general reasoning abilities that can be applied to any cognitive task. Recall the *modular view of the mind,* introduced earlier in this chapter, prompted by the remarkable competencies of infants and the rapid development of many structures during the first few years. According to this nativist, domain-specific perspective, we begin life with well-defined, special-purpose knowledge systems, hardwired into the brain. (Return to page 234 to review this perspective, along with questions raised about it.)

In sum, although Piaget's description of development is no longer fully accepted, researchers are a long way from consensus on how to modify or replace it. Some have begun to search for points of contact among the alternative perspectives just mentioned. These investigators are identifying both domain-specific changes and periods of broad, stage-wise change. They are also blending Piaget's emphasis on the child as an active agent with a stronger role for *context*—the objects, events, and people in the child's life (Fischer & Bidell, 1998; Fischer & Hencke, 1996). Turn back to Chapter 1, page 30, and notice how the *dynamic systems perspective* integrates these diverse elements. And Vygotsky's theory, to which we now turn, places special emphasis on social and cultural contexts of children's thinking.

Despite wide disagreement on how to characterize cognitive development, the field of child development continues to draw inspiration from Piaget's lifelong quest to understand how children acquire new capacities. As Flavell (1985) points out, "Perhaps what the field needs is another genius like Piaget to show us how, and to what extent, all those cognitive developmental strands within the growing child are really knotted together" (p. 297).

Piaget and Education

iaget's theory has had a major impact on education, especially at the preschool and early elementary school levels. Three educational principles have served as the foundation for a variety of Piagetian-based curricula:

■ *An emphasis on discovery learning.* In a Piagetian classroom, children are encouraged to discover for themselves through spontaneous interaction with the environment. Instead of presenting ready-made knowledge verbally, teachers provide a rich variety of activities designed to promote exploration and discovery—arts and crafts materials, puzzles, table games, dress-up clothing, building blocks, books, measuring tools, musical instruments, and more.

■ *Sensitivity to children's readiness to learn.* A Piagetian classroom does not try to speed up development. Instead, Piaget believed that appropriate learning experiences build on children's current level of thinking. Teachers watch and listen to their pupils, introducing experiences that permit them to practice newly discovered schemes and that are likely to challenge their incorrect ways of viewing the world. But new skills are not imposed before children indicate that they are interested or ready, since this leads to superficial acceptance of adult formulas rather than true understanding (Johnson & Hooper, 1982).

■ *Acceptance of individual differences.* Piaget's theory assumes that all children go through the same sequence of development, but they may do so at different rates. Therefore, teachers must plan activities for individuals and small groups rather than just for the total class (Ginsburg & Opper, 1988). In addition, teachers evaluate educational progress by comparing each child to his or her own previous development. They are less interested in how children measure up to normative standards, or the average performance of same-age peers.

Educational applications of Piaget's theory, like his stages, have met with criticism. Perhaps the greatest challenge has to do with his emphasis on action as the major mode of learning to the neglect of other important avenues, such as verbal communication. Nevertheless, Piaget's influence on education has been powerful (Vergnaud, 1996). He gave teachers new ways to observe, understand, and enhance young children's development and offered strong theoretical justification for child-oriented approaches to classroom teaching and learning.

BRIEF REVIEW

n Piaget's formal operational stage, the capacity for abstraction appears, as indicated by hypothetico-deductive reasoning and propositional thought. New cognitive powers lead to the imaginary audience and personal fable. Recent research shows that abstract reasoning is not well developed until after age 11. Adolescents and adults are most likely to display abstract thinking in areas in which they have had extensive experience. In many village and tribal cultures, adults do not master formal operational tasks. These findings challenge Piaget's view of formal operations as resulting from independent discovery.

Major criticisms of Piaget's theory include the vagueness of his ideas about cognitive change, inaccuracies in his account of the timetable of development, and evidence that children's cognition is not as broadly stagelike and domain general as he assumed. Piaget's theory has had a powerful influence on education, promoting discovery learning, sensitivity to children's readiness to learn, and acceptance of individual differences.

ASK YOURSELF . . .

◆ *Thirteen-year-old Cassie insisted that she had to have high-heeled shoes to wear to the school dance. "No way I can wear those low heels, Mom. They'll make me look way too short, and the whole evening will be ruined!" Why is Cassie so concerned about a detail of her appearance that most people would be unlikely to notice?*

◆ CONNECTIONS
The transition to abstract thinking at adolescence is widely regarded as stagelike. After reviewing the concept of stage in Chapter 1 (see page 8), cite evidence that supports this conclusion.

Vygotsky's Sociocultural Theory

ccording to Piaget, the most important source of cognition is the child himself—a busy, self-motivated explorer who forms ideas and tests them against the world, without external pressure. Lev Vygotsky also believed that children are active seekers of knowledge, but he did not view them as solitary agents. In his theory, rich social and cultural contexts profoundly affect the way children's cognitive world is structured.

Early events in Vygotsky's life contributed to his vision of human cognition as inherently social and language based. As a young boy in Russia, he was instructed at home by a private tutor, who conducted lessons using the Socratic dialogue—an interactive, question-and-answer approach that challenges current conceptions to promote heightened understanding. By the time Vygotsky entered the University of Moscow, his primary interest was a verbal field—literature. After graduating, he was first a teacher; only later did he turn to psychology (Kozulin, 1990).

Vygotsky died of tuberculosis when he was 37 years old. Although he wrote prolifically, he had little more than a decade to formulate his ideas. Consequently, his theory is not as completely specified as Piaget's. Nevertheless, the field of child development is

During the preschool years, children frequently talk to themselves as they play and explore the environment. Research supports Vygotsky's theory that children use private speech to guide their behavior when faced with challenging tasks. With age, private speech is transformed into silent, inner speech, or verbal thought.

(Kopstein/Monkmeyer Press)

private speech Self-directed speech that children use to plan and guide their own behavior.

experiencing a burst of interest in Vygotsky's sociocultural perspective. The major reason for his appeal lies in his rejection of an individualistic view of the developing child in favor of a socially formed mind (Rogoff, 1998; Wertsch & Tulviste, 1992).

According to Vygotsky, infants are endowed with basic perceptual, attentional, and memory capacities that they share with other animals. These undergo a natural course of development during the first 2 years through direct contact with the environment. But once children become capable of mental representation, especially through language, their ability to participate in social dialogues while engaged in culturally important tasks is enhanced. Soon young children start to communicate with themselves in much the same way they converse with others. As a result, basic mental capacities are transformed into uniquely human, higher cognitive processes. Let's see how this happens, as we explore in greater detail the controversy between Piaget and Vygotsky introduced at the beginning of this chapter.

PRIVATE SPEECH

Watch preschoolers as they go about their daily activities, and you will see that they frequently talk out loud to themselves as they play and explore the environment. For example, as a 5-year-old worked a puzzle at preschool one day, I heard him say, "Where's the red piece? I need the red one. Now a blue one. No, it doesn't fit. Try it here."

■ **PIAGET'S VIEW.** Piaget (1923/1926) called these utterances *egocentric speech*, a term expressing his belief that they reflect the preoperational child's inability to imagine the perspectives of others. For this reason, Piaget said, young children's talk is often "talk for self" in which they run off thoughts in whatever form they happen to occur, regardless of whether they are understandable to a listener.

Piaget believed that cognitive maturity and certain social experiences—namely, disagreements with peers—eventually bring an end to egocentric speech. Through arguments with agemates, children repeatedly see that others hold viewpoints different from their own. As a result, egocentric speech declines and is replaced by social speech, in which children adapt what they say to their listeners.

■ **VYGOTSKY'S VIEW.** Vygotsky (1934/1986) voiced a powerful objection to Piaget's conclusion that young children's language is egocentric and nonsocial. He reasoned that children speak to themselves for self-guidance and self-direction. Because language helps children think about their own behavior and select courses of action, Vygotsky regarded it as the foundation for all higher cognitive processes, including controlled attention, deliberate memorization and recall, categorization, planning, problem solving, abstract reasoning, and self-reflection. As children get older and find tasks easier, their self-directed speech declines and is internalized as silent, inner speech—the verbal dialogues we carry on with ourselves while thinking and acting in everyday situations.

Over the past three decades, researchers have carried out many studies to determine which of these two views—Piaget's or Vygotsky's—is correct. Almost all the findings have sided with Vygotsky (Berk, 1999). As a result, children's "speech to self" is now called **private speech** instead of egocentric speech. Research shows that children use more of it when tasks are difficult, after they make errors, or when they are confused about how to proceed (Berk, 1994b). Also, just as Vygotsky predicted, private speech goes underground with age, changing into whispers and silent lip movements (Bivens & Berk, 1990; Duncan & Pratt, 1997). Furthermore, children who use private speech when faced with challenging tasks are more attentive and involved and show greater improvement in performance than their less talkative agemates (Behrend, Rosengren, & Perlmutter, 1992; Berk & Spuhl, 1995).

Finally, compared to their normally achieving agemates, children with learning problems engage in higher rates of private speech over a longer developmental period. They seem to call on private speech to help compensate for the impairments in cognitive processing and attention that make academic tasks more difficult for them (Berk & Landau, 1993, 1997; Diaz & Berk, 1995).

Where does private speech come from? Vygotsky's answer to this question highlights the social origins of cognition, his main difference of opinion with Piaget.

SOCIAL ORIGINS OF COGNITIVE DEVELOPMENT

Vygotsky (1930–1935/1978) believed that all higher cognitive processes develop out of social interaction. Through joint activities with more mature members of society, children come to master activities and think in ways that have meaning in their culture. A special concept, the **zone of proximal** (or potential) **development,** explains how this happens. It refers to a range of tasks that the child cannot yet handle alone but can accomplish with the help of adults and more skilled peers.

Consider the joint activity of 4-year-old Sammy and his mother, who assists him in putting together a difficult puzzle:

Sammy: "I can't get this one in." *[Tries to insert a piece in the wrong place]*

Mother: "Which piece might go down here?" *[Points to the bottom of the puzzle]*

Sammy: "His shoes." *[Looks for a piece resembling the clown's shoes but tries the wrong one]*

Mother: "Well, what piece looks like this shape?" *[Pointing again to the bottom of the puzzle]*

Sammy: "The brown one." *[Tries it, and it fits; then attempts another piece and looks at his mother]*

Mother: "Try turning it just a little." *[Gestures to show him]*

Sammy: "There!" *[Puts in several more pieces. His mother watches.]*

Sammy's mother keeps the puzzle within his zone of proximal development—at a manageable level of difficulty—by questioning, prompting, and suggesting strategies. Within the zone, interaction constantly adjusts to fit Sammy's changing competencies and his mother's insights into what will best help him learn. Eventually, children take the language of these dialogues, make it part of their private speech, and use this speech to organize their own thinking and behavior.

■ **EFFECTIVE SOCIAL INTERACTION.** Although Vygotsky was not explicit about the features of dialogues that promote transfer of cognitive processes to children, contemporary researchers believe that two characteristics are important.

INTERSUBJECTIVITY. The first is **intersubjectivity,** the process whereby two participants who begin a task with different understandings arrive at a shared understanding (Newson & Newson, 1975). Intersubjectivity creates a common ground for communication, as each partner adjusts to the perspective of the other. Adults try to promote it when they translate their own insights in ways that are within the child's grasp. As the child stretches to understand the interpretation, she is drawn into a more mature approach to the situation (Rogoff, 1998).

The concept of intersubjectivity is applicable to many contexts—parent–child and teacher–child interaction, family discussions, and peer relations. The capacity for intersubjectivity is present early—in the young baby's mutual gaze, exchange of emotional signals, and imitation of the caregiver. Yet intersubjectivity changes with development. Language, permitting greater clarity of communication, facilitates it. By the second year of life, children are active in seeking others' help and in directing that assistance to ensure that it is beneficial (Whitington & Ward, 1998).

In sum, intersubjectivity reminds us that children and adults *jointly* manage shared endeavors. The contributions of both create the zone of proximal development.

SCAFFOLDING AND GUIDED PARTICIPATION. Another feature of social interaction that fosters development is **scaffolding** (Bruner, 1983; Wood, 1989). It refers to a changing quality of support over the course of a teaching session. Adults who offer an effective scaffold for children's independent mastery adjust the assistance they provide to fit the child's current level of performance. When the child has little notion of how to proceed, the adult uses direct instruction, breaking the task down into manageable units and calling the child's attention to specific features. As the child's competence increases, effective scaffolders gradually and sensitively withdraw support, turning over responsibility to the child.

zone of proximal development In Vygotsky's theory, a range of tasks that the child cannot yet handle alone but can do with the help of more skilled partners.

intersubjectivity A process whereby two participants who begin a task with different understandings arrive at a shared understanding.

scaffolding A changing quality of support over a teaching session in which adults adjust the assistance they provide to fit the child's current level of performance. Direct instruction is offered when a task is new; less help is provided as competence increases.

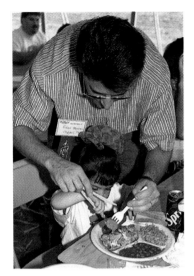

This father scaffolds his 3-year-old daughter's efforts to master a cultur-ally meaningful task. By holding the fork while she cuts with the knife, he breaks the task down into manageable units, ensuring that it is within the girl's zone of proximal development.

(Bob Daemmrich/Stock Boston)

Scaffolding best captures the form of teaching interaction that occurs as children work on school or school-like tasks, when adults typically structure the learning situation. It may not apply to communication in other contexts that are just as vital for cognitive development—for example, play or everyday activities, during which adults often support children's efforts without deliberately instructing. To account for children's diverse opportunities to learn through involvement with others, Barbara Rogoff (1990, 1994) has suggested the term **guided participation,** a broader concept than scaffolding. It calls attention to both adult and child contributions to a cooperative dialogue, without conveying a particular model of communication. Consequently, it allows for situational and cultural variation.

■ **RESEARCH ON SOCIAL INTERACTION AND COGNITIVE DEVELOPMENT.** Is there evidence to support Vygotsky's ideas on the role of social interaction in cognitive development? As early as the first few months, intersubjectivity, in the form of finely tuned emotional communication and joint gazing at objects, is related to advanced play, language, and problem-solving skills during the second year (Bornstein et al., 1992b; Frankel & Bates, 1990; Tamis-LeMonda & Bornstein, 1989).

In early childhood, parents who are effective scaffolders in teaching their child to solve a challenging problem have children who use more private speech and are more successful when asked to do a similar task by themselves (Behrend, Rosengren, & Perlmutter, 1992; Berk & Spuhl, 1995; Conner, Knight, & Cross, 1997). Furthermore, many studies support the social origins of private speech. For example, social and private utterances are positively correlated during the preschool years, suggesting that they have common roots. And socially rich contexts seem to foster private speech, since children talk to themselves more when they have access to social partners—either peers or adults (Berk, 1992a).

Finally, reducing children's access to their sociocultural world and the opportunities it affords for dialogues with others limits the extent to which they engage in dialogues with themselves, manage their own behavior, and acquire new skills. Consult the Variations box on the following page for a striking example.

VYGOTSKY'S VIEW OF MAKE-BELIEVE PLAY

In accord with his emphasis on social experience and language as vital forces in cognitive development, Vygotsky (1930–1935/1978) granted make-believe play a prominent place in his theory. He regarded it as a unique, broadly influential zone of proximal development in which *children advance themselves* as they try out a wide variety of challenging skills.

How does make-believe lead development forward? According to Vygotsky, it does so in two ways. First, as children create imaginary situations in play, they learn to act in accord with internal ideas, not just in response to external stimuli. Substitute objects are crucial in this process. When children use a stick to represent a horse or a folded blanket to represent a sleeping baby, they change an object's usual meaning. Gradually they realize that thinking (or the meaning of words) is separate from the actions and objects for which it stands and that ideas can be used to guide behavior.

A second feature of make-believe—its rule-based nature—also strengthens children's capacity to think before they act. Pretend play, Vygotsky pointed out, constantly demands that children act against their impulses because they must follow social rules to execute the play scene. For example, a child pretending to go to sleep follows the rules of bedtime behavior. Another child imagining himself to be a father and a doll to be a child conforms to the rules of parental behavior. As children enact rules in make-believe, they come to better understand social norms and expectations and strive to follow them.

Vygotsky regarded the fantasy play of the preschool years as essential for further development of play—specifically, for movement toward game play in middle childhood. The games that captivate school-age children increasingly emphasize rules, providing additional instruction in setting goals and regulating one's behavior in pursuit of those goals. Make-believe, in Vygotsky's theory, provides crucial preparation for cooperative and productive participation in social life.

Was Vygotsky correct that make-believe serves as a zone of proximal development, supporting the emergence and refinement of a wide variety of competencies? Much evidence fits with Vygotsky's conclusion. Turn back to page 237 to review findings that

guided participation A concept that accounts for children's diverse opportunities to learn through involvement with others. Calls attention to both adult and child contributions to a cooperative dialogue, without conveying a particular model of communication.

Parent–Child Interaction and Cognitive Development of Deaf Children

VYGOTSKY EXTENDED HIS sociocultural approach to the development of children with disabilities. He believed that the greatest problem for such children is not the original disability but how it affects the child's interaction with adults and peers (Gindis, 1995). When a child cannot participate fully in social life, development of higher cognitive processes is compromised.

Yet the consequences of a disability vary with social context. Deafness, for example, has profound implications for cognitive development. Because it interferes with verbal communication, it can prevent children from using language to guide behavior unless special steps are taken to enrich the deaf child's social world (Vygotsky, 1925/1993). Comparisons of deaf children of hearing parents with deaf children of deaf parents highlight this chain of events.

Over 90 percent of deaf children have hearing parents. During the preschool years, these children are often delayed in language progress (both other-directed and self-directed communication) and in complex make-believe play. In middle childhood, many achieve poorly in school and are deficient in social skills. Yet deaf children of deaf parents escape these difficulties! Their language (use of sign) and play maturity are on a par with hearing children's, and their self-directed signs resemble hearing children's private speech. After school entry, deaf children of deaf parents learn easily and get along well with adults and peers (Jamieson, 1995b; Spencer & Lederberg, 1997).

These differences can be traced to early parent–child communication. As early as the first year of life, hearing parents of deaf children are less positive, less effective at achieving joint attention and turn taking, and more directive and intrusive (Meadow-Orlans & Steinberg, 1993; Spencer &

Meadow-Orlans, 1996). While helping their deaf preschoolers solve a challenging puzzle, hearing parents do not scaffold effectively; they have trouble adjusting their verbal and nonverbal assistance to the child's needs (Jamieson, 1994, 1995a). In contrast, the quality of interaction between deaf children of deaf parents is similar to that of hearing children of hearing parents.

Children with limited and less sensitive parental interaction are behind their agemates in achieving verbal control over their behavior. Deaf children of hearing parents frequently display impulse-control problems (Harris, 1978).

Hearing parents are not at fault for their deaf child's problems. Instead, they lack experience with visual communication, which enables deaf parents to respond readily to a deaf child's needs. Deaf parents know that they must wait for the child to turn toward them before interacting (Spencer, Bodner-Johnson, & Gutfreund, 1992). Hearing parents tend to speak or gesture while the child's attention is directed elsewhere—a strategy that works with a hearing but not with a deaf partner. When their child is confused or unresponsive, hearing parents often feel overwhelmed and become more controlling (Jamieson, 1994, 1995a). Furthermore, learning sign language is an immense task that requires years of effort, and few hearing parents become fluent.

The impact of deafness on cognitive development can best be understood by considering its effects on parents and other significant people in the child's life. Deaf children need access to language models—deaf adults and peers—to create a natural language-learning situation. And their hearing parents benefit from social support along with training in how to interact sensitively with a nonhearing partner.

---

make-believe enhances a diverse array of cognitive and social skills. Pretend play is also rich in private speech—a finding that supports its role in helping children bring action under the control of thought (Krafft & Berk, 1998). And in a recent study, preschoolers who engaged in more complex sociodramatic play showed greater gains in following classroom rules over a 4-month period (Elias & Berk, 1999).

Finally, Vygotsky took issue with Piaget's view that make-believe arises spontaneously in the second year of life. Instead, Vygotsky argued that the elaborate pretending of the preschool years, like other higher cognitive processes, has social origins (Berk, 1994a; Nicolopoulou, 1993). New evidence, reviewed in the Cultural Influences box on page 264, supports the view that children initially learn to pretend under the supportive guidance of experts.

Vygotsky and Education

ygotsky's theory offers new visions of teaching and learning—ones that emphasize the importance of social context and collaboration. Today, educators are eager to use his ideas.

Piagetian and Vygotskian classrooms clearly have features in common, such as opportunities for active participation and acceptance of individual differences. Yet Vygotsky differed from Piaget in that he believed education does not just refine structures that have

Social Origins of Make-Believe Play

O NE OF MY husband Ken's shared activities with our two sons when they were young was to bake pineapple upside-down cake, a favorite treat. I remember well one Sunday afternoon when a cake was in the making. Little Peter, then 21 months old, stood on a chair at the kitchen sink, busily pouring water from one cup to another.

"He's in the way, Dad!" complained 4-year-old David, trying to pull Peter away from the sink.

"Maybe if we let him help, he'll give us some room," Ken suggested. As David stirred the batter, Ken poured some into a small bowl for Peter, moved his chair to the side of the sink, and handed him a spoon.

"Here's how you do it, Petey," instructed David, with an air of superiority. Peter watched as David stirred, then tried to copy his motion. When it was time to pour the batter, Ken helped Peter tip the small bowl so its contents flowed into the pan.

"Time to bake it," said Ken.

"Bake it, bake it," repeated Peter, as he watched Ken slip the pan into the oven.

Several hours later, we observed one of Peter's earliest instances of make-believe play. He got his pail from the sandbox and, after filling it with a handful of sand, carried it into the kitchen and put it down on the floor in front of the oven. "Bake it, bake it," Peter called to Ken. Together, father and son lifted the pretend cake inside the oven.

Until recently, most researchers studied make-believe play apart from the social environment in which it occurs, while children played alone. Probably for this reason, Piaget and his followers concluded that toddlers discover make-believe independently, as soon as they are capable of representational schemes. Vygotsky's theory has challenged this view. He believed that society provides children with opportunities to represent culturally meaningful activities in play. Make-believe, like other mental functions, is initially learned under the guidance of expert partners (Garvey, 1990). In the example just described, Peter's capacity to represent daily events was extended when Ken drew him into the baking task and helped him act it out in play.

New evidence supports the idea that early make-believe is the combined result of children's readiness to engage in it and social experiences that promote it. In one observational study of middle-class American toddlers, 75 to 80 percent of make-believe involved mother–child interaction. At 12 months, make-believe was fairly one-sided; almost all play episodes were initiated by caregivers. By the end of the second year, caregivers and children displayed mutual interest in getting make-believe started; half of pretend episodes were initiated by each. At all ages, caregivers elaborated on the

In Mexico, where sibling caregiving is common, make-believe play is more frequent as well as complex with older siblings than with mothers. This 5-year-old provides rich, challenging stimulation to her younger sister within a pretend-play scene.
(Karen Halverson/Omni-Photo Communications)

child's contribution, resulting in both partners' active participation in an imaginative dialogue. Over time, the adult gradually released responsibility to the child for creating and guiding the fantasy theme (Haight & Miller, 1993).

When adults participate in toddlers' make-believe, it is more elaborate and advanced (O'Reilly & Bornstein, 1993). For example, play themes are more varied. And toddlers are more likely to combine schemes into complex sequences, as Peter did when he put the sand in the bucket ("making the batter"), carried it into the kitchen, and (with Ken's help) put it in the oven ("baking the cake").

In many cultures, adults do not spend much time playing with young children. Instead, older siblings take over this function. For example, in Indonesia and Mexico, where extended-family households and sibling caregiving are common, make-believe is more frequent as well as more complex with older siblings than with mothers. As early as 3 to 4 years of age, children provide rich, challenging stimulation to their younger brothers and sisters. The fantasy play of these toddlers is just as well developed as that of their middle-class American counterparts (Farver, 1993; Farver & Wimbarti, 1995a; Gaskins, 1994).

Make-believe is a major means through which children extend their cognitive skills and learn about important activities in their culture. Vygotsky's theory, and the findings that support it, tell us that providing a stimulating environment is only part of what is necessary to promote early cognitive development. In addition, toddlers must be invited and encouraged by their elders to become active participants in the social world around them.

already emerged. Instead, it leads development forward as children form new structures through collaboration with more expert partners. Consequently, a Vygotskian classroom goes beyond independent discovery; it promotes *assisted discovery.* Teachers guide children's learning, carefully tailoring their interventions to each child's zone of proximal development. Assisted discovery is also fostered by *peer collaboration.* Classmates with varying abilities work in groups, teaching and helping one another.

Vygotsky's major educational message regarding the preschool years was to provide many challenging activities that promote teacher–child and child–child interaction. In addition, much time should be devoted to imaginative play—the ultimate means of fostering the self-discipline required for mastery of academic tasks after school entry (Berk, 1994a). Once formal schooling begins, Vygotsky placed special emphasis on literacy activities (Bodrova & Leong, 1996; John-Steiner & Mahn, 1996). As children talk about reading and writing in literature, mathematics, science, and social studies, they begin to reflect on their thought processes. As they do so, they develop the capacity to consciously manipulate and control the symbolic systems of their culture, and they shift to a higher level of cognitive activity.

Let's look at three Vygotsky-based educational innovations, each of which incorporates assisted discovery and peer collaboration.

RECIPROCAL TEACHING

Originally designed to improve reading comprehension in pupils achieving poorly, **reciprocal teaching** has been adapted to other subjects, such as social studies and science, and as a useful model for all school-age children (Palincsar, 1992). A teacher and two to four pupils form a collaborative learning group and take turns leading dialogues on the content of a text passage. Within the dialogues, group members flexibly apply four cognitive strategies: questioning, summarizing, clarifying, and predicting.

The dialogue leader (at first the teacher, later a pupil) begins by *asking questions* about the content of the text passage. Pupils offer answers, raise additional questions, and in case of disagreement, reread the original text. Next, the leader *summarizes* the passage, and children discuss the summary and *clarify* ideas that are unfamiliar to any group members. Finally, the leader encourages pupils to *predict* upcoming content based on prior knowledge and clues in the passage (Palincsar & Klenk, 1992).

Elementary and junior high school students exposed to reciprocal teaching show impressive gains in reading comprehension compared to controls taught in other ways with the same reading materials (Palincsar, Brown, & Campione, 1993; Rosenshine & Meister, 1994). Notice how reciprocal teaching creates a zone of proximal development in which children gradually assume more responsibility for comprehending complex text passages. Reciprocal teaching also keeps reading activities whole rather than breaking them down into isolated skills (Engliert & Palincsar, 1991). In line with Vygotsky's theory, the method ensures that children learn in a culturally meaningful context and acquire skills vital for success in everyday life.

COOPERATIVE LEARNING

Although reciprocal teaching uses peer collaboration, a teacher is present to guide it, helping to ensure its success. According to Vygotsky (1930–1935/1978), more expert peers can also spur children's development, as long as they adjust the help they provide to fit the less mature child's zone of proximal development. Recall that Piaget, too, thought that peer interaction could contribute to cognitive change. In fact, he regarded discussion with agemates as more valuable than discussion with adults, since a child might superficially accept an adult's perspective without critically examining it, out of an unquestioning belief in the adult's authority. Piaget also asserted that clashing viewpoints—arguments jarring the young child into noticing a peer's point of view—were necessary for peer interaction to foster logical thought (Tudge & Winterhoff, 1993).

Today, peer collaboration is used in many classrooms, but evidence is mounting that it fosters development only under certain conditions. A crucial factor is **cooperative learning**—structuring the peer group so that students work toward a common goal. Conflict and disagreement seem less important than the extent to which peers achieve intersubjectivity—by resolving differences of opinion, sharing responsibility, and engaging in cooperative dialogues (Forman & McPhail, 1993; Kobayashi, 1994; Tudge, 1992). For example, in a study of fifth graders solving math problems cooperatively, partners were far more likely to move toward correct strategies if they explained and considered one another's ideas (Ellis, Klahr, & Siegler, 1994). And in line with Vygotsky's theory, children's

reciprocal teaching A method of teaching based on Vygotsky's theory in which a teacher and two to four pupils form a collaborative learning group. Dialogues occur that create a zone of proximal development in which reading comprehension improves.

cooperative learning A learning environment structured into groups of peers who work together toward a common goal.

planning and problem solving improve most when their peer partner is an "expert"—especially capable at the task (Azmitia, 1988; Radziszewska & Rogoff, 1988).

Cultural values and practices influence pupils' ability to learn cooperatively. Working in groups comes more easily to children reared in collectivist than individualistic cultures. For example, Navajo children do so more readily than do Caucasian-American children (Ellis & Gauvain, 1992). Japanese classroom practices, in which children solve problems by building on one another's ideas, are situated in a larger culture that values interdependence in family and work life (Hatano, 1994). In contrast, cultural-majority children in the United States typically consider competition and independent work to be natural—a perspective that interferes with their ability to attain intersubjectivity in groups (Forman & McPhail, 1993).

THE CLASSROOM AS A COMMUNITY OF LEARNERS

Recognizing that collaboration requires a supportive context, a new Vygotsky-inspired educational approach makes it a school-wide value. Classrooms are transformed into communities of learners where no distinction is made between adult and child contributions; all collaborate and develop. The **community-of-learners model** is based on the assumption that different people have different areas of expertise that can be helpful to other members of the community, depending on the task at hand. Projects, not lessons, are the focus of classroom activities—complex real-world problems requiring many steps in which children and adults draw on one another's expertise and that of others within and outside the school (Strauss, 1998).

In one science program, elementary school pupils studied animal–habitat relationships so they could design an animal of the future, suited to environmental changes. The class formed small research groups, each of which selected a subtopic—for example, defense against predators, protection from the elements, reproduction, or food getting. Each group member assumed responsibility for part of the subtopic, consulting diverse experts and preparing teaching materials. Then group members taught one another, assembled their respective contributions, and brought them to the community as a whole so that the knowledge gathered could be used to solve the problem (Brown, 1997; Brown & Campione, 1994). The result was a multifaceted understanding of the topic that would have been difficult and time consuming for any learner to attain alone.

In the community-of-learners model, collaboration is created from within by teachers and children and supported from without by the culture of the school. As a result, the approach broadens Vygotsky's concept of the zone of proximal development, from a single child in collaboration with a more expert partner (adult or peer) to multiple, interrelated zones.

Evaluation of Vygotsky's Theory

Piaget and Vygotsky shared the belief that children arrive at knowledge through actively participating in the world around them. Yet in granting social experience a fundamental role in cognitive development, Vygotsky's theory is unique in helping us understand the wide cultural variation in cognitive skills. Unlike Piaget, who emphasized universal cognitive change, Vygotsky's theory leads us to expect highly variable development, depending on the child's social and cultural experiences.

For example, the reading, writing, and mathematical activities of children who go to school in literate societies generate cognitive capacities that differ from those in nonliterate cultures. Yet the elaborate spatial skills of Australian Aborigines, whose food-gathering missions require that they find their way through barren desert regions, or the proportional reasoning of Brazilian fishermen, promoted by their navigational experiences, are no less advanced (Carraher, Schliemann, & Carraher, 1988; Kearins, 1981). Instead, each is a unique form of thinking required by activities that make up a culture's way of life (Rogoff, 1998; Tulviste, 1991).

Vygotsky's theory, like Piaget's, has not gone unchallenged. Although Vygotsky acknowledged the role of diverse symbol systems (such as pictures, maps, and algebraic ex-

community-of-learners model
A Vygotsky-inspired educational approach in which collaboration is a school-wide value; classrooms become learning communities in which adults and children jointly work on complex, real-world problems, drawing on many sources of expertise within and outside the school.

pressions) in the development of higher cognitive processes, he elevated language to highest importance. However, verbal dialogue and scaffolded instruction are not the only means, or even the most important means, through which thought develops in some cultures.

In a recent study, Barbara Rogoff and her collaborators (1993) asked caregivers to help young children with challenging tasks (getting dressed and operating novel toys) in four communities—two middle-income urban areas, one in Turkey and one in the United States; a Mayan town in Guatemala; and a tribal village in India. In the middle-income communities, parents assumed much responsibility for children's motivation and involvement in the tasks. They often verbally instructed, conversed, and interacted playfully with the child. Their communication resembled the teaching that takes place in school, where their children will spend years preparing for adult life. In contrast, in the Mayan and Indian communities, adults expected toddlers to take greater responsibility for acquiring new skills through keen observation. As the child showed attentive interest, caregivers offered responsive assistance, often nonverbally. This style of interaction, which depended heavily on demonstration and gesture, appeared well suited to conditions in which young children learn by participating in daily activities of adult life.

In cultures everywhere, caregivers guide children's mastery of the practices of their community. Yet the type of assistance offered varies greatly, depending on the nature of adult–child involvement and the tasks essential for success in each society. So we are reminded once again that children learn in many ways, and as yet, no single theory provides a complete account of cognitive development.

Finally, recall that Vygotsky stated that the natural and cultural lines of development join, forming a single developmental path. In focusing on the cultural line, he said little about the natural line—far less than did Piaget or information processing, to which we now turn. Consequently, we cannot tell from Vygotsky's theory exactly how elementary cognitive processes contribute to higher cognitive processes. For example, Vygotsky's theory does not address the way children's developing motor, perceptual, and cognitive capacities actually spark changes in their social world, from which more advanced skills spring (Moll, 1994; Wertsch & Tulviste, 1992). It is intriguing to speculate about the broader theory that might exist today had these two giants of cognitive development had the chance to meet and weave together their extraordinary accomplishments.

This young Peruvian girl watches intently as her mother weaves an elaborately patterned cloth. Compared with children growing up in middle-income urban communities, she depends more on parental demonstration and gesture and less on finely tuned, scaffolded instruction.

(Inga Spence/The Picture Cube)

ASK YOURSELF . . .

◆ *Review the interaction between Sammy and his mother on page 261. Is Sammy's mother engaging in scaffolding? How might her assistance to change as Sammy improves at the task? How would it differ were she and Sammy engaged in make-believe play?*

SUMMARY

PIAGET'S COGNITIVE-DEVELOPMENTAL THEORY

According to Piaget, how do the child's schemes develop?

◆ Influenced by his background in biology, Piaget viewed cognitive development as an adaptive process. By acting directly on the environment, children move through four stages, in which internal structures achieve a better fit with external reality. According to Piaget, cognitive development is a matter of **domain-general** rather than **domain-specific** changes, and infants begin life with little in the way of built-in structures; they must **construct** virtually all knowledge about their world.

◆ In Piaget's theory, psychological structures, or **schemes,** change in two ways. The first is through **adaptation,** which consists of two complementary activities: **assimilation** and **accommodation.** The second is through **organization,** the internal rearrangement of schemes to form a strongly interconnected cognitive system. **Equi-**

libration sums up the changing balance of assimilation and accommodation that gradually leads to more effective schemes. Piaget assumed that the stages are invariant and universal.

THE SENSORIMOTOR STAGE (BIRTH TO 2 YEARS)

Describe the major cognitive achievements of the sensorimotor stage.

◆ Piaget's **sensorimotor stage** is divided into six substages. Through the **circular reaction,** the newborn baby's reflexes are gradually transformed into the more flexible action patterns of the older infant. During Substage 4, infants develop **intentional,** or **goal-directed, behavior** and begin to understand **physical causality** and **object permanence.** Substage 5 brings a more flexible, exploratory approach, and infants no longer make the **AB search error.** By Substage 6, they become capable of **mental representation,** as shown by sudden solutions to sensorimotor problems, mastery of **invisible displacement, deferred imitation,** and **make-believe play.**

What does recent research have to say about the accuracy of Piaget's sensorimotor stage?

◆ Piaget's focus on full-blown rather than partial attainments led him to underestimate many infant capacities. Secondary circular reactions and aspects of physical reasoning, as revealed by the **violation-of-expectation method**—including a grasp of object permanence, object substance, effects of gravity, and physical causality—are present earlier than Piaget assumed. In addition, even young infants are capable of representation—in the form of deferred imitation, categorization, and **analogical problem solving.**

◆ Today, investigators believe that newborns have more built-in equipment for making sense of their world than Piaget assumed. Some researchers speculate that infants begin life with a set of perceptual procedures that they use to construct new understandings. Others advocate a **nativist, modular view of the mind** that grants newborns substantial built-in, domain-specific knowledge.

THE PREOPERATIONAL STAGE (2 TO 7 YEARS)

Describe advances in mental representation and cognitive limitations of the preoperational stage.

◆ Rapid advances in mental representation, including language, make-believe play, drawing, and understanding of spatial symbols, mark the beginning of the **preoperational stage.** With age, make-believe becomes increasingly complex, evolving into **sociodramatic play.** Preschoolers' make-believe not only reflects but contributes to cognitive development.

◆ According to Piaget, preschoolers are not yet capable of **operations** because of **egocentrism,** an inability to distinguish the perspectives of others from one's own. This leads to **animistic thinking, centration, perception-bound thought,** a focus on **states rather than transformations,** and **irreversibility.** In addition, preoperational children engage in **transductive reasoning** rather than truly causal reasoning. Because of these difficulties, they fail **conservation** and **hierarchical classification** (class inclusion) tasks.

What are the implications of recent research for the accuracy of Piaget's preoperational stage?

◆ When given simplified problems relevant to their everyday lives, preschoolers show few of the illogical features of thought just mentioned. Their language reflects accurate causal reasoning and hierarchical classification, and they form many categories based on nonobvious features. These findings indicate that rather than being absent, logical thinking develops gradually over the preschool years.

THE CONCRETE OPERATIONAL STAGE (7 TO 11 YEARS)

What are the major characteristics of the concrete operational stage?

◆ During the **concrete operational stage,** thought is far more logical and organized than it was during the preschool years. The ability to conserve indicates that children can decenter and reverse their thinking. In addition, they are better at hierarchical classification and **seriation,** including **transitive inference,** which they may master by drawing on their capacity for analogical problem solving.

◆ School-age children have an improved understanding of distance and can give clear directions. **Cognitive maps** become more organized and accurate during middle childhood.

◆ Concrete operational thought is limited in that children can reason logically only about concrete, tangible information; they have difficulty with abstractions. Piaget used the term **horizontal décalage** to describe the school-age child's gradual mastery of logical concepts, such as conservation.

Discuss recent research on concrete operational thought and its implications for the accuracy of Piaget's concrete operational stage.

◆ Recent evidence indicates that cultural practices, schooling, and the phrasing of questions can have a profound effect on Piagetian task performance. Concrete operations may not emerge universally in middle childhood and seems to be greatly affected by training, context, and cultural conditions.

THE FORMAL OPERATIONAL STAGE (11 YEARS AND OLDER)

Describe major features of abstract thought during the formal operational stage and the consequences of new reasoning powers for thinking about the relation between self and other.

◆ In Piaget's **formal operational stage,** abstract thinking appears. Adolescents engage in **hypothetico-deductive reasoning.** When faced with a problem, they think of all possibilities, including ones that are not obvious, and test them systematically against reality. **Propositional thought** also develops. Young people can evaluate the logic of verbal statements without considering them against real-world circumstances.

◆ Early in this stage, two distorted images of the relation between self and other appear: the **imaginary audience** and the **personal fable.** Research suggests that these visions of the self result from advances in perspective taking rather than a return to egocentrism.

Discuss recent research on formal operational thought and its implications for the accuracy of Piaget's formal operational stage.

◆ Recent evidence reveals that school-age children display the beginnings of abstraction, but they are not as competent as adolescents and adults. School-age children cannot sort out evidence that bears on three or more variables at once, and they do not yet grasp the **logical necessity** of propositional reasoning.

◆ Many college students think abstractly only in situations in which they have had extensive experience, and formal operational tasks are not mastered in many tribal and village societies. These findings indicate that Piaget's highest stage is reached gradually and is affected by specific learning opportunities, including direct teaching in school.

LARGER QUESTIONS ABOUT PIAGET'S THEORY

Summarize questions raised about Piaget's theory, along with current alternatives to his view of development.

◆ Research reveals that Piaget's theory has a variety of shortcomings. Some ideas, such as his explanation of cognitive change, are not clearly spelled out. Others, such as the timetable of development, are not entirely accurate.

- ◆ Some researchers reject Piaget's stages but retain his view of cognitive development as an active, constructive process. Others argue that Piaget's strict stage definition needs to be modified into a less tightly knit concept. Still others deny both Piaget's stages and his conception of domain-general change in favor of a modular view of the mind. The future is likely to bring compromises among these clashing viewpoints—identification of both domain-specific and domain-general changes and greater emphasis on social and cultural contexts of children's thinking.

PIAGET AND EDUCATION

Describe educational implications of Piaget's theory.

- ◆ Piaget's theory has had a lasting impact on educational programs for young children. A Piagetian classroom promotes discovery learning, sensitivity to children's readiness to learn, and acceptance of individual differences.

VYGOTSKY'S SOCIOCULTURAL THEORY

Explain Vygotsky's view of cognitive development, noting the importance of social experience and language.

- ◆ In Vygotsky's theory, the child and the social environment collaborate to mold cognition in culturally adaptive ways. When children become capable of mental representation, especially through language, the natural line of development is transformed by the social line, leading to uniquely human, higher cognitive processes.
- ◆ Whereas Piaget believed that language does not play a major role in cognitive development, Vygotsky regarded it as crucial. As children engage in cooperative dialogues with more skilled partners while engaged in tasks within the **zone of proximal development,** they integrate the language of these dialogues into their **private speech** and use it to organize their independent efforts.

Describe features of social interaction that promote transfer of culturally adaptive ways of thinking to children, and discuss Vygotsky's view of the role of make-believe play in development.

- ◆ **Intersubjectivity** and **scaffolding** are features of social interaction that promote transfer of cognitive processes to children. The term **guided participation** recognizes cultural and situational variations in the way adults support children's efforts.
- ◆ According to Vygotsky, make-believe play is a unique, broadly influential zone of proximal development. As children create imaginary situations and follow the rules of the make-believe scene, they learn to act in accord with internal ideas rather than on impulse. In Vygotsky's theory, make-believe play, like other higher cognitive processes, is the product of social collaboration.

VYGOTSKY AND EDUCATION

Describe educational implications of Vygotsky's theory.

- ◆ A Vygotskian classroom emphasizes assisted discovery through teachers' verbal guidance and peer collaboration. Imaginative play in the preschool years and literacy activities during middle childhood foster important cognitive advances. Educational practices consistent with Vygotsky's theory include **reciprocal teaching, cooperative learning,** and the **community-of-learners model.**

EVALUATION OF VYGOTSKY'S THEORY

Cite strengths and limitations of Vygotsky's theory.

- ◆ Vygotsky's theory helps us understand wide cultural variation in cognitive skills. However, verbal dialogues that scaffold children's efforts may not be the only means, or even the most important means, through which thought develops in some cultures. Piaget emphasized the natural line, Vygotsky the cultural line of development. A broader theory might exist today had these two contemporaries had the chance to meet and weave together their extraordinary contributions.

IMPORTANT TERMS AND CONCEPTS

AB search error (p. 226)
accommodation (p. 223)
adaptation (p. 223)
analogical problem solving (p. 231)
animistic thinking (p. 240)
assimilation (p. 223)
centration (p. 241)
circular reaction (p. 225)
cognitive maps (p. 251)
community-of-learners model (p. 266)
concrete operational stage (p. 249)
conservation (p. 240)
constructivist approach (p. 222)
cooperative learning (p. 265)
deferred imitation (p. 227)
domain-general changes (p. 222)
domain-specific changes (p. 222)
egocentrism (p. 240)

equilibration (p. 223)
formal operational stage (p. 254)
guided participation (p. 262)
hierarchical classification (p. 242)
horizontal décalage (p. 252)
hypothetico-deductive reasoning (p. 254)
imaginary audience (p. 255)
intentional, or goal-directed, behavior (p. 225)
intersubjectivity (p. 261)
invisible displacement task (p. 227)
logical necessity (p. 257)
make-believe play (p. 227)
mental representation (p. 226)
modular view of the mind (p. 234)
nativist approach (p. 222)
object permanence (p. 225)
operations (p. 240)
organization (p. 223)

perception bound (p. 241)
personal fable (p. 255)
physical causality (p. 225)
preoperational stage (p. 235)
private speech (p. 260)
propositional thought (p. 254)
reciprocal teaching (p. 265)
reversibility (p. 241)
scaffolding (p. 261)
scheme (p. 222)
sensorimotor stage (p. 225)
seriation (p. 249)
sociodramatic play (p. 236)
states rather than transformations (p. 241)
transductive reasoning (p. 241)
transitive inference (p. 249)
violation-of-expectation method (p. 227)
zone of proximal development (p. 261)

Cognitive Development: An Information-Processing Perspective

RATHER THAN A SINGLE, unified theory of children's cognitive development, information processing is an approach followed by researchers studying a wide variety of aspects of cognition. Their goal is to find out how children and adults operate on different kinds of information, detecting, transforming, storing, accessing, and modifying it further as it makes its way through the cognitive system.

This chapter provides an overview of the information-processing perspective. First, we review general and developmental models of the human cognitive system that have served as major forces in research. Next, we turn to two basic operations that enter into all human thinking: attention and memory. We also consider how children's growing knowledge of the world and awareness of their own mental activities affect these basic operations.

As we examine each of these topics, we will return to a theme that surfaced many times in Chapter 6: the role of task demands and cultural contexts in cognitive performance. Consider the experience of one researcher, who interviewed Kpelle farmers of Liberia about how they would sort a set of 20 familiar objects as an aid to remembering them (Glick, 1975). Adults in this nonliterate society arranged the objects by function. For example, they placed a knife with an orange and a hoe with a potato rather than putting all the tools in one pile and the food items in another, as the researcher expected them to do. Puzzled that Kpelle adults would approach this task much like young children in Western nations, the researcher asked for an explanation. Many Kpelle replied that a wise person would do it that way. In exasperation, the researcher finally blurted out, "How would a fool do it?" Right away, he got the kinds of object groupings he had been looking for!

The Kpelle study suggests that societal definitions of skilled performance can mold information processing in certain directions. In this chapter, we pay special attention to how schooling, with its emphasis on literacy, mathematics, scientific reasoning, and retention of discrete pieces of information, channels cognition in culturally specific ways. Although information-processing theorists are especially interested in internal, self-generated changes that take place with age, they also want to find out how external influences—from the organization of learning environments to teaching techniques to cultural values—affect the way children and adults approach various tasks. Our discussion concludes with an evaluation of the strengths and limitations of information processing as a framework for understanding cognitive development.

The Information-Processing Approach

Most information-processing theorists view the mind as a complex symbol-manipulating system through which information flows, much like a computer. Information from the environment is *encoded,* or taken in by the system and retained in symbolic form. Then a variety of internal processes operate on it, *recoding* it, or revising its symbolic structure into a more effective representation, and then *decoding* it, or interpreting its meaning by comparing and combining it with other information in the system. When these cognitive operations are complete, individuals use the information to make sense of their experiences and to solve problems.

Consider this brief description of information processing, and perhaps you can see why researchers have found the computer analogy of human mental functioning so attractive. It shares with Piaget's theory a view of the mind as an active processor of information. But beyond this, the computer model offers clarity and precision in a way that many Piagetian concepts do not. Using computerlike diagrams and flowcharts, investigators can map the exact series of steps children and adults execute when faced with a task or problem. Some do so in such detail that the same mental operations can be programmed into a computer. Then computer simulations are used to test predictions about how children and adults approach a variety of tasks.

Other information-processing investigators do not rely on computer simulations to test their ideas. Instead, they draw from other methods, such as tracking eye movements, analyzing error patterns, and examining self-reports of mental activity. But all share a strong commitment to explicit models of cognitive functioning, each component of which must be thoroughly tested with research (Klahr, 1992; Siegler, 1998).

General Models of Information Processing

Most investigators interested in the development of information processing adopt—either directly or indirectly—a general, computerlike view of the cognitive system that emerged in the late 1960s and early 1970s (Klahr & MacWhinney, 1998). It led to two influential models of adult information processing, which have inspired a wealth of research on children's thinking.

☐ THE STORE MODEL

Figure 7.1 depicts Atkinson and Shiffrin's (1968) influential **store model** of the information-processing system. It is called a store model because information is assumed to be held, or stored, in three parts of the system for processing: the sensory register; working, or short-term, memory; and long-term memory. These stores are assumed to be inborn and universal. You can think of them as the *hardware* of the mental system. Each is limited in the *speed* with which it can process information. In addition, the sensory register and short-term memory are limited in *capacity.* They can hold onto only a certain amount of information for a brief period until it fades away entirely.

As information flows through each store, we can operate on and transform it using **mental strategies**—the *software* of the system. Strategies are learned procedures that increase the efficiency of thinking and the chances that we will retain information for later use. They also permit us to think flexibly, adapting information to changing circumstances. To understand this more clearly, let's take a brief look at each component of the mental system.

■ **COMPONENTS OF THE STORE MODEL.** First, information enters the **sensory register.** Here, sights and sounds are represented directly but cannot be held for long. For example, look around you, and then close your eyes. An image of what you saw probably persists for a few moments, but then it decays or disappears, unless you use mental strategies to preserve it. For example, you can *attend to* some information more carefully than

store model Model of mental functioning that views information as being held in three parts of the system for processing: the sensory register, short-term memory, and long-term memory.

mental strategies Learned procedures that operate on and transform information, thereby increasing the efficiency and flexibility of thinking and that chances that information will be retained.

sensory register The first part of the mental system, where sights and sounds are represented directly but held only briefly.

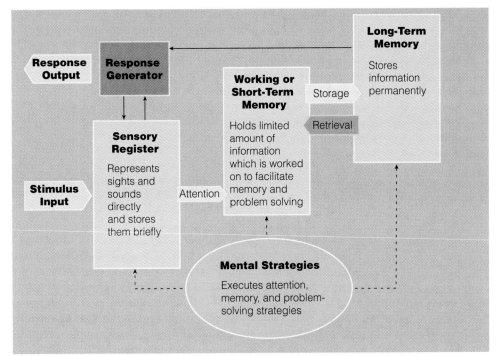

FIGURE 7.1

Store model of the human information processing system. Information flows through three parts of the mental system: the sensory register; working, or short-term memory; and long-term memory. In each, mental strategies can be used to manipulate information, increasing the efficiency of thinking and the chances that information will be retained. Strategies also permit us to think flexibly, adapting information to changing circumstances.

others, thereby increasing the chances that it will transfer to the next step of the information-processing system.

The second part of the mind is **working,** or **short-term, memory.** It is the central processing unit, the conscious part of our mental system, where we actively "work" on a limited amount of information. For example, if you are studying this book effectively, you are constantly applying mental strategies, manipulating input to ensure that it will be retained for future use. Perhaps you are attending to certain information that seems most important. Or you may be using a variety of memory strategies, such as taking notes, repeating information to yourself, or grouping pieces of information together, as the Kpelle farmers were asked to do in the study described at the beginning of this chapter.

Think, for a moment, about why you apply strategies to retain information in working memory. The sensory register, although also limited, can take in a wide panorama of information. But when input reaches working memory, a bottleneck occurs. Once the limited space in working memory is occupied, either new information cannot enter the system, or if it does, it will push out existing information. However, the capacity limit of working memory is not a matter of physical pieces of information but of *meaningful chunks.* Therefore, by connecting separate pieces through strategy use, you can increase your memory capacity. And the longer information is retained in working memory, the greater the likelihood that it will be transferred to the third, and largest, storage area of the system.

Unlike the sensory register and working memory, the amount of information that can be held in **long-term memory,** our permanent knowledge base, is limitless. In fact, so much input is stored in long-term memory that we sometimes have problems in *retrieval,* or getting information back from the system. To aid retrieval, we apply strategies in long-term memory just as we do in working memory. For example, think about how information in your long-term memory is arranged. It is categorized according to a master plan based on contents, much like a library shelving system based on the contents of books. When information is filed in this way, it can be retrieved quite easily by following the same network of associations used to store it in the first place.

So far, we have depicted the human thinker as a *sequential* processor—first taking in information; then operating on, storing, and retrieving it; and finally responding. Some tasks, such as memorizing a list, planning a trip, or solving a math problem, require this step-by-step form of processing. But others, like reading, typing, or playing basketball, demand that the sensory, memory, and motor parts of the system operate in a *simultaneous,* integrated fashion, with information flowing continuously and rapidly from stimulus

working, or short-term, memory The conscious part of the mental system, where we actively "work" on a limited amount of information to ensure that it will be retained.

long-term memory The part of the mental system that contains our permanent knowledge base.

input to response output (Klahr & MacWhinney, 1998). The cognitive system depicted in Figure 7.1 engages in both sequential and simultaneous processing, depending on the type of task.

■ **RESEARCH EVALUATING THE STORE APPROACH.** The well-known **serial position effect,** which occurs when you try to memorize a list of items, supports the distinction between working and long-term memory. Items in the middle are less likely to be remembered than those at the beginning or the end. Over time, however, items at the end decay from memory, whereas those at the beginning continue to be retained. Researchers believe that this happens because items learned last are held only temporarily in working memory. Those learned first have had enough time to transfer to the long-term store. When exposed to a list of three stimuli and then tested for recognition a short time later, even 3-month-old infants show the serial position effect (Merriman, Rovee-Collier, & Wilk, 1997).

Other findings raise questions about the store approach. The capacity limits of the sensory register and short-term memory vary widely from study to study. For example, retention of visual information in the sensory register ranges from milliseconds to several hours and, at times, even months. Working memory, once thought to be limited to 7 slots or pieces of information, usually varies from about 2 to 20 (Baddeley, 1994; Lockhart & Craik, 1990). And when strategies are applied very effectively, capacity can expand greatly. In one case, extended practice in recoding number digits into meaningful sequences led to a working-memory capacity of 80 digits! Difficulties in identifying the precise size of these "hardware units" have led some researchers to turn toward a levels-of-processing view.

THE LEVELS-OF-PROCESSING MODEL

The **levels-of-processing model** abandons the idea of fixed-capacity stores. Instead, it assumes that transfer of information from working to long-term memory depends on the depth to which it is processed. For example, we could encode a written word superficially, by attending to how it looks or sounds. In these instances, we might notice whether the word is printed in upper- or lower-case letters or repeat the word aloud to ourselves. To process deeply, we would encode the word according to its meaning, or *semantic features,* relating it to other information already in our systems (Craik & Lockhart, 1972; Lockhart & Craik, 1990). In the levels-of-processing model, information that is analyzed in a shallow way is soon forgotten. In contrast, information interpreted meaningfully and linked to existing knowledge is retained much longer.

According to the levels-of-processing view, rather than a fixed number of slots, working memory is a limited pool of attentional resources from which our information-processing activities draw. Our difficulty handling many pieces of information at once has to do with the extent to which we can distribute attention across multiple activities (Baddeley, 1992). The amount of attention a person must allocate to an activity depends on **automatization**—how well learned, or automatic, the cognitive processes required by it happen to be. Unskilled individuals must devote more attention. As a result, attentional resources are drawn away from other activities they might do at the same time. In contrast, automatic cognitive processes demand little or no attentional resources, and individuals can engage in other tasks simultaneously.

Consider two children, one a novice bicycle rider and the other an expert. The novice's attention is entirely consumed by efforts to steer, control the pedals, and maintain balance. Indeed, parents are best off insisting that this child practice in traffic-free areas, since little or no attentional resources remain to watch out for cars and pedestrians. In contrast, the practiced bicyclist can ride easily around the neighborhood, delivering papers and conversing with a nearby rider at the same time.

IMPLICATIONS FOR DEVELOPMENT

When applied to development, the information-processing models just reviewed suggest that two broad aspects of the cognitive system may change with age: its hardware, or the absolute size of its processing units; and its software, or the extent and effectiveness of strat-

serial position effect In memory tasks involving lists of items, the tendency to remember those at the beginning and the end better than those in the middle. Over time, items at the end decay, whereas those at the beginning continue to be retained.

levels-of-processing model A model of mental functioning in which retention of information depends on the depth to which it is processed. Attentional resources determine processing capacity.

automatization The extent to which cognitive processes are well learned, or automatic, and therefore require little or no attentional resources.

egy use. That is, what develops may be both a bigger system and a wider array of programs, or strategies, which leads to more efficient use of processing resources (Guttentag, 1997).

Research we will consider throughout this chapter indicates that without a doubt, strategy use improves with age. Children gradually acquire a variety of procedures for efficiently allocating space, or attention, within their limited-capacity systems. They also process information more deeply—an important cause of age-related memory gains (Ornstein, 1995).

Does the hardware of the system also expand? Although researchers disagree on this issue, evidence on speed of processing suggests that absolute capacity does increase. Robert Kail (1991, 1993, 1997) gave individuals between 7 and 22 years of age a variety of basic cognitive tasks in which they had to respond as quickly as possible. For example, in a visual search task, participants were shown a single digit and asked to signal if it was among a set of digits that appeared on a screen. In a mental rotation task, they were given pairs of letters in any of six different orientations and asked to decide whether the letters were identical or mirror images. And in a mental addition task, participants were presented with addition problems and answers, and they had to indicate whether or not the solution was correct.

Kail found that processing time decreased with age for all tasks. But even more important, rate of change was the same across many activities—a fairly rapid decline that trailed off around 12 years of age (see Figure 7.2). This pattern was also evident when participants performed perceptual–motor tasks, such as releasing a button or tapping as fast as possible—activities that do not rely on mental strategies (Kail, 1991).

The changes in processing speed shown in Figure 7.2 have been found in Canada, Korea, and the United States (Fry & Hale, 1996; Kail & Park, 1992). Similarity in development across a diverse array of tasks in several cultures implies an age-related gain in basic information-processing resources, possibly due to myelinization or synaptic pruning

Is this third grader processing deeply, encoding new material by relating it to what she already knows? The levels-of-processing model emphasizes that interpreting material meaningfully, in terms of existing knowledge, leads it to be retained much longer.

(Nita Winter/The Image Works)

FIGURE 7.2

Decline in processing time from childhood to adolescence, illustrated for mental addition (a) and tapping (b). The rate of change is the same across many tasks—even perceptual–motor activities, such as tapping as fast as possible, that do not rely on mental strategies. This common trend implies an age-related gain in basic processing capacity, or size of the cognitive system.

(Part a from R. Kail, 1988, "Developmental Functions for Speeds of Cognitive Processes," Journal of Experimental Child Psychology, 45, p. 361. Copyright © 1988 by Academic Press. Reprinted by permission of the publisher and author. Part b from R. Kail, 1991, "Processing Time Declines Exponentially During Childhood and Adolescence,"Developmental Psychology, 27, p. 265. Copyright © 1991 by the American Psychological Association. Adapted by permission of the publisher and author.)

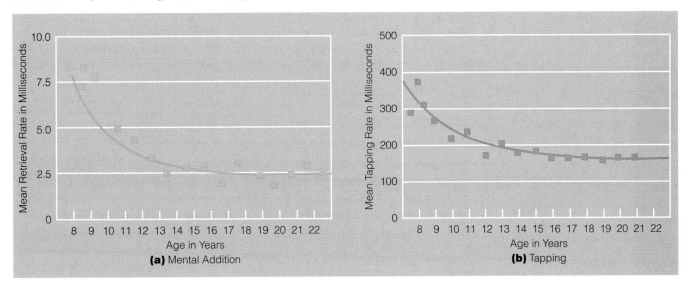

in the brain (see Chapter 5) (Kail & Salthouse, 1994; Miller & Vernon, 1997). As a result, older children and adults can hold more information in their cognitive systems at once, scan it more quickly, and generate faster responses in a wide range of situations. Kail reminds us, however, that older individuals are more adept at strategies, which also contribute to more efficient information processing (Kail & Park, 1994).

In sum, although the precise capacity limits of the cognitive system are hard to pin down, *both* its hardware and its software seem to expand with age. As we turn now to developmental models of information processing, we will see efforts to integrate these two aspects—the first emphasizing brain development, the second experience in transforming information—into an overall picture of how the cognitive system changes with age.

Developmental Theories of Information Processing

Although the store and levels-of-processing models have implications for development, neither focuses directly on how children's thinking changes with age. However, several *developmental* approaches, each of which borrows ideas from adult information processing, are attracting widespread attention. We will take up three of these views, which study cognitive change from strikingly different vantage points.

The first is a *neo-Piagetian perspective* (Case, 1992; Fischer & Pipp, 1984; Halford, 1993). To create an overall vision of development, these theorists use Piaget's theory as a starting point, reinterpreting it within an information-processing framework. Case's theory is the most prominent neo-Piagetian view.

The second approach is *connectionism* (Elman et al., 1996; Plunkett et al., 1997). These theorists focus, not on broad changes in cognition, but on the most basic processing units and their connections, using computer simulations to model the way neurons work in the brain. Computer simulations of the functioning of these cognitive building blocks are used to test hypotheses about how children master specific skills.

Finally, we will consider an approach that draws on evolutionary concepts of variation and selection to explain the great diversity in children's cognition and its ever-changing nature—Siegler's *model of strategy choice.* In different ways, each of these theories aims to fulfill a central goal of information processing: explaining, more precisely than ever before, just how development occurs.

CASE'S NEO-PIAGETIAN THEORY

Robbie Case's (1992a, 1998) **neo-Piagetian theory** accepts Piaget's stages but views change within each, as well as movement from one stage to the next, as due to increases in information-processing capacity. Each major stage involves a distinct type of cognitive structure—in infancy, sensory input and physical actions; in early childhood, internal representations of events and actions; in middle childhood, simple transformations of representations; and in adolescence, complex transformations of representations. As children become more efficient cognitive processors, the amount of information they can hold onto and combine in working memory expands, making this sequence of development possible.

■ **MECHANISMS OF CHANGE.** According to Case, three factors are responsible for gains in the capacity of working memory:

■ *Brain development.* Recall our discussion of brain growth spurts in Chapter 5—changes in EEG activity of the cerebral cortex that coincide with major gains in cognitive competence (see page 191). Case believes that synaptic growth, synaptic pruning, and myelinization, which underlie these growth spurts, improve the efficiency of thought, leading to readiness for each stage. In this way, biology imposes a system-wide ceiling on cognitive development. At any given time, the child cannot exceed a certain upper limit of processing capacity without further brain development.

neo-Piagetian theory A theory that reinterprets Piaget's stages within an information-processing framework.

■ *Practice with schemes and automatization.* According to Case, Piagetian schemes constitute the child's mental strategies. As the child repeatedly uses schemes, they become more automatic and require less attention. This frees up resources in working memory for combining existing schemes and generating new ones. Notice how these mechanisms of change offer an equivalent, but clarified, view of Piaget's concepts of assimilation and accommodation. *Practicing schemes* (assimilation) leads to *automatization,* which *releases attentional resources* for other activities, permitting *scheme combination and construction* (accommodation).

■ *Formation of central conceptual structures.* Once the schemes of a Piagetian stage become sufficiently automatized, enough working-memory capacity is available to consolidate them into an improved representational form. As a result, children acquire **central conceptual structures,** networks of concepts and relations that permit them to think about a wide range of situations in more advanced ways. Consequently, processing capacity expands further, since these structures permit more efficient approaches to interpreting experience and solving problems (Case, 1996, 1998). When children form new central conceptual structures, they move up to the next stage of development.

Case's neo-Piagetian theory explains children's mastery of conservation in information-processing terms. As these children pour water from one container to another, their understanding of what happens to the height and width of the liquid becomes better coordinated, and conservation of liquid is achieved. Once this logical idea becomes automatic, enough working-memory capacity is available to form a central conceptual structure—a general representation of conservation that can be applied to a wide range of situations.
(Lawrence Migdale/Stock Boston)

Let's take a familiar set of tasks—conservation—to illustrate Case's ideas. Imagine a 5-year-old who cannot yet conserve liquid but who has some isolated schemes, such as (1) after water is poured from a tall into a short glass, the height of the water level is reduced; and (2) after water is poured from a thin into a wide glass, the width of the water increases. As the child gains experience transferring liquids from one container to another, these schemes become automatic, and she combines them into a conserving response. A similar sequence of development occurs in other conservation situations, such as length, mass, and weight. Eventually the child coordinates several task-specific conserving responses into a new, broadly applicable principle—a central conceptual structure. When this happens, cognition moves to a higher level of functioning—from simple to complex transformations of representations, or from concrete to formal operational thought.

Case and his colleagues have applied his theory to many tasks, including solving arithmetic word problems, understanding stories, drawing pictures, sight-reading music, handling money, and interpreting social situations (Case, 1992, 1998; Case & Okamoto, 1996). In each, preschoolers' central conceptual structures focus on one dimension. In understanding stories, for example, they grasp only a single story line. In drawing pictures, they depict objects separately, ignoring their spatial arrangement. By the early school years, central conceptual structures coordinate two dimensions. Children combine two story lines into a single plot, and they create drawings that show both the features of objects and the relationship of objects to one another. Around 9 to 11 years, central conceptual structures integrate multiple dimensions. Children tell coherent stories with a main plot and several subplots. And their drawings follow a set of rules for representing perspective and, therefore, include several points of reference, such as near, midway, and far (see Figure 7.3 on page 278).

Case's theory offers an information-processing account of the horizontal décalage—that many understandings appear in specific situations at different times rather than being mastered all at once. First, different forms of the same logical insight, such as conservation of liquid and weight, may vary in the processing demands they make of the child. As a result, each successive task requires more working-memory resources for mastery. Second,

central conceptual structures
In Case's neo-Piagetian theory, networks of concepts and relations that permit children to think about a wide range of situations in more advanced ways. Formation of new central conceptual structures marks the transition to a new Piagetian stage.

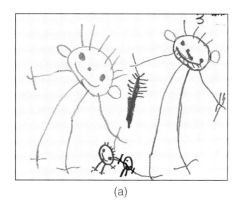
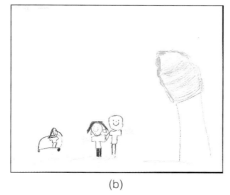

(a)   (b)   (c)

FIGURE 7.3

Development of central conceptual structures in Case's neo-Piagetian theory. Case identified the same general sequence in children's performance on many tasks. Here, it is shown for drawings. Children were asked to "draw a picture of a mother and a father holding hands in a park, with their little baby on the grass in front of them, and a tree far off behind." (a) Preschoolers focused on one dimension. They depicted objects separately, ignoring their spatial arrangement. (b) During the early school years, children coordinated two dimensions. Their drawings showed both the features of objects and their relationship to one another. (c) Nine- to 11-year-olds integrated multiple dimensions. They used perspective to represent several points of reference, such as near, midway, and far.

(From R. Case & Y. Okamoto, 1996, "The Role of Central Conceptual Structures in the Development of Children's Thought," *Monographs of the Society for Research in Child Development, 61*[246, 1–2], p. 106. © The Society for Research in Child Development, Inc. Adapted by permission. Courtesy of Robbie Case.)

connectionism An approach that tries to explain development in terms of artificial neural networks, which are programmed into computers, set up to learn, and presented with tasks that children encounter. If the system's pattern of responses resembles that of children, then researchers conclude that the artificial network is a good model of how children learn.

children's task-specific experiences vary widely. A child who often listens to and tells stories but rarely draws pictures would display more advanced central conceptual structures in the story domain than in the drawing domain.

■ **EVALUATION OF CASE'S THEORY.** Case's theory is a domain-general approach, since similar changes in central conceptual structures are observed across many tasks. At the same time, he acknowledges greater domain-specificity in development than did Piaget, attributing it to variations in the complexity of tasks and children's experiences. Consequently, his theory is better able to account for the gradual and uneven nature of cognitive development, discussed in Chapter 6. To identify both domain-general and domain-specific change, Case advocates detailed study of children's learning in specific contexts—a research strategy he shares with other information-processing theorists.

Case's (1998) theory still needs to be tested in many more task domains. But so far, it is unique in offering an integrated picture of how basic capacity, practice with strategies, and children's constructive efforts to reorganize their thinking interact to produce development.

CONNECTIONISM

Connectionism tries to explain development by means of computer-simulated learning tasks, using large numbers of interconnected simple processing units, which are organized in layers, much like the brain's neurological structure. These *artificial neural networks* are programmed into computers, set up to learn, and presented with tasks that children encounter.

A typical network includes an *input layer*, which encodes the task; one or more *hidden layers*, which combine information from input units into internal representations; and an *output layer*, which generates a response to the situation. As in the brain, a particular processing unit sends a signal when the stimulation it receives from other units connected to it reaches a certain strength. And because task-relevant knowledge is distributed throughout the system—over all the units and the strengths of their connections, acting in parallel (simultaneously)—these computer-simulated learners are sometimes called *parallel distributed processing systems*.

How does the system "learn"? Researchers program it with a learning procedure—typically, one in which the system receives input, generates a response, observes the discrepancy between that response and the correct answer, and then adjusts the strengths of connections (represented as weights in the hidden units) so they are more likely to yield an improved response in the future. By varying the learning environment (input to the system) and the learning procedure (adjustments of connections in response to errors), investigators can study how interactions between a self-organizing learner and its context lead to new skills (Elman et al., 1996). The system's pattern of responses is compared with that of children confronted with a similar task. If the two are alike, then researchers conclude that the artificial network is a good model of how children learn.

■ **CONNECTIONIST MODELING: AN EXAMPLE.** Connectionists have succeeded in depicting children's development on a variety of tasks. These include object permanence; early vocabulary growth; mastery of certain grammatical forms, such as the past tense; and understanding how a balance scale works (Mareschal, Plunkett, & Harris, 1995; Mc-Clelland, 1989, 1995; Plunkett et al., 1992). Let's take the balance-scale problem, a Piagetian formal operational task, as an example.

Robert Siegler (1981) showed 3- to 18-year-olds varying weights placed on a balance scale's arms at varying distances from the center. In each instance, he asked whether or not the scale would balance and, if not, whether its right or left arm would go down. Children's patterns of responses revealed the following stages of development:

Stage 1. *Preschoolers notice only weight on each side, ignoring distance.* If the number of weights is equal, they predict the scale will balance. Otherwise, they say the scale will not balance.

Stage 2. *School-age children continue to focus on weight, except when the weights on both sides are equal.* Under these conditions, they predict that the scale will balance only if the two distances are the same.

Stage 3. *Adolescents consider both weight and distance.* If one dimension is equal and the other is not, they base their decision on the unequal dimension and say the scale will not balance. If both dimensions are unequal, they are confused and simply guess.

Stage 4. *A few adolescents master the concept of torque, mostly through direct teaching.* They realize that only when the product of weight × distance on both sides of the scale is equal will the scale balance.

To explore the mechanisms of change underlying this sequence, James McClelland (1989, 1995) set up an artificial neural network. Figure 7.4 shows the network's structure. Notice how it reflects the preschool child's initial knowledge—ability to distinguish weight and distance, as indicated by different input units for each. McClelland presented the network with

FIGURE **7.4**

Connectionist artificial neural network used to simulate mastery of the balance scale. Examples of problems are shown on the left. The network structure for unequal weight–unequal distance (the bottom balance scale) is shown on the right. Different *input units* for weight and distance reflect preschoolers' initial knowledge. The *hidden units* combine information from input units into internal representations of connection strengths, which send signals to the *output units,* one for the left (L) and the other for the right (R) side of the scale. If the activity of one output unit exceeds that of the other by a certain amount, then the "side" of the scale whose unit is most active "goes down." Otherwise, the scale balances. On the basis of feedback about response accuracy, the hidden units adjust the strengths of connections so the output units are more likely to yield an improved response on future problems.

(Right side of figure adapted from K. Plunkett, A. Karmiloff-Smith, E. Bates, J. L. Elman, & M. H. Johnson, 1997, "Connectionism and Developmental Psychology," *Journal of Child Psychology and Psychiatry,* 38, p. 64. © Association for Child Psychology and Psychiatry. Reprinted by permission.)

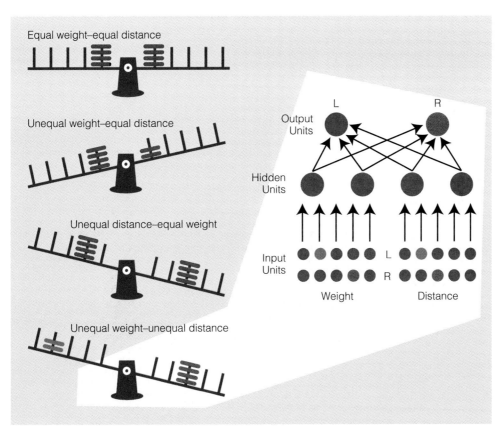

Equal weight–equal distance

Unequal weight–equal distance

Unequal distance–equal weight

Unequal weight–unequal distance

Output Units
L   R
Hidden Units
Input Units
L
R
Weight   Distance

hundreds of balance-scale problems involving many weight and distance combinations. The problems varied weight more often than distance—a characteristic of the environment thought to account for younger children's greater focus on weight in this type of task.

This learner–task environment combination produced a changing pattern of responses that mirrored findings with children and adolescents. At first, weight connections strengthened, due to more frequent weight variations in the balance-scale problems (Stage 1). Gradually, the system gained experience with distance variations, and distance connections grew stronger. Eventually, they reached a point at which the system responded to distance when weights were equal (Stage 2). With further training, distance connections became strong enough to trigger responses under unequal-weight conditions (Stage 3). However, the system never fully attained the highest level of development—responses consistent with the concept of torque (Stage 4). Adolescents, as well, rarely grasp this idea without being taught.

Neural-network mastery of the balance scale and other tasks reveals that continuous learning can yield stagelike shifts in performance (Plunkett et al., 1997). Notice how the system first focuses on one dimension (weight), later notices the second dimension (distance), and finally, begins to integrate the two. Yet within each stage, the network is constantly attending to feedback about the accuracy of its responses and adjusting the strength of its connections. Connectionist models highlight this gradual, internal learning as essential for changes in many skills that appear abrupt when viewed from outside the system.

■ **EVALUATION OF CONNECTIONISM.** Connectionist models provide a detailed look at what might be happening at the most fundamental level as children master particular tasks. The approach shows how just a few built-in procedures can get learning "off the ground"—detecting the structure of complex learning environments and acquiring a variety of skills. Consequently, connectionists argue that their findings present a powerful argument against the nativist, modular view of the mind (see Chapter 6, page 234). Instead, connectionists claim, the human cognitive system is a domain-general processor that gradually attains domain-specific competencies with exposure to specific learning opportunities.

At the same time, connectionism has a variety of shortcomings that make its account of mechanisms of development incomplete. These difficulties are of three main kinds:

- Artificial neural networks learn slowly, usually requiring many more exposures to a task than do children and adults, who sometimes show sudden insights (Raijamkers, Koten, & Molenaar, 1996). This difficulty may result from the relatively passive nature of connectionist models, which exist in artificial, preprogrammed environments over which the learner has no control. People, in contrast, have goals, often select their own environments, and interact with others, who assist them in making new discoveries.

- The internal representations of connectionist systems are limited to connection strengths. Artificial neural networks do not construct plans, hypotheses, or propositions, which foster complex, highly efficient human learning (recall that in mastering balance-scale problems, the network never attained the torque concept). Perhaps for this reason, connectionist explanations are limited to specific skills. They do not provide an overall view of how a child learns about the physical world, acquires language, or reasons scientifically. So it seems crucial to add mechanisms of development at higher levels to neural-network models (Karmiloff-Smith, 1992a, 1992b).

- We cannot be certain that artificial neural networks actually mirror the operation of the human brain. Indeed, their learning procedures do not fully capture how humans make use of feedback. For example, we will see when we turn to the next developmental theory, strategy choice, that children are great experimenters. To arrive at the most efficient means of solving a problem, they change their strategies not just after they make errors (as artificial neural networks do) but even after they succeed!

Still, connectionism reminds us that a full specification of children's cognitive development must take into account the operation of its most basic units. Currently, connectionists are trying to devise more realistic models of brain functioning and the contexts in which children learn (Elman et al., 1996). More than any other information-

model of strategy choice
Siegler's evolutionary theory of cognitive development, which states that variation and selection characterize children's mental strategies, yielding adaptive problem-solving techniques and an overlapping-waves pattern of development.

processing approach, connectionists are responding to current urgings that theories of cognitive development take the brain as seriously as the mind (Bjorklund, 1997).

SIEGLER'S MODEL OF STRATEGY CHOICE

In Chapter 1, we noted that many theories of development have drawn inspiration from Darwin's theory of evolution. Robert Siegler's (1995a, 1996) **model of strategy choice** is one of several current efforts to apply an evolutionary perspective to children's cognition. When given challenging problems, children generate a *variety* of strategies for solving them. With experience, some strategies are *selected*; they become more frequent and "survive." Others become less frequent and "die off." As in the biological context, *variation* and *selection* characterize children's mental strategies, yielding adaptive problem-solving techniques.

■ **TRYING OUT STRATEGIES.** To study children's strategy use, Siegler used the microgenetic research design (see Chapter 2, page 63), presenting children with a large number of problems over an extended time, recording their strategies and the circumstances in which each emerged and declined. He found that children try out diverse strategies on many types of problems, including number conservation, time telling, memory for lists of items, word decoding in early reading, spelling, basic math facts, and even tic-tac-toe (Siegler, 1995b, 1996).

How do children choose adaptively among strategies? Let's illustrate with 5-year-olds' learning of basic addition. When given a problem like 2 + 4, children use the following strategies: guess, without applying a procedure; count from 1 on their fingers (1, 2, 3, 4, 5, 6); hold up 4 fingers on one hand, 2 on the other, and recognize 6 as the total; start with the lower digit, 2, and "count on" (2, 3, 4, 5, 6); start with the higher digit, 4, and "count on" (4, 5, 6), a strategy called "min" because it minimizes the work involved; or automatically retrieve the answer from memory.

Siegler found that strategy use for basic math facts—and many other types of problems—does not progress in a stagelike way. Instead, it follows the *overlapping-waves pattern* shown in Figure 7.5. Multiple strategies are present throughout learning, with some becoming less frequent, others more frequent, and still others rising and falling over time. The strategy choices children make are adaptive in two respects:

■ Trying out a variety of strategies encourages children to consider why some approaches work well, others work less well, and still others are unsuccessful. As a result, children build up a repertoire of effective strategies they can use when faced with new problems.

■ The way strategies change suggests that children evaluate them on the basis of two criteria: *efficiency* and *accuracy*. Those that result in rapid, correct solutions are favored—in the case of basic addition, the "min" strategy. As children practice and "home in" on more successful strategies, they learn more about the problems at hand. As a result, correct answers become more strongly associated with problems, and children acquire the most efficient strategy: automatic retrieval.

How do children move from less to more efficient strategies? Often they discover a faster procedure as a result of success with a more time-consuming technique. For example, children frequently put up their fingers to solve addition problems. Eventually they become proficient at recognizing the number of fingers that are up without counting them. Once they can do this, they soon move to the "min" strategy (Siegler & Jenkins, 1989). Also, certain problems dramatize the need for a better strategy. Children who have used "min" at least once recognize its usefulness on problems like 3 + 22, where counting is tedious. Reasoning about number concepts also

FIGURE 7.5

Overlapping-waves pattern of development in Siegler's model of strategy choice. Children generate multiple strategies, each represented by a wave. Several strategies overlap at any given time. Use of each strategy, depicted by the height of the wave, is constantly changing. Over time, the most adaptive strategy, based on efficiency and accuracy, wins out.

(From R. S. Siegler, 1996, *Emerging Minds: The Process of Change in Children's Thinking*, New York: Oxford University Press, p. 238. © Oxford University Press. Reprinted by permission.)

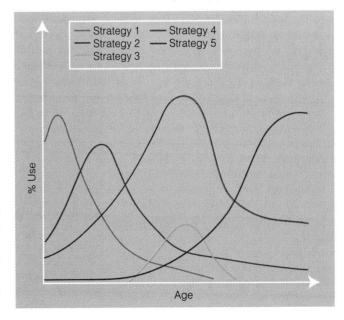

— Strategy 1 — Strategy 4
— Strategy 2 — Strategy 5
— Strategy 3

% Use

Age

fosters efficiency (Canobi, Reeve, & Pattison, 1998). First graders more often use the "min" strategy after they realize that regardless of the order in which two sets are combined, they yield the same results ($2 + 4 = 6$ and $4 + 2 = 6$). Finally, teaching children an effective strategy usually leads them to include the new technique in their strategy repertoire, although initially they do not generalize it to new types of problems (Alibali, 1999).

Even when they are aware of a more adaptive strategy, children do not always take advantage of it. As we will see in later sections, using a new strategy requires considerable effort, taxing working-memory resources. Furthermore, children are often reluctant to give up a well-established strategy for a new one, perhaps because gains in efficiency are small until children have had time to practice the new technique. Clearly, strategy development is very gradual on many types of tasks.

■ EVALUATION OF SIEGLER'S THEORY. Most theories of cognitive development try to identify *the* way children think at different ages—in Piagetian and neo-Piagetian theories, how children think across a broad range of problems; in information-processing theories, how they think while engaged in a particular task. Yet Siegler's model reveals that no child thinks in just one way, even on the same task. A child given the same problem on two occasions often uses different approaches. Even on a single item, children may generate varying procedures, as indicated by occasions in which their words and gestures differ (see the From Research to Practice box on the following page to find out about the significance of these mismatches).

Siegler's theory underscores that strategy variability is vital for devising new, more adaptive ways of thinking, which "evolve" through extensive experience solving problems. At present, mechanisms that lead children to choose among strategies are clearer than those that produce strategy variation. And the model has yet to be tested on tasks in which strategies are less well defined, such as telling stories and drawing pictures—those used earlier to illustrate Case's neo-Piagetian theory.

At the same time, the model of strategy choice offers a powerful image of development that overcomes deficiencies of the stage approach in accounting for both diversity and constant change in children's thinking. In this new view, each new way of thinking is seen "as a wave approaching a seashore, with several waves (ways of thinking) overlapping at any given time, with the height of each wave (frequency of use of the ways of thinking) continuously changing, with different waves being most prominent at different times, and with some waves never being the most prominent but still influencing other waves and contributing to the tide" (Siegler, 1996, pp. 237–238).

ASK YOURSELF . . .

◆ A researcher gave 5-year-old Kayla several conservation-of-number problems and told her whether her answer was right or wrong. On the first one, she gave a nonconserving response. On the second one, she said, "The rows have the same number because you didn't add any pennies." On the third one, she said, "I counted the pennies. The rows have the same number." Why is it beneficial for Kayla to use several strategies? Which strategy is she likely to emphasize over time, and why?

◆ CONNECTIONS
Return to Chapter 6, page 239, to review the drawings of nonschooled Jimi 10- to 15-year-olds of Papua New Guinea. Use Case's theory to explain why these drawings resemble the one-dimensional artwork of much younger children. Are these Jimi children likely to be one-dimensional thinkers on many other tasks? Explain.

BRIEF REVIEW

nformation-processing researchers are committed to explicit models of cognitive functioning that map the precise steps children and adults use when faced with a task or problem. Two general models of adult information processing have influenced research on children's cognition. Atkinson and Shiffrin's store model regards the limited capacity of our mental systems as due to fixed-size sensory and working memory stores. The levels-of-processing view emphasizes allocation of attention in working memory as responsible for capacity limitations. Research indicates that both gains in size of the system and more effective strategy use contribute to an age-related increase in children's ability to hold onto and operate on more information at once.

Developmental approaches borrow ideas from adult information processing. In Case's neo-Piagetian theory, greater working-memory capacity—due to brain development, practice with schemes and automatization, and formation of central conceptual structures—account for both continuous and stagewise changes. Connectionism explains cognitive development at the level of interconnected basic processing units, akin to neurons in the brain. Computerized artificial neural networks are programmed with learning procedures and presented with specific tasks. Their changing patterns of responses are compared with those of children to see if the network's functioning can serve as a good model of children's thinking. Siegler's model of strategy choice borrows evolutionary concepts to explain cognitive development. Wide variation in strategy use is adaptive, leading to more efficient, accurate problem solving.

Speech-Gesture Mismatches: Using the Hand to Read the Mind

FROM RESEARCH TO PRACTICE

MR. BEAL INTRODUCED his fourth-grade class to the concept of equivalence—that the quantity on one side of an equals sign is the same as the quantity on the other side. Then he watched as several children stepped up to the blackboard to work the following problem: $5 + 3 + 4 = \_\_ + 4$.

Kerry tried first. "I added $5 + 3 + 4 + 4$ equals 16," she said, pointing at each number as she mentioned it, then at the blank as she gave her answer. Kerry's speech and gestures were consistent; both revealed an incorrect strategy.

Noel went next. She gave the same incorrect explanation as Kerry did, but her gestures sent a different message. While she spoke, she pointed to each number on the left, next touched the equals sign, then moved to the 4 on the right, and finally rested her finger on the blank. Noel showed a speech–gesture mismatch. Her hand movements suggested she knew more than she could say. Over the next few weeks, Noel mastered equivalence problems more rapidly than did Kerry. How can we account for Noel's faster progress?

According to Susan Goldin-Meadow and her colleagues (1993), children who produce speech–gesture mismatches are in a transitional state. Their behavior indicates that they are considering two contradictory strategies at once, a sign of readiness to learn. In a microgenetic study, the researchers identified two groups of children who did not have a full understanding of addition-based equivalence problems: speech–gesture matched and speech–gesture mismatched. Then, as the children worked more problems, some in each group received feedback on the accuracy of their answers along with instruction that explained the equivalence principle, whereas others received no intervention. Finally, children's learning was assessed as they worked problems on their own (Alibali & Goldin-Meadow, 1993).

Speech–gesture mismatch children who received instruction were more likely than others to move out of that state to a correct answer, based on a speech–gesture match. They also more often generalized their new knowledge to multiplication-based equivalence problems ($5 \times 3 \times 4 = 5 \times \_\_$). Interestingly, the few speech–gesture match children who improved with instruction generalized what they learned only if they first passed through a speech–gesture mismatch phase. Correct strategies first appeared in gesture, only later in speech.

As this fifth grader works a math problem at the blackboard, do her hand gestures suggest that she knows more than she can say? Speech–gesture mismatches indicate that children are considering two contradictory strategies and are particularly open to teaching. (Myrleen Ferguson Cate/Photo Edit)

Gesturing during problem solving serves a vital function, since nongesturing children typically progress more slowly than gesturing children do. Children on the verge of learning appear to have a variety of strategies accessible to gesture but not to speech. In Vygotsky's terms, such children are in a *zone of proximal development*. They are particularly open to teaching, which helps them make explicit in speech what they already know implicitly in gesture.

Goldin-Meadow's findings reveal that at times, gesture captures children's progress better than speech does. Although children are rarely aware of their hand movements, gestures may promote cognitive change in ways that do not require awareness (McNeill, 1992). Perhaps speech–gesture mismatches indicate that the neural pathways of interest to connectionists are growing stronger and about to reach a critical juncture. Parents and teachers who are attuned to children's gestures can use that information to adjust their interaction, providing development-enhancing instruction at the most opportune moment.

Attentional Processing

The central sections of this chapter address a wealth of evidence on children's processing in the major parts of the cognitive system. In the following sections, we consider how children of different ages encode information, operate on it in working memory so it will transfer to long-term memory, and retrieve it so they can think about the world and solve problems.

We begin with research on the development of attention. Attention is fundamental to human thinking, since it determines the information that will be considered in any task. Parents and teachers are quick to notice that young children spend only short times

The capacity to engage in complex play supports sustained attention, which increases during the preschool years. This 2-year-old's engrossed play provides the foundation for selective and adaptable attentional strategies, which will improve during the school years.

(Erik Skagestad)

involved in tasks, have difficulty focusing on details, and are easily distracted. Attention improves greatly during early and middle childhood, becoming more selective, adaptable, and planful.

SELECTIVITY AND ADAPTABILITY

Watch young children at play, and you are likely to see that attention becomes more sustained with age. In a recent study, infants and preschoolers were seated at a table with toys. Concentrated involvement rose between 1 and 4 years. Infants' and older children's patterns of attention also differed. After playing for a short time with a toy, babies tended to habituate. Their attention was externally controlled by the physical properties of objects. In contrast, preschoolers became increasingly attentive as the play session progressed. Their capacity to engage in complex play supported engagement with objects (Ruff & Lawson, 1990).

As sustained attention improves, children become better at deliberately focusing on just those aspects of a situation that are relevant to their task goals, ignoring other information. Researchers study this increasing selectivity of attention by introducing irrelevant stimuli into a task. Then they see how well children attend to its central elements (Lane & Pearson, 1982). In a typical experiment, school-age children and adults sorted decks of cards as fast as possible on the basis of shapes on each card—for example, circles in one pile and squares in another. Some decks contained no irrelevant information. Others included either one or two irrelevant stimuli, such as lines running across the shapes or stars appearing above or below them. Ability to ignore unnecessary information was determined by seeing how much longer sorting took when decks had irrelevant stimuli. As Figure 7.6 indicates, keeping attention on central features of the task improved sharply over middle childhood (Strutt, Anderson, & Well, 1975).

Older children are also more adaptable, flexibly adjusting their attention to the momentary requirements of situations. For example, in judging whether pairs of stimuli are the same or different, sixth graders quickly shift their basis of judgment (from size to shape to color) when asked to do so. Second graders have trouble with this type of task (Pick & Frankel, 1974). Furthermore, with age, children adapt their attention to changes in their own learning. When given lists of items to learn and allowed to select half for further study, first graders do not choose systematically. But by third grade, children show a strong tendency to select those they had previously missed (Masur, McIntyre, & Flavell, 1973). For more complex information, such as prose passages, the ability to allocate attention on the basis of previous performance continues to improve into the college years (Brown, Smiley, & Lawton, 1978).

How do children acquire and perfect attentional strategies that focus on relevant information and adapt to task requirements? Gains in two factors—cognitive inhibition and effectiveness of attentional strategies—are important.

■ **COGNITIVE INHIBITION.** Selective attention depends on **cognitive inhibition**—the ability to control internal and external distracting stimuli. Individuals who are skilled at cognitive inhibition can prevent the mind from straying to alternative attractive thoughts. They can also keep stimuli that are unrelated to a current goal from capturing their attention. By ensuring that working memory will not be cluttered with irrelevant stimuli, cognitive inhibition fosters performance on a wide variety of tasks. Besides helping children remember, reason, and solve problems, it can assist them in controlling behavior in social situations (Dempster, 1993, 1995; Bjorklund & Harnishfeger, 1990, 1995). In later chapters, we will see that to get along with others, children must learn to restrain impulses, keep negative emotions in check, and resist temptation.

The ability to inhibit thoughts and behavior increases with age. Recall from Chapter 4 that very young infants have difficulty disengaging from a visual stimulus and redirecting their attention. And in Chapter 6, we saw that infants younger than 12 months may make the AB search error because they cannot inhibit a previously rewarded response. Overcoming this error coincides with rapid development of the frontal lobes of the cerebral cortex at the end of the first year (see page 228).

cognitive inhibition The ability to control internal and external distracting stimuli, preventing them from capturing attention and cluttering working memory with irrelevant information.

Gains in cognitive inhibition are particularly marked from early to middle childhood; further improvements occur in adolescence. Researchers believe that the frontal lobes, among the last brain regions to reach full maturity (see Chapter 5), are largely responsible. EEG recordings reveal that brain waves in the frontal lobes involved in evaluating stimuli and preparing responses become more pronounced from 5 to 12 years of age (Ridderinkhof & Molen, 1997). When the frontal lobes are damaged, children and adults find it very hard to ignore irrelevant information (Dempster, 1995).

In sum, by clearing unnecessary stimuli from working memory, cognitive inhibition is yet another mechanism that enhances processing capacity. As we will see next, greater capacity opens the door to effective strategy use, which increases capacity further.

■ **EFFECTIVENESS OF ATTENTIONAL STRATEGIES.** Patricia Miller and her colleagues found that development of a selective attentional strategy follows a predictable sequence. They showed 3- to 9-year-olds a large box with rows of doors that could be opened. Half the doors had pictures of cages on them, signifying that behind each was a different animal. The other half had pictures of houses, indicating that they contained a variety of household objects. Children were asked to remember the precise location of all the objects in one group (DeMarie-Dreblow & Miller, 1988; Miller et al., 1986; Woody-Ramsey & Miller, 1988).

Emergence and refinement of the attentional strategy occurred in four phases:

1. **Production deficiency.** Preschoolers fail to use a strategy in situations in which it could be helpful. On the task just described, the youngest children simply opened all the doors, regardless of the pictures on them.

2. **Control deficiency.** Early elementary school children sometimes produce a helpful strategy, but not consistently. They fail to *control*, or execute, strategies effectively. For example, 5-year-olds began to apply a selective attentional strategy, opening only relevant doors. But they did not always use it; at times, they reverted to opening irrelevant doors.

3. **Utilization deficiency.** Slightly later, children apply a strategy consistently, but their performance does not improve. For many 6- and 7-year-olds, opening just the relevant doors did not result in improved memory for locations of objects.

4. **Effective strategy use.** By the mid-elementary school years, children use a strategy consistently, and performance improves.

The phases just described apply to strategies on many types of tasks. For example, we will encounter this trend again when we take up memory. Recall from our discussion of Siegler's model of strategy choice that initially, applying a strategy takes so much of children's attentional resources that they do not have enough to both execute the strategy and perform the task well (Miller et al., 1991; Miller, Woody-Ramsey, & Aloise, 1991). In support of this interpretation, reducing the demands of the task by having an adult perform the strategy for the child (by opening relevant doors) led to substantial gains in memory for object locations (DeMarie-Dreblow & Miller, 1988).

Yet another reason a new strategy may not lead to performance gains is that young children are not good at monitoring their task performance (Schneider & Bjorklund, 1998). Because they fail to keep track of how well a strategy is working, they do not apply it consistently or refine it in other ways.

PLANNING

With age, yet another change in children's attention is apparent: It becomes more planful. **Planning** involves thinking out a sequence of acts ahead of time and allocating attention accordingly to reach a goal (Scholnick, 1995). The seeds of effective planning are present in infancy. When researchers showed 2- and 3-month-olds a series of pictures that alternated in a predictable left–right sequence, they quickly learned to shift their focus

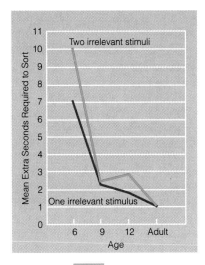

FIGURE **7.6**

Improvement in selective attention during middle childhood. Children and adults sorted decks of cards on the basis of shapes (circles and squares) appearing on each card. Six-year-olds took much longer to sort when the decks contained irrelevant stimuli (lines and stars) than when they did not. By age 9, sorting speed was only slightly affected by the presence of irrelevant information.

(From G. F. Strutt, D. R. Anderson, & A. D. Well, 1975, "A Developmental Study of the Effects of Irrelevant Information on Speeded Classification," *Journal of Experimental Child Psychology, 20,* p. 132. Copyright © 1975 by Academic Press. Adapted by permission of the publisher and author.)

production deficiency The failure to produce a mental strategy when it could be helpful.

control deficiency The inability to execute a mental strategy effectively.

utilization deficiency The failure of performance to improve after consistently using a mental strategy.

effective strategy use Consistent use of a mental strategy that leads to improvement in performance.

planning Thinking out a sequence of acts ahead of time and allocating attention accordingly to reach a goal.

FIGURE **7.7**

Play grocery store used to investigate children's planning. Five- to 9-year-olds were given "shopping lists" consisting of five cards, each with a picture of a food item on it. Along the walls and on the shelves of the doll-sized store were pictures of food items that could be picked up by moving a figurine called the "shopper" down the aisles. Researchers recorded children's scanning of the store before starting on a shopping trip and along the way. The length of the route used to gather the items served as the measure of planning effectiveness.

(Adapted from Szepkouski, Gauvain, & Carberry, 1994.)

to the location of the next stimulus before it appeared—a response not apparent when picture locations were random (Wentworth & Haith, 1992, 1998). Even the attention of very young babies seems to be "future oriented," as indicated by their ability to anticipate routine events (Haith, 1997).

During the preschool years, children encounter circumstances that require deliberate planning. As long as tasks are familiar and not too complex, they sometimes generate and follow a plan. For example, by age 4, they search for a lost object in a play yard systematically and exhaustively, looking only in locations between where they last saw the object and where they discovered it missing (Wellman, Somerville, & Haake, 1979).

Nevertheless, planful attentional strategies have a long way to go. When asked to compare detailed pictures, school-age children's scanning is more thorough (Vurpillot, 1968). And on complex tasks that require coordinating many acts, they make decisions about what to do first and what to do next in a more orderly fashion. For example, when researchers gave 5- to 9-year-olds lists of items to obtain from a doll-sized grocery store, older children took more time to scan the store thoroughly before starting on a shopping trip. They also paused more often along the way to look for each item before moving to get it (see Figure 7.7). Consequently, they followed shorter routes through the aisles (Gauvain & Rogoff, 1989; Szepkouski, Gauvain, & Carberry, 1994).

The development of planning illustrates how attention becomes coordinated with other cognitive processes. To solve problems involving multiple steps, children must postpone action in favor of mentally weighing alternatives, organizing task materials (such as items in a grocery list), and remembering the steps of their plan so they can attend to each one in sequence. Along the way, they must monitor how well the plan is working and revise it if necessary.

Clearly, planning places heavy demands on attentional resources. Not surprisingly, even when young children do plan, they often forget to implement important steps. Opportunities to observe others planning help children understand its components and benefits, increasing the likelihood they will apply this knowledge. When parents organize daily life into predictable routines and often talk about what they are going to do next, children are more likely to plan. As planning is practiced and requires less effort, children narrow the gap between their plans and actual behavior (Friedman & Scholnick, 1997; Scholnick, 1995).

The selective, adaptable, and planful attentional strategies we have just considered are crucial for success in school. Unfortunately, some school-age children have great difficulty paying attention. See the Variations box on pages 288–289 for a discussion of the serious learning and behavior problems of children with attention-deficit hyperactivity disorder.

BRIEF REVIEW

Attention improves greatly from early to middle childhood. Preschoolers show gains in sustained, focused attention while playing. Over the school years, the ability to attend to relevant information and ignore irrelevant stimuli and adapt attention to momentary requirements of a task increases. Gains in cognitive inhibition, largely due to development of the frontal lobes of the cerebral cortex, and in the effectiveness of attentional strategies contribute greatly to selectivity and adaptability of attention. Older children are also better at deciding what to do first and what to do next in a planful fashion, monitoring the success of their plan, and modifying it accordingly.

ASK YOURSELF . . .

♦ *At age 7, Jonah played each of his piano pieces from beginning to end instead of picking out the hard parts for extra practice. Around age 8, he began to devote more time to sections he knew least well, but his performance did not improve for several months. What explains Jonah's gradual strategy development and gains in performance?*

♦ **CONNECTIONS**
How can bidirectional influences between child and environment explain the development of defiant, aggressive behavior in about one-third of children with ADHD? In what ways do the child-rearing experiences of such children resemble those known to foster aggression? (See Chapter 1, page 27, and Chapter 12, pages 512–514.)

Working Memory

As attention improves with age, so do memory strategies, deliberate mental activities we use to increase the likelihood of holding information in working memory and transferring it to our long-term knowledge base. As we will see in the following sections, although memory strategies start to emerge during the preschool years, at first they are not very successful. In middle childhood, these techniques take a giant leap forward.

STRATEGIES FOR STORING INFORMATION

Researchers have studied the development of three strategies that enhance memory for new information: rehearsal, organization, and elaboration.

■ **REHEARSAL.** The next time you have a list of things to learn, such as a phone number, major cities in your state or country, or items to buy at the grocery store, take note of your behavior. You are likely to repeat the information to yourself, a memory strategy called **rehearsal.**

Preschoolers show the beginnings of rehearsal. When asked to remember a set of familiar toys, they name, look at, and manipulate them more and play with them less than when not instructed to remember them. However, they do not name the toys consistently, and their rehearsal efforts have little impact on memory until about age 6 (Baker-Ward, Ornstein, & Holden, 1984). Furthermore, when young children are given less familiar materials, they rarely rehearse. In a well-known study, researchers presented 6- and 10-year-olds with pictures of objects to remember. Many more older than younger children audibly repeated the objects' names or moved their lips. Those who rehearsed recalled far more objects (Keeney, Canizzo, & Flavell, 1967).

Why are young children not very adept at rehearsal? Look closely at the findings reviewed so far, and you will see that both *production* and *control deficiencies* are evident. Studies in which nonrehearsing children have been taught to rehearse highlight an early production deficiency. Training improves recall on the task at hand. But when given an opportunity to rehearse later without prompting, most trained children abandon the strategy (Bjorklund et al., 1997).

In addition, when children first use the strategy spontaneously, they show *control* and *utilization deficiencies,* since their efforts are neither efficient nor very successful (Bjorklund & Coyle, 1995). Eight-year-olds commonly repeat items one by one. After being

rehearsal The memory strategy of repeating information.

Children with Attention-Deficit Hyperactivity Disorder

WHILE THE OTHER fifth graders worked quietly at their desks, Calvin squirmed in his seat, dropped his pencil, looked out the window, fiddled with his shoelaces, and talked out. "Hey Joey," he yelled over the top of several desks, "wanna play ball after school?"

Joey didn't answer. He and the other children weren't eager to play with Calvin. Out on the playground, Calvin was a poor listener and failed to follow the rules of the game. He had trouble taking turns at bat. In the outfield, he tossed his mitt up in the air and looked elsewhere when the ball came his way. Calvin's desk at school and his room at home were a chaotic mess. He often lost pencils, books, and other materials necessary for completing assignments. And very often, he had difficulty remembering his assignments and when they were due.

SYMPTOMS OF ADHD. Calvin is one of 3 to 5 percent of school-age children with **attention-deficit hyperactivity disorder (ADHD)** (American Psychiatric Association, 1994). Boys are diagnosed five to ten times more often than girls. However, many girls with ADHD may be overlooked because their symptoms are usually not as flagrant (Gaub & Carlson, 1997).

Children with ADHD have great difficulty staying on task for more than a few minutes. In addition, they often act impulsively, ignoring social rules and lashing out with hostility when frustrated. Many (but not all) are *hyperactive.* They charge through their days with excessive motor activity, leaving parents and teachers frazzled and other children annoyed. ADHD youngsters have few friends; they are soundly rejected by their classmates. According to one view that has amassed substantial research support, these diverse symptoms are unified by a common theme: an impairment in inhibition, which makes it hard for them to delay action in favor of thought (Barkley, 1997b; Schachar et al., 1995).

The intelligence of ADHD children is normal, and they show no signs of serious emotional disturbance. Instead, because they have trouble thinking before they act, they do poorly on laboratory tasks requiring sustained attention and find it hard to ignore irrelevant information. Their distractibility results in poor encoding of essential information, which may underlie their forgetfulness and difficulties with planning, reasoning, and problem solving in academic and social situations. Children with ADHD are behind their agemates in development of many information-processing capacities (Barkley, 1997b; Denckla, 1996). Although some outgrow these difficulties, most continue to have problems concentrating and finding friends into adolescence and adulthood (Claude & Firestone, 1995).

ORIGINS OF ADHD. Heredity plays a major role in ADHD, since the disorder runs in families, and identical twins share it more often than do fraternal twins. Also, an adopted child who is inattentive and hyperactive is likely to have a biological parent (but not an adoptive parent) with similar symptoms (Sherman, Iacono, & McGue, 1997; Zametkin, 1995). Recent psychophysiological research, including EEG and fMRI studies, reveals differences in brain functioning between children with and without ADHD. These include, in children with ADHD, reduced electrical activity and blood flow in the frontal lobes and a smaller corpus callosum, which transfers information from one cerebral hemisphere to the other (Lyoo et al., 1996; Novak, Solanto, & Abikoff, 1995; Riccio et al., 1993).

At the same time, ADHD is associated with a variety of environmental factors. These children are somewhat more

---

given the word "cat" in a list of items, they say, "Cat, cat, cat." In contrast, older children combine previous words with the newest item, saying, "Desk, man, yard, cat," an approach that greatly improves recall (Kunzinger, 1985; Ornstein, Naus, & Liberty, 1975). With age, children become better at varying the strategy to fit the material to be learned. For example, 9- and 10-year-olds tend to rehearse repeatedly when given a random list of numbers (such as "5, 7, 3, 4, 6") but only once or not at all when given a serially ordered list ("4, 5, 6, 7, 8"), since they can rely on counting to retain it. In contrast, 5- and 6-year-olds usually fail to note a list's features before deciding how to memorize (McGilly & Siegler, 1990).

The preschool child's minimal use of rehearsal and the young elementary school child's less effective execution of it reveal that becoming skilled at this strategy is a gradual process. After much time and practice, it becomes more automatic, and it can be used adaptively in a wide range of situations.

attention-deficit hyperactivity disorder A childhood disorder involving inattention, impulsivity, and excessive motor activity. Often leads to academic failure and social problems.

organization The memory strategy of grouping information into meaningful chunks.

■ ORGANIZATION. If, in trying to remember items, you group them into meaningful chunks, you are using a second memory strategy, called **organization.** It causes memory to improve dramatically.

Like rehearsal, the beginnings of organization can be seen in very young children. For example, when circumstances permit, they use spatial organization to aid their memories. In one study, an adult placed either an M&M or a wooden peg in each of 12 identical containers and handed them one by one to preschoolers, asking them to remember where the candy was hid-

The boy on the right frequently engages in disruptive behavior, disturbing his classmates while they try to work. Children with ADHD have great difficulty staying on task and often act impulsively, ignoring social rules.
(Elena Rooraid/PhotoEdit)

likely to come from homes in which marriages are unhappy and family stress is high (Bernier & Siegel, 1994). But researchers agree that a stressful homelife rarely causes ADHD. Instead, the behaviors of these children can contribute to family problems, which (in turn) are likely to intensify the child's pre-existing difficulties. Furthermore, prenatal teratogens (particularly those involving long-term exposure, such as illegal drugs, alcohol, and cigarettes) are linked to inattention and hyperactivity (Milberger et al., 1997). Dietary causes, such as food additives and sugar, have also been sug-

gested, but there is little evidence that they play important roles (Hynd et al., 1991).

TREATING ADHD. Calvin's doctor eventually prescribed stimulant medication, the most common treatment for ADHD. As long as dosage is carefully regulated, these drugs reduce activity level and improve attention, academic performance, and peer relations for 70 percent of children who take them (Barkley, 1997a; Rapport & Kelly, 1993). Researchers do not know precisely why stimulants are helpful. Some speculate that they change the chemical balance in brain regions that inhibit impulsiveness and hyperactivity, thereby decreasing the child's need to engage in off-task and self-stimulating behavior.

Although stimulant medication is relatively safe, its impact is only short term. Drugs cannot teach children ways of compensating for inattention and impulsivity. Combining medication with interventions that model and reinforce appropriate academic and social behavior seems to be the most effective approach to treatment (Barkley, 1997a; Pelham & Hoza, 1996). Teachers can also create conditions in classrooms that support these pupils' special learning needs. Short work periods followed by a chance to get up and move around help them concentrate.

Finally, family intervention is particularly important. Inattentive, overactive children strain the patience of parents, who are likely to react punitively and inconsistently in return—a child-rearing style that strengthens inappropriate behavior. Breaking this cycle is as important for ADHD children as it is for the defiant, aggressive youngsters we will discuss in Chapter 12. In fact, at least 35 percent of the time, these two sets of behavior problems occur together (Lahey & Loeber, 1997).

den. By age 4, children put the candy containers in one place and the peg containers in another, a strategy that almost always led to perfect recall (DeLoache & Todd, 1988). But preschoolers do not yet use *semantic organization*—grouping objects or words into meaningful categories—to aid recall. With intensive instruction they can be taught to do so, but training does not always improve performance (Carr & Schneider, 1991; Lange & Pierce, 1992).

Once children semantically organize, the quality of their organizational strategies improves. Before age 9 or 10, children divide their lists into a greater number of categories and change their groupings from one trial to the next (Moely, 1977). Also, they tend to link items by function. For example, a 7- to 8-year-old is likely to say "hat–head," "shoes–feet," "banana–monkey," and "carrot–rabbit." Older children and adults group these items into clothing, body parts, food, and animals. The first approach is less deliberate; it depends on involuntary associations between items. In other words, when asked to think of something that goes with "hat," we are more likely to say "head" than "shoes" because we see hat and head together in everyday life. Indeed, unless items are highly familiar and strongly associated, children age 8 and younger do not group them at all (Best & Ornstein, 1986; Bjorklund & Jacobs, 1985).

Young children's use of unstable, functional categories reduces the power of organization, and they retain little information. Experience with materials that form clear categories helps children organize more effectively, notice the strategy, and begin to apply it under less obvious task conditions. Still, utilization deficiencies remain. Only after considerable practice does organization lead to substantial gains in memory (Best, 1993; Bjorklund et al., 1994).

Once organization is well established, it becomes more flexible. Between second and fourth grade, children more often combine organization with other memory strategies, such as rehearsal and stating the category name of a set of items—a multiple-strategy technique that greatly improves recall (Coyle & Bjorklund, 1997). And adolescents choose semantic organization for object names but switch to spatial organization for object–location pairings. In contrast, children approach both recall tasks similarly (Plumert, 1994). Observing the effectiveness of organization in a variety of situations gradually leads to more discriminating strategy use.

■ **ELABORATION.** Sometimes information cannot be categorized easily. For example, suppose "fish" and "pipe" are among a list of words you need to learn. If you imagined a fish smoking a pipe, you used a memory strategy called **elaboration.** It involves creating a relationship, or shared meaning, between two or more pieces of information that are not members of the same category.

Compared to other strategies, elaboration is a late-developing skill. It rarely appears before age 11. Once children discover this memory technique, they find it so effective that it tends to replace other strategies. The very reason elaboration is so successful helps explain why it is late to develop. To use elaboration, we must translate items into images and think of a relationship between them. Children's working memories must expand before they can carry out these activities at the same time (Schneider & Pressley, 1997).

Perhaps for this reason, teaching children under age 11 to elaborate is not very successful. When they do try to use the strategy, they usually produce static images, such as "The dog had a car"—an approach that reflects control and utilization deficiencies. In contrast, adolescents and adults generate active images that are more memorable, as in "The dog raced the car through town" (Reese, 1977). Increased knowledge of ways items can be combined in memory undoubtedly contributes to more successful use of elaboration.

As these Guatemalan Mayan boys practice the intricate art of mat weaving, they demonstrate keen memory for information embedded in meaningful contexts. Yet when given a list-memory task of the kind American children often perform in school, they do poorly.
(Adam Woolfitt/Corbis)

CULTURAL AND SITUATIONAL INFLUENCES ON MEMORY STRATEGIES

In most of the laboratory studies reviewed so far, children were asked to learn discrete bits of information, and memorizing was the only goal of their activity. In everyday life, people rarely learn listlike material. Rather, they participate in daily activities that yield excellent memory as a natural byproduct of the activity itself (Rogoff & Chavajay, 1995). In a study illustrating this idea, 4- and 5-year-olds were told either to play with a set of toys or to remember them. The play condition produced far better recall. Rather than just naming or touching objects, children instructed to play engaged in many spontaneous organizations that helped them recall. These included functional use of objects (pretending to eat a banana or putting a shoe on a doll) and narrating their activities, as in "I'm squeezing this lemon" or "Fly away in this helicopter, doggie" (Newman, 1990).

These findings help explain why the Kpelle farmers, described at the beginning of this chapter, viewed functional grouping as "the wise way" to organize familiar objects. Much like young children, people in non-Western cultures who have no formal schooling rarely use or benefit from instruction in memory strategies (Rogoff & Mistry, 1985). They may seldom use the memorizing techniques we have discussed because they see little reason to remember information for its own sake.

In contrast, tasks that require learning of lists are common in classrooms, and they provide children with a great deal of motivation to use memory strategies. In fact, Western children get so much practice in acquiring discrete bits of information that they apply memory strategies inappropriately when trying to recall information in meaningful contexts (Mistry, 1997). For example, Guatemalan Mayan 9-year-olds do slightly better than their American agemates when told to remember the placement of 40 familiar objects in a play scene. American children often rehearse object names when it is more effective to keep track of spatial relations (Rogoff & Waddell, 1982). The skill shown by Mayan children in remembering contextually organized information contrasts sharply with their poorer performance on list memory tasks.

Looked at in this way, the development of memory strategies is not just a matter of a more competent information-processing system. It is also a product of task demands and cultural circumstances.

roduction, control, and utilization deficiencies characterize young children's use of memory strategies. Preschoolers seldom engage in deliberate efforts to improve their memory, nor do they show lasting gains from training. During the elementary school years, children use rehearsal and organization more effectively, and over time their efforts lead to better retention of information. Elaboration emerges later, after age 11. The need to learn isolated bits of information, a typical requirement of schooling, influences the development of memory strategies.

ASK YOURSELF . . .

◆ Cite research findings that show utilization deficiencies as children master each of the memory strategies discussed in the preceding sections.

◆ CONNECTIONS
How can gains in cognitive inhibition during middle childhood support the development of memory strategies? (See page 284.)

Long-Term Memory

o far, we have discussed strategies for putting information into memory. Once it enters our long-term knowledge base, it must be *retrieved*, or recovered, to be used again. In the following sections, we consider how children retrieve information from long-term memory. Then we turn to their expanding long-term knowledge base and its impact on memory performance.

RETRIEVAL OF INFORMATION

Information can be retrieved from memory in three ways: through recognition, recall, and reconstruction. As we discuss the development of these approaches to remembering, we will also take up an intriguing, universal memory problem: our inability to recollect experiences that occurred during the first few years of our lives.

■ **RECOGNITION**. Try showing a young child a set of 10 pictures or toys. Then mix them up with some unfamiliar items and ask the child to point to the ones in the original set. Noticing that a stimulus is identical or similar to one previously experienced is called **recognition.** It is the simplest form of retrieval, since the material to be remembered is fully present during testing to serve as its own retrieval cue.

As the habituation–dishabituation research discussed in Chapter 4 shows, even young infants are capable of recognition. The ability to recognize a larger number of stimuli over longer delays improves steadily from infancy through early childhood. By age 4, recognition memory is highly accurate. After viewing a series of 80 pictures, children of this age correctly discriminated 90 percent from pictures not in the original set (Brown & Campione, 1972).

Because recognition appears early and preschoolers' performance approaches that of adults, it is probably a fairly automatic process that does not depend on a deliberate search of long-term memory. Nevertheless, the ability of older individuals to apply strategies during storage, such as systematic scanning of visual stimuli and rehearsal, increases the number of items recognized later, especially when they are complex and unfamiliar (Mandler & Robinson, 1978). Also, growth in general knowledge undoubtedly supports gains in recognition memory. With age, children encounter fewer stimuli with which they have no experience (Perlmutter, 1984).

■ **RECALL**. Now, try giving the child a more challenging task. While keeping the 10 items out of view, ask the child to name them. This requires **recall**—generating a mental image of an absent stimulus. Perhaps there are only a few cues as to what it is, or none at all beyond the context in which the information was previously experienced.

elaboration The memory strategy of creating a relationship between two or more pieces of information that are not members of the same category.

recognition A type of memory that involves noticing whether a stimulus is identical or similar to one previously experienced.

recall A type of memory that involves generating a mental image of an absent stimulus.

The beginnings of recall appear before 1 year of age as long as memories are strongly cued. Think back to our discussion of deferred imitation in Chapter 6. Its presence in infancy is good evidence for recall. Researchers have also asked parents to keep diary accounts of their babies' memories. Many examples of recall for people, places, and objects appear in the records. The following diary entry of a 7-month-old's memory of his father is an example:

> My husband called from work and I let him talk to Rob. (Rob) looked puzzled for a while and then he turned and looked at the door. Rob thought of the only time he hears his dad's voice when he knows Dad isn't home is when his Dad just got home. He heard his dad's voice and based on past experiences, he reasoned that his dad must be home, so he looked at the door. (Ashmead & Perlmutter, 1980, p. 4)

In other studies, children between 1½ and 4 years recalled events many months and even years earlier, from a time before they had learned to talk (Bauer, 1996, 1997). However, what young children recall about an event that happened long ago is only part of what could be remembered. In one longitudinal study, sixth graders were asked to tell what happened when they went to an archaeological museum in kindergarten. They said much less about the experience than when they were asked the same question 6 weeks after the museum trip actually occurred. But in response to specific retrieval cues, including photos of the event, sixth graders remembered a great deal. And in some respects, their recall was more accurate. For example, they inferred that adults had hidden artifacts in a sandbox for them to find, whereas in kindergarten they simply recalled digging for relics (Hudson & Fivush, 1991).

When younger and older children are asked to recall information after an identical time lapse, older children's recall is considerably more accurate and complete. In fact, compared to recognition, recall shows much greater improvement with age. One reason is that older individuals are much better at strategic processing (Schneider & Bjorklund, 1998). During the school years, semantic organization of the knowledge base increases. Children develop more consistent and stable categories, which they arrange into more elaborate hierarchies. When stimuli are deeply processed at encoding so they are connected with other information in long-term memory, then a wide variety of internal retrieval cues can be used to recall them later.

■ **RECONSTRUCTION.** Read the following passage about George, a convict who has escaped from prison. Then close your book and try to write the story down or tell it to a friend:

> George was alone. He knew they would soon be here. They were not far behind him when he left the village, hungry and cold. He dared not stop for food or shelter for fear of falling into the hands of his pursuers. There were many of them; they were strong and he was weak. George could hear the noise as the uniformed band beat its way through the trees not far behind him. The sense of their presence was everywhere. His spine tingled with fear. Eagerly he awaited the darkness. In darkness he would find safety. (Brown et al., 1977, p. 1456)

Now compare your version with the original. Is it a faithful reproduction?

When people are given complex, meaningful material to remember, condensations, additions, and distortions appear that are not just the result of memory failure. Instead, they are due to a radical transformation of the information. This suggests that we do not always copy material into the system at storage and faithfully reproduce it at retrieval. Instead, much information we encounter in our daily lives, such as written and spoken language, is selected and interpreted in terms of our existing knowledge. And once the material is transformed, we often have difficulty distinguishing it from the original (Bartlett, 1932). Notice how this *constructivist* approach to information processing is consistent with Piaget's theory, especially his notion of assimilating new information to existing schemes (Schneider & Bjorklund, 1998).

Constructive processing can take place during any phase of information processing. It can occur during storage. In fact, the memory strategies of organization and elaboration are within the province of constructive memory, since both require us to generate relationships between stimuli. Yet earlier we saw that young children rarely use these strategies. Constructive processing can also involve **reconstruction** of information while it is in the system or being retrieved. Do children reconstruct stored information? The answer is clearly yes.

Children's reconstructive processing has been studied by asking them to recall prose material. Like adults, when children retell a story, they condense, integrate, and add information. By age 6 or 7, children recall the important features of a story and forget the unimportant ones, combine information into more tightly knit units, and reorder the sequence of events to make it more logical (Bischofshausen, 1985; Mandler, 1984). And they often report information that fits with the meaning of a passage but that was not really presented.

For example, after elementary school pupils listened to the story of George, the escaped convict, the following statements appeared in their reconstructions: "All the prison guards were chasing him." "He climbed over the prison walls." "He was running so the police would be so far away that their dogs would not catch his trail" (Brown et al., 1977, p. 1459). In revising the information in meaningful ways, children provide themselves with a wealth of helpful retrieval cues that can be used during recall. Over time, school-age children become more adept at drawing *inferences* about actors and actions—that is, adding information not in the story that helps make sense of it, as the statements just cited illustrate (Thompson & Myers, 1985). This increases the coherence of reconstructed information and, therefore, its memorableness.

Since inference making is vital for comprehending and recalling complex information, are there ways to facilitate it? Think back to our discussion of reciprocal teaching in Chapter 6. Discussions aimed at clarifying prose content and predicting what might happen next require pupils to make inferences—one reason this method has been so successful. Other strategies for recalling prose, such as identifying and summarizing main ideas, are not produced spontaneously until the high school years (Bjorklund & Douglas, 1997).

■ **ANOTHER VIEW OF RECONSTRUCTION: FUZZY-TRACE THEORY.** So far, we have emphasized deliberate reconstruction of meaningful material by using the long-term knowledge base to interpret it. According to C. J. Brainerd and Valerie Reyna's (1990, 1993) **fuzzy-trace theory,** when we first encode information, we reconstruct it automatically, creating a vague, fuzzy version called a **gist,** which preserves essential content without details and is especially useful for reasoning. At the same time, we retain a verbatim version for answering questions about specifics. For example, consider the following statement: "Farmer Brown owns many animals. He has 3 dogs, 5 sheep, 7 chickens, 9 horses, and 11 cows." Besides holding the precise numerical information in memory, you create a gist, such as "cows the most; dogs the least; horses, chickens, and sheep in the middle."

Fuzzy-trace theorists take issue with the assumption that all reconstructions are transformations of verbatim memory. Instead, they believe that both verbatim and gist memories are present from the outset and are stored separately so they can be used for different purposes. In support of this idea, shortly after being read a brief story, children can discriminate sentences they actually heard from ones they did not hear but that are consistent with the story's gist. Only over time, as the complete, verbatim memory decays more quickly than the efficiently represented gist, do children begin to say that statements consistent with but not in the story were ones they heard (Reyna & Kiernan, 1994). Fuzzy-trace theory also helps us understand why children (and adults) often reason effectively without recalling specifics. For example, when asked, "Which of Farmer Brown's animals are the most, cows or horses?" your gist memory yields the answer quickly and easily.

With age, children rely less on verbatim memory and more on fuzzy, reconstructed gists. In a recent study, researchers presented children with the description of Farmer Brown's barnyard and asked questions requiring only gist information (like the one just given) as well as questions requiring verbatim knowledge, such as "How many cows does Farmer Brown own, 11 or 9?" Preschoolers were better at answering verbatim- than gist-dependent questions, whereas the reverse was true for second graders (Brainerd & Gordon, 1994). Notice how relying on gist eases mental effort. Compared to a detailed statement, a fuzzy trace consumes less working memory, freeing attentional resources for the steps involved in thinking. Of course, for certain tasks, such as mental arithmetic, we need to have verbatim information. But in everyday life, the gist is often sufficient, and if

reconstruction A type of memory in which complex, meaningful material is reinterpreted in terms of existing knowledge.

fuzzy-trace theory A theory that proposes two types of encoding, one that automatically reconstructs information into a fuzzy version called a *gist,* which is especially useful for reasoning; and a second, verbatim version that is adapted for answering questions about specifics.

gist A fuzzy representation of information that preserves essential content without details, is less likely to be forgotten than a verbatim version, and requires less mental effort to use.

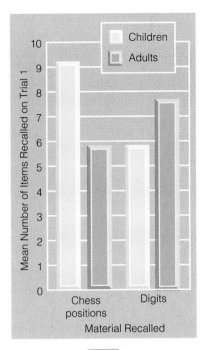

FIGURE 7.8

Performance of skilled child chess players and adults on two tasks: memory for complex chessboard arrangements and memory for numerical digits. The child chess experts recalled more on the chess task, the adults on the digit task. These findings show that size of the knowledge base contributes to memory performance. (Adapted from Chi, 1978.)

necessary, we can supplement it by referring to notes, lists, and other records (Reyna & Brainerd, 1992).

Fuzzy-trace theory adds to our understanding of reconstruction by pointing out that it can occur immediately, as soon as information is encoded, without distorting verbatim memories. The extent to which gist and verbatim representations undergo further reconstructive processing depends on the nature of the meaningful material, the type of task (telling an entire story versus answering a single question), and the passage of time. Fuzzy-trace research reveals that although memory is vital for reasoning, it is only loosely dependent on it. Getting bogged down in detail (as young children are prone to do) can interfere with effective cognitive processing. And since fuzzy traces are less likely than verbatim memories to be forgotten, gists may serve as enduring retrieval cues, contributing (along with strategy use) to improved recall with age (Brainerd & Reyna, 1995).

KNOWLEDGE AND MEMORY PERFORMANCE

At several points in our discussion, we suggested that children's expanding knowledge may promote improved memory. Many researchers believe that cognitive development is largely a matter of acquiring domain-specific knowledge—knowledge in a specific area that makes new, related information more meaningful so it is easier to store and retrieve (Schneider, 1993).

To test this idea, Michelene Chi (1978) looked at how well third- through eighth-grade chess experts could remember complex chessboard arrangements. The children recalled the configurations considerably better than did adults who knew how to play chess but were not especially knowledgeable. These findings cannot be explained by the selection of very bright youngsters with exceptional memories. On a task in which the same participants had to recall a list of numbers, the adults did better. The children showed superior memory only in the domain of knowledge in which they were expert (see Figure 7.8).

In Chi's study of chess-playing children, better memory was credited to a larger knowledge base. Experts also have more deeply and elaborately structured knowledge that permits them to retrieve items more adeptly. To illustrate this idea, Wolfgang Schneider and David Bjorklund (1992) classified elementary school children as experts or novices in knowledge of soccer. Then both groups were given lists of soccer and nonsoccer items to learn. As in Chi's study, experts remembered far more items on the soccer list (but not on the nonsoccer list) than did nonexperts. In observing how fourth graders studied soccer items, the researchers found that both groups used organizational strategies. But experts were more likely to apply these strategies during retrieval (as indicated by clustering of items during recall). And within each category searched, experts remembered more items.

Higher levels of organization at retrieval rather than storage suggests that very knowledgeable children apply strategies in their domain of expertise with little or no effort. Their recall has become *automatized,* through rapid associations of new items with the large number they already know. Consequently, experts can devote more working-memory resources to using easily recollected information to reason and solve problems. Several studies contrasting expert children (in soccer or baseball) with novices show much better memory for experts when lists of items are in their domain of expertise but little difference between the groups in use of strategies while learning the new information (Bjorklund & Douglas, 1997).

However, knowledge must be quite broad and well structured before it can facilitate memory. A brief series of lessons designed to increase knowledge in a particular area does not affect children's ability to recall information in that domain (DeMarie-Dreblow, 1991). Until children have enough knowledge and have time to connect it into stable, well-formed hierarchies, they may not be able to apply it to new memory problems.

Finally, knowledge is not the only factor involved in strategic memory processing. Children who are expert in a particular area, whether it be chess, math, social studies, or spelling, are usually highly motivated. Faced with new material, they say to themselves, "What can I do to clarify the meaning of this information so I can learn it more easily?" As a result, they not only acquire knowledge more quickly, but they actively use what they know to add more. In contrast, academically unsuccessful children fail to ask how previously stored information can clarify new material. This, in turn, interferes with the development of a broad knowledge base (Schneider, 1993). Consequently, knowledge acquisition and use of memory strategies are intimately related and support one another.

SCRIPTS: BASIC BUILDING BLOCKS OF STRUCTURED KNOWLEDGE

Think back to research on children's ability to categorize in Chapter 6. It shows that a structured long-term knowledge base begins to form in infancy. How do children build a coherent network of knowledge, and in what ways does it change with age?

As these dinosaur enthusiasts enlarge their knowledge about various species and connect it into stable, well-formed hierarchies, they will be able to commit dinosaur information to memory with little or no effort. Extensive, well-structured knowledge makes recall automatic, through rapid associations of new items with the large number already known. (Steven Rubin/The Image Works)

Our vast, intricately organized general knowledge system, which for purposes of clarity we now refer to as **semantic memory,** must grow out of the young child's **episodic memory,** or memory for many personally experienced events. How semantic memory emerges from a foundation of specific, real-world experiences is one of the most puzzling questions about memory development.

Like adults, preschoolers remember familiar events—what you do when you get up in the morning, go to day care, or get ready for bed—in terms of **scripts,** general representations of what occurs and when it occurs in a particular situation. For very young children, scripts begin as a structure of main acts. For example, when asked to tell what happens when you go to a restaurant, a 3-year-old might say, "You go in, get the food, eat, and then pay." Although children's first scripts contain only a few acts, as long as events in a situation take place in a logical order, they are almost always recalled in correct sequence (Fivush, Kuebli, & Clubb, 1992). This is true even for 1- and 2-year-olds, who cannot yet verbally describe events but who act them out with toys (Bauer, 1997). With age, children can form a script on the basis of fewer repetitions of an event. Their scripts also become more elaborate, as in the following restaurant account given by a 5-year-old child: "You go in. You can sit in the booths or at a table. Then you tell the waitress what you want. You eat. If you want dessert, you can have some. Then you pay and go home" (Farrar & Goodman, 1992; Hudson, Fivush, & Kuebli, 1992).

Scripts are a special form of reconstructive memory, providing yet another example of continuity in memory processing from early childhood to adulthood. When we experience repeated events, we fuse them into the same script representation. Then any specific instance of a scripted experience becomes hard to recall. For example, unless it was out of the ordinary, you probably cannot remember exactly what you had for dinner two days ago. The same is true for young children. By the second day of kindergarten, 5-year-olds have difficulty recalling specific events that occurred on the first day of class, although they can describe what happened in general terms (Fivush, 1984).

Once held in long-term memory, a script can be used to predict what will happen on similar occasions in the future. In this way, scripts serve as a basic means through which children (and adults) organize and interpret everyday experiences. For example, young children rely on scripts in make-believe play and when listening to and telling stories. They recall more events from stories that are based on familiar event sequences than on unfamiliar ones (Hudson & Nelson, 1983). Script structures also support children's earliest efforts at planning by helping them represent sequences of actions that lead to goals in familiar situations (Hudson, Sosa, & Shapiro, 1997).

Scripts may be the developmental link between early episodic memory and a semantically organized long-term memory store (Lucariello, 1998). In several studies, preschoolers remembered script-related items (such as peanut butter, bologna, cheese—foods often eaten at lunchtime) in clustered form and recalled them more easily than a typical categorical list (toast, cheese, ice cream—foods) (Lucariello, Kyratzis, & Nelson, 1992; Yu & Nelson, 1993). Once children develop an array of script sequences, objects that share the same function but occur in different scripts (eating toast for breakfast, peanut butter for lunch) are joined together in a single, more typical semantic category (food). Diverse

semantic memory The vast, intricately organized knowledge system in long-term memory.

episodic memory Memory for personally experienced events.

scripts General representations of what occurs and when it occurs in a particular situation. A basic means through which children organize and interpret familiar everyday experiences.

Children's memory for everyday experiences improves greatly during early childhood. This girl cannot remember the details of what she did on a particular day when she washed her hands at preschool. Instead, she recalls the event in script form—in terms of what typically occurs when you get ready for lunch. Her account will become more elaborate with age. Scripts help us predict what will happen on similar occasions in the future.

(Will Faller)

samples of children—African American, Caucasian American, and Korean—display this shift in basis of organization by the early school years.

AUTOBIOGRAPHICAL MEMORY

A special form of episodic memory is **autobiographical memory,** representations of one-time events that are long lasting and particularly meaningful in terms of the life story each of us creates about ourselves. For example, perhaps you recall the day a sibling was born, the first time you took an airplane, a hospitalization, or a move to a new house. Memory for autobiographical events begins in early childhood. Practically none of us can retrieve experiences that happened to us before age 3—a phenomenon called **infantile amnesia.** Between ages 3 and 6, autobiographical memory becomes clearer and more detailed (Pillemer & White, 1989). Why do we experience infantile amnesia, and how do autobiographical events differentiate from other episodic memories and stand out for a lifetime?

■ **THE MYSTERY OF INFANTILE AMNESIA.** Some researchers speculate that brain maturation brings an end to the period of infantile amnesia. Perhaps growth of the frontal lobes of the cortex along with other structures is necessary before experiences can be stored in ways that permit them to be retrieved many years later (Boyer & Diamond, 1992).

Several psychological accounts of infantile amnesia are consistent with this explanation. For example, one hypothesis is that two levels of memory exist, one that operates unconsciously and automatically, another that is conscious and intentional. Infants' memories may be largely of the first kind, children's and adults' memories of the second; but the second system cannot access events stored by the first. In support of this idea, 9- and 10-year-olds shown pictures of their preschool classmates react physiologically in ways consistent with remembering, even when they do not consciously recall the child (Newcombe & Fox, 1994). Another conjecture is that adults often use verbal means for storing information, whereas infants' processing is nonverbal—an incompatibility that may prevent us from retrieving our earliest experiences (Pillemer & White, 1989).

Yet the idea of vastly different approaches to remembering in younger and older individuals has been questioned. Turn back to our discussion of recall on pages 291–292, and you will see that 1½- to 4-year-olds can describe their memories verbally and sometimes recall events that happened to them as preverbal infants. A growing number of researchers believe that rather than a radical change in the way experience is represented, two other developmental milestones lead to the offset of infantile amnesia.

First, for episodic memories to become autobiographical, the child must have a well-developed image of the self. In Chapter 11, we will see that the "psychological self" has only begun to emerge by age 3. In the first few years of life, it is not yet mature enough to serve as an anchor for one-time events, which become more difficult to retrieve over time if they do not take on personal meaning (Howe & Courage, 1993, 1997). Second, an autobiographical memory requires that children organize personally relevant events in narrative form so they become part of a life story. Recent evidence indicates that children learn to structure memories as narratives during the preschool years by talking about them with others (Nelson, 1993).

■ **FORMING AN AUTOBIOGRAPHICAL NARRATIVE: TALKING ABOUT THE PAST.** As early as 1½ to 2 years, children begin to talk about the past, guided by adults who expand on their fragmented recollections. In these conversations, adults ask "who," "what," "when," "where," "how," and "why" questions and expand on children's responses. For example, here is a short excerpt of a mother talking with her nearly 3-year-old daughter about a recent Halloween celebration:

Child: Once on Halloween the kids was over and I had a princess dress on me.

Adult: You had a princess dress on? Did you get any candy? Did you go door to door? What happened?

Child: We went treating.

autobiographical memory Representations of special, one-time events that are long lasting because they are imbued with personal meaning.

infantile amnesia The inability of older children and adults to remember experiences that happened before age 3.

Adult: You went treating! And who took you?

Child: Andrea's mother took us. And my mom . . . and we brought a pumpkin too.

Adult: What did you do with the pumpkin?

Child: We lighted it.

Adult: What did it look like? Was it scary?

Child: Uh-huh. Dad made cuts in it with a razor. He made a face too. That was funny.

(Fivush & Hamond, 1990, p. 223)

As children participate in these dialogues, they gradually adopt the narrative thinking generated in them, in the same way that Vygotsky indicated higher cognitive processes emerge out of social interaction with more expert partners (see Chapter 6).

Research reveals that parents use two styles of eliciting autobiographical narratives from children. In the *elaborative style,* they ask many, varied questions; add information to children's statements; and volunteer their own recollections and evaluations of events—as the mother did in the conversation just given. In contrast, parents who use the *repetitive style* provide little information and ask the same short-answer questions over and over, as in, "Do you remember the zoo?" "What did we do at the zoo?" "What did we do there?" The elaborative style is considerably better at fostering narrative skill, since 2- and 3-year-olds who experience it produce more coherent and detailed personal stories when followed up 1 to 2 years later (McCabe & Peterson, 1991; Reese, Haden, & Fivush, 1993).

The complexity of parents' conversations about the past increases as their preschoolers' language skills become more sophisticated. Between 3 and 6 years, children's descriptions of special, one-time occurrences become better organized, elaborate, and evaluative (and therefore imbued with personal meaning). Older children also add more background information, placing events in the larger context of their lives (Fivush, Haden, & Adam, 1995; Haden, Haine, & Fivush, 1997).

Interestingly, girls are more advanced than boys in this sequence. And Western children produce narratives with more talk about thoughts, emotions, and preferences than do Asian children. These differences fit with variations in parent–child conversations. Talk about the past is more elaborative and evaluative with daughters (Reese, Haden, & Fivush, 1996). And collectivist cultural values lead Asian parents to discourage children from engaging in excessive talk about themselves (Han, Leichtman, & Wang, 1998). Perhaps because their early experiences were integrated into more coherent narratives, women report an earlier age of first memory and more vivid early memories than do men. Similarly, the earliest memories of Caucasian-American adults are, on the average, 6 months earlier than those of Asians (Mullen, 1994).

In sum, as children share and retain memories in socially and personally meaningful ways, autobiographical memory appears and expands in early childhood. As a result, children enter into the history of their family and community (Fivush, 1995). Children's narrative skill is important for other cognitive and social advances. For example, it helps them make the transition from oral to written language. And it provides a means of telling others about events in an organized way, fostering gratifying social interaction (McCabe, 1997).

The accuracy and completeness of children's autobiographical memories have recently taken on special applied significance. Increasingly, children are being called on to testify in court cases in which their recollections play a critical role in legal decisions affecting their own welfare. How reliable are children's memories under these conditions? See the Social Issues box on pages 298–299 for a discussion of this topic.

Parents who talk about the past help their children build an autobiographical narrative of personally meaningful experiences. As this boy discusses photos in the family album with his father, he recalls significant events and integrates them into his life story.
(Jeff Greenberg/The Picture Cube)

Children's Eyewitness Memory

RENATA, A PHYSICALLY abused and neglected 8-year-old, was taken from her parents and placed in foster care. There, she was seen engaging in sexually aggressive behavior toward other children, including grabbing their sex organs and using obscene language. Renata's foster mother suspected that sexual abuse had taken place in her natural home. She informed the child protective service worker, who met with Renata to gather information. But Renata seemed anxious and uncomfortable. She did not want to answer any questions.

Increasingly, children are being called on to testify in court cases involving child abuse and neglect, child custody, and other matters. Having to provide such information can be difficult and traumatic. Almost always, children must report on events that were highly stressful. In doing so, they may have to speak against a parent or other relative to whom they feel a strong sense of loyalty. In some family disputes, they may fear punishment for telling the truth. In addition, child witnesses are faced with a strange and unfamiliar situation—at the very least, an interview in the judge's chambers, and at most, an open courtroom with judge, jury, spectators, and the possibility of unsympathetic cross-examination. Not surprisingly, there is considerable debate about the accuracy of children's recall under these conditions.

AGE DIFFERENCES. Until recently, it was rare for children under age 5 to be asked to testify, whereas those age 6 and older often did so. Children between ages 10 and 14 have historically been assumed competent to testify. Yet, as a result of societal reactions to rising rates of child abuse and difficulties in prosecuting perpetrators (see Chapter 14), legal requirements for child testimony have been relaxed in Canada and the United States. In recent years, children as

Will this 6-year-old boy recount events accurately and completely on the witness stand? The answer to this question depends on many factors—his cognitive maturity, the way he is questioned, how long ago the events occurred, whether adults in his life have tried to influence his response, how the doll is used to prompt his recall, and his understanding of the courtroom process.
(Stacy Pick/Stock Boston)

young as age 3 have frequently served as witnesses (Ceci & Bruck, 1998).

Compared to preschoolers, school-age children are better able to give detailed descriptions of past experiences and make accurate inferences about others' motives and intentions. Older children are also more resistant to misleading questions of the sort asked by attorneys when they probe for more information or, in cross-examination, try to influence the content of the child's response (Ceci & Bruck,

---

ASK YOURSELF . . .

◆ Given a list of baseball players' names to learn, Tyrone, a baseball expert, recalled many more than did Hal, who knows little about baseball, even though both boys used an organizational strategy in learning the items. Explain Tyrone's superior memory.

◆ What characteristics of the parent–child conversation about the past on pages 296–297 are likely to promote the development of autobiographical memory? Explain.

◆ CONNECTIONS
Review the development of deferred imitation on page 230 of Chapter 6. What does it tell us about gains in recall memory during the first 2 years?

BRIEF REVIEW

During infancy, retrieval changes from recognition of previously experienced stimuli to include recall in the presence of salient retrieval cues. Recall improves steadily in childhood and adolescence as knowledge increases and memory strategies are applied more effectively. Children, like adults, often recall complex, meaningful information in reconstructed form. Gains in reconstructive processing occur as the ability to draw inferences expands, a change that permits children to better understand and recall prose material. In addition, reconstruction often occurs at encoding, in the form of fuzzy traces called gists. With age, children rely less on verbatim memory and more on gist, which contributes to improved reasoning and recall with age.

Growth in size and structure of the knowledge base has a major impact on memory performance. Like adults, young children remember everyday experiences in terms of scripts—general representations that become more elaborate with age. Scripts may serve as the developmental link between episodic memory and our semantically organized, general knowledge system. As preschoolers' self-image and language skills develop, they form a personal narrative by talking about the past with adults. As a result, infantile amnesia gives way to autobiographical memory.

1993; Goodman & Tobey, 1994). Nevertheless, when properly questioned, even 3-year-olds can recall recent events accurately—including ones that were highly stressful (Baker-Ward et al., 1993; Goodman et al., 1991).

SUGGESTIBILITY. Yet court testimony often involves repeated interviews. When adults lead children by suggesting incorrect facts ("He touched you there, didn't he?"), they increase the likelihood of incorrect reporting, especially among preschoolers. Yet even school-age children, whose descriptions are usually elaborate and dependable, can succumb to suggestion. Falsely reported events in response to leading questions can be quite fantastic. In one study, after a visit to a doctor's office, children said yes to questions about events that not only never occurred but that connoted abuse—"Did the doctor lick your knee?" "Did the nurse sit on top of you?" (Ornstein et al., 1997).

By the time children come to court, it is weeks, months, or even years after the occurrence of the target events. When a long delay is combined with suggestions about what happened and stereotyping of the accused ("He's in jail because he's been bad"), children can easily be misled into giving false information (Ceci, Leichtman, & Bruck, 1994; Leichtman & Ceci, 1995). A frightening legal setting further compromises children's ability to report past events completely and accurately (Saywitz & Nathanson, 1993).

To ease the task of providing testimony, special interviewing methods have been devised for children. In many child sexual abuse cases, anatomically correct dolls are used to prompt children's recall. However, serious concerns have been raised about this method, since it can encourage reports of physical and sexual contact that did not happen (Ceci & Bruck, 1998). For example, several studies assessed 3- and 4-year-olds' recall of a just-completed medical exam in which half the participants had received a genital exam (Bruck et al., 1995). When given an anatomically correct doll and asked to show how the doctor had touched them, many children engaged in inaccurate touching of the doll's genitals—even some who had not had a genital exam! When anatomical dolls are combined with repeated interviewing, false reporting increases further (Steward & Steward, 1996).

INTERVENTIONS. Child witnesses need to be prepared so that they understand the courtroom process and know what to expect. Before age 8, children have little grasp of the differing roles of judge, attorney, and police officer. Many regard the court negatively, as "a room you pass through on your way to jail" (Saywitz, 1989, p. 149). In some places, "court schools" exist, in which children are taken through the setting and given an opportunity to role-play court activities. As part of this process, children can be encouraged to admit not knowing an answer rather than guessing or going along with what an adult expects of them. At the same time, legal professionals need to take steps to lessen the risk of suggestibility—by limiting the number of times children are interviewed; asking questions in open-ended, nonleading ways; and being warm and patient (Ceci & Bruck, 1993).

If a child is likely to experience emotional trauma or later punishment (in a family dispute), then courtroom procedures can be adapted to protect them. For example, Renata eventually testified over closed-circuit TV so she would not have to face her abusive father. When it is not wise for a child to participate directly, expert witnesses can provide testimony that reports on the child's psychological condition and includes important elements of the child's story. But for such testimony to be worthwhile, witnesses must be impartial and carefully trained in how to question children in ways that minimize false reporting (Bruck, Ceci, & Hembrooke, 1998).

Metacognition

Throughout this chapter, we have mentioned many ways in which cognitive processing becomes more reflective and deliberate with age. These trends suggest that another form of knowledge may influence how well children remember and solve problems. The term **metacognition** refers to awareness and understanding of various aspects of thought.

During early and middle childhood, metacognition expands greatly. A wealth of research suggests that children construct a naive **theory of mind,** a coherent understanding of people as mental beings, which they revise as they encounter new evidence (Gopnik & Wellman, 1994). Most investigations into theory of mind have addressed children's ability to be "mind readers"—to appreciate their own and other people's perceptions, thoughts, and feelings. We will take up this aspect when we consider emotional and social understanding in Chapters 10 and 11. A second facet of metacognitive research concerns children's knowledge of mental activity, or *what it means to think.* To work most effectively, the information-processing system must be aware of itself. It must arrive at such realizations as "I'd better write that phone number down or I'll

metacognition Awareness and understanding of various aspects of thought.

theory of mind A coherent understanding of people as mental beings, which children revise as they encounter new evidence. Includes knowledge of mental activity and awareness that people can have different perceptions, thoughts, and feelings about the same event.

forget it" and "This paragraph is complicated; I'll have to read it again to grasp the author's point."

For metacognitive knowledge to be helpful, children must apply it on a moment-by-moment basis. They must monitor what they do, calling on what they know about thinking to overcome difficulties. In the following sections, we consider these higher-level, "executive" aspects of information processing.

METACOGNITIVE KNOWLEDGE

With age, knowledge of mental activities expands in three ways. Children become increasingly conscious of cognitive capacities, strategies for processing information, and task variables that facilitate or impede performance.

■ **KNOWLEDGE OF COGNITIVE CAPACITIES.** Listen closely to the conversations of young children, and you will find evidence that awareness of mental activity emerges remarkably early. Such words as "think," "remember," and "pretend" are among the first verbs in children's vocabularies. After age 2½, they use these words appropriately to refer to internal states, as when they say, "I thought the socks were in the drawer, 'cept they weren't" (Wellman, 1990). By age 3, children distinguish thinking from other activities. They realize that it takes place inside their heads and that a person can think about something without seeing it, talking about it, or touching it (Flavell, Green, & Flavell, 1995; Woolley & Wellman, 1992).

But when questioned further, preschoolers' view of the workings of the mind appears limited. Without strong situational cues (a challenging task and a thoughtful expression), 3- and 4-year-olds deny that a person is thinking. They indicate that the minds of people waiting, looking at pictures, listening to stories, or reading books, are "empty of thoughts and ideas" (see Figure 7.9). They do not realize that people are constantly talking to themselves and engaged in thought, even when there are no stimuli to perceive and no problems to solve (Flavell, Green, & Flavell, 1993, 1995; Flavell et al., 1997).

Furthermore, preschoolers pay little attention to the *process* of thinking but, instead, focus on outcomes of thought. For example, 3-year-olds use the word *know* to refer to acting successfully (finding a hidden toy) and the word *forget* to refer to acting unsuccessfully (not finding the toy), even when a person is guessing at the toy's location (Lyon & Flavell, 1994; Perner, 1991). And children younger than age 6 have trouble recalling what they were thinking just moments before. In one study, right after being taught a new fact, 4- and 5-year-olds claimed they had known it for a long time (Taylor, Esbensen, & Bennett, 1994). Finally, preschoolers believe that all events must be observed directly to be known. They do not understand that *mental inferences* can be a source of knowledge (Carpendale & Chandler, 1996).

Even though their grasp of mental activities is incomplete, young children realize that the mind is a limited-capacity device, and both internal and external factors affect its functioning. Three- and 4-year-olds know that noise, lack of interest, and thinking about other things can interfere with attention to a task (Miller & Zalenski, 1982). And by age 5, most children understand that information briefly presented or that must be retained for a long time is more likely to be forgotten (Kreutzer, Leonard, & Flavell, 1975).

Nevertheless, school-age children have a more complete grasp of the impact of psychological factors on performance. For example, they recognize that doing well on a task depends on focusing attention—concentrating, wanting to do it, and not being tempted by anything else (Miller & Bigi, 1979). They also distinguish mental activities on the basis of the certainty of their knowledge. They realize that if you "remember," "know," or "understand," then you are more certain than if you "guessed," "estimated," or "compared" (Schwanenflugel, Fabricius, & Noyes, 1996).

How, then, should we describe the difference between the young child's understanding of cognitive capacities and that of the older

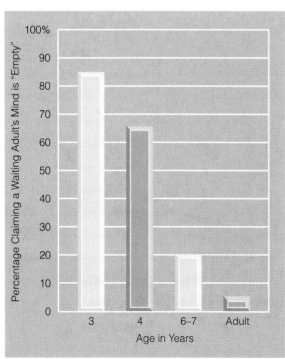

FIGURE **7.9**

Age-related changes in awareness of an active mind. As an adult sat waiting in a chair, an experimenter asked 3-, 4-, and 6- to 7-year-olds, as well as adults, "How about her mind right now? Is she having some thoughts and ideas, or is her mind empty of thoughts and ideas?" Many more preschoolers than school-age children claimed that the adult's mind was "empty." (Adapted from Flavell, Green, & Flavell, 1993.)

child? Preschoolers know that we have an internal mental life, but they seem to view the mind as a passive container of information. Before age 4 or 5, they believe that physical experience determines mental experience. Consequently, they greatly underestimate the amount of mental activity that goes on in people and are poor at inferring what people know or are thinking about. In view of their limited awareness of how knowledge is acquired, it is not surprising that preschoolers rarely engage in planning or use memory strategies. In contrast, older children regard the mind as an active, constructive agent, capable of selecting and transforming information (Chandler & Carpendale, 1998; Pillow, 1995). Look again at the findings we have discussed, and note how they illustrate this change.

What promotes this more reflective, process-oriented view of the mind? Perhaps children become aware of mental activities through quiet-time observation of their own thinking and through exposure to talk about the mind in active terms, as when they hear people say, "I was thinking a lot" or "My mind wandered" (Wellman & Hickling, 1994). Formal schooling probably contributes as well. Instructing children to keep their minds on what they are doing and remember mental steps calls attention to the workings of the mind. And as children read, write, and solve math problems, they often use private speech, at first speaking aloud and later silently, inside their heads. As they "hear themselves think," they may detect many aspects of mental life (Astington, 1995; Flavell, Green, & Flavell, 1995).

School-age children show improved metacognitive knowledge. This child is aware that writing down a phone message is a very effective strategy for overcoming the limits of memory capacity.
(Will Faller)

■ **KNOWLEDGE OF STRATEGIES AND TASK VARIABLES.** Consistent with their more active view of the mind, school-age children are far more conscious of strategies for processing information than are preschoolers. For example, they know quite a bit about effective memory techniques. When shown video clips depicting two children using different recall strategies and asked which one is likely to produce better memory, kindergarten and young elementary school children recognize gross differences in strategy effectiveness—that rehearsing or categorizing is better than looking or naming. Older children are aware of more subtle differences—that categorizing is better than rehearsing (Justice, 1986; Schneider, 1986). By third grade, children realize that in studying material for later recall, it is helpful to devote the most effort to items you know least well (Kreutzer, Leonard, & Flavell, 1975).

Older children also have a more complete understanding of task variables that affect performance. Kindergartners are aware of a few factors that make a memory task easy or hard—the number of items, their familiarity, how much study time is available, and whether they must recognize or recall them (Speer & Flavell, 1979). But by the mid-elementary school years, children know much more—for example, that a list of semantically related items is easier to remember than unrelated items and that recalling prose material word for word is more difficult than paraphrasing it (Kreutzer, Leonard, & Flavell, 1975).

Once children become conscious of the many factors that influence mental activity, they combine them into an integrated understanding. At the end of middle childhood, children take account of interactions between variables—how age and motivation of the learner, effective use of strategies, and nature and difficulty of the task work together to affect cognitive performance (Wellman, 1990). In this way, metacognition truly becomes a comprehensive theory.

COGNITIVE SELF-REGULATION

Although knowledge of mental activity expands, many studies report that it is only modestly related to task performance (Pressley, 1995b). This suggests that school-age children have difficulty with the second aspect of metacognition mentioned earlier: putting what they know into action. They are not yet good at **cognitive self-regulation,** the process of continuously monitoring progress toward a goal, checking outcomes, and redirecting unsuccessful efforts.

One way cognitive self-regulation can be assessed is by looking at the impact of children's awareness of memory strategies on their recall, a relationship that grows stronger over the elementary school years. Younger school-age children implement their memory-strategy knowledge only on simple, familiar memory tasks. Older children, in contrast, are better able to apply it on tasks that are complex and new to them (Hasselhorn, 1992;

cognitive self-regulation The process of continuously monitoring progress toward a goal, checking outcomes, and redirecting unsuccessful efforts.

This boy's cognitive self-regulatory capacities are evident as he practices the piano. When he makes a mistake, does he ignore it, or does he isolate that passage for further study and practice? The boy's parents and piano teacher can foster his self-regulatory skills by pointing out the special demands of the piece he is learning, showing him how to use strategies to master it, and encouraging him to monitor his progress.

(Elizabeth Crews)

Schneider & Pressley, 1997). Furthermore, children who can explain why a memory strategy works seem to use it more effectively, since they show better recall (Justice et al., 1997).

The difficulties children experience in engaging in self-regulation on complex tasks are evident in their *comprehension monitoring*—sensitivity to how well they understand a spoken or written message. In one study, fourth and sixth graders listened to short essays containing missing or inconsistent information, as in the following passage:

> Janet decided to play some CDs. She looked through all the songs and picked out her favorite. It was a song called "As Time Goes By." She said to herself, "I haven't played this one in a long time." She played it quietly so she would not disturb her family. She was out of practice so it sounded funny sometimes. Janet sang along with the music. She knew some of the words and she hummed the rest. The last verse of the song was the part she liked the best. After that song was finished she played another CD. (Beal, 1990, p. 249)

Sixth graders detected more text problems than did fourth graders. In fact, many school-age children also fail to notice gaps and contradictions in prose that they produce themselves—a major reason they rarely revise their writing (Fitzgerald, 1987).

Current evidence indicates that cognitive self-regulation develops slowly. This is not surprising, since monitoring learning outcomes is a cognitively demanding activity, requiring constant evaluation of effort and progress. By the time young people reach secondary school, self-regulation is a strong predictor of academic success (Joyner & Kurtz-Costes, 1997). Students who do well know when they possess a skill and when they do not. If they run up against obstacles, such as poor study conditions, a confusing text passage, or an unclear class lecture, they take steps to organize the learning environment, review the material, or seek other sources of support. This active, purposeful approach contrasts sharply with the passive orientation of students who do poorly (Zimmerman & Risemberg, 1997).

Parents and teachers can foster children's self-regulatory skills by pointing out the special demands of tasks, encouraging the use of strategies, and emphasizing the value of self-correction. As adults ask children questions and help them monitor their own behavior in circumstances where they are likely to encounter difficulties, children internalize these procedures (Pressley, 1995a).

Think about these practical suggestions for fostering self-regulation. Do they resemble Vygotsky's theory of the social origins of higher cognitive processes? In fact, Vygotsky's theory has been a source of inspiration for *metacognitive training*. Many studies show that providing children with instructions to check and monitor their progress toward a goal has a substantial impact on their learning. In addition, training that goes beyond demonstrating a strategy to emphasizing why it is effective enhances children's use of it in similar situations (Pressley & El-Dinary, 1993; Schunk & Zimmerman, 1994). When adults tell children why and not just what to do, they provide a rationale for future action. Then children learn not only how to get a particular task done but what to do when faced with new problems.

As we turn now to development within academic skill areas, notice how the importance of cognitive self-regulation is ever-present. But before we consider these domains of learning, you may find to helpful to review the Milestones table on the following page, which summarizes the diverse changes in information processing we have considered.

ASK YOURSELF . . .

◆ *"Mom, let's go!" pleaded 4-year-old Tom, waiting for his mother to take him to the park. "Tom, just a minute. I'm thinking about where I put my keys." Tom responded, "You can't think about keys that way. You're just standing there." What does Tom's statement reveal about his metacognitive knowledge?*

◆ CONNECTIONS
Self-regulation develops in other domains besides cognition. For example, children must learn how to regulate their emotions. Why is emotional self-regulation important? (See Chapter 10, pages 404–406).

BRIEF REVIEW

Children's metacognitive knowledge changes from a passive to an active, constructive view of mental functioning as awareness of cognitive capacities, strategies, and task variables expands. Cognitive self-regulation improves slowly during childhood and adolescence; with age, children are more likely to apply their metacognitive understanding to more complex tasks. Teaching children self-regulatory skills can have broad effects on their learning.

Development of General Information Processing

Age	Basic Capacities	Strategies	Knowledge	Metacognition
2–5 years	■ Organization of the mental system into sensory register, working memory, and long-term memory is adultlike. ■ Many basic processing skills are evident, including attention, recognition, recall, and reconstruction. ■ Overall capacity, or size, of the system increases.	■ Attention becomes more focused and sustained. ■ Beginnings of memory strategies are present, but they are seldom used spontaneously and have little impact on performance. ■ Variability and adaptive selection among problem-solving strategies is evident.	■ Knowledge expands and takes on adultlike organization. ■ Familiar events are remembered in terms of scripts, which become more elaborate. ■ Autobiographical memory emerges and becomes more detailed.	■ Differentiation of thinking from other activities occurs. ■ Awareness of a limited-capacity mental system is present, but preschoolers view the mind as a passive container of information.
6–10 years	■ Overall capacity, or size, of the system continues to increase.	■ Attention becomes more selective, adaptable, and planful. ■ Cognitive inhibition improves markedly. ■ Memory strategies of rehearsal and semantic organization are used spontaneously and more effectively. ■ Ability to apply multiple strategies increases. ■ Ability to draw inferences in reconstructive processing improves. ■ Reliance on fuzzy, reconstructed gists for reasoning increases.	■ Knowledge continues to expand and become better organized, which facilitates retrieval.	■ View of the mind as an active, constructive agent develops. ■ Knowledge of different types of cognitive processes and the impact of psychological factors on performance increases. ■ Knowledge of the impact of task variables on performance increases and is integrated with psychological factors. ■ Cognitive self-regulation improves gradually.
11 years–adulthood	■ Overall capacity, or size, of the system continues to increase, but at a slower pace than in childhood.	■ Memory strategy of elaboration appears and improves.	■ Knowledge expands further and becomes more intricately organized.	■ Metacognitive knowledge and cognitive self-regulation continue to improve.

Applications of Information Processing to Academic Learning

ver the past 2 decades, interest in information processing has been extended to children's mastery of academic skills in different subject-matter areas. Because paths to competence vary across knowledge domains, each area has been studied separately. Nevertheless, the research has features in common. First, investigators identify the cognitive capacities and strategies necessary for skilled performance, try to trace their development, and pinpoint the ways in which good and poor learners differ. Then, using this information, they design and test instructional procedures to improve children's learning. In the following sections, we discuss a sampling of these efforts in reading, mathematics, and scientific reasoning.

READING

While reading, we use a large number of skills at once, taxing all aspects of our information-processing systems. We must perceive single letters and letter combinations, translate them into speech sounds, learn to recognize the visual appearance of many common words, hold chunks of text in working memory while interpreting their meaning, and combine the meanings of various parts of a text passage into an understandable whole. In fact, reading is so demanding that most or all of these skills must be done automatically. If one or more are poorly developed, they will compete for space in our limited working memories, and reading performance will decline (Perfetti, 1988). Becoming a proficient reader is a complex process that begins in the preschool years.

■ **EARLY CHILDHOOD.** Preschoolers understand a great deal about written language long before they begin to read and write in conventional ways. This is not surprising when we consider that children in industrialized nations live in a world filled with written symbols. Each day, they observe and participate in activities involving storybooks, calendars, greeting cards, lists, and signs, to name just a few. As part of these experiences, children try to figure out how written symbols convey meaning. Their active efforts to construct literacy knowledge through informal experiences are called **emergent literacy.**

Young preschoolers search for units of written language as they "read" memorized versions of stories and recognize familiar signs, such as "PIZZA" at their favorite fast food counter. But their early ideas about how written language is related to meaning are quite different from our own. For example, many preschoolers think that a single letter stands for a whole word or that each letter in a person's signature represents a separate name (Sulzby, 1985). Gradually, children revise these ideas as their perceptual and cognitive capacities improve, as they encounter writing in many different contexts, and as adults help them with various aspects of written communication.

Soon, preschoolers become aware of some general characteristics of written language. As a result, their own writing takes on features of real print, as in the "story" and "grocery list" written by a 4-year-old in Figure 7.10. Eventually children figure out that letters are parts of words and are linked to sounds in systematic ways. You can see this in the invented spellings that are typical between ages 5 and 7. At first, children rely heavily on the names

FIGURE 7.10

A story (a) and a grocery list (b) written by a 4-year-old child. This child's writing has many features of real print. It also reveals an awareness of different kinds of written expression.

(From L. M. McGee & D. J. Richgels, 1996, *Literacy's Beginnings* [2nd ed.], Boston: Allyn and Bacon, p. 81. Reprinted by permission.)

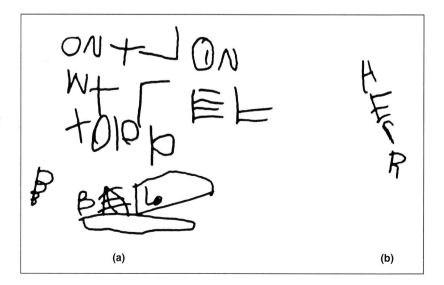

(a)   (b)

of letters: "ADE LAFWTS KRMD NTU A LAVATR" ("eighty elephants crammed into a[n] elevator"). Over time, they switch to conventional spelling (McGee & Richgels, 1996).

Literacy development builds on a broad foundation of spoken language and general knowledge about the world. The more literacy-related experiences young children have in their everyday lives, the better prepared they are to tackle the complex tasks involved in becoming skilled readers. Storybook reading, in which caregivers engage preschoolers in dialogues about books, and adult-supported writing activities focusing on connected discourse are related to reading readiness scores and literacy progress after school entry (Crain-Thoreson & Dale, 1992; Purcell-Gates, 1996).

In this first-grade whole-language classroom, children acquire a sight vocabulary and learn to read through exposure to whole, meaningful text. Research indicates that kindergartners just starting to read benefit from an emphasis on whole language. In the early grades, combining the whole-language and basic-skills approaches seems most effective. (Will Hart)

■ **MIDDLE CHILDHOOD.** Look again at the literacy developments of early childhood. Do they remind you of Siegler's *strategy-choice model*? Children seem to experiment with and choose adaptively among strategies in learning to decode written symbols. In support of this idea, Siegler (1988, 1996) found that each time children encounter a combination of letters they cannot yet read, they resort to diverse strategies, such as sounding out the word, looking up the spelling of a possible word in the dictionary, or asking for help. With practice, the appearance of each word becomes more strongly associated with its meaning in long-term memory. When this happens, children gradually give up capacity-consuming strategies in favor of automatic retrieval.

Currently, psychologists and educators are engaged in a "great debate" about how to teach beginning reading. On one side are those who take a **whole-language approach** to reading instruction. They argue that reading should be taught in a way that parallels natural language learning. From the very beginning, children should be exposed to text in its complete form—stories, poems, letters, posters, and lists—so they can appreciate the communicative function of written language. According to these experts, as long as reading is kept whole and meaningful, children will be motivated to discover the specific skills they need as they gain experience with the printed word (Watson, 1989). On the other side of the debate are those who advocate a **basic-skills approach.** According to this view, children should be given simplified text materials. At first, they should be coached on *phonics*—the basic rules for translating written symbols into sounds. Only later, after they have mastered these skills, should they get complex reading material (Rayner & Pollatsek, 1989).

As yet, research does not show clear-cut superiority for either of these approaches (Stahl, McKenna, & Pagnucco, 1994). In fact, a third group of experts believes that children learn best when they receive a balanced mixture of both (Pressley, 1994; Stahl, 1992). Kindergartners benefit from an emphasis on whole language, with gradual introduction of phonics as reading skills improve (Sacks & Mergendoller, 1997). In the early grades, balancing the two methods seems most effective. In one study, 7-year-old poor readers showed greater reading gains when assigned to a "phonics/meaningful reading" intervention than to either a "phonics alone" or a "reading alone" teaching condition (Hatcher, Hulme, & Ellis, 1994).

Why might combining phonics with whole language work best? Learning the basics—relations between letters and sounds—enables children to decode words they have never seen before. As this process becomes more automatic, it releases children's attention to the higher-level activities involved in comprehending the text's meaning (Adams, Treiman, & Pressley, 1998). Yet if practice in basic skills is overemphasized, children may lose sight of the goal of reading: understanding. Many teachers report cases of pupils who can read aloud fluently but who comprehend very little. These children might have been spared serious reading problems if they had received meaning-based instruction with attention to basic skills.

Around age 7 to 8, a major shift occurs from "learning to read" to "reading to learn" (Ely, 1997). As decoding and comprehension skills reach a high level of efficiency, adolescent readers can become actively engaged with the text. They adjust the way they read to fit their current purpose—at times seeking new facts and ideas, at other times questioning, agreeing, or disagreeing with the writer's viewpoint.

emergent literacy Young children's active efforts to construct literacy knowledge through informal experiences.

whole-language approach An approach to beginning reading instruction that parallels children's natural language learning and keeps reading materials whole and meaningful.

basic-skills approach An approach to beginning reading instruction that emphasizes training in phonics—the basic rules for translating written symbols into sounds—and simplified reading materials.

MATHEMATICS

Mathematical reasoning, like reading, builds on informal knowledge. Habituation–dishabituation research shows that newborn babies are sensitive to differences in the sizes of small sets—for example, two versus three items (Antell & Keating, 1983). By 5 months, infants can keep track of the number of items, up to three, that a hand hides behind a screen; they dishabituate to quantities inconsistent with the hand's behavior (Wynn, 1992). Twelve- to 18-month-olds display a beginning grasp of **ordinality,** or order relationships between quantities, such as three is more than two and two is more than one (Strauss & Curtis, 1984). These remarkably early numerical sensitivities serve as the basis for more complex understandings.

■ **EARLY CHILDHOOD.** In the early preschool years, children start to attach verbal labels (such as *lots, little, big,* and *small*) to different amounts and sizes. And between ages 2 and 3, many begin to count. However, at first counting is little more than a memorized routine. Often numbers are recited in an unbroken string like this: "Onetwothreefourfivesix!" Or children repeat a few number words while vaguely pointing toward objects they have seen others count (Fuson, 1992).

Very soon, however, counting strategies become more precise. Most 3- to 4-year-olds have established an accurate one-to-one correspondence between a short sequence of number words and the items they represent (Gallistel & Gelman, 1992; Geary, 1994). Sometime between ages 4 and 5, they grasp the vital principle of **cardinality.** They understand that the last word in a counting sequence indicates the quantity of items in a set (Bermejo, 1996). They also know that if two groups of objects match up (for example, every jar has its own spoon or every doll its own cup), then each set contains the same number of items (Sophian, 1988).

Mastery of cardinality quickly increases the efficiency of children's counting. By age 4, children use counting to solve arithmetic problems. At first, their strategies are tied to the order of numbers as presented; when given 2 + 4, they "count on" from 2 (Ginsburg, Klein, & Starkey, 1998). Soon they begin to experiment with various strategies (refer back to our discussion of Siegler's model of strategy choice, page 283, for examples) in both addition and subtraction. As a result, the "min" strategy, a more efficient approach, appears in their repertoire of procedures.

Cross-cultural evidence suggests that the basic arithmetic knowledge just described emerges universally around the world, although ways of representing number vary. For example, among the Oksapmin, an agricultural society of Papua New Guinea, counting is mapped onto 27 body parts, which serve as number terms. To count as Oksapmins do, start with the thumb on one hand and move around the upper body, ending on the little finger of the opposite hand (see Figure 7.11). Using this system, Oksapmin children keep track of quantities, measure, and play number games. When they start school, they can be seen pointing to body parts instead of counting on fingers, creating complex calculation procedures that tailor their already existing skills to new problems (Saxe, 1985).

Depending on the extent to which informal counting experiences are available in children's everyday lives, children may acquire early number understandings at different rates. In homes and preschools where adults provide many occasions and requests for quantification, children construct these basic concepts sooner (Geary, 1994). Then they are solidly available as supports for the wide variety of mathematical skills that are taught in school.

■ **MIDDLE CHILDHOOD.** Mathematics instruction builds on yet greatly enriches children's informally acquired knowledge. Written notation systems and formal computational techniques enhance children's ability to represent number and compute. Over the early elementary school years, children acquire basic math facts through a combination of frequent drill and reasoning about number concepts. (Return to page 282 for research supporting the importance of both extended practice and a grasp of concepts.) Eventually children retrieve answers automatically and apply this knowledge to more complex problems.

Counting on fingers is an early, spontaneous approach that children use to experiment with strategies for solving basic math facts. As they try out various routes to solution and select those that are efficient and accurate, answers become more strongly associated with problems. Soon children give up counting on fingers in favor of retrieving the right answer.

(Myrleen Ferguson Cate/PhotoEdit)

ordinality A principle specifying order (more-than and less-than) relationships among quantities.

cardinality A principle specifying that the last number in a counting sequence indicates the quantity of items in the set.

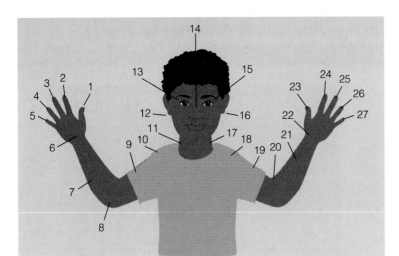

FIGURE 7.11

Sequence of body parts used for counting by the Oksapmin of Papua New Guinea. In the Oksapmin language, there are no terms for numbers aside from the body part names themselves (for example, "nose" represents "fourteen"). Children begin to use this system in the preschool years. Instead of counting on fingers, they can often be seen pointing to body parts. With age, they adapt the technique to handle more complex computation.

(From G. B. Saxe, 1985, "Effects of schooling on arithmetical understandings: Studies with Oksapmin children in Papua New Guinea," *Journal of Educational Psychology, 77,* p. 505. Copyright © 1985 by the American Psychological Association. Reprinted by permission of the publisher and author.)

Arguments about how to teach mathematics resemble the positions discussed earlier in the area of reading. Extensive speeded practice to promote automatic retrieval is pitted against "number sense," or understanding. Yet once again, a blend of these two approaches is most beneficial. In learning basic math facts, poorly performing pupils move too quickly toward trying to retrieve answers automatically. Their responses are often wrong because they have not used strategies long enough to build strong associations between problems and correct solutions (Siegler, 1988). And when asked to explain math concepts, their performance is weak (Canobi, Reeve, & Pattison, 1998). This suggests that encouraging pupils to apply strategies and making sure they understand why certain strategies work well are vital for solid mastery of basic math.

A similar picture emerges when we look at more complex skills, such as carrying in addition, borrowing in subtraction, and operating with decimals and fractions. Children's mistakes indicate that they draw on their experience with easier problems and invent strategies, which do not always work. Or they try to use a procedure they have been taught but do not understand the basis for it. For example, look at the following subtraction errors:

$$
\begin{array}{r}
427 \\
-138 \\
\hline
311
\end{array}
\qquad
\begin{array}{r}
^{6}\!\!\not{7}00^{1}2 \\
5445 \\
\hline
1447
\end{array}
$$

In the first problem, the child consistently subtracts a smaller from a larger digit, regardless of which is on top. In the second, columns with zeros are repeatedly skipped in a borrowing operation, and whenever there is a zero on top, the bottom digit is written as the answer. Researchers believe that an overemphasis on drill-oriented math that discourages children from using their naturally acquired counting strategies to grasp new skills underlies these difficulties (Fuson, 1990; Resnick, 1989).

Cross-cultural evidence suggests that American math instruction may have gone too far in emphasizing computational drill over numerical understanding. As we will see in greater detail in Chapter 15, children in Asian nations are ahead of American pupils in mathematical development at all levels of schooling. As the Cultural Influences box on page 308 illustrates, Asian children receive a variety of supports for acquiring mathematical knowledge that are not available to American children. The result is deeper processing—the formation of secure numerical concepts that provide a firm foundation for mastery of new skills.

SCIENTIFIC REASONING

During a free moment in physical education class, 13-year-old Heidi wondered why more of her tennis serves and returns seemed to pass the net and drop in her opponent's court when she used a particular brand of balls. "Maybe it's something about their color or size? Hmm, possibly it's their surface texture, which might affect their bounce," she thought to herself as she carefully inspected and bounced several balls.

Asian Children's Understanding of Multidigit Addition and Subtraction

LEMENTARY SCHOOL PUPILS in the United States find multidigit addition and subtraction problems requiring trades between columns very difficult. Many American children try to solve these problems by rote, without grasping crucial aspects of the procedure. They seem to have a confused, single-digit conception of multidigit numbers. For example, they tend to view the 3 in 5,386 as being just 3 rather than 300. As a result, when they carry to or borrow from this column, they are likely to compute the value incorrectly.

Chinese, Japanese, and Korean children, by contrast, are highly accurate at multidigit addition and subtraction. What accounts for their superior performance? To find out, Karen Fuson and Youngshim Kwon (1992) asked Korean second and third graders to solve a set of two- and three-digit problems, observed their methods, and asked questions about their knowledge. The performance of the children was excellent. For example, even though second graders had not yet received formal instruction on three-digit problems, their scores in addition were nearly perfect. In subtraction, they solved 78 percent of three-digit problems correctly.

Quantitative understanding of multidigit numbers was clearly responsible for the Korean pupils' exceptional competence. Almost all identified the tens' and hundreds' columns correctly as they described how to solve problems. And no Korean child viewed a "1" mark signaling trading to the tens column as "one," as American children typically do. Instead, they clearly identified it as "ten" if it came from the ones' column (addition) and "one hundred" if it came from the hundreds' column (subtraction). Especially remarkable were third graders' clear explanations of how to perform complex, multistep trading operations that stump their American agemates. Here are two examples:

> I borrowed one hundred. And I gave nine tens to the tens' column and the remainder, ten, to the ones' column.

> As four becomes three, the zero in the tens' column becomes nine and the zero in the ones' column becomes ten. (Fuson & Kwon, 1992, p. 502)

In fact, most Korean third graders no longer wrote extra marks when solving problems like this one. They could handle intricate trading procedures mentally.

Researchers point to several cultural and language-based factors that contribute to the sharp skill advantage of Asian over American pupils. First, use of the metric system in Asian countries, which presents one, ten, hundred, and thousand values in all areas of measurement, helps children think in ways consistent with place value. Second, English words for two-digit numbers (such as twelve and thirteen) are irregular and do not convey the idea of tens and ones. Asian-language number words ("ten two," "ten three") make this composition obvious. Number words are also shorter and more quickly pronounced. This facilitates counting strategies, since more digits can be held in working memory at once. It also increases the speed with which children can retrieve math facts from long-term memory (Geary et al., 1996; Jensen & Whang, 1994).

Cultural and language-based factors contribute to Asian children's skill at manipulating multidigit numbers. The abacus supports these Japanese pupils' understanding of place value. Ones, tens, hundreds, and thousands are each represented by a different column of beads, and calculations are performed by moving the beads to different positions. As children become skilled at using the abacus, they generate mental images that assist them in solving complex arithmetic problems.
(Fuji Fotos/The Image Works)

Asian instructional practices support rapid mastery of multidigit problems as well. For example, teachers use phrases that explicitly describe the trading operation. Instead of carrying, they say "raise up," and instead of borrowing, they say "bring down." Textbooks also do a good job of helping children discriminate place values. Hundreds', tens', and ones' columns have separate color codes, and pictures depicting their relative sizes are often linked to addition and subtraction problems (Fuson, 1992). Finally, multidigit problems are introduced earlier in Asian schools. American pupils spend more time on problems requiring no trading, increasing the chances that they will apply single-digit strategies inappropriately to multidigit numbers.

In sum, what appears at first glance to be the same cognitive task is actually quite different for American than for Asian pupils. These findings highlight several ways adults in the United States might ease children's mastery of numerical concepts.

The heart of scientific reasoning is coordinating theories with evidence. A scientist can clearly describe the theory that he or she favors, knows what evidence is needed to support it and what would refute it, and can explain how pitting evidence against available theories led to the acceptance of one theory as opposed to others.

Deanna Kuhn has conducted extensive research into the development of scientific reasoning, using problems that resemble tasks used by Piaget in that several variables might affect an outcome. In one series of studies, third, sixth, and ninth graders; adults of mixed educational backgrounds; and professional scientists were provided with evidence, sometimes consistent and sometimes conflicting with theories. Then they were asked questions about the accuracy of each theory.

For example, participants were given a problem much like the one Heidi posed. They were asked to theorize about which of several features of sports balls—size (large or small), color (light or dark), surface texture (rough or smooth), or presence or absence of ridges—influences the quality of a player's serve. Next, they were told about the theory of Mr. (or Ms.) S, who believes that size is important, and the theory of Mr. (or Ms.) C, who thinks that color makes a difference. Finally, the interviewer presented evidence by placing balls with certain characteristics in two baskets labeled "good serve" and "bad serve" (see Figure 7.12).

■ **AGE-RELATED CHANGE.** Kuhn and her collaborators (1988) found that the capacity to reason like a scientist improved with age. The youngest participants often ignored conflicting evidence or distorted it in ways consistent with their theory. When one third grader, who judged that size was causal (with large balls producing good serves and small balls, bad serves), was shown incomplete evidence (a single, large, light-colored ball in the good-serve basket and no balls in the bad-serve basket), he insisted on the accuracy of Mr. S's theory (which was also his own). Asked to explain, he stated flatly, "Because this ball is big . . . the color doesn't really matter" (Kuhn, 1989, p. 677).

These findings, and others like them, reveal that instead of viewing evidence as separate from and bearing on a theory, children often blend the two into a single representation of "the way things are." The ability to distinguish theory from evidence and use logical rules to examine their relationship in complex, multi-variable situations improves from childhood into adolescence and adulthood (Foltz, Overton, & Ricco, 1995; Kuhn et al., 1995; Schauble, 1996).

■ **HOW SCIENTIFIC REASONING DEVELOPS.** What factors support skill at coordinating theory with evidence? Greater processing capacity, permitting a theory and the effects of several variables to be compared at once, is vital. Beyond this, *metacognition—* thinking about thought—is especially important (Kuhn, 1989, 1993). Individuals must be able to represent the theory as an object of thought rather than a mirror image of reality. And they must also set aside their own preference for the theory and consider what the evidence says as their sole basis for judgment.

How does skill in coordinating theory with evidence increase? Performance is strongly influenced by years of schooling, whether individuals grapple with traditional scientific tasks or tasks in the social domain—for example, justify a theory about what causes children to fail in school (Kuhn, 1993). But even at advanced levels of education, scientific reasoning is rarely taught directly. Instead, in all subject-matter areas, students receive practice in setting aside their own experiences and beliefs to infer conclusions that follow from information given. Research reveals that repeated opportunities to pit theory against evidence prompt children and adolescents to reflect on their current strategies, revise them, and think more scientifically (Kuhn et al., 1995; Schauble, 1996).

Return to page 276, and review Robbie Case's information-processing view of Piaget's stages. Do Case's ideas about extensive practice with schemes leading to the formation of *central conceptual structures* remind you of the metacognitive advances just described? Piaget himself emphasized the role of metacognition in formal operational thought when he spoke of "operating on operations" (see Chapter 6, page 254). But recent findings indicate that scientific reasoning is not the result of an abrupt, stagewise change. Instead, it develops gradually out of many specific experiences that require individuals to match theories against evidence and reflect on and evaluate their thinking.

FIGURE 7.12

Example of evidence in the sports ball problem. Participants were asked to tell which of four features of sports balls—size, color, surface texture, or presence or absence of ridges—influences the quality of a player's serve. This set of evidence suggests that color might be important, since light-colored balls are largely in the good-serve basket and dark-colored balls in the bad-serve basket. But the same is true for texture! The good-serve basket has mostly smooth balls, the bad-serve basket rough balls. Since all light-colored balls are smooth and all dark-colored balls are rough, we cannot tell whether color or texture makes a difference. However, we can deduce that size and presence or absence of ridges are not important, since these variables are equally represented in the good-serve and bad-serve baskets.

(From D. Kuhn, E. Amsel, & M. O'Loughlin, 1988, *The Development of Scientific Thinking Skills*, Orlando, FL: Academic Press, p. 140. Reprinted by permission.)

ASK YOURSELF . . .

♦ *Using information-processing mechanisms of development and research discussed in this chapter, explain why attention to both basic skills and understanding is important in reading and math instruction.*

♦ *Review Heidi's thinking about the impact of diverse variables on the bounce of her tennis balls on page 307. What features of her reasoning suggest that she is beginning to reason scientifically?*

♦ CONNECTIONS
Describe cultural values, child-rearing attitudes and practices, and educational methods that lead Asian children to outperform American children in math achievement (See Chapter 15, page 638.)

BRIEF REVIEW

nformation-processing researchers have turned their attention to children's academic learning. Reading involves integrating a variety of skills, many of which must be done automatically. It builds on a firm foundation of spoken language and informal literacy-related knowledge acquired during the preschool years. Similarly, young children's spontaneously constructed number concepts and counting strategies serve as the foundation for formal mathematics instruction in school. Siegler's strategy-choice model explains how children use diverse strategies adaptively to master basic knowledge in reading and math. In both domains, instruction that provides balanced attention to basic skills and understanding seems most beneficial. Extensive practice in coordinating theory with evidence promotes the metacognitive skills necessary for scientific reasoning on diverse types of tasks.

Evaluation of the Information-Processing Approach

major strength of the information-processing approach is its explicitness and precision in breaking down complex cognitive performance into its components. Information processing has provided a wealth of detailed evidence on how younger versus older and more skilled versus less skilled individuals attend, remember, reason, and solve problems. Compared to Piaget's theory, it also offers a more precise account of cognitive change. Because information-processing researchers view thinking as a collection of separate skills rather than a single entity, they rely on many mechanisms to explain development. The most important ones are summarized in Table 7.1. As you review them, think back to the theories and research evidence discussed in this chapter that illustrate the role of each. Finally, information processing is helping to clarify which aspects of cognitive development are domain specific, which are domain general, and how they work together. In doing so, it is contributing to our understanding of variations in development.

TABLE 7.1

Mechanisms of Cognitive Change from the Information-Processing Perspective

Mechanism	Description
Basic processing capacity	Size of the mental system increases as a result of brain development.
Processing efficiency	Speed of basic operations increases, consuming less capacity in working memory and freeing up resources for other mental activities.
Encoding of information	Encoding, in the form of attention, becomes more thorough and better adapted to task demands.
Cognitive inhibition	Ability to prevent internal and external distracting stimuli from capturing attention improves, freeing up resources in working memory for remembering, reasoning, and solving problems.
Strategy execution	Strategies become more effective, improving storage, representation, and retrieval of information.
Knowledge	Amount and structure of domain-specific knowledge increase, making new, related information more meaningful so it is easier to store and retrieve.
Metacognition	Awareness and understanding of cognitive processes expand and self-regulation improves, leading strategies to be applied more effectively in a wider range of situations.

Nevertheless, the information-processing perspective has several limitations that prevent it from serving as a complete account of cognitive development. The first, ironically, stems from its central strength: by analyzing cognition down to its components, information processing has had difficulty putting them back together into a broad, comprehensive theory of development. For this reason, many child development specialists resist turning away from Piaget's view in favor of it. In fact, we have seen that the neo-Piagetian perspective is a major effort to build a general theory by retaining Piaget's stages while drawing on information-processing mechanisms to explain cognitive change.

Furthermore, the computer metaphor, although bringing precision to research on the human mind, has drawbacks. Computer models of cognitive processing, although complex in their own right, do not reflect the richness of real-life learning experiences. For example, they tell us little about aspects of cognition that are not linear and logical, such as imagination and creativity (Greeno, 1989). In addition, computers do not have desires, interests, and intentions. And they cannot engage in interaction with others in the same way children do when learning from parents, teachers, and peers. Perhaps because of the narrowness of the computer metaphor, information processing has not yet told us much about the links between cognition and other areas of development. Currently, researchers are intensely interested in whether information processing can enhance our understanding of how children think about their social world. We will see some examples of this emphasis in later chapters. But it is still true that extensions of Piaget's theory prevail when it comes to research on children's social and moral development.

Finally, information-processing research has been slow to respond to the growing interest in the biological bases of cognitive development. Connectionist theories have begun to fill this gap by creating computer simulations that model human information processing at a neural level, helping us understand how infants and young children with little initial knowledge might acquire complex skills. Evolutionary ideas, as well, have started to appear in information-processing theories, building bridges between biological evolution and cognitive development, as Siegler's model of strategy choice illustrates. And studies of the psychophysiological bases of certain cognitive changes, such as gains in cognitive inhibition, are enlarging our appreciation of the central role of brain development in children's processing capacity.

Despite its shortcomings, the information-processing approach holds great promise for the future. New breakthroughs in understanding the joint operation of mechanisms of cognitive development, neurological changes that underlie various mental activities, and instructional methods that support children's learning are likely to take place in the years to come.

SUMMARY

THE INFORMATION-PROCESSING APPROACH

What unique features characterize the information-processing approach to cognitive development?

◆ The information-processing approach views the mind as a complex, symbol-manipulating system through which information flows, operating much like a computer. The computer analogy helps researchers analyze thought into separate components, each of which can be studied thoroughly to yield a detailed understanding of what children and adults do when faced with a task or problem.

GENERAL MODELS OF INFORMATION PROCESSING

Describe the store and levels-of-processing models, noting their implications for cognitive development.

◆ Atkinson and Shiffrin's **store model** assumes that information moves through three parts of the system, where **mental strategies** operate on it so that it can be retained and used efficiently. The **sensory register** and **working,** or **short-term, memory** are limited in capacity. **Long-term memory,** our permanent knowledge base, is limitless. The **serial position effect** supports the distinction between working and long-term memory.

◆ According to the **levels-of-processing model,** retention depends on the depth to which information is processed by the system. Working memory is a conscious pool of attentional resources from which our information-processing activities draw. The amount of attention that must be allocated to a task depends on how well learned, or automatic, its cognitive operations are. As **automatization** increases, attentional resources are freed for other activities.

◆ Although the precise capacity limits of the cognitive system are difficult to identify, similar changes in processing speed across many tasks suggest an age-related increase in basic cognitive resources. In addition, improved strategy use contributes greatly to gains in processing capacity.

DEVELOPMENTAL THEORIES OF INFORMATION PROCESSING

Describe and evaluate three developmental theories of information processing: Case's neo-Piagetian theory, connectionism, and Siegler's model of strategy choice.

◆ According to Case's **neo-Piagetian theory,** development is due to an increase in working-memory capacity. Brain maturation and automatization of strategies due to practice release attentional resources for the child to combine old schemes and generate new ones. When schemes are consolidated into **central conceptual structures,** working memory expands further, and the child moves up to a new Piagetian stage. Case's theory accounts for domain-specific change through variations in the complexity of tasks and children's experiences. His powerful ideas need to be tested in additional task domains.

◆ **Connectionism** examines cognitive development at the level of simple processing units, much like neurons in the brain. Researchers program artificial neural networks into computers, equip them with simple learning procedures, and compare their pattern of learning to that of children on a variety of tasks. Neural-network modeling reveals that continuous change in the strength of connections can yield stagelike shifts in performance. Although these artificial systems learn more slowly than do children and cannot fully explain cognitive change, they remind us that a complete account of cognitive development must consider brain functioning.

◆ Siegler's **model of strategy choice** applies an evolutionary perspective to children's cognition. Strategy development follows an overlapping-wave pattern. Faced with a challenging problem, children try a variety of strategies, gradually selecting those that are most efficient and accurate. Siegler's findings reveal that no child thinks in just one way, even on the same task. His model has yet to be tested on problems in which strategies are not well defined.

ATTENTIONAL PROCESSING

Describe the development of attention in terms of selective, adaptable, and planful strategies, noting the role of gains in processing capacity.

◆ Attention becomes more sustained and selective with age. Older children are also better at adapting attention to the momentary requirements of situations. Gains in **cognitive inhibition,** believed to be due to development of the frontal lobes of the cerebral cortex, are particularly marked in middle childhood. They lead to expansion of processing capacity and underlie children's greater selectivity of attention.

◆ Attentional (and memory) strategies develop in a four-step sequence as working memory expands: (1) **production deficiency** (failure to use the strategy); (2) **control deficiency** (failure to execute the strategy consistently); (3) **utilization deficiency** (consistent use of the strategy, but no improvement in performance); and (4) **effective strategy use.**

◆ During middle childhood, children become better at **planning.** On tasks that require systematic visual search or the coordination of many acts, school-age children are more likely than preschoolers to decide ahead of time how to proceed and allocate their attention

accordingly. The serious attentional difficulties of children with **attention-deficit hyperactivity disorder** (ADHD), which may be due to an impairment in inhibition, lead to both academic and social problems.

WORKING MEMORY

Describe the development of memory strategies of rehearsal, organization, and elaboration, noting the influence of task demands and culture.

◆ Although the beginnings of memory strategies can be seen during the preschool years, young children seldom engage in **rehearsal** or **organization** when given unfamiliar materials. As use of these strategies improves, they gradually become more flexible; children vary them to fit the demands of the material to be learned. **Elaboration** is a late-developing memory strategy that rarely appears before age 11.

◆ Like young children, people in non-Western cultures who have no formal schooling do not spontaneously use or benefit from instruction in memory strategies. Tasks requiring children to memorize discrete bits of information in school promote deliberate memorization in middle childhood.

LONG-TERM MEMORY

Describe the development of three approaches to memory retrieval: recognition, recall, and reconstruction.

◆ **Recognition,** the simplest form of retrieval, is a fairly automatic process that is highly accurate by the preschool years. In contrast, **recall,** or generating an image of an absent stimulus, is more difficult and shows much greater improvement with age.

◆ Even young children engage in **reconstruction** when remembering complex, meaningful material. Over middle childhood, the ability to draw inferences from prose material expands. According to **fuzzy-trace theory,** information is reconstructed automatically at encoding into a vague, fuzzy version called a **gist,** which is stored separately from the verbatim version. With age, children rely less on verbatim and more on gist memory, which contributes to improved reasoning and recall.

How do gains in knowledge enhance memory performance?

◆ Gains in the quantity and structure of domain-specific knowledge enhance memory performance by making new, related information easier to store and retrieve. However, children differ not only in what they know but in how well they use their knowledge to acquire new information. Knowledge and memory strategies support one another.

Describe the development and function of scripts and autobiographical memory.

◆ Like adults, young children remember familiar experiences in terms of **scripts**—general representations of what occurs and when it occurs in a particular situation. Scripts permit children to predict what might happen on future, similar occasions and may be the developmental link in the transition from **episodic** to **semantic memory.**

◆ During the preschool years, **infantile amnesia** subsides as children's self-image develops and language skills permit them to talk about the past with adults. Gradually, children adopt the narrative thinking generated in these dialogues, forming an **autobiographical memory.** Parents who use an elaborative rather than repetitive style in discussing past events have children who produce more coherent and detailed personal stories.

METACOGNITION

Describe the development of metacognitive knowledge and cognitive self-regulation, and explain why self-regulation is vital for success on complex tasks.

◆ **Metacognition** improves as children construct a naive **theory of mind,** a coherent understanding of people as mental beings. Children's awareness of cognitive capacities, strategies, and task variables becomes more accurate and complete and changes from a passive to an active view of mental functioning in middle childhood.

◆ **Cognitive self-regulation**—using metacognitive knowledge to monitor performance—develops slowly over childhood and adolescence, as indicated by children's **comprehension monitoring** while processing spoken or written prose. Instruction that demonstrates self-regulatory strategies and explains why they are effective helps children generalize them to new situations. By secondary school, cognitive self-regulation is a strong predictor of academic performance.

APPLICATIONS OF INFORMATION PROCESSING TO ACADEMIC LEARNING

Discuss development in reading, mathematics, and scientific reasoning, noting the implications of research findings for teaching in each academic domain.

◆ Reading requires executing many cognitive skills simultaneously, taxing all aspects of the information-processing system. **Emergent literacy** reveals that young children understand a great deal about written language before they read and write in conventional ways. Preschoolers gradually revise incorrect ideas about the meaning of written symbols as their perceptual and cognitive capacities improve, as they encounter writing in many different contexts, and as adults help them make sense of written information.

◆ School-age children experiment and choose adaptively among strategies in learning to decode written symbols. Experts disagree on whether a **whole-language approach** or **basic-skills approach** should be used to teach beginning reading. Research suggests that a balanced mixture of both is most effective.

◆ Like reading, mathematical reasoning builds on a foundation of informally acquired knowledge. Toddlers display a beginning grasp of **ordinality,** which serves as the basis for more complex understandings. As preschoolers experiment with counting strategies, they grasp **cardinality,** which increases the efficiency of counting.

◆ During the early school years, children apply diverse strategies adaptively to learn basic math facts. Children's mistakes in solving more complex problems reveal that they sometimes apply strategies incorrectly because they do not understand the basis for them. Mathematics instruction that combines practice in basic skills with conceptual understanding is best.

◆ Children (and to a lesser degree, adolescents and adults) have difficulty coordinating theories with evidence. They often blend the two, instead of viewing evidence as separate from and bearing on a theory. Tasks that offer repeated practice in pitting theories against evidence promote the metacognitive skills necessary for scientific reasoning.

EVALUATION OF THE INFORMATION-PROCESSING APPROACH

Summarize the strengths and limitations of the information-processing approach.

◆ A major strength of the information-processing approach is its precision in breaking down cognition into separate elements so each can be studied thoroughly. As a result, information processing has uncovered a variety of explicit mechanisms of cognitive change. It has also helped clarify domain-specific and domain-general aspects of development and how the two work together.

◆ Nevertheless, information processing has not yet led to a comprehensive theory nor told us much about the links between cognition and other areas of development. Although information-processing researchers have been slow to integrate their findings with research on the developing brain, they are making strides in this area.

IMPORTANT TERMS AND CONCEPTS

attention-deficit hyperactivity disorder (ADHD) (p. 288)
autobiographical memory (p. 296)
automatization (p. 274)
basic-skills approach (p. 305)
cardinality (p. 306)
central conceptual structures (p. 277)
cognitive inhibition (p. 284)
cognitive self-regulation (p. 301)
connectionism (p. 278)
control deficiency (p. 285)
effective strategy use (p. 285)
elaboration (p. 291)
emergent literacy (p. 305)

episodic memory (p. 295)
fuzzy-trace theory (p. 293)
gist (p. 293)
infantile amnesia (p. 296)
levels-of-processing model (p. 274)
long-term memory (p. 273)
mental strategies (p. 272)
metacognition (p. 299)
model of strategy choice (p. 280)
neo-Piagetian theory (p. 276)
ordinality (p. 306)
organization (p. 288)
planning (p. 285)
production deficiency (p. 285)

recall (p. 291)
recognition (p. 291)
reconstruction (p. 293)
rehearsal (p. 287)
scripts (p. 295)
semantic memory (p. 295)
sensory register (p. 272)
serial position effect (p. 274)
store model (p. 272)
theory of mind (p. 299)
utilization deficiency (p. 285)
whole-language approach (p. 305)
working, or short-term, memory (p. 273)

Intelligence

FIVE-YEAR-OLD JERMAINE, an African-American child, sat in a small, unfamiliar testing room while Nora, an adult whom he had met only moments ago, prepared to give him an intelligence test. Eager to come when Nora had arrived at his kindergarten classroom, Jermaine became confused once the testing session began.

Starting with some word definitions, Nora asked, "Jermaine, how are wood and coal alike? How are they the same?"

Jermaine's eyebrows wrinkled in puzzlement. He shrugged his shoulders and said, "Well, they're both hard."

Nora continued, "And an apple and a peach?"

"They taste good," responded Jermaine, looking up at Nora's face for any sign that he was doing all right.

Nora looked back pleasantly but moved along in a businesslike way. "A ship and an automobile?"

Jermaine paused, unsure of what Nora meant. "They're hard," he finally replied, returning to his first response.

"Iron and silver?"

"They're hard," Jermaine repeated, still trying to figure out what these questions were all about. (Adapted from Miller-Jones, 1989, p. 362)

The **psychometric approach** to cognitive development is the basis for the wide variety of intelligence tests available for assessing children's mental abilities. As Nora's testing of Jermaine illustrates, compared to Piagetian, Vygotskian, and information-processing views, the psychometric perspective is far more product oriented than process oriented. For the most part, it focuses on outcomes and results—how many and what kinds of questions children can answer correctly at different ages. How children arrive at solutions to problems is emphasized less. Researchers interested in intelligence testing ask such questions as these: What factors, or dimensions, make up intelligence, and how do they change with age? How can cognitive development be measured so that scores are useful for predicting future academic achievement, career attainment, and other aspects of intellectual success? To what extent do children of the same age differ in intelligence, and what factors explain these differences?

As we examine these issues, we will quickly become immersed in the IQ nature–nurture debate, waged over the course of this century. We will look closely at genetic and environmental influences on intelligence, as well as the controversy over whether intelligence tests yield biased estimates of the abilities of low-income and ethnic minority children. As our discussion proceeds, we will see that the cognitive perspectives we have considered in previous chapters, as well as the work of many investigators examining contextual influences on development, have added much to our understanding of children's test performance.

TABLE 8.1

Five Traits Most Frequently Mentioned by College Students as Characterizing Intelligence at Different Ages

6-Month-Olds	2-Year-Olds	10-Year-Olds	Adults
1. Recognition of people and objects	1. Verbal ability	1. Verbal ability	1. Reasoning
2. Motor coordination	2. Learning ability	2, 3, 4. Learning ability; problem solving; reasoning (all three tied)	2. Verbal ability
3. Alertness	3. Awareness of people and environment		3. Problem solving
4. Awareness of environment	4. Motor coordination		4. Learning ability
5. Verbalization	5. Curiosity	5. Creativity	5. Creativity

Source: R. S. Siegler & D. D. Richards. 1980, "College students' Prototypes of Children's Intelligence." Paper presented at the annual meeting of the American Psychological Association, New York. Adapted by permission of the author.

Our discussion concludes with the development of creativity and special talents. Although these are among the most highly valued human characteristics, they are not represented on current intelligence tests for children.

Definitions of Intelligence

Take a moment to jot down a list of behaviors you view as typical of people who are highly intelligent. Did you come up with just one or two characteristics or a great many? When Robert Sternberg asked nearly 500 laypeople and 24 experts to complete a similar exercise, he found that their responses were surprisingly similar. Both groups viewed intelligence as a complex construct made up of verbal ability, practical problem solving, and social competence (Sternberg, 1982; Sternberg & Detterman, 1986). These findings indicate that most people do not think of intelligence as a single ability. Instead, their definitions include a variety of attributes.

The problem of defining children's intelligence is especially challenging, since behaviors that reflect intelligent behavior change with age. To illustrate, list five traits of intelligent 6-month-olds, 2-year-olds, 10-year-olds, and adults. The responses of students in an introductory psychology course are shown in Table 8.1. Notice how sensorimotor responsiveness became less important, whereas verbal ability, problem solving, and reasoning became more important, in much the same way that Piagetian, Vygotskian, and information-processing research suggests intelligence changes with age (Siegler & Richards, 1980).

The researchers also asked college students to estimate correlations between the mental abilities mentioned for each age. Students thought there would be some close connections, but they predicted considerable distinctiveness as well. As we will see in the following sections, scientific theories underlying the measurement of intelligence reveal this same tension between a single, overarching ability versus a collection of only loosely related skills.

ALFRED BINET: A HOLISTIC VIEW

The social and educational climate of the late nineteenth and early twentieth centuries sparked the intelligence testing movement. The most important influence was the beginning of universal public education in Europe and the United States. Once schools opened their doors to children of all social classes—not just society's privileged—educators called for methods to help them identify pupils who could not profit from regular classroom instruction. The first successful intelligence test, completed by French psychologist Alfred Binet and his colleague Theodore Simon in 1905, responded to this need.

Binet was asked by the French Ministry of Instruction to devise an objective method for assigning pupils with mental retardation to special classes. The goal was to prevent un-

psychometric approach A product-oriented approach to cognitive development that focuses on the construction of tests to assess mental abilities (see page 315).

fair exclusion of disruptive pupils from regular education on the basis of their behavior rather than their intellectual ability. Other researchers had tried to assess intelligence using simple laboratory measures of sensory responsiveness and reaction time (Cattell, 1890; Galton, 1883). Binet believed that very different kinds of test items were needed—ones that did not dissect intelligence into elementary processes but instead required complex functions involved in intelligent behavior, such as memory, good judgment, and abstraction. Consequently, Binet and Simon devised a test of "general mental ability" that included a variety of verbal and nonverbal reasoning tasks. Their test was also the first *developmental* approach to test construction. Items varied in difficulty, and each was classified according to the age at which a typical child could first pass it (Brody, 1992).

Behaviors that reflect intelligent behavior change with age. These children, ages 6 months and 3 years, demonstrate their intelligence in very different ways. After infancy, sensorimotor responsiveness becomes less important and problem solving and reasoning become more important.
(Spencer Grant/Stock Boston)

The Binet test was so successful in predicting school performance that it became the basis for new intelligence tests developed in other countries. In 1916, Lewis Terman at Stanford University adapted it for use with American schoolchildren. Since then, the American version has been known as the Stanford-Binet Intelligence Scale. The Stanford-Binet has been revised several times over this century. Later we will see that it no longer provides just a single, holistic measure of intelligence. Nevertheless, many of its items continue to resemble those on Binet's original scale.

THE FACTOR ANALYSTS: A MULTIFACETED VIEW

As Figure 8.1 on page 318 shows, a wide variety of tasks typically appear on intelligence tests for children. Psychologists and educators became increasingly aware that a single score might not adequately represent human mental functioning. Researchers seeking clearer definitions of intelligence had to confront the issue of whether it really is a holistic trait or a collection of many different abilities.

To resolve this dilemma, a special technique was used to analyze the performances of individuals on intelligence tests. **Factor analysis** is a complicated statistical procedure in which scores on many separate items are combined into a few factors, which substitute for the separate scores. Then the researcher gives each factor a name, based on common characteristics of items that are closely correlated with the factor. For example, if vocabulary, verbal comprehension, and verbal analogies items all correlate highly with the same factor, it might be labeled "verbal ability." Using this method, many efforts were made to identify the underlying mental abilities that contribute to successful performance on intelligence tests.

■ **EARLY FACTOR ANALYSTS.** The first influential factor analyst was British psychologist Charles Spearman (1927), who found that all test items he examined correlated to some degree with one another. Therefore, Spearman proposed the existence of a common underlying **general factor,** called "**g**." At the same time, he noticed that test items were not perfectly correlated. In other words, they varied in the extent to which they tapped "g." Consequently, he suggested that each item or set of similar items also measured a **specific factor,** called "**s**," that was unique to the task. Spearman's identification of "g" and "s" led his view of mental abilities to be called the *two-factor theory of intelligence.*

Spearman viewed "g" as central and supreme, and he was especially interested in its psychological characteristics. With further study, he concluded that "g" represented some kind of abstract reasoning power. Test items that required individuals to form relationships and apply general principles were the strongest correlates of "g," and they were also the best predictors of cognitive performance outside the testing situation.

Louis Thurstone (1938), an American contemporary of Spearman, soon took issue with his emphasis on "g." Instead, Thurstone argued, separate, unrelated intellectual abilities exist. Thurstone gave over 50 intelligence tests to a large sample of college students; their scores produced seven clear factors. As a result, he concluded that intelligence consists of seven distinct **primary mental abilities:** verbal meaning, perceptual speed, reasoning, number, rote memory, word fluency, and spatial visualization.

factor analysis A complicated statistical procedure that combines scores from many separate test items into a few factors, which substitute for the separate scores. Used to identify mental abilities that contribute to performance on intelligence tests.

general factor, or "g" In Spearman's theory of intelligence, a common factor representing abstract reasoning power that underlies a wide variety of test items.

specific factor, or "s" In Spearman's theory of intelligence, a mental ability factor that is unique to a particular task.

primary mental abilities In Thurstone's theory of intelligence, seven distinct mental abilities identified through factor analysis (verbal meaning, perceptual speed, reasoning, number, rote memory, word fluency, and spatial visualization).

FIGURE 8.1

Sample items similar to those that appear on common intelligence tests for children. In contrast to verbal items, nonverbal items do not require reading or direct use of language. Performance items are also nonverbal, but they require the child to draw or construct something rather than merely give a correct answer. As a result, they appear only on individually administered intelligence tests.

(Logical reasoning, picture oddities, and spatial visualization examples are adapted with permission of The Free Press, a division of Macmillan, Inc., from A. R. Jensen, 1980, *Bias in Mental Testing*, New York: The Free Press, pp. 150, 154, 157.)

Item Type	Typical Verbal Items
Vocabulary	Tell me what "carpet" means.
General Information	How many ounces make a pound? What day of the week comes right after Thursday?
Verbal Comprehension	Why are police officers needed?
Verbal Analogies	A rock is hard; a pillow is _____ .
Logical Reasoning	Five girls are sitting side by side on a bench. Jane is in the middle and Betty sits next to her on the right. Alice is beside Betty, and Dale is beside Ellen, who sits next to Jane. Who are sitting on the ends?
Number Series	Which number comes next in the series? 4 8 6 12 10 ___

Typical Nonverbal Items

Picture Oddities	Which picture does not belong with the others?

Spatial Visualization	Which of the boxes on the right can be made from the pattern shown on the left?

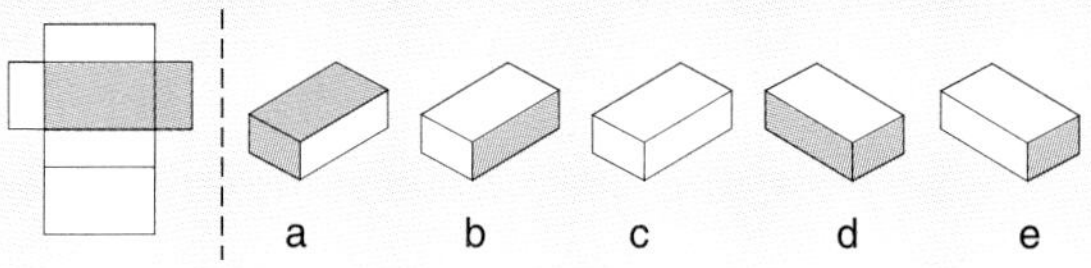

Typical Performance Items

Picture Series	Put the pictures in the right order so that what is happening makes sense.

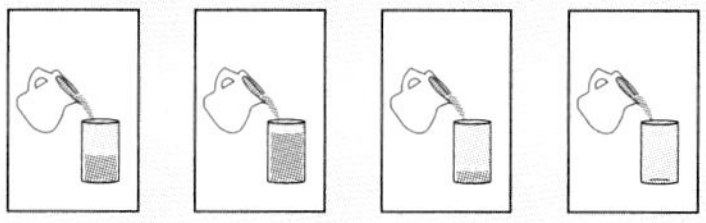

Puzzles	Put these pieces together so they make a wagon.

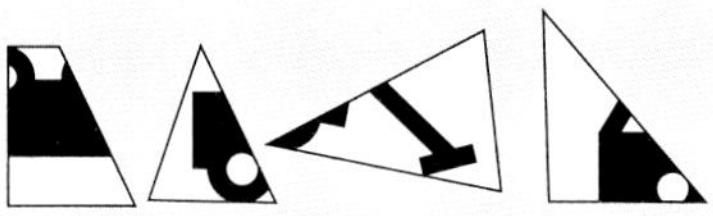

Spearman's and Thurstone's findings represent two ways of thinking about intelligence. Today, each is supported by research and accounts for part of the story. Current theorists and test designers reconcile these two views by proposing *hierarchical models* of mental abilities. At the highest level is "g," assumed to be present to a greater or lesser degree in all specialized factors. These factors, in turn, are measured by subtests, or groups of related items. Subtest scores provide information about a child's strengths and weaknesses, and they can also be combined into an overall index of general intelligence (Brody, 1992).

■ **MODERN FACTOR ANALYSTS.** Several modern mental ability theorists have extended the efforts of the early factor analysts. The two most influential are R. B. Cattell and John Carroll. Each offers a unique, multifaceted perspective on intelligence.

R. B. CATTELL'S CRYSTALLIZED VERSUS FLUID INTELLIGENCE. Raymond B. Cattell (1971, 1987) accepts the existence of "g" but divides it into two factors. **Crystallized intelligence**

crystallized intelligence In Cattell's theory, a form of intelligence that depends on culturally loaded, fact-oriented information.

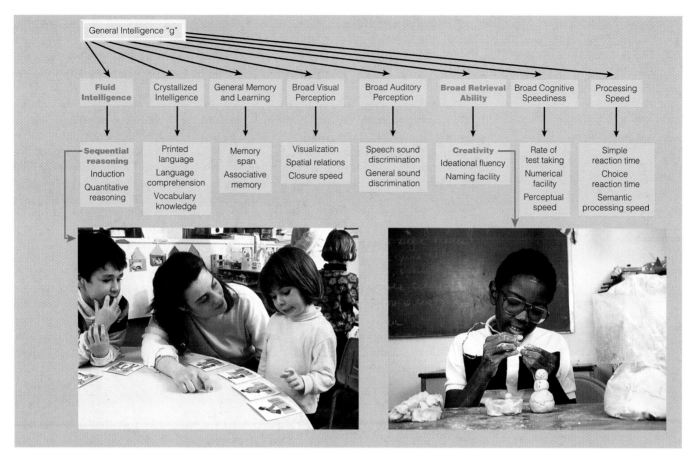

FIGURE 8.2

Carroll's three-stratum theory of intelligence. Second-stratum abilities are arranged from left to right in terms of their decreasing strength of relationship with "g." The photos depict specific manifestations of second-stratum factors, listed at the lowest stratum. The child on the left completes a sequential reasoning task in which she arranges pictures to tell a story—a type of fluid intelligence. The child on the right uses art materials creatively to build a snowman, applying her broad retrieval ability.

(From J. B. Carroll, 1993, *Human Cognitive Abilities: A Survey of Factor-Analytic Studies,* New York: Cambridge University Press, p. 626. Adapted by permission.)

(Left, Will Faller; right, Myrleen Ferguson Cate/PhotoEdit)

depends on culturally loaded, fact-oriented information. Tasks highly correlated with it include vocabulary, general information, and arithmetic problems. In contrast, **fluid intelligence** requires very little specific knowledge. It involves the ability to see complex relationships and solve problems, as in the number series, spatial visualization, and figure matrix items shown in Figure 8.1.

Among children who are similar in cultural and educational background, crystallized and fluid intelligence are highly correlated, and it is difficult to distinguish them. In these instances, the strong relationship is probably due to the fact that children who are high in fluid intelligence acquire specific information with greater ease. But when children who differ greatly in cultural and educational experiences are tested, the two abilities are easier to identify; children with the same fluid capacity may perform quite differently on tests that emphasize crystallized tasks. As these findings suggest, Cattell's theory has important implications for the issue of cultural bias in intelligence testing (Horn, 1994). We will see later that tests aimed at reducing culturally specific content usually emphasize fluid over crystallized items.

CARROLL'S THREE-STRATUM THEORY OF INTELLIGENCE. John Carroll (1993, 1997) used improved factor-analytic techniques to reanalyze hundreds of studies of relationships between mental abilities. His findings yielded a **three-stratum theory of intelligence** that elaborates the models proposed by Spearman, Thurstone, R. B. Cattell, and others. As Figure 8.2 shows, Carroll represents the structure of intelligence as a pyramid, with "g" at the

fluid intelligence In Cattell's theory, a form of intelligence that requires very little specific knowledge but involves the ability to see complex relationships and solve problems.

three-stratum theory of intelligence Carroll's theory, which represents the structure of intelligence as a pyramid, with "g" at the top; eight broad, biologically based abilities at the second stratum; and narrower manifestations of these abilities at the lowest stratum that result from experience with particular tasks. The most comprehensive classification of mental abilities to be confirmed by factor-analytic research.

top and eight broad abilities in the second stratum, arranged from left to right in terms of their decreasing strength of relationship with "g." Each broad ability is believed to be a basic, biological human characteristic that can influence a wide variety of behaviors. At the lowest stratum are narrow abilities—specific manifestations of second-stratum factors that result from experience with particular tasks.

Carroll's model is the most comprehensive classification of mental abilities to be confirmed by factor-analytic research. As we will see in the next section, it provides a useful framework for researchers seeking to understand mental test performance in cognitive processing terms. The three-stratum theory highlights the multiplicity of intellectual factors sampled by current mental tests. Currently, no single test measures all of Caroll's factors (Kranzler, 1997). Because they are so diverse, we can expect that a large proportion of the population can become quite good at one or several, and perhaps a great many.

Recent Advances in Defining Intelligence

lthough factor analysis has been the major approach to defining mental abilities, many researchers believe its usefulness will remain limited unless it is combined with other theoretical approaches to human cognition. Factor analysts have been criticized for devoting too much attention to identifying factors and too little to clarifying the cognitive processes that underlie them. Once we discover exactly what separates individuals who can solve certain mental test items from those who cannot, we will know much more about why a particular child does well or poorly and what skills must be worked on to improve performance.

COMBINING PSYCHOMETRIC AND INFORMATION-PROCESSING APPROACHES

To overcome the limitations of factor analysis, some researchers have combined psychometric and information-processing approaches. These investigators conduct **componential analyses** of children's test scores by correlating them with laboratory measures designed to assess the speed and effectiveness of information processing. In this way, they hope to provide process-oriented explanations of mental test performance.

Which information-processing components have turned out to be good predictors of intelligence? Many studies reveal that basic efficiency of thinking is correlated with the "g" factor. For example, speed of processing—measured in terms of reaction time to visual or auditory stimuli or through more complex tasks requiring scanning of information in working memory or retrieval from long-term memory—is moderately related to general intelligence and to gains in mental test performance over time (Deary, 1995; Deary & Stough, 1996; Fry & Hale, 1996; Neubauer & Bucik, 1996). In fact, as early as 3 months of age, reaction time to visual stimuli predicts preschool intelligence test scores (Dougherty & Haith, 1997).

These findings suggest that individuals whose nervous systems function more efficiently have an edge when it comes to intellectual skills. Because they can take in and manipulate information more quickly, they have more attentional resources available to solve problems. In support of this interpretation, nerve conduction velocity and the quickness and amplitude[1] of event-related potentials (ERPs, or EEG responses to specific stimulation) are modestly correlated with speed of processing and mental test scores (Rijsdijk & Boomsma, 1997; Vernon, 1993; Vernon & Mori, 1992). In addition, brain-imaging research reveals that the metabolic rate of the cortex when solving complex tasks is lower for more intelligent people, suggesting that they need to expend less mental effort (Haier et al., 1988, 1992).

Nevertheless, rapid responding is not the only processing correlate of mental test performance. Strategy use also makes a difference, and it explains some of the association be-

componential analysis A research procedure aimed at clarifying the cognitive processes responsible for intelligence test scores by correlating them with laboratory measures designed to assess the speed and effectiveness of information processing.

[1]The rapidity of ERPs is a measure of how quickly the brain responds to stimulation, and the amplitude reflects the amount of electrical activity that stimulation evokes. Both are associated with general intelligence.

tween response speed and intelligence (Miller & Vernon, 1992). In one study, researchers used Siegler's model of strategy choice (see Chapter 7, page 283) to see if the way 4- to 6-year-olds apply strategies to simple addition problems is related to mental test scores. Adaptive strategy users—children who retrieved answers accurately, used other strategies (such as counting) when they could not retrieve a math fact, and seldom guessed—did considerably better on a measure of general intelligence and on subtests of mathematical and spatial abilities than did their less adaptive agemates (Geary & Burlingham-Dubree, 1989). As we saw in Chapter 7, children who apply strategies adaptively develop the capacity for fast, accurate retrieval—a skill that seems to carry over to performance on intelligence test items.

Componential research has also highlighted cognitive processes that appear unrelated to test performance but that children can rely on to compensate for tested mental ability. Recent evidence suggests that certain aspects of metacognition—awareness of problem-solving strategies and organizational and planning skills—are not good predictors of general intelligence (Alexander & Schwanenflugel, 1996; Alexander, Carr, & Schwanenflugel, 1995). In one study, fourth and fifth graders who were average in mental ability but high in metacognitive knowledge about problem solving did far better on Piagetian formal operational tasks (such as the pendulum problem) than did highly intelligent classmates who knew little about effective problem-solving techniques (Swanson, 1990).

As these findings illustrate, componential analyses are beginning to isolate specific cognitive skills on which training might be especially helpful to some children. Nevertheless, the componential approach has one major shortcoming. It attributes intelligence entirely to causes within the child. Yet throughout Chapter 7, we showed that cultural and situational factors profoundly affect children's thinking. Robert Sternberg has expanded the componential approach into a comprehensive theory that views intelligence as a product of both internal and external forces.

STERNBERG'S TRIARCHIC THEORY

Sternberg's (1985, 1988, 1997) **triarchic theory of intelligence** is made up of three interacting subtheories (see Figure 8.3). The first, the *componential subtheory,* spells out the information-processing skills that underlie intelligent behavior. You are already familiar with its main elements—strategy application, knowledge acquisition, metacognition, and self-regulation—from reading Chapter 7.

This boy solves a math problem with the help of a special set of small blocks. Children who apply strategies adaptively, using backup procedures when they cannot recall an answer rather than guessing, develop the capacity for fast, accurate retrieval and score higher on intelligence tests. (Stephen Marks)

Componential Subtheory

Metacognition
Strategy application
Knowledge acquisition

Intelligence

Experiential Subtheory

Novelty of task
Automatization of skills

Contextual Subtheory

Adapting skills to fit current contexts
Shaping contexts to meet personal goals
Selecting contexts consistent with personal goals

FIGURE 8.3

Sternberg's triarchic theory of intelligence.

triarchic theory of intelligence Sternberg's theory, which states that information processing skills, prior experience with tasks, and contextual (or cultural) factors interact to determine intelligent behavior.

According to Sternberg, children's use of these components is not just a matter of internal capacity. It is also a function of the conditions under which intelligence is assessed. The *experiential subtheory* states that highly intelligent individuals, compared to less intelligent ones, process information more skillfully in novel situations. When given a relatively new task, the bright person learns rapidly, making strategies automatic so working memory is freed for more complex aspects of the situation.

Think, for a moment, about the implications of this idea for measuring children's intelligence. To accurately compare children in brightness—in ability to deal with novelty and learn efficiently—all children would have to be presented with equally unfamiliar test items. Otherwise, some children will appear more intelligent than others simply because of their past experiences, not because they are really more cognitively skilled. These children start with the unfair advantage of prior practice on the tasks.

This point brings us to the third part of Sternberg's model, the *contextual subtheory*. It proposes that intelligent people skillfully *adapt* their information-processing skills to fit with their personal desires and the demands of their everyday worlds. When they cannot adapt to a situation, they try to *shape,* or change, it to meet their needs. If they cannot shape it, they *select* new contexts that are consistent with their goals. The contextual subtheory emphasizes that intelligent behavior is never culture free. Because of their backgrounds, some children come to value behaviors required for success on intelligence tests, and they easily adapt to the tasks and testing conditions. Others with different life histories misinterpret the testing context or reject it entirely because it does not suit their needs. Yet such children may display very sophisticated abilities in daily life—for example, telling stories, engaging in elaborate artistic activities, accomplishing athletic feats, or interacting skillfully with other people (Sternberg, 1988).

Sternberg's theory emphasizes the complexity of human mental skills—in particular, their sensitivity to environmental contexts—and the limitations of current tests in assessing that complexity. Like Cattell's distinction between crystallized and fluid intelligence, Sternberg's ideas are relevant to the controversy surrounding cultural bias in intelligence testing, a topic we return to later in this chapter.

GARDNER'S THEORY OF MULTIPLE INTELLIGENCES

Howard Gardner's (1983, 1993, 1998a) **theory of multiple intelligences** provides yet another view of how information-processing skills underlie intelligent behavior. But unlike the componential approach, it does not begin with existing mental tests and try to isolate the processing elements required to succeed on them. Instead, Gardner believes that in-

According to Gardner, children are capable of at least eight distinct intelligences. As these children classify wildflowers they collected during a walk through a forest and meadow, they enrich their naturalist intelligence.

(B. Daemmrich/The Image Works)

TABLE 8.2

Gardner's Multiple Intelligences

Intelligence	Processing Operations	End-State Performance Possibilities
Linguistic	Sensitivity to the sounds, rhythms, and meanings of words and the different functions of language	Poet, journalist
Logico-mathematical	Sensitivity to, and capacity to detect, logical or numerical patterns; ability to handle long chains of logical reasoning	Mathematician
Musical	Ability to produce and appreciate pitch, rhythm (or melody), and aesthetic-sounding tones; understanding of the forms of musical expressiveness	Violinist, composer
Spatial	Ability to perceive the visual-spatial world accurately, to perform transformations on those perceptions, and to re-create aspects of visual experience in the absence of relevant stimuli	Sculptor, navigator
Bodily-kinesthetic	Ability to use the body skillfully for expressive as well as goal-directed purposes; ability to handle objects skillfully	Dancer, athlete
Naturalist	Ability to recognize and classify all varieties of animals, minerals, and plants	Biologist
Interpersonal	Ability to detect and respond appropriately to the moods, temperaments, motivations, and intentions of others	Therapist, salesperson
Intrapersonal	Ability to discriminate complex inner feelings and to use them to guide one's own behavior; knowledge of one's own strengths, weaknesses, desires, and intelligences	Person with detailed, accurate self-knowledge

Sources: Gardner, 1983, 1993, 1998b.

telligence should be defined in terms of distinct sets of processing operations that permit individuals to solve problems, create products, and discover new knowledge in a diverse array of culturally valued activities. Accordingly, Gardner dismisses the idea of a single overarching mental ability, or "g," and proposes eight independent intelligences, which are described in Table 8.2.

Gardner acknowledges that if tests were available to assess all these abilities, factor analysis should yield low correlations between them. But he regards neurological support for their separateness as more persuasive. Research indicating that damage to a certain part of the adult brain influences only one ability (such as linguistic or spatial) while sparing others suggests that the affected ability is independent. The existence of prodigies, who show precocious development in only one area, such as language, mathematics, music, or visual arts, also fits with Gardner's belief in distinct abilities. (You may wish to review findings on the development of prodigies on page 51 of Chapter 2.)

Finally, Gardner argues that each intelligence has a unique biological potential, a distinct course of development, and different expert, or "end-state," performances. At the same time, he stresses that a lengthy process of education is required to transform any raw intellectual potential into a mature social role (Gardner, 1998a; Gardner, Hatch, & Torff, 1997). This means that cultural values and learning opportunities have a great deal to do with the extent to which a child's strengths are realized and the ways they are expressed.

Does Gardner's theory remind you of the modular view of the mind discussed in Chapter 6? Indeed, he is sympathetic to this position. Gardner's work has been especially helpful in efforts to understand and nurture children's special talents, a topic we will take up at the end of this chapter. At the same time, reservations have been raised about his theory. Neurological support for the independence of his intelligences is weak. Logico-mathematical ability, in particular, seems to be governed by many brain regions, not just one, and to be linked to spatial intelligence (Casey et al., 1995; Casey, Nuttall, & Pezaris, 1997). Furthermore, exceptionally gifted individuals exist whose abilities are broad rather than limited to a particular domain (Feldman & Goldsmith, 1991; Winner, 1996). Finally,

theory of multiple intelligences Gardner's theory, which identifies eight independent intelligences on the basis of distinct sets of processing operations applied in culturally meaningful activities (linguistic, logico-mathematical, musical, spatial, bodily-kinesthetic, naturalist, interpersonal, intrapersonal).

current mental tests do tap several of Gardner's intelligences (linguistic, logico-mathematical, and spatial), and evidence for "g" suggests that they have some common features.

In sum, Gardner's list of abilities has yet to be firmly grounded in research. Nevertheless, his ideas have been powerful enough to reawaken the debate over a unitary versus multifaceted human intelligence. Still, without clear evidence in favor of one side or the other, most test designers (as we will see in the following sections) strike a balance between these two views.

ASK YOURSELF . . .

◆ *Use the experiential and contextual subtheories of Sternberg's triarchic theory to explain why a child might do poorly on an intelligence test but display superior mental abilities in everyday life.*

◆ CONNECTIONS
In his second-grade classroom, Tony can often be seen experimenting with strategies in reading, spelling, and math. How might Tony's adaptive strategy use contribute to both his speed of processing and his intelligence test performance? (See Chapter 7, page 281.)

Cite similarities between Gardner's theory of multiple intelligences and the modular view of the mind. (See Chapter 6, page 234.) What questions raised about the modular view also apply to Gardner's theory?

BRIEF REVIEW

Binet and Simon's first successful intelligence test provided a single score designed to identify children who required assignment to special school classes. Factor analysts sought answers to the question of whether intelligence is a holistic trait or a collection of many different abilities. Their findings led to the identification of a general factor, or "g," and a wide variety of distinct mental abilities. Recently, researchers have combined the psychometric and information-processing approaches, conducting componential analyses aimed at uncovering the processing skills that predict mental test scores. Sternberg has expanded this approach into a triarchic theory that views intelligence as the combined result of processing skills, experience with tasks, and contextual (or cultural) influences. According to Gardner's theory of multiple intelligences, eight distinct domains of ability, each defined by unique processing operations, represent the diversity of human intelligence.

Representative Intelligence Tests for Children

A wide variety of tests are currently available to assess children's intelligence. Those that pupils take every two or three years in their classrooms are *group-administered tests*. They permit many children to be tested at once and require very little training of teachers who give them. Group tests are useful for instructional planning and identifying pupils who require more extensive evaluation with *individually administered tests*. Unlike group tests, individually administered ones demand considerable training and experience to give well. The examiner not only considers the child's answers but carefully observes the child's behavior, noting such reactions as attention to and interest in the tasks and wariness of the adult. These observations provide insights into whether the test score is accurate or underestimates the child's ability.

Two individual tests—the Stanford-Binet and the Wechsler—are most often used to identify highly intelligent children and diagnose those with learning problems.

THE STANFORD-BINET INTELLIGENCE SCALE

The **Stanford-Binet Intelligence Scale,** the modern descendant of Binet's first successful test, is appropriate for individuals between 2 years of age and adulthood. Its latest version measures both general intelligence and four intellectual factors: verbal reasoning, quantitative reasoning, abstract/visual (spatial) reasoning, and short-term memory (Thorndike, Hagen, & Sattler, 1986). Within these factors are 15 subtests that permit a detailed analysis of each child's mental abilities. The verbal and quantitative factors emphasize crystallized intelligence (culturally loaded, fact-oriented information), such as the child's knowledge of vocabulary and comprehension of sentences. In contrast, the abstract/visual reasoning factor taps fluid intelligence. It is believed to be less culturally biased because it requires little in the way of specific information.

Like many current tests, the Stanford-Binet is designed to be sensitive to ethnic minority children and children with physical disabilities and to reduce gender bias. Pictures

Stanford-Binet Intelligence Scale An individually administered intelligence test that is the modern descendent of Alfred Binet's first successful test for children. Measures general intelligence and four factors: verbal reasoning, quantitative reasoning, abstract/visual (spatial) reasoning, and short-term memory.

of children from different ethnic groups, a child in a wheelchair, and "unisex" figures that can be interpreted as male or female are included.

THE WECHSLER INTELLIGENCE SCALE FOR CHILDREN

The **Wechsler Intelligence Scale for Children–III (WISC–III)** is the third edition of a widely used test for 6- through 16-year-olds. A downward extension of it, the *Wechsler Preschool and Primary Scale of Intelligence–Revised (WPPSI–R)*, is appropriate for children 3 through 8 (Wechsler, 1989, 1991). The Wechsler tests offered both a measure of general intelligence and a variety of separate factor scores long before the Stanford-Binet. As a result, over the past two decades, many psychologists and educators have come to prefer the WISC and the WPPSI for individual assessment of children.

Both the WISC–III and the WPPSI–R measure two broad intellectual factors: verbal and performance. Each contains 6 subtests, yielding 12 separate scores in all. Performance items (look back at Figure 8.1 on page 318 for examples) require the child to arrange materials rather than talk to the examiner. Consequently, these tests provided one of the first means through which non-English-speaking children and children with speech and language disorders could demonstrate their intellectual strengths.

The Wechsler tests were also the first to be standardized on children representing the total population of the United States, including ethnic minorities. Their broadly representative standardization samples have served as models for many other tests, including the most recent version of the Stanford-Binet.

INFANT INTELLIGENCE TESTS

Accurately measuring the intelligence of infants is an especially challenging task. Unlike children, babies cannot answer questions or follow directions. All we can do is present them with stimuli, coax them to respond, and observe their behavior. In addition, infants are not necessarily cooperative subjects. They are likely to become distracted, fatigued, or bored during testing. Some tests depend heavily on information supplied by parents to compensate for the uncertain behavior of these young test-takers.

Most infant measures consist largely of perceptual and motor responses. For example, the *Bayley Scales of Infant Development,* a commonly used test for children between 1 month and 3½ years, was inspired by the early normative work of Arnold Gesell (see Chapter 1, page 14). It consists of two parts: (1) the Mental Scale, which includes such items as turning to a sound, looking for a fallen object, building a tower of cubes, and naming pictures; and (2) the Motor Scale, which assesses fine and gross motor skills, such as grasping, sitting, drinking from a cup, and jumping (Bayley, 1993).

Despite careful construction, infant tests emphasizing these types of items are poor predictors of intelligence during the childhood years, at least for samples of normal babies. The consistency of this finding has led researchers to conclude that infant perceptual and motor behaviors do not represent the same aspects of intelligence assessed in childhood.

To increase its predictive validity, the most recent version of the Bayley test includes a few items that emphasize infant memory, problem solving, categorization, and other complex cognitive skills—responses that, as we will see in a moment, are far more likely to correlate with later mental test scores. Nevertheless, traditional infant tests do show somewhat better long-term prediction for very low-scoring babies (Colombo, 1993). As a result, they are largely used for *screening*—helping to identify for further observation and intervention infants whose low scores mean that they are likely to have developmental problems in the future (Kopp, 1994).

Recall from Chapter 4 that speed of habituation and dishabituation to visual stimuli is an effective infant correlate of childhood intelligence. Unlike typical infant test items, the habituation–dishabituation response seems to tap aspects of cognitive processing (speed of thinking and attention, memory, and response to novelty) that are important in the verbal, conceptual, and problem-solving skills assessed at later ages. Consequently, a test made up entirely of habituation–dishabituation items, the *Fagan Test of Infant Intelligence,* has been constructed. To take it, the infant sits on the mother's lap and views a series of pictures. After exposure to each one, the examiner records looking time toward

Wechsler Intelligence Scale for Children–III (WISC–III)
An individually administered intelligence test that includes a measure of both general intelligence and a variety of verbal and performance scores.

a novel picture that is paired with the familiar one. Besides predicting childhood IQ, the Fagan test is highly effective in identifying babies who (without intervention) will soon show serious delays in mental development (Fagan & Detterman, 1992).

Infant tests based on Piaget's theory are also available. For example, Užgiris and Hunt's (1975) *Infant Psychological Development Scale* contains eight subtests, each of which assesses an important sensorimotor milestone, such as imitation and object permanence. Like habituation–dishabituation, object permanence is a better predictor of later IQ than traditional infant tests, perhaps because it, too, reflects a basic cognitive process—problem solving (Wachs, 1975).

The Computation and Distribution of IQ Scores

cores on intelligence tests, whether designed for infants, children, or adults, are usually arrived at in the same way—by computing an **intelligence quotient (IQ),** which indicates the extent to which the raw score (number of items passed) deviates from the typical performance of same-age individuals. When a test is constructed, it is given to a large, representative sample of individuals. Performances at each age level form a *normal, or bell-shaped, curve* in which most people fall near the center and progressively fewer fall out toward the extremes. Two important features of the normal curve are its *mean,* or the average score, and its *standard deviation,* which provides a measure of the average variability, or "spread-outness," of the scores from the mean.

Most intelligence tests convert their raw scores so that the mean is set at 100 and the standard deviation at 15. As Figure 8.4 shows, knowing the mean and standard deviation, we can determine the percentage of individuals at each age who fall above or below a certain score. Then, when we speak of a particular IQ, we know exactly what it means. For example, as Table 8.3 makes clear, a child with an IQ of 100 does better than 50 percent of same-age children. A child with an IQ of 85 does better than only 16 percent of her agemates, whereas a child with an IQ of 130 outperforms 98 percent of them. Look at Figure 8.4 once more, and notice how most scores cluster near the mean. The IQs of the great majority of people (95.5 percent) fall between 70 and 130; only a few achieve higher or lower scores.

What and How Well Do Intelligence Tests Predict?

lready we have seen that infant perceptual and motor tasks are poor predictors of later intellectual performance. What about the more frequently given childhood tests? Psychologists and educators who use test scores to make decisions about the educational placement of children assume that they are good indicators of future intelligence and scholastic performance. How well does IQ actually fare as a predictive measure?

FIGURE 8.4

The normal curve, with the baseline scaled in both IQ and standard deviation (SD) units. Areas under the curve are given in percentages. By summing the percentages to the left of an individual's IQ, we can obtain a percentile rank, which refers to the proportion of people of the same age that scored lower than the individual did on the test.

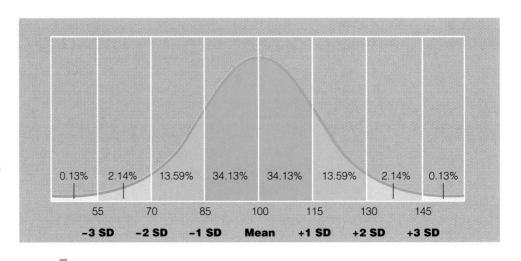

TABLE 8.3

Meaning of Different IQ Scores

Score	Percentile Rank (Child Does Better Than _____ Percent of Same-Age Children)	
70	2	
85	16	
100 (average IQ)	50	
115	84	
130	98	

STABILITY OF IQ SCORES

Stability refers to how effectively IQ predicts itself from one age to the next. Do children who obtain a particular IQ at 3 or 4 years perform about the same during elementary school and again when tested in high school? To answer this question, researchers rely on longitudinal studies in which the same children have been tested repeatedly over many ages.

■ **CORRELATIONAL STABILITY.** One way of examining the stability of IQ is to correlate scores obtained from repeated testings. This tells us whether children who score low or high in comparison to their agemates at one age continue to do so later. Examining these correlations, researchers have identified two generalizations about the stability of IQ:

1. *The older the child at time of first testing, the better the prediction of later IQ.* For example, in one longitudinal study, the correlation between scores at 2 and 5 years was only .32. It rose to .70 between ages 5 and 8, and .85 between 9 and 12 (Honzik, Macfarlane, & Allen, 1948). Preschool IQs do not predict school-age scores as well as do later measures, but after age 6, there is good stability, with many correlations in the .70s and .80s. Relationships between two testings obtained in adolescence are as high as the .80s and .90s (Hayslip, 1994; Humphreys, 1989).

2. *The closer in time two testings are, the stronger the relationship between the scores.* For example, a 4-year-old IQ correlates with a 5-year-old score at .72, but prediction drops by age 6 to .62. By age 18, it has declined to .42 (Honzik, Macfarlane, & Allen, 1948).

Taken together, these findings indicate that before 5 or 6 years, IQ is largely a measure of present ability, not a dependable, enduring measure. Why do preschool scores predict less well than later scores? One frequently cited reason is similar to the one we discussed with respect to infant tests: differences in the nature of test items. Concrete knowledge tends to be tested at younger ages, abstract problem solving later. Success on the first may require different skills than success on the second. Another explanation is that during early periods of rapid development, one child may spurt ahead of another and reach a plateau, whereas a second child, moving along slowly and steadily from behind, may catch up with and eventually overtake the first. Because children frequently change places in a distribution during periods of rapid change, all measures of developmental progress, including height and weight, are less stable and predictable at these times. IQ is no exception.

■ **STABILITY OF ABSOLUTE SCORES.** So far, we have looked at IQ stability in terms of how well children maintain their relative standing among agemates over time. We can also view stability in absolute terms—by examining each child's profile of IQ scores on a series

intelligence quotient (IQ)
A score that permits an individual's performance on an intelligence test to be compared to the typical performance of same-age individuals.

A wealth of research indicates that IQ predicts scholastic performance. However, researchers disagree on the underlying basis of this relationship, and the correlation is far from perfect. Other factors, such as motivation and personality characteristics, are just as important as IQ in accounting for children's learning in school.

(Dennis MacDonald/The Picture Cube)

environmental cumulative deficit hypothesis A view that attributes the age-related decline in IQ among poverty-stricken ethnic minority children to the compounding effects of under-privileged rearing conditions.

of repeated testings. Longitudinal research reveals that the majority of children show substantial IQ fluctuations over childhood and adolescence—in most cases, 10 to 20 points, and sometimes much more (McCall, 1993).

Children who change the most tend to have orderly profiles in which scores either increase or decrease with age. A close look at their characteristics and life experiences highlights factors that may be responsible for these varying IQ trends. Gainers were more independent and competitive about doing well in school. In addition, their parents were more interested in their intellectual accomplishments, applied greater pressure to succeed, and used rational, democratic discipline. In contrast, decliners tended to have parents who made little effort to stimulate them and who showed extremes in child rearing, using either very severe or very lax discipline (Honzik, Macfarlane, & Allen, 1948; McCall, Appelbaum, & Hogarty, 1973; Sontag, Baker, & Nelson, 1958).

When ethnic minority children and other youngsters who live in poverty are selected for special study, many show IQ declines. Both genetic and environmental factors contribute to children's IQ profiles (Cardon et al., 1992). Yet environment seems to be the overriding factor in the decreasing scores of poverty-stricken children. According to the **environmental cumulative deficit hypothesis,** the effects of underprivileged rearing conditions worsen the longer children remain in them. As a result, early cognitive deficits lead to more deficits that become harder to overcome as children get older (Klineberg, 1963). This idea has served as the basis for many early intervention programs, which are intensive efforts to offset these declines.

What evidence exists to support the environmental cumulative deficit? In a study of African-American children growing up under severely depressed conditions in the rural South, older siblings consistently obtained lower IQs than their younger brothers and sisters. But no such relation appeared for less economically disadvantaged African-American children living in California (Jensen, 1974). This finding is consistent with the environmental cumulative deficit rather than a genetically determined IQ profile. To fit with a genetic explanation, both the rural South- and California-reared groups should have displayed age-related IQ declines.

In sum, many children show substantial changes in the absolute value of IQ that are the combined result of personal characteristics, child-rearing practices, and living conditions. Nevertheless, once IQ becomes reasonably stable in a correlational sense, it predicts a variety of outcomes, as we will see in the following sections.

IQ AS A PREDICTOR OF SCHOLASTIC PERFORMANCE

Thousands of studies reveal that intelligence tests have accomplished their goal of predicting academic achievement. Correlations range from .40 to .70 and are typically around .50 (Brody, 1992). Children with higher IQs also get better grades and stay in school longer. As early as age 7, IQ is moderately correlated with adult educational attainment (McCall, 1977).

Why is IQ an effective predictor of scholastic performance? Researchers differ in how they answer this question. Some believe that both IQ and achievement depend on the same abstract reasoning processes that underlie Spearman's "g." A child well endowed with "g" is better able to acquire knowledge and skills taught in school. That IQ correlates best with achievement in the more abstract school subjects, such as English, mathematics, and science, is consistent with this interpretation (Jensen, 1998).

Other researchers argue that both IQ and achievement sample from the same pool of culturally specific information. From this point of view, an intelligence test is partly an achievement test, and a child's past experiences affect performance on both measures. Support for this view comes from evidence that crystallized intelligence (which reflects acquired knowledge) does a much better job of predicting academic achievement than does its fluid counterpart (Kaufman, Kamphaus, & Kaufman, 1985).

Does Schooling Influence IQ?

T IS WIDELY accepted that intelligence affects achievement in school, but how important is schooling in the development of intelligence? Stephen Ceci (1990, 1991; Ceci & Williams, 1997) reviewed hundreds of studies addressing this question. Taken together, they suggest that events taking place in classrooms have a profound effect on mental test performance.

Consider, first, the small but consistent drop in IQ that occurs over the summer months, especially among low-income children, whose summer activities least resemble school tasks. For economically advantaged children, whose vacation pursuits (such as academic-type camps) are often like those of school, the summer decline does not occur (Heyns, 1978).

Research dating back to the early part of this century reveals that irregular school attendance has an even greater impact on IQ. In one study, test scores of children growing up in "hollows" of the Blue Ridge Mountains were compared. All were descendants of Scottish-Irish and English immigrants, whose families had lived in the hollows for generations. One hollow was located at the foot of the mountains and had schools in session nine months of the year. In the other, more isolated hollows, schooling was irregular. Children's IQs varied substantially with amount of schooling available. Those who received the most had a 10- to 30-point advantage (Sherman & Key 1932).

Delayed entry into school is similarly related to test scores. In the Netherlands during World War II, many schools were closed as a result of the Nazi occupation. The IQs of children who started school several years late dropped about 7 points (DeGroot, 1951). Similar findings come from a study of children of Indian settlers in South Africa, whose schooling was postponed up to 4 years because their villages did not have teachers. Compared to Indian children in nearby villages who attended school, they showed a loss of 5 IQ points per year (Ramphal, 1962).

Dropping out of school also has a detrimental effect on IQ. In a Swedish study, a large random sample of 13-year-old boys were given intelligence tests. At age 18, they were retested as part of the country's national military registration. The impact of dropping out was determined by comparing children who were similar in IQ, social class, and school grades at age 13. Each year of high school not completed

During Serbian air raids over Zagreb, Yugoslavia, these children and their families took refuge in an air raid shelter, where school continued as usual. Daily classes provided the children with a sense of order and hopefulness and protected their intellectual development. (Donna Binder/Impact Visuals)

amounted to a loss of 1.8 IQ points, up to a maximum of 8 points for all 4 years of high school (Härnqvist, 1968).

Yet another illustration of the impact of schooling on IQ is the contrast between children born during the first 9 months of the year and those born during the last 3 months. Because most states have birth-date cutoffs for school entry, children in the first group usually enter school a year earlier than those in the second. And their IQ is higher—a difference entirely explained by their having attended school 1 year longer (Heckman, 1995).

Although many factors contribute to individual differences in mental test performance, schooling clearly emerges as a major force. Ceci (1991) believes that it influences IQ in at least three ways: (1) by teaching children factual knowledge relevant to test questions; (2) by promoting information-processing skills, such as memory strategies and categorization, that are tapped by test items; and (3) by encouraging attitudes and values that foster successful test taking, such as listening carefully to an adult's questions, answering under time pressure, and trying hard.

As you can probably imagine, researchers who believe heredity plays a crucial role in individual differences in IQ prefer the first of these explanations. Those who favor the power of environment prefer the second. Since the IQ–achievement correlation is stronger among identical than fraternal twins, heredity does seem to be important (Thompson, Detterman, & Plomin, 1991). But children's experiences also contribute. For example, findings reviewed in the Cultural Influences box above indicate that IQ not only predicts future achievement but is itself increased by years of schooling! Clearly, the relationship between intelligence and achievement is complex and determined by multiple factors.

Finally, although IQ predicts achievement better than any other tested measure, notice that the correlation is far from perfect. Other factors, such as motivation and personality characteristics that lead some children to try hard and want to do well in school, are just as important in accounting for individual differences in scholastic performance (Neisser et al., 1996).

IQ AS A PREDICTOR OF OCCUPATIONAL ATTAINMENT AND PERFORMANCE

Psychologists and educators would probably be less concerned with IQ scores if they were unrelated to long-term indicators of life success. But research indicates that childhood IQ predicts adult occupational attainment just about as well as it correlates with academic achievement. By second grade, pupils with the highest IQs are those who are most likely to enter prestigious professions, such as medicine, science, law, and engineering (McCall, 1977). Furthermore, IQ is modestly related to how successful a person is likely to be within an occupation. Employees who score higher on mental tests tend to receive higher job competence ratings from supervisors in a wide range of occupations (Hunter & Hunter, 1984).

Once again, however, we must keep in mind that the relationship between IQ and occupational attainment is far from perfect. Factors related to family background, such as parental encouragement, modeling of career success, and connections in the world of work, also predict occupational choice and attainment (Grotevant & Cooper, 1988). Furthermore, the influence of IQ on occupational status is partly due to the fact that test scores affect access to higher education. Educational attainment is a stronger predictor of occupational success and income than is IQ (Ceci & Williams, 1997; Featherman, 1980).

Personal variables also figure prominently into occupational achievement. In 1923, Lewis Terman initiated a longitudinal study of over 1,500 children with IQs above 135, who were followed well into mature adulthood. By middle age, more than 86 percent of the men in the sample had entered high-status professional and business occupations, a higher percentage than would have been expected for a random sample of individuals from similar home backgrounds (Terman & Oden, 1959).[2] But not all were professionally successful. Looking closely at those who fared best compared to those who fared worst, Terman found that their IQs were similar, averaging around 150. But the highly successful group appeared to have "a special drive to succeed, a need to achieve, that had been with them from grammar school onward" (Goleman, 1980, p. 31). They also experienced more intellectually stimulating home lives and a lower rate of family disruption due to parental divorce—factors that may have contributed to their achievement-oriented style.

Finally, once a person enters an occupation, abilities grouped under the label **practical intelligence** (because they are apparent in the real world but not in testing situations) predict on-the-job performance at least as well as or better than IQ. Practical intelligence involves "knowing how" rather than "knowing that" (Sternberg et al., 1995). It can be seen in the assembly line worker who discovers the fewest moves needed to complete a product or the business manager who increases productivity by making her subordinates feel valued. Unlike IQ, practical intelligence does not vary with ethnicity. And a growing body of evidence reveals that the two types of intelligence do not correlate with one another and make independent contributions to job success (Ceci & Liker, 1986; Scribner, 1986; Wagner, 1994, 1997).

In sum, occupational outcomes are a complex function of traditionally measured intelligence, education, motivation, family influences, special opportunity, and practical know-how. Current evidence indicates that IQ is not more important than these other factors.

IQ AS A PREDICTOR OF PSYCHOLOGICAL ADJUSTMENT

Is IQ so influential that it predicts indicators of life success beyond school and the workplace, such as emotional and social adjustment? During middle childhood, children with

practical intelligence Abilities apparent in the real world, not in testing situations, that involve "knowing how" rather than "knowing that."

[2]Born in the early part of this century during an era quite different from our own, nearly half the women in Terman's sample became housewives. However, of those who had professional careers, there were examples of outstanding accomplishments. Among them were scientists (one of whom contributed to the development of the polio vaccine), several novelists and journalists, and highly successful businesswomen (Terman & Oden, 1959).

higher IQs tend to be better liked by their agemates (Hartup, 1983). But the reasons for this association are not clear. A child's social competence is also related to child-rearing practices, health, physical appearance, and personality, all of which are correlated with IQ.

Another way of exploring the relationship between IQ and psychological adjustment is to look at the mental test performance of children who are clearly poorly adjusted, such as highly aggressive children who engage in norm-violating acts. Chronic delinquents have IQs that are, on the average, about 8 points lower than those of nondelinquents (Coie & Dodge, 1998). A lower IQ increases the risk of school failure, which is associated with delinquency. But a more likely direction of influence is that a history of aggressive behavior prevents children from taking advantage of classroom and other experiences that promote academic learning. In support of this view, longitudinal research in China and the United States reveals that early aggression predicts later academic difficulties. But the reverse is not true; early academic difficulties do not predict later aggression (Chen, Rubin, & Li, 1997; Masten et al., 1995). Hostile, defiant young people who fail in school are likely to conclude that traditional routes to occupational success will be closed to them. Consequently, they may seek alternative sources of reward, turning to antisocial peer groups and criminal behavior (Neisser et al., 1996; Patterson, Reid, & Dishion, 1992).

Finally, many adjustment disorders, such as high anxiety, social withdrawal, and depression, are unrelated to mental test scores. When we look at the evidence as a whole, we must conclude that a high IQ offers little guarantee of happiness and life satisfaction. And its imperfect prediction of other indicators of success, such as scholastic performance and occupational attainment, provides strong justification for never relying on IQ alone to forecast a child's future or make important educational placement decisions.

BRIEF REVIEW

ntelligence tests for children typically measure overall intelligence and a variety of separate factors. The Stanford-Binet and Wechsler scales are the most commonly used individually administered tests. Traditional infant tests, which consist largely of perceptual and motor responses, predict childhood intelligence poorly. Because tests measuring speed of habituation–dishabituation and object permanence tap basic cognitive processes, they are better predictors. The IQ score permits a direct comparison of a child's performance with a representative sample of same-age children.

Research consistently shows that IQ is an effective predictor of scholastic performance and occupational attainment. It is also linked to some aspects of psychological adjustment. However, a wide variety of personal, familial, and experiential factors also contribute to these outcomes. Although a high IQ does offer certain advantages, IQ alone tells us little that is definite about a child's chances for future success.

ASK YOURSELF . . .

◆ Fifteen-month-old Joey's score on the Bayley Scales of Infant Development is 115. His parents want to know exactly what this means and whether the score is likely to forecast Joey's childhood IQ. How would you respond to these questions?

◆ Seven-year-old Scott's father is concerned about how high his son's IQ is, since he wants Scott to go to college and enter a high-status occupation. What other factors in addition to IQ are likely to contribute to Scott's life success?

◆ CONNECTIONS
What family experiences linked to poverty probably contribute to the environmental cumulative deficit in IQ? (See Chapter 14, page 569.)

Ethnic and Socioeconomic Variations in IQ

eople in industrialized nations are stratified on the basis of what they do at work and how much they earn for doing it—factors that determine their social position and economic well-being. Researchers assess a family's standing on this continuum through an index called **socioeconomic status (SES)**. It combines three interrelated, but not completely overlapping, variables: (1) years of education and (2) the prestige of and skill required by one's job, both of which measure social status; and (3) income, which measures economic status.

In searching for the roots of socioeconomic disparities in the population, researchers have compared the IQ scores of SES and ethnic groups, since certain ethnicities are heavily represented at lower SES levels (for example, African American and Hispanic) and others at middle and upper SES levels (for example, Caucasian and Asian American). These findings are responsible for the IQ nature–nurture debate. If group differences in IQ exist, then either there must be genetic differences that vary with SES and ethnicity, or certain

socioeconomic status (SES) A measure of a family's social position and economic well-being that combines three interrelated, but not completely overlapping, variables: (1) years of education and (2) the prestige of and skill required by one's job, both of which measure social status; and (3) income, which measures economic status.

What are the origins of ethnic and SES differences in intelligence? Research aimed at answering this question has been the subject of heated controversy.

(Michael Newman/PhotoEdit)

groups must have fewer opportunities to acquire the skills needed for successful test performance.

In the 1970s, the IQ nature–nurture controversy escalated, after psychologist Arthur Jensen (1969) published a controversial article in the *Harvard Educational Review,* entitled "How Much Can We Boost IQ and Scholastic Achievement?" Jensen's answer to this question was "not much." He argued that heredity is largely responsible for individual, ethnic, and SES differences in IQ, a position he continues to maintain (Jensen, 1980, 1985, 1998).

Jensen's work received widespread public attention. It was followed by an outpouring of responses and research studies. In addition, there were ethical challenges from scientists deeply concerned that his conclusions would be used inappropriately to fuel social prejudices. Recently, the controversy was rekindled in Richard Herrnstein and Charles Murray's (1994) *The Bell Curve.* Like Jensen, these authors concluded that the contribution of heredity to individual and SES differences in IQ is substantial. At the same time, they stated that the relative role of heredity and environment in the black–white IQ gap (the main focus of investigations into ethnicity) remains unresolved.

Herrnstein and Murray's book, like Jensen's 1969 article, prompted heated debate. Some researchers praised it; other deplored it, underscoring the damaging social consequences of using uncertain evidence to claim that IQ variations are largely determined by heredity. Before we consider relevant research, let's look at group differences in IQ scores, since they are at the heart of the controversy.

DIFFERENCES IN GENERAL INTELLIGENCE

American black children score, on the average, 15 points below American white children on measures of general intelligence, although the difference has been shrinking (Nisbett, 1995; Suzuki & Valencia, 1997). Hispanic children fall midway between black and white children. Asian Americans score only slightly higher than their white counterparts—about 3 points (Ceci, Rosenblum, & Kumpf, 1998).

SES differences in IQ also exist. In one large-scale study, low-SES children scored 9 points below children in the middle of the SES distribution (Jensen & Figueroa, 1975). Since 42 percent of African-American children live in poverty compared to 22 percent of all American children, a reasonable question is whether economic status fully accounts for the black–white IQ difference. It accounts for some but not all of it. When black and white children are matched on family income, the black–white IQ gap is reduced by about a third (Jencks, 1972; Jensen & Reynolds, 1982).

No ethnic differences exist on infant measures of dishabituation to visual stimuli, which are good predictors of later IQ (Fagan & Singer, 1983). But before the third year of life, African-American children lag behind their white peers on other mental tests, a difference that persists into adulthood (Peoples, Fagan, & Drotar, 1995). Still, there is great variability in IQ *within* each ethnic and SES group. For example, as Figure 8.5 shows, the IQ distributions of blacks and whites overlap greatly. About 16 percent of blacks score above the white mean, and the same percentage of whites score below the black mean. In fact, ethnicity and SES account for only about one-fourth of the total variation in IQ. Nevertheless, these group differences are large enough and serious enough that they cannot be ignored.

DIFFERENCES IN SPECIFIC MENTAL ABILITIES

Are ethnic and SES differences limited to certain kinds of mental abilities? Arthur Jensen believes so. In his **Level I–Level II theory,** Jensen distinguishes two types of intelligence. Level I refers to items emphasizing short-term and rote memory, such as digit span and

Level I–Level II theory Jensen's controversial theory, which states that ethnic and social-class differences in IQ are due to genetic differences in higher-order, abstract forms of intelligence (Level II) rather than basic memory skills (Level I).

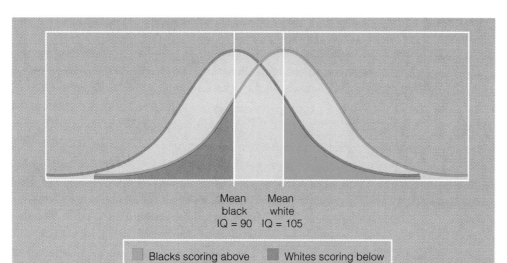

FIGURE 8.5

IQ score distributions for black and for white children. The means represent approximate values obtained in studies of children reared by their biological parents.

Mean
black
IQ = 90

Mean
white
IQ = 105

Blacks scoring above
the white IQ mean

Whites scoring below
the black IQ mean

recall of basic arithmetic facts. In contrast, Level II involves abstract reasoning and problem solving—items strongly correlated with Spearman's "g," such as vocabulary, verbal comprehension, spatial visualization, and figure matrices. (Turn back to Figure 8.1 on page 318 to review examples of these items.)

According to Jensen, black–white and (to a lesser extent) SES differences in IQ are due to Level II abilities; the groups are about the same in Level I intelligence (Jensen, 1988, 1998). Furthermore, Jensen indicated that among Level II abilities, black children do worst on the least culturally loaded, fluid-type items (such as figure matrices) and best on crystallized tasks (such as vocabulary). Therefore, he argued, black–white IQ differences cannot be caused by cultural bias in the tests. Jensen's conclusion—that blacks are less well endowed than whites with higher-order, abstract forms of intelligence—intensified public outcries over the racist implications of his work.

Is there support for Jensen's Level I–Level II theory? In reviewing a large number of studies, one researcher judged that most were consistent with it (Vernon, 1981, 1987). But others have not been able to confirm the theory. For example, Nathan Brody (1987) found that test items strongly correlated with "g" did not always produce the largest black–white IQ differences. A second group of researchers reported that both Level I and Level II scores declined similarly with SES (Stankov, Horn, & Roy, 1980).

These findings suggest that "g" contributes to ethnic and SES differences in IQ, but it is not the only basis for them. At present, the evidence on specific mental abilities is not clear enough to favor either a genetic or cultural-bias explanation. To explore the basis for individual and group differences in IQ, we must turn to a very different set of findings.

Explaining Individual and Group Differences in IQ

Over the past 2 decades, researchers have conducted hundreds of studies aimed at uncovering the origins of individual, ethnic, and SES differences in mental abilities. The research falls into three broad classes: (1) investigations addressing the importance of heredity; (2) those that look at whether IQ scores are biased measures of low-SES and minority children's true abilities; and (3) those that examine the quality of children's home environments as a major influence on their mental test performance.

GENETIC INFLUENCES

Recall from Chapter 3 that behavioral geneticists examine the relative contributions of heredity and environment to complex human characteristics by conducting *kinship studies,* in which they compare individuals of differing degrees of genetic relationship to one another. Let's look closely at what they have discovered about genetic influences on IQ.

■ **HERITABILITY OF INTELLIGENCE.** In Chapter 3, we introduced the most common method for studying the role of heredity in IQ—the *heritability estimate*. To briefly review, first the IQs of pairs of family members who vary in the extent to which they share genes are correlated. Then, using a complicated statistical procedure, the correlations are compared to arrive at an index of heritability, ranging from 0 to 1, that indicates the proportion of variation among individuals in a specific population due to genetic factors.

Let's begin our consideration of the importance of heredity by looking closely at the correlations on which heritability estimates are based. Table 8.4 summarizes worldwide findings on IQ correlations between kinship pairs. Notice that the greater the genetic similarity between family members, the more they resemble one another in IQ. In fact, two of the correlations reveal that heredity is, without question, partially responsible for individual differences in mental test performance. The correlation for identical twins reared apart (.76) is much higher than for fraternal twins reared together (.55).

When researchers look at how these kinship correlations change with age, they find additional support for the importance of heredity. Greater IQ similarity for identical than fraternal twins is evident by 2 years of age (Petrill et al., 1998). And as Figure 8.6 shows, correlations for identical twins increase modestly into adulthood, whereas those for fraternal twins drop sharply at adolescence. Do these trends remind you of the *niche-picking* idea discussed in Chapter 3? Common rearing experiences support the similarity of fraternal twins during childhood. But as they get older and are released from the influence of their families, each fraternal twin follows a course of development, or finds a niche, that fits with his or her unique genetic makeup. As a result, their IQ scores diverge. In contrast, the genetic likeness of identical twins leads them to seek out similar niches in adolescence and adulthood. Consequently, their IQ resemblance is even greater than it was during childhood. Other studies confirm that the contribution of heredity to IQ strengthens with development (Loehlin, Horn, & Willerman, 1997; McGue et al., 1993).

Although kinship research underscores the importance of heredity, a careful review of the correlations in Table 8.4 reveals that environment is clearly involved. Comparisons of twin and sibling pairs reared together and apart reveal that in each instance, the correla-

TABLE 8.4

Worldwide Summary of IQ Correlations between Kinship Pairs

Kinship Pair	Average Weighted Correlation	Total Number of Kinship Pairs Included
Identical twins reared together	.86	4,672
Identical twins reared apart	.76	158
Fraternal twins reared together	.55	8,600
Fraternal twins reared apart	.35	112
Siblings reared together	.47	26,473
Siblings reared apart	.24	203
Parent–biological child living together	.42	8,433
Parent–biological child living apart	.22[a]	814
Nonbiological siblings (adopted–natural pairings)	.29	345
Nonbiological siblings (adopted–adopted pairings)	.34	369
Parent–adopted child	.19	1,397

[a]This correlation, reported by Bouchard and McGue (1981), is lower than the values obtained in three subsequent adoption studies, which reported correlations of .31, .37, and .43 (Horn, 1983; Phillips & Fulker, 1989; Scarr & Weinberg, 1983).

Sources: Bouchard & McGue, 1981; Scarr, 1997.

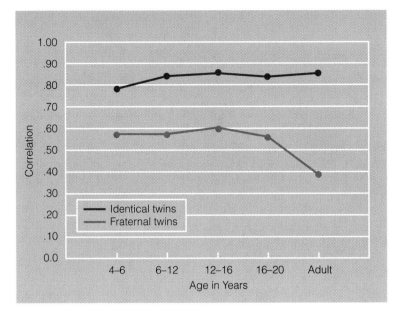

Cross-sectional age-related changes in IQ correlations, derived from published studies including thousands of twin pairs. Correlations for identical twins increase modestly into adulthood, whereas those for fraternal twins drop sharply at adolescence. Similar trends appear when twins are followed longitudinally and IQ correlations are computed at successive ages.

(From M. McGue, T. J. Bouchard, Jr., W. G. Iacono, & D. T. Lykken, 1993, "Behavioral Genetics of Cognitive Ability: A Life-Span Perspective," in R. Plomin & G. E. McClearn, Eds., *Nature, Nurture, and Psychology,* p. 63. Washington, DC: American Psychological Association. Copyright © 1993 by the American Psychological Association. Adapted by permission.)

tion for "reared together" is stronger. Similarly, for parents and biological children, the correlation for "living together" is stronger than that for "living apart." Finally, parents and adopted children, as well as unrelated siblings, show low positive correlations, again providing support for the effects of common rearing conditions.

As we indicated in Chapter 3, heritability estimates are usually computed using correlations for identical and fraternal twins. The typical value in recent research in Western industrialized nations is about .50, which means that half the variation in IQ is due to individual differences in heredity (Plomin, 1994c). This is a much more modest figure than the estimate of .80 arrived at by Jensen as part of his controversial 1969 article.

Furthermore, we noted in Chapter 3 that even this moderate value may be too high, since twins reared together often experience very similar overall environments. And even when they are reared apart, they are often placed in foster and adoptive homes that are advantaged and alike in many ways. When the range of environments to which twins are exposed is restricted, heritabilities underestimate the role of environment and overestimate the role of heredity. So although heritability research offers convincing evidence that genetic factors contribute to IQ, disagreement persists over how large the role of heredity really is (Waldman, 1997).

■ DO HERITABILITY ESTIMATES EXPLAIN ETHNIC AND SES DIFFERENCES IN IQ?

Despite the limitations of the heritability estimate, Jensen (1969, 1998) relied on it to support the argument that ethnic and SES differences in IQ have a strong genetic basis. This line of reasoning is widely regarded as inappropriate. Although heritability estimates computed within black and white populations are similar, they provide no direct evidence on what is responsible for between-group differences in IQ (Plomin et al., 1997; Suzuki & Valencia, 1997). And recall from Chapter 3 that the heritability of IQ is *higher* under advantaged (higher-SES) than disadvantaged (lower-SES) rearing conditions (Bronfenbrenner & Morris, 1998). Factors associated with low income and poverty, including weak or absent prenatal care, family stress, low-quality schools, and lack of community supports for effective child rearing, prevent children from attaining their genetic potential.

In a well-known example, Richard Lewontin (1976) showed that using within-group heritabilities to explain between-group differences is like comparing different seeds in different soil. Suppose we take a handful of corn seeds (which vary in genetic make-up) and plant them in the same pot with a rich supply of fertilizer designed to promote plant growth. Then we take another handful of seeds and grow them under quite different conditions, in a pot with half as much fertilizer. We find that although the plants in each group vary in height, the first group, on the average, grows taller than the second group. Within each group, individual differences in plant height are largely due to heredity, since growth environments of all plants were much the same. But the between-group

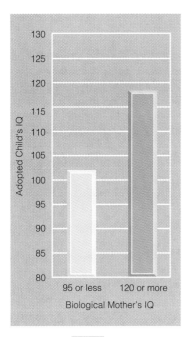

FIGURE 8.7

IQs of adopted children as a function of biological mothers' IQ in the Texas Adoption Project. In this study, selective placement was not great enough to account for the large difference between the two groups.

(Adapted from Willerman, 1979.)

difference is probably environmental, since the fertilizer given to the second group was far less plentiful.

To be sure of this conclusion, we could design a second study in which we expose the second group of seeds to a full supply of fertilizer and see if they reach an average height that equals that of the first group. If they do, then we would have more powerful evidence that environment is responsible for the previous group difference. In the next section, we will see that researchers have conducted natural experiments of this kind by studying the IQs of children adopted into homes very different from their family of origin.

■ **ADOPTION RESEARCH.** Adoption studies provide a wider range of information than the twin evidence on heritability considered so far. Correlations of children with their biological and adoptive family members can be examined for the relative contribution of heredity and environment. Even more important, researchers can gain insight into how malleable IQ is by looking at changes in the absolute value of test scores as the result of growing up in an advantaged family.

One of the earliest and best-known of these investigations was carried out nearly a half century ago by Marie Skodak and Harold Skeels (1949). They repeatedly tested the intelligence of one hundred children who had been placed in adoptive homes before 6 months of age. Although the biological parents were largely low income, the adoptive parents were well above average in earnings and education. Children's scores remained above the population mean throughout middle childhood and into adolescence, suggesting that IQ is highly malleable! Nevertheless, children's IQs still showed substantial correlation with the scores of their biological mothers, providing support for the influence of heredity.

Skodak and Skeels's groundbreaking study suffered from an important limitation. Selective placement of adoptees took place. That is, children with the best-off biological parents tended to be placed with the most advantaged adoptive families. When this occurs, genetic and environmental influences on children's IQ scores cannot be separated completely.

But more recent adoption research, in which selective placement was judged to be minimal, agrees with Skodak and Skeels's findings. The Texas Adoption Project resulted from the discovery of a large private adoption agency that had routinely given IQ tests to unwed mothers staying in its residence until they gave birth. Children of two extreme groups of mothers—those with IQs below 95 and those with IQs above 120—were chosen for special study. As Figure 8.7 shows, when tested in middle childhood, both groups of adopted children scored above average in IQ. But children of the low-IQ biological mothers did not do nearly as well as children of brighter mothers who were placed in similar adoptive families (Horn, 1983). And when correlations were examined, adopted children showed an increasing resemblance to their biological mothers as they grew older and a decreasing resemblance to their adoptive parents (Loehlin, Horn, & Willerman, 1997). In sum, adoption research shows that both environment and heredity contribute significantly to IQ.

The fact that adopted children have consistently been found to score above average in IQ suggests that the SES difference in intelligence has a substantial environmental component. But concluding that it is entirely explained by environment is probably too extreme. Although children of low-IQ biological mothers adopted into middle-SES families attain above-average IQs, they generally score somewhat lower than their adoptive parents' natural children, with whom they share equally privileged rearing conditions. This difference could be due to heredity, to environmental influences prior to adoption (such as prenatal conditions), or to both (Devlin et al., 1995). In addition, adoption studies repeatedly reveal stronger correlations between the IQ scores of biological than adoptive relatives (Horn, 1983; Plomin & DeFries, 1983; Scarr & Weinberg, 1983). On the basis of these findings, several researchers have concluded that the SES–IQ relationship is partly genetic (Bouchard, 1997; Scarr, 1997).

What about the black–white IQ gap? In this case, adoption research suggests that it is environmental; it cannot be assigned to racially linked, inferior genes. See the Variations box on the following page for a description of this important research.

Transracial Adoption: When Black Children Grow Up in White Homes

TWO TRANSRACIAL ADOPTION studies, both focusing on the development of black children growing up in white middle-SES homes, shed light on the origins of IQ differences between black and white children. If Jensen's claim that black children are limited in potential is correct, then IQs of black adoptees should remain considerably below those of other children growing up in advantaged white families. If black children are as well equipped genetically as white children, then their IQs should rise when they are reared by white parents "in the culture of the tests and schools."

Sandra Scarr and Richard Weinberg (1976, 1983) gave IQ tests during childhood and adolescence to more than 100 transracially adopted black children. Two-thirds were placed during the first year of life, one-third after 12 months of age. The white adoptive parents had high-average to superior IQs, were well above average in occupational status and income, and had four to five more years of education than did the children's biological parents. When tested in childhood, the adoptees attained an average IQ of 106, considerably above the general population mean. The scores of those who had been adopted within the first 12 months were even higher. They averaged 110, 20 points above the mean of children growing up in low-income black communities. Scarr and Weinberg concluded that heredity cannot account for black children's typically depressed intelligence test scores.

A decade later, the researchers restudied the sample. They found that IQ scores declined in adolescence, probably due to use of different tests at the two ages and to the emotional challenge of establishing an ethnic identity that blends birth and rearing backgrounds (DeBerry, Scarr, & Weinberg, 1996). Otherwise, earlier favorable findings persisted. Interracially adopted young people remained substantially above the IQ average for low-SES African-Americans, and they scored slightly above the national norm in academic achievement. In sum, the adoptees continued to show the beneficial effects of their rearing environments (Waldman, Weinberg, & Scarr, 1994; Weinberg, Scarr, & Waldman, 1992).

A second transracial study lends insight into cultural experiences that contributed to Scarr and Weinberg's findings. Elsie Moore (1986) compared the test-taking behavior and parent–child interaction of two groups of black adoptees: one growing up in white and the other growing up in black middle-SES families. Tested between 7 and 10 years of age, the traditionally adopted children did well, attaining a mean IQ of 104. But scores of their transracially adopted counterparts were much higher, averaging 117.

Consistent with their superior scores, the transracially adopted group approached the test with attitudes and strategies conducive to success. They were more task involved and persistent, and their responses were more elaborate. When they did not know an answer, they rarely attributed

When black children grow up "in the culture of the tests and schools," they perform substantially above the population mean in IQ. Transracial adoption research supports the view that rearing environment is responsible for the black–white IQ gap.
(Tony Freeman/PhotoEdit)

failure to their own inability. The transracially adopted group's greater test-taking confidence was, in turn, related to their mothers' special support of problem-solving behavior. When asked to teach their children a difficult task, the white mothers displayed more encouragement and enthusiasm for children's efforts.

These findings support the position that rearing environment accounts for the black–white IQ gap. However, the researchers were careful to point out that their findings are not an endorsement for widespread adoption of black children into white homes. Instead, they call for more research on ways in which ethnically different families promote a diverse array of cognitive skills.

ARE ETHNIC GROUPS BIOLOGICALLY BASED?

The dramatic rise in IQ that results from granting black children born into poverty the child-rearing advantages of white middle-SES children is consistent with the conclusions of biologists that ethnicity is not biologically based. DNA analyses reveal wide genetic variation *within* ethnic groups and insignificant variation *between* them (Cavalli-Sforza, Menozzi, & Piazza, 1994). The ethnicities that have been the focus of the IQ nature–nurture controversy share experiences and opportunities, not biology.

Nevertheless, many people assume that genetic, racial differences determine ethnic differences in psychological traits. A closer look reveals that racial labels assumed to have genetic meaning are often arbitrary. For example, "black" designates people with dark skin in the United States. It refers to hair texture, eye color, and stature in Brazil and Peru, where many African Americans would be called "white." Asians and the !Kung of Botswana, Africa, could be regarded as one race, since they have similarly shaped eyes. Alternatively, Asians, Native Americans, and Swedes could be grouped together because of their similarly shaped teeth (Begley, 1995; Renzetti & Curran, 1998).

Changes in ethnic and racial designations over time underscore their unclear boundaries. On the U.S. Census form, ten racial categories appeared in 1930, only five in 1990. And in research on ethnicity and psychological traits, people self-identify, expressing a sense of group belonging and cultural heritage; they are not categorized on the basis of genetic similarity. Finally, ethnic mixing is extensive in countries as culturally diverse as the United States. Consider this Hawaiian native's description of his ethnicity: "I'm Asian on my birth certificate and the U.S. Census form, but I'm really multiracial. My mother's parents were Japanese, my father's mother was Filipino, and my father's father was Irish."

As one scholar of race relations recently summed up, "Classification of human beings into races is in the end a futile exercise" (Payne, 1998, p. 32). An ever-present danger of perpetuating the belief that some ethnic groups are genetically inferior in IQ is continued unfair allocation of resources, making an unfounded assumption seem true.

ETHNICITY AND TEST BIAS

A controversial question raised about ethnic differences in IQ has to do with whether they are an artifact of test content and administration procedures. If a test samples culturally specific knowledge and skills that not all groups of children have had equal opportunity to learn, then is it a fair measure of the intelligence of all children?

Some experts reject the idea that intelligence tests are biased, claiming that they were intended to represent important aspects of success in the common culture. According to this perspective, since current mental tests predict scholastic performance equally well for majority and minority children, they are fair measures for both groups (Jensen, 1980, 1998; Oakland & Parmelee, 1985). Others take a broader view of test bias. They believe that lack of prior exposure to test content, language customs, and testing conditions lead IQ scores to underestimate the abilities of certain ethnic minority groups and low-SES children (Ceci & Williams, 1997; Ogbu, 1997; Sternberg 1997). To evaluate this position, let's look at each of these factors.

■ **PRIOR EXPOSURE TO TEST CONTENT.** Many researchers argue that IQ scores are affected by specific information acquired as part of majority-culture upbringing. Unfortunately, efforts to make tests fairer to ethnic minorities, either by basing them on more familiar content or by eliminating crystallized items and using only fluid tasks, have not raised the scores of these children very much (Reynolds & Kaiser, 1990). For example, Raven Progressive Matrices is one of the most commonly used tests of fluid intelligence. To see a typical item, look back at the figure matrix task in Figure 8.1. Yet low-SES minority children continue to perform more poorly on the Raven test, and others like it, than do their white middle-SES agemates (Jensen, 1980).

Nevertheless, it is possible that high scores on fluid tests depend on subtle learning opportunities. In one study, children's performance on a spatial reasoning subscale of the WISC was related to the extent to which they had played a popular but expensive game that (like the test items) required them to arrange blocks to duplicate a design as quickly as possible (Dirks, 1982). Playing videogames that require fast responding and mental rotation of visual images also fosters success on spatial test items (Subrahmanyam & Greenfield, 1996). Low-income minority children, who often grow up in more "people-oriented" than "object-oriented" homes, may lack play materials that promote certain intellectual skills. In line with this possibility, when a large, ethnically diverse sample of parents were asked about characteristics important to their idea of an intelligent first grader, Anglo-Americans valued cognitive traits over noncognitive ones. In contrast, ethnic minorities (Cambodian, Filipino, Vietnamese, and Mexican immigrants)

saw noncognitive attributes—motivation, self-management, and social skills—as equally or more important than cognitive skills. Mexican parents, especially, highly valued the social component of intelligence (Okagaki & Sternberg, 1993).

Finally, recall the evidence presented earlier in this chapter that the more time children spend in school, the higher their IQ scores. It also supports the conclusion that exposure to specific information resembling the content of intelligence tests affects performance on a wide range of mental ability tasks (Ceci, 1991).

How does this Hispanic girl tell a story to her classmates? Ethnic minority children often use distinct narrative structures derived from listening to and telling stories at home. Their narrative style may not match the topic-focused formula valued in school.

(Michael Newman/PhotoEdit)

■ **LANGUAGE CUSTOMS.** Ethnic minority families often foster unique language skills that do not match the expectations of most classrooms and testing situations. Shirley Brice Heath (1982, 1989), an anthropologist who spent many hours observing in low-SES black homes in a southeastern American city, found that adults asked black children very different kinds of questions than is typical in white middle-SES families. From an early age, white parents ask knowledge-training questions, such as "What color is it?" and "What's this story about?" that resemble the questioning style of tests and classrooms. In contrast, the black parents asked only "real" questions—ones that they themselves did not know the answer to. Often these were analogy questions ("What's that like?") or story-starter questions ("Didja hear Miss Sally this morning?") that called for elaborate responses about personal experiences and no single right answer.

Heath and other researchers report that these experiences lead low-SES black children to develop complex verbal skills at home, such as storytelling and exchanging quick-witted remarks. But their language differs from that of white middle-SES children in emphasizing social and emotional topics rather than facts about the world (Blake, 1994). Not surprisingly, black children may be confused by the "objective" questions they encounter in classrooms and withdraw into silence.

The impact of culture on language style is apparent in children's narratives. Most school-age children's narratives increasingly follow a *topic-focused formula.* They build toward a high point, describe a critical event, and then resolve it. African-American children, however, often tell *topic-associating stories,* which blend several similar experiences and therefore include multiple shifts in time and setting. One 9-year-old, for example, related having a tooth pulled, then described seeing her sister's tooth pulled, next told how she removed one of her baby teeth before a test at school, and concluded with her offer to take out her cousin's baby tooth: "So I told him, 'I'm a pullin' teeth expert. . . . if you need somebody to do it, call me, and I'll be over" (McCabe, 1997, p. 164). When teachers criticize this approach as "disorganized," they devalue the child's culture (McCabe, 1998).

Other minority youngsters also develop distinct language styles. For example, children of Hispanic immigrants are taught to respect adult authority rather than express their own knowledge and opinions. Yet American teachers, who value self-assertive speaking, typically equate the silence of Hispanic children with having a negative attitude toward learning (Greenfield & Suzuki, 1998). As the child listens politely but does not answer out of deference to the adult, a culturally valued style of communicating quickly leads to unfair, negative evaluations in school and on mental tests.

The pace of conversation customary in the child's ethnic group can disrupt communication with majority-culture adults. Navajo Indian children speak slowly and rhythmically, leaving much time between phrases and sentences. Teachers and testers often think these children have finished responding when they have only paused. In contrast, Native Hawaiian children prefer rapid-fire, overlapping speech. Non-Hawaiian adults may interpret this style as rude interruption, although in Hawaiian society it signals interest and involvement (Tharp, 1989, 1994).

During testing, the minority child may look to the examiner for cues about how to respond. Yet most intelligence tests permit tasks to be presented in only one way, and they allow no feedback. Consequently, minority children may simply give the first answer that comes to mind, not one that truly represents what they know. Turn back to the beginning of this chapter and review Jermaine's responses to Nora's questions. Jermaine appeared to repeat his first answer because he had trouble figuring out the task's meaning, not because he was unable to classify objects. Had Nora prompted him to look at the questions in a different way, his performance might have been better.

■ REACTIONS TO TESTING CONDITIONS. When tested by an unfamiliar adult, children from poverty backgrounds often reply, "I don't know," to the simplest of questions, including "What's your name?" The response does not reflect lack of ability. Instead, it is due to wariness of the examiner and the testing situation. As a result, the fearful child behaves in ways aimed at minimizing interaction and terminating the unpleasant experience as quickly as possible (Zigler & Finn-Stevenson, 1992). Besides feeling discomfort in the presence of strangers, many low-SES minority children do not define testing conditions in achievement terms. They may be more concerned with attention and approval from the adult than in answering as many questions correctly as possible (Zigler & Seitz, 1982).

When testing conditions are modified so that the minority child has a chance to become familiar with the examiner, is praised frequently, and is given easier items after incorrect responses to minimize the emotional consequences of failure, IQ scores improve. Although these procedures ease adjustment of young children to the testing situation, over time many low-SES minority children suffer from deep-seated motivational difficulties. As they experience repeated academic failure, they are likely to develop a self-defeating style marked by withdrawal and reduced effort that severely affects their approach to tests and school tasks. Recent evidence indicates a growing discrepancy over the school years between high- and low-achieving children in their motivation to excel on standardized tests (Paris et al., 1991). As a result, IQs may become especially inaccurate indicators of these youngsters' learning potential at older ages.

REDUCING TEST BIAS

Although not all experts agree, today there is greater acknowledgment that IQ scores can underestimate the intelligence of culturally different children. A special concern exists about incorrectly labeling minority children as slow learners and assigning them to remedial classes. These special educational experiences are far less stimulating than regular classes and are linked to high rates of negative educational outcomes, including school failure and drop out.

Because of the danger of restricting minority children's educational opportunities and life chances, precautions are advised when evaluating children for educational placement. Besides test scores, assessments of children's adaptive behavior—their ability to cope with the demands of their everyday environments—should be obtained (Landesman & Ramey, 1989). The child who does poorly on an IQ test yet displays considerable practical intelligence by playing a complex game on the playground, figuring out how to rewire a broken TV, or caring for younger siblings responsibly is unlikely to be mentally deficient.

In addition, test designers are becoming more aware that minority children are often capable of the cognitive operations called for by test items. But because they are used to thinking in other ways in daily life, they may not access the required operation (Greenfield, 1997). Consequently, alternative testing procedures are being tried. **Dynamic testing,** an innovative approach consistent with Vygotsky's concept of the zone of proximal development, tries to narrow the gap between actual and potential test performance. In-

dynamic testing An approach to testing consistent with Vygotsky's concept of the zone of proximal development, in which purposeful teaching is introduced into the testing situation to see what the child can do with social support.

Dynamic testing introduces purposeful teaching into the testing situation
to find out what the child can attain
with social support. Many ethnic
minority children perform more
competently on test items after adult
assistance. And the approach helps
identify the teaching style to which
the child is most responsive.
(Bob Daemmrich/Stock Boston)

stead of emphasizing previously acquired knowledge and skills, it introduces purposeful
teaching into the testing situation to find out what the child can attain with social support. Three factors distinguish dynamic testing from traditional, static approaches:

- a focus on the *processes* involved in learning and development (rather than on intellectual *products*);

- provision of feedback after each task (rather than no feedback); and

- an examiner–child relationship based on teaching and helping that is individualized
for each child (rather than a neutral relationship that is identical for all children).
(Grigorenko & Sternberg, 1998)

Several dynamic testing models exist, each of which uses a pretest–intervene–retest
procedure (Lidz, 1991, 1997). The best known of these is Reuben Feuerstein's (1979, 1980)
Learning Potential Assessment Device. Using traditional intelligence test items, the adult
tries to find the teaching style to which the child is most responsive and communicates
principles and strategies that the child can generalize to new situations. Other dynamic
assessment models do not use intelligence test items. Rather, the examiner observes and
tries to facilitate cognitive change on academic tasks children encounter in classrooms
(Campione & Brown, 1987).

Evidence on the effectiveness of dynamic testing reveals that the IQs of ethnic minority children underestimate their ability to perform intellectual tasks after adult assistance.
Instead, children's receptiveness to teaching and their capacity to transfer what they have
learned to novel problems add to the prediction of future task success (Brown & Ferrara,
1985; Rand & Kaniel, 1987; Tzuriel & Feuerstein, 1992). As yet, dynamic testing is not
more effective in predicting academic achievement than are traditional tests. But better
correspondence may emerge in classrooms where teaching resembles procedures integral
to the dynamic testing approach—namely, individualized, responsive interaction on tasks
carefully selected to help the child move beyond his or her current level of development
(Grigorenko & Sternberg, 1998). Bridging the gap between high-quality classroom learning experiences and mental testing is at the heart of another innovative assessment approach, discussed in the From Research to Practice box on page 342.

Dynamic testing presents challenges much greater than those faced in traditional, static assessment. The approach is time consuming and requires extensive knowledge of cultural values and practices to work well with minority children. Until we have the resources
to implement these procedures broadly, should we suspend the use of intelligence testing
in schools? Most experts regard this solution as unacceptable, since important educational
decisions would be based only on subjective impressions—a policy that could increase the

Authentic Assessment

FROM RESEARCH TO PRACTICE

AT CENTRAL PARK East Secondary School in New York City, students working toward a high school diploma do not focus on passing tests. Instead, they are absorbed in preparing a portfolio that represents their accomplishments in a wide range of subjects over a 2- to 3-year period. Here is a sampling of required portfolio contents:

- An autobiography, involving reflection on the past and plans for the future

- A list of texts read and samples of essays demonstrating a capacity to reflect on literary products and ideas

- Competency test scores in mathematics and a special project using complex mathematical reasoning for either a scientific or practical purpose

- School and community service accomplishments, documented through essays, videos, work samples, or other demonstrations

The portfolio is evaluated by a committee, composed of teachers with diverse expertise, an outside examiner, and a student peer. Before deciding on readiness to graduate, the committee hears the student's oral defense of the portfolio and asks a wide range of questions about the process of compiling its contents and the student's knowledge and conclusions.

The portfolio is only one of many ways to conduct **authentic assessment,** an approach that measures intellectual progress by examining students' real performance in school over time. In the early grades, for example, teachers often observe and take notes as students work. They also compile and comment on samples of reading, writing, and oral work, documenting children's attainment of valued school goals. In some cases, assessment is so firmly embedded in everyday learning that the two cannot be distinguished (Darling-Hammond, Ancess, & Falk, 1995).

Administrators and teachers turning to alternative assessment realize that traditional tests do not tap many important aspects of learning. They want to find out how well students perform on tasks that mirror real-world challenges.

In addition, they want to inspire improvements in teaching. Placing a high value on intelligence and achievement test scores often encourages teachers to focus on training isolated facts and skills. Authentic assessment, in contrast, fosters educational experiences that require complex thinking needed in everyday life—framing problems, finding information, evaluating alternatives, and generating new ideas and products. An important goal of authentic assessment is self-assessment—helping students evaluate their own work on the basis of public standards and revise it to make it better (Newmann, 1996; Wiggins, 1993).

Can authentic assessment promote high achievement for all pupils? In a recent study of 24 elementary, middle, and high schools selected for their innovative practices, researchers gave each class an "instruction score" based on the extent to which classroom experiences required students to (1) construct knowledge rather than just reproduce it, (2) strive for depth of understanding by relating diverse pieces of information, and (3) communicate their ideas in ways valued beyond school (Newmann, Marks, & Gamoran, 1996). The classrooms varied widely; even in these progressive schools, many teachers did not foster complex, real-life thinking. Yet the more they did, the better students performed on an authentic assessment. Neither SES, ethnicity, nor gender affected the relationship of classroom experiences to authentic academic achievement; children from all social backgrounds benefited similarly from challenging but meaningful learning activities. And although traditional achievement test scores were positively correlated with authentic assessment scores, the relationship was modest. Authentic assessment seemed to be tapping aspects of learning not picked up by traditional measures.

More research is needed on how well authentic assessment measures cognitively complex skills and motivates students with diverse backgrounds to perform at their best (Linn & Baker, 1996; Wiggins, 1998). Until that evidence is available, authentic procedures can be combined with traditional test scores. When a child does well on authentic tasks but poorly on an intelligence or achievement test, then educators must consider carefully whether the traditional score is a biased measure of that child's mental ability.

---

discriminatory placement of minority children. Intelligence tests are useful as long as they are interpreted carefully by examiners who are sensitive to cultural influences on test performance. And despite their limitations, IQ scores continue to be valid measures of school learning potential for the majority of Western children.

HOME ENVIRONMENT AND IQ

Ethnic and SES differences are not the only IQ variations with environmental explanations. As we indicated earlier, children of the *same* ethnic and SES background also vary in IQ. Many studies support the conclusion that home environmental factors contribute to these differences.

Researchers divide home influences into two broad types. The first, called **shared environmental influences,** are factors that pervade the general atmosphere of the home

authentic assessment An approach that measures intellectual progress by examining students' real performance in school over time.

shared environmental influences Environmental influences that pervade the general atmosphere of the home and affect all children living in it to the same extent.

TABLE 8.5

Home Observation for Measurement of the Environment (HOME) Subscales

Infancy Version	Preschool Version	Middle Childhood Version
1. Emotional and verbal responsiveness of the parent	1. Pride, affection, and warmth	1. Emotional and verbal responsiveness of the parent
2. Acceptance of the child	2. Avoidance of physical punishment	2. Emotional climate of the parent–child relationship
3. Involvement with the child	3. Language stimulation	3. Encouragement of social maturity
4. Organization of the physical environment	4. Stimulation of academic behavior	4. Provision for active stimulation
5. Provision of appropriate play materials	5. Stimulation through toys, games, and reading material	5. Growth-fostering materials and experiences
6. Variety in daily stimulation	6. Modeling and encouragement of social maturity	6. Family participation in developmentally stimulating experiences
	7. Variety in daily stimulation	7. Physical environment: safe, clean, and conducive to development
	8. Physical environment: safe, clean, and conducive to development	8. Parental involvement in child rearing

Sources: Bradley & Caldwell, 1979; Bradley et al., 1988; Elardo, Bradley, & Caldwell, 1975.

and, therefore, affect all children living in it to the same extent. The availability of stimulating toys and books and parental modeling of intellectual activities are good examples. The second type, **nonshared environmental influences,** are factors that make siblings different from one another. Examples include unique treatment by parents, birth order and spacing, as well as certain events, such as moving to a new neighborhood, that affect one sibling more than another. Let's see what research says about each of these classes of environmental events.

■ **SHARED ENVIRONMENTAL INFLUENCES.** Two types of research shed light on the role of shared environmental influences: (1) studies in which researchers observe home environmental qualities and relate them to IQ scores; and (2) research examining the impact of family attitudes toward intellectual success on student performance.

OBSERVATIONS OF HOME ENVIRONMENTAL QUALITIES. Bettye Caldwell and Robert Bradley developed the **Home Observation for Measurement of the Environment (HOME),** a checklist for gathering information about the quality of children's home lives through observation and parental interviews (Caldwell & Bradley, 1994). Separate infancy preschool, and middle childhood versions exist. Table 8.5 shows the subscales measured by each.

Evidence on HOME confirms the findings of many years of research—that stimulation provided by parents is linked to mental development. All infant and preschool subscales are moderately correlated with IQ, although the most important factors change with age. In infancy, organization of the physical environment and variety in daily stimulation show strongest relationships with mental test scores. During the preschool years, warmth, stimulation of language and academic behavior, and provision of appropriate play materials are the best predictors (Bradley & Caldwell, 1976; Elardo, Bradley, & Caldwell, 1975, 1977). Furthermore, high HOME scores during infancy are associated with IQ gains between 1 and 3 years of age, whereas low HOME scores predict declines as large as 15 to 20 points (Bradley et al., 1989).

The association between HOME and IQ decreases in middle childhood, perhaps because older children spend longer periods of time in other settings, such as school. Nevertheless, the relationship is still present (Luster & Dubow, 1992). And two middle-childhood HOME scales are especially strong predictors of academic achievement: provision for active stimulation (for example, encouraging hobbies and organizational memberships) and

nonshared environmental influences Environmental influences that make children living in the same family different from one another.

Home Observation for Measurement of the Environment (HOME) A checklist for gathering information about the quality of children's home lives through observation and parental interviews. Infancy, preschool, and middle childhood versions exist.

family participation in developmentally stimulating experiences (visiting friends, attending theater performances) (Bradley, Caldwell, & Rock, 1988).

When home environments within SES and ethnic groups are examined, a stimulating environment, encouragement of achievement, and affection are repeatedly linked to IQ, no matter what the child's background (Bradley & Caldwell, 1981, 1982; Bradley et al., 1989; Luster & Dubow, 1992). The extent to which parents talk to their young children seems to be particularly important. In a longitudinal study of children highly diverse in ethnic and SES background, amount of verbal interaction in the home during the first 3 years was a powerful predictor of early language progress. Preschoolers' language competence, in turn, contributed substantially to verbal intelligence and academic achievement in elementary school, after SES was controlled (Hart & Risley, 1995; Walker et al., 1994).

Yet we must be cautious about interpreting these correlational findings. In all the studies, children were reared by their biological parents, with whom they share not just a common environment but also a common heredity. Parents who are genetically more intelligent might provide better experiences as well as give birth to genetically brighter children. In addition, brighter children may evoke more parental stimulation. Note that these hypotheses refer to genetic–environmental correlation (see Chapter 3, page 122).

Indeed, there is support for a genetic contribution to the HOME–IQ relationship. The correlation is not as strong for adopted children as it is for biological children (Braungart, Fulker, & Plomin, 1992; Cherny, 1994). This suggests that parent–child genetic similarity elevates the relationship. Using complicated statistical procedures, researchers estimate that as much as half the correlation between HOME and IQ is due to heredity (Coon et al., 1990; Scarr, 1997). But so far, these findings are based only on white middle-SES families. We do not yet know whether they apply to all SES and ethnic groups.

Furthermore, it is clear that heredity does not account for all of the association between home environment and mental test scores. In several studies, family living conditions—HOME scores and affluence of the surrounding neighborhood—continued to predict children's IQ beyond the effect of maternal intelligence and education. These findings that highlight the importance of environment (Chase-Lansdale et al., 1997; Klebanov et al., 1998; Sameroff et al., 1993). Also, one HOME subscale—organization of the physical environment—is unrelated to parental intelligence. Yet a measure of it in infancy predicts children's IQ well into middle childhood (Coon et al., 1990).

FAMILY ATTITUDES TOWARD INTELLECTUAL SUCCESS. Support for achievement is greater in high-SES families where both parent and child IQs are higher, making it difficult to isolate the impact of family attitudes on children's performance. But SES and IQ alone cannot explain the high valuing of educational endeavors among immigrant families to the United States. Research suggests that regardless of SES, newly arrived families from the Caribbean, Central America, India, and Southeast Asia place great emphasis on intellectual success (Caplan, Choy, & Whitmore, 1991; Suarez-Orozco, 1989; Waters, 1994).

In a recent study of over 1,300 ethnic minority adolescents, those who were immigrants (foreign-born with foreign-born parents) outperformed their native-born agemates in English and math courses (Fuligni, 1997). The academic success of immigrants was particularly noteworthy, since they were more likely to come from homes in which English was not spoken. Students from immigrant families were also exposed to a stronger emphasis on education—greater valuing of academic success, more rigorous achievement standards, and higher expectations for educational attainment. These attitudes, apparent in each ethnic group studied, were far more powerful predictors of academic performance than were parental education and occupational status.

Is IQ responsible for immigrant adolescents' superior performance in school? Probably not, since recent arrivals are unlikely to be more intelligent than individuals who came a decade or two earlier. Rather, immigrant parents' belief that education is the surest way to improve life chances seems to play a profound role in the academic performance of their children, even in ethnic groups (such as Mexican and Southeast Asian) that face considerable economic hardship (Kao & Tienda, 1995).

SES and IQ alone cannot explain the high valuing of education endeavors widespread among immigrant families to the United States. Although these Vietnamese parents speak little English, they place great emphasis on learning and expect their son and daughter to study hard and succeed. (Michael Newman/PhotoEdit)

■ **NONSHARED ENVIRONMENTAL INFLUENCES.** Although children growing up in the same family are affected by common environments, in many ways their experiences are decidedly different. Parents may favor one child over another. Each child experiences sibling relationships differently. And children may be assigned special roles—for example, one expected to achieve, a second to get along well with others (Dunn & Plomin, 1990).

Kinship research suggests that nonshared environmental factors are more powerful than shared influences. Turn back to Table 8.4 on page 334. Notice the relatively low correlations between nonbiological siblings—a direct estimate of the effect of shared environment on IQ. Recall, also, that in adolescence the IQ resemblance between fraternal twins drops (see page 335). This trend also characterizes nontwin siblings. And it is particularly marked for nonbiological siblings, whose IQs at adolescence are no longer correlated (Jensen, 1997; Scarr & Weinberg, 1983). On the basis of these findings, some researchers have concluded that the impact of the shared environment on IQ is greatest in childhood (Loehlin, Horn, & Willerman, 1997; Rowe, 1994; Scarr, 1997). Thereafter, it gives way to nonshared influences, as young people spend more time away from home, encounter experiences unlike those of their siblings, and seek environmental niches consistent with their genetic makeup.

Nevertheless, very few studies have examined nonshared environmental influences on IQ. The most extensively studied factors are birth order and spacing between siblings. According to one theory, earlier birth order and wider spacing should yield higher IQs because they grant children more parental attention and stimulation (Zajonc, 1976; Zajonc & Mullally, 1997). In a well-known study that included almost all males born in the Netherlands at the end of World War II, IQ did decline with birth order (see Figure 8.8). Notice, also, the drop in IQ with increasing family size—another trend highlighting the impact of parental attention (Belmont & Marolla, 1973). Yet the findings depicted in Figure 8.8 are not entirely consistent. Only children, who have more opportunity for parental contact than do firstborns with siblings, do not necessarily have higher IQs. And overall, birth order and family size effects amount to no more than a few IQ points—barely enough to be meaningful.

As these results illustrate, attempts to identify the systematic impact of nonshared influences on IQ in large-scale studies have been disappointing. This has led some investigators to conclude that the most potent ones are unpredictable, one-time events. A particularly inspiring English teacher, a summer at a special camp, or a period of intense rivalry with a sibling are examples. To understand the role of these nonshared factors in mental development, we need more intensive case studies of children growing up in the same family than have been accomplished to date (Brody, 1992; McCall, 1993).

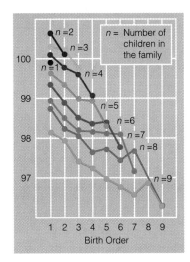

FIGURE 8.8

IQ as a function of family size and birth order among 19-year-old males born in the Netherlands at the end of World War II.

(From L. Belmont & F. A. Marolla, 1973, "Birth Order, Family Size, and Intelligence," *Science*, 182, p. 1097. Copyright © 1973 by the AAAS. Reprinted by permission.)

BRIEF REVIEW

The existence of ethnic and SES differences in intelligence test performance has sparked the IQ nature–nurture debate. Heritability estimates indicate that genetic factors account for about half of the variation among individuals in mental test scores. The contribution of heredity to IQ strengthens with development. However, heritabilities cannot explain ethnic and SES differences in IQ. Adoption research reveals that IQ is highly malleable. At the same time, heredity remains important, since adopted children's scores are more strongly correlated with the IQs of their biological than adoptive relatives. Consistent with the conclusions of biologists that ethnicity is not biologically based, black children adopted into white middle-SES homes show a dramatic rise in IQ.

Researchers who view mental tests as biased point to test content, language customs, and reactions to testing conditions that can lead IQs to underestimate the intelligence of low-SES and ethnic minority children. Supplementing IQs with measures of adaptive behavior and adjusting testing procedures to take into account cultural differences, as in dynamic testing, are ways of reducing test bias.

Shared environmental influences, including a stimulating home environment and parental warmth and encouragement of achievement, consistently predict higher mental test scores. The superior academic performance of immigrant over native-born ethnic minority adolescents highlights the contribution of family attitudes to intellectual success. As children spend more time away from the family, nonshared environmental influences on IQ strengthen. The most potent may be unpredictable, one-time events.

ASK YOURSELF . . .

♦ *IQ correlations for fraternal twins and siblings decline from childhood to adolescence. What does this suggest about the impact of shared and nonshared environmental influences on IQ?*

♦ *Desiree, an African-American child, was quiet and withdrawn while taking an intelligence test. Later, she remarked to her mother, "I can't understand why that lady asked me all those questions. She's a grown-up. She must know what a ball and stove are for!" Explain Desiree's reaction to the testing situation. Why is her score likely to underestimate her intelligence?*

♦ **CONNECTIONS**
Explain how dynamic testing is consistent with Vygotsky-based concepts, including the zone of proximal development and scaffolding. (See Chapter 6, page 261.)

Early Intervention and Intellectual Development

In the 1960s, during a decade in which the United States launched a "war on poverty," a wide variety of early intervention programs for economically disadvantaged preschoolers were initiated. They were based on the assumption that learning problems were best treated early, before the beginning of formal schooling, as well as the hope that early enrichment would offset the declines in IQ and achievement common among children from low-SES and ethnic minority backgrounds.

Project Head Start, begun by the federal government in 1965, is the most extensive of these experiments. A typical Head Start program provides children with a year or two of preschool, along with nutritional and medical services. Parent involvement is central to the Head Start philosophy. Parents serve on policy councils and contribute to program planning. They also work directly with children in classrooms, attend special programs on parenting and child development, and receive services directed at their own social, emotional, and vocational needs. Currently, over 1,300 Head Start centers located around the country enroll about 720,000 children each year (Currie & Thomas, 1997).

BENEFITS OF EARLY INTERVENTION

Over two decades of research establishing the long-term benefits of early intervention helped Head Start survive. The most important of these studies was coordinated by the Consortium for Longitudinal Studies, a group of investigators who combined data from seven university-based interventions. Results showed that children who attended programs scored higher in IQ and achievement than did controls during the first 2 to 3 years of elementary school. After that time, differences in test scores declined (Lazar & Darlington, 1982).

Nevertheless, children who received intervention remained ahead on measures of real-life school adjustment into adolescence. As Figure 8.9 shows, they were less likely to be placed in special education classes or retained in grade, and a greater number graduated from high school. There were also lasting benefits in attitudes and motivation. Children who attended programs were more likely to give achievement-related reasons (such as school or job accomplishments) for being proud of themselves, and their mothers held higher vocational aspirations for them. A separate report on one program suggested benefits extending into young adulthood, including a reduction in crime and teenage pregnancy and a greater likelihood of employment (Barnett, 1993; Berrueta-Clement et al., 1984).

FIGURE 8.9

Benefits of preschool intervention programs. Low-income children who received intervention fared better than controls on real-life indicators of school adjustment.
(Adapted from Royce, Darlington, & Murray, 1983.)

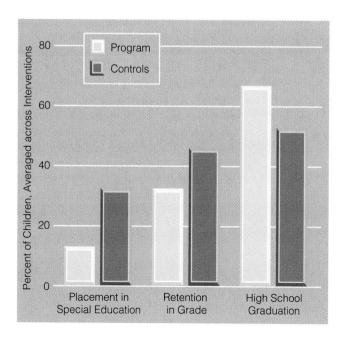

Project Head Start A federal program that provides low-income children with a year or two of preschool, along with nutritional and medical services, and that encourages parent involvement in children's development.

EVALUATIONS OF HEAD START

Do these findings on outstanding university-based programs generalize to Head Start centers located in American communities? Although some studies report only minimal benefits, new evidence reveals that they are biased by one very important factor: Because not all poverty-stricken children can be served, Head Start typically enrolls the most economically disadvantaged preschoolers. Controls to whom they are compared often do not come from such extremely impoverished families (Schnur, Brooks-Gunn, & Shipman, 1992).

An investigation of Head Start programs in two large cities took this into account. It also looked carefully at the effectiveness of Head Start by comparing it to other preschool alternatives as well as to no preschool at all. Results showed that Head Start children, compared to "other preschool" and "no preschool" groups, had less educated mothers, came from more crowded households, and were more likely to be growing up in single-parent homes. Before entering the program, they scored well below the other groups on mental tests. Yet at the end of a year's intervention, Head Start children showed greater gains than both comparison groups (Lee, Brooks-Gunn, & Schnur, 1988; Lee et al., 1990).

A consistent finding of research on Head Start is that almost all children experience an eventual **washout effect.** In other words, improvements in IQ and achievement do not last for more than a few years. One reason is that former Head Start attendees enter public schools substantially lower in quality than do their "no preschool" counterparts. This difference is even greater when Head Start graduates are compared to "other preschool" peers (Lee & Loeb, 1995). Improvements in mental test scores due to Head Start fade especially rapidly for African-American children; they are more likely to be sustained for Caucasian-American and Mexican-American children.

This discouraging outcome is at least partly due to black children's higher likelihood of enrolling in inferior, inner-city schools (Currie & Thomas, 1995, 1997). The benefits of Head Start are easily undermined when children do not have access to high-quality educational supports throughout the school years. When intervention begun at age 4 is extended until third grade, African-American children show achievement gains in reading and math still evident in junior high (Reynolds & Temple, 1998). More intensive programs that start earlier yield enduring IQ gains, as indicated by another intervention effort, the Carolina Abecedarian Project, described in the Social Issues box on page 348.

Despite declining test scores, graduates of high-quality Head Start centers (like those of university-based programs) show an improved ability to meet basic school requirements. Although researchers are not sure how these effects are achieved, one possibility is that they are partly the result of changes in parents, who create better rearing environments for their children (White, Taylor, & Moss, 1992). In a recent study, parents of kindergartners who had attended Head Start expressed great optimism about their children's academic skills and future educational prospects. The more positive these parental beliefs were, the better children's attitudes toward school, expectations for academic success, and achievement test scores (Galper, Wigfield, & Seefeldt, 1997). These findings highlight the importance of enhancing parents' life circumstances and involvement in their children's learning. Consequently, new interventions are being conceived as two-generation models.

A TWO-GENERATION PROGRAM STRATEGY

A typical parent component of early intervention emphasizes teaching parenting skills and providing other supports that encourage parents to act as supplementary intervenors for their child. Some researchers believe these efforts may not be enough. By expanding intervention to include developmental goals for *both* parents and children, program benefits might be extended (Smith, 1995). A parent helped to move out of poverty with education, vocational training, and other social services is likely to gain in psychological well-being,

These economically disadvantaged 4-year-olds benefit from the comprehensive early intervention services of Project Head Start. A rich, stimulating preschool experience is an essential part of the program. As parents like this classroom volunteer participate, they improve their own life circumstances as well as their children's development.
(Elizabeth Crews)

washout effect The loss of IQ and achievement gains resulting from early intervention within a few years after the program ends.

The Carolina Abecedarian Project: A Model of Early Intervention

N THE 1970S, an experiment was begun to find out if educational enrichment starting at a very early age could prevent the declines in mental development that affect children born into extreme poverty. The Carolina Abecedarian Project identified over 100 African-American infants at serious risk for school failure, based on parent education and income, a history of poor school achievement among older siblings, and other family problems. Shortly after birth, the babies were randomly assigned to either a treatment or a control group.

Between 3 weeks and 3 months of age, infants in the treatment group were enrolled in a full-time, year-round child-care program, where they remained until they entered school. During the first 3 years, the children received stimulation aimed at promoting motor, cognitive, language, and social skills. After age 3, the goals of the program expanded to include prereading and math concepts.

At all ages, special emphasis was placed on adult-child communication. Teachers were trained to engage in informative, helpful, and nondirective interaction with the children, who were talked to and read to daily. Both treatment and control children received nutrition and health services. The primary difference between them was the day-care experience, designed to support the treatment group's mental development.

Intelligence test scores were gathered on the children regularly, and (as Figure 8.10 indicates) by 12 months the performance of the two groups began to diverge. Treatment children scored higher than controls throughout the preschool years. Although the high-risk backgrounds of both groups led their IQs to decline over middle childhood, follow-up testing at ages 8, 12, and 15 revealed that treatment children maintained their advantage in IQ over controls (see Figure 8.10). In addition, at ages 12 and 15, treatment youngsters were achieving considerably better, especially in reading and mathematics. By age 18, rate of graduation from high school was higher for the treatment than the control group (67 versus 51 percent) (Campbell & Ramey, 1991, 1994, 1995).

When the Carolina Abecedarian children entered elementary school, the researchers conducted a second experiment to compare the impact of early and later intervention. From kindergarten through second grade, half the treatment and half the control group were provided with a special resource teacher. She introduced supplementary educational activities into the home addressing the child's specific learning needs. School-age intervention had little impact on IQ (refer again to Figure 8.10). And although it enhanced children's academic achievement, the effects were weaker than the impact of very early intervention (Campbell & Ramey, 1994, 1995). The Carolina Abecedarian Project shows that providing children with continuous, high-quality enrichment from infancy through the preschool years is an effective way to reduce the devastating impact of poverty on children's mental development.

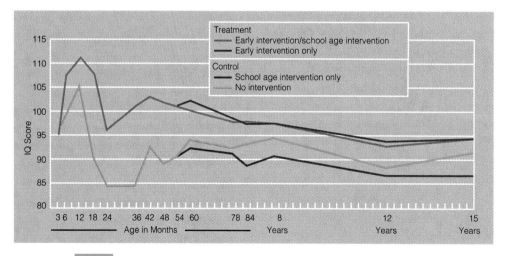

FIGURE 8.10

IQ scores of treatment and control children from 6 months to 15 years in the Carolina Abecedarian Project. To compare the impact of early and later intervention, half the treatment and half the control group were provided with supplementary educational activities suited to their learning needs from kindergarten through second grade. School-based intervention had little impact on age-related changes in IQ; the effects of early intervention were far more powerful.

(From F. A. Campbell & C. T. Ramey, 1995, "The Cognitive and School Outcomes for High-Risk African-American Students at Middle Adolescence: Positive Effects of Early Intervention," *American Educational Research Journal*, 32, p. 757. Reprinted by permission of the American Educational Research Association.)

planning for the future, and beliefs and behaviors that foster children's efforts in school. When combined with child-centered intervention, these gains should translate into exceptionally strong benefits for children (Ramey & Ramey, 1998; Zigler & Styfco, 1994).

At present, the two-generation approach is too new to have yielded much research on long-term benefits (McLoyd 1998). But one pioneering effort, New Chance, is cause for optimism. In it, teenage mothers received a variety of services for themselves and their babies, including education, employment, family planning, life management, parent training, and child health care. A follow-up when children were 5 years old revealed that parent participants were less likely to be on welfare and had higher family earnings than did controls receiving less intensive intervention. In addition, program children experienced warmer and more stimulating home environments, were more likely to have enrolled in Head Start, and had higher verbal IQs (Quint, Box, & Polit, 1997).

THE FUTURE OF EARLY INTERVENTION

Although over one-fifth of American preschoolers are eligible for Head Start by virtue of their poverty level, at present the program serves only about one-third of these children. Yet Head Start and other interventions like it are highly cost effective. Program expenses are far less than the funds required to provide special education, treat delinquency, and support welfare dependency. Because of its demonstrated returns to society, a move is under way to expand Head Start to reach all eligible children (Currie & Thomas, 1997; Hofferth, 1995).

Nevertheless, the distance in IQ and school achievement between Head Start graduates and their more economically advantaged peers remains considerable. As early intervention becomes more widespread, there is a need to find ways of increasing and sustaining the short-term cognitive gains that result from one- and two-year efforts. Programs that begin in infancy, extend through the preschool years, ensure high-quality elementary and secondary education, and focus on the development of both parents and children offer hope of reaching these goals.

Development of Creativity

Throughout this chapter, we have seen that the concept of intelligence means much more than mental abilities that predict success in school. Today, educators recognize that gifted children—those who display exceptional intellectual strengths—have diverse characteristics. Some are high-IQ youngsters with scores above 130—the standard definition of giftedness based on intelligence test performance (Gardner, 1998b). High-IQ children, as we have seen, are particularly quick at academic work. They have keen memories and an exceptional capacity to solve challenging problems rapidly and accurately. Yet recognition that intelligence tests do not sample the entire range of human mental skills has led to an expanded conception of giftedness, which includes creativity (Feldhusen, 1986; Renzulli, 1986; Sternberg, 1986).

Creativity is the ability to produce work that is *original*—that others have not thought of before. Yet novelty is not enough for a product to be creative. It must also be *appropriate*—sensible or useful in some way. If a product is unusual but does not serve a social need, then it is not creative; it is, instead, an irrelevant response (Barron, 1988; Ochse, 1990; Sternberg & Lubart, 1991b). Besides quality of the product, the process of arriving at it affects judgments of creativity. Rather than following established rules, a creative work pulls together previously disparate ideas. And it typically involves hard work and overcoming obstacles on the way to the final product (Amabile, 1983; Weisberg, 1993).

Creativity is of great value to individuals on the job and in daily life. In addition, it is vital for societal progress. Without it, there would be no new inventions, scientific findings, movements in art, or social programs. Therefore, understanding its ingredients and nurturing them from childhood is paramount. As we will see in the following sections, ideas about creativity have changed radically over the past decade.

creativity The ability to produce work that *is* original (that others have not thought of before) and that *is* appropriate (sensible or useful in some way).

Until recently, a purely cognitive perspective dominated research on creativity. Commonly used tests tapped **divergent thinking**—the generation of multiple and unusual possibilities when faced with a task or problem. Divergent thinking contrasts sharply with **convergent thinking,** which involves arriving at a single correct answer and is emphasized on intelligence tests (Guilford, 1985).

Recognizing that highly creative children (like high-IQ children) are often better at some types of tasks than others, researchers devised verbal, figural, and "real-world-problem" tests of divergent thinking (Runco, 1992a, 1993; Torrance, 1988). A verbal measure might ask children to name as many uses for common objects (such as a newspaper) as they can. A figural measure might ask them to come up with as many drawings based on a circular motif as possible (see Figure 8.11). A "real-world problem" measure either gives children everyday problems or requires them to think of such problems and then suggest solutions. Responses to all these tests can be scored for the number of ideas generated and their originality. For example, on a verbal test, saying that a newspaper can be used "as handgrips for a bicycle" would be more unusual than saying it can be used "to clean things."

Because tests of divergent thinking permit comparisons between people on a standard "creativity" scale, they are referred to as the *psychometric approach to creativity* (Lubart, 1994). Yet critics of these measures point out that at best, they are imperfect predictors of creative accomplishment in everyday life, since they tap only one of the complex cognitive contributions to creativity. In addition, they say nothing about personality traits, motivational factors, and environmental circumstances that determine whether people will realize their creative potential (Amabile, 1983; Sternberg, 1989). Although divergent-thinking tests are incomplete measures of creativity, they do tap relevant skills, have been the major focus of research on children, and (as we will see shortly) have enhanced our understanding of the development of creativity.

FIGURE 8.11

Responses of an 8-year-old who scored high on a figural measure of divergent thinking. This child was asked to make as many pictures as she could from the circles on the page. The titles she gave her drawings, from left to right, are as follows: "Dracula," "one-eyed monster," "pumpkin," "Hula-Hoop," "poster," "wheelchair," "earth," "moon," "planet," "movie camera," "sad face," "picture," "stoplight," "beach ball," "the letter O," "car," and "glasses." Tests of divergent thinking tap only one of the complex cognitive contributions to creativity.

(Test form copyright © 1980 by Scholastic Testing Service, Inc. Reprinted by permission of Scholastic Testing Service, Inc., from *The Torrance Tests of Creative Thinking* by E. P. Torrance.)

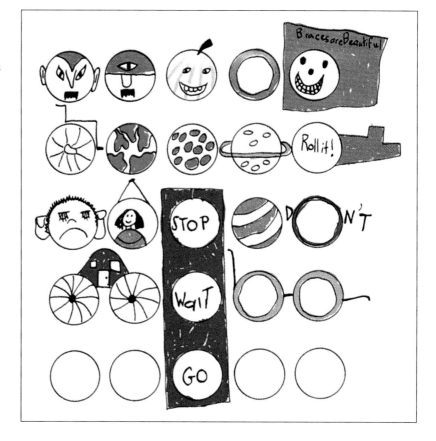

TABLE 8.6

Resources Necessary for Creativity

Cognitive	Personality	Motivational	Environmental
Problem finding	Innovative style of thinking	Task focused rather than goal focused	Availability of stimulating activities
Problem definition			Emphasis on intellectual curiosity
Divergent thinking	Tolerance of ambiguity		Acceptance of child's individual characteristics
Convergent thinking	Perseverance		Provision of systematic instruction relevant to child's talent
Insight processes	Willingness to take intellectual risks		Availability of time to reflect on ideas
Evaluation of competing ideas	Courage of one's convictions		Encouragement of flexible and original use of knowledge
Knowledge			Provision of challenging, extended assignments that promote tolerance of ambiguity, perseverance, and risk taking
			Emphasis on task-focused motivators

Sources: Sternberg & Lubart, 1991b, 1996.

A MULTIFACETED VIEW

Recent theories agree that many elements must converge for creativity to occur (Amabile, 1983; Csikszentmihalyi, 1988; Simonton, 1988; Weisberg, 1993). One influential multi-faceted approach that represents this view is Robert Sternberg and Todd Lubart's (1991b, 1996) **investment theory of creativity.** According to Sternberg and Lubart, people can invest in a variety of projects. Pursuing those that are novel (and therefore currently un-dervalued by others) will increase the chances of devising a creative, highly valued prod-uct. But whether a person invests in novelty—initiates an original project and brings it to fruition—depends on the availability of diverse intellectual, personality, motivational, and environmental resources, summarized in Table 8.6. Each must be present at a mini-mum level to catalyze creativity, although strength in one (such as perseverance) can com-pensate for weakness in another (an environment that is lukewarm toward novel ideas).

Contrary to popular belief, creativity is neither determined at birth nor the prized possession of an elite few. Instead, many people can develop it to varying degrees, and it is likely to reach greater heights when fostered from an early age. Let's look closely at the components of creativity and how we can strengthen them in children.

■ **COGNITIVE RESOURCES.** Creative work brings together a variety of high-level cognitive skills. Rather than just problem solving, it requires *problem finding*—detecting a gap in current knowledge, a need for a new product, or a deficiency with existing pro-cedures. Once a problem is found, *the ability to define it*—to move it from a vague to a clearly specified state—becomes important. In both children and adults, the more effort devoted to defining the problem, the more original the final product (Getzels & Csik-szentmihalyi, 1976; Runco & Okuda, 1988). In one study, elementary school pupils were asked to choose an object and write an essay about it. Children who explored more ob-jects, investing heavily in problem discovery and definition, wrote more fluent and origi-nal essays (Moore, 1985).

Divergent thinking is essential for generating novel solutions to problems. But the successful creator must also be able to set aside fruitless options in favor of the best responses. Therefore, rather than emphasizing only one mode of reasoning, creativity involves *alternating between divergent and convergent thinking* at opportune moments. And in narrowing the range of possibilities, creative individuals rely on *insight processes*—ones that combine and restructure elements in sudden but useful ways. For example, using analogies and metaphors to identify unique connections is common among people who have made outstanding creative contributions to literature, art, science, business, and

divergent thinking The genera-tion of multiple and unusual possi-bilities when faced with a task or problem. Associated with creativity.

convergent thinking The gener-ation of a single correct answer to a problem. Type of cognition em-phasized on intelligence tests.

investment theory of creativ-ity Sternberg and Lubart's theory, in which investment in novel pro-jects depends on the availability of diverse intellectual, personality, motivational, and environmental resources, each of which must be present at some minimum level.

How can we nurture creativity? According to investment theory, learning environments that encourage children to come up with new ideas and to implement them are crucial. This 11-year-old holds a model of the human eye that she made with household objects. At a regional science fair, she used the model's efficient design, which grants easy access to inner visual structures, to teach others how we see. Her work illustrates two vital facets of creativity: originality (novelty) and appropriateness (usefulness).

(Gary Watts/The Image Works)

other fields (Barron, 1988). At an early age, children are capable of this kind of thinking (see Chapter 6, page 245, and Chapter 9, page 376). Furthermore, *evaluating competing ideas* to select the most promising keeps creative problem solving moving efficiently toward a high-quality solution. School-age children's evaluative ability is related to their performance on divergent thinking tasks and can be enhanced by instructions to critically assess the originality of ideas (Runco, 1992b).

Finally, *knowledge* is necessary to make a creative contribution to any field, since without it, people cannot recognize or understand new ideas. Perhaps for this reason more than any other, individuals usually demonstrate creativity in only one or a few related domains. When researchers ask children and adults to describe their creative achievements or complete creativity tasks in several areas, cross-domain correlations between their performances are typically quite low, averaging about .20 (Baer, 1991; Lubart & Sternberg, 1995). Similarly, eminent creators rarely produce enduring work in more than one or two fields (Gray, 1966). Consequently, high creativity is usually manifested as a special talent.

Consider these multiple cognitive ingredients, and you will see why numerous studies report only a low positive correlation between IQ and creativity, typically around .20 to .30 (Baer, 1991; Torrance, 1988). Although some cognitive requirements for creativity overlap with factors on intelligence tests, others do not. Beyond a minimum level of general intelligence, the presence of other variables determines creative giftedness—which is quite distinct from the academic giftedness best predicted by IQ.

■ **PERSONALITY RESOURCES.** Personality characteristics foster the cognitive components of creativity, ensuring that they will be applied and reach fruition (Lubart, 1994; Sternberg & Lubart, 1996). The following traits are crucial:

▨ *Innovative style of thinking.* Creative people not only have the capacity to see things in new ways but like to do so. They prefer loosely structured activities permitting innovative problem finding rather than already defined tasks. In a study of thinking styles in middle schools, teachers in the lower grades were more encouraging of the type of thinking linked to creativity, and pupils tended to match their teachers' preferred style (Sternberg & Grigorenko, 1993). These findings suggest that creative thinking is at least partially taught.

▨ *Tolerance of ambiguity and perseverance.* Creative goals inevitably bring periods of uncertainty, when pieces of the problem do not fit together. During those times, we may feel pressure to give up or pursue the first available (but not the best) solution. Encouraging patience and persistence in the face of obstacles can help children think creatively.

▨ *Willingness to take risks.* Creativity requires a willingness to "deviate from the crowd," to undertake challenge when outcomes are uncertain. Inducing a risk-oriented state of mind enhances divergent thinking scores (Glover, 1977).

▨ *The courage of one's convictions.* Because their ideas are novel, creators may at times doubt them, especially when skeptical teachers or peers criticize them. Independence of judgment and high self-esteem are necessary for creative endeavors.

■ **MOTIVATIONAL RESOURCES.** Motivation for creativity must be *task focused* rather than *goal focused.* Task-focusing motivators, such as the desire to succeed at a high standard, energize work and keep attention on the problem itself. Goal-focusing motivators, often extrinsic rewards such as grades and prizes, divert attention from the task to other goals, thereby impairing performance. In one study, 7- to 11-year-old girls worked on collages, some competing for prizes and others expecting that the prizes would be raffled off. The products of those in the first group were much less creative (Amabile, 1982).

Extrinsic rewards are not always detrimental to creativity. They convey its social value and can encourage children to embark on innovative projects when they otherwise might not do so. But when rewards are overemphasized, children see only "the carrot at the end of the stick," and creativity suffers (Lubart, 1994).

■ **ENVIRONMENTAL RESOURCES.** Environments can provide physical and social conditions that help new ideas form and develop, or they can stifle them. This means that a child can appear creatively gifted in one context but quite ordinary in another.

Studies of the backgrounds of talented children and highly accomplished adults often reveal homes rich in reading materials and other stimulating activities and parents who emphasize intellectual curiosity and are highly accepting of their youngster's individual characteristics (Albert, 1994; Perleth & Heller, 1994). In addition, such parents recognize their child's creative potential and provide systematic instruction (in the form of out-of-school lessons), assistance with the child's learning, and (as the talent develops) apprenticeship under inspiring teachers (Feldman & Goldsmith, 1991; Winner, 1996).

Classrooms in which children can take risks, challenge the instructor, and have time to reflect on ideas without being rushed to the next assignment are also facilitating. Elementary school teachers who are neither directive nor nondirective but who balance structure with freedom of choice have pupils who score higher in divergent thinking (Thomas & Berk, 1981). Unfortunately, creativity is discouraged in many classrooms. Knowledge acquisition is usually stressed over using knowledge originally, leading children's thinking to become *entrenched,* or limited to commonplace associations that produce correct answers. Assignments, which are usually short and well defined, do not promote the tolerance of ambiguity, perseverance, and risk taking necessary to sustain creative work. And goal-focusing motivators (grades and the desire to appear competent in front of teachers, parents, and peers) are widespread (Sternberg & Lubart, 1991a).

Although programs for the gifted exist in many schools, debate about their effectiveness typically focuses on factors irrelevant to creativity—whether to provide enrichment in regular classrooms, to pull children out for special instruction (the most common practice), or to advance brighter pupils to a higher grade. Children of all ages fare well academically and socially within each of these models (Moon & Feldhusen, 1994; Southern, Jones, & Stanley 1994). Yet the extent to which they foster creativity depends on opportunities to acquire relevant skills.

Recently, Gardner's theory of multiple intelligences has served as the basis for several model programs that provide domain-specific enrichment to all pupils. A wide variety of meaningful activities, each tapping a specific intelligence or set of intelligences, serve as contexts for assessing strengths and weaknesses and, on that basis, teaching new knowledge and original thinking. For example, linguistic intelligence might be fostered and evaluated through storytelling or playwriting; spatial intelligence through drawing, sculpting, or taking apart and reassembling objects; and kinesthetic intelligence through dance or pantomime (Gardner, 1993).

Evidence is still needed on how effectively these programs nurture children's talents (Plucker, Callahan, & Tomchin, 1996). But so far, they have succeeded in one way—by highlighting the strengths of some pupils who previously had been considered unexceptional or even at risk for school failure. Consequently, they may be especially useful in identifying talented ethnic minority children, who are underrepresented in school programs for the gifted (Suzuki & Valencia, 1997). How best to maximize the creative resources of the coming generation—the future poet and scientist as well as the everyday citizen—is a challenge for future research.

ASK YOURSELF

◆ *Explain why educational programs inspired by Gardner's theory of multiple intelligences require authentic assessment of children's intellectual accomplishments. (Refer to the From Research to Practice box on page 342.)*

◆ **CONNECTIONS**
Using what you learned about brain development in Chapter 5 (see pages 186–191), explain why intensive intervention for poverty-stricken children beginning in the first 2 years has a greater impact on IQ than intervention at a later age.

How do findings on factors that contribute to creativity fit with research on the development of prodigies? (See Chapter 2, page 51.)

DEFINITIONS OF INTELLIGENCE

Describe changing definitions of intelligence, from Binet's first successful test to the modern factor analysts.

- The **psychometric approach** to cognitive development is the basis for the wide variety of intelligence tests used to assess individual differences in children's mental abilities. In the early 1900s, Alfred Binet developed the first successful test, which provided a single, holistic measure of intelligence.

- **Factor analysis** emerged as a major means for determining whether intelligence is a single trait or a collection of many different abilities. The research of Spearman and Thurstone led to two schools of thought. The first, supporting Spearman, regarded test items as having in common one **general factor,** or "**g,**" but acknowledged the existence of **specific factors,** or "**s.**" The second, supporting Thurstone, viewed intelligence as a set of distinct **primary mental abilities.**

- Modern factor analysts have extended the work of Spearman and Thurstone. Cattell's distinction between **crystallized** and **fluid intelligence** has influenced many attempts to create culture-fair tests. Carroll's **three-stratum theory of intelligence** is the most comprehensive classification of mental abilities to be confirmed by factor-analytic research.

RECENT ADVANCES IN DEFINING INTELLIGENCE

Why have researchers conducted componential analyses of test scores, and how have Sternberg's triarchic theory and Gardner's theory of multiple intelligences expanded contemporary definitions of intelligence?

- To provide process-oriented explanations of mental test performance, some researchers conduct **componential analyses** of children's scores by correlating them with laboratory measures of information processing. Findings reveal that basic efficiency of thinking and adaptive strategy use are related to measures of general intelligence. Sternberg's **triarchic theory of intelligence** extends these efforts. It views intelligence as a complex interaction of information-processing skills, specific experiences, and contextual (or cultural) influences.

- According to Gardner's **theory of multiple intelligences,** mental abilities should be defined in terms of unique sets of processing operations applied in culturally meaningful activities. His eight distinct intelligences have been influential in efforts to understand and nurture children's special talents, although they have yet to be firmly grounded in research.

REPRESENTATIVE INTELLIGENCE TESTS FOR CHILDREN

Cite commonly used intelligence tests for children, and discuss prediction of later IQ from infant tests.

- The **Stanford-Binet Intelligence Scale** and the **Wechsler Intelligence Scale for Children–III (WISC–III)** are most often used to identify highly intelligent children and diagnose those with learn-

ing problems. Each provides an overall IQ as well as a profile of subtest scores.

- Traditional infant tests, which consist largely of perceptual and motor responses, predict childhood IQ poorly. The Fagan Test of Infant Intelligence, made up entirely of habituation–dishabituation items, taps aspects of cognitive processing and is an effective predictor of childhood IQ. Measures of object permanence also correlate better with later IQ than do traditional infant tests.

THE COMPUTATION AND DISTRIBUTION OF IQ SCORES

How are IQ scores computed and distributed?

- Scores on intelligence tests are arrived at by computing an **intelligence quotient (IQ).** It compares a child's raw score to the scores of a large, representative sample of same-age children, which form a normal, or bell-shaped, curve.

WHAT AND HOW WELL DO INTELLIGENCE TESTS PREDICT?

Discuss the stability of IQ and its prediction of scholastic performance, occupational attainment, and psychological adjustment.

- IQs obtained after age 6 show substantial correlational stability. Nevertheless, most children display considerable age-related change in the absolute value of their scores. Poverty-stricken ethnic minority children often experience declines due to an **environmental cumulative deficit,** or the compounding effects of underprivileged rearing conditions.

- IQ is an effective predictor of scholastic performance, occupational attainment and on-the-job performance, and certain aspects of psychological adjustment. However, the underlying causes of these correlational findings are complex. Besides IQ, home background, personality, motivation, education, and **practical intelligence** contribute substantially to academic and life success.

ETHNIC AND SOCIOECONOMIC VARIATIONS IN IQ

Describe ethnic and socioeconomic variations in IQ, including evidence on Jensen's Level I–Level II theory.

- Black children and children of low **socioeconomic status (SES)** score lower on intelligence tests than do white and middle-SES children, findings responsible for kindling the IQ nature–nurture debate. Jensen's **Level I–Level II theory** attributes the poorer scores of these children largely to a genetic deficiency in higher-order, abstract forms of ability. However, his theory has been challenged by subsequent research.

EXPLAINING INDIVIDUAL AND GROUP DIFFERENCES IN IQ

Describe and evaluate the contributions of heredity and environment to individual and group differences in IQ.

- Heritability estimates support a moderate role for heredity in individual differences in IQ. The contribution of heredity strengthens with development. However, heritabilities cannot be used to explain ethnic and SES differences in test scores.
- Adoption studies indicate that advantaged rearing conditions can raise the absolute value of children's IQs substantially. At the same time, adopted children's scores correlate more strongly with those of their biological than adoptive relatives, providing support for the influence of heredity. Research on black children reared in white middle-SES homes reveals that the black–white IQ gap is environmentally determined. No evidence supports the assumption that genetic, racial differences underlie ethnic differences that have been the focus of the IQ nature–nurture debate.

Evaluate evidence on whether IQ is a biased measure of the intelligence of ethnic minority children, and discuss efforts to reduce test bias.

- Experts disagree on whether intelligence tests yield biased measures of the mental abilities of low-income minority children. IQ predicts academic achievement equally well for majority and minority children. However, lack of familiarity with test content, language customs, and reactions to testing conditions can lead test scores to underestimate minority children's intelligence.
- Assessments of children's adaptive behavior can serve as safeguards against test scores that underestimate minority children's intelligence. By introducing purposeful teaching into the testing situation, **dynamic testing** narrows the gap between a child's actual and potential performance.

Summarize the impact of shared and nonshared environmental influences on IQ.

- **Shared** and **nonshared environmental influences** contribute to individual differences in intelligence. Research with the **Home Observation for Measurement of the Environment (HOME)** indicates that overall quality of the home—a shared environmental influence—consistently predicts mental development. Although the HOME–IQ relationship is partly genetic, a warm, stimulating family environment does promote higher test scores. Family valuing of intellectual success exerts a powerful impact on academic performance, as indicated by the superior achievement of immigrant over native-born ethnic minority adolescents.

- Kinship research suggests that the impact of the shared environment on IQ is strongest in childhood, giving way to nonshared influences in adolescence and adulthood. Birth order and spacing are linked to IQ. However, these relationships are weak. The most potent nonshared factors may be unpredictable, one-time events. Understanding the role of nonshared factors requires intensive study of children growing up in the same family.

EARLY INTERVENTION AND INTELLECTUAL DEVELOPMENT

Discuss the impact of early intervention on intellectual development.

- Research on high-quality university-based early interventions as well as **Head Start** programs located in American communities shows that immediate IQ gains **wash out** with time. However, lasting benefits occur in school adjustment. Participants are less likely to be placed in special education classes or retained in grade and more likely to graduate from high school.
- To induce larger and longer-lasting cognitive gains, early intervention must start earlier, last longer, and be more intensive. In addition, it must be followed by high-quality public school education. Two-generation programs with developmental goals for both parents and children are being tried to see if they lead to more powerful long-term outcomes.

DEVELOPMENT OF CREATIVITY

Describe and evaluate evidence on the development of creativity, including the psychometric view and the multifaceted approach of investment theory.

- Recognition that intelligence tests do not sample the full range of human mental skills has led conceptions of giftedness to expand to include **creativity.** The psychometric approach to creativity, which emphasizes the distinction between **divergent and convergent thinking,** is too narrow an approach to predict real-life creative accomplishment. Consequently, it has given way to new, multifaceted approaches.
- According to Sternberg and Lubart's **investment theory of creativity,** a wide variety of intellectual, personality, motivational, and environmental resources are necessary to catalyze creative projects and bring them to fruition. Each of these resources can be fostered in children's homes and schools.

IMPORTANT TERMS AND CONCEPTS

authentic assessment (p. 342)
componential analysis (p. 320)
convergent thinking (p. 351)
creativity (p. 349)
crystallized intelligence (p. 318)
divergent thinking (p. 351)
dynamic testing (p. 340)
environmental cumulative deficit
   hypothesis (p. 328)
factor analysis (p. 317)
fluid intelligence (p. 319)

general factor, or "g" (p. 317)
Home Observation for Measurement
   of the Environment (HOME) (p. 343)
intelligence quotient (IQ) (p. 327)
investment theory of creativity (p. 351)
Level I–Level II theory (p. 332)
nonshared environmental influences (p. 343)
practical intelligence (p. 330)
primary mental abilities (p. 317)
Project Head Start (p. 346)
psychometric approach (p. 316)

shared environmental influences (p. 342)
socioeconomic status (SES) (p. 331)
specific factor, or "s" (p. 317)
Stanford-Binet Intelligence Scale (p. 324)
theory of multiple intelligences (p. 323)
three-stratum theory of intelligence (p. 319)
triarchic theory of intelligence (p. 321)
washout effect (p. 347)
Wechsler Intelligence Scale for Children–III
   (WISC–III) (p. 325)

Language Development

"BAH-BAH!" SHOUTS 1-YEAR-OLD Mark while waving good-bye as his mother backs the car out of the driveway at his grandmother's house. As his mother pulls onto the freeway and heads for home, Mark calls out insistently, "Bel! Bel!" He tugs at the seat belt, looking alternately at it and his mother beside him.

"The seat belt, Mark?" his mother responds. "Let's keep it on. Look!" she says. "Here's something," handing him a cracker.

"Caa-ca. Caa-ca," says Mark, who begins to eat contentedly.

"Can you shut the front door?" Susan's father shouts from upstairs to his 3-year-old daughter.

"There, I shutted it, Dad," calls Susan after closing the door. "No more wind's in here now."

Four-year-old Connie reaches for a piece of toast as she looks over the choices of jams and jellies at the breakfast table. "Mama, there's no more honey, is there?" she says.

"That's right, we ran out," her mother acknowledges. "We need to buy some more."

"There's a beehive at Uncle Joe's farm, so we could get some there," suggests Connie.

"We won't be seeing Uncle Joe until next summer," explains Connie's mother. "I'll get a jar at the store while you're at nursery school."

Language—the most awesome of universal human achievements—develops with extraordinary speed during the early childhood years. At age 1, Mark uses single words to name familiar objects and convey his desires. Three-year-old Susan grasps subtle conventions of human communication. Although her father's message is phrased as a question, she knows that he intends it to be a directive and willingly complies by closing the door. In her report of the accomplished act, Susan combines words into meaningful sentences she has never heard before. Even her mistakes, such as "shutted," attest to her active, rule-oriented approach to language. Four-year-old Connie produces longer utterances and more sophisticated language structures, such as negatives, tag questions, and connectives that join sentences. In making timely, topic-relevant comments in a short exchange with her mother, Connie shows that she is a skilled conversationalist.

Children's amazing linguistic accomplishments raise some of the most puzzling questions about development. How are a vast vocabulary and an intricate grammatical system acquired in such a short time? Is language a separate capacity—an innate *module* with its own prewired, special-purpose neural system in the brain? Or is it governed by powerful general cognitive capacities that humans also apply to other aspects of their physical and social worlds? Without exposure to a rich verbal environment, will young children invent their

To engage in effective verbal communication, these preschoolers must combine four components of language that have to do with sound, meaning, overall structure, and everyday use. How children accomplish this feat so rapidly raises some of the most puzzling questions about development.

(Laura Dwight)

own language? Do all children acquire language in the same way, or are there individual and cultural differences?

To explore these questions, this chapter follows the common practice of dividing language into four components. By examining each separately, we can more fully appreciate the diverse skills children must master to become competent communicators. Our discussion of development opens with the fiery theoretical debate of the 1950s between behaviorist B. F. Skinner and linguist Noam Chomsky, which inspired the burst of research since that time. Then we turn to infant preparatory skills that set the stage for the child's first words during the second year of life. Next, for each component of language, we first describe what develops and then treat the more controversial question of how children acquire so much in so little time. We conclude with the challenges and benefits of bilingualism—mastering two languages—in childhood.

Components of Language

When children learn language, exactly what is it that they must learn? Language consists of several subsystems that have to do with sound, meaning, overall structure, and everyday use. Knowing language entails mastering each of these aspects and combining them into a flexible communicative system.

The first component, **phonology,** refers to the rules governing the structure and sequencing of speech sounds. If you have ever visited a foreign country in which you did not know the language, you probably wondered how anyone could analyze the rapid flow of speech into organized strings of words. Yet in English, you easily apply an intricate set of rules to comprehend and produce complicated sound patterns. How you acquired this ability is the story of phonological development.

Semantics involves vocabulary, or the way underlying concepts are expressed in words and word combinations. As we will see later, when young children first use a word, it often does not mean the same thing as it does to an adult. To build a versatile vocabulary, preschoolers must refine the meanings of thousands of words and connect them into elaborate networks of related terms. With age, children not only use many words correctly but become consciously aware of what they mean. As a result, they can define and experiment with words in imaginative ways.

Once mastery of vocabulary is under way, children begin to combine words and modify them in meaningful ways. Knowledge of **grammar** consists of two main parts: *syntax,* the rules by which words are arranged into sentences; and *morphology,* the use of grammatical markers that indicate number, tense, case, person, gender, active or passive voice, and other meanings (the "-s" and "-ed" endings are examples in English).

Finally, **pragmatics** refers to the communicative side of language. To interact effectively, children must learn to take turns, maintain topic relevance, and state their meaning clearly. In addition, they must figure out how gestures, tone of voice, and the context in which an utterance is spoken clarify meaning. Pragmatics also involves *sociolinguistic knowledge,* since society dictates how language should be spoken. To be successful communicators, children must acquire certain interaction rituals, such as verbal greetings and leave-takings. They must also adjust their speech to mark important social relationships, such as differences in age and status.

As we take up each of the four aspects of language, you will see that they are really interdependent. Acquisition of each one facilitates mastery of the others.

Theories of Language Development

During the first half of this century, research on language development was primarily descriptive—aimed at establishing norms of development. The first studies identified milestones that applied to children around the globe:

phonology The component of language concerned with the rules governing the structure and sequencing of speech sounds.

semantics The component of language concerned with understanding the meaning of words and word combinations.

grammar The component of language concerned with *syntax,* the rules by which words are arranged into sentences, and *morphology,* the use of grammatical markers that indicate number, tense, case, person, gender, active or passive voice, and other meanings.

pragmatics The component of language concerned with how to engage in effective and appropriate communication with others.

all babbled around 6 months, said their first words at about 1 year, combined words at the end of the second year, and were in command of a vast vocabulary and most grammatical constructions by 4 to 5 years of age. The regularity of these achievements suggested a process largely governed by maturation. Yet at the same time, language seemed to be learned, since without exposure to a spoken language, children who were born deaf or who were severely neglected did not acquire verbal communication. This apparent contradiction set the stage for a nature–nurture debate as intense as any that has been waged in the field of child development. By the end of the 1950s, two major figures had taken opposite sides in the controversy.

THE BEHAVIORIST PERSPECTIVE

Well-known behaviorist B. F. Skinner (1957) proposed that language, just like any other behavior, is acquired through *operant conditioning*. As the baby makes sounds, parents reinforce those that are most like words with smiles, hugs, and speech in return. For example, at 12 months, my older son, David, could often be heard babbling something like this: "book-a-book-a-dook-a-dook-a-book-a-nook-a-book-aaa." One day while he babbled away, I held up his picture book and said, "Book!" Very soon, David was saying "book-aaa" in the presence of books.

Some behaviorists rely on *imitation* to explain how children rapidly acquire complex utterances, such as whole phrases and sentences (Whitehurst & Vasta, 1975). And imitation can combine with reinforcement to promote language, as when a parent coaxes, "Say 'I want a cookie,'" and delivers praise and a treat after the child responds correctly.

As these examples indicate, reinforcement and imitation contribute to early language learning. Yet only a few researchers cling to the behaviorist perspective today (see, for example, Moerk, 1992). Think, for a moment, about the process of language development just described. Adults must engage in intensive language tutoring—continuously modeling and reinforcing so that by age 6, children have an extensive vocabulary and produce an enormous number of complex sentences. This seems like a physically impossible task, even for the most conscientious parents. Furthermore, we have already seen that children create novel utterances that could not have been copied from or reinforced by others, such as Susan's use of "shutted" at the beginning of this chapter. This suggests that instead of learning specific sentences, young children develop a working knowledge of grammatical rules.

Nevertheless, the ideas of Skinner and other behaviorists should not be dismissed entirely. Throughout this chapter, we will see how adult responsiveness and example support children's language learning, even though they do not fully explain it. Behaviorist principles are also valuable to speech and language therapists in their efforts to help children with serious language delays and disabilities overcome their problems (Ratner, 1997).

THE NATIVIST PERSPECTIVE

Linguist Noam Chomsky's (1957) critical review of Skinner's theory first convinced the scientific community that children assume much responsibility for their own language learning. In contrast to behaviorists, Chomsky (1959) argued that mental structures are at the heart of our capacity to interpret and generate language. His alternative theory is a nativist account that regards language as a biologically based, uniquely human accomplishment.

Focusing on children's grammatical achievements, Chomsky reasoned that the rules for sentence organization are too complex to be directly taught to or discovered by cognitively immature young children. Instead, humans are born with a **language acquisition device (LAD)**, a biologically based, innate module for picking up language that needs only to be triggered by verbal input from the environment. The LAD permits children, as soon as they have acquired sufficient vocabulary, to combine words into grammatically consistent, novel utterances and to understand the meaning of sentences they hear.

How can a single LAD account for children's mastery of diverse languages around the world? According to Chomsky (1976), within the LAD is a *universal grammar,* a built-in storehouse of rules that apply to all human languages. Young children use this knowledge

language acquisition device (LAD) In Chomsky's theory, a biologically based, innate module for picking up language that permits children, as soon as they have acquired sufficient vocabulary, to combine words into grammatically consistent, novel utterances and to understand the meaning of sentences they hear.

to decipher grammatical categories and relationships in any language to which they are exposed. In proposing a universal grammar, Chomsky's theory emphasizes features that the world's languages have in common. It assumes that wide variation in their structural properties can be reduced to the same underlying set of rules. Furthermore, since the LAD is specifically suited for language processing, sophisticated cognitive capacities are not required to master the structure of language. Instead, children do so spontaneously with only limited language exposure. Therefore, in sharp contrast to the behaviorist view, the nativist perspective regards deliberate training by parents as unnecessary for language development. Instead, the LAD ensures that language will be acquired early and swiftly, despite its complexity (Pinker, 1994).

■ **SUPPORT FOR THE NATIVIST PERSPECTIVE.** Are children biologically primed to acquire language? Research reviewed in the Cultural Influences box on page 361, which suggests that children have a remarkable ability to invent new language systems, provides some of the most powerful support for this perspective. And three additional sets of evidence—efforts to teach nonhuman primates language systems, localization of language functions in the human brain, and investigations into whether a sensitive period exists for language development—are also consistent with Chomsky's view that humans are prepared for language in a specialized way. Let's look at each in turn.

CAN GREAT APES ACQUIRE LANGUAGE? Is the ability to master a grammatically complex language system a uniquely human attribute? To find out, many attempts have been made to teach language to chimpanzees, who are closest to humans in the evolutionary hierarchy. In some instances, researchers created artificial languages in which plastic tokens or computer keyboards are used to generate strings of visual symbols (Premack, 1976; Rumbaugh, 1977). In other cases, chimps have been trained in American Sign Language, a gestural communication system used by the deaf that is as elaborate as any spoken language (Gardner & Gardner, 1969; Terrace et al., 1980).

Findings reveal that the ability of apes to acquire a humanlike language system is limited. Many months and sometimes years of training and reinforcement are necessary to get them to master a basic vocabulary. And although their two-sign combinations resemble the two-word utterances of human toddlers, there is no convincing evidence that chimpanzees can master complex grammatical forms. Sign strings longer than two generally do not conform to a rule-based structure. For example, one chimp named Nim either repeated information or combined words nonsensically in his three- and four-word utterances. "Eat Nim eat" and "Play me Nim play" are typical examples (Terrace et al., 1980).

In the wild, chimpanzees do not seem to use symbols acquired through observing and imitating others. Instead, their vocal and gestural behaviors are limited to rituals that signal what they might do next. For example, a young chimp might push on his mother's back to lower it so he can climb on. The next time he touches her back, she anticipates his desire by lowering her body. Soon a light touch of the back signals the infant chimp's intentions to the mother. But a touch of the back is not a symbol understood in reciprocal communication (Tomasello & Camaioni, 1997). In a study in which researchers observed human 2- and 3-year-olds' and adult apes' reactions to novel symbols that indicated under which of three covers a reward could be found, children mastered the symbolic meanings quickly and easily. But as Figure 9.1 on the following page shows, the apes (both chimps and orangutans) had great difficulty making use of the symbols, even after three times as many trials in which to learn their significance (Tomasello, Call, & Gluckman, 1997).

Still, these findings do not tell us for sure that humans are endowed with a specialized language

Nim, a chimp taught American Sign Language, built a vocabulary of more than one hundred signs over several years of training. In addition, his two-sign combinations, such as "groom me," "hug Nim," and "Nim book," were similar to those of human toddlers. But for sign strings longer than two, Nim's productions showed little resemblance to human grammar.
(Susan Kuklin/Photo Researchers, Inc.)

Children Invent Language: Homesign and Hawaiian Creole English

C AN INSTANCES BE found in which children develop complex language systems with only minimal language input? If so, this evidence would serve as strong support for Chomsky's idea that human beings are born with a biological program for language development.

DEAF CHILDREN INVENT HOMESIGN. In a series of studies, Susan Goldin-Meadow and her colleagues followed deaf children over the preschool years whose parents discouraged manual signing and addressed them verbally. Yet none of the children were making progress in acquiring spoken language or used even the most common American Sign Language gestures. Nevertheless, they spontaneously produced a gestural communication system, called *homesign*, strikingly similar to hearing children's verbal language.

The deaf children developed stable gestural vocabularies with distinct forms for nouns and verbs that they combined into novel sentences conforming to simple grammatical rules (Goldin-Meadow, Mylander, & Butcher, 1995; Goldin-Meadow et al., 1994). For example, to describe a large bubble he had just blown, one child first pointed at a bubble jar and then used two open palms with fingers spread to denote the act of "blowing up big." Another child indicated that footballs were for kicking by pointing at a picture of a football and forming a kicking motion with his fingers.

Language becomes a flexible means of communication when it is used to talk about nonpresent objects and events, permitting us to convey memories, speculate about the future, and express abstract and imagined concepts. In referring to the nonpresent, the deaf children followed the same sequence of development as did hearing children—first denoting objects and events in the recent past or anticipated but imminent future, next the more remote past and future, and finally hypothetical and fantasized events (Morford & Goldin-Meadow, 1997). Homesigning children conversed in the nonpresent far more often than their parents did. One homesigning child pointed to the top of his head and shrugged his shoulders to ask where his missing hat was. Another pointed over his shoulder to signify the past, then pointed to a picture of a poodle, and finally pointed to the floor in front of him, saying, "I used to have a poodle!"

Hearing children reach language milestones earlier than do children acquiring homesign, indicating that a rich language environment fosters the attainments just mentioned. But without access to conventional language, deaf children appear to generate their own language system and follow a path of early development much like that of their hearing counterparts. Nevertheless, some critics claim that subtle gestural exchanges with parents might explain homesigning children's linguistic competencies (Bohannon & Bonvillian, 1997).

IMMIGRANT CHILDREN INVENT HAWAIIAN CREOLE ENGLISH. The study of *creoles* offers another test of the nativist perspective. Creoles are languages that arise rapidly from *pidgins*, which are minimally developed "emergency" tongues that result when several language communities migrate to the same area and no dominant language exists to support interaction between them. In 1876, large numbers of immigrants from China, Japan, Korea, the Philippines, Puerto Rico, and Portugal came to Hawaii to work in the sugar industry. The

These children are descendants of immigrants who came from many parts of the world to work in the sugar industry in Hawaii in the 1870s. The multilingual population began to speak Hawaiian Pidgin English, a simplified communication system that permitted them to "get by" in everyday life. Yet the next generation spoke a new complex language, Hawaiian Creole English, believed to have been invented by children. The existence of creoles is among the most powerful evidence for Chomsky's idea that humans are born with a biological program for language development.
(Joe Carini/Pacific Stock)

multilingual population quickly outnumbered other residents—English speakers and native Hawaiians alike. Out of this melting pot, Hawaiian Pidgin English emerged, a communication system with a small vocabulary and narrow range of grammatical options that permitted new immigrants to "get by" in everyday life. Pidgin English, however, was so limited that it may have offered young children too little language input from which to learn. Yet within 20 to 30 years, a new complex language, Hawaiian Creole English, which borrowed vocabulary from its pidgin and foreign-language predecessors, became widespread. How could this remarkable linguistic achievement have occurred?

Derek Bickerton (1981, 1990) concludes that the next generation of children must have invented the language, relying on innate mechanisms. Support for this conclusion is of two kinds. First, the structure of creole languages is similar around the world, suggesting that a common genetic program underlies them. Second, creole grammar resembles the linguistic structures children first use when acquiring any language and their incorrect hypotheses about complex grammatical forms. For example, expressions like "He no bite you" and "Where he put the toy?" are perfectly correct in Hawaiian Creole English.

According to Bickerton, the child's biological language is always there, under the surface, ready to reemerge when cultural language is shattered. However, no one has yet been able to observe the language development of first-generation creole children directly. Some researchers claim that without such evidence, we cannot be entirely sure that adult input plays little role in the creation of creole (Tomasello, 1995).

FIGURE 9.1

Game used to test the ability of adult apes to interpret novel symbols. (a) The ape sat in front of three distinct containers. After the ape was taught that a piece of orange or sweet potato would be hidden in one of them, an adult "communicator" used one of three types of gestures (pointing, placing a wooden block on top of the correct container, or holding up an exact model of the correct container) to indicate where the reward was hidden. (b) Compared with 2- and 3-year-old children who played a similar game, apes did poorly. No chimp or orangutan demonstrated above-chance responding for the wooden block (shown above) or any other novel sign, whereas the children performed well.

(Adapted from Tomasello, Call, & Gluckman, 1997.)

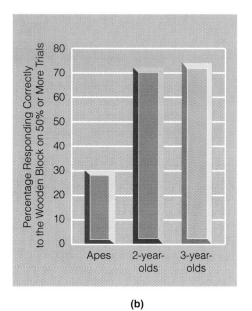

(a) (b)

capacity. Perhaps cognitive abilities or social and motivational factors account for the linguistic gap between chimpanzees and humans. For example, Michael Tomasello (1999) believes that unlike human toddlers, apes fail to understand that others are intentional beings who want to share experiences with them through symbols. Furthermore, not all species of apes have been studied as extensively as the common chimp, the subject of the research just described.

Recently, researchers began to study pygmy chimps, who are more intelligent and sociable than common chimps. When taught to comprehend many expressions before producing them (a sequence of language learning like that of human children), pygmy chimps show more rapid vocabulary development and better comprehension of novel sentences than ever before attained by nonhuman primates (Savage-Rumbaugh et al., 1993). Still, even pygmy chimps require several extra years of experience to attain the basic linguistic understandings of human 2- to 3-year-olds.

LANGUAGE AREAS IN THE BRAIN. Humans have evolved specialized regions in the brain that support language skills. Recall from Chapter 5 that for most individuals, language is housed in the left hemisphere of the cerebral cortex. Within it are two language-specific structures (see Figure 9.2). **Broca's area,** located in the frontal lobe, controls language production. Damage to it results in a specific *aphasia,* or communication disorder, in which the person has good comprehension but speaks in a slow, labored, ungrammatical, and emotionally flat fashion. In contrast, **Wernicke's area,** located in the

FIGURE 9.2

Language-specific structures in the left hemisphere of the cerebral cortex. *Broca's area* controls language production by creating a detailed program for speaking, which it sends to the face area of the cortical region that controls body movement and coordination. *Wernicke's area* interprets language by receiving impulses from the primary auditory area, where sensations from the ears are sent. To produce a verbal response, Wernicke's area communicates with Broca's area through a bundle of nerve fibers, represented by dotted lines in the figure.

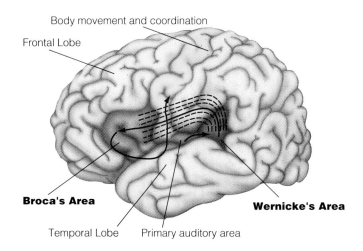

362 PART III / COGNITIVE AND LANGUAGE DEVELOPMENT

temporal lobe, is responsible for interpreting language. When it is damaged, speech is fluent and grammatical, but it contains many nonsense words. Comprehension of others' speech is also impaired.

Although some lateralization is present at birth, as children acquire language, the brain becomes increasingly specialized for language processing. When researchers recorded event-related potentials (ERPs) as toddlers listened to words within their vocabularies, between 13 and 17 months electrical activity was broadly distributed over both hemispheres of the cerebral cortex. But by 20 months, it was concentrated in certain left-hemispheric regions, a trend that was stronger for children advanced in vocabulary development (Mills, Coffey-Corina, & Neville, 1993, 1997). This relationship between language competence and lateralization has also been found among language-impaired children and among adults acquiring a second language (Neville et al., 1993; Weber-Fox & Neville, 1992). It is certainly consistent with the idea that a language module develops in a specific part of the brain.

IS THERE A SENSITIVE PERIOD FOR LANGUAGE DEVELOPMENT? Erik Lenneberg (1967) first proposed that children must acquire language during the age span of brain lateralization, which he believed to be complete by puberty. If this idea is correct, it would provide further support for the nativist position that language development has unique biological properties.

To test this sensitive period idea, researchers have tracked the recovery of severely abused children who experienced little human contact in childhood. The most recent thorough study is of Genie, a child isolated at 20 months in the back room of her parents' house and not discovered until she was 13½ years old.[1] Genie's early environment was linguistically and emotionally impoverished. No one was permitted to talk to her, and she was beaten when she made any noise. Over several years of training with dedicated caregivers, Genie's language developed, but not nearly to the same extent as that of normal children. Although she eventually acquired a large vocabulary and good comprehension of everyday conversation, her grammatical and pragmatic abilities were limited (Curtiss, 1977, 1989). Genie's case, along with several other similar ones, fits with Lenneberg's hypothesis that first-language learning is optimal during the period of brain lateralization, although an exact age cut-off for a decline in language competence has not been established.

What about acquiring a second language? Is this task harder during adolescence and adulthood, after a sensitive period for language development has passed? In a study of Chinese and Korean adults who had immigrated to the United States at varying ages, those who began mastering English between 3 and 7 years scored as well as native speakers on a test of grammatical knowledge (see Figure 9.3 on page 364). As age of arrival in the United States increased through adolescence, test scores gradually declined. Similar outcomes occur for adults who had become deaf in childhood or adolescence and learned American Sign Language at different ages (Mayberry, 1994; Newport, 1991). These and other findings indicate that younger second-language learners do better in the long run on a wide range of linguistic skills. But the capacity to acquire a second language does not cease at puberty. It extends into adulthood, although ultimate attainment is not as great (Harley & Wang, 1997).

■ **LIMITATIONS OF THE NATIVIST PERSPECTIVE.** Chomsky's theory has had a major impact on current views of language development. It is now widely accepted that a uniquely human biological predisposition plays a powerful role in language learning. Still, Chomsky's account of development has been challenged on several grounds.

First, comparisons between languages reveal vastly different grammatical systems. Chomsky (1981) and others have attempted to specify an underlying universal grammar, but as yet a single set of rules that encompasses all languages has not been identified. Even

Broca's area A language structure located in the frontal lobe of the cerebral cortex that controls language production.

Wernicke's area A language structure located in the temporal lobe of the cortex that is responsible for interpreting language.

---

[1]Medical records of Genie's early infancy suggest that she was an alert, responsive baby. Her motor development was normal, and she said her first words just before her confinement, after which all language disappeared. Therefore, mental retardation is an unlikely explanation for the course of her development.

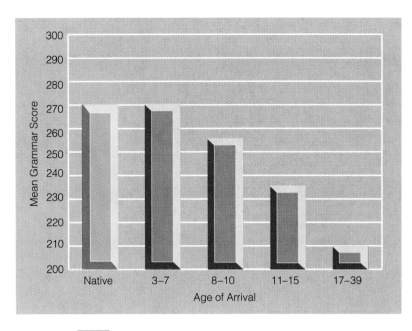

FIGURE 9.3

Relationship between age of arrival of Chinese and Korean immigrants in the United States and performance on a test of English grammar. Individuals who began learning English in early childhood attained the competence of native speakers. With increasing age, scores declined.

(Adapted from Johnson & Newport, 1989.)

seemingly simple grammatical distinctions, such as *the* versus *a* in English, are made in quite different ways around the world. For example, several African languages rely on tone patterns to designate definite versus indefinite articles. In Japanese and Chinese, they are inferred entirely from sentence context. In Finnish, *en* is attached to the front of a word to signify *the,* to the back of a word to signify *a.* In Turkish, marking this distinction is highly complex; it depends on a noun's grammatical use and pronunciation. Critics of Chomsky's theory doubt the existence of a universal grammar that can account for such varied approaches to conveying the same grammatical forms (Karmiloff-Smith, 1992a; Maratsos, 1998; Tomasello, 1995).

Second, Chomsky's assumption that grammatical knowledge is innately determined does not fit with certain observations of language development. Although extraordinary strides are made during preschool years, children's acquisition of many sentence constructions is not immediate but steady and gradual. Complete mastery of some forms (such as the passive voice) is not achieved until well into middle childhood, and very subtle aspects of grammar continue to be refined into the adult years (Tager-Flusberg, 1997). This suggests that more learning and discovery are involved in grammatical development than Chomsky assumed.

Third, although certain regions of the cerebral cortex are specialized for language, our knowledge of which parts deal with which language functions is very limited. Look back at the deficits resulting from damage to Broca's and Wernicke's areas, and you will see that several aspects of language—not just grammar—are involved in each. Other evidence reveals that additional parts of the cortex (for example, frontal lobe regions that permit us to relate concepts to one another) must support these specialized areas for effective language functioning (Bates, 1995; Blumstein, 1995). Furthermore, as we noted in Chapter 5, for infants with left-hemispheric damage and children who learn sign language, language is housed in the right hemisphere. At present, the biological basis of Chomsky's LAD is far from clear.

Dissatisfaction with Chomsky's theory has also arisen from its lack of comprehensiveness. For example, in focusing on language structure at the sentence level, it cannot explain how children weave statements together into connected discourse and develop strategies for sustaining meaningful conversations. Perhaps because Chomsky did not dwell on the pragmatic side of language, his theory grants little attention to quality of language input and social experience in supporting language development. Furthermore, we have already noted that the nativist perspective does not regard children's cognitive capacities as important. Yet in Chapter 6, we saw that attainment of cognitive milestones is involved in children's early vocabulary growth. And studies of children with mental retardation (see the Variations box on the following page) show that cognitive development has at least some effect on children's ability to detect grammatical structure as well.

THE INTERACTIONIST PERSPECTIVE

In recent years, new theories of language development have arisen, emphasizing interactions between inner predispositions and environmental inputs, replacing the dichotomy that grew out of the Skinner–Chomsky debate. Although several interactionist models exist, virtually all stress the social context of language learning. An active child, well endowed for acquiring language, observes and engages in social exchanges with others. Out of this experience, the child builds a communication system that relates the form and content of language to its social meaning. According to this view, native capacity, a strong desire to interact with others, and a rich linguistic and social environment combine to assist

Language Development in Children with Williams Syndrome

WILLIAMS SYNDROME IS a rare disorder, occurring once in every 20,000 to 50,000 births, that is caused by deletion of genetic material on the seventh chromosome. Affected individuals have facial, heart, and kidney abnormalities and mild to serious mental retardation, with IQ scores typically ranging from 50 to 70 (Tass-abehji et al., 1996).

Yet poor planning, problem solving, and spatial skills do not place expected limits on language development in Williams syndrome. When individuals with Williams syndrome and Down syndrome are matched on age and IQ, the language skills of the Williams syndrome group are far more advanced (Bellugi & Wang, 1999). For many years, this apparent "decoupling" of cognition and language was taken as strong evidence that language is modular, or controlled by an innate LAD (Pinker, 1994). To see if this conclusion is warranted, let's take a closer look at language attainments linked to this disorder.

Infants with Williams syndrome are strongly oriented toward the social world—fascinated by faces and voices rather than objects (Mervis et al., 1998). Although their language development is delayed, it is impressive. During the preschool years, the sentences of children with Williams syndrome are more accurately pronounced and more grammatically complex than are those of children with Down syndrome (Harris et al., 1997). For example, the longest sentence of one Williams syndrome 3-year-old was, "Please have some grapes in my cup right now." Her Down syndrome counterpart said, "Here-ya-go" and "Hold me" (Jarrold, Baddeley, & Hewes, 1998, p. 361). By adolescence, individuals with Williams syndrome have a remarkably large vocabulary that contains many unusual words. When asked to name as many animals as possible, one Williams syndrome teenager said "weasel, newt, salamander, Chihuahua, ibex, yak" (Bellugi et al., 1992, p. 11).

Yet careful testing reveals that Williams syndrome does not leave language fully intact. Affected individuals score low on tests of general grammatical knowledge because they have trouble with highly challenging rules of language. For example, French-speaking adolescents with Williams syndrome do poorly on grammatical gender assignment—matching masculine and feminine articles (such as *un* versus *une*) with nouns by attending to word endings and noting exceptions. Yet normally developing French children master this gender system by age 4 (Karmiloff-Smith et al., 1997). In one study of Italian-speaking adults with Williams syndrome, grammatical errors in word order and use of prepositions, among others, occurred often (Volterra et al., 1996). In another study of English-speaking adults, difficulties with subtle verb forms (*he struggled with the dog*, not *he struggle the dog*) appeared (Karmiloff-Smith et al., 1998).

Why does Williams syndrome lead to an uneven language profile—areas of both strength and weakness? According to Annette Karmiloff-Smith (1997), the cognitive deficits of Williams syndrome profoundly affect language development, altering its course. Children with the disorder are relatively

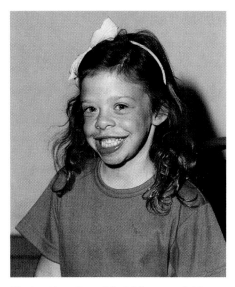

The impish smile and facial features of this child, who has Williams syndrome, suggest that she is strongly oriented toward the social world. In keeping with their sociability, children with Williams syndrome display impressive language skills given their mild to serious mental retardation. Yet the cognitive deficits of Williams syndrome impair children's ability to master the most complex rules of language.

(The Williams Syndrome Association)

good at memorizing but poor at rule learning. To compensate for this weakness, they capitalize on their social strengths, focusing on faces and voices and acquiring as much language by rote as they can.

Recall that experience influences brain development. Karmiloff-Smith believes that more of the Williams syndrome brain may specialize in language than in other cognitive abilities. The more space devoted to language, the less emphasis on grammatical rules because of abundant resources for storing individual items. Over time, children with the disorder acquire the most obvious rules, but they fail to grasp highly complex ones. And they frequently lapse into grammatical errors.

In support of this rote approach to language learning, unlike normally developing infants, infants with Williams syndrome do not build their early vocabularies on intentional gestures (such as pointing) and advances in categorization, as normally developing children do (Mervis et al., 1998). Instead, they seem to rely heavily on mimicking others. According to some parent reports, children with the disorder even speak without fully comprehending what they are saying (Harris et al., 1997). In sum, although the language of individuals with Williams syndrome is impressive in view of their cognitive limitations, it is impaired in significant ways.

children in discovering the functions and regularities of language (Bohannon & Bonvillian, 1997).

Although all interactionists regard the child as an active communicative being, debate continues over the precise nature of children's innate abilities. Some theorists accept a modified view of Chomsky's position, which states that although children are primed to make sense of language, they formulate and refine hypotheses about its structure based on input they receive (Slobin, 1985). Other theorists are impressed by the remarkable cognitive capacities of infants and preschoolers that we discussed in earlier chapters. They believe that children make sense of their complex language environments by applying powerful tools of a general cognitive kind rather than ones that are specifically tuned to language (Bates, 1995; Tomasello, 1995).

As we chart the course of language development, we will describe some of these new views, but we must keep in mind that none are completely verified yet. Indeed, even interactionist theories have not escaped the critical eye of modern researchers. Because interactionists assume that language competence grows out of communicative experience, we should not be able to find children who show large disparities between pragmatics and other aspects of language skill. Yet recall that Genie's development was quite uneven in this respect. And studies of children with mental retardation reveal that their conversational skills often lag behind other language achievements (Levy, 1996; Yamada, 1990).

Today there is increasing acknowledgment that biology, cognition, and social experience may operate in different balances with respect to each component of language. And to complicate matters further, the relative contributions of these factors may change with age (Owens, 1996). Research on children's language continues to face many theoretical puzzles. We still know much more about the course of language development than precisely how language acquisition takes place.

ASK YOURSELF . . .

♦ How does research on acquiring a second language support the existence of a sensitive period for language development? What practical implications do these findings have for teaching foreign languages in school?

♦ CONNECTIONS
Cite research, in this chapter and in Chapter 5, supporting the conclusion that the brain is not fully specialized for language at birth. Instead, areas of the cortex become increasingly committed to language processing with age. Relate these findings to the concept of brain plasticity. (See pages 188–189.)

BRIEF REVIEW

In mastering language, children acquire four components—phonology, semantics, grammar, and pragmatics—that they combine into a flexible communication system. Three theories provide different accounts of how children develop language. According to Skinner and other behaviorists, language is learned through operant conditioning and imitation. However, these principles cannot account for the speed of early language development or children's novel, rule-based utterances. In contrast, Chomsky's nativist view regards children as biologically equipped with a language acquisition device (LAD) that supports rapid early mastery of the structure of language. Although much evidence supports a biological contribution to language development, Chomsky's theory cannot explain many aspects of language learning. Interactionist theories offer a compromise between these two views, stressing that innate abilities and social contexts combine to promote language development.

Prelinguistic Development: Getting Ready to Talk

From the very beginning, infants are prepared to acquire language. During the first year of life, inborn capabilities, cognitive and social milestones, and environmental supports pave the way for the onset of verbal communication.

RECEPTIVITY TO LANGUAGE

Recall from Chapter 4 that newborns are especially sensitive to the pitch range of the human voice and find speech to be more pleasing than other sounds. In addition, they have an astonishing ability to make fine-grained distinctions between the sounds of virtually any human language. Because this skill may help them crack the phonological code of their native tongue, let's look at it more closely.

■ **LEARNING NATIVE-LANGUAGE SOUND CATEGORIES AND PATTERNS.** As adults, we analyze the speech stream into **phonemes,** the smallest sound units with distinctive features that can signal a difference in meaning, such as the difference between the consonant sounds in "pa" and "ba." Phonemes are not the same across all languages. For example, "ra" and "la" are separate sounds to English speakers, but Japanese individuals hear them as the same. Similarly, English speakers have trouble perceiving the difference between the two "p" sounds used in the Thai language. This tendency to perceive as identical a range of sounds that belong to the same phonemic class is called **categorical speech perception.** Like children and adults, 1-month-olds are capable of it. But unlike older individuals, they are sensitive to a much wider range of categories than exists in their own language environment (Aslin, Jusczyk, & Pisoni, 1998; Jusczyk, 1995).

Within the first few days after birth, babies distinguish and prefer the overall sound pattern of their native tongue to that of other languages (Mehler et al., 1996; Moon, Cooper, & Fifer, 1993). As infants continue to listen actively to the talk of people around them, they learn to focus on meaningful sound variations. By 6 months of age, long before they are ready to talk, babies start to organize speech into the phonemic categories of their own language. That is, they stop attending to many sound distinctions that are not useful in their language community (Kuhl et al., 1992; Polka & Werker, 1994).

In the second half of the first year, infants focus on larger speech units that are crucial for making sense of what they hear. They recognize familiar words in spoken passages (Jusczyk & Aslin, 1995; Jusczyk & Hohne, 1997). Older infants can also detect clauses and phrases in sentences. In one study, researchers recorded two versions of a mother telling a story. In the first, she spoke naturally, with pauses occurring between clauses, like this: "Cinderella lived in a great big house [pause], but it was sort of dark [pause] because she had this mean stepmother." In the second version, the mother inserted pauses in unnatural places—in the middle of clauses: "Cinderella lived in a great big house, but it was [pause] sort of dark because she had [pause] this mean stepmother." Like adults, 7-month-olds clearly preferred speech with natural breaks (Hirsh-Pasek et al., 1987).

Around 9 months, infants extend this rhythmic sensitivity to individual words. They listen much longer to speech with stress patterns and phoneme sequences common in their own language (Jusczyk, Charles-Luce, & Luce, 1994; Jusczyk, Cutler, & Redanz, 1993; Morgan & Saffran, 1995). And they use these cues to divide the speech stream into word-like segments. Dutch-learning infants of this age can distinguish sound patterns that typically begin words from those that do not (Friederici & Wessels, 1993). English learners often rely on the onset of a strong syllable to indicate new words. By 10 months, they can detect words that start with weak syllables, such as "surprise," by listening for sound regularities before and after the words (Jusczyk, 1997).

■ **ADULT SPEECH TO YOUNG LANGUAGE LEARNERS.** The findings just reviewed reveal that by the second half of the first year, infants have begun to analyze the internal structure of sentences and words—information that will be vital for linking speech units with their meanings in the second year. Certain features of adult talk assist babies in making sense of a complex speech stream. Adults in many countries speak to infants and toddlers in **child-directed speech (CDS),** a form of language made up of short sentences with high-pitched, exaggerated expression, clear pronunciation, and distinct pauses between speech segments (Fernald et al., 1989). Deaf mothers show a similar style of communication with their babies. They form signs at a slower tempo and exaggerate the movements associated with each (Masataka, 1992).

Parents do not seem to be deliberately trying to teach infants to talk when they use CDS, since many of the same speech qualities appear when adults communicate with foreigners. CDS probably arises from adults' unconscious desire to keep young children's attention and ease the task of understanding, and it works effectively in these ways. From birth on, infants prefer to listen to CDS over other kinds of adult talk (Cooper & Aslin, 1994). By 5 months, they are more emotionally responsive to it and can discriminate the tone quality of CDS with different meanings—for example, approving from soothing

phoneme The smallest sound unit with distinctive features that can signal a difference in meaning.

categorical speech perception The tendency to perceive as identical a range of sounds that belong to the same phonemic class as identical.

child-directed speech The form of language adults use to speak to infants and toddlers that consists of short sentences with high-pitched, exaggerated expression, clear pronunciation, and distinct pauses between speech segments.

utterances (Moore, Spence, & Katz, 1997; Werker, Pegg, & McLeod, 1994). The emotional quality of CDS helps young babies process social information visually. At the sound of CDS, they turn toward the human face, looking more intently when a voice–face "emotional match" is made (Kaplan et al., 1997).

Parents constantly fine-tune CDS, adjusting the length and content of their utterances to fit with children's cognitive needs. In a study of "baby talk" in four cultures, American, Argentinean, French, and Japanese mothers tended to speak to 5-month-olds in affect-laden ways, emphasizing greetings, repeated sounds, and terms of endearment. At 13 months, when toddlers began to understand as well as respond, a greater percentage of maternal speech in each culture was information-laden—concerned with giving directions, asking questions, and describing what was happening at the moment (Bornstein et al., 1992a). The more effectively parents modify speech complexity over the first year, the better their children's language comprehension at 18 months of age (Murray, Johnson, & Peters, 1990).

This Nepalese mother speaks to her baby daughter in short, clearly pronounced sentences with high-pitched, exaggerated intonation. Adults in many countries use this form of language, called child-directed speech, with infants and toddlers. It eases the task of early language learning.

(David Austen/Stock Boston)

FIRST SPEECH SOUNDS

Around 2 months, babies begin to make vowel-like noises, called **cooing** because of their pleasant "oo" quality. Gradually, consonants are added, and around 4 months **babbling** appears, in which infants repeat consonant–vowel combinations in long strings, such as "babababababa" and "nanananana."

The timing of early babbling seems to be due to maturation, since babies everywhere (even those who are deaf) start babbling at about the same age and produce a similar range of early sounds (Stoel-Gammon & Otomo, 1986). But for babbling to develop further, infants must be exposed to human speech. Around 7 months, babbling starts to include the sounds of mature spoken languages. However, if a baby is hearing impaired, these speechlike sounds emerge several months to years later and, in the case of deaf infants, are totally absent (Eilers & Oller, 1994; Oller & Eilers, 1988). But babbling is not restricted to the spoken modality. When deaf infants are exposed to sign language from birth, they babble manually in much the same way hearing infants do through speech (Petitto & Marentette, 1991).

Although language input is necessary for babbling to be sustained, maturation continues to affect its development through the second half of the first year. Adults cannot change a baby's babbled sounds through reinforcement and modeling, although they can, to some extent, influence the overall amount of babbling (Dodd, 1972). Also, the development of babbling follows a universal pattern. Regardless of whether infants are reared in low-SES or middle-SES homes and hear one or two languages, at first they produce a limited number of sounds, which expand to a much broader range by 12 months of age. Babbling continues for 4 or 5 months after infants say their first words (Oller et al., 1997).

Nevertheless, a careful look at babbling reveals that infants are applying the knowledge they have gained from many months of listening to their native tongue. By 1 year of age, babbling reflects the consonant–vowel and intonation patterns of the child's language community, some of which are transferred to their first words (Boysson-Bardies & Vihman, 1991; Levitt & Utmann, 1992). Listen to an older baby babble, and you are likely to notice that certain sounds appear in particular contexts—for example, when exploring objects, looking at books, and walking upright (Blake & Boysson-Bardies, 1992). Through babbling, infants experiment with the sound system and meaning of language before they speak in conventional ways.

BECOMING A COMMUNICATOR

cooing Pleasant vowel-like noises made by infants beginning around 2 months of age.

babbling Repetition of consonant–vowel combinations in long strings, beginning around 4 months of age.

At birth, infants are prepared for some aspects of conversational behavior. For example, newborn babies can initiate interaction by making eye contact and terminate it by looking away. Around 4 months, they start to gaze in the same direction adults are looking, a skill that increases and becomes more accurate between 12 and 15 months of age (Tomasello, 1999). Adults follow the baby's line of vision as well, often commenting on what the infant sees. In this way, the environment is labeled for the baby.

This kind of joint attention is quite important for early language development. Mothers who maintain high levels during play have babies who comprehend more language, produce meaningful gestures and words earlier, and show faster vocabulary development. In contrast, mothers who are intrusive—that is, who often interrupt, redirect, or restrict the baby's attention and activities—sometimes have infants whose language develops slowly (Baumwell, Tamis-LeMonda, & Bornstein, 1997; Carpenter, Nagell, & Tomasello, 1998; Duchan, 1989).

By 3 months, the beginnings of conversation can be seen. At first, the mother vocalizes at the same time as the baby—an event that may help infants realize that others attend to their speech sounds (Elias & Broerse, 1996). Soon, a turn-taking pattern emerges. The baby vocalizes, the caregiver vocalizes in return, waits for a response, and vocalizes again. At first, the adult is responsible for sustaining these vocal exchanges, but as they increase over the first 2 years, infants play a more active role. Similarly, around 6 months, turn-taking games, such as pat-a-cake and peekaboo, appear, in which the parent starts the game and the infant is an amused observer. But by 12 months, infants participate actively, exchanging roles with the parent. As they do so, they practice the turn-taking pattern of human conversation, and they also hear words paired with the actions they perform (Bruner, 1983). Infants' play maturity and vocal behavior during games predict their language progress between 1 and 2 years of age (Rome-Flanders & Cronk, 1995; Vibbert & Bornstein, 1989).

At the end of the first year, as infants become capable of intentional behavior and begin to realize that others' attention can be influenced in various ways, they use two forms of preverbal gestures to influence the behavior of others. The first is the **protodeclarative,** in which the baby touches an object, holds it up, or points to it while looking at others to make sure they notice. In the second, the **protoimperative,** the infant gets another person to do something by reaching, pointing, and often making sounds at the same time (Carpenter, Nagell, & Tomasello, 1998; Fenson et al., 1994). Over time, some of these gestures become explicitly representational—much like those that appear in children's early make-believe play (see Chapter 6). For example, a 1- to 2-year-old might sniff to refer to flowers, lift her arms over her head to indicate big, and flap her arms to refer to a butterfly. In this way, gestural communication provides yet another context in which young children learn about the functions of language—that meanings can be symbolized and conveyed to others (Acredolo & Goodwyn, 1990).

Early in the second year, turn-taking and gestural communication come together, especially in situations in which children's messages do not communicate clearly. When adults respond to babies' reaching and pointing gestures and also label them ("Oh, you want a cookie!"), infants learn that using language quickly leads to desired results. Soon toddlers utter words along with gestures, the gestures recede, and words become the dominant symbolic form (Iverson, Capirci, & Caselli, 1994; Namy & Waxman, 1998).

A final note: Throughout our discussion, we have stressed that progress toward spoken language is encouraged by caregivers who involve infants in dialoguelike exchanges. Yet in some cultures, such as the Kaluli of Papua New Guinea and the people of Western Samoa, adults rarely treat infants as communicative partners and never play social games with them. Not until infants crawl and walk do sibling caregivers take charge, talk to babies, and respond to their vocalizations. Yet Kaluli and Samoan children acquire language within the normal time frame of development (Ochs, 1988; Schieffelin & Ochs, 1987). These findings suggest that adult molding of infant communication may not be essential. Nevertheless, when it occurs, it clearly supports the transition from the preverbal phase to the much longer linguistic period of childhood.

This 1-year-old infant uses the proto-declarative to attract his mother's attention to the flowers. As she labels her son's pointing gesture, she promotes the transition to verbal language.

(Laura Dwight)

protodeclarative A preverbal gesture through which infants make an assertion about an object by touching it, holding it up, or pointing to it.

protoimperative A preverbal gesture in which infants point, reach, and make sounds to get another person to do something.

ASK YOURSELF . . .

◆ Cite findings indicating that both infant capacities and the child's language environment contribute to prelinguistic development.

◆ CONNECTIONS
Explain how parents' use of child-directed speech fits with Vygotsky's concept of the zone of proximal development. (See Chapter 6, page 261.)

Research indicates that infants advanced in language development have mothers who often establish joint attention and comment on what the baby sees. How is this quality of interaction similar to parental behavior that fosters secure attachment? (See Chapter 10, pages 426–427.)

BRIEF REVIEW

During infancy, biological predispositions, cognitive development, and a responsive social environment join to prepare the child for language. Newborn babies have a built-in capacity to detect a wide variety of sound categories in human speech. By the second half of the first year, they become increasingly sensitive to the phonemes, words, and sentence structure of their native tongue. Cooing begins at about 2 months, babbling around 4 months. By 1 year, babbling reflects the sound and intonation patterns of the native language, and infants use preverbal gestures to influence the behavior of others. When adults use child-directed speech, engage infants in turn-taking exchanges, and respond to babies' preverbal gestures, they support the transition to verbal communication.

Phonological Development

Think about the sounds you might hear if you listened in on a 1- or 2-year-old trying out her first handful of words. You probably imagined an assortment of interesting pronunciations, such as "nana" for banana, "oap" for soap, and "weddy" for ready, as well as some puzzling productions that the child uses like words but that do not resemble adult forms. For "translations" of these, you have to ask the child's parent. Phonological development is a complex process that depends on the child's ability to attend to the sound sequences of speech, produce sounds voluntarily, and combine them into understandable words and phrases. Between 1 and 4 years of age, children make considerable progress at this task.

Experts in phonology view children mastering the pronunciation of their language as young problem solvers. In trying to figure out how to talk like people around them, they adopt a variety of temporary strategies for producing sounds that bring adult words within their current range of physical and cognitive capabilities (Stoel-Gammon & Menn, 1997). Let's see how they do so.

THE EARLY PHASE

Children's first words are limited by the small number of sounds they can control. The easiest sound sequences start with consonants, end with vowels, and include repeated syllables, as in "mama," "dada," "bye-bye," and "nigh-nigh" (for "night-night"). In other instances, young speakers may use the same sound to represent a variety of words, a feature that makes their speech hard to understand. For example, one toddler substituted "bat" for as many as 12 different words, including "bad," "bark," "bent," and "bite" (Ingram, 1986).

These observations reveal that early phonological and semantic development are related. The words children choose to say are influenced partly by what they can pronounce (Hura & Echols, 1996; Vihman, 1996). Interestingly, languages cater to young children's phonological limitations. Throughout the world, sounds resembling "mama," "dada," and "papa" refer to parents, so it is not surprising that these are among the first words children everywhere produce. Also, when speaking child-directed speech, adults often use simplified words to talk about things of interest to toddlers. For example, rabbit becomes "bunny," stomach becomes "tummy," and train becomes "choo-choo." These word forms support the child's first attempts to talk.

APPEARANCE OF PHONOLOGICAL STRATEGIES

By the middle of the second year, children can be heard experimenting with sounds, sound patterns, and speech rhythms. One 21-month-old pronounced "juice" as "du," "ju," "dus," "jus," "sus," "zus," "fus," "tfus," "jusi," and "tfusi" within a single hour (Fee, 1997). This marks an intermediate phase of development in which pronunciation is partly right and partly wrong. A close look reveals that children's errors are fairly consistent. They apply systematic strategies to words so they fit with their phonological capacities yet resemble adult utterances. Although individual differences exist in the precise strategies children adopt (see Table 9.1 for examples), they follow a general developmental pattern (Vihman, 1996).

At first, children produce *minimal words,* in which they focus on the stressed syllable and try to pronounce its consonant–vowel combination ("du" or "ju" for "juice"). Soon they add ending consonants ("jus"), adjust vowel length ("beee" for "please"), and add unstressed syllables ("mae-do" for "tomato"). Finally, they produce the full word with a correct stress pattern, although they may still need to refine its sounds ("timemba" for "remember," "pagetti" for "spaghetti") (Demuth, 1996; Salidis & Johnson, 1997).

The errors children make are similar across a range of languages, including Cantonese, Czech, English, French, Italian, Quiché (a Mayan language), Spanish, and Swedish. However, differences in rate of phonological progress exist, depending on the complexity of a language's sound system. Cantonese-speaking children, for example, develop more quickly than English-speaking children. In Cantonese, many words are single syllables. Although a change in tone of a syllable can lead to a change in meaning, Chinese children master this tone system by age 2 (So & Dodd, 1995).

Over the preschool years, children's pronunciation improves greatly. Maturation of the vocal tract and the child's active problem-solving efforts are largely responsible, since children's phonological errors are very resistant to adult correction. One father I know tried repeatedly to get his 2½-year-old daughter to pronounce the word "music," but each time she persisted with "ju-jic." Like other young children, she was well aware of the difference between her immature pronunciation and the correct version. When her father made one last effort, she replied, "Wait 'til I big. Then I say ju-jic, Daddy!"

LATER PHONOLOGICAL DEVELOPMENT

Although phonological development is largely complete by the time children go to school, a few syllable stress patterns that signal subtle differences in meaning are acquired in middle childhood and adolescence. For example, when shown pairs of pictures and asked to identify which is the "greenhouse" and which is the "green house," most children recognized the correct label by third grade and produced it between fourth and sixth grade (Atkinson-King, 1973). Changes in syllabic stress after certain abstract words take on endings—for example, "humid" to "humidity" and "method" to "methodical"—are not mastered until adolescence (Camarata & Leonard, 1986).

These late developments are probably affected by the semantic complexity of the words to which they apply. Even among young children, pronunciation is best for easily understood words. As we indicated in Chapter 7, the capacity of the human information-processing system is limited. Working on the sound and meaning of a new word simulta-

TABLE 9.1

Common Phonological Strategies Used by Young Children to Simplify Pronunciation of Adult Words

Strategy	Example
Repeating the first consonant-vowel in a multisyllable word	"TV" becomes "didi," "cookie" becomes "gege."
Deleting unstressed syllables in a multisyllable word	"Banana" becomes "nana," "giraffe" becomes "raffe."
Replacing fricatives (hissing sounds) with stop consonant sounds	"Sea" becomes "tea," "say" becomes "tay."
Replacing consonant sounds produced in the rear and palate area of the vocal tract with ones produced in the frontal area	"Shoe" becomes "zue," "goose" becomes "doose."
Replacing liquid sounds ("l" or "r") with glides ("y" or "w")	"Lap" becomes "yap," "ready" becomes "weddy."
Reducing consonant-vowel-consonant words to a consonant-vowel form by deleting the final consonant	"Bike" becomes "bai," "more" becomes "muh."
Replacing an ending consonant syllable with a vowel	"Apple" becomes "appo," "bottom" becomes "bada."
Replacing a consonant cluster to a single consonant	"Clown" becomes "cown," "play" becomes "pay."

Source: Ingram, 1986.

neously may overload the system, leading children to sacrifice sound temporarily until the word's meaning is better understood.

Semantic Development

aternal reports indicate that on the average, children say their first word at 12 months of age. By age 6, they have a vocabulary of about 10,000 words. To accomplish this extraordinary feat, children learn about 5 new words each day (Anglin, 1993; Bloom, 1998).

The semantic achievements of early childhood are even more awesome if we consider that from infancy on, children's **comprehension,** the language they understand, develops ahead of **production,** or the language they use. For example, toddlers follow many simple directions, such as "Bring me your book" or "Don't touch the lamp," even though they cannot yet express all these words in their own speech. There is a 5-month lag between the time children comprehend 50 words (around 13 months) and the time they produce this many (around 18 months) (Menyuk, Liebergott, & Schultz, 1995).

Why is language comprehension ahead of production? Think back to the distinction we made in Chapter 7 between two types of memory: recognition and recall. Comprehension requires only that children recognize the meaning of a word, whereas production demands that they recall, or actively retrieve from their memories, the word as well as the concept for which it stands (Kuczaj, 1986). Language production is clearly a more difficult task. Failure to say a word does not mean that toddlers do not understand it. As we discuss semantic development, we need to keep both processes in mind. If we rely only on what children say, we will underestimate their language progress.

THE EARLY PHASE

Learning words is a matter of identifying which concept each label picks out in a particular language community. Ask several parents of toddlers to tell you which words appeared first in their children's vocabularies. You will quickly see that early language builds on the sensorimotor foundations Piaget described and on categories children construct during the first 2 years (see Chapter 6). First words refer to important people ("Mama," "Dada"), objects that move or can be acted on ("ball," "car," "cat," "shoe"), familiar actions ("bye-bye," "more," "up"), or outcomes of familiar actions ("dirty," "hot," "wet"). As Table 9.2 reveals, in their first 50 words, toddlers rarely name things that just sit there, such as table or vase (Nelson, 1973).

TABLE 9.2

Types of Words Appearing in Toddlers' 50-Word Vocabularies

Word Type	Description	Typical Examples	Percentages of Total Word [a]
Object word	Words used to refer to the "thing world"	*Apple, ball, bird, boat, book, car, cookie, Dada, doggie, kitty, milk, Mama, shoe, snow, truck*	66
Action words	Words that describe, demand, or accompany action or that express attention or demand attention	*Bye-bye, go, hi, look, more, out, up*	13
State words (modifiers)	Words that refer to properties or qualities of things or events	*All gone, big, dirty, hot, mine, pretty, outside, red, uh-oh, wet*	9
Personal/social words	Words that express emotional states and social relationships	*No, ouch, please, want, yes, thank you*	8
Function words	Words that fill a solely grammatical function	*For, is, to, what, where*	4

[a]Average percentages are given, based on a sample of 18 American toddlers.
Source: Nelson, 1973.

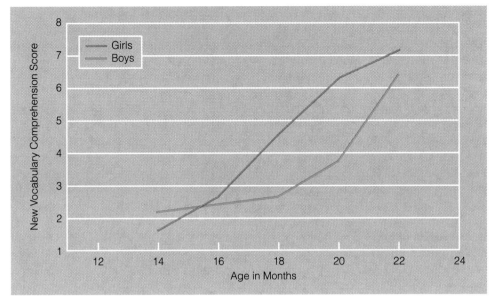

Spurt in vocabulary growth between 18 and 24 months, averaged over 24 English-speaking children. Although the graph is based on a measure of language comprehension, a similar spurt appears when language production is assessed. Boys lag behind girls in size of their early vocabularies and in timing of the spurt.

(From J. S. Reznick & B. A. Goldfield, 1992, "Rapid Change in Lexical Development in Comprehension and Production," *Developmental Psychology, 28*, p. 410. Copyright © 1992 by the American Psychological Association. Reprinted by permission.)

In Chapter 6, we noted that certain early words are linked to specific cognitive achievements. Recall that about the time children master advanced object permanence problems, they start to use disappearance terms, like "all gone." And when they solve sensorimotor problems suddenly (in Piaget's Substage 6), success and failure expressions, such as "there!" and "uh-oh!" appear in their vocabularies. As one pair of researchers concluded, "Children seem to be motivated to acquire words that are relevant to the particular cognitive problems they are working on at the moment" (Gopnik & Meltzoff, 1986, p. 1052).

Besides cognition, emotion influences early word learning. At first, toddlers' talk focuses on people, objects, and events that their feelings are about rather than on the feelings themselves. When acquiring a word, 1½-year-olds say it rather neutrally; they need to listen carefully to learn, and strong emotion diverts their attention. As words become better learned, toddlers integrate talking and expressing feelings (Bloom, 1993, 1998). "Shoe!" said one enthusiastic 22-month-old as her mother tied her shoelaces before an outing. At the end of the second year, children begin to label their emotions with words like "happy," "mad," and "sad"—a development we will consider further in Chapter 10.

Young toddlers add to their vocabularies slowly, at a rate of 1 to 3 words a month. Over time, the number of words learned accelerates. As Figure 9.4 shows, between 18 and 24 months, a spurt in vocabulary usually takes place (Fenson et al., 1994; Reznick & Goldfield, 1992). Many children add 10 to 20 new words a week, a rise that (as we mentioned in Chapter 6) occurs at about the time their understanding of categories accelerates. An improved ability to pronounce words and retrieve them from memory also adds to this "naming explosion" (Gershoff-Stowe & Smith, 1997; Plunkett, 1993). And a more flexible capacity to represent experience contributes. In the middle of the second year, talk about nonpresent objects and events emerges and increases (McCune, 1995; Morford & Goldin-Meadow, 1997).

How do children build their vocabularies so quickly? Researchers have discovered that they can connect a new word with an underlying concept after only a brief encounter, a process called **fast-mapping.** When an adult labeled an oddly shaped plastic ring with the nonsense word "koob" during a game, children as young as 2 picked up the word's meaning (Dollaghan, 1985). Toddlers also acquire new labels rapidly. In another study, researchers paired the nonsense words "bard" and "sarl" with pictures of unfamiliar objects. Then they presented the pictures side by side, together with a label that matched one of them or neither of them ("geek"). Fifteen-month-olds spent more time looking at an image when they heard the word for it (Schafer & Plunkett, 1998). Nevertheless, these very young language learners need more object-label pairings to acquire a word than do preschoolers, who are better at remembering and categorizing speech-based information (Woodward, Markman, & Fitzsimmons, 1994).

Preschoolers even fast-map new words they hear on television (Rice & Woodsmall, 1988). However, TV-watching is not sufficient for language development. Hearing children

comprehension In language development, the words and word combinations that children understand.

production In language development, the words and word combinations that children use.

fast-mapping Connecting a new word with an underlying concept after only a brief encounter.

reared by deaf parents and exposed to spoken language only on TV do not acquire normal speech (Bonvillian, Nelson, & Charrow, 1976). As research on individual differences (to which we now turn) reveals, a variety of factors combine to determine vocabulary growth—the cognitive foundations we have considered, rate of neurological maturation, personal styles of children, and the quantity and quality of adult–child communication.

■ **INDIVIDUAL AND CULTURAL DIFFERENCES.** Although the average age at which the first word is spoken is 12 months, the range is large, from 8 to 18 months. Individual differences in rate of language development have long been recognized. Many studies show that girls are slightly ahead of boys in vocabulary growth until 2 years of age, when boys gradually catch up. (Look again at Figure 9.4 to see these trends.) The most common explanation is girls' faster rate of physical maturation, believed to promote earlier development of the left cerebral hemisphere. Besides the child's sex, temperament makes a difference. Toddlers who are very reserved and cautious often wait until they understand a great deal before trying to speak. When they finally do speak, their vocabularies increase rapidly (Nelson, 1973).

But these child characteristics are also related to the surrounding language environment. For example, mothers talk much more to toddler-age girls than boys (Leaper, Anderson, & Sanders, 1998). The more words caregivers use when talking to young children, the greater the number integrated into the child's vocabulary (Hart, 1991; Huttenlocher et al., 1991). Because lower-SES children experience less verbal stimulation in their homes than do higher-SES children, their vocabularies tend to be smaller, regardless of the child's sex and ethnicity (Hart & Risley, 1995; Hoff-Ginsberg, 1994).

Besides rate of development, striking individual differences in style of early language learning exist. In an intensive study of 18 children from 1 to 2½ years of age, Katherine Nelson (1973) noticed wide variation in the kinds of words produced. The majority fit a **referential style.** Their vocabularies consisted of many words that referred to objects. A smaller number of children used an **expressive style.** Compared to referential children, they used many more pronouns and social formulas, such as "Stop it," "Thank you," and "I want it," uttered as compressed phrases, much like single words (as in "Iwannit"). Toddlers who use these styles have different early ideas about the functions of language. Referential children think that words are for naming objects, whereas expressive children believe they are for talking about the feelings and needs of themselves and other people. The vocabularies of referential-style children grow faster, since all languages contain many more object labels than social phrases (Bates et al., 1994).

What accounts for a toddler's choice of a particular language style? Once again, both biological and environmental factors seem to be involved. Rapidly developing, referential-style children often have an especially active interest in exploring objects and parents who eagerly respond with names of things to their children's first attempts to talk. And these children freely imitate words they hear others say, a strategy that supports swift vocabulary growth because it helps children remember new labels (Masur, 1995). In contrast, expressive-style children spend more time watching people, and their parents more often use verbal routines ("How are you?" "It's no trouble") designed to support social relationships (Goldfield, 1987).

The two language styles are also linked to culture. For example, in Western societies, many mothers stress object labels to children, but Vietnamese toddlers first learn an honorific pronoun system conveying respect for their elders (Nelson, 1981). And compared to American mothers, Japanese mothers more often engage young children in social routines, probably because their culture stresses the importance of membership in the social group (Fernald & Morikawa, 1993). African mothers of Mali, Mauritania, and Senegal respond verbally to their infant's glances and vocalizations to other people, not to the baby's exploration of objects (Jamin, 1994). When we consider these findings as a whole, early vocabulary development supports the interactionist's emphasis on the combined impact of children's inner dispositions and their linguistic and social worlds.

■ **TYPES OF WORDS.** Three types of words—object, action, and state—are most common in young children's vocabularies. Careful study of each provides important information about the course of semantic development.

referential style A style of early language learning in which toddlers use language mainly to label objects.

expressive style A style of early language learning in which toddlers use language mainly to talk about the feelings and needs of themselves and other people.

OBJECT AND ACTION WORDS. Although children differ in the first words they choose to learn, many early language learners have more object than action words in their beginning vocabularies (Au, Dapretto, & Song, 1994; Caselli et al., 1995). If actions are an especially important means through which infants find out about their world, then why this early emphasis on naming objects?

One reason is that concepts referred to by nouns are perceptually distinct and therefore very salient to young children. As a result, when they start to talk, they easily match objects with their appropriate labels. In contrast, verbs are cognitively more complex in that they require an understanding of the relationship between objects and actions (Gentner & Rattermann, 1991). Nevertheless, characteristics of the linguistic environment affect toddlers' relative use of object and action words. For example, the structure of English emphasizes nouns more than do some non-Western languages, and (as mentioned earlier) Western mothers like to talk about objects with their children. In Chinese, Japanese, and Korean, nouns are often omitted entirely from adult sentences, and verbs are stressed. In line with this difference, Asian toddlers typically acquire action words first and use them far more often than do their English-speaking counterparts (Choi, 1991; Gopnik & Choi, 1995; Tardif, 1996).

When English-speaking children first refer to actions, they often use a variety of words to represent them. For example, a toddler might use a noun, such as "door," or a preposition, such as "out," to convey the idea that she wants to open something. As their vocabularies expand at the end of the second and the beginning of the third year, English-speaking children use many more verbs to refer to actions (Bates et al., 1994).

STATE WORDS. Between 2 and 2½ years, children's use of state (or modifier) words expands to include labels for attributes of objects, such as size and color ("big," "red") as well as possession ("my toy," "Mommy purse"). Words referring to the functions of objects appear soon after (for example, "dump truck," "pickup truck") (Nelson, 1976).

When state words are related in meaning, general distinctions (which are cognitively easier) appear first. For example, among words referring to the size of objects, children acquire "big–small" first, followed by "tall–short," "high–low," and "long–short," and finally "wide–narrow" and "deep–shallow." The same is true for temporal terms, which modify actions. Between ages 3 and 5, children first master "now" versus "then" and "before" versus "after," followed by "today" versus "yesterday" and "tomorrow" (Clark, 1983; Stevenson & Pollitt, 1987).

State words referring to the location and movement of objects provide additional examples of how cognition influences vocabulary development. Before age 2, children can easily imitate an adult's action in putting an object "in" or "on" another object, but they have trouble imitating the placement of one object "under" another. These terms appear in children's vocabularies in just this order, with all three achieved around 2½ years of age (Clark, 1973). With respect to motion words, those that describe an object's source ("out," "off") and path of movement ("up," "down") appear before ones that refer to the place an object comes to rest ("here," "there"). The reason is that describing the end point of an object's motion demands that children grasp the relationship between all three concepts—where an object started, how it moved, and where it ended (Stockman & Vaughn-Cooke, 1992).

State terms serve a vital communicative function. Because they refer to the qualities of objects and actions, children can use them to express many more concepts than they could previously. As preschoolers master more of these words, their language becomes increasingly flexible.

■ UNDEREXTENSIONS AND OVEREXTENSIONS. When young children first learn new words, they often do not use them just the way we do. Sometimes

In Western societies, many mothers stress object labels to young language learners. In contrast, these African mothers of Botswana respond verbally to their toddlers' glances and vocalizations to other people, not to exploration of objects.
(DeVore/Anthro-Photo File)

Cognitive development influences young children's mastery of state (or modifier) words. This toddler is likely to say "in" the cup and "on" the table before she says "under" the table. But adult labeling of experiences like this one will help her acquire more challenging terms referring to object location by age 2½. (Nancy Sheehan)

they apply the word too narrowly, an error called **underextension.** For example, at 16 months, my younger son used the word "bear" to refer only to a special teddy bear to which he had become attached. A more common error between 1 and 2½ years of age is **overextension**—applying the word to a wider collection of objects and events than is appropriate. For example, a toddler might use the word "car" to refer to a great many objects, including buses, trains, trucks, and fire engines.

Overextensions are yet another illustration of very young children's sensitivity to categorical relations. Children do not overextend words randomly. Instead, they apply them to similar referents—for example, using "dog" to refer to a variety of furry, four-legged animals, or "open" to mean opening a door, peeling fruit, and undoing shoe laces (Behrend, 1988). Furthermore, children overextend many more words in production than they do in comprehension. That is, a 2-year-old may refer to trucks, trains, and bikes as "cars" but point to these objects correctly when given their names in a comprehension task (Naigles & Gelman, 1995). This suggests that children sometimes overextend deliberately because they cannot recall or have not acquired a suitable word. In addition, when a word is hard to pronounce, toddlers are likely to substitute a related one they can say (Elsen, 1994). As vocabulary and phonology expand, overextensions gradually disappear.

■ WORD COINAGES AND METAPHORS. To fill in for words they have not yet learned, children as young as age 2 coin new words based on ones they already know. At first, children operate on whole words, as in the technique of compounding. For example, a child might say "break-machine" for a machine that breaks things and "plant-man" for a gardener. Later they convert verbs into nouns and nouns into verbs, as in one child's use of "needle it" for mending something. Soon after, children discover more specialized word coinage techniques, such as adding "-er" to identify the doer of a particular action—for example, "crayoner" for a child using crayons instead of paints. Children give up coined words as soon as they acquire conventional labels for their intended meanings (Clark, 1995). Still, their ability to invent these expressions is evidence for a remarkable, rule-governed approach to language.

Preschoolers also extend language meanings through metaphor. Some very clever ones appear in their everyday language. For example, one 3-year-old used the expression "fire engine in my tummy" to describe a stomachache (Winner, 1988). Not surprisingly, the metaphors young preschoolers use and understand are based largely on concrete, sensory comparisons, such as "clouds are pillows" and "leaves are dancers." Once their vocabulary and knowledge of the world expand, they start to appreciate ones based on nonsensory comparisons, such as "Friends are like magnets" (Karadsheh, 1991; Keil, 1986). Metaphors permit children to communicate in especially vivid and memorable ways. And sometimes metaphors are the only means we have to convey what we want to say.

LATER SEMANTIC DEVELOPMENT

Because the average 6-year-old's vocabulary is already quite large, parents and teachers are less aware of gains in middle childhood and adolescence. Between the start of elementary school and adolescence, vocabulary increases fourfold, eventually exceeding 40,000 words, a rate of growth that exceeds that of early childhood. In addition, as we saw in Chapter 7, the knowledge base that underlies school-age children's vocabulary becomes better organized. This permits them to use words more precisely and think about them differently than they did at younger ages.

If you look carefully at children's word definitions, you will see examples of this change. Five- and 6-year-olds give very concrete descriptions that refer to functions or

underextension An early vocabulary error in which a word is applied too narrowly, to a smaller number of objects or events than is appropriate.

overextension An early vocabulary error in which a word is applied too broadly, to a wider collection of objects and events than is appropriate.

appearance—for example, "knife: when you're cutting carrots"; "bicycle: it's got wheels, a chain, and handlebars." By the end of elementary school, synonyms and explanations of categorical relationships appear—for example, "knife: Something you could cut with. A saw is like a knife. It could also be a weapon" (Litowitz, 1977; Wehren, De Lisi, & Arnold, 1981). This advance reflects the older child's ability to deal with word meanings on an entirely verbal plane. Fifth and sixth graders no longer need to be shown what a word refers to in order to understand it. They can add new words to their vocabulary simply by being given a definition (Dickinson, 1984).

School-age children's more reflective, analytical approach to language permits them to appreciate the multiple meanings of words. For example, they recognize that many words, such as "cool" or "neat," have psychological as well as physical meanings: "What a cool shirt!" or "That movie was really neat!" This grasp of double meanings permits 8- to 10-year-olds to comprehend subtle, mental metaphors, such as "sharp as a tack," "spilling the beans," and "left high and dry" (Nippold, Taylor, & Baker, 1996; Wellman & Hickling, 1994). It also leads to a change in children's humor. By the mid-elementary school years, riddles and puns requiring children to go back and forth between different meanings of the same key word are common:

"Hey, did you take a bath?" "No! Why, is one missing?"

"Why did the old man tiptoe past the medicine cabinet?" "Because he didn't want to wake up the sleeping pills."

Preschoolers may laugh at these statements because they are nonsensical. But they cannot tell a good riddle or pun, nor do they understand why these jokes are funny (Ely & McCabe, 1994).

The capacity for abstract reasoning permits adolescents to add such words as "counterintuitive," "incredible," and "philosophy" to their vocabularies. They can also understand subtle nonliteral word meanings. As a result, they become masters of sarcasm and irony (Winner, 1988). "Don't have a major brain explosion," one 16-year-old commented to his sister when she complained about having to write an essay for school. And when his mother fixed a dish for dinner that he disliked, he quipped, "Oh boy, my favorite!" School-age children sometimes realize that a sarcastic remark is insincere if it is said in a very exaggerated, mocking tone of voice (Capelli, Nakagawa, & Madden, 1990). And they can generate ironic endings to stories that strongly suggest irony, such as a character who discovers that the game she wants for her birthday is very boring (Lucariello & Mindolovich, 1995). But adolescents and adults need only notice the discrepancy between a statement and its context to grasp sarcasm. And they can comprehend and produce irony in a wide range of circumstances.

IDEAS ABOUT HOW SEMANTIC DEVELOPMENT TAKES PLACE

Research shows that adult feedback facilitates semantic development. When adults go beyond correcting and provide an explanation ("That's not a car. It's a truck. See, it has a place to put things in"), toddlers are more likely to move toward conventional word meanings (Chapman, Leonard, & Mervis, 1986). Still, there is no way that adults can tell children exactly what concept each new word picks out. For example, if an adult points to a dog and calls it a "doggie," it is not clear whether the word refers to four-legged animals, the dog's shaggy ears, the shape of its wagging tail, or its barking sound. Therefore, the child's cognitive processing must play a major role in vocabulary development.

■ **THE INFLUENCE OF MEMORY.** A special part of working memory, a **phonological store** that permits us to retain speech-based information, supports young children's fast-mapping. The more rapidly 4-year-olds can repeat back nonsense words to an experimenter (a measure of phonological memory skill), the greater their vocabulary growth over the following year (Gathercole, 1995). This suggests that a child with good phonological memory produces traces of new words that are clear and persistent enough to increase their chances of being transferred to long-term memory and linked with relevant concepts.

phonological store A special part of working memory that permits us to retain speech-based information. Supports early vocabulary development.

But phonological memory does not provide a full account of word learning. After age 5, semantic knowledge influences how quickly children form phonological traces, and both factors support the ability to learn new words (Gathercole et al., 1997). And even at younger ages (as we will see next), there is good evidence that children rely heavily on words they already know to detect the meanings of new ones.

■ **STRATEGIES FOR WORD LEARNING.** Recently, Eve Clark (1990, 1993, 1995) proposed an explanation of semantic development called **lexical contrast theory.** It assumes that two principles govern vocabulary growth. The first is *conventionality,* children's natural desire to acquire words and word meanings of their language community. The second is *contrast,* which explains how new word meanings are added. According to Clark, children assume that the meaning of each word they hear is unique. Therefore, when they hear a new label, they try to figure out its meaning by contrasting it with words they know and assigning it to a gap in their vocabulary.

Many researchers have criticized lexical contrast theory for not being specific about the hypotheses young children use to determine new word meanings (Gathercole, 1987; Golinkoff et al., 1992). Yet exactly how they discover which concept each word picks out is not yet fully understood. Ellen Markman (1989, 1992) believes that in the early phases of vocabulary growth, children adopt a **principle of mutual exclusivity.** They assume that words refer to entirely separate (nonoverlapping) categories. The principle of mutual exclusivity works well as long as available referents are perceptually very distinct. For example, when 2-year-olds are told the names of two very different novel objects (a clip and a horn), they assign each label correctly, to the whole object and not a part of it (Waxman & Senghas, 1992).

But mutual exclusivity cannot account for what young children do when adults call a single object by more than one name. Under these conditions, they look for cues in the adult's behavior to determine whether the new word refers either to a higher- or lower-order category or to particular features, such as a part of the object, its shape, its color, or a proper name (Hall, 1996; Tomasello & Barton, 1994; Waxman & Hatch, 1992). When no such cues are available, children as young as 2 demonstrate remarkable flexibility in their word learning strategies. They abandon the mutual exclusivity principle and treat the new word as a second name for the object (Mervis, Golinkoff, & Bertrand, 1994).

Although these findings tell us something about how children master object labels, they say little about strategies used for other types of words. Children often draw on other components of language for help in these instances. According to one proposal, children deduce many word meanings by observing how words are used in syntax, or the structure of sentences—a hypothesis called **syntactic bootstrapping** (Gleitman, 1990). Consider an adult who says, "This is a *citron* one," while showing a child a yellow car. As early as age 21 months, children interpret a novel word used as an adjective as a property of the object (such as its color) (Waxman & Markow, 1998). Similarly, syntactic cues strongly affect preschoolers' interpretations of new verbs. After seeing puppets act out a scene in which a rabbit pushed an elephant, 3- and 4-year-olds who heard "The rabbit is *ziking* the elephant" interpreted *ziking* as "pushing." Those who heard "The elephant is *ziking*" said *ziking* meant "falling" (Fisher et al., 1994).

Finally, children also rely on pragmatic cues to identify nonobject words. In one study, an adult performed an action on an object and then used a new label while looking back and forth between the child and the object, as if to invite the child to play. Two-year-olds capitalized on this social information to conclude that the label referred to the action, not the object (Tomasello & Akhtar, 1995). Young preschoolers can even infer verb meaning when a person intends an action but cannot complete it. After demonstrating several activities (for example, a platform that catapulted Big Bird into the air), an adult put the toys away. Then the adult took out one toy (the platform) and announced, "Let's *meek* Big Bird now," but pretended Big Bird was lost. Two-year-olds used their knowledge of the adult's previous behavior to infer that *meek* meant "launch" from the platform (Akhtar & Tomasello, 1996).

As these examples illustrate, children draw on many sources of information to guide word learning, all of which are not clearly specified (Woodward & Markman, 1998). We still have much to discover about the processes responsible for the phenomenal pace of semantic development.

lexical contrast theory A theory that assumes two principles govern semantic development: conventionality, children's natural desire to acquire the words and word meanings of their language community; and contrast, children's discovery of meanings by contrasting new words with ones they know and assigning them to gaps in their vocabulary.

principle of mutual exclusivity The assumption by children in the early stages of vocabulary growth that words refer to entirely separate (nonoverlapping) categories.

syntactic bootstrapping Observing how words are used syntactically, in the structure of sentences, to deduce their meanings.

emantic development takes place with extraordinary speed as young children fast-map thousands of words into their vocabularies. Although individual differences exist, object words are emphasized first. Action and state words increase later. Errors of underextension and overextension gradually decline as preschoolers enlarge and refine their vocabularies. During middle childhood, understanding of word meanings becomes more flexible and precise. Adolescents acquire many abstract words and grasp subtle, nonliteral word meanings. Adult feedback assists with word learning, but the child's cognitive processing is crucial. Lexical contrast theory is a recent account of how semantic development takes place. Research indicates that children use a wide variety of strategies to infer word meanings, including contrasting new words with ones they know and attending to syntactic and pragmatic cues.

Grammatical Development

rammar requires that children use more than one word in a single utterance. In studying grammatical development, researchers have puzzled over the following questions: Do very young children use a consistent grammar, and if so, is it like adults'? Is grammatical learning special, or does it depend on general cognitive processes? What is the role of adult teaching—in particular, corrective feedback for grammatical errors? Perhaps you noticed that these questions have been prompted by Chomsky's theory. If a nativist account is plausible, then grammar should appear early, and the role of adult input should be minimal. We will consider evidence on these issues as we chart the course of grammatical development.

FIRST WORD COMBINATIONS

Sometime between 1½ and 2½ years, shortly after the vocabulary spurt and when more verbs have been added to the child's single-word vocabulary, first sentences appear (Bloom, 1998). Children combine two words, such as "Mommy shoe," "Go car," and "More cookie," in **telegraphic speech.** Like a telegram, children focus on high-content words and leave out smaller, less important ones, such as "can," "the," and "to." For children learning languages that emphasize word order (such as English and French), endings like "-s" and "-ed" are not yet present. In languages where word order is flexible and small grammatical markers are stressed, children's first sentences include them from the start (de Villiers & de Villiers, 1992).

Even though the two-word utterance is very limited, children the world over use it to express a wide variety of meanings (see Table 9.3). In doing so, are they already applying a consistent grammar? At least to some extent they are, since children rarely engage in gross violations of the structure of their language. For example, English-speaking children usually say "Daddy eat" rather than "eat Daddy" and "my chair" rather than "chair my" (Bloom, 1990).

Yet controversy exists over the extent to which children at the two-word stage grasp the grammatical categories of their language. According to some investigators, a more complete, and perhaps full adultlike, grammar lies behind these two-word sentences (Gleitman et al., 1988; Pinker, 1994; Valian, 1991). Consistent with this view, children often use the same construction to express different underlying propositions. For example, a child might say "Mommy cookie" when he sees his mother eating a cookie and use the same phrase on another occasion to indicate that he wants his mother to give him a cookie (Bloom, 1970). Perhaps the more elaborate structure is present in the child's mind, but an inability to remember and produce a longer word string prevents him from displaying it.

Other researchers disagree, arguing that two-word sentences are based on a very limited structure that differs from the grammar of adults (Maratsos & Chalkley, 1980). For example, Jonathan, a child studied by Martin Braine (1976), produced several actor–action

ASK YOURSELF . . .

◆ *Eric's first words included "see," "give," and "thank you," and his vocabulary grew slowly during the second year. What style of early language learning did he display, and what factors might explain it?*

◆ CONNECTIONS
Toddlers experiment with sounds, sound patterns, and speech rhythms in trying to pronounce words. Explain how Siegler's model of strategy choice can help us understand why such experimentation is adaptive. (See Chapter 7, page 281.)

What cognitive advances during middle childhood probably support school-age children's astounding growth in vocabulary? (See Chapter 7, pages 294 and 301.)

telegraphic speech Children's two-word utterances that, like a telegram, leave out smaller and less important words.

TABLE 9.3

Common Meanings Expressed by Children's Two-Word Utterances

Meaning	Example
Agent–action	"Tommy hit"
Action–object	"Give cookie"
Agent–object	"Mommy truck" (meaning Mommy push the truck)
Action–location	"Put table" (meaning put X on the table)
Entity–location	"Daddy outside"
Possessor–possession	"My truck"
Attribution–entity	"Big ball"
Demonstrative–entity	"That doggie"
Notice–noticed object	"Hi mommy," "Hi truck"
Recurrence	"More milk"
Nonexistence–nonexistent or disappeared object	"No shirt," "No more milk"

Source: Brown, 1973

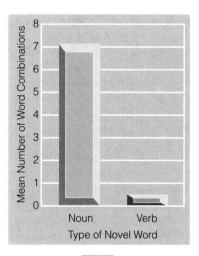

FIGURE 9.5

Number of word combinations with novel nouns and verbs produced by 18- to 23-month-olds. After learning the meaning of several noun and verb nonsense words, toddlers often combined the new nouns with other words. They seldom formed word combinations with the verbs, suggesting that their two-word utterances were not based on subject–verb and verb–object structures, which are the foundation of grammar.

(Adapted from Tomasello et al., 1997.)

combinations, such as "Mommy sit," "Daddy sleep," and "Daddy work." However, these utterances did not reflect a general understanding of subject–verb relations, since Jonathan used the structure only in specific situations—when a person was moving from one place to another (such as his father going to bed or leaving for work). Also, many creative combinations that children produce during the two-word period do not conform to adult grammatical restrictions. For example, Andrew, another child studied by Braine, said "more hot" and "more read." He seemed to apply a rule—"more + X"—in generating these utterances. But the combinations he created are not acceptable in English grammar.

Still other researchers claim even less consistency in first word combinations. Michael Tomasello argues that word-order regularities in children's two-word utterances are merely copies of adult language. For example, as adults say, "How about some *more sandwich?*" and "Let's see if you can *eat the berries,*" children copy the "more + X" and "eat + X" patterns (Tomasello & Brooks, 1999). In support of this view, Tomasello taught children just beginning to combine words several noun and verb nonsense words (for example, "meek" for a doll and "gop" for a snapping action). Then he gave them opportunities to use the new words in novel ways. As Figure 9.5 shows, although the children frequently combined the new nouns with words they knew well (as in "more meek" or "my meek"), they seldom formed word combinations with novel verbs (Tomasello et al., 1997). Tomasello concluded that very young children do not yet grasp subject–verb and verb–object structures, which are the foundation of grammar.

These findings suggest that in first combining words, children are preoccupied with figuring out the meanings of words and using their limited vocabularies in whatever way possible to get their thoughts across to others (Maratsos, 1983, 1998). However, as we will see in the next section, it does not take long for children to grasp the basic structure of their language.

FROM TWO-WORD UTTERANCES TO COMPLEX SPEECH

Between 2 and 3 years of age, three-word sentences appear that, in English-speaking children, follow the subject–verb–object word order. Although at one time this sequence was thought to be a universal grammatical structure and to represent a natural order of thoughts, we now know that it is not. Instead, young children adopt the word orders of the adult speech to which they are exposed (Maratsos, 1998). For example, for "It is broken," a German 2-year-old says, "Kaputt is der" (literally translated as "Broken is it"). Yet

TABLE 9.4

Order of Acquisition of English Grammatical Morphemes

Morpheme	Example
1. Verb present progressive ending ("-ing")	"He singing."
2. Preposition "on"	"On horsie."
3. Preposition "in"	"In wagon."
4. Noun plural ("-s")	"Cats."
5. Verb irregular past tense	"He ran." "It broke."
6. Noun possessive	"Daddy's hat."
7. Verb uncontractible "be" form used with adjective, preposition, or noun phrase	"Are kitties sleepy?"
8. Articles "a" and "the"	"A cookie." "The bunny."
9. Verb regular past tense ending ("-ed")	"He kicked it."
10. Verb present tense, third person singular irregular ending	"He likes it."
11. Verb present tense, third person singular irregular ending	"She has [from *have*] a cookie." "He does [from *do*] a good job."
12. Auxiliary verb uncontractible "be" forms	"Are you eating?"
13. Verb contractible "be" forms used with adjective, preposition, or noun phrase	"He's inside." "They're sleepy."
14. Auxiliary verb contractible "be" forms	"He's coming." "Doggie's eating."

Source: Brown, 1973.

German children find their native tongue no more difficult to learn than do children born into English-speaking homes.

■ **DEVELOPMENT OF GRAMMATICAL MORPHEMES.** As children move beyond two-word utterances, their speech reflects the grammatical categories of their language. In a study of the verbalizations of young preschoolers, by 2½ years children created sentences in which adjectives, articles, nouns, verbs, prepositions, and prepositional phrases appeared in the same structural form as adults generate them (Valian, 1986).

At about the same time, a grammatical explosion takes place. Children add **grammatical morphemes**[2]—small markers that change the meaning of sentences, as in "John's dog" and "he *is* eating." A striking finding is that these morphemes are acquired in a regular sequence by English-speaking 2- and 3-year-olds (Brown, 1973; de Villiers & de Villiers, 1973). It is shown in Table 9.4. Although children make mistakes in applying morphemes for months or years after they first appear, their errors are surprisingly few given the difficulty of the task (Maratsos, 1998).

Why does this regular sequence of development occur? Since adults' use of grammatical morphemes is unrelated to children's learning, language input cannot be responsible (Pinker, 1981). Instead, two characteristics of morphemes themselves play important roles. The first is *structural complexity.* For example, adding the endings "-ing" or "-s" is structurally less complex than using various forms of the verb "to be." In these, the child has to take account of different forms that express tense and make the verb agree with the subject (for example, "I am coming" versus "They are coming"). Second, grammatical morphemes differ in *semantic complexity,* or the number and difficulty of the meanings they express. For example, adding "-s" to a word requires only one semantic distinction—the difference between one and more than one. In contrast, using the various forms of "to

[2]A *morpheme* is the smallest unit of meaning in speech; any further division violates the meaning or produces meaningless units. Both "dog" and "-s" are morphemes; "-s" is a grammatical morpheme.

grammatical morphemes Small markers that change the meaning of sentences, as in "John's dog" and "he *is* eating."

be" involves many more, including an understanding of person, number, and time of occurrence (Brown, 1973).

Research on children acquiring different languages illustrates the impact of both factors. For example, children learning English, Italian, and Turkish acquire morphemes that denote location (in English, these would be prepositions, such as "in" and "on") sooner than do children learning Serbo-Croatian, in which expressing location is structurally more complex (Johnston & Slobin, 1979). At the same time, semantic complexity is clearly involved, since across languages, there is considerable similarity in the order in which children acquire grammatical morphemes with the same meaning (Slobin, 1982).

■ **OVERREGULARIZATION.** Look again at Table 9.4, and you will see that some morphemes with irregular forms are acquired before those with regular forms. For example, children use past tense irregular verbs, such as "ran" and "broke," before they acquire the regular "-ed" ending. But once children grasp a regular morphological rule, they extend it to words that are exceptions, a type of error called **overregularization.** "My toy car breaked," "I runned faster than you," and "We each have two foots" are expressions that begin to appear between 2 and 3 years of age. Overregularization occurs only occasionally—in about 5 to 8 percent of instances in which children use irregular forms, a rate that remains constant into middle childhood. It shows that children apply grammatical rules creatively, since they do not hear mature speakers overregularize (Marcus, 1995; Marcus et al., 1992).

At this point, you may be wondering: Why do children use some correct irregular forms before they start to overregularize? In all languages, irregular forms are assigned to important, frequently used words. Since young children hear them often, they probably learn these instances by rote memory. But when they grasp a morphological rule, they apply it broadly, making their language more orderly than it actually is. Sometimes children even impose the rule on well-learned exceptions—for example, when they say "ated" or "felled" (Bybee & Slobin, 1982). At other times, children's memory for an irregular morpheme may fail. Then they call on the rule to generate the form, and overregularization results (Marcus, 1995).

DEVELOPMENT OF COMPLEX GRAMMATICAL FORMS

Once children master the auxiliary verb "to be," the door is open to a variety of new expressions. In English, auxiliary verbs play important roles in many sentence structures that are variations on the basic subject–verb–object form. Negatives and questions are examples.

■ **NEGATIVES.** Three types of negation exist, which appear in the following order in children learning languages as different as English and Tamil (spoken in India): (1) *nonexistence,* in which the child remarks on the absence of something, such as "no cookie" or "all gone crackers"; (2) *rejection,* in which the child expresses opposition to something, such as "no take bath"; and (3) *denial,* in which the child denies the truthfulness of something, such as "That not my kitty" (Bloom, 1970; Clancy, 1985; Vaidyanathan, 1991).

As these examples illustrate, before age 3, children tend to use the rule "no + utterance" to express nonexistence and rejection, but they use an internal form of negation to express denial. Their early constructions probably result from listening to parental speech. When parents express nonexistence or rejection, they often put "no" at the beginning of the sentence, as in "No more cookies" or "No, you can't have another cracker." Around 3 to 3½ years, children add auxiliary verbs to their sentences and become sensitive to the way they combine with negatives. As a result, appropriate grammatical constructions of all three kinds appear, such as, "There aren't any more cookies" (nonexistence), "I don't want a bath" (rejection), and "That isn't my kitty" (denial) (Tager-Flusberg, 1997).

■ **QUESTIONS.** Like negatives, questions first appear during the early preschool years and show an orderly pattern of development. English-speaking children can use rising intonation to convert an utterance into a yes/no question, as in "Mommy baking cookies?" As a result, they produce them earlier than do children learning languages in which the structure of yes/no questions is more complex (Bowerman, 1973).

overregularization Application of regular grammatical rules to words that are exceptions.

Correct question form requires that children invert the subject and auxiliary verb. In the case of *wh-* questions—ones that begin with "what," "where," "which," "who," "when," "why," and "how"—the *wh-* word must also be placed at the beginning of the sentence. When first creating questions, English-speaking children cling to the subject–verb–object word order that is so basic to the English language. As a result, they do not make the inversion. A 2-year-old is likely to say, "What you doing?" and "Where Daddy going?" A little later, children include the auxiliary without inverting, as in "What you are doing?" Finally, they can apply all the rules for producing a question. Among English-, Korean-, and Tamil-speaking preschoolers, correct question form appears first for yes/no questions and later for *wh-* questions, which are semantically and structurally more difficult (Clancy, 1989; Vaidyanathan, 1988).

Like English-speaking children, these Korean-speaking preschoolers will master yes/no questions before wh-questions, which are both semantically and structurally more difficult. (Dana White/PhotoEdit)

■ **OTHER COMPLEX CONSTRUCTIONS.** Between ages 3 and 6, children begin to use increasingly complex grammatical forms. First, connectives appear that join whole sentences ("Mom picked me up, *and* we went to the park") and verb phrases ("I got up *and* ate breakfast"). The most general connective, "and," is used first, followed by connectives expressing more specific meanings, such as "then" and "when" for temporal relations, "because" and "so" for causal relations, "if" for conditionals, and "but" for opposition (Bloom et al., 1980).

Later, children produce embedded sentences ("I think *he will come*"), tag questions ("Dad's going to be home soon, *isn't he?*"), indirect object–direct object structures ("He showed *his friend* the present"), and passive sentences ("The dog was patted by the girl"). As the preschool years draw to a close, children use most of the grammatical structures of their native language competently (Tager-Flusberg, 1997).

LATER GRAMMATICAL DEVELOPMENT

Although preschoolers have an impressive mastery of grammar, development is not yet complete. During the school years, children's grasp of some constructions improves. The passive voice is one example. At all ages, children produce more abbreviated passives ("It got broken" or "They got lost") than full passives ("The glass was broken by Mary"). However, full passives are rarely used by English-speaking 3- to 6-year-olds, who seldom hear them in adult speech. Three-year-olds can be trained to produce full passives, but they cannot do so flexibly and often make errors (Brooks & Tomasello, 1999). Passive constructions increase steadily during middle childhood and early adolescence (Horgan, 1978).

Older children also apply their understanding of the passive voice to a wider range of nouns and verbs. Preschoolers comprehend the passive best when the subject of the sentence is an animate being and the verb is an action word ("The *boy is kissed* by the girl"). Over the school years, the passive form extends to inanimate subjects, such as *hat* ("The *hat* was worn by the man") and experiential verbs, such as *see* or *know* ("the dog *was seen* by the cat") (Lempert, 1990; Pinker, Lebeaux, & Frost, 1987). What accounts for this developmental trend? Recall that action is salient to young children in mastering vocabulary, a bias that may also influence their early acquisition of grammatical rules. But learning is also affected by input from the environment. Preschoolers rarely hear adults use experiential passives in everyday life, yet when exposed to them in the laboratory, they willingly integrate them into their own speech (Gordon & Chafetz, 1990).

Another grammatical achievement of middle childhood is an advanced understanding of pronoun reference. Consider the two sentences "Mickey told Barney that he liked

Wonderwoman" and "Mickey told Barney that Wonderwoman liked him." In the first, the pronoun "he" can refer to Mickey, but in the second, the pronoun "him" cannot. Children's difficulties with these complex rules have been interpreted in many ways. One study revealed that an improved ability to take the perspective of others facilitates mastery. When 5- to 8-year-olds used a puppet representing the speaker to demonstrate the meaning of each sentence (thereby getting the child to take the role of the speaker), performance improved substantially (Smyth, 1995).

Like vocabulary, later grammatical achievements are fostered by children's cognitive development and improved ability to analyze and reflect on language. Older children can deal with more complex relationships and are more attentive to subtle linguistic and situational cues. These capacities play major roles in helping them understand the most intricate grammatical forms.

IDEAS ABOUT HOW GRAMMATICAL DEVELOPMENT TAKES PLACE

In view of the complexity of what is learned, preschoolers' mastery of most of the grammar of their language is truly astounding. How to explain this feat is perhaps the most disputed issue in the study of language development.

■ **STRATEGIES FOR ACQUIRING GRAMMAR.** Evidence that grammatical development is an extended rather than sudden process has raised questions about Chomsky's strict nativist account. Some experts have concluded that grammar is largely a product of general cognitive development, or children's tendency to search the environment for consistencies and patterns of all sorts (Bates & MacWhinney, 1987; Bloom, 1991; Maratsos, 1983, 1998; Budwig, 1995). Yet among these theorists, there is intense debate about how children acquire the structure of their language.

According to one view, young children rely on the semantic properties of words to figure out basic grammatical regularities—an approach called **semantic bootstrapping.** For example, children might begin by grouping together words with "agent qualities" (entities that cause actions) as subjects and words with "action qualities" as verbs and then merge these semantic categories with observations of how words are used in sentences (Bates & MacWhinney, 1987; Braine, 1994). In this way, children lay down a basic grammatical framework, which they modify over time to take into account exceptions. A major problem for semantic bootstrapping is that in some languages, semantic categories (such as "agent") and basic grammatical structures (such as "subject") do not match up. In Tagalog, a language spoken in the Philippines, certain agents can be subjects, but others cannot! Yet Tagalog-speaking children acquire the main grammar of their language by age 3 (Maratsos, 1998).

Other theorists believe that children master grammar through direct observation of the structure of language. That is, they notice which words appear in the same positions in sentences, take the same morphological endings, and are similarly combined with other words and, over time, group them into the same grammatical class (Braine, 1992; Maratsos & Chalkley, 1980). Connectionist models, discussed in Chapter 7 (see pages 278–281), have tested this idea by seeing whether artificial neural networks exposed to language input like that of children show a similar course of grammatical development. So far, neural-network mastery of regular and irregular past tense and certain aspects of syntax comes close to children's patterns of learning (Elman, 1993; Plunkett & Marchman, 1993, 1996). But the correspondence is not perfect, and no current neural-network system offers a comprehensive account of grammatical development (Klahr & MacWhinney, 1998). It is possible that a combination of semantic and structural analysis leads children to acquire the grammar of their language.

Still other theorists, while also focusing on processing mechanisms, agree with the essence of Chomsky's position that children are specially tuned for language learning. For example, Dan Slobin (1985) proposes that children do not start with an innate knowledge of grammatical rules, as Chomsky believed. However, they do have a special **language-making capacity**—a set of procedures for analyzing the language they hear, which supports the discovery of grammatical regularities. Studying the development of children acquiring over 40 different languages, Slobin found common patterns suggesting that a

semantic bootstrapping Relying on the semantic properties of words to figure out basic grammatical regularities.

language-making capacity (LMC) According to Slobin's theory, a built-in set of cognitive procedures for analyzing language that supports the discovery of grammatical regularities.

expansions Adult responses that elaborate on a child's utterance, increasing its complexity.

recasts Adult responses that restructure a child's incorrect speech into appropriate form.

basic set of strategies exists. Yet we have seen that grammatical structures differ drastically across languages. Controversy continues over whether there is a universal, built-in language-processing device or whether children in different parts of the world develop unique strategies influenced by the specific language they hear (de Villiers & de Villiers, 1992; Maratsos, 1998).

■ **ENVIRONMENTAL SUPPORT FOR GRAMMATICAL DEVELOPMENT.** Besides investigating the child's capacities, researchers have been interested in what aspects of the language environment might ease the task of mastering grammar. Research consistently shows that although adults correct children's semantics, they rarely provide direct feedback about grammar. For example, an early study reported that when a child said, "There's an animal farmhouse," the parent quickly explained that the building was really a lighthouse. In contrast, the statement "her curling my hair" was met with an approving response because the parent was, in fact, curling the child's hair (Brown & Hanlon, 1970). These findings confirm that young children must figure out the intricacies of grammar largely on their own.

Nevertheless, adults could be offering subtle, indirect feedback about grammatical errors through two techniques, which they generally use in combination: **expansions** and **recasts.** For example, a parent hearing a child say, "I gotted new red shoes," might respond, "Yes, you got a pair of new red shoes," *expanding* the complexity of the child's statement as well as *recasting* its incorrect features into appropriate form. Parents and nonparents alike tend to respond in these ways after children make errors. When sentences are well formed, adults usually continue the topic of conversation or repeat exactly what the child just said (Bohannon & Stanowicz, 1988; Penner, 1987). Furthermore, children often imitate adult recasts, but they rarely imitate adult repetitions of their correct speech (Bohannon & Symons, 1988). Notice how expansions and recasts highlight the difference between a missing grammatical structure in the child's utterance and an adult sentence containing it.

However, the impact of such feedback has been challenged. Critics argue that it is not provided to all children in all cultures. And even when it is given, it may not be offered frequently enough and across a broad enough range of mistakes to serve as an important source of grammatical development (Marcus, 1993; Valian, 1996). Furthermore, whereas some studies report that parents' reformulations have a corrective effect, others show no impact on children's use of grammatical forms (Farrar, 1990; Morgan, Bonama, & Travis, 1995). Rather than eliminating specific errors, perhaps expansions and recasts serve the broader purpose of modeling a variety of grammatical alternatives and encouraging children to experiment with them.

In sum, virtually all investigators agree that young children are amazing processors of linguistic structure. But the extent to which factors in the language environment help young children correct errors and take the next grammatical step forward remains a hotly contested issue in child language research.

ASK YOURSELF . . .

♦ *One day, 3-year-old Jason's mother explained that the family would take a vacation in Miami. The next morning, Jason emerged from his room with belongings spilling out of a suitcase and remarked, "I gotted my bags packed. When are we going to Your-ami?" What do Jason's errors reveal about his approach to mastering grammar?*

♦ **CONNECTIONS**
Explain why connectionists, who compare children's mastery of grammatical structures to that of artificial neural networks, argue against a nativist, modular view of grammatical development like Chomsky's? (See Chapter 7, page 280.)

BRIEF REVIEW

Children are active, rule-oriented learners whose earliest word combinations begin to reflect the word order of their native tongue. As children move beyond two-word utterances, their speech reflects the grammatical categories of their language. They also add grammatical morphemes in a regular sequence influenced by the semantic and structural complexity of the forms to be learned. By age 6, children have mastered most of the grammar of their language. They continue to refine certain complex forms in middle childhood. Powerful processing strategies are largely responsible for young children's grammatical achievements, but researchers disagree on whether they are of a general cognitive kind or specially tuned to language. Adult feedback may support children's mastery of grammar, but its influence continues to be debated.

Pragmatic Development

esides phonology, vocabulary, and grammar, children must learn to use language effectively in social contexts. For a conversation to go well, participants must take turns, stay on the same topic, state their messages clearly, and conform to cultural rules that govern how individuals are supposed to interact. During the preschool years, children make considerable headway in mastering the pragmatics of language.

ACQUIRING CONVERSATIONAL SKILLS

At the beginning of early childhood, children are already skilled conversationalists. In face-to-face interaction with peers, they take turns, make eye contact, respond in a timely fashion to their partner's remarks, and maintain a topic over time (Garvey, 1974; Podrouzek & Furrow, 1988). Additional conversational strategies are added at later ages. One of these is the **turnabout,** in which the speaker not only comments on what has just been said but also adds a request to get the partner to respond again. Turnabouts increase over the preschool years. Very young children may not use them because they cannot yet generate many words in each turn (Goelman, 1986). Between ages 5 and 9, more advanced conversational strategies appear, such as **shading,** in which a change of topic is initiated gradually rather than abruptly by modifying the focus of discussion (Wanska & Bedrosian, 1985).

Effective conversation also depends on understanding the **illocutionary intent** of utterances—that is, what a speaker means to say, regardless of whether the form of the utterance is perfectly consistent with it. For example, the statement "Would you like to make cookies?" can be a request for information, an offer to provide an activity, or a directive to do something, depending on its context. By age 3, children comprehend a variety of utterances as requests for action even when they are not directly expressed that way, such as "I need a pencil" or "Why don't you tickle me?" (Garvey, 1974). During middle childhood, illocutionary knowledge develops further. For example, in the context of having forgotten to do his chore of taking the garbage out, an 8-year-old understands that his mother's statement "The garbage is beginning to smell" really means, "Take the garbage out!" Appreciating form–intention pairings like this one requires children to make subtle inferences between content and utterance that are beyond preschoolers' cognitive capacities (Ackerman, 1978).

Still, surprisingly advanced conversational abilities are present at a very early age, and the way caregivers interact with young children encourages and sustains them. For example, when adults respond to children's utterances in a timely manner and continue the child's topic of conversation, 2-year-olds are more likely to reply in kind (Dunham et al., 1991; Dunham & Dunham, 1996). Expansions are an especially effective strategy for helping very young children learn to converse with others. When a child says "truck" and the caregiver responds, "That's a big truck!", the adult expansion scaffolds the child's focus of attention on the topic while modeling how to maintain it in a conversational reply (Tomasello, 1992). See the From Research to Practice box on the following page for evidence on how three-way conversations—an adult with two children—foster early pragmatic skills.

In fact, opportunities to converse with adults, either at home or in preschool, are consistently related to general measures of language progress (Hart & Risley, 1995; Helburn, 1995). Engaging young children in dialogues during picture-book reading enhances the language skills of both middle- and low-SES preschoolers (Arnold et al., 1994; Lange & Carroll, 1997; Whitehurst et al., 1994). Through these conversations, preschoolers learn much about communicating in a clear, coherent narrative style—a skill that undoubtedly contributes to the association between joint storybook reading and literacy development (see Chapter 7, page 305).

Shared reading with parents is particularly powerful, perhaps because parents are better able than teachers to read to the child often and tailor conversations to the child's interests and abilities. In a 6-week intervention for low-SES 3- and 4-year-olds comparing shared reading with teachers at preschool, shared reading with parents at home, and a combined condition, all three groups gained in descriptive use of language compared to no-treatment controls. But children experiencing home reading improved the most (Lonigan & Whitehurst, 1998).

turnabout A conversational strategy in which the speaker not only comments on what has just been said but also adds a request to get the partner to respond again.

shading A conversational strategy in which a change of topic is initiated gradually by modifying the focus of discussion.

illocutionary intent What a speaker means to say, regardless of whether the form of the utterance is perfectly consistent with it.

Language Learning in Parent-Toddler-Sibling Conversations

M OST RESEARCH ON the role of social interaction in language development has focused
on mother–child pairs. Later-born children
and twins, however, typically spend their first few years in
the presence of siblings. Only on rare occasions do these
youngsters have the attention of a parent all to themselves.

Several studies report that the presence of another child
reduces the quantity and quality of parent–child interaction.
Mothers of more than one child address each with fewer utterances, use more commands, and provide fewer comments
and questions—factors thought to account for the slower
early vocabulary growth of twins and, to a lesser extent,
later-born children (Jones & Adamson, 1987; Tomasello,
Mannle, & Kruger, 1986).

But vocabulary is only one aspect of language development. Research suggests that participating in parent–
toddler–sibling conversations may have certain positive
consequences. Michelle Barton and Michael Tomasello
(1991) brought 19- to 25-month-old toddlers, their mothers, and their 3- to 5-year-old siblings into a laboratory and
asked them to play with some novel toys. Even the youngest
toddlers closely monitored the actions of their mothers and
siblings, frequently establishing joint attention with them.
When they did so, toddlers were especially likely to join in
the interaction, sparking elaborate verbal exchanges. As Figure 9.6 shows, mother–toddler–sibling conversations were

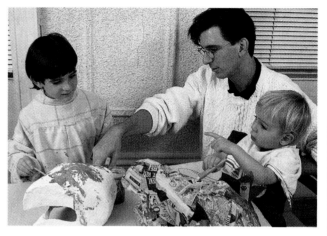

Parent–toddler–sibling interaction seems to offer a unique context
for acquiring the pragmatics of language. The toddler in this family
may become especially skilled at joining in conversations and adapting his speech to the needs of his listeners.
(Laura Dwight)

almost three times longer than either mother–toddler or
mother–sibling conversations. When all three interacted together, each participant took more turns. These unique features are not due to participation of an older sibling, since
similar findings occur when toddler twins interact with their
mothers (Barton & Strosberg, 1997).

Parent–toddler–sibling interaction seems to offer a
unique context for acquiring the pragmatics of language.
For example, successfully joining an ongoing conversation
requires a toddler to understand the other speakers' topic
and think of a way to add to it rather than just stating
whatever comes to mind. Furthermore, as toddlers listen
to the conversations of others, they are exposed to models
that may be especially important for certain skills, such as
use of personal pronouns ("I" versus "you"), which are more
common in the first 50 to 100 words of younger than older
siblings (Pine, 1995). Finally, communicating with siblings
requires children to adapt their utterances to partners
who may be far less willing than caregivers to give in to
their wishes.

In sum, young children appear to profit in different
ways from single- and multi-child language learning environments, and both are important for development. Although
homes with siblings and twins may reduce adult sensitivity to
individual children, they provide a rich variety of linguistic
stimulation that helps children learn to use language for
social purposes.

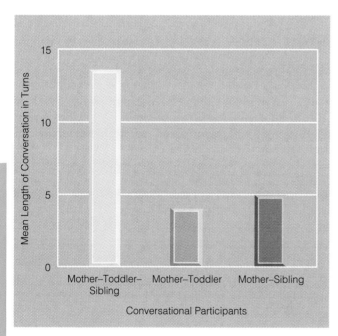

FIGURE 9.6

**Average number of turns in mother-toddler-sibling
conversations.** When all three interacted together, conversations
almost tripled in length, and each participant took more turns.
(Adapted from Barton & Tomasello, 1991.)

Context affects young children's referential communication skills. When talking on the telephone, this 4-year-old is likely to have trouble communicating clearly because she lacks the supports available in face-to-face interaction, such as visual access to her partner's reaction and to objects that are topics of conversation.

(Oscar Burriel/Science Photo Library)

LEARNING TO COMMUNICATE CLEARLY

Effective communication requires the ability to produce clear verbal messages as well as to recognize when messages we receive are unclear so we can ask for more information. These aspects of language are called **referential communication skills.**

Laboratory tasks designed to assess children's ability to communicate clearly typically present them with challenging situations in which they must describe one object among a group of very similar objects to a listener. For example, in one study, 3- to 10-year-olds were shown several eight-object arrays. In each, objects were similar in size, shape, and color. Children were asked to indicate which object they liked best as a birthday present for an imaginary friend. Most 3-year-olds gave ambiguous descriptions. When asked for clarification, they relied heavily on gestures, such as pointing. The ability to send clear messages improved steadily with age (Deutsch & Pechmann, 1982).

These findings may remind you of Piaget's notion of *egocentric speech*—that young children have difficulty taking the perspective of others (see Chapter 6). However, when preschoolers are given simpler communication tasks or engage in face-to-face interaction with familiar people, they adjust their speech to the needs of their listeners quite competently. This suggests that context has much to do with the clarity of young children's messages—a conclusion borne out by their telephone conversations. Have you tried talking on the phone with a 4-year-old lately? Here is an excerpt of one grandfather's attempt to do so:

> *Grandfather:* "How old will you be?"
>
> *John:* "Dis many." *[Holding up four fingers.]*
>
> *Grandfather:* "Huh?"
>
> *John:* "Dis many." *[Again holding up four fingers.]*
>
> *Grandfather:* "How many is 'at?"
>
> *John:* "Four. I'm gonna change ears, okay?"
>
> *Grandfather:* "Okay. Was one of your ears gettin' tired?"
>
> *John:* "Yeah. This one is." *[points to his left ear]*
>
> (Warren & Tate, 1992, pp. 259–260)

John used gestures that his grandfather could not see, and when his grandfather signaled that he could not understand ("Huh?"), John did not revise his message. Over time, children become more adept at communicating clearly in unfamiliar, challenging situations where they cannot see their listeners' reactions or rely on typical conversational aids, such as toys and objects to talk about (Lloyd, Boada, & Forns, 1992).

Children's ability to evaluate the adequacy of messages they receive also improves with age. Around age 3, preschoolers start to ask others to clarify ambiguous messages (Revelle, Karabenick, & Wellman, 1981). At first, children recognize when a message provides a poor description of a concrete object (Ackerman, 1993). Only later do they become good at telling when a message is inconsistent with something said earlier. Detection of this kind of difficulty requires the listener to retrieve previous discourse from memory and match it against currently spoken information. It depends on the comprehension monitoring skills we discussed in Chapter 7 and is a late-developing achievement, improving gradually during middle childhood and adolescence (Sonnenschein, 1986a).

SOCIOLINGUISTIC UNDERSTANDING

Language adaptations to social expectations are called **speech registers.** As early as the preschool years, children are sensitive to them. In one study, 4- to 7-year-olds were asked to act out different roles with hand puppets. Even the youngest children showed that they understood the stereotypic features of different social positions. They used more commands when playing socially dominant and male roles, such as teacher, doctor, and father, and more politeness routines and indirect requests when playing less dominant and feminine roles, such as pupil, patient, and mother (Anderson, 1992).

referential communication skills The ability to produce clear verbal messages and to recognize when the meaning of others' messages is unclear.

speech registers Language adaptations to social expectations.

Speech adjustments based on familiarity and age also appear during the preschool and early elementary school years. Children give fuller explanations to an unfamiliar listener than to someone with whom they share common experiences, such as a friend or family member (Sonnenschein, 1986b). They also simplify their speech when talking to a very young child (see Chapter 6, page 243). These abilities are refined in middle childhood. For example, when communicating with an unfamiliar listener or a 2-year-old, fourth graders include more redundant information than do first graders. Older children apply their more advanced referential communication skills to their speech register adjustments, taking extra steps to accommodate the needs of their listeners (Sonnenschein, 1988).

The importance of register adjustments is reflected in how often parents teach social routines as part of the child's first communicative acts. Infants are encouraged to wave "bye-bye" before they can grasp the meaning of the gesture. By age 2, when children fail to say "please," "thank you," or "hi" and "good-bye," parents usually model and demand an appropriate response (Becker, 1990). In some cultures, much greater emphasis is placed on tutoring young children in social routines than in language per se. For example, Kaluli mothers of New Guinea model socially appropriate statements, terminating their utterance with the word *ellema* (say it). If the child is too young to imitate, the mother may pitch her voice higher and repeat the routine, as if the infant or toddler were speaking (Schieffelin & Ochs, 1987).

Parents everywhere seem to realize that a child can get by in the world without perfectly correct pronunciation, grammar, and a large vocabulary. But failing to use socially acceptable speech can lead to scorn and rejection, causing a child's message not to be received at all.

BRIEF REVIEW

During early and middle childhood, children acquire a variety of pragmatic skills that permit them to engage in more sustained and effective conversation with others. Over this same period, referential communication in unfamiliar, highly demanding situations improves. Sensitivity to speech registers is present during the preschool years. Parents the world over realize the importance of socially appropriate communication and tutor children in social routines from an early age.

ASK YOURSELF . . .

◆ *Return to the illustrations of children's language at the beginning of this chapter. What pragmatic skills are reflected in Susan's and Connie's utterances? How do the children's parents support their pragmatic development?*

◆ CONNECTIONS
Do boys and girls acquire different speech registers for interacting with peers? Describe these registers, and explain why they contribute to children's preference for playmates of their own sex. (See Chapter 13, pages 536–537.)

Development of Metalinguistic Awareness

In previous sections, we noted several times that older children's more reflective and analytical approach to language is involved in later linguistic achievements. The ability to think about language as a system is called **metalinguistic awareness.** Researchers have been especially interested in when it emerges and the role it plays in a variety of language-related accomplishments.

Consider the following exchange between a mother and her 4-year-old child:

Child: What's that?

Mother: It's a typewriter.

Child: (frowning) No, you're the typewriter, that's a typewrite.

(Karmiloff-Smith et al., 1996)

As the child's remark clearly illustrates, the beginnings of metalinguistic awareness are present in early childhood. This preschooler is conscious of word endings; she expected "-er" to signify an animate agent, like "baker" and "dancer."

By age 4, children are also aware that word labels are arbitrary and not part of the objects to which they refer. When asked whether an object could be called by a different name in a new language, they respond "yes." Four-year-olds can also make some conscious syntactic judgments—for example, that a puppet who says, "Nose your touch" or "Dog the pat," is saying his sentences backward (Chaney, 1992). And by age 5, children have a good sense of the word concept. When an adult reads a story and stops to ask, "What was

metalinguistic awareness The ability to think about language as a system.

Language Development

Age	Phonology	Semantics
Birth–1 year	■ Categorical speech perception is present. ■ Speech sounds become organized into phonemic categories of native language. ■ Intonation and sound patterns of babbling begin to resemble those of native language.	■ Preference for sound pattern of native tongue is evident. ■ Sensitivity to stress patterns and phoneme sequences in words of native language develops. ■ Preverbal gestures develop.
1–2 years	■ Systematic strategies to simplify word pronunciation appear.	■ First words are produced; vocabulary builds to several hundred words. ■ Object words are emphasized first; action and state words follow soon after.
3–5 years	■ Pronunciation improves greatly.	■ Word-coinage forms expand. ■ Metaphors based on concrete, sensory comparisons appear.
6–10 years	■ Pronunciations signaling subtle differences in meaning are mastered.	■ At school entry, vocabulary includes about 10,000 words. ■ Meanings of words are grasped on the basis of definitions. ■ Appreciation of multiple meanings of words enhances understanding of metaphors and humor.
11 years–adulthood	■ Changes in syllabic stress after certain difficult words take on endings are mastered.	■ Vocabulary builds to over 40,000 words and includes many abstract terms. ■ Understanding of subtle, nonliteral word meanings, as in irony and sarcasm, improves.

the last word I said?" they almost always answer correctly for all parts of speech. They do not say "on-the-floor" instead of "floor" or "isa" instead of "a" (Karmiloff-Smith et al., 1996). These early metalinguistic understandings are good predictors of vocabulary and grammatical development during the preschool years (Smith & Tager-Flusberg, 1982).

Nevertheless, young children view language primarily as a means of communication, and they seldom treat it as an object of thought. Full flowering of metalinguistic skills does not take place until middle childhood. For example, around age 8, children can identify phonemes (all the sounds in a word) (Tunmer & Nesdale, 1982). They can also judge the grammatical correctness of a sentence even if its meaning is false or senseless, whereas preschoolers cannot (Bialystok, 1986). School-age children's metalinguistic knowledge is also evident in their improved ability to define words and appreciate their multiple meanings in puns, riddles, and metaphors—skills that continue to be refined into adolescence.

Grammar	Pragmatics	Metalinguistic Awareness
■ Sensitivity to natural phrase units develops.	■ Joint attention with caregiver is established. ■ Ability to engage in vocal exchanges and turn-taking games develops.	
■ Two-word utterances, in the form of telegraphic speech, appear. ■ First grammatical morphemes are added.	■ Conversational turn-taking and topic maintenance are present.	
■ Sentences clearly reflect an appreciation of adult grammatical categories. ■ Grammatical morphemes continue to be added in a regular order. ■ Many complex grammatical structures are added.	■ Conversational strategies, such as the turnabout, appear. ■ Grasp of illocutionary intent is present. ■ Ability to adjust speech in accord with social expectations develops.	■ The beginnings of metalinguistic awareness emerge.
■ A few complex grammatical structures, such as the passive voice and infinitive phrases, continue to be refined.	■ Advanced conversational strategies, such as shading, appear. ■ Understanding of illocutionary intent expands. ■ Referential communication in unfamiliar, highly demanding contexts improves.	■ Metalinguistic awareness develops rapidly.
■ Refinement of complex grammatical structures continues.	■ Referential communication—especially detection of unclear messages received—continues to improve.	■ Metalinguistic awareness continues to be refined.

Metalinguistic awareness emerges as language use becomes more automatic, freeing children from the immediate linguistic context so they can attend to how messages are communicated. As early as the preschool years, *phonological awareness*—the ability to reflect on the sound structure of spoken language—predicts reading and spelling success. Young children who can categorize words on the basis of similar sounds and rhyming syllables make good use of this knowledge when they get to school and must map printed text onto oral language (Busink, 1997). Once reading and spelling are under way, they enhance more fine-grained aspects of phonological understanding, such as the ability (mentioned earlier) to divide words into phonemes (Morrison, Smith, & Dow-Ehrensberger, 1995). Training children in phonological awareness is a promising technique for encouraging early literacy development.

As we will see in the final section of this chapter, bilingual children are advanced in metalinguistic awareness (as well as other cognitive skills). But before we conclude with this topic, you may find it helpful to turn to the Milestones table above, which provides an overview of the many aspects of language development we have discussed throughout this chapter.

Bilingualism: Learning Two Languages in Childhood

An estimated 6 million American school-age children speak a language other than English in their homes and neighborhoods. Bilingualism enhances many cognitive and linguistic skills.

(John Nordell/The Image Works)

Most American children speak only one language, their native tongue of English. Yet throughout the United States and the world, many children grow up bilingual. They learn two languages, and sometimes more than two, during childhood. An estimated 6 million American school-age children speak a language other than English at home, a figure expected to increase steadily in the twenty-first century (U.S. Bureau of the Census, 1998).

Children can become bilingual in two ways: (1) through *simultaneous acquisition,* by acquiring both languages at the same time in early childhood, or (2) through *sequential acquisition,* by learning a second language after mastering the first. Children of bilingual parents who teach them both languages in early childhood show no special problems with language development. For a time, they appear to develop more slowly because they mix the two languages. They often apply the grammar of one language to the vocabulary of the other, and they occasionally mix the two phonological systems.

But this is not a sign of confusion, since 1- and 2-year-olds use each language more with the parent who customarily speaks that language (Genesee, Nicoladis, & Paradis, 1995). And bilingual parents rarely maintain strict language separation either! Instead, early language mixing reflects the young child's strong desire to use any means available to communicate. These simultaneous bilingual learners acquire normal native ability in the language of their surrounding community and good to native ability in the second language, depending on their exposure to it. When children acquire a second language sequentially, after they already speak another language, it generally takes them 3 to 5 years to become about as fluent in the second language as native-speaking agemates (Ramirez et al., 1991).

Until recently, a commonly held belief among Americans was that childhood bilingualism led to cognitive and linguistic deficits as well as a sense of personal rootlessness, since the bilingual child was thought to identify only weakly with mainstream American culture. This negative attitude has been fueled by ethnic prejudices, since bilingualism in the United States is strongly associated with low-SES minority status. In addition, during the early part of this century, the view was bolstered by findings of seriously flawed research.

A large body of carefully conducted investigations now shows that bilingualism has a positive impact on development. Children who are fluent in two languages do better than their single-language agemates on tests of analytical reasoning, concept formation, and cognitive flexibility (Hakuta, Ferdman, & Diaz, 1987). And as mentioned earlier, their metalinguistic skills are particularly well developed. They are more aware that words are arbitrary symbols, more conscious of language structure and detail, and better at noticing errors of grammar and meaning in spoken and written prose—capacities that enhance their reading achievement (Bialystok, 1997; Campbell & Sais, 1995; Ricciardelli, 1992).

The advantages of bilingualism provide strong justification for bilingual education programs in American schools. The Social Issues box on the following page describes the current controversy over bilingual education in the United States. As you will see, bilingual children rarely receive support for their native language in classrooms. Yet bilingualism provides one of the best examples of how language, once learned, becomes an important tool of the mind and fosters cognitive development. In fact, the goals of schooling could reasonably be broadened to include helping all children become bilingual, thereby fostering the cognitive, language, and cultural enrichment of the entire nation (Mohanty & Perragaux, 1997).

ASK YOURSELF . . .

◆ *Explain why development of metalinguistic awareness expands greatly in middle childhood. What might foster more rapid metalinguistic progress in bilingual children?*

◆ CONNECTIONS
How can bilingual education support the development of a healthy ethnic identity? (See Chapter 11, page 461.)

Bilingual Education

INCENTE, A 7-YEAR-OLD boy who recently immigrated from Mexico to the United States, attends a bilingual education classroom in a large American city. His teacher, Serena, is fluent in both Spanish and English. At the beginning of the year, Serena instructed Vincente and his classmates in their native tongue. As the children mixed with English-speaking youngsters at school and in the community, they quickly picked up English phrases, such as "My name is . . . ," "I wanna," and "Show me."

Serena reinforced her pupils' first efforts to speak English, helping them feel confident about communicating in a second language. Gradually, she introduced more English into classroom learning experiences. At the same time, she continued to strengthen the children's native language and culture.

Vincente is enrolled in one of many bilingual education programs serving the growing number of American children with limited proficiency in English. Yet the question of how Vincente and his classmates should be taught continues to be hotly debated.

On one side of the controversy are those who believe that Vincente should be instructed only in English. According to this view, time spent communicating in the child's native tongue subtracts from English language achievement, which is vital for forging national unity and easing communication in education, business, and everyday life.

On the other side are educators like Serena, who are committed to truly *bilingual* education—developing Vincente's native language while fostering his mastery of English. Supporters of this view believe that providing instruction in the native tongue lets minority children know that their heritage is respected (McGroarty, 1992). In addition, by avoiding abrupt submersion in an English-speaking environment, bilingual education prevents *semilingualism,* or inadequate proficiency in both languages. When minority children experience a gradual decline of the first language as a result of being taught the second, they end up limited in both languages for a period of time, a circumstance that leads to serious academic difficulties. Semilingualism is one factor believed to contribute to the high rates of school failure and dropout among low-income Hispanic youngsters, who make up nearly 50 percent of the American language minority population.

At present, public opinion sides with the first of these two viewpoints. Many states have passed laws declaring

These Pueblo children attend a bilingual education program in which they receive instruction in their native language and in English. In classrooms where both the first and the second language are integrated into the curriculum, ethnic minority children are more involved in learning, participate more actively in class discussions, and acquire the second language more easily.
(Robert E. Daemmrich/Tony Stone Images)

English to be their official language, creating conditions in which schools have no obligation to teach minority pupils in languages other than English. In 1998, California voters passed a law that eliminated bilingual education in favor of a one-year, English-only immersion course for non-English-speaking pupils, a move expected to spread to other states. Yet research underscores the value of instruction in the child's native tongue. In classrooms where both languages are integrated into the curriculum, minority children are more involved in learning, participate more actively in class discussions, and acquire the second language more easily. In contrast, when teachers speak only a language their pupils can barely understand, children display frustration, boredom, withdrawal, and academic failure (Crawford, 1995, 1997).

English-only supporters often point to Canada, which recognizes the linguistic rights of its French-speaking minority but where friction between English- and French-speaking groups is intense. Nevertheless, both English and French are official languages, and most Canadian children become fluent in both—ideal conditions for building greater ethnic harmony (Piatt, 1993).

COMPONENTS OF LANGUAGE

What are the four components of language?

◆ Language consists of four subsystems—**phonology, semantics, grammar,** and **pragmatics**—that children combine into a flexible communication system.

THEORIES OF LANGUAGE DEVELOPMENT

Describe and evaluate three major theories of language development.

◆ According to the behaviorist perspective, language is learned through operant conditioning and imitation. Behaviorism has difficulty accounting for the speed of language progress and for children's novel, rule-based utterances. However, it has been helpful in treating children with language delays and disabilities.

◆ Chomsky's nativist perspective proposes a **language acquisition device (LAD)** that permits children, as soon as they have sufficient vocabulary, to speak grammatically and comprehend sentences. Consistent with this theory, research indicates that a complex language system is unique to humans, that language functions are housed in **Broca** and **Wernicke's areas,** and that a sensitive period for first- and second-language development exists. However, vast diversity among the world languages and children's gradual acquisition of many constructions has raised questions about Chomsky's ideas.

◆ Interactionist theories stress that innate abilities and social contexts combine to promote language development. Today, there is acknowledgment that biology, cognition, and social experience may operate in different balances for each component of language. Debate continues over the precise nature of children's innate abilities.

PRELINGUISTIC DEVELOPMENT: GETTING READY TO TALK

Describe receptivity to language, development of speech sounds, and conversational skills during infancy.

◆ Infants are specially prepared for language learning. Newborns are capable of **categorical speech perception** and sensitive to a wider range of **phonemes** than are children and adults. By 6 months, infants focus more intently on the sound categories of their own language. In the second half of the first year, they start to detect clauses, phrases, and words. **Child-directed speech (CDS)** eases the young child's task of making sense of language.

◆ Infants begin **cooing** at about 2 months; **babbling,** around 4 months. Over the first year, the range of babbled sounds expands. Then, as infants get ready to talk, intonation and sound patterns start to resemble those of the child's native language. Certain patterns of babbles appear in particular contexts, suggesting that infants are experimenting with the semantic function of language.

◆ Conversation emerges in the first few months, as infants and caregivers establish joint attention and the adult comments on what the baby sees. Turn-taking is present in early vocal exchanges. By the end of the first year, babies become active participants in turn-taking games and use two preverbal gestures, the **protodeclarative** and **protoimperative,** to influence others' behavior. Soon, words are ut-

tered and gestures diminish as children make the transition to verbal communication.

PHONOLOGICAL DEVELOPMENT

Describe the course of phonological development.

◆ First words are influenced partly by what children can pronounce. When learning to talk, children experiment with sounds, sound patterns, and speech rhythms and apply systematic phonological strategies to simplify adult pronunciations. Gradually, minimal words are refined into a full word with a correct stress pattern.

◆ Pronunciation improves greatly as the vocal tract matures and preschoolers engage in active problem solving. Accent patterns signaling subtle differences in meaning are not mastered until middle childhood and adolescence.

SEMANTIC DEVELOPMENT

Describe the course of semantic development, noting individual differences.

◆ Vocabulary increases rapidly in early childhood; language **comprehension** develops ahead of **production.** First words build on early cognitive and emotional foundations. Between 18 and 24 months, a vocabulary spurt usually takes place. To build vocabulary quickly, children engage in **fast-mapping.**

◆ Girls show faster early vocabulary growth than do boys, and reserved, cautious toddlers may wait for a time before beginning to speak. Because lower-SES children experience less verbal stimulation, their vocabularies tend to be smaller. Most toddlers use a **referential style** of language learning. Those who use an **expressive style** have vocabularies that grow more slowly.

◆ Early vocabularies typically emphasize object words; action and state words appear soon after, an order influenced by cognitive development. When first learning new words, children make errors of **underextension** and **overextension.** Word coinages and metaphors permit children to expand the range of meanings they can express.

◆ Vocabulary growth in middle childhood exceeds that of the preschool years. School-age children can grasp word meanings from definitions, and comprehension of metaphor and humor expands. Adolescents' ability to reason abstractly leads to an enlarged vocabulary and appreciation of subtle meanings, as in irony and sarcasm.

Discuss ideas about how semantic development takes place, including the influence of memory and strategies for word learning.

◆ A special part of working memory, a **phonological store** that permits us to retain speech-based information, supports vocabulary growth in early childhood. After age 5, semantic knowledge influences how quickly children form phonological traces, and both factors influence word learning.

◆ According to **lexical contrast theory,** children figure out the meaning of a new word by contrasting it with ones they already know and assigning it to a gap in their vocabulary. The **principle of mutual exclusivity** explains children's acquisition of some, but not all, early words. Children may deduce many word meanings through **syntactic bootstrapping** and pragmatic cues.

GRAMMATICAL DEVELOPMENT

Describe the course of grammatical development.

◆ Between 1½ and 2½ years, children combine two words to express a variety of meanings. These first sentences are called **telegraphic speech,** since they leave out smaller, less important words. Early two-word combinations probably do not reflect adult grammatical rules.

◆ As children move beyond two-word utterances, a grammatical explosion takes place. Their speech conforms to the grammatical categories of their language. English-speaking children add **grammatical morphemes** in a consistent order that is a product of both structural and semantic complexity. Once children acquire a regular morphological rule, they occasionally **overregularize,** or extend it to words that are exceptions. New expressions based on auxiliary verbs, such as negatives and questions, are soon mastered.

◆ Between ages 3 and 6, a variety of complex constructions are added. Still, certain forms, such as the passive voice and subtle pronoun reference, continue to be refined in middle childhood.

Discuss ideas about how grammatical development takes place, including strategies and environmental supports for mastering new structures.

◆ Some experts believe that grammar is a product of general cognitive development. According to one view, children engage in **semantic bootstrapping,** relying on common meanings of words to figure out grammatical regularities.

◆ Others believe that children master grammar through direct observation of language structure. Connectionist models have tested this idea, but no current artificial neural-network system fully accounts for grammatical development.

◆ Still others agree with the essence of Chomsky's theory that children are specially tuned for language learning. One speculation is that children have a **language-making capacity,** or set of procedures for analyzing language, which supports the discovery of grammatical regularities.

◆ Adults provide children with indirect feedback about grammatical errors through **expansions** and **recasts.** However, the impact of such feedback on grammatical development has been challenged.

PRAGMATIC DEVELOPMENT

Describe the course of pragmatic development, including social influences.

◆ Young children are effective conversationalists—early skills that are fostered through caregiver–child interaction. Conversations with adults consistently predict general measures of language progress.

◆ Strategies that help sustain interaction, such as the **turnabout** and **shading,** are added in early and middle childhood. During this time, children's understanding of **illocutionary intent** improves, and they also acquire more effective **referential communication skills.** Preschoolers are sensitive to **speech registers.** Parents tutor children in social routines at an early age, emphasizing the importance of adapting language to social expectations.

DEVELOPMENT OF METALINGUISTIC AWARENESS

Describe the development of metalinguistic awareness, noting its influence on language and literacy skills.

◆ Preschoolers show the beginnings of **metalinguistic awareness,** and their understandings are good predictors of vocabulary and grammatical development. Major advances in metalinguistic skills take place in middle childhood. Phonological awareness predicts reading and spelling achievement. Literacy, in turn, enhances metalinguistic understanding.

BILINGUALISM: LEARNING TWO LANGUAGES IN CHILDHOOD

How does bilingualism affect language and cognitive development, and what evidence supports bilingual education?

◆ Historically, Americans have held negative attitudes toward childhood bilingualism, a view fueled by ethnic prejudices. Children fluent in two languages score higher in analytical reasoning, concept formation, cognitive flexibility, and metalinguistic awareness. These advantages provide strong justification for bilingual education.

IMPORTANT TERMS AND CONCEPTS

babbling (p. 368)
Broca's area (p. 363)
categorical speech perception (p. 367)
child-directed speech (CDS) (p. 367)
comprehension (p. 373)
cooing (p. 368)
expansions (p. 384)
expressive style (p. 374)
fast-mapping (p. 373)
grammar (p. 358)
grammatical morphemes (p. 381)
illocutionary intent (p. 386)
language acquisition device (LAD) (p. 359)

language-making capacity (p. 384)
lexical contrast theory (p. 378)
metalinguistic awareness (p. 389)
overextension (p. 376)
overregularization (p. 382)
phoneme (p. 367)
phonological store (p. 377)
phonology (p. 358)
pragmatics (p. 358)
principle of mutual exclusivity (p. 378)
production (p. 373)
protodeclarative (p. 369)
protoimperative (p. 369)

recasts (p. 384)
referential communication skills (p. 388)
referential style (p. 374)
semantic bootstrapping (p. 384)
semantics (p. 358)
shading (p. 386)
speech registers (p. 388)
syntactic bootstrapping (p. 378)
telegraphic speech (p. 379)
turnabout (p. 386)
underextension (p. 376)
Wernicke's area (p. 363)

Emotional Development

ON A SPRING DAY, 4-month-old Zach, cradled in the arms of his father, followed by 13-month-old Emily and 23-month-old Brenda, led by their mothers, arrived at the door of my classroom, transformed into a playroom for the
morning. My students and I spent the next hour watching closely for the wide
variety of capacities that develop during the first 2 years. Especially captivating were the children's emotional reactions to people and things around them.
As Zach's dad bounced him energetically on his knee and lifted him up in the
air, Zach responded with a gleeful grin. A tickle followed by a lively kiss on the
tummy produced an excited giggle. When I held a rattle in front of Zach, his
brows knit, his face sobered, and he eyed it intently as he mobilized all his energies to reach for it.

Transferred to my arms and then to the laps of several students, Zach remained at ease with a variety of adults (although he reserved an unusually
broad smile for his father). In contrast, Emily and Brenda were wary of this
roomful of strangers. I held out a toy and coaxed Emily toward it. She pulled
back and glanced at her mother, as if to check whether the new adult and tantalizing object were safe to explore. When her mother grinned and encouraged, Emily approached cautiously and accepted the toy. A greater capacity to
understand the situation combined with her mother's explanations helped
Brenda adjust quickly, and soon she was engrossed in play. During the hour,
Brenda displayed a whole new range of emotional reactions, including embarrassment at seeing chocolate on her chin in a mirror and pride as I remarked on the tall block tower she had built.

Although the emotional side of development was overshadowed by cognition for several decades, today great excitement surrounds the topic. An explosion of research reveals that emotions play a central role in all aspects of
human experience. Our discussion brings together several lines of evidence.
First, we discuss the functions of emotions and chart age-related changes in
emotional expression and understanding. As we do so, we will account for
Zach, Emily, and Brenda's expanding range of emotional capacities. Next, our
attention turns to individual differences in temperament and personality. We
examine biological and environmental contributions to these differences and
their consequences for future development. Finally, we take up attachment to
the caregiver, the child's first affectional tie that emerges during infancy. We
will see how the feelings of security that grow out of this important bond provide a vital source of support for the child's exploration, sense of independence, and expanding social relationships.

The Functions of Emotions

onsider events in your life that generate emotion. In the last day or so, you may have felt happy, sad, fearful, or angry in response to a grade on a test, a conversation with a friend, or the story line of a movie. These events, and others, generate emotion because, at least for the moment, you care about their outcome. The emotion experienced, in turn, prepares you for action. For example, happiness leads you to approach a situation, sadness to passively withdraw, fear to actively move away, and anger to overcome obstacles. An **emotion,** then, expresses your readiness to establish, maintain, or change your relation to the environment on a matter of importance to you (Saarni, Mumme, & Campos, 1998).

New theories, gathered together under the **functionalist approach,** emphasize that the broad function of emotions is to prompt action in the service of personal goals (Barrett & Campos, 1987; Bretherton et al., 1986; Campos et al., 1994; Izard, 1991; Lazarus, 1991). Events can become personally relevant in several ways. First, you may already have a goal in mind, such as doing well on a test, so the test situation prompts strong emotion. Second, others' social behavior may alter a situation's significance for you, as when your friend visits and you respond contagiously to her warm greeting or react to her report of good or bad news. Third, sensations and states of mind—any sight, sound, taste, smell, touch, memory, or imagining—can become personally relevant, yielding positive emotion if it is pleasant and negative emotion if it is unpleasant. Your emotional reaction affects your desire to repeat the experience.

Indeed, functionalist theorists view emotions as central forces in all aspects of human activity—cognitive processing, social behavior, and even physical health. To clarify this idea, let's examine the functions of emotions—the way they organize and regulate experience in each of these domains.

EMOTIONS AND COGNITIVE PROCESSING

Emotional reactions can lead to learning that is crucial for survival. For example, a newly walking toddler does not need to receive a shock from an electric outlet or to fall down a staircase to learn to avoid these dangerous situations. Instead, the caregiver's highly charged command is enough to get the child to acquire these self-protective behaviors (Campos et al., 1983).

To illustrate further, think about your own feelings on occasions in which you did poorly on a test or oral presentation, even though you spent many hours preparing. Did anxiety affect your performance? Among children and adults, very high or low anxiety leads to poorer outcomes on cognitive tasks than does moderate anxiety, which can be facilitating (Sarason, 1980). Emotions also have powerful effects on memory. For example, children highly upset by an inoculation at the doctor's office remembered the event more clearly than did less stressed children (Goodman et al., 1991). At the same time, negative emotion can impair children's encoding of information from the broader environment (Bugental et al., 1992).

Most functionalist theorists view the relationship between emotion and cognition as bidirectional. Michael Lewis and his colleagues found evidence for this dynamic interplay as early as the first half-year of life. Two- to 8-month-olds were trained to pull a string attached to their wrists, which produced a slide of a smiling baby and a recording of a children's song. By tracking facial expressions, the researchers found that interest, happiness, and surprise increased as the infants learned the task—expressions that reflected pleasure at mastery of a new contingency. Next, a short nonreinforcement period followed in which pulling the string no longer activated the attractive stimuli. The babies' emotional reactions quickly changed—for most to anger but for a few to sadness. When the contingency was reinstated, babies who had reacted angrily to nonreinforcement showed renewed interest and enjoyment, pulling eagerly to produce the stimuli. In contrast, sad babies withdrew, displaying reduced involvement in the task (Lewis, Sullivan, & Ramsay, 1992). Emotions were intimately interwoven with cognitive processing, serving both as outcomes of mastery and as the foundation for infants' approach to the next learning phase.

emotion An expression of readiness to establish, maintain, or change one's relation to the environment on a matter of personal importance.

functionalist approach A perspective emphasizing that the broad function of emotions is to prompt action in the service of personal goals and that emotions are central forces in all aspects of human activity.

EMOTIONS AND SOCIAL BEHAVIOR

Children's emotional signals, such as smiling, crying, and attentive interest, affect others' behavior in powerful ways. Similarly, emotional reactions of others regulate children's social behavior.

For example, careful analyses of caregiver–infant face-to-face interaction reveal that by 3 months, a complex communication system is in place in which each partner responds in an appropriate and carefully timed fashion to the other's cues (Tronick & Cohn, 1989). In several studies, this exchange of emotional signals was disrupted by having the parent assume either a still-faced, unreactive pose or a depressed emotional state. Infants tried facial expressions, vocalizations, and body movements to get their mother or father to respond again. When these efforts failed, they reacted to the parent's sad, vacant gaze by turning away, frowning, and crying (Hernandez & Carter, 1996; Segal et al., 1995). The still-face reaction is identical in American, Canadian, and Chinese babies, suggesting that it might be a built-in withdrawal response to caregivers' lack of communication (Kisilevsky et al., 1998). To find out more about the powerful impact of maternal depression on children's emotional and social functioning, refer to the From Research to Practice box on page 400.

EMOTIONS AND PHYSICAL HEALTH

Much research indicates that emotions influence children's physical well-being. For example, in Chapter 5 we discussed two childhood growth disorders—nonorganic failure to thrive and deprivation dwarfism—that result from emotional deprivation. And other studies indicate that temporary or permanent separation from a loved one depresses the immune response and is associated with a variety of health difficulties from infancy into adulthood (Laudenslager & Reite, 1984).

In a dramatic demonstration of the emotion–health relationship, researchers examined the archives of Terman's longitudinal study of high-IQ children, who were followed into old age (Friedman et al., 1995). They found that experiencing parental divorce in childhood and marital instability in adulthood were powerful predictors of age of death. Average life expectancy was 76 for men whose parents divorced, 80 for men whose parents stayed married. For women, the corresponding figures were 82 and 86 years. At age 40, participants who were steadily married (had one lasting marriage) or who had never married were at lowest risk for premature death. Risk increased considerably for those who were "inconsistently married" (remarried after divorce), and it was highest for those who were separated, divorced, or widowed.

The bright participants in Terman's study faced unique life challenges and developed in a particular historical context, so we should be cautious about generalizing these results. Nevertheless, they fit well with other evidence on the relationship of emotional stress to physical health.

OTHER FEATURES OF THE FUNCTIONALIST APPROACH

Besides the central role of emotions in cognitive, social, and physical experience, the functionalist approach views emotions as important in the emergence of self-awareness. For example, the interest and excitement that babies display when acting on novel objects helps them develop a *sense of self-efficacy*—an awareness that they are capable of affecting events in their surrounding world (Alessandri, Sullivan, & Lewis, 1990). Once a beginning sense of self appears, the door is open to new emotional reactions. Recall Brenda's expressions of pride and embarrassment—two feeling states that have to do with evaluations of the self's goodness or badness (Barrett & Campos, 1987).

The functionalist approach also stresses that to adapt to their physical and social worlds, children must gradually gain voluntary control over their emotions, just as they do over motor, cognitive, and social behavior. At the same time, emotional expressions gradually become socialized, as children learn the circumstances in which it is acceptable to communicate feelings in their culture. As a result, by late childhood few emotions are

Emotions have a profound impact on cognitive processing. This toddler's interest and delight at the sight, sound, and feel of autumn leaves motivate him to approach, explore, and learn about his surroundings.
(David J. Sams/Stock Boston)

Maternal Depression and Child Development

PPROXIMATELY 8 TO 10 percent of women experience chronic depression—mild to severe feelings of sadness and withdrawal that continue for months or years. Often the beginnings of this gloomy, distressed emotional state cannot be pinpointed; it has simply become a part of the person's daily life. In other instances, it emerges or strengthens after childbirth but fails to subside as the new mother adjusts to hormonal changes in her body and gains confidence in caring for her baby. Stella experienced this type—called *postpartum depression.* Although genetic makeup increases the risk of depressive illness, Stella's case shows that social and cultural factors are also involved.

During Stella's pregnancy, her husband Kyle's lack of interest in the baby caused her to worry that having a child might be a mistake. Shortly after Lucy was born, Stella's mood plunged. She was anxious and weepy, overwhelmed by Lucy's needs, and angry that she no longer had control over her own schedule. When Stella approached Kyle about her own fatigue and his unwillingness to help with the baby, he snapped that she overreacted to every move he made. Stella's friends, who did not have children, stopped by once to see Lucy and did not call again.

Children of depressed parents are two to five times more likely to develop behavior problems than are children of nondepressed parents (Cummings & Davies, 1994b). Although heredity may be partly responsible (see Chapter 3, page 120), quality of parenting—in particular, less positive, responsive interaction—plays a major role. The more extreme the depression and the greater the number of stressors in a mother's life (such as marital discord, little or no social support, and poverty), the more the parent-child relationship suffers (Goodman et al., 1993). Stella, for example, rarely smiled and talked to Lucy, who responded to her mother's sad, vacant gaze by turning away, crying, and often looking sad or angry herself (Campbell, Cohn, & Meyers, 1995; Murray & Cooper, 1997). Each time this happened, Stella felt inadequate as a mother, and her depression deepened. By 6 months of age, Lucy showed emotional symptoms common in babies of depressed mothers—a negative, irritable mood and attachment difficulties (Teti et al., 1995).

When maternal depression persists, the parent-child relationship worsens. Depressed parents use inconsistent discipline—sometimes lax, at other times too forceful—a pattern that reflects their disengaged as well as hostile behavior (Zahn-Waxler et al., 1990). As we will see in later chapters, children who experience these maladaptive parenting practices often have serious adjustment problems. To avoid their parent's insensitivity, they sometimes withdraw into a depressive mood themselves. Or they mimic their parent's anger and become impulsive and antisocial (Conger, Patterson, & Ge, 1995). Children of depressed parents may inherit a tendency to develop emotional and behavior prob-

Depression combined with the stresses of poverty disrupts this mother's capacity to engage in positive, responsive interaction with her children. They respond in kind to her sad, vacant expression and are at risk for serious adjustment problems.

(Kevin Horan/Tony Stone Images)

lems. But clearly, quality of parenting is a major factor in their adjustment.

Over time, the parenting behaviors just described lead children to develop a negative world view—one in which they perceive their parents and other people as a threat to their well-being. Children who constantly feel in danger and whose parents have not helped them learn how to manage negative feelings are likely to become overly aroused in stressful situations, easily losing control in the face of cognitive or social challenges (Cummings & Cicchetti, 1990). Depressed parents are also more likely to have unhappy marriages. Repeated exposure to parental arguments sensitizes children to conflict, increasing their distress and aggression (Cummings & Zahn-Waxler, 1992). Impairments in regulating emotion (see page 404) compound these children's cognitive and social difficulties.

Early treatment of maternal depression is vital, to prevent the disorder from interfering with the parent-child relationship and harming children. Stella described her tearfulness, fatigue, and inability to comfort Lucy to her doctor. He referred her to a special program for depressed mothers and their babies, where a counselor worked with the family, helping Stella and Kyle with their marital problems and encouraging them to be more sensitive and patient with Lucy. In most cases of postpartum depression, treatment is successful (Cooper & Murray, 1997). When depressed mothers do not respond easily to treatment, a warm relationship with the father or another caregiver and efforts to reduce the many stressors that typically accompany depression can safeguard children's development.

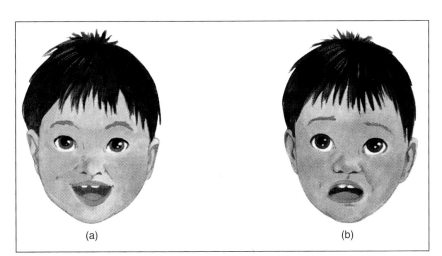

FIGURE 10.1

Which emotions are these babies displaying?
The MAX (Maximally Discriminative Facial Movement) System is a widely used method for classifying infants' emotional expressions. Facial muscle movements are carefully rated to determine their correspondence with basic feeling states, since people around the world associate different facial gestures with emotions in the same way. For example, cheeks raised and corners of the mouth pulled back and up signal happiness (a). Eyebrows raised, eyes widened, and mouth opened with corners pulled straight back denote fear (b).
(From Izard, 1979.)

expressed as openly and freely as they were in the early years of life (Thompson, 1990a). With these factors in mind, let's chart the course of emotional development.

Development of Emotional Expression

ince infants cannot describe their feelings, determining exactly which emotions they are experiencing is a challenge. Although vocalizations and body movements provide some information, facial expressions seem to offer the most reliable cues. Cross-cultural evidence reveals that people around the world associate photographs of different facial gestures with emotions in the same way (Ekman & Friesen, 1972). These findings, which suggest that emotional expressions are built-in social signals, inspired researchers to carefully analyze infants' facial patterns to determine the range of emotions they display at different ages. A commonly used method for doing so, the MAX System, is illustrated in Figure 10.1.

Do infants come into the world with the ability to express **basic emotions**—those that can be directly inferred from facial expressions, such as happiness, interest, surprise, fear, anger, sadness, and disgust? Most researchers agree that signs of almost all these emotions are present in early infancy (Izard et al., 1995; Malatesta-Magai, Izard, & Camras, 1991; Sroufe, 1979). Over time they become clear, well-organized signals.

The *dynamic systems perspective* helps us understand how this happens. Recall from Chapter 4 that according to this view, children coordinate separate skills into more effective systems as the central nervous system develops and the child's goals and experiences change. Videotaping the facial expressions of her daughter from 6 to 14 weeks, Linda Camras (1992) observed that in the early weeks, the infant displayed a fleeting angry face as she was about to cry and a sad face as her crying waned. These expressions first appeared on the way to or away from full-blown distress and were not clearly linked to the baby's experiences and desires. With age, she was better able to sustain an angry signal as she encountered a blocked goal and a sad signal when she could not overcome an obstacle.

Around 6 months, face, gaze, voice, and posture form distinct, coherent patterns that vary meaningfully with environmental events. For example, babies typically respond to their mother's playful interaction with a joyful face, positive vocalizations, and mouthing of body parts. In contrast, an unresponsive mother is likely to evoke a sad face and fussy vocalizations (sending the message "I'm overwhelmed") or an angry face, crying, and "pick-me-up" gestures (as if to say, "Change this unpleasant event!"). In sum, by the middle of the first year, emotional expressions are well organized and specific—and therefore able to tell us a great deal about the infant's internal state (Weinberg & Tronick, 1994, 1996).

Four emotions—happiness, anger, sadness, and fear—have received the most research attention. Let's see how they develop as the baby's capacities and physical and social contexts change.

basic emotions Emotions that can be directly inferred from facial expressions, such as happiness, interest, surprise, fear, anger, sadness, and disgust.

CHAPTER TEN / EMOTIONAL DEVELOPMENT   **401**

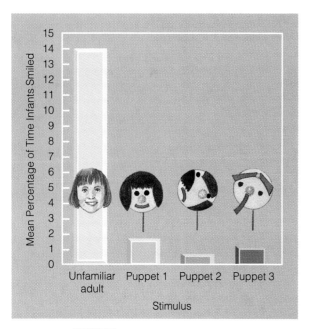

FIGURE **10.2**

Three-month-old infants' smiling at an unfamiliar adult and three hand puppets varying in resemblance to the human face. All stimuli responded contingently to the baby's behavior. Although the infants looked with just as much interest at the puppets as at the adult, they spent much more time smiling at the human stimulus.

(From C. P. Ellsworth, D. W. Muir, & S. M. J. Hains, 1993, "Social Competence and Person–Object Differentiation: An Analysis of the Still-Face Effect," *Developmental Psychology, 29,* p. 70. Copyright © 1993 by the American Psychological Association. Reprinted by permission.)

social smile The smile evoked by the stimulus of the human face. First appears between 6 and 10 weeks.

HAPPINESS

Happiness—first in terms of blissful smiles and later through exuberant laughter—contributes to many aspects of development. Infants smile and laugh when they achieve new skills, expressing their delight in cognitive and motor mastery. The smile also encourages caregivers to be affectionate as well as stimulating, so the baby will smile even more. Happiness binds parent and baby into a warm, supportive relationship that fosters the infant's developing competence.

During the early weeks, newborn babies smile when full, during REM sleep, and in response to gentle touches and sounds, such as stroking of the skin, rocking, and the mother's soft, high-pitched voice. Already, the relation between smiling and tension release is present. EEG waves indicate that these early smiles are associated with spontaneous neural discharge in the limbic system, a set of brain structures involved in the regulation of emotional behavior (Sroufe & Waters, 1976).

By the end of the first month, infants start to smile at interesting sights, but these must be dynamic, eye-catching events, such as a bright object jumping suddenly across the baby's field of vision. Between 6 and 10 weeks, the human face evokes a broad grin called the **social smile,** which is soon accompanied by pleasurable cooing (Sroufe & Waters, 1976). Perhaps you can already tell that early changes in smiling parallel the development of infant perceptual capacities—in particular, babies' increasing sensitivity to visual patterns, including the human face—that we discussed in Chapter 4.

By 3 months, infants smile most often when interacting with people. In one study, babies were presented with four facial stimuli, each of which responded contingently to their behavior: an unfamiliar adult and three hand puppets that varied in resemblance to the human face. Although infants looked with just as much interest at the moving, "talking" puppets as they did at the responsive adult, they rarely smiled at a puppet stimulus, even when it had humanlike features (see Figure 10.2). In contrast, they directed frequent grins (as well as more vocalizations) toward the adult, indicating that they clearly identified human beings as having unique, social qualities (Ellsworth, Muir, & Hains, 1993).

Laughter, which appears around 3 to 4 months, reflects faster processing of information than does smiling. But like smiling, the first laughs occur in response to very active stimuli, such as the mother saying playfully, "I'm gonna get you!" and kissing the baby's tummy. As infants understand more about their world, they laugh at events that contain more subtle elements of surprise, such as a soundless game of peekaboo or the caregiver walking like a penguin (Sroufe & Wunsch, 1972).

By the middle of the first year, infants smile and laugh more when interacting with familiar people, a preference that supports and strengthens the parent–child bond. As preverbal gestures develop (see Chapter 9), the smile becomes a deliberate social signal. During the second year, toddlers break their play with an interesting toy to turn around and communicate their delight to an attentive adult (Jones & Raag, 1989).

ANGER AND SADNESS

Newborn babies respond with generalized distress to a variety of unpleasant experiences, including hunger, painful medical procedures, changes in body temperature, and too much or too little stimulation (see Chapter 4). From 4 to 6 months into the second year, angry expressions increase in frequency and intensity. Older infants react with anger in a wider range of situations—for example, when an interesting object or event is removed, their arms are restrained, the caregiver leaves for a brief time, or they are put down for a nap (Camras et al., 1992; Stenberg & Campos, 1990).

Why do angry reactions increase with age? Cognitive and motor development are intimately involved. As infants acquire the capacity for intentional behavior (see Chapter 6), they start to value control over their own actions and the effects they produce (Alessandri, Sullivan, & Lewis, 1990). Older infants are also better at identifying the agent of a painful stimulus or blocked goal. Consequently, their anger is particularly intense when a familiar caregiver from whom they have come to expect warm behavior causes discomfort (Stenberg, Campos, & Emde, 1983). The rise in anger is also adaptive. New motor capacities permit babies to use the energy mobilized by anger to defend themselves or overcome obstacles. At the same time, anger is a powerful social signal that motivates caregivers to ease a baby's distress, and in the case of separation, may discourage them from leaving again soon.

Expressions of sadness also occur in response to pain, removal of an object, and brief separations, but they are less frequent than anger (Alessandri, Sullivan, & Lewis, 1990; Izard, Hembree, & Huebner, 1987; Shiller, Izard, & Hembree, 1986). In contrast, sadness is common when caregiver–infant communication is seriously disrupted (refer again to the From Research to Practice box on page 400). Extreme sadness can also be seen in infants separated from their familiar caregiver who do not experience the care of a sensitive adult (Gaensbauer, 1980).

This newly walking 1-year-old explores unfamiliar territory confidently, as long as her mother serves as a secure base to which she can return should she become uneasy or frightened. The rise in fear after 7 months of age holds in check infants' compelling urge to venture away from the caregiver.
(David H. Wells/The Image Works)

FEAR

Fear is rare during early infancy, since young babies do not yet have the motor skills to protect themselves from dangerous situations; they must rely on caregivers to do so (Izard & Malatesta, 1987). Like anger, the incidence of fear rises during the second half of the first year. Older infants hesitate before playing with a new toy that they would have grasped immediately at an earlier age. And as we saw in Chapter 4, newly crawling infants soon show fear of heights. But the most frequent expression of fear is to unfamiliar adults, a reaction called **stranger anxiety.**

Many infants and toddlers are quite wary of strangers, although the reaction does not always occur. It depends on several factors: the infant's temperament (some babies are generally more fearful), past experiences with strangers, and the situation in which baby and stranger meet (Thompson & Limber, 1991). When an unfamiliar adult approaches and picks up the infant in a new situation, stranger anxiety is likely. But if the adult sits still while the baby moves around and a parent remains nearby, infants often show positive and curious behavior toward unfamiliar adults, although they rarely initiate physical contact (Horner, 1980). The stranger's style of interaction also makes a difference. Holding out an attractive toy, playing a familiar game, or approaching slowly rather than abruptly reduces the baby's fear (Trause, 1977).

Furthermore, culture can modify fear of strangers through infant-rearing practices. Maternal mortality is very high among the Efe hunters and gatherers of Zaire, Africa. To ensure infant survival, a collective caregiving system exists in which Efe babies are passed from one adult to another—relatives and nonrelatives alike. Consequently, Efe infants show little stranger anxiety (Tronick, Morelli, & Ivey, 1992). In contrast, in Israeli kibbutzim (cooperative agricultural settlements), frequent terrorist attacks have led to widespread wariness of strangers. By the end of the first year, when (as we will see later) infants look to others for cues about how to respond emotionally, kibbutz babies display far greater stranger anxiety than do their city-reared counterparts (Saarni, Mumme, & Campos, 1998).

The impact of context on stranger anxiety helps us understand the significance of greater fearfulness around 7 months of age. It holds in check the baby's compelling urge to venture away from the caregiver that comes with independent movement. Once wariness develops, babies start to use the familiar caregiver as a **secure base** from which to explore and a haven of safety when distress occurs. As part of this adaptive system, encounters with strangers lead to two conflicting tendencies in the baby: approach (indicated by interest and friendliness) and avoidance (indicated by fear). The infant's behavior is a matter of a balance between the two (Thompson & Limber, 1991).

Eventually, stranger anxiety declines as cognitive development permits toddlers to discriminate more effectively between threatening and nonthreatening people. This change is also adaptive, since adults other than caregivers will be important in children's development, and in later life many interactions will take place with unfamiliar people (Bornstein & Lamb, 1992). Fear also wanes as children acquire a wider array of strategies for coping with it, as we will see when we discuss emotional self-regulation shortly.

stranger anxiety The infant's expression of fear in response to unfamiliar adults. Appears in many babies after 7 months of age.

secure base The use of the familiar caregiver as a base from which the infant confidently explores the environment and to which the infant returns for emotional support.

SELF-CONSCIOUS EMOTIONS

Besides basic emotions, humans are capable of a second, higher-order set of feelings, including shame, embarrassment, guilt, envy, and pride. These are called **self-conscious emotions** because each involves injury to or enhancement of our sense of self. For example, when we are ashamed or embarrassed, we feel negatively about our behavior or accomplishments, and we want to retreat so others will no longer notice our failings. In contrast, pride reflects delight in the self's achievements, and we are inclined to tell others what we have accomplished (Saarni, Mumme, & Campos, 1998).

Self-conscious emotions appear at the end of the second year, as the sense of self emerges. Between 18 and 24 months, children can be seen feeling ashamed and embarrassed as they lower their eyes, hang their heads, and hide their faces with their hands. Pride also emerges around this time, and envy and guilt are present by age 3 (Lewis et al., 1989; Sroufe, 1979).

Besides self-awareness, self-conscious emotions require an additional ingredient: adult instruction in when to feel proud, ashamed, or guilty. The situations in which adults encourage these feelings vary from culture to culture. In most of the United States, children are taught to feel pride over personal achievement—throwing a ball the farthest, winning a game, and getting good grades. Among the Zuni Indians, shame and embarrassment occur in response to purely individual success, whereas pride is evoked by generosity, helpfulness, and sharing (Benedict, 1934b). In Japan, violating cultural standards of concern for others—a parent, a teacher, or an employer—is cause for intense shame (Lewis, 1992).

By 3 years of age, self-conscious emotions are clearly linked to self-evaluation (Lewis, 1995). In one study, parents were asked to give their 3-year-olds easy and difficult problems to solve. Children showed much more pride when they succeeded on difficult than easy tasks and much more shame when they failed simple than hard tasks (Lewis, Alessandri, & Sullivan, 1992). In contrast, basic emotions of joy and sadness accompany success or failure, regardless of the challenge involved. They do not depend on judgments of self-worth.

Nevertheless, the conditions under which children experience self-conscious emotions do change with age. For example, young children are likely to feel guilty for any act that can be described as wrongdoing, even if it was accidental (Graham, Doubleday, & Guarino, 1984). Also, the presence of an audience seems to be necessary for preschoolers to experience self-conscious emotions. In the case of pride, they depend on external recognition, such as a parent or teacher saying, "That's a great picture you drew" or "You did a good job picking up your toys today." And they are likely to experience guilt and shame only if their misdeeds are observed or detected by others (Harter & Whitesell, 1989).

Self-conscious emotions play an important role in children's achievement-related and moral behavior. Since preschoolers are still developing standards of excellence and conduct, they depend on instruction, feedback, and example from adults to know when to feel proud, guilty, or ashamed. As children develop guidelines for good behavior (see Chapters 11 and 12), the presence of others will no longer be necessary to evoke these emotions. In addition, pride and guilt will be limited to situations in which children feel personally responsible for an outcome, whereas shame will more often be experienced when violating a standard is unintentional—accidentally dropping spaghetti on one's shirt or forgetting an appointment (Mascolo & Fischer, 1995; Stipek, Recchia, & McClintic, 1992; Stipek, 1995).

EMOTIONAL SELF-REGULATION

Besides expressing a wider range of emotions, children acquire a variety of ways to manage their emotional experiences. **Emotional self-regulation** refers to the strategies we use to adjust our emotional state to a comfortable level of intensity so we can accomplish our goals. It requires several cognitive capacities we discussed in Chapter 7—attention focusing and shifting as well as the ability to inhibit thoughts and behavior (Eisenberg et al.,

self-conscious emotions
Emotions that involve injury to or enhancement of the sense of self. Examples are shame, embarrassment, guilt, envy, and pride.

emotional self-regulation
Strategies for adjusting our emotional state to a comfortable level of intensity so we can accomplish our goals.

1995b; Thompson, 1994). If you reminded yourself that an anxiety-provoking event would be over soon, resolved not to think about someone who makes you feel angry, or decided not to see a horror movie because it might frighten you, you were engaging in emotional self-regulation.

■ **INFANCY.** In the early months of life, infants have only a limited capacity to regulate their emotional states. Although they gradually become better at turning away from unpleasant stimulation and can mouth and suck when their feelings get too intense, they are easily overwhelmed by internal and external stimuli. As a result, they depend on the soothing interventions of caregivers—lifting the distressed infant to the shoulder, rocking, and talking softly—for help in adjusting their emotional reactions.

Rapid development of the cerebral cortex increases the baby's tolerance for stimulation. Between 2 and 4 months, caregivers start to build on this capacity by engaging in face-to-face play and encouraging attention to objects. In these interactions, parents arouse pleasure in the baby while adjusting the pace of their own behavior so the infant does not become overwhelmed and distressed. As a result, the baby's tolerance for stimulation increases further (Field, 1994). By 4 months of age, infants' ability to shift attention helps them control stimulation. Babies who more readily turn away from unpleasant events are rated by their mothers as less fearful, less prone to anger, and more easily soothed (Johnson, Posner, & Rothbart, 1991). At the end of the first year, crawling and walking enable infants to regulate feelings more effectively by approaching or retreating from various stimuli.

As caregivers help infants regulate their emotions, they contribute to the child's style of emotional self-regulation. For example, a parent who waits to intervene until an infant has become extremely agitated reinforces the baby's rapid rise to intense distress (Thompson, 1990a). This makes it harder for the parent to soothe the baby in the future—and for the baby to learn to calm herself.

By the end of the second year, gains in representation and language lead to new ways of regulating emotion. Although children of this age often succeed at redirecting their attention for short periods when they are distressed, they are not yet good at using language to comfort themselves (Grolnick, Bridges, & Connell, 1996). But by describing their internal states, they can guide caregivers in ways that will help them feel better. For example, while listening to a story about monsters, one 22-month-old whimpered, "Mommy, scary." Her mother put down the book and gave her a consoling hug.

■ **EARLY CHILDHOOD.** After age 2, children frequently talk about their feelings and engage in active efforts to control them. For example, they might try to blunt emotional arousal by restricting sensory input (covering their eyes or ears to block out an unpleasant sight or sound), talking to themselves ("Mommy said she'll be back soon"), or changing their goals (deciding that they don't want to play anyway after being excluded from a game). Children's increasing awareness and use of these strategies means that emotional outbursts become less frequent over the preschool years (Thompson, 1990a).

Nevertheless, preschoolers' vivid imaginations combined with their difficulty separating appearance from reality make fears of monsters, ghosts, darkness, thunder, and lightning common in early childhood. Parents may need to limit exposure to frightening stories in books and on TV, keep a night-light burning at bedtime, and offer extra emotional support until the child is better able to distinguish the way things really are from the way they appear (see Chapter 6 page 247).

As these interventions suggest, the social environment powerfully affects children's capacity to cope with stress. By watching adults handle their own feelings, preschoolers pick up strategies for regulating emotion. When parents have difficulty controlling anger

Self-conscious emotions appear at the end of the second year. This Guatemalan 2-year-old undoubtedly feels a sense of pride as she helps care for her elderly grandmother—an activity highly valued in her culture. (Celia Roberts/Earth Images)

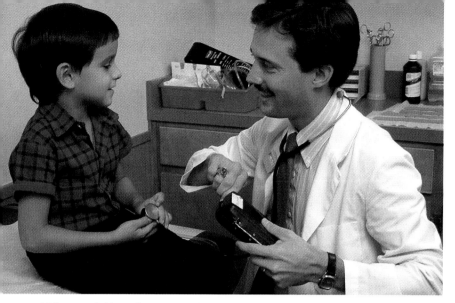

Talking to children about potentially frightening experiences helps them develop effective strategies for emotional self-regulation. This doctor puts a young child at ease by explaining what will happen during a physical examination.

(Bob Daemmrich/Stock Boston)

and hostility, children have problems as well (Cummings & Davies, 1994a). Adult–child conversations also provide techniques for regulating feelings. When parents prepare children for difficult experiences by describing what to expect and ways to handle anxiety, they offer coping strategies that children can use on their own.

Besides parenting, temperament affects the development of emotional self-regulation. Children who experience negative emotion very intensely find it harder to inhibit their feelings and shift their focus of attention away from disturbing events. As early as the preschool years, they are more likely to respond with irritation to others' distress and get along poorly with peers (Eisenberg et al., 1996, 1997a, 1997b). As we will see when we turn to the topic of temperament in a later section, because emotionally reactive children are difficult to rear, they often evoke ineffective parenting—a circumstance that compounds their poor emotional self-regulation.

■ **MIDDLE CHILDHOOD AND ADOLESCENCE.** Rapid gains in emotional self-regulation occur after school entry. As children's accomplishments are compared with their classmates' and they care more about peer approval, they must learn to manage negative emotion that threatens their sense of self-worth. Common fears of the school years include poor academic performance and rejection by classmates. And as children begin to understand the realities of the wider world, the possibility of personal harm (being robbed, stabbed, or shot) and media events (war and disasters) often trouble them (Silverman, La Greca, & Wasserstein, 1995).

School-age children's fears are shaped in part by their culture. For example, in China, where self-restraint and complying with social standards are highly valued, more children mention failure and adult criticism as salient fears than in Australia or the United States. Chinese children, however, are not more fearful overall. The number and intensity of fears they report resemble those of Western children (Ollendick et al., 1996).

By age 10, most children have an adaptive set of techniques for managing emotion (Kliewer, Fearnow, & Miller, 1996). In situations in which they have some control over an outcome (a difficult test at the end of the week or a friend who is angry at them), they view problem solving and seeking social support as the best strategies. When outcomes are beyond their control (having received a bad grade or awaiting a painful injection at the doctor's office), they opt for distraction or redefining the situation in ways that help them accept current conditions ("Things could be worse. There'll be another test") (Aldwin, 1994; Compas, Phares, & Ledoux, 1989). Compared with preschoolers, school-age children more often use internal strategies to manage emotion, a change fostered by metacognitive gains in middle childhood (Brenner & Salovey, 1997). Consequently, fears decline steadily over the school years (Gullone & King, 1997).

The capacity to generate a diverse array of self-regulatory techniques and flexibly adjust them to situational demands permits adolescents to handle unanticipated daily stresses more effectively than they could at younger ages. When the development of emotional self-regulation has gone along well, young people acquire a sense of *emotional self-efficacy*—a feeling of being in control of their emotional experience (Saarni, 1997). This fosters a favorable self-image and an optimistic outlook, which assist them further in the face of emotional challenges.

ACQUIRING EMOTIONAL DISPLAY RULES

In addition to regulating internal emotional states, children must learn to distinguish them from external emotional expression so they can control what they communicate to others. Young preschoolers have some ability to modify their expressive behavior. For example, when denied a cookie before dinnertime, one 2-year-old paused, picked up her blanket, and walked from the hard kitchen floor to the soft family-room carpet where she could comfortably throw herself on the floor and howl loudly!

At first, children modify emotional expressions to serve personal needs, and they exaggerate their true feelings (as this child did to get attention and a cookie). Soon, they learn to damp down their expressive behavior and substitute other expressions, such as smiling when feeling anxious or disappointed. Besides satisfying their own desires, children need to become skilled at controlling emotional displays to get along in their society, as all cultures have **emotional display rules** that specify when, where, and how it is appropriate to express emotions.

As early as the first few months of life, infants are encouraged to suppress negative emotion. In several studies, researchers watched middle-SES mothers play with their 2- to 7-month-olds. The mothers frequently imitated positive expressions of interest, happiness, and surprise, but they rarely imitated anger and sadness (Malatesta et al., 1986; Malatesta & Haviland, 1982).

At slightly older ages, children receive direct instruction in emotional display rules. Peggy Miller and Linda Sperry (1987) studied the everyday interactions of three mother–toddler pairs in an urban working-class neighborhood. Consistent with the values of their community, the mothers encouraged children to express anger and aggression in self-defense—for example, when a playmate grabbed a toy—but not under other conditions.

Although caregiver shaping of emotional behavior begins early, only gradually are children able to conform to display rules. Not until age 3 can they pose an expression they do not feel. These emotional "masks" are largely limited to positive feelings of happiness and surprise. Children of all ages (and adults as well) find it harder to act angry, sad, or disgusted than pleased (Lewis, Sullivan, & Vasen, 1987). Over the school years, children become increasingly adept at suppressing negative affect, although the extent to which they do so varies with the situation. For example, they are more likely to suppress anger in the presence of an authority figure, such as a teacher, than a peer (Underwood, Coie, & Herbsman, 1992). At the same time, they more often keep negative emotions hidden from peers than from parents, whom they count on to accept their feelings (Zeman & Garber, 1996).

Social pressures are responsible for these trends. To foster harmonious relationships, most cultures teach children to communicate positive feelings and inhibit unpleasant emotional displays. Societies that stress collective over individual needs place particular emphasis on these rules. For example, compared with Americans, Japanese and Asian Indian adults think that masking negative feelings is more important, and they are more emotionally controlled (Matsumoto, 1990; Roland, 1988). Cultures also vary in how children are taught to control negative emotions. In rural Nepal, Tamang 6- to 9-year-olds, who are steeped in the Buddhist value of inner peace, often say they would feel *tiken* (calm) in an emotionally charged situation, such as peer aggression or parents arguing. In contrast, Hindi children, who are taught to recognize negative feelings and suppress them, are more likely to say they would be upset but would try hard to hide their emotions from others (Cole & Tamang, 1998).

Besides greater conformity to display rules, conscious awareness and understanding of them emerge in middle childhood. When given hypothetical stressful situations (for example, a child who has boasted to a friend about his skating ability but who then falls down), 10-year-olds can think of more display rules to handle them than can 6- and 8-year-olds. Also, older children justify display rules by referring to social norms ("It's impolite to show you feel that way"), whereas younger children justify them as a way to avoid scolding and ridicule.

These findings suggest that at first, children obey display rules to avoid punishment and gain approval from others. Gradually, they see that each rule is followed by members of their culture, and they come to understand its value as a culturally accepted standard for expressive behavior (Saarni, 1995). School-age children who justify following emotional display rules by referring to concern for others' feelings are rated by their teachers as especially helpful, cooperative, and socially responsive (Garner, 1996).

emotional display rules Rules that specify when, where, and how it is culturally appropriate to express emotions.

ccording to the functionalist approach, emotions prompt action in the service of personal goals. Functionalist theorists view emotions as central forces in all aspects of human activity, including cognitive processing, social behavior, and physical health; as important in the emergence of self-awareness; and as becoming increasingly voluntary and socialized.

The development of emotional expression is a gradual process that begins in infancy and continues into adolescence. Changes in happiness, anger, sadness, and fear reflect infants' developing cognitive capacities and serve social as well as survival functions. At the end of the second year, self-conscious emotions emerge. By middle childhood, these self-evaluative feelings occur in the absence of adult monitoring and are clearly linked to personal responsibility. Emotional self-regulation begins in infancy and is supported by central nervous system maturation, cognitive and language development, and sensitive parenting. During the preschool years, children start to conform to the emotional display rules of their culture. In middle childhood, they become consciously aware of these rules.

Understanding and Responding to the Emotions of Others

hildren's emotional expressiveness is intimately tied to their ability to recognize and interpret the feelings of others. Already we have seen that in the first few months, infants match the feeling tone of the caregiver in face-to-face communication. Early on, babies detect others' emotions through a fairly automatic process of *emotional contagion,* just as we tend to feel happy or sad when we sense these emotions in others. Resonating in this way to another's feelings suggests that babies are beginning to discriminate emotional states.

In Chapter 4, we saw that at 3 months, infants respond to variations in emotional messages conveyed through tone of voice. And their reaction to the still face of a previously responsive adult indicates that the same is true in the visual modality. Between 7 and 10 months, infants perceive facial expressions as organized patterns, and they can match the emotion in a voice with the appropriate face of a speaking person (see pages 163 and 166).

Responding to emotional expressions as organized wholes rather than in component parts indicates that these signals have become meaningful to babies. Soon they realize that an emotional expression not only has meaning but is a meaningful reaction to a specific object or event (Bornstein & Lamb, 1992; Walker-Andrews, 1997). Once these understandings are in place, infants actively seek emotional information from trusted caregivers and use it to guide their own behavior.

SOCIAL REFERENCING

Social referencing involves relying on another person's emotional reaction to appraise an uncertain situation. Besides the ability to interpret emotional signals, the tendency of 8- to 10-month-olds to evaluate objects and events in terms of their safety and security leads to the emergence of this capacity. Many studies show that a caregiver's emotional expression (happy, angry, or fearful) influences whether a 1-year-old will show wariness of strangers, play with an unfamiliar toy, or cross the deep side of the visual cliff (Repacholi, 1998; Rosen, Adamson, & Bakeman, 1992; Sorce et al., 1985).

Mothers and fathers are equally effective sources of emotional information for babies. When parents are absent, infants and toddlers turn to other familiar adults, especially those who interact with them in an emotionally expressive way (Camras & Sachs, 1991). In fact, a caregiver's emotional cues during moments of uncertainty may be a major reason that she serves as a secure base for exploration. In an unfamiliar playroom, babies show a strong desire to remain within "eyeshot" of the caregiver. If she turns away, they will leave an attractive set of toys to relocate within her visual field so they have access to her facial and vocal cues (Carr, Dabbs, & Carr, 1975).

Social referencing provides yet another example of how adults help children regulate their emotional experiences. And parents can capitalize on social referencing to teach their youngster, whose capacity to explore is rapidly expanding, how to react to a great many everyday events.

Social referencing also permits toddlers to compare their own assessments of events with those of others. By the middle of the second year, they begin to appreciate that others' emotional reactions may differ from their own. In a recent study, an experimenter showed 14- and 18-month-olds broccoli and crackers. In one condition, she acted delighted with the taste of broccoli but disgusted with the taste of crackers. In the other condition, she showed the reverse preference. When asked to share the food, 14-month-olds offered only the type of food they themselves preferred—usually crackers. In contrast, 18-month-olds gave the experimenter whichever food they saw she liked, regardless of their own preferences (Repacholi & Gopnik, 1997).

In sum, social referencing helps young children move beyond simply reacting to others' emotional messages. They use those signals to find out about others' internal states and preferences and to guide their own actions (Saarni, Mumme, & Campos, 1998).

EMOTIONAL UNDERSTANDING IN CHILDHOOD

During the preschool years, children's emotional understanding expands rapidly, as their everyday talk about emotions reveals. Here are some excerpts from conversations in which 2-year-olds and 6-year-olds commented on emotionally charged experiences:

Two-year-old: (After father shouted at child, she became angry, shouting back.) "I'm mad at you, Daddy. I'm going away. Good-bye."

Two-year-old: (Commenting on another child who refused to take a nap and cried.) "Mom, Annie cry. Annie sad."

Six-year-old: (In response to mother's comment, "It's hard to hear the baby crying.") "Well, it's not as hard for me as it is for you." *(When mother asked why)* "Well, you like Johnny better than I do! I like him a little, and you like him a lot, so I think it's harder for you to hear him cry."

Six-year-old: (Trying to comfort a small boy in church whose mother had gone up to communion) "Aw, that's all right. She'll be right back. Don't be afraid. I'm here."

(Bretherton et al., 1986, pp. 536, 540, 541)

As these examples show, early in the preschool years, children refer to causes, consequences, and behavioral signs of emotion, and over time their understanding becomes more accurate and complex.

■ COGNITIVE DEVELOPMENT AND EMOTIONAL UNDERSTANDING. By age 4 to 5, children correctly judge the causes of many basic emotional reactions. When asked why a nearby playmate is happy, sad, or angry, they describe events similar to those identified by adults, such as "He's happy because he's swinging very high" or "He's sad because he misses his mother." However, they are likely to emphasize external factors over internal states as explanations—a balance that changes with age (Fabes et al., 1991). For example, before age 7, children believe that people respond with anger when they have been wronged but can change the situation, whereas older children and adults associate anger with intent to do harm (Levine, 1995). Nevertheless, preschoolers realize that thinking and feeling are interconnected. For example, 4- and 5-year-olds know that a person reminded of a previous sad experience is likely to feel sad (Lagattuta, Wellman, & Flavell, 1997).

Preschoolers are also good at predicting what a person expressing a certain emotion might do next. Four-year-olds say that an angry child might hit someone and that a happy child is more likely to share (Russell, 1990). They are even aware that a lingering mood can affect a person's behavior for some time in the future (Bretherton, 1986).

An improved ability to consider multiple sources of information when explaining others' emotions develops during middle childhood. In situations with conflicting cues about how a person is feeling, preschoolers have difficulty making sense of what is going on. For example, when asked what might be happening in a picture showing a happy-faced child with a broken bicycle, 4- and 5-year-olds tended to rely only on the emotional expression ("He's happy because he likes to ride his bike"). By age 8 to 9, children more often reconciled the two cues (He's happy because his father promised to help fix his broken bike") (Gnepp, 1983; Hoffner & Badzinski, 1989).

Similarly, older children recognize that people can experience more than one emotion at a time—in other words, that they can have "mixed feelings," each of which may be positive or negative and may differ in intensity (Wintre & Vallance, 1994). Preschoolers staunchly deny that two emotions can occur at once, in much the same way that they do not integrate two variables (height and width) in a Piagetian conservation-of-liquid task. When asked about the feelings of a child who pushed a playmate off a swing to get a turn for himself, 4-year-olds report positive emotions—"happy" or "good" because he got what he wanted. By age 8, children spontaneously explain that in addition to feeling good, the naughty child also feels "sad," "bad," or "angry" because he did harm to another (Arsenio & Kramer, 1992).

The capacity to make sense of conflicting emotional cues enables school-age children to appreciate that people's expressions need not reflect their true feelings (Saarni, 1997). Notice how thinking about emotions resembles the development of metacognition, or thinking about thought, discussed in Chapter 7. Striking gains in both domains take place in middle childhood.

■ SOCIAL EXPERIENCE AND EMOTIONAL UNDERSTANDING. Although cognitive development fosters emotional understanding, social experience also contributes. The more mothers label emotions and explain them while conversing with their preschoolers, the more emotion words children use in these discussions. Maternal prompting of emotional thoughts ("What makes him afraid?") is a good predictor of 2-year-olds' emotion language. Later in the preschool years, explanations ("He's sad because his dog ran away") are more predictive (Cervantes & Callanan, 1998). Does this remind you of the concept of *scaffolding*— that to be effective, adult teaching must adjust to children's increasing competence?

Preschoolers growing up in families that frequently talk about feelings are better at judging the emotions of others when tested at later ages (Denham, Zoller, & Couchoud, 1994; Dunn et al., 1991). Discussions in which family members disagree about feelings are particularly helpful. These dialogues seem to help children step back from the experience of emotion and reflect on its causes and consequences.

As preschoolers learn more about emotion from conversing with adults, they transfer this knowledge to other contexts, engaging in more emotion talk with siblings and friends, especially during sociodramatic play (Brown, Donelan-McCall, & Dunn, 1996; Hughes & Dunn, 1998). Make-believe, in turn, contributes to emotional understanding, especially when children play with siblings. The intense nature of the sibling relationship, combined with frequent acting out of feelings in make-believe, makes this an excellent context for early learning about emotions (Youngblade & Dunn, 1995).

Emotional knowledge helps children greatly in their efforts to get along with others. As early as 3 to 5 years of age, it is related to friendly, considerate behavior, willingness to make amends after harming another, and peer acceptance (Cassidy et al., 1992; Dunn, Brown, & Maguire, 1995; Garner, Jones, & Miner, 1994).

EMPATHY

empathy The ability to understand another's emotional state and feel with that person, or respond emotionally in a similar way.

In **empathy,** understanding and expression of emotions are interwoven, since both awareness of the emotions of another and vicariously experiencing those emotions are required for an empathic response. Current theorists agree that empathy involves a complex interaction of cognition and affect: the ability to detect different emotions, to take another's perspective in order to comprehend that person's emotional state, and to *feel with* that person, or respond emotionally in a similar way (Zahn-Waxler & Radke-Yarrow, 1990).

Beginning in the preschool years, empathy is an important motivator of **prosocial, or altruistic, behavior**—actions that benefit another person without any expected reward for the self (Eisenberg & Fabes, 1998). Yet empathy does not always yield acts of kindness and helpfulness. In some children, the emotion aroused by an upset adult or peer escalates into personal distress. In trying to reduce these feelings, the child focuses on himself rather than the person in need. Consequently, empathy does not give way to **sympathy**—*feelings of concern or sorrow for another person's plight.*

■ **DEVELOPMENT OF EMPATHY.** Empathy has roots early in development. Newborn babies tend to cry in response to the cry of another baby, a reaction that may be the primitive beginnings of an empathic response (Dondi, Simion, & Caltran, 1999). In sensitive, face-to-face communication, infants "connect" emotionally with their caregivers—experiences believed to be the foundation for empathy and concern for others (Zahn-Waxler, 1991).

Empathy increases over the elementary school years, due to the older child's ability to accurately detect the feelings of others and imagine the self in another's place. The boy on the left translates empathy into sympathetic concern for his friend, a response fostered by the capacity to regulate negative emotion.
(Susan Johns/Photo Researchers)

Like the self-conscious emotions we discussed earlier, true empathy requires children to understand that the self is distinct from other people. As self-awareness develops, children nearing 2 years of age begin to empathize. They not only sense another's unhappiness but often try to relieve it, using methods that become more varied with age. For example, one 21-month-old reacted to his mother's simulated sadness by offering comforting words, giving her a hug, trying to distract her with a hand puppet, and asking the experimenter to help (Zahn-Waxler & Radke-Yarrow, 1990).

As language develops, children rely more on words to console others, a change that indicates a more reflective level of empathy. A 6-year-old said this to his mother after noticing she was distressed at not being able to find a motel after a long day's travel: "You're pretty upset, aren't you, Mom? You're pretty sad. Well, I think it's going to be all right. I think we'll find a nice place and it'll be all right" (Bretherton et al., 1986, p. 540).

Empathic responding increases over the elementary school years. Children's understanding of a wider range of emotions and ability to take multiple cues into account in assessing another's feelings underlie this change (Ricard & Kamberk-Kilicci, 1995). During late childhood and adolescence, advances in perspective taking permit an empathic response not just to people's immediate distress but also to their general life condition. According to Martin Hoffman (1984), the ability to empathize with the poor, oppressed, and sick is the most mature form of empathy. It requires an advanced form of perspective taking in which the child understands that people lead continuous emotional lives beyond the current situation.

■ **INDIVIDUAL DIFFERENCES.** Whether empathy prompts a personally distressed, self-focused response or sympathetic, prosocial behavior is related to temperament. Preschool and school-age children who are sociable, assertive, and good at regulating emotion are more likely to help, share, and comfort others in distress. In contrast, children who frequently display negative emotion and who are poor emotion regulators less often display sympathetic concern and prosocial behavior (Eisenberg et al., 1992, 1996, 1998).

These differences are evident in children's facial and psychophysiological responses to empathy-inducing situations. In a series of studies, Nancy Eisenberg, Richard Fabes, and their colleagues showed children videotapes of people in need, such as two children who had fallen from a playground climber lying on the ground, crying. Children who reacted with facial or physiological markers of sympathy—either a concerned expression or a decrease in heart rate, suggesting orienting and attention—tended to behave prosocially when offered a chance to help the person in the film or similar people. In contrast, children who showed evidence of facial and physiological distress—frowning, lip biting, and

prosocial, or altruistic, behavior Actions that benefit another person without any expected reward for the self.

sympathy Feelings of concern or sorrow for another's plight.

a rise in heart rate and skin conductance—were less prosocial (Fabes, Eisenberg, & Eisenbud, 1993; Fabes et al., 1994; Miller et al., 1996).

Recall that parenting has a profound impact on emotional self-regulation, and it affects empathy and sympathy as well. Parents who are nurturant and encouraging and who show sensitive, empathic concern for their preschoolers have children who are more likely to react in a concerned way to the distress of others—relationships that persist into adolescence and young adulthood (Eisenberg & McNally, 1993; Koestner, Franz, & Weinberger, 1990). But empathy and sympathy are fostered not just by modeling. Setting clear limits is also important. Parental intervention when children display inappropriate emotion and direct teaching about the importance of kindness predict high levels of sympathetic responding (Eisenberg et al., 1991; Zahn-Waxler & Radke-Yarrow, 1990).

In contrast, angry, punitive parenting is related to disruptions in empathy and sympathy at an early age (Miller et al., 1989). In one study, severely physically abused toddlers were observed at a day-care center to see how they reacted to other children's distress. Compared to their nonabused counterparts, they rarely showed signs of concern. Instead, they responded with fear, anger, and physical attacks (Klimes-Dougan & Kistner, 1990). By the second year of life, the reactions of abused children already resemble the behavior of their parents, since both respond with anger and aversion to others' distress.

These findings—as well as others discussed so far—reveal wide variations in children's emotional dispositions. As we take a closer look at these individual differences in the next section, we will discover that they are the combined result of biological and environmental influences. Even in the case of empathy, twin studies suggest a modest genetic contribution (Emde et al., 1992; Plomin et al., 1993; Zahn-Waxler, Robinson, & Emde, 1992). But before we delve into the topic of temperament, turn to the Milestones table on the following page for an overview of the emotional attainments we have just considered.

ASK YOURSELF . . .

♦ As 4-year-old Tia attended a carnival with her mother, the heat of the afternoon caused her balloon to pop. When Tia started to cry, her mother said, "Oh, Tia, we'll get another balloon on a cooler day. If you cry, you'll mess up your beautiful face painting." What aspect of emotional development is Tia's mother trying to promote? Why might her intervention also foster the development of empathy?

♦ CONNECTIONS
School-age children can take multiple cues into account in interpreting others' emotions and are aware that people do not always express their true feelings. Relate these advances to cognition and metacognition in middle childhood. (See Chapter 6, page 249, and Chapter 7, pages 277 and 301.)

temperament Stable individual differences in quality and intensity of emotional reaction, activity level, attention, and emotional self-regulation.

BRIEF REVIEW

The ability to meaningfully interpret others' emotional expressions emerges at the end of the first year. Around this time, infants start to engage in social referencing, actively seeking emotional information from caregivers in uncertain situations. Over early and middle childhood, emotional understanding expands, a change influenced by cognitive and language development, family experiences involving discussion of feelings, and make-believe play with siblings. School-age children rely on multiple cues to evaluate the emotions of others, and they realize that people can experience more than one emotion at a time.

Gains in empathy from infancy into adolescence are supported by cognitive development and advances in perspective taking. A calm, sociable temperament, good emotional self-regulation, sensitive child rearing, and parental teaching of kindness increase the chances that children's empathy will motivate sympathetic concern and prosocial behavior.

Temperament and Development

When we describe one person as cheerful and upbeat, another as active and energetic, and still others as calm, cautious, or prone to angry outbursts, we are referring to **temperament**—stable individual differences in quality and intensity of emotional reaction, activity level, attention, and emotional self-regulation (Rothbart & Bates, 1998). Researchers have become increasingly interested in temperamental differences among infants and children, since the psychological traits that make up temperament are believed to form the cornerstone of the adult personality.

The New York Longitudinal Study, initiated in 1956 by Alexander Thomas and Stella Chess, is the longest and most comprehensive study of temperament to date. A total of 141 children were followed from the first few months of life over a period that now extends well into adulthood. Results showed that temperament is a major factor in increas-

Emotional Development

Age	Emotional Expressiveness	Emotional Understanding
Birth–6 months	■ Signs of almost all basic emotions are present. ■ Social smile emerges. ■ Laughter appears. ■ Expressions of happiness are greater when interacting with familiar people. ■ Emotional expressions are well organized and clearly related to social events.	■ Capacity to match the feeling tone of the caregiver in face-to-face communication is present.
7–12 months	■ Anger and fear, especially stranger anxiety, increase. ■ Use of caregiver as a secure base emerges. ■ Emotional self-regulation improves as crawling and walking permit approach and retreat from stimulation.	■ Ability to detect the meaning of others' emotional signals emerges. ■ Social referencing develops.
1–2 years	■ Self-conscious emotions appear but depend on the presence of others.	■ Appreciation that others' emotional reactions may differ from one's own emerges. ■ Vocabulary of words for talking about feelings expands. ■ Empathy appears.
3–6 years	■ As representation and language improve, active strategies for regulating emotion develop. ■ Ability to conform to display rules by posing a positive emotion one does not feel emerges.	■ Understanding of causes, consequences, and behavioral signs of emotion improves in accuracy and complexity. ■ As language develops, empathy becomes more reflective.
7–11 years	■ Self-conscious emotions become integrated with inner standards for right action. ■ Strategies for engaging in emotional self-regulation increase in variety, become more internal, and are adjusted to situational demands. ■ Conformity to and conscious awareness of emotional display rules improve.	■ Ability to consider multiple sources of information when explaining others' emotions appears. ■ Awareness that people can have mixed feelings and that their expressions may not reflect their true feelings emerges. ■ Empathy increases as emotional understanding improves.

Note: These milestones represent overall age trends. Individual differences exist in the precise age at which each milestone is attained.

This mother wants her 3-year-old son to put his toys away and turn to another activity—perhaps lunch time or an errand. Transitions seem like crises for this difficult child, who reacts negatively and intensely to disruptions and new experiences.
(B. Daemmrich/The Image Works)

easy child A child whose temperament is such that he or she quickly establishes regular routines in infancy, is generally cheerful, and adapts easily to new experiences.

difficult child A child whose temperament is such that he or she is irregular in daily routines, is slow to accept new experiences, and tends to react negatively and intensely.

slow-to-warm-up child A child whose temperament is such that he or she is inactive, shows mild, low-key reactions to environmental stimuli, is negative in mood, and adjusts slowly to new experiences.

ing the chances that a child will experience psychological problems or, alternatively, be protected from the effects of a highly stressful home life. However, Thomas and Chess (1977) also found that temperament is not fixed and unchangeable. Parenting practices can modify children's emotional styles considerably.

These findings stimulated a growing body of research on temperament, including its stability, its biological roots, and its interaction with child-rearing experiences. Let's begin to explore these issues by looking at the structure, or makeup, of temperament and how it is measured.

THE STRUCTURE OF TEMPERAMENT

Thomas and Chess's nine dimensions, listed in Table 10.1, served as the first influential model of temperament, inspiring all others that followed. When detailed descriptions of infants' and children's behavior obtained from parental interviews were rated on these dimensions, certain characteristics clustered together, yielding three types of children that described the majority of their sample:

- The **easy child** (40 percent of the sample): This child quickly establishes regular routines in infancy, is generally cheerful, and adapts easily to new experiences.

- The **difficult child** (10 percent of the sample): This child has irregular daily routines, is slow to accept new experiences, and tends to react negatively and intensely.

- The **slow-to-warm-up child** (15 percent of the sample): This child is inactive, shows mild, low-key reactions to environmental stimuli, is negative in mood, and adjusts slowly to new experiences.

Note that 35 percent of the children did not fit any of these categories. Instead, they showed unique blends of temperamental characteristics.

Of the three temperamental types, the difficult pattern has sparked the most interest, since it places children at high risk for adjustment problems. In the New York Longitudinal Study, 70 percent of young preschoolers classified as difficult developed behavior problems by school age, whereas only 18 percent of the easy children did (Thomas, Chess, & Birch, 1968). And other longitudinal findings indicate that infant difficultness predicts both anxious withdrawal and aggressive behavior in early and middle childhood (Bates, Wachs, & Emde, 1994).

Unlike difficult children, slow-to-warm-up children do not present many problems in the early years. They encounter special challenges later, after they enter school and peer groups in which they are expected to respond actively and quickly. Thomas and Chess found that by middle childhood, 50 percent of these children began to show adjustment difficulties, in the form of excessive fearfulness and slow, constricted behavior (Chess & Thomas, 1984).

A second model of temperament, devised by Mary Rothbart and Jennifer Mauro (1990), is also shown in Table 10.1. It combines dimensions of Thomas and Chess and other researchers that overlap. For example, "distractibility" and "attention span and persistence" are considered opposite ends of the same dimension and called "attention span/persistence." Rothbart and Mauro also include a dimension not identified by Thomas and Chess—"irritable distress"—that emphasizes emotional self-regulation. Overall, the temperamental characteristics shown in Table 10.1 provide a fairly complete picture of the traits most often studied.

MEASURING TEMPERAMENT

To measure temperament, researchers typically select from a variety of methods that assess children's behavior. But new techniques are focusing on physiological reactions in an effort to identify biological processes at the heart of temperamental styles.

■ **ASSESSMENTS OF BEHAVIOR.** Temperament is often assessed through interviews or questionnaires given to parents, although behavior ratings by pediatricians, teachers, and

TABLE 10.1

Two Models of Temperament

Thomas and Chess		Rothbart and Mauro	
Dimension	**Description and Example**	**Dimension**	**Description**
Activity level	Proportion of active periods to inactive ones. Some babies are always in motion. Others move about very little.	Activity level	Level of gross motor activity
Rhythmicity	Regularity of body functions. Some infants fall asleep, wake up, get hungry, and have bowel movements on a regular schedule, whereas others are much less predictable.	Rhythmicity	Regularity of functions, such as sleep, wakefulness, hunger, and excretion
Distractibility	Degree to which stimulation from the environment alters behavior. Some hungry babies stop crying temporarily if offered a pacifier or a toy to play with. Others continue to cry until fed.	Attention span/ persistence	Duration of orienting or interest
Approach/ withdrawal	Response to a new object or person. Some babies accept new foods and smile and babble at strangers, whereas others pull back and cry on first exposure.	Fearful distress	Wariness and distress in response to intense or novel stimuli, including time taken to adjust to new situations
Adaptability	Ease with which the child adapts to changes in the environment. Although some infants withdraw when faced with new experiences, they quickly adapt, accepting the new food or person on the next occasion. Others continue to fuss and cry.	Irritable distress	Fussing, crying, and showing distress when desires are frustrated
Attention span and persistence	Amount of time devoted to an activity. Some babies watch a mobile or play with a toy for a long time, whereas others lose interest after a few minutes.	Positive affect	Frequency of expression of happiness and pleasure
Intensity of reaction	Intensity or energy level of response. Some infants laugh and cry loudly, whereas others react only mildly.		
Threshold of responsiveness	Intensity of stimulation required to evoke a response. Some babies startle at the slightest change in sound or lighting. Others take little notice of these changes in stimulation.		
Quality of mood	Amount of friendly, joyful behavior as opposed to unpleasant, unfriendly behavior. Some babies smile and laugh frequently when playing and interacting with people. Others fuss and cry often.		

Sources: Rothbart & Mauro, 1990; Thomas & Chess, 1977.

others familiar with the child, as well as direct observations by researchers, have also been used. Parental reports have been emphasized because of their convenience and parents' depth of knowledge about the child.

At the same time, information from parents has been criticized for being biased and subjective. For example, parents' prebirth expectations for their infant's temperament affect their reports after the infant arrives (Diener, Goldstein, & Mangelsdorf, 1995). And mothers who are anxious, depressed, and low in self-esteem tend to regard their babies as more difficult (Mebert, 1991; Vaughn et al., 1987). Nevertheless, parental ratings are moderately related to observations of children's behavior (Rothbart & Bates, 1998). And parent perceptions are useful for understanding the way parents view and respond to their child.

■ **ASSESSMENTS OF PHYSIOLOGICAL REACTIONS.** To explore the biological basis of temperament, researchers are turning to psychophysiological measures. Besides providing insights into the origins of temperament, psychophysiological indices (like direct observations) are not hampered by the subjective elements of parental reports.

Most efforts have focused on **inhibited,** or **shy, children,** who react negatively to and withdraw from novel stimuli, and **uninhibited,** or **sociable, children,** who display positive emotion to and approach novel stimuli. As the Variations box on the following page reveals, heart rate, hormone levels, and EEG waves in the frontal region of the cerebral cortex differentiate children with inhibited and uninhibited temperaments.

Investigators do not yet know how or when these psychophysiological measures become interrelated—information that may shed new light on the integrated role of various brain structures in shyness and sociability. And, as we will see in the following sections, more research is needed to clarify how brain mechanisms combine with experience to support consistency and change in children's temperamental styles.

STABILITY OF TEMPERAMENT

It would be difficult to claim that temperament really exists if children's emotional styles were not stable over time. Indeed, many studies provide support for the stability of temperament. Infants and young children who score low or high on attention span, irritability, sociability, or shyness are likely to respond similarly when assessed again several months to a few years later and, occasionally, even into the adult years (Caspi & Silva, 1995; Kochanska & Radke-Yarrow, 1992; Pedlow et al., 1993; Rothbart, Derryberry, & Posner, 1994; Ruff et al., 1990).

When the evidence as a whole is examined carefully, however, temperamental stability from one age period to the next is generally low to moderate (Rothbart & Bates, 1998). Although quite a few children remain the same, a good number have changed when assessed again. In fact, some characteristics, such as shyness and sociability, are stable over the long term only in children at the extremes—those who are very shy or very outgoing to begin with (Kerr et al., 1994; Sanson et al., 1996).

Why is temperament not more stable? A major reason is that temperament itself develops with age; early behaviors reorganize into new, more complex systems. To illustrate, let's look at irritability and activity level. Recall from Chapter 4 that the early months are a period of fussing and crying for most babies. As infants become better at regulating their attention and emotions, many who initially seemed irritable become calm and content. In the case of activity level, the meaning of the behavior changes. At first, an active, wriggling infant tends to be highly aroused and uncomfortable, whereas an inactive baby is often alert and attentive. As infants move on their own, the reverse is so! An active crawler is usually alert and interested in exploration, whereas a very inactive baby might be fearful and withdrawn.

These inconsistencies help us understand why long-term prediction from early temperament is best achieved from the second year of life and after, when styles of responding are better established (Caspi, 1998; Lemery et al., 1999). At the same time, the changes shown by many youngsters in childhood suggest that biologically based temperamental traits can be modified by experience (although children rarely change from one extreme to another—that is, a shy toddler practically never becomes highly sociable). With these ideas in mind, let's turn to genetic and environmental contributions to temperament and personality.

GENETIC AND ENVIRONMENTAL INFLUENCES

The word *temperament* implies a genetic foundation for individual differences in emotional style. In recent years, many kinship studies have compared individuals of different degrees of genetic relationship to determine the extent to which temperament and personality are heritable. As with the heritability of intelligence, the most common approach has been to compare identical and fraternal twins.

■ **HERITABILITY.** Identical twins are more similar than fraternal twins across a wide range of temperamental traits (activity level, sociability, shyness, distress to limitations, intensity of emotional reaction, attention span, and persistence) and personality measures (introversion, extroversion, anxiety, agreeableness, and impulsivity) (DiLalla, Kagan, & Reznick, 1994; Emde et al., 1992; Goldsmith, Buss, & Lemery, 1997; Saudino & Eaton,

inhibited, or shy, child A child whose temperament is such that he or she reacts negatively to and withdraws from novel stimuli.

uninhibited, or sociable, child A child whose temperament is such that he or she displays positive emotion to and approaches novel stimuli.

Biological Basis of Shyness and Sociability

T AGE 4 months, Larry and Mitch visited the laboratory of Jerome Kagan, who observed their reactions to a variety of unfamiliar experiences. When exposed to new sights and sounds, such as a moving mobile decorated with colorful toys, Larry tensed his muscles, moved his arms and legs with agitation, and began to cry. Mitch's body remained relaxed and quiet, and he smiled and cooed pleasurably at the excitement around him.

Larry and Mitch returned to the laboratory as toddlers. This time, each experienced a variety of procedures designed to induce uncertainty. For example, electrodes were placed on their bodies and blood pressure cuffs on their arms to measure heart rate; highly stimulating toy robots, animals, and puppets moved before their eyes; and unfamiliar people entered and behaved in atypical ways or wore novel costumes. Larry whimpered and quickly withdrew, seeking his mother's protection. Mitch watched with interest, laughed at the strange sights, and approached the toys and strangers.

On a third visit, at age 4½ years, Larry barely talked or smiled during an interview with an unfamiliar adult. In contrast, Mitch asked questions and communicated his pleasure at each intriguing activity. In a playroom with two unfamiliar peers, Larry pulled back, keeping an anxious eye on the other children. Mitch made friends quickly.

In longitudinal research on several hundred Caucasian children, Kagan (1998a) found that about 20 percent of 4-month-old babies were easily upset by novelty (like Larry), whereas 40 percent were comfortable, even delighted, with new experiences (like Mitch). About 30 percent of these extreme groups retained their temperamental styles as they grew older. Those resembling Larry tended to become fearful, inhibited toddlers and preschoolers; those resembling Mitch developed into outgoing, uninhibited youngsters.

PHYSIOLOGICAL CORRELATES OF SHYNESS AND SOCIABILITY. Kagan believes that individual differences in arousal of the *amygdala*, an inner brain structure that controls avoidance reactions, contribute to these contrasting temperamental styles. In shy, inhibited children, novel stimuli easily excite the amygdala and its connections to the cerebral cortex and sympathetic nervous system, which prepares the body to act in the face of threat. The same level of stimulation evokes minimal neural excitation in highly sociable, uninhibited children. In support of this theory, several physiological responses of shy children resemble those of highly timid animals and are known to be mediated by the amygdala:

- *Heart rate.* As early as the first few weeks of life, the heart rates of shy children are consistently higher than those of sociable youngsters, and they speed up further in response to unfamiliar events (Snidman et al., 1995).

- *Cortisol.* Saliva concentration of cortisol, a hormone that regulates blood pressure and is involved in resistance to stress, tends to be higher in shy than sociable children (Gunnar & Nelson, 1994; Kagan & Snidman, 1991).

- *Pupil dilation and blood pressure.* Compared with sociable children, shy children show greater pupil dilation and rise in blood pressure when faced with novelty and challenge (Kagan, 1994).

The shy boy on the far right retreats while his peers engage in active play. A strong physiological response to uncertain situations prompts his social withdrawal.
(Laura Dwight)

Yet another physiological correlate of approach–withdrawal to people and objects is the pattern of EEG waves in the frontal region of the cerebral cortex. Recall from Chapter 5 that the left cortical hemisphere is specialized to respond with positive emotion, the right hemisphere with negative emotion. Shy infants and preschoolers show greater right than left frontal brain wave activity; their sociable counterparts show the opposite pattern (Calkins, Fox, & Marshall, 1996; Fox, Bell, & Jones, 1992; Fox, Calkins & Bell, 1994). Neural activity in the amygdala is transmitted to the frontal lobes and may influence these patterns.

LONG-TERM CONSEQUENCES. According to Kagan (1998a), children who are extremely shy or sociable inherit a physiology that biases them toward a particular temperamental style. Among Caucasians, shy children are more likely to have certain physical traits—blue eyes and thin faces—known to be affected by heredity (Arcus & Kagan, 1995). The genes controlling these characteristics may also influence the excitability of the amygdala.

Yet heritability research indicates that genes make only a modest contribution to shyness and sociability. They share power with experience. When early inhibition persists, it can lead to adjustment difficulties, such as excessive cautiousness, social withdrawal, and loneliness (Caspi & Silva, 1995; Rubin, Stewart, & Coplan, 1995). At the same time, many inhibited infants and children cope with novelty more effectively as they get older, although few become highly sociable.

Child-rearing practices affect the chances that an emotionally reactive baby will become a fearful child. Warm, supportive parenting reduces cortisol production in inhibited babies, buffering the child's fear, whereas cold, intrusive parenting heightens the cortisol response (Gunnar, 1998). In addition, when parents protect infants who dislike novelty from minor stresses, they make it harder for the child to overcome an urge to retreat from unfamiliar events. In contrast, parents who make appropriate demands for their baby to approach new experiences help the child overcome fear (Park et al., 1997; Rubin et al., 1997). In sum, for children to develop their best, parenting must be tailored to their temperaments—a theme we will encounter again in this and later chapters.

TABLE **10.2**

Kinship Correlations for Temperament, Personality, and Intelligence

Kinship Pair	Temperament in Infancy	Personality in Childhood and Adulthood	Intelligence
Identical twins reared together	.36	.52	.86
Fraternal twins reared together	.18	.25	.55
Biological siblings reared together	.18	.20	.47
Nonbiological siblings (adopted–natural pairings)	−.03	.05	.29

Note: Correlations are averages across a variety of temperament and personality characteristics.
Sources: Braungart et al. (1992) and Emde et al. (1992) for temperament in infancy; Nichols (1978) and Plomin, Chipuer, & Loehlin (1990) for personality in childhood and adulthood; and Scarr (1997) for intelligence.

1991). Table 10.2 reveals that twin resemblance for temperament and personality is considerably lower than for intelligence. Nevertheless, when heritability estimates are computed by comparing the correlations of identical and fraternal twins, they are moderate, averaging around .50 (Rothbart & Bates, 1998).

■ **NONSHARED ENVIRONMENT.** Recall from earlier chapters that adoption research is useful in unraveling the relative contribution of heredity and environment to complex traits. The few such studies available for temperament and personality report very low correlations for both biological and nonbiological siblings, despite the fact that they are reared together in the same family (refer again to Table 10.2).

In Chapter 8, we discussed a similar pattern of kinship correlations for IQ (see page 345). To explain it, we distinguished two broad classes of environmental factors: *shared environmental influences,* those that affect all children living in the same home to the same extent, and *nonshared environmental influences,* those that make siblings different from one another. That siblings growing up in the same family show little or no resemblance in temperament and personality suggests that shared environmental factors, such as the overall climate of the home, do not make an important contribution. Instead, behavioral geneticists believe that nonshared environmental factors—those that bring out each child's uniqueness—are especially salient in personality development (Braungart et al., 1992; Emde et al., 1992; Plomin, 1994d).

How might these nonshared influences operate? Behavioral geneticists claim that when it comes to children's personalities, parents look for and emphasize differences. This is reflected in the comments many parents make after the birth of a second baby: "He's so much calmer," "She's a lot more active," or "He's more sociable." In one study, parents' descriptions of their children as temperamentally easy or difficult showed a sharp contrast effect. When one child was seen as easy, another was likely to be perceived as difficult (Schachter & Stone, 1985). Each child, in turn, evokes responses from caregivers that are consistent with parental beliefs and the child's actual temperamental style.

Besides different experiences within the family, siblings have unique experiences with peers, teachers, and others in their community that profoundly affect development. Furthermore, as they get older, siblings often actively seek ways in which they can be different from one another. For these reasons, both identical and fraternal twins tend to become more distinct in personality in adulthood (McCartney, Harris, & Bernieri, 1990; Rose et al., 1988). The less contact twins have with one another, the stronger this effect—additional support for the power of the nonshared environment.

However, not everyone agrees that nonshared influences are supreme in personality development. In Chapter 14, we will see that researchers who have assessed shared factors directly, such as family stress and child-rearing styles, report that they do affect children's personalities. As Lois Hoffman (1991, 1994) points out, we must think of temperament and personality as resulting from many different inputs. For some qualities, child-specific experiences may be important. For others, the general family environment may be important. And for still others, both nonshared and shared factors may be involved.

■ **CULTURAL VARIATIONS.** Consistent ethnic differences in early temperament exist. Compared to Caucasian infants, Chinese and Japanese babies tend to be less active, irritable, and vocal, more easily soothed when upset, and better at quieting themselves (Kagan et al., 1994; Lewis, Ramsay, & Kawakami, 1993). Although these variations may have biological roots, cultural beliefs and practices support them. When Japanese mothers are asked about their approach to child rearing, they respond that babies come into the world as independent beings who must learn to rely on their mothers through close physical contact. American mothers are likely to believe just the opposite—that they must wean the baby away from dependence into autonomy (Kojima, 1986). Consistent with these beliefs, Asian mothers interact gently, soothingly, and gesturally with their babies, whereas Caucasian mothers use a more active, stimulating, verbal approach—behaviors that enhance early temperamental differences between their infants (Fogel, Toda, & Kawai, 1988).

Chinese infants are less active, irritable, and vocal, more easily soothed when upset, and better at quieting themselves than are Caucasian infants. Although these variations may have biological roots, cultural variations in child rearing support them. (Alan Oddie/PhotoEdit)

Taken together, research on the nature–nurture issue in the realm of temperament and personality indicates that the importance of heredity cannot be ignored. At the same time, individual differences in personality can be understood only in terms of complex interdependencies between genetic and environmental factors.

TEMPERAMENT AS A PREDICTOR OF CHILDREN'S BEHAVIOR

In the first part of this chapter, we saw many examples of how emotions serve as powerful determinants of cognitive and social functioning. Since temperament represents an individual's emotional style, it should predict behaviors that emotions organize and regulate.

■ **TEMPERAMENT AND COGNITIVE PERFORMANCE.** Temperamental characteristics of interest and persistence are related to learning and cognitive performance almost as soon as they can be measured. For example, persistence during the first year correlates with infant mental test scores and preschool IQ (Matheny, 1989). During middle childhood, persistence, in the form of teacher-rated task orientation, continues to predict IQ as well as grades in school and teacher estimates of academic competence. In contrast, distractibility and high activity level are associated with poor school achievement (Martin, Olejnik, & Gaddis, 1994).

■ **TEMPERAMENT AND SOCIAL BEHAVIOR.** Temperament also predicts important variations in social behavior. For example, highly active preschoolers are very sociable with peers, but they also become involved in more conflict than do their less active agemates. Emotionally sensitive, excitable preschoolers tend to interact physically by hitting, touching, and grabbing objects from peers. Shy, inhibited children do more watching of classmates and engaging in anxious behaviors that discourage interaction, such as pushing other children away and speaking to them less often (Broberg, Lamb, & Hwang, 1990; Hinde, Stevenson-Hinde, & Tamplin, 1985). And as we will see in Chapter 12, temperament influences moral development. Inhibited youngsters' high anxiety leads them to be more prone to discomfort after wrongdoing and to feel a greater sense of responsibility to others. As a result, early fearfulness protects children against the development of aggression (Caspi & Silva, 1995). In contrast, irritable, impulsive children are at risk for aggressive and antisocial conduct.

In some cases, social behavior seems to be a direct result of temperament, as is the case with shy children. In other instances, it is due to the way people respond to the child's

The adaptiveness of temperament varies with cultural circumstances. When a famine swept the homeland of the Masai people of Kenya and Tanzania, many more difficult babies than easy babies survived. The irritable behavior of the difficult infants may have ensured that they were better fed.

(Diane M. Love/Stock Boston)

goodness-of-fit model Thomas and Chess's model, which states that an effective match, or "good fit," between child-rearing practices and a child's temperament leads to favorable development and psychological adjustment. When a "poor fit" exists, the outcome is distorted development and maladjustment.

emotional style. For example, active children are often targets of negative interaction, which leads to conflict. This is illustrated by research on sibling relationships; arguments between siblings increase when one member of a sibling pair is emotionally intense or highly active (Brody, Stoneman, & McCoy, 1994; Dunn, 1994). Conflict-ridden exchanges with parents, siblings, and peers probably underlie the tendency for active children to develop into disagreeable young adults who are quick to lash out at others (Caspi, 1998). And as Chapter 12 will make clear, the link between early impulsivity and later lawbreaking and aggressive acts has much to do with the inept parenting that distractible, headstrong children often evoke. In sum, temperamental styles often stimulate certain reactions in other people, which, in turn, mold the child's development.

TEMPERAMENT AND CHILD REARING: THE GOODNESS-OF-FIT MODEL

We have already indicated that the temperaments of many children change with age. This suggests that environments do not always act in the same direction as a child's temperament. If a child's disposition interferes with learning or getting along with others, then it is important for adults to gently but consistently counteract the child's maladaptive behavior.

Thomas and Chess (1977) proposed a **goodness-of-fit model** to describe how temperament and environmental pressures can work together to produce favorable outcomes. Goodness of fit involves creating child-rearing environments that recognize each child's temperament while encouraging more adaptive functioning.

Goodness of fit helps explain why children with difficult temperaments are at high risk for later behavior problems. These children, at least in Western middle-SES families, frequently experience parenting that fits poorly with their dispositions. Without encouragement to try new experiences, their dislike of novelty can translate into to overwhelming anxiety in the face of academic and social challenges. In addition, difficult infants are less likely to receive sensitive caregiving (van den Boom & Hoeksma, 1994). By the second year, their parents often resort to angry, punitive discipline. In response, the child reacts with defiance and disobedience. Then parents often behave inconsistently, rewarding the child's noncompliant behavior by giving in (Lee & Bates, 1985). The difficult child's temperament combined with harsh, inconsistent child rearing forms a poor fit that maintains and even increases the child's irritable, conflict-ridden style. In contrast, when parents are positive and involved with their babies and establish a happy, stable home life despite their child's negative behavior, infant difficultness declines (Belsky, Fish, & Isabella, 1991).

According to the goodness-of-fit model, caregiving is not just responsive to the child's temperament. It also depends on life conditions and cultural values. During a famine in Africa, difficult temperament was associated with infant survival—probably because difficult babies demanded and received more maternal attention and food (deVries, 1984). In low-SES Puerto Rican families, difficult children are treated with sensitivity and patience; they are not at risk for adjustment problems (Gannon & Korn, 1983).

Similarly, in Western nations, shy, withdrawn children are regarded as socially incompetent, yet Chinese adults evaluate such children positively—as advanced in social maturity and understanding (Chen, Rubin, & Li, 1995). Expectations for restrained, persistent child behavior are so strong in Thailand that Thai teachers regard children as inattentive and unmotivated who would be seen as quite normal in the United States (Weisz et al., 1995).

In cultures where particular temperamental styles are linked to adjustment problems, an effective match between rearing conditions and child temperament is best accomplished early, before unfavorable temperament–environment relationships have had a chance to produce maladjustment that is hard to undo. Both difficult and shy children benefit from warm, accepting parenting that makes firm but reasonable demands for mastering new experiences. In the case of reserved, inactive infants and toddlers, highly stimulating maternal behavior (frequent questioning, instructing, and pointing out objects) fosters exploration of the environment. Yet these same parental behaviors inhibit exploration in very active babies. For these children, too much adult intervention dampens their natural curiosity (Gandour, 1989; Miceli et al., 1998).

The goodness-of-fit model reminds us that infants come into the world with unique dispositions that adults need to accept. Parents can neither take full credit for their children's virtues nor be blamed for all their faults. But parents can turn an environment that exaggerates a child's problems into one that builds on the youngster's strengths, helping each child master the challenges of development.

In the following sections, we will see that goodness of fit is also at the heart of infant–caregiver attachment. This first intimate relationship grows out of interaction between parent and baby, to which the emotional styles of both partners contribute.

BRIEF REVIEW

Children's unique temperamental styles are apparent in infancy, through assessments of children's behavior and psychophysiological reactions. However, the stability of temperament is only weak to moderate because temperament itself develops with age. Long-term prediction is best achieved from the second year of life and after. Heredity influences temperament, but child-rearing experiences affect whether a child's emotional style is sustained or modified over time. Nonshared environmental influences—experiences within and beyond the family that differ for each sibling—appear especially salient in personality development.

Temperamental traits are good predictors of cognitive and social functioning. A good fit between parenting practices and child temperament helps children whose temperaments predispose them to adjustment problems function more adaptively. Cultural values affect the meaning of temperamental traits, parents' and teachers' reaction to those traits, and their consequences for children's development.

ASK YOURSELF . . .

◆ *Slow-to-warm-up children are at risk for becoming withdrawn and constricted, whereas difficult children are at risk for both anxious withdrawal and defiant, aggressive behavior. Explain these relationships by considering the characteristics of each temperamental style and the parenting practices it often evokes.*

◆ **CONNECTIONS**
About 35 percent of children with attention-deficit hyperactivity disorder (ADHD) become defiant and aggressive. Using your knowledge of temperament and child rearing, explain why these children often display antisocial behavior. (See Chapter 7, page 289.)

Development of Attachment

Attachment is the strong, affectional tie we feel for special people in our lives that leads us to feel pleasure and joy when we interact with them and to be comforted by their nearness during times of stress. By the second half of the first year, infants have become attached to familiar people who have responded to their needs for physical care and stimulation. Watch babies of this age, and notice how parents are singled out for special attention. A whole range of responses are reserved just for them. For example, when the mother enters the room, the baby breaks into a broad, friendly smile. When she picks him up, he pats her face, explores her hair, and snuggles against her body. When he feels anxious, he crawls into her lap and clings closely.

EARLY THEORIES OF ATTACHMENT

Freud first suggested that the infant's emotional tie to the mother provides the foundation for all later relationships. We will see shortly that research on the consequences of attachment is consistent with Freud's idea. But attachment has also been the subject of intense theoretical debate. Turn back to the description of Freud's and Erikson's theories in Chapter 1 (see pages 16–18), and notice how *psychoanalytic theory* regards feeding as the central context in which caregivers and babies build this close emotional bond. *Behaviorism,* too, emphasizes the importance of feeding, but for different reasons. According to a well-known behaviorist *drive reduction explanation,* as the caregiver satisfies the baby's hunger (*primary drive*), her presence becomes a *secondary* or *learned drive* because it is paired with tension relief. As a result, the baby prefers all kinds of stimuli that accompany feeding, including the parent's soft caresses, warm smiles, and tender words of comfort (Sears, Maccoby, & Levin, 1957).

Although feeding is an important context in which mothers and babies build a close relationship, attachment does not depend on hunger satisfaction. In the 1950s, a famous experiment showed that rhesus monkeys reared with terry cloth and wire mesh "surrogate mothers" spent their days clinging to the terrycloth substitute, even though the wire mesh "mother" held the bottle and infants had to climb on it to be fed (Harlow & Zimmerman, 1959). Observations of human infants also reveal that they become attached to family

attachment The strong affectional tie that humans feel toward special people in their lives.

Baby monkeys reared with "surrogate mothers" from birth preferred to cling to a soft terry cloth "mother" instead of a wire mesh "mother" that held a bottle. These findings reveal that the drive-reduction explanation of attachment, which assumes that the mother-infant relationship is based on feeding, is incorrect.

(Martin Rogers/Stock Boston)

ethological theory of attachment A theory formulated by Bowlby, which views the infant's emotional tie to the familiar caregiver as an evolved response that promotes survival.

separation anxiety An infant's distressed reaction to the departure of the familiar caregiver.

internal working model A set of expectations derived from early caregiving experiences concerning the availability of attachment figures, their likelihood of providing support during times of stress, and the self's interaction with those figures that affect all future close relationships.

Strange Situation A procedure involving short separations from and reunions with the parent that assesses the quality of the attachment bond.

members who seldom feed them, including fathers, siblings, and grandparents. And perhaps you have noticed that toddlers in Western cultures who sleep alone and experience frequent daytime separations from their parents sometimes develop strong emotional ties to cuddly objects, such as blankets or teddy bears (Passman, 1987). Yet such objects have never played a role in infant feeding!

Another problem with drive reduction and psychoanalytic accounts of attachment is that a great deal is said about the caregiver's contribution to the attachment relationship. But much less attention is given to the importance of the infant's characteristics and behavior.

BOWLBY'S ETHOLOGICAL THEORY

Today, **ethological theory of attachment** is the most widely accepted view of the infant's emotional tie to the caregiver. Recall from Chapter 1 that according to ethology, many human behaviors have evolved over the history of our species because they promote survival. John Bowlby (1969), who first applied this idea to the infant–caregiver bond, was originally a psychoanalyst. In his theory, he retained the psychoanalytic idea that quality of attachment to the caregiver has profound implications for the child's feelings of security and capacity to form trusting relationships.

At the same time, Bowlby was inspired by Konrad Lorenz's studies of imprinting in baby geese (see Chapter 1). He believed that the human infant, like the young of other animal species, is endowed with a set of built-in behaviors that help keep the parent nearby, increasing the chances that the infant will be protected from danger. Contact with the parent also ensures that the baby will be fed, but Bowlby was careful to point out that feeding is not the basis for attachment. Instead, the attachment bond has strong biological roots. It can best be understood within an evolutionary framework in which survival of the species is of utmost importance.

According to Bowlby, the infant's relationship to the parent begins as a set of innate signals that call the adult to the baby's side. Over time, a true affectional bond develops, which is supported by new emotional and cognitive capacities as well as a history of warm, sensitive care. The development of attachment takes place in four phases:

1. The *preattachment phase* (birth to 6 weeks). A variety of built-in signals—grasping, smiling, crying, and gazing into the adult's eyes—help bring newborn babies into close contact with other humans. Once an adult responds, infants encourage her to remain nearby, since they are comforted when picked up, stroked, and talked to softly. Babies of this age can recognize their own mother's smell and voice (see Chapter 4). However, they are not yet attached to her, since they do not mind being left with an unfamiliar adult.

2. The *"attachment-in-the-making"* phase (6 weeks to 6–8 months). During this phase, infants start to respond differently to a familiar caregiver than to a stranger. For example, the baby smiles, laughs, and babbles more freely when interacting with the mother and quiets more quickly when she picks him up. As infants engage in face-to-face interaction with the parent and experience relief from distress, they learn that their own actions affect the behavior of those around them. They begin to develop a sense of trust—the expectation that the caregiver will respond when signaled. But babies still do not protest when separated from the parent, despite the fact that they can distinguish her from unfamiliar people.

3. The *phase of "clear-cut" attachment* (6–8 months to 18 months–2 years). Now attachment to the familiar caregiver is evident. Babies of this period show **separation anxiety,** in that they become upset when the adult on whom they have come to rely leaves. Separation anxiety appears universally around the world after 6 months of age, increasing until about 15 months (see Figure 10.3). Its appearance suggests that infants have a clear understanding that the caregiver continues to exist when not in view. Consistent with this idea, babies who have not yet mastered Piagetian object permanence usually do not become anxious when separated from their mothers (Lester et al., 1974).

Besides protesting the parent's departure, older infants and toddlers act more deliberately to maintain her presence. They approach, follow, and climb on her in preference to others. And they use her as a secure base from which to explore, venturing into the environment and then returning for emotional support, as indicated earlier in this chapter.

4. *Formation of a reciprocal relationship* (18 months–2 years and on). By the end of the second year, rapid growth in representation and language permits toddlers to understand some of the factors that influence the parent's coming and going and to predict her return. As a result, separation protest declines. Now children start to negotiate with the caregiver, using requests and persuasion to alter her goals rather than crawling after and clinging to her. For example, one 2-year-old asked her mother to read a story before leaving her with a babysitter. The extra time with her mother, along with an explanation of where she was going ("to a movie with Daddy") and when she would be back ("right after you go to sleep") helped this child withstand her mother's absence.

This infant becomes upset when her mother hands her to a caregiver and starts to leave for work. After 6 months of age, separation anxiety appears universally around the world. (Laura Dwight/PhotoEdit)

According to Bowlby (1980), out of their experiences during these four phases, children construct an enduring affectional tie to the caregiver that permits them to use the attachment figure as a secure base across time and distance. This inner representation becomes a vital part of personality. It serves as an **internal working model,** or set of expectations about the availability of attachment figures, their likelihood of providing support during times of stress, and the self's interaction with those figures. This image becomes the model, or guide, for all future close relationships—through childhood and adolescence and into adult life (Bretherton, 1992).

MEASURING THE SECURITY OF ATTACHMENT

Although virtually all family-reared babies become attached to a familiar caregiver by the second year, the quality of this relationship differs greatly from child to child. Some infants appear especially relaxed and secure in the presence of the caregiver; they know they can count on her for protection and support. Others seem more anxious and uncertain.

A widely used technique for measuring the quality of attachment between 1 and 2 years of age is the **Strange Situation.** In designing it, Mary Ainsworth and her colleagues (1978) reasoned that if the development of attachment has gone along well, infants and toddlers should use the parent as a secure base from which to explore an unfamiliar playroom. In addition, when the parent leaves for a brief period of time, the child should show

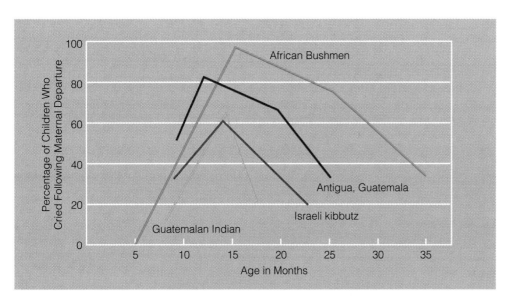

FIGURE 10.3

Development of separation anxiety. In cultures around the world, separation anxiety emerges in the second half of the first year, increasing until about 15 months and then declining.

(From J. Kagan, R. B. Kearsley, & P. R. Zelazo, 1978, *Infancy: Its Place in Human Development,* Cambridge, MA: Harvard University Press, p. 107. Copyright © 1978 by the President and Fellows of Harvard College. All rights reserved. Reprinted by permission.)

TABLE 10.3

Episodes in the Strange Situation

Episode	Events	Attachment Behaviors Observed
1	Experimenter introduces parent and baby to playroom and then leaves.	
2	Parent is seated while baby plays with toys.	Parent as a secure base
3	Stranger enters, is seated, and talks to parent.	Reaction to unfamiliar adult
4	Parent leaves room. Stranger responds to baby and offers comfort if upset.	Separation anxiety
5	Parent returns, greets baby and offers comfort if necessary. Stranger leaves room.	Reaction to reunion
6	Parent leaves room.	Separation anxiety
7	Stranger enters room and offers comfort.	Ability to be soothed by stranger
8	Parent returns, greets baby, offers comfort if necessary, and tries to reinterest baby in toys.	Reaction to reunion

Note: Episode 1 lasts about 30 seconds; the remaining episodes each last about 3 minutes. Separation episodes are cut short if the baby becomes very upset. Reunion episodes are extended if the baby needs more time to calm down and return to play.
Source: Ainsworth et al., 1978.

separation anxiety, and an unfamiliar adult should be less comforting than the parent. As summarized in Table 10.3, the Strange Situation takes the baby through eight short episodes in which brief separations from and reunions with the parent occur.

Observing the responses of infants to these episodes, researchers have identified a secure attachment pattern and three patterns of insecurity (Ainsworth et al., 1978; Main & Solomon, 1990). They are as follows:

- **Secure attachment.** These infants use the parent as a secure base. When separated, they may or may not cry, but if they do, it is due to the parent's absence, since they show a strong preference for her over the stranger. When the parent returns, they actively seek contact, and their crying is reduced immediately. About 65 percent of American babies show this pattern.

- **Avoidant attachment.** These infants seem unresponsive to the parent when she is present. When she leaves, they are usually not distressed, and they react to the stranger in much the same way as to the parent. During reunion, they avoid or are slow to greet the parent, and when picked up, they often fail to cling. About 20 percent of American babies show this pattern.

- **Resistant attachment.** Before separation, these infants seek closeness to the parent and often fail to explore. When she returns, they display angry, resistive behavior, sometimes hitting and pushing. In addition, many continue to cry after being picked up and cannot be comforted easily. About 10 to 15 percent of American infants show this pattern.

- **Disorganized/disoriented attachment.** This pattern reflects the greatest insecurity. At reunion, these infants show a variety of confused, contradictory behaviors. For example, they might look away while being held by the parent or approach her with flat, depressed emotion. Most of these babies communicate their disorientation with a dazed facial expression. A few cry out unexpectedly after having calmed down or display odd, frozen postures. About 5 to 10 percent of American infants show this pattern.

Infants' reactions in the Strange Situation closely resemble their use of the parent as a secure base and their response to separation at home (Blanchard & Main, 1979). For this reason, the procedure is a powerful tool for assessing attachment security.

Recently, an alternative, more efficient method has become popular: the **Attachment Q-Sort** (Waters et al., 1995). It is suitable for children between 1 and 5 years of age. An observer—the parent or an expert informant—sorts a set of 90 descriptors of attachment-related behaviors (such as "Child greets mother with a big smile when she enters the room" and "If mother moves very far, child follows along") into nine categories, ranging

secure attachment The quality of attachment characterizing infants who are distressed by parental separation and easily comforted by the parent when she returns.

avoidant attachment The quality of insecure attachment characterizing infants who are usually not distressed by parental separation and who avoid the parent when she returns.

resistant attachment The quality of insecure attachment characterizing infants who remain close to the parent before departure and display angry, resistive behavior when she returns.

disorganized/disoriented attachment The quality of insecure attachment characterizing infants who respond in a confused, contradictory fashion when reunited with the parent.

Attachment Q-Sort An efficient method for assessing the quality of the attachment bond, in which a parent or an expert informant sorts a set of 90 descriptors of attachment-related behaviors on the basis of how well they characterize the child. A score permits children to be assigned to securely or insecurely attached groups.

from highly descriptive to not at all descriptive of the child. Then a score is computed that permits children to be assigned to securely or insecurely attached groups. Q-Sort responses of expert observers correspond well with Strange Situation attachment classifications (Pederson et al., 1998). And when mothers are carefully trained and supervised, their responses are reasonably consistent with those of expert observers (Seifer et al., 1996; Teti & McGourty, 1996).

STABILITY OF ATTACHMENT

Studies assessing the stability of attachment patterns between 1 and 2 years of age yield a wide range of findings. In some, the percentage of children who continue to respond to the parent in a similar fashion is as low as 30 to 40 percent; in others, it is as high as 70 to 90 percent. Reviewing the evidence, Ross Thompson (1998) concludes, "[A]ttachment security cannot generally be presumed to be temporally consistent" (p. 56).

A closer look at which infants change and which ones stay the same yields a more consistent picture. Securely attached babies more often maintain their attachment status than do insecure babies, whose relationship with the caregiver is, by definition, fragile and unreliable. In addition, for middle-SES families with stable life conditions, quality of attachment is usually secure and fairly stable. But for low-SES families with many daily stresses, attachment status is more unstable (Owen et al., 1984; Vaughn et al., 1979). And for families undergoing major life changes, such as a shift in employment or marital status, quality of attachment is also likely to change, sometimes positively and sometimes negatively (Thompson, Lamb, & Estes, 1982).

Yet in a recent study that looked at family circumstances between two Strange Situation assessments during the second year, this stability and instability remained hard to explain (Belsky et al., 1996). As Thomspon (1998) points out, family stress and major life changes may not, by themselves, be responsible for shifts in attachment quality over time. Instead, parents' capacity to cope with such changes and maintain a stable relationship with the child may be the crucial factor. When we take up factors that predict attachment security, we will consider evidence in agreement with this idea.

The research just described reveals substantial, early short-term instability in attachment quality. Yet two studies, one carried out in Germany and one in the United States, reported high long-term stability: More than 80 percent of children assessed in the Strange Situation in infancy responded similarly to the parent when reobserved in a laboratory reunion situation at age 6 (Main & Cassidy, 1988; Wartner et al., 1994). These children were from middle-SES homes, and they may have encountered few disruptions in their parental relationships. And perhaps the development of inner representations of attachment quality introduced greater stability, at least during the preschool years. In sum, much remains to be discovered about the stability of attachment and the complex array of factors that contribute to it.

CULTURAL VARIATIONS

Cross-cultural evidence indicates that attachment patterns may have to be interpreted differently in other cultures. For example, as Figure 10.4 reveals, German infants show considerably more avoidant attachment than American babies do. But German parents encourage their infants to be nonclingy and independent, so the baby's behavior may be an intended outcome of cultural beliefs and practices (Grossmann et al., 1985). An unusually high number of Japanese infants display a resistant response, but the reaction may not represent true insecurity. Japanese mothers rarely leave their babies in the care of unfamiliar people, so the Strange Situation probably creates far greater stress for them than it does for infants who frequently experience maternal separations (Miyake, Chen, & Campos, 1985; Takahashi, 1990).

FIGURE 10.4

A cross-cultural comparision of infants' reactions in the Strange Situation. A high percentage of German babies seem avoidantly attached, whereas a substantial number of Japanese infants appear resistantly attached. Note that these responses may not reflect true insecurity. Instead, they are probably due to cultural differences in rearing practices.

(Adapted from van IJzendoorn & Kroonenberg, 1988.)

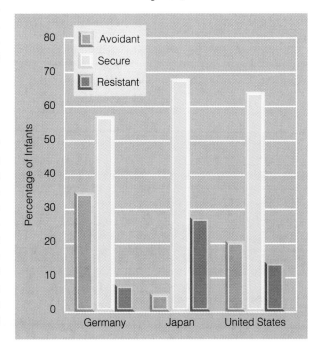

Despite these cultural variations, the secure pattern is still the most common attachment classification in all societies studied to date (van IJzendoorn & Kroonenberg, 1988). And when the Attachment Q-Sort is used to assess conceptions of the ideal child, mothers in diverse cultures—China, Germany, Israel, Japan, Norway, and the United States—prefer that their young children express their feelings of attachment by using the mother as a secure base for exploration (Posada et al., 1995).

FACTORS THAT AFFECT ATTACHMENT SECURITY

What factors might influence attachment security? First, simply having an opportunity to establish a close relationship with one or a few caregivers should be crucially important. Second, warm, responsive parenting should lead to greater attachment security. Third, since babies actively contribute to the attachment relationship, an infant's characteristics should make a difference in how well it proceeds. And finally, because children and parents are embedded in larger contexts, family circumstances and parents' internal working models should influence attachment quality. In the following sections, we examine each of these factors.

■ **MATERNAL DEPRIVATION.** The powerful effect of the baby's affectional tie to the familiar caregiver is most evident when it is absent. In a series of landmark studies, René Spitz (1946) observed institutionalized infants who had been given up by their mothers between the third month and the end of the first year. The babies were placed on a large ward where they shared a nurse with at least seven other babies. In contrast to the happy, outgoing behavior they had shown before separation, they wept and withdrew from their surroundings, lost weight, and had difficulty sleeping. If a caregiver whom the baby could get to know did not replace the mother, the depression deepened rapidly.

These institutionalized infants experienced emotional difficulties because they were prevented from forming a bond with one or a few adults (Rutter, 1996). A more recent study of maternally deprived children supports this conclusion. Researchers followed the development of infants reared in an institution that offered a good caregiver–child ratio and a rich selection of books and toys. However, staff turnover was so rapid that the average child had a total of 50 different caregivers by the age of 4½! Many of these children became "late adoptees" who were placed in homes after age 4. Most developed deep ties with their adoptive parents, indicating that a first attachment bond can develop as late as 4 to 6 years of age (Tizard & Rees, 1975).

But throughout childhood and adolescence, these youngsters were more likely to display emotional and social problems, including an excessive desire for adult attention, "overfriendliness" to unfamiliar adults and peers, and few friendships (Hodges & Tizard, 1989; Tizard & Hodges, 1978). Although follow-ups into adulthood are necessary to be sure, these results leave open the possibility that fully normal development depends on establishing close bonds with caregivers during the first few years of life.

■ **QUALITY OF CAREGIVING.** What kind of parental behavior promotes attachment? Research reveals that **sensitive caregiving** distinguishes securely from insecurely attached infants. Examining 66 studies involving over 4,000 mother–infant pairs, investigators reported that the extent to which mothers responded promptly, consistently, and appropriately to infant signals and held their babies tenderly and carefully was moderately related to attachment security (De Wolff & van IJzendoorn, 1997). In contrast, insecurely attached infants tend to have mothers who engage in less physical contact, handle them awkwardly, behave in a "routine" manner, and are sometimes negative, resentful, and rejecting (Ainsworth et al., 1978; Isabella, 1993; Pederson & Moran, 1996).

Are there additional caregiver behaviors that support babies' feelings of trust? In several studies, a special form of communication called **interactional synchrony** separated the experiences of secure from insecure babies (Isabella & Belsky, 1991; Isabella, Belsky, & von Eye, 1989; Kochanska, 1998). It is best described as a sensitively tuned "emotional dance," in which caregiver–infant interaction appears to be mutually rewarding. The caregiver responds to infant signals in a well-timed, appropriate fashion. In addition, both partners match emotional states, especially the positive ones.

sensitive caregiving Caregiving involving prompt, consistent, and appropriate responding to infant signals.

interactional synchrony A sensitively tuned "emotional dance," in which the caregiver responds to infant signals in a well-timed, appropriate fashion and both partners match emotional states, especially the positive ones.

But more evidence is needed to document the link between interactional synchrony and secure attachment. Other research reveals that only 30 percent of the time are exchanges between mothers and their babies perfectly "in sync" with one another. The remaining 70 percent of the time, interactive errors occur (Tronick, 1989). Perhaps warm, sensitive caregivers and their babies become especially skilled at repairing these errors and returning to a synchronous state.

Furthermore, finely tuned, coordinated interaction and matching of positive emotional states do not always predict attachment security (Kochanska, 1998). And these features do not characterize mother–infant interaction everywhere. Among the Gusii people of Kenya, mothers rarely cuddle, hug, and interact playfully with their babies, although they are very responsive to their infants' needs (LeVine et al., 1994). This suggests that secure attachment depends on attentive caregiving, but its association with moment-by-moment contingent interaction is probably limited to certain cultures.

Compared with securely attached infants, avoidant babies tend to receive overstimulating, intrusive care. Their mothers might, for example, talk energetically to a baby who is looking away or falling asleep. By avoiding the mother, these infants appear to be escaping from overwhelming interaction. Resistant infants often experience inconsistent care. Their mothers are minimally involved in caregiving and unresponsive to infant signals. Yet when the baby begins to explore, these mothers interfere, shifting the infant's attention back to themselves. As a result, the baby shows exaggerated dependence as well as anger and frustration at the mother's lack of involvement (Cassidy & Berlin, 1994; Isabella & Belsky, 1991).

When caregiving is extremely inadequate, it is a powerful predictor of disruptions in attachment. Child abuse and neglect (topics we will consider in Chapter 14) are associated with all three forms of attachment insecurity. Among maltreated infants, the most worrisome classification—disorganized/disoriented attachment—is especially high (Lyons-Ruth & Block, 1996). Infants of depressed mothers also show the uncertain behaviors of this pattern, mixing closeness, resistance, and avoidance while looking very sad and depressed themselves (Lyons-Ruth et al., 1990; Teti et al., 1995).

■ INFANT CHARACTERISTICS. Since attachment is the result of a *relationship* that builds between two partners, infant characteristics should affect how easily it is established. In Chapter 3, we saw that prematurity, birth complications, and newborn illness make caregiving more taxing for parents. In poverty-stricken, stressed families, these infant conditions are linked to attachment insecurity (Wille, 1991). But when parents have the time and patience to care for a baby with special needs and the infant is not very sick, at-risk newborns fare quite well in attachment security (Pederson & Moran, 1995).

Infants also vary considerably in temperament, but its role in attachment security has been intensely debated. Some researchers believe that infants who are irritable and fearful may simply react to brief separations with intense anxiety, regardless of the parent's sensitivity to the baby (Kagan, 1989, 1998a). Consistent with this view, proneness to distress in early infancy is moderately related to later insecure attachment (Seifer et al., 1996; Vaughn et al., 1992).

But other evidence argues for temperament as only a modest influence! First, quality of attachment to the mother and the father is often similar, a resemblance that could be due to parents' tendency to react similarly to their baby's temperament (Fox, Kimmerly, & Schafer, 1991; Rosen & Rothbaum, 1993). Yet quite a few infants establish distinct attachment relationships with each parent and with their professional caregivers (Goossens & van IJzendoorn, 1990). If infant temperament were very powerful, we would expect attachment classification to be more constant across familiar adults than it is.

Second, caregiving seems to be involved in the relationship between irritability and attachment security. In one study, distress-prone infants who became insecurely attached

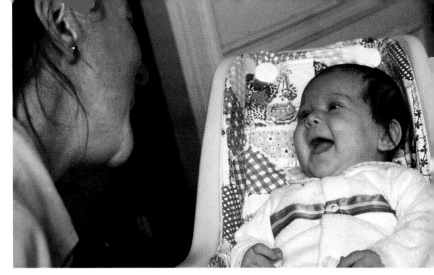

This mother and baby engage in a sensitively tuned form of communication called interactional synchrony in which they match emotional states, especially the positive ones. Interactional synchrony may support the development of secure attachment, but it does not characterize mother–infant interaction in all cultures.

(Julie O'Neil/The Picture Cube)

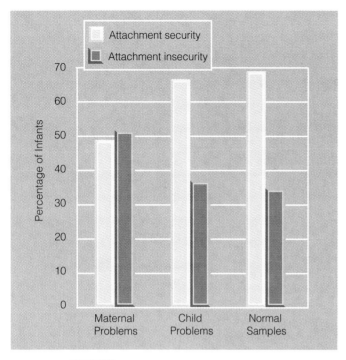

FIGURE 10.5

Comparison of the effects of maternal and child problem behaviors on the attachment bond. Maternal problems were associated with a sharp rise in attachment insecurity. In contrast, child problems had little impact on the rate of attachment security and insecurity, which resembled that of normal samples.

(Adapted from van IJzendoorn et al., 1992.)

tended to have rigid, controlling mothers who probably had difficulty altering their immediate plans to comfort a baby who often cried (Mangelsdorf et al., 1990). And in another study, an intervention that taught mothers how to respond sensitively to their irritable 6-month-olds led to gains in maternal responsiveness and in children's attachment security, exploration, cooperativeness, and sociability that were still present at 3½ years of age (van den Boom, 1995).

Finally, extensive research confirms that caregiving can override the impact of infant characteristics on attachment security. When researchers combined data from over 34 studies including more than a thousand mother–infant pairs, they found that maternal problems—such as mental illness, teenage parenthood, and child abuse—were associated with a sharp rise in attachment insecurity (see Figure 10.5). In contrast, child problems—ranging from prematurity and developmental delays to serious physical disabilities and psychological disorders—had little impact on attachment quality (van IJzendoorn et al., 1992).

Infants with cleft lip and palate offer a dramatic illustration of the relative contribution of infant traits and caregiving to attachment. These babies' facial deformities lead to feeding difficulties and frequent ear infections—factors that promote infant irritability and reduced social responsiveness. Although the cleft lip is usually repaired by age 3 to 4 months and the palate by age 2 years, the surgeries are highly stressful and require many follow-up medical interventions. Yet by 1 year of age, rate of attachment security for infants with clefts is just as high as for other babies (Speltz et al., 1997).

A major reason that temperament and other child characteristics do not show strong relationships with attachment quality may be that their influence depends on goodness of fit. From this perspective, *many* child attributes can lead to secure attachment as long as the caregiver sensitively adjusts her behavior to fit the baby's needs (Seifer & Schiller, 1995; Sroufe, 1985). But when a parent's capacity to do so is strained—for example, by her own personality or by stressful living conditions—then difficult infants are at greater risk for attachment problems.

■ **FAMILY CIRCUMSTANCES.** We have already indicated, in this and previous chapters, that quality of caregiving can be fully understood only in terms of the larger social environment in which parent and child are embedded. Job loss, a failing marriage, financial difficulties, and other stressors can undermine attachment by interfering with the sensitivity of parental care. Or they can affect babies' sense of security directly, by exposing them to angry adult interactions or unfavorable child-care arrangements (Owen & Cox, 1997; Thompson, 1998).

The arrival of a new sibling illustrates how family circumstances can affect attachment quality. In one study, firstborn preschoolers as a group decreased in attachment security after the birth of the baby. But children who responded this way often had mothers who were depressed, anxious, or hostile just before the birth. These maternal symptoms were associated with a rise in marital friction (which the firstborns probably sensed) as well as with unfavorable mother–firstborn interaction. When mothers coped well with the birth and stayed affectionately involved with their older child, preschoolers maintained a secure attachment bond (Teti et al., 1996).

The availability of social supports, especially a good marriage and assistance with caregiving, reduces family stress and predicts greater attachment security (Pianta, Sroufe, & Egeland, 1989). Unfortunately, not all parents have access to supportive family ties. In one study of poverty-stricken depressed and abusive mothers, home visitors provided an accepting, trustworthy relationship, offered help in making use of community resources, and modeled and reinforced more effective caregiving over a 9- to 18-month period. Home-visited babies scored ten points higher than controls in mental development and were twice as likely to be securely attached. The longer lasting the intervention, the more involved high-risk mothers were with their babies (Lyons-Ruth et al., 1990).

■ **PARENTS' INTERNAL WORKING MODELS.** Parents bring to the family context a long history of attachment experiences, out of which they construct internal working models that they apply to the bonds established with their babies. To assess parents' "state of mind" with respect to attachment, Carol George, Nancy Kaplan, and Mary Main (1985) devised the Adult Attachment Interview. It asks adults to recall and evaluate childhood attachment experiences. Parents' *interpretations*, rather than the positive or negative nature of the events themselves, provide an overall impression of the adult's working model. Four types of attachment representations, summarized in Table 10.4, have been identified.

Quality of maternal working models is clearly related to attachment in infancy and early childhood—results replicated in studies carried out in Canada, Germany, Great Britain, the Netherlands, and the United States. Autonomous/secure mothers typically have secure infants, dismissing mothers have avoidant infants, preoccupied mothers have resistant infants, and unresolved mothers have disorganized infants (Benoit & Parker, 1994; van IJzendoorn, 1995a). Caregiving behavior helps explain these associations. Mothers with autonomous/secure representations are warmer and more sensitive with their babies. They are also more likely to be supportive and to encourage learning and mastery in their older children, who, in turn, are more affectionate and comfortably interactive with them (Cohn et al., 1992; Pederson et al., 1998).

Fathers' responses to the Adult Attachment Interview are less clearly related to attachment than are mothers' responses, perhaps because fathers typically spend less time with infants (van IJzendoorn & Bakermans-Kranenburg, 1996). Nevertheless, the quality of fathers' marital and parental relationships predicts their attitudes toward their babies. This suggests that working models also provide an important foundation for infant–father emotional ties (Cox et al., 1992).

But we must be careful not to assume any direct transfer of parents' childhood experiences to quality of attachment with their own children. Internal working models are *reconstructed memories* affected by many factors, including relationship experiences over the life course, personality, and current life satisfaction. Consequently, adults with unhappy upbringings are not destined to become insensitive parents. Rather, the way parents *view* their childhoods—their ability to integrate new information into their working models, to come to terms with negative life events, and to look back on their own parents in an understanding, forgiving way—is much more influential in how they rear their children than is the actual history of care they received (van IJzendoorn, 1995b).

TABLE **10.4**

Relationship of Mothers' Internal Working Models to Infant Attachment Security

Type of Maternal Working Model	Description	Infant Attachment Classifications[a]
Autonomous/ secure	These mothers show objectivity and balance in discussing their childhood experiences, whether they were positive or negative. They neither idealize their parents nor feel angry about the past. Their explanations are coherent and believable.	Secure
Dismissing	These mothers devalue the importance of their attachment relationships. They tend to idealize their parents without being able to recall specific experiences. What they do recall is discussed intellectually, with little emotion.	Avoidant
Overinvolved	These mothers talk about their childhood experiences with highly charged emotion, sometimes expressing anger toward their parents. They appear overwhelmed and confused about their early attachments and cannot discuss them coherently.	Resistant
Unresolved	These mothers show characteristics of any of the three other patterns. At the same time, they reason in a disorganized and confused way when loss of a loved one or experiences of physical or sexual abuse are discussed.	Disorganized/ disoriented

Note: [a]Correspondences between type of maternal working model and infant attachment classification hold for 60 to 70 percent of mother–infant pairs.
Sources: Benoit & Parker, 1994; Main & Goldwyn, 1994; Pederson et al, 1998.

MULTIPLE ATTACHMENTS: THE FATHER'S SPECIAL ROLE

We have already indicated that babies develop attachments to a variety of familiar people—not just mothers, but fathers, siblings, grandparents, and professional caregivers. Although Bowlby (1969) made room for multiple attachments in his theory, he believed that infants are predisposed to direct their attachment behaviors to a single special person, especially when they are distressed. Consistent with this view, when an anxious, unhappy 1-year-old is permitted to choose between the mother and the father as a source of comfort and security, the infant usually chooses the mother (Lamb, 1997). Yet this preference declines over the second year of life until, around 18 months, it is no longer present. And when babies are not distressed, they approach, touch, ask to be held by, vocalize to, and smile at both parents equally (Clarke-Stewart, 1978).

Fathers are salient figures in the lives of babies, building relationships with them shortly after birth. Observations of and interviews with fathers reveal that most are overjoyed at the infant's arrival; characterize the experience as "awesome," "indescribable," or "unforgettable"; and display intense interest and involvement in their newborn child (Bader, 1995). Regardless of SES or participation in childbirth classes, fathers touch, look at, talk to, and kiss their newborn babies just as much as mothers do (Parke & Tinsley, 1981).

Like mothers', fathers' sensitive caregiving predicts secure attachment—an effect that becomes stronger the more time they spend with their babies (Cox et al., 1992; van IJzendoorn & De Wolff, 1997). Also, fathers of 1- to 5-year-olds enrolled in full-time day care because both parents are employed report feeling just as much anxiety about separating from their child and just as much concern about the impact of these daily separations on the child's welfare as do mothers. Today, many fathers seem to "share anxieties that mothers have traditionally borne alone" (Deater-Deckard et al., 1994, p. 346).

As infancy progresses, mothers and fathers from a variety of cultures—Australia, Israel, India, Italy, Japan, and the United States—relate to babies in different ways. Mothers devote more time to physical care and expressing affection. In contrast, fathers spend more time in playful interaction (Lamb, 1987; Roopnarine et al., 1990). Also, mothers and fathers tend to play differently with babies. Mothers more often provide toys, talk to infants, and initiate conventional games like pat-a-cake and peekaboo. In contrast, fathers tend to engage in more exciting, highly physical bouncing and lifting games, especially with their infant sons (Yogman, 1981). In view of these differences, it is not surprising that babies prefer their mothers when distressed and their fathers for playful stimulation.

However, this picture of "mother as caregiver" and "father as playmate" has changed in some families as a result of the revised work status of women. Employed mothers tend to engage in more playful stimulation of their babies than do unemployed mothers, and their husbands are somewhat more involved in caregiving (Cox et al., 1992). When fathers are the primary caregivers, they usually retain their arousing play style (Lamb & Oppenheim, 1989). Such highly involved fathers are less gender stereotyped in their beliefs; have sympathetic, friendly personalities; and regard parenthood as an especially enriching experience (Lamb, 1987; Levy-Shiff & Israelashvili, 1988).

A warm, gratifying marital relationship supports both parents' involvement with babies, but it is particularly important for fathers (Belsky, 1996). See the Cultural Influences box for cross-cultural evidence that supports this conclusion.

ATTACHMENT AND LATER DEVELOPMENT

According to psychoanalytic and ethological theories, the inner feelings of affection and security that result from building an early, healthy attachment relationship support all aspects of psychological development. Many researchers have addressed the link between infant–mother attachment and cognitive, emotional, and social development.

When playing with their babies, especially sons, fathers tend to engage in highly physical bouncing and lifting games.
(Steve Starr/Stock Boston)

Father–Infant Relationships Among the Aka

MONG THE AKA hunters and gatherers of Central Africa, fathers devote more time to infants than in any other known society. Observations reveal that Aka fathers are within arm's reach of their babies more than half the day. They pick up and cuddle their babies at least five times more often than do fathers in other African hunting-and-gathering societies.

Why are Aka fathers so involved with their babies? Research shows that when husband and wife help each other with many tasks, fathers assist more with infant care. The relationship between Aka husband and wife is unusually cooperative and intimate. Throughout the day, they share hunting, food preparation, and social and leisure activities. Babies are brought along on hunts, and mothers find it hard to carry them long distances. This explains, in part, why fathers spend so much time holding their infants. But when the Aka return to the campground, fathers continue to devote many hours to infant caregiving. The more Aka parents are together, the greater the father's interaction with his baby (Hewlett, 1992).

This Aka father spends much time in close contact with his baby. In Aka society, husband and wife share many tasks of daily living and have an unusually cooperative and intimate relationship. Infants are generally within arms reach of their fathers, who devote many hours to caregiving.

(Barry Hewlett)

In the most extensive longitudinal study of this kind, Alan Sroufe and his collaborators reported that preschoolers who were securely attached as babies showed more elaborate make-believe play and greater enthusiasm, flexibility, and persistence in problem solving by 2 years of age. At age 4, such children were rated by their preschool teachers as high in self-esteem, socially competent, cooperative, popular, and empathic. In contrast, their avoidantly attached agemates were viewed as isolated and disconnected, and those who were resistantly attached were regarded as disruptive and difficult. Studied again at age 11 in summer camp, children who were secure as infants had more favorable relationships with peers, closer friendships, and better social skills, as judged by camp counselors (Elicker, Englund, & Sroufe, 1992; Matas, Arend, & Sroufe, 1978; Shulman, Elicker, & Sroufe, 1994).

These findings have been taken by some researchers to mean that secure attachment in infancy causes improved cognitive, emotional, and social competence during later years. Yet more evidence is needed before we can be certain of this conclusion. Other short-term longitudinal studies yield a mixed picture; secure infants do not always show more favorable development than their insecure counterparts (Belsky & Cassidy, 1994). And one long-term study revealed that attachment at age 1 did not predict psychological adjustment at age 18 (Lewis, 1997).

Why is research on the long-term consequences of attachment quality as yet unclear? Michael Lamb and his colleagues (1985) suggest that *continuity of caregiving* determines whether attachment security is linked to later development. When parents respond sensitively not just in infancy but during later years, children are likely to develop favorably. In contrast, children of parents who react insensitively for a long time are at increased risk for maladjustment. In support of this interpretation, a closer look at Sroufe's longitudinal study reveals that in the few instances in which securely attached infants did develop later behavior problems, their mothers became less positive and supportive in early childhood. Similarly, the handful of insecurely attached babies who became well-adjusted preschoolers had mothers who were sensitive and provided their young children with clear structure and guidance (Egeland et al., 1990; Thompson, 1998).

Do these findings remind you of our discussion of *resiliency* in Chapter 1? A child whose parental caregiving improves or who has other compensating affectional ties can bounce back from adversity. In contrast, a child who experiences tender care in infancy but who lacks sympathetic ties later is at risk for problems. In sum, efforts to create warm, sensitive rearing environments are not just important in infancy and toddlerhood; they are crucial throughout childhood and adolescence.

Drive reduction (behaviorist) and psychoanalytic theories have been criticized for overemphasizing feeding and paying little attention to the baby's active role in establishing an attachment bond. According to ethological theory, infant–caregiver attachment has evolved because it promotes survival. In early infancy, babies' innate signals help keep the parent nearby. By 6 to 8 months, separation anxiety and use of the mother as a secure base indicate that a true attachment has formed. Representation and language help older children tolerate brief separations from the parent as they begin to rely for security on an internal working model of the attachment bond.

Research on infants deprived of a consistent caregiver suggests that fully normal development depends on establishing a close affectional bond in the first few years of life. Caregiving that is sensitive to babies' needs supports the development of secure attachment; insensitive care is linked to attachment insecurity. Infant illness and irritable and fearful temperamental styles make attachment security harder to achieve, but good parenting can override the impact of infant characteristics. By affecting caregiving, family conditions and parents' internal working models also contribute to attachment quality.

Fathers are influential attachment figures, often relating to babies through physically active play. When attachment security predicts later cognitive, emotional, and social competence, continuity of caregiving may be largely responsible.

ASK YOURSELF . . .

♦ *Fifteen-month-old Caleb's mother tends to overwhelm him with questions and instructions that are not related to his on-going actions. How would you expect Caleb to respond in the Strange Situation? Explain.*

♦ *Around Emily's first birthday, her father lost his job, and her parents argued constantly over how they would pay bills. To look for employment, several times Emily's mother left her with a familiar baby-sitter. Emily, who had previously taken such separations well, cried desperately when her mother left and both clung and pushed her mother away after she returned. Describe the change in Emily's attachment pattern, and explain what may have caused it.*

♦ **CONNECTIONS**

How does attachment security contribute to early peer sociability? (See Chapter 15, page 599.)

Attachment and Social Change: Maternal Employment and Child Care

Over the past three decades, women have entered the labor force in record numbers. Today, over 60 percent of American mothers with a child under age 2 are employed (U.S. Bureau of the Census, 1998). In response to this trend, researchers and lay people alike have raised questions about the impact of child care and daily separations of infant from parent on the attachment bond.

The Social Issues box on the following page reviews the current controversy over whether child care threatens the emotional security of young children. As you will see, the weight of evidence suggests that *quality of care,* both at home and in the child-care setting, rather than child care itself is the important factor. Research consistently shows that infants and young children exposed to poor-quality child care, regardless of whether they come from middle- or low-SES homes, score lower on measures of cognitive and social skills of life. In one American study, children who entered poor-quality child care during the first year of life and remained there over the preschool years were rated by teachers as distractible, low in task involvement, and inconsiderate of others when they reached kindergarten. (Howes, 1990).

In contrast, good child care can reduce the negative impact of a stressed, poverty-stricken home life, and it sustains the benefits of growing up in an economically advantaged family (Burchinal et al., 1996; Lamb, 1998). This conclusion is strengthened by longitudinal research in Sweden, where child care is nationally regulated and liberally funded to ensure its high quality. Compared with children reared fully at home, Swedish children enrolled in out-of-home child care before their second birthday scored higher in

Is Child Care in Infancy a Threat to Attachment Security?

RECENT RESEARCH SUGGESTS that American infants placed in full-time child care before 12 months of age are more likely than babies who remain at home to display insecure attachment—especially avoidance—in the Strange Situation. Does this mean that infants who experience daily separations from their employed parents and early placement in child care are at risk for developmental problems? Some researchers think so (Belsky, 1989, 1992; Sroufe, 1988), whereas others disagree (Clarke-Stewart, 1992; Scarr, Phillips, & McCartney, 1990). Yet a close look at the evidence reveals that we should be cautious about concluding that child care is harmful to infants.

First, in studies reporting a child care–attachment association, the rate of insecurity among child-care infants is somewhat higher than that of non–child-care infants (36 versus 29 percent), but it nevertheless resembles the overall rate of insecurity reported for children in industrialized countries around the world (Lamb, Sternberg, & Prodromidis, 1992). In fact, most infants of employed mothers are securely attached! Furthermore, not all investigations report a difference in attachment quality between child-care and home-reared infants (NICHD Early Child Care Research Network, 1997; Roggman et al., 1994).

Second, we have seen that family conditions affect attachment security. Many employed women find the pressures of handling two full-time jobs (work and motherhood) stressful. Some respond less sensitively to their babies because they are fatigued and harried, thereby risking the infant's security (Stifter, Coulehan, & Fish, 1993). Other employed mothers probably value and encourage their infant's independence. Or their babies are unfazed by brief separations in the Strange Situation because they are used to separating from their parents. In these cases, avoidance in the Strange Situation may represent healthy autonomy rather than insecurity (Lamb, 1998). As yet, there is no evidence that "avoidant" child-care infants show problems in development as they get older.

Third, poor-quality child care may contribute to a higher rate of insecure attachment among infants of employed mothers. In the NICHD Study of Early Child Care—the largest longitudinal study to date, including one thousand infants and their mothers in ten areas of the country—child care alone did not contribute to attachment insecurity. But when babies were exposed to combined home and child-care risk factors—insensitive caregiving at home with insensitive caregiving in child care, long hours in child care, or more than one child-care arrangement—the rate of insecurity increased (NICHD Early Child Care Research Network, 1997).

Finally, when young children first enter child care, they must adjust to new routines and daily separations from the parent. Under these conditions, signs of distress are expected. But after a few months, infants and toddlers enrolled in high-quality programs become more comfortable. They smile, play actively, seek comfort from sensitive caregivers they have come to know well, and begin to interact with agemates (Barnas & Cummings, 1994; Fein, Gariboldi, & Boni, 1993).

These findings reveal that assessing attachment security during the period of adaptation to child care may not provide an accurate picture of its effects on early emotional adjustment. Findings of the NICHD Study indicate that parenting has a far stronger impact on preschoolers' problem behavior than does early, extensive child care (NICHD Early Child Care

This caregiver works in a child-care center that meets rigorous, professionally established standards of quality. A generous caregiver-child ratio, a limited number of children in each room, and training in child development enable him to respond to infants' and toddlers' needs to be held, comforted, and stimulated.

(Laura Berk)

Research Network, 1998). Indeed, having the opportunity to form a warm bond with a stable professional caregiver seems to be particularly helpful to infants whose relationship with one or both parents is insecure. When followed into the preschool and early school years, such children show higher self-esteem and socially skilled behavior than do their insecurely attached agemates who did not attend day care (Egeland & Hiester, 1995).

Taken together, research suggests that some infants may be at risk for attachment insecurity due to inadequate child care and the joint pressures of full-time employment and parenthood experienced by their mothers. However, using this as evidence to justify a reduction in infant child-care services is inappropriate. When family incomes are limited or mothers who want to work are forced to stay at home, children's emotional security is not promoted.

Instead, it makes sense to increase the availability of high-quality child care and to educate parents about the vital role of sensitive caregiving in early emotional development. Look again at the signs of developmentally appropriate child care for infants and toddlers, listed in Table 10.5. For child care to foster attachment security, the professional caregiver's relationship with the baby is vital. When caregiver–child ratios are generous, group sizes are small, and caregivers are educated about child development and child rearing, caregivers' interactions are more positive (NICHD Early Child Care Research Network, 1996). Child care with these characteristics can become part of an ecological system that relieves rather than intensifies parental and child stress, thereby promoting healthy attachment and development.

FIGURE 10.6

Quality ratings of child care for infants, toddlers, and pre-schoolers in the United States. Visits were made to 400 randomly selected child-care centers in California, Colorado, Connecticut, and North Carolina. Centers were classified as (1) *inadequate*—children's needs for health and safety are not met, and there is no warmth, support, and encouragement of learning; (2) *mediocre*—children's health and safety needs are met, and there is minimal to moderate warmth, support, and encouragement of learning; or (3) *developmentally appropriate*—children's health and safety needs are met, and warmth, support, and encouragement of learning are plentiful.

(From Cost, Quality, and Outcomes Study Team, 1995, "Cost,Quality, and Child Outcomes in Child Care Centers: Key Findings and Recommendations," *Young Children 50*[4], p. 41. © Cost, Quality, and Outcomes Study Team. Adapted by permission of the author.)

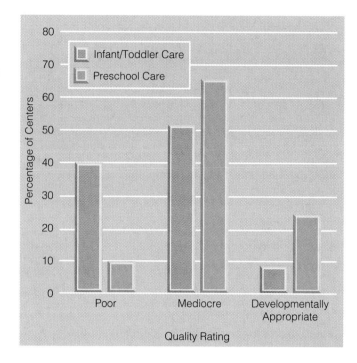

cognitive, emotional, and social competence during middle childhood and adolescence (Andersson, 1989, 1992; Broberg et al., 1997).

Recall from Chapter 1 that in contrast to most Western nations, the quality of American child care is cause for deep concern (see page 34). Standards are set by the states, and they vary greatly across the nation. In some places, caregivers need no special training in child development, and one adult is permitted to care for as many as 6 to 12 babies at once (Children's Defense Fund, 1999). Large numbers of infants and toddlers attend unlicensed child-care homes, where no one checks to see that even minimum health and safety standards are met.

In a study of several hundred randomly selected child-care centers in California, Colorado, Connecticut, and North Carolina, researchers judged that only 1 in 7 provided a level of care sufficient to promote healthy psychological development. As Figure 10.6 shows, the quality of programs for infants and toddlers was abysmal; the large majority were either mediocre or poor (Helburn, 1995). Similar conclusions have been reached about child-care homes (Galinsky et al., 1994). Unfortunately, children most likely to receive inadequate child care come from low-SES families. Their parents cannot afford to pay for the kind of services they need (Phillips et al., 1994). As a result, these children receive a double dose of vulnerability, both at home and in the child-care environment.

Table 10.5 lists signs of high-quality care that can be used in choosing a child-care setting for an infant or toddler, based on standards for **developmentally appropriate practice** devised by the National Association for the Education of Young Children (Bredekamp & Copple, 1997). These standards specify program characteristics that meet the developmental and individual needs of young children of varying ages, based on current research and the consensus of experts. Child-care centers in states with more stringent regulations offer children more stimulating and supportive daily experiences. And when centers exceed minimum state standards by meeting standards for developmentally appropriate practice, children's learning opportunities and the warmth, sensitivity, and stability of their caregivers are especially high (Helburn, 1995; Phillips, Howes, & Whitebook, 1992).

Of course, for parents to select child care that is developmentally appropriate, there must be enough good child care available. Child care in the United States is affected by a macrosystem of individualistic values and weak government regulation and funding. Furthermore, many parents think that their children's child-care experiences are higher in quality than they really are. Over 90 percent rate programs in which their children are enrolled as very good, whereas trained observers rate most of the same programs as

developmentally appropriate practice A set of standards devised by the National Association for the Education of Young Children that specifies program characteristics that meet the developmental and individual needs of young children of varying ages, based on current research and the consensus of experts.

TABLE 10.5

Signs of High-Quality Infant and Toddler Child Care

Program Characteristic	Signs of Quality
Physical setting	Indoor environment is clean, in good repair, well lighted, and well ventilated. Fenced outdoor play space is available. Setting does not appear overcrowded when children are present.
Toys and equipment	Play materials are appropriate for infants and toddlers and stored on low shelves within easy reach. Cribs, highchairs, infant seats, and child-sized tables and chairs are available. Outdoor equipment includes small riding toys, swings, slide, and sandbox.
Caregiver–child ratio	In child-care centers, caregiver–child ratio is no greater than 1 to 3 for infants and 1 to 6 for toddlers. Group size (number of children in one room) is no greater than 6 infants with 2 caregivers and 12 toddlers with 2 caregivers. In child-care homes, caregiver is responsible for no more than 6 children; within this group, no more than 2 are infants and toddlers. Staffing is consistent, so infants and toddlers can form relationships with particular caregivers.
Daily activities	Daily schedule includes times for active play, quiet play, naps, snacks, and meals. It is flexible rather than rigid, to meet the needs of individual children. Atmosphere is warm and supportive, and children are never left unsupervised.
Interactions among adults and children	Caregivers respond promptly to infants' and toddlers' distress; hold, talk to, sing, and read to them; and interact with them in a contingent manner that respects the individual child's interests and tolerance for stimulation.
Caregiver qualifications	Caregiver has at least some training in child development, first aid, and safety.
Relationships with parents	Parents are welcome anytime. Caregivers talk frequently with parents about children's behavior and development.
Licensing and accreditation	Child-care setting, whether a center or a home, is licensed by the state. Accreditation by the National Academy of Early Childhood Programs or the National Association for Family Child Care is evidence of an especially high-quality program.

Sources: Bredekamp & Copple, 1997; National Association for the Education of Young Children, 1998.

mediocre and poor (Helburn, 1995). Inability to identify good care means that many parents do not demand it, thereby leaving child-care providers with little incentive to improve quality. Consumer education efforts to help parents recognize signs of high-quality child care are desperately needed.

Recognizing that American child care is in a state of crisis, in recent years Congress allocated additional funds to subsidize its cost, especially for low-income families (see Chapter 1, page 38). Although far from meeting the total need, the increase in resources has had a positive impact on child-care quality and accessibility (Children's Defense Fund, 1999). This is a hopeful sign, since good child care is a cost-effective means of supporting the well-being of all children, and it can serve as effective early intervention for children whose development is at risk, much like the programs we discussed in Chapter 8. We will revisit the topics of parental employment and child care in Chapter 14, when we consider their consequences for development during childhood and adolescence in greater detail.

ASK YOURSELF . . .

♦ *In view of evidence on the development of attachment security, explain why each of the following indicators of child-care quality is important: caregiver stability, generous caregiver–child ratio, small group size, and frequent caregiver–parent communication.*

♦ CONNECTIONS
Explain the impact of cultural values on the status of child care in the United States compared with other Western nations. (See Chapter 1, page 36.)

SUMMARY

THE FUNCTIONS OF EMOTIONS

Describe the functionlist approach to emotional development.

♦ According to the **functionalist approach,** the broad function of **emotions** is to prompt action in the service of personal goals. Functionalist theorists regard emotions as central, adaptive forces in all aspects of human activity, including cognitive processing, social behavior, and physical health. In addition, emotions are viewed as important in the emergence of self-awareness, which opens the door to new, self-evaluative emotions. Furthermore, to adapt to their

physical and social worlds, children must gradually gain voluntary control over their emotions.

DEVELOPMENT OF EMOTIONAL EXPRESSION

How does the expression of happiness, anger, sadness, and fear change during infancy?

♦ Signs of almost all the **basic emotions** are present in early infancy and are gradually coordinated into more effective systems. By the middle of the first year, emotional expressions are well organized and meaningfully related to social events.

- Happiness strengthens the parent-child bond and reflects as well as supports cognitive and physical mastery. As infants' sensitivity to visual patterns improves, the **social smile** appears between 6 and 10 weeks. By 3 months, infants smile most often when interacting with familiar people. Soon laughter, associated with faster information processing, emerges.

- Anger and fear, especially in the form of **stranger anxiety,** increase in the second half of the first year as infants become better able to evaluate objects and events. These emotions have special adaptive value as infants' motor capacities improve. Once fear develops, infants start to use the familiar caregiver as a **secure base** from which to explore. Expressions of sadness appear in response to pain, removal of an object, brief separations, and disruptions of caregiver–infant communication, but they are less frequent than anger.

Describe the development of self-conscious emotions, emotional self-regulation, and conformity to emotional display rules.

- At the end of the second year, self-awareness and adult instruction provide the foundation for **self-conscious emotions,** such as shame, embarrassment, and pride. With age, self-conscious emotions become more internally governed. The presence of others is no longer necessary to evoke them, and pride, guilt, and shame are limited to situations in which children feel personally responsible for an outcome.

- **Emotional self-regulation** emerges from the early infant–caregiver relationship. As motor, cognitive, and language development proceed, children gradually acquire more effective self-regulatory strategies. Adult modeling and conversations with children about emotional challenges foster emotional self-regulation. Children who experience negative emotion intensely find it harder to inhibit their feelings.

- During the preschool years, children start to conform to the **emotional display rules** of their culture, but only gradually do they become adept at doing so. In middle childhood, they become consciously aware of these rules and come to understand their value.

UNDERSTANDING AND RESPONDING TO THE EMOTIONS OF OTHERS

Describe the development of emotional understanding from infancy into adolescence.

- As infants develop the capacity to meaningfully interpret emotional expressions, they actively seek emotional information from trusted caregivers. **Social referencing** appears at the end of the first year. By the middle of the second year, toddlers begin to appreciate that others' emotional reactions may differ from their own.

- Preschoolers have an impressive understanding of the causes, consequences, and behavioral signs of emotion. The capacity to consider multiple sources of information when explaining others' feelings develops during middle childhood. Older children also realize that people can experience mixed emotions.

- Both cognitive development and social experience contribute to emotional understanding. Conversations with family members and make-believe play with siblings are excellent contexts for learning about emotions.

Distinguish empathy and sympathy, and describe the development of empathy from infancy into adolescence, noting factors that influence individual differences.

- The development of **empathy** involves a complex interaction of cognition and affect. Empathy is an important motivator of **prosocial,** or altruistic, **behavior.** Yet if the emotion aroused by an upset other escalates into personal distress, empathy is unlikely to prompt **sympathy** and resulting acts of kindness and helpfulness.

- As self-awareness emerges, toddlers begin to empathize. Gains in language, emotional understanding, and perspective taking support an increase in empathic responding during childhood and adolescence. Eventually, empathy is evoked not just by people's immediate distress but by their general life condition.

- Temperament affects whether empathy gives way to sympathy. Children who are sociable, assertive, and good at regulating emotion are more likely to behave prosocially than are children who often display negative emotion. Parents who are nurturant, display empathic concern, and set clear limits on children's display of inappropriate emotion foster the development of empathy and sympathy. In contrast, angry, punitive parenting disrupts these capacities at an early age.

TEMPERAMENT AND DEVELOPMENT

What is temperament, and how is it measured?

- Children differ greatly in **temperament,** or quality and intensity of emotion, activity level, attention, and emotional self-regulation. Three patterns of temperament—the **easy child,** the **difficult child,** and the **slow-to-warm-up child**—were identified in the New York Longitudinal Study. Rothbart and Mauro's model of temperament combines dimensions of other researchers and adds one that emphasizes emotional self-regulation.

- Temperament is often assessed through parental self-reports, although behavior ratings by others familiar with the child and direct observations are also used. Researchers have begun to use psychophysiological measures to distinguish temperamental styles, such as **inhibited,** or shy, **children** from **uninhibited,** or sociable, **children.**

Discuss the role of heredity and environment in the stability of temperament, the relationship of temperament to cognitive and social functioning, and the goodness-of-fit model.

- Because temperament itself develops with age and can be modified by experience, stability from one age period to the next is generally low to moderate. Long-term prediction from early temperament is best achieved from the second year of life and after, when styles of responding are better established.

- Kinship studies reveal that temperament is moderately heritable. They also suggest that nonshared environmental influences are more important than are shared influences in contributing to temperament. Although ethnic differences in temperament may have biological roots, cultural beliefs and practices support them.

- Temperament is consistently related to cognitive performance and social behavior. The **goodness-of-fit model** describes how temperament and environmental pressures work together to affect later development. Parenting practices that create a good fit with the child's temperament help difficult, shy, and highly active children achieve more adaptive functioning.

DEVELOPMENT OF ATTACHMENT

What are the unique features of ethological theory of attachment?

◆ The development of **attachment,** the strong affectional tie we feel for special people in our lives, has been the subject of intense theoretical debate. Although psychoanalytic and drive reduction (behaviorist) explanations exist, the most widely accepted perspective is **ethological theory of attachment.** It views babies as biologically prepared to contribute actively to ties established with their caregivers, which promote survival.

◆ In early infancy, a set of built-in behaviors encourages the parent to remain close to the baby. Around 6 to 8 months, **separation anxiety** and use of the parent as a secure base indicate that a true attachment bond has formed. As representation and language develop, preschoolers better understand the parent's goals, and separation anxiety declines. Out of early caregiving experiences, children construct an **internal working model** that serves as a guide for all future close relationships.

Cite the four attachment patterns assessed by the Strange Situation and the Attachment Q-Sort, and discuss factors that affect the development of attachment.

◆ A widely used technique for measuring the quality of attachment between 1 and 2 years of age is the **Strange Situation.** A more efficient method is the **Attachment Q-Sort.** Four attachment patterns have been identified: **secure, avoidant, resistant,** and **disorganized/disoriented.**

◆ The stability of attachment varies widely from one study to the next. Infants who are securely attached and reared in middle-SES families with stable life conditions more often maintain their attachment status. For infants in low-SES families with many daily stresses or in families undergoing major life changes, quality of attachment often changes. Cultural conditions must be considered in interpreting reactions to the Strange Situation.

◆ A variety of factors affect attachment security. Infants deprived of affectional ties with one or a few adults show lasting emotional and social problems. **Sensitive caregiving** is moderately related to secure attachment. **Interactional synchrony** also separates the experiences of secure from insecure babies, but its importance is probably limited to certain cultures.

◆ Even ill and temperamentally irritable infants are likely to become securely attached if parents adapt their caregiving to suit the baby's needs. Family circumstances influence caregiving behavior and the attachment bond. Parents' internal working models show substantial correspondence with their own children's attachment status in infancy and early childhood. Internal working models are reconstructed memories; transfer of parents' childhood experiences to quality of attachment with their own children is indirect and affected by many factors.

Discuss fathers' attachment relationships with their infants and the role of early attachment quality in later development.

◆ Infants establish attachment relationships with a variety of familiar people. Fathers' affectional bonds with their babies are just as emotionally intense as are mothers', and their sensitive caregiving predicts attachment security. When interacting with infants, mothers typically devote more time to physical care and expressing affection, fathers to stimulating, playful interaction.

◆ Evidence for the impact of early attachment quality on cognitive, emotional, and social competence in later years is mixed. Continuity of caregiving may be the crucial factor that determines whether attachment security is linked to later development.

ATTACHMENT AND SOCIAL CHANGE: MATERNAL EMPLOYMENT AND CHILD CARE

Discuss the effects of maternal employment and child care in infancy on attachment security and psychological development.

◆ The majority of mothers with children under age 2 are employed. Poor-quality child care and stressful conditions in some families with employed mothers are associated with insecure attachment and less favorable cognitive, emotional, and social development. In contrast, good child care can foster children's development and well-being.

◆ Quality of infant and toddler child care in the United States is mediocre to poor. When child-care centers meet professionally accepted standards for **developmentally appropriate practice,** children's learning opportunities and the warmth, sensitivity, and stability of their caregivers is especially high.

IMPORTANT TERMS AND CONCEPTS

attachment (p. 421)
Attachment Q-Sort (p. 424)
avoidant attachment (p. 424)
basic emotions (p. 401)
developmentally appropriate practice (p. 434)
difficult child (p. 415)
disorganized/disoriented attachment (p. 424)
easy child (p. 415)
emotion (p. 398)
emotional display rules (p. 407)
emotional self-regulation (p. 404)

empathy (p. 410)
ethological theory of attachment (p. 422)
functionalist approach (p. 398)
goodness-of-fit model (p. 420)
inhibited, or shy, child (p. 416)
interactional synchrony (p. 426)
internal working model (p. 422)
prosocial, or altruistic, behavior (p. 411)
resistant attachment (p. 424)
secure attachment (p. 424)
secure base (p. 403)

self-conscious emotions (p. 404)
sensitive caregiving (p. 426)
separation anxiety (p. 422)
slow-to-warm-up child (p. 415)
social referencing (p. 408)
social smile (p. 402)
Strange Situation (p. 425)
stranger anxiety (p. 403)
sympathy (p. 411)
temperament (p. 412)
uninhibited, or sociable, child (p. 416)

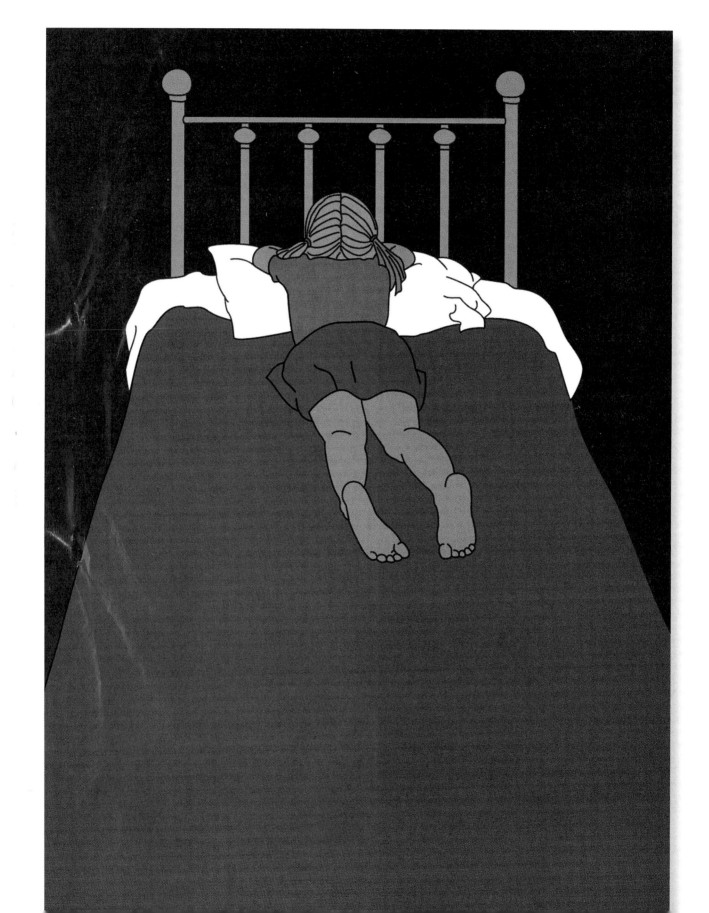

Self and Social Understanding

"GRANDPA, LOOK AT my new shirt!" exclaimed 4-year-old Ellen at her family's annual reunion. "See, it's got Barney and Baby Bop on it and. . . ."

Ellen's voice trailed off as she realized all eyes were turned toward her 1-year-old cousin, who was about to take his first steps. As little David tottered forward, the grownups laughed and cheered. No one, not even Grandpa, who was usually so attentive and playful, took note of Ellen and her new shirt.

Ellen felt a twinge of jealousy and retreated to the bedroom, where she threw a blanket over her head. Arms outstretched, she peered through the blanket's loose weave and made her way back to the living room, where she saw Grandpa leading David about the room. "Here I come, the scary ghost," announced Ellen as she purposefully bumped into David, who toppled over and burst into tears.

Pulling off the blanket, Ellen quickly caught her mother's disapproving expression. "I couldn't see him, Mom! The blanket was over my face," Ellen sheepishly explained.

Ellen's mother insisted that Ellen help David up and apologize at once. At the same time, she marveled at Ellen's skillful capacity for trickery.

This chapter addresses the development of **social cognition,** or how children come to understand their multifaceted social world. Like our discussion of cognitive development in Chapters 6 and 7, the changes to which we now turn are concerned with matters of thinking about and interpreting experience. But the experience of interest is no longer the child's physical surroundings. Instead, it is the inner characteristics of the self and other people.

Researchers interested in social cognition seek answers to questions like these: When do infants first discover they are separate beings, distinct from other people and objects? How does children's understanding of their own and others' mental lives change with age? For example, what new realizations underlie Ellen's creative act of deception? When a 10-year-old calls another child "my best friend," what does he mean? In what ways are his ideas about friendship different from those of preschoolers, and how will they change during adolescence?

As we answer these and other questions, you will see that many of the trends we identified for nonsocial thinking apply to children's understanding of their social world. Like nonsocial cognition, social cognition develops from *concrete* to *abstract.* Children first notice observable characteristics—the appearance and behavior of themselves and other people. Soon after, they become aware of internal processes—the existence of desires, beliefs, intentions, abilities, and attitudes. Social cognition also becomes *better organized* with age, as children gather together separate behaviors into an appreciation of their own and others' personalities and identities. In addition, children revise their ideas about the causes of people's behavior—from *simple, one-sided explanations* to *complex interacting relationships* that take into account both the person and the situation. Finally, social cognition moves toward a *metacognitive level of understanding*. As children get older, their thinking is no longer limited to social reality. They also think about their own and other people's social thoughts.

Although nonsocial and social cognition share many features, they differ in important respects. Consider, for a moment, how much easier it is to predict the motions of physical objects, such as a rolling ball, than the actions of people. Movements of things can be fully understood from the physical forces that act on them. In contrast, the behavior of people is not simply the result of others' actions toward them. It is also determined by inner states that cannot be observed directly.

In view of this complexity, we might expect social cognition to develop more slowly than nonsocial cognition. Yet surprisingly, it does not. We will see that children demonstrate some sophisticated understandings at early ages, even though others take a long time to develop. Unique features of social experience probably help children make early sense of its complexity. First, the fact that people are animated beings and objects of deep emotional investment makes them especially interesting to think about. Second, social experience continually presents children with discrepancies between behaviors they expect and those that occur, which prompts them to revise their thoughts about social concerns. Finally, children and the people with whom they interact are all human beings, with the same basic nervous system and a background of similar experiences. This means that interpreting behavior from the self's point of view often helps us understand others' actions. When it does not, humans are equipped with a unique capacity—*perspective taking*—that permits them to imagine what another's thoughts and feelings might be. Perspective taking is so important for psychological development that we have already mentioned it many times in earlier parts of this book, and we will devote considerable attention to it in this chapter.

Our discussion is organized around three aspects of development: thinking about the self, thinking about other people, and thinking about relationships between people. Perhaps you have noticed that we have already considered some social–cognitive topics in previous chapters. Good examples are referential communication skills in Chapter 9 and emotional understanding in Chapter 10. Children's sense of morality is another important social–cognitive topic, but research on it is so extensive that it merits a chapter of its own. We will consider the development of moral reasoning in Chapter 12.

Thinking About the Self

Virtually all investigators agree that two distinct aspects of the self, identified by philosopher William James (1890/1963) over a century ago, emerge and become more refined with age:

- The **I-self,** a sense of self as *subject,* or *agent,* who is separate from but attends to and acts on objects and other people. It includes the following realizations: that the self is separate from the surrounding world; can act on and gain a sense of control over its environment; has a private, inner life not accessible to others; and maintains a continuous existence over time.

- The **me-self,** a *reflective observer* who treats the self as an object of knowledge and evaluation by sizing up its diverse features. The me-self consists of all qualities that make the self unique—*material characteristics,* such as physical appearance and possessions; *psychological characteristics,* including desires, attitudes, beliefs, thought processes, and personality traits; and *social characteristics,* such as roles and relationships with others.

Self-understanding begins with the dawning of self-awareness in the second year of life and gradually evolves into a rich, multifaceted view of the self's characteristics and capacities over childhood and adolescence. As we trace the blossoming of this increasingly elaborate and organized image of the self, we will see that the I-self and me-self are intimately intertwined and influence each other.

social cognition Thinking about the self, other people, and social relationships.

I-self A sense of self as subject, or agent, who is separate from but attends to and acts on objects and other people.

me-self A reflective observer who treats the self as an object of knowledge and evaluation.

self-recognition Perception of the self as a separate being, distinct from other people and objects.

SELF-AWARENESS

As early as the first few months of life, infants smile and return friendly behaviors to their reflection in a mirror. At what age do they realize that the charming baby gazing and grinning back is really the self?

■ **BEGINNINGS OF THE I-SELF.** To answer this question, researchers have conducted clever laboratory observations in which they expose infants and toddlers to images of themselves in mirrors, on videotapes, and in photographs. When shown their own video-taped image next to that of a peer, 3-month-olds look longer at the peer's image. This suggests that at least for babies with access to mirrors, discrimination of self from others is under way in the first few months of life (Bahrick, Moss, & Fadil, 1996).

Researchers agree that the earliest aspect of the self to emerge is the *I-self*. According to many theorists, its beginnings lie in infants' recognition that their own actions cause objects and people to react in predictable ways (Harter, 1998). In support of this idea, securely attached toddlers, whose parents have responded to their signals consistently and sensitively, are advanced in performance on agency tasks requiring them to engage in self- and mother-directed actions during make-believe play, such as pretending to eat and to feed the mother (Pipp, Easterbrooks, & Brown, 1993).

Then, as infants act on the environment, they notice different effects that may help them sort out self from other people and objects. For example, batting a mobile and seeing it swing in a pattern different from the infant's own actions informs the baby about the relation between self and physical world. Smiling and vocalizing at a caregiver who smiles and vocalizes back helps specify the relation between self and social world. And watching the movements of one's own hand provides still another kind of feedback—one under much more direct control than other people or objects. The contrast between these experiences may help infants build an image of self as separate from external reality.

■ **BEGINNINGS OF THE ME-SELF.** During the second year, toddlers start to construct the me-self. Consequently, they become consciously aware of the self's physical features. In one study, 9- to 24-month-olds were placed in front of a mirror. Then, under the pretext of wiping the baby's face, each mother was asked to rub red dye on her child's nose. Younger infants touched the mirror as if the red mark had nothing to do with any aspect of themselves. But by 15 months, toddlers began to rub their strange-looking little red noses, a response that indicated keen awareness of their unique visual appearance (Lewis & Brooks-Gunn, 1979). In addition, some toddlers act silly or coy in front of the mirror, playfully experimenting with the way the self looks (Bullock & Lutkenhaus, 1990).

Around age 2, **self-recognition**—perception of the self as a separate being, distinct from other people and objects—is well established. Children look and smile more at a photo of themselves than one of another child. And almost all use their name or a personal pronoun ("I" or "me") to refer to themselves (Lewis & Brooks-Gunn, 1979). Like the I-self, the me-self seems to be fostered by sensitive caregiving. Securely attached toddlers display more complex featural knowledge of themselves and their parents (such as labeling their own and their parents' body parts) than do their insecurely attached agemates (Pipp, Easterbrooks, & Brown, 1993).

■ **SELF-AWARENESS AND EARLY EMOTIONAL AND SOCIAL DEVELOPMENT.** Self-awareness quickly becomes a central part of children's emotional and social lives. Recall from Chapter 10 that self-conscious emotions depend on toddlers' emerging sense of self. Self-awareness also leads to the child's first efforts to appreciate another's perspective. For example, it is associated with the beginnings of empathy (see page 411) and self-conscious behavior—bashfully looking away or hiding behind the parent in response to

This infant notices the correspondence between his own movements and the movements of the image in the mirror, a cue that helps him figure out that the grinning baby is really himself.

(Paul Damien/Tony Stone Images)

A firmer sense of self permits young children to cooperate in solving simple problems. These 3-year-olds work together to sweep up spilled sand in their preschool classroom.
(Laura Dwight)

attention from others. Furthermore, mirror self-recognition precedes the appearance of sustained, mutual imitation in play—a partner banging an object, the toddler copying the behavior, the partner imitating back, and the toddler copying again (Asendorpf, Warkentin, & Baudonniere, 1996). These exchanges indicate that the toddler is not only interested in the playmate but realizes that the playmate is interested in him or her.

At first, children's sense of self is so bound up with particular possessions and actions that they spend much time asserting their rights to objects. In one study, 2-year-olds' ability to distinguish between self and other was assessed. Then each child was observed interacting with a peer in a laboratory playroom. The stronger 2-year-olds' self-definitions, the more possessive they tended to be about objects, claiming them as "Mine!" (Levine, 1983).

A firmer sense of self also permits children to cooperate for the first time in resolving disputes over objects, playing games, and solving simple problems (Brownell & Carriger, 1990; Caplan et al., 1991). Adults might take both of these capacities into account when trying to promote friendly peer interaction. For example, teachers and parents can accept the young child's possessiveness as a sign of self-assertion ("Yes, that's your toy") and then encourage compromise ("but in a little while, would you give someone else a turn?"), rather than simply insisting on sharing.

THE CATEGORICAL AND REMEMBERED SELVES

Language is a powerful tool in self-development (Lewis, 1994). Because it permits children to represent and express the me-self more clearly, it greatly enhances young preschoolers' self-awareness.

Between 18 and 30 months, children develop a **categorical self** as they classify themselves and others according to salient ways in which people differ, such as age ("baby," "boy," or "man"), sex ("boy" versus "girl" and "woman" versus "man"), physical characteristics ("big," "strong"), and even goodness and badness ("I good girl." "Tommy mean!"). They also start to refer to the self's competencies ("Did it!" "I can't") (Stipek, Gralinski, & Kopp, 1990).

In Chapter 7, we noted that conversations with adults about the past and the beginnings of a "psychological self" lead to an autobiographical memory. This life-story narrative grants the child a **remembered self**—a more coherent and enduring portrait than offered by the isolated, episodic memories of the first few years. As early as age 2, parents use these discussions to impart rules and standards and include much descriptive and evaluative information about the child ("You were a big boy when you did that!"). Consequently, they serve as a rich source of self-knowledge and a major means through which the me-self is imbued with cultural values.

For example, examining ethnographic records of everyday talk with 2-year-olds in middle-SES families, Peggy Miller and her colleagues discovered striking cultural variations. Compared with Caucasian-American mothers, Chinese mothers more often told stories about the child's past misdeeds (see Figure 11.1). Consistent with the Confucian parental duty, "The deeper the love, the greater the correction," these narratives were conveyed in an atmosphere of warmth and caring. They often occurred right after the child committed another transgression and typically ended with direct teaching of proper behavior ("Saying dirty words is not good"). In the few instances in which Caucasian-American stories referred to children's misbehavior, mothers de-emphasized these acts, attributing them to the child's spunk and assertiveness (Miller, Fung, & Mintz, 1996; Miller et al., 1997). As a result, the early me-selves of Chinese and Caucasian-American children are likely to differ—the former stressing obligations to others, the latter more autonomous (Markus, Mullally, & Kitayama, 1997).

categorical self Early classification of the self according to salient ways people differ, such as age, sex, physical characteristics, and goodness and badness.

remembered self Life-story narrative constructed from conversations with adults about the past that leads to an autobiographical memory.

THE INNER SELF: YOUNG CHILDREN'S THEORY OF MIND

As children think more about themselves and others, they begin to elaborate the I-self by forming a naive *theory of mind*—a coherent understanding of their own and other's rich mental lives. Recall from Chapter 7 that after age 2½, children refer to mental states, such as "want," "think," and "pretend," frequently and appropriately in everyday language. Although they confuse certain mental terms (see page 300), young preschoolers are clearly aware of an **inner self** of private thoughts and imaginings.

What is the young child's view of the inner self like, and how does it change with age? Investigators are interested in this question because ideas about the mind are powerful tools in predicting and explaining our own and others' everyday behavior. Despite a vocabulary of mentalistic terms, 2-year-olds have only a beginning grasp of the distinction between mental life and behavior. They think that people always behave in ways consistent with their desires and do not understand that beliefs affect their actions (Bartsch & Wellman, 1995).

According to Henry Wellman, from age 3 or 4 on, children's ideas about how the mind works are differentiated, organized, and accurate enough to qualify as a theory (Gopnik & Wellman, 1994; Wellman, 1990). Older preschoolers know that both *beliefs* and *desires* determine *actions,* and they understand the relationship between these three constructs. Turn back to the beginning of this chapter, and notice how 4-year-old Ellen deliberately tried to alter her mother's *belief* about the real motive behind her pretending—in hopes of warding off any *desire* on her mother's part to punish her. Wellman labels Ellen's more sophisticated view of the mind a **belief–desire theory**—a conception of mentality that closely resembles the everyday psychology of adults.

■ **DEVELOPMENT OF BELIEF–DESIRE REASONING.** One way researchers study belief–desire reasoning is to tell children stories about actors desiring or not desiring an outcome and believing or not believing that it would happen. Then the outcome either happens or does not happen. Here is one example:

> Lisa wants it to be sunny today because she wants to play on her new swingset. But, Lisa thinks it's going to rain today. She thinks it's going to rain because she heard the weather man say it might rain. Look, it rains. (Wellman & Banerjee, 1991, p. 194)

Children are asked to indicate how Lisa would feel—happy or unhappy (a desire-related emotion) and surprised or unsurprised (a belief-related emotion). Both 3- and 4-year-olds easily give the appropriate desire-related feeling. They know that Lisa will be happy if she gets the weather she wants and unhappy if she does not (Hadwin & Perner, 1991; Wellman & Bartsch, 1988). And when the interviewing method is changed to clarify the meaning of emotional terms (preschoolers often confuse surprise with happiness), even 3-year-olds display some awareness that surprise occurs in situations that violate prior beliefs, a response that becomes consistent around age 4 (Wellman & Banerjee, 1991).

A more dramatic illustration of belief–desire reasoning comes from games in which preschoolers are asked to mislead an adult. By age 4, children realize that people can hold *false beliefs* that combine with desire to determine behavior (Perner, 1991). In one study, 2½- to 4-year-olds were asked to hide the driver of a toy truck underneath one of five cups in a sandbox so that an adult, who was out of the room, could not find it (see Figure 11.2 on page 444). An experimenter showed the child how the truck left telltale tracks in the sand as a sign of where it had been. Most 2- and 3-year-olds needed explicit prompts to hide the evidence—smoothing over the tracks and returning the truck to its starting place. In contrast, 4-year-olds thought of doing these things on their own. They were also more likely to trick the adult by laying false tracks or giving incorrect information about where the driver was hidden (Sodian et al., 1991). Other research confirms that children's understanding of the role of false belief in guiding their own and others' actions strengthens over the preschool years, becoming more secure between ages 4 and 6 (Flavell & Miller, 1998).

Mastery of false belief is a remarkable achievement. It signals a major advance in representation—the ability to view beliefs as *interpretations,* not just reflections, of reality. Does this remind you of school-age children's more active view of the mind, discussed in

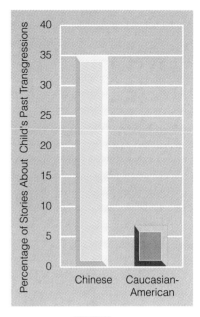

FIGURE 11.1

Percentage of mothers' stories about child's past transgressions in Chinese and Caucasian-American families. Chinese mothers were far more likely to focus on 2-year-olds' misdeeds in their narratives than were Caucasian-American mothers. In this way, the Chinese child's remembered self is imbued with obligations to others.
(Adapted from Miller et al., 1997.)

inner self Awareness of the self's private thoughts and imaginings.

belief–desire theory of mind The theory of mind that emerges around age 3 to 4 in which both beliefs and desires determine behavior and that closely resembles the everyday psychology of adults.

FIGURE 11.2

Game used to assess belief–desire reasoning. The child hides the driver of a toy truck underneath one of five cups in a sandbox so that an adult, who is out of the room, cannot find it. The experimenter points out that the truck leaves tell-tale tracks in the sand as a sign of where it has been. Children who understand that people can hold false beliefs think of smoothing over the tracks to the driver's actual location, returning the truck to its starting place, and even laying false tracks to mislead the adult.

(Adapted from Sodian et al., 1991.)

Chapter 7? Perhaps belief–desire reasoning marks the beginnings of this overall change (Leekam, 1993).

■ **WHERE DOES A THEORY OF MIND ORIGINATE?** How do children manage to develop a theory of mind at such a young age? Various speculations and findings suggest that social experience is profoundly important:

■ *Early forms of communication.* Perhaps an understanding of others' beliefs originates in certain early forms of communication, such as joint attention and social referencing, which require a beginning ability to represent another's mental state (Sigman & Kasari, 1995).

■ *Imitation.* Imitation may also contribute to an early grasp of mental life. Infants' primitive plan to copy an action, located inside the body, has much of the character of mental states. At the same time, imitation teaches infants that other people are like themselves. Perhaps this prompts them to conclude that others are also mental beings (Meltzoff & Gopnik, 1993).

■ *Make-believe play.* Make-believe play provides another possible foundation for thinking about the mind. As children play at various roles and use one object to represent another, they notice that the mind can change what objects mean. These experiences may trigger an awareness that beliefs influence behavior. In support of this idea, preschoolers who engage in extensive fantasy play are more advanced in their understanding of false belief and other aspects of the mind (Astington & Jenkins, 1995; Taylor & Carlson, 1997).

■ *Language.* Understanding the mind requires the ability to reflect on thoughts, made possible by language. A grasp of false belief is related to language ability equivalent to that of an average 4-year-old or higher (Jenkins & Astington, 1996).
    A mental state vocabulary is also necessary. Among the Quechua of the Peruvian highlands, adults refer to mental states such as "think" and "believe" indirectly, since their language lacks mental state terms. Quechua children have difficulty with false belief tasks for years after children in industrialized nations have mastered them (Vinden, 1996).

self-concept The set of attributes, abilities, attitudes, and values that an individual believes defines who he or she is.

■ *Social interaction.* Preschoolers with older siblings are advanced in performance on false-belief tasks. And those with several older siblings do better than those with only one (Ruffman et al., 1998). Having older siblings may allow for many interactions that highlight the influence of beliefs on behavior—through teasing, trickery, make-believe play, and discussing feelings.

Besides sibling relationships, preschool friendships may foster an appreciation of mentality. The more 3- and 4-year-olds engage in mental-state talk with friends, the better their performance on false-belief tasks more than a year later (Hughes & Dunn, 1998). Interacting with more mature members of society is also helpful. In a study of Greek preschoolers with large networks of extended family and neighbors, daily contact with many adults and older children predicted mastery of false belief (Lewis et al., 1996). These encounters probably offer extra opportunities to observe different points of view and talk about inner states.

Having older siblings fosters an understanding of false belief, probably because sibling interactions often highlight the influence of beliefs on behavior—through teasing, trickery, make-believe play, and discussing feelings.

(Tony Freeman/PhotoEdit)

Many researchers believe that to profit from the social experiences just described, children must be biologically prepared to develop a theory of mind. Consistent with this assumption, children with *infantile autism,* who are indifferent to other people and display poor knowledge of social rules, seem to be impaired in mental understanding and in the early capacities believed to underlie it. See the Variations box on page 446 to find out more about the biological basis of reasoning about the mind.

At older ages, children distinguish more clearly between different cognitive and emotional states (see Chapters 7 and 10) and between their own mental state and that of others, as we will see when we take up the development of perspective taking in a later section. Theorizing about the mind is a long developmental process, and we will add to our understanding of it throughout this chapter.

SELF-CONCEPT

As children develop an appreciation of their inner mental world, they think more intently about themselves. During early childhood, the me-self expands as children begin to construct a **self-concept,** the set of attributes, abilities, attitudes, and values that an individual believes defines who he or she is.

Preschoolers' self-concepts emphasize observable characteristics—the child's name, physical appearance, possessions, and everyday behaviors. If asked to tell about herself, this 4-year-old might say, "I can help water the plants with my sprinkling can!" In a few years, she will begin to mention personality traits, such as "I'm helpful and responsible."

(Robert Brenner/PhotoEdit)

■ **EARLY CHILDHOOD.** Ask a 3- to 5-year-old to tell you about him- or herself, and you are likely to hear something like this: "I'm Tommy. See, I got this new red T-shirt. I'm 4 years old. I can brush my teeth, and I can wash my hair all by myself. I have a new Tinkertoy set, and I made this big, big tower." As these statements indicate, preschoolers' self-concepts are very concrete. Usually they mention observable characteristics, such as their name, physical appearance, possessions, and everyday behaviors (Harter, 1996; Watson, 1990).

By age 3½, children also describe themselves in terms of typical emotions and attitudes, as in "I'm happy when I play with my friends" or "I don't like being with grownups" (Eder, 1989). And when asked to tell whether statements are true of themselves (a much easier task than producing a self-description), 3½-year-olds often respond consistently. For example, a child who says that she "doesn't push in front of other people in line" is also likely to indicate that she "feels like being quiet when angry" and "usually does what Mommy or the teacher says," as if she recognizes that she is high in self-control (Eder, 1990). This suggests that young children have a beginning understanding of their unique psychological characteristics.

■ **MIDDLE CHILDHOOD.** Over time, children organize these internal states and behaviors into dispositions that they can verbalize to others. Between ages 8 and 11, a major shift takes place in children's self-descriptions. They begin to

"Mindblindness" and Infantile Autism

SIDNEY STOOD AT the water table in his preschool classroom, repeatedly filling a plastic cup and dumping out its contents. Dip-splash, dip-splash, dip-splash he went, until his teacher came over and redirected his actions. Without looking at his teacher's face, Sidney moved to a new repetitive pursuit: pouring water from one cup into another and back again. As other children entered the play space and conversed, Sidney hardly noticed. He rarely spoke, and when he did, he usually used words to get things he wanted, not to exchange ideas.

Sidney has *infantile autism,* the most severe behavior disorder of childhood. The term *autism* means "absorbed in the self," an apt description of Sidney. Like other children with the disorder, Sidney is impaired in emotional and gestural (nonverbal) behaviors required for successful social interaction. In addition, his language is delayed and stereotyped; some autistic children do not speak at all. Sidney's interests, which focus on the physical world, are narrow and overly intense. For example, one day he sat for more than an hour making a toy ferris wheel go round and round. When Leslie showed the children a movie about wild animals, Sidney watched the projector, not the screen.

Autism is highly heritable; its concordance is much greater for identical than for fraternal twins. A growing body of evidence suggests that one psychological factor involved is a severely deficient or absent theory of mind. Long after they reach the intellectual level of an average 4-year-old, autistic children have great difficulty with false-belief tasks. Most cannot attribute mental states to others or to themselves. Such words as "believe," "think," "know," and "pretend" are rarely part of their vocabularies (Happé, 1995; Tager-Flusberg & Sullivan, 1994; Yirmiya, Solomonica-Levi, & Shulman, 1996).

As early as the second year, autistic children show deficits in capacities believed to contribute to an understanding of mentality (see page 444). For example, they less often establish joint attention, engage in social referencing, or imitate an adult's novel behaviors than do normal children (Charman et al., 1997; Sigman et al., 1992). Furthermore, they are relatively insensitive to a speaker's gaze as a cue to what he or she is talking about. Instead, autistic children often assume that an adult's verbal expression refers to what they themselves are attending to—a possible reason that they use many nonsensical expressions (Baron-Cohen, Baldwin, & Crowson, 1997). Finally, autistic children engage in much less make-believe play than do age- and mental-ability matched comparison groups—both normal children and children with other developmental problems (Hughes, 1998).

Do these findings indicate that autism is due to an impairment in an innate social-cognitive brain module, which leaves the child "mindblind" and therefore unable to engage in human sociability? Some researchers think so (Baron-Cohen, 1993). A second, related speculation is that infantile autism results from a deficit in comprehending emotion, which is essential for understanding others. In support of this view, autistic children have trouble interpreting emotional stimuli, such as facial expressions (Hobson, 1993).

This autistic girl does not take note of a speaker's gaze as a cue to what he or she is talking about. For this reason, the girl's teacher takes extra steps to capture her attention in a science lesson. Researchers disagree on whether autistic children's "mindblindness" is due to an impairment in an innate social-cognitive brain module or to a general memory deficit.
(Will Hart)

Yet a third conjecture is that autism is due to a general memory deficit, which makes it hard to retain the parts of complex tasks (Bennetto, Pennington, & Rogers, 1996). Perhaps this explains autistic children's preoccupation with simple, repetitive acts. It may also account for their difficulty with problems, such as conservation, that require them to integrate several contexts at once (before, during, and after the transformation of a substance) (Yirmiya & Shulman, 1996). A memory deficit would also interfere with understanding the social world, since social interaction takes place quickly and requires integration of information from various sources.

At present, it is not clear which of these hypotheses is correct. Although researchers agree that the disorder stems from abnormal brain functioning, several regions may be involved, including the limbic system—a set of structures specialized for processing emotional information—and the frontal lobes of the cerebral cortex, which support memory by inhibiting attention to distracting stimuli (see Chapter 7) (Dawson et al. 1998). Perhaps several biologically based deficits underlie the tragic social isolation of children like Sidney.

mention personality traits, which increase with age. The following response from an 11-year-old reflects this change:

> My name is A. I'm a human being. I'm a girl. I'm a truthful person. I'm not pretty. I do so-so in my studies. I'm a very good cellist. I'm a very good pianist. I'm a little bit tall for my age. I like several boys. I like several girls. I'm old-fashioned. I play tennis. I am a very good swimmer. I try to be helpful. I'm always ready to be friends with anybody. Mostly I'm good, but I lose my temper. I'm not well-liked by some girls and boys. I don't know if I'm liked by boys or not. (Montemayor & Eisen, 1977, pp. 317–318)

Notice that instead of specific behaviors, this child emphasizes competencies, as in "I'm a very good cellist" (Damon & Hart, 1988). In addition, she clearly describes her personality, acknowledging the existence of both positive and negative attributes—"truthful" but "not pretty," a "good cellist [and] pianist" but only "so-so in my studies." Unlike their younger counterparts, older school-age children are far less likely to describe themselves in all-or-none ways (Harter, 1996).

During the school years, children's self-concepts expand to include feedback from a wider range of people as they spend more time in settings beyond the home. Scouting and its associated qualities of friendliness, helpfulness, and kindness are probably important aspects of the self-definitions of these boys.

(B. Daemmrich/The Image Works)

■ **ADOLESCENCE.** In early adolescence, young people unify separate traits, such as "smart" and "creative," into higher-order, abstract descriptors, such as "intelligent." But these generalizations about the self are not yet interconnected, and often they appear contradictory. For example, 12- to 14-year-olds might mention such opposing traits as "intelligent" versus "airhead" or "shy" versus "outgoing." These disparities result from social pressures to display different selves in different relationships—with parents, classmates, close friends, and romantic partners. As adolescents' social world expands, contradictory self-descriptions increase, and teenagers frequently agonize over "which is the real me" (Harter, 1998; Harter & Monsour, 1992).

By middle to late adolescence, teenagers combine their various traits into an organized system. And they begin to use qualifiers ("I have a fairly quick temper," "I'm not thoroughly honest"), which reveal their awareness that psychological qualities often change from one situation to the next. Older adolescents also add integrating principles, which make sense of formerly troublesome contradictions. For example, one young person remarked, "I'm very adaptable. When I'm around my friends, who think that what I say is important, I'm very talkative; but around my family I'm quiet because they're never interested enough to really listen to me" (Damon, 1990, p. 88).

Compared with school-age children, teenagers also place more emphasis on social virtues, such as being friendly, considerate, kind, and cooperative. Adolescents are very preoccupied with being liked and viewed positively by others, and their statements about themselves reflect this concern. In addition, personal and moral values appear as key themes in older adolescents' self-concepts. For example, here is how Ben, a 16-year-old boy, described himself in terms of honesty to himself and others:

> I like being honest like with yourself and with everyone. . . . [A person] could be, in the eyes of everyone else the best person in the world, but if I knew they were lying or cheating, in my eyes they wouldn't be. . . . When I'm friendly, it's more to tell people that it's all right to be yourself. Not necessarily don't conform, but just whatever you are, you know, be happy with that. . . . So I'm not an overly bubbly person that goes around, "Hi, how are you?" . . . But if someone wants to talk to me, you know, sure. I wouldn't like, not talk to someone. (Damon & Hart, 1988, pp. 120–121)

Ben's well-integrated account of his personal traits and values is quite different from the fragmented, listlike self-descriptions of children. Notice how Ben's *I-self* weaves several of his *me-selves* into a coherent narrative. As adolescents revise their views of themselves to include enduring beliefs and plans, they move toward the kind of unity of self that is central to identity development.

COGNITIVE, SOCIAL, AND CULTURAL INFLUENCES ON SELF-CONCEPT

What factors are responsible for these revisions in self-concept? Cognitive development certainly affects the changing *structure* of the self. School-age children, as we saw in Chapter 6, are better at coordinating several aspects of a situation in reasoning about their physical world. They show improved ability to relate separate observations in the social realm as well. Consequently, they combine typical experiences and behaviors into stable psychological dispositions and acknowledge both positive and negative traits. In middle childhood, children also gain a clearer understanding of traits as linked to specific desires (a "generous" person *wants* to share) and, therefore, as causes of behavior (Yuill & Pearson, 1998). For this reason, they may mention traits more often. And formal operational thought transforms the adolescent's vision of the self into a complex, well-organized, internally consistent picture (Harter, 1996, 1998).

The changing *content* of the self is a product of both cognitive capacities and feedback from others. Early in this century, sociologist George Herbert Mead (1934) described the self as a blend of what we imagine important people in our lives think of us. He believed that a psychological self emerges when the child's I-self comprehends the attitudes of significant others and adopts a view of the me-self that resembles those attitudes. Mead called this reflected self the **generalized other.** Mead's ideas indicate that *perspective-taking skills*—in particular, an improved ability to infer what other people are thinking—are crucial in the development of a self-concept based on personality traits. Indeed, as we will see later, perspective taking improves greatly over middle childhood and adolescence. Young people become better at "reading" messages they receive from others and incorporating these into their self-definitions.

During middle childhood, children look to more people for information about themselves as they enter a wider range of settings in school and community. This is reflected in children's frequent reference to social groups in their self-descriptions (Livesley & Bromley, 1973). "I'm a Boy Scout, a paper boy, and a Prairie City soccer player," one 10-year-old remarked when asked to describe himself. Gradually, as children move into adolescence, their sources of self-definition become more selective. Although parents remain strongly influential, between ages 8 and 15, peers become more important. And over time, self-concept becomes increasingly vested in feedback from close friends (Oosterwegel & Oppenheimer, 1993).

Keep in mind, however, that the changes just described are based on interviews with North American and Western European children. Other evidence indicates that the development of self-concept does not follow the same path in all societies. Recall from earlier chapters that Asian parents stress harmonious interdependence, whereas Western parents emphasize the person's separateness and the importance of asserting the self. Consequently, in China and Japan, the self is defined in relation to the social group. In the United States, the self usually becomes the "property" of a self-contained individual (Markus & Kitayama, 1991). Turn back to page 442, and notice this difference in mothers' conversations about the past with their 2-year-old children.

A strong collectivist theme is also reflected in the values of many subcultures in Western nations. In one study, the self-descriptions of children in a Puerto Rican fishing village were compared with those of children in an American town. The Puerto Rican children more often described themselves as "polite," "nice," "respectful," and "obedient" and justified these social traits by noting the positive reactions they evoke from others. In contrast, the American children more often mentioned individualistic traits, such as interests, preferences, and skills (Damon, 1988). In characterizing themselves, children from individualistic cultures seem to be more egoistic and competitive, those from collectivist cultures more concerned with the welfare of others—a finding that underscores the powerful impact of the social environment on the makeup of self-concept.

SELF-ESTEEM: THE EVALUATIVE SIDE OF SELF-CONCEPT

So far, we have focused on how the general structure and content of self-concept change with age. Another component of self-concept is **self-esteem,** the judgments we make about our own worth and the feelings associated with those judgments. According to Morris Rosenberg (1979), "a person with high self-esteem is fundamentally satisfied with the type of person he is, yet he may acknowledge his faults while hoping to overcome them" (p. 31). High self-esteem implies a realistic evaluation of the self's characteristics and competencies, coupled with an attitude of self-acceptance and self-respect.

generalized other A blend of what we imagine important people in our lives think of us; contributes to a self-concept comprising personality traits.

self-esteem The aspect of self-concept that involves judgments about one's own worth and the feelings associated with those judgments.

Self-esteem ranks among the most important aspects of self-development, since evaluations of our own competencies affect emotional experiences, future behavior, and long-term psychological adjustment. As soon as a categorical self with features that can be judged positively or negatively is in place, children start to become self-evaluative beings. Around age 2, they call a parent's attention to an achievement, such as completing a puzzle, by pointing and saying something like "Look, Mom!" In addition, 2-year-olds are likely to smile when they succeed at a task set for them by an adult and look away or frown when they fail (Stipek, Recchia, & McClintic, 1992). Furthermore, recall from Chapter 10 that by age 3, self-conscious emotions of pride and shame are clearly linked to self-evaluation (see page 404). Self-esteem originates early, and (as we will see in the next section) its structure becomes increasingly elaborate with age.

■ **ONE SELF-ESTEEM OR MANY?** Take a moment to think about your own self-esteem. Besides a global appraisal of your worth as a person, you have a variety of separate self-judgments concerning how well you perform at different activities.

Researchers have studied the multifaceted nature of self-esteem in the same way they have explored the question of whether there is one intelligence or many: by applying factor analysis[1] to children's ratings of themselves on many characteristics. For example, Susan Harter (1982, 1986) asked children to indicate the extent to which a variety of statements, such as "I am good at homework," "I'm usually the one chosen for games," and "Most kids like me," are true of themselves. Her findings reveal that preschoolers distinguish how well others like them (social acceptance) from how "good" they are at doing things (competence). And when procedures are specially adapted for young children by questioning them individually and encouraging them to seek clarification of any statement they do not understand, their sense of self-worth appears even more differentiated (Marsh, Craven, & Debus, 1991, 1998).

The structure of self-esteem depends on both information available to children and the ability to process that information. By 6 to 7 years, children have formed at least three separate self-esteems—academic, physical, and social—that become more refined with age. For example, academic self-worth divides into performance in different school subjects, social self-worth into peer and parental relationships (Marsh, 1990). In fact, children seem to develop an array of separate self-esteems first. The ability to view the self in terms of stable dispositions permits school-age children to combine their separate self-evaluations into a general psychological image of themselves—an overall sense of self-esteem (Harter, 1990, 1998). Consequently, self-esteem takes on the hierarchical structure shown in Figure 11.3 on page 450.

Separate self-evaluations, however, do not contribute equally to general self-esteem. Instead, as children attach greater importance to some aspects, those self-judgments are weighted more heavily in the total picture. Although individual differences exist in aspects of the self deemed most important, at all ages perceived physical appearance correlates more strongly with global self-worth than any other self-esteem factor (Harter, 1990, 1998). As we noted in Chapter 5, the emphasis that society and the media place on appearance has major implications for overall satisfaction with the self.

With the arrival of adolescence, several new dimensions of self-esteem are added—close friendship, romantic appeal, and job competence—that reflect important concerns of this period. Furthermore, the hierarchical structure of self-esteem is reflected even more clearly in factor analytic studies, and it is similar across different SES and ethnic groups (Byrne & Shavelson, 1996; Cauce, 1987; Harter, 1990). Finally, adolescents become more discriminating in the people they look to for validation of their self-esteem. Some rely more on parents, others on teachers, and still others on peers—differences that reflect the extent to which teenagers believe people in each context are interested in and respect them as a person (Harter, Waters, & Whitesell, 1998).

■ **CHANGES IN LEVEL OF SELF-ESTEEM: THE ROLE OF SOCIAL COMPARISONS.** Once self-esteem is established, does it remain stable or does it fluctuate? Longitudinal

[1]If you need to review the meaning of factor analysis, return to Chapter 8, page 317.

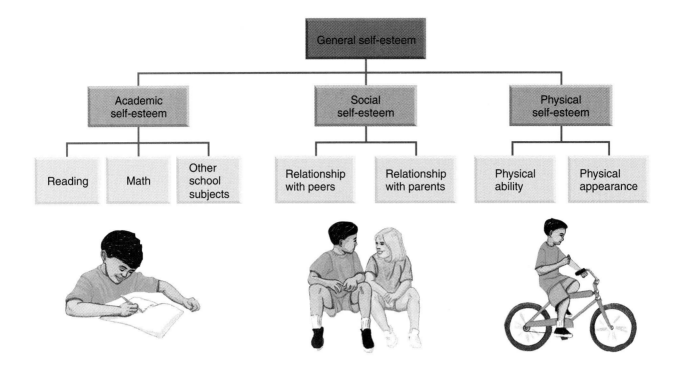

```
                    ┌─────────────────────┐
                    │  General self-esteem │
                    └─────────────────────┘
```

| Academic self-esteem | Social self-esteem | Physical self-esteem |

| Reading | Math | Other school subjects | | Relationship with peers | Relationship with parents | | Physical ability | Physical appearance |

FIGURE 11.3

Hierarchical structure of self-esteem in middle childhood.
From their experiences in different settings, children form at least three separate self-esteems—academic, social, and physical. These differentiate into additional self-evaluations and combine to form an overall sense of self-worth.

and cross-sectional evidence shows that self-esteem is very high during early childhood. Then it drops over the first few years of elementary school (Marsh, Craven & Debus, 1998; Wigfield et al., 1997). This decline in self-esteem occurs as children start to make **social comparisons**—that is, judge their abilities, behavior, appearance, and other characteristics in relation to those of others (Marsh et al., 1984; Stipek & MacIver, 1989).

Although 4- to 6-year-olds can engage in social comparison and use this information as the basis for self-evaluation, they do so only in very simple, two-instance situations—their own performance in relation to that of one other peer (Butler, 1998). In middle childhood, children are better able to compare multiple individuals, including themselves—a capacity fostered by grades and other feedback they receive in school (Ruble & Frey, 1991). As a result, self-esteem adjusts to a more realistic level that matches the opinions of others as well as objective performance. Over time, children also become aware of the benefits and costs of social comparison—its potential for self-enhancement as well as damage to one's own and others' self-esteem. Between first and fourth grade, they shift from overt comparisons in everyday talk ("My picture is better than yours") to subtle techniques ("What problem are you on?"). In this way, they protect themselves from the negative social consequences of bragging about their accomplishments (Pomerantz et al., 1995).

To shield their self-worth, most children eventually balance social comparison information with personal achievement goals (Ruble & Flett, 1988). Perhaps for this reason, the drop in self-esteem in the early school years is not great enough to be harmful. In fact, from fourth grade on, self-esteem rises and remains high for the majority of young people, who feel especially good about their peer relationships and athletic capabilities (Nottelmann, 1987; Zimmerman et al., 1997). The only exceptions to this trend are a decline in self-worth for some adolescents after transition to junior high and high school. Entry into a new school, accompanied by new teacher and peer expectations, may temporarily interfere with the ability to make realistic judgments about behavior and performance. In Chapter 15, we will take up these school transition effects in greater detail.

The increase in self-esteem just described is yet another reason that researchers question the widespread assumption discussed in Chapter 5—that adolescence is a time of emotional turmoil. To the contrary, for most young people, becoming an adolescent leads to feelings of pride and self-confidence (Powers, Hauser, & Kilner, 1989).

social comparisons Judgments of one's own abilities, behavior, appearance, and other characteristics in relation to those of others.

INFLUENCES ON SELF-ESTEEM

Up to this point, we have discussed general trends in the development of self-esteem. Wide individual differences exist that are strongly correlated with everyday behavior. For example, academic self-esteem predicts children's school achievement as well as their willingness to try hard at challenging tasks (Marsh, Smith, & Barnes, 1985). Children with high social self-esteem are better liked by peers (Harter, 1982). And as we saw in Chapter 5, boys come to believe they have more athletic talent than do girls, and they are more advanced in a variety of physical skills.

By adolescence, positive overall self-esteem predicts favorable psychological adjustment, including good grades in school and resistance to peer pressure and deviant activities (Zimmerman et al., 1997). Because self-esteem is related to so many outcomes, researchers have been intensely interested in uncovering factors that cause it to be high for some children and low for others. If ways can be found to improve children's sense of self-worth, then many aspects of development might be enhanced as well.

Self-esteem rises during adolescence. These young people participate in building a new home for a needy family under the auspices of Habitat for Humanity. They appear optimistic about life and proud of their new competencies.
(Mary Kate Denny/PhotoEdit)

■ **CULTURE.** Cultural forces profoundly affect self-esteem. For example, recall from Chapter 5 that during adolescence, early maturing girls and late maturing boys tend to feel poorly about themselves—outcomes influenced by cultural standards of physical beauty. Gender-stereotyped expectations for physical attractiveness and achievement have a detrimental effect on the self-esteem of many girls. Beginning in adolescence, they score lower than do boys in overall sense of self-worth—partly because girls worry more about their appearance and partly because they feel more insecure about their abilities (Crain, 1996).

Furthermore, the role of social comparison in self-esteem varies from culture to culture. An especially strong emphasis on social comparison may underlie the finding that Chinese and Japanese children score lower in self-esteem than do American children, despite their higher academic achievement (Chiu, 1992–1993; Hawkins, 1994). In Asian classrooms, competition is tough and achievement pressure is high. At the same time, Asian children less often call on social comparisons to bolster their own self-esteem. Because their culture places a high value on modesty and social harmony, they tend to be reserved about judging themselves positively but generous in their praise of others (Falbo et al., 1997; Heine & Lehman, 1995).

■ **CHILD-REARING PRACTICES.** Children and adolescents whose parents are warm and accepting and provide reasonable expectations for behavior feel especially good about themselves (Deković & Meeus, 1997; Feiring & Taska, 1996; Steinberg, Darling, & Fletcher, 1995). Warm, positive parenting lets young people know that they are accepted as competent and worthwhile. And firm but appropriate expectations, backed up with explanations, help them make sensible choices and evaluate their own behavior against reasonable standards.

In contrast, when parental support is *conditional* (withheld unless the young person meets very high standards), adolescents frequently engage in behaviors they consider "false"—not representative of their true self. Although most teenagers report acting "phony" from time to time, they usually do so to win temporary approval or to experiment with new roles. Those who display false-self behavior—"expressing things you don't really believe" or "putting on an act"—because others (and therefore they) devalue their true self suffer from low self-esteem, depression, and pessimism about the future (Harter et al., 1996).

Furthermore, children and adolescents who experience coercive parenting suffer severe assaults to their self-esteem. Harsh, forceful techniques communicate a sense of inadequacy to children—that their behavior needs to be controlled by adults because they are ineffective in managing it themselves. Finally, overly tolerant, indulgent parenting that promotes a feel-good attitude no matter how children behave creates a false sense of self-esteem, which is detrimental to development as well (see the From Research to Practice box on page 452).

Although parental acceptance and maturity demands are undoubtedly important ingredients of high self-esteem, we must keep in mind that these findings are correlational.

How Should Parents Boost Their Children's Self-Esteem?

ARED, A BRIGHT adolescent growing up in a well-to-do American family, earned C's and D's in academic courses because he seldom turned in homework or studied for exams. His parents tried paying Jared for good grades, but to no avail. Next, they threatened to ground him. When Jared's report card again showed no improvement, his parents gave in to his pleas for weekend privileges, blaming his weak school performance on low self-esteem.

"If only Jared liked himself better," his father reasoned, "he'd work harder in school and choose friends with more serious interests. We've *got* to find a way to make Jared feel better about himself!" Over the next 6 months, Jared's grades dropped further, and he and two of his friends were arrested for property destruction at a shopping mall.

Will parenting that boosts children's self-esteem help increasing numbers of young people like Jared, who lack character and direction? Or is Jared's parents' child-centeredness at the heart of his problems? According to William Damon (1995), the child-centered philosophy was a major breakthrough when it was first introduced. It made parents and teachers aware that children have unique developmental needs and benefit from warmth and encouragement. But, Damon argues, modern child-centeredness has been stretched to the point of indulgence. Many American parents are convinced that a child cannot develop meaningful goals and respect others without first coming to love himself. This idea is based on the assumption that self-esteem *precedes* healthy development. It must be built before anything else, through generous praise and unconditional acceptance.

Yet children with highly inflated self-esteem—self-perceptions much more favorable than the judgments of others—often have serious adjustment problems. In a recent study, second and third graders identified by their teachers as aggressive (frequently teasing, starting fights, telling mean lies, or excluding others) were far more likely than their classmates to rate themselves as perfect on a self-esteem

measure. Their distorted view of their own competence appeared to undermine any motivation to improve their behavior (Hughes, Cavell, & Grossman, 1997).

Damon maintains that self-esteem that fosters favorable development must be *the result of* prior accomplishment. From this perspective, it cannot be gained through its own pursuit; it must be earned through socially useful commitment and responsibility. Instead of insisting on mastery of meaningful skills, too many American parents assure their children, regardless of circumstances, that they are "okay" in every way. Compliments, such as "you're great," "you're terrific," that have no basis in real attainment disrupt children's potential for development. In Damon's view, sooner or later children see through them, come to mistrust the adults who repeat them, and begin to doubt themselves.

Cross-cultural evidence supports the view that genuine self-esteem is the product (not the producer) of real accomplishment. As we will see in Chapter 15, the academic achievement of children in the United States falls behind that of children in Asian nations, such as Japan and Taiwan. Yet even though Japanese and Taiwanese high school students report higher parental expectations for school performance, they feel less stress and anxiety than do their American agemates and display low rates of deviant behavior. Contrary to popular belief, Asian pupils do not attain their impressive levels of achievement at expense to their psychological well-being. Indeed, the highest Asian achievers report the fewest psychological symptoms. Strong parental support for achievement seems to contribute to Asian students' ability to meet rigorous academic standards while remaining well adjusted (Chen & Stevenson, 1995; Crystal et al., 1994).

According to Damon, parents serve children best when they guide them toward worthwhile activities and goals that result in credible self-esteem. Parents serve children poorly when they promote in them a false sense of self-regard. Had Jared's parents helped him sustain effort in the face of difficulty and insisted that he meet his responsibilities years earlier, they might have prevented the current situation.

We cannot really separate the extent to which child-rearing styles are causes of or reactions to children's characteristics and behavior. Research addressing the precise content of adults' messages to children has been far more successful at isolating factors that affect children's sense of self-worth. Let's see how these messages mold children's evaluations of themselves in achievement contexts.

ACHIEVEMENT-RELATED ATTRIBUTIONS

Attributions are our common, everyday explanations for the causes of behavior—the answers we provide to the question "Why did I (or another person) do that?" We group the causes of our own and others' behavior into two broad categories: external, environmental causes and internal, psychological causes. Then we further divide the category of psychological causes into two types: ability and effort. In assigning a cause, we use certain rules. If a behavior occurs for many people but only in a single situation (the whole class gets *A*'s on Mrs. Apple's French test), we conclude that it is externally caused (the test was easy). In

attributions Common, everyday explanations for the causes of behavior.

contrast, if an individual displays a behavior in many situations (Sally always gets *A*'s on French tests), we judge the behavior to be internally caused—by ability, effort, or both.

In Chapter 8, we showed that although intelligence predicts school achievement, the relationship is far from perfect. Differences among children in **achievement motivation**—the tendency to persist at challenging tasks—explain why some less intelligent pupils do better in school than their more intelligent classmates and why children who are equal in ability often respond differently in achievement situations. Today, researchers regard achievement-related attributions as the main reason some children are competent learners who display initiative when faced with obstacles to success, whereas others give up easily when their goals are not immediately achieved.

■ **EMERGENCE OF ACHIEVEMENT-RELATED ATTRIBUTIONS.** In earlier chapters, we showed that infants express great pleasure at acquiring new skills—satisfaction that reinforces their efforts. Babies are naturally driven toward mastery of activities that support their development (White, 1959). Achievement motivation is believed to have roots in this early drive.

"I did it!" this boy seems to exclaim, after filling his basket in an Easter egg hunt. Preschoolers are "learning optimists" who believe they can succeed if they keep on trying. Their attributions support initiative in the face of challenging tasks.
(Erik Skagestad)

By the end of the second year, children turn to adults for evaluations of their accomplishments, picking up information about the meaning of competence in their culture (Stipek, Recchia, & McClintic, 1992). And around age 3, they begin making attributions about their successes and failures. These attributions affect their expectancies of success. Expectancies, in turn, influence the extent to which children try hard in the future.

Many studies show that preschoolers are "learning optimists" who rate their own ability very high, often underestimate task difficulty, and hold positive expectancies of success. When asked to react to a situation in which one person does worse on a task than another, young children indicate that the lower-scoring person can still succeed if she keeps on trying (Schuster, Ruble, & Weinert, 1998). Although preschoolers sometimes get frustrated or angry when a task is hard, most recover easily. Their attributions support a continuation of the initiative they displayed during infancy.

One reason that young children's attributions are usually optimistic is that cognitively, they cannot yet distinguish the precise cause of their successes and failures. Instead, they view all good things as going together: A person who tries hard is also a smart person who is going to succeed (Nicholls, 1978). Belief in positive outcomes is also supported by the patience and encouragement of adults. Most parents realize that a preschooler who has trouble riding a tricycle or cutting with scissors is likely to be able to do so a short time later. Preschoolers, too, know that they are growing larger and stronger, and they see that failure on one occasion often precedes success on another.

Nevertheless, by age 4 some children give up easily when faced with a challenge, such as working a hard puzzle or building a tall block tower. They conclude that they cannot do the task and are discouraged after failing (Cain & Dweck, 1995; Smiley & Dweck, 1994). When these young nonpersisters are asked to act out with dolls an adult's reaction to failure, they often respond, "He's punished because he can't do the puzzle" or "Daddy's mad and is going to spank her." In contrast, persisters make an adult doll say, "He worked hard but just couldn't finish. He wants to try again" (Burhans & Dweck, 1995).

Furthermore, nonpersisting 4- to 6-year-olds are likely to see themselves as bad and deserving of negative feedback. And they often report that their parents would berate them for making minor mistakes (Dweck, 1991; Heyman, Dweck, & Cain, 1992). These children seem to base their self-worth entirely on others' judgments, not on inner standards. Consequently, they show early signs of maladaptive achievement behaviors that become more common during the school years, when performance evaluations increase.

■ **MASTERY-ORIENTED VERSUS LEARNED-HELPLESS CHILDREN.** During middle childhood, children begin to distinguish ability, effort, and external factors in explaining their performance (Skinner, 1995). Those who are high in achievement motivation develop **mastery-oriented attributions.** They believe that their successes are due to ability—a characteristic they can improve through trying hard and can count on when faced with

achievement motivation The tendency to persist at challenging tasks.

mastery-oriented attributions Attributions that credit success to high ability and failure to insufficent effort. Leads to high expectancies of success and a willingness to approach challenging tasks.

Repeated negative evaluations about their ability can cause children to develop learned helplessness—low expectancies of success and debilitating anxiety when faced with challenging tasks. This learned-helpless boy is overwhelmed by a poor grade. He seems to have concluded that there is little he can do to improve his performance.

(MacDonald Photography/Envision)

incremental view of ability The view that ability can be improved through trying hard.

learned helplessness Attributions that credit success to external factors, such as luck, and failure to low ability. Leads to low expectancies of success and anxious loss of control in the face of challenging tasks.

entity view of ability The view that ability is a fixed characteristic and cannot be changed.

new challenges. This **incremental view of ability**—that it can be altered—influences the way mastery-oriented children interpret and respond to negative events (Heyman & Dweck, 1998). When failure hits, they attribute it to factors that can be changed or controlled, such as insufficient effort or a very difficult task. So regardless of whether these children succeed or fail, they take an industrious, persistent approach to learning.

Unfortunately, children who develop **learned helplessness** give very discouraging explanations for their performance. They attribute their failures, not their successes, to ability. When they succeed, they are likely to conclude that external events, such as luck, are responsible. Furthermore, unlike their mastery-oriented counterparts, learned-helpless children hold an **entity view of ability**—that it is a fixed characteristic and cannot be changed. They do not think that competence can be improved by trying hard. So when a task is difficult, these children experience an anxious loss of control. They quickly give up, saying "I can't do this," before they have really tried (Elliott & Dweck, 1988).

Children's attributional styles affect their goals in learning situations. Mastery-oriented children focus on *learning goals*—increasing ability through effort and seeking information on how to do so. In contrast, the interests of learned-helpless children are much narrower. They focus on *performance goals*—obtaining positive and avoiding negative evaluations of their fragile sense of ability.

Over time, the ability of learned-helpless children no longer predicts their performance. Many are very bright pupils who have concluded that they are incompetent (Wagner & Phillips, 1992). Because they fail to make the connection between effort and success, learned-helpless children do not develop the metacognitive and self-regulatory skills that are necessary for high achievement (see Chapter 7). Lack of effective learning strategies, reduced persistence, and a sense of being controlled by external forces sustain one another in a vicious cycle (Heyman & Dweck, 1992).

In adolescence, young people attain a fully differentiated understanding of the relation between ability and effort. They realize that two people varying in ability can achieve the same outcome with different degrees of effort (Butler, 1999). When they view their own ability as fixed and low, they conclude that mastering a challenging task is not worth the cost—extremely high effort. To protect themselves from painful feelings of failure and to keep their inferior ability from being revealed to others, these learned-helpless young people select less challenging tasks and, eventually, less challenging courses and even less demanding careers. As Figure 11.4 shows, learned helplessness prevents children from pursuing tasks they are capable of mastering and from realizing their potential.

■ **INFLUENCES ON ACHIEVEMENT-RELATED ATTRIBUTIONS.** What accounts for the very different attributions of mastery-oriented and learned-helpless children? Adult communication plays a key role. Children who display a learned-helpless style tend to have parents who set unusually high standards yet believe that their child is not very capable and has to work harder than others to succeed (Parsons, Adler, & Kaczala, 1982; Phillips, 1987). When the child fails, the adult might say, "You can't do that, can you? It's okay if you quit" (Hokoda & Fincham, 1995). And when the child succeeds, the adult might respond, "Gee, I'm surprised you got that *A*," again leading the child to doubt his ability. Or the adult might give feedback evaluating the child's traits, as in "You're so smart." When used continuously, trait statements promote an entity view of ability, which encourages children to focus on performance goals, question their competence in the face of setbacks, and respond helplessly (Erdley et al., 1997).

Experimental research confirms the powerful impact of adult feedback on children's attributional styles. In one study, elementary school children were led to believe that their ability to do a task was either high or low. Then they were given one of two types of instructions: a message that emphasized a performance goal ("You'll be graded by experts on this task") or a message that highlighted a learning goal ("This task sharpens the mind and will help you with your studies"). Children who were told that they had low ability and for whom a performance goal was emphasized responded to mistakes in a learned-helpless fashion—by giving up, displaying negative affect, and remarking on their lack of talent. In contrast, children who were encouraged to pursue a learning goal behaved in a mastery-oriented fashion, persisting in attempts to find solutions regardless of their perceived ability (Elliott & Dweck, 1988).

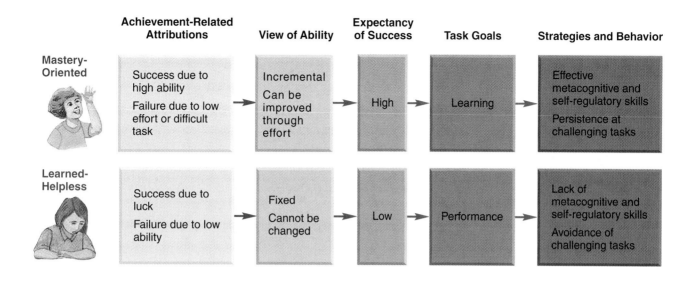

	Achievement-Related Attributions	View of Ability	Expectancy of Success	Task Goals	Strategies and Behavior
Mastery-Oriented	Success due to high ability Failure due to low effort or difficult task	Incremental Can be improved through effort	High	Learning	Effective metacognitive and self-regulatory skills Persistence at challenging tasks
Learned-Helpless	Success due to luck Failure due to low ability	Fixed Cannot be changed	Low	Performance	Lack of metacognitive and self-regulatory skills Avoidance of challenging tasks

FIGURE 11.4

Consequences of mastery-oriented and learned-helpless attributional styles.

A recent longitudinal study following 1,600 third to eighth graders over a three-year period highlights the vital role of teacher communication in fostering a mastery-oriented approach (Skinner, Zimmer-Gembeck, & Connell, 1998). Pupils who viewed their teachers as warm and as providing consistent, fair learning conditions (for example, making expectations clear, checking to see that the child understands) worked harder on assignments and participated more in class. Active engagement, in turn, predicted better academic performance, which sustained the child's belief in the effectiveness of effort. In contrast, children who experienced their teachers as unsupportive were more likely to regard their performance as externally controlled (by powerful teachers or luck). This predicted classroom disengagement and declining achievement. These negative outcomes led children to doubt their ability and believe even more strongly in the power of external forces.

Some children are especially likely to have their performance undermined by adult feedback. Girls more often than boys blame their ability for poor performance. Girls also tend to receive messages from teachers and parents that their ability is at fault when they do not do well (Ruble & Martin, 1998). Low-income ethnic minority children are vulnerable to learned helplessness as well. In several studies, African-American and Mexican-American children received less favorable teacher feedback than did other children (Aaron & Powell, 1982; Irvine, 1986; Losey, 1995). Furthermore, when ethnic minority children observe that adults in their own family are not rewarded by society for their achievement efforts, they may give up themselves. Many African-American children may come to believe that even if they do try in school, social prejudice will prevent them from succeeding in the end (Ogbu, 1997).

Finally, cultural values affect the likelihood that children will develop learned helplessness. Compared to Americans, Chinese and Japanese parents and teachers believe that success in school depends much more on effort than ability—a message they transmit to children (Tuss, Zimmer, & Ho, 1995). And Israeli children growing up on *kibbutzim* (cooperative agricultural settlements) are shielded from learned helplessness by classrooms that emphasize mastery and interpersonal harmony rather than ability and competition (Butler & Ruzany, 1993).

■ FOSTERING A MASTERY-ORIENTED APPROACH. Attribution research suggests that at times, well-intended messages from adults undermine children's competence. **Attribution retraining** is an effective approach to intervention that encourages learned-helpless children to believe they can overcome failure if only they exert more effort. Most often, children are given tasks that are hard enough that they will experience some failure. Then they get repeated feedback that helps them revise their attributions, such as "You can do it if you try harder." Children are also taught to view success as due to both ability and

attribution retraining An approach to intervention that uses adult feedback to modify the attributions of learned-helpless children, thereby encouraging them to believe they can overcome failure if only they exert more effort.

Ways to Foster a Mastery-Oriented Approach to Learning and Prevent Learned Helplessness

Technique	Description
Provision of tasks	Select tasks that are meaningful, responsive to a diversity of pupil interests, and appropriately matched to current competence so that the child is challenged but not overwhelmed.
Parent and teacher encouragement	Communicate warmth, confidence in the child's abilities, the value of achievement, and the importance of effort in success.
	Model high effort in overcoming failure.
	(For teachers) Communicate often with parents, suggesting ways to foster children's effort and progress.
	(For parents) Monitor schoolwork; provide scaffolded assistance that promotes knowledge of effective strategies and self-regulation.
Performance evaluations	Make evaluations private; avoid publicizing success or failure through wall posters, stars, privileges to "smart" children, and prizes for "best" performance.
	Stress individual progress and self-improvement.
School environment	Offer small classes, which permit teachers to provide individualized support for mastery.
	Provide for cooperative learning and peer tutoring, in which children assist each other; avoid ability grouping, which makes evaluations of children's progress public.
	Accommodate individual and cultural differences in styles of learning.
	Create an atmosphere that values academics and sends a clear message to teachers, parents, and children that all pupils can learn.

Sources: Ames, 1992; Eccles, Wigfield, & Schiefele, 1998.

effort rather than chance by giving them additional feedback after they succeed, such as "You're really good at this" or "You really tried hard on that one" (Schunk, 1983).

Another approach is to teach low-effort children to focus less on grades and more on learning for its own sake. A large-scale study showed that classrooms emphasizing the intrinsic value of acquiring new knowledge led to impressive gains in failing pupils' academic self-esteem and motivation (Ames, 1992). Learned-helpless children also need instruction in metacognition and self-regulation to make up for development lost in this area and to ensure that renewed effort will pay off (Borkowski & Muthukrisna, 1995).

To work well, attribution retraining is best begun early, before children's views of themselves become hard to change (Eccles, Wigfield, & Schiefele, 1998). An even better approach is to prevent learned helplessness before it happens. Table 11.1 lists a variety of ways to foster a mastery-oriented approach to learning.

CONSTRUCTING AN IDENTITY

Adolescents' well-organized self-descriptions and more differentiated sense of self-esteem provide the cognitive foundation for forming an **identity,** first recognized by psychoanalyst Erik Erikson (1950, 1968) as a major personality achievement and as a crucial step toward becoming a productive, happy adult. Constructing an identity involves defining who you are, what you value, and the directions you choose to pursue in life. One expert described it as an explicit theory of oneself as a rational agent—one who acts on the basis of reason, takes responsibility for those actions, and can explain them (Moshman, 1998). This search for what is true, real, and indispensable to the self is the driving force behind many commitments—to a sexual orientation (see Chapter 5); to a vocation; to interpersonal relationships and community involvement; to ethnic group membership; and to moral, political, religious, and cultural ideals.

Erikson regarded successful psychosocial outcomes in infancy and childhood as paving the way toward a coherent, positive identity. (Return to Chapter 1, page 19, to review Erikson's stages.) Although the seeds of identity formation are planted early, not until adolescence do young people become absorbed in this task. According to Erikson, in complex societies, teenagers experience an *identity crisis*—a temporary period of distress as they experiment with alternatives before settling on a set of values and goals. During this period, what adolescents once took for granted they question. Those who go through a process of inner soul-searching eventually arrive at a mature identity. They sift through characteristics that defined the self in childhood and combine them with new commitments. Then they mold these into a solid inner core that provides a sense of sameness as they move through different roles in daily life.

Current theorists agree with Erikson that questioning of values, plans, and priorities is necessary for a mature identity, but they no longer refer to this process as a "crisis" (Grotevant, 1998). The term suggests a sudden, intense upheaval of the self. For some young people, identity development is traumatic and disturbing, but for most it is not. "Exploration" better describes the typical adolescent's experience. Identity formation usually proceeds in a very gradual, uneventful way. The many daily choices teenagers make—"whom to date, whether or not to break up, having intercourse, taking drugs, going to college or working, which college, what major, studying or playing, being politically active"—and the reasons for them are gradually put together into an organized self-structure (Marcia, 1980, p. 161; Moshman, 1999).

Erikson described the negative outcome of adolescence as *identity confusion*. Some young people appear shallow and directionless, either because earlier conflicts have been resolved negatively or society restricts their choices to ones that do not match their abilities and desires. As a result, they are unprepared for the psychological challenges of adulthood.

Is there research to support Erikson's ideas about identity development? In the following sections, we will see that adolescents go about the task of defining the self in ways that closely match Erikson's description.

As these adolescents exchange opinions about a recent news event, they become more aware of a diversity of viewpoints. A flexible, open-minded approach to grappling with competing beliefs and values fosters identity development.

(Tony Freeman/PhotoEdit)

■ **PATHS TO IDENTITY.** Using a clinical interviewing procedure, researchers group adolescents into four categories, called *identity statuses,* which show the progress they have made toward forming a mature identity. Table 11.2 on page 458 summarizes these identity statuses: **identity achievement, moratorium, identity foreclosure,** and **identity diffusion.**

Adolescents often shift from one status to another until identity is achieved. Cross-sectional and longitudinal research reveals that many young people start out as identity foreclosed and diffused, but by late adolescence they have moved toward moratorium and identity achievement (Archer, 1982; Meilman, 1979). College triggers increased exploration as young people are exposed to new career options and lifestyles. Most teenagers who go to work right after high school graduation settle on a self-definition earlier than do college-bound youths (Munro & Adams, 1977). But those who find it difficult to realize their occupational goals because of lack of training or vocational choices are at risk for identity foreclosure or diffusion (Archer, 1989b).

At one time, researchers thought that adolescent girls postponed the task of establishing an identity and, instead, focused their energies on Erikson's next stage, intimacy development. We now know that this is not so. Girls do show more sophisticated reasoning in identity areas related to intimacy, such as sexuality and family–career priorities. In this respect, they are actually ahead of boys in identity development. Otherwise, the process and timing of identity formation are the same for boys and girls (Archer, 1989a; Archer & Waterman, 1994).

■ **IDENTITY STATUS AND PSYCHOLOGICAL WELL-BEING.** Identity achievement and moratorium are psychologically healthy routes to a mature self-definition, whereas foreclosure and diffusion are maladaptive. Young people who are identity achieved or actively exploring have a higher sense of self-esteem, are more likely to engage in abstract and critical thinking, report greater similarity between their ideal self (what they hoped to become) and their real self, and are advanced in moral reasoning (Josselson, 1994; Marcia et al., 1993). Although they report spending more time thinking about themselves than do adolescents who lag behind in identity development, they are also more secure about revealing their true selves to others (O'Connor, 1995).

Adolescents who get stuck in foreclosure or diffusion have adjustment difficulties. Foreclosed individuals tend to be dogmatic, inflexible, and intolerant. Some use their

identity A well-organized conception of the self made up of values, beliefs, and goals to which the individual is solidly committed.

identity achievement The identity status of individuals who have explored and committed themselves to self-chosen values and goals.

moratorium The identity status of individuals who are exploring alternatives in an effort to find values and goals to guide their life.

identity foreclosure The identity status of individuals who have accepted ready-made values and goals that authority figures have chosen for them.

identity diffusion The identity status of individuals who do not have firm commitments to values and goals and are not actively trying to reach them.

TABLE 11.2

The Four Identity Statuses

Identity Status	Description	Example
Identity achievement	Having already explored alternatives, identity-achieved individuals are committed to a clearly formulated set of self-chosen values and goals. They feel a sense of psychological well-being, of sameness through time, and of knowing where they are going.	When asked how willing she would be to give up going into her chosen occupation if something better came along, the adolescent responds, "I might, but I doubt it. I've thought long and hard about law as a career. I'm pretty certain it's for me."
Moratorium	*Moratorium* means delay or holding pattern. These individuals have not yet made definite commitments. They are in the process of exploration—gathering information and trying out activites, with the desire to find values and goals to guide their life.	When asked if he had ever had doubts about his religious beliefs, the adolescent answers, "Yes, I guess I'm going through that right now. I just don't see how there can be a god and yet so much evil in the world."
Identity foreclosure	Identity-foreclosed individuals have committed themselves to values and goals without taking time to explore alternatives. Instead, they accept a ready-made identity that authority figures (usually parents but sometimes teachers, religious leaders, or romantic partners) have chosen for them.	When asked if she had ever reconsidered her religious beliefs, the adolescent states, "No, not really; our family is pretty much in agreement on these things."
Identity diffusion	Identity-diffused individuals lack clear direction. They are not committed to values and goals, nor are they actively trying to reach them. They may have never explored alternatives, or they may have tried to do so but found the task too threatening and overwhelming.	When asked about his attitude toward nontraditional gender roles, the adolescent responds, "Oh, I don't know. It doesn't make much difference to me. I can take it or leave it."

commitments defensively, regarding any difference of opinion as a threat. Most are afraid of rejection by people on whom they depend for affection and self-esteem (Berzonsky, 1993; Kroger, 1995). A few foreclosed teenagers who are alienated from their families and society may join cults or other extremist groups, uncritically adopting a way of life that is different from their past.

Long-term diffused teenagers are the least mature in identity development. They typically entrust themselves to luck or fate, have an "I don't care" attitude, and tend to passively go along with whatever the "crowd" is doing at the moment. As a result, they are most likely to use and abuse drugs. At the heart of their apathy is often a sense of hopelessness about the future (Archer & Waterman, 1990). Many of these young people are at risk for serious depression and suicide—problems that rise sharply during adolescence (see the Social Issues box on the following page).

■ **FACTORS THAT AFFECT IDENTITY DEVELOPMENT.** Adolescent identity is the beginning of a lifelong process of refinement in personal commitments that reflect a dynamic blend of personality with situational context. Whenever the individual or the context changes, the possibility for reformulating identity exists (Grotevant, 1998). A wide variety of factors affect identity development.

PERSONALITY. In the previous section, we showed that identity status is linked to personality characteristics. The attributes considered are both cause and consequence of identity development. In particular, a flexible, open-minded approach to grappling with competing beliefs and values is important. Adolescents who assume that absolute truth is always attainable tend to be foreclosed, whereas those who lack confidence in the prospect of ever knowing anything with certainty are more often identity diffused or in a state of moratorium. Adolescents who appreciate that rational criteria can be used to choose among alternative visions are likely to be identity achieved (Boyes & Chandler, 1992).

FAMILY. Recall that infants who develop a healthy sense of agency have parents who provide both emotional support and freedom to explore. A similar link between parenting and identity exists at adolescence. When the family serves as a "secure base" from which teenagers can confidently move out into the wider world, identity development is enhanced.

Adolescent Suicide: Annihilation of the Self

THE SUICIDE RATE increases over the lifespan. As Figure 11.5 shows, it is lowest in childhood and highest in old age, but it jumps sharply at adolescence. Currently, suicide is the third-leading cause of death among young people, after motor vehicle injuries and homicides. It is a growing national problem, having tripled over the past 30 years, perhaps because teenagers face more stresses and have fewer supports than they did in decades past. Adolescent suicide has also risen throughout Europe, although not as much as it has in the United States (U.S. Department of Health and Human Services, 1998c).

FACTORS RELATED TO ADOLESCENT SUICIDE. Striking sex-related differences in suicidal behavior exist. The number of boys who kill themselves exceeds the number of girls by 4 or 5 to 1. This may seem surprising, since girls show a higher rate of depression. Yet the findings are not inconsistent. Girls make more unsuccessful suicide attempts and use methods with a greater likelihood of revival, such as a sleeping pill overdose. In contrast, boys tend to select more active techniques that lead to instant death, such as firearms or hanging. Gender-role expectations may account for these differences. There is less tolerance for feelings of helplessness and failed efforts in males than females (Garland & Zigler, 1993).

Compared to the white majority, certain nonwhite, ethnic minority teenagers, including African Americans and Hispanics, have lower suicide rates—a difference that increases in adulthood. Higher levels of support through extended families may be responsible. In contrast, suicide among Native American and Canadian Aboriginal youths is several times higher than the national average. It appears to be linked to high rates of profound family poverty, alcohol use, depression, and a sense of hopelessness (Strickland, 1997).

Suicidal adolescents often show signs of extreme despondency during the period before the suicidal act. Many verbalize the wish to die, lose interest in school and friends, neglect their personal appearance, and give away treasured possessions. These warning signs appear in two types of young people. In the first group are highly intelligent teenagers who are solitary, withdrawn, and unable to meet their own high standards or those of important people in their lives. A second, larger group show antisocial tendencies. These young people express their unhappiness through bullying, fighting, stealing, and increased risk-taking and drug use (Lehnert, Overholser, & Spirito, 1994). Besides turning their anger and disappointment inward, they are hostile and destructive toward others.

Family turmoil, parental emotional problems, and marital breakup are common in the backgrounds of suicidal teenagers, who typically feel distant from parents and peers (Shagle & Barber, 1993). Their fragile self-esteem disintegrates in the face of stressful life events. Common circumstances just before a suicide include the breakup of an important peer relationship or the humiliation of having been caught engaging in irresponsible, antisocial acts (King, 1997).

Why is suicide rare in childhood but on the rise in adolescence? Teenagers' improved ability to plan ahead seems to be involved. Few successful suicides are sudden and impulsive. Instead, young people at risk usually take purposeful steps toward killing themselves. The cognitive changes of

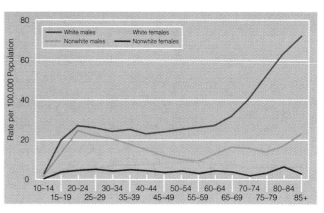

FIGURE 11.5

Suicide rates over the lifespan in the United States. Although teenagers do not commit suicide as often as adults and the aged, the suicide rate rises sharply from childhood to adolescence. Rates are greater for males than females and for white majority than nonwhite, ethnic minority individuals.

(From U.S. Bureau of the Census, 1998.)

adolescence also contribute to the age-related increase in suicide. Belief in the personal fable (see Chapter 6) leads many depressed young people to conclude that no one could possibly understand the intense pain they feel. As a result, their despair, hopelessness, and isolation deepen.

PREVENTION AND TREATMENT. Picking up on the signals that a troubled teenager sends is a crucial first step in preventing suicide. Parents and teachers need to be trained in warning signs. Schools can help by providing sympathetic counselors, peer support groups, and information about telephone hotlines. Once a teenager takes steps toward suicide, staying with the young person, listening, and expressing sympathy and concern until professional help can be obtained is essential.

Intervention with depressed and suicidal adolescents takes many forms, from antidepressant medication to individual, family, and group therapy. Sometimes hospitalization is necessary to ensure the teenager's safety and swift entry into treatment. Until the adolescent improves, parents are usually advised to remove weapons, knives, razors, scissors, and drugs from the home. On a broader scale, gun-control legislation that limits adolescents' access to the most frequent and deadly suicide method would greatly reduce both the number of suicides and the high teenage homicide rate (Clark & Mokros, 1993).

After a suicide, family and peer survivors need support to assist them in coping with grief, anger, and guilt for not having been able to help the victim. Teenage suicides often take place in clusters. When one occurs, it increases the likelihood of others among peers who knew the young person or heard about the death through the media. In view of this trend, an especially watchful eye must be kept on vulnerable adolescents after a suicide happens. Restraint by journalists in reporting teenage suicides on television or in newspapers can also aid in preventing them (Diekstra, Kienhorst, & de Wilde, 1995).

Adolescents who feel attached to their parents but who are also free to voice their own opinions tend to be identity achieved or in a state of moratorium (Grotevant & Cooper, 1985, 1998; Hauser, Powers, & Noam, 1991). Foreclosed teenagers usually have close bonds with parents, but they lack opportunities for healthy separation. And diffused young people report the lowest levels of warm, open communication at home (Papini, 1994).

SCHOOL AND COMMUNITY. Identity development also depends on schools and communities offering young people rich and varied opportunities for exploration. Erikson (1968, p. 132) noted that it is "the inability to settle on an occupational identity which most disturbs young people." Classrooms that promote high-level thinking; extracurricular and community activities that enable teenagers to take on responsible roles; teachers and counselors who encourage low-SES and ethnic minority students to go to college; and vocational training programs that immerse adolescents in the real world of adult work foster identity achievement (Cooper, 1998).

Variations in opportunity can lead to regional differences in identity development. For example, between ages 13 and 17, exploration increases among Australian adolescents living in urban environments, whereas it decreases among youths in rural areas. Lack of educational and vocational options in Australian rural regions is undoubtedly responsible (Nurmi, Poole, & Kalakoski, 1996). Regardless of where young people live, a chance to talk with adults and older peers who have worked through identity questions can be helpful (Waterman, 1989).

LARGER SOCIETY. The larger cultural context and historical time period affect identity development. Among today's adolescents, exploration and commitment take place earlier in the identity domains of gender-role preference and vocational choice than in religious and political values. Yet a generation ago, when the Vietnam War divided Americans and disrupted the lives of thousands of young people, the political beliefs of American youths took shape sooner (Archer, 1989b). Societal forces are also responsible for the special problems that gay and lesbian youths (see Chapter 5) and ethnic minority adolescents face in forming a secure identity, as the Cultural Influences box on the following page describes.

BRIEF REVIEW

The earliest aspect of the self to emerge is the I-self, evident in infants' recognition that their own actions cause objects and people to react in predictable ways. In the second year, toddlers become aware of the self's physical features, indicating that they have begun to construct a me-self. During the preschool years, language development leads to clearer representation and expression of the me-self, in the form of categorical and remembered selves. Awareness of an inner self is evident in young preschoolers' talk about mental states. By age 4, children form a theory of mind in which they understand the relationship of beliefs and desires to behavior.

Self-concept evolves from an emphasis on observable characteristics and typical emotions and attitudes in the preschool years to stable personality traits in middle childhood. By middle to late adolescence, teenagers combine their various traits into an integrated picture. During the early school years, self-esteem differentiates, becomes hierarchically organized, and declines as children make social comparisons and evaluate their performance at different activities. From fourth grade on, self-esteem rises for the majority of young people. Adult communication affects children's attributions for success and failure in achievement contexts, leading some children to become mastery oriented and others to be learned helpless when faced with challenging tasks.

Four identity statuses describe the degree of progress that adolescents have made toward constructing a mature identity. Identity achievement and moratorium are adaptive statuses associated with psychological well-being. Teenagers in a long-term state of identity foreclosure or diffusion tend to have adjustment difficulties. Identity development is fostered by a rational approach to choosing among competing beliefs and values, by parents who provide emotional support and freedom to explore, by schools and communities that are rich in opportunities, and by societies that permit young people from all backgrounds to realize their personal goals.

ASK YOURSELF . . .

◆ At age 13, Jeremy described himself as both "cheerful" and "glum." At age 16, he said, "Sometimes I'm cheerful, at other times I'm glum, so I guess I'm kind of moody." What accounts for this change in Jeremy's self-concept?

◆ Several parents want to know what they can do to promote their child's self-esteem. What advice would you give them, and why?

◆ CONNECTIONS
Recall from Chapter 6 (see page 244) that between 4 and 8 years, children figure out who is really behind the activities of Santa Claus and the Tooth Fairy, and they realize that magicians use trickery. How might these understandings relate to development of a theory of mind?

During middle childhood, children emphasize personality traits in their self-descriptions and distinguish ability, effort, and external factors in their causal explanations of behavior. What cognitive changes underlie these capacities? (See Chapter 6, page 249, and Chapter 7, page 277.)

Identity Development Among Ethnic Minority Adolescents

ALTHOUGH MOST CAUCASIAN-AMERICAN adolescents are aware of their cultural ancestry, it is not a matter of intense concern for them (Phinney, 1993). For minority teenagers, ethnicity is central to the quest for identity, and it presents difficult, sometimes overwhelming challenges. As they develop cognitively and become more sensitive to feedback from the social environment, minority youths become painfully aware that they are targets of discrimination and inequality. This discovery complicates their efforts to develop a sense of cultural belonging and a set of personally meaningful life goals.

Minority adolescents often feel caught between the standards of the larger society and the traditions of their culture. Some respond by rejecting aspects of their ethnic background. In one study, Asian-American 15- to 17-year-olds were more likely than blacks and Hispanics to hold negative attitudes toward their subcultural group. Perhaps the absence of a social movement stressing ethnic pride of the kind available to black and Hispanic teenagers underlies this finding (Phinney, 1989). Some parents are overly restrictive of their teenagers out of fear that assimilation into the larger society will undermine their cultural traditions, and their youngsters rebel. One Southeast-Asian refugee described his daughter's behavior, "She complains about going to the Lao temple on the weekend and instead joined a youth group in a neighborhood Christian Church. She refused to wear traditional dress on the Lao New Year. The girl is setting a very bad example for her younger sisters and brothers" (Nidorf, 1985, pp. 422–423).

Other minority teenagers react to years of shattered self-esteem, school failure, and barriers to success in the American mainstream by defining themselves in contrast to majority values. A Mexican-American teenager who had given up on school commented, "Mexicans don't have a chance to go on to college and make something of themselves." Another, responding to the question of what it takes to be a successful adult, pointed to his uncle, leader of a local gang, as an example (Matute-Bianche, 1986, p. 250–251).

The challenges of blending mainstream and ethnic-group values are apparent in the experiences of academically successful African-American adolescents. To avoid being labeled white by their peers, they may reduce their academic effort or conceal their accomplishments. Because it is painful and confusing, minority high school students often dodge the task of forming an ethnic identity. Many are diffused or foreclosed on ethnic identity issues (Markstrom-Adams & Adams, 1995).

Yet some economically disadvantaged minority students do not react this way. A case study of six poverty-stricken African-American adolescents who were high-achieving and optimistic about their future revealed that they were intensely aware of oppression but believed in striving to alter their social position. How did they develop this sense of agency? Parents, relatives, and teachers had convinced them through discussion and example that injustice should not be tolerated and that together, blacks could overcome it. David, whose family was on welfare and lived in rundown housing, illustrates the experiences of these achievement-oriented, ethnically identified young people:

> My 20-year-old brother, he talks about it a lot. The way that Blacks have been treated as time went on. And he stress a lot that it [racism] still goes on—is alive and well. And he talks about it. He says you always have to give back and maintain. Never forget where you came from. Make our selves one—make Whites stand up and take notice—'cause that's the only way we [Blacks] going to get out of the situation we always been in. (O'Connor, 1997, p. 618)

Research indicates that adolescents who use a proactive style to deal with prejudice and discrimination, including self-affirmation and attempts to disprove stereotypes, are more likely to have a committed sense of their ethnic group membership (Phinney & Chavira, 1995).

How can society help minority adolescents resolve identity conflicts constructively? A variety of efforts are relevant, including

- reducing poverty;

- promoting effective parenting, in which children and adolescents benefit from family ethnic pride yet are encouraged to explore the meaning of ethnicity in their own lives;

- ensuring that schools respect minority youths' native language and unique learning styles; and

- fostering multicultural knowledge, contact, and respect between ethnic groups in integrated schools and neighborhoods. (García-Coll & Magnuson, 1997)

A secure ethnic identity is associated with better psychological adjustment. But forming a **bicultural identity**—by exploring and adopting values from *both* the subculture and the dominant culture—offers added benefits. Biculturally identified adolescents tend to be achieved in other areas of identity as well. They also have a higher sense of self-esteem, a greater sense of mastery over the environment, and more positive relations with members of other ethnic groups (Phinney & Kohatsu, 1997). In sum, ethnic-identity achievement enhances many aspects of emotional and social development.

These Native-American adolescents dress in traditional costume in preparation for demonstrating a ceremonial dance to citizens of a small Wyoming town. When minority youths encounter respect for their cultural heritage in schools and communities, they are more likely to retain ethnic values and customs as an important part of their identities.

(John Eastcott/Yva Momatiuk/The Image Works)

Thinking About Other People

Children's understanding of other people—the inferences they make about others' behavior, mental states, and personality traits—has much in common with their developing understanding of themselves. This facet of social cognition also becomes increasingly differentiated and well organized with age.

UNDERSTANDING INTENTIONS

Accurately interpreting others' behavior and deciding how to react to it often depend on distinguishing actions that are intentional from those that are accidental. By age 2, children say "gonna," "hafta," and "wanna" to announce behaviors they are about to perform. Preschoolers often rely on this grasp of purposefulness to defend themselves. After being scolded for bumping into a playmate or spilling a glass of milk, they exclaim, "It was an accident!" or "I didn't do it on purpose!"

Between 2½ and 3 years, this understanding extends to others. Preschoolers become sensitive to behavioral cues that help them tell if another person is acting intentionally. At first, they focus on the person's statements. If a person says he is going to do something and then does it, 3-year-olds judge the behavior as deliberate. If statements and actions do not match, then the behavior was not intended (Abbott, Lee, & Flavell, 1998; Astington, 1993).

Around age 4, children move beyond this view of intention-in-action. They start to appreciate intention as an internal mental state that guides but can be distinguished from action. Consequently, they realize that a desired outcome can be achieved deliberately (as intended) or accidentally. In one study, preschoolers heard two stories. In one, a girl threw bread crumbs, and birds ate them. In the other, a girl accidentally dropped bread crumbs, and birds ate them. When asked which girl meant for the birds to eat the crumbs, 3-year-olds were equally likely to choose either girl. In contrast, 4- and 5-year-olds correctly chose the first girl, even though both girls acted similarly (Astington, 1991). Older preschoolers also have a beginning grasp of make-believe as intentional action. They say that an involuntary behavior (sneezing, coughing, or yawning) is intentional if someone is pretending to do it (Joseph, 1998).

By the end of early childhood, children draw on a wide range of information to judge intentionality. For example, 5-year-olds note whether a person is concentrating on what she is doing; whether her action leads to positive or negative outcomes (negative ones are usually not intended); whether she looks surprised, disappointed, or puzzled at an outcome; and whether some external cause can account for the person's behavior (Smith, 1978).

Human intentional acts extend beyond the ones just considered. For example, we can deliberately refrain from acting but pretend that our lack of response was unintentional, by saying something like "I forgot all about it!" Between ages 5 and 9, children rely increasingly on a *verbal–nonverbal consistency rule* to evaluate the sincerity of such statements about intentions. For example, older children understand quite well that telling another person you like something when you look neutral or unhappy probably means you are not telling the truth (Rotenberg, Simourd, & Moore, 1989). The ability to detect more subtle efforts to conceal intentions depends on awareness of fine-grained features of a situation as well as sophisticated perspective-taking skills, a topic we will take up shortly.

Finally, children differ in how accurately they interpret others' intentions. Those who get along well with adults and peers make these judgments easily. In contrast, highly aggressive children show striking biases in inferring intentions; they often see hostility where it does not exist (Dodge & Price, 1994). As we will see in Chapter 12, such children require special help in learning how to evaluate and respond appropriately to others' behavior.

PERSON PERCEPTION

Person perception concerns how we size up the attributes of people with whom we are familiar in everyday life. To study it, researchers use methods similar to those that focus on children's self-concepts: asking them to describe people they know, such as "Can you tell me what kind of person _____ is?"

bicultural identity The identity constructed by adolescents who explore and adopt values from both their subculture and the dominant culture (see page 461).

person perception The way individuals size up the attributes of people with whom they are familiar in everyday life.

■ **UNDERSTANDING PEOPLE AS PERSONALITIES.** Like their self-descriptions, before age 8, children's descriptions of others focus on commonly experienced emotions and attitudes, concrete activities, and behaviors. Over time, children discover consistencies in the actions of people they know and mention personality traits.

At first, these references are closely tied to behavior and consist of implied dispositions, such as "He is always fighting with people" or "She steals and lies" (Rholes, Newman, & Ruble, 1990). Later, children mention traits directly, but they are vague and stereotyped—for example, "good," "nice," or "acts smart." At times, children's predictions of behavior based on these traits are too broad, as when a child says a "nice" person is better at schoolwork than a "not-nice" person. At other times, predictions are too narrow due to school-age children's limited awareness that a person can express a trait in a range of related behaviors. Gradually, sharper trait descriptions appear, such as "honest," "trustworthy," "generous," "polite," and "selfish," and children become more convinced of the stability of such dispositions (Droege & Stipek, 1993; Ruble & Dweck, 1995).

About the time they begin comparing themselves to others, children start to make comparisons between people. These also change from concrete to abstract. At first, children cast comparisons in behavioral terms: "Billy runs a lot faster than Jason." Around age 10 to 12, after children have had sufficient experience inferring personality traits, they integrate these into social comparisons: "Paul's a lot more considerate than thick-headed Del" (Barenboim, 1981, p. 133).

During adolescence, as abstract thinking becomes better established, inferences about others' personalities are drawn together into organized character sketches (O'Mahoney, 1989). As a result, between ages 14 and 16, teenagers present much richer accounts of people they know that combine physical traits, typical behaviors, and inner dispositions.

■ **UNDERSTANDING ETHNICITY AND SOCIAL CLASS.** Person perception also includes making sense of diversity and inequality among people. Most 3- and 4-year-olds have formed basic concepts of race and ethnicity, in that they can apply labels of black and white to pictures, dolls, and people. Indicators of social class—education and occupational prestige—are not accessible to young children. Nevertheless, they can distinguish rich from poor on the basis of physical characteristics, such as clothing, residence, and possessions (Ramsey, 1991).

By the early school years, children absorb prevailing attitudes toward social groups. Since race, ethnicity, and social class are closely related in the United States, American children quickly connect power and privilege with white people and poverty and subordinate status with people of color (Ramsey, 1995).

Children are more likely to hold negative attitudes toward groups to which they themselves do not belong—a bias that also characterizes adults. Yet recall that with age, children pay more attention to dispositions and make finer distinctions between people. The capacity to classify the social world in multiple ways permits school-age children to understand that people can be both "the same" and "different"—that those who look different need not think, feel, or act differently (Bigler & Liben, 1993; Doyle & Aboud, 1995). Consequently, prejudice declines in middle childhood.

Nevertheless, children vary in the extent to which they hold racial, ethnic, and social-class biases. Although adults with intolerant personalities (who hold a wide array of negative stereotypes) exist, traitlike prejudice is rare among children. Five- to 12-year-olds' ethnic bias does not predict their gender bias or their dislike of overweight people (Powlishta et al., 1994). This suggests that childhood prejudice is the product of specific learning experiences. The following three factors are influential:

■ *A fixed view of personality traits.* Children who come to believe that personality is fixed tend to make rigid judgments of people as good or bad and ignore the intentions behind their behavior. These trait-stability endorsers, compared to children who see personality as changeable, are more likely

Contact with members of other races and ethnic groups reduces the chances that children will classify the social world on the basis of race and ethnicity. When children sort people in these ways, they are likely to rate members of their own group positively and members of outgroups negatively—beginning signs of prejudice.

(Chip Henderson/Tony Stone Images)

to agree that "a new girl at school who makes up a lie to try to get other kids to like her" is a bad kid and that "if someone is really friendly and shares her toys with other kids, she will always act this way" (Heyman & Dweck, 1998).

■ *High self-esteem.* A surprising finding is that children (and adults) with very high self-esteem are more likely to hold unfair racial and ethnic biases. Individuals who think well of themselves seem to compare themselves to lower-status, less advantaged individuals or groups as a way of confirming their favorable self-evaluation (Gagnon & Morasse, 1995). As yet, researchers are not sure what motivates people to use this means of maintaining a positive self-image.

■ *A social world in which people are sorted into groups.* The more obvious group distinctions are, the greater the chances of own-group preference and out-group discrimination. When children in a summer school program were sorted into "blue" and "yellow" groups that teachers used as the basis for seating arrangements and assigned tasks, they were more likely than controls to rate members of their own group positively and members of the out-group negatively (Bigler, Jones, & Lobliner, 1997).

Children and adolescents with a tolerant outlook may still display prejudice in their behavior. As we will see later, racial, ethnic, and SES segregation is common in children's friendships at all ages. Contact and collaboration among different groups in neighborhoods, schools, and communities are the best ways to overcome these biases—in both thought and action (Ramsey, 1995).

PERSPECTIVE TAKING

In this and previous chapters, we have emphasized that **perspective taking**—the capacity to imagine what other people may be thinking and feeling—is important for a wide variety of social-cognitive achievements, including referential communication skills (Chapter 9), understanding others' emotions (Chapter 10), self-concept and self-esteem, person perception, and inferring intentions.

Recall that Piaget regarded egocentrism—preschoolers' inability to take the viewpoint of another—as the major feature responsible for the immaturity of their thought, in both the physical and social domains. Yet we have seen that young children have some capacity for perspective taking as soon as they become consciously self-aware in the second year of life. Nevertheless, Piaget's ideas inspired a wealth of research on children's capacity to take another's perspective, which improves steadily over childhood and adolescence.

■ **SELMAN'S STAGES OF PERSPECTIVE TAKING.** Robert Selman developed a five-stage model of children's perspective-taking skill. He asked preschool through adolescent youngsters to respond to social dilemmas in which the characters have differing information and opinions about an event. Here is one example:

Holly is an 8-year-old girl who likes to climb trees. She is the best tree climber in the neighborhood. One day while climbing down from a tall tree she falls off the bottom branch but does not hurt herself. Her father sees her fall. He is upset and asks her to promise not to climb trees anymore. Holly promises. Later that day, Holly and her friends meet Sean. Sean's kitten is caught up in a tree and cannot get down. Something has to be done right away or the kitten may fall. Holly is the only one who climbs trees well enough to reach the kitten and get it down, but she remembers her promise to her father (Selman & Byrne, 1974, p. 805)

After the dilemma is presented, children answer questions that highlight their ability to interpret the story from varying points of view, such as

Does Sean know why Holly cannot decide whether or not to climb the tree?

What will Holly's father think? Will he understand if she climbs the tree?

Does Holly think she will be punished for climbing the tree? Should she be punished for doing so?

perspective taking The capacity to imagine what other people may be thinking and feeling.

TABLE 11.3

Selman's Stages of Perspective Taking

Stage	Approximate Age Range	Description	Typical Response to "Holly" Dilemma
Level 0: Undifferentiated perspective taking	3–6	Children recognize that self and other can have different thoughts and feelings, but they frequently confuse the two.	The child predicts that Holly will save the kitten because she does not want it to get hurt and believes that Holly's father will feel just as she does about her climbing the tree: "Happy; he likes kittens."
Level 1: Social-informational perspective taking	4–9	Children understand that different perspectives may result because people have access to different information.	When asked how Holly's father will react when he finds out that she climbed the tree, the child responds, "If he didn't know anything about the kitten, he would be angry. But if Holly shows him the kitten, he might change his mind."
Level 2: Self-reflective perspective taking	7–12	Children can "step into another person's shoes" and view their own thoughts, feelings, and behavior from the other person's perspective. They also recognize that others can do the same.	When asked whether Holly thinks she will be punished, the child says, "No. Holly knows that her father will understand why she climbed the tree." This response assumes that Holly's point of view is influenced by her father being able to "step into her shoes" and understand why she saved the kitten.
Level 3: Third-party perspective taking	10–15	Children can step outside a two-person situation and imagine how the self and other are viewed from the viewpoint of a third, impartial party.	When asked whether Holly should be punished, the child says, "No, because Holly thought it was important to save the kitten. But she also knows that her father told her not to climb the tree. So she'd think she shouldn't be punished only if she could get her father to understand why she had to climb the tree." This response steps outside the immediate situation to view both Holly's and her father's perspectives simultaneously.
Level 4: Societal perspective taking	14–adult	Individuals understand that third-party perspective taking can be influenced by one or more systems of larger societal values.	When asked if Holly should be punished, the individual responds, "No. The value of humane treatment of animals justifies Holly's action. Her father's appreciation of this value will lead him not to punish her."

Sources: Selman, 1976; Selman & Byrne, 1974.

Table 11.3 summarizes Selman's five stages of perspective taking. As you can see, at first children have only a limited idea of what other people might be thinking and feeling. Over time, they become more conscious of the fact that people can interpret the same event in different ways. Soon, children can "step into another person's shoes" and reflect on how that person might regard their own thoughts, feelings, and behavior. Finally, they can examine the relationship between two people's perspectives simultaneously, at first from the vantage point of a disinterested spectator and later by making reference to societal values.

■ **SUPPORT FOR SELMAN'S STAGES.** Both cross-sectional and longitudinal research provide support for Selman's stages (Gurucharri & Selman, 1982; Selman, 1980). Even so, perspective-taking skill differs greatly among children of the same age. These differences have much to do with everyday experiences in which adults and peers clarify their viewpoints, encouraging children to look at situations from another's perspective. Consistent with this idea, children in collectivist cultures, which emphasize the importance of cooperation and group harmony, do better on perspective-taking tasks than do children in individualistic cultures (Keats & Fang, 1992).

Attainment of Selman's stages is also related to cognitive development—findings that offer additional support for his developmental progression. Individuals who fail Piaget's

FIGURE 11.6

In viewing each of these pictures for the first time, can a baby or a child tell that the object depicted is a horse? Four-year-olds thought that both observers could recognize the horse, even from a nondescript part. Not until age 6 did they realize that prior experience (having seen the full picture) as well as greater knowledge (being older and familiar with horses) affects an individual's ability to interpret pictures. (Adapted from Taylor, Cartwright, & Bowden, 1991.)

recursive thought The self-embedded form of perspective taking that involves thinking about what another person is thinking.

concrete operational tasks tend to be at Selman's Level 0; those who pass concrete but not formal operational tasks tend to be at Levels 1 and 2; and those who are increasingly formal operational tend to be at Levels 3 and 4 (Keating & Clark, 1980; Krebs & Gillmore, 1982). Furthermore, each set of Piagetian tasks tends to be mastered somewhat earlier than its related perspective-taking level (Walker, 1980).

These findings suggest that Piagetian milestones are a necessary but not sufficient condition for gains in perspective taking. As a close look at Selman's stages reveals, advances depend on the capacity to consider several pieces of information at once and to think abstractly. At the same time, additional social-cognitive capacities are required, as we will see in the following section.

■ **PERSPECTIVE-TAKING GAMES.** According to several researchers, preschoolers' limited perspective-taking skills are largely due to their passive view of the mind—their assumption that what a person knows is the result of simply observing rather than actively interpreting experience (Chandler & Carpendale, 1998; Pillow, 1995). In agreement with this idea, when asked to play a special "privileged-information game," preschoolers run into difficulty.

In one study, an experimenter showed 4- to 6-year-olds pictures of objects and then covered them so either a nondescript part or an identifiable part was left showing (see Figure 11.6). Next, children were asked whether two observers—a baby and a child—who had never seen the full pictures could recognize the objects from the incomplete versions. Four-year-olds often said that an observer could tell from a nondescript part what the object was. And although they were well aware that children know more than babies, they did not apply this understanding to the perspective-taking game. They thought that a baby would be able to recognize pictures of nondescript and identifiable object parts just as easily as would an older child, even when the objects (a horse or a teeter-totter) were unfamiliar to infants. Not until age 6 did children realize that prior experience and knowledge affect the ability to interpret a picture (Taylor, Cartwright, & Bowden, 1991). Around 6 to 8 years, children understand that besides knowledge, people's beliefs and expectations can lead to quite different views of new information (Pillow, 1991).

Other gamelike tasks have focused on **recursive thought,** the self-embedded form of perspective taking that involves thinking about what another person is thinking. Selman's stages suggest that thinking recursively (Levels 3 and 4) improves over the adolescent years, a trend that is supported by research. Patricia Miller, Frank Kessel, and John Flavell (1970) asked first through sixth graders to describe cartoon drawings showing one- and two-loop recursive thought (see Figure 11.7). By sixth grade, only 50 percent of children had mastered one-loop recursions, and two-loop recursions were rare. Not until midadolescence do young people grasp the complexities of recursive understanding (Flavell et al., 1968).

Recursive thought makes human interaction truly reciprocal. People often call on it to clear up misunderstandings, as when they say, "I thought you would think I was just kidding when I said that." Recursive thinking is also involved in our attempts to disguise our real thoughts and feelings, when we reason in ways like this: "He'll think I'm jealous if I tell him I don't like his new car, so I'll pretend I do" (Perner, 1988). Finally, the capacity to think recursively contributes to the intense self-focusing and concern with the imaginary audience typical of early adolescence (see Chapter 6). As Miller, Kessel, and Flavell (1970) point out, "Often to their pain, adolescents are much more gifted at this sort of wondering than first graders are" (p. 623).

■ **PERSPECTIVE TAKING AND SOCIAL BEHAVIOR.** Children's developing perspective-taking skills help them get along with other people. When we anticipate another person's point of view, social relationships become more predictable. We can also respond to the needs of others more effectively. Good perspective takers are more likely to display empathy and sympathy, and they are better at thinking of effective ways to handle difficult social situations (Eisenberg, Murphy, & Shepard, 1997; Marsh, Serafica, & Barenboim, 1981). For these reasons, they tend to be especially well liked by peers (LeMare & Rubin, 1987).

Although good perspective taking is a crucial ingredient of mature social behavior, it does not always result in prosocial acts. How children apply their ability to imagine another person's viewpoint depends on the situation. In a competitive task, skilled perspec-

FIGURE 11.7

Cartoon drawings depicting recursive thought. Not until midadolescence do young people master the complexities of this self-embedded form of perspective taking.

(From P. H. Miller, F. S. Kessel, & J. H. Flavell, 1970, "Thinking About People Thinking About People Thinking About . . . : A Study of Social Cognitive Development," *Child Development, 41*, p. 616. © The Society for Research in Child Development, Inc. Reprinted by permission.)

One-loop recursion
"The boy is thinking that he is thinking about himself."

Two-loop recursion
"The boy is thinking that the girl is thinking of the father thinking of the mother."

tive takers are often as good at defending their own viewpoint as they are at cooperating. Also, even when children appreciate another person's thoughts and feelings, additional factors, such as temperament, influence whether they will act on their social awareness. Recall from Chapter 10 that children who have learned to regulate their emotions effectively are more likely to help others in distress and handle social conflicts constructively. Assertive, sociable children also engage in higher rates of prosocial behavior.

Finally, children and adolescents with very poor social skills—in particular, the angry, aggressive styles that we will take up in Chapter 12—have great difficulty imagining the thoughts and feelings of others. They often mistreat adults and peers without experiencing the guilt and remorse prompted by awareness of another's point of view. Interventions that provide coaching and practice in perspective taking help reduce antisocial behavior and increase prosocial responding (Chalmers & Townsend, 1990; Chandler, 1973).

BRIEF REVIEW

The ability to infer intentions from others' behavior emerges in early childhood. By the end of the preschool years, children begin to view intention as an internal mental state that guides but can be distinguished from action. During middle childhood, children detect subtle efforts to conceal intentions.

Like self-concept, person perception shifts from a focus on concrete activities and behaviors in early childhood to an emphasis on personality traits during the school years. In describing others, adolescents produce organized character sketches. Preschoolers form basic concepts of race and ethnicity and distinguish rich and poor on the basis of physical characteristics. As school-age children begin to classify the social world in multiple ways, they realize that people who look different need not think, feel, or act differently, and prejudice declines. Children who believe that personality is fixed are more likely to make rigid social judgments than are those who view it as changeable.

Perspective taking undergoes vast changes from early childhood into adolescence. It begins with limited awareness of others' thoughts and feelings and evolves into advanced recursive and societal perspective-taking skills. Perspective taking is fostered by experiences in which adults and peers encourage children to look at situations from another's point of view. It also builds on cognitive milestones and children's awareness that the mind actively interprets experience. Perspective taking is related to a wide variety of social skills.

ASK YOURSELF . . .

◆ *Ten-year-old Marla is convinced that her classmate, Bernadette, who often doesn't turn in her homework, is lazy and will never be any good at her studies. Jane thinks that Bernadette tries but can't concentrate because her parents are getting a divorce. Why is Marla more likely than Jane to harbor social prejudices?*

◆ CONNECTIONS
Review the section on children's understanding of emotion in Chapter 10 (pages 408–411). List examples of age-related changes in the ability to take the emotional perspective of another and relate them to Selman's stages of perspective taking.

How are advances in perspective taking related to the emergence of the imaginary audience and personal fable in early adolescence? (See Chapter 6, page 255.)

Thinking About Relations Between People

s children develop, they apply their insights into the inner psychological worlds of themselves and others to an understanding of relations between people. Most research on this aspect of social cognition has to do with reasoning about friendship and interpersonal conflicts.

UNDERSTANDING FRIENDSHIP

To an adult, friendship is not a one-sided relationship. You can like someone without being a friend to that person, since your liking may not be returned. Instead, friendship is a mutual relationship involving companionship, sharing, understanding of thoughts and feelings, and caring for and comforting one another in times of need. In addition, mature friendships endure over time and survive occasional conflicts.

Children's ideas about friendship do not start out this way. On the basis of interviews with children, several theories of the development of friendship understanding have emerged. All emphasize that friendship begins as a concrete relationship based on pleasurable activity and evolves into a more abstract relationship based on mutual consideration and psychological satisfaction. William Damon (1977, 1988) has combined the work of other investigators into a three-stage sequence.

■ **LEVEL 1: FRIENDSHIP AS A HANDY PLAYMATE[2] (ABOUT 4 TO 7 YEARS).** Preschoolers already understand something about the uniqueness of friendship. They know that a friend is someone "who likes you," with whom you spend a lot of time playing, and with whom you share toys. As yet, there is little sense of appreciating another person's personality traits, since (as we saw earlier) young children are only beginning to size up their own and others' dispositions.

Because friendship is viewed concretely, in terms of play and exchange of material goods, young children regard it as easily begun—for example, by meeting in the neighborhood and saying, "Hi." However, friendship does not yet have a long-term, enduring quality. Level 1 children say that a friendship can dissolve when one partner refuses to share, hits, or is not available to play. A 5-year-old's answer to the question "What makes a good friend?" sums up the young child's view of friendship: "Boys play with boys, trucks play with trucks, dogs play with dogs." When the interviewer probed, "Why does that make them good friends?" the child answered, "Because they do the same things" (Selman, 1980, p. 136).

■ **LEVEL 2: FRIENDSHIP AS MUTUAL TRUST AND ASSISTANCE (ABOUT 8 TO 10 YEARS).** During middle childhood, children's concepts of friendship become more complex and psychologically based. Look closely at the responses of this 8-year-old to questions about what makes a best friend:

> *Who's your best friend?* Shelly. *Why is Shelly your best friend?* Because she helps me when I'm sad, and she shares. . . . *What makes Shelly so special?* I've known her longer, I sit next to her and got to know her better. . . . *How come you like Shelly better than anyone else?* She's done the most for me. She never disagrees, she never eats in front of me, she never walks away when I'm crying, and she helps me on my homework. . . . *How do you get someone to like you?* . . . If you're nice to [your friends], they'll be nice to you. (Damon, 1988, pp. 80–81)

As these statements show, friendship is no longer just a matter of engaging in the same activities. Instead, it is a mutually agreed-on relationship in which children like each other's personal qualities and respond to one another's needs and desires. Since friendship is a matter of both children wanting to be together, getting it started takes more time and effort than it did at earlier ages.

Once a friendship forms, *trust* becomes its defining feature. School-age children state that a good friendship is based on acts of kindness that signify each person can be counted

[2]I have provided titles for each of the stages to help you remember them.

on to support the other. Consequently, events that break up a friendship are quite different than they were during the preschool years. Older children regard violations of trust, such as not helping when others need help, breaking promises, and gossiping behind the other's back, as serious breaches of friendship. And once a rift occurs, it cannot be patched up as easily as it could at younger ages—by playing nicely after a conflict. Instead, apologies and explanations are necessary (Damon, 1977; Selman, 1980).

■ **LEVEL 3: FRIENDSHIP AS INTIMACY AND LOYALTY (11 TO 15 YEARS AND OLDER).** By early adolescence, friendship takes on greater depth. When asked to comment on the meaning of friendship, teenagers stress two characteristics. The first, and most important, is *intimacy.* Adolescents seek psychological closeness and mutual understanding from their friends. Second, more than younger children, teenagers want their friends to be *loyal*—to stick up for them and not to leave them for somebody else (Buhrmester, 1996).

Because friendship has this depth dimension to it, adolescents regard it as a relationship formed over time by "getting to know someone." In addition, friends are viewed as important in relieving psychological distress, such as loneliness, sadness, and fear. And because true mutual understanding implies forgiveness, only an extreme falling out can lead relationships to dissolve. Here is how one teenager described his best friendship:

> *Well, you need someone you can tell anything to, all kinds of things that you don't want to spread around. That's why you're someone's friend.* Is that why Jimmy is your friend? Because he can keep a secret? *Yes, and we like the same kinds of things. We speak the same language. My mother says we're two peas in a pod. . . .* Do you ever get mad at Jimmy? *Not really.* What if he did something that got you really mad? *He'd still be my best friend. I'd tell him what he did wrong and maybe he'd understand. I could be wrong too, it depends.* (Damon, 1977, p. 163)

■ **RESEARCH ON CHILDREN'S DEVELOPING UNDERSTANDING OF FRIENDSHIP.** Both cross-sectional and longitudinal research confirm the sequence of friendship understanding just described (Bigelow, 1977; Keller & Wood, 1989). Also, virtually every study shows that even after a psychological appreciation of friendship emerges, early concepts, such as sharing common activities, are not abandoned. Instead, they are integrated into more mature concepts. Furthermore, friendship reasoning is related to advances in perspective taking (Selman, 1981). We would certainly expect this to be so, since a more advanced appreciation of friendship implies greater awareness of others' thoughts and feelings.

■ **ARE CHILDREN'S CONCEPTS OF FRIENDSHIP RELATED TO FEATURES OF THEIR REAL FRIENDSHIPS?** If social cognition plays a vital role in everyday behavior, then children's developing ideas about friendship should predict qualities of their real friendships. There is good evidence for this in three areas: friendship stability, interaction, and resemblance.

STABILITY OF FRIENDSHIPS. We would expect greater friendship stability as mutual trust and loyalty become more important in children's expectations of their friends. Indeed school-age children are more selective about their friendships. Preschoolers say they have lots of friends—sometimes everyone in their class! By age 8 or 9, children have only a handful of people they call friends and, very often, only one best friend. Girls, especially, are more exclusive in their friendships because (as we will see shortly) they typically demand greater closeness than do boys (Parker & Asher, 1993).

Although friendship stability does increase with age, children's friendships are remarkably stable at all ages. However, lasting friendships at younger ages are more a function of the constancy of social environments, such as preschool and neighborhood, than of social cognition. At older ages, friendships endure for psychological reasons, although they often undergo temporary shifts in the strength of each partner's commitment (Cairns et al., 1995). And as children approach puberty, varying rates of development and new interests often lead to a temporary period of change in choice of friends (Berndt, 1988).

INTERACTION BETWEEN FRIENDS. A more mature understanding of friendship should lead older children to behave with more mutual responsiveness and sensitivity toward

During middle childhood, concepts of friendship become more psychologically based. Although these boys enjoy playing baseball, they want to spend time together because they like each other's personal qualities. Mutual trust is a defining feature of their friendship. Each child counts on the other to provide support and assistance.

(Richard Hutchings/PhotoEdit)

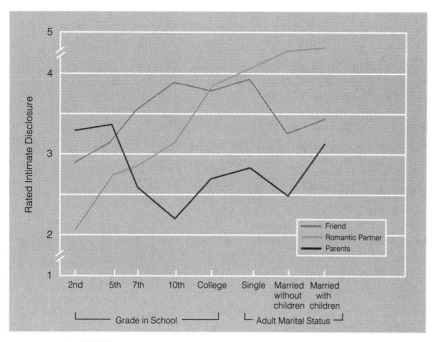

FIGURE 11.8

Age changes in reported self-disclosure to parents and peers, based on data from several studies. Self-disclosure to friends increases steadily during adolescence, reflecting intimacy as a major basis of friendship. Self-disclosure to romantic partners also rises. However, not until the college years does it surpass intimacy with friends. Self-disclosure to parents declines in early adolescence, a time of mild parent–child conflict. As family relationships readjust to the young person's increasing autonomy, self-disclosure to parents rises.

(From D. Buhrmester, 1996, "Need Fulfillment, Interpersonal Competence, and the Developmental Contexts of Early Adolescent Friendship," in W. M. Bukowski, A. F. Newcomb, & W. W. Hartup, Eds., *The Company They Keep: Friendship During Childhood and Adolescence*, New York: Cambridge University Press, p. 168. Reprinted by permission.)

friends. Actually, interactions between friends have a unique quality at all ages. Preschoolers give twice as much reinforcement, in the form of greetings, praise, and compliance, to children whom they identify as friends, and they also receive more from them. Friends are also more emotionally expressive—talking, laughing, and looking at each other more often—than are nonfriends (Hartup, 1996). Apparently, spontaneity, intimacy, and sensitivity characterize rewarding friendships very early, although children are not able to say until much later that these qualities are essential to a good friendship.

Prosocial behavior toward friends does increase with age. When working on a task together, school-age friends help, share, refer to each other's comments, and spend more time focused than first-grade friends do (Hartup, 1996; Newcomb & Bagwell, 1995). Cooperation, generosity, mutual affirmation, and self-disclosure (see Figure 11.8) continue to rise into adolescence—trends that may reflect greater effort and skill at preserving the relationship, increased sensitivity to a friend's needs, and intimacy as a basis for friendship (Buhrmester, 1996; Windle, 1994). Teenagers are also less possessive of their friends than they were in childhood. They recognize that friends need a certain degree of autonomy, which they also desire for themselves (Rubin, Bukowski, & Parker, 1998).

Friends do not just behave more prosocially. They get into more conflicts and compete with each other more than do nonfriends. Since children regard friendship as based on equality, they seem especially concerned about losing a contest to a friend. Also, when children hold differing opinions, friends are more likely to voice them than are nonfriends (Fonzi et al., 1997). As early as middle childhood, friends realize that close relationships can survive disagreements if both parties are secure in their liking for one another (Laursen, Hartup, & Koplas, 1996). As a result, friendship provides an important context in which children learn to tolerate criticism and resolve disputes.

Yet the extent to which friendships support children's development depends on the company they keep. Children who bring kindness and compassion to their friendships strengthen their prosocial tendencies. When aggressive children make friends, the relationship often becomes a context for magnifying antisocial acts. The friendships of aggressive girls are high in self-disclosure but full of jealousy, conflict, and betrayal. These girls frequently elicit personal information from their friends and then use it to gain control over the relationship by threatening to reveal confidences. In contrast, aggressive boys are seldom hostile toward friends. Instead, they expect their friends to join them in aggressive acts against peers outside the relationship (Grotpeter & Crick, 1996).

These findings indicate that the social problems of aggressive children operate within their closest peer ties. When we take up the development of aggression in Chapter 12, we will return to these sex-related differences in ways of expressing hostility.

RESEMBLANCE BETWEEN FRIENDS. The value adolescents attach to feeling especially "in sync" with their friends suggests that friendship pairs should become increasingly similar in attitudes and values with age. Actually, the attributes on which friends are most alike throughout childhood and adolescence are race, ethnicity, sex, and SES. But friends also resemble one another in personality (sociability, shyness, aggression, and depression), peer popularity, academic achievement, and prosocial behavior (Haselager et al., 1998; Kupersmidt, DeRosier, & Patterson, 1995). And by adolescence, they tend to be alike in educational aspirations, political beliefs, and willingness to try drugs and engage in lawbreaking acts. Perhaps children and adolescents choose companions like themselves to increase the supportiveness of friendship. Once they do so, friends influence each other.

Adolescent friends become more alike in attitudes, values, school grades, and social behavior over time (Berndt & Keefe, 1995; Savin-Williams & Berndt, 1990).

Still, we must keep in mind that some aspects of friendship similarity are due to the way the social world is organized. Most children and adolescents live in neighborhoods that are segregated by income, ethnicity, and belief systems. In one study of friendships in an integrated junior high school, over 50 percent of seventh to ninth graders reported at least one close other-race friend. But these friendships seldom extended to out-of-school contexts unless adolescents lived in integrated neighborhoods (Du-Bois & Hirsch, 1990).

In integrated schools and neighborhoods, many children form close other-race friendships.

(Carol Palmer/The Picture Cube)

■ **SEX-RELATED DIFFERENCES IN FRIENDSHIPS.** Ask several girls and boys age 8 or older to describe their close friendships, and you are likely to find a consistent difference. Emotional closeness and trust are more common in girls' talk about friends than in boys' (Buhrmester & Prager, 1995). Whereas girls frequently get together to "just talk," boys more often gather for an activity—usually sports and competitive games that foster control, power, and excitement. When boys talk, their discussions often focus on recognition and mastery issues, such as the accomplishments of sports figures or their own achievements in sports and school (Buhrmester, 1996).

In a study illustrating this difference, 12- to 15-year-olds were telephoned each evening over 5 days and asked to report their social experiences of the previous 24 hours. For each interaction lasting 10 minutes or longer, participants judged the extent of self-disclosure and emotional support. Girls reported more frequent interaction with friends, and they rated their friendship interactions substantially higher on these qualities (Buhrmester & Carbery, 1992).

Because of gender-role expectations, boys and girls seem to enter friendships with different social needs. Then their friendships nurture those needs further—girls toward communal concerns, boys toward achievement and status concerns. This does not mean that boys rarely form close friendship ties. They often do, but the quality of their friendships is more variable. The intimacy of boys' friendships is related to gender identity. Boys who identify strongly with the traditional masculine role are less likely to form close friendships than are those with flexible gender-related preferences (Jones & Dembo, 1989).

■ **BENEFITS OF FRIENDSHIPS.** By adolescence, warm, gratifying friendships are related to many aspects of psychological health and competence (Buhrmester, 1996). Although young people who are well adjusted to begin with are better able to form and sustain close peer ties, supportive friendships further their emotional and social development. The reasons are several:

■ *Close friendships provide opportunities to explore the self and develop a deep understanding of another.* Through open, honest communication, friends become sensitive to each other's strengths and weaknesses, needs and desires. They get to know themselves and their friend especially well, a process that supports the development of self-concept, perspective taking, identity, and intimate ties beyond the family. Look again at Figure 11.8, and you will see that self-disclosure to friends precedes disclosure to romantic partners. The lengthy, often emotionally laden psychological discussions between adolescent friends appear to prepare the young person for love relationships (Savin-Williams & Berndt, 1990; Sullivan, 1953).

■ *Close friendships provide support in dealing with the stresses of everyday life.* Because friendship enhances sensitivity to and concern for another, it increases the likelihood of empathy, sympathy, and prosocial behavior. Adolescents with supportive friendships report fewer daily hassles and more "uplifts" than do others (Kanner et al., 1987). As a result, anxiety and loneliness are reduced while self-esteem and sense of well-being are fostered.

■ *Close friendships can improve attitudes toward and involvement in school.* Young people with satisfying friendships tend to do well in school. The link between friendship and academic performance depends, of course, on the extent to which each friend values achievement. But overall, close friendship ties promote good school adjustment in both middle- and low-SES students. When children and adolescents enjoy interacting with friends at school, perhaps they begin to view all aspects of school life more positively (Berndt & Keefe, 1995; Vandell & Hembree, 1994).

UNDERSTANDING CONFLICT: SOCIAL PROBLEM SOLVING

Children, even when they are best friends, sometimes come into conflict with one another. Recall that Piaget (1923/1926) granted social conflict an important role in development. He believed that arguments and disagreements help children notice others' viewpoints, which leads to a decline in egocentrism. In Chapter 6, we noted that resolution of conflict, rather than conflict per se, promotes development. Indeed, even preschoolers seem to handle most quarrels constructively. Only rarely do conflicts lead to intensely hostile encounters. Instead, brief refusals, denials, and opposition that children settle themselves are much more common. Furthermore, conflicts are not very frequent when compared to children's friendly, cooperative interactions (Hay, 1984).

Despite their infrequency and brevity, peer conflicts are important. Watch children work out their disputes over play objects ("That's mine!" "I had it first!"), entry into and control over play activities ("I'm on your team, Jerry." "No, you're not!"), and disagreements over facts, ideas, and beliefs ("I'm taller than he is." "No, you aren't!"). You will see that they take these matters quite seriously. Recent research reveals that social conflicts offer children invaluable learning opportunities in **social problem solving.** In their efforts to resolve conflicts effectively—in ways that are both acceptable to others and beneficial to the self—children must bring together a variety of social-cognitive skills. These include encoding and interpreting social cues, clarifying a social goal, generating strategies for reaching the goal, evaluating the effectiveness of each strategy in preparation for choosing one, and enacting it.

Kenneth Dodge regards social problem solving as a special, interpersonal form of the more general problem-solving process. He organizes the steps of social problem solving into the circular model shown in Figure 11.9. Notice how this flowchart takes an *information-processing approach* to social cognition. It clarifies the exact series of steps a child

Although not very frequent when compared to friendly interaction, conflicts between children do occur. To solve social problems effectively, children must bring together a variety of social-cognitive skills: accurately encoding and interpreting social cues, formulating social goals that take into account both their own and others' needs, generating and evaluating problem-solving strategies, and enacting an adaptive response.

(Jonathan Nourok/PhotoEdit)

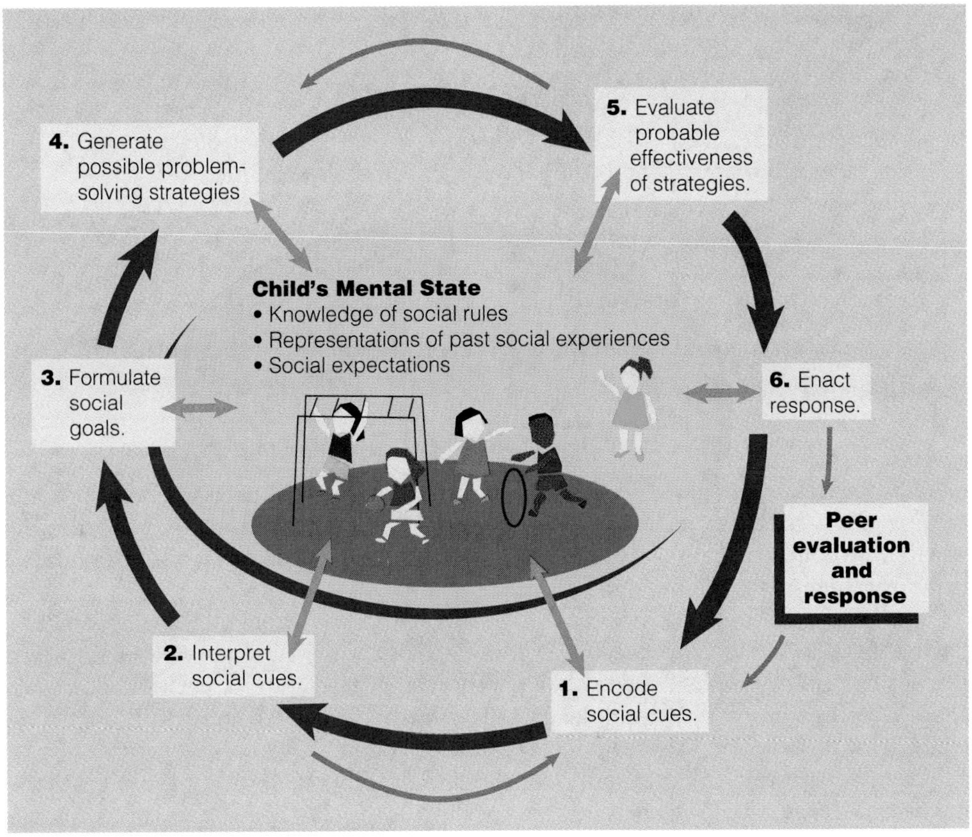

FIGURE 11.9

Dodge's information-processing model of social problem solving. The model is circular, since children often engage in several information-processing activities at once—for example, interpreting information as they encode it and continuing to consider the meaning of another's behavior while they generate and evaluate problem-solving strategies. The model also takes into account the impact of mental state on social information processing—in particular, children's knowledge of social rules, their representations of past social experiences, and their expectations for future experiences. Peer evaluations and responses to enacted strategies, along with the way children think about those responses, are also important factors in social problem solving.

(Adapted from N. R. Crick & K. A. Dodge, 1994, "A Review and Reformulation of Social Information-Processing Mechanisms in Children's Social Adjustment," *Psychological Bulletin, 115,* 74–101. Copyright © 1994 by the American Psychological Association. Adapted by permission.)

might use in grappling with a social problem and arriving at a solution. Once these are known, then specific processing deficits can be identified, and treatment programs can be tailored to meet children's individual needs (Crick & Dodge, 1994; Dodge, 1985).

Researchers are especially interested in social problem solving because of its profound impact on social competence. Well-adjusted children who get along with peers interpret social cues accurately, formulate goals that enhance relationships (such as being helpful to peers), and have a repertoire of effective strategies that they apply adaptively. In contrast, maladjusted children who are disliked by peers, either because they are highly aggressive or because they are anxious and withdrawn, have great difficulty solving social problems. They attend selectively to certain social cues, such as hostile acts, and hold biased expecations for how a situation is going to proceed. Their social goals (getting even with or avoiding a peer) often lead to strategies that damage relationships (Crick & Dodge, 1994; Rose & Asher, 1999). When social problem-solving skills improve, both children and adolescents show gains in academic, emotional, and social functioning (Dubow et al., 1991; Elias et al., 1986).

■ **DEVELOPMENT OF SOCIAL PROBLEM SOLVING.** Most research on social problem solving focuses on strategy generation—by asking young children to think of ways to deal with hypothetical conflicts, such as wanting to play with a toy someone else has. Findings reveal that the quantity and quality of children's strategies improve with age. Younger children, as well as children with poor peer relations, describe strategies that impulsively meet their needs, such as grabbing, hitting, or ordering another child to obey. Older children and those with good peer relations assert their needs in ways that take into account the needs of others. They rely on friendly persuasion and compromise, sometimes suggesting that a conflict might be solved by creating new mutual goals. In doing so, they recognize that solutions to immediate problems have an important bearing on the future of the relationship (Downey & Walker, 1989; Yeates, Schultz, & Selman, 1991).

Other researchers have expanded the study of social problem solving to find out at what points, besides strategy generation, socially competent children differ from less

social problem solving Resolving social conflicts in ways that are both acceptable to others and beneficial to the self. Involves encoding and interpreting social cues, clarifying a social goal, generating and evaluating strategies, and enacting a response.

competent children. Dodge and his collaborators (1986) assessed school-age children's skillfulness at five of the problem-solving steps in Figure 11.9. A videotape dramatized a problem involving entry into a play group. In the first scene, two children played a board game, and the researchers measured each participant's ability to *encode and interpret social cues* about the video characters' willingness to let the child join the game. Then children *generated strategies* for joining the game, and their responses were coded in the following ways:

- *Competent:* polite requests to play and other friendly comments

- *Aggressive:* threats, physical force, and barging in without asking

- *Self-centered:* statements about the self, such as "Hey, I know how to play that!"

- *Passive:* shy, hovering responses, such as waiting and "hanging around"

- *Appeals to authority:* for example, "The teacher said I could play"

Next, participants viewed five more scenes in which a child tried to enter the game using each of these strategies, and they engaged in *strategy evaluation* by indicating whether or not the technique would succeed. Finally, participants *enacted a response* by demonstrating a way of joining the game.

In a separate session, the investigators assessed children's actual social competence by having them gain entry into a real peer group activity in the laboratory. Results showed that all five social problem-solving skills were related to children's performance. Each social-cognitive measure also predicted how effectively children joined play activities while being observed on their school playground.

Over the early elementary school years, the various components of social problem solving become more strongly associated with socially competent behavior. As children move through the first few years of schooling, they confront increasingly complex social situations, which demand more sophisticated social information-processing skills. These, in turn, become increasingly important for getting along with others (Dodge & Price, 1994).

■ **TRAINING SOCIAL PROBLEM SOLVING.** Intervening with children who are poor social problem solvers can enhance development in several ways. Besides improving peer relations, effective social problem solving provides children with a sense of mastery and self-worth in the face of stressful life events. It reduces the risk of adjustment difficulties in children from low-income and troubled families (Downey & Walker, 1989; Goodman, Gravitt, & Kaslow, 1995).

George Spivack and Myrna Shure (1974) devised a widely applied social problem-solving training program. For several months, preschoolers and kindergartners participate in daily sessions in which puppets act out social problems and children discuss ways to resolve them. In addition, teachers intervene as conflicts arise in the classroom, pointing out consequences of children's behavior and suggesting alternative strategies. In several studies, trained pupils, in contrast to untrained controls, improved in both social reasoning and teacher-rated adjustment—gains still evident months after the program ended (Shure, 1997). Older elementary school children benefit from similar interventions (Gettinger, Doll, & Salmon, 1994).

At present, researchers are not sure which ingredients of social problem-solving training are most effective. Some evidence suggests that social-cognitive training must be accompanied by practice in enacting responses. When children have had many opportunities to engage in maladaptive behaviors, repeated rehearsal of new techniques may be necessary to overcome their habitual responses (Mize & Ladd, 1988). Also, current programs have not been tailored to fit the social-cognitive deficits of particular children. But it is in precisely these ways that the information-processing approach to social problem solving promises to make a unique contribution.

On a final note, social-cognitive training is not the only means for helping socially incompetent children. Because their parents often model poor social-problem solving skills and use ineffective child-rearing practices, family intervention may be necessary—a topic we will return to several times in later chapters. The Milestones table on the following page provides an overview of the changes in social cognition we have considered.

ASK YOURSELF . . .

♦ *Review the sections on interaction between friends and benefits of friendships on pages 469 and 471. Cite ways that warm, gratifying friendships can serve as contexts for development of effective social problem-solving skills.*

♦ **CONNECTIONS**
How do the family experiences of aggressive children promote poor social problem solving? (See Chapter 12, page 514.)

Does temperament contribute to children's social problem solving? Explain, using examples. (See Chapter 10, pages 414–420.)

Age	Thinking About the Self	Thinking About Other People	Thinking About Relations Between People
1–2 years	■ Self-recognition emerges and becomes well established. ■ By age 2, a categorical self develops. ■ Self-evaluative statements appear.	■ By age 2, ability to categorize people according to salient characteristics develops. ■ Beginnings of perspective taking emerge.	
3–5 years	■ A remembered self, in the form of a life-story narrative, emerges. ■ A belief-desire theory of mind emerges. ■ Self-concept emphasizes observable characteristics and commonly experienced emotions and attitudes. ■ Self-esteem is typically high and has begun to differentiate. ■ Achievement-related attributions appear.	■ Understanding of intention as an internal mental state distinct from action develops. ■ Person perception emphasizes concrete characteristics and commonly experienced emotions and attitudes. ■ Perspective taking is limited; children assume that what people observe determines their perspective.	■ Friendship is viewed concretely, in terms of play and exchange of material goods. ■ Social problem-solving strategies increase.
6–10 years	■ Self-concept emphasizes personality traits. ■ Self-esteem becomes hierarchically organized: at least three dimensions (academic, physical, and social) are present, which differentiate into additional self-evaluations and combine into an overall impression. ■ Self-esteem declines as children make social comparisons, then rises. ■ Achievement-related attributions differentiate into ability, effort, and external factors.	■ Detection of efforts to conceal intentions improves. ■ Person perception emphasizes personality traits and social comparisons. ■ Prevailing attitudes about racial, ethnic, and social-class groups are acquired; prejudice declines. ■ Perspective taking expands; children understand that people can interpret the same event in different ways.	■ Friendship emphasizes mutual trust and assistance. ■ Quantity and quality of social problem-solving strategies improve. ■ Components of social problem solving become more strongly associated with socially competent behavior.
11 years– adulthood	■ Self-concept becomes an organized system of personality traits. ■ New aspects of self-esteem are added (close friendship, romantic appeal, and job competence). ■ Self-esteem continues to rise. ■ Achievement-related attributions reflect full differentiation of ability and effort. ■ Identity develops.	■ Person perception consists of organized character sketches. ■ Recursive and societal perspective taking develops.	■ Friendship emphasizes intimacy and loyalty.

"Peter is nicer than you!"

Note: These milestones represent overall age trends. Individual differences exist in the precise age at which each milestone is attained.

What is social cognition, and how does it differ from non-social cognition?

◆ Researchers interested in the development of **social cognition** study how children's understanding of themselves, other people, and relationships between people changes with age. Compared to nonsocial cognition, social cognition involves the challenge of comprehending how both inner states and external forces affect people's behavior.

THINKING ABOUT THE SELF

Describe the development of self-awareness in infancy and toddlerhood and its consequences for young children's emotional and social capacities.

◆ The earliest aspect of the self to emerge is the **I-self,** a sense of self as subject, or agent. Its beginnings lie in infants' recognition that their own actions cause objects and people to react in predictable ways. During the second year, toddlers start to construct the **me-self,** a reflective observer that treats the self as an object of knowledge and evaluation.

◆ By the end of the second year, **self-recognition** is well established, as indicated by reactions of toddlers to their own image and use of language to refer to themselves. Self-awareness underlies the emergence of self-conscious emotions, perspective taking, empathy, sustained imitative play, and peer competition and cooperation.

Describe the development of the categorical, remembered, and inner selves, and cite factors that may contribute to preschoolers' belief–desire theory of mind.

◆ Language development permits young preschoolers to construct a **categorical self** as they classify themselves and others on the basis of salient characteristics, such as age, sex, physical characteristics, and goodness and badness. Conversations with adults about the past lead to an autobiographical memory—a life-story narrative that grants the child a **remembered self** imbued with cultural values.

◆ Early in the preschool years, the I-self elaborates to include an **inner self** of private thoughts and imaginings. Around age 4, children's theory of mind becomes a **belief–desire theory,** as mastery of false-belief tasks reveals. Many factors appear to contribute to young children's belief–desire reasoning, including early forms of communication, such as joint attention and social referencing; imitation; make-believe play; language development; and social interaction with siblings, friends, and adults. Some researchers believe that the normal human brain is biologically prepared to develop a belief–desire theory. Others think that it is supported by general cognitive development.

Discuss the development of self-concept from early childhood through adolescence, noting cognitive, social, and cultural influences.

◆ The me-self expands as preschoolers begin to construct a **self-concept,** or set of beliefs about their own characteristics. In middle childhood, self-concept changes from an appreciation of observable characteristics and typical beliefs, emotions, attitudes to an emphasis on personality traits. In adolescence, self-descriptions become more abstract and form an organized system that

places greater emphasis on social virtues and personal and moral values.

◆ Changes in self-concept are supported by cognitive development, perspective-taking skills (as suggested by Mead's concept of the **generalized other**), and feedback from others. In describing themselves, children tend to be more egoistic and competitive in individualistic cultures, more concerned with the welfare of others in collectivist cultures.

Discuss changes in self-esteem from early childhood through adolescence, including the role of social comparison, culture, and child-rearing practices.

◆ **Self-esteem,** the judgments we make about our own worth, differentiates, becomes hierarchically organized, and declines over the first few years of elementary school as children start to make **social comparisons.** Except for a temporary drop associated with school transition, self-esteem rises from fourth grade on. For most young people, becoming an adolescent leads to feelings of pride and self-confidence.

◆ Self-esteem is influenced by cultural forces, as illustrated by variations in the role of social comparison in children's judgments of self-worth. Child-rearing practices that are warm and accepting and that provide reasonable expectations for mature behavior are consistently related to high self-esteem.

Discuss the development of achievement-related attributions, noting the influence of cognitive development and adults' messages to children, and suggest ways to prevent learned helplessness and foster a mastery-oriented style.

◆ Research on achievement-related **attributions** has identified adult messages that affect children's self-esteem and **achievement motivation.** During middle childhood, children begin to distinguish ability, effort, and external factors in attributions for success and failure.

◆ Children with **mastery-oriented attributions** credit their successes to high ability and failures to insufficient effort. They hold an **incremental view of ability**—that it can be improved through trying hard. In contrast, children with **learned helplessness** attribute their successes to luck and failures to low ability. They hold an **entity view of ability**—that it is fixed and cannot be changed.

◆ Adolescents have a fully differentiated understanding of the relation of ability and effort. Those with learned helplessness quickly conclude that mastering a challenging task is not worth the cost—extremely high effort. In this way, they fail to realize their potential.

◆ Children who experience negative feedback about their ability, other messages evaluating their traits, pressure to focus on performance goals, and unsupportive teachers are likely to develop learned helplessness. Cultural values emphasizing the importance of effort and classrooms that stress interpersonal harmony shield children from learned helplessness.

◆ **Attribution retraining,** which encourages learned-helpless children to believe they can overcome failure if only they exert more effort, has succeeded in improving the self-evaluations and task performance of learned-helpless children. Teaching children to focus less on grades and more on mastering tasks for their own sake also leads to impressive gains in failing pupils' academic self-esteem and motivation.

Describe the quest for identity, the four identity statuses, and factors that influence identity development.

◆ Erikson first recognized **identity**—the construction of a solid self-definition consisting of self-chosen values and goals—as the major personality achievement of adolescence. In complex societies, a period of exploration is necessary to form a personally meaningful identity. **Identity achievement** and **moratorium** are psychologically healthy identity statuses. Long-term **identity foreclosure** (commitment without exploration) and **identity diffusion** (absence of clear direction) are related to adjustment difficulties.

◆ Adolescents who have a flexible, open-minded approach to grappling with competing beliefs and values and who feel attached to parents but free to disagree are likely to be advanced in identity development. Schools and communities that provide young people of all backgrounds with rich and varied options for exploration support the search for identity. Ethnic minority youths who construct a **bicultural identity** are advantaged in many aspects of emotional and social development.

THINKING ABOUT OTHER PEOPLE

Discuss gains in understanding intentions and in person perception, including children's appreciation of others' personalities, ethnicity, and social class.

◆ Over the preschool years, children become increasingly skilled at distinguishing intentional from unintentional acts. By age 4, they move beyond a view of intention-in-action to an understanding of intention as an internal mental state that guides but can be distinguished from action. During middle childhood, they begin to detect efforts to conceal intentions.

◆ **Person perception** concerns how we size up the attributes of people with whom we are familiar. Like their self-concepts, children's descriptions of other people place greater emphasis on personality traits and become more differentiated and organized with age.

◆ Basic concepts of race and ethnicity emerge in the preschool years, and children distinguish rich from poor on the basis of physical characteristics. By the early school years, children absorb prevailing attitudes toward social groups and tend to hold negative attitudes toward members of groups to which they do not belong. The capacity to classify the social world in multiple ways leads prejudice to decline in middle childhood. Children who view personality as fixed, have high self-esteem, and experience a social world in which people are sorted into groups are more likely to harbor prejudices.

Cite major changes in perspective taking from early childhood into adolescence, and explain the role of perspective-taking skill in children's social behavior.

◆ **Perspective taking** improves greatly from childhood to adolescence, as Selman's five-stage sequence indicates. Mastery of Piagetian tasks and a view of the mind as an active interpreter of experience are related to advances in perspective taking. During adolescence, **recursive thought** is mastered.

◆ The ability to understand the viewpoints of others contributes to a wide variety of social skills. Angry, aggressive young people have great difficulty imagining the thoughts and feelings of others. Interventions that teach perspective-taking skills reduce antisocial behavior and increase prosocial responding.

THINKING ABOUT RELATIONS BETWEEN PEOPLE

Describe the development of friendship understanding, its implications for children's real friendships, and the benefits of close friendship ties.

◆ Children's friendship understanding evolves from a concrete relationship based on shared activities and material goods to a mutual relationship based on trust in middle childhood and intimacy and loyalty in adolescence. In line with this change, children's real friendships are characterized by greater stability, prosocial responding, and similarity in attitudes and values with age. For aggressive children, however, friendships often become a context for magnifying antisocial acts.

◆ Girls emphasize emotional closeness and trust in their friendships more than boys do. Close friendships foster a wide variety of social-cognitive skills, provide support in dealing with everyday stresses, and can improve attitudes toward and involvement in school.

Describe the components of social problem solving, the development of social problem-solving skills, and ways to help children who are poor social problem solvers.

◆ With age, children become better at resolving conflict through **social problem solving.** Components of the social problem-solving process—encoding and interpreting social cues, clarifying social goals, generating and evaluating strategies, and enacting responses—become more strongly linked to socially competent behavior during middle childhood. Training in social problem solving leads to gains in psychological adjustment for both preschool and school-age children.

IMPORTANT TERMS AND CONCEPTS

Moral Development

IN CULTURES AS diverse as the American middle class, Vietnamese immigrants to California, and the Fiji Islanders of the South Pacific, a profound change takes place during the latter half of the second year. Toddlers start to show concern with deviations from the way people should behave, reacting with distress to actions that are aggressive or that might otherwise endanger their own or another's welfare. By age 2, language includes references to standards of conduct, such as "broken," "dirty," or "boo-boo," and evaluations of behavior as "good" or "bad" (Kochanska, Casey, & Fukumoto, 1995). Empathy and sympathetic concern also emerge around this time (see Chapter 10). And children of this age can be seen sharing toys, helping with household tasks, and cooperating in games (see Chapter 11)—early indicators of a considerate, responsible attitude.

As these observations reveal, accompanying the emergence of self-awareness and new representational capacities in the second year is another crowning achievement: The child becomes a moral being. Throughout the world, adults take note of this budding capacity to distinguish right from wrong and to accommodate to the needs of others. In some cultures, special terms are used to describe it. The Utku Indians of Hudson Bay say the child develops *ihuma* (reason). The Fijians believe that *vakayalo* (sense) appears. In response, parents hold children more responsible for their behavior (Kagan, 1998b).

What accounts for the early emergence of morality and children's expanding appreciation of standards of conduct? Philosophers have pondered this question for centuries, and modern investigators have addressed it with such intensity that research on moral development exceeds that on all other aspects of social development.

The determinants of morality can be found at both societal and individual levels. In all cultures, morality is promoted by an overarching social organization that specifies rules for good conduct. At the same time, it has roots in each major aspect of our psychological makeup. First, as we indicated in Chapter 10, morality has an *emotional component,* since powerful feelings cause us to empathize with another's distress or feel guilty when we are the cause of it. Second, morality has an important *cognitive component.* As we showed in Chapter 11, humans think about their social experiences, and children's developing social understanding permits them to make more profound judgments about actions they believe to be right or wrong. Third, morality has a vital *behavioral component,* since experiencing morally relevant thoughts and feelings only increases the chances, but does not guarantee, that people will act in accord with them.

Traditionally, these three facets of morality have been studied separately: biological and psychoanalytic theories focused on emotions, cognitive-developmental theory on moral thought, and social learning theory on moral behavior. Today, a growing body of research reveals that all three facets are interrelated. Still, major theories continue to disagree on which is primary. We will see that the aspect a theory emphasizes has major implications for how it conceptualizes the basic age trend of moral development: the shift from superficial, or externally controlled, responses to behavior that is based on inner standards. Truly moral individuals do not just do the right thing for the sake of social conformity or when authority figures are around. Instead, they have developed compassionate concerns and principles of good conduct, which they follow in a wide variety of situations.

Our discussion of moral development takes a close look at the theories just mentioned, highlighting the strengths and limitations of each based on current research. Then we consider self-control. The development of a personal resolve to keep the self from doing anything it feels like doing—from painting on the walls and playing with matches in the young preschooler to ignoring chores, insulting a playmate, or breaking a promise in the older child—is crucial for translating moral commitments into action. We conclude with a discussion of the "other side" of self-control—the development of aggression.

Morality as Rooted in Human Nature

During the 1970s, biological theories of human social behavior became prominent, spurred by a controversial new field called **sociobiology.** It suggested that many morally relevant prosocial behaviors, such as helping, sharing, and cooperating, are rooted in the genetic heritage of our species (Wilson, 1975). This view was supported by the work of ethologists, who observed animals aiding other members of their species, often at great risk to their own safety. For example, some small birds, including robins and thrushes, use a special call that warns others of an approaching predator, even though the sound might betray the caller's presence. Certain species of insects, such as ants, bees, and termites, show extremes of self-sacrifice. Large numbers will sting or bite an animal that threatens the hive, a warlike response that often results in their own death. Among primates, chimpanzees often share meat after a cooperative hunt and practice adoption when a baby loses its mother (Goodall, 1990). On the basis of this evidence, sociobiologists reasoned that evolution must have made similar provisions for prosocial acts in human beings.

How might genes influence behaviors that protect the social group and, thereby, the survival of the species? Although researchers admit that they do not fully understand this process, many believe that prewired emotional reactions are involved (Hoffman, 1981, 1991a; Trivers, 1971). In Chapter 10, we noted that newborns cry when they hear another baby cry, a possible precursor of empathy. By the second year, empathic concern is present, and toddlers react with distress to behaviors that threaten not just their own well-being but that of others. Perhaps these emotions underlie early sharing as well as other prosocial acts. Indeed, 2-year-olds in a play group share more often when toys are scarce than when they are plentiful (Hay et al., 1991). Consistent with sociobiological theory, the tendency to sacrifice personal gain in favor of group welfare is present at an early age.

But like most other human behaviors, morality cannot be fully explained by its biological foundations. Recall from Chapter 10 that morally relevant emotions, such as pride, guilt, empathy, and sympathy, require strong caregiving supports to develop. And their mature expression depends on cognitive development. Furthermore, in Chapter 10 we noted that the child's capacity to regulate negative affect has a bearing on whether an empathic response leads to sympathetic concern. Finally, although emotion is one basis for moral action, it is not a complete account, since following our sympathetic feelings is not always moral. For example, most of us would question the behavior of a parent who decides not to take a sick child to the doctor out of sympathy for the child's fear and anxiety.

According to sociobiologists, many morally relevant prosocial behaviors, such as helping, sharing, and cooperating, are rooted in the genetic heritage of our species. These chimpanzees retreat to a safe, secluded spot in a tree to share meat after a cooperative hunt.

(Baron Hugo Van Lawick/National Geographic Society Image Collection)

Still, the biological perspective on morality is useful, since it reminds us of the adaptive significance of moral behavior. Because the capacity to serve the self's needs is present early, nature seems to have made sure that counteracting tendencies are also in place that limit disruptive acts and promote concern for the well-being of others.

Morality as the Adoption of Societal Norms

The two perspectives we are about to discuss, psychoanalytic and social learning theory, offer quite different accounts of how children become moral beings. Yet both regard moral development as a matter of **internalization:** adopting societal standards for right action as one's own. Each view focuses on how morality moves from society to individual—that is, how children acquire norms, or prescriptions for good conduct, widely held by members of their social group (Gibbs & Schnell, 1985).

Our examination of these theories will reveal that internalization is not just a straightforward process of taking over externally imposed prescriptions. Several factors jointly affect the child's willingness to adopt societal standards:

- the parent's style of discipline, which varies with the type of misdeed;

- the child's characteristics, including age and temperament;

- the parent's characteristics; and

- the child's view of both the misdeed and the reasonableness of parental demands.

The last of these factors—*the child's perspective*—suggests that for internalization to occur, the child must "move beyond the parent's specific position to one of his or her own"— that is, adopt societal standards with conviction (Grusec & Goodnow, 1994, p. 4).

We will see that parents who are effective in promoting conscience development help children acquire reasoning skills so they can take initiative in situations involving moral choice. Consistent with the active view of the child now broadly accepted in the field, today internalization is regarded as the combined result of factors within the child and in the rearing environment. Most likely, when the process goes along well, "external forces reinforce and facilitate the emergence and refining of [the child's] propensities" (Turiel, 1998, p. 878). In the following sections, we will see many examples of this idea.

PSYCHOANALYTIC THEORY

According to Sigmund Freud, morality emerges between ages 3 and 6, during which the well known Oedipus and Electra conflicts arise (see Chapter 1, page 17). Young children desire to possess the parent of the other sex—feelings that lead to intense anxiety, since children fear punishment and loss of parental love for their unacceptable wishes. To master anxiety, avoid punishment, and maintain the affection of parents, children form a *superego,* or conscience, by *identifying* with the same-sex parent, whose moral standards they take into their personality. Finally, children turn the hostility previously aimed at the same-sex parent toward themselves, which leads to painful feelings of guilt each time the superego is disobeyed (Freud, 1925/1961).

In sum, Freud believed that morality is transferred from parents to children, who act in accord with moral prescriptions to avoid punitive feelings of guilt from a harsh, restrictive superego. He viewed moral development as largely complete by age 5 or 6, with some strengthening of the superego in middle childhood.

■ **IS FREUD'S THEORY SUPPORTED BY RESEARCH?** Today, most child development researchers disagree with Freud's account of conscience development on several grounds. First, Freud's view of guilt as a hostile impulse redirected toward the self is no longer widely accepted. As we will see, high levels of self-blame are not associated with moral internalization. Instead, guilt arises when a person intentionally engages in an unacceptable act and feels personally responsible for the outcome. From this perspective, children cannot experience a mature form of guilt without several cognitive capacities. These include

sociobiology A field that assumes many morally relevant prosocial behaviors are rooted in our genetic heritage and have evolved because of their survival value.

internalization The process of adopting societal standards for right action as one's own.

awareness of themselves as autonomous beings who make choices about actions and the ability to distinguish intentional from unintentional acts. In Chapters 10 and 11, we saw that these understandings emerge during the preschool years and are refined in middle childhood. Although this is the same period Freud assigned to conscience formation, the basis of the guilt response differs sharply from his theory.

Second, look carefully at the Oedipus and Electra conflicts, and you will see that discipline promoting fear of punishment and loss of parental love is assumed to motivate young children to behave morally (Hoffman, 1988; Kochanska, 1993). Yet children whose parents frequently use threats, commands, or physical force tend to violate normative standards often and feel little guilt after harming others. In the case of love withdrawal—for example, when a parent refuses to speak to or actually states a dislike for the child—children often respond with high levels of self-blame after misbehaving. They might think to themselves, "I'm no good" or "Nobody loves me." Eventually, these children may protect themselves from overwhelming feelings of guilt by denying the emotion when they do something wrong. So they, too, develop a weak conscience (Kochanska, 1991; Zahn-Waxler et al., 1990).

THE POWER OF INDUCTIVE DISCIPLINE. In contrast, a special type of discipline called **induction** does support conscience formation. It involves pointing out the effects of the child's misbehavior on others. At younger ages, referring to simple, direct outcomes works best, as in, "If you keep pushing him, he'll fall down and cry." Later, parents can explain why the child's action was inappropriate, perhaps by referring to the other person's intentions: "Don't yell at him. He was only trying to help." And with further cognitive advances, more subtle psychological explanations can be given: "He feels proud of his tower and you knocked it down" (Hoffman, 1983, p. 246). As long as the explanation matches the child's ability to understand and the child's attention is elicited by generally nurturant parents, induction is effective as early as 2 years of age. In one study, mothers who consistently used inductive reasoning had preschoolers who were more likely to make up for their misdeeds. They also showed more prosocial behavior, in that they spontaneously gave hugs, toys, and verbal sympathy to others in distress (Zahn-Waxler, Radke-Yarrow, & King, 1979).

The success of induction may lie in its power to cultivate the child's active commitment to moral norms (Turiel, 1998). How does it do so? First, induction tells children how to behave so they can call on this information in future situations. Second, by pointing out the impact of the child's actions on others, parents encourage empathy and sympathetic concern, which motivate use of the inductive information in prosocial behavior (Krevans & Gibbs, 1996). Third, providing children with reasons for changing their behavior invites them to judge the appropriateness of parental expectations, which fosters adoption of standards because they make sense.

In contrast, discipline that relies too heavily on threats of punishment or love withdrawal produces such high levels of fear and anxiety that children cannot think clearly enough to figure out what they should do. These practices may stop unacceptable behavior temporarily, but in the long run they do not get children to internalize moral norms.

This teacher uses inductive discipline to explain to a child the impact of her transgression on others. Induction supports conscience development by clarifying how the child should behave, encouraging empathy and sympathetic concern, and permitting the child to grasp the reasons behind parental expectations.

(Nancy Sheehan)

However, mild warnings and disapproval may sometimes be necessary to get children to listen to an inductive message.

Furthermore, Freud's theory places a heavy burden on parents, who must ensure through their disciplinary practices that children develop an internalized conscience. The research we have reviewed indicates that parental discipline is vitally important. Yet parent–child interaction is a two-way street; children's characteristics can affect the success of parenting techniques. Turn to the From Research to Practice box on the following page for recent findings on temperament and moral internalization.

THE ROLE OF GUILT IN MORAL ACTION. Although there is little support for Freudian conceptions of guilt or conscience development, Freud was correct that guilt can be an important motivator of moral action. In one study, 4- to 11-year-olds were asked to complete ambiguous stories in which a

Temperament and Moral Internalization in Young Children

WHEN HER MOTHER reprimanded her sharply for pouring water on the floor as she played in her bath, 2-year-old Katherine burst into tears. An anxious, sensitive child, Katherine was so distressed that it took her mother 10 minutes to calm her down. Outside in the front yard the next day, Katherine's mother watched as her next-door-neighbor patiently asked her 3-year-old son, who was about to pick the first tulips to blossom in the garden, not to touch the flowers. Alex, an active, adventurous child, paid no attention. As he pulled at another tulip, Alex's mother grabbed him, scolded him harshly, and carried him inside. Alex responded by kicking, hitting, and screaming, "Let me down, let me down!"

What explains Katherine and Alex's very different reactions to firm parental discipline? Grazyna Kochanska (1993, 1995) points out that children's temperaments affect the parenting practices that best promote responsibility and concern for others. She found that for temperamentally inhibited 2- and 3-year-olds, maternal gentle discipline—reasoning, polite requests, suggestions, and distractions—predicted conscience development at age 5, measured in terms of not cheating in some games and completing stories about moral issues with prosocial themes (saying "I'm sorry," not taking someone else's toys, helping a child who is hurt). In contrast, for relatively fearless, impulsive children, mild disciplinary tactics showed no relationship to moral internalization. Instead a secure attachment bond with the mother predicted a mature conscience (Kochanska, 1997a).

According to Kochanska, inhibited children like Katherine, who are prone to anxiety, are easily overcome by intense psychological discipline. Mild, patient tactics are suf-ficient to motivate them to internalize parental messages. In fact, research indicates that inhibited toddlers exposed to gentle intervention continue to show a more firmly internalized conscience, in the form of self-reported guilt and willingness to make amends after a transgression, during the school years (Kochanska, 1991). But impulsive children, such as Alex, may not respond to gentle interventions with enough discomfort to promote internalization. Yet frequent use of power-assertive methods is not effective either, since these techniques spark anger and resentment, which interfere with the child's processing of parental messages.

Why is secure attachment predictive of conscience development in nonanxious children? Kochanska suggests that when children are so low in anxiety that typically effective disciplinary practices fail, a close bond with the caregiver provides an alternative foundation for conscience formation. It motivates children unlikely to experience negative emotion to internalize rules as a means of preserving a spirit of affection and cooperation with the parent.

To foster early moral development, parents must tailor their child-rearing strategies to their child's temperament. In Katherine's case, a soft-spoken correction would probably be effective. For Alex, taking extra steps to build a warm, caring relationship during times when he behaves well is likely to promote moral internalization. Although Alex's parents need to use firmer and more frequent discipline than Katherine's do, emphasizing power assertion is counterproductive for both children. Do these findings remind you of the notion of *goodness of fit*, discussed in Chapter 10? Return to page 420 to review this idea.

---

child like themselves could have caused another person's distress. Children who made reference to empathy-related guilt reactions (expressions of personal responsibility, such as "She's sorry she pushed him down") were far more likely to help an adult in need in the laboratory (Chapman et al., 1987). Furthermore, 10- to 12-year-olds often end such stories by having the main character resolve to be less selfish and more considerate in the future. In older children, guilt may contribute to moral behavior by triggering a general motive to act morally that goes well beyond the immediate situation (Hoffman, 1980).

Despite the effectiveness of guilt in prompting moral action, Freud's theory is one-sided in viewing it as the only force that compels us to act morally. In addition, a wealth of research we will review later in this chapter indicates that contrary to what Freud believed, moral development is not an abrupt event that is virtually complete by the end of the preschool years. Instead, it is a far more gradual process, beginning in early childhood and extending into adulthood.

■ **RECENT PSYCHOANALYTIC IDEAS.** Recognizing the limitations of Freud's theory, recent psychoanalytic ideas underscore the importance of a positive parent–child relationship and much earlier development of morality. According to Robert Emde, sensitive emotional exchanges between caregiver and infant that support the attachment bond serve as a vital foundation for acquiring moral standards. Toddlers who feel a secure sense of connection with the parent are more likely to be responsive to adult messages about how to behave, which increase in the second year of life (Emde et al., 1991; Kochanska &

induction A type of discipline in which the effects of the child's misbehavior on others are communicated to the child.

Aksan, 1995). (Return to the From Research to Practice box on page 483, and notice the strong role of attachment in impulsive children's moral internalization.)

Furthermore, current psychoanalytic theorists believe that the superego children build from parental teachings consists not just of prohibitions or "don'ts" (as Freud emphasized), but also of positive guidelines for behavior, or "do's." After formulating a punitive superego, Freud acknowledged that conscience includes a set of ideals based on love rather than threats of punishment, but he placed less emphasis on this aspect.[1] The positive side of conscience probably develops first, out of toddlers' participation in morally relevant activities with caregivers, such as helping to wipe up spilled milk or move a delicate object from one place to another. In these situations, parents offer generous praise, and the small child smiles broadly with pride—an early sign of internalization of parental moral standards.

A short time later, parents' warnings and disapproval of forbidden acts evoke shame along with "hurt feelings"—blends of sadness, anger, and pouting—that may be the forerunners of guilt. Soon, toddlers use their capacity for social referencing to check back with the parent, searching for emotional information that can serve as a guide for moral conduct. With a disapproving glance or shake of the head, parents respond with subtle but powerful messages about the moral meaning of the child's actions. Around age 3, guilt reactions are clearly evident (see Chapter 10) (Emde & Oppenheim, 1995).

Notice how recent psychoanalytic formulations retain continuity with Freud's theory in regarding emotion as the primary basis for early moral development. Although little attention is paid to young children's reasoning about moral norms, values, or decisions (the emphasis of cognitive-developmental theory), it is possible that early morally relevant feelings are the platform on which a mature understanding of and commitment to moral principles is built (Hoffman, 1991b).

SOCIAL LEARNING THEORY

Unlike psychoanalytic theory, the social learning perspective does not consider morality to be a special form of human activity that follows a unique course of development. Instead, moral behavior is acquired just like any other set of responses: through reinforcement and modeling.

■ **THE IMPORTANCE OF MODELING.** Operant conditioning—following up children's "good behavior" with positive reinforcement in the form of approval, affection, and other rewards—is not enough for children to acquire moral responses. For a behavior to be reinforced, it must first occur spontaneously. Yet many prosocial acts, such as sharing, helping, or comforting an unhappy playmate, do not occur often enough at first for reinforcement to explain their rapid development in early childhood. Instead, social learning theorists believe that children learn to behave morally largely through *modeling*—by observing and imitating adults who demonstrate appropriate behavior (Bandura, 1977; Grusec, 1988). Once children acquire a moral response, such as sharing or telling the truth, reinforcement in the form of praising the act ("That was a nice thing to do") and attributing good behavior to the child's character ("You're a very kind and considerate boy") increases its frequency (Mills & Grusec, 1989).

Many studies show that models who behave helpfully or generously increase young children's prosocial responses. The model's characteristics affect children's willingness to imitate in the following ways:

■ *Warmth and responsiveness.* Preschoolers are more likely to copy the prosocial actions of an adult who is warm and responsive rather than one who is cold and

---

[1]Erik Erikson's psychosocial theory, which builds on Freud's stage sequence, accepts the restrictive side of the superego but also views it as a positive, constructive force in development. For example, Erikson described the outcome of the phallic stage as a sense of initiative, which provides the foundation for ambition and purpose in life (see Chapter 1, page 19). In addition, Erikson (1968) believed that conscience development extends into the adult years. Recall from Chapter 11 that an important part of identity development involves the search for a set of moral values. These are selected during late adolescence as identity is achieved, and they are refined during adulthood.

distant (Yarrow, Scott, & Waxler, 1973). Warmth seems to make children more attentive and receptive to the model. Also, warm, affectionate behavior is an example of a prosocial response, and part of what children may be imitating is this aspect of the model's behavior.

■ *Competence and power.* Children admire and therefore tend to select competent, powerful models to imitate—the reason they are especially willing to copy the behavior of older peers and adults (Bandura, 1977).

■ *Consistency between assertions and behavior.* When models say one thing and do another—for example, announce that "it's important to help others" but rarely engage in helpful acts—children generally choose the most lenient standard of behavior that adults demonstrate (Mischel & Liebert, 1966).

Models exert their strongest influence during the preschool years. At the end of early childhood, children who have a history of consistent exposure to caring adults tend to behave prosocially regardless of whether a model is present. By that time, they have internalized prosocial rules from repeated observations of and encouragement by others (Mussen & Eisenberg-Berg, 1977). In contrast, younger children are still acquiring norms and finding out the conditions under which to apply them. Consequently, they look to adult models for information about where, when, and what kinds of prosocial behaviors are appropriate (Peterson, 1982).

So far, we have seen that children can pick up many positive behaviors through observing others. Can modeling also help children learn to inhibit unfavorable acts? Research suggests that it can under certain conditions. Joan Grusec and her colleagues (1979) had a person first try to lure an adult model and then 5- to 8-year-olds away from a boring task to play with toys that the experimenter had forbidden them to touch. A model who verbalized that she was resisting temptation and clearly stated her reason for doing so ("I can't come play with the toys because I'm here to sort cards, and I always try to do what's right") was more effective in promoting children's self-restraint than a model who merely did not touch the toys. These findings indicate that to inspire resistance to temptation, models need to make their own efforts explicit by verbalizing them. The explanation also provides a rationale for self-restraint that children can call on when similar situations arise in the future.

■ **EFFECTS OF PUNISHMENT.** Most parents are aware of the limited usefulness of punishment, such as scolding, criticism, and spankings for misbehavior, and apply it sparingly. Using sharp reprimands or physical force to restrain or move a child is justified when immediate obedience is necessary—for example, when a 3-year-old is about to run into the street. In fact, parents are most likely to use forceful methods under these conditions. When they are interested in fostering long-term goals, such as acting kindly toward others, they tend to rely on warmth and reasoning (Kuczynski, 1984). Furthermore, parents often combine power assertion with reasoning in response to very serious transgressions, such as lying and stealing (Grusec & Goodnow, 1994).

Indeed, a great deal of research shows that when used frequently, punishment promotes only momentary compliance, not lasting changes in children's behavior. Children who are repeatedly criticized, shouted at, or slapped are likely to display the unacceptable response again as soon as adults are out of sight and they can get away with it. In fact, children of highly punitive parents are known to be especially aggressive and defiant outside the home (Strassberg et al., 1994).

Harsh punishment also has undesirable side effects. First, when parents spank, they often do so in response to children's aggression (Holden, Coleman, & Schmidt, 1995). Yet the punishment itself models aggression! Second, children who are frequently punished soon learn to avoid the punishing adult. When children refrain from interacting with adults who are responsible for their upbringing, those adults have little opportunity to teach desirable behaviors. Finally, as punishment "works" to stop children's misbehavior temporarily, it offers immediate relief to adults, and they are reinforced for using coercive discipline. For this reason, a punitive adult is likely to punish with greater frequency over time, a course of action that can spiral into serious abuse.

Time out is an effective disciplinary technique when a child is out of control and other effective methods of discipline cannot be applied at the moment. But the best way to motivate good conduct is to let children know ahead of time how to act and praise them when they behave well. Then time out will seldom be necessary.

(Goodman/Monkmeyer Press)

■ **ALTERNATIVES TO HARSH PUNISHMENT.** Alternatives to criticism, slaps, and spankings can reduce the side effects of punishment. A technique called **time out** involves removing children from the immediate setting—for example, by sending them to their rooms—until they are ready to act appropriately. Time out is useful when a child is out of control and other effective methods of discipline cannot be applied at the moment (Betz, 1994). It usually requires only a few minutes to change children's behavior, and it also offers a "cooling off" period for angry parents. Another approach is *withdrawal of privileges,* such as allowance, going to the movies, or watching a favorite TV program. Removing privileges often generates some resentment in children, but it allows parents to avoid harsh techniques that could easily intensify into violence.

Although its usefulness is limited, punishment can play a valuable role in moral development. Earlier we noted that mild warnings and disapproval are occasionally necessary if induction is to be effective. And recall William Damon's (1995) argument, discussed in Chapter 11, that parents must be willing to assert their authority to avoid the dangers of excessive child-centeredness (see page 452).

When parents do decide to use punishment, they can increase its effectiveness in several ways:

▨ *Consistency.* Punishment that is unpredictable is related to especially high rates of disobedience in children. In a study in which researchers had mothers carry on a 12-minute telephone conversation while their toddlers played, reprimanding half of the children's inappropriate demands for attention ("Please don't interrupt me") and giving in to the other half led to a dramatic increase in children's negative affect and intrusive behaviors—crying while standing next to the mother, climbing on the mother's lap, banging toys, and pulling the phone cord (see Figure 12.1) (Acker & O'Leary, 1996). When parents scold children on some occasions but permit them to act inappropriately on others, children are confused about how to behave, and the unacceptable act persists.

▨ *A warm parent–child relationship.* Children of involved, caring parents find the interruption in parental affection that accompanies punishment to be especially unpleasant. As a result, they want to regain the warmth and approval of parents as quickly as possible.

▨ *Explanations.* Explanations help children recall the misdeed and relate it to expectations for future behavior. Consequently, pairing reasons with mild punishment (such as time out) leads to a far greater reduction in misbehavior than using punishment alone (Larzelere et al., 1996). Yet not all reasons adults offer are equally effective, since children evaluate their appropriateness in relation to the type of

FIGURE 12.1

How does inconsistent punishment affect children's behavior? To find out, researchers conducted an experiment in which they had mothers talk on the telephone while their toddlers played. Mothers in the "reprimand/give in" condition (who reprimanded half of their child's inappropriate demands and gave into the other half) had toddlers with far higher rates of negative affect and intrusive behaviors than did mothers in the "reprimand" condition (who reprimanded every inappropriate demand) and mothers in the "reprimand/ignore" condition (who reprimanded half of the inappropriate demands and ignored the other half).

(Adapted from Acker & O'Leary, 1996.)

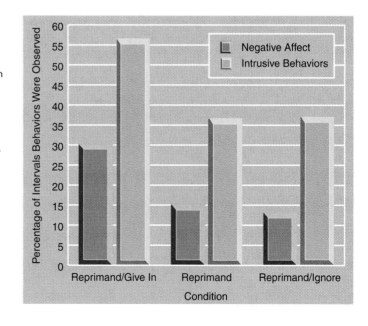

transgression. For example, with respect to stealing from or hitting a classmate, children grant little legitimacy to a teacher who emphasizes obeying rules. When teachers point to fairness or others' welfare, children are much more responsive (Killen, 1991). Furthermore, children listen more closely if they know that the adult regards the misdeed or value as very important (Goodnow, 1992).

■ **POSITIVE DISCIPLINE.** The most effective forms of discipline encourage good conduct. Instead of waiting for children to misbehave, parents can build a positive, cooperative relationship with the child, serve as good examples, let children know ahead of time how to act, and praise children when they behave well (Zahn-Waxler & Robinson, 1995).

When sensitivity, cooperation, and shared positive affect are evident in joint activities between mothers and their 2-year-olds, children more often follow maternal directives to clean up toys and not touch attractive objects in a laboratory play room. And they continue to obey after the mother steps out of the room and an adult tries to get them to violate maternal standards. These indicators of moral internalization are still present a year later (Kochanska, 1997b). Early, mutually responsive parent–child ties lead children to want to heed parental demands because they feel a sense of commitment to the relationship. This reduces the need for coercive discipline, freeing parents to focus on encouraging children's competent behavior.

One- to 3-year-olds whose parents use this proactive approach to discipline are more likely to comply and less likely to display behavior problems at age 5 (Kuczynski & Kochanska, 1995). Their parents also do much to reduce opportunities for misbehavior. For example, on a long car trip, they bring along back-seat activities that relieve children's restlessness and boredom. At the supermarket, where exciting temptations abound, they engage young children in conversations and encourage them to help with shopping (Holden, 1983; Holden & West, 1989). When adults help children acquire acceptable behaviors that they can use to replace forbidden acts, the need for punishment is greatly reduced.

Sensitivity, cooperation, and shared positive affect between parent and child support conscience development. This boy feels a sense of commitment to the relationship with his father. This eases the parent's task of encouraging competent behavior.
(Ariel Skelley/The Stock Market)

LIMITATIONS OF "MORALITY AS THE ADOPTION OF SOCIETAL NORMS" PERSPECTIVE

Adoption of and personal commitment to societal norms are, without question, essential aspects of moral development. Without a shared moral code, people would disregard each other's rights whenever their desires conflicted. Furthermore, external sanctions are not enough to ensure morality. The emphasis that psychoanalytic and social learning theories place on internalization is vital, since people must continuously govern their own behavior in countless everyday situations in which moral violations would remain unobserved and undetected by others (Bandura, 1991).

Nevertheless, a major criticism of theories that treat morality as entirely a matter of internalization of societal norms is that prevailing standards sometimes are at odds with important ethical principles and social goals. Under these conditions, deliberate violation of norms is not immoral. It is justifiable and courageous. Think, for a moment, about historical figures who rose to greatness because they refused to accept the validity of prevailing societal norms. Abraham Lincoln's opposition to slavery, Susan B. Anthony's leadership in the crusade for women's suffrage, and Martin Luther King, Jr.'s campaign to end racial prejudice are only a few examples. Yet the conduct of each was seriously at odds with widely accepted standards.

With respect to children, internalization is often accompanied by other parental goals. At times, parents regard noncompliance as desirable if the child provides a reasonable justification (Kuczynski & Hildebrandt, 1997). Consider a boy who violated a parental prohibition by cutting a cake reserved for a family celebration and giving a piece to a hungry playmate. As the parent began to reprimand, the boy explained that the playmate had not

time out A form of mild punishment in which children are removed from the immediate setting until they are ready to act appropriately.

eaten all day and that the refrigerator was nearly empty, leaving no alternative. In this instance, many parents would value the morality of the boy's claims along with his reasoning and negotiation skills.

Cognitive-developmental theorists believe that neither identification with parents nor teaching, modeling, and reinforcement are the major means through which children become moral. Instead of internalizing existing rules and expectations, the cognitive-developmental approach assumes that individuals develop morally through **construction**—actively attending to and interrelating multiple perspectives on situations in which social conflicts arise and deriving new moral understandings. In other words, children make moral judgments on the basis of concepts they construct about justice and fairness (Gibbs, 1991).

The cognitive-developmental position on morality is unique in its view of the child as a thinking moral being who wonders about right and wrong and searches for moral truth. We will see in the following sections that cognitive-developmental theorists differ in the methods they use to study moral understanding and in their timing of certain moral advances. But all agree that changes in children's reasoning are at the heart of moral development.

ASK YOURSELF . . .

◆ Alice and Wayne want their two young children to develop a strong, internalized conscience and to become generous, caring individuals. List as many parenting practices as you can that would promote these goals.

◆ Nanette told her 3-year-old son, Darren, not to go into the front yard without asking, since the house faces a busy street. An impulsive child, Darren disobeyed several times. How would you recommend that Nanette discipline Darren, and why? Considering Darren's temperament, what kind of parent–child relationship is likely to help him internalize parental standards?

◆ CONNECTIONS
What social-cognitive capacities are probably fostered by inductive discipline? (See Chapter 11, pages 445 and 465.)

BRIEF REVIEW

According to sociobiology, morality is grounded in our genetic heritage through prewired emotional reactions. However, morally relevant emotions, such as pride, guilt, empathy, and sympathy, cannot fully explain moral action. Although psychoanalytic and social learning theories offer different accounts of development, both emphasize internalization—children's adoption of societal standards. Current evidence reveals that internalization is the combined result of factors within the child and in the rearing environment. Children contribute actively to this process, adopting moral prescriptions with conviction.

Contrary to predictions from Freudian theory, power assertion and love withdrawal do not promote conscience formation. Instead, induction, against a backdrop of nurturance, is far more effective. Social learning theorists have shown that modeling combined with reinforcement in the form of praise is effective in encouraging prosocial acts. In contrast, harsh punishment promotes only temporary compliance, not lasting changes in children's behavior. The most effective forms of discipline encourage and reward good conduct through a warm, cooperative parent–child relationship.

A major criticism of theories that view morality as entirely a matter of internalization is that sometimes violating normative prescriptions is ethically valid. The cognitive-developmental perspective regards construction—actively thinking about right and wrong in situations in which social conflicts arise and deriving new moral understandings—as central to moral development.

Morality as Social Understanding

According to the cognitive-developmental perspective, cognitive maturity and social experience lead to advances in moral understanding, from a superficial orientation to physical power and external consequences toward a more profound appreciation of interpersonal relationships, societal institutions, and lawmaking systems. As their grasp of social cooperation expands, children's ideas about what ought to be done when the needs and desires of people conflict also change, toward increasingly just, fair, and balanced solutions to moral problems (Gibbs, 1995).

PIAGET'S THEORY OF MORAL DEVELOPMENT

Piaget's (1932/1965) early work on children's moral judgments was the original inspiration for the cognitive-developmental perspective and continues to stimulate new research. To study children's ideas about morality, Piaget relied on open-ended clinical interviews, questioning Swiss children between ages 5 and 13 about their understanding of rules in the game of marbles. In addition, he gave children stories in which characters' intentions to engage in right or wrong action and the consequences of their behavior were varied. In the best known of these stories, children were asked which of two boys—well-intentioned John, who breaks 15 cups while on his way to dinner, or ill-intentioned Henry, who breaks 1 cup while stealing some jam—is naughtier and why. From children's responses, Piaget identified two broad stages of moral understanding.

■ HETERONOMOUS MORALITY (ABOUT 5 TO 10 YEARS). *Heteronomous* means under the authority of another. As the term **heteronomous morality** suggests, children of this stage view rules as handed down by authorities (God, parents, and teachers), as having a permanent existence, as unchangeable, and as requiring strict obedience. For example, young children state that the rules of the game of marbles cannot be changed, explaining that "God didn't teach [the new rules]," "you couldn't play any other way," or "it would be cheating. . . . A fair rule is one that is in the game" (Piaget, 1932/1965, pp. 58, 59, 63).

According to Piaget, two factors limit children's moral understanding: (1) the power of adults to insist that children comply, which promotes unquestioning respect for rules and those who enforce them; and (2) cognitive immaturity, especially egocentrism. Because young children think that all people view rules in the same way, their moral understanding is characterized by **realism**—that is, they regard rules as external features of reality rather than as cooperative principles that can be modified at will.

Together, adult power, egocentrism, and realism result in superficial moral understandings. In judging an act's wrongness, younger children focus on objective consequences rather than on intent to do harm. For example, in the story about John and Henry mentioned earlier, they regard John as naughtier because he broke more cups, despite his innocent intentions.

■ AUTONOMOUS MORALITY, OR THE MORALITY OF COOPERATION (ABOUT 10 YEARS AND OLDER). Cognitive development, gradual release from adult control, and peer interaction lead children to make the transition to **autonomous morality.** Piaget regarded peer disagreements as especially facilitating (see Chapter 6). Through them, children become aware that people can have different perspectives about moral action and that intentions, not objective consequences, should serve as the basis for judging behavior.

Furthermore, as children interact as equals with peers, they learn to settle conflicts in mutually beneficial ways. Gradually, they start to use a standard of fairness called **reciprocity,** in which they express the same concern for the welfare of others as they do for themselves. Most of us are familiar with reciprocity in the form of the Golden Rule: "Do unto others as you would have them do unto you." But Piaget found that the way to the Golden Rule must be paved with a "cruder" form of reciprocity: "You scratch my back and I'll scratch yours." It defines the beginning of the morality of cooperation.

According to Piaget, reciprocity helps children realize that rules are flexible, socially agreed-on principles that can be revised to suit the will of the majority. It also leads to a new perspective on punishment, which should be reciprocity based, or fit the seriousness of the transgression and, whenever possible, be a logical consequence of it—for example, a cheater whom no one will play with or a liar whom no one will believe anymore, even when he tells the truth. Finally, punishment should be meted out in a fair, even-handed fashion to everyone responsible for an offense, guaranteeing equal justice for all.

EVALUATION OF PIAGET'S THEORY

Follow-up research on Piaget's theory indicates that it describes the general direction of change in moral judgment fairly well. In many studies, some conducted in different cultures, the diverse characteristics that distinguish heteronomous from autonomous reasoning are related to age. Also, much evidence confirms Piaget's conclusion that moral understanding is supported by cognitive maturity, gradual release from adult control, and peer interaction (Lickona, 1976). We will consider these findings when we turn to extensions of Piaget's work by Lawrence Kohlberg and his followers. Nevertheless, several aspects of Piaget's theory have been questioned because they underestimate the moral capacities of young children.

construction The process of moral development in which children actively attend to and interrelate multiple aspects of situations in which social conflicts arise and derive new moral understandings.

heteronomous morality Piaget's first stage of moral development, in which children view rules as handed down by authorities, as having a permanent existence, as unchangeable, and as requiring strict obedience.

realism A view of rules as external features of reality rather than cooperative principles that can be modified at will. Characterizes Piaget's heteronomous stage.

autonomous morality Piaget's second stage of moral development, in which children view rules as flexible, socially agreed-on principles that can be revised to suit the will of the majority.

reciprocity A standard of fairness in which individuals express the same concern for the welfare of others as they do for themselves.

■ **INTENTIONS AND MORAL JUDGMENTS.** Look again at the story about John and Henry on page 489. Because bad intentions are paired with little damage and good intentions with a great deal of damage, Piaget's method yields a conservative picture of young children's ability to make moral judgments. When questioned about moral issues in a way that makes a person's intent stand out as strongly as the harm he does, preschool and early school-age children are quite capable of judging ill-intentioned people as naughtier than well-intentioned ones (Nelson-Le Gall, 1985; Yuill & Perner, 1988).

As further evidence, by age 4, children clearly recognize the difference between two morally relevant intentional behaviors: truthfulness and lying. They approve of telling the truth and disapprove of lying, even when a lie remains undetected (Bussey, 1992). And by age 7, children integrate their judgments of lying and truth telling with prosocial and antisocial intentions. Influenced by collectivist values of social harmony and self-effacement, Chinese children are more likely than Canadian children to rate lying favorably when an intention involves modesty—for example, when a pupil who generously picks up the garbage in the school yard says, "I didn't do it." In contrast, both Chinese and Canadian children rate lying about antisocial acts as "very naughty" (Lee et al., 1997).

Nevertheless, an advanced understanding of the morality of intentions does await the emergence of autonomous morality. Young elementary school children interpret statements of intention in a rigid, heteronomous fashion. They believe that once you say you will do something, you are obligated to follow through, even if uncontrollable circumstances (such as an accident) make it difficult or impossible for you to do so. By age 9 or 10, children realize that not keeping your word is much worse in some situations than in others—namely, when you are able to do so and permit another person to count on your actions (Mant & Perner, 1988). Appeals to intangible considerations, such as trust (as opposed to external, physical consequences) are also much more prevalent among older children (Peterson, Peterson, & Seeto, 1983). In sum, Piaget was partly right and partly wrong about this aspect of moral reasoning.

■ **REASONING ABOUT AUTHORITY.** Research on young children's understanding of authority reveals that they do not regard adults with the unquestioning respect Piaget assumed. Even preschoolers judge certain acts, such as hitting and stealing, to be wrong regardless of the opinions of authorities. When asked to explain, 3- and 4-year-olds express concerns about harming other people rather than obeying adult dictates (Nucci & Turiel, 1978; Smetana, 1981, 1985).

By age 4, children have differentiated notions about the legitimacy of authority figures that they refine during the school years. In several studies, kindergartners through sixth graders were asked questions designed to assess their view of how broad an adult's authority should be. Pupils of all ages did not conceive of adults as having general authority—even when they held positions of status and power, such as teacher or school principal. For example, most rejected a principal's right to set rules and issue directives in settings other than his own school (Laupa, 1995).

With respect to nonmoral concerns, such as the rules to be followed in a game, children base legitimacy on a person's knowledge of the situation, not social position. And when a directive is fair and caring (for example, telling children to stop fighting, to return lost money to its owner, or to share candy), children view it as right, regardless of who states it—a principal, a teacher, a class president, or a child. This is even true for Korean children, whose culture places a high value on respect for and deference to adults. Korean 7- to 11-year-olds evaluate negatively a teacher's or principal's order to keep fighting, to steal, or to refuse to share—a response that strengthens with age (Kim, 1998; Kim & Turiel, 1996).

As these findings reveal, adult status is not required for preschool and school-age children to view someone as an authority. Peers who are very knowledgeable or who act to protect others' rights and welfare are regarded as just as legitimate, and sometimes more legitimate, than adults. And at times, children regard a peer's or adult's social position as the basis for authority because of its organizational function—for example, a safety patrol member directing children at a street corner and a principal determining procedures in his school (Laupa, 1991, 1995).

In sum, in reasoning about authority, preschool and young elementary school children place somewhat greater weight on power and status than do older children. Nevertheless, several factors are coordinated at a much earlier age than Piaget anticipated—the attributes of the individual, the type of behavior to be controlled, and the context in which it occurs.

■ **STAGEWISE PROGRESSION.** An additional point about Piaget's theory is that the characteristics associated with each stage do not correlate highly, as we would expect if each represented a general, unifying organization of moral judgment. As Thomas Lickona (1976) puts it, "The child's moral thought, as it unfolds in Piagetian interviews, is not all of a piece but more of a patchwork of diverse parts" (p. 240). But in fairness, Piaget (1932/1965) observed a mixture of heteronomous and autonomous reasoning in the responses of many children and recommended that the two moralities be viewed as fluid, overlapping phases rather than tightly knit stages.

Finally, moral development is currently regarded as a more extended process than Piaget believed. In fact, Kohlberg's six-stage sequence, to which we now turn, identifies three stages beyond the first appearance of autonomous morality. Nevertheless, Kohlberg's theory is a direct continuation of the research Piaget began—the search for universal moral stages and the study of how moral understanding is intimately tied to cognitive growth.

KOHLBERG'S EXTENSION OF PIAGET'S THEORY

Like Piaget, Kohlberg used a clinical interviewing procedure to study moral development, but he based his stage sequence on situations quite different from Piaget's stories. Whereas Piaget asked children to judge the naughtiness of a character who had already decided on a moral course of action, Kohlberg presented people with **moral dilemmas** and asked them to decide both what the main actor should do and why. Perhaps as a result, he obtained a clearer picture of the reasoning on which moral decisions are based. Today, Kohlberg's clinical interviewing procedure is widely used to assess moral understanding. More efficient, questionnaire approaches have also been devised.

■ **THE CLINICAL INTERVIEW.** Each of Kohlberg's dilemmas presents a genuine crisis that pits one moral value against another. The best known of these is the "Heinz dilemma," which asks individuals to choose between the value of obeying the law (not stealing) and the value of human life (saving a dying person):

> In Europe, a woman was near death from cancer. There was one drug the doctors thought might save her. A druggist in the same town had discovered it, but he was charging ten times what the drug cost him to make. The sick woman's husband, Heinz, went to everyone he knew to borrow the money, but he could only get together half of what it cost. The druggist refused to sell it cheaper or let Heinz pay later. So Heinz got desperate and broke into the man's store to steal the drug for his wife. Should Heinz have done that? Why or why not? (paraphrased from Colby et al., 1983, p. 77)

Kohlberg emphasized that it is the *structure* of the answer—the way an individual reasons about the dilemma—and not the *content* of the response (whether to steal or not to steal) that determines moral maturity. Individuals who believe that Heinz should take the drug and those who think he should not can be found at each of Kohlberg's first four stages. To bring out the structure of moral understanding, the interview is lengthy and free-ranging. After a dilemma is presented, follow-up questions elicit views on such issues as obedience to laws and authority figures and understanding of higher moral values, such as respect for human life.

Although structure is the primary consideration for determining an individual's moral progress, at the highest two stages content is also relevant. Morally mature individuals do not just agree on why certain actions are justified. They also agree on what people ought to do when faced with a moral dilemma. Given a choice between obeying the law and preserving individual rights, the most advanced moral thinkers support individual rights (in the Heinz dilemma, stealing the drug to save a life). As we look at development in Kohlberg's scheme, we will see that moral reasoning and content are at first

This fourth grader bows her head as her principal discusses the importance of obeying school rules. Yet her understanding of authority is not limited to unquestioning respect for adults, as Piaget assumed. She respects the principal's right to govern in his school, and she probably views his expectations for fair and caring behavior as appropriate in any situation. But if he ordered her to behave immorally—to fight, steal, or refuse to share—undoubtedly she would resist.

(Ellen B. Senisi/Photo Researchers, Inc.)

moral dilemma A conflict situation presented to research participants, who are asked to decide both what the main actor should do and why. Used to assess the development of moral reasoning.

independent, but eventually they are integrated into a coherent ethical system (Kohlberg, Levine, & Hewer, 1983).

Does this remind you of adolescents' efforts to construct a sound, well-organized set of personal values in identity development, discussed in Chapter 11? According to some theorists, the development of identity and moral understanding are part of the same process (Blasi, 1994b; Davidson & Youniss, 1991).

■ THE SOCIOMORAL REFLECTION MEASURE–SHORT FORM. The most recently devised questionnaire instrument for assessing moral understanding is the **Sociomoral Reflection Measure–Short Form (SRM–SF).** Like Kohlberg's clinical interview, the SRM–SF asks individuals to evaluate the importance of moral values and produce moral reasoning. Here are four of its eleven questions:

▨ Let's say a friend of yours needs help and may even die, and you're the only person who can save him or her. How important is it for a person (without losing his or her own life) to save the life of a friend?

▨ What about saving the life of anyone? How important is it for a person (without losing his or her own life) to save the life of a stranger?

▨ How important is it for people not to take things that belong to other people?

▨ How important is it for people to obey the law? (Gibbs, Basinger, & Fuller, 1992, pp. 151–152)

After reading each question, participants rate the importance of the value it addresses (as "very important," "important," or "not important") and write a brief explanation of their rating. The explanations are coded according to a revised rendition of Kohlberg's stages.

The SRM–SF is far less time consuming than clinical interviewing because it does not require people to read and think about lengthy moral dilemmas. Instead, they merely evaluate moral values and justify their evaluations. Nevertheless, scores on the SRM–SF correlate well with those obtained from clinical interviews (Basinger, Gibbs, & Fuller, 1995). Apparently, moral judgment can be measured without using dilemmas—a discovery that is likely to ease the task of conducting moral development research.

■ KOHLBERG'S STAGES OF MORAL UNDERSTANDING. Kohlberg organized his six stages into three general levels and made strong statements about the properties of this sequence. First, he regarded the stages as invariant and universal—a sequence of steps that people everywhere move through in a fixed order. Second, he viewed each new stage as building on reasoning of the preceding stage, resulting in a more logically consistent and morally adequate concept of justice. Finally, he saw each stage as an organized whole—a qualitatively distinct structure of moral thought that a person applies across a wide range of situations (Colby & Kohlberg, 1987). Recall from Chapter 6 that these characteristics are the very ones Piaget used to describe his cognitive stages.

Furthermore, Kohlberg believed that moral understanding is promoted by the same factors that Piaget thought were important for cognitive development: (1) disequilibrium, or actively grappling with moral issues and noticing weaknesses in one's current thinking; and (2) gains in perspective taking, which permit individuals to resolve moral conflicts in more complex and effective ways. As we examine Kohlberg's developmental sequence and illustrate it with responses to the Heinz dilemma, look for changes in cognition and perspective taking that each stage assumes.

THE PRECONVENTIONAL LEVEL. At the **preconventional level,** morality is externally controlled. As in Piaget's heteronomous stage, children accept the rules of authority figures, and actions are judged by their consequences. Behaviors that result in punishment are viewed as bad, and those that lead to rewards are seen as good.

▨ *Stage 1: The punishment and obedience orientation.* Children at this stage find it difficult to consider two points of view in a moral dilemma. As a result, they ignore people's intentions and instead focus on fear of authority and avoidance of punishment as reasons for behaving morally.

Sociomoral Reflection Measure–Short Form (SRM–SF) A questionnaire for assessing moral understanding in which individuals rate the importance of moral values addressed by brief questions and explain their ratings. Does not require research participants to read and think about lengthy moral dilemmas.

preconventional level Kohlberg's first level of moral development, in which moral understanding is based on rewards, punishment, and the power of authority figures.

Prostealing: "If you let your wife die, you will get in trouble. You'll be blamed for not spending the money to help her, and there'll be an investigation of you and the druggist for your wife's death." (Kohlberg, 1969, p. 381)

Antistealing: "You shouldn't steal the drug because you'll be caught and sent to jail if you do. If you do get away, [you'd be scared that] the police would catch up with you any minute." (Kohlberg, 1969, p. 381)

■ *Stage 2: The instrumental purpose orientation.* Awareness that people can have different perspectives in a moral dilemma appears, but at first this understanding is very concrete. Individuals view right action as what satisfies their needs or otherwise results in a personal advantage, and they believe that others also act out of self-interest. Reciprocity is understood as equal exchange of favors—"you do this for me and I'll do that for you."

Prostealing: "The druggist can do what he wants and Heinz can do what he wants to do. . . . But if Heinz decides to risk jail to save his wife, it's his life he's risking; he can do what he wants with it. And the same goes for the druggist; it's up to him to decide what he wants to do." (Rest, 1979, p. 26)

Antistealing: "[Heinz] is running more risk than it's worth [to save a wife who is near death]." (Rest, 1979, p. 27)

THE CONVENTIONAL LEVEL. At the **conventional level,** individuals continue to regard conformity to social rules as important, but not for reasons of self-interest. They believe that actively maintaining the current social system is important for ensuring positive human relationships and societal order.

■ *Stage 3: The "good boy—good girl" orientation, or the morality of interpersonal cooperation.* The desire to obey rules because they promote social harmony first appears in the context of close personal ties. Stage 3 individuals want to maintain the affection and approval of friends and relatives by being a "good person"—trustworthy, loyal, respectful, helpful, and nice. The capacity to view a two-person relationship from the vantage point of an impartial, outside observer supports this new approach to morality. At this stage, the individual understands reciprocity in terms of the Golden Rule.

Prostealing: "No one will think you're bad if you steal the drug, but your family will think you're an inhuman husband if you don't. If you let your wife die, you'll never be able to look anyone in the face again." (Kohlberg, 1969, p. 381)

Antistealing: "It isn't just the druggist who will think you're a criminal, everyone else will too. After you steal it, you'll feel bad thinking how you brought dishonor on your family and yourself; you won't be able to face anyone again." (Kohlberg, 1969, p. 381)

■ *Stage 4: The social-order-maintaining orientation.* At this stage, the individual takes into account a larger perspective—that of societal laws. Moral choices no longer depend on close ties to others. Instead, rules must be enforced in the same evenhanded fashion for everyone, and each member of society has a personal duty to uphold them. The Stage 4 individual believes that laws cannot be disobeyed under any circumstances because they are vital for ensuring societal order.

Prostealing: "He should steal it. Heinz has a duty to protect his wife's life; it's a vow he took in marriage. But it's wrong to steal, so he would have to take the drug with the idea of paying the druggist for it and accepting the penalty for breaking the law later."

Antistealing: "It's a natural thing for Heinz to want to save his wife but. . . . You have to follow the rules regardless of how you feel or regardless of the special circumstances. Even if his wife is dying, it's still his duty as a citizen to obey the law. No one else is allowed to steal, why should he be? If everyone starts breaking the law in a jam, there'd be no civilization, just crime and violence." (Rest, 1979, p. 30)

THE POSTCONVENTIONAL OR PRINCIPLED LEVEL. Individuals at the **postconventional level** move beyond unquestioning support for the rules and laws of their own society.

conventional level Kohlberg's second level of moral development, in which moral understanding is based on conforming to social rules to ensure positive human relationships and societal order.

postconventional level Kohlberg's highest level of moral development, in which individuals define morality in terms of abstract principles and values that apply to all situations and societies.

They define morality in terms of abstract principles and values that apply to all situations and societies.

- *Stage 5: The social-contract orientation.* At Stage 5, individuals regard laws and rules as flexible instruments for furthering human purposes. They can imagine alternatives to their social order, and they emphasize fair procedures for interpreting and changing the law when there is a good reason to do so. When laws are consistent with individual rights and the interests of the majority, each person follows them because of a social-contract orientation—free and willing participation in the system because it brings about more good for people than if it did not exist.

Prostealing: "Although there is a law against stealing, the law wasn't meant to violate a person's right to life. Taking the drug does violate the law, but Heinz is justified in stealing in this instance. If Heinz is prosecuted for stealing, the law needs to be reinterpreted to take into account situations in which it goes against people's natural right to keep on living."

- *Stage 6: The universal ethical principle orientation.* At this highest stage, right action is defined by self-chosen ethical principles of conscience that are valid for all humanity, regardless of law and social agreement. These values are abstract, not concrete moral rules like the Ten Commandments. Stage 6 individuals typically mention such principles as equal consideration of the claims of all human beings and respect for the worth and dignity of each person.

Prostealing: "If Heinz does not do everything he can to save his wife, then he is putting some value higher than the value of life. It doesn't make sense to put respect for property above respect for life itself. [People] could live together without private property at all. Respect for human life and personality is absolute and accordingly [people] have a mutual duty to save one another from dying." (Rest, 1979, p. 37)

FIGURE 12.2

Longitudinal trends in moral reasoning at each stage in Kohlberg's 20-year study of adolescent boys.

(From A. Colby, L. Kohlberg, J. C. Gibbs, & M. Lieberman, 1983, "A Longitudinal Study of Moral Judgement," *Monographs of the Society for Research in Child Development,* 48 [1–2, Serial No. 200], p. 46. © The Society for Research in Child Development, Inc. Reprinted by permission.)

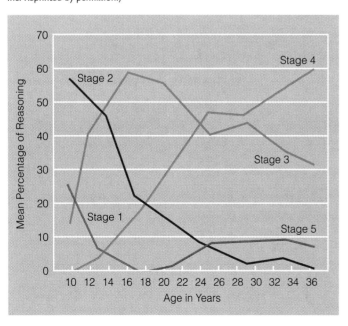

RESEARCH ON KOHLBERG'S STAGES

Is there support for Kohlberg's developmental sequence? If so, movement through the stages should be related to age, cognitive development, and gains in perspective taking. Also, moral reasoning should conform to the strict stage properties that Kohlberg assumed.

■ **AGE-RELATED CHANGE AND INVARIANT STAGES.** A wealth of longitudinal and cross-sectional research reveals that progress through Kohlberg's stages is consistently related to age. The most convincing evidence comes from a 20-year continuation of Kohlberg's first study of adolescent boys, in which participants were reinterviewed at 3- to 4-year intervals. The correlation between age and moral maturity was strong, at .78. In addition, the stages formed an invariant sequence. Almost all participants moved through them in the predicted order, without skipping steps or returning to less mature reasoning once a stage had been attained (Colby et al., 1983). Other longitudinal findings confirm the invariance of Kohlberg's stages (Rest, 1986; Walker, 1989; Walker & Taylor, 1991b).

A striking finding is that development of moral reasoning is very slow and gradual. Figure 12.2 shows the extent to which individuals used each stage of moral reasoning between ages 10 and 36 in the longitudinal study just described. Notice how Stages 1 and 2 decrease in early adolescence, whereas Stage 3 increases through mid-adolescence and then declines. Stage 4 rises over the teenage years until, by early adulthood, it is the typical response. Few people move beyond it to Stage 5. In fact, postconventional morality is so rare that there is no clear evidence that Kohlberg's Stage 6 actually follows Stage 5. The highest stage of moral development is still a matter of speculation.

Will the 14-year-old girls on the left decide to accept a peer's offer of a cigarette? How will they justify their decision? Real-life moral dilemmas bring out the motivational and emotional side of moral judgment along with a variety of strategies for resolving conflicts. These teenagers may talk the matter through with each other or call on intuition, since they must make an on-the-spot decision. (Elizabeth Zuckerman/PhotoEdit)

■ **ARE KOHLBERG'S STAGES ORGANIZED WHOLES?** As you read the Heinz dilemma, you probably came up with your own solution to it. Now try to think of a moral problem you recently faced in everyday life. How did you solve it, and what factors influenced your choice? Did your reasoning fall at the same stage as your thinking about Heinz and his dying wife? If each of Kohlberg's stages forms an organized whole, then we should use the same level of moral reasoning across many tasks and situations.

In focusing on hypothetical dilemmas, Kohlberg's interviewing procedure emphasizes rationally weighing alternatives to the neglect of other influences on moral judgment. When researchers asked adolescents and adults to recall and discuss a real-life moral dilemma, the most frequent strategy advocated for resolving it *was* reasoning it out. But participants also posed other strategies, such as talking through issues with others, relying on intuition that their decision was right, and calling on notions of religion and spirituality. Especially striking were expressions of anguish in working through everyday dilemmas. People mentioned feeling drained, confused, and torn by temptation—a motivational and emotional side of moral judgment not tapped by hypothetical situations (Walker & Hennig, 1997; Walker et al., 1995).

Although everyday moral reasoning corresponds to Kohlberg's scheme, it typically falls at a lower stage than do responses to hypothetical dilemmas (Walker & Moran, 1991). Real-life problems—whether to continue helping a friend when she's taking advantage of you, whether to live with mother or father following their separation, whether to challenge a supervisor's negative evaluation of a co-worker—seem to elicit reasoning below a person's actual capacity because they bring out the many practical considerations involved in an actual moral conflict. Hypothetical situations, in contrast, evoke the upper limits of adolescents' and adults' moral thought because they allow reflection without the interference of personal risks. As one participant in a study involving both types of dilemmas observed, "It's a lot easier to be moral when you have nothing to lose" (Walker et al., 1995, pp. 381–382).

The influence of situational factors on moral reasoning suggests that like Piaget's cognitive stages, Kohlberg's moral stages are best viewed in terms of a loose rather than strict concept of stage. Rather than developing in a neat, stepwise fashion, people seem to draw on a range of moral responses that vary with context. With age, this range shifts upward as less mature moral reasoning is gradually replaced by more advanced moral thought (Rest, 1979; Siegler, 1996).

■ **COGNITIVE PREREQUISITES FOR MORAL REASONING.** Moral maturity, whether based on Piaget's or Kohlberg's theories, is positively correlated with IQ, performance on Piagetian cognitive tasks, and perspective-taking skill (Lickona, 1976; Walker & Hennig, 1997). Kohlberg (1976) argued that each moral stage requires certain cognitive and perspective-taking capacities, but these are not enough to ensure moral advances. In addition, reorganization of thought unique to the moral domain is necessary. In other words, Kohlberg hypothesized that cognitive and perspective-taking attainments are *necessary but not sufficient conditions* for each of the moral stages.

Recall from Chapter 11 that the "necessary but not sufficient" criterion also applies to the relation between Piaget's cognitive and Selman's perspective-taking stages, so Kohlberg's hypothesis is an expansion of this idea. Although no single study has examined all the stage relationships in Table 12.1 on page 496, research shows that cognitive, perspective-taking, and moral development are related in ways consistent with Kohlberg's predictions (Krebs & Gillmore, 1982; Selman, 1976). For example, in a study of fourth through seventh graders, with only one exception all children at Stage 3 moral reasoning scored at either a higher stage or the matching stage of cognition and perspective taking (Walker, 1980). Furthermore, attempts to increase moral reasoning reveal that it cannot be stimulated beyond the stage for which an individual has the appropriate cognitive prerequisites (Walker & Richards, 1979).

TABLE 12.1

Relations Among Kohlberg's Moral, Piaget's Cognitive, and Selman's Perspective-Taking Stages

Kohlberg's Moral Stage	Description	Piaget's Cognitive Stage	Selman's Perspective-Taking Stage
Punishment and obedience orientation	Fear of authority and avoidance of punishment are reasons for behaving morally.	Preoperational, early concrete operational	Social-informational
Instrumental purpose orientation	Satisfying personal needs determines moral choice.	Concrete operational	Self-reflective
"Good boy–good girl" orientation	Maintaining the affection and approval of friends and relatives motivates good behavior.	Early formal operational	Third-party
Social-order-maintaining orientation	A duty to uphold laws and rules for their own sake justifies moral conformity.	Formal operational	Societal
Social-contract orientation	Fair procedures for changing laws to protect individual rights and the needs of the majority are emphasized.		
Universal ethical principle orientation	Abstract universal principles that are valid for all humanity guide moral decision making.		

ENVIRONMENTAL INFLUENCES ON MORAL REASONING

What other factors besides the attainment of Piaget's and Selman's stages might promote moral maturity? Earlier we mentioned Kohlberg's belief that actively grappling with moral issues is vital for moral change. As we will see in the following sections, many environmental factors are related to moral understanding, including peer interaction, child-rearing practices, schooling, and aspects of culture.

The weakness of this research is one we have mentioned many times: Correlational studies cannot tell us for sure that an important cause of moral reasoning has been isolated. Fortunately, in some cases, experiments have been conducted demonstrating the role of certain experiences in moral development. Furthermore, a growing body of evidence suggests that these experiences work by inducing disequilibrium—presenting young people with cognitive challenges, which stimulate them to think about moral problems in more complex ways.

■ **PEER INTERACTION.** Research supports Piaget's belief that interaction with agemates can promote moral understanding. Maturity of moral reasoning is correlated with peer popularity, participation in social organizations, and service in leadership roles (Enright & Sutterfield, 1980; Harris, Mussen, & Rutherford, 1976). Studies conducted in Africa underline the importance of exposure to diverse peer value systems for stimulating moral thought. Kenyan and Nigerian students enrolled in ethnically and racially mixed high schools and colleges were advanced in moral development compared with those enrolled in homogeneous settings (Edwards, 1978; Maqsud, 1977).

As Piaget suggested, peer conflict probably contributes to gains in moral reasoning by making children aware of others' perspectives. But as we noted in Chapter 6, conflict resolution, rather than conflict per se, may be the feature of peer disagreements that stimulates cognitive development—nonmoral and moral alike. Peers typically require one another to justify their actions—a feature that reduces conflict. When children engage in negotiation and compromise, they realize that social life can be based on cooperation between equals rather than authority relations (Damon, 1988; Killen & Nucci, 1995). Recall from Chapter 11 that within children's friendships, conflicts often arise but are worked out collaboratively. The mutuality and intimacy of friendship, which foster decisions based on consensual agreement, may contribute importantly to moral development.

Peer experiences have provided the framework for many interventions aimed at improving moral understanding. Most involve peer discussion and role playing of moral problems. A study by Moshe Blatt and Lawrence Kohlberg (1975) yielded particularly impressive findings. After participating in either teacher- or student-led classroom discussions of moral dilemmas for one semester, many sixth and tenth graders moved partially or totally to the next moral stage, a change not found in pupils who did not receive the intervention. A year later, these differences were still evident.

Which aspects of peer discussion stimulate moral development? Once again, give-and-take and compromise, involving efforts to comprehend another's viewpoint, appear important. In one study, college students who confronted, critiqued, and attempted to clarify one another's statements gained in moral maturity. In contrast, nongainers made assertions, told personal anecdotes, or expressed confusion about the task (Berkowitz & Gibbs, 1983). However, because moral development is a gradual process, it usually takes many peer interaction sessions over weeks or months to produce moral change.

Discussions about moral issues in which peers confront, critique, and attempt to clarify one another's statements lead to gains in moral understanding.
(Kopstein/Monkmeyer Press)

■ **CHILD-REARING PRACTICES.** Child-rearing practices associated with mature moral reasoning reflect rational, democratic processes. Lawrence Walker and John Taylor (1991a) assessed level of moral reasoning and interaction styles of mothers and fathers as they discussed moral dilemmas with their first- through tenth-grade children. Parents who created a supportive atmosphere by listening sensitively, asking clarifying questions, presenting higher-level reasoning, and using praise and humor had children who gained most in moral understanding when interviewed 2 years later. In contrast, parents who lectured, used threats, or made sarcastic remarks had children who changed little or not at all.

Other research reveals that parents who use low levels of power assertion and high levels of warmth and inductive discipline and who encourage participation in family decision making have morally mature children (Boyes & Allen, 1993; Parikh, 1980). In sum, the kind of parent who facilitates moral understanding is verbal, rational, and affectionate and promotes a cooperative style of family life. Notice that these are the very characteristics, discussed earlier in this chapter, that foster moral internalization in young children.

■ **SCHOOLING.** Years of schooling completed is one of the most powerful predictors of moral understanding. Moral reasoning advances in late adolescence and young adulthood only as long as a person remains in school (Rest & Narvaez, 1991; Speicher, 1994). Perhaps higher education has a strong impact on moral development because it introduces young people to social issues that extend beyond personal relationships to entire political or cultural groups. Consistent with this idea, college students who report more academic perspective-taking opportunities (for example, classes that emphasize open discussion of opinions) and who indicate that they have become more aware of social diversity tend to be advanced in moral reasoning (Mason & Gibbs, 1993a, 1993b).

■ **CULTURE.** Cross-cultural research reveals that individuals in technologically advanced, urban cultures move through Kohlberg's stages more rapidly and advance to a higher level than do individuals in nonindustrialized, village societies. Stages 4 and above are not reached by members of these small, collectivist communities, whereas they are attained by high school– and college-educated adolescents and adults in developed nations (Snarey, 1995). (Recall, however, that Stages 5 and 6 are not commonly reached even by adults in industrialized countries.)

Why these cultural differences exist is a matter of considerable debate. One explanation addresses the role of societal institutions in advanced moral understanding. In village cultures, moral cooperation is based on direct relations between people. Yet Stage 4 to 6 reasoning depends on understanding the role of laws and government institutions in resolving moral conflict (Kohlberg, 1969). In support of this view, in cultures where young people participate in the institutions of their society at early ages, moral reasoning is advanced. For example, on kibbutzim, small but technologically complex agricultural settlements in Israel, children receive training in the governance of their community beginning in middle childhood. By third grade, they mention more concerns about societal laws and rules when discussing moral conflicts than do Israeli city-reared or American children (Fuchs et al., 1986). During adolescence and adulthood, a greater

Young people growing up on Israeli kibbutzim receive training in the governance of their society at an early age. As a result, they understand the role of societal laws and rules in resolving moral conflict and are advanced in moral reasoning.

(Louis Goldman/Photo Researchers, Inc.)

percentage of kibbutz than American individuals reach Kohlberg's Stages 4 and 5 (Snarey, Reimer, & Kohlberg, 1985).

A second possible reason for cultural variation is that Kohlberg's dilemmas are not well suited to certain cultures. At times, people respond in ways not easily scorable in Kohlberg's scheme. Recall from Chapter 11 that self-concepts in collectivist cultures (including village societies) are more other-directed than in Western Europe and North America. This very difference seems to characterize moral reasoning as well (Miller, 1994, 1997). In village societies, moral statements that portray the individual as vitally connected to the social group through a deep sense of community responsibility are common. For example, one New Guinea village leader placed the blame for the Heinz dilemma on the entire social group, stating, "If I were the judge, I would give him only light punishment because he asked everybody for help but nobody helped him" (Tietjen & Walker, 1985, p. 990).

Similarly, members of Eastern nations with a collectivist orientation grant interpersonal moral obligations greater weight than do people in Western individualistic societies. In one study, East Indian and American adults were presented with interpersonal transgressions (a son refusing to care for his elderly parents, a man leaving his wife and children for another woman) and justice issues (a college student cheating on an exam because family responsibilities prevented him from studying, a man leaving the city without paying back a loan). Both groups viewed the justice issues as morally wrong. But East Indians were more likely than Americans to condemn the interpersonal transgressions and to view them as moral offenses rather than matters of personal choice (Miller & Luthar, 1989).

In addition, East Indians less often hold individuals accountable for moral violations. In their view, the self is intimately connected to the physical and social context. Therefore, behaviors are often explained in contextual rather than personal terms (Miller, 1994; Miller & Bersoff, 1995). This perspective is evident even among well-educated East Indian adults, who would be expected to be postconventional in Kohlberg's scheme. In discussing the Heinz dilemma, they rarely appeal to personal ethical principles. Instead, they resist choosing a course of action, explaining that a moral solution should be the burden not of a single individual but of the entire society. As one woman explained,

> The problems that Heinz is up against are not individual problems that are affecting one or two Heinzes of the world. These are social problems. Forget Heinz in Europe, just come to India. . . . Heinz's story is being repeated all around us all the time with wives dying, with children dying, and there is no money to save them. . . . So Heinz in his individual capacity—yes, okay, steal the drug, but it's not going to make any difference on a large scale. . . . I don't think in the final analysis a solution can be worked out on an individual basis. . . . It will probably have to be tackled on a macro level. (Vasudev & Hummel, 1987, p. 110)

These findings raise the question of whether Kohlberg's highest stages represent a culturally specific rather than universal way of thinking—one limited to Western societies that emphasize individual rights and an appeal to an inner, private conscience. But recall that although East Indians place a high priority on interpersonal responsibilities, they (like Americans) recognize certain moral issues as matters of justice. Perhaps a justice morality and an interpersonal morality coexist but vary in prominence across cultures and, within individuals, from one situation to another. As we turn to the topic of sex-related differences in moral reasoning, we will revisit this idea.

ARE THERE SEX-RELATED DIFFERENCES IN MORAL REASONING?

Carol Gilligan (1982) is the most well-known figure among those who have argued that Kohlberg's theory—originally formulated on the basis of interviews with males—does not adequately represent the morality of females. She believes that feminine morality emphasizes an "ethic of care," but Kohlberg's system devalues it. Return to the description of Kohlberg's stages on pages 492–494 and notice how Stage 3 is based on interpersonal obligations. In contrast, Stages 4 to 6 stress justice—an abstract, rational commitment to moral ideals that, according to Gilligan, tends to be encouraged in males. In her view, a concern for others is a *different*, not less valid, basis for moral judgment than a focus on impersonal rights.

Many studies have tested Gilligan's claim that Kohlberg's approach underestimates the moral maturity of females, and most do not support it (Turiel, 1998). On hypothetical dilemmas as well as everyday moral problems, adolescent and adult females do not fall behind males in development. Also, themes of justice and caring appear in the responses of both sexes, and when girls do raise interpersonal concerns, they are not downscored in Kohlberg's system (Jadack et al., 1995; Kahn, 1992; Walker, 1995). These findings suggest that although Kohlberg emphasized justice rather than caring as the highest of moral ideals, his theory does include both sets of values.

Still, Gilligan's claim that research on moral development has been limited by too much attention to rights and justice (a "masculine" ideal) and too little attention to care and responsiveness (a "feminine" ideal) is a powerful one. Some evidence shows that although the morality of males and females taps both orientations, females do tend to stress care, or empathic perspective taking, whereas males either stress justice or use justice and care equally (Galotti, Kozberg, & Farmer, 1991; Garmon et al., 1996; Wark & Krebs, 1996). The difference in emphasis appears most often on real-life rather than hypothetical dilemmas. Consequently, it may be largely a function of men's and women's daily lives. In support of this idea, one study found that restricting moral problems to child-rearing concerns eliminated gender differences in reasoning between mothers and fathers. As the researchers noted, men "only needed to have their attention drawn to an important part of their lives to manifest the care concerns already abundantly present" (Clopton & Sorell, 1993, p. 99).

Although current evidence indicates that justice and caring are not gender-specific moralities, Gilligan's work has had the effect of broadening conceptions of the highly moral person. Mary Brabeck (1983) notes,

> When Gilligan and Kohlberg's theories are taken together, the moral person is seen as one whose moral choices reflect reasoned and deliberate judgments that ensure justice be accorded each person while maintaining a passionate concern for the well-being and care of each individual. Justice and care are then joined . . . and the need for autonomy and for interconnection are united in an enlarged and more adequate conception of morality. (p. 289)

Perhaps Piaget (1932/1965) himself said it best: "Between the more refined forms of justice . . . and love properly so called, there is no longer any real conflict" (p. 324).

MORAL REASONING AND BEHAVIOR

A central assumption of the cognitive-developmental perspective is that moral understanding should affect moral motivation. As young people grasp the underlying moral "logic" of human social cooperation, they are upset when this logic is violated. As a result, they gradually realize that behaving in line with the way one thinks is an important part of creating and maintaining a just social world (Gibbs, 1995; Narvaez & Rest, 1995). On the basis of this idea, Kohlberg predicted a very specific relationship between moral thought and behavior: The two should come closer together as individuals move toward the higher stages of moral understanding (Blasi, 1994a).

Consistent with Kohlberg's prediction, advanced moral reasoning is related to many aspects of social behavior. Higher-stage adolescents more often engage in prosocial acts, such as helping, sharing, and defending victims of injustice (Gibbs et al., 1986). They are also more honest. For example, they are less likely to cheat on assignments and tests in school (Harris, Mussen, & Rutherford, 1976). Conversely, lower-stage adolescents are likely to be less honest and to engage in antisocial behavior (Gregg, Gibbs, & Basinger, 1994).

Yet even though a clear connection between moral thought and action exists, it is only moderate. We have already seen that moral behavior is also influenced by noncognitive factors, including the emotions of empathy and guilt, individual differences in temperament, and a long history of experiences that affect moral choice and decision making. Personality traits, such as the degree to which morality is central to self-concept, are also involved. A study of African-American and Hispanic adolescents displaying exceptional levels of prosocial behavior revealed that compared to controls, their actual and ideal selves showed a closer match, and their self-descriptions more often included moral traits and goals. The two groups did not differ in stage of moral reasoning (Hart & Fegley, 1995). Researchers have yet to discover how all these complex facets of morality work together.

FURTHER QUESTIONS ABOUT KOHLBERG'S THEORY

Although there is much support for Kohlberg's theory, it continues to face challenges. The most important of these concerns Kohlberg's conception of moral maturity and the appropriateness of his stages for characterizing the moral reasoning of young children.

A key controversy has to do with Kohlberg's belief that moral maturity is not achieved until the postconventional level. Yet if people had to reach Stages 5 and 6 to be considered truly morally mature, few individuals anywhere would measure up! John Gibbs (1991) believes that "postconventional morality" should not be viewed as the standard against which other levels are judged immature. Instead, he regards such reasoning as a reflective, philosophical orientation beyond the realm of spontaneous, everyday moral thought. Gibbs finds maturity in a revised understanding of Stages 3 and 4—specifically, appeals to ethically ideal relationships (Stage 3) and society (Stage 4). These stages are not necessarily "conventional" or based on social conformity, as Kohlberg assumed. Instead, Stages 3 and 4 require vital moral constructions—an understanding of mutual trust as the basis for obligations between people and of widely accepted moral standards as necessary for society.

Finally, Kohlberg's stages largely describe changes in moral reasoning during adolescence and adulthood. They tell us little about moral understanding in early and middle childhood. Indeed, Kohlberg's moral dilemmas are remote from the experiences of most children and may not be clearly understood by them. When children are given moral problems related to their everyday lives, their responses indicate that Kohlberg's preconventional level, much like Piaget's heteronomous morality, underestimates their moral reasoning. In sum, Kohlberg's belief in an early, externally governed morality meant that he failed to uncover young children's internally based judgments of right and wrong. We take a close look at this evidence in the following sections.

ASK YOURSELF . . .

♦ Tam grew up in a small village culture, Lydia in a large industrial city. At age 15, Tam reasons at Kohlberg's Stage 2, Lydia at Stage 4. What factors might account for the difference?

♦ CONNECTIONS
In Chapter 11 (page 447), we noted that compared with school-age children, adolescents place more emphasis in their self-descriptions on social virtues, such as being friendly, considerate, kind, and cooperative. They also stress personal moral values as key themes. How do these changes in self-concept relate to stagewise advances in moral reasoning, described on page 493?

BRIEF REVIEW

According to Kohlberg's three-level, six-stage theory, morality changes from concrete, externally oriented reasoning to more abstract, principled justifications for moral choices. Each moral stage builds on cognitive and perspective-taking capacities. Research suggests a powerful role for environmental contexts in the development of moral understanding. Advanced moral reasoning is not attained unless supports exist on many levels, including family, peers, schooling, and wider society. Although Kohlberg's theory emphasizes a morality of justice rather than a morality of care, it does not underestimate the moral maturity of females. As individuals advance through Kohlberg's stages, moral reasoning becomes better related to behavior. Recent challenges to Kohlberg's theory question its definition of moral maturity and its view of the moral reasoning of young children.

Moral Reasoning of Young Children

Researchers using moral dilemmas specifically designed for children have addressed three facets of their moral understanding: (1) their ability to distinguish moral obligations from social conventions and matters of personal choice; (2) their ideas about fair distribution of rewards; and (3) their prosocial reasoning—how they choose between self-interest and meeting the needs of others. Besides being relevant to children's real-life experiences, the moral problems used in these studies differ from Kohlberg's in that the role of laws and the possibility of punishment are de-emphasized. When dilemmas are formulated in these ways, young children reveal surprisingly advanced moral judgments.

DISTINGUISHING MORAL, SOCIAL-CONVENTIONAL, AND PERSONAL DOMAINS

As early as age 3, children have a beginning grasp of justice. Many studies reveal that preschool and young grade school children distinguish **moral imperatives,** which protect people's rights and welfare, from two other domains of action: **social conventions,** customs determined solely by consensus, such as table manners, dress styles, and rituals of social interaction; and **matters of personal choice,** which do not violate rights or harm others, are not socially regulated, and therefore are up to the individual (Nucci, 1996; Smetana, 1995; Tisak, 1995).

■ **MORAL VERSUS SOCIAL-CONVENTIONAL DISTINCTIONS.** In one study, 2- and 3-year-olds were interviewed about drawings depicting familiar moral and social-conventional violations. For example, a moral picture showed a child stealing an agemate's apple; a social-conventional picture showed a child eating ice cream with fingers. By 34 months, children viewed moral transgressions as more generalizably wrong (not OK, regardless of the setting in which they are committed). And by 42 months, they indicated that moral (but not social-conventional) violations would still be wrong if an adult did not see them and no rules existed to prohibit them (Smetana & Braeges, 1990).

As these findings illustrate, the distinction between moral and social-conventional transgressions sharpens during early childhood. Four-year-olds judge immoral acts as wrong in any context, whether or not rules or authorities prohibit them. (Note that research on children's reasoning about authority, reported on page 490, yields similar results.) These understandings are, at first, limited to familiar experiences. By age 9 to 10, children apply them more broadly, to both familiar and unfamiliar events. See the Social Issues box on page 502 for evidence that older school-age children extend morality to the entire natural environment.

According to Elliott Turiel (1998), children separate moral from social-conventional matters by actively making sense of their experiences in both types of situations. They observe that people respond differently to violations of moral rules than to breaks with social convention. When a moral offense occurs, children describe their own injury or loss, tell another child to stop, or retaliate. And an adult who intervenes is likely to call attention to the rights, needs, and feelings of the victim. In contrast, children often do not respond to violations of social convention. And in these situations, adults may demand obedience without explanation, as when they state, "Say the magic word!" or "Don't eat with your fingers." Or they focus on obeying rules, keeping order, and other aspects of social organization (Turiel, Smetana, & Killen, 1991).

Compared with social-conventional transgressions, moral violations prompt intensely negative emotions, which serve as vital cues to their justice implications. When researchers presented school-age children with descriptions of emotional reactions and asked them to select from alternative events that might have elicited them, 5- to 12-year-olds attributed very negative responses to victims of a moral violations (such as having a toy stolen) (Arsenio & Fleiss, 1996).

Yet children do not rely only on emotions in forming moral judgments. For example, they say that an adult would react negatively to a child who breaks a school dress code, but they do not regard the child as having breached the adult's rights or welfare. Furthermore, even young children differentiate the emotions of moral victims and perpetrators, who they say might feel happy because of material gain. Older school-age children's grasp of the relation between emotion and moral transgression is more mature. They realize that a victim's unhappiness can affect the perpetrator, producing a mixture of positive and negative emotion (Arsenio & Kramer, 1992; Arsenio & Lover, 1995).

moral imperatives Standards that protect people's rights and welfare.

social conventions Customs determined solely by consensus, such as table manners, dress styles, and rituals of social interaction.

matters of personal choice Concerns that do not violate rights or harm others, are not socially regulated, and therefore are up to the individual.

Children's Environmental Moral Reasoning

OES CHILDREN'S MORAL reasoning extend to the connection between humans and nature—to the welfare of animals, trees, water, landscapes, and the earth as a whole? If so, what is the structure of such reasoning, and how does it change with age?

In a series of studies, Peter Kahn sought answers to these questions by interviewing school-age children about environmental concerns. Some were second through eighth graders from families of diverse ethnic and SES backgrounds in Houston, Texas (Kahn, 1997b; Kahn & Friedman, 1995). Others were urban and rural Brazilian fifth graders—from Manaus, the largest city within the Amazon rain forest, and from Novo Ayrao, a small, remote Amazon village (Howe, Kahn, & Friedman, 1996).

Despite the fact that many Houston children faced harsh living conditions in poverty-stricken African-American neighborhoods, the majority reported that animals, plants, and open spaces were important to their lives. And most talked about environmental issues with their families and engaged in practices to improve the environment, such as recycling and picking up litter (Kahn, 1997a).

To assess environmental moral reasoning, the children were asked questions about pollution of their local waterway—a bayou in Texas, a river in Brazil. And shortly after the 1990 Exxon Valdez oil spill, which sparked worldwide attention to the ecological devastation wrought by 11 million gallons of oil flowing into Alaskan waters, the Texas children were questioned about its potentially harmful effects.

In both cultures, children regarded polluting the environment as a moral violation—that is, as not all right, even if you live in another country and a law lets you do it. Over the school years, more children claimed that people are morally obliged not to pollute.

A close look at children's justifications indicated that environmental moral reasoning takes three forms:

- *anthropocentric:* explanations that focus on how spoiling the environment affects people, including interfering with (1) their personal interests ("animals matter to me because we need more pets"), (2) their aesthetics ("the beauty of all the plants"), and (3) their physical, material, and psychological welfare ("making people sick")

- *biocentric:* explanations that appeal to the larger ecological community of which humans are a part by emphasizing (1) the intrinsic value and rights of nature ("without animals, the world is incomplete, like a paper that's not finished"), and (2) respect or fair treatment of nature ("every creature has a right to live")

- unelaborated *harm to nature:* explanations focusing on harm, with no clear reference to anthropocentric or biocentric orientations ("if animals die, the land wouldn't be fertilized to grow plants, and animals need plants to eat").

In each study, anthropocentric and biocentric reasoning increased with age, whereas unelaborated harm explanations declined. This indicates that a nonspecific concern for the well-being of nature gradually gives way to both human-oriented and nature-oriented justice considerations. And some older children integrated anthropocentric and biocentric concerns into a wider structure referring to the entire ecological system, as in this eighth grader's reaction to the Exxon Valdez oil spill: "There's people, nature, and animals . . . you're killing one third of the environment that way [killing animals]. I don't think that's right" (Kahn, 1997b, p. 1095).

A striking finding was that environmental moral reasoning was highly similar across cultures, despite wide variation in American and Brazilian children's experiences. Even though Amazonian children lived close to nature, they did not give more biocentric justifications than did their American agemates. Instead, anthropocentric reasoning was more common among all children.

These findings are consistent with other cross-cultural evidence indicating that justifications referring to fairness, rights, and welfare may represent a universal aspect of moral thought. As yet, researchers know little about factors that promote environmental moral reasoning. Perhaps children must first construct interpersonal moral obligations, which they transfer and adapt to the natural world. Alternatively, children's natural and interpersonal moral concepts may develop simultaneously, each fostering the other in a bidirectional fashion.

In sum, societal discourse about the environment has firm roots in childhood. During the school years, children develop a rich appreciation for nature and a moral commitment to its preservation.

■ ARE MORAL VERSUS SOCIAL-CONVENTIONAL DISTINCTIONS CULTURALLY UNIVERSAL? A strong case exists for early emergence of distinct moral and social-conventional domains of understanding. Yet the very criticism of Kohlberg's theory mentioned earlier—that it overemphasizes individual rights—has also been leveled at the moral–social-conventional distinction (Witherell & Edwards, 1991).

To examine this claim, researchers have conducted cross-cultural research, which reveals that children and adolescents in many societies—not just Western nations, but diverse non-Western cultures, such as Brazil, Korea, Indonesia, Nigeria, and Zambia—use the same criteria to separate moral concerns from social conventions (Bersoff & Miller, 1993; Nucci, Camino, & Sapiro, 1996; Tisak, 1995). Certain behaviors are classified differently across

distributive justice Beliefs about how to divide resources fairly.

cultures. For example, East Indian Hindu children believe that eating chicken the day after a father's death is morally wrong, whereas American children do not (Shweder, Mahapatra, & Miller, 1990). But Hindu religious teachings specify that eating chicken causes harm by preventing the father's soul from receiving salvation! In India, as in many developing countries, practices with profound moral significance strike Western outsiders as arbitrary because they do not understand the intentions behind those practices.

When asked about acts that obviously lead to harm or violate rights, such as breaking promises, destroying another's property, or kicking harmless animals, cultural differences diminish (Turiel, 1998). We are reminded, once again, that justice considerations appear to be a universal feature of moral thought.

Children in diverse cultures use the same criteria to separate moral concerns from social conventions. Certain behaviors are classified differently across cultures because of the intentions behind those practices. This Hindu Indian girl is likely to say that eating chicken the day after a father's death is an immoral act. In her world view, doing so would inflict harm on the father by preventing his soul from receiving salvation.
(Renato Rotolo/Liaison Agency)

■ **RELATION OF PERSONAL AND MORAL DOMAINS.** In Western and non-Western cultures, children and adolescents identify a unique domain of personal matters. For example, they are likely to argue that hairstyle, choice of friends, and the contents of a diary are up to the individual—a view that strengthens between ages 8 and 16 (Nucci, 1996; Nucci, Camino, & Sapiro, 1996).

The personal domain emerges with self-awareness in the early preschool years. By age 2, children engage in efforts to establish boundaries between the self and others through claims of ownership ("That's mine!") and personal choice ("I'm gonna wear *this* shirt!"). Children quickly learn that parents are willing to compromise on personal issues and, at times, on social-conventional matters, but not on moral concerns. Likewise, when children and adolescents challenge parental authority, they typically do so within the personal domain (Nucci & Weber, 1995). As insistence that parents not intrude on the personal arena strengthens at adolescence, disputes over personal issues increase. Disagreements are sharpest on matters that are both personal and social-conventional and therefore subject to interpretation—for example, a messy bedroom, which can be viewed as individual and communal space (Smetana & Asquith, 1994).

When asked, mothers say that they grant their preschoolers control over certain activities to encourage a sense of autonomy and agency (Nucci & Smetana, 1996). According to Larry Nucci (1996), children's grasp of their own and others' agency serves as a vital foundation for morality because it leads to concepts of rights and freedom. By adolescence, young people in both individualistic and collectivistic cultures think more intently about conflicts between personal freedom and community obligation—for example, whether, and under what conditions, it is permissible for governments to restrict speech, religion, marriage, childbearing, and other individual rights (Helwig, 1995; Wainryb, 1997). Although answers vary, personal, social-conventional, and moral matters coexist and interact in all societies. As adolescents realize that personal and social-conventional claims can have moral implications (for example, when free speech incites prejudice or violating a custom offends someone), moral understanding is enhanced.

These five school-age children have figured out how to divide up two pizzas fairly among themselves. Already, they have a well-developed sense of distributive justice.
(Will Faller)

DISTRIBUTIVE JUSTICE

In everyday life, children frequently experience situations that involve **distributive justice**—beliefs about how to divide resources fairly. Heated discussions take place over how much weekly allowance is to be given to siblings of different ages, who has to sit where in the family car on a long trip, and in what way an eight-slice pizza is to be shared by six hungry playmates. William Damon (1977, 1988) has studied changing concepts of distributive justice over early and middle childhood. His developmental sequence, which is supported by both cross-sectional and longitudinal evidence, reveals, once again, that children construct complex notions of fairness much earlier than Piaget and Kohlberg believed (Enright et al., 1984; Enright, Franklin, & Manheim, 1980).

TABLE **12.2**

Damon's Sequence of Distributive Justice Reasoning

Basis of Reasoning	Age	Description
Equality	5–6	Fairness involves strictly equal distibution of goods. Special considerations, such as merit and need, are not considered.
Merit	6–7	Fairness is based on deservingness. Children recognize that some people should get more because they have worked harder.
Benevolence	8	Fairness includes special consideration for those who are disadvantaged. More should be given to people in need.

Source: Damon, 1977, 1988.

Even 4-year-olds recognize the importance of sharing, but their reasons often seem contradictory and self-serving: "I shared because if I didn't, she wouldn't play with me" or "I let her have some, but most are for me because I'm older." These rather arbitrary and egocentric explanations are not surprising when we recall preschoolers' "undifferentiated perspective-taking" responses to such problems as Selman's "Holly dilemma" (see Chapter 11, page 464).

As children enter middle childhood, they start to express more mature notions of distributive justice (see Table 12.2). At first, their ideas of fairness are based on *equality.* Children in the early school grades are intent on making sure that each person gets the same amount of a treasured resource, such as money, turns in a game, or a delicious treat. This strict-equality approach resembles young children's rigidity in other areas, such as the morality of intentions (return to page 490 to review).

A short time later, children start to view fairness in terms of *merit.* Extra rewards should be given to someone who has worked especially hard or otherwise performed in an exceptional way. Finally, around 8 years, children can reason on the basis of *benevolence.* They recognize that special consideration should be given to those at a disadvantage. Older children say that an extra amount might be given to a child who cannot produce as much or does not get any allowance from his parents. They also adapt their basis of fairness to the situation—for example, relying more on merit when interacting with strangers and more on benevolence when interacting with friends (McGillicuddy-De Lisi, Watkins, & Vinchur, 1994).

According to Damon (1988), parental advice and encouragement support these developing standards of justice, but the give-and-take of peer interaction is especially important. Peer disagreements, along with efforts to resolve them, make children more sensitive to others' perspectives, and this supports their developing ideas of fairness (Kruger, 1993). Advanced distributive justice reasoning, in turn, is associated with more effective social problem solving and a greater willingness to help and share with others (Blotner & Bearison, 1984; McNamee & Peterson, 1986).

PROSOCIAL MORAL REASONING

Return for a moment to Kohlberg's Heinz dilemma, and notice that to help his wife, Heinz has no choice but to break the law and steal. In most everyday situations in which children must decide whether to act prosocially, the cost is not disobeying the law or an authority figure. Instead, it is not satisfying one's own wants or needs. Nancy Eisenberg asked preschoolers through twelfth graders to respond to prosocial dilemmas in which the primary sacrifice in aiding another person is giving up personal desires. Here is a typical scenario given to younger children:

> One day a girl named Mary was going to a friend's birthday party. On her way she saw a girl who had fallen down and hurt her leg. The girl asked Mary to go to her house and get her parents so the parents could come and take her to the doctor. But

if Mary did run and get the child's parents, she would be late for the birthday party and miss the ice cream, cake, and all the games. What should Mary do? Why? (Eisenberg, 1982, p. 231)

Conducting both cross-sectional and longitudinal research, Eisenberg found that responses formed the age-related sequence summarized in Table 12.3 (Eisenberg, 1986; Eisenberg et al., 1991, 1995a).

Notice how Eisenberg's developmental levels resemble Kohlberg's stages. For example, her hedonistic, pragmatic orientation is like Kohlberg's Stage 2, her approval-focused and empathic orientations are like Kohlberg's Stage 3, and her internalized values orientation includes forms of reasoning that seem to match Kohlberg's Stages 4 to 6. Furthermore, child-rearing practices that foster moral internalization and higher-level reasoning in Kohlberg's system—warmth, reasonable expectations for maturity, and explanations— also promote advanced prosocial moral understanding (Janssens & Deković, 1997). But certain features of Eisenberg's findings depart from Kohlberg's. Punishment- and authority-oriented reasoning is rare in children's responses. Also, prosocial moral understanding is clearly advanced when compared with the timing of Kohlberg's stages.

Finally, prosocial dilemmas bring out a form of moral reasoning that Eisenberg calls "empathic." By the late elementary school years, children realize that empathy is an important motivator of prosocial behavior. In one study, 9- and 10-year-olds who easily empathized advanced to higher levels of prosocial understanding during early adolescence (Eisenberg et al., 1987). According to Eisenberg, empathic feelings may encourage more mature prosocial thought and strengthen its realization in everyday behavior. In line with this idea, children and adolescents at higher prosocial moral levels do tend to act more prosocially than do agemates who are less advanced (Eisenberg et al., 1995; Eisenberg, Losoya, & Guthrie, 1997; Miller et al., 1996).

The research reviewed in the preceding sections reveals that moral understanding in childhood is a rich, diverse phenomenon not completely described by any single theory. Children's responses to a wide range of moral problems, including ones that focus on justice, fair distribution, and prosocial behavior, are needed to comprehensively represent the development of moral thought.

TABLE 12.3

Eisenberg's Levels of Prosocial Reasoning

Level	Approximate Age	Description
Hedonistic, pragmatic orientation	Preschool, early elementary school	Right behavior satisfies one's own needs. Reasons for helping or not helping refer to gains for the self—for example, "I wouldn't help because I might be hungry."
"Needs of others" orientation	Preschool, elementary school	Concern for the physical, material, and psychological needs of others is expressed in simple terms, without clear evidence of perspective taking or empathic feeling—for example, "He needs it."
Stereotyped, approval-focused orientation	Elementary school and secondary school	Stereotyped images of good and bad persons and concern for approval justify behavior—for example, "He'd like him more if he helped."
Empathic orientation	Later elementary school and secondary school	Reasoning reflects an emphasis on perspective taking and empathic feeling for the other person—for example, "I'd feel bad if I didn't help because he'd be in pain."
Internalized values orientation	Small minority of secondary school students, no elementary school pupils	Justifications for moral choice are based on internalized values, norms, desire to maintain contractual obligations, and belief in the dignity, rights, and equality of all individuals—for example, "I would feel bad if I didn't help because I'd know that I didn't live up to my values."

Source: Eisenberg, 1982.

ASK YOURSELF . . .

◆ *At preschool, 3-year-old Dahlia noticed that her classmate, Claude, reacted angrily when another child snatched his toy. Later, at the snack table, Dahlia watched the teacher tell Claude to use his napkin. Claude complied unemotionally. During outdoor play, Dahlia listened as Claude asked to play on the jungle gym. "You can do whatever you like," the teacher responded. Explain how these events help Dahlia and Claude differentiate moral imperatives, social conventions, and matters of personal choice.*

◆ CONNECTIONS
Older school-age children's grasp of the relation between emotion and moral transgression includes the realization that a victim's unhappiness can affect the perpetrator, producing a mixture of positive and negative emotion. How is this finding related to changes in emotional understanding in middle childhood? (See Chapter 10, page 410.)

BRIEF REVIEW

hen children are asked to reason about moral problems in which the role of laws and the possibility of punishment are deemphasized, they display moral judgments that are considerably more advanced than predicted by Piaget and Kohlberg. Even preschoolers have a beginning grasp of justice in that they distinguish moral imperatives from social conventions and matters of personal choice. With age, children apply these understandings to a wider range of experiences. The personal domain serves as the foundation for morally relevant concepts of rights and freedom. By adolescence, young people realize that personal and social-conventional claims can have moral implications.

During middle childhood, children's notions of distributive justice become more differentiated and adapted to the requirements of situations. At first, fair division of resources is based on equality. Soon children view fairness in terms of merit and, eventually, benevolence.

Prosocial moral dilemmas yield earlier attainment of advanced forms of moral reasoning than Kohlberg's sequence suggests. Empathy may foster prosocial moral thought and its realization in everyday behavior.

Development of Self-Control

he study of moral reasoning tells us what people think they should do and why when faced with a moral problem. But we have already indicated that people's good intentions often fall short. Whether children and adults act in accord with their beliefs depends in part on characteristics we call willpower, firm resolve, or, put more simply, **self-control.** Self-control in the moral domain involves inhibiting an impulse to engage in behavior that violates a moral standard. Sometimes it is called *resistance to temptation.*

In the first part of this chapter, we noted that inductive discipline and models who demonstrate as well as verbalize self-controlled behavior foster children's self-control. These practices become effective only when children develop the ability to resist temptation. When and how does the child's capacity for self-control develop?

BEGINNINGS OF SELF-CONTROL

The beginnings of self-control are supported by achievements of the second year, discussed in earlier chapters. To behave in a self-controlled fashion, children must have some ability to think of themselves as separate, autonomous beings who can direct their own actions. And they must have the representational and memory skills to recall a caregiver's directive and apply it to their own behavior (Kopp, 1987). Gains in cognitive inhibition, supported by development of the frontal lobes of the cortex (see Chapter 7), also contribute to resistance to temptation. And as we will see shortly, emotional self-regulation—strategies children acquire that prevent them from being overwhelmed by negative emotion—are intimately involved in self-control (see Chapter 10).

As these capacities emerge, the first glimmerings of self-control appear in the form of **compliance.** Between 12 and 18 months, children start to show clear awareness of caregivers' wishes and expectations and can voluntarily obey simple requests and commands (Kaler & Kopp, 1990). And, as every parent knows, they can also decide to do just the opposite! Earlier we noted that one way toddlers assert their autonomy is by resisting adult directives. But among toddlers who experience warm, sensitive caregiving and reasonable expectations for mature behavior, opposition is far less common than eager, willing compliance (Kochanska, Aksan, & Koenig, 1995). For most toddlers, resistance is gradually transformed into polite refusals and skilled efforts to negotiate compromises with parents over the preschool years (Kuczynski & Kochanska, 1990).

self-control Inhibiting an impulse to engage in behavior that violates a moral standard.

compliance Voluntary obedience to requests and commands.

delay of gratification Waiting for a more appropriate time and place to engage in a tempting act or obtain a desired object.

Parents are usually delighted at toddlers' newfound ability to comply, since it indicates that they are ready to learn the rules of social life. Nevertheless, control of the child's actions during the second year depends heavily on caregiver support. According to Vygotsky (1934/1986), children cannot guide their own behavior until they integrate standards represented in adult–child dialogues into their own speech and use it to instruct the self. Recall from Chapter 6 that this self-directed form of language is called *private speech*. The development of compliance quickly leads to toddlers' first consciencelike verbalizations—for example, correcting the self by saying "no, can't" before touching a light socket, jumping on the sofa, or taking candy from a forbidden dish (Kochanska, 1993).

Researchers typically study self-control by creating situations in the laboratory much like the ones just mentioned. Notice how each calls for **delay of gratification**—waiting for a more appropriate time and place to engage in a tempting act or obtain a desired object. In one study, toddlers were given three delay-of-gratification tasks. In the first, they were asked not to touch an interesting toy telephone that was within arm's reach. In the second, raisins were hidden under cups, and the toddlers were instructed to wait until the experimenter said it was all right to pick up a cup and eat a raisin. In the third, they were told not to open a gift until the experimenter had finished her work. As Figure 12.3 shows, on all three problems, the ability to wait increased steadily between 18 and 30 months of age. Consistent with Vygotsky's theory, toddlers who were especially self-controlled were also advanced in language development (Vaughn, Kopp, & Krakow, 1984).

As children's ability to engage in socially approved behaviors and to inhibit undesirable behaviors improves, caregivers' expectations increase. Heidi Gralinski and Claire Kopp (1993) asked mothers what they require or encourage their young children to do and what they insist they not do between 13 and 30 months of age. As Figure 12.4 reveals, rules expanded from a narrow focus on safety, property, and respect for others to a broader emphasis on the realities of living in a social world. Gradually, mothers placed

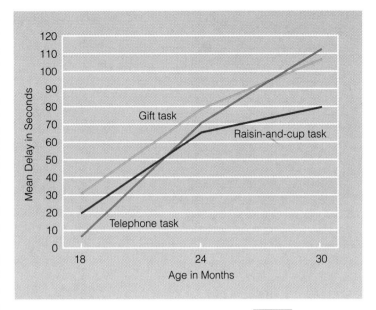

FIGURE 12.3

Age changes in delay of gratification between 18 and 30 months. The capacity for self-control increases dramatically during this period.

(Adapted from Vaughn, Kopp, & Krakow, 1984.)

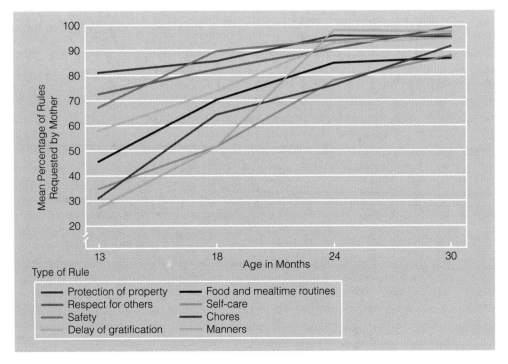

FIGURE 12.4

Rules mothers reported asking of their 13- to 30-month-old children. Mothers emphasized safety, property, and respect for rules early. As children's capacity for self-control increased, mothers introduced a wider array of rule expectations related to the realities of living in a social world.

(From J. H. Gralinski & C. B. Kopp, 1993, "Everyday Rules for Behavior: Mothers' Requests to Young Children," *Developmental Psychology, 29*, p. 579. Copyright © 1993 by the American Psychological Association. Reprinted by permission.)

The development of self-control is well under way by the time children enter school, where they are frequently required to delay gratification. Waiting to be called on is a common event in the lives of these pupils, who have developed strategies for being patient.

(D. Wells/The Image Works)

more emphasis on issues related to family routines, self-care, and independence until, at 30 months, all rules were stressed to the same degree. If you compare these trends with the gains depicted in Figure 12.3, you will see that overall, mothers' expectations dovetail nicely with children's emerging capacity for self-control.

DEVELOPMENT OF SELF-CONTROL IN CHILDHOOD AND ADOLESCENCE

Although the capacity for self-control is in place by the third year, it is not complete. Cognitive development—in particular, gains in attention and mental representation—permits children to use a variety of effective self-instructional strategies to resist temptation. As a result, delay of gratification improves during childhood and adolescence.

■ **STRATEGIES FOR SELF-CONTROL.** Walter Mischel (1996) has studied exactly what children think and say to themselves that promotes gains in resistance to temptation. In several studies, preschoolers were shown two rewards: a highly desirable one that they would have to wait for and a less desirable one that they could have anytime during the waiting period. The most self-controlled preschoolers used any technique they could think of to divert their attention from the desired objects, including covering their eyes, singing, and even trying to go to sleep!

In everyday situations, preschoolers find it difficult to keep their minds off tempting activities and objects for long. When their thoughts do turn to an enticing but prohibited goal, the way children mentally represent it has much to do with their success at self-control. Mischel found that teaching children to transform the stimulus in ways that deemphasize its arousing qualities promotes delay of gratification. In one study, some preschoolers were told to think about marshmallows imaginatively as "white and puffy clouds." Others were asked to focus on their realistic, "sweet and chewy properties." Children in the stimulus-transforming, imaginative condition waited much longer before eating the marshmallow reward (Mischel & Baker, 1975).

In the study just described, an experimenter taught young children to use delay-enhancing strategies. When an adult refrains from giving preschoolers instructions in how to resist temptation, their ability to wait in delay-of-gratification tasks declines considerably. In contrast, first and second graders do just as well whether or not an adult provides them with strategies (Toner & Smith, 1977). Beginning in the elementary school years, children become better at thinking up their own strategies for resisting temptation. By this time, self-control has been transformed into a flexible capacity for **moral self-regulation**—the ability to monitor one's own conduct, constantly adjusting it as circumstances present opportunities to violate inner standards (Bandura, 1991; Kopp, 1987).

moral self-regulation The ability to monitor one's own conduct, constantly adjusting it as circumstances present opportunities to violate inner standards.

instrumental aggression Aggression aimed at obtaining an object, privilege, or space with no deliberate intent to harm another person.

hostile aggression Aggression intended to harm another person.

overt aggression A form of hostile aggression that harms others through physical injury or the threat of such injury—for example, hitting, kicking, or threatening to beat up a peer.

relational aggression A form of hostile aggression that damages another's peer relationships, as in social exclusion or rumor spreading.

■ **KNOWLEDGE OF STRATEGIES.** In Chapter 7, we indicated that metacognitive knowledge, or awareness of strategies, plays an important role in the development of self-regulation. When interviewed about situational conditions and self-instructions likely to help them delay gratification, over middle childhood children suggested a broader array of successful, arousal-reducing strategies. But not until the late elementary school years did they mention techniques involving transformations of rewards or their own arousal states. For example, one 11-year-old recommended saying, "The marshmallows are filled with an evil spell." Another said he would tell himself, "I hate marshmallows, I can't stand them. But when the grown-up gets back, I'll tell myself 'I love marshmallows' and eat it" (Mischel & Mischel, 1983, p. 609). Perhaps awareness of transforming ideation appears late in development because it requires the abstract, hypothetical reasoning powers of formal operational thought. But once this advanced metacognitive understanding emerges, it facilitates moral self-regulation (Rodriguez, Mischel, & Shoda, 1989).

■ **INDIVIDUAL DIFFERENCES.** Longitudinal research reveals modest stability in children's capacity to manage their behavior in a morally relevant fashion. Mischel and his collaborators found that 4-year-olds able to wait longer in delay-of-gratification tasks were especially adept as adolescents in applying metacognitive skills to their behavior. Their parents saw them as more verbally fluent and responsive to reason, as better at concentrating and planning ahead, and as coping with stress more maturely. When applying to college, those who had been self-controlled preschoolers scored somewhat higher on the Scholastic Aptitude Test (SAT), although they were no more intelligent than children less able to resist temptation (Mischel, Shoda, & Peake, 1988; Shoda, Mischel, & Peake, 1990). Furthermore, children who are better at delaying gratification can wait long enough to interpret social cues accurately, which supports effective social problem solving and positive peer relations (Gronau & Waas, 1997).

Researchers believe that these enduring individual differences are the combined result of temperament and child-rearing practices. Consistent with this idea, impulsive preschoolers, who often act without thinking and are hot-tempered when they do not get their way, tend to show deficits in moral self-regulation (Barkley, 1997a; Kochanska et al., 1994). In contrast, preschoolers high in ability to inhibit behavior are advanced in internalization of standards and in moral reasoning when followed up during the early school years (Kochanska, Murray, & Coy, 1997). Recall that a mismatch between a child's temperamental style and parenting practices can undermine psychological adjustment. As we will see in the final section of this chapter, when temperamentally vulnerable children are exposed to highly power-assertive, inconsistent discipline, they display long-term, serious problems in moral conduct.

Before we turn to the topic of aggression, you may find it helpful to review the moral changes discussed throughout this chapter, summarized in the Milestones table on page 510.

The Other Side of Self-Control: Development of Aggression

Beginning in late infancy, all children display aggression from time to time, and as opportunities to interact with siblings and peers increase, aggressive outbursts occur more often. But recall from Chapter 11 that conflicts between young children are far less frequent than friendly, cooperative interaction. An occasional aggressive act is normal and to be expected, and these encounters often become important learning experiences as adults intervene and teach children alternative ways of satisfying desires. Furthermore, aggression is not always antisocial. At times, it serves prosocial ends when there is no other way to stop a victimizer from harming others.

Nevertheless, the large majority of human aggressive acts are clearly antisocial (Coie & Dodge, 1998). As early as the preschool years, some children show abnormally high rates of hostility. They lash out with verbal insults and physical assaults with little or no provocation. Allowed to continue, their belligerent behavior can lead to lasting deficits in moral development and self-control and to an antisocial lifestyle. To understand this process, let's see how aggression develops during childhood and adolescence.

An occasional expression of aggression is normal among young children. These preschoolers display instrumental aggression as they struggle over an attractive toy. Instrumental aggression declines with age as preschoolers' improved ability to delay gratification helps them avoid grabbing others' possessions.

(Laura Dwight)

EMERGENCE OF AGGRESSION

During the second half of the first year, infants develop the cognitive capacity to identify sources of anger and frustration and the motor skills to lash out at them (see Chapter 10). By the early preschool years, two general types of aggression emerge. The most common is **instrumental aggression.** In this form, children want an object, privilege, or space, and in trying to get it, they push, shout at, or otherwise attack a person who is in the way. The other type, **hostile aggression,** is meant to hurt another person.

Hostile aggression comes in at least two varieties. The first is **overt aggression,** which harms others through physical injury or the threat of such injury—for example, hitting, kicking, or threatening to beat up a peer. The second is **relational aggression,** which damages another's peer relationships, as in social exclusion or rumor spreading. Relational aggression may be confrontational ("Go away, I'm not

Moral Development

Age	Moral Internalization	Moral Construction	Self-Control
1½–2 years	■ Concern with deviations from standards emerges. ■ Modeling of a wide variety of prosocial acts begins.		■ Compliance and delay of gratification emerge.
3–6 years	■ Guilt reactions to transgressions emerge. ■ By the end of this period, internalization of many prosocial standards and prohibitions has occurred.	■ Sensitivity to intentions when making moral judgments is evident. ■ Complex, differentiated notions about the legitimacy of authority figures are formed. ■ Distinctions between moral imperatives, social conventions, and matters of personal choice are applied to familiar experiences. ■ Distributive justice and prosocial moral reasoning are self-serving. ■ At the end of this period, distributive justice is based on equality.	■ Delay of gratification improves. ■ Adult-provided strategies assist with self-control; children can generate only a few strategies on their own. ■ Self-control is transformed into a flexible capacity for moral self-regulation.
7–11 years	■ Internalization of societal norms continues.	■ Preconventional responses to Kohlberg's hypothetical moral dilemmas, focusing on rewards, punishment, and the power of authority figures, are common. ■ Distinctions between moral imperatives, social conventions, and matters of personal choice extend to unfamiliar experiences. ■ Distributive justice reasoning includes merit and, eventually, benevolence; basis of fairness is adapted to situations. ■ Prosocial moral reasoning reflects concern with others' needs and approval.	■ Generation of self-control strategies expands. ■ Awareness of effective self-control strategies and why they work improves.
12–adulthood		■ Conventional responses to Kohlberg's hypothetical moral dilemmas, emphasizing human relationships and societal order, increase. ■ Moral thought and action become integrated as individuals move toward Kohlberg's higher stages. ■ Postconventional responses to Kohlberg's hypothetical moral dilemmas, reflecting abstract principles and values, appear among a few highly educated individuals. ■ Prosocial moral reasoning reflects empathic feelings, norms, and abstract values.	■ Moral self-regulation continues to improve.

Note: These milestones represent overall age trends. Individual differences exist in the precise age at which each milestone is attained. See Chapter 10, page 413, for additional milestones related to the morally relevant emotions of empathy and guilt.

your friend anymore!") or nonconfrontational ("Don't play with Margie, she's a nerd"). Nonconfrontational aggression has also been called *covert* aggression (Loeber & Schmaling, 1985).

AGGRESSION IN EARLY AND MIDDLE CHILDHOOD

Both the form of aggression and the way it is expressed change during the preschool years. In a classic study, mothers were asked to keep records of their children's angry outbursts. Physical aggression was gradually replaced by verbal aggression after age 2 (Goodenough, 1931). Rapid language development contributes to this change, but it is also due to adults' and peers' strong negative reactions to pushing, hitting, and biting. Furthermore, instrumental aggression occurs less often as preschoolers' improved ability to delay gratification helps them avoid grabbing others' possessions. In contrast, hostile, person-oriented outbursts increase. Although tattling, criticism, and ridicule seldom provoke aggression in 4- and 5-year-olds, they often do in 6- and 7-year-olds (Hartup, 1974). Older children seem better able to "read" malicious behavior in others and, as a result, more often respond with a hostile retaliation.

By the school years, aggression lessens for most children. However, on the average, boys are more overtly aggressive than girls, a trend that appears in many cultures (Whiting & Edwards, 1988a). In Chapter 13, when we take up sex-related differences in aggression in greater detail, we will see that biological factors—in particular, male sex hormones, or androgens—are influential. At the same time, the development of gender roles is important. As soon as 2-year-olds become dimly aware of gender stereotypes—that males and females are expected to behave differently—aggression drops off more sharply for girls than for boys (Fagot & Leinbach, 1989).

But preschool and school-age girls are not less aggressive than boys! Instead they are likely to express their hostility differently—through relational aggression (Crick, Casas, & Mosher, 1997; Crick & Grotpeter, 1995). When trying to harm a peer, children seem to do so in ways especially likely to thwart that child's social goals. Boys more often attack physically to block the dominance goals that are typical of boys. Girls resort to relational aggression because it interferes with the close intimate bonds especially important to girls.

AGGRESSION AND DELINQUENCY IN ADOLESCENCE

Although most young people decline in teacher- and peer-rated aggression in adolescence, the teenage years are accompanied by a rise in delinquent acts. Adolescents under the age of 21 account for a large proportion of police arrests in the United States—about 30 percent (U.S. Department of Justice, 1998). When teenagers are asked directly, and confidentially, about lawbreaking, almost all admit that they are guilty of an offense of one sort or another (Farrington, 1987). Most of the time, they do not commit major crimes. Instead, they engage in petty stealing and disorderly conduct.

Both police arrests and self-reports show that these acts rise over the early teenage years, remain high during middle adolescence, and then decline into young adulthood. What accounts for this trend? The desire for peer approval increases antisocial behavior among young teenagers. Over time, peers become less influential, moral reasoning improves, and young people enter social contexts (such as marriage, work, and career) that are less conducive to lawbreaking.

For most adolescents, a brush with the law does not forecast long-term antisocial behavior. But repeated arrests are cause for concern. Teenagers are responsible for 27 percent of violent crimes (homicide, rape, robbery, and assault) and 42 percent of property crimes (burglary and theft (U.S. Department of Justice, 1998). A small percentage commit most of them, developing into recurrent offenders. Some enter a life of crime.

In adolescence, the gender gap in overt aggression widens. Depending on the estimate, about three to eight times as many boys as girls commit major crimes. Although SES and ethnicity are strong predictors of arrests, they are only mildly related to teenagers' self-reports of antisocial acts. The difference is due to biases in the juvenile justice system—in particular the tendency to arrest, charge, and punish low-SES, ethnic minority youths more often than their higher-SES white and Asian counterparts (Elliott, 1994).

Most of the time, juvenile delinquency involves petty stealing, disorderly conduct, and acts that are illegal only for minors, such as underage drinking. Usually two or more peers commit these acts together. In early adolescence, the desire for peer approval increases antisocial behavior among people.

(Smith/Monkmeyer Press)

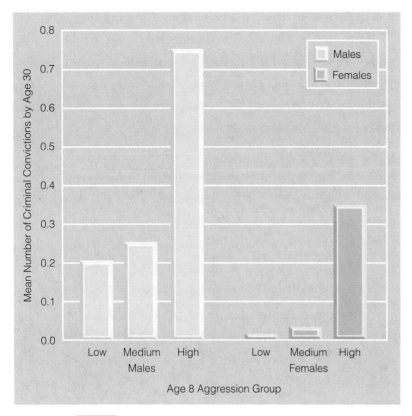

FIGURE 12.5

Relationship of childhood aggression to criminal behavior in adulthood for males and females.

(From L. R. Huesmann, L. D. Eron, M. M. Lefkowitz, & L. O. Walder, 1984, "Stability of Aggression over Time and Generations," *Developmental Psychology, 20,* p. 1125. Copyright © 1984 by the American Psychological Association. Reprinted by permission.)

STABILITY OF AGGRESSION

From middle childhood on, aggression is a highly stable personality characteristic. In a longitudinal investigation spanning 22 years, very aggressive 8-year-olds became 30-year-olds who were more likely to score high in aggressive inclinations on a personality test, use severe punishment with their children, and be convicted of criminal offenses (see Figure 12.5). In this study, the researchers also tracked the aggressive tendencies of participants' family members and found strong continuity across generations. Highly aggressive children were more likely to have parents and grandparents who were antisocial themselves and whose behavior problems were apparent in their own childhoods (Huesmann et al., 1984). As the Variations box on the following page reveals, childhood-onset conduct problems are far more likely to persist than are conduct problems that first appear in adolescence.

In recent years, researchers have made considerable progress in identifying individual and environmental factors that sustain aggressive behavior. Although some children—especially those who are impulsive and overactive—are clearly at risk for high aggression, whether or not they become so depends on child-rearing conditions. Strife-ridden families, poor parenting practices, aggressive peers, and televised violence are strongly linked to antisocial acts. In this chapter, we focus on family and peer influences, reserving the topic of television for Chapter 15. We will also see that community and cultural influences can heighten or reduce children's risk of acquiring a hostile interpersonal style.

THE FAMILY AS TRAINING GROUND FOR AGGRESSIVE BEHAVIOR

The same child-rearing practices that undermine moral internalization and self-control are correlated with aggression. Love withdrawal, power assertion, physical punishment, and inconsistent discipline are linked to antisocial behavior from early childhood through adolescence, in children of both sexes (Coie & Dodge, 1998). These ineffective and destructive techniques are often found together in the same family, compounding their harmful consequences.

Home observations of aggressive children reveal that anger and punitiveness quickly spread from one family member to another, creating a conflict-ridden family atmosphere and an "out-of-control" child. As Figure 12.7 on page 514 shows, the pattern begins with forceful discipline, which is made more likely by stressful life experiences (such as economic hardship or an unhappy marriage), a parent's own personality, or a temperamentally difficult child. Once the parent threatens, criticizes, and punishes, then the child whines, yells, and refuses until the parent finds the child's behavior to be too much and "gives in." The sequence is likely to be repeated, since at the end of each exchange, both parent and child get relief for stopping the unpleasant behavior of the other. The next time the child misbehaves, the parent is even more coercive and the child more defiant until one member of the pair "begs off." As these cycles become more frequent, they generate anxiety and irritability among other family members, who soon join in the hostile interactions (Dodge, Pettit, & Bates, 1994; Patterson, 1995, 1997).

Boys are more likely than girls to be targets of angry, inconsistent discipline because they are more active and impulsive and therefore harder to control. When children extreme in these characteristics are exposed to inept parenting, aggression rises during childhood, is transformed into criminality by adolescence, and persists into adulthood (refer again to the Variations box).

Two Routes to Adolescent Delinquency

P ERSISTENT ADOLESCENT DELINQUENCY follows two paths of development, one with an onset of conduct problems in childhood, the second with an onset in adolescence. Longitudinal research reveals that the early-onset type is far more likely to lead to a life-course pattern of aggression and criminality. The late-onset type usually does not persist beyond the transition to young adulthood (Loeber & Stouthamer-Loeber, 1998).

Childhood-onset and adolescent-onset youths look very similar during the teenage years. They both show comparable levels of serious offenses, involvement with deviant peers, substance abuse, unsafe sex, dangerous driving, and time spent in correctional facilities. Why does antisocial activity more often persist and escalate into violence in the first group than in the second? Longitudinal research extending from childhood into early adulthood sheds light on this question. So far, investigations have focused only on boys because of their greater involvement in delinquent activity.

EARLY-ONSET TYPE. A difficult temperament distinguishes these boys; they are emotionally negative, restless, and willful as early as age 3. In addition, they show subtle deficits in cognitive functioning that seem to contribute to disruptions in the development of language, memory, and self-regulation (Moffitt et al., 1996; Moffitt, Lynam, & Silva, 1994). Some have attention-deficit hyperactivity disorder (ADHD), which compounds their learning and self-control problems (see Chapter 7, page 288) (Moffitt, 1990; White et al., 1996).

Yet these biological risks are not sufficient to sustain antisocial behavior, since about half of early-onset boys do not display serious delinquency followed by adult criminality. Among those who follow the life-course path, inept parenting transforms their undercontrolled style into hostility and defiance. As they fail academically and are rejected by peers,

they befriend other deviant youths, who provide the attitudes and motivations for violent behavior (see Figure 12.6) (Simons et al., 1994). Compared with their adolescent-onset counterparts, early-onset teenagers feel distant from their families and leave school early (Moffitt et al., 1996). Their limited cognitive and social skills result in high rates of unemployment, contributing further to their antisocial involvements.

LATE-ONSET TYPE. A larger number of youths begin to display antisocial behavior around the time of puberty, gradually increasing their involvement. Their conduct problems arise from the peer context of early adolescence, not from biological deficits and a history of unfavorable development. For some, quality of parenting may decline for a time, perhaps due to family stresses or the challenges of disciplining an unruly teenager. When age brings gratifying adult privileges, they draw on prosocial skills mastered before adolescence and give up their antisocial ways (Moffitt et al., 1996).

A few late-onset youths, however, continue to engage in antisocial acts. The seriousness of their adolescent offenses seems to act as a "snare," trapping them in situations that rule out opportunities for responsible behavior. In one study, finding a steady, well-paying job and entering a happy marriage led to a large reduction in repeat offending. One former delinquent commented, "I worked steadily to support [my family] and take care of my responsibilities. I never had any time to get into trouble." In contrast, the longer antisocial young people spent in prison, the more likely they were to sustain a life of crime (Sampson & Laub, 1993).

These findings suggest a need for a fresh look at policies aimed at stopping youth crime. Keeping adolescent and young adult offenders locked up for many years disrupts their vocational and marital lives during a crucial period of development, committing them to a future that is bleak.

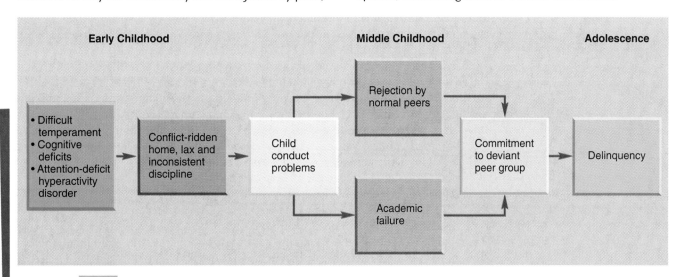

FIGURE 12.6

Developmental path to chronic delinquency for adolescents with childhood-onset antisocial behavior. Difficult temperament and deficits in cognitive functioning characterize many of these youths in early childhood; some have attention-deficit hyperactivity disorder. But these risks are not sufficient to sustain antisocial behavior. Instead, inept parenting transforms biologically based self-control difficulties into hostility and defiance.

(Adapted from Patterson, DeBaryshe, & Ramsey, 1989.)

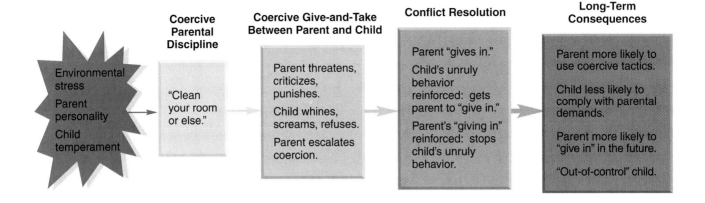

Coercive Parental Discipline	Coercive Give-and-Take Between Parent and Child	Conflict Resolution	Long-Term Consequences
"Clean your room or else."	Parent threatens, criticizes, punishes. Child whines, screams, refuses. Parent escalates coercion.	Parent "gives in." Child's unruly behavior reinforced: gets parent to "give in." Parent's "giving in" reinforced: stops child's unruly behavior.	Parent more likely to use coercive tactics. Child less likely to comply with parental demands. Parent more likely to "give in" in the future. "Out-of-control" child.

(Environmental stress, Parent personality, Child temperament →)

FIGURE 12.7

Coercive interaction pattern that promotes and sustains aggression between family members.

Besides fostering aggression directly, parents can encourage it indirectly, through poor supervision of children. Unfortunately, children from conflict-ridden homes who already display serious antisocial tendencies are most likely to experience inadequate parental monitoring. As a result, few if any limits are placed on out-of-home activities and peer associations that further their hostile style of responding. Aggressive children typically select antisocial friends like themselves. Talk between them contains frequent coercive statements and attacks, even during videotaping in a laboratory. These friendships provide yet another context in which to practice and strengthen hostile behavior (Dishion, Andrews, & Crosby, 1995; Dishion, Patterson, & Griesler, 1994).

SOCIAL-COGNITIVE DEFICITS AND DISTORTIONS

Children who are products of the family processes just described soon acquire a violent and callous view of the social world. Aggressive children often see hostile intent where it does not exist—in situations where a peer's intentions are unclear, where harm is accidental, and even where a peer is trying to be helpful (Dodge, 1985; Dodge & Somberg, 1987). As a result, they make many unprovoked attacks, which trigger aggressive retaliations. Recall, also, that young people high in antisocial behavior fall behind their agemates in perspective-taking skill, and they are delayed in moral understanding as well (Gregg, Gibbs, & Basinger, 1994; Trevethan & Walker, 1989).

Furthermore, compared to their nonaggressive agemates, aggressive children are convinced that there are more benefits and fewer costs for engaging in hostile acts. They are more likely to think that aggression "works" to produce tangible rewards and reduce teasing, taunting, and other unpleasant behaviors by others (Perry, Perry, & Rasmussen, 1986). And when tempted to aggress, they are more concerned about achieving control, less concerned about a victim's suffering or being disliked by peers, and less likely to evaluate themselves negatively (Boldizar, Perry, & Perry, 1989).

If the sociobiological perspective is correct, however, even these children retain a basic tendency to respond empathically. According to Gibbs (1993), antisocial children may neutralize empathy by using such cognitive-distortion techniques as blaming their victims. As a result, they retain a positive self-evaluation even after behaving aggressively (Liau, Barriga, & Gibbs, 1998). Looking back on his burglaries, one delinquent reflected, "If I started feeling bad, I'd say to myself, 'Tough rocks for him. He should have had his house locked better and the alarm on' " (Samenow, 1984, p. 115).

Yet another biased feature of many aggressive children's social cognition is overly high self-esteem (see Chapter 11, page 452). Despite their academic and social failings, chronic aggressors commonly believe that they are superior, competent beings. When their arrogant, cocky behavior inevitably results in challenges to their inflated but vulnerable self-image, they react with anger and lash out at others (Baumeister, Smart, & Boden, 1996).

Social-cognitive deficits and distortions add to the maintenance of aggressive behavior. In a longitudinal study, biased social cognitions were already present in 4-year-olds who had been physically abused. These same children displayed high rates of aggression after entering kindergarten 6 months later (Dodge, Bates, & Pettit, 1990).

COMMUNITY AND CULTURAL INFLUENCES

Children's tendency to engage in destructive, injurious behavior increases under certain environmental conditions. When the peer group atmosphere is tense and competitive rather than friendly and cooperative, hostility is more likely (DeRosier et al., 1994). These group characteristics are more common in poverty-stricken neighborhoods with a wide range of stressors, including poor-quality schools, limited recreational and employment opportunities, and negative adult role models.

Among low-SES, ethnic minority youths, such neighborhoods predict aggression beyond family influences (Kupersmidt et al., 1995). Children and adolescents have easy access to deviant peers and are especially likely to be recruited into antisocial gangs. Furthermore, schools in these locales typically fail to meet students' developmental needs. Large classes, weak instruction, and rigid rules are associated with higher rates of law-breaking, even after other influences are controlled (Hawkins & Lam, 1987).

Harsh living conditions are far more prevalent in some societies than in others. Cross-national comparisons reveal that the United States ranks first in the industrialized world in interpersonal violence and homicides. Glorification of violence in popular culture, ready availability of handguns, and a high poverty rate are believed to be responsible (Hill et al., 1994; Sheley & Wright, 1995).

Ethnic and political prejudices that keep certain groups at the margins of society further magnify the risk of angry, combative responses. In inner-city ghettos and in war-torn areas of the world, large numbers of children live in midst of constant danger, chaos, and deprivation. As the Cultural Influences box on page 516 reveals, these youngsters are at risk for severe emotional stress, deficits in moral reasoning, and behavior problems.

HELPING CHILDREN AND PARENTS CONTROL AGGRESSION

Help for aggressive children must break the cycle of hostilities between family members and promote effective ways of relating to others. Interventions with preschool and school-age children have been most successful. Once antisocial patterns persist into adolescence, so many factors act to sustain them that treatment is far more difficult.

■ **COACHING, MODELING, AND REINFORCING ALTERNATIVE BEHAVIORS.** Procedures based on social learning theory have been devised to interrupt destructive family interaction. Gerald Patterson (1982) designed a successful parent training program of this kind. A therapist observes inept practices, models alternatives, and has parents practice them. Parents learn not to give in to an acting-out child and not to escalate forceful attempts to control misbehavior. In addition, they are taught to pair commands with reasons and to replace verbal insults and spankings with more effective punishments, such as time out and withdrawal of privileges. After only a few weeks of such training, antisocial behavior declines and parents view their children more positively—gains still evident a year later (Patterson & Fleishman, 1979).

On the child's side, interventions that teach alternative ways of resolving conflict that are incompatible with aggression are helpful. Sessions in which children model and role-play cooperation and sharing and see that these behaviors lead to rewarding social outcomes reduce aggression and increase positive social behavior (Zahavi & Asher, 1978). Many aggressive children also need help with language delays and deficits that interfere with the development of self-control. Encouraging parents to converse with their young children, especially about how to regulate strong negative emotion, helps children develop internalized controls.

Once aggressive children begin to change, parents need to be reminded to give them attention and approval for prosocial acts. The coercive cycles of parents and aggressive

The Impact of Ethnic and Political Violence on Children

O N MAY 27, 1992, Zlata Filipovic, a 10-year-old Bosnian girl, recorded the following reactions to the intensifying Serb attack on the city of Sarajevo in her diary:

> SLAUGHTER! MASSACRE! HORROR! CRIME! BLOOD! SCREAMS! TEARS! DESPAIR!
>
> That's what Vaso Miskin Street looks like today. Two shells exploded in the street and one in the market. Mommy was nearby at the time. . . . Daddy and I were beside ourselves because she hadn't come home. I saw some of it on TV but I still can't believe what I actually saw. . . . I've got a lump in my throat and a knot in my tummy. HORRIBLE. They're taking the wounded to the hospital. It's a madhouse. We kept going to the window hoping to see Mommy, but she wasn't back. . . . Daddy and I were tearing our hair out. . . . I looked out the window one more time and . . . I SAW MOMMY RUNNING ACROSS THE BRIDGE. As she came into the house she started shaking and crying. Through her tears she told us how she had seen dismembered bodies. . . . Thank God, Mommy is with us. Thank God. (Filipovic, 1994, p. 55)

Violence stemming from ethnic and political tensions is being felt increasingly around the world. Today, virtually all armed conflicts are internal civil wars in which well-established ways of life are threatened or destroyed and children are frequently victims (Mays et al., 1998).

Children's experiences under conditions of armed conflict are diverse. Some may participate in the fighting, either because they are forced or because they want to please adults. Others are kidnapped, terrorized, or tortured. Those who are bystanders often come under direct fire and may be killed or physically maimed for life. And as Zlata's diary entry illustrates, many children of war watch in horror as family members, friends, and neighbors flee, are wounded, or die (Ladd & Cairns, 1996).

When war and social crises are temporary, most children are comforted by caregivers' reassuring messages and do not show long-term emotional difficulties. But chronic danger requires children to make substantial adjustments, and their psychological functioning can be seriously impaired. Many children of war lose their sense of safety, become desensitized to violence, are haunted by terrifying memories, and build a pessimistic view of the future (Cairns, 1996).

The extent to which children are negatively affected by war depends on mediating factors. Closeness to wartime events increases the chances of maladjustment. For example,

These traumatized ethnic Albanian refugee children from Kosovo are victims of the Serbian program of "ethnic cleansing." Here they receive humanitarian aid at a refugee center. Some of the children have seen their homes burned and family members wounded or killed. Without special support from caring adults, they are likely to show lasting emotional problems.
(Hidajet Delic/AP/Wide World Photos)

an estimated 50 percent of traumatized 6- to 12-year-old Cambodian war refugees continued to show intense stress reactions when they reached young adulthood (Kinzie et al., 1989). The support and affection of parents is the best safeguard against lasting problems. Unfortunately, many children of war are separated from family members. Sometimes the child's community can offer protection. For example, Israeli children who lost a parent in battle fared best when they lived in kibbutzim, where many adults knew the child well and felt responsible for his or her welfare (Lifschitz et al., 1977).

When wartime drains families and communities of resources, international organizations must step in and help children. Until we know how to prevent war, efforts to preserve children's physical, psychological, and educational well-being may be the best way to stop transmission of violence to the next generation in many parts of the world.

children are so pervasive that these children often get punished when they do behave appropriately (Strassberg, 1995).

■ **SOCIAL-COGNITIVE INTERVENTIONS.** The social-cognitive deficits and distortions of aggressive children prevent them from sympathizing with another person's pain and suffering—an important inhibitor of aggressive behavior. Furthermore, since aggressive children have few opportunities to witness family members acting in sensitive, caring ways, they miss early experiences that are vital for promoting empathy and sympathy (see

Chapter 10). In such children, these responses may have to be directly taught. In one program, sessions in which children practiced identifying others' feelings and expressing their own reduced hostility between peers and increased cooperation, helping, and generosity (Feshbach & Feshbach, 1982).

Other social-cognitive treatments focus on improving social information processing in antisocial youths. For example, in a program designed to remediate social problem-solving deficits, adolescents were taught to attend to relevant, nonhostile social cues; seek additional information before acting; and evaluate potential responses in terms of their effectiveness. The intervention led to increased skill in solving social problems, decreased endorsement of beliefs supporting aggression, and reduced hostile, impulsive behaviors (Guerra & Slaby, 1990).

Training in empathy, sympathy, and social information processing necessarily involves taking the perspectives of others. In Chapter 11, we noted that the antisocial acts of troubled youths can be reduced through coaching and practice in perspective taking. Perhaps this approach is helpful because it promotes sympathetic concern and accurate interpretation of social cues, which deter aggressive behavior.

■ **COMPREHENSIVE APPROACHES.** According to some researchers, effective treatment for antisocial children and adolescents must be multifaceted, encompassing parent training, social understanding, relating to others, and self-control (Kazdin, 1993). Although only a few comprehensive efforts have been tried, their success supports the power of a comprehensive approach.

In a program called EQUIP, *positive peer culture*—an adult-guided but youth-conducted small-group approach designed to create a climate in which prosocial acts replace antisocial behavior—served as the basis for treatment. By themselves, peer culture groups do not reduce antisocial behavior and, in one study, they increased it (Guerra, Attar, & Weissberg, 1997). But in EQUIP, the approach was supplemented with social skills training, anger management training, training to correct cognitive distortions (such as blaming the victim), and moral discussions to promote "catch-up" to age-appropriate moral reasoning (Gibbs, Potter, & Goldstein, 1995). Juvenile delinquents who participated in EQUIP displayed improved social skills and conduct during the following year relative to controls receiving no intervention. Also, the more advanced moral reasoning that emerged during group meetings appeared to have a long-term impact on antisocial youths' ability to inhibit lawbreaking behavior (Leeman, Gibbs, & Fuller, 1993).

Yet even multidimensional treatments can fall short if young people remain embedded in hostile home lives, antisocial peer groups, and violent neighborhood settings. Intensive efforts to create nonaggressive environments—at the family, community, and cultural levels—are needed to support the interventions just described and to ensure optimal development of all children. We will return to this theme in later chapters.

ASK YOURSELF . . .

◆ *Throughout his school years, Mac had difficulty learning, was disobedient, and picked fights with peers. At age 16, he was arrested for burglary. Zeke had been a well-behaved child in elementary school, but around age 13, he started spending time with the "wrong crowd." At age 16, he was arrested for property damage. Which boy is more likely to become a long-term offender, and why?*

◆ CONNECTIONS
Read the section on teenage pregnancy in Chapter 5 (page 214), adolescent suicide in Chapter 11 (page 459), and substance abuse in Chapter 15 (page 614). What factors do these problems have in common with delinquency? How would you explain the finding that teenagers who experience one of these difficulties are likely to display others?

SUMMARY

MORALITY AS ROOTED IN HUMAN NATURE

Describe and evaluate the biological perspective on morality advanced by sociobiologists.

◆ The biological perspective on moral development is represented by a controversial field called **sociobiology.** It assumes that morality is grounded in the genetic heritage of our species, perhaps through prewired emotional reactions. Although human morality cannot be fully explained in this way, the biological perspective reminds us of the adaptive significance of moral behavior.

MORALITY AS THE ADOPTION OF SOCIETAL NORMS

Describe and evaluate the psychoanalytic perspective on moral development.

◆ Psychoanalytic and social learning theories regard moral development as a matter of **internalization:** the adoption of societal standards for right action as one's own. Internalization is not just a straightforward process of taking over externally imposed prescriptions. Instead, children actively participate, taking initiative in acquiring norms and engaging in good conduct.

- According to Freud, morality emerges with the resolution of the Oedipus and Electra conflicts during the preschool years. Fear of punishment and loss of parental love lead children to form a super-ego through identification with the same-sex parent and to redirect hostile impulses toward the self in the form of guilt.

- Although guilt is an important motivator of moral action, Freud's interpretation of it is no longer widely accepted. In contrast to Freudian predictions, power assertion and love withdrawal do not foster conscience development. Instead, **induction** is far more effective. Recent psychoanalytic ideas place greater emphasis on a positive parent–child relationship and earlier beginnings of morality. However, they retain continuity with Freud's theory in regarding emotion as the basis for moral development.

Describe and evaluate the social learning perspective on moral development, including the importance of modeling, the effects of punishment, and alternatives to harsh discipline.

- Social learning theory views moral behavior as acquired in the same way as other responses: through modeling and reinforcement. Young children readily imitate morally relevant behaviors, including resistance to temptation, if models make their efforts explicit by verbalizing them. Effective models are warm and powerful and display consistency between what they say and what they do.

- Harsh punishment does not promote moral internalization and socially desirable behavior. Instead, it provides children with aggressive models, leads them to avoid the punishing adult, and can spiral into serious abuse. Alternatives, such as **time out** and withdrawal of privileges, can reduce these undesirable side effects, as long as parents apply them consistently, maintain a warm relationship with the child, and offer explanations that fit the transgression.

- The most effective forms of discipline encourage good conduct. Parents who build a positive relationship with the child have children who want to adopt parental standards because they feel a sense of commitment to the relationship.

MORALITY AS SOCIAL UNDERSTANDING

Describe Piaget's theory of moral development, and evaluate its accuracy.

- In contrast to psychoanalytic and social learning theories, Piaget's cognitive-developmental perspective assumes that morality develops through **construction**—actively thinking about multiple aspects of situations in which social conflicts arise and deriving new moral understandings.

- Piaget's work was the original inspiration for the cognitive-developmental perspective. He identified two stages of moral understanding: **heteronomous morality,** in which children view moral rules in terms of **realism** and as fixed dictates of authority figures; and **autonomous morality,** in which children use **reciprocity** as a standard of fairness and regard rules as flexible, socially agreed-on principles.

- Although Piaget's theory describes the general direction of moral development, it underestimates the moral capacities of young children. Preschool and early school-age children take intentions into account in making moral judgments, although they interpret intentions in a rigid fashion. Furthermore, they have differentiated notions about the legitimacy of authority figures. With respect to nonmoral issues, they base authority on knowledge, not social po-

sition. When a directive is morally valid, they regard it as important, regardless of whether an authority figure endorses it.

Describe Kohlberg's extension of Piaget's theory, and evaluate its accuracy.

- According to Kohlberg, moral development is a gradual process that extends beyond childhood into adolescence and adulthood. By examining responses to **moral dilemmas,** Kohlberg found that moral reasoning advances through three levels, each of which contains two stages: (1) the **preconventional level,** in which morality is viewed as controlled by rewards, punishments, and the power of authority figures; (2) the **conventional level,** in which conformity to laws and rules is regarded as necessary to preserve positive human relationships and societal order; and (3) the **postconventional level,** in which individuals define morality in terms of abstract, universal principles of justice. Besides Kohlberg's clinical interview, efficient questionnaires for assessing moral understanding exist. The most recently devised is the **Sociomoral Reflection Measure–Short Form (SRM–SF).**

- Kohlberg's stages are strongly related to age and form an invariant sequence. In focusing on hypothetical moral dilemmas, Kohlberg's theory overlooks other strategies, besides rationally weighing alternatives, that affect moral judgment. Because situational factors affect moral reasoning, Kohlberg's stages are best viewed in terms of a loose rather than strict concept of stage.

- Piaget's cognitive and Selman's perspective-taking stages are necessary but not sufficient conditions for each advance in moral reasoning. Many experiences contribute to maturity of moral thought, including peer interaction that resolves conflict through give-and-take and compromise; warm, rational child-rearing practices; and years of schooling.

Evaluate claims that Kohlberg's theory does not represent morality in all cultures and underestimates the moral maturity of females, and describe the relationship of moral reasoning to moral behavior.

- Cross-cultural research indicates that a certain level of societal complexity is required for Kohlberg's highest stages. Although his theory does not encompass the full range of moral reasoning, a common justice morality is evident in the moral dilemma responses of individuals from vastly different cultures. Kohlberg's theory does not underestimate the moral maturity of females. Instead, justice and caring moralities coexist but vary in prominence across cultures, between males and females, and from one situation to the next.

- Maturity of moral reasoning is moderately related to a wide variety of moral behaviors. Many other factors also influence moral behavior, including emotions, temperament, personality, and history of morally relevant experiences.

MORAL REASONING OF YOUNG CHILDREN

Explain how children separate moral imperatives from social conventions and matters of personal choice, and trace changes in their understanding from childhood into adolescence.

- Even preschoolers have a beginning grasp of justice in that they distinguish **moral imperatives** from **social conventions** and **mat-**

ters of personal choice. From actively making sense of people's everyday social experiences and emotional reactions, children in diverse cultures come to view moral transgressions as wrong in any context, regardless of whether rules or authorities prohibit them. The personal domain emerges with self-awareness in the early preschool years and strengthens from middle childhood into adolescence. It supports young children's sense of autonomy and agency and leads to moral concepts of rights and freedom.

Describe the development of distributive justice and prosocial moral reasoning, noting factors that foster mature understanding.

◆ Children's concepts of **distributive justice** change over middle childhood, from equality to merit to benevolence. Peer disagreements, along with efforts to resolve them, make children more sensitive to others' perspectives, which fosters their developing ideas of fairness.

◆ Although levels of prosocial moral reasoning resemble Kohlberg's stages, children show more advanced understandings when responding to prosocial dilemmas. Empathy seems to foster prosocial moral thought and its relationship to prosocial behavior.

DEVELOPMENT OF SELF-CONTROL

Trace the development of self-control from early childhood into adolescence, noting the implications of individual differences for cognitive and social competencies.

◆ The emergence of **self-control** is supported by self-awareness and by the representational and memory capacities of the second year. The first glimmerings of self-control appear in the form of **compliance.** The ability to **delay gratification** increases steadily over the third year. Language development—in particular, use of self-directed speech to guide behavior—fosters self-control.

◆ During the preschool years, children profit from adult-provided self-control strategies. Over middle childhood, they produce an increasing variety of strategies themselves and become consciously aware of which ones work well and why, leading to a flexible capacity for **moral self-regulation.** Individual differences in delay of gratification, believed to be due to both temperament and child-

rearing practices, predict a wide variety of cognitive and social competencies.

THE OTHER SIDE OF SELF-CONTROL: DEVELOPMENT OF AGGRESSION

Discuss the development of aggression from infancy into adolescence, noting individual, family, community, and cultural influences, and describe successful interventions.

◆ Aggression first appears in late infancy. During the preschool years, physical forms are replaced by verbal forms, and **instrumental aggression** declines, whereas **hostile aggression** increases. Two types of hostile aggression appear: **overt aggression,** which is more common among boys, and **relational aggression,** which is more common among girls. By the school years, aggression lessens for most children.

◆ The teenage years are accompanied by a rise in delinquent acts, although only a few adolescents become recurrent offenders. The gender gap in overt aggression widens, and many more boys than girls commit major crimes. From middle childhood on, aggression is a highly stable personality trait. Childhood-onset conduct problems are far more likely to persist than are conduct problems that first appear in adolescence.

◆ Although impulsive, overactive children are at risk for high aggression, whether or not they become so depends on child-rearing conditions. Strife-ridden family environments and power-assertive, inconsistent discipline promote self-perpetuating cycles of aggressive behavior. Children who are products of these family processes develop social-cognitive deficits and distortions that add to the long-term maintenance of aggression. Widespread poverty, harsh living conditions, schools that fail to meet students' developmental needs, and cultural glorification of violence increase antisocial acts among children and adolescents.

◆ Among interventions designed to reduce aggression, training parents in child discipline and teaching children alternative ways of resolving conflict are helpful. Social-cognitive interventions, including empathy, social problem solving, and perspective-taking training, have yielded benefits as well. However, the most effective treatments are comprehensive, addressing the multiple factors that sustain antisocial behavior.

IMPORTANT TERMS AND CONCEPTS

autonomous morality (p. 489)
compliance (p. 506)
construction (p. 489)
conventional level (p. 493)
delay of gratification (p. 506)
distributive justice (p. 502)
heteronomous morality (p. 489)
hostile aggression (p. 508)
induction (p. 483)

instrumental aggression (p. 508)
internalization (p. 481)
matters of personal choice (p. 501)
moral dilemma (p. 491)
moral imperatives (p. 501)
moral self-regulation (p. 508)
overt aggression (p. 508)
postconventional level (p. 493)
preconventional level (p. 492)

realism (p. 489)
reciprocity (p. 489)
relational aggression (p. 508)
self-control (p. 506)
social conventions (p. 501)
sociobiology (p. 481)
Sociomoral Reflection Measure–Short Form (SRM–SF) (p. 492)
time out (p. 487)

Development of Sex-Related Differences and Gender Roles

ON A TYPICAL morning, I observed the following scene during a free-play period at our university laboratory preschool:

> Four-year-old Jenny eagerly entered the housekeeping corner and put on a frilly long dress and grown-up-looking high heels. Karen, setting the table nearby, produced whimpering sound effects for the baby doll in the crib. Jenny lifted the doll, sat down in the rocking chair, gently cradled the baby in her arms, and whispered, "You're hungry, aren't you?" A moment later, Jenny announced to Karen, "This baby won't eat. I think she's sick. Ask Rachel if she'll be the nurse." Karen ran off to find Rachel, who was coloring at the art table.
>
> Meanwhile, Nathan called to Tommy, "Wanna play traffic?" Both boys dashed energetically toward the cars and trucks in the block corner. Soon David joined them. "I'll be policeman first!" announced Nathan, who pulled a chair into the center of the block area and climbed on it. "Green light, go!" shouted the young police officer. With this signal, Tommy and David scurried on all fours around the chair, each pushing a large wooden truck. "Red light," exclaimed Nathan, and the trucks screeched to a halt.
>
> "My truck beat yours," announced Tommy to David.
>
> "Only 'cause I need gas," David responded as he pulled off to the side and pretended to fill the tank.
>
> "Let's build a runway for the trucks," suggested Nathan. The three construction engineers began to gather large blocks and boards for the task.

The activity choices and behaviors of these young children reveal that they have already adopted many of the gender-linked standards of their culture. Jenny, Karen, and Rachel used dresses, dolls, and household props to act out a stereotypically feminine scene of nurturance. In contrast, Nathan, Tommy, and David's play is active, competitive, and masculine in theme. And already, these preschoolers interact more often with children of their own sex than of the other sex.

What causes young children's play and social preferences to become so strongly gender typed, and how do these attitudes and behaviors change with age? Do societal expectations affect the way children think about themselves as masculine and feminine beings, thereby limiting their potential? To what extent do widely held beliefs about the characteristics of males and females reflect reality? Is it true that the average boy is aggressive, competitive, and good at spatial and mathematical skills, whereas the average girl is passive, nurturant, and good at verbal skills? How large are differences between the sexes, and in what ways do biological and environmental factors contribute to them? These are the central questions asked by researchers who study gender typing, and we will answer each of them in this chapter.

Perhaps more than any other area of child development, the study of gender typing has responded to societal change. Largely because of progress in women's rights, over the past 30 years major shifts have occurred in how sex-related differences are regarded. Until the early 1970s, the adoption of gender-typed beliefs and behavior was viewed as a desirable goal of child rearing and essential for healthy psychological adjustment. Today, many people recognize that some gender-typed characteristics, such as extreme aggressiveness and competitiveness on the part of males and passivity and conformity on the part of females, are serious threats to mental health.

Consistent with this realization, theoretical revision marks the study of gender typing. At one time, psychoanalytic theory offered an influential account of how children acquired "masculine" and "feminine" traits. According to Freud, these attitudes and behaviors were adopted in the same way as other societal standards—through identification with the same-sex parent during the preschool years. Today we know that interactions with other-sex parents, siblings, teachers, and peers, along with examples of gender-appropriate behavior in the surrounding culture, also play powerful roles.

Furthermore, recent research shows that gender typing begins earlier and lasts much longer than Freud believed, continuing into adolescence and even adulthood. Finally, Freud's theory, as well as Erikson's extension of it, regards gender typing as a natural outcome of biological differences between the sexes. Although debate continues over this assumption, firm commitment to it has not been helpful in the quest to discover how children might be released from gender-based definitions of appropriate behavior. As a result, most researchers have abandoned the psychoanalytic approach in favor of other perspectives.

Social learning theory, with its emphasis on modeling and reinforcement, and cognitive-developmental theory, with its focus on children as active thinkers about their social world, are major current approaches to gender typing. However, neither is sufficient by itself. We will see that an information-processing view, *gender schema theory,* combines elements of both theories to explain how children acquire gender-typed knowledge and behavior.

Along with new theories have come new terms. Considerable controversy surrounds the labels *sex* and *gender.* Some researchers use these words interchangeably. Others use the term *sex* for biologically based differences, *gender* for socially influenced differences. Still others object to this convention because our understanding of many differences is still evolving. Also, it perpetuates too strong a dichotomy between nature and nurture (Unger & Crawford, 1993). I use another system that avoids these problems. In this book, **sex related** refers to comparisons between males and females in which a difference simply exists. I use this term when I am making no inferences about the source of the difference. In contrast, **gender** is used when judgments are being made about biological or environmental influences or both (Deaux, 1993).

Throughout this chapter, you will encounter additional terms. Two of them involve the public face of gender in society. **Gender stereotypes** are widely held beliefs about characteristics deemed appropriate for males and females. **Gender roles** are the reflection of these stereotypes in everyday behavior. **Gender identity** is the private face of gender. It refers to perception of the self as relatively masculine or feminine in characteristics. Finally, **gender typing,** a term already mentioned, is the process of developing gender-linked beliefs, gender roles, and a gender identity. As we explore this process, you will see that biological, cognitive, and social factors are involved.

Gender Stereotypes and Gender Roles

 ender stereotypes have appeared in religious, philosophical, and literary works for centuries. Consider the following literary excerpts, from ancient times to the present:

■ "Woman is more compassionate than man and has a greater propensity to tears. . . . But the male . . . is more disposed to give assistance in danger, and is more courageous than the female." (Aristotle, cited in Miles, 1935)

sex-related In this book, characterization of differences between males and females in which no inferences are being made about the source of the difference.

gender In this book, characterization of differences between males and females in which judgments are being made about either biological or environmental influences.

gender stereotypes Widely held beliefs about characteristics deemed appropriate for males and females.

gender roles The reflection of gender stereotypes in everyday behavior.

gender identity The perception of oneself as relatively masculine or feminine in characteristics.

gender typing The process of developing gender-linked beliefs, gender roles, and a gender-role identity.

- "A man will say what he knows, a woman says what will please." (Jean Jacques Rousseau, *Emile*, 1762)

- "Man with the head and woman with the heart;
  Man to command and woman to obey;
  All else confusion." (Alfred, Lord Tennyson, *Home They Brought Her Warrior*, 1842)

- "Love is a mood—no more—to a man,
  And love to a woman is life or death." (Ella Wheeler Wilcox, *Blind*, 1882)

- "Women ask: How do you get a man to open up?
  Men ask: Why does she always want to talk about the relationship?" (Gray, *Mars and Venus on a Date*, 1997)

Although the past three decades have brought a new level of awareness about the wide range of roles possible for each gender, strong beliefs about differences between males and females remain. In the 1960s, researchers began to ask people what personality characteristics they consider typical of men and women. Widespread agreement emerged in many studies. As Table 13.1 illustrates, **instrumental traits,** reflecting competence, rationality, and assertiveness, were regarded as masculine; **expressive traits,** emphasizing warmth, caring, and sensitivity, were viewed as feminine.

Despite intense political activism over gender equality during the 1970s and 1980s, these stereotypes have remained essentially the same (Lueptow, Garovich, & Lueptow, 1997; Lutz & Ruble, 1995; Ruble & Martin, 1998). In a study in which undergraduate students were asked how typical personality traits were of boys and girls, they rated all gender-stereotyped items as distinguishing the sexes. In fact, the college students even rated many supposedly neutral (nonstereotyped) items as separating boys and girls! For example, they characterized boys as more conceited, girls as more likable, truthful, and reliable. On questions addressing the desirability of each trait, boys scored higher on competitive, dominant, and independent; girls scored higher on gentle, helpful, sympathetic, and well-mannered (Martin, 1995). Furthermore, cross-cultural research conducted in 30 nations reveals that the instrumental–expressive dichotomy is a widely held stereotype around the world (Williams & Best, 1990).

Besides personality traits, other gender stereotypes exist. These include physical characteristics (tall, strong, and sturdy for men; soft, dainty, and graceful for women), occupations (truck driver, insurance agent, and chemist for men; elementary school teacher, secretary, and nurse for women), and activities or behaviors (good at fixing things and leader in groups for men; good at child care and decorating the home for women) (Biernat, 1991a; Deaux & Lewis, 1984). The variety of attributes consistently identified as masculine or feminine, their broad acceptance, and their stability over time suggest that gender stereotypes are deeply ingrained patterns of thinking. When do children become aware of them, and what implications do they have for gender-role adoption?

GENDER STEREOTYPING IN EARLY CHILDHOOD

Recall from Chapter 11 that around age 2, children label their own sex and that of other people, using such words as "boy" versus "girl" and "woman" versus "man." As soon as these categories are established, children start to sort out what they mean in terms of activities and behaviors. As a result, a wide variety of gender stereotypes are mastered.

Preschoolers associate many toys, articles of clothing, tools, household items, games, occupations, and even colors (pink and blue) with one sex as opposed to the other (Ruble & Martin, 1998). In a study illustrating the range of gender stereotypes acquired at an early age, children as young as 2½ were shown pictures of boys and girls. As each was presented, an adult described it by making a statement about a gender-stereotyped behavior,

TABLE 13.1

Personality Traits Regarded as Stereotypically Masculine and Feminine

Masculine Traits	Feminine Traits
Active	Aware of others' feelings
Acts as a leader	Considerate
Adventurous	Cries easily
Aggressive	Devotes self to others
Ambitious	Emotional
Competitive	Excitable in a major crisis
Doesn't give up easily	Feelings hurt easily
Dominant	Gentle
Feels superior	Home oriented
Holds up well under pressure	Kind
Independent	Likes children
Makes decisions easily	Neat
Not easily influenced	Needs approval
Outspoken	Passive
Rough	Tactful
Self-confident	Understanding of others
Takes a stand	Warm in relations with others

instrumental traits Masculine-stereotyped personality traits that reflect competence, rationality, and assertiveness.

expressive traits Feminine-stereotyped personality traits that reflect warmth, caring, and sensitivity.

By age 1½, gender-stereotyped game and toy choices are present, becoming increasingly consistent with age. Already, these 3-year-olds play in highly gender-stereotyped ways.
(E. Zuckerman/PhotoEdit)

physical characteristic, activity, or future role—for example, "I can hit you," "I look nice," "I like to play ball," and "When I grow up, I'll be a nurse." Children of both sexes indicated that girls "like to play with dolls," "talk a lot," "never hit," say "I need some help," and later on as grown-ups will "clean the house" and "be a nurse." They also believed that boys "like to help father," say "I can hit you," and as future adults will "be boss" and "mow the grass" (Kuhn, Nash, & Brucken, 1978).

Even before children can label their own sex and match up statements and objects with male and female figures, they prefer "gender-appropriate" activities. By 1½ years, gender-stereotyped game and toy choices are present (Caldera, Huston, & O'Brien, 1989; Fagot, Leinbach, & Hagan, 1986). By age 3, these preferences become highly consistent for both boys and girls (O'Brien & Huston, 1985).

A striking feature of preschoolers' gender stereotypes is that they operate like blanket rules rather than flexible guidelines. In several studies, researchers labeled a target child as a boy or girl and then provided either gender-typical or gender-atypical information about the target's characteristics. Next, children were asked to rate the target on additional gender-stereotypic attributes. Preschoolers usually relied on only the gender label in making these judgments, ignoring the specific information. For example, when told, "Tommy is a boy. Tommy's best friend is a girl, and Tommy likes to play house," children under age 6 nevertheless said that Tommy would much prefer to play with cars and train engines than sewing machines and dolls (Biernat, 1991a; Martin, 1989).

The rigidity of preschoolers' gender stereotypes helps us understand some commonly observed everyday behaviors. Shown a picture of a Scottish bagpiper wearing a kilt, a 4-year-old is likely to say, "Men don't wear skirts!" At preschool, children can be heard exclaiming that girls don't drive fire engines and can't be police officers and boys don't take care of babies and can't be the teacher. These one-sided judgments are a joint product of gender stereotyping in the environment and young children's cognitive limitations—in particular, their difficulty integrating conflicting sources of information. Most preschoolers do not yet realize that characteristics *associated with* one's sex—activities, toys, occupations, hairstyle, and clothing—do not *determine* whether a person is male or female. As we will see later, young children have trouble understanding that males and females can be different in terms of their bodies yet similar in many other ways.

GENDER STEREOTYPING IN MIDDLE CHILDHOOD AND ADOLESCENCE

By age 5, gender stereotyping of activities and occupations is well established. During middle childhood and adolescence, knowledge of stereotypes expands and strengthens in the less obvious areas of personality traits and achievement (Signorella, Bigler, & Liben, 1993). At the same time, older children begin to realize that gender-stereotypic attributes are associated, not defining, features of gender. As a result, beliefs about characteristics and capacities possible for males and females become more flexible.

gender-stereotype flexibility
Belief that both genders can display a gender-stereotyped personality trait or activity.

■ **PERSONALITY TRAITS.** To assess stereotyping of personality traits, researchers ask children to assign "masculine" adjectives (such as tough, rational, and cruel) and "feminine" adjectives (such as gentle, affectionate, and dependent) to either a male or female stimulus figure. Recall from Chapter 11 that not until middle childhood are children good at sizing up people in terms of psychological dispositions. This same finding carries over to awareness of gender stereotypes.

Research in many countries, including Canada, France, Germany, Great Britain, India, Korea, the Netherlands, and the United States, reveals that stereotyping of personality traits increases steadily in middle childhood, becoming adultlike around age 11 (Beere, 1990; Best et al., 1977). A large Canadian study examined the pattern of children's trait learning and found that the stereotypes acquired first reflected "own-sex favoritism."

Kindergartners through second graders had greatest knowledge of trait stereotypes that portrayed their own gender in a positive light. Once trait stereotyping was well under way, elementary school pupils were most familiar with "positive feminine" traits and "negative masculine" traits (Serbin, Powlishta, & Gulko, 1993). In addition to learning specific stereotypes, children seemed to pick up a widely held general impression—that of girls as "sugar and spice and everything nice" and boys as "snakes and snails and puppy dog tails."

■ **ACHIEVEMENT AREAS.** Shortly after entering elementary school, children figure out which academic subjects and skill areas are "masculine" and which are "feminine." Throughout the school years, they regard reading, art, and music as more for girls and mathematics, athletics, and mechanical skills as more for boys (Eccles, Jacobs, & Harold, 1990; Jacobs & Weisz, 1994). This is despite the fact that girls' grades are higher in both feminine- and masculine-stereotyped subjects during elementary school.

Similar achievement stereotypes can also be found in other cultures. When school-age children in Japan, Taiwan, and the United States were asked to name the school subject they liked best, girls were more likely to choose reading and boys mathematics in all three countries. Asked to predict how well they would do in these subjects once they reached high school, boys thought they would do better in mathematics than did girls. In contrast, no sex-related difference in favor of girls emerged in predictions about reading (Lummis & Stevenson, 1990). These findings suggest that by the mid-elementary school years, children have acquired a more general stereotype of achievement as a "masculine" pursuit.

■ **TOWARD GREATER FLEXIBILITY.** Clearly, school-age children are knowledgeable about a wide variety of gender stereotypes. At the same time, they develop a more open-minded view of what males and females *can do*, a trend that continues into adolescence.

Look back at how researchers assessed gender stereotyping in the studies described earlier. You will see that almost all used a forced-choice technique in which children had to assign a characteristic to either one gender or the other. In some instances, researchers have asked whether both genders can display a personality trait or activity— a response that provides a measure of **gender-stereotype flexibility.** In the Canadian study mentioned on the previous page, stereotype knowledge and flexibility were assessed, and as Figure 13.1 reveals, both increased from kindergarten to sixth grade (Serbin, Powlishta, & Gulko, 1993).

Gender stereotypes become more flexible as children develop the cognitive capacity to integrate conflicting social cues. Consequently, they no longer rely on only a gender label to predict what a person will be like; they also consider the individual's unique characteristics. Unlike preschoolers, when school-age children and adolescents are told about a child named Tommy who likes to play house, they notice both his sex and his interest. Realizing that many attributes are shared by boys and girls, older participants say that Tommy would probably enjoy several other "cross-gender" activities and some gender-typical ones as well (Biernat, 1991a; Martin, 1989).

Accompanying gender-stereotype flexibility is a greater tendency during the school years to view gender differences as socially rather than biologically influenced. In one study, 4- to 10-year-olds and adults were told stories about hypothetical boy and girl babies reared on an island either by members of their own sex or by members of the

FIGURE 13.1

Changes in knowledge and flexibility of gender stereotypes from kindergarten to sixth grade in a cross-sectional study of more than 500 Canadian children.

(From L. A. Serbin, K. K. Powlishta, & J. Gulko, 1993, "The Development of Sex Typing in Middle Childhood," *Monographs of the Society for Research in Child Development*, 58[2, Serial No. 232], p. 35. © The Society for Research in Child Development, Inc. Adapted by permission.)

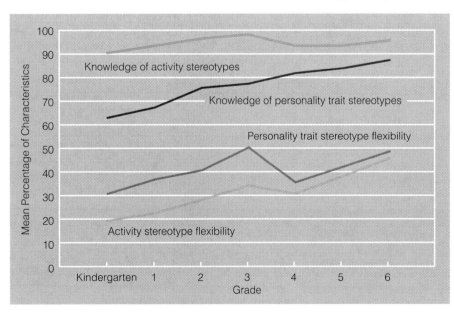

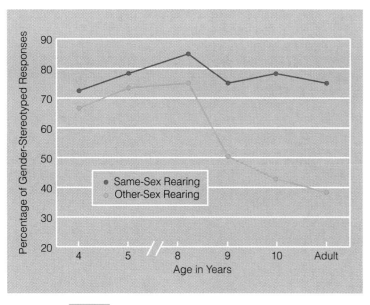

other sex. Then they were asked what "masculine" and "feminine" properties each child would develop. As Figure 13.2 on page 526 shows, preschool and younger school-age children believed that gender-stereotyped characteristics would emerge, regardless of rearing environment. Not until ages 9 and 10 did children think that a child reared by the other sex would be non-stereotyped in many ways (Taylor, 1996).

Nevertheless, acknowledging that boys and girls *can* cross gender lines does not mean that children always *approve* of doing so. In one study, preschoolers, school-age children, and adults were asked how much they would like being friends with an agemate who violated gender-role expectations for behavior (such as a male wearing a dress or a female playing football) and how bad they thought such "transgressions" were. Children and adults were fairly tolerant of "feminine" violations. But most judged "masculine" violations quite harshly— as just as bad as violating a moral rule! Clearly, evaluations of certain "cross-gender" behaviors on the part of males are negative at all ages—a finding that reflects greater social pressure on boys and men to conform to gender roles (Levy, Taylor, & Gelman, 1995).

FIGURE 13.2

Gender-typed responses of 4- to 10-year-olds and adults to stories about hypothetical boy and girl babies reared on an island either by members of their own sex or by members of the other sex. Younger children thought that gender-stereotyped characteristics would emerge, regardless of rearing environment. Beginning at ages 9 and 10, children viewed gender typing as socially rather than biologically influenced. They thought that other-sex rearing would produce far less stereotyped children than would same-sex rearing.

(Adapted from Taylor, 1996.)

INDIVIDUAL, SEX-RELATED, AND ETHNIC DIFFERENCES IN GENDER STEREOTYPING

Almost all children acquire extensive knowledge of gender stereotypes by middle childhood. But while they are developing, children differ widely in the makeup of their understanding. The various components of gender stereotyping—activities, behaviors, occupations, and personality traits—do not correlate highly. A child very knowledgeable in one area may not be very knowledgeable in the others (Serbin, Powlishta, & Gulko, 1993). This suggests that gender typing is not unitary. Instead, it is more like "an intricate puzzle that the child pieces together in a rather idiosyncratic way" (Hort, Leinbach, & Fagot, 1991, p. 196). To build a coherent notion of gender, children must assemble many elements, including gender labels, diverse stereotypes, and evaluations of the appropriateness of each. The precise pattern in which they acquire the pieces, the rate at which they do so, and the flexibility of their beliefs vary greatly from child to child.

Group differences in gender stereotyping also exist. The strongest of these is sex related: boys hold more rigid gender-stereotyped views throughout childhood and adolescence—in studies carried out in the United States and in other nations (Archer, 1992; Levy, Taylor, & Gelman, 1995; Turner, Gervai, & Hinde, 1993). In addition, boys are more likely than girls to devalue the achievements of females, to regard gender equality as unimportant, and to attribute gender differences to biological rather than social causes (Antill et al., 1996; Smith & Russell, 1984). However, in a few recent studies, boys and girls did not always differ in these ways (Biernat, 1991b; Serbin, Powlishta, & Gulko, 1993; Taylor, 1996). One heartening possibility is that boys are beginning to view gender roles as encompassing more varied possibilities.

Research including ethnic minorities reveals that black children hold less stereotyped views of females than do white children (Bardwell, Cochran, & Walker, 1986). Perhaps this finding is due to aspects of African-American family life. For example, more black than white women with children under age 18 are employed (U.S. Bureau of the Census, 1998). This means that African-American children are more likely to have mothers whose lives reflect less traditional gender roles.

Finally, although no SES differences in gender stereotyping are present in childhood, higher-SES individuals tend to hold more flexible gender-stereotyped views than their lower-SES counterparts in adolescence and adulthood (Lackey, 1989; Serbin, Powlishta, & Gulko, 1993). Years of schooling along with a wider array of life options may contribute to this difference.

Do children's gender-stereotyped patterns of thinking influence gender-role adoption, thereby restricting their experiences and potential? The evidence on this issue is mixed. Gender-typed preferences and behaviors increase sharply over the preschool years—the same period in which children rapidly acquire a wide variety of stereotypes. In addition, boys—the more stereotyped of the two sexes—show greater conformity to their gender role (Bussey & Bandura, 1992; Ruble & Martin, 1998).

But these parallel patterns of development do not tell us for sure that stereotyping shapes children's behavior. Indeed, research suggests that the relationship is not that clear-cut. Children well versed in gender-related expectations are not always highly gender typed in everyday life (Downs & Langlois, 1988; Serbin, Powlishta, & Gulko, 1993; Weinraub et al., 1984).

Why might this be so? First, some gender-role preferences, such as the desire to play with "gender-appropriate" toys and same-sex playmates, are acquired before children know much about stereotypes. Second, we have already seen that children master the components of gender-stereotyped knowledge in diverse ways, each of which may have different implications for their behavior. Finally, by middle childhood, virtually all children know a great deal about gender stereotypes—knowledge so universal that it cannot predict variation in gender-role adoption.

According to Aletha Huston (1983), gender-typed knowledge and behavior may develop along different lines during the preschool years, perhaps coming together in middle childhood. In support of this idea, stereotype flexibility (rather than knowledge) is a good predictor of gender-role adoption during the school years. Children who believe that many stereotyped characteristics are actually appropriate for both sexes are more likely to cross gender lines in the activities, playmates, and occupational roles they choose for themselves (Serbin, Powlishta, & Gulko, 1993; Signorella, Bigler, & Liben, 1993).

The impact of stereotypes on behavior becomes more powerful as children incorporate these ideas into their gender-role identities—self-perceptions about what they can and should do at play, in school, and as future participants in society. But the development of gender identity is a topic we treat later in this chapter. For now, let's turn to various influences that promote children's gender-typed beliefs and behavior.

BRIEF REVIEW

During the preschool years, children acquire a wide variety of gender stereotypes about activities, behaviors, and occupations. Stereotypes involving personality traits and achievement areas are added in middle childhood. At the same time, a more flexible view of what males and females can do emerges, a trend that continues into adolescence. Children master the components of gender stereotyping in diverse ways, and they differ widely in the flexibility of their beliefs. Group differences in stereotyping also exist. In most studies, boys hold more rigid gender-stereotyped views than girls, and black children hold less stereotyped views of females than do white children. In adolescence and adulthood, higher-SES individuals show greater gender-stereotype flexibility. Children with a flexible view of gender stereotypes are less gender typed in their preferences and behavior.

Influences on Gender Stereotyping and Gender-Role Adoption

According to social learning theorists, direct teaching is the way gender-stereotyped knowledge and behaviors are transmitted to children. We will see shortly that much research is consistent with this view. Nevertheless,

ASK YOURSELF . . .

◆ Four-year-old Trixie announced to her 8-year-old sister, Natasha, that girls can't drive police cars. Natasha responded, "Yes they can. If mom can drive our car, she can drive a police car." Explain how cognitive development supports Natasha's flexible view of gender stereotypes.

◆ Dennis discovered that he was the only boy in a home-economics cooking class. "How are we supposed to be your friends if that's where you spend your time?" Tom and Bill complained at lunchtime. Cite research that sheds light on Tom and Bill's negative reaction to Dennis's "cross-gender" behavior.

◆ CONNECTIONS
Cite parallels between the development of gender stereotyping and children's understanding of ethnicity and social class. (See Chapter 11, page 463.)

Great diversity exists in the extent to which societies promote instrumental traits in males and expressive traits in females. These boys of the Dinka tribe in Kenya are assigned "feminine" tasks—grinding corn and looking after younger siblings. Consequently, they are less likely to be gender stereotyped in personality traits than are most boys in other cultures.

(Akhtar Hussein/Woodfin Camp & Associates)

some people argue that biological makeup leads each sex to be uniquely suited to fill particular roles and that most societies do little more than encourage gender differences that are genetically based. Is there evidence to support this idea?

THE CASE FOR BIOLOGY

Although practically no modern theorist would claim that "biology is destiny," serious questions about biological influences on gender typing remain. Two sources of evidence have been used to support the role of biology: (1) cross-cultural similarities in gender stereotypes and gender-role adoption, and (2) the influence of hormones on gender-role behavior. Let's examine each in turn.

■ **HOW MUCH CROSS-CULTURAL SIMILARITY EXISTS IN GENDER TYPING?** Earlier in this chapter, we noted that the instrumental–expressive dichotomy is reflected in the gender stereotyping of many national groups. Although this finding fits with the idea that social influences simply build on genetic differences between the sexes, we must be cautious in drawing this conclusion.

A close look at cross-cultural findings reveals that most societies promote instrumental traits in males and expressive traits in females, but great diversity exists in the magnitude of this difference (Hendrix & Johnson, 1985; Whiting & Edwards, 1988b). Consider Nyansongo, a small agricultural settlement in Kenya. Nyansongo mothers, who work 4 to 5 hours a day in the gardens, assign the care of young children, the tending of the cooking fire, and the washing of dishes to older siblings. Since children of both sexes perform these duties, girls are relieved of total responsibility for "feminine" tasks and have more time to interact with agemates. Their greater freedom and independence leads them to score higher than girls of other tribal and village cultures in dominance, assertiveness, and playful roughhousing. In contrast, boys' caregiving responsibilities mean that they often display help-giving and emotional support (Whiting & Edwards, 1988a). Among industrialized nations, Sweden is widely recognized as a society in which traditional gender beliefs and behaviors are considerably reduced (see the Cultural Influences box on the following page).

Furthermore, cultural reversals of traditional gender typing exist. Anthropologist Margaret Mead (1935/1963) conducted a classic study of three tribal societies in New Guinea. Among the Arapesh, both men and women were cooperative and nurturant. Among the Mundugamor, both sexes tended to be ruthless and aggressive. And among the Tchambuli, women were dominant and assertive whereas men were passive and dependent.

These examples indicate that experience can have a profound impact on gender typing. Nevertheless, follow-up investigations have challenged the extent of role reversals in the New Guinea societies Mead studied (Daly & Wilson, 1988). And it can be argued that deviations from traditional gender roles are more the exception than the rule. Biological pressures may still be operating, appearing in behavior as long as cultural pressures against them are not extreme. Because cross-cultural findings are inconclusive, scientists have turned to a more direct test of the importance of biology: research on the impact of sex hormones on gender-role adoption.

■ **SEX HORMONES AND GENDER-ROLE ADOPTION.** In Chapters 3 and 5, we discussed how genetic makeup, mediated by hormones, regulates sexual development and body growth in males and females. Sex hormones also affect brain development and neural activity in many animal species, and they do so in humans as well (Hines & Green, 1991). Are hormones, which so pervasively affect body structures, also important in gender-role adoption?

PLAY STYLES AND PREFERENCE FOR SAME-SEX PEERS. Experiments with animals reveal that exposure to sex hormones during certain sensitive periods does affect behavior. For example, prenatally administered androgens (male sex hormones) increase active play in

Sweden's Commitment to Gender Equality

O F ALL NATIONS in the world, Sweden is unique in its valuing of gender equality and its social programs that translate this commitment into action. Over a century ago, Sweden's ruling political party adopted equality as a central goal. One social class was not to exploit another, nor one gender another. In the 1960s, Sweden's expanding economy required that women enter the labor force in large numbers. When the question arose as to who would help sustain family life, the Swedish people called on the principle of equality and answered: fathers, just like mothers.

The Swedish "equal roles family model" maintains that husband and wife should have the same opportunity to pursue a career and be equally responsible for housework and child care. To support this goal, child-care centers had to be made available outside the home. Otherwise, a class of less privileged women might be exploited for caregiving and domestic work—an outcome that would contradict the principle of equality. And since full-time employment for both parents often strains a family with young children, Sweden mandated that mothers and fathers with children under age 8 could reduce the length of their working day to 6 hours, with a corresponding reduction in pay but not in benefits (Sandqvist, 1992).

According to several indicators, Sweden's family model is very successful. Maternal employment is extremely high; over 80 percent of mothers with infants and preschoolers work outside the home. Child-care centers are numerous, of high quality, and heavily subsidized by the government (Kallós & Broman, 1997). And although Swedish fathers do not yet share housework and child care equally with mothers, they are more involved than are fathers in North America and other Western European nations.

Has Sweden's progressive family policy affected the gender beliefs and behaviors of its youths? A study of Swedish and American adolescents found that the "masculine" role was more highly valued than the "feminine" role in both countries. However, this difference was less pronounced in Sweden, where young people regarded each gender as a

Sweden places a high value on gender equality. Swedish parents try especially hard to be sensitive and empathic, to ensure participation in decision making, and to spend most of their free time with their children. Compared to fathers in North America and other Western European nations, Swedish fathers are more involved in housework and child care.

(Bo Zaunders/The Stock Market)

blend of instrumental and expressive traits. Furthermore, Swedish girls felt considerably better about their gender—a difference that might be due to greater equalization in men's and women's pay scales and a widespread attitude in Sweden that "feminine" work is important to society. Finally, compared to American adolescents, Swedish young people more often viewed gender roles as a matter of learned tasks and domains of expertise than inborn traits or rights and duties (Intons-Peterson, 1988).

Traditional gender typing is not eradicated in Sweden. But great progress has been made as a result of steadfastly pursuing a program of gender equality for several decades.

---

both male and female mammals. Androgens also promote male-typical sexual behavior and aggression and suppress maternal caregiving in a wide variety of species (Beatty, 1992).

Eleanor Maccoby (1990a) argues that at least some of these hormonal effects extend to humans. In the introduction to this chapter, we noted that as early as the preschool years, children seek out playmates of their own sex—a preference observed in a wide variety of cultures and many mammalian species (Beatty, 1992; Whiting & Edwards, 1988a). At age 4, children already spend three times as much time with same-sex as with other-sex playmates. By age 6, this ratio climbs to 11 to 1 (Maccoby & Jacklin, 1987). Throughout the school years, children continue to show a strong preference for same-sex peers, a trend that declines in adolescence when puberty triggers an interest in the other sex (Hayden-Thomson, Rubin, & Hymel, 1987; Serbin, Powlishta, & Gulko, 1993).

Why is gender segregation so widespread and persistent? According to Maccoby, early on, hormones affect play styles, leading to rough, noisy movements among boys and calm, gentle actions among girls. Then, as children begin to interact with peers, they choose

Beginning in the preschool years, children seek out playmates of their own sex. Sex hormones are believed to influence children's play styles, leading to calm, gentle actions in girls and rough, noisy movements in boys. Then preschoolers naturally choose same-sex partners who share their interests and behavior. Social pressures for "gender-appropriate" play and the tendency to evaluate members of one's own sex more positively are also believed to promote gender segregation.

(Left, Merritt Vincent/PhotoEdit; right, Michael Newman/PhotoEdit)

partners whose interests and behaviors are compatible with their own. By age 2, girls already appear overwhelmed by boys' rambunctious behavior. When paired with a boy in a laboratory play session, the girl is likely to stand idly by while he explores the toys (Jacklin & Maccoby, 1978). Nonhuman primates react similarly. When a male juvenile initiates rough, physical play, male peers join in, whereas females withdraw (Beatty, 1992).

As children increasingly seek out same-sex playmates, girls can be seen playing in pairs and triads because of a common preference for quieter interaction (Benenson, 1993). After age 5, boys come to prefer larger-group play with other boys, who respond positively to one another's desire to run, climb, play-fight, and build up and knock down (Benenson, Apostoleris, & Parnass, 1997). Play-style preferences are especially powerful in boys' choice of playmates. When asked whether they would prefer playing with a girl who likes rough, active games or a boy who likes calm, quiet games, preschool and school-age boys choose on the basis of play style rather than gender. Girls' responses are less consistent (Alexander & Hines, 1994).

Social pressures for "gender-appropriate" play and cognitive factors—in particular, gender stereotyping and the tendency to evaluate members of one's own sex more positively—are also believed to contribute to gender segregation. But sex hormones are involved—a conclusion that receives further support from studies of exceptional sexual development in humans.

EXCEPTIONAL SEXUAL DEVELOPMENT. For ethical reasons, we cannot experimentally manipulate hormones to see how they affect human behavior. But cases do exist in which hormone levels varied naturally or were modified for medical reasons.

John Money, Anke Ehrhardt, and their collaborators conducted research on children with *congenital adrenal hyperplasia (CAH)*, a disorder in which a genetic defect causes the adrenal system to produce unusually high levels of androgens from the prenatal period onward. Although the physical development of boys remains unaffected, CAH girls are usually born with masculinized external genitals. Most undergo surgical correction in infancy or childhood; a few experience it in later life. Continuous drug therapy is used to correct the hormone imbalance (Ehrhardt & Baker, 1974; Money & Ehrhardt, 1972).

Interviewing CAH children and their family members, the researchers found that girls liked cars, trucks, and blocks better than dolls; preferred boys as playmates; were uninterested in fantasizing about traditional feminine roles (such as bride and mother); and were less concerned with matters of physical appearance (clothing, jewelry, and hairstyle) than were non-CAH girls. Also, both boys and girls with CAH showed higher activity levels, as indicated by greater participation in active sports and outdoor games.

Recent interview and observational studies lend additional weight to Money and Ehrhardt's conclusion that prenatal androgen exposure supports certain aspects of "masculine" gender-role behavior. Compared to controls, CAH women asked to reflect on their childhoods recalled less comfort with their sense of femininity and more "masculine" toy, peer, and fantasy-role preferences (Zucker et al., 1996). Videotaped records of CAH children at play revealed that CAH girls preferred vehicle and building toys and, to a lesser extent, boys as play partners. However, they did not engage in rough or physically assaulting play more often than did control girls; in fact, regardless of CAH exposure, girls scored lower than control boys on these measures (Berenbaum & Hines, 1992; Berenbaum & Snyder, 1995; Hines & Kaufman, 1994).

Critics point out that subtle environmental pressures may contribute to the "masculine" play styles of CAH girls. One speculation is that genital abnormalities, in some cases not corrected until well beyond infancy, may have caused family members to perceive affected girls as boyish and unfeminine and to treat them accordingly. However, in the studies just described, CAH girls with masculinized genitals were not more "masculine" in toy or playmate preferences than other CAH girls. Nevertheless, in the course of their medical treatment, girls with CAH were probably told that as adults they might have difficulty conceiving a child. Perhaps they showed little interest in "feminine" play themes of marriage and motherhood because they were unsure of these possibilities in their own lives.

Other research on individuals reared as members of the other sex because they had ambiguous genitals indicates that in most cases, gender typing is consistent with sex of rearing, regardless of genetic sex (Money, 1985). In instances in which these individuals do decide to switch gender roles, they usually move from "feminine" to "masculine"—to the gender associated with more highly valued characteristics. Consider some striking findings on genetic males born with female-looking genitals because of a prenatal androgen deficiency. In four villages in the Dominican Republic, where this defect is common, all but one of those reared as a girl changed to a masculine gender role in adolescence and young adulthood (Imperato-McGinley et al., 1979). Although the researchers inferred that "androgens make a strong and definite contribution to gender typing" (p. 1236), additional research questions this conclusion. Among the Sambia of Papua New Guinea, sexually ambiguous males reared as females switched gender roles only in response to social pressures—when it became clear that they could not fulfill their cultural destiny of bearing children (Herdt & Davidson, 1988).

Studies of individuals whose mothers took synthetic androgens to prevent miscarriage but whose genitals were unaffected yield mixed results. Some report a rise in "masculine" attributes, including play interests, independence, self-confidence, and aggressive solutions to social problems (Ehrhardt, 1975; Reinisch, 1981). But others show no clear effects (Hines, 1982).

Taken together, research on the impact of sex hormones suggests that they affect some aspects of gender typing. The most uniform findings involve activity level and a preference for "gender-appropriate" play and toys (Collaer & Hines, 1995). Since other behavioral outcomes are neither large nor consistent, biological makeup probably plays little role. Finally, it is important to keep in mind that even biological factors can be modified by experience. For example, in animal research, social dominance and environmental stress increase androgen production (Macrides, Bartke, & Dalterio, 1975; Rose, Holaday, & Bernstein, 1976).

THE CASE FOR ENVIRONMENT

A wealth of evidence reveals that environmental factors provide powerful support for gender-role development. As we will see in the following sections, adults view boys and girls differently, and they treat them differently. In addition, children's social contexts—home, school, and community—offer many opportunities to observe people behaving in ways consistent with gender stereotypes. And as soon as children enter the world of the peer group, their agemates encourage conformity to gender roles.

■ **PERCEPTIONS AND EXPECTATIONS OF ADULTS.** When adults are asked to observe neutrally dressed infants who are labeled as either boy or girl, they "see" qualities that fit with the baby's artificially assigned sex. In research of this kind, adults tend to rate infants' physical features and (to a lesser extent) their personality traits in a gender-stereotyped fashion (Stern & Karraker, 1989; Vogel et al., 1991). Among new parents, these gender-biased perceptions may be even stronger. In one study, mothers and fathers were

Will this high school valedictorian realize her talents and vocational aspirations? Gender-stereotyped messages underlie a decline in academically talented females' achievements and career expectations during high school and college. *(Dana White/PhotoEdit)*

interviewed 24 hours after the birth of their first child. Although male and female newborns did not differ in length, weight, or Apgar scores, parents perceived them differently. They rated sons as firmer, larger featured, better coordinated, more alert, stronger, and hardier and daughters as softer, finer featured, more delicate, more awkward, and more inattentive (Rubin, Provenzano, & Luria, 1974).

During childhood and adolescence, parents continue to hold different perceptions and expectations of their sons and daughters. They interpret children's behavior in stereotyped ways, want their preschoolers to play with "gender-appropriate" toys, and say that boys and girls should be reared differently. For example, when asked about their child-rearing values, parents tend to emphasize achievement, competitiveness, and control of emotion as important for sons and warmth, "ladylike" behavior, and close supervision of activities as important for daughters. These differences have changed very little over the past several decades (Block, 1983; Brooks-Gunn, 1986; Turner & Gervai, 1995).

■ **TREATMENT BY PARENTS.** Do adults actually treat children in accord with their stereotypical beliefs? A combined analysis of 172 studies reported that on the whole, differences in the way parents socialize boys and girls are not large (Lytton & Romney, 1991). However, this does not mean that parental treatment is unimportant. It simply says that if we sum across age periods and behaviors, we find only a few clear trends. When the evidence is examined closely, consistent age effects emerge. Younger children receive more direct training in gender roles than do older children—a finding that is not surprising, since gender typing takes place especially rapidly during early childhood (Fagot & Hagan, 1991). And wide variation from study to study suggests that some parents practice differential treatment much more intensely than do others.

INFANCY AND EARLY CHILDHOOD. In infancy and early childhood, parents encourage a diverse array of "gender-appropriate" play activities and behaviors. As early as the first few months of life—before children can express their own preferences—parents begin to create different environments for boys and girls. Bedrooms are decorated with distinct colors and themes. Parents give guns, cars, tools, and footballs to boys; dolls, tea sets, jewelry, and jump ropes to girls. A child who makes a special request for a birthday or Christmas present is far more likely to receive it if it is a "gender-consistent" toy (Etaugh & Liss, 1992; Pomerleau et al., 1990). Parental purchase of gender-typed toys is stronger for boys, especially if the child asks for the item (Fisher-Thompson, 1993).

Parents also actively reinforce gender-role conformity in young children. For example, they react more positively when a young son as opposed to a daughter plays with cars and trucks, demands attention, runs and climbs, or tries to take toys from others. In contrast, they more often direct play activities, provide help, encourage participation in household tasks, and refer to emotions when interacting with a daughter (Fagot, 1978; Fagot & Hagan, 1991; Kuebli, Butler, & Fivush, 1995). Furthermore, the way parents converse with preschool boys and girls differs. Mothers more often *label emotions* when talking to girls. In doing so, they seem to teach daughters to "tune in" to others' feelings. In contrast, mothers more often *explain emotions*, noting causes and consequences, when talking to boys—an approach that emphasizes why it is important to control the expression of emotion (Cervantes & Callanan, 1998; Fivush, 1989).

Early in development, then, parents provide experiences that encourage assertiveness, exploration, engagement with the physical world, and emotional control in boys. In contrast, they promote imitation, dependency, and emotional sensitivity in girls.

MIDDLE CHILDHOOD. During middle childhood, issues of achievement become more salient to parents as children's skills expand. Observations of mothers and fathers interacting with their school-age children in teaching situations reveal that they demand greater independence from boys. For example, when a child requests help, parents more often ignore or refuse to respond to a son, whereas they offer help right away to a daughter (Rothbart & Rothbart, 1976). And the way parents provide help to each sex differs. They behave in a more mastery-oriented fashion with sons, setting higher standards and pointing out important features of the task. In contrast, they frequently stray from task goals to joke and play with daughters (Block, Block, & Harrington, 1975). During conversations, parents are likely to interrupt daughters but permit sons to finish their statements, subtly delivering the message that what a boy has to say is more important (Greif, 1979).

Parents also hold gender-differentiated perceptions of and expectations for children's competencies in various school subjects. In longitudinal research on over 2,100 families with school-age children, Jacqueline Eccles, Janis Jacobs, and Rena Harold (1990) found that parents rated daughters as more competent in English than sons; the reverse was true for mathematics and sports. These beliefs were stronger than actual skill differences among the children. In fact, boys and girls in this sample performed equally well in the two academic areas, based on grades and achievement test scores. What else besides overt performance influenced parents' judgments? The researchers discovered that parents' stereotypes about the abilities of males and females played a significant role. The more parents endorsed the idea of gender-specific abilities, the more likely they were to believe that their child was naturally talented in a gender-typical field and would find "cross-gender" pursuits to be difficult. These judgments, in turn, influenced children's self-perceptions of ability, the effort they devoted to mastering particular skills, and their later performance (Jacobs, 1991; Jacobs & Eccles, 1992). The researchers speculated that this chain of events is likely to affect the occupations that males and females seek out and qualify for. As the Social Issues box on page 534 reveals, gender inequality continues to exist in many vocational domains.

Differential treatment by parents extends to the freedom granted children in their everyday lives. Parents use more directive speech (imperatives and specific suggestions) with girls than with boys (Leaper, Anderson, & Sanders, 1998). Furthermore, although mothers' self-reported use of control tactics to ensure that children meet their daily responsibilities is similar for boys and girls, mothers of sons more often pair control with autonomy granting. That is, they tend to ask boys to make decisions themselves, and they communicate confidence in boys when praising them for meeting a standard, as in "you must enjoy your work" (see Figure 13.3) (Pomerantz & Ruble, 1998b). School-age children generously interpret parental control without autonomy granting (for example, the parent making decisions for the child) as well-intentioned guidance. But they also say that such control makes them feel incompetent (Pomerantz & Ruble, 1998a).

Yet another sign of boys' greater freedom is parental willingness to let them range farther from home without supervision. Assignment of chores reflects this trend. In many cultures, girls are given tasks, such as food preparation, cleaning, and baby-sitting, that keep them close to home, whereas boys are given responsibilities that take them into the

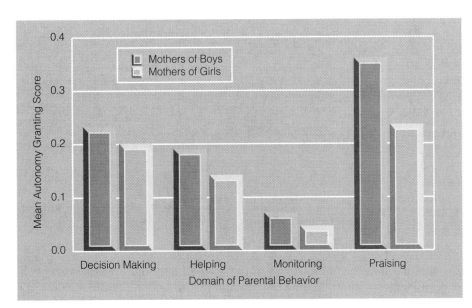

FIGURE 13.3

Mothers' autonomy granting in the context of control tactics aimed at getting 6- to 11-year-olds to meet their daily responsibilities. Autonomy granting was assessed in four domains of parental behavior: *decision making, helping* (with homework and other projects), *monitoring* (overseeing completion of homework, out-of-school projects, and chores), and *praising* (communicating confidence in the child). In each, mothers granted boys more autonomy.

(Adapted from Pomerantz & Ruble, 1998b.)

Sex-Related Differences In Vocational Development

OVER THE PAST three decades, high school boys' vocational preferences have remained strongly gender stereotyped, whereas girls have expressed increasing interest in occupations traditionally held by men (Gottfredson, 1996). Nevertheless, women's progress in entering and excelling at male-dominated professions has been slow. As Table 13.2 shows, the percentage of women engineers, lawyers, and doctors increased between 1972 and 1997 in the United States, but it falls far short of equal representation. Women remain heavily concentrated in the less well-paid, traditionally feminine professions of literature, social work, education, and nursing (U.S. Bureau of the Census, 1998). In virtually all fields, their achievements lag behind those of men, who write more books, make more discoveries, hold more positions of leadership, and produce more works of art.

TABLE 13.2

Percentage of Females in Various Professions, 1972, 1984, 1997

Profession	1972	1984	1997
Engineering	0.8	5.8	9.6
Law	3.8	15.8	26.6
Medicine	9.3	15.8	26.2
Business—executive and managerial	17.6	32.4	43.0[a]
Writing, art, entertainment	31.7	42.7	49.3
Social work	55.1	64.3	69.3
Elementary and secondary education	70.0	70.9	75.7
Higher education	28.0	36.3	42.7
Library, museum curatorship	81.6	84.4	77.1
Nursing	92.6	95.8	93.5

Source: U.S. Bureau of the Census, 1998.

Note: [a]This percentage includes executives and managers at all levels. Women make up only 10 percent of senior management at big firms, although that figure represents a three-fold increase in the past decade.

As we will see in the final section of this chapter, ability cannot account for these dramatic differences. Instead, gender-stereotyped messages play a key role. Although girls' grades are higher than boys', girls reach adolescence less confident of their ability and more likely to underestimate their achievement (Bornholt, Goodnow, & Cooney, 1994). Over time, the proportion of girls in gifted programs decreases. Girls make up about half the population in these programs in elementary school. By secondary school, they account for less than 30 percent, and their presence continues to drop during high school. Those who remain do not develop their talents to the same degree as boys, either educationally or vocationally (Winner, 1996).

When high school students were asked what discouraged them from continuing in gifted programs, parental and peer pressures and attitudes of teachers and counselors ranked high on girls' lists (Read, 1991). Some parents still regard vocational accomplishment as unnecessary for girls and as risking their chances for marriage and motherhood. At times, counselors advise girls not to enroll in advanced math and science courses for similar reasons. Furthermore, teachers tend to view girls as less skilled than boys in math and science. And they view gifted girls, who violate their expectations, more negatively than other children (Kramer, 1991; Shepardson & Pizzini, 1992). Once communicated, these beliefs can be reinforced by peers.

During college, the career aspirations of academically talented females decline further. In one longitudinal study, high school valedictorians were followed over a 10-year

period—through college and into the work world. By their sophomore year, women showed a decline in estimates of their intelligence, whereas men did not. Women also shifted their expectations toward less demanding careers because of concerns about combining work with child rearing and unresolved questions about their ability. Even though female valedictorians outperformed their male counterparts in college courses, they achieved at lower levels after career entry (Arnold, 1994). Another study reported similar results. Educational aspirations of mathematically talented females declined considerably during college, as did the number majoring in the sciences (Benbow & Arjimand, 1990). The underrepresentation of women in physical-science careers is severe. They constitute only 9 percent of employed engineers and physicists (U.S. Bureau of the Census, 1998).

These findings reveal a pressing need for programs that sensitize parents, teachers, and school counselors to the special problems girls face in developing and maintaining high career aspirations. Research shows that academically talented girls' aspirations rise in response to career guidance that encourages them to set high goals—ones that match their abilities, interests, and values (Kerr, 1983). Those who continue to achieve usually have four experiences in common:

- a college environment that values and supports the accomplishments of women;

- frequent interaction with faculty and professionals in their chosen fields;

- the opportunity to test their abilities in a nurturing environment; and

- models of accomplished women who have successfully dealt with family—career role conflict (Arnold, 1994; Schroeder, Blood, & Maluso, 1993).

surrounding world, such as yard work and errands (Whiting & Edwards, 1988a). As we noted earlier, when cultural circumstances require children to perform "cross-gender" chores (as in Nyansongo), the range of behaviors practiced expands.

Although these findings might be taken to suggest that children in Western cultures be assigned more gender-atypical tasks, the consequences of doing so are not so straightforward. For example, when fathers hold stereotypical views and their sons engage in "feminine" housework, boys experience strain in the father–child relationship, feel stressed by their responsibilities, and judge themselves to be less competent (McHale et al., 1990).

In contrast, a match between parental values and nontraditional child-rearing practices leads to benefits for children. In one study, 6-year-olds growing up in countercultural families that were committed to gender equality were compared to age-mates living in conventional homes or experiencing other countercultural alternatives (for example, communes emphasizing spiritual and pronature values but not gender equality). Children in gender-countercultural homes were less likely to classify objects and occupations in stereotypical ways, and girls more often aspired to nontraditional careers (Weisner & Wilson-Mitchell, 1990).

This Lapp boy of Norway wanders far from home as he tends his family's sled reindeer. The freedom he is granted promotes independence and self-reliance. Because his sisters are given household tasks, they spend much more time under the watchful eye of adults.

(Bryan and Cherry Alexander)

MOTHERS VERSUS FATHERS. In most aspects of differential treatment of boys and girls, fathers are the ones who discriminate the most. For example, in Chapter 10 we saw that fathers tend to engage in more physically stimulating play with their infant sons than with their infant daughters, whereas mothers tend to play in a quieter way with infants of both sexes. In childhood, fathers more than mothers encourage "gender-appropriate" behavior, and they place more pressure to achieve on sons than on daughters (Gervai, Turner, & Hinde, 1995; Lytton & Romney, 1991).

Parents also seem especially committed to ensuring the gender typing of children of their own sex. While mothers go on shopping trips and bake cookies with their daughters, fathers play catch, help coach the Saturday morning soccer game, and go fishing with their sons. This same-sex-child bias is another aspect of gender-role training that is more pronounced for fathers (Parke, 1996). When asked whether certain aspects of child rearing are the domain of one parent rather than the other, parents of boys indicated that fathers have a special responsibility to serve as a role model and play companion to their sons (Fagot, 1974).

■ TREATMENT BY TEACHERS. In some ways, preschool and elementary school teachers reinforce children of both sexes for "feminine" rather than "masculine" behavior. In classrooms, obedience is usually valued and assertiveness is discouraged—by male and female teachers alike (Fagot, 1985a; Oettingen, 1985; Robinson & Canaday, 1978). This "feminine bias" is believed to promote discomfort for boys in school, but it may be equally or even more harmful for girls, who willingly conform, with possible long-term negative consequences for their sense of independence and self-esteem.

Teachers also act in ways that maintain and even extend gender roles taught at home. They often segregate children by sex, as when they say, "Will the girls line up on one side and the boys on the other?" and "Boys, I wish you'd quiet down like the girls!" (Thorne, 1993). At the same time, teachers follow parents' lead in interrupting girls more often than boys during conversation, thereby promoting boys' social dominance and girls' passivity. By age 4, children react in kind: Boys interrupt their female teachers more often than girls do (see Figure 13.4 on page 536) (Hendrick & Stange, 1991).

At older ages, teachers react to children's achievement and social behaviors in terms of gender stereotypes. They praise boys for their knowledge, girls for their obedience. And although they discourage aggression and other forms of misbehavior in all children, they do so more frequently and forcefully in boys. Teachers' greater scolding of boys seems to

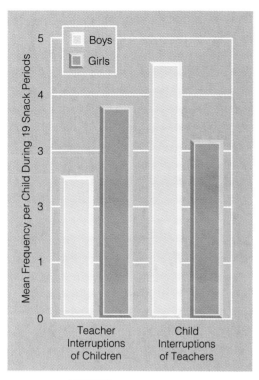

FIGURE 13.4

Interruptions by teachers of children and by children of teachers at snack time in preschool. Children were observed in groups of two boys and two girls at a table with a female teacher. Teachers interrupted girls' conversations more often than boys'. Boys responded in kind; compared to girls, they more often interrupted teachers.

(Adapted from Hendrick & Stange, 1991.)

result from an expectation that boys will misbehave more often than girls—a belief based partly on boys' actual behavior and partly on gender stereotypes. When teachers reprimand girls, it is usually for giving a wrong answer (Good & Brophy, 1996).

Just as teachers can promote gender typing, they can do the opposite by modifying the way they communicate with children. For example, when teachers introduce new materials in a non-gender-biased fashion, praise all pupils for independence and persistence, and ignore attention seeking and dependency, children's activity choices and behavior change accordingly (Serbin, Connor, & Citron, 1978; Serbin, Connor, & Iler, 1979). However, girls are more responsive to these interventions than boys are. And most of the time, changes in children's behavior are short lived. As soon as the usual interaction patterns resume in the classroom, children return to their prior ways of responding. Like nontraditional families, schools that are successful in modifying gender typing have clearly articulated philosophies about gender equality that pervade all aspects of classroom life (Bianchi & Bakeman, 1978; Gash & Morgan, 1993).

■ **OBSERVATIONAL LEARNING.** In addition to direct pressures from adults, numerous gender-typed models are available in children's environments. Although American society has changed to some degree, children come in contact with many real people who conform to traditional gender-role expectations.

Reflections of gender in the media are also stereotyped. As we will see in Chapter 15, the way males and females are represented in television programs has changed very little in recent years (Huston & Wright, 1998; Ruble & Martin, 1998). Also, analyses of the content of children's storybooks and textbooks reveal that they continue to portray males and females stereotypically. Boys and men outnumber girls and women as main characters, and males take center stage in most of the exciting and adventurous plot activities. Females, when they do appear as important characters, are often engaged in housekeeping and caring for children. The availability of gender-equitable reading materials for children is increasing, but school texts at the high school level have been especially slow to change (Noddings, 1992).

When children are exposed to nonstereotyped models, they are less traditional in their beliefs and behaviors. Children who often see their parents cross traditional gender lines—mothers who are employed or who engage in "masculine" household tasks (repairing appliances, washing the car) and fathers who engage in "feminine" household tasks (ironing, cooking, child care)—less often endorse gender stereotypes (Turner & Gervai, 1995; Updegraff, McHale, & Crouter, 1996). Girls with career-oriented mothers show special benefits. They more often engage in typically masculine activities (such as physically active play), have higher educational aspirations, and hold nontraditional vocational goals (Hoffman, 1989). Finally, among children of divorced parents, boys in father-absent homes and girls in mother-absent homes are less gender typed, perhaps because they have fewer opportunities to observe traditional gender roles than they would in a two-parent household (Brenes, Eisenberg, & Helmstadter, 1985; Williams, Radin, & Allegro, 1992).

■ **PEERS.** Earlier we noted that children's preference for same-sex peers is widespread. Once formed, sex-segregated peer associations become powerful environments for strengthening traditional beliefs and behaviors.

Observations of preschoolers reveal that by age 3, same-sex peers positively reinforce one another for "gender-appropriate" play by praising, approving, imitating, or joining in the activity of an agemate (Fagot & Patterson, 1969; Langlois & Downs, 1980). In contrast, when preschoolers display "gender-inappropriate" play—for example, when boys play with dolls, or girls with woodworking tools—they are criticized and rebuffed. Peer rejection is greater for boys who frequently engage in "cross-gender" behavior. Their male peers ignore them even when they do enter "masculine" activities (Fagot, 1977).

Boys and girls also develop different styles of social influence in gender-segregated peer groups. To get their way with male peers, boys more often rely on commands, threats, and physical force. In contrast, girls learn to emphasize polite requests and persuasion. These strategies succeed with other girls but not with boys, who start to ignore girls' gentle tactics (Leaper, 1994; Neppl & Murray, 1997). Consequently, an additional reason that girls may stop interacting with boys is that they do not find it very rewarding to communicate with an unresponsive social partner (Maccoby, 1988, 1990a).

Although children prefer same-sex playmates, mixed-sex interaction does occur, and adults can promote it. When teachers comment approvingly, interaction between boys and girls is sustained on a short-term basis (Serbin, Tonick, & Sternglanz, 1977). Also, changing the design of the preschool classroom by joining gender-typed activity areas (such as blocks and housekeeping) increases mixed-sex play (Kinsman & Berk, 1979). Interaction between boys and girls is encouraged on a long-term basis in classrooms where teaching nonstereotyped values is an important part of the school curriculum (Lockheed, 1986).

Some educators believe that fostering mixed-sex interaction in preschool and elementary school is a vital means for reducing gender stereotyping and broadening developmental possibilities for both sexes (Lloyd & Smith, 1985). However, to be successful, interventions may also need to modify the styles of social influence acquired by children in their same-sex peer relations. Otherwise, boys are likely to dominate and girls to react passively, thereby strengthening traditional gender roles and the stereotypes each sex holds of the other (Lockheed & Harris, 1984).

By secondary school, athletics becomes a major context in which gender stereotypes are fostered (Eder & Parker, 1987). The high status of male athletes and female cheerleaders leads the peer culture to value competition and toughness for boys and physical attractiveness and support of male prowess for females.

■ **SIBLINGS.** Growing up with siblings of the same or other sex also affects gender typing. But compared to peer influences, sibling effects are more complex because their impact depends on birth order and family size (Wagner, Schubert, & Schubert, 1993).

If sibling effects operated just like peer influences, we would expect a family of same-sex siblings to promote traditional gender roles and a family of mixed-sex siblings to do just the opposite. In an observational study of the play behaviors of 4- to 9-year-olds in their homes, the activities of same-sex siblings were highly "gender appropriate." But among mixed-sex siblings, play choices were determined by the sex of the older child. In fact, this effect was so strong that boys with older sisters actually played "house" and "dolls" as much as pairs of sisters did. In contrast, boys with older brothers never engaged in these "feminine" pursuits (Stoneman, Brody, & MacKinnon, 1986).

But curiously, other research contradicts these findings. For example, when 8- and 9-year-olds were videotaped playing with toys in a laboratory, preference for "other-gender" toys was more common among children whose siblings were all of their own sex (Tauber, 1979). And individuals with same-sex siblings seem to be less stereotyped in their interests and personality characteristics than are those from mixed-sex families (Grotevant, 1978).

How can these conflicting results be explained? Recall from Chapter 10 that an important nonshared family environmental influence on personality development is that siblings often strive to be different from one another. This effect is strongest when children are of the same sex and come from large families. A close look at the research just described reveals that studies reporting a modeling and reinforcement effect (an increase in gender typing among same-sex siblings) were limited to children from small, two-child families. In contrast, those reporting a differentiation effect included children from large families. In homes with many children, a younger child may not emulate an older sibling out of a need to stand out as unique.

In addition, parents may sometimes relax pressures toward gender typing when their children are all of the same sex. Consistent with this idea, mothers are more willing to give their child a gender-atypical toy as a gift if a child has an older, same-sex sibling (Stoneman, Brody, & MacKinnon, 1986). Also, in all-girl and all-boy families, children are more likely to be assigned "cross-gender" chores because no "gender-appropriate" child is available to do the job. Therefore, families in which siblings are all of the same sex may provide some special opportunities to step out of traditional gender roles.

When siblings are the same sex, they are more likely to be assigned "cross-gender" chores. These brothers help with dishes after a family meal—a responsibility typically reserved for girls.
(Spencer Grant/Stock Boston)

ASK YOURSELF . . .

♦ One day, Pat and Chris each announced to their mothers that they had to do a science project. Pat's mother said, "Perhaps you'd like to go to the library tonight to choose your topic." Chris's mother said,"You'd better get started right away. We already have some books on whales, so you can do it on that." Is Pat more likely to be a boy or a girl? How about Chris? Explain, using research findings.

♦ CONNECTIONS

Girls are more susceptible than boys to learned helplessness in achievement situations. Explain why this is so, using research in this chapter (see page 533) and in Chapter 11 (see page 455).

Describe gender-stereotyped messages conveyed to children on television. (See Chapter 15, page 619.)

Cross-cultural similarities in gender typing suggest a role for biology but are not conclusive. Research on sex hormones and gender-role adoption reveals that prenatally administered androgens promote a variety of "masculine" behaviors in animal species. Studies of children with congenital adrenal hyperplasia (CAH) suggest similar effects in humans for activity level and "masculine" play and toys.

At the same time, powerful environmental influences on gender typing exist. Beginning in infancy, adults view and treat boys and girls differently. Parents—especially fathers—actively promote "gender-appropriate" play activities and behavior in young children. During middle childhood, parents demand greater independence from boys in achievement situations, hold gender-stereotyped beliefs about children's abilities in school subjects, and grant boys more freedom in their everyday lives. Adoption of traditional gender roles receives further support from teachers, same-sex peers, and models in the surrounding environment. Sibling effects on gender typing are jointly influenced by sex of siblings, birth order, and family size.

Gender Identity

Besides biological and environmental influences, another factor eventually comes to influence gender stereotyping and gender-role behavior: *gender identity,* a person's perception of the self as relatively masculine or feminine in characteristics. By middle childhood, researchers can measure gender identity by asking children to rate themselves on personality traits, since at that time, self-concepts begin to emphasize psychological dispositions over concrete behaviors (see Chapter 11). Table 13.3 shows some sample items from a gender identity questionnaire for school-age children, who evaluate each statement on a four-point scale, from "very true of me" to "not at all true of me" (Boldizar, 1991). Similar methods for assessing gender identity are used with adults (Bem, 1974; Spence, Helmreich, & Stapp, 1975).

Individuals differ considerably in the way they respond to these questionnaires. A child or adult with a "masculine" identity scores high on traditionally masculine items (such as ambitious, competitive, and self-sufficient) and low on traditionally feminine ones (such as affectionate, cheerful, and soft-spoken). Someone with a "feminine" identity does just the reverse. Although the majority of individuals view themselves in gender-typed terms, a substantial minority (especially females) have a type of gender identity called **androgyny.** They score high on *both* masculine and feminine personality characteristics (Bem, 1974; Boldizar, 1991).

Gender identity is a good predictor of psychological adjustment. Masculine and androgynous children and adults have a higher sense of self-esteem, whereas feminine individuals often think poorly of themselves (Alpert-Gillis & Connell, 1989; Boldizar, 1991). In line with their flexible self-definitions, androgynous individuals are more adaptable in behavior—for example, able to show masculine independence or feminine sensitivity, depending on the situation (Taylor & Hall, 1982). They also show greater maturity of moral judgment than do individuals with other gender-role orientations (Bem, 1977).

However, a close look at these findings reveals that the masculine component of androgyny is largely responsible for the superior psychological health of androgynous women over those with traditional identities (Taylor & Hall, 1982; Whitley, 1983).

TABLE **13.3**

Sample Items from a Gender Identity Questionnaire for School-Age Children

Personality Trait	Item
Masculine	
Ambitious	I'm willing to work hard to get what I want.
Assertive	It's easy for me to tell people what I think, even when I know they will probably disagree with me.
Competitive	When I play games, I really like to win.
Self-sufficient	I can take care of myself.
Feminine	
Affectionate	When I like someone, I do nice things for them to show them how I feel.
Cheerful	I am a cheerful person.
Soft-spoken	I usually speak softly.
Yielding	When there's a disagreement, I usually give in and let others have their way.

Source: J. P. Boldizar, 1991, "Assessing Sex Typing and Androgyny in Children: The Children's Sex Role Inventory," *Developmental Psychology, 27,* p. 509. Copyright © 1991 by the American Psychological Association. Reprinted by permission.

Feminine women seem to have adjustment difficulties because many of their traits are not valued highly by society. Nevertheless, the existence of an androgynous identity demonstrates that masculinity and femininity are not opposites, as many people believe. Children can acquire a mixture of positive qualities traditionally associated with each gender—an orientation that may best help them realize their potential. And in a future society in which feminine characteristics are socially rewarded to the same extent as masculine ones, androgyny may very well represent the ideal personality.

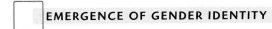

EMERGENCE OF GENDER IDENTITY

How do children develop gender identities that consist of varying mixtures of masculine and feminine characteristics? Both social learning and cognitive-developmental answers exist.

According to *social learning theory*, behavior comes before self-perceptions. Preschoolers first acquire gender-typed responses through modeling and reinforcement. Only later do they organize these behaviors into society's gender-role expectations, which they accept as appropriate for themselves. In contrast, *cognitive-developmental theory* emphasizes that self-perceptions come before behavior. Over the preschool years, children first acquire a cognitive appreciation of the permanence of their sex. They develop **gender constancy,** the understanding that sex remains the same even if clothing, hairstyle, and play activities change. Then children use this idea to guide their actions, and a preference for gender-typed activities appears.

Social learning and cognitive-developmental theories lead to strikingly different predictions about gender-role development. But before we look at what research has to say about the accuracy of each, let's trace the development of gender constancy during the preschool years.

■ **DEVELOPMENT OF GENDER CONSTANCY.** Lawrence Kohlberg (1966) first proposed that before age 6 or 7, children cannot maintain the constancy of their gender, just as they cannot pass Piagetian conservation problems. Only gradually do they attain this understanding, by moving through three stages of development:

1. **Gender labeling.** During the early preschool years, children can label their own sex and that of others correctly. But when asked such questions as "When you (a girl) grow up, could you ever be a daddy?" or "Could you be a boy if you wanted to?" young children freely answer yes (Slaby & Frey, 1975). In addition, when shown a doll whose hairstyle and clothing are transformed before their eyes, children indicate that the doll's sex is no longer the same (McConaghy, 1979).

2. **Gender stability.** At this stage, children have a partial understanding of the permanence of sex. They grasp its stability over time. But even though they know that male and female babies will eventually become boys and girls and men and women, they continue to insist, as they did at younger ages, that changing hairstyle, clothing, or "gender-appropriate" activities will lead a person to switch sexes as well (Fagot, 1985b; Slaby & Frey, 1975).

3. **Gender consistency.** During the late preschool and early school years, children become certain of the situational consistency of sex. They know that sex remains constant even if a person decides to dress in "cross-gender" clothes or engage in nontraditional activities (Emmerich, 1981; McConaghy, 1979).

Many studies confirm that gender constancy emerges in the sequence just described. In addition, mastery of gender constancy is associated with attainment of conservation, as Kohlberg assumed (De Lisi & Gallagher, 1991). Yet cognitive immaturity is not the only reason for preschoolers' poor performance on gender constancy tasks. It also results from limited social experience—in particular, lack of opportunity to learn about genital differences between the sexes. In many households in Western cultures, young children do not see members of the other sex naked. Therefore, they distinguish males and females using the only information they do have—the way each gender dresses and behaves. As Figure 13.5 shows, children as young as 3 who are aware of genital characteristics usually answer gender-constancy questions correctly (Bem, 1989).

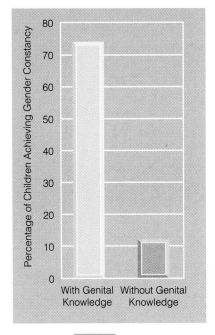

F I G U R E 13.5

Percentage of preschoolers with and without genital knowledge who achieved gender constancy in a study of 3- to 5-year-olds.
(Adapted from Bem, 1989.)

androgyny A type of gender identity in which the person scores high on both masculine and feminine personality characteristics.

gender constancy The understanding that sex remains the same even if clothing, hairstyle, and play activities change.

gender labeling Kohlberg's first stage of gender understanding, in which preschoolers can label the gender of themselves and others correctly.

gender stability Kohlberg's second stage of gender understanding, in which preschoolers have a partial understanding of the permanence of sex; they grasp its stability over time.

gender consistency Kohlberg's final stage of gender understanding, in which children master gender constancy.

Is cognitive-developmental theory correct that gender constancy is responsible for children's gender-typed behavior? From findings discussed earlier in this chapter, perhaps you have already concluded that evidence for this assumption is weak. Long before most preschoolers appreciate the permanence of their sex, they show a wide variety of gender-typed responses and are especially attentive to same-sex models (Bussey & Bandura, 1984). "Gender-appropriate" behavior appears so early in the preschool years that modeling and reinforcement must account for its initial appearance. In line with social learning theory, a cross-sectional study found that preschoolers first acquired "gender-consistent" play behavior and clear awareness of peer disapproval of "cross-gender" activities. Only later, around age 4, did they apply these social standards to themselves, anticipating feeling good for play with "gender-appropriate" toys and bad for play with "gender-inappropriate" toys. Once these self-evaluations were established, children seemed to use them to guide their own actions. Gender-linked self-evaluations predicted preference for gender-typed play activities (Bussey & Bandura, 1992).

Although gender constancy does not initiate gender-role conformity, the cognitive changes that lead up to it do seem to facilitate gender typing. Preschoolers who reach the stage of gender labeling early show especially rapid development of "gender-appropriate" play preferences and are more knowledgeable about gender stereotypes than are their late-labeling peers (Fagot & Leinbach, 1989; Fagot, Leinbach, & O'Boyle, 1992). Similarly, understanding of gender stability is related to gender stereotyping, preference for same-sex playmates, and choice of "gender-consistent" toys (Martin & Little, 1990). These findings suggest that as soon as children acquire basic gender categories, they use them as the basis for acquiring gender-relevant information and modifying their own behavior.

If a complete understanding of gender constancy is not necessary for gender-role adoption, then just what is its function in development? Considerable debate surrounds this issue. Some studies report that gender constancy leads to a rise in "gender-appropriate" activity choices (Frey & Ruble, 1992; Luecke-Aleksa et al., 1995). Others find that it predicts gender-stereotype flexibility (Ullian, 1976; Urberg, 1979). And still others report that gender constancy has no impact on preschoolers' already well-developed gender-role preferences (Bussey & Bandura, 1992; Lobel & Menashri, 1993). Whichever position is correct, the impact of gender constancy on gender typing is not great. As we will see in the following section, gender-role adoption is more powerfully affected by children's beliefs about how tight the connection needs to be between their own gender and behavior (Maccoby, 1990b).

GENDER IDENTITY DURING MIDDLE CHILDHOOD

During middle childhood, boys' and girls' gender identities follow different paths of development. Self-ratings on personality traits reveal that from third to sixth grade, boys strengthen their identification with the "masculine" role. In contrast, girls' identification with "feminine" characteristics declines. Although girls' overall orientation still leans toward the feminine side, they are clearly the more androgynous of the sexes (Boldizar, 1991; Serbin, Powlishta, & Gulko, 1993).

Children's activity preferences and behaviors follow a similar pattern. Unlike boys, girls do not increase their preference for gender-typed activities in middle childhood. Instead, they experiment with a wider range of options. Besides cooking, sewing, and baby-sitting, they join organized sports teams, take up science projects, and build forts in the backyard.

These changes are due to a mixture of cognitive and social forces. We have already seen that society attaches greater prestige to "masculine" characteristics. Girls undoubtedly become aware of this as they grow older. As a result, in middle childhood they start to identify with "masculine" traits and are attracted to some typically mas-

During middle childhood, girls feel freer than boys to engage in "cross-gender" activities. This 10-year-old perfects her lasso technique.
(Bob Daemmrich/Stock Boston)

culine activities (Thorne, 1993). Messages from adults and agemates are also influential. Parents (especially fathers) are far less tolerant when sons as opposed to daughters cross gender lines. Similarly, a tomboyish girl can make her way into boys' activities without losing status with her female peers, but a boy who hangs out with girls is likely to be ridiculed and rejected.

GENDER IDENTITY DURING ADOLESCENCE

In early adolescence, the gender identities of both sexes become more traditional, a trend that is somewhat stronger for girls, since they were more androgynous than boys during childhood. Although overall, young teenage girls continue to be less gender typed than boys, they feel less free to experiment with "other-gender" activities and behavior than they did earlier (Galambos, Almeida, & Petersen, 1990; Huston & Alvarez, 1990).

What accounts for this period of **gender intensification?** Biological, social, and cognitive factors are involved. Puberty magnifies sex differences in appearance, causing teenagers to spend more time thinking about themselves in gender-linked ways. Pubertal changes also prompt gender-typed pressures from others. Parents—especially those with traditional gender-role beliefs—may encourage "gender-appropriate" activities and behavior to a greater extent than they did in middle childhood (Crouter, Manke, & McHale, 1995). And when adolescents start to date, they often become more gender typed as a way of increasing their attractiveness to other-sex peers (Crockett, 1990). Finally, cognitive changes—in particular, greater concern with what others think—make young teenagers more responsive to gender-role expectations.

As young people move toward a mature personal identity, they become less concerned with others' opinions of them and more involved in finding meaningful values to include in their self-definitions (see Chapter 11). As a result, highly stereotypic self-perceptions decline, especially when parents and teachers encourage adolescents to question the value of gender stereotypes for themselves and their society.

Early adolescence is a period of gender intensification. Puberty magnifies gender differences in appearance, causing teenagers to begin thinking about themselves in gender–linked ways. And when adolescents start to date, they often become more gender typed as a way of increasing their attractiveness to the other sex.

(Bob Daemmrich/Stock Boston)

INDIVIDUAL DIFFERENCES

Although gender identity follows the general path of development just described, individual differences exist at all ages, and they are moderately related to gender-role behavior. A more masculine and less feminine identity is associated with better performance on spatial and mathematical tasks (Newcombe & Dubas, 1992; Signorella & Jamison, 1986). Although girls with feminine orientations are more popular with agemates, masculine-oriented children of both sexes are more assertive and less dependent (Hall & Halberstadt, 1980). At present, androgynous children are not especially advantaged in any of these areas. Instead, a gender identity that leans toward the masculine side seems to be the key factor in the majority of positive outcomes for children.

Since these relationships are correlational, we cannot really tell whether masculine and feminine self-perceptions *arise from particular behaviors* (as social learning theory assumes) or *serve as guides for behavior* (as cognitive-developmental theory predicts). According to recent theory and research, the answer is both, as we will see in the following section.

GENDER SCHEMA THEORY

Gender schema theory is an information-processing approach to gender typing that combines social learning and cognitive-developmental features. It also integrates the various elements of gender typing—stereotyping, gender identity, and gender-role adoption—into a unified picture of how masculine and feminine orientations emerge and are often strongly maintained (Bem, 1981, 1983; Martin, 1993; Martin & Halverson, 1987).

At an early age, children respond to instruction from others, picking up gender-typed preferences and behaviors. At the same time, they start to organize their experiences into

gender intensification Development of more traditional gender identities in early adolescence.

gender schema theory An information-processing approach to gender typing that combines social learning and cognitive-developmental features to explain how social pressures and cognitions work together to affect stereotyping, gender-role identity, and gender-role adoption.

FIGURE 13.6

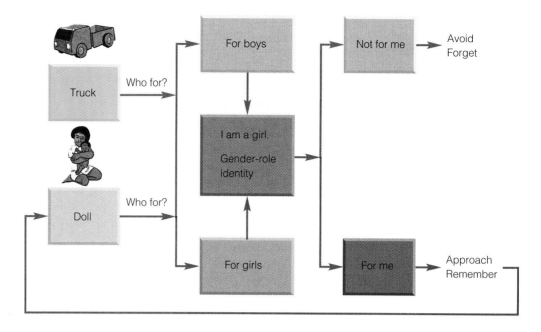

Impact of gender schemas on gender-typed preferences and behaviors. This girl's network of gender schemas leads her to approach and explore "feminine" toys, such as dolls, and to avoid "masculine" toys, such as trucks.

(From C. L. Martin & C. F. Halverson, Jr., 1981, "A Schematic Processing Model of Sex Typing and Stereotyping in Children," *Child Development*, 52, p. 1121. © The Society for Research in Child Development, Inc. Adapted by permission.)

gender schemas, or masculine and feminine categories, that they use to interpret their world. As soon as children can label their own sex, they select gender schemas that are consistent with it, applying those categories to themselves. As a result, self-perceptions become gender typed and serve as additional gender schemas that children use to process information and guide their own behavior.

Figure 13.6 shows exactly how this network of gender schemas strengthens gender-typed preferences and behaviors. Let's consider a child who has been taught that "dolls are for girls" and "trucks are for boys." She also knows that she is a girl. The child uses this information to make decisions about how to behave. Because her schemas lead her to conclude that "dolls are for me," when given a doll she approaches it, explores it, and learns more about it. In contrast, on seeing a truck, she uses her gender schemas to conclude that "trucks are not for me" and responds by avoiding the "gender-inappropriate" toy (Martin & Halverson, 1981).

In research examining this pattern of reasoning, 4- and 5-year-olds were shown gender-neutral toys varying in attractiveness and asked how much they, other girls, and other boys would like each toy. Children made gender-based predictions. For example, if a girl liked a toy, she assumed that other girls would like it more and boys would like it less, even if it was highly attractive! Next, the researchers showed another group of 4- and 5-year-olds the toys, but this time they labeled some as boys' toys and others as girls' toys and left a third group unlabeled. Once again, children engaged in gender-based reasoning, relying on the label to guide their own liking and their expectations of others. Highly attractive toys lost their appeal when they were labeled as for the other gender (Martin, Eisenbud, & Rose, 1995).

Gender schema theory explains why gender stereotypes and gender-role preferences are self-perpetuating and how they restrict children's alternatives. Children attend to and approach schema-consistent information, whereas they ignore, misinterpret, or reject schema-inconsistent information. For example, when shown a picture of a boy cooking at a stove, many children recall the picture as a girl rather than a boy. And when shown a film that includes a male nurse, they remember him as a doctor (Liben & Signorella, 1993; Martin & Halverson, 1983). Over time, children increase their knowledge of "things for me" that fit with their gender schemas, but they learn much less about "cross-gender" activities and behaviors.

Would these children continue playing if an adult labeled marbles as a boys' toy or a girls' toy? Powerful gender schemas lead children to like a toy or game less if they believe it is for the other gender.

(Charles Thatcher/Tony Stone Images)

Reducing Gender-Schematic Thinking with Cognitive Interventions

FROM RESEARCH TO PRACTICE

O N THE FIRST day of school, Mrs. Brown taped blue tags with boys' names and pink tags with girls' names to the corner of each desk in her second-grade classroom. When explaining classroom routines, she told boys and girls to form separate lines at lunch and recess. During daily lessons, Mrs. Brown made frequent reference to gender. "All the boys should be sitting down!" she exclaimed when the class got too noisy. And as an art activity was about to begin, she directed, "Leanne, please get paper for the girls. Jack, I'd like you to be a good helper for the boys."

Rebecca Bigler (1995) had some teachers create "gender classrooms" like Mrs. Brown's by emphasizing gender categories. Other teachers in "control classrooms" were told to refer to children only by their names or treat the class as a unit. After 4 weeks, 6- to 10-year-olds in "gender classrooms" endorsed more gender stereotypes than did controls. They also had a more homogeneous view of each gender group in that they judged all or most members as very similar in personality traits and abilities. An additional consequence of group labeling is a positive view of one's own group and a negative view of the out-group (see Chapter 11, page 464).

Yet as Figure 13.7 shows, the impact of "gender classrooms" was largely limited to rigid thinkers—children who had trouble understanding that a person can belong to more than one social category at once. According to gender schema theory, environmental influences on gender typing are sustained by cognitive forces. When children who are one-dimensional thinkers encounter an exception to their gender schemas (such as a girl who is good at baseball), they are unlikely to process it, since they cannot separate the activity category "baseball" from the gender category "male." Recall that operational thought enables children to classify flexibly by the end of middle childhood (see Chapter 6, page 249).

Bigler's findings suggest that it is especially important for teachers to avoid grouping children on the basis of gender during the early years of schooling, when classification skills are limited and gender stereotypes are forming. At the same

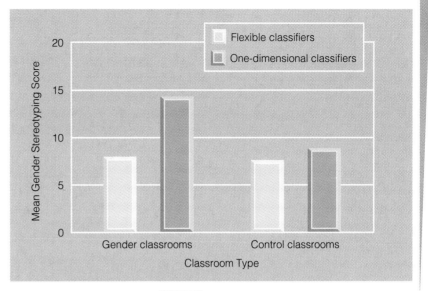

FIGURE 13.7

Children's gender stereotyping in "gender" and "control classrooms." "Gender classrooms" had a powerful impact on 6- to 10-year-olds who were one-dimensional thinkers—unable to see that a person can belong to more than one social category at once. These children endorsed many more stereotypes than did classmates who could classify flexibly.

(Adapted from Bigler, 1995.)

time, training in multiple classification can reduce gender-biased thinking. When 5- to 10-year-olds were taught that ability and interest, not gender, determine whether a person can do a job well, they gained in stereotype flexibility and memory for "gender-inconsistent" information (story characters engaged in "cross-gender" tasks). Interestingly, classification training with gender-neutral stimuli that required children to sort objects into two categories at once had the same effect (Bigler & Liben, 1992). Interventions that promote logical reasoning about gender and other aspects of knowledge can help children develop a more gender-equitable view of the world.

Among children with strong stereotypical beliefs, self-perceptions, and activity preferences, gender-schematic thinking is especially extreme (Carter & Levy, 1991). But gender-schematic thinking could not operate to limit behavior and learning opportunities if society did not teach children a wide variety of gender-linked associations. Currently, researchers are experimenting with ways to reduce children's tendency to view the world in gender-schematic terms. As the From Research to Practice box above reveals, training in cognitive skills that counteract powerful social messages about gender has produced some impressive results.

ASK YOURSELF . . .

♦ *Geraldine cut her 3-year-old daughter Fern's hair very short for the summer, When Fern looked in the mirror, she said, "I don't wanna be a boy," and began to cry. Why is Fern upset about her short hairstyle, and what can Geraldine do to help?*

♦ *When 4-year-old Roger was in the hospital, he was cared for by a male nurse named Jared. After Roger recovered, he told his friends about Dr. Jared. Using gender schema theory, explain why Roger remembered Jared as a doctor, not a nurse.*

♦ CONNECTIONS
Describe gains in perspective taking that lead young teenagers to be very concerned with what others think, thereby contributing to gender intensification. (See Chapter 11, page 466.)

ccording to social learning theory, behavior precedes self-perceptions in the development of gender identity. In contrast, cognitive-developmental theory assumes that self-perceptions emerge first and guide children's behavior. In contrast to cognitive-developmental predictions, gender-typed behavior is present so early that gender constancy cannot explain it; modeling and reinforcement must account for its initial appearance. Several cognitive achievements—gender labeling, gender stability, and gender-linked self-evaluations—promote gender-role adoption. During middle childhood, boys strengthen their identification with the "masculine" role, whereas girls become more androgynous. Early adolescence is a period of gender intensification, in which gender identity becomes more traditional. As young people move toward a mature personal identity, highly stereotypic self-perceptions subside.

Gender schema theory is an information-processing approach to gender typing that combines social learning and cognitive-developmental features. It explains how social pressures and children's cognitions work together to perpetuate gender-linked perceptions and behavior.

To What Extent Do Boys and Girls *Really* Differ in Gender-Stereotyped Attributes?

o far, we have examined the relationship of biological, social, and cognitive factors to children's gender-typed preferences and behavior. But we have said little about the extent to which boys and girls actually differ in mental abilities and personality traits on which we might expect them to differ, given pervasive gender stereotypes. Over the past several decades, there have been thousands of efforts to measure sex-related differences in these characteristics. At the heart of these studies is the age-old nature–nurture debate. Researchers have looked for stable differences between males and females and, from there, have searched for the biological and environmental roots of each variation.

Many literature reviews of sex-related differences have been conducted. To avoid basing conclusions on small and potentially biased samples, researchers often reanalyze the data of many investigations together. This approach has another advantage. Besides telling us whether a sex-related difference exists, it provides an estimate of its size. Table 13.4 summarizes differences between boys and girls in mental abilities and personality traits, based on current evidence. The majority of findings listed in the table are small to moderate in size, making them fairly typical in magnitude for psychological research.[1] Nevertheless, as we will see shortly, a few sex-related differences are large (Eagly, 1995; Hyde & Plant, 1995).

In considering the size of sex-related differences, we must keep in mind that some have changed over time. For example, during the past several decades, the gender gap has narrowed in all areas of mental ability for which differences have been identified except upper-level mathematics, where boys' advantage has remained constant (Feingold, 1988, 1993; Linn & Hyde, 1989). This trend is a reminder that sex-related differences are not fixed for all time. The general picture of how boys and girls differ may not be the same in a few decades as it is today.

MENTAL ABILITIES

Sex-related differences in mental abilities have sparked almost as much controversy as the ethnic and SES differences in IQ considered in Chapter 8. Although boys and girls do not differ in general intelligence, they do vary in specific mental abilities. Many researchers

[1]Sex usually accounts for about 5 to 10 percent of individual differences, leaving most to be explained by other factors. This means that on virtually every ability and personality characteristic, the distributions of boys' and girls' scores overlap greatly. Yet even small to moderate differences are meaningful. For example, in instances in which sex is responsible for only 5 percent of individual variation, about 60 percent of one group but only 40 percent of the other group would score above average.

TABLE 13.4

Sex-Related Differences in Mental Abilities and Personality Traits

Characteristic	Sex-Related Difference
Verbal abilities	Girls show faster early language development and are advantaged in reading achievement throughout the school years.
Spatial abilities	Boys outperform girls in certain spatial skills by middle childhood, a difference that persists throughout the lifespan.
Mathematical abilities	Beginning in adolescence, boys do better than girls on tests of mathematical reasoning. The difference is greatest among high-achieving pupils. Many more boys perform exceptionally well in math.
School achievement	Girls get better grades than boys in all academic subjects in elementary school, after which the difference declines. In junior high, boys start to show an advantage in mathematics.
Achievement motivation	Sex-related differences in achievement motivation are linked to type of task. Boys perceive themselves as more competent and have higher expectancies of success in "masculine" achievement areas, such as mathematics, sports, and mechanical skills. Girls have higher expectancies and set higher standards for themselves in "feminine" areas, such as reading, writing, literature, and art.
Emotional sensitivity	Girls are more effective senders and receivers of emotional information and score higher on self-report measures of empathy and sympathy. Girls' advantage in prosocial behavior is greatest for kindness and considerateness, very small for helping behavior.
Fear, timidity, and anxiety	Girls are more fearful and timid than boys, a difference that is present in the first year of life. In school, girls are more anxious about failure and try harder to avoid it. In contrast, boys are greater risk takers, a difference reflected in their higher injury rates throughout childhood and adolescence.
Compliance and dependency	Girls are more compliant than boys in response to directives from adults or peers. They also seek help from adults more often and score higher in dependency on personality tests. In contrast, boys are more dominant and assertive.
Activity level	Boys are more active than girls.
Depression	Adolescent girls are more likely to show depressive symptoms than are adolescent boys.
Aggression	Boys display more overt aggression, girls more relational aggression. Adolescent boys are far more likely than girls to become involved in antisocial behavior and violent crime.
Developmental problems	Many types of developmental problems are more common among boys, including speech and language disorders, reading disabilities, and behavior problems such as hyperactivity, hostile acting-out behavior, and emotional and social immaturity. More boys than girls are born with genetic disorders, physical disabilities, and mental retardation.

Sources: Bielinksi & Davison, 1998; Campbell, Voelkl, & Donahue, 1997; Cicchetti & Toth, 1998; Crick & Grotpeter, 1995; Eisenberg & Lennon, 1983; Eisenberg & Fabes, 1998; Feingold, 1994; Hall & Halberstadt, 1981; Hyde, Fenema, & Lamon, 1990; Lubinski & Benbow, 1994; Prior et al., 1993; Reznick et al., 1989; Saarni, 1993; Wichstrøm, 1999; Zahn-Waxler et al., 1992.

believe that heredity is involved in the disparities, and they have attempted to identify the specific biological processes responsible. But no biological factor operates in an experiential vacuum. For each ability we will consider, environment plays an important role.

■ **VERBAL ABILITIES.** Early in development, girls are ahead in language progress. They begin to talk earlier and show faster vocabulary growth during the second year, after which boys catch up (see Chapter 9). Throughout the school years, girls attain higher scores on reading and writing achievement tests and account for a lower percentage of children referred for remedial reading instruction (Campbell, Voelkl, & Donahue, 1997; Halpern, 1992). Girls' advantage on tests of general verbal ability is still present in adolescence. However, it has declined considerably since the 1970s and is so slight that it is not really meaningful (Hyde & Linn, 1988).

In Chapter 9, we noted that girls' early advantage in language skills may be fostered by their faster rate of physical maturation, believed to promote earlier development of the left cerebral hemisphere, where language functions are housed for most people (see Chapter 5). In animals and humans, the left side of the cortex is slightly larger and more mature in females than in males (Diamond et al., 1983).

Although biology may contribute to girls' superior language and reading performance, experience also seems to be important. Recall that mothers talk much more to toddler-age girls than to toddler-age boys (see Chapter 9). Furthermore, children think of reading as a feminine subject, parents rate daughters as more competent at it, and elementary school

Sex-Related Differences in Spatial Abilities

VARIATIONS

SPATIAL ABILITIES HAVE become a key focus of researchers' efforts to explain the male advantage in mathematical reasoning. Clear sex differences in spatial skills exist, but they occur only on certain types of tasks (see Figure 13.8). The gender gap favoring males is large for *mental rotation tasks,* in which individuals must rotate a three-dimensional figure rapidly and accurately inside their heads. In addition, males do considerably better on *spatial perception tasks,* in which people must determine spatial relationships by considering the orientation of the surrounding environment. Sex-related differences on *spatial visualization tasks,* involving analysis of complex visual forms, are weak or nonexistent, perhaps because many strategies can be used to solve them. Both sexes may come up with effective procedures (Linn & Petersen, 1985; Voyer, Voyer, & Bryden, 1995).

Sex-related differences in spatial abilities emerge by middle childhood and persist throughout the lifespan (Kerns & Berenbaum, 1991). The pattern is consistent enough to suggest a biological explanation. One hypothesis is that heredity, perhaps through prenatal exposure to androgen hormones, enhances right hemispheric functioning, granting males a spatial advantage. (Recall that for most people, spatial skills are housed in the right hemisphere of the cerebral cortex.) Consistent with this idea, girls and women whose prenatal androgen levels were abnormally high show superior performance on mental rotation tasks (Collaer & Hines, 1995). And people with severe prenatal deficits in either male or female hormones have difficulty

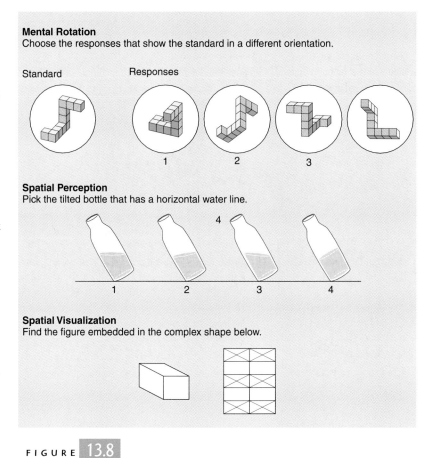

Mental Rotation
Choose the responses that show the standard in a different orientation.

Standard   Responses

Spatial Perception
Pick the tilted bottle that has a horizontal water line.

Spatial Visualization
Find the figure embedded in the complex shape below.

FIGURE **13.8**

Types of spatial tasks. Large sex differences favoring males appear on mental rotation, and males do considerably better than females on spatial perception. In contrast, sex differences on spatial visualization are weak or nonexistent.

(From M. C. Linn & A. C. Petersen, 1985, "Emergence and Characterization of Sex Differences in Spatial Ability: A Meta-Analysis," *Child Development, 56,* pp. 1482, 1483, 1485. © The Society for Research in Child Development, Inc. Reprinted by permission.)

classrooms are feminine-biased settings in which boys' greater activity level and noncompliance lead them to be targets of teacher disapproval. Consistent with this idea, girls' tendency to learn to read more quickly is reduced in countries where reading and early school learning are regarded as well suited to the masculine gender role (Preston, 1962). Perhaps girls write more fluently than do boys because they read books more frequently and generalize what they learn to written expression (Hedges & Nowell, 1995).

■ **MATHEMATICAL ABILITIES.** The male advantage in mathematics is clearly evident by high school, although among highly gifted youngsters, it is present earlier—by age 13. When all students are considered, the size of the difference is small. But among the most capable, the gender gap is considerable. In widely publicized research on thousands of bright seventh and eighth graders who were invited to take the Scholastic Aptitude Test (SAT) long before they needed to do so for college admission, boys outscored girls on the mathematics subtest year after year. Twice as many boys as girls had scores above 500; 13 times as many scored over 700 (Benbow & Stanley, 1983; Lubinski & Benbow, 1994). Sex-related differences are not present on all test items. Boys and girls do equally well on tests of basic math knowledge, and girls do better in computational skills. The difference ap-

with spatial reasoning (Hier & Crowley, 1982; Temple & Carney, 1995).

However, research on hormone variations within normal range is less clear. Two studies report a link between prenatal androgens and spatial abilities during the preschool years, but only for girls and in the opposite direction expected: The greater the hormone exposure, the lower the spatial score (Finegan, Niccols, & Sitarenios, 1992). Prenatal hormones seem to affect spatial skills but not in a straightforward fashion.

Although biology is involved in males' superior spatial performance, experience also makes a difference. Children who engage in manipulative activities, such as block play, model building, and carpentry, do better on spatial tasks (Baenninger & Newcombe, 1995). Furthermore, playing video games that require rapid mental rotation of visual images enhances spatial scores of boys and girls alike (Okagaki & Frensch, 1996; Subrahmanyam & Greenfield, 1996). Yet boys spend far more time at all these pursuits than do girls.

Do superior spatial skills contribute to the greater ease with which males solve complex math problems? Research indicates that they do (Casey et al., 1995). Yet in a recent study of high-ability college-bound adolescents, *both* mental rotation ability and self-confidence at doing math predicted higher scores on the math subtest of the SAT (Casey, Nuttall, & Pezaris, 1997). Boys are advantaged not only in mental rotation but in math self-confidence. Even when their grades are poorer than girls', boys judge themselves to be better at math (Eccles et al., 1993a). In sum, biology and environment *jointly* determine variations in spatial and math performance—within and between the sexes.

This girl is probably the only female enrolled in her high school metal shop class. Experience with manipulative activities, including model building and carpentry, contribute to gender differences in spatial abilities. Superior spatial skills and confidence at doing math, in turn, contribute to the ease with which young people solve complex math problems. (Bob Daemmrich/Stock Boston)

pears on tests of mathematical reasoning, primarily on complex word problems and geometry (Bielinski & Davison, 1998; Hyde, Fenema, & Lamon, 1990).

Some researchers believe that the gender gap in mathematics—especially the tendency for many more boys to be extremely talented in math—is genetic. One common assumption is that sex-related differences in mathematical ability are rooted in boys' biologically based superior spatial reasoning. See the Variations box above for a discussion of this issue.

Although heredity is involved, social pressures also contribute to girls' underrepresentation among the mathematically talented. The mathematics gender gap is related to pupil attitudes and self-esteem. Earlier in this chapter, we noted that long before sex-related differences in math achievement are present, children view math as a masculine subject, and parents believe that boys are better at it. Furthermore, girls' tendency to attribute their academic failures to low ability (rather than insufficient effort) reduces their self-confidence and promotes high anxiety in achievement situations (see Chapter 11). Girls display this learned-helpless style particularly strongly in mathematics. Over time, girls start to regard math as less useful for their future lives and are more likely than boys to stop taking math courses when they are not mandatory (Byrnes & Takahira, 1993; Catsambis, 1994). The result of this chain of events is that girls—even those who are highly talented academically—are less likely to develop abstract mathematical concepts and effective problem-solving strategies.

A positive sign is that sex-related differences in mathematical reasoning, as in the verbal arena, have declined steadily over the past several decades. Paralleling this change is an increase in girls' enrollment in advanced high school math and science courses, although girls still take fewer of these courses than do boys (Campbell, Voelkl, & Donahue, 1997; Davenport et al., 1998).

Clearly, extra steps must be taken to promote girls' interest in and confidence at math and science. By the end of high school, sex-related differences in attitudes are much larger than in test performance. Many more girls have the capacity to study advanced math and science than choose to do so. When parents hold nonstereotyped gender-role values, daughters are less likely to show declines in math and science achievement at adolescence (Updegraff, McHale, & Crouter, 1996). In schools, teachers need to do a better job of demonstrating the relevance of math and science to everyday life. Girls, especially, respond positively toward math and science taught from an applied, hands-on perspective than from a purely book-learning approach (Eccles, 1994). At the same time, teachers must ensure that girls participate fully in hands-on group activities and are not reduced to a passive role by boys' more assertive style of peer interaction (Jovanovic & King, 1998).

Finally, a common assumption is that girls show better math and science achievement in single-sex secondary schools, where they may encounter fewer stereotyped messages and more same-sex role models. Although past research supported this belief, recent evidence indicates that sex-segregated schools do not enhance boys' or girls' learning or self-esteem (Bryk, Lee, & Holland, 1993; LePore & Warren, 1997). Perhaps because both single-sex and coeducational schools are sharpening their focus on reducing gender discrimination, the makeup of the student body is less relevant today than it once was for girls' academic development.

PERSONALITY TRAITS

Sex-related differences in personality are in line with gender stereotypes. Traits most often studied include emotional sensitivity, compliance and dependency, depression, and aggression.

■ **EMOTIONAL SENSITIVITY.** Females are more emotionally sensitive than are males, a difference that appears quite early. Beginning in the preschool years, girls perform slightly better than boys when asked to make judgments of others' emotional states using nonverbal cues (Hall, 1978). Except for anger, girls also express feelings more freely and intensely, using language and facial and body gestures (Hall & Halberstadt, 1981; Saarni, 1993).

It would be reasonable to expect these differences to extend to empathy, sympathy, and prosocial behavior, but so far the evidence is mixed. On self-report measures, girls and women consistently score higher than boys and men. But when observed for behavioral signs, 1- to 2-year-old girls display greater concern for a distressed person than do boys, but preschool-through adolescent-age youngsters show no difference. Girls show a slight advantage in prosocial responding. It is greatest for being kind and considerate, very small for helping another (Eisenberg & Fabes, 1998; Eisenberg & Lennon, 1983; Zahn-Waxler et al., 1992).

As with other attributes, both biological and environmental explanations for sex-related differences in emotional sensitivity exist. One possibility is that females are genetically prewired to be more emotionally sensitive as a way of ensuring that they will be well prepared for the caregiving role. Yet research suggests that girls are not naturally more nurturant. Before age 5, boys and girls spend equal amounts of time talking to and playing with babies (Fogel et al., 1987). In middle childhood, boys' willingness to relate to infants declines, but they continue to respond with just as much care and affection to pets and elderly relatives (Melson & Fogel, 1988). Furthermore, sex-related differences in emotional sensitivity are not present in adulthood when parents interact with their own babies. In Chapter 10, we saw that fathers are very affectionate with their infants and are just as competent caregivers as are mothers. And in Chapter 4, we noted that men and women react similarly to the sound of a crying baby.

Cultural expectations that girls be warm and expressive and boys be distant and controlled seem largely responsible for the gender gap in emotional sensitivity. In infancy, mothers respond more often to a girl's happiness and distress than to a boy's (Malatesta et al., 1986). And during childhood, parents are more likely to rely on inductive discipline with girls (which promotes sympathetic concern) and to pressure them to be kind and considerate (Block, 1978; Zahn-Waxler, Cole, & Barrett, 1991). In addition, recall that parents more often label emotions when conversing with daughters. They are also more willing to discuss sadness with girls (Kuebli & Fivush, 1992). Taken together, these findings suggest that girls receive far more encouragement to express and reflect on feelings than do boys.

Girls' greater emotional sensitivity is probably environmentally determined, since boys are just as caring and affectionate in certain situations— for example, when interacting with a cherished pet.
(Camille Tokerud/Photo Researchers, Inc.)

■ **COMPLIANCE AND DEPENDENCY.** Beginning in the preschool years, girls are more compliant than are boys, to both adult and peer demands. Girls also seek help and information from adults more often and score higher in dependency on personality tests (Feingold, 1994). There is widespread agreement that these patterns of behavior are learned, and they have much to do with activity environments in which boys and girls spend their time.

From an early age, girls are encouraged to participate in adult-structured activities at home and in preschool and, consequently, spend more time near adults. In contrast, boys are attracted to activities in which adults are minimally involved or entirely absent (Powlishta, Serbin, & Moller, 1993). As a result, boys and girls engage in very different social behaviors. Compliance and bids for help and attention appear more often in adult-structured contexts, whereas assertiveness, leadership, and creative use of materials occur more often in unstructured pursuits (Carpenter, 1983).

Ideally, boys and girls should experience a balanced array of activities to develop both the capacity to lead and assert as well as to comply with others' directives. In one study, the assertive and compliant tendencies of preschoolers of both sexes were easily modified by assigning them to classroom activities that differed in degree of adult structure (Carpenter, Huston, & Holt, 1986).

FIGURE 13.9

Change in depressive symptoms from age 12 to 20 in a cross-sectional study of over 12,000 Norwegian adolescents. Girls showed a more rapid rise in depression around the time of puberty than did boys. Similar trends occur in other industrialized nations.

(From L. Wichstrøm, 1999, "The Emergence of Gender Difference in Depressed Mood During Adolescence: The Role of Intensified Gender Socialization," *Developmental Psychology, 35,* p. 237. Copyright © 1999 by the American Psychological Association. Reprinted by permission of the publisher and author.)

■ **DEPRESSION.** Depression—feeling sad, frustrated, and hopeless about life, accompanied by loss of pleasure in most activities and disturbances in sleep, appetite, concentration, and energy—is the most common psychological problem of adolescence. About 15 to 20 percent of teenagers have had one or more major depressive episodes (a rate comparable to that of adults); from 2 to 8 percent are chronically depressed—gloomy and self-critical for many months and sometimes years (Birmaher et al., 1996; Kessler et al., 1994). Depression is not absent in the first decade of life; about 1 to 2 percent of children are seriously depressed, 70 to 75 percent of whom continue to display severe depression in adolescence (Kovacs et al., 1994). Yet as Figure 13.9 shows, depressive symptoms start to increase around the time of puberty. They occur twice as often in adolescent girls as in adolescent boys—a difference sustained throughout the lifespan.

Researchers believe that diverse combinations of biological and environmental factors lead to depression; the precise blend differs from one individual to another. As we saw in Chapter 3, kinship studies reveal that heredity plays an important role, since the concordance rate for severe depression is higher among identical than fraternal twins. Genes can promote depression by affecting the balance of neurotransmitters in the brain, the development of brain regions involved in inhibiting negative emotion, or the body's hormonal response to stress (Cicchetti & Toth, 1998a).

But experience can also activate depression, promoting any of the biological changes just described. Parents of depressed children

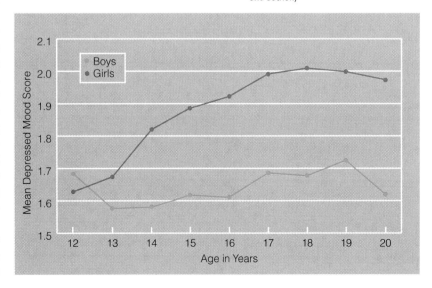

and adolescents have a high incidence of depression and other psychological disorders. Although a genetic risk may be passed from parent to child, in earlier chapters we saw that depressed or otherwise stressed parents often engage in maladaptive parenting. As a result, their child's emotional self-regulation, attachment, and self-esteem may be impaired, with serious consequences for many cognitive and social skills (Garber, Braafladt, & Weiss, 1995; Garber et al., 1991). Depressed youths usually display a learned-helpless attributional style, in which they view positive academic and social outcomes as beyond their control. Consequently, myriad events can spark depression in a vulnerable young person. Sometimes depression follows a profound loss, such as parental divorce or the end of a close friendship or dating relationship. At other times, failing at something important sets it off.

Why are girls more prone to depression? Biological changes at puberty cannot account for the gender gap, since it is limited to industrialized nations. In developing countries, rates of depression are similar for males and females and occasionally higher for males (Culbertson, 1997).

Instead, the developmental challenges of adolescence combined with gender-typed coping styles seem to be responsible. Early maturing girls, who often have a negative body image (see Chapter 5), are prone to depression, especially when they face other life stresses. (Recall from Chapter 11 that perceived physical appearance is the strongest contributor to overall self-esteem.) At the same time, the gender intensification that girls experience in early adolescence often strengthens passivity, dependency, and selflessness—maladaptive approaches to the tasks expected of teenagers in complex cultures and to stressful life events (Nolen-Hoeksema & Girgus, 1994). Consistent with this explanation, adolescents who identify strongly with "feminine" traits are more depressed, regardless of their sex (Hart & Thompson, 1996; Wichstrøm, 1999). And girls with either an androgynous or masculine gender identity show a much lower rate of depressive symptoms—one no different from that of masculine-identified boys (Wilson & Cairns, 1988).

Severely depressed teenagers are prone to suicidal thoughts, which all too often are translated into action (see Chapter 11, page 459). Adolescent depression is also associated with persistent anxiety, poor school performance, drug abuse, lawbreaking, auto accidents, and future problems in employment, marriage, and child rearing (Harrington, Rutter, & Fombonne, 1996; Kovacs, 1996). Unfortunately, teachers and parents tend to overlook teenagers' depressive symptoms; 70 to 80 percent do not receive any treatment. Because of the popular stereotype of adolescence as a period of storm and stress, many adults interpret depressive reactions as just a passing phase (Strober, McCracken, & Hanna, 1990).

■ **AGGRESSION.** Aggression has attracted more research attention than any other sex-related difference. In Chapter 12, we noted that boys are more *overtly aggressive* than are girls. Beginning in the preschool years, they engage in more physical and verbal attacks. By adolescence, they are far more likely to be involved in antisocial behavior and violent crime.

But recall that preschool and school-age girls exceed boys in another form of hostility—*relational aggression.* As Figure 13.10 shows, the percentage of girls who often engage in rumor spreading and social exclusion is just as great as the percentage of boys who frequently engage in direct attacks (Crick & Grotpeter, 1995). Since most research focuses on physical and verbal assaults, it underestimates girls' aggressiveness.

Look again at Figure 13.10, and you will see that a few children are gender-atypical: girls who display high overt aggression, boys who display high relational aggression. Overt aggression is associated with *externalizing forms* of adjustment problems—defiance in the face of parental discipline, blaming others for one's own wrongdoing, inflated self-esteem, and lack of concern with victims' suffering (see Chapter 12). Notice that these are mascu-

FIGURE 13.10

Percentage of boys and girls who often used overt and relational aggression in a study of third through sixth graders. Boys expressed their antagonism directly, through physical and verbal attacks. In contrast, girls used indirect forms of aggression aimed at damaging another's peer relationships. When both types of aggression are considered, girls are just as aggressive as boys. (Adapted from Crick & Grotpeter, 1995.)

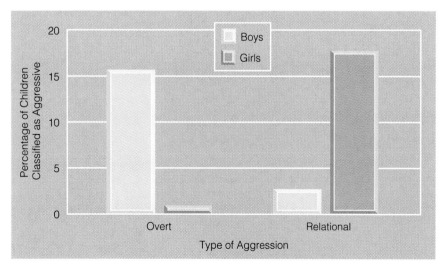

line-stereotyped attributes in exaggerated form. Relational aggression also predicts externalizing difficulties. But relationally aggressive children often have *internalizing problems* as well—high anxiety and low self-esteem, which are feminine-stereotyped attributes (Crick, 1997; Crick & Grotpeter, 1995).

Compared with gender-typical aggressive children, gender-atypical aggressors have more severe emotional and behavior problems (Crick, 1997). Children who violate their gender role in the realm of aggression may be targets of especially intolerant and rejecting feedback from adults and peers—reactions that compound their adjustment difficulties.

Our discussion of the origins of sex-related differences in aggression focuses on overt verbal and physical acts. At present, little is known about factors that contribute to the development of relational aggression.

BIOLOGICAL INFLUENCES. Because males' greater overt aggression is evident early in life, generalizes across cultures, and is found in many animal species, almost all researchers agree that biology must be involved. Earlier we mentioned that androgen hormones are related to aggression in animals; they are also believed to play a role in humans. But think back to our discussion of children with CAH. Although they were exposed prenatally to abnormally high levels of androgens, they were not more aggressive. This suggests that in humans, only a predisposition for aggression results from androgen exposure. Researchers currently believe that the impact of male sex hormones is indirect. They affect certain behaviors that, when combined with situational influences, lead to a higher likelihood of aggressive outcomes.

One possibility is that prenatal androgens promote physical activity, which may or may not be translated into aggression, depending on the situation (Archer, 1994). For example, a very active child who often participates in large-group physical activities, such as water fights and tackle football, is likely to become more overtly aggressive than a child who participates in nonaggressive pursuits, such as small-group quiet play and track or swimming.

Another hypothesis is that prenatal hormones influence brain functioning in ways that affect children's emotional reactions. According to this view, hormone levels might induce more frequent displays of excitement, anger, or anxiety, which have an increased likelihood of resulting in aggression in the presence of certain environmental conditions. Indeed, there is evidence that early hormone levels (measured at birth from umbilical cord blood samples) predict excited emotional states for boys during the first 2 years of life, although no relationships exist for girls (Marcus et al., 1985).

Besides the prenatal period, adolescence is a second phase in which hormonal changes have implications for aggressive behavior. Adolescent boys who are high in androgens are more dominant and, perhaps for this reason, more likely to respond with aggression when provoked by peers (Olweus et al., 1988; Tremblay et al., 1997). In one study, higher estrogens and androgens were linked to more frequent expressions of anger by adolescent girls in a laboratory discussion session with their parents (Inoff-Germain et al., 1988).

Although much more research is needed, current evidence suggests that multiple pathways exist between sex hormones and overt aggression, that each involves a complex series of steps, and that each may vary with the sex and age of the child. It is also clear that whether hormonally induced responses, such as activity level or emotional state, are channeled into aggressive acts depends on environmental conditions.

ENVIRONMENTAL INFLUENCES. In Chapter 12, we showed how coercive child-rearing practices and strife-ridden families promote aggressive behavior. For several reasons, boys are more likely to be affected by these interaction patterns than are girls. Parents more often use physical punishment with boys, which encourages them to adopt the same tactics in their own relationships. In addition, parents are less likely to interpret fighting as aggressive when it occurs among boys. The stereotype reflected in the familiar saying "Boys will be boys" may lead many adults to overlook male hostility unless it is extreme. This sets up conditions in which it is encouraged, or at least tolerated (Condry & Ross, 1985). In view of these findings, it is not surprising that school-age boys expect less parental disapproval and report feeling less guilty for overt aggression than do girls (Perry, Perry, & Weiss, 1989).

Furthermore, arguing between husband and wife, although stimulating aggression among all family members, more often triggers hostility in boys. In a study in which 2-year-olds overheard angry verbal exchanges between adults while playing with a familiar peer in a laboratory, girls tended to show fearful, withdrawing reactions, such as freezing in place and covering or hiding their faces. In contrast, boys engaged in more aggression, lashing out at their playmates (Cummings, Iannotti, & Zahn-Waxler, 1985). During the school years, boys report feeling more hostile than do girls after observing angry exchanges between adults (Hennessy, Rabideau, & Cicchetti, 1994).

Putting together all the evidence, we can see that boys have a higher likelihood of becoming embroiled in circumstances that serve as training ground for aggressive and antisocial behavior. Biological predispositions and encouragement from the social environment, acting in complex combination, are responsible.

BRIEF REVIEW

Boys and girls differ in a variety of mental abilities and personality traits. Girls show more rapid early language development and higher reading achievement. They are also more emotionally sensitive, compliant, dependent, prone to depression, and relationally aggressive. Boys are advantaged in certain spatial skills and complex mathematical reasoning and engage in more overt aggression.

Although biological factors are involved in some characteristics, both boys and girls can acquire all of them, and social experience affects the size of each difference. Finally, in view of the many ways it is possible for human beings to vary, our overall conclusion must be that males and females are more alike in developmental potential than they are different from each other.

ASK YOURSELF . . .

◆ *Thirteen-year-old Donna reached puberty early and feels negatively about her physical appearance. She also has a feminine gender identity. Explain why Donna is at risk for depression.*

◆ **CONNECTIONS**
Return to Chapter 11, page 471, and review sex-related differences in children's friendships. Can the nature of girls' friendships shed light on why they tend to express hostility through relational aggression? (Hint: Consult Chapter 12, page 511.)

Describe the consequences of overt and relational aggression for children's peer acceptance. (See Chapter 15, page 606.)

Developing Non-Gender-Stereotyped Children

The Milestones table on the following page provides an overview of changes in gender typing considered in this chapter. We have seen that children's developmental possibilities can be seriously limited by persistent gender stereotypes in their culture. Although many researchers and laypeople recognize the importance of rearing children who feel free to express their human qualities without fear of violating gender-role expectations, no easy recipe exists for accomplishing this difficult task. It must be tackled on many fronts—in the home, at school, and in the wider society.

Throughout our discussion, we have mentioned ways in which gender stereotyping and gender-role adoption can be reduced. But even children who are fortunate enough to grow up in homes and schools that minimize stereotyping will eventually encounter it in the media and in what men and women typically do in their communities. Consequently, children need early experiences that repeatedly counteract their readiness to absorb our culture's extensive network of gender-linked associations.

Sandra Bem (1993, 1998) suggests that parents and teachers make a special effort to delay young children's learning of gender-stereotyped messages, since preschoolers readily assume that cultural practices determine a person's sex. Adults can begin by eliminating traditional gender roles from their own behavior and from the alternatives they provide for children. For example, mothers and fathers can take turns making dinner, bathing children, and driving the family car, and they can provide sons and daughters with both trucks and dolls and pink and blue clothing. Teachers can make sure that all children spend some time each day in adult-structured and unstructured activities. Also, efforts can be made to shield children from media presentations that indicate males and females differ in what they can do.

Once children notice the wide array of gender stereotypes in their society, parents and teachers can point out exceptions. For example, they can arrange for children to see men and women pursuing nontraditional careers. And they can reason with children, explaining that interests and skills, not sex, should determine a person's occupation. Furthermore, older children can be told about the historical roots and current consequences of gender inequalities—why, for example, there have been few female presidents and prime ministers, why fathers rarely stay home with their children, and why stereotyped views of men and women are hard to change. As these efforts help children build concepts

Gender Typing

Age	Gender Stereotyping and Gender-Role Adoption	Gender Identity	Sex-Related Differences in Mental Abilities and Personality Traits
1½–5 years	■ "Gender-appropriate" play preferences emerge and increase. ■ Gender stereotyping of activities, occupations, and behaviors develops. ■ Preference for same-sex peers emerges and increases.	■ Gender constancy develops in a three-stage sequence: gender labeling, gender stability, and gender consistency. ■ By the end of this period, gender-linked self-evaluations develop.	■ Girls show more rapid language development during the second year, after which boys catch up. ■ Girls' greater emotional sensitivity emerges and persists into adulthood. ■ Girls' greater compliance and dependency is evident and persists into adulthood. ■ Boys' greater overt aggression and girls' greater relational aggression emerge and persist into adulthood.
6–11 years	■ Knowledge of gender stereotypes expands, especially in areas of personality traits and achievement. ■ Gender stereotyping becomes more flexible. ■ Large-group play emerges among boys. ■ Girls experiment with "cross-gender" activities; boys' preference for "masculine" pursuits increases.	■ "Masculine" gender identity strengthens among boys; girls' gender identity becomes more androgynous.	■ Girls are ahead in reading achievement throughout the school years. ■ Boys' advantage in certain spatial abilities emerges and persists throughout the lifespan.
12–20 years	■ Gender-role conformity increases in early adolescence and then declines, especially for girls. ■ Preference for same-sex peers becomes less pronounced after puberty.	■ Gender identities of both sexes become more traditional in early adolescence, a trend that gradually declines, especially for girls.	■ Boys' advantage in mathematical reasoning emerges. ■ Depressive symptoms increase, occurring more often in girls than in boys. ■ Boys' greater overt aggression translates into much higher involvement in antisocial behavior and violent crime, a trend accounted for by a small number of adolescents.

Note: These milestones represent overall age trends. Individual differences exist in the precise age at which each milestone is attained and in the extent of gender typing.

of themselves and their social world that are not limited by a masculine–feminine dichotomy, they contribute to the transformation of societal values. And they bring us closer to a time when people will be released from the constraints of traditional gender roles.

SUMMARY

Explain how the study of gender typing has responded to societal change.

♦ Largely because of progress in women's rights, the adoption of gender-typed beliefs and behavior is no longer regarded as essential for healthy psychological development. Researchers are more interested in how children might be released from gender-based definitions of appropriate behavior. In this text, **sex-related** refers to comparisons between males and females that make no inferences about the source of the difference, **gender** to judgments about biological and environmental influences.

GENDER STEREOTYPES AND GENDER ROLES

Cite examples of gender stereotypes, and describe the development of gender stereotyping from early childhood into adolescence.

♦ Despite recent progress in women's rights, gender stereotypes have remained essentially the same. **Instrumental traits** continue to be regarded as masculine, **expressive traits** as feminine—a dichotomy that is widely held around the world. Stereotyping of physical characteristics, occupations, and activities is also common.

♦ Children begin to acquire **gender stereotypes** and **gender roles** early in the preschool years. By middle childhood, they are aware of many stereotypes, including activities, occupations, personality traits, and achievement areas. Preschoolers' understanding of gender stereotypes is inflexible. Gains in **gender-stereotype flexibility** occur during middle childhood and adolescence; children develop a more open-minded view of what males and females can do, although they often do not approve of males who violate gender-role expectations.

Cite individual, sex-related, and ethnic differences in gender stereotyping, and discuss the relationship of gender stereotyping to gender-role adoption.

♦ Children acquire the components of gender stereotyping—activities, behaviors, occupations, and personality traits—in different patterns and to different degrees. Boys hold more rigid gender-stereotyped views than do girls, white children more than black children. Although SES differences do not exist in childhood, middle-SES adolescents and adults hold more flexible views than do their lower-SES counterparts.

♦ Awareness of gender stereotypes is only weakly related to gender-role adoption. Stereotype flexibility, however, is a moderately good predictor of children's willingness to cross gender lines during the school years.

INFLUENCES ON GENDER STEREOTYPING AND GENDER-ROLE ADOPTION

Discuss the role of biology in gender stereotyping and gender-role adoption, including cross-cultural evidence and the influence of hormones.

♦ Cross-cultural similarities in gender stereotypes and gender-role adoption have been used to support the role of biology in **gender typing.** However, great diversity exists in the extent to which cultures endorse the instrumental–expressive dichotomy, and cases of traditional gender-role reversal exist.

♦ Prenatal androgen levels may underlie sex-related differences in play styles, which contribute to children's preference for same-sex playmates. Research on children with congenital adrenal hyperplasia (CAH) supports the role of androgens in certain aspects of "masculine" gender-role adoption. CAH girls prefer vehicle and building toys and, to a lesser extent, boys as play partners. However, other gender-role preferences of CAH children may be due to environmental pressures. In instances in which children are reared as members of the other sex because of ambiguous genitals, gender typing is usually consistent with sex of rearing, regardless of genetic sex.

Discuss environmental influences on gender stereotyping and gender-role adoption, including expectations and treatment by parents, teachers, and peers; observational learning; and the impact of siblings.

♦ Beginning in infancy, parents hold gender-stereotyped perceptions and expectations of boys and girls and create different environments for them. By the preschool years, parents reinforce their children for many "gender-appropriate" play activities and behaviors. During middle childhood, they demand greater independence from boys in achievement situations, hold gender-stereotyped beliefs about children's abilities in various school subjects, and grant boys more freedom in their everyday lives. Fathers differentiate between boys and girls more than mothers do. Also, each parent takes special responsibility for the gender typing of the same-sex child.

♦ Teachers reinforce children of both sexes for "feminine" behavior and also act in ways that promote traditional gender roles. Besides direct pressure from adults, children have many opportunities to observe gender-typed models in the surrounding environment. When children are exposed to nonstereotyped models, such as parents who cross traditional gender lines in household tasks or career choice, they are less traditional in their beliefs and behaviors.

♦ When interacting with children of their own sex, boys and girls receive further reinforcement for "gender-appropriate" play and develop different styles of social influence. Boys more often rely on commands, threats, and physical force, girls on polite requests and persuasion—differences that strengthen sex segregation.

♦ The impact of siblings on gender typing varies with birth order and family size. In small, two-child families, younger children tend to imitate the gender-role behavior of their older sibling. In large families, same-sex siblings often strive to be different from one another. Consequently, they are likely to be less stereotyped in their interests and personality characteristics.

GENDER IDENTITY

Explain the meaning of androgyny, and describe and evaluate the accuracy of social learning and cognitive-developmental views of the development of gender identity in early childhood.

- Researchers measure **gender identity** by asking children and adults to rate themselves on "masculine" and "feminine" personality traits. Although most people have traditional identities, some are **androgynous,** scoring high on both masculine and feminine characteristics. At present, the masculine component of androgyny is largely responsible for its association with superior psychological adjustment.
- According to social learning theory, preschoolers first acquire gender-typed responses through modeling and reinforcement and only later organize them into cognitions about themselves. Cognitive-developmental theory suggests that **gender constancy** must be achieved before children can develop gender-typed behavior.
- Children master gender constancy by moving through three stages: **gender labeling, gender stability,** and **gender consistency.** Understanding of gender constancy is associated with attainment of conservation and opportunities to learn about genital differences between the sexes. In contrast to cognitive-developmental predictions, "gender-appropriate" behavior is acquired long before gender constancy. However, other cognitive attainments—gender labeling, gender stability, and gender-linked self-evaluations—strengthen preschoolers' gender-role adoption.

What changes in gender identity typically occur in middle childhood and adolescence?

- During middle childhood, boys strengthen their identification with the "masculine" role, whereas girls become more androgynous. The greater prestige of "masculine" characteristics makes them attractive to girls. At the same time, parents and peers are more tolerant of girls as opposed to boys crossing gender lines.
- Early adolescence is a period of **gender intensification:** the gender identities of both sexes become more traditional. Physical and cognitive changes prompt young teenagers to spend more time thinking about themselves in gender-linked ways, and gender-typed pressures from parents and peers increase. As young people move toward a mature personal identity, highly stereotypic self-perceptions decline. Individual differences in gender identity persist that are moderately related to gender-role behavior.

Explain how gender schema theory accounts for the persistence of gender stereotypes and gender-role preferences.

- **Gender schema theory** is an information-processing approach to gender typing that combines social learning and cognitive-developmental features. As children learn gender-typed preferences and behaviors, they form masculine and feminine categories, or gender schemas, that they apply to themselves and use to interpret their world. Schema-consistent information is attended to and approached, whereas schema-inconsistent information is ignored, misinterpreted, or actively rejected. As a result, children learn much more about "gender-appropriate" than "gender-inappropriate" activities and behaviors.

TO WHAT EXTENT DO BOYS AND GIRLS *REALLY* DIFFER IN GENDER-STEREOTYPED ATTRIBUTES?

Describe sex-related differences in mental abilities and personality attributes, noting factors that contribute to those differences.

- Girls are ahead in early language development, score better in reading and writing achievement, and are more emotionally sensitive, compliant, dependent, prone to depression, and relationally aggressive. Boys are advantaged in certain spatial skills and complex mathematical reasoning and engage in more overt aggression.
- Biological factors contribute to sex-related differences in language development and spatial and math performance. At the same time, adult encouragement and learning opportunities play a strong role. Girls' greater emotional sensitivity, compliance, and dependency are largely due to gender-stereotyped expectations and child-rearing practices.
- Depression is the most common psychological problem of the teenage years. The higher rate of severe depression in adolescent girls is the combined result of the challenges of adolescence and gender-typed coping styles. Gender intensification in early adolescence often strengthens passivity, dependency, and selflessness in girls, which interfere with their mastery of developmental tasks and their ability to handle stressful life events.
- Prenatal and pubertal hormones seem to contribute to greater overt aggression in males. However, hormones exert their effects indirectly, by influencing activity level, emotional reactions, or dominance, which increase the likelihood of aggressive behavior under certain conditions. Powerful environmental influences on aggression include coercive child-rearing practices and strife-ridden families. Parents are more likely to use physical punishment with boys and to overlook their aggressive acts. In addition, boys react with greater hostility to parental arguments than do girls.

DEVELOPING NON-GENDER-STEREOTYPED CHILDREN

Cite ways to reduce gender stereotyping in children.

- Parents and teachers can counteract young children's readiness to absorb gender-linked associations by eliminating traditional gender roles from their own behavior and from the alternatives they provide for children. They can also shield children from gender-stereotyped media messages. Once children notice gender stereotypes, adults can point out exceptions and discuss the arbitrariness of many gender inequalities in society.

IMPORTANT TERMS AND CONCEPTS

androgyny (p. 539)

expressive traits (p. 523)

gender (p. 522)

gender consistency (p. 539)

gender constancy (p. 539)

gender identity (p. 522)

gender intensification (p. 541)

gender labeling (p. 539)

gender roles (p. 522)

gender schema theory (p. 541)

gender stability (p. 539)

gender stereotypes (p. 522)

gender-stereotype flexibility (p. 524)

gender typing (p. 522)

instrumental traits (p. 523)

sex related (p. 522)

The Family

THINK BACK TO your own childhood, and jot down a brief description of the first ten memories that come to mind. When I ask my students to do this, about half the events they list involve their families. This emphasis on the family is not surprising, since it is the child's first and longest-lasting context for development. Recall from Chapter 5 that compared with other species, human children develop slowly, requiring years of support and teaching before they are ready to be independent. Our gradual journey to maturity has left an imprint on human social organization everywhere: Families are pervasive, and parents are universally important in the lives of children.

Of course, other contexts also mold children's development, but in power and breadth of influence, none equals the family. In previous chapters, we saw that the family introduces children to the physical world through the opportunities it provides for play and exploration of objects. It also creates unique bonds between people. The attachments children form with parents and siblings usually last a lifetime, and they serve as models for relationships in the wider world of neighborhood and school. Within the family, children experience their first social conflicts. Discipline by parents and arguments with siblings provide important lessons in compliance and cooperation and opportunities to learn how to influence the behavior of others. Finally, within the family, children learn the language, skills, and social and moral values of their culture.

We begin our discussion of the family by examining the reasons that this social unit came into being and has survived for thousands of years. Then we describe the current view of the family as a *social system* with many interacting influences on the child. Next, we look closely at the family as the core socializing agency of society. We consider parents' child-rearing styles, the many factors that shape them, and their consequences for children's development.

In the second half of this chapter, we take up the significance for child development of recent social changes that have led to a diversity of family lifestyles. And families of all walks of life are affected by high rates of divorce and remarriage, the dramatic increase in employed mothers, and the need for high-quality child care. Finally, the modern family is especially vulnerable to a breakdown in protective, emotionally supportive parent–child relationships. We conclude by considering the origins and consequences of child maltreatment.

Evolutionary Origins

The family in its most common form—a lifelong commitment between a man and woman who feed, shelter, and nurture their children until they reach maturity—arose tens of thousands of years

A lifelong commitment between a man and woman who care for their young until they reach maturity arose tens of thousands of years ago among our hunting-and-gathering ancestors because it enhanced survival. This modern hunting-and-gathering mother of Central Africa cracks recently gathered nuts with her children while the father hunts for game.

(I. DeVore/Anthro-Photo)

ago among our hunting-and-gathering ancestors. Many other species live in social groups, but only rarely do they organize themselves into familylike units. Only 3 percent of birds and mammals, for example, form families (Emlen, 1995). Even among apes and monkeys, our closest evolutionary ancestors, families are almost nonexistent. Most of the time, primates cling to and are nursed by their mothers until they can move about independently. After that time, they travel with the larger group for protection but, unlike human children, must forage to feed themselves (Lancaster & Witten, 1980).

Anthropologists believe that bipedalism—the ability to walk upright on two legs—was an important evolutionary step that led to the human family unit. Once arms were freed to carry things, our ancestors found it easier to cooperate and share, especially in providing for the young. Men usually traveled in search of game; women gathered fruit and vegetables that served as a temporary food supply when hunting was unsuccessful. The human family pattern in which a man and woman assumed special responsibility for their own children emerged because it enhanced survival. It ensured a relatively even balance of male hunters and female gatherers within a social group, thereby creating the greatest possible protection against starvation during times when game was scarce (Lancaster & Whitten, 1980).

Kinship groups expanded to include ties with other relatives, such as grandparents, aunts, uncles, and cousins, because larger kin networks offered greater protection in the face of competition with other humans for resources. Within these clans, elders no longer able to reproduce helped their children and other younger relatives reproduce successfully by assisting with mate selection and child care. In this way, they increased the chances that their own genetic heritage would continue (Davis & Daly, 1997). Furthermore, the economic and social obligations of family members to one another were so important to the survival of early humans that they could not be entrusted to rational thinking alone. The capacity for strong emotional bonds evolved to foster long-term commitment among parents, children, and other family members (Nesse, 1990; Williams, 1997).

Ninety-nine percent of the history of our species was spent in the hunting-and-gathering stage. Although this form of society no longer characterizes most contemporary cultures, it has left a lasting imprint on family life (Brown, 1991). Indeed, hunters and gatherers who live today as they did in prehistoric times vary in many of the same ways that families in industrialized nations do: in their rate of divorce; in the extent to which men and women share work roles; in fathers', grandparents', and other relatives' involvement in child rearing; and in their kindness toward children (Hewlett, 1992a).

Functions of the Family

Besides promoting survival of its own members, the family unit of our evolutionary ancestors performed vital services for society. Each of the following functions must be carried out for a society to survive:

▒ *Reproduction.* Replacements for dying members must be provided.

▒ *Economic services.* Goods and services must be produced and distributed.

▒ *Social order.* Procedures must exist for reducing conflict and maintaining orderly conduct.

▒ *Socialization.* The young must be trained by mature members to become competent, participating members of society.

- *Emotional support.* Procedures must exist for binding individuals together, dealing with emotional crises, and fostering a sense of commitment and purpose in each person.

In the early history of our species, families probably served all or most of these functions. But as societies became more complex, the demands placed on the family became too much for it to sustain alone. Consequently, other institutions developed to assist with certain functions, and families became linked to larger social structures. For example, political and legal institutions assumed responsibility for ensuring societal order, and schools built on the family's socialization function. Religious institutions supplemented both child-rearing and emotional support functions by offering family members educational services and a set of common beliefs that enhanced their sense of purpose and shared goals (Parke & Kellam, 1994).

Finally, although some family members still carry out economic tasks together (as in family-run farms and businesses), this function has largely been taken over by institutions that make up the world of work. The modern family consumes far more goods and services than it produces. Consequently, whereas children used to be important contributors to the family's economic well-being, today they are economic liabilities. According to a conservative estimate, today's new parents will spend about $250,000 to rear a child from birth through 4 years of college—one factor that has contributed to the declining birth rate in modern industrialized nations (U.S. Department of Labor, 1999).

Although some functions have been taken over by or are shared with other institutions, three important ones—reproduction, socialization, and emotional support—remain primarily the province of the family. These functions are especially concerned with children, since they include giving birth to, rearing, and nurturing the young. Researchers interested in finding out how modern families fulfill these functions take a **social systems perspective,** viewing the family as a complex set of interacting relationships influenced by the larger social context.

The Family as a Social System

The social systems perspective on family functioning grew out of researchers' efforts to describe and explain the complex patterns of interaction between family members. As we review its features, you will see that it has much in common with Bronfenbrenner's ecological systems theory, discussed in Chapter 1.

When child development specialists first studied the family in the middle part of this century, they investigated in a very limited way. Most research focused on the mother–child relationship and emphasized one-way effects of child-rearing practices on children's behavior. Today, family systems theorists recognize that children are not mechanically shaped by their parents. You already know from earlier chapters that *bidirectional influences* exist in which the behaviors of each family member affect those of others. The very term *family system* implies that the responses of all family members are interrelated (Parke & Buriel, 1998; Sameroff, 1994). These system influences operate both directly and indirectly.

DIRECT INFLUENCES

Recently, as I passed through the checkout counter at the supermarket, I witnessed the following two episodes, in which parents and children directly influenced each other:

- Little Danny stood next to tempting rows of candy as his mother lifted groceries from the cart onto the counter. "Pleeeease, can I have it, Mom?" begged Danny, holding up a large package of bubble gum. "Do you have a dollar? Just one?"
  "No, not today," his mother answered softly. "Remember, we picked out your special cereal. That's what I need the dollar for." Danny's mother handed him the cereal while gently taking the bubble gum from his hand and returning it to the shelf. "Here, let's pay the man," she said, as she lifted Danny into the empty grocery cart where he could see the checkout counter.

social systems perspective A view of the family as a complex set of interacting relationships influenced by the larger social context.

▓ Three-year-old Meg sat in the cart while her mother transferred groceries to the counter. Meg turned around, grabbed a bunch of bananas, and started to pull them apart.

"Stop it, Meg!" shouted her mom, who snatched the bananas from Meg's hand. Meg reached for a chocolate bar from a nearby shelf while her mother wrote the check. "Meg, how many times have I told you, DON'T TOUCH!" Loosening the candy from Meg's tight little grip, Meg's mother slapped her hand. Meg's face turned red with anger as she began to wail. "Keep this up, and you'll get it when we get home," threatened Meg's mom as they left the store.

These observations fit with a wealth of research on the family system. Many studies show that when parents are firm but patient (like Danny's mom), children tend to comply with their requests. And when children cooperate, their parents are likely to be warm and gentle in the future. In contrast, parents who discipline with harshness and impatience (like Meg's mom) have children who refuse and rebel. And because children's misbehavior is stressful for parents, they may increase their use of punishment, leading to more unruliness by the child (Dodge, Pettit, & Bates, 1994; Patterson, Reid, & Dishion, 1992). In these examples, the behavior of one family member helps sustain a form of interaction in another that either promotes or undermines children's well-being.

INDIRECT INFLUENCES

The impact of family relationships on child development becomes even more complicated when we consider that interaction between any two members is affected by others present in the setting. Recall from Chapter 1 that Bronfenbrenner called these indirect influences the effect of *third parties.* Researchers have become intensely interested in how a range of relationships—mother with father, parent with sibling, grandparent with parent—modifies the child's direct experiences in the family. In fact, as the From Research to Practice box on the following page reveals, a child's birth has a third-party impact on parents' interaction, which returns to affect the child's development and well-being.

Third parties can serve as effective supports for children's development, or they can undermine children's well-being. For example, when parents' marital relationship is warm and considerate, mothers and fathers praise and stimulate their children more and nag and scold them less. In contrast, when a marriage is tense and hostile, parents are likely to express anger, criticize, and punish (Erel & Burman, 1995; Harold & Conger, 1997). Disputes between parents over child-rearing issues seem to be particularly harmful. They are linked to a rise in child behavior problems over and above the increase associated with non-child-related marital difficulties (Jouriles et al., 1991).

Yet even when parental disagreements strain children's adjustment, other family members may help restore effective interaction. Grandparents are a case in point. As we will see later, they can promote children's development in many ways—both directly, by responding warmly to the child and assisting with caregiving, and indirectly, by providing parents with child-rearing advice, models of child-rearing skill, and even financial assistance (Cherlin & Furstenberg, 1986). Of course, like any indirect influence, grandparents can sometimes be harmful. When quarrelsome relations exist between grandparents and parents, children may suffer.

ADAPTING TO CHANGE

Think back to the *chronosystem* in Bronfenbrenner's theory (see page 30). To make matters even more complicated, the interplay of forces within the family must constantly adapt to the development of its members, since each changes throughout the lifespan.

As children acquire new skills, parents adjust the way they treat their more competent youngsters. To cite just one example, turn back to Chapter 4, page 144, and review how babies' mastery of crawling leads parents to engage in more game playing and expressions of affection as well as restriction of the child's activities. Then changes in child rearing pave the way for new achievements and further modifications in family relationships. Can you think of other illustrations of this idea, discussed in earlier chapters?

Parents' development affects children as well. Later we will see that the mild increase in parent–child conflict that often occurs in early adolescence is not solely due to teen-

The Transition to Parenthood

THE EARLY WEEKS after a new baby enters the family are full of profound changes. Disrupted sleep schedules, less time for husband and wife to devote to each other, and new financial responsibilities often lead to a mild decline in a couple's marital happiness. In addition, the roles of husband and wife often become more traditional, even for couples who are strongly committed to gender equality and were used to sharing household tasks. Mothers spend more time at home with the baby, whereas fathers focus more on their provider role (Cowan & Cowan, 1997; Huston & Vangelisti, 1995).

This movement toward traditional roles is hardest on new mothers who have been used to active involvement in a career. The larger the difference in men's and women's responsibilities, the greater the rise in conflict and decline in marital satisfaction and mental health after childbirth, especially for women, with negative consequences for parent–infant interaction (Hawkins et al., 1993; Levy-Shiff, 1994).

Violated expectations about jointly caring for a new baby contribute to the decline in marital happiness. Women, especially, count on far more help from their partners than they usually get (Hackel & Ruble, 1992). Postponing childbearing until the late twenties or thirties eases the transition to parenthood. Waiting permits couples to pursue occupational goals and gain life experience. Under these circumstances, men are more enthusiastic about becoming fathers and therefore more willing to participate. And women whose careers are under way are more likely to encourage their husbands to share housework and child care (Coltrane, 1990).

Special interventions exist to ease the transition to parenthood. For parents who are not at high risk for problems, couples' groups led by counselors are highly effective (Cowan & Cowan, 1995). In one program, first-time expectant couples gathered once a week for 24 weeks, with their babies joining the group as they were born. Sessions focused on partners' dreams for the family and changes in relationships sparked by the baby's arrival. Eighteen months after the program ended, participating fathers described themselves as more involved with their child than did fathers assigned to a no-intervention condition. Perhaps because of fathers' caregiving assistance, participating mothers maintained their prebirth satisfaction with family and work roles. Three years after the birth, the marriages of all participating couples were still intact and just as happy as they had been before parent-

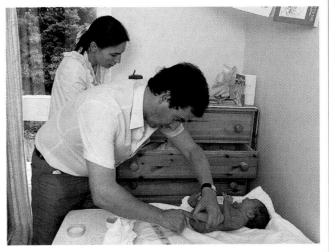

The demands of new parenthood, from baby care to added financial responsibilities, often lead to a mild decline in marital satisfaction. This father's involvement can limit marital unhappiness by freeing up time for the mother to attend to her personal needs and for the couple to spend time together—factors that return to benefit the parent-infant relationship.

(Nancy Durrell McKenna/Photo Researchers, Inc.)

hood. In contrast, 15 percent of couples receiving no intervention had divorced (Cowan & Cowan, 1997).

For high-risk parents struggling with poverty or the birth of a child with disabilities, interventions must be more intensive. Programs in which a trained intervener makes regular home visits for several months, focusing on enhancing social support and the parent–child relationship, yield improved parent–infant interaction and benefits for children's cognitive and social development up to 5 years after the intervention (Meisels, Dichtelmiller, & Liaw, 1993).

At least 12 weeks of paid maternal employment leave is crucial for easing the transition to parenthood (see Chapter 3, page 117). Flexible work hours are also helpful. When favorable workplace policies exist and couples try to support each other's needs, the stress caused by the birth of a baby stays at manageable levels. Family relationships are worked out after a few months, and most infants flourish, bringing great satisfaction to their parents and making the sacrifices of this period worthwhile.

agers' striving for independence and desire to explore new values and goals. Most parents of adolescents have reached middle age and are reconsidering their own commitments. They are very conscious that their youngsters will soon leave home and establish their own lives (Grotevant, 1998). Consequently, while the adolescent presses for greater autonomy, the parent may press for more togetherness. This imbalance promotes friction that is gradually resolved as parent and teenager accommodate to changes in one another (Collins, 1997). In sum, no other social unit is required to adjust to such vast changes in its members as is the family.

THE FAMILY SYSTEM IN CONTEXT

The social systems perspective, as we noted earlier, views the family as affected by surrounding social contexts. As the *mesosystem* and *exosystem* in Bronfenbrenner's model make clear, connections to the neighborhood and the larger community—in terms of *formal organizations,* such as school, workplace, child-care center, and church or synagogue, as well as *informal social networks* of relatives, friends, and neighbors—influence parent–child relationships.

For example, child adjustment problems, particularly those related to parent conflict, are more common in urban than rural settings. Although population density and poverty con-

According to the social systems perspective, ties to the community are essential for families to function at their best. These parents and children participate in a city project in which they plant trees along an expressway. As they do so, they beautify their community and form networks of social support.

(Cathlyn Melloan/Tony Stone Images)

tribute to this finding, fragmented communication networks are also responsible. Psychological disturbance is highest in inner-city neighborhoods where families move often, parks and playgrounds are in disarray, and community centers providing leisure-time activities do not exist. In contrast, when family ties to the surrounding social context are strong—as indicated by regular church attendance and frequent contact with friends and relatives—family stress and child adjustment problems are reduced (Garbarino & Kostelny, 1993).

How do neighborhood and community ties reduce stress and foster child development? The answer lies in their provision of social support, which leads to the following benefits:

- *Parental interpersonal acceptance.* A neighbor or relative who listens and tries to relieve a parent's concern enhances her self-esteem. The parent, in turn, is likely to behave more sensitively toward her children. In one study of families experiencing economic strain, social networks affected parenting indirectly by reducing mothers' feelings of depression (Simons et al., 1993).

- *Parental access to valuable information and services.* A friend who suggests where a job or housing might be found or who looks after children while the parent attends to other pressing needs helps make the multiple roles of spouse, provider, and caregiver easier to fulfill.

- *Child-rearing controls and role models.* Friends, relatives, and other community members may encourage and demonstrate effective ways of interacting with children and discourage ineffective practices (Cochran, 1993).

- *Direct assistance with child rearing.* As children participate in their parents' social networks and in child-oriented community activities, other adults can influence children directly through warmth, stimulation, and exposure to a wider array of competent models.

Neighborhood resources have a greater impact on young people growing up in economically disadvantaged than well-to-do areas—an effect that strengthens with age (McLeod & Shanahan, 1996). Families residing in affluent sections of cities and in suburbs are not as dependent on their immediate surroundings for social supports and leisure pursuits. They can afford to reach beyond the streets near their home, transporting their children to activities and entertainment in distant parts of the community (Elliott et al., 1996). In low-income areas, neighborhood organization and informal social activity predict many aspects of adolescents' psychological functioning, including self-confidence, school performance, and educational aspirations (Gonzales et al., 1996).

No single researcher could possibly study all aspects of family functioning included in the social systems perspective at once. However, as we address each piece of the family puzzle in the course of this chapter, we will continually see examples of the many interlocking parts that combine to influence children's development.

authoritative style A parenting style that is demanding and responsive. A rational, democratic approach in which both parents' and children's rights are respected.

The human family originated with our hunting and gathering ancestors, for whom it helped ensure cooperation in providing for the young and sufficient food during times of scarcity. Ties with other relatives offered increased protection in the face of competition for resources. Within larger kin networks, elders promoted the continuation of their genetic heritage by assisting the younger generation with mate selection and child care. Important functions of the contemporary family include reproduction, socialization, and emotional support.

According to the social systems perspective, the family consists of a complex network of bidirectional relationships that continually readjust as family members change over time. The quality of these relationships, and therefore children's development, depends in part on links established with formal and informal social supports in the surrounding neighborhood and community.

ASK YOURSELF . . .

◆ On one of your trips to a local shopping center, you see a father getting very angry at his young son. Using the social systems perspective on family functioning, list as many factors as you can that might account for the father's behavior.

◆ CONNECTIONS
Review research on the goodness-of-fit model (see Chapter 10, page 420). How does it illustrate bidirectional influences between parent and child?

Explain how disintegration of family ties to neighborhood and community promotes delinquency in adolescence. (See Chapter 12, page 515.)

Socialization Within the Family

Among functions of the family, socialization has been of greatest interest to child development researchers. In previous chapters, we discussed many ways in which parents can foster children's competence—by building a parent–child relationship based on sensitivity, cooperation, and shared positive affect; by serving as warm models and reinforcers of mature behavior; by using reasoning, explanation, and inductive discipline to promote morality and self-control; and by attributing children's failures to lack of effort rather than low ability, thereby encouraging a mastery-oriented approach to challenging tasks.

Socialization begins in earnest during the second year, once children are first able to comply with parental directives (see Chapter 12). Effective caregivers pace their demands so they fit with children's capacities. For example, they do not impose a range of "don'ts" on infants. Instead, they put away breakable objects, place barriers across steep staircases, and physically remove babies when they behave in ways that endanger themselves or disturb others. As socialization pressures increase in early childhood, parents vary greatly in how they go about the task. Let's combine the various elements of good child rearing we have already considered into an overall view of effective parenting.

STYLES OF CHILD REARING

In a landmark series of studies, Diana Baumrind gathered information on child rearing by watching parents interact with their preschoolers. Two broad dimensions of parenting emerged. The first is *demandingness*. Some parents establish high standards for their children and insist that their youngsters meet those standards. Other parents demand very little and rarely try to influence their child's behavior. The second dimension is *responsiveness*. Some parents are accepting of and responsive to their children. They frequently engage in open discussions and verbal give-and-take. Others are rejecting and unresponsive.

As Figure 14.1 shows, the various combinations of demandingness and responsiveness yield four styles of parenting. Baumrind's research focused on three of them: authoritative, authoritarian, and permissive. The fourth type, the uninvolved style, has been studied by other researchers.

■ **AUTHORITATIVE CHILD REARING.** The **authoritative style** is the most adaptive approach to child rearing. Authoritative parents make reasonable demands for maturity, and they enforce them by setting limits and insisting that the child obey. At the same time, they

FIGURE 14.1

A two-dimensional classification of child-rearing styles. The various combinations of demandingness and responsiveness yield four styles of child rearing: authoritative, authoritarian, permissive, and uninvolved.

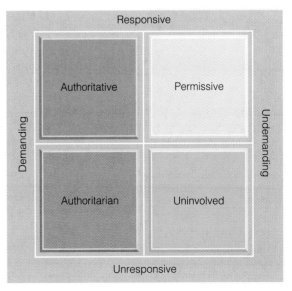

express warmth and affection, listen patiently to their child's point of view, and encourage participation in family decision making. In sum, authoritative child rearing is a rational, democratic approach that recognizes and respects the rights of both parents and children.

Baumrind's findings revealed that children of authoritative parents were developing especially well. Ratings by psychologists indicated that they were lively and happy in mood, self-confident in their mastery of new tasks, and self-controlled in their ability to resist engaging in disruptive behavior. These children also seemed less gender typed. Girls scored particularly high in independence and the desire to master new tasks and boys in friendly, cooperative behavior (Baumrind & Black, 1967). Other evidence confirms a positive association between authoritative parenting and emotional and social skills during the preschool years (Denham, Renwick, & Holt, 1991).

At older ages, authoritative parenting continues to be linked to many aspects of competence. These include high self-esteem, social and moral maturity, involvement in school learning, academic achievement in high school, and educational attainment (Eccles et al., 1997; Herman et al., 1997; Luster & McAdoo, 1996; Steinberg, Darling, & Fletcher, 1995).

■ **AUTHORITARIAN CHILD REARING.** Parents who use an **authoritarian style** are also demanding, but they place such a high value on conformity that they are unresponsive—even outright rejecting—when children are unwilling to obey. "Do it because I say so!" is the attitude of these parents. As a result, they engage in very little give-and-take with children, who are expected to accept an adult's word in an unquestioning manner. If the child does not, authoritarian parents resort to force and punishment. The authoritarian style is clearly biased in favor of parents' needs; children's self-expression and independence are suppressed.

Baumrind found that preschoolers with authoritarian parents were anxious, withdrawn, and unhappy. When interacting with peers, they tended to react with hostility when frustrated (Baumrind, 1967). Boys, especially, showed high rates of anger and defiance. Girls were dependent and lacking in exploration, and they retreated from challenging tasks (Baumrind, 1971).

In adolescence, young people with authoritarian parents continue to be less well adjusted than those reared with an authoritative style (Steinberg et al., 1994). Nevertheless, teenagers used to authoritarian child rearing do better in school and are less likely to engage in antisocial acts than are those with undemanding parents—that is, parents who use either of the two styles we are about to discuss (Baumrind, 1991; Kurdek & Fine, 1994; Lamborn et al., 1991).

■ **PERMISSIVE CHILD REARING.** The **permissive style** of child rearing is nurturant and accepting, but it avoids making demands or imposing controls of any kind. Permissive parents allow children to make many of their own decisions at an age when they are not yet capable of doing so. They can eat meals and go to bed when they feel like it and watch as much television as they want. They do not have to learn good manners or do any household chores. Although some permissive parents truly believe that this approach is best, many others lack confidence in their ability to influence their child's behavior and are disorganized and ineffective in running their households.

Baumrind found that children of permissive parents were very immature. They had difficulty controlling their impulses and were disobedient and rebellious when asked to do something that conflicted with their desires. They were also overly demanding and dependent on adults, and they showed less persistence at tasks in preschool than did children of parents who exerted more control. The link between permissive parenting and dependent, nonachieving behavior was especially strong for boys (Baumrind, 1971).

In adolescence, parental indulgence continues to be related to poor self-control. Permissively reared teenagers are less involved in school learning and use drugs more frequently than do teenagers whose parents communicate clear standards for behavior (Baumrind, 1991; Kurdek & Fine, 1994; Lamborn et al., 1991).

■ **UNINVOLVED CHILD REARING.** The **uninvolved style** combines undemanding with indifferent, rejecting behavior. Uninvolved parents show little commitment to caregiving beyond the minimum effort required to feed and clothe the child. Often they are emotionally detached and depressed and so overwhelmed by the many stresses in their

authoritarian style A parenting style that is demanding but low in responsiveness to children's rights and needs. Conformity and obedience are valued over open communication.

permissive style A parenting style that is responsive but undemanding. An overly tolerant approach to child rearing.

uninvolved style A parenting style that is both undemanding and unresponsive. Reflects minimal commitment to child rearing.

lives that they have little time and energy to spare for children. As a result, they may respond to the child's demands for easily accessible objects, but any efforts that involve long-term goals, such as establishing and enforcing rules about homework and acceptable social behavior, are weak and fleeting (Maccoby & Martin, 1983).

At its extreme, uninvolved parenting is a form of child maltreatment called *neglect*. It is likely to characterize depressed parents with many stresses in their lives, such as marital conflict, little or no social support, and poverty. Especially when it begins early, it disrupts virtually all aspects of development, including attachment, cognition, play, and emotional and social skills (See Chapter 10, page 400).

Even when parental disengagement is less extreme, it is linked to adjustment problems. Adolescents whose parents rarely interact with them, take little interest in their life at school, and do not monitor their whereabouts show poor emotional self-regulation and school performance and are prone to frequent drug use and delinquency (Baumrind, 1991; Kurdek & Fine, 1994; Lamborn et al., 1991; Pulkkinen, 1982).

WHAT MAKES THE AUTHORITATIVE STYLE EFFECTIVE?

Table 14.1 summarizes outcomes associated with each of the child-rearing styles just considered. But like other correlational findings, the relationship between the authoritative style and children's competence is open to different interpretations. Perhaps parents of mature children use demanding tactics because their youngsters have cooperative, obedient dispositions, not because firm control is an essential ingredient of effective parenting (Lewis, 1981). Yet Baumrind (1983) points out that children often resisted adult directives in authoritative homes, but parents neither gave in nor responded harshly and arbitrarily. Rather, they handled children's unreasonable demands patiently and rationally. Baumrind emphasizes that not just firm control, but *rational and reasonable* use of firm control, facilitates development.

Nevertheless, children's characteristics contribute to the ease with which parents can apply the authoritative style. Recall from Chapter 10 that temperamentally difficult children are more likely to receive coercive discipline. And when children resist, some parents respond inconsistently, at first by being punitive and later by giving in, thereby reinforcing the child's unruly behavior. Children of parents who go back and forth between authoritarian and uninvolved styles are especially aggressive and irresponsible and do very poorly in school (see Chapter 12). Over time, the relationship between parenting and children's characteristics becomes increasingly bidirectional. An impulsive, noncompliant child makes it very hard for parents to be firm, rational, and consistent. Yet child-rearing practices can either strengthen or reduce difficult behavior (Stice & Barrera, 1995).

How might authoritative child rearing support children's competence and help bring children's recalcitrant behavior under control? Although research has yet to clarify how

TABLE **14.1**

Relationship of Child-Rearing Styles to Development and Adjustment

Child-Rearing Style	Outcomes	
	Childhood	Adolescence
Authoritative	Lively and happy mood; high self-esteem and self-control; less gender typed	High self-esteem, social and moral maturity, academic achievement, and educational attainment
Authoritarian	Anxious, withdrawn, and unhappy mood; hostile when frustrated	Less well adjusted than agemates reared with the authoritative style, but better school performance than agemates reared with permissive or uninvolved styles
Permissive	Impulsive, disobedient, and rebellious; demanding and dependent on adults; poor persistence at tasks	Poor self-control and school performance; frequent drug use
Uninvolved	Deficits in attachment, cognition, play, and emotional and social skills; aggressive, acting-out behavior	Poor emotional self-regulation and school performance; frequent drug use; delinquency

parenting *styles* are linked to everyday parenting *practices* that promote development, the following processes may be at work:

- Control that appears fair and reasonable to the child, not arbitrary, is far more likely to be complied with and internalized (see Chapter 12).

- Nurturant parents who are secure in the standards they hold for their children provide models of caring concern as well as confident, self-controlled behavior. Perhaps for this reason, children of such parents are advanced in emotional self-regulation and emotional and social understanding—factors linked to social competence with peers (Eisenberg & Fabes, 1994; Parke, 1994).

- Parents who combine warmth with rational and reasonable control are likely to be more effective reinforcing agents, praising children for striving to meet their expectations and making good use of disapproval, which works best when applied by an adult who has been warm and caring (see Chapter 12).

- Authoritative parents make demands that fit with children's ability to take responsibility for their own behavior. As a result, these parents let children know that they are competent individuals who can do things successfully for themselves, thereby fostering high self-esteem and cognitive and social maturity (see Chapter 11).

- Supportive aspects of the authoritative style, including parental warmth, involvement, and discussion, help protect children from the negative effects of family stress and poverty (Petit, Bates, & Dodge, 1997).

ADAPTING CHILD REARING TO CHILDREN'S DEVELOPMENT

Since authoritative parents continually adapt to children's growing competence, their practices change with age. In the following sections, we will see that a gradual lessening of direct control supports development, as long as it is built on continuing parental warmth and involvement in child rearing.

■ PARENTING IN MIDDLE CHILDHOOD: COREGULATION. In middle childhood, the amount of time children spend with parents declines dramatically. The child's growing independence means that parents must deal with new issues. As one mother commented, "I've struggled with how many chores to assign, how much allowance to give, whether their friends are good influences, and what to do about problems at school. And then there's the challenge of how to keep track of them when they're out of the house or even when they're home and I'm not there to see what's going on."

Although parents face a new set of concerns, child rearing becomes easier for those who established an authoritative style during the early years. Reasoning works more effectively with school-age children because of their greater capacity for logical thinking and increased respect for parents' expert knowledge and skill (Braine et al., 1991). Of course, older children sometimes use their cognitive powers to bargain and negotiate. Fortunately, parents can appeal to their child's better developed sense of self-esteem, humor, and morality to resolve these difficulties. Perhaps because parents and children have, over time, learned how to resolve conflicts, coercive discipline declines during middle childhood (Collins, Harris, & Susman, 1996).

As children demonstrate that they can manage daily activities and responsibilities, effective parents gradually shift control from adult to child. This does not mean that they let go entirely. Instead, they engage in **coregulation,** a transitional form of supervision in which they exercise general oversight while permitting children to be in charge of moment-by-moment decision making. Coregulation supports and protects children, who are not yet ready for total independence. At the same time, it prepares them for adolescence, when they will make many important decisions themselves.

Coregulation grows out of a cooperative relationship between parent and child—one based on give-and-take and mutual respect. Here is a summary of its critical ingredients:

First, [parents] must monitor, guide, and support their children at a distance—that is, when their children are out of their presence; second, they must effectively use the times when di-

coregulation A transitional form of supervision in which parents exercise general oversight while permitting children to be in charge of moment-by-moment decision making.

rect contact does occur; and third, they must strengthen in their children the abilities that will allow them to monitor their own behavior, to adopt acceptable standards of [good] conduct, to avoid undue risks, and to know when they need parental support and guidance. Children must be willing to inform parents of their whereabouts, activities, and problems so that parents can mediate and guide when necessary. (Maccoby, 1984, pp. 191–192)

Although school-age children often press for greater independence, they know how much they need their parents' continuing support. In one study, fifth and sixth graders described parents as the most influential people in their lives. They often turned to mothers and fathers for affection, advice, enhancement of self-worth, and assistance with everyday problems (Furman & Buhrmester, 1992).

Adolescent autonomy is best achieved in the context of warm parenting. This mother and father support their daughter's desire to try new experiences, relaxing control in accord with her readiness to take on new responsibilities. The girl's beaming smile as she introduces her prom date suggests a healthy balance of togetherness and independence.
(Michael Newman/PhotoEdit)

■ **PARENTING IN ADOLESCENCE: FOSTERING AUTONOMY.** During adolescence, young people in complex societies deal with the need to choose from many options by seeking **autonomy**—establishing themselves as separate, self-governing individuals. Autonomy extends beyond school-age children's capacity to regulate their own behavior in the absence of parental monitoring. It has a vital *emotional component*—relying more on oneself and less on parents for support and guidance. And it also has an important *behavioral component*—making decisions independently by carefully weighing one's own judgment and the suggestions of others to arrive at a well-reasoned course of action (Hill & Holmbeck, 1986; Steinberg & Silverberg, 1986). Autonomy is closely related to the quest for identity. Adolescents who successfully establish personally meaningful values and life goals are autonomous. They have given up childish dependence on parents for a more mature, responsible relationship (Frank, Pirsch, & Wright, 1990).

Autonomy receives support from a variety of changes within the adolescent. In Chapter 5, we saw that puberty triggers psychological distancing from parents. In addition, as young people look more mature, they are granted more independence and responsibility. Cognitive development also paves the way toward autonomy. Abstract thinking permits teenagers to solve problems and foresee the consequences of their actions more effectively. And an improved ability to reason about social relationships leads adolescents to *deidealize* their parents, viewing them as "just people." Consequently, they no longer bend as easily to parental authority as they did at earlier ages.

How can parents foster this readiness for autonomy? Controversy surrounds this question. Think back to Erikson's psychosocial theory, discussed in Chapter 1. Autonomy is a central task of toddlerhood, and it resurfaces at adolescence, when social expectations demand a new level of self-reliance. Research reveals that autonomy can be arrived at in different ways. When young people feel autonomous yet characterize their relationship with parents as unsupportive, they appear better adjusted than do teenagers in conflict-ridden families who do not feel autonomous. This suggests that adolescents in troubled homes benefit when they can separate themselves emotionally from stressful parent–child interaction (Fuhrman & Holmbeck, 1995). But overall, autonomy achieved in the context of warm, supportive parent–child ties is most adaptive. It predicts high self-reliance, work orientation, academic competence, and gains in self-esteem during the adolescent years (Allen et al., 1994; Lamborn & Steinberg, 1993).

Why do many parents report that living with adolescents is stressful? Recall that the family is a system that must adapt to changes in its members. But when development is very rapid, adjustment is harder. Earlier we noted that many parents of adolescents, who have reached their forties, are changing as well. While teenagers face a boundless future and a wide array of choices, their parents must come to terms with the fact that half their life is over and possibilities are narrowing. In addition, parents of adolescents are often caught in a "middle-generation squeeze"—faced with competing demands of children, aging parents, and employment. As a result, they have a harder time caring for themselves.

The pressures experienced by each generation act in opposition to one another (Holmbeck & Hill, 1991). Parents often can't understand why the adolescent wants to skip family activities to be with peers. And teenagers fail to appreciate that parents want the family to be together as often as possible because an important stage in adult life—parenthood—will soon be over. In addition, parents and adolescents—especially early adolescents—differ sharply on the appropriate time the young person should be granted certain responsibilities and privileges, such as control over clothing, school courses, and

autonomy A sense of oneself as a separate, self-governing individual. An important developmental task of adolescence that is closely related to the quest for identity.

going out with friends (Collins et al., 1997). Parents typically say that the young person is not yet ready for these signs of independence, whereas teenagers think that they should have been granted long ago!

As adolescents move closer to adulthood, the task for parents and children is not one of just separating. They must establish a blend of togetherness and independence—a relationship in which parental control gradually relaxes without breaking the parent–child bond. This means establishing guidelines that are flexible, open to discussion, and implemented in an atmosphere of concern and fairness. The mild parent–child conflict that typically occurs facilitates adolescent identity and autonomy by helping family members learn to express and tolerate disagreement (Steinberg, 1990, 1999). Conflicts also inform parents of adolescents' changing needs and expectations, signaling them that adjustments in the parent–child relationship are necessary.

The diminishing time that teenagers spend with their family actually has less to do with conflict than with expanding opportunities—being able to drive, having a part-time job, and being allowed to stay out later. After a decline in early adolescence, positive parent–child interaction is on the rise (Larson et al., 1996).

SOCIOECONOMIC AND ETHNIC VARIATIONS IN CHILD REARING

Research examining parenting in over 180 societies reveals that a style that is responsive but moderately demanding is the most common pattern around the world (Rohner & Rohner, 1981). Nevertheless, consistent variations in child rearing exist that are linked to SES and ethnicity.

■ **SOCIOECONOMIC STATUS.** Recall that SES is an index that combines years of education, prestige and skill required by one's job, and income. As SES rises and falls, parents and children face changing circumstances that profoundly affect family functioning.

When asked about qualities they would like to encourage in their children, parents who work in skilled and semiskilled manual occupations (for example, machinists, truck drivers, and custodians) tend to place a high value on external characteristics, such as obedience, neatness, and cleanliness. In contrast, parents in white-collar and professional occupations tend to emphasize inner psychological traits, such as curiosity, happiness, and self-control. These differences in values are reflected in parenting behaviors. Parents higher in SES talk to and stimulate their infants more and grant them greater freedom to explore (Luster, Rhoades, & Haas, 1989). When their children are older, they use more warmth, explanations, inductive discipline, and verbal praise. In contrast, commands, such as "You do that because I told you to," as well as criticism and physical punishment occur more often in low-SES households (Dodge, Pettit, & Bates, 1994).

These differences in child rearing can be understood in terms of the life conditions of families. Low-SES parents often feel a sense of powerlessness and lack of influence in their relationships beyond the home. For example, at work they must obey the rules of others in positions of power and authority. When they get home, their parent–child interaction seems to duplicate these experiences, only with them in the authority roles. In contrast, higher-SES parents have a greater sense of control over their own lives. At work, they are used to making independent decisions and convincing others of their point of view. At home, they teach these skills to their children (Greenberger, O'Neil, & Nagel, 1994).

Education also contributes to SES differences in child rearing. Higher-SES parents' interest in verbal stimulation and in developing their children's inner characteristics is supported by years of schooling, during which they acquired advanced verbal skills and learned to think about abstract, subjective ideas. In research carried out in Mexico, where female school enrollment has recently increased, the more years of education a mother had, the more she stimulated her young child through face-to-face conversation (Richman, Miller, & LeVine, 1992; Uribe, LeVine, & LeVine, 1994).

Furthermore, the greater economic security of higher-SES parents frees them from the burden of having to worry about making ends meet on a daily basis. They can devote more energy and attention to their own inner characteristics and those of their children. And they can also provide many more experiences—from toys to special outings to after-school lessons—that encourage these characteristics.

■ **POVERTY.** When families slip into poverty, effective parenting and children's development are seriously threatened. Shirley Brice Heath (1990), an anthropologist who has spent many years studying children and families of poverty, describes the case of Zinnia Mae, who grew up in Trackton, a close-knit black community located in a small southeastern American city. As unemployment struck Trackton in the 1980s and citizens moved away, 16-year-old Zinnia Mae caught a ride to Atlanta. Two years later, Heath visited her there. By then, Zinnia Mae was the mother of three children—a 16-month-old daughter named Donna and 2-month-old twin boys. She had moved into a high-rise public housing project, one of eight concrete buildings surrounding a dirt plot scattered with broken swings, seesaws, and benches.

Each of Zinnia Mae's days was much the same. She watched TV and talked with her girlfriends on the phone. The children had only one set meal (breakfast) and otherwise ate whenever they were hungry or bored. Their play space was limited to the living-room sofa and a mattress on the floor. Toys consisted of scraps of a blanket, spoons and food cartons, a small rubber ball, a few plastic cars, and a roller skate abandoned in the building. Zinnia Mae's most frequent words were "I'm so tired." She worried about how to get papers to the welfare office, where to find a baby-sitter so she could go to the laundry or grocery, and what she would do if she located the twins' father, who had stopped sending money.

At Heath's request, Zinnia Mae agreed to tape record her interactions with her children over a 2-year period. In 500 hours of tape (other than simple directions or questions about what the children were doing), Zinnia Mae started a conversation with Donna and the boys only 18 times. Cut off from community ties and preoccupied with day-to-day survival, Zinnia Mae had little energy to join in activities with her children. As a result, Donna and her brothers experienced a barren, understimulating home life—one very different from the family and community in which Zinnia Mae herself had grown up.

The constant stresses that accompany poverty gradually weaken the family system. Poor families have many daily hassles—bills to pay, the car breaking down, loss of welfare and unemployment payments, something stolen from the house, to name just a few. When daily crises arise, parents become depressed, irritable, and distracted; marital conflict rises; parenting becomes less nurturant and involved; and children's development suffers (Conger et al., 1992; Garrett, Ng'andu, & Ferron, 1994; McLoyd, 1998b). These outcomes are especially severe in single-parent families, in families living in poor housing and dangerous neighborhoods, and in homeless families—circumstances that make everyday existence even more difficult while reducing social supports that assist in coping with economic hardship (Duncan, Brooks-Gunn, & Klebanov, 1994; McLoyd et al., 1994). The earlier poverty begins and the longer it lasts, the more devastating its effects on children's physical and mental health, intelligence, and school achievement (Korenman, Miller & Sjaastad, 1995; McLeod & Shanahan, 1996).

■ **ETHNICITY.** Despite broad agreement on the advantages of authoritative child rearing, ethnic groups often have distinct child-rearing beliefs and practices. Some involve variations in demandingness that appear to be adaptive when viewed in light of cultural values and family circumstances.

For example, compared with Caucasian Americans, Chinese adults describe their own parenting techniques and those they experienced as children as more demanding (Berndt et al., 1993). As Figure 14.2 shows, this greater emphasis on control continues to characterize immigrant Chinese parents in the United States, who are more directive in teaching and scheduling their children's time beginning in early childhood (Huntsinger, Jose, & Larson, 1998). But high control in Chinese families does not have the same meaning as authoritarian child rearing in Western culture. Instead, it reflects the Confucian belief in strict discipline, respect for elders, and socially desirable behavior, taught by parents who are deeply concerned and involved in the lives of their children (Chao, 1994).

Homelessness in the United States has risen over the past two decades. Families like this one travel from place to place in search of employment and a safe and secure place to live. Because of constant stress and few social supports, homeless children are usually behind in development, have frequent health problems, and show poor psychological adjustment. (Tony Freeman/PhotoEdit)

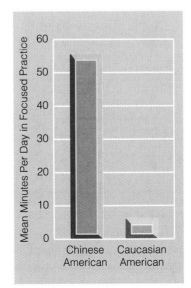

FIGURE 14.2

Daily time spent by Chinese-American and Caucasian-American preschoolers and kindergartners in focused practice on a task (usually math, music, or drawing), as reported by parents. Chinese-American young children exceeded their Caucasian-American agemates by nearly ten fold. In addition, Chinese-American parents indicated that they were more likely to set aside daily periods for such practice and taught their children in more formal ways. (Adapted from Huntsinger, Jose, & Larson, 1998.)

In Hispanic and Asian Pacific Island families, firm insistence on respect for parental authority, particularly that of the father, is paired with unusually high maternal warmth. As in Chinese families, this combination reflects parental commitment rather than authoritarianism. It is believed to promote compliance, identification with parents and close relatives, and strong feelings of family loyalty (Fracasso & Busch-Rossnagel, 1992; Harrison et al., 1994).

Although wide variation exists in African-American families, black mothers (especially those who are younger, single, and less educated) often rely on an adult-centered approach in which they expect immediate obedience from children (Kelley, Power, & Wimbush, 1992). Strict demands for compliance, however, make sense under certain conditions. When parents have few social supports and live in dangerous neighborhoods, forceful discipline may be necessary to protect children from becoming victims of crime or involved in antisocial activities. Other research suggests that black parents use very firm child rearing for broader reasons—to promote self-reliance, self-control, and a vigilant approach to risky surroundings (Brody & Flor, 1998).

Consistent with this view, low-SES, ethnic minority parents who use more controlling strategies tend to have more cognitively and socially competent children (Baldwin, Baldwin, & Cole, 1990; Brody, Stoneman, & Flor, 1995, 1996). And in several studies, physical discipline in early childhood predicted aggression and other conduct problems during the school years only for Caucasian-American children, not for African-American children (Deater-Deckard & Dodge, 1997; Deater-Deckard et al., 1996). This does not mean that slaps and spankings are effective strategies. But it does suggest the possibility of ethnic differences in how children view parental behavior that can modify its consequences. When physical discipline within a subculture is common but not excessively harsh, children may regard it as a sign of parent involvement rather than rejection. African-American parents who use strict, "no-nonsense" discipline, including physical punishment, typically combine it with warmth and support, which predict favorable adjustment among both black and white children (Petit, Bates, & Dodge, 1998; Staples & Johnson, 1993).

The family structure and child-rearing customs of many ethnic minorities buffer the stress and disorganization caused by poverty. As the Cultural Influences box on the next page indicates, the African **extended-family household,** in which one or more adult relatives live with the parent–child **nuclear family unit,** is a vital feature of black family life that has enabled its members to survive, despite a long history of prejudice and economic deprivation. Active and involved extended families also characterize Asian-American, Native American, and Hispanic subcultures (Harrison et al., 1994). These families illustrate the remarkable ability of the family unit to use its cultural traditions to support its members under conditions of high life stress.

ASK YOURSELF . . .

◆ *Don teaches in a school district serving many ethnic minority families. He notices that the parents are very strict, insisting that children comply with adult directives immediately. Why should Don ask the parents to explain their approach to child rearing rather than simply concluding that they are authoritarian?*

◆ CONNECTIONS
How might adolescents' view of personal versus social-conventional issues contribute to parent–child conflict? (See Chapter 12, page 503)

Review Figure 11.8 on page 470. What might explain the decline in self-disclosure to parents in early adolescence, followed by the rise from tenth grade through college?

BRIEF REVIEW

Two broad dimensions, demandingness and responsiveness, yield four styles of child rearing: authoritative, authoritarian, permissive, and uninvolved. The authoritative style is linked to many aspects of competence; children experiencing uninvolved child rearing fare least well. Although authoritative parents handle children's unreasonable demands patiently and rationally, children's characteristics contribute to the ease with which parents can apply the authoritative style.

Authoritative parents continually adapt to children's changing capacities. During middle childhood, they engage in coregulation, a transitional form of supervision in which parents exercise general oversight while granting children more decision-making power. In adolescence, warm, supportive parenting in which control is gradually relaxed in accord with adolescents' readiness for greater freedom fosters mature autonomy and positive adjustment.

Consistent SES differences in child rearing exist: Lower-SES parents tend to be more coercive, whereas higher-SES parents use more warmth, explanations, inductive discipline, and verbal praise. The constant stresses that accompany poverty undermine effective parenting and children's development. Ethnic variations in child rearing can be understood in terms of cultural values and the contexts in which families live.

The African-American Extended Family

THE AFRICAN-AMERICAN extended family can be traced to the African heritage of most black Americans. In many African societies, newly married couples do not start their own households. Instead, they marry into a large extended family that assists its members with all aspects of daily life. This tradition of a broad network of kin ties traveled to the United States during the period of slavery. Since then, it has served as a protective shield against the destructive impact of poverty and racial prejudice on African-American family life (McAdoo, 1993). Today, more black than white adults have relatives other than their own children living in the same household. African-American parents also see more kin during the week and perceive them as more important figures in their lives, respecting the advice of relatives and caring deeply about what they think is important (Wilson et al., 1995).

By providing emotional support and sharing income and essential resources, the African-American extended family helps reduce the stress of poverty and single parenthood. In addition, extended-family members often help with the rearing of children (Pearson et al., 1990). The presence of grandmothers in the households of many African-American teenagers and their infants protects babies from the negative influence of an overwhelmed and inexperienced mother. In one study, black grandmothers displayed more sensitive interaction with the babies of their teenage daughters than did the teenage mothers themselves. The grandmothers also provided basic information about infant development to these young mothers (Stevens, 1984). Furthermore, black adolescent mothers living in extended families are more likely to complete high school and get a job and less likely to be on welfare than are mothers living on their own—factors that return to benefit children's well-being (Trent & Harlan, 1994).

For single mothers who were very young at the time of their child's birth, extended family living is associated with more positive adult–child interaction during infancy and the preschool years. Otherwise, establishing an independent household with the help of nearby relatives is related to improved child rearing. Perhaps this arrangement permits the more mature mother who has developed effective parenting skills to implement them (Chase-Lansdale, Brooks-Gunn, & Zamsky, 1994). In families rearing adolescents, kinship support increases the likelihood of effective parenting, which, in turn, is related to self-reliance, emotional well-being, and reduced delinquency (Taylor & Roberts, 1995).

Finally, the African-American extended family plays an important role in transmitting black cultural values to chil-

Strong bonds with extended-family members have helped to protect many African-American children growing up under conditions of poverty and single parenthood.
(Karen Kasmauski/Woodfin Camp & Associates)

dren. Compared with African Americans who live in nuclear family households (which include only parents and their children), extended-family arrangements place more emphasis on cooperation and moral and religious values (Tolson & Wilson, 1990). Older black adults, such as grandparents and great-grandparents, are also more likely to possess a strong ethnic identity and to regard educating children about their African heritage as an important part of socialization (Thornton & Taylor, 1988). These influences strengthen family bonds, protect children's development, and increase the chances that the extended-family lifestyle will carry over to the next generation.

Family Lifestyles and Transitions

Families in industrialized nations have become more pluralistic than ever before—a trend that is particularly marked in the United States. Today, there are fewer births per family unit, more adults who want to adopt, more lesbian and gay parents who are open about their sexual orientation, and more never-married parents.

extended-family household A household in which parent and child live with one or more adult relatives.

nuclear family unit The part of the family that consists of parents and their children.

In addition, transitions in family life over the past several decades—a dramatic rise in marital breakup, remarried parents, and employed mothers—have reshaped the family system.

In the following sections, we discuss these changes in the family, emphasizing how each affects family relationships and, ultimately, children's development. In reading about some of these shifts in family life, you may wonder, as many people do, whether the family is in a state of crisis. Family transitions have always existed; they are simply more numerous and visible today than in the past. Yet rapid social change has intensified pressures on the family.

As you consider the diverse array of contemporary family forms, think back to the social systems perspective and Bronfenbrenner's ecological model. Notice how children's well-being continues to depend on the quality of family interaction, which is sustained by supportive ties to kin and community and favorable policies at the level of the larger culture.

FROM LARGE TO SMALL FAMILIES

In the mid-1950s, the peak of the post–World War II baby boom, the average number of children in an American family was 3.8. Today, it is 2.1, a downward trend expected to continue. In many developed countries, the birth rate is already less than two children per family—for example, 1.9 in Australia and Canada; 1.6 in Austria and the Netherlands; 1.5 in Japan; and 1.3 in Germany (Bellamy, 1998). Compared with several decades ago, there are more one- and two-child families, as well as couples opting to have no children.

Family size has declined for several reasons. Improved contraception along with legalized abortion have made the current period one of greater choice with respect to having children. Also, many more women are experiencing the economic and personal rewards of a career. A family size of one or two children is certainly more compatible with a woman's decision to divide her energies between work and family. Furthermore, more couples are delaying the birth of their first child until they are well established professionally and secure economically (see Chapter 3). Adults who postpone parenthood are likely to have fewer children. Finally, marital instability is another reason families are smaller. More couples today get divorced before their childbearing plans are complete.

■ **FAMILY SIZE AND CHILD REARING.** Overall, a smaller family size enhances parent–child interaction. Parents of fewer children are more patient and less punitive. They also have more time to devote to each child's activities, schoolwork, and other special needs. Furthermore, in smaller families, siblings are more likely to be widely spaced (born more than 2 years apart), which adds to the attention and resources parents can invest in each child. Together, these findings may account for the fact that children who grow up in smaller families are healthier, have somewhat higher intelligence test scores, do better in school, and attain higher levels of education (Blake, 1989; Grant, 1994).

Children's problem behavior also varies with family size. Parents of one or two children sometimes pressure their youngsters too much. As a result, anxiety is more common in small families. In contrast, coercive discipline and reduced supervision probably contribute to higher rates of antisocial behavior and delinquency in families with many children (Wagner, Schubert, & Schubert, 1985).

However, these findings require an important qualification. Large families are usually less well off economically. Factors associated with low income—crowded housing, poor nutrition, and parental stress—may be responsible for the negative relationship between family size and children's well-being. In a study of black South African families experiencing economic hardship, parents who could provide greater residential stability and less crowded housing had children who were developing more favorably—physically, cognitively, emotionally, and socially (Goduka, Poole, & Aotaki-Phenice, 1992). Furthermore, when children grow up in large, well-to-do families, the unfavorable outcomes typically associated with large family size are reduced (but not eliminated) (Powell & Steelman, 1993).

■ **GROWING UP WITH SIBLINGS.** Despite a declining family size, 80 percent of American children still grow up with at least one sibling. Siblings exert important influences on development, both directly, through relationships with each other, and indirectly, through the effects an additional child has on the behavior of parents. In previous chapters, we examined some consequences of having brothers and sisters, including effects on intelligence, language development, personality, self and social understanding, and gender typing. Now let's look more closely at the quality of the sibling relationship itself.

EMERGENCE OF SIBLING RELATIONSHIPS. When adults think of sibling ties, images of rivalry often come to mind—brothers and sisters competing for parental attention and material resources. The common assumption that jealousy is a key element in sibling interaction originated with psychoanalytic theory, which stressed that each child desires to monopolize the parents' love. Today we know that conflict is only one feature of a rich emotional relationship that starts to build between siblings after a baby's birth.

Although the arrival of a baby brother or sister is a difficult experience for most preschoolers, a rich emotional relationship quickly builds between siblings. This toddler is already actively involved in play with his 4-year-old brother, and both derive great pleasure from the interaction. (Ericka Stone/Photo Researchers, Inc.)

Longitudinal research on the early development of sibling ties shows that a drop in maternal involvement with the older preschool child occurs after the birth of a baby. As a result, jealousy is often an element in the firstborn's feelings toward the new arrival. Many young children become demanding and clingy for a time and engage in instances of deliberate naughtiness. But expressions of affection and sympathetic concern also occur. The older child can be seen kissing, patting, and calling out when the baby cries, "Mom, he needs you." By the end of the baby's first year, siblings typically spend much time together, with the preschooler helping, sharing toys, imitating, and expressing friendliness in addition to anger and ambivalence. During the second year, the younger sibling often imitates and joins in play with the older child. Already, older siblings have become powerful agents of socialization (Dunn & Kendrick, 1982).

Because of their frequency and emotional intensity, sibling interactions become unique contexts in which social competence expands. Between their second and fourth birthdays, younger siblings take a more active role in play. As a result, sibling conversations increase, and their content differs from parent–child interaction. Mothers' statements typically emphasize caregiving and control—for example, providing comforting words, acknowledging children's hurts and fears, and referring to feelings as a way of stopping inappropriate behavior. In contrast, siblings talk more about emotions in playful or humorous ways and call attention to their own wants and needs when conflicts arise (Brown & Dunn, 1992). At least when they are close in age, siblings relate to each other on a more equal footing, much like peers. The skills acquired during sibling interaction contribute to perspective taking, moral maturity, and competence in relating to other children. Consistent with these outcomes, positive sibling ties predict favorable adjustment, even among hostile children at risk for social difficulties (Dunn et al., 1994; Stormshak et al., 1996).

Wide individual differences in the quality of sibling relationships appear in the first few weeks after the second child's birth that remain modestly stable from early into middle childhood (Dunn, 1989, 1992). In Chapter 10, we noted that temperament affects how positive or conflict ridden sibling interaction will be. Parenting also makes a difference. Typically, mothers are more positive and playful with second-borns than first-borns and discipline the older preschooler more—behaviors that can spark feelings of rivalry and behavior problems in the older child along with less friendliness toward the baby (Dunn & Kendrick, 1982; Moore, Cohn, & Campbell, 1997; Volling & Elins, 1998). Early parental differential treatment of siblings marks the beginning of the powerful impact of nonshared environmental influences on personality development, discussed in Chapter 10.

Other research reveals that secure infant–mother attachment and parental warmth toward both children predict positive sibling interaction. Cold, intrusive child rearing is associated with sibling antagonism (MacKinnon-Lewis et al., 1997; Stocker & McHale, 1992). Once established, this match between parent–child and sibling relationships is self-sustaining. Warm parenting fosters considerate sibling interaction, which prompts positive parental behavior in the future. When parents are hostile and coercive, aggression is promoted among all family members and spreads to adult and peer relationships beyond the home (see Chapter 12).

SIBLING RELATIONSHIPS IN MIDDLE CHILDHOOD AND ADOLESCENCE. During middle childhood, sibling conflict tends to increase. At times, it is evoked by one child making new friends, sparking jealousy in a sibling who feels left out (Dunn, 1996). Also, as children participate in a wider range of activities, parents often compare siblings' traits and accomplishments. The child who gets less parental affection, more disapproval, or fewer material resources is likely to resent a sibling who receives more favorable treatment (Brody, Stoneman, & McCoy, 1994; McHale et al., 1995).

When siblings are close in age and the same sex, parental comparisons are more frequent, resulting in more quarreling and antagonism. This effect is particularly strong when fathers prefer one child. Perhaps because fathers spend less time with children, their favoritism is more noticeable and triggers greater anger (Brody, Stoneman, & McCoy, 1992; Brody et al., 1992). Of course, what is best for one sibling may not serve another well. When parents discipline one child more, they are usually responding to that child's unique characteristics. And younger siblings tend to react more strongly to a less favored status, objecting to privileges legitimately granted to older children.

Although conflict rises during the school years, siblings continue to rely on each other for companionship, emotional support, and assistance with everyday tasks. Because of the uniqueness of the sibling relationship, older siblings provide an effective scaffold for children's learning. When researchers had either a sibling or a good friend of the sibling teach a younger child how to build a windmill out of small, interlocking pieces, siblings offered more explanations, encouragement, and control over the task. In part, this occurred because younger children observed, imitated, consulted, asked for explanations, and exerted pressure for task control to a greater extent with siblings. As a result, children taught by siblings performed better on the task (Azmitia & Hesser, 1993).

Like parent–child relationships, sibling interactions adapt to development at adolescence. As younger children mature and become more self-sufficient, they are no longer willing to accept as much direction from their brothers and sisters. Consequently, older siblings' influence declines during the teenage years. Sibling relationships also become less intense during adolescence, in both positive and negative feelings. As teenagers become more involved in friendships and romantic partnerships, they invest less time and energy in siblings, who are part of the family from which they are trying to establish autonomy (Furman & Buhrmester, 1992; Stocker & Dunn, 1994). An overly intrusive older sibling, much like a coercive parent, undermines self-esteem and promotes adjustment difficulties during adolescence (Conger, Conger, & Scaramella, 1997).

Despite a drop in companionship, attachment between siblings, like closeness to parents, remains strong for most young people. The quality of sibling interaction at adolescence continues to be affected by other relationships, both within and outside the family. Teenagers whose parents are warm and supportive have more positive sibling ties (Brody et al., 1992). And for children who have difficulty making friends at school, a gratifying sibling relationship can provide compensating emotional supports (East & Rook, 1992).

ONE-CHILD FAMILIES

Sibling relationships bring many benefits, but they are not essential for healthy development. Contrary to popular belief, only children are not spoiled and selfish. Instead, they are just as well-adjusted and socially competent as other children and advantaged in some respects. Children growing up in one-child families score higher in self-esteem and achievement motivation. Consequently, they do better in school and attain higher levels of education (Falbo, 1992). A major reason may be that only children have somewhat closer relationships with their parents, who exert more pressure for mastery and accomplishment (Falbo & Polit, 1986).

Favorable development also characterizes only children in the People's Republic of China, where a one-child family policy is strictly enforced to control overpopulation. Today, over 90 percent of Chinese children in urban areas and 50 to 60 percent in rural

Limiting family size is a basic national policy in the People's Republic of China. In urban areas, the majority of couples have no more than one child.

(Marc Bernheim/Woodfin Camp & Associates)

TABLE 14.2

Advantages and Disadvantages of a One-Child Family

Advantages		Disadvantages	
Mentioned by Parents	**Mentioned by Children**	**Mentioned by Parents**	**Mentioned by Children**
Having time to pursue one's own interests and career	Avoiding sibling rivalry	Walking a "tightrope" between family attention and overindulgence	Not getting to experience the closeness of a sibling relationship
Less financial pressure	Having more privacy		
	Enjoying greater affluence	Having only one chance to "make good" as a parent	Feeling too much pressure from parents to succeed
Not having to worry about "playing favorites" among children	Having a closer parent–child relationship		
		Being left childless in case of the child's death	Having no one to help care for parents when they get old

Source: Hawke & Knox, 1978.

regions have no siblings. Compared with agemates who have brothers and sisters, Chinese only children are advanced in variety of mental abilities and in academic achievement (Falbo & Poston, 1993; Jiao, Ji, & Jing, 1996). They also feel more emotionally secure, perhaps because government disapproval promotes tension and unhappiness in families with more than one child (Falbo & Poston, 1993; Yang et al., 1995). Although many Chinese adults remain convinced that the one-child family policy breeds self-centered "little emperors," Chinese only children do not differ from children with siblings in social skills and peer acceptance (Chen, Rubin, & Li, 1995).

Nevertheless, the one-child family has both pros and cons, as does every family lifestyle. In a survey in which American only children and their parents were asked what they liked and disliked about living in a single-child family, each mentioned a set of advantages and disadvantages, which are summarized in Table 14.2. The list is useful for Western parents to consider when deciding how many children would best fit their own personal and family life plans.

ADOPTIVE FAMILIES

Adults who are infertile, who are likely to pass along a genetic disorder, or who are older and single but want a family are turning to adoption in increasing numbers. Adoption agencies try to find parents of the same ethnic and religious background as the child. Where possible, they also try to choose parents who are the same age as most natural parents. Because the availability of healthy babies has declined (since fewer young unwed mothers give up their babies than in the past), more people are adopting from foreign countries or taking children who are older or who have developmental problems.

Although adoptive families are highly diverse, they face common challenges. Waiting many years for parenthood and having no control over when they will get a child leads some people to question their entitlement to be parents, including their right to discipline. And different heredity means that adoptive parents and children are less alike in intelligence and personality than are biological relatives—resemblances that contribute to family harmony. Partly for these reasons, adopted children and adolescents—whether born in a foreign country or the country of their adoptive parents—have more learning and emotional difficulties than do their nonadopted agemates in childhood and adolescence (Verhulst, Althaus, & Versluis-Den Bieman, 1990; Verhulst & Versluis-Den Bieman, 1995).

Yet when we consider that many adopted children had poor prenatal care and stressful early lives, they fare surprisingly well. In a Swedish longitudinal study, researchers followed over 600

This transracially adopted African-American baby plays with her Caucasian older sisters. Will she develop an identity that is a healthy blend of her birth and rearing backgrounds? The answer depends on the extent to which her adoptive parents expose her to her African-American heritage.

(Jim Pickerell/Stock Boston)

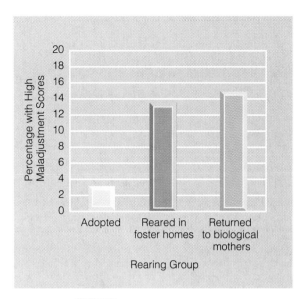

FIGURE 14.3

Percentage of 15-year-olds with high maladjustment scores who were adopted, placed in foster homes, or returned to their biological mothers shortly after birth, according to a Swedish longitudinal study. All adolescents had been candidates for adoption when they were born. Compared with the other two groups, adopted young people were rated by teachers as having far fewer problems, including anxiety, withdrawal, aggression, inability to concentrate, peer difficulties, and poor school motivation.

(Adapted from Bohman & Sigvardsson, 1990.)

infant candidates for adoption into adolescence and young adulthood. Some were adopted shortly after birth; some were reared in foster homes; and some were reared by their biological mothers, who changed their minds about giving them up. As Figure 14.3 shows, adoptees developed much more favorably than did children reared in foster families or returned to their birth mothers (Bohman & Sigvardsson, 1990). Furthermore, children with special needs usually benefit, even when they are adopted at older ages. From 70 to 80 percent of their parents report high satisfaction with the adoptive experience—a rate that equals that of families adopting healthy infants (Rosenthal, 1992).

By adolescence, adoptees' lives are often complicated by unresolved curiosity about their roots. Some have difficulty accepting the possibility that they may never know their birth parents. Others worry about what they would do if their birth parents suddenly reappeared. Nevertheless, the decision to search for birth parents is usually postponed until young adulthood, when marriage and childbirth may trigger it (Schaffer & Kral, 1988). Despite concerns about their origins, most adoptees appear optimistic and well adjusted as adults. By that time, their higher rate of adjustment problems disappears.

Young people who were transracially or transculturally adopted typically develop identities that are healthy blends of their birth and rearing backgrounds (Simon, Altstein, & Melli, 1994). However, this favorable outcome depends on parents' willingness to help their child learn about his or her heritage. In a longitudinal study of African-American children whose Caucasian parents tended to avoid racial issues, ethnic identity was often weak at adolescence—a factor that contributed to adjustment difficulties (DeBerry, Scarr, & Weinberg, 1996).

Clearly, adoption is a satisfying family alternative for most parents and children who experience it. The outcomes are good because of careful pairing of children with parents and guidance provided to adoptive families by well-trained social service professionals.

GAY AND LESBIAN FAMILIES

Several million American gay men and lesbians are parents, most through heterosexual marriages that ended in divorce, a few through adoption or reproductive technologies (Patterson, 1996). In the past, laws assuming that homosexuals could not be adequate parents led those who divorced a heterosexual partner to lose custody of their children. Today, several states hold that sexual orientation is irrelevant to custody. In others, fierce prejudice against homosexual parents still prevails.

Families headed by a homosexual parent or a gay or lesbian couple are very similar to those of heterosexuals. Gay and lesbian parents are as committed to and effective at the parental role, and sometimes more so. Indeed, some research indicates that gay fathers are more consistent in setting limits and more responsive to their children's needs than are heterosexual fathers, perhaps because gay men's less traditional gender identity fosters involvement with children (Bigner & Jacobsen, 1989). In lesbian families, quality of mother–child interaction is as positive as in heterosexual families. And children of lesbian mothers regard their mother's partner as very much a parent (Brewaeys et al., 1997). Whether born to or adopted by their parents or conceived through donor insemination, children in homosexual families are as well adjusted as other children, and the large majority are heterosexual (Bailey et al., 1995; Chan, Raboy, & Patterson, 1998; Golombok & Tasker, 1996).

When extended-family members have difficulty accepting them, homosexual mothers and fathers often build "families of choice" through friends, who assume the roles of relatives. But most of the time, parents of gays and lesbians cannot endure a permanent rift. With time, interactions of homosexual parents with their families of origin become more positive and serve as supports for child rearing (Hare, 1994).

Partners of homosexual parents usually take on some caregiving responsibilities and are attached to the children. But their involvement varies with the way children were brought into the relationship. When children were adopted or conceived through reproductive technologies, partners tend to be more involved than when children resulted from a previous heterosexual relationship (Hare & Richards, 1993).

Overall, children of homosexuals can be distinguished from other children only by issues related to living in a nonsupportive society. The greatest concern of gay and lesbian parents is that their children will be stigmatized by their parents' sexual orientation (Hare, 1994).

NEVER-MARRIED SINGLE-PARENT FAMILIES

Children of never-married parents make up 10 percent of the child population in the United States. Of these, 89 percent are mothers and 11 percent, fathers (U.S. Bureau of the Census, 1998). Although still few in number, more single women over age 30 in high-status occupations have become parents in recent years, often (as mentioned earlier) through adoption or through donor insemination (see Chapter 3). Little is known about how their children fare in comparison with children entering families the same way but reared by two parents.

The largest group of never-married parents are African-American young women. In 1996, over 60 percent of births to black women in their twenties were out of wedlock, compared with only 18 percent to white women. African-American women postpone marriage more and childbirth less than do all other American ethnic groups (Glick, 1997; U.S. Bureau of the Census, 1998). Overall, more black young children are being reared by never-married mothers than by married couples or divorced mothers—a trend partly due to the high rate of African-American teenage childbearing (see Chapter 5).

A cultural shift toward later marriage over the past 20 years has contributed to a rise in never-married motherhood among all ethnic groups. But job loss, persisting unemployment, and consequent inability of many black men to support a family have led this increase to be particularly marked for African Americans (Rice, 1994). Never-married black mothers tap the extended family, especially their own mothers, for help in caring for children. For most, marriage occurs several years after birth of the first child, not necessarily to the child's biological father. Nevertheless, these couples function much like other first-marriage parents. Their children are often unaware that the father is a stepfather, and couples do not report the child-rearing difficulties associated with remarriage that we will take up shortly (Ganong & Coleman, 1994).

Perhaps because they are shielded from marital strife, children of never-married mothers show slightly better academic performance and emotional adjustment than do children of divorced or remarried mothers. But they do not do as well as children in first-marriage families (Demo & Acock, 1996). Never-married parenthood among low-income women is costly, since living in a single-mother household makes it more difficult to overcome poverty. Many children in these homes display developmental problems associated with economic hardship. In addition, compared with children in low-income, two-parent families, children reared by never-married mothers experience less warmth, communication, monitoring, and connection with a male parental figure—factors linked to poor school achievement and antisocial behavior (Coley, 1998; Florsheim, Tolan, & Gorman-Smith, 1998). Strengthening social support, education, and employment opportunities for low-income parents would encourage marriage as well as help never-married mothers rear their children.

DIVORCE

Parental separation and divorce are extremely common in the lives of American children. Between 1960 and 1985, the divorce rate in the United States doubled and then stabilized. Currently, it is the highest in the world (see Figure 14.4 on page 578). About half of American marriages end in divorce, three-fourths of which involve children. This means that at any given time, about 1 in 4 American children live in single-parent households. Although the large majority (85 percent) reside with their mothers, the number in father-headed households has increased over the past decade, from 9 to 14 percent (Hetherington & Stanley-Hagan, 1997).

These adopted children spend a quiet hour watching television with their two fathers. Homosexual parents are as committed to and effective at child rearing as are heterosexual parents. Their children are well adjusted, and the large majority develop a heterosexual orientation. (S. Grazin/The Image Works)

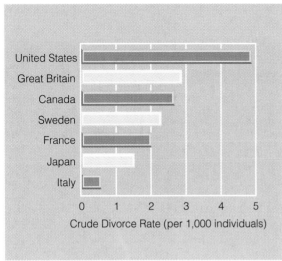

FIGURE 14.4

Divorce rate in seven industrialized nations. The divorce rate in the United States is the highest in the world.

(Adapted from McKenry & Price, 1995.)

United States
Great Britain
Canada
Sweden
France
Japan
Italy

0   1   2   3   4   5
Crude Divorce Rate (per 1,000 individuals)

Children spend an average of 5 years in a single-parent home, or almost a third of their total childhood. For many, divorce eventually leads to new family relationships. About two-thirds of divorced parents marry a second time. Half of these children eventually experience a third major change—the end of their parents' second marriage (Hetherington & Henderson, 1997).

These figures reveal that divorce is not a single event in the lives of parents and children. Instead, it is a transition that leads to a variety of new living arrangements, accompanied by changes in housing, income, and family roles and responsibilities. Since the 1960s, many studies have reported that marital breakup is quite stressful for children (Hetherington, Bridges, & Insabella, 1998). But the research also reveals wide individual differences in how children respond. The custodial parent's psychological health, the child's characteristics, and social supports within the family and surrounding community contribute to children's adjustment.

Our understanding of the impact of divorce has been enriched by several longitudinal studies as well as many short-term investigations. As we consider current evidence, you may find it helpful to refer to the summary in Table 14.3.

■ **IMMEDIATE CONSEQUENCES.** Family conflict often rises around the time of divorce as parents try to settle disputes over children, finances, and personal belongings. Once one parent moves out, additional events threaten supportive interaction between parents and children. Mother-headed households typically experience a sharp drop in income. Three-fourths of divorced mothers in the United States get less than the full amount of child support or none at all from the absent father (Children's Defense Fund, 1999). They often have to move to new housing for economic reasons, reducing supportive ties to neighbors and friends.

These life circumstances often lead to high maternal stress, depression, and anxiety and to a disorganized family situation called "minimal parenting" (Hetherington, 1989; Wallerstein & Kelly, 1980). Predictable events and routines—scheduled meals and bedtimes, household chores, and joint parent–child activities—usually disintegrate. As children react with distress and anger to their less secure home lives, discipline may become harsh and inconsistent as mothers try to recapture control of their upset youngsters. Noncustodial fathers usually spend considerable time with children immediately after divorce,

TABLE 14.3

Factors Related to Children's Adjustment to Divorce

Factor	Description
Custodial parents' psychological health	A mature, well-adjusted parent is better able to handle stress, shield the child from conflict, and engage in authoritative parenting.
Child characteristics	
Age	Preschool and early school-age children often blame themselves and show intense separation anxiety. Older children and adolescents may also react strongly by engaging in disruptive, antisocial acts. However, some display unusually mature, responsible behavior.
Temperament	Children with difficult temperaments are less able to withstand stress and show longer-lasting difficulties.
Sex	Boys in mother-custody homes experience more severe and longer lasting problems than do girls.
Social supports	The ability of parents to set aside their hostilities; contact with the noncustodial parent; and positive relationships with extended-family members, teachers, and friends lead to improved outcomes for children.

but often this contact wanes. About 20 percent of American children of divorce have little or no paternal contact (Hetherington, Bridges, & Insabella, 1998). When fathers see their children only occasionally, they are inclined to be permissive and indulgent. This often conflicts with the mother's style of parenting and makes her task of managing the child on a day-to-day basis even more difficult.

In view of these changes, it is not surprising that children experience painful emotional reactions. But the intensity of their feelings and the way they are expressed vary with the child's age, temperament, and sex.

CHILDREN'S AGE. The cognitive immaturity of preschool and early school-age children makes it difficult for them to grasp the reasons behind their parents' separation. Because they tend to blame themselves and take the marital breakup as a sign that they could be abandoned by both parents, younger children are often profoundly upset. They may whine and cling, displaying intense separation anxiety. Preschoolers are especially likely to fantasize that their parents will get back together (Hetherington, 1989; Wallerstein, Corbin, & Lewis, 1988).

Older children are better able to understand the reasons behind their parents' divorce. They recognize that strong differences of opinion, incompatible personalities, and lack of caring for one another are responsible (Mazur, 1993). The ability to accurately assign blame may reduce some of the pain that children feel. Still, many school-age and adolescent youngsters react strongly to the end of their parents' marriage, particularly when family conflict is high and parental supervision of children is low (Forehand et al., 1991). Some escape into undesirable peer activities, such as running away, truancy, early sexual activity, and delinquent behavior (Simons & Chao, 1996; Tasker & Richards, 1994).

However, not all older children react this way. For some—especially the oldest child in the family—divorce can trigger more mature behavior. These youngsters may willingly take on extra burdens, such as household tasks, care and protection of younger siblings, and emotional support of a depressed, anxious mother. But if these demands are too great, older children may eventually become resentful and withdraw from the family into some of the more destructive behavior patterns just described (Hetherington, 1993, 1999).

CHILDREN'S TEMPERAMENT AND SEX. When temperamentally difficult children are exposed to stressful life events and inadequate parenting, their problems are magnified. In contrast, easy children are less often targets of parental anger and are also better at coping with adversity when it hits. After a moderately stressful divorce, some easy children (usually girls) actually emerge with enhanced coping skills (Hetherington, 1993).

These findings help us understand sex-related differences in children's response to divorce. Girls sometimes respond with crying, self-criticism, and withdrawal. At other times, they show demanding, attention-getting behavior. But in mother-custody families, boys typically experience more serious adjustment problems. Recall from Chapter 13 that boys are more active, assertive, and noncompliant—behaviors that increase with exposure to parental conflict and inconsistent discipline. Longitudinal studies in Great Britain and the United States reveal that long before the marital breakup, many sons of divorcing couples were impulsive and defiant—behaviors that may have contributed to as well as been caused by their parents' marital problems. As a result, these boys entered the period of turmoil surrounding divorce with a reduced capacity to cope with family stress (Cherlin et al., 1991; Hetherington, 1991).

Perhaps because their behavior is so unruly, boys of divorcing parents receive less emotional support from mothers, teachers, and peers. Furthermore, the coercive cycles of interaction that boys often establish with their divorced mothers soon spread to sibling relations (MacKinnon, 1989). These outcomes compound boys' difficulties. Children of both sexes show declines in achievement during the aftermath of divorce, but school problems are greater for boys (Guidubaldi & Cleminshaw, 1985).

■ **LONG-TERM CONSEQUENCES.** The majority of children show improved adjustment by 2 years after divorce. Yet for a few, persisting emotional distress and declines in school achievement contribute to serious adjustment difficulties into young adulthood (Chase-Lansdale, Cherlin, & Kiernan, 1995).

After parents divorce, most children reside with their mothers. Those who also stay involved with their fathers fare best in development. For girls, a good father–daughter relationship appears to contribute to heterosexual development. For boys, it seems to play a crucial role in overall psychological well-being.

(Will Hart)

Because they are more often exposed to ineffective child rearing, boys and children with difficult temperaments are especially likely to drop out of school and display antisocial behavior in adolescence, but some girls also show these lasting problems (Hetherington, 1993; McLanahan & Sandefur, 1994). The most consistent long-term effects for girls involve heterosexual behavior—a rise in sexual activity at adolescence, in teenage childbearing, and in risk of divorce in adulthood (Cherlin, Kiernan, & Chase-Lansdale, 1995; Hetherington, 1997).

The overriding factor in positive adjustment following divorce is effective parenting—in particular, how well the custodial parent handles stress, shields the child from family conflict, and engages in authoritative parenting (Hetherington, 1991; Simons & Johnson, 1996). Contact with noncustodial fathers is also important. For girls, a good father–child relationship appears to contribute to heterosexual development. For boys, it seems to affect overall psychological well-being.

In fact, several studies indicate that outcomes for sons are better when the father is the custodial parent (Camara & Resnick, 1988; Clarke-Stewart & Hayward, 1996). Most of the time, custodial fathers are financially better off than custodial mothers—one reason that fathers report less child-rearing stress. But even when income is controlled, boys in father-custody families are better adjusted. Fathers are more likely to praise a boy's good behavior and less likely to ignore his disruptiveness. The father's image of greater power and authority may also help him obtain more compliance from a son.

Although divorce is painful for children, there is clear evidence that remaining in a high-conflict intact family is much worse than making the transition to a low-conflict, single-parent household (Amato, Loomis, & Booth, 1995). When divorcing parents put aside their disagreements and support each other in their child-rearing roles, children have the best chance of growing up competent, stable, and happy. Caring extended-family members, positive sibling relationships, and warm friendships can also reduce the likelihood that divorce will result in long-term disruption (Grych & Fincham, 1997).

Schools make a difference as well. Cognitive and social outcomes are improved if teachers of preschool and school-age children create a democratic classroom atmosphere in which warmth is combined with reasonable demands for mature behavior (Hetherington, Bridges, & Insabella, 1998; Peres & Pasternack, 1991). Note that these very factors are linked to favorable adjustment in intact families. Children of divorce clearly benefit from a nurturant, predictable school environment when these experiences are not available at home.

■ **INTERVENTIONS.** Awareness that divorce is highly stressful for parents and children has led to community-based services aimed at helping them through this difficult time. Parents Without Partners is a national organization with a membership of 180,000. It provides publications, telephone referrals, and programs through local chapters designed to relieve the problems of single parents. Support groups for children are also available, often sponsored by churches, synagogues, schools, and mental health agencies, in which children share fears and concerns and learn coping skills. Evaluations of the effectiveness of these programs suggest that they can reduce stress and promote improved communication between family members (Emery, 1988).

Another recently developed intervention is **divorce mediation.** It consists of a series of meetings between divorcing adults and a trained professional, who tries to help them settle disputes, such as property division and child custody. Its purpose is to avoid legal battles that intensify family conflict. Research reveals that it increases out-of-court settlements, compliance with agreements, and feelings of well-being among divorcing parents (Emery, Mathews, & Kitzmann, 1994). By reducing family hostilities, divorce mediation has great benefits for children. In one study, parents randomly assigned to mediation reported more frequent contact by the noncustodial parent and more positive communication about child-related matters 9 years later than did parents who ended their marriages in a courtroom battle (Dillon & Emery, 1996).

divorce mediation A series of meetings between divorcing adults and a trained professional, who tries to help them settle disputes. Aimed at avoiding legal battles that intensify family conflict.

To encourage both parents to stay involved with children, today courts more often award **joint custody,** which grants mother and father equal say in important decisions about the child's upbringing. Nevertheless, many experts have raised questions about the practice. Joint custody results in a variety of living arrangements. In most instances, children reside with one parent and see the other on a fixed schedule, much like the typical sole-custody situation. But in other cases, parents share physical custody, and children must move between homes and sometimes schools and peer groups. These transitions introduce a new kind of instability that may be especially hard on some children (Johnston, Kline, & Tschann, 1989). The success of joint custody requires a cooperative relationship between divorcing parents. If they continue to quarrel, it prolongs children's exposure to a hostile family atmosphere (Furstenberg & Cherlin, 1991).

For this reason, *grandparent visitation rights* can also create difficulties for children. All 50 U.S. states permit grandparents to seek legal visitation judgments. The policy arose out of a well-intentioned desire to foster children's access to social supports and a belief in the specialness of the grandparent–grandchild relationship. But when parents are divorcing, the behavior of grandparents varies greatly, from constructive help to entanglement in parental battles (Bostock, 1994). Unfortunately, intense conflict usually lies behind the legal petitions of grandparents who fail to work out visitation informally. Because children are in danger of becoming embroiled in yet another family dispute, the courts are wise to exercise restraint in awarding grandparent visitation privileges in divorce cases.

Finally, many single-parent families depend on child support from the absent parent to relieve financial strain. In response to federal law, all states have established procedures for withholding wages from parents who fail to make these payments. Although child support is usually not enough to lift a single-parent family out of poverty, it can ease the burden substantially. An added benefit is that a noncustodial father is more likely to maintain contact with his children if he pays child support (Garfinkel & McLanahan, 1995).

BLENDED FAMILIES

Life in a single-parent home is often a temporary condition. Many parents remarry within a few years. Others *cohabit,* or share an intimate sexual relationship and a residence with a partner outside of marriage. Some cohabiting couples eventually marry and some do not. In either case, parent, stepparent, and children form a new family structure called the **blended,** or **reconstituted, family.**

For some children, this expanded family network is a positive turn of events that brings with it greater adult attention. But for most, it presents difficult adjustments. Stepparents often use different child-rearing practices than the child was used to, and having to switch to new rules and expectations can be stressful. In addition, children often regard steprelatives as "intruders" into the family (Hetherington & Jodl, 1994). But how well children adapt is, once again, related to the overall quality of family functioning. This often depends on which parent forms a new relationship and on the age and sex of the child. As we will see, older children and girls seem to have the hardest time (refer to Table 14.4 on page 582).

■ **MOTHER–STEPFATHER FAMILIES.** The most frequent form of blended family is a mother–stepfather arrangement, since mothers generally retain custody of the child. Boys usually adjust quickly. They welcome a stepfather who is warm and involved, who refrains from exerting his authority too quickly, and who offers relief from the coercive cycles of interaction that tend to build with their divorced mothers. Mothers' friction with sons also declines due to greater economic security, another adult to share household tasks, and an end to loneliness (Stevenson & Black, 1995). In contrast, girls adapt less favorably when custodial mothers find new partners. Stepfathers disrupt the close ties many girls have established with their mothers in the single-parent family, and girls often react to the new arrangement with sulky, resistant behavior (Hetherington, 1993; Vuchinich et al., 1991).

Note, however, that age affects these findings. Early adolescents of both sexes find it harder to adjust to blended families (Bray & Berger, 1993; Hetherington, 1993). Young

joint custody A child custody arrangement following divorce in which the court grants both parents equal say in important decisions about the child's upbringing.

blended, or reconstituted, family A family structure resulting from cohabitation or remarriage that includes parent, stepparent, and children.

TABLE 14.4

Factors Related to Children's Adjustment to Blended Families

Factor	Description
Form of blended family	Children living in father–stepmother families display more adjustment difficulties than do those in mother–stepfather families, perhaps because father-custody children start out with more problems.
Child characteristics	
Age	Early adolescents find it harder to adjust, perhaps because the presence of a stepparent makes it more difficult for them to deal with sexuality and autonomy. Also, compared to children, they are more aware of the impact of remarriage on their own lives.
Sex	Girls display more severe reactions than do boys because of interruptions in close bonds with custodial parents and greater conflict with stepmothers.
Repeated marital transitions	The more marital transitions, the greater the risk of severe and long-lasting adjustment problems.
Social supports	(See Table 14.3 on page 578.)

teenagers are in the midst of dealing with their own budding sexuality and establishing autonomy. The presence of a stepparent may make these tasks more difficult. And perhaps because they are more aware of the impact of remarriage on their own lives, they challenge some aspects of it that children simply accept, creating more relationship issues with their steprelatives.

About one-third of adolescent boys and one-fourth of adolescent girls disengage from their stepfamilies, spending little time at home. Instead, they may turn to a friend's family (as a "surrogate"), extracurricular activities, a job, or peers. When disengagement leads to positive relationships with adults and constructive pursuits, teenagers fare quite well. When it results in involvement with antisocial peers and little adult supervision, it is linked to serious difficulties—poor achievement, school dropout, sexual activity, substance abuse, and delinquency (Hetherington & Jodl, 1994).

■ **FATHER–STEPMOTHER FAMILIES.** Research reveals more confusion for children in father–stepmother families. In the case of noncustodial fathers, remarriage often leads to reduced contact. They tend to withdraw from their "previous" families, more so if they have daughters rather than sons (Hetherington, 1997). When fathers have custody, children typically react negatively to remarriage. One reason is that children living with fathers often start out with more problems. Perhaps the biological mother could no longer handle the unruly child (usually a boy), so the father and his new wife are faced with a youngster who has serious behavior problems. In other instances, the father is granted custody because of a very close relationship with the child, and his remarriage disrupts this bond (Buchanan, Maccoby, & Dornbusch, 1996).

Girls, especially, have a hard time getting along with their stepmothers (Hobart & Brown, 1988). Sometimes (as just mentioned) this occurs because the girl's relationship with her father is threatened by the remarriage. In addition, girls often become entangled in loyalty conflicts between their two mother figures. Noncustodial mothers (unlike fathers) are likely to maintain regular contact with children, but frequent visits by mothers are associated with less favorable stepmother–stepdaughter relations. The longer girls live in father–stepmother households, the more positive their interaction with stepmothers becomes. With time and patience they do adjust, and eventually girls benefit from the support of a second mother figure (Hetherington & Jodl, 1994).

■ **SUPPORT FOR BLENDED FAMILIES.** In blended families, as in divorce, there are multiple pathways leading to diverse outcomes. Family life education and therapy can help parents and children adapt to the complexities of their new circumstances. Effective approaches encourage stepparents to move into their new roles gradually rather than abruptly. Only when a warm bond has formed between stepparents and stepchildren is more active parenting possible. In addition, couples often need help in forming a "parenting coalition"—cooperation and consistency in child rearing (Visher, 1994). By limiting loyalty conflicts, this allows children to benefit from stepparent relationships and increased diversity in their lives.

■ **REPEATED MARITAL TRANSITIONS.** Unfortunately, many children do not have a chance to settle into a happy blended family, since the divorce rate for second marriages is higher than for first marriages. In a study of fourth-grade boys, the more marital transitions children experienced, the more severe and prolonged their adjustment difficulties (see Figure 14.5). Furthermore, parents with poor child-rearing skills and antisocial tendencies (as indicated by arrest records, drug use, and personality tests) were particularly likely to undergo several divorces and remarriages. In the process, they exposed their children to recurring episodes of high family conflict and inconsistent parenting (Capaldi & Patterson, 1991).

When marital transitions pile up, they become part of a cluster of negative life events that severely disrupt children's development. As the Variations box on page 584 reveals, the problems of these and other highly troubled parents have led to a rise in yet another family form, in which grandparents take full responsibility for rearing children.

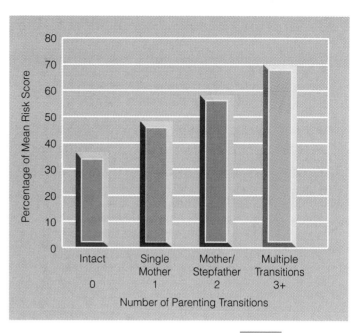

FIGURE 14.5

Boys' risk for poor adjustment by number of parenting transitions. Risk was determined by averaging seven adjustment measures: antisocial behavior, drug use, deviant peer associations, peer rejection, poor academic skills, low self-esteem, and depression. The greater the number of transitions, the higher the risk score.

(Adapted from Capaldi & Patterson, 1991.)

MATERNAL EMPLOYMENT AND DUAL-EARNER FAMILIES

For many years, divorce has been associated with a high rate of maternal employment, due to financial strains experienced by single mothers. But over the last several decades, women of all sectors of the population—not just those who are single and poor—have gone to work in increasing numbers. Today, single and married mothers are in the labor market in nearly equal proportions. For children of any age, over 60 percent of their mothers are employed. This figure rises from 64 percent in the preschool years to over 70 percent in middle childhood (U.S. Bureau of the Census, 1998).

In Chapter 10, we discussed the impact of maternal employment on attachment and concluded that for babies, the consequences depend on the quality of child care and the continuing parent–child relationship. This same conclusion applies during later years. In addition, several factors—the mother's work satisfaction, the support she receives from her husband, and the child's sex—have a bearing on how children fare.

■ **MATERNAL EMPLOYMENT AND CHILD DEVELOPMENT.** As long as mothers want to work, like their jobs, and have satisfactory child-care arrangements, employment is associated with greater life satisfaction for both low-SES and middle-SES mothers (Beyer, 1995; Goldberg & Easterbrooks, 1988). Children of mothers who enjoy working and remain committed to parenting show very favorable adjustment—a higher sense of self-esteem, more positive family and peer relations, less gender-stereotyped beliefs, and better grades in school (Williams & Radin, 1993). Outcomes are especially positive for girls, who profit from the image of female competence. African-American adolescent girls whose mothers worked during the daughter's early years are more likely to stay in school (Wolfer & Moen, 1996). And overall, children of employed mothers have higher educational aspirations and, in college, are more likely to choose nontraditional careers, such as law, medicine, and physics (Hoffman, 1989).

These diverse benefits undoubtedly result from parenting practices. Employed mothers who value their parenting role are more likely to use authoritative child rearing (Greenberger & Goldberg, 1989). Also, children in dual-earner households devote more daily hours to doing homework under parental guidance. And contrary to popular belief,

Grandparents Rearing Grandchildren: The Skipped-Generation Family

N EARLY 1.5 MILLION American children and adolescents—2 percent of the child population—live with grandparents but apart from parents, in **skipped-generation families** (U.S. Bureau of the Census, 1998). The number of grandparents rearing grandchildren has increased over the past decade. The arrangement occurs in all ethnic groups, although more often among African-American and Hispanic children than among Caucasian-American children (Szinovacz, 1998).

The following grandmother's account illustrates the circumstances in which skipped-generation families form:

> I think [the child's mother] is doing an awful lot of drugs. I don't know if it's serious drugs, but enough that she wasn't doing a good job. They were doing an awful lot of partying, and I just finally went to her one day and said, "Your life is messed up, let me take the baby for a while so you can get your life together." And it was just because we wanted her [the granddaughter] out of there. She had become our main priority. (Jendrek, 1994, p. 209)

Usually, grandparents step in because substance abuse, emotional problems, or physical illness prevent the child's parents, most often the mother, from engaging in competent child rearing (Burton, 1992; Woodworth, 1996). At times, child welfare authorities, out of a preference for placing the child with relatives rather than in a foster home, approach the grandparent, who assumes temporary or permanent legal custody. In most instances, grandparents offer their assistance, sometimes with and sometimes without legal responsibility. Most say they took action to protect the child only when the parents' situation became intolerable.

Because the skipped-generation family structure is not freely chosen, many grandparents face a highly stressful child-rearing situation. Previous family experiences have left their mark, in the form of high rates of learning difficulties, depression, and antisocial behavior (Pinson-Millburn et al., 1996). These children are not only challenging to rear but introduce financial burdens into households, many of which are already low income. Grandparents struggle daily with dilemmas—wanting to be grandparents, not parents; wanting the parent to be present in the child's life but fearing for the child's well-being if the parent returns and cannot provide good care. Daily child-rearing tasks mean that grandparents have less time for spouse, friends, and leisure when they had expected to have more time. Many report feeling tired,

Many grandparents are taking on the responsibility of rearing the third and sometimes the fourth generation of their families. They come to care for grandchildren through a variety of circumstances—most often, parental substance abuse, emotional problems, or physical illness. Grandparents in skipped-generation families face myriad problems, including children who are challenging to rear, shattered dreams of relaxation and freedom at this time in their lives, and significant financial burdens.

(Linda Rosier/NYT Pictures)

emotionally drained, and depressed (Goldberg-Glen et al., 1998; Minkler et al., 1997).

Skipped-generation families have a tremendous need for social and financial support. Despite the burdens, these grandparents seem to realize their widespread image as "silent saviors." A survey of a large representative sample of U.S. families revealed that compared with children in divorced, single-parent families and in blended families, children reared by grandparents were better behaved in school, less susceptible to physical illness, and doing just as well academically (Solomon & Marx, 1995).

---

maternal employment does not reduce the amount of time school-age children and adolescents spend with their mothers. But it does result in more time with fathers, who take on greater child-care responsibility (Richards & Duckett, 1994; Coltrane, 1996). More paternal contact is related to higher intelligence and achievement test scores, mature social behavior, and gender-stereotype flexibility (Gottfried, 1991; Radin, 1994).

However, when employment places heavy demands on the mother's schedule, children are at risk for ineffective parenting. Working long hours and spending little time with children are associated with less favorable cognitive and social competence (Moorehouse, 1991). In contrast, part-time employment seems to have benefits for children of all ages,

skipped-generation family A family structure in which children live with grandparents but apart from parents.

probably because it prevents work overload, thereby helping mothers meet children's needs (Lerner & Abrams, 1994; Williams & Radin, 1993).

As long as this employed mother enjoys her job, remains committed to parenting, and finds satisfactory child care arrangements, her child is likely to develop high self-esteem, positive family and peer relations, and flexible beliefs about gender. But when employment places heavy demands on the mother's schedule and she receives little or no help from the father, children are at risk for ineffective parenting and less favorable cognitive and social outcomes. (Jonathan Nourok/Tony Stone Images)

■ **SUPPORT FOR EMPLOYED MOTHERS AND FATHERS.** When mothers have the necessary supports to engage in effective parenting, maternal employment offers children many advantages. In dual-earner families, the husband's willingness to share responsibilities is crucial. Although men assist to a greater extent than they did in the past, women still shoulder most household and child-care tasks (Parke & Buriel, 1998). If the father helps very little or not at all, the mother carries a double load, at home and at work, leading to fatigue, distress, and reduced time and energy for children.

Employed mothers and dual-earner parents need the assistance of work settings, communities, and government policies. Part-time employment and time off when children are ill would help them juggle the demands of work and child rearing. Although these workplace supports are widely available in Canada and Western Europe, at present only unpaid employment leave is mandated by U.S. federal law (see Chapter 3, page 117). Equal pay and equal employment opportunities for women are also important. Because these policies enhance financial status and morale, they improve the way mothers feel and behave when they arrive home at the end of the working day. Finally, high-quality child care is vital for parents' peace of mind and children's healthy development, as we will see in the following section.

CHILD CARE

Preschoolers spend even more time away from their parents than infants and toddlers do. Over the last 30 years, the number of young children in child care has steadily increased. Figure 14.6 on page 586 shows the varied ways American 3- and 4-year-olds are cared for while their parents are at work. About 39 percent spend most of these hours in their own home, cared for by a relative or nonrelative. Of settings designed for child care, child-care homes serve approximately 12 percent of 3- and 4-year-olds. A much larger proportion— 40 percent—attend child-care centers, which usually specialize in preschoolers; fewer take infants and toddlers or provide before- and after-school care for 5- to 13-year-olds. Figure 14.6 also reflects the shortage of affordable child care in the United States. Five percent of employed mothers of 3- and 4-year-olds get by without any child-care arrangements, a figure that is similar for infants and toddlers and that rises to 51 percent for school-age children (Lombardi, 1993).

■ **CHILD-CARE QUALITY AND CHILDREN'S DEVELOPMENT.** Recall from Chapter 8 that early intervention can enhance the development of economically disadvantaged children. However, as we noted in Chapter 10, much child care in the United States is not of this high quality (see Figure 10.6 on page 434). Preschoolers in poor-quality child care score lower on measures of cognitive and social skills, whereas those in high-quality care develop more favorably, regardless of whether they come from low-SES or middle-SES homes (Hausfather et al., 1997; Howes, 1988b, 1990; Lamb, 1998; Phillips et al., 1994).

What are the ingredients of high-quality child care for preschoolers? Several large-scale studies of center- and home-based care reveal that the following factors are important: group size (number of children in a single space), caregiver–child ratio, caregivers' educational preparation, and caregivers' personal commitment to learning about and caring for children. When these characteristics are favorable, adults are more verbally stimulating and sensitive to preschoolers' needs, and children do especially well on measures of intelligence, language, and social development (Galinsky et al., 1994; Helburn, 1995; Howes, Phillips, & Whitebook, 1992). Other research shows that spacious, well-equipped environments and

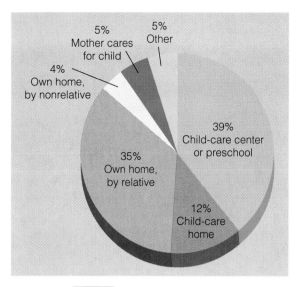

5%
Mother cares
for child

5%
Other

4%
Own home,
by nonrelative

39%
Child-care center
or preschool

35%
Own home,
by relative

12%
Child-care
home

FIGURE 14.6

Who's minding America's pre-schoolers? The chart refers to settings in which 3- and 4-year-olds spend most time while their parents are at work. Over one-fourth of 3- and 4-year-olds experience more than one type of child care, a fact not reflected in the chart.
(U.S. Bureau of the Census, 1997.)

a rich variety of developmentally appropriate activities also contribute to positive outcomes (Howes, 1988b).

Table 14.5 summarizes characteristics of high-quality child care for preschoolers, based on standards of developmentally appropriate practice devised by the National Association for the Education of Young Children. (Return to Chapter 10, page 435, to review signs of high-quality child care for infants and toddlers.) When these ingredients are absent, children's well-being is compromised. Parents who place their preschoolers in low-quality child care tend to lead stressful lives and use inappropriate child-rearing techniques—a combination of factors that poses an especially serious risk to children's development (Howes, 1990).

■ **CHILD-CARE POLICIES IN THE UNITED STATES AND OTHER INDUSTRIALIZED NATIONS.** As we noted in Chapters 1 and 10, the overall state of American child care is alarmingly inadequate. Many caregivers have little or no specialized education for teaching young children, and in some states, one adult is permitted to supervise as many as 12 to 15 preschoolers. From 75 to 90 percent of child-care homes are unlicensed and therefore not monitored for quality. Caregivers' salaries typically fall below the poverty line, with few if any fringe benefits. As a result, over 40 percent leave their jobs annually (Willer et al., 1991; Zigler & Gilman, 1993). Tax relief to help American parents pay for child care has increased in recent years, but many have difficulty affording the weekly expense. At current rates, child-care fees consume more than 25 percent of the annual earnings of a minimum-wage worker with one young child (Maynard & McGinnis, 1993). Although publicly funded centers for low-income families exist, they fall far short of the need. In some places, waiting lists have swelled into the thousands (Children's Defense Fund, 1999).

TABLE 14.5

High-Quality Child Care for Preschool Children

Program Characteristics	Signs of Quality
Physical setting	Indoor environment is clean, in good repair, and well ventilated. Classroom space is divided into richly equipped activity areas, including make-believe play, blocks, science, math, games and puzzles, books, art, and music. Fenced outdoor play space is equipped with swings, climbing equipment, tricycles, and sandbox.
Group size	In preschools and day-care centers, group size is no greater than 18 to 20 children with 2 teachers.
Caregiver–child ratio	In day-care centers, teacher is responsible for no more than 8 to 10 children. In family day-care homes, caregiver is responsible for no more than 6 children.
Daily activities	Most of the time, children work individually or in small groups. Children select many of their own activities and learn through experiences relevant to their own lives. Teachers facilitate children's involvement, accept individual differences, and adjust expectations to children's developing capacities.
Interactions between adults and children	Teachers move between groups and individuals, asking questions, offering suggestions, and adding more complex ideas. They use positive guidance techniques, such as modeling and encouraging expected behavior and redirecting children to more acceptable activities.
Teacher qualifications	Teachers have college-level specialized preparation in early childhood development, early childhood education, or a related field.
Relationships with parents	Parents are encouraged to observe and particiapte. Teachers talk frequently with parents about children's behavior and development.
Licensing and accreditation	Program is licensed by the state. If a preschool or day-care center, accreditation by the National Academy of Early Childhood Programs is evidence of an especially high-quality program. If a day-care home, accreditation by the National Association for Family Child Care is evidence of high-quality experiences for children.

Sources: Bredekamp & Copple, 1997; National Association for the Education of Young Children, 1998.

Child care for school-age children is widely available in Australia but rare in the United States. These Australian children have access to special lessons as part of a government-supported after-school program. Low-SES children, who otherwise would have few opportunities for such enrichment activities, benefit greatly—in school performance, peer relations, and psychological adjustment.

(Carly Wolinsky/Stock Boston)

In Australia and Western Europe, government-supported child care up to the age of school entry is widely available. Caregivers are usually paid on the same scale as elementary school teachers, and they receive health insurance and other benefits just like any other citizen. Standards for child care are rigorously set and enforced. Center-based care is the most common form, but many governments also support child-care homes by paying caregivers directly, providing training for them, and inspecting for health and safety. Since programs are heavily subsidized, parents pay only a small income-related fee, usually less than 10 percent of the average woman's wages (Ebbeck & Ebbeck, 1999; Kamerman, 1993; Scarr et al., 1993).

Child care is a legal right and nearly as accessible as public schooling in Australia and Western Europe. It is one element in a wide array of policies designed to attract mothers to the labor force while fostering children's development. Because the United States does not yet have a national child-care policy, it lags far behind other industrialized nations in supply, quality, and affordability of child care.

SELF-CARE

Care for school-age children of employed parents also has important implications for development. In recent years, much public concern has been voiced about the estimated 3.5 million 5- to 12-year-olds in the United States who regularly look after themselves during after-school hours (Belle, 1997).

Research on these **self-care children** reveals inconsistent findings. Some studies report that they suffer from low self-esteem, antisocial behavior, poor academic achievement, and fearfulness, whereas others show no such effects (Padilla & Landreth, 1989). What explains these contradictions? The way self-care children spend their time seems to be the crucial factor. Children who have a history of authoritative child rearing, are monitored from a distance by telephone calls, and have regular after-school chores appear responsible and well adjusted. In contrast, those left to their own devices are more likely to bend to peer pressures and engage in antisocial behavior (Steinberg, 1986).

Parents must consider children's maturity before deciding on self-care. Before age 8 or 9, children should not be left unsupervised because most are not yet competent to deal with emergencies (Galambos & Maggs, 1991). Unfortunately, when children are not mature enough to handle the self-care arrangement, many employed parents have no alternative. After-school programs for 6- to 13-year-olds are rare in American communities. Enrolling children in poor-quality after-school care can undermine their academic and social competence (Vandell & Corasaniti, 1988). In contrast, where high-quality programs exist, low-SES children who otherwise would have few opportunities for enrichment activities (scouting, music lessons, and organized sports) show improved school performance, peer relations, and psychological adjustment (Posner & Vandell, 1994).

self-care children Children who regularly look after themselves during after-school hours.

ASK YOURSELF . . .

♦ *"How come you don't study hard and get good grades like your sister?" a mother exclaimed in exasperation after seeing her son's poor report card. What impact do remarks like this have on sibling interaction, and why?*

♦ *What advice would you give divorcing parents of two school-age sons about how to help their children adapt to life in a single-parent family?*

♦ *Eight-year-old Bobby's mother has just found employment, so Bobby takes care of himself after school. What factors are likely to affect Bobby's adjustment to this arrangement?*

♦ CONNECTIONS
Review research on resilient children in Chapter 1 (see page 10). Are factors that foster resiliency similar to those that promote favorable adjustment to divorce and remarriage? Explain.

BRIEF REVIEW

Rapid changes in family life have taken place in industrialized nations. The trend toward a smaller family size is associated with more favorable parenting and child development. Nevertheless, most children continue to grow up with at least one sibling. Although unequal treatment by parents promotes sibling rivalry, sibling relationships serve as important sources of companionship, emotional support, and assistance. Only children are just as well adjusted and socially competent as children with siblings, and they are advantaged in self-esteem, academic achievement, and educational attainment. Compared to their nonadopted agemates, adopted children have more emotional and learning difficulties in childhood—a difference that disappears by adulthood. Children of gay and lesbian parents develop as favorably as other children, and the majority are heterosexual. Because of economic hardship, many children of never-married mothers display developmental problems.

Large numbers of American children experience the divorce of their parents. Although many adjust well by 2 years after the divorce, boys and temperamentally difficult children are likely to experience more severe and lasting problems. Effective parenting is the most important factor in helping children adapt to life in a single-parent family. When parents cohabit or remarry, daughters, early adolescents, and children living in father–stepmother families have a harder time.

Maternal employment is related to high self-esteem, mature social behavior, reduced gender stereotyping, and better grades in school. Outcomes are especially favorable for girls, but they depend on the demands of the mother's job and the father's participation in child rearing. High-quality child care during the preschool years fosters cognitive, language, and social development. Unfortunately, much child care in the United States is substandard and poses serious risks to children's development. The impact of self-care on school-age children varies with parenting practices and how children spend their time after school.

Vulnerable Families: Child Maltreatment

Families, as we indicated in the first part of this chapter, contribute to the maintenance of society by serving as contexts in which children are loved, protected, and encouraged to develop into competent, caring adults. Throughout our discussion of family transitions, we encountered examples of many factors, both within and outside the family, that contribute to parents' capacity to be warm, consistent, and appropriately demanding. As we turn now to the topic of child maltreatment, we will see that when these vital supports for effective child rearing break down, children as well as their parents can suffer terribly.

INCIDENCE AND DEFINITIONS

Child maltreatment is as old as the history of humankind, but only recently has there been widespread acceptance that the problem exists and research aimed at understanding it. Perhaps this increase in public and professional concern has occurred because child maltreatment is especially common in large industrialized nations. It happens so often in the United States that a recent government committee called it "a national emergency." Three million cases were reported to juvenile authorities in 1997, an increase of 132 percent over the previous decade (U.S. Department of Health and Human Services, 1999). The true figure is surely much higher, since most cases, including ones in which children suffer serious physical injury, go unreported.

Child maltreatment takes the following forms:

- *Physical abuse:* assaults on children that produce pain, cuts, welts, bruises, burns, broken bones, and other injuries

- *Sexual abuse:* sexual comments, fondling, intercourse, and other forms of exploitation

- *Physical neglect:* living conditions in which children do not receive enough food, clothing, medical attention, or supervision

- *Emotional neglect:* failure of caregivers to meet children's needs for affection and emotional support

- *Psychological abuse:* actions, such as ridicule, humiliation, scapegoating, or terrorizing, that damage children's cognitive, emotional, or social functioning

Although all experts recognize that these five types exist, they do not agree on how frequent and intense an adult's actions must be to be called maltreatment. Consensus is important, since without a definition of abuse and neglect, researchers are hampered in studying their origins and consequences for children and designing effective interventions. The greatest problems arise in the case of subtle, ambiguous behaviors (Barnett, Manly, & Cicchetti, 1993). All of us can agree that broken bones, cigarette burns, and bite marks are abusive, but the decision is harder to make in instances in which an adult touches or makes degrading comments to a child.

Some investigators regard psychological and sexual abuse as the most destructive forms. The rate of psychological abuse may be the highest, since it accompanies most other types. Yet definitions of psychological abuse are especially complex and serious in their consequences. If they are too narrow and include only the most severe instances of mental cruelty, they allow many harmful actions toward children to continue unchecked and untreated. If they are too lenient, they can result in arbitrary, disruptive legal intrusions into family life. More than 200,000 cases of child sexual abuse are reported each year (U.S. Department of Health and Human Services, 1999). Yet this statistic greatly underestimates the actual number, since affected children may feel frightened, confused, and guilty and are usually pressured into silence. (See the Social Issues box on pages 590–591.)

Children learn by repetition.

You don't have to hit to hurt.

San Francisco Child Abuse Council
(415) 668-0494

This poster reminds adults that degrading remarks can hit as hard as a fist. Public service announcements help prevent child abuse by educating people about the problem and informing them of where to seek help.

(Courtesy San Francisco Child Abuse Council)

ORIGINS OF CHILD MALTREATMENT

When child maltreatment first became a topic of research in the 1960s, it was viewed as rooted in adult psychological disturbance. The first studies indicated that adults who abused or neglected their children usually had a history of maltreatment in their own childhoods, unrealistic expectations that children would satisfy their own emotional needs, and poor control of aggressive impulses (Kempe et al., 1962; Spinetta & Rigler, 1972).

It soon became clear that although child maltreatment was more common among disturbed parents, a single "abusive personality type" did not exist. Sometimes, even "normal" parents harmed their children! Also, parents who were abused as children did not always repeat the cycle with their own youngsters (Buchanan, 1996; Simons et al., 1991).

For help in understanding child maltreatment, researchers turned to the social systems perspective on family functioning. They discovered that child abuse and neglect are affected by many interacting variables—at the family, community, and cultural levels. Table 14.6 on page 592 summarizes factors associated with child maltreatment. The more that are present, the greater the risk that abuse or neglect will occur. Let's examine each set of influences in turn.

■ **THE FAMILY.** Within the family, certain children—those whose characteristics make them more of a challenge to rear—are more likely to become targets of abuse. These include premature or very sick babies and children who are temperamentally difficult, are inattentive or overactive, or have other developmental problems. But whether such children actually are maltreated depends on characteristics of parents (Belsky, 1993). In one study, temperamentally difficult children who were physically abused had mothers who believed that they could do little to control the child's behavior. Instead, they attributed the child's unruliness to a stubborn or bad disposition, an interpretation that led them to move quickly toward physical force when the child misbehaved (Bugental, Blue, & Cruzcosa, 1989).

Once child abuse gets started, it quickly becomes part of a self-sustaining family relationship. The small irritations to which abusive parents react—a fussy baby, a preschooler

Child Sexual Abuse

U NTIL RECENTLY, CHILD sexual abuse was viewed as a rare occurrence. When children came forward with it, adults often thought that they had fantasized the experience and did not take their claims seriously. In the 1970s, efforts by professionals along with widespread media attention caused child sexual abuse to be recognized as a serious and widespread problem. More than 200,000 cases are reported in the United States each year (U.S. Department of Health and Human Services, 1999).

CHARACTERISTICS OF ABUSERS AND VICTIMS. Sexual abuse is committed against children of both sexes, but more often against girls than boys. Reported cases are highest in middle childhood, but sexual abuse also occurs at younger and older ages. Few children experience only a single episode. For some, the abuse begins early in life and continues for many years (Burkhardt & Rotatori, 1995; Holmes & Slap, 1998).

Generally, the abuser is male—a parent or someone whom the parent knows well. Often it is a father, stepfather, or live-in boyfriend; somewhat less often, an uncle or older brother. In a few instances, mothers are the offenders, more often with sons than daughters. If the abuser is a nonrelative, the person is usually someone the child has come to know and trust (Kolvin & Trowell, 1996).

In the overwhelming majority of cases, the abuse is serious—vaginal or anal intercourse, oral–genital contact, fondling, and forced stimulation of the adult. Abusers make the child comply in a variety of distasteful ways, including deception, bribery, verbal intimidation, and physical force (Gomez-Schwartz, Horowitz, & Cardarelli, 1990).

You may be wondering how any adult—especially, a parent or close relative—could possibly violate a child sexually. Many offenders deny their own responsibility. They blame the abuse on the willing participation of a seductive youngster. Yet children are not capable of making a deliberate, informed decision to enter into a sexual relationship! Even at older ages, they are not free to say yes or no. Instead, abusers tend to have characteristics that predispose them toward sexual exploitation of children. They have great difficulty controlling their impulses, may suffer from psychological disorders, and are often addicted to alcohol and drugs. Often they pick out children who are unlikely to defend themselves—children who are physically weak, emotionally deprived, and socially isolated (Faller, 1990).

Reported cases of child sexual abuse are strongly linked to poverty, marital instability, and resulting weakening of family ties. Children who live in homes with a history of constantly changing characters—repeated marriages, separations, and new partners—are especially vulnerable. But community surveys reveal that children in economically advantaged, stable families are also victims; they are simply more likely to escape detection. Intense pressure toward secrecy and feelings of confusion and guilt prevent most children from seeking help (Gomez-Schwartz, Horowitz, & Cardarelli, 1990).

CONSEQUENCES OF SEXUAL ABUSE. The adjustment problems of child sexual abuse victims are often severe. Depression, low self-esteem, mistrust of adults, and anger and hostility can persist for years after the abusive episodes. Younger children react with sleep difficulties, loss of appetite, and generalized fearfulness and anxiety. Adolescents may run away or show suicidal reactions, substance abuse, and delinquency (Kendall-Tackett, Williams, & Finkelhor, 1993; Tebbutt et al., 1997).

Sexually abused children frequently display sexual knowledge and behavior beyond their years. They have learned from their abusers that sexual overtures are acceptable ways to get attention and rewards. As they move toward young adulthood, they tend to be promiscuous and to enter into unhealthy relationships. Women are likely to choose partners who abuse both them and their children (Faller, 1990). As mothers, they often show poor parenting skills, abusing and neglecting their youngsters (Pianta, Egeland, & Erickson, 1989). In these ways, the harmful impact of sexual abuse is transmitted to the next generation.

who knocks over a glass of milk, or a child who will not mind immediately—soon become bigger ones. Then the harshness of parental behavior increases. By the preschool years, abusive and neglectful parents seldom interact with their children. When they do, they rarely express pleasure and affection; the communication is almost always negative (Trickett et al., 1991).

Most parents, however, have enough self-control not to respond to their children's misbehavior with abuse, and not all children with developmental problems are mistreated. Other factors must combine with these conditions to prompt an extreme parental response. Unmanageable parental stress is strongly associated with all forms of maltreatment. Abusive parents respond to stressful situations with high emotional arousal. At the same time, such factors as low income, unemployment, marital conflict, overcrowded living conditions, frequent moves, substance abuse, and extreme household disorganization are common in abusive homes (Garbarino, 1997; Magura & Laudet, 1996). These personal and situational conditions increase the chances that parents will be so overwhelmed that

PREVENTION AND TREATMENT. Treating child sexual abuse is difficult. The reactions of family members—anxiety about harm to the child, anger toward the abuser, and sometimes hostility toward the victim for telling—can increase children's distress. Since sexual abuse typically appears in the midst of other serious family problems, long-term therapy with both children and parents is usually necessary (Doyle, 1994; Gomez-Schwartz, Horowitz, & Cardarelli, 1990).

The best way to reduce the suffering of child sexual abuse victims is to prevent it from continuing. Today, courts are prosecuting abusers (especially nonrelatives) more vigorously and taking children's testimony more seriously (see Chapter 7). Special efforts are needed to help sexually abused boys, who are less likely than girls to speak about the experience and receive therapy and court protection (Holmes & Slap, 1998).

Educational programs can teach children to recognize inappropriate sexual advances and show them where to go for help. Yet because of controversies over teaching children about sexual abuse, few schools offer these interventions. New Zealand is the only country in the world with a national, school-based prevention program targeting sexual abuse. In *Keeping Ourselves Safe*, 5- to 13-year-olds learn that when abuse occurs, someone close to them, not a stranger, is usually responsible. Parent involvement ensures that home and school work together in teaching children self-protection skills (Sanders, 1997). Evaluations reveal that virtually all New Zealand parents and children support the program and that it has helped many children avoid or report abuse (Briggs & Hawkins, 1996, 1999).

they cannot meet basic child-rearing responsibilities or will vent their frustrations by lashing out at their children.

■ **THE COMMUNITY.** The majority of abusive and neglectful parents are isolated from both formal and informal social supports in their communities. There are at least two causes of this social isolation. First, because of their own life histories, many of these parents have learned to mistrust and avoid others. They do not have the skills necessary for establishing and maintaining positive relationships with friends and relatives (Polansky et al., 1985). Second, maltreating parents are more likely to live in poverty-stricken neighborhoods with high resident mobility that provide few links between family and community, such as parks, child-care centers, preschool programs, recreation centers, and churches (Coulton et al., 1995; Garbarino & Kostelny, 1993). For these reasons, they lack "lifelines" to others and have no one to turn to for help during particularly stressful times.

TABLE 14.6

Factors Related to Child Maltreatment

Factor	Description
Parent characteristics	Psychological disturbance; alcohol and drug abuse; history of abuse as a child; belief in harsh, physical discipline; desire to satisfy unmet emotional needs through the child; unreasonable expectations for child behavior; young age (most under 30); low educational level
Child characteristics	Premature or very sick baby; difficult temperament; inattentiveness and overactivity; other developmental problems
Family characaeristics	Low income; poverty; homelessness, marital instability; social isolation; physical abuse of mother by husband or boyfriend; frequent moves; large families with closely spaced children; overcrowded living conditions; disorganized household; lack of steady employment; other signs of high life stress
Community	Characterized by social isolation; few parks, day-care centers, preschool programs, recreation centers, and churches to serve as family supports
Culture	Approval of physical force and violence as ways to solve problems

Sources: Belsky, 1993; Cicchetti & Toth, 1998a.

■ **THE LARGER CULTURE.** One final set of factors—cultural values, laws, and customs—profoundly affects the chances that child maltreatment will occur when parents feel overburdened. Societies that view violence as an appropriate way to solve problems set the stage for child abuse. These conditions exist in the United States. Although all 50 states have laws designed to protect children from maltreatment, strong support still exists for the use of physical force with children. For example, during the past 30 years, the U.S. Supreme Court twice upheld the right of school officials to use corporal punishment to discipline children. Crime rates are high in American cities, and television sets beam graphic displays of violence into family living rooms.

In view of the widespread acceptance of violent behavior in American culture, it is not surprising that over 90 percent of American parents report using slaps and spankings at one time or another to discipline their children (Staub, 1996). In countries where physical punishment is not accepted, such as China, Japan, Luxembourg, and Sweden, child abuse is rare (Zigler & Hall, 1989).

CONSEQUENCES OF CHILD MALTREATMENT

The family circumstances of maltreated children impair the development of emotional self-regulation, empathy and sympathy, self-concept, and social skills. Over time, these youngsters show serious learning and adjustment problems, including academic failure, severe depression, difficulties with peers, substance abuse, and delinquency (Cicchetti & Toth, 1998).

How do these damaging consequences occur? Think back to our discussion in Chapter 12 of the effects of hostile cycles of parent–child interaction, which are especially severe for abused children. Indeed, a family characteristic strongly associated with child abuse is domestic violence, in which mothers are repeatedly brutalized (physically and psychologically) by their partners (Holden, Geffner, & Jouriles, 1998). Clearly, the home lives of abused children overflow with opportunities to learn to use aggression as a way of solving problems. The low warmth and control to which neglected children are exposed also promote aggressive, acting-out behavior (Miller et al., 1993).

Furthermore, demeaning parental messages, in which children are ridiculed, humiliated, rejected, or terrorized, result in low self-esteem, high anxiety, self-blame, and efforts to escape from extreme psychological pain—at times severe enough to lead to attempted suicide in adolescence (Sternberg et al., 1993; Toth & Cicchetti, 1996). At school, maltreated children are serious discipline problems. Their noncompliance, poor motivation, and cognitive immaturity interfere with academic achievement—an outcome that further undermines their chances for life success (Eckenrode, Laird, & Doris, 1993).

Finally, the trauma of repeated abuse can lead to psychophysiological changes, including abnormal EEG activity and altered production of stress hormones (Hart, Gunnar, & Cicchetti, 1995; Pollack et al., 1997). These effects on brain functioning increase the likelihood that adjustment problems will endure.

PREVENTING CHILD MALTREATMENT

Since child maltreatment is embedded within families, communities, and society as a whole, efforts to prevent it must be directed at each of these levels. Many approaches have been suggested, including interventions that teach high-risk parents effective child-rearing and disciplinary strategies, high school child development courses that include direct experience with children, and broad social programs that have as their goal full employment and better economic conditions for low-SES families.

We have already seen that providing social supports to families is very effective in easing parental stress. This approach sharply reduces child maltreatment as well. Research indicates that a trusting relationship with another person is the most important factor in preventing mothers with childhood histories of abuse from repeating the cycle with their own youngsters (Caliso & Milner, 1992; Egeland, Jacobvitz, & Sroufe, 1988). Parents Anonymous, a national organization that has as its main goal helping child-abusing parents learn constructive parenting practices, does so largely through providing social supports. Its local chapters offer self-help group meetings, daily phone calls, and regular home visits to relieve social isolation and teach alternative child-rearing skills.

Crisis intervention services also exist in many communities. Nurseries offer temporary child care when parents feel they are about to lose control, and telephone hot lines provide immediate help to parents under stress and refer them to appropriate community agencies when long-term assistance is warranted.

Other preventive approaches include announcements in newspapers and magazines and on television and radio that are designed to educate people about child maltreatment and tell them where to seek help. Besides these efforts, changes are needed in American culture. Many experts believe that child maltreatment cannot be eliminated as long as violence is widespread and corporal punishment is regarded as an acceptable child-rearing alternative. In addition, combating poverty and its diverse correlates—family stress and disorganization, inadequate food and medical care, teenage childbearing, low-birth-weight babies, and parental hopelessness—would do much to reduce child maltreatment.

Although more cases reach the courts than in decades past, child maltreatment remains a crime that is difficult to prove. Most of the time, the only witnesses are the child victims or other loyal family members. Even in court cases in which the evidence is strong, judges hesitate to impose the ultimate safeguard against further harm: permanently removing the child from the family.

There are several reasons for this reluctant attitude. First, in American society, government intervention into family life is viewed as a last resort, to be used only when there is near certainty that a child will be denied basic care and protection. Second, despite destructive family relationships, maltreated children and their parents are usually attached to one another. Most of the time, neither desires separation. Finally, the American legal system tends to regard children as parental property rather than as human beings in their own right, and this also has stood in the way of court-ordered protection.

Even with intensive treatment, some adults persist in their abusive acts. An estimated 1,500 American children (half of them under 1 year of age) die from maltreatment each year (U.S. Department of Health and Human Services, 1999). When parents are unlikely to change their behavior, the drastic step of separating parent from child and legally terminating parental rights is the only reasonable course of action.

Child maltreatment is a distressing and horrifying topic. When we consider how often it occurs in the United States, a society that claims to place a high value on the dignity and worth of the individual, it is even more appalling. Yet there is reason to be optimistic. Great strides have been made over the past several decades in understanding and preventing child maltreatment.

ASK YOURSELF . . .

◆ Chandra heard a news report that ten severely neglected children, living in squalor in an inner-city tenement, were discovered by Chicago police. Chandra thought to herself, "What could possibly lead parents to mistreat their children so badly?" How would you answer Chandra's question?

◆ CONNECTIONS
Can the U.N. Convention on the Rights of the Child help prevent child maltreatment? Explain, drawing on the concept of the macrosystem in Bronfenbrenner's ecological model. (See Chapter 1, pages 29 and 39.)

After reviewing factors linked to teenage parenthood, explain why it places children at risk for child abuse and neglect. (See Chapter 5, pages 214–216.)

EVOLUTIONARY ORIGINS

Discuss the evolutionary origins and adaptive value of the family among our hunting-and-gathering ancestors.

◆ The human family in its most common form can be traced to our hunting-and-gathering ancestors. When bipedalism evolved and arms were freed to carry things, our ancestors found it easier to co-operate and share, especially in providing food for the young. A man became committed to a woman and their joint offspring, a re-lationship that enhanced survival. Kinship groups expanded, offer-ing greater protection in the face of competition with other humans for resources.

FUNCTIONS OF THE FAMILY

Cite the functions modern families perform for society.

◆ Besides promoting the survival of its own members, the family per-forms essential functions for society. As societies became more complex, other institutions developed to assist with certain func-tions. Responsibilities of modern families are largely restricted to reproduction, socialization, and emotional support.

THE FAMILY AS A SOCIAL SYSTEM

Describe the social systems perspective on family functioning, including its view of family interaction and the influence of surrounding social contexts.

◆ Contemporary researchers view the family from a **social systems perspective**—as a complex set of interacting relationships affected by the larger social context. Bidirectional influences exist in which the behaviors of each family member affect those of others—an in-terplay of forces that must constantly adapt to the development of its members. Connections to the community—through formal or-ganizations and informal social networks—grant parents and chil-dren social support, thereby promoting effective family interaction and children's development.

SOCIALIZATION WITHIN THE FAMILY

Discuss the influence of four child-rearing styles on develop-ment, and explain how effective parents adapt child rearing to children's growing competence during middle childhood and adolescence.

◆ Two dimensions, demandingness and responsiveness, describe varia-tions in the way parents socialize children. When combined, they yield four styles of parenting. The **authoritative style,** which is both de-manding and responsive, promotes cognitive, emotional, and social competence from early childhood into adolescence. The **authoritarian style,** which is high in demandingness but low in responsiveness, is as-sociated with anxious, withdrawn, dependent child behavior. The **per-missive style** is responsive but undemanding; children who experience it typically show poor self-control and achievement. The **uninvolved style** is low in both demandingness and responsiveness. It disrupts virtually all aspects of development. Children's characteristics con-tribute to the ease with which parents can apply an authoritative style.

◆ As children get older, a gradual lessening of control supports devel-opment, as long as parental warmth and involvement in child rear-ing are maintained. In middle childhood, effective parents engage in **coregulation,** exerting general oversight while permitting chil-dren to be in charge of moment-by-moment decision making. Dur-ing adolescence, mature **autonomy** is fostered by parenting that grants young people independence in accord with their readiness while maintaining close family ties.

Describe socioeconomic and ethnic variations in child rear-ing, including the impact of poverty.

◆ The authoritative style is the most common pattern of child rearing in many cultures around the world. Nevertheless, consistent varia-tions in child rearing exist that are linked to SES and ethnicity. Higher-SES parents are more verbal and stimulating and rely more on warmth and explanations; low-SES parents use more commands, criticism, and physical punishment. Certain ethnic groups, includ-ing Chinese, Hispanic, Asian Pacific Island, and African American, rely on high levels of parental control that appear adaptive when viewed in light of cultural values and family circumstances.

◆ Effective parenting, along with children's development, is seriously undermined by the stress and disorganization of living in poverty. **Extended-family households,** in which one or more adult relatives live with the parent–child **nuclear family unit,** are common among ethnic minorities and protect children's development under condi-tions of high life stress.

FAMILY LIFESTYLES AND TRANSITIONS

Describe the influence of family size on child rearing, and explain how sibling relationships change with age and affect development.

◆ Over the past several decades, family lifestyles in industrialized na-tions have become more diverse. The trend toward smaller families has positive consequences for child rearing, in terms of attention, patience, and resources invested in children. Most children still grow up with at least one sibling. Because of their frequency and emotional intensity, sibling interactions promote many aspects of social competence. Unequal parental treatment increases sibling ri-valry. During adolescence, sibling relationships become less intense, but attachment to siblings remains strong for most young people.

◆ Contrary to popular belief, only children are as well adjusted as are children with siblings, and they are advantaged in self-esteem, school achievement, and educational attainment.

How do children fare in adoptive families, gay and lesbian families, and never-married single-parent families?

◆ Infertile couples and older, single individuals often turn to adop-tion as a way of starting a family. Although adopted children have more learning and emotional difficulties than do their nonadopted agemates, by adulthood this difference disappears. Most parents who adopt children with physical or psychological problems report high satisfaction with the adoptive experience. When parents help them learn about their heritage, transracially or transculturally adopted young people typically develop healthy identities that com-bine their birth and rearing backgrounds.

- Gay and lesbian parents are as committed to and effective at child rearing as are heterosexuals, and sometimes more so. Their children are well adjusted and largely heterosexual.
- The largest group of never-married parents are African-American young women, due to the inability of many black men to support a family. Children of never-married mothers show slightly better academic performance and emotional adjustment than do children of divorced or remarried mothers, but they do not do as well as children in first-marriage families. Many display developmental problems associated with economic hardship.

What factors influence children's adjustment to divorce and blended-family arrangements?

- Divorce is extremely common in the lives of American children. Although painful emotional reactions usually accompany the period surrounding divorce, children with difficult temperaments and boys in mother-custody homes react more strongly and are more likely to show lasting adjustment problems. The most consistent long-term effects for girls involve heterosexual behavior—a rise in sexual activity at adolescence, in teenage childbearing, and in risk of divorce in adulthood.
- The overriding factor in positive adjustment following divorce is effective parenting. Outcomes with sons tend to be better when the father is the custodial parent. Because **divorce mediation** helps parents resolve their disputes, it has great benefits for children. **Joint custody** is a controversial practice that requires a cooperative relationship between divorcing parents to be successful. Intense conflict usually lies behind grandparents' legal petitions for visitation rights, so courts are wise to exercise restraint in granting them.
- When divorced parents enter new relationships through cohabitation or remarriage, children must adapt to a **blended, or reconstituted, family.** How well children do depends on which parent forms a new relationship and on the age and sex of the child. Girls, older children, and children in father–stepmother families display the greatest problems.
- Because repeated marital transitions expose children to recurring episodes of family conflict and inconsistent parenting, they severely disrupt development. Highly troubled parents who cannot engage in competent child rearing have led to a rise in **skipped-generation families,** in which grandparents take full responsibility for rearing children.

How do maternal employment and life in dual-earner families affect children's development?

- As long as mothers enjoy their work and remain committed to parenting, maternal employment is associated with favorable consequences for children, including a higher sense of self-esteem, more

positive family and peer relations, and less gender-stereotyped beliefs. In dual-earner families, the father's willingness to share household and child-care tasks is vital. The availability of workplace supports, such as part-time employment and time off when children are ill, help mothers juggle the multiple demands of work and child rearing.

Discuss the influence of child-care quality on preschoolers' development, the status of child care in the United States compared to other industrialized nations, and the impact of self-care on school-age children's adjustment.

- American children experience a diverse array of child-care arrangements while their parents are at work. Center-based care is the most common form during the preschool years. When group size is small, caregiver–child ratios are generous, and caregivers are well educated and personally committed to caring for children, adults communicate in more stimulating and responsive ways. As a result, children do especially well on measures of intelligence, language, and social development. The United States lags far behind other Western nations in supply, quality, and affordability of child care.
- During middle childhood, millions of children look after themselves during out-of-school hours. When **self-care children** have a history of authoritative child rearing and are monitored from a distance, they fare well. In contrast, children left to their own devices are at risk for antisocial behavior. High-quality after-school care is not widely available in the United States.

VULNERABLE FAMILIES: CHILD MALTREATMENT

Discuss the multiple origins of child maltreatment, its consequences for development, and prevention strategies.

- Child maltreatment is related to factors within the family, community, and larger culture. Child and parent characteristics often feed on one another to produce abusive behavior. Unmanageable parental stress and social isolation greatly increase the chances that abuse and neglect will occur. When a society approves of force and violence as appropriate means for solving problems, child abuse is promoted.
- Maltreated children are impaired in the development of emotional self-regulation, self-concept, social skills, and learning in school. Over time, they show a wide variety of serious adjustment problems. Successful prevention of child maltreatment requires efforts at the family, community, and cultural levels, including social supports for parents, crisis intervention services, public education about the problem and information on how to seek help, and a reduction in societal violence and poverty.

IMPORTANT TERMS AND CONCEPTS

authoritarian style (p. 564)
authoritative style (p. 562)
autonomy (p. 567)
blended, or reconstituted, family (p. 581)
coregulation (p. 566)

divorce mediation (p. 580)
extended-family household (p. 571)
joint custody (p. 581)
nuclear family unit (p. 571)
permissive style (p. 564)

self-care children (p. 587)
skipped-generation family (p. 584)
social systems perspective (p. 559)
uninvolved style (p. 564)

Peers, Media, and Schooling

FOUR PUPILS ARE gathered around a computer in their first-grade classroom, using LOGO, a flexible computer language in which numerical instructions yield geometric shapes, to draw a snowman on the screen. As John assumes control of the keyboard, the children consider how large to make the snowman's hat. Their conversation is richly woven with ideas and joint efforts at problem solving:

> *Kevin:* Small.
>
> *John:* Two [referring to units specifying size in LOGO].
>
> *Andrew:* Shh, listen to what Cathie says. What number?
>
> *Cathie:* I don't know. John, I think you should decide. It's your hat.
>
> *Kevin:* Should take four.
>
> *Cathie:* I think that would be too big, wouldn't it?
>
> *Kevin:* You've never took four before.
>
> *Andrew:* Do three . . . It'll be too big.
>
> *John:* I say two.
>
> *Cathie:* If you say two, put in two, John. Put in two. [John draws the square.] That's fine, isn't it? [Now the children decide on a length for the brim.] (Hughes & Macleod, 1986, pp. 197–198)

In creating the snowman, these young children cooperate to reach a common goal, generate alternative strategies, extend their knowledge of mathematical estimation, and begin to master a technology that is central to the economic and leisure life of their society. Their cognitive and social competencies illustrate the importance of three contexts for development. Beginning at an early age, socialization in the family is supplemented by experiences in the wider world of peers, media, and school.

In all human societies, children spend many hours in one another's company; in no culture are they reared entirely by adults. In Chapter 11, we saw how a special peer relationship, friendship, contributes uniquely to development. In this chapter, we take a broader look at how peer sociability changes with age, the factors that support it, and its profound significance for psychological adjustment. Next we turn to television and computers, reviewing what is known about the effects of these captivating electronic devices on children's cognitive and social skills. Finally, our discussion addresses the school, an institution established to assist the family in transmitting culturally valued knowledge to the next generation. We consider how class and school size, educational philosophy, teacher–pupil interaction, and the ability mix of pupils affect educational experiences. We conclude with an evaluation of the success of American schools in equipping young people to keep pace with their counterparts in other industrialized nations and in preparing them for productive work lives.

The Importance of Peer Relations

Are peer relations crucial for development, and how do they add to children's experiences with caring adults? To find out for sure, we would need to study a group of children reared only by parents, comparing their competencies to children growing up under typical conditions. In humans, these circumstances rarely occur naturally and are unethical to arrange experimentally. But scientists who have conducted such studies with nonhuman primates report that although peer bonds are usually not as intense as attachments to parents, they are vital for social competence. For example, maternally reared rhesus monkeys with no peer contact display immature play, excessive aggression and fearfulness, and less cooperation at maturity (Harlow, 1969).

Parent and peer associations seem to complement one another. The parent–child bond emphasizes caregiving and affection, providing children with the security they need to enter the world of peers. Peer interaction, in turn, consists mainly of play and socializing, permitting children to expand social skills first acquired within the family (Hartup & Moore, 1990). Peer relations are also flexible enough so that they can fill in, at least to some extent, for the early parent–child bond. In a special type of investigation called **peer-only rearing,** researchers reared rhesus monkey infants in groups without adults. When given a choice between their preferred peer (the one they sought closeness to during rearing), a familiar peer, and an unfamiliar peer, peer-only reared monkeys spent most time near the preferred peer. In addition, the preferred peer served as a source of security, reducing distress more effectively than did other agemates (Higley et al., 1992).

Nevertheless, peer-only reared monkeys do not develop as well as their counterparts with typical parental and peer upbringing. In novel environments, they spend much of their time either clinging to or hovering near their preferred agemate, constantly seeking reassurance. Perhaps for this reason, peer-only reared monkeys display behavior problems as they get older, including increased dominant and submissive (as opposed to friendly) interaction with unfamiliar agemates, reduced exploration, and deficient sexual behavior (Goy & Goldfoot, 1974). Nevertheless, within their familiar peer group, peer-only reared monkeys develop socially competent behavior. And they are far better off than monkeys reared in isolation (Suomi & Harlow, 1978).

Do these findings generalize to human children? A unique parallel to peer-only rearing research suggests that in large measure, they do. In the 1940s, Anna Freud and Sophie Dann (1951) studied six young German-Jewish orphans whose parents had been murdered in the Nazi gas chambers shortly after the children's birth. The children remained together in a concentration camp for several years, without close ties to adults. When World War II ended, they were brought to England and cared for in a country house until they could adjust to their new surroundings. Observations revealed that they were passionately attached to members of their group, becoming upset when separated, even for brief moments. They were also intensely prosocial, freely sharing, comforting, and offering assistance to one another. At the same time, they showed many anxious symptoms, including intense thumb sucking, restlessness, immature play, and aggression toward as well as excessive dependency on their caregivers. As they built trusting relationships with adults, the children's play, language, and exploration developed rapidly.

In sum, peers serve as vital sources of security in threatening situations and contribute to many aspects of development. But they do so more effectively when they are preceded by a warm, supportive relationship with a caregiver.

Development of Peer Sociability

In cultures where infants and toddlers have regular contact with agemates, peer sociability begins early, gradually evolving into the more complex, better coordinated social exchanges of the childhood and adolescent years. The develop-

peer-only rearing A type of study in which nonhuman primates are reared together from birth without adults.

nonsocial activity Unoccupied, onlooker behavior and solitary play.

parallel play A form of limited social participation in which the child plays near other children with similar materials but does not try to influence their behavior.

associative play A form of true social participation in which children engage in separate activities but interact by exchanging toys and commenting on one another's behavior.

cooperative play A form of true social participation in which children's actions are directed toward a common goal.

ment of peer sociability is supported by and contributes to the cognitive, language, and emotional milestones discussed in previous chapters.

INFANT AND TODDLER BEGINNINGS

When pairs of infants are brought together in a laboratory, looking accompanied by touching is present at 3 to 4 months, peer-directed smiles and babbles by 6 months. These isolated social acts increase until by the end of the first year, an occasional reciprocal exchange occurs in which babies grin, gesture, or otherwise imitate a playmate's behavior (Vandell & Mueller, 1995; Vandell, Wilson, & Buchanan, 1980).

Between 1 and 2 years, coordinated interaction occurs more often, largely in the form of mutual imitation involving jumping, chasing, or banging a toy. Through these imitative, turn-taking games, children create joint understandings that aid in verbal communication. Around age 2, toddlers begin to use words to talk about and influence a peer's behavior, as when they say "Let's play chase," and after the game gets going, "Hey, good running!" (Eckerman & Didow, 1996). They also begin to engage in complementary roles in make-believe, such as feeding a doll that another child is holding (Eckerman, Davis, & Didow, 1989; Howes & Matheson, 1992). Reciprocal play and positive emotion are especially frequent in toddlers' interactions with familiar agemates, suggesting that they are building true peer relationships (Ross et al., 1992).

Although quite limited, peer sociability is present in the first 2 years, and it is fostered by the early caregiver–child bond. From interacting with sensitive adults, infants and toddlers learn how to send and interpret emotional signals in their first peer associations (Vandell & Mueller, 1995). Consistent with this idea, toddlers with a warm parental relationship engage in more extended peer exchanges. These children, in turn, display more socially competent behavior during the preschool years (Howes, 1988a; Howes & Matheson, 1992; Vandell & Wilson, 1987). And for young children in child care, a secure attachment to a stable professional caregiver predicts advanced play and peer behavior (Howes & Hamilton, 1993).

THE PRESCHOOL YEARS

Between ages 2 and 5, as children become increasingly self-aware, more effective at communicating, and better at understanding the thoughts and feelings of others, the amount and quality of peer interaction changes greatly. Early in this century, Mildred Parten (1932) observed young children in nursery school and noticed a dramatic rise with age in joint, interactive play. She concluded that social development proceeds in a three-step sequence. It begins with **nonsocial activity**—unoccupied, onlooker behavior and solitary play. Then it shifts to a form of limited social participation called **parallel play,** in which a child plays near other children with similar materials but does not try to influence their behavior. At the highest level, preschoolers engage in two forms of true social interaction. The first is **associative play,** in which children engage in separate activities, but they interact by exchanging toys and commenting on one another's behavior. The second is **cooperative play**—a more advanced type of interaction in which children orient toward a common goal, such as acting out a make-believe theme or working on the same product, for example, a sand castle or painting.

Recent longitudinal evidence indicates that these play forms emerge in the order suggested by Parten, but they do not form a developmental sequence in which later-appearing ones replace earlier ones (Howes & Matheson, 1992). Instead, all types coexist during the preschool years (see Table 15.1). Furthermore, although nonsocial activity declines with age, it is still the most frequent form of behavior among 3- to 4-year-olds. Even among kindergartners it

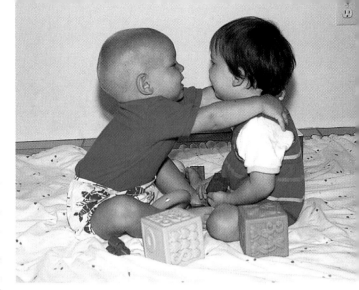

The beginnings of peer sociability emerge in infancy, in the form of touches, smiles, and babbles that gradually develop into coordinated interaction in the second year. Early peer sociability is fostered by a warm, sensitive caregiver–child bond.
(Nancy Sheehan)

TABLE **15.1**

Changes in Parten's Social Play Types from Preschool to Kindergarten

Play Type	Preschool 3–4 Years	Kindergarten 5–6 Years
Nonsocial activity	41%	34%
Unoccupied, onlooker behavior	(19)	(14)
Solitary play	(22)	(20)
Parallel play	22	23
Cooperative play	37	43

Sources: Preschool percentages are averages of those reported by Barnes (1971); Rubin, Maioni, & Hornung (1976); Rubin, Watson, & Jambor (1978); and Smith (1978). Kindergarten figures are averages of those reported by Barnes (1971) and Rubin, Watson, & Jambor (1978).

TABLE 15.2

Developmental Sequence of Cognitive Play Categories

Play Category	Description	Examples
Functional play	Simple, repetitive motor movements with or without objects. Especially common during the first 2 years of life.	Running around a room, rolling a car back and forth, kneading clay with no intent to make something
Constructive play	Creating or constructing something. Especially common between 3 and 6 years.	Making a house out of toy blocks, drawing a picture, putting together a puzzle
Make-believe play	Acting out everyday and imaginary roles. Especially common between 2 and 6 years.	Playing house, school, or police officer; acting out storybook or television characters
Games with rules	Understanding and following rules in play activities.	Playing board games, cards, hopscotch, baseball

Source: Rubin, Fein, & Vandenberg, 1983.

continues to take up as much as a third of children's free-play time. Also, solitary and parallel play remain fairly stable from 3 to 6 years, accounting for as much of the young child's play as highly social, cooperative interaction. Social development during the preschool years is not just a matter of eliminating nonsocial and partially social activity from the child's behavior.

We now understand that it is the *type*, rather than the amount, of solitary and parallel play that changes during early childhood. In studies of preschoolers' play in Taiwan and the United States, researchers rated the *cognitive maturity* of nonsocial, parallel, and cooperative play by applying the categories shown in Table 15.2. Within each of Parten's play types, older children engaged in more cognitively mature behavior than did younger children (Pan, 1994; Rubin, Watson, & Jambor, 1978).

These findings are helpful in responding to the concerns of some parents, who wonder if a young child who spends much time playing alone is developing normally. Only *certain kinds* of nonsocial activity—aimless wandering, hovering near peers, and functional play involving immature, repetitive motor action—are cause for concern (Coplan et al., 1994; Rubin & Coplan, 1998). Most nonsocial play of preschoolers is not of this kind. Instead, it is positive and constructive, and teachers encourage it when they set out art materials, puzzles, and building toys during free play. Children who spend much time in these activities are not maladjusted. Instead, they are bright children who, when they do play with peers, show socially skilled behavior.

In Chapter 6, we noted that *sociodramatic play* becomes especially common during the preschool years. This advanced form of cooperative play requires sophisticated cognitive, emotional, and social skills, and it also enhances them. In joint make-believe, preschoolers act out and respond to one another's pretend feelings. Their play is rich in references to emotional states. Young children also explore and gain control of fear-arousing experiences when they play doctor or dentist or pretend to search for monsters in a magical forest. As a result, they are better able to understand others' feelings and regulate their own. Finally, to collectively create and manage complex plots, preschoolers must resolve their disputes through negotiation and compromise—experiences that contribute greatly to their ability to get along with others (Garvey, 1990; Howes, 1992).

These children are engaged in parallel play. Although they sit side by side and use similar materials, they do not try to influence one another's behavior. Parallel play remains frequent and stable over the preschool years. Working puzzles or engaging in other similar activities encourages it. (George Doodwin/Monkmeyer Press)

MIDDLE CHILDHOOD AND ADOLESCENCE

When formal schooling begins, children are exposed to agemates who differ in many ways, including achievement, ethnicity, religion, interests, and personality. Contact with a wider variety of peers probably contributes to school-age children's increasing awareness that others have viewpoints different from their own (see Chapter 11). Peer communication, in turn, profits from improved perspective taking. Children of this age are better at accurately interpreting others' emotions and intentions and taking them into account in peer dialogues. In addition, their ability to understand the complementary roles of several players in relation to a set of rules permits the transition to rule-oriented games in middle childhood (refer again to Table 15.2).

School-age children apply their greater awareness of prosocial norms to peer interaction. Recall from Chapter 12 that sharing, helping, and other prosocial acts increase in middle childhood. In addition, younger and older children differ in how they help agemates. Kindergartners move right in and give assistance, regardless of whether it is desired. In contrast, school-age children offer to help and wait for a peer to accept it before behaving prosocially. During adolescence, agemates work on tasks more cooperatively—staying on task, exchanging ideas freely, asking for opinions, and acknowledging one another's contributions (Hartup, 1983). In line with children's greater sensitivity to prosocial expectations, the overall incidence of aggression drops off in middle childhood, although (as we indicated in Chapter 13) its form makes a difference. Overt verbal aggression among boys and relational aggression among girls persist into adolescence, whereas physical attacks decline.

As children enter middle childhood, another form of peer interaction becomes common. Watch children at play in a public park or schoolyard, and you will see that they sometimes wrestle, roll, hit, and run after one another while smiling and laughing. This friendly chasing and play-fighting is called **rough-and-tumble play.** Research indicates that it is a good-natured, sociable activity that is quite distinct from aggressive fighting. Children in many cultures engage in it with peers whom they like especially well, and they continue interacting after a rough-and-tumble episode rather than separating, as they do at the end of an aggressive encounter (Costabile et al., 1991; Smith & Hunter, 1992).

Children's rough-and-tumble play is similar to the social behavior of young mammals of many species. It seems to originate in parents' physical play with babies, especially fathers with sons (see Chapter 10). Similarly, childhood rough-and-tumble is more common among boys, although girls also display it. Girls' rough-and-tumble largely consists of running, chasing, and brief physical contact. Boys engage in more playful wrestling, restraining, and hitting (Boulton, 1996).

Does rough-and-tumble play have an adaptive function? One speculation is that in our evolutionary past, it may have been important for the development of fighting skill. Consistent with this idea, by age 11 children choose rough-and-tumble partners who are similar in strength to themselves, permitting safer practice of fighting techniques (Humphreys & Smith, 1987). A second possibility is that rough-and-tumble assists children, especially boys, in establishing dominance relations, a topic we will consider when we take up peer groups. Through rough-and-tumble, children can assess their own and others' strength before challenging a peer's dominance (Pellegrini & Smith, 1998). And at times, children may use rough-and-tumble to display their strength—for example, by pinning a partner to the ground. Indeed, 12- and 13-year-old boys who often play-fight are rated as "tougher" by their classmates (Pellegrini, 1995). As adolescents reach physical maturity, individual differences in strength become clear, and rough-and-tumble play declines.

Over middle childhood, children interact increasingly often with peers until, by midadolescence, more time is spent with them than with any other social partners (Csikszentmihalyi & Larson, 1984). Common interests, novel play activities, and opportunities to interact on an equal footing make peer interaction especially gratifying. As adolescence draws to a close, most young people emerge from their peer experiences proficient in many complex social behaviors.

Rough-and-tumble play can be distinguished from aggression by its good-natured quality. In our evolutionary past, it may have been important for the development of fighting skill and dominance relations. (Tony Freeman/PhotoEdit)

rough-and-tumble play A form of peer interaction involving friendly chasing and play-fighting that, in our evolutionary past, may have been important for the development of fighting skill.

Influences on Peer Sociability

What can adults do to promote peer sociability? In the following sections, we will see that parental encouragement affects peer interaction. So do situational factors that adults can influence, such as play materials and the age mix of children. Cultural values make a difference as well.

PARENT ENCOURAGEMENT

Outside of preschool and child care, young children are limited in their ability to find playmates. They depend on parents to help them establish rewarding peer associations. Parents influence children's peer relations in many ways. One is through the neighborhood they choose to live in. When children live some distance from one another and cannot gather on their own, parents must act as social planners and "booking agents," scheduling play at home, taking children to community settings such as the library or pool, and enrolling them in organized activities (Parke et al., 1994). Parents who frequently arrange informal peer contact tend to have preschoolers with larger peer networks and who are more socially skilled (Ladd, LeSieur, & Profilet, 1993). In providing opportunities for peer play, parents show children how to initiate their own peer contacts and encourage them to be good "hosts" who are concerned about their playmates' needs.

Parents also influence children's social relations by offering guidance and effective examples of how to act toward others. Parents who phrase their directives positively and politely ("Please . . ." or "Why don't you try . . ." instead of "Don't" or "No, you can't") have preschoolers who are less aggressive and more successful at influencing peers (Kochanska, 1992). And parents' skillful advice on how to solve peer problems, such as entering an ongoing play group, is associated with preschoolers' social competence and peer acceptance (Laird et al., 1994; Mize & Pettit, 1997).

Parents' style of interaction while playing with their child also makes a difference. The quality of parent–child physical and nonphysical play forecasts early peer relationships. Cooperation and frequent exchange of positive affect predict good social skills and favorable peer ties; high control, conflict, noncompliance, and negative affect predict aggression, peer difficulties, and feelings of loneliness (Barth & Parke, 1993; Gottman, Katz, & Hooven, 1996; Harrist et al., 1994; Mize & Pettit, 1997).

PLAY MATERIALS

Quantity of play materials affects young children's peer interaction. Fights and quarrels increase when preschoolers are confined to a relatively small space and there are not enough toys to go around (Smith & Connolly, 1980).

Peer interaction also varies with the toys available. Art, construction materials, blocks, and puzzles tend to be associated with solitary and parallel play, open-ended and relatively unstructured objects with cooperative play (Farver, Kim, & Lee, 1995). Type of open-ended materials is influential as well. Preschoolers use realistic toys (trucks, dolls, and tea sets) to act out everyday roles, such as mother, doctor, and baby. In contrast, nonspecific materials (pipe cleaners, cardboard cylinders, and paper bags) encourage fantastic role play, such as pirate and creature from outer space. Fantastic roles, in turn, prompt more complex social interaction, especially planning statements, as in "I'll be the pirate and you be the prisoner." Since fantastic make-believe does not follow familiar scripts, children devote more time to planning each episode and explaining what they are doing to peer companions (McLoyd, Warren, & Thomas, 1984).

AGE MIX OF CHILDREN

When observed in age-graded settings, such as child-care centers, schools, and summer camps, children typically interact with children close in age. Yet in the neighborhood, more than half their contacts are with children who differ in age by at least a year (Ellis,

Rogoff, & Cromer, 1981). And in cultures where children are not segregated by age for schooling and recreation, cross-age interaction is even more common.

The theories of Piaget and Vygotsky, discussed in Chapter 6, suggest different benefits from same- versus different-age peer interaction. Piaget emphasized experiences with children equal in status who challenge one another's viewpoints, thereby fostering cognitive, social, and moral development. In contrast, Vygotsky believed that children profit from interacting with older, more capable peers, who encourage more advanced skills.

Beginning in infancy, contact with older children seems to foster peer interaction. Babies with older siblings are more socially responsive to same-age playmates, both positively and negatively. They more often laugh and imitate as well as hit, push, and grab than do infants without brothers and sisters (Vandell & Mueller, 1995). And 12-month-olds who are around older children at least once a week are more likely to make social contact with a peer (Vandell, 1996). As skills in relating to agemates improve, they return to enhance other relationships. Preschoolers whose interactions with a best friend are especially cooperative develop more positive relationships with younger siblings (Kramer & Gottman, 1992).

Children interact differently with same-age and different-age youngsters. In several studies, preschool and school-age children played or worked on problem-solving tasks. Mixed-age conditions led to a greater quantity and complexity of interaction by younger children, along with special accommodations by older children, who reduced their rate of communication and assumed more responsibility for the task (Brody, Graziano, & Musser, 1983; Howes & Farver, 1987). Nevertheless, the oldest school-age children in mixed-age settings prefer same-age companions, perhaps because they have more compatible interests and experience more cooperative interaction. Younger children's interaction with same-age partners is also more intense and harmonious, but they often turn to older peers because of their superior knowledge and exciting play ideas.

In early adolescence, mixed-age interaction increases (Gray & Feldman, 1997). As young people seek companions similar in pubertal status to themselves (see Chapter 5), many turn to older or younger companions. Also, compared with childhood, in adolescence cognitive and social competence depends less on age, making mixed-age relationships more satisfying.

Children clearly profit from both same-age and mixed-age relationships. From interacting with coequals, they learn to cooperate and resolve conflicts, and they develop important moral notions of reciprocity and justice (see Chapters 11 and 12). In addition, younger children acquire new competencies from their older companions. And when more mature youngsters teach their less mature counterparts, they practice nurturance, guidance, and other prosocial behaviors.

CULTURAL VALUES

Culture shapes children's interaction and play activities. In collectivist societies that stress group harmony, peer sociability takes different forms than in individualistic cultures like the United States. For example, children in India generally play in large groups that require high levels of cooperation. Much of their behavior during sociodramatic play and early games is imitative, occurs in unison, and involves close physical contact. In a game called Atiya Piatiya, children sit in a circle, join hands, and swing while they recite a jingle. In Bhatto Bhatto, they act out a script about a trip to the market, touching each other's elbows and hands as they pretend to cut and share a tasty vegetable (Roopnarine et al., 1994).

Cultural beliefs about the importance of play also affect the quantity and quality of peer associations. Caregivers who view play as mere entertainment are less likely to provide props and encourage pretend than those who value its cognitive and educational benefits (Farver & Wimbarti, 1995a, 1995b). Korean-American parents, who emphasize task persistence as the means to academic success, have preschoolers who spend less time at joint make-believe and more time unoccupied and in parallel play than do their Caucasian-American counterparts. A cultural

These Chinese girls demonstrate an intricate hand-clapping game in which they must respond quickly and in unison. Preschoolers in the People's Republic of China frequently perform such games for classmates and parents. Their play reflects the value their culture places on group harmony.
(Jeff Greenberg/PhotoEdit)

deemphasis on individuality and self-expression may also contribute to Korean-American children's reduced involvement in sociodramatic play (Farver, Kim, & Lee, 1995).

In all cultures, peer contact rises in adolescence, a trend that is particularly strong in industrialized nations, where young people spend most of each weekday with agemates in school. Teenagers also spend much out-of-class time together, especially in the United States. American teenagers average 18 nonschool hours per week with peers, compared with 12 hours for Japanese and 9 hours for Taiwanese adolescents (Fuligni & Stevenson, 1995). Higher rates of maternal employment and less demanding academic standards probably account for this difference.

BRIEF REVIEW

Experiments with rhesus monkeys reveal that peer interaction is a vital source of social competence. Peer sociability begins in infancy as isolated smiles, gestures, and babbles evolve into coordinated interaction. During the preschool years, cooperative play increases, but solitary and parallel play are also common. Within each of these play types, children's activities become more cognitively complex. During middle childhood and adolescence, gains in communication skills and greater awareness of social norms contribute to advances in peer interaction. Rough-and-tumble play increases in middle childhood and declines in adolescence. In our evolutionary past, it may have been important for the development of fighting skill and dominance relations.

Parents influence young children's peer relations by arranging peer play activities and teaching and modeling effective social skills. Richly equipped play environments, nonspecific toys, and same-age peers promote highly positive, cooperative child–child interaction. Mixed-age contact permits older children to practice prosocial skills and younger children to learn from more mature partners. Cultural values influence the quantity and quality of peer associations.

ASK YOURSELF . . .

◆ *Three-year-old Bart lives in the country, where there are no other preschoolers nearby. His parents wonder whether it is worth driving Bart into town once a week to play with his 3-year-old cousin. What advice would you give Bart's parents, and why?*

◆ CONNECTIONS
What aspects of adult–child interaction probably contribute to the relationship between attachment security and young children's peer sociability? (See Chapter 10, page 431.)

Explain how peer interaction contributes to young children's concepts of distributive justice and to their capacity to distinguish moral from social-conventional and personal matters. (See Chapter 12, pages 501 and 503.)

sociometric techniques Self-report measures that ask peers to evaluate one another's likability.

popular children Children who get many positive votes on sociometric measures of peer acceptance.

rejected children Children who are actively disliked and get many negative votes on sociometric measures of peer acceptance.

controversial children Children who get a large number of positive and negative votes on sociometric measures of peer acceptance.

neglected children Children who are seldom chosen, either positively or negatively, on sociometric measures of peer acceptance.

Peer Acceptance

As we know from our own childhoods, some children are more desirable peer companions than others. *Peer acceptance* refers to likability—the extent to which a child is viewed by agemates as a worthy social partner. Researchers usually assess peer acceptance with self-report measures called **sociometric techniques.** For example, children may be asked to nominate several peers in their class whom they especially like or dislike, to indicate for all possible pairs of classmates which one they prefer to play with, or to rate each peer on a scale from "like very much" to "like very little." Children as young as age 4 can answer these questions reliably (Rubin, Bukowski, & Parker, 1998).

Sociometric techniques yield four different categories of social acceptance: **popular children,** who get many positive votes; **rejected children,** who are actively disliked; **controversial children,** who get a large number of positive and negative votes; and **neglected children,** who are seldom chosen, either positively or negatively. About two-thirds of pupils in a typical elementary school classroom fit one of these categories. The remaining one-third are *average* in peer acceptance; they do not receive extreme scores (Coie, Dodge, & Coppotelli, 1982).

Peer acceptance is a powerful predictor of current as well as future psychological adjustment. Rejected children, especially, are unhappy, alienated, poorly achieving children with a low sense of self-esteem. Both teachers and parents view them as having a wide range of emotional and social problems. Peer rejection during middle childhood is also strongly associated with poor school performance, absenteeism, dropping out, antisocial behavior, and delinquency in adolescence and criminality in young adulthood (Bagwell, Newcomb, & Bukowski, 1998; Parker & Asher, 1987; Parker et al., 1995).

Although rejected status predicts and may contribute to a variety of later life problems, keep in mind that the evidence is correlational. Preceding influences—children's characteristics, child-rearing experiences, or some combination of the two—may explain the link between peer relations and psychological adjustment. For example, temperamentally difficult children and shy, inhibited children are at risk for peer problems (see Chapter 10). And on the parents' side, warmth, explanations, and well-coordinated communication characterize the parenting of popular children; high life stress, power-assertive discipline, and insensitive, conflict-ridden dialogue tend to characterize the home lives of rejected children (Black & Logan, 1995; Deković & Janssens, 1992; Pettit et al., 1996).

At the same time, popular and rejected children prompt very different reactions from agemates. Let's look closely at factors in the peer situation that increase the chances that a child will fall into one rather than another peer acceptance category.

ORIGINS OF ACCEPTANCE IN THE PEER SITUATION

To find out what leads one child to be liked, a second to be disliked, and a third to evoke neither positive nor negative peer reactions, researchers have correlated many child characteristics with sociometric scores. They have also conducted short-term longitudinal research to isolate factors that lead up to peers' positive and negative evaluations. Their findings reveal that children's physical appearance and social behavior are important determinants of peer acceptance.

■ **PHYSICAL APPEARANCE.** Recall from Chapter 5 that children and adolescents who deviate from society's standards of physical beauty as a result of obesity or pubertal timing are less well accepted by peers. In Chapter 11, we noted that physical attractiveness is highly salient for children; their physical self-judgments correlate more strongly with overall self-worth than any other self-esteem factor.

Although the strong preference in our culture for a lithesome female body and a muscular male physique is probably learned, partiality for certain facial features emerges so early that it may be built in. Three- to 6-month-old infants look longer at faces judged attractive as opposed to unattractive by adults, regardless of the age, race, and sex of the model (Langlois et al., 1991). By 12 months, babies direct more positive affect and involved play toward an attractive than an unattractive unfamiliar adult (Langlois, Roggman, & Rieser-Danner, 1990).

During early and middle childhood, children have different expectations of attractive and unattractive agemates. When asked to guess the characteristics of unfamiliar peers from their photographs, they attribute friendliness, smartness, and niceness to those who are good-looking and aggressiveness and other negative behaviors to those who are unattractive (Langlois & Stephan, 1981). Attractiveness is also associated with popularity and behavior ratings among children who know each other well, although these relationships are stronger for girls than boys (Langlois & Styczynski, 1979). Parents and teachers show a "beauty-as-best" bias in their attitudes and behavior toward children as well (Langlois et al., 1995; Ritts, Patterson, & Tubbs, 1992).

Do children derive their opinions from the way attractive and unattractive agemates actually behave or from stereotypes held by adults? To investigate this question, Judith Langlois and Chris Downs (1979) assigned 3- to 5-year-olds to the following same-age, same-sex pairs: two attractive children, two unattractive children, and one attractive and one unattractive child. Then they observed each pair in a laboratory play session. By age 5, unattractive children actually displayed some of the negative behaviors that peers attributed to them: They more often aggressed against their partners than attractive children did. However, since differences did not appear until the end of the preschool years, it is possible that unattractive children responded as they did because of others' prior reactions to their physical appearance.

In sum, beginning early in life, a preference for attractive over unattractive children translates into differential adult and peer treatment. Then children may respond in kind to the way they are treated, thereby sustaining the prejudices of their social world.

■ **SOCIAL BEHAVIOR.** A wealth of research indicates that social behavior is the most powerful determinant of peer acceptance. Popular, rejected, controversial, and neglected children interact with agemates in distinct ways.

Popular children have very positive social skills. They are sensitive, friendly, cooperative, and appropriately assertive; they rarely behave in ways that interfere with others' goals. When they do not understand another child's reaction, they ask for an explanation. If they disagree with a play partner in a game, they go beyond voicing their displeasure; they suggest what the other child could do instead. When they want to enter an ongoing play group, they adapt their behavior to the flow of peer activity (Dodge, McClaskey, & Feldman, 1985; Newcomb, Bukowski, & Pattee, 1993).

Rejected children, in contrast, display a wide range of negative social behaviors. But not all of these disliked children look the same. At least two subtypes exist:

■ **Rejected-aggressive children,** the largest subgroup, show severe conduct problems— high rates of conflict, hostility, and hyperactive, inattentive, and impulsive behavior. These children are deficient in regulation of negative emotion and in social understanding. For example, they are more likely than are other children to be poor perspective takers, to misinterpret the innocent behaviors of peers as hostile, to blame others for their social difficulties, and to act on their angry feelings (Crick & Ladd, 1993; Deković & Gerris, 1994; Rubin et al., 1995). Furthermore, in studies carried out in Italy and the United States, both overtly aggressive and relationally aggressive children were rejected by their classmates (Crick, 1996; Tomada & Schneider, 1997).

■ **Rejected-withdrawn children,** a smaller subgroup, are passive and socially awkward. These inhibited, timid children are also poor emotion regulators; overwhelmed by social anxiety, they withdraw in the face of social challenges (Rubin et al., 1995). As a result, they feel lonely, hold negative expectations for how peers will treat them, and are very concerned about being scorned and attacked (Boivin & Hymel, 1997; Rabiner, Keane, & MacKinnon-Lewis, 1993; Stewart & Rubin, 1995). Because of their inept, submissive style, rejected-withdrawn children are at risk for abuse at the hands of bullies (see the Variations box on the following page).

In addition to being disliked by many peers, rejected children have few friends, and occasionally none at all. They are likely to befriend younger children and agemates who are also unpopular, and their friendships are less caring and intimate and more conflict-ridden than are those of their peers (George & Hartmann, 1996; Parker & Asher, 1993). These friendship qualities further limit rejected children's chances of acquiring effective social skills.

Consistent with the mixed peer opinion they engender, controversial children display a blend of positive and negative social behaviors. Like rejected-aggressive children, they are hostile and disruptive, but they also engage in positive, prosocial acts. Even though some peers dislike them, controversial children have some qualities that protect them from social exclusion. As a result, they have as many friends as do popular children and are relatively happy with their peer relationships. The social status of controversial children often changes over time (Newcomb, Bukowski, & Pattee, 1993; Parkhurst & Asher, 1992).

Finally, perhaps the most surprising finding on peer acceptance is that neglected children, once thought to be in need of treatment, are usually well adjusted. Because they engage in low rates of interaction, they are considered shy by their classmates. But unlike rejected-withdrawn children, neglected children do not display social anxiety and are neither lonely nor unhappy about their social life. Instead, when they want to, they can break away from their usual pattern of playing by themselves, and they are just as socially skilled as are average children (Crick & Ladd, 1993; Harrist et al., 1997; Wentzel & Asher, 1995). Perhaps for this reason, socially neglected status (like controversial status) is highly unstable, even over short periods.

Neglected children remind us that there are other paths to emotional well-being besides the outgoing, gregarious personality style so highly valued in our culture. In Chapter 10, we noted that in China, adults view cautious, inhibited children as advanced in social maturity! In accord with this standard, shyness and sensitivity are associated with peer acceptance and teacher-rated social competence and leadership among Chinese 8- to 10-year-olds (Chen, Rubin, & Li, 1995).

rejected–aggressive children A subgroup of rejected children who engage in high rates of conflict, hostility, and hyperactive, inattentive, and impulsive behavior.

rejected–withdrawn children A subgroup of rejected children who are passive and socially awkward.

peer victimization A destructive form of peer interaction in which certain children become frequent targets of verbal and physical attacks or other forms of abuse.

Peer Victimization

OLLOW THE ACTIVITIES of aggressive children over a school day, and you will see that they reserve their hostilities for certain peers. A particularly destructive form of interaction that emerges during middle childhood is **peer victimization,** in which certain children become frequent targets of verbal and physical attacks or other forms of abuse. What sustains repeated assault–retreat cycles between pairs of children, leading one member to become an attacker and the other a victim of abuse?

In one of the most comprehensive studies of the aggressor–victim relationship, Dan Olweus (1978, 1984) asked Swedish teachers to list adolescent male bullies, their "whipping boys," and well-adjusted classmates. Then judgments of each group's characteristics were obtained from teachers, mothers, peers, and the boys themselves. Compared with bullies and well-adjusted adolescents, whipping boys were chronically anxious (at home and at school), low in self-esteem, ostracized by peers, physically weak, and afraid to defend themselves.

These findings suggest that victimized children are attacked more than others because they are perceived as weak and likely to provide their aggressors with rewarding consequences. Indeed, the majority of victimized children reinforce bullies by giving in to their demands, crying, assuming defensive postures, and failing to fight back. Biologically based traits—an inhibited, fearful temperament and a frail physical appearance—contribute to their behavior. But they also have histories of resistant attachment; overly intrusive, controlling child rearing; and (among boys) maternal overprotectiveness. These parenting behaviors prompt anxiety, low self-esteem, and dependency, resulting in a passive, fearful demeanor that radiates vulnerability (Ladd & Ladd, 1998; Olweus, 1993).

By elementary school, 10 percent of children are harassed by aggressive agemates, and peers view these targets differently. They expect victims to give up desirable objects, show signs of distress, and fail to retaliate far more often than nonvictims. In addition, children (especially those who are aggressive) feel less discomfort at the thought of causing pain and suffering to victims than nonvictims, thereby minimizing the possibility of harmful consequences (Perry, Williard, & Perry, 1990). Although bullies and victims are most often boys, at times they are girls who bombard a vulnerable classmate with relational hostility (Crick & Grotpeter, 1996). As early as kindergarten, victimization leads to a variety of adjustment difficulties, including sadness and depression, loneliness, and dislike and avoidance of school (Boulton & Underwood, 1992; Ladd, Kochenderfer, & Coleman, 1997).

Children who are bullied by agemates have characteristics that make them easy targets. They are highly anxious, physically weak, rejected by peers, and afraid to defend themselves. Both temperamental traits and child-rearing experiences underlie their cowering behavior, which reinforces their attackers' abusive acts.
(Aloma/Monkmeyer Press)

Aggression and victimization are not polar opposites. A small number of extreme victims are also aggressive, picking arguments and fights (Boulton & Smith, 1994). Perhaps these children foolishly provoke stronger agemates, who then prevail over them. Although both aggressive and victimized children are rejected by peers, these highly aggressive–highly abused youngsters are the most despised, placing them at severe risk for maladjustment.

Interventions that change victimized children's negative opinions of themselves and that teach them to respond in nonreinforcing ways to their attackers are vital. Nevertheless, victimized children's behavior should not be taken to mean that they are to blame for their abuse. Instead, the responsibility lies with bullies who brutally attack and adults who supervise children's interactions. Developing a school code against bullying, enlisting parents' assistance in changing both bullies' and victims' behavior, and moving aggressive children to another class or school can greatly reduce bully–victim problems, which account for a substantial portion of peer aggression in middle childhood (Olweus, 1995).

Yet another way to help victimized children is to assist them in acquiring the social skills to form and maintain a gratifying friendship. Anxious, withdrawn children who have a mutual best friend seem better equipped to withstand peer attacks. They show fewer adjustment problems than do victims with no close friends (Hodges et al., 1999).

HELPING REJECTED CHILDREN

A variety of interventions exist to improve the peer relations and psychological adjustment of rejected children. Most involve coaching, modeling, and reinforcing positive social skills, such as how to begin interacting with a peer, cooperate in games, and respond to another child with friendly emotion and approval. Several of these programs have produced gains in social competence and peer acceptance still present from several weeks to a year later (Asher & Rose, 1997; Lochman et al., 1993; Mize & Ladd, 1990).

Some researchers believe that these interventions might be even more effective when combined with other treatments. Often rejected-aggressive children's impulsivity contributes to a maladaptive learning style, including distractibility and poor planning and organization. As early as first grade, many are poor students, and their low academic self-esteem magnifies their negative reactions to teachers and classmates (O'Neil et al., 1997). Intensive academic tutoring improves both school achievement and social acceptance (Coie & Krehbiel, 1984). In addition, techniques aimed at reducing rejected-aggressive children's antisocial behavior are helpful. In one study, including verbal prohibitions against antisocial acts and negative consequences for engaging in them in a social-skills coaching program led to better social acceptance than a program focusing only on teaching positive social behaviors (Bierman, Miller, & Stabb, 1987).

Social-cognitive interventions, such as training in perspective taking and social problem solving, have also produced favorable outcomes. Still another approach is to increase expectancies for social success. Many rejected-withdrawn children develop a *learned helpless* approach to peer acceptance. They conclude, after repeated rebuffs, that no matter how hard they try, they will never be liked (Rubin, Bukowski, & Parker, 1998; Toner & Munro, 1996). In contrast, rejected-aggressive children tend to externalize their combative behaviors with such claims as "They made me do it!" (Coie & Dodge, 1998). Both types of youngsters need help in attributing their peer difficulties to internal, changeable causes.

Finally, we have seen that rejected children's socially incompetent behaviors often originate in a poor fit between the child's temperament and parenting practices. Therefore, interventions that focus on the child alone are unlikely to be sufficient. If the quality of parent–child interaction is not changed, rejected children may soon return to their old behavior patterns.

ASK YOURSELF . . .

♦ In kindergarten, Miranda prefers to draw pictures, work puzzles, and look at books by herself. She rarely plays with other children. Jezebel is also a solitary child, but she spends most of the day wandering around the room, anxiously hovering near peers without joining their play. Which child is likely to have a neglected social status? How about a rejected-withdrawn status? Explain.

♦ CONNECTIONS
How can parents help shy, inhibited children overcome their social wariness, thereby reducing their risk for peer rejection and later maladjustment? (See Chapter 10, pages 417 and 420.)

BRIEF REVIEW

Peer acceptance is a powerful predictor of current and future psychological adjustment. Rejected children, especially, display serious academic and behavior problems. Physical attractiveness is related to likability. Differential treatment of physically attractive and unattractive children may affect the way they behave, thereby sustaining peer opinion.

Children's social behavior is a major determinant of peer acceptance. Popular children interact in a cooperative, friendly fashion; rejected children behave antisocially and ineptly; and controversial children display a mixture of positive and negative social behaviors. Although neglected children engage in low rates of peer interaction, they are usually socially competent and well adjusted. Interventions that train social skills, improve academic performance, reduce antisocial behavior, and increase social understanding lead to improved social acceptance of rejected children.

Peer Groups

Watch children in the schoolyard or neighborhood, and you will see that groups of three to a dozen often gather. The organization of these collectives changes greatly with age. By the end of middle childhood, children display a strong desire for group belongingness. Together, they generate unique values and standards for behavior. They also create a social structure of leaders and followers that ensures group goals will be met. When these characteristics are present, a **peer group** is formed.

In Chapter 11, we saw how friendships contribute to the development of trust and sensitivity. Children's experiences in peer groups also provide a unique context for social learning—one in which children practice cooperation, leadership, and followership and develop a sense of loyalty to collective goals. Through these experiences, children experiment with and learn about the functioning of social organizations.

PEER GROUP FORMATION

A classic study by Muzafer Sherif and his colleagues (1961), called the Robbers Cave experiment, illustrates how peer groups form and their functions in children's lives. Fifth-grade boys were brought to a summer campground called Robbers Cave, divided into two clusters of 11 members each, and removed to separate campsites. Although friendships developed quickly, a strong group structure emerged only after the camp staff arranged activities requiring cooperation. Backpacking trips and opportunities to improve swimming and athletic areas led the campers to create a division of labor. Soon several boys with superior skills took on greater status—one for his cooking, another for his athletic ability, and a third for his entertaining personality. Over time, a clear ranking of leaders and followers appeared.

As the group structure took shape, the boys at each campsite developed distinct notions of appropriate behavior and ways of doing things. For example, one group generated a "norm of toughness" in which they engaged in rowdiness and swearing and suppressed any signs of pain when injured. In contrast, a "norm of good behavior" emphasizing clean language and helpfulness arose in the other group. Eventually the groups took names for themselves: the Rattlers and the Eagles. The boys in each displayed a strong group identity.

The next phase of Sherif's study showed that a group's norms and social structures develop further, based on its relationship with "outsiders." The camp counselors arranged for a tournament of competitive games. Sparked by intergroup rivalry, new leaders and normative behaviors appeared. Among the Rattlers, a large bully emerged as a hero, who led the group in insulting and retaliating against the outgroup, with each successful attack intensifying group solidarity. Over time, the Rattlers and Eagles stereotyped each other as nasty and sneaky, reactions that further magnified the social distance between the groups.

In the final phase of the study, the camp staff planned events with superordinate goals, and intergroup hostility subsided. In one instance, the water supply "broke down," and in another, a truck preparing to get food for the hungry campers "stalled." As a result, all campers joined forces to solve common problems, negative stereotyping declined, and new friendships emerged that cut across group lines.

The Robbers Cave experiment reveals that peer groups form when individuals perceive that others share similar goals. Norms and social structures emerge and change in the service of common motivations. Although racial, ethnic, and gender differences often promote out-group prejudice and stereotyping (see Chapters 11 and 13), Sherif's study shows that competition for highly desired resources is enough to evoke deep-seated hostilities. Superordinate goals can reduce intergroup hatred and promote positive attitudes and relationships.

Let's look closely at two features that are essential for peer group cohesion: norms and social structures.

GROUP NORMS

Group norms are evident by the end of middle childhood and strengthen during the teenage years, when peer groups become more tightly knit and exclusive. Late childhood and adolescent peer groups are organized around **cliques,** small groups of about five to seven members who are good friends and, therefore, usually alike in age, sex, ethnicity, SES, personality, and attitudes and values (see Chapter 11). The cliques within a typical high school can be identified by their interests and social status, as the well-known

peer group Peers who form a social unit by generating unique values and standards of behavior and a social structure of leaders and followers.

clique A small group of about five to seven members who are good friends.

These high school international club members form a crowd. Unlike the more intimate clique, the larger, more loosely organized crowd grants adolescents an identity within the larger social structure of the school.
(Will Faller)

"popular" and "unpopular" groups reveal (Cairns et al., 1995; Gillmore et al., 1997). Once formed, cliques develop dress codes, ways of speaking, and behaviors that separate them from one another and from the adult world.

Adolescents also form larger, more loosely organized groups called **crowds.** Unlike the more intimate clique, membership in a crowd is based on reputation and stereotype. Whereas the clique serves as the main context for direct interaction, the crowd grants the adolescent an identity within the larger social structure of the school. In a typical high school, for example, the "jocks" are very involved in athletics; the "brains" worry about their grades; and the "workers" have part-time jobs and lots of spending money. The "druggies" use drugs on more than a one-time basis, while the "greasers" wear dark jackets, cross the street to smoke cigarettes, and feel alienated from most aspects of school life (Brown, 1990; Urberg et al., 1995).

What influences the assortment of teenagers into cliques and crowds? In addition to adolescent personality and interests, family factors are important. In a study of 8,000 ninth to twelfth graders, adolescents who described their parents as authoritative (warm and demanding) were members of "brain," "jock," and "popular" groups that accepted both the adult and peer reward systems of the school. In contrast, boys with permissive parents (warm but undemanding) valued interpersonal relationships and aligned themselves with the "fun culture" or "partyer" crowd. And teenagers who viewed their parents as uninvolved (low in warmth and demandingness) more often affiliated with "partyer" and "druggie" crowds, suggesting lack of identification with adult reward systems (Durbin et al., 1993).

Cultural variations in group norms also exist. The strong emphasis Asian parents place on academic achievement and interpersonal harmony carries over to peer affiliations. Among Chinese young people, scholastic rank, cooperation, politeness, hard work, and restrained behavior are especially salient bases of peer group membership (Leung, 1996).

These findings indicate that many peer group norms are extensions of ones acquired at home. But once adolescents join a clique or crowd, it can modify their beliefs and behaviors. For example, when adolescents associate with peers who have authoritative parents, their friends' competence "rubs off" on them in terms of better academic performance and lower levels of delinquency and substance abuse (Fletcher et al., 1995). However, the positive impact of having academically and socially skilled peers is greatest for teenagers whose own parents are authoritative. And the negative impact of having antisocial, drug-using friends is strongest for teenagers whose parents use less effective child-

crowd A large, loosely organized peer group in which membership is based on reputation and stereotype.

rearing styles (Mounts & Steinberg, 1995). In sum, family experiences affect the extent to which adolescents become like their peers over time.

In early adolescence, as interest in dating increases, boys' and girls' cliques come together. The merger takes place slowly. At junior high school dances and parties, clusters of boys and girls can be seen standing on opposite sides of the room, watching but seldom interacting. As mixed-sex cliques form, they provide a supportive context for boys and girls to get to know each other. Cliques offer models of how to interact with the other sex and opportunities to do so without having to be intimate. Gradually, the larger group divides into couples, several of whom spend time together, going to parties and movies. By late adolescence, boys and girls feel comfortable enough approaching each other directly that the mixed-sex clique is no longer needed and disappears (Padgham & Blyth, 1990).

Just as cliques gradually decline in importance, so do crowds. As older adolescents formulate their own personal values and goals, they no longer feel a strong need to wear a "badge" that broadcasts—through dress, language, and preferred activities—who they are. Nevertheless, both cliques and crowds serve vital functions during the teenage years. The clique provides a context for acquiring new social skills and for experimenting with values and roles in the absence of adult monitoring. The crowd offers adolescents the security of a temporary identity as they separate from the family and begin to construct a coherent sense of self (Brown, 1990).

GROUP SOCIAL STRUCTURES

In all groups, members differ in power or status, an arrangement that fosters division of responsibilities and smooth, cooperative interaction. Group norms and social structures are related. Leaders are generally the major norm setters, and the ideas of high-status peers are usually sufficient to alter the group's opinion (Adler & Adler, 1995). How do leaders and followers emerge in children's groups?

As our earlier discussion of rough-and-tumble play revealed, group social structures are sometimes based on toughness or assertiveness. A **dominance hierarchy** is a stable ordering of individuals that predicts who will win when conflict arises between group members. Observations of arguments, threats, and physical attacks between children reveal a

Peer groups form by the end of middle childhood. These boys have probably established a social structure of leaders and followers as they gather often for joint activities, such as bike riding and basketball. Their body language suggests that they feel a strong sense of group belonging.
(R. Sidney/The Image Works)

dominance hierarchy A stable ordering of group members that predicts who will win when conflict arises between group members.

consistent lineup of winners and losers as early as the preschool years. This hierarchy becomes increasingly stable during middle childhood and adolescence, especially among boys (Pettit et al., 1990). Recall from Chapter 13 that after age 5, boys play in larger groups than girls do. Boys' popularity (an indicator of dominance) is strongly related to the size of their friendship networks. In contrast, girls interact in small clusters, irrespective of social status (Benenson, Apostoleris, & Parnass, 1998).

Like dominance relations among animals, those among human children serve the adaptive function of limiting aggression among group members. Once a dominance hierarchy is clearly established, hostility is rare. When it occurs, it is very restrained, often taking the form of playful verbal insults that can be accepted cheerfully by the target (Fine, 1980). This gradual replacement of friendly insults for more direct hostility may help children and adolescents learn how to control their aggressive impulses.

Think back to the Robbers Cave study, and you will see that when group goals focus on conquest or exclusion of "outsiders," a structure based on dominance is likely to emerge, as it did when the Rattlers and Eagles played competitive games. Parents and teachers often express concern about the exclusiveness of cliques, common to both boys' and girls' peer cultures. Adolescents report that the strategies used by some clique leaders to recruit "acceptable" members and reject or cast out the "unworthy" rank among their most anxious and (for those expelled) emotionally painful experiences. At times, clique dynamics teach unfortunate lessons in power, manipulation, submission, and prejudice (Adler & Adler, 1995).

At other times, qualities other than dominance are the basis for group leadership. In a study of fourth- to sixth-grade Girl Scout troups, girls who emerged as informal leaders had traits reflecting an effective managerial style. They were friendly, thoughtful, organized, and quick to suggest new ideas. Often they were popular and physically attractive as well (Edwards, 1994). Many group structures also depend on talents that support important normative activities, such as knowing what to do on a camp-out or being a skilled athlete or debater (Savin-Williams, 1980). Since peer groups vary widely in their normative concerns, high status accrues to different young people in different situations.

Peer Relations and Socialization

eer interaction contributes to a wide variety of skills that help children and adolescents adapt successfully to their social worlds. Just how do peers socialize one another? As we will see in the following sections, they use some of the same techniques that parents do: reinforcement, modeling, and direct pressures to conform to certain expectations.

PEER REINFORCEMENT AND MODELING

Children's responses to one another serve as reinforcers, modifying the extent to which they display certain behaviors. Turn back to Chapter 13, page 536, to review how peers reinforce gender-role behavior. Peer reinforcement begins early and increases with age. Children often use it for positive ends. Those who engage in attentive, approving, and affectionate social acts are likely to receive similar behaviors in return (Kindermann, 1998).

Children are just as receptive to peer reinforcement for antisocial behavior as they are for prosocial acts. In the Variations box on page 607, we showed that the hostile acts of bullies are repeatedly reinforced by the passivity of their victims. Children who retaliate and succeed at getting an aggressor to retreat punish that child's actions. At the same time, their own behavior is rewarded. A striking finding is a steady increase in aggression by initially nonaggressive children who counterattack in the face of peer hostility (Patterson, Littman, & Bricker, 1967). Peer feedback is an important means through which children's aggression is enhanced as well as controlled, and even mild-mannered children can learn to behave aggressively from being targets of peer hostility.

Besides dispensing reinforcers, peers model a broad array of social behaviors. Peer imitation occurs more often between familiar than unfamiliar peers. A sense of similarity and closeness increases children's willingness to model another's behavior. Being imitated, in turn, fosters feelings of connection to others and may be an important means through which peer ties form and strengthen (Kindermann, 1998). Imitation is also one reason that friends become more alike over time (see Chapter 11).

The powerful effects of peer reinforcement and modeling have led researchers to experiment with peers as agents of behavior change. Socially competent children can be trained to encourage social skills in less competent peers, and both show gains in social maturity (Strain, 1977). Peers can also tutor less knowledgeable children at school, teaching, modeling, and reinforcing academic skills. Carefully planned peer tutoring programs, in which tutors are trained and supervised by adult teachers, lead to benefits in academic achievement and self-esteem for both tutors and tutees (Renninger, 1998).

PEER CONFORMITY

Conformity to peer pressure is greater during adolescence than in childhood or young adulthood—a finding that is not surprising when we consider how much time teenagers spend together. But contrary to popular belief, adolescence is not a period in which young people blindly do what their peers ask. Peer conformity is a complex process that varies with the adolescent's age and need for social approval and with the situation.

In one study of nearly 400 junior and senior high students, adolescents reported that they felt greatest pressure to conform to the most obvious aspects of the peer culture—dressing and grooming like everyone else and participating in social activities, such as dating and going to parties (see Figure 15.1). Peer pressure to engage in proadult behavior, such as getting good grades and cooperating with parents, was also strong. Although pressure toward misconduct rose in early adolescence, compared with other areas it was low. Many teenagers said that their friends actively discouraged antisocial acts. These findings show that peers and parents often act in concert, toward desirable ends! Finally, peer pressures were only modestly related to teenagers' values and behaviors. Clearly, these young people did not always follow the dictates of peers (Brown, Lohr, & McClenahan, 1986).

Perhaps because of their greater concern with what their friends think of them, early adolescents are more likely than younger or older individuals to give in to peer pressure (Brown, Clasen, & Eicher, 1986). Yet when parents and peers disagree, even young teenagers do not consistently rebel against their families. Instead, parents and peers differ in their spheres of greatest influence. Parents have more impact on teenagers' basic life values and educational plans (Sebald, 1986). Peers are more influential in short-term,

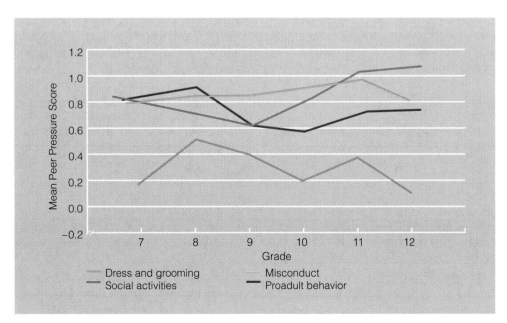

FIGURE 15.1

Grade changes in perceived peer pressure in four areas of behavior in a cross-sectional study of junior and senior high school students. Overall, teenagers felt the greatest pressure to conform to dress and grooming styles and social activities. Pressure to engage in proadult behavior was also high. Although peer pressure toward misconduct peaked in early adolescence, it was relatively low.

(From B. B. Brown, M. J. Lohr, & E. L. McClenahan, 1986, "Early Adolescents' Perceptions of Peer Pressure," *Journal of Early Adolescence, 6*, p. 147. Reprinted by permission.)

Adolescent Substance Use and Abuse

N THE UNITED States, teenage alcohol and drug use is pervasive—higher than in any other industrialized nation. By age 14, 56 percent of young people have tried smoking, 81 percent drinking, and 39 percent at least one illegal drug (usually marijuana). By the end of high school, 16 percent are regular cigarette users, 30 percent have engaged in heavy drinking at least once, and over 45 percent have experimented with illegal drugs. Of these, about one-third have tried at least one highly addictive and toxic substance, such as amphetamines, cocaine, phencyclidine (PCP), or heroin (U.S. Department of Health and Human Services, 1998a).

These high figures represent a steady increase in alcohol and drug use over the past few years, after a decade of decline (see Figure 15.2). Why do so many young people subject themselves to the health risks of these substances? Part of the reason is cultural. Modern adolescents live in a drug-dependent society. They see adults using caffeine to wake up in the morning, cigarettes to cope with daily hassles, a drink to calm down in the evening, and other remedies to relieve stress, depression, and physical illness. Reduced parental, school, and media attention to the hazards of drugs as the epidemic of the 1980s subsided may explain the recent upsurge in adolescent drug taking.

For most young people, drug use simply reflects their intense curiosity about "adultlike" behaviors. Research reveals that the majority of teenagers dabble in alcohol as well as tobacco and marijuana. These minimal *experimenters* are not headed for a life of decadence and addiction. Instead, they

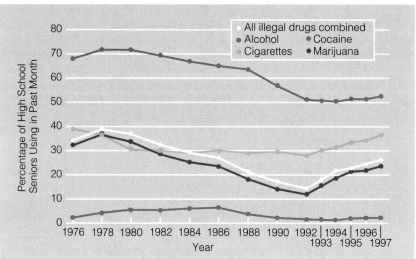

FIGURE 15.2

Percentages of high school seniors reporting use of alcohol, cigarettes, and illegal drugs in the past month, 1976–1997. Substance use continues to be widespread among adolescents. Although it declined from 1982 to 1992, a sharp increase during the past few years—largely accounted for by marijuana and cigarette smoking—has sounded a note of alarm.
(From U.S. Department of Health and Human Services, 1998a.)

are psychologically healthy, sociable, curious young people (Shedler & Block, 1990). In a society in which substance use is commonplace, it appears that some involvement with drugs is normal and to be expected.

---

day-to-day matters, such as type of dress, taste in music, and choice of friends. Adolescents' personal characteristics also made a difference. Young people who feel competent and worthwhile are less likely to fall in line behind peers who engage in early sex, delinquency, and frequent drug use (see the From Research to Practice box above).

Finally, authoritative parenting is consistently related to resistance to unfavorable peer pressure (Fletcher et al., 1995; Mason et al., 1996). In contrast, adolescents who experience extremes of parental behavior—either too much restrictiveness or two little monitoring—tend to be highly peer oriented. They more often rely on friends for advice about their personal lives and future and are more willing to break their parents' rules, ignore their schoolwork, and hide their talents to be popular with agemates (Fuligni & Eccles, 1993). Supportive ties to parents protect adolescents from peer antisocial involvements even under conditions of high life stress. In a study of poverty-stricken Brazilian street youths, those who worked at street jobs but returned to their families at night or on weekends reported more social supports and fewer problem behaviors than did homeless youths with fragmented family ties. Family support served as an antidote to unfavorable peer pressures on the street, with profound consequences for development.

Before we turn to the impact of media on children and adolescents, you may find it helpful to examine the Milestones table on page 616, which summarizes the development of peer relations.

Yet adolescent drug experimentation should not be taken lightly. Because most drugs impair perception and thought processes, a single heavy dose can lead to permanent injury or death. And a worrisome minority of teenagers move from substance *use* to *abuse*—taking drugs regularly, requiring increasing amounts to achieve the same effect, and finding themselves unable to stop.

CORRELATES AND CONSEQUENCES OF ADOLESCENT SUBSTANCE ABUSE. In contrast to experimenters, drug abusers are seriously troubled young people who are inclined to express their unhappiness through antisocial acts. Their impulsive, disruptive style is often evident in early childhood and seems to be perpetuated by a variety of other interrelated factors, including low SES, family mental health problems, parental and older sibling drug abuse, lack of parent involvement and support, and poor school performance. By early adolescence, peer encouragement—friends who use drugs, urge the young person to do so, and provide access to illegal substances—is a strong predictor of substance abuse. Once an adolescent associates with deviant, drug-using peers, his or her own substance use approaches their level (Chassin et al., 1996; Wills et al., 1996).

Adolescent substance abuse often has lifelong consequences. When teenagers depend on alcohol and hard drugs to deal with daily stresses, they fail to learn responsible decision-making skills and alternative coping techniques. These young people show serious adjustment problems, including depression and antisocial behavior (Luthar & Cushing, 1997). They often enter into marriage, childbearing, and the work world prematurely and fail at them readily—painful outcomes that encourage further addictive behavior.

PREVENTION AND TREATMENT. School-based programs that promote effective parenting (including monitoring of teenagers' activities) and that teach adolescents skills for resisting peer pressure reduce drug experimentation to some degree (Steinberg, Fletcher, & Darling, 1994). But some drug taking seems to be inevitable. Therefore, interventions that prevent adolescents from endangering themselves and others when they do experiment are essential. Many communities offer weekend on-call transportation services that any young person can contact for a safe ride home, with no questions asked. Providing appealing substitute activities, such as drug-free video arcades, dances, and sports activities, is also helpful. And educating teenagers about the dangers of drugs and alcohol is vital, since an increase in perceived risk closely paralleled the decline in substance use in the 1980s and early 1990s (O'Malley, Johnston, & Bachman, 1995).

Drug abuse, as we have seen, occurs for quite different reasons than does occasional use. Therefore, different prevention strategies are required. One approach is to work with parents early, reducing family adversity and improving parenting skills, before children are old enough to become involved with drugs (Luthar, Cushing, & McMahon, 1997). Programs that teach at-risk teenagers strategies for handling life stressors and that build competence through community service have been found to reduce alcohol and drug use, just as they reduce teenage pregnancy (see Chapter 5) (Richards-Colocino, McKenzie, & Newton, 1996).

When an adolescent becomes a drug abuser, hospitalization is often a necessary and even lifesaving first step. Once the young person is weaned from the drug, therapy to treat low-self-esteem, anxiety, and impulsivity and academic and vocational training to improve life success are generally needed. Not much is known about the best way to treat adolescent drug abuse. Even the most comprehensive programs have relapse rates that are alarmingly high—from 35 to 70 percent (Newcomb & Bentler, 1989; Segal & Stewart, 1996).

BRIEF REVIEW

By the end of middle childhood, peer groups form, through which children and adolescents learn about the functioning of social organizations. Group norms foster a sense of belongingness and are often extensions of values acquired at home. Group social structures lead to a division of responsibility and offer practice in leader and follower roles. Adolescent peer groups are organized around cliques and crowds. The clique provides a setting in which adolescents learn social skills and try out new values and roles. The crowd offers a temporary identity as teenagers work on constructing their own. When group goals focus on conquest and exclusion of outsiders, dominance often determines leader–follower roles. Otherwise, leadership is based on managerial skills and talents that support important normative activities.

Peers socialize one another through reinforcement, modeling, and direct pressure to conform to certain expectations. The powerful effects of peer reinforcement and modeling have inspired peer social skills training and tutoring programs. Conformity to peer pressure rises in adolescence, but teenagers do not mindlessly "follow the crowd." Peers have a more powerful impact on everyday matters of dress and social behavior, parents on basic life values and educational plans. Authoritative parenting protects adolescents against unfavorable peer pressures.

ASK YOURSELF . . .

◆ *Phyllis likes her 14-year-old daughter Farrah's friends, but she wonders what Farrah gets out of hanging out with them at Jake's Pizza Parlor on Friday and Saturday evenings. Explain to Phyllis what Farrah is learning.*

◆ **CONNECTIONS**
Consider what children learn from participating in large peer networks versus interacting with one or two close friends. How might boys' preference for large groups and girls' preference for small clusters contribute to sex-related differences in friendship quality and personality traits? (See Chapter 11, page 471, and Chapter 13, pages 548–552.)

Development of Peer Relations

MILESTONES

Age	Peer Sociability	Peer Groups	Peer Socialization
Birth–2 years	■ Isolated social acts increase over the first year and are gradually replaced by coordinated interaction.		■ At the end of this period, peer reinforcement and modeling are evident.
2½–6 years	■ At the beginning of this period, children use words to affect a peer's behavior. ■ Parallel play appears, remains stable from 3 to 6 years, and becomes more cognitively mature. ■ Cooperative play increases—especially sociodramatic play. ■ Rough-and-tumble play emerges.	■ Dominance hierarchies emerge.	■ Peer modeling and reinforcement increase.
7–11 years	■ Peer communication skills improve, including interpreting and responding to the emotions and intentions of others. ■ Ability to understand the complementary roles of several players improves, permitting the transition to rule-oriented games. ■ Peer interaction becomes more prosocial, and aggression (in the form of physical attacks) declines. ■ Rough-and-tumble play becomes more common.	■ Peer groups with distinct norms and social structures emerge. ■ Dominance hierarchies become more stable.	■ As children internalize social rules, peer modeling declines.
12–20 years	■ Peer interaction becomes more cooperative. ■ Rough-and-tumble play declines. ■ More time is spent with peers than with any other partners.	■ Peer groups become more tightly knit and exclusive, organized around cliques. ■ Large, loosely organized crowds form, based on reputation and stereotype. ■ As interest in dating increases, mixed-sex cliques form.	■ Conformity to peer pressure increases and gradually declines.

Note: These milestones represent overall age trends. Individual differences exist in the precise age at which each milestone is attained.

Television

xposure to television is almost universal in the United States and other Western industrialized nations. Ninety-eight percent of American homes have at least one television set, over 50 percent have two or more, and a TV set is switched on in a typical household for 7.1 hours per day (Comstock, 1993). Although the popularity of television is widespread, there is good reason to be concerned about its impact on children and youths. In an unusual investigation, residents of a small Canadian town were studied just before TV reception became available in their community and then 2 years later. School-age children showed a decline in reading ability and creative thinking, a rise in gender-stereotyped beliefs, and an increase in verbal and physical aggression during play. In addition, a sharp drop in adolescents' community participation followed the arrival of television (Williams, 1986).

Worrisome findings like these have been reported in hundreds of studies. But they are not an inherent part of the medium itself. Instead, they result from the way it is used in our society. As our discussion proceeds, we will see that television has as much potential for good as for ill. If the content of TV programming were improved and adults capitalized on it to enhance children's interest in their everyday worlds, television could be a powerful, cost-effective means of strengthening cognitive, emotional, and social development.

HOW MUCH TELEVISION DO CHILDREN VIEW?

The amount of time children in the United States devote to television is extraordinary. Regular viewing typically begins between 2 and 3 years of age at about 1½ hours a day, rises to 4 hours by age 12, and then declines slightly during adolescence. The average American school-age child watches TV 28 hours per week (Comstock, 1993). When we consider how much time the set is on during school holidays and summer vacations, children spend more time watching television than they do in any other waking activity, including going to school and interacting with family members or peers.

Children differ in their attraction to television. In early and middle childhood, boys watch slightly more TV than do girls. Low-SES, ethnic minority children and children from large families are also more frequent viewers, perhaps because their parents are less able to pay for out-of-home entertainment or their neighborhoods provide few alternative activities. And if parents tend to watch a lot of TV, their children usually do so as well (Huston & Wright, 1998). Excessive TV viewing is associated with family and peer difficulties. Parents with high life stress often escape into television viewing, and their children may do so as well (Anderson et al., 1996).

DEVELOPMENT OF TELEVISION LITERACY

When watching TV programs, children are confronted with a rapid stream of people, objects, places, words, and sounds. Television, or film, has its own specialized code of conveying information. Researchers liken the task of cracking this code to that of learning to read, calling it **television literacy.** Although the symbolic learning required to understand television is not as great as that demanded by reading, it is still considerable.

Television literacy has two parts. The first involves understanding the form of the message. Children must master the meaning of a variety of visual and auditory effects, such as camera zooms, panoramic views, fade-outs, split screens, instant replays, and sound effects. Second, they must process the content of the message, constructing an accurate story line by integrating scenes, character behavior, and dialogue. These two parts are really interdependent, since television form provides essential cues to a program's content (Fitch, Huston, & Wright, 1993).

During early and middle childhood, children are captivated by TV's salient perceptual features. When a program contains quickly paced character movement, special effects, loud music, nonhuman speech, or children's voices, they become highly attentive. At other times, they look away, play with toys, or talk to others in the same room (Rice, Huston, &

television literacy The task of learning television's specialized symbolic code of conveying information.

Wright, 1982). While involved in other activities, preschoolers follow the TV soundtrack. They turn back to the set when they hear cartoon characters and puppets speaking and certain words, such as "Big Bird" and "cookie," that signal the content is likely to be interesting and meaningful to them (Alwitt et al., 1980).

Clearly, young children are selective and strategic processors of televised information, but how much do they really understand? Not a great deal. Before age 8, children have difficulty integrating separate scenes into a continuous story line. As a result, they often do not relate a TV character's behavior to prior intentions and later consequences (Collins et al., 1978). Other TV forms are confusing as well, such as fades, which signal the passage of time, and instant replays, which preschoolers take as repeated events (Anderson & Smith, 1984; Rice, Huston, & Wright, 1986).

Furthermore, young children find it hard to judge the reality of TV material. At ages 2 and 3, they do not discriminate televised images from real objects; they say a bowl of popcorn on television would spill if the TV were turned upside down (Flavell et al., 1990). By age 4 they have mastered this distinction, and they judge TV reality according to whether the images resemble people and objects in their everyday world. Consequently, they consider human actors "real" and cartoon characters "unreal." Around age 5, children start to make finer distinctions about television reality. They say that news and documentaries depict real events and that fictional programs are "just for TV." But not until age 7 do they fully grasp the unreality of TV fiction—that characters do not retain their roles in real life and that their behavior is scripted and rehearsed (Wright et al., 1994).

Cognitive development and experience with TV lead to gains in television literacy. Grasp of cinematic forms and memory for information important to plot comprehension increase sharply from middle childhood to adolescence. In addition, older children can draw inferences about televised material. For example, fifth to eighth graders recognize that a character who at first seems like a "good guy" but who unexpectedly behaves callously and aggressively is really a double-dealing "bad guy" in the end. In contrast, younger children find it difficult to reconcile their initially positive expectations with the character's eventual bad behavior. Consequently, they evaluate the character and his actions much more favorably (Collins, 1983).

In sum, preschool and early school-age children assimilate televised information piecemeal, have an incomplete understanding of its reality, and are unable to critically evaluate it. These factors increase the chances that they will imitate and believe what they see on the screen. Let's look at the impact of TV on children's social learning.

TELEVISION AND SOCIAL LEARNING

Since the 1950s, researchers and public citizens have been concerned about the attitudes and behaviors that television cultivates in young viewers. Most studies have focused on the implications of TV violence for the development of antisocial conduct. Still others have addressed the power of TV to teach undesirable gender and ethnic stereotypes. And growing evidence illustrates TV's potential to contribute to children's cognitive and social competence.

■ AGGRESSION. The National Television Violence Study, a recent large-scale survey of the amount, nature, and context of TV violence in the United States, concluded that violence pervades American TV (see Figure 15.3). Fifty-seven percent of programs between 6 A.M. and 11 P.M. contain violent scenes, often in the form of repeated aggressive acts against a victim that go unpunished. In fact, most violent portrayals do not show victims experiencing any serious physical harm, and few condemn violence or depict alternative ways of solving problems. To the contrary, over one-third of violent TV scenes are embedded in humor, a figure that rises to two-thirds for children's shows. Violent content is 9 percent above average in children's programming, and cartoons are the most violent TV fare of all (Center for Communication and Social Policy, 1998).

Reviewers of thousands of studies have concluded that television violence provides children with "an extensive how-to course in aggression" (Comstock & Paik, 1994; Huston et al., 1992; Slaby et al., 1995, p. 163). The case is strengthened by the fact that re-

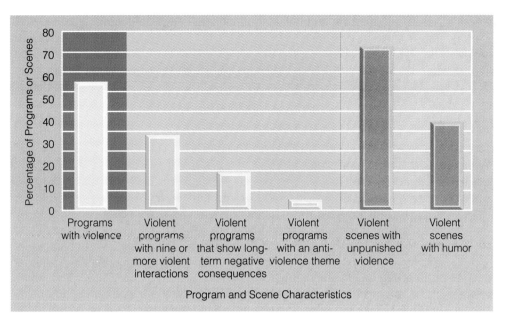

FIGURE 15.3

Violent characteristics of American television programming, based on a large, representative sample of more than 3,000 programs broadcast between 6 A.M. and 11 P.M. Violence occurs in the majority of programs. It often consists of repeated aggressive acts that go unpunished and that are embedded in humor. Only rarely do programs show long-term negative consequences of violence or present it in the context of an antiviolence theme.

(Adapted from Center for Communication and Social Policy, 1998.)

search using a wide variety of research designs, methods, and participants has yielded similar findings. In addition, the relationship of TV violence to hostile behavior remains the same after many factors that might otherwise account for this association are controlled, such as IQ, SES, school achievement, and child-rearing practices (Donnerstein, Slaby, & Eron, 1994).

Violent programming creates both short-term and long-term difficulties in family and peer relations. Longitudinal research reveals that highly aggressive children have a greater appetite for violent TV. As they watch more, they become increasingly likely to resort to hostile ways of solving problems, a spiraling pattern of learning that contributes to serious antisocial acts by adolescence and young adulthood (Slaby et al., 1995). In the most extensive longitudinal study conducted to date, boys who watched many violent programs at age 8 were more likely to be rated by peers as highly aggressive at age 19 and to have committed serious criminal acts by age 30 (see Figure 15.4) (Huesmann, 1986; Lefkowitz et al., 1972).

Television violence also "hardens" children to aggression, making them more willing to tolerate it in others. Heavy TV viewers believe that there is much more violence and danger in society, an effect that is especially strong for children who perceive televised aggression as realistic and relevant to their own lives (Donnerstein, Slaby, & Eron, 1994). As these findings indicate, violent television modifies children's attitudes toward social reality so they increasingly match what children see on TV. They begin to see the world as a mean and scary place where aggressive acts are a normal and acceptable means for solving problems.

■ **ETHNIC AND GENDER STEREOTYPES.** Although educational programming for children is highly sensitive to issues of equity and diversity, commercial entertainment TV conveys ethnic and gender stereotypes. African Americans and other ethnic minorities are underrepresented; only 33 percent of entertainment shows include at least one main character from a minority group. When minorities appear, they are usually depicted in subservient roles or as villains or victims of violence (Graves, 1993; Williams & Cox, 1995).

Similarly, women appear less often than men in TV entertainment fare, filling only one-fourth to one-third of character roles. Compared to a decade ago, women are more often shown as involved in careers (Allan & Coltrane, 1996). But overall, they continue to be portrayed as young, attractive, caring, emotional, victimized, and in romantic and family

FIGURE 15.4

Relationship between boys' violent television viewing at age 8 and seriousness of criminal convictions by age 30. Longitudinal research showed that boys who watched many violent programs were more likely to commit serious criminal acts in adolescence and early adulthood.

(From L. R. Huesmann, 1986, "Psychological Processes Promoting the Relation Between Exposure to Media Violence and Aggressive Behavior by the Viewer," *Journal of Social Issues, 42,* p. 129. Reprinted by permission.)

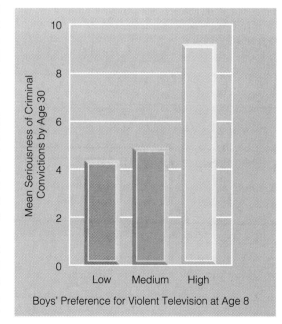

contexts. In contrast, men are depicted as dominant and powerful (Signorielli, 1993; Zillman, Bryant, & Huston, 1994). Gender roles are especially stereotypic in entertainment programs for children and youths. For example, male cartoon characters are usually problem solvers, whereas females are sweet, childlike followers (Huston et al., 1992). Music television (MTV), designed for teenagers but also viewed by many children, includes males twice as often as females. When women appear, they tend to be dressed in revealing clothing and to be the object of sexual advances (Sommers-Flanagan, Sommers-Flanagan, & Davis, 1993).

Do TV's stereotyped portrayals mold children's beliefs? Much like the association between televised violence and aggressive behavior, a bidirectional relationship between TV viewing and gender stereotyping may exist. Adolescents who hold strong gender-stereotyped beliefs are especially attracted to TV programs with stereotyped characters (Friedrich-Cofer et al., 1978). At the same time, television viewing is linked to gains in children's endorsement of many gender stereotypes (Signorielli, 1993).

Nevertheless, several studies show that nonstereotypic images on TV can reduce children's ethnic and gender biases. For example, girls' television viewing predicts greater attraction to nontraditional careers, such as law, often depicted on TV (Wroblewski & Huston, 1987). And positive portrayals of African Americans and other ethnic minorities lead to more favorable views and greater willingness to form ethnically diverse friendships (Graves, 1993).

■ **CONSUMERISM.** Television commercials directed at children "work" by increasing product sales. Although children can distinguish a TV program from a commercial as early as 3 years of age, below age 8 they seldom grasp the selling purpose of the ad. They think that commercials are well-intentioned efforts by filmmakers to be helpful to viewers (Levin, Petros, & Petrella, 1982). Around age 8 or 9, most children understand that commercials are meant to persuade, and by age 11, they realize that advertisers will resort to clever techniques to sell their products. As a result, children become increasingly skeptical of the truthfulness of commercial messages (Ward, Wackman, & Wartella, 1977).

Nevertheless, even older children and adolescents find many commercials alluring. In a study of 8- to 14-year-old boys, celebrity endorsement of a racing toy made the product more attractive, and live racetrack images led to exaggerated estimates of the toy's positive features (Ross et al., 1984). Combining ads with educational footage for viewing at school seems to lend authority to the ads. Students exposed to these programs in their classrooms, compared with those who are not, express more positive attitudes toward advertised products and more often say they intend to buy them (Brand & Greenberg, 1994). The ease with which television advertising can manipulate children's beliefs and preferences has raised questions about whether child-directed commercials constitute fair and ethical practice by the broadcasting industry.

Although television has the potential to support development, too often it teaches negative lessons. Heavy viewers learn that aggression is an acceptable way to solve problems and are taken in by TV advertising. Programs with violent content, including syndicated shows with toys as main characters, are detrimental to imaginative play.

(Mary Kate Denny/PhotoEdit)

■ **PROSOCIAL BEHAVIOR.** Many TV programs include acts of cooperating, helping, and comforting. A large-scale review leaves little doubt that television with prosocial content can increase children's prosocial behavior (Hearold, 1986). But the evidence also highlights some important qualifications. Almost all of the findings are short term and limited to situations quite similar to those shown on TV. In addition, television programs often mix prosocial and antisocial intentions and behavior. Recall that young children have difficulty integrating these elements. As a result, they usually attend to the characters' aggressions and miss the prosocial message, and their antisocial behavior rises accordingly. Prosocial TV has positive effects only when it is free of violent content (Liss, Reinhardt, & Fredriksen, 1983).

Finally, parents who use authoritative child rearing have children who watch more prosocial programs (Abelman,

1985). Consequently, children from families that already promote social and moral maturity probably benefit most from prosocial television.

TELEVISION, ACADEMIC LEARNING, AND IMAGINATION

Since the early days of television, educators have been interested in its potential for strengthening school performance, especially among low-SES children who enter kindergarten behind their higher-SES peers. "Sesame Street" was created for public television with this goal in mind. It uses fast-paced action, lively sound effects, and humorous puppet characters to stress letter and number recognition, counting, vocabulary, and basic concepts. Today, more than 75 percent of American preschool children and 60 percent of kindergartners watch "Sesame Street" at least once a week, and it is broadcast in more than 40 countries around the world (Zill, Davies, & Daly, 1994).

Research shows that "Sesame Street" works well as an academic tutor. The more children watch, the higher they score on tests of vocabulary and basic academic knowledge designed to measure the program's learning goals (Rice et al., 1990; Wright & Huston, 1995; Zill, Davies, & Daly, 1994). In other respects, however, the rapid-paced format of "Sesame Street" and other children's programs has been criticized. When different types of programs are compared, ones with slow-paced, nonviolent action and easy-to-follow story lines lead to more elaborate make-believe play. Those presenting quick, disconnected bits of information do not (Huston-Stein et al., 1981; Tower et al., 1979).

Programs with violent content are particularly detrimental to imaginative play as children mimic aggressive themes (van der Voort & Valkenberg, 1994). The rise over the past two decades in syndicated shows that feature toys as main characters also dampens children's imagination. These programs, designed to get children to buy, follow predictable formulas and are high in violence. When children play with the featured toys, they tend to imitate what they saw on TV rather than experiment with ideas (Greenfield et al., 1990).

Some experts argue that because television presents such complete data to the senses, in heavy doses it encourages reduced mental effort and shallow information processing. Too much television also takes up time children would otherwise spend in activities that require sustained concentration and active thinking, such as reading, playing, and interacting with adults and peers (Singer & Singer, 1990). However, television can support cognitive development as long as children's viewing is not excessive and programs meet their developmental needs.

IMPROVING CHILDREN'S TELEVISION

Improving children's television is an especially challenging task. Over time, high-quality programming has dropped off and advertising has risen as commercial broadcasting stations have tried to reach larger audiences and boost profits. Public broadcasting and cable TV offer some excellent programs for children. But government funding for public television has declined during the past 2 decades, and cable (which depends on user fees) is less available to low-income families. Furthermore, there are fewer restrictions than there once were on program content and advertising for children.

Professional organizations and citizens groups have pressed for government regulation of TV, but without success. Until children's television improves, parents must be informed about the dangers of excessive TV viewing and how to control it, and children must be taught critical viewing skills. See the Social Issues box on pages 622–623 for more information on protecting children from harmful TV.

Computers

Today, computers are a familiar fixture in the everyday lives of children and adolescents, offering a wide range of learning and entertainment tools. By 1997, almost all American public schools had integrated computers into their instructional programs, and 78 percent could access the Internet (Collis et al., 1996). And

THE AVERAGE AMERICAN child finishing elementary school has seen more than 100,000 violent acts on television, a figure that climbs to over 200,000 by the end of the teenage years (Gerbner & Signorielli, 1990). TV violence on commercial television has remained relatively constant over the past two decades. But recent changes in the media world have increased children's exposure. Over 65 percent of American families are cable subscribers, and about 82 percent own VCRs—rates that are rapidly increasing (U.S. Bureau of the Census, 1998). Children with cable or VCR access can see films with far more graphic violence and sexual content than are shown on commercial TV (Huston et al., 1992). Although the greatest concern is with violence, we have seen that TV messages fostering ethnic and gender stereotyping and uncritical consumerism are also damaging to children.

Many organizations concerned with the well-being of children and families have recommended governmental regulation of TV. But the First Amendment right to free speech has made the federal government reluctant to place limits on television content. Consequently, professionals and committed public officials have sought ways to counteract the negative impact of television that are consistent with the First Amendment.

Broadcasters, whose profits are at risk, are against any governmental restrictions. Whereas other industries must face the scrutiny of the media, the television industry has been able to control the way TV violence research is presented. To protect itself, it has perpetuated a variety of myths—that violent programming is simply a reflection of society, a response to popular demand, or a problem of parental irresponsibility. Consequently, the gap between research and public understanding has been far greater for television than for other public health threats, such as cigarette smoking and drunk driving (Donnerstein, Slaby, & Eron, 1994).

Instead of regulatory control, the federal government now requires broadcasters to provide at least 3 hours per week of educational programming for children. In addition, broadcasters must rate television content and manufacturers must build the V-Chip (also called the Violence-Chip) into new TV sets so viewers can program ratings codes into their TVs to block out undesired violent and sexual material.

Although the V-Chip eases parental control, it is far from a complete solution. The rating system is largely based on

Using television to promote children's prosocial behavior and active engagement with their surroundings is a great challenge for American parents, given the antisocial content of many programs. Here a trip to the zoo brings to life an educational TV program on wildlife. (Paul Damien/Tony Stone Images)

frequency of offensive content, not harmfulness. Yet research indicates that *the context of violent acts*—their realism, intensity, motivation, and consequences—affects children's emotional reactions, evaluations, and imitation. Furthermore, although ratings may reduce the appropriateness of programs in parents' eyes, they may make shows more appealing to young audiences—a hypothesis supported for boys (Cantor & Harrison, 1997). Children may go to other homes to watch

as computer technology became more affordable, the number of American homes with at least one computer increased 39-fold between 1981 and 1997, from 750,000 to 29 million (U.S. Bureau of the Census, 1998).

These trends are also apparent in other industrialized nations. How do computers affect children's cognitive development, academic achievement, everyday activities, and social behavior? Let's address this question by examining children's classroom- and home-based computer use.

COMPUTERS IN CLASSROOMS

Most research on computers and child development has been carried out in schools, where computer use can be easily observed. Findings reveal that computers can have rich

TABLE 15.3

Strategies for Regulating Children's TV Viewing

Strategy	Description
Limit TV viewing.	Avoid using TV as a baby-sitter. Provide clear rules that limit what children can watch—for example, an hour a day and only certain programs—and stick to the rules.
Refrain from using TV as a reinforcer.	Do not use television to reward or punish children, a practice that increases its attractiveness.
Encourage child-appropriate viewing	Encourage children to watch programs that are child-appropriate, informative, and prosocial.
Explain televised information to children.	As much as possible, watch with children, helping them understand what they see. When adults express disapproval of on-screen behavior, raise questions about the realism of televised information, and encourage children to discuss it, they teach children to evaluate TV content rather than accept it uncritically.
Link televised content to everyday learning.	Build on TV programs in constructive ways, encouraging children to move away from the set into active engagement with their surroundings. For example, a program on animals might spark a trip to the zoo, a visit to the library for books about animals, or new ways of observing and caring for the family pet.
Model good viewing practices.	Avoid excess television viewing, especially violent programs, yourself. Parental viewing patterns influence children's viewing patterns.
Use a warm, rational approach to child rearing.	Respond to children with warmth and reasonable demands for mature behavior. Children who experience these practices prefer programs with prosocial content and are less attracted to violent TV.

Source: Slaby et al., 1995.

programs they cannot see at home. And it will take years for the V-Chip to reach every TV.

Sometimes it takes a tragedy to mobilize action to protect children. In 1992, a Canadian teenager, who believed that TV violence contributed to his sister's rape and murder, organized a petition to reduce violent TV programming. More than 1 million people signed it (Dubow & Miller, 1996). The Canadian television industry responded with a voluntary code that bans gratuitous violence (unnecessary to the plot) and that requires the consequences of violence to be shown in children's programs. Still, programs from the United States that violate the code slip through on Canadian cable TV.

Parents face an awesome task in monitoring children's TV viewing, given the extent of harmful messages on the screen. Table 15.3 lists some strategies they can use. At the same time, the television industry must take a more responsible attitude toward limiting such content. Public education about the impact of television on children's development is vital, since consumer pressure is a powerful instrument of change. Government regulation consistent with the First Amendment combined with public insistence that broadcasters generate their own remedies would transform TV into part of the solution to violence and other social ills in the United States.

educational and social benefits. Children as young as 3 years of age like computer activities and can type in simple commands on a standard keyboard. Yet they do not find the computer so captivating that it diverts them from other worthwhile classroom activities (Campbell & Schwartz, 1986).

Furthermore, preschool and elementary school pupils prefer to use computers socially. Small groups often gather around the machine, and children more often collaborate when working with the computer than with paper and pencil (Clements, Nastasi, & Swaminathan, 1993). The common belief that computers channel children into solitary pursuits is unfounded.

■ **COMPUTER-ASSISTED INSTRUCTION, WORD PROCESSING, AND PROGRAMMING.**
Computers in classrooms are used in a variety of ways. In *computer-assisted instruction*

(CAI), specially designed educational software permits children to practice academic skills and acquire new knowledge. Most CAI programs provide drill on basic skills; a few emphasize discovery learning, reasoning, and problem solving. When children use programs regularly for several months, they gain in reading and math achievement. Benefits are greatest for younger pupils and those with learning difficulties (Clements & Nastasi, 1992; Fletcher-Flinn & Gravatt, 1995). However, overemphasizing drill activities can undermine children's willingness to learn through active experimentation (Clements, Nastasi, & Swaminathan, 1993).

As soon as children begin to read and write, they can use the computer for *word processing.* It permits them to write freely without having to struggle with handwriting at the same time. In addition, children can plan and revise the text's meaning and style as well as check their spelling. As a result, they worry less about making mistakes, and their written products tend to be longer and of higher quality (Clements, 1995). However, computers by themselves do not help children master the mechanics of writing (such as spelling and grammar) (Cunningham & Stanovich, 1990). So it is best to use computers to build on and enhance, not replace, other classroom writing experiences.

Programming offers children the highest degree of control over the computer, since they must tell it what to do. Specially designed computer languages, such as LOGO, are available to introduce children to programming skills. Computer programming leads to improvements in concept formation, problem solving, and creativity (Clements, 1995; Clements & Nastasi, 1992). Also, since children must detect errors in their programs to get them to work, programming helps them reflect on their thought processes, leading to gains in metacognitive knowledge and self-regulation (Clements, 1990).

In the research just described, teachers encouraged and supported children's efforts. They questioned, prompted, and modeled, providing a vital scaffold for acquiring word processing and programming skills. Furthermore, in open-ended programming contexts like LOGO, children are especially likely to devise and solve problems collaboratively, persist in the face of challenge, and display positive attitudes toward learning (Nastasi & Clements, 1992, 1994). Consistent with Vygotsky's theory, social interaction surrounding challenging computer tasks fosters children's mastery of a wide variety of higher cognitive processes.

Computers in classrooms provide learning environments that are cognitively stimulating and socially interactive. Children are far more likely to collaborate when working with the computer than when working with paper and pencil.

(Ed Block/The Stock Market)

■ **THE INTERNET AT SCHOOL.** New communications technology is available through electronic mail (e-mail) and the World Wide Web. As a result, teachers are developing website-based learning activities, and children can access information and interact with people around the world (Windschitl, 1998). Although little research exists on the learning potential of these experiences, one study highlights their power to enhance understanding of other cultures. Groups of six to nine classrooms, from the United States and foreign countries, formed "learning circles." Each class planned a project and consulted with their circle to complete it. E-mail messages revealed a broadening of horizons about other people and places. For example, pupils in Persian Gulf nations wrote candidly about their fears as one circle discussed world security and peace (Reis, 1992).

HOME COMPUTERS

About 40 percent of American families own a personal computer; one-third of these have access to the Internet (Kraut et al., 1998a). When home computers extend the CAI, word processing, programming, and collaborative problem-solving pursuits typically offered at school, children reap additional cognitive and social benefits. Yet computers appear most often in the homes of economically well-off children. And parents of sons are more likely than parents of daughters to install a computer in the home (Cocking & Greenfield, 1996). Consequently, some experts believe that computers are widening cognitive performance gaps between low- and higher-SES children and between girls and boys.

Furthermore, children and adolescents spend much time using home computers for entertainment purposes—especially playing video games, but also "surfing the net" and communicating through e-mail and chatrooms. As with TV, these computer activities have raised concerns about possible harmful effects.

■ **VIDEOGAMES.** Most videogames emphasize speed and action in violent plots in which children advance by shooting at and evading the enemy. Children also play more complex exploratory and adventure games, such as *Dungeons and Dragons* (again with themes of conquest and aggression) and sports games, such as football and soccer.

Speed-and-action videogames foster attentional and spatial skills in boys and girls alike. Experience in playing them leads to better performance on tasks in which children must divide their visual attention (respond to a stimulus that could appear in two locations on a computer screen) and engage in spatial reasoning (see Chapter 13, page 547) (Greenfield et al., 1994; Okagaki & Frensch, 1996; Subrahmanyam & Greenfield, 1996).

Yet game software is unappealing to girls because of its themes of violence and male-dominated sports. And a growing number of studies indicate that playing violent videogames duplicates the effects of violent TV—that is, promotes aggression and desensitizes children to violence (Cocking & Greenfield, 1996; Goldstein, 1994; Irwin & Gross, 1995). Furthermore, videogames are full of ethnic and gender stereotypes (Kinder, 1996).

Many parents express another concern about videogames—that their children will become overly involved in these fast-paced, violent amusements. About 5 percent become "passionate," or excessive, players (Phillips et al., 1995). Compared with infrequent users, children captivated by videogames spend time less productively, more often watching cartoons and less often reading (Wright & Huston, 1995).

■ **THE INTERNET AT HOME.** Think back to the study described on page 617, in which a decline in community participation followed the introduction of TV into a small Canadian town. Home computing may also alter social interaction. For example, in several studies, the purchase of a home computer was associated with a decline in leisure time spent with family members (Kohut, 1994; Vitalari, Venkatesh, & Gronhaug, 1985).

Yet debate surrounds the implications of home-based Internet access for family interaction, since most people use the Internet for interpersonal communication (Kraut et al., 1998a). Are social relationships on the Internet equivalent to social ties in other settings? To find out, researchers provided over 90 families, many of whom had teenagers, with their first Internet experience by giving each a computer, a telephone line, and free Internet access in exchange for allowing automatic tracking of their Internet use (Kraut et al., 1998b). Before gaining access and 1 to 2 years later, participants completed a questionnaire assessing social involvement and psychological well-being.

Findings revealed that teenagers used the Internet more hours than did adults, although (unlike other computer activities) males did not differ from females. Regardless of age, greater Internet use predicted a drop in time spent communicating with family members and in size of nearby and distant social networks. Also, those who used the Internet more reported feeling lonelier and more depressed at a later date. Because initial social involvement and psychological well-being were unrelated to time on-line, the investigators concluded that heavy Internet use negatively affected emotional and social adjustment. It probably did so by displacing social activity with relatives, friends, and neighbors—stronger, more supportive ties than typically form through e-mail or in chatrooms.

The Internet's potential for causing disengagement from real life must be weighed against its value for acquiring computer skills and information and enabling convenient communication. Parents are wise to oversee how much their children use the home computer—and when they use the Internet, just how they spend their time.

ASK YOURSELF . . .

◆ *"I can't control him, he's impossible," Robbie's mother complained, referring to his impulsive, aggressive behavior. At home, Robbie often turns on the TV and watches prime-time shows with high doses of violence. Why might Robbie be attracted to violent television? Suggest some strategies his parents can use to shield him from harmful TV messages.*

◆ CONNECTIONS
How can excessive TV viewing negatively affect children's health? (See Chapter 5, page 197.)

American children spend more time watching TV than they do in any other waking activity. Before age 8, children have difficulty processing televised information accurately. Heavy TV viewing promotes aggressive behavior, indifference to real-life violence, a fearful view of the world, ethnic and gender stereotypes, and a naive belief in the truthfulness of advertising. Although the right kind of televised content can encourage prosocial behavior, academic skills, and imaginative thinking, the positive potential of the TV medium remains largely untapped.

Computers have become increasingly common in children's lives. At school, children often collaborate on computer activities. Computer-assisted instruction, word processing, programming, and electronic communications each offer unique educational benefits. Home computers are more available to economically well-off children, particularly boys. Although videogames foster attentional and spatial skills, their highly violent content duplicates the negative effects of violent TV. Heavy home Internet use by adolescents and adults leads to declines in social involvement and psychological well-being.

Schooling

Unlike the informal world of peer relations, the school is a formal institution designed to transmit knowledge and skills children need to become productive members of society. Children spend many hours in school—6 hours a day, 5 days a week, 36 weeks of the year—totaling, altogether, about 15,000 hours by high school graduation. In earlier chapters, we noted that schools are vital forces in children's development, affecting their motivation to learn and modes of remembering, reasoning, problem solving, and social and moral understanding. How do schools exert such a powerful impact? Research looking at schools as complex social systems—their class and student body size, educational philosophies, teacher–pupil interaction patterns, and the larger cultural context in which they are embedded—provides important insights into this question.

CLASS AND STUDENT BODY SIZE

The physical plants of all schools are similar: Each has classrooms, hallways, a playground, and a lunchroom. But they also vary widely in the number of pupils they accommodate in each class and in the school as a whole.

Is there an optimal class size for effective learning? In a large-scale field experiment, over 6,000 kindergartners in 76 Tennessee elementary schools were randomly assigned to three class types: small (13 to 17 pupils), regular (22 to 25 pupils), and regular with a full-time teacher's aide. These arrangements continued into third grade. Small-class pupils scored higher in reading and math achievement each year, an effect that was particularly strong for minority pupils. Placing teacher's aides in regular-size classes had no consistent impact. Finally, even after all pupils returned to regular-size classes in fourth and fifth grades, children who had experienced the small classes remained ahead in achievement (Mosteller, 1995).

Why is small class size beneficial? Teachers of fewer children spend less time disciplining and more time giving individual attention, and children's interactions with one another are more positive and cooperative. Also, when class size is small, teachers and pupils are more satisfied with their school experiences. The learning advantages of small classes are greatest in the early years of schooling, when children require more adult assistance (Blatchford & Mortimore, 1994).

By the time students reach secondary school, they no longer spend most of their time in a single, self-contained classroom. Instead, they move from class to class and have access to many activities outside regular instruction. As a result, the relevant physical context for adolescents is the school as a whole. Student body size profoundly affects their life at school. A greater percentage of students in small than large high schools are actively involved in the extracurricular life of their schools. Schools of 500 to 700 students or less promote personalized conditions because there are fewer people to ensure that clubs, sports events, and social activities will function. As a result, young people enter a greater number and variety of activities and hold more positions of responsibility and leadership. In contrast, plenty of students are available to fill activity slots in large schools, so only a small elite are genuinely active (Barker & Gump, 1964; Berk, 1992b).

In view of these findings, it is not surprising that adolescents in small schools report a greater sense of personal responsibility, competence, and challenge from their extracurricular experiences. This is true even for "marginal" students—those with low IQs, academic difficulties, and poverty-stricken backgrounds—who otherwise display little school commitment. A special advantage of small schools is that potential dropouts are far more likely to join in activities, gain recognition for their abilities, and remain until graduation (Mahoney & Cairns, 1997). The sense of social obligation engendered in small high schools seems to carry over to classroom learning. In a sample of over 11,000 sophomores attending 830 high schools, smaller school size predicted better achievement in reading, math, history, and science—relationships that were stronger for low-SES students (Lee & Smith, 1995).

EDUCATIONAL PHILOSOPHIES

Each teacher brings to the classroom an educational philosophy that plays a major role in children's learning experiences. Two philosophical approaches—traditional and open classrooms—have received the most research attention. They differ in what children are taught, the way they are believed to learn, and how their progress is evaluated.

■ **TRADITIONAL VERSUS OPEN CLASSROOMS.** In a **traditional classroom,** children are relatively passive in the learning process. The teacher is the sole authority for knowledge, rules, and decision making and does most of the talking. Pupils spend most of their time at their desks—listening, responding when called on, and completing teacher-assigned tasks. Their progress is evaluated by how well they keep pace with a uniform set of standards for all pupils in their grade.

In contrast, in an **open classroom,** children are viewed as active agents in their own development. The teacher assumes a flexible authority role, sharing decision making with pupils, who learn at their own pace. Children are evaluated by considering their progress in relation to their own prior development. How well they compare to other same-age pupils is of lesser importance. A glance inside the door of an open classroom reveals richly equipped learning centers, small groups of pupils working on tasks they choose themselves, and a teacher who moves from one area to another, guiding and supporting in response to children's individual needs.

During the past few decades, the pendulum in American education has swung back and forth between these two views. In the 1960s and early 1970s, open education gained in popularity, inspired by Piaget's vision of the child as an active, motivated learner. When concern over the academic progress of American children and youths became widespread, a "back to basics" movement arose. Classrooms returned to traditional, teacher-directed instruction, a style still prevalent today.

The combined results of many studies reveal that older pupils in traditional classrooms have a slight edge in academic achievement. But open settings are associated with other benefits. Open-classroom pupils are more critical thinkers, and they value and respect individual differences in their classmates more. Pupils in open environments also like school better than do those in traditional classrooms (Walberg, 1986).

Whole-class, teacher-directed instruction, previously not encountered until first grade or later, has filtered down to American preschools and kindergartens. When young children spend much time passively sitting and doing worksheets as opposed to being actively engaged in learning centers, they are less confident of their abilities and more likely to retreat from challenging problems (Stipek et al., 1995). They also display more stress behaviors, such as wiggling, withdrawal, and talking out. Follow-ups reveal that traditional-

traditional classroom A classroom based on the educational philosophy that children are passive learners who acquire information presented by teachers. Pupils are evaluated on the basis of how well they keep pace with a uniform set of standards for all pupils in their grade.

open classroom A classroom based on the educational philosophy that children are active agents in their own development and learn at different rates. Teachers share decision making with pupils. Pupils are evaluated in relation to their own prior development.

classroom kindergartners achieve less well in grade school than do their open-classroom counterparts (Burts et al., 1992; Hart et al., 1998). These outcomes are strongest for low-SES children. Yet teachers tend to prefer a traditional approach for economically disadvantaged pupils—a disturbing trend in view of its negative impact on motivation and learning (Eccles et al., 1993b; Stipek & Byler, 1997).

■ **NEW VYGOTSKY-INSPIRED DIRECTIONS.** Although much research has focused on the traditional–open dichotomy, it oversimplifies the real world of classroom differences. The philosophies of some teachers fall in between. These teachers want to foster high achievement as well as critical thinking, positive social relationships, and excitement about learning. New experiments in elementary education, grounded in Vygotsky's sociocultural theory, represent this point of view (Forman, Minick, & Stone, 1993). In Chapter 6, we considered several Vygotsky-inspired educational innovations, including reciprocal teaching, cooperative learning, and classrooms as communities of learners (see pages 265–266). Each is consistent with one or more of the following themes:

■ *Teachers and children as partners in learning.* Classrooms rich in dialogue, between teachers and children and between children themselves, foster transfer of culturally valued, higher cognitive processes to children.

■ *Experience with many types of symbolic communication in meaningful activities.* As children master reading, writing, and quantitative reasoning, they become aware of their culture's communication systems, reflect on their own thinking, and bring it under voluntary control.

■ *Teaching adapted to each child's zone of proximal development.* Providing assistance that is responsive to current understandings but that encourages children to take the next step forward helps ensure that each pupil will make the best progress possible.

The most well-known and extensive educational reform effort based on these principles is the *Kamehameha Elementary Education Program* (KEEP). To foster development, KEEP instruction is organized around activity settings specially designed to enhance teacher–child and child–child interaction. In each setting, children work on a project that ensures that their learning will be active and directed toward a meaningful goal. For example, they might read a story and discuss its meaning or draw a map of the playground to promote an understanding of geography.

All children enter a focal activity setting, called "Center One," at least once each morning for scaffolding of challenging literacy skills. Text content is carefully selected to relate to children's experiences, and instruction builds on children's ideas. The precise organization of each KEEP classroom is adjusted to fit the unique learning styles of its pupils, creating culturally responsive environments (Au, 1997; Tharp, 1993, 1994).

Thousands of low-SES minority children have attended KEEP classrooms in the public schools of Hawaii, on a Navajo reservation in Arizona, and in Los Angeles. Research suggests that the approach is highly effective. In KEEP schools, minority pupils performed at their expected grade level in reading achievement, much better than children of the same background enrolled in traditional schools (see Figure 15.5). Furthermore, KEEP pupils more often participated actively in class discussion, used elaborate language structures, and supported one another's

Active engagement in learning centers in preschool and kindergarten fosters a relaxed, confident approach to challenging problems and better achievement in grade school, especially for low-SES children.
(Will Hart)

learning than did non-KEEP controls (Tharp & Gallimore, 1988). As the KEEP model becomes more widely applied, perhaps it will prove successful with all types of children because of its comprehensive goals and effort to meet the learning needs of a wide range of pupils.

■ **A FULL-SERVICE APPROACH.** In addition to efforts to reform classroom experiences, many schools have begun to collaborate with community agencies to provide children and adolescents at risk for poor achievement with the health and social services they need to benefit fully from education. These **full-service schools** offer medical and dental checkups and treatment, individual counseling, social skills training, substance abuse treatment, parent education and support, and other interventions on school grounds or in other easily accessible locations, increasing the chances of comprehensive, integrated services. The approach dramatically improves parent and community involvement in schools; teacher morale; and student attendance, classroom performance, and graduation rates (Dryfoos, 1996; Holtzman, 1997).

SCHOOL TRANSITIONS

Besides size and educational philosophy, an additional structural feature of schooling has implications for pupils' achievement and psychological adjustment: the timing of transitions from one school level to the next. Many 5- and 6-year-olds are already accustomed to school-like settings, since they have attended preschool and child-care centers. Still, entering kindergarten is a major milestone. Parents take pride in their children's readiness for more independence and responsibility but worry about how ready their children are for formal schooling. Children, in turn, must accommodate to new physical settings, adult authorities, daily schedules, peer companions, and academic challenges.

■ **EARLY ADJUSTMENT TO SCHOOL.** In a study of factors that predict effective transition to kindergarten, Gary Ladd and Joseph Price (1987) gathered observational and interview data on children at the end of preschool and during their kindergarten year. Both child and setting characteristics ensuring supportive ties to peers promoted favorable school adjustment. Children who engaged in cooperative play and friendly interaction with agemates in preschool seemed to transfer these skills to kindergarten. They were better liked by peers and more involved in classroom life. The presence of preschool friends in kindergarten also enhanced adaptation. Perhaps familiar agemates served as a secure base from which to develop new ties, enhancing children's peer acceptance and feelings of comfort in the classroom. Finally, children who retained more out-of-school friends viewed kindergarten more favorably. The continuity of these nonschool ties may have provided children with a greater sense of stability in their otherwise changing social environments.

In further research following children over the kindergarten year, additional factors emerged as contributors to school adjustment. Pupils with more preschool experience scored higher on school readiness tests and showed increasingly positive school attitudes as kindergarten progressed. In addition, the extent to which children made new friends, were accepted by their classmates, and formed a warm relationship with their teacher predicted gains in achievement (Birch & Ladd, 1997; Ladd, 1990; Ladd, Kochenderfer, & Coleman, 1997). As children forge new bases of social support, they seem to integrate themselves into the environment in ways that foster academic competence.

In contrast, negative, nonsupportive relationships—with either peers or teachers—threaten favorable adaptation to school. Kindergarten boys who report conflict-ridden friendships are more likely to say they dislike and feel lonely at school. Perhaps friendship conflict threatens boys' adjustment more than girls' because boys have fewer close friends. Therefore, when one friendship goes awry, they are less able to turn to others for support.

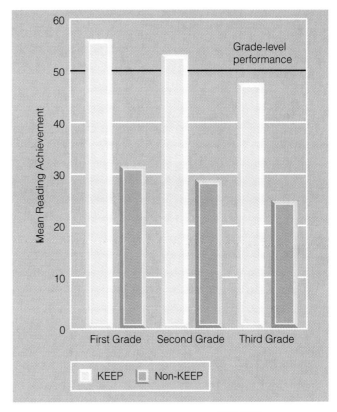

FIGURE 15.5

Reading achievement of KEEP-instructed and traditionally instructed first- through third-grade low-income minority pupils. The KEEP children performed at grade level; the non-KEEP pupils performed substantially below grade level.

(Adapted from R. G. Tharp & R. Gallimore, 1988, *Rousing Minds to Life: Teaching, Learning, and Schooling in Social Context,* New York: Cambridge University Press, P. 116. Adapted by permission.)

full-service schools Schools that collaborate with community agencies to provide children and adolescents at risk for poor achievement with the health and social services they need to benefit fully from education.

Alternatively, boys who often argue and fight with friends may be more noncompliant and aggressive, prompting difficulties in friendships as well as other aspects of school life (Ladd, Kochenderfer, & Coleman, 1996).

Consistent with this idea, overtly aggressive children (mostly boys) tend to establish conflict-ridden relationships with teachers, which further impair their adjustment to school. And peer-avoidant children often become overly dependent on teachers, clinging and asking for help when they do not need it (Birch & Ladd, 1998). If, at the start of kindergarten, these socially anxious children become victims of peer abuse, they soon seek ways to avoid the classroom, which threatens their sense of safety and security (return to Variations box on page 607 to review).

■ **HELPING KINDERGARTNERS ADJUST TO SCHOOL.** These findings suggest a variety of ways to assist children in meeting the challenges of kindergarten: encouraging positive social skills, arranging for children to attend preschool, helping them establish supportive friendships both in and out of school, and intervening quickly in peer victimization. In planning the composition of kindergarten classrooms, educators might also consider grouping children to maximize contact with friends. As we will see shortly, gratifying peer ties continue to be important in successful adaptation to school change at later ages.

■ **SCHOOL TRANSITIONS IN ADOLESCENCE.** Early adolescence is a second important period of school transition, when students typically move from an intimate, self-contained elementary school classroom to a much larger, impersonal secondary school in which they must shift from one class to the next throughout the day. These changes can drastically alter academic and social experiences, creating new adjustment problems.

Research reveals that with each school change—from elementary to middle or junior high and then to high school—adolescents' course grades decline. The drop is partly due to tighter academic standards. At the same time, the transition to secondary school often brings with it less personal attention, more whole-class instruction, and less chance to participate in classroom decision making (Eccles, Lord, & Buchanan, 1996).

In view of these changes, it is not surprising that students rate their junior-high learning experiences less favorably than their elementary school experiences (Wigfield & Eccles, 1994). They also report that their junior-high teachers care less about them, are less friendly, grade less fairly, and stress competition more and mastery and improvement less. Consequently, many young people feel less academically competent and show a drop in motivation (Anderman & Midgley, 1997; Eccles et al., 1993c).

Inevitably, the transition to secondary school requires students to readjust their feelings of self-confidence and self-worth as academic expectations are revised and students enter a more complex social world. A comprehensive study revealed that the timing of school transition is important, especially for girls (Simmons & Blyth, 1987). Over 300 adolescents living in a large Midwestern city were followed from sixth to tenth grade. Some were enrolled in school districts with a 6–3–3 grade organization (a K–6 elementary school, a 3-year junior high, and a 3-year high school). These students made two school changes, one to junior high and one to high school. A comparison group attended schools with an 8–4 grade organization. They made only one school transition, from a K–8 elementary school to high school.

For the sample as a whole, grade point average dropped and feelings of anonymity increased after each transition. Participation in extracurricular activities declined more in the 6–3–3 than in the 8–4 arrangement, although the drop was greater for girls. Sex-related differences in self-esteem were even more striking. As Figure 15.6 shows, boys' self-esteem increased throughout junior high and high school, except in 6–3–3 schools, where it leveled off after entry into high school. Girls in the 6–3–3 arrangement fared especially poorly. Their self-esteem declined with each school change. In contrast, their 8–4 counterparts gained in sense of self-worth throughout secondary school.

These findings show that any school transition is likely to temporarily depress adolescents' psychological well-being, but the earlier it

Moving from a small, self-contained elementary school classroom to a large, impersonal secondary school is stressful for adolescents. School grades decline and feelings of anonymity increase, as this junior-high hallway suggests. Girls' extracurricular participation and self-esteem are also likely to suffer.

(B. Daemmrich/The Image Works)

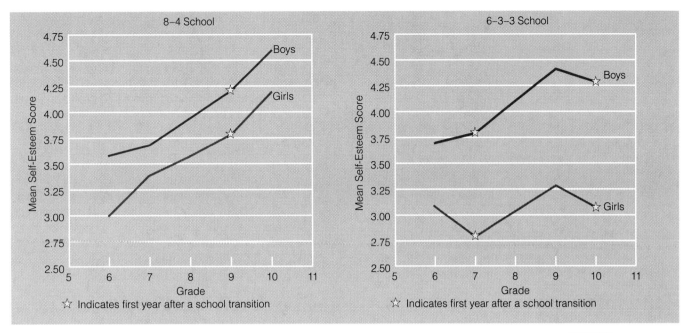

FIGURE 15.6

Self-esteem from sixth to tenth grade by school type for boys and girls. In this longitudinal study of more than 300 adolescents, self-esteem increased steadily for both sexes in the 8–4 school arrangement. Girls in 6–3–3 schools fared especially poorly. Their self-esteem dropped sharply after each school change. *(Adapted from Simmons & Blyth, 1987.)*

occurs, the more dramatic and long lasting its impact. Girls in 6–3–3 schools fared poorest, the researchers argued, because moving to junior high tended to coincide with other life changes—namely, the onset of puberty and dating. Adolescents who face added transitions, such as family disruption, parental unemployment, or a shift in residence around the time they change schools, are at greatest risk for academic and emotional difficulties (Flanagan & Eccles, 1993).

Poorly achieving and poverty-stricken young people show an especially sharp drop in school performance after the transition to junior high school. These students are likely to turn to peers, whose values they describe as becoming increasingly antisocial, for the support they lack in other spheres of school life (Seidman et al., 1994). For some, school transition initiates a downward spiral in academic performance and school involvement that eventually leads to failure and dropping out (Simmons, Black, & Zhou, 1991).

■ **HELPING ADOLESCENTS ADJUST TO SCHOOL TRANSITIONS.** Consider the findings just reviewed, and you will see that school transitions often lead to environmental changes that fit poorly with adolescents' developmental needs. They disrupt close relationships with teachers at a time when adolescents need adult support. They emphasize competition during a period of heightened self-focusing. They reduce decision making and choice as the desire for autonomy is increasing. And they interfere with peer networks at a time of increased concern with peer acceptance.

Fortunately, there are ways to ease the strain of moving from elementary to secondary school. Since most students do better in an 8–4 school arrangement, school districts thinking about reorganization should seriously consider this plan.[1] When early school transitions cannot be avoided, smaller social units can be formed within large schools, permitting closer relations with teachers and peers and greater extracurricular involvement (Berk, 1992b; Seidman & French, 1997). In addition, students can be assigned to classes with several familiar peers or a constant group of new peers—arrangements that promote emotional security and social support. In one study, high school freshmen experiencing these interventions showed much better academic performance and psychological adjustment at the end of the school year than did controls. And a follow-up after 4 years revealed that only half as many students in the intervention group had dropped out of school (Felner & Adan, 1988).

[1]Recall from Chapter 5 (page 207) that girls who reach puberty early fare better in K–6 schools, where they are relieved of pressures from older adolescents to become involved in dating, sexual activity, and drug experimentation before they are ready. Although the 8–4 organization is best for the majority of adolescents, early maturing girls require special support under these conditions.

The quality of teachers' instructional messages affects pupils' involvement in academic lessons. Emphasizing higher-level thinking—analyzing, synthesizing, and applying ideas and concepts—promotes participation and learning.
(Stephen Marks)

Finally, successful transitions are most likely to occur in schools that foster adolescents' growing capacity for autonomy and responsibility. Rigid school rules that strike young people as unfair and punitive frustrate their developmental needs, contributing to long-term dissatisfaction with school life (Eccles et al., 1993b).

TEACHER–PUPIL INTERACTION

The classroom is a complex social system in which myriad interactions take place each day. Teachers play a central role in this highly social environment, engaging in as many as 1,000 exchanges with pupils from the time the bell rings in the morning until dismissal in the afternoon (Jackson, 1968). A vast amount of research exists on teacher–pupil interaction, most focusing on its significance for academic achievement.

■ **CLASSROOM MANAGEMENT AND QUALITY OF INSTRUCTION.** Class time devoted to instruction and pupil involvement in academic work are consistently related to achievement test scores. But for pupils to learn effectively in an environment as crowded and distracting as the classroom, teachers must make work possible (Good & Brophy, 1996). Effective classroom managers arrange conditions in which activities flow easily from one to the next and few discipline problems arise. As a result, pupils spend more time learning, which is reflected in their achievement test scores.

Besides management skills, the quality of teachers' instructional messages affects children's task involvement and learning. A disappointing finding is that American teachers emphasize rote, repetitive drill more than higher-level thinking, such as analyzing, synthesizing, and applying ideas and concepts (Campbell, Voelkl, & Donahue, 1997). In a study of fifth-grade social studies and math lessons, students were far more attentive when teachers emphasized high-level thinking than basic memory exercises (Stodolsky, 1988). And in a longitudinal investigation of over 5,000 seventh graders, those attending schools with a more demanding academic climate showed better attendance and larger gains in math achievement during the following 2 years (Phillips, 1997).

As we have already seen, teachers do not interact in the same way with all children. Some pupils get more attention, encouragement, and praise than others. Well-behaved, high-achieving pupils typically experience positive interactions with teachers. In contrast, many teachers actively dislike children who achieve poorly and are also disruptive. These unruly pupils are often criticized and are rarely called on to contribute to class discussion. When they seek special help or permission, their requests are usually denied (Good & Brophy, 1996).

■ **TEACHER EXPECTATIONS FOR CHILDREN'S PERFORMANCE.** Unfortunately, once teachers' attitudes toward pupils are established, they are in danger of becoming more extreme than is warranted by children's behavior. If teachers rigidly treat pupils in ways that match their impressions, they may engage in discriminatory practices that have long-term consequences for children's motivation and achievement. A special concern is that an **educational self-fulfilling prophecy**[2] can be set in motion: Children may adopt teachers' positive or negative views and start to live up to them.

Self-fulfilling prophecies interact in complex ways with teacher and student characteristics. When teachers emphasize competition and public comparisons between pupils, children are very aware of teacher opinion, increasing the chances that it will affect their performance (Weinstein et al., 1987). Furthermore, teachers who fear losing control of their class are especially likely to initiate negative self-fulfilling prophecies. They do so by avoiding public communication with disruptive, low-achieving pupils and giving them

educational self-fulfilling prophecy The idea that pupils may adopt teachers' positive or negative attitudes toward them and start to live up to these views.

[2]Most research on self-fulfilling prophecies focuses on the teacher–pupil relationship, but the effect can occur in other social contexts, such as parent–child and peer interaction. Try to think of other findings we have discussed in this and earlier chapters that can be viewed as self-fulfilling prophecies.

feedback that is abrupt, inconsistent, and not based on the quality of their work (Cooper, 1979). Withdrawn children may also be prime candidates for biased teacher expectations. Since they rarely approach teachers, they provide little information about what they are like as learners. This makes it easier for teachers who hold inappropriate expectancies to sustain them (Jones & Gerig, 1994).

Furthermore, when teachers hold inaccurate views, poorly achieving students are more affected. In a longitudinal study of over 1,500 middle-school students, teacher overestimates and underestimates of sixth graders' math talent, effort, and performance (determined by comparing teacher ratings to the previous year's math achievement) had a greater impact on future math achievement for low than high achievers (Madon, Jussim, & Eccles, 1997). High-achieving pupils have less room to improve when teachers think well of them, and they can fall back on their long history of success experiences when a teacher is critical.

In the study just described, teacher overestimates had a stronger impact on future achievement than did teacher underestimates (see Figure 15.7). When teachers are optimistic, many children respond with improved performance. Unfortunately, biased teacher judgments are usually slanted in a negative direction, resulting in more unfavorable classroom experiences and achievement than would otherwise occur (Brophy, 1983).

■ TEACHERS' REACTIONS TO CHILDREN'S ETHNIC AND SES BACKGROUNDS. Teachers sometimes respond in stereotyped ways to low-SES and ethnic minority pupils, making them especially susceptible to negative self-fulfilling prophecies. In Chapter 11, we noted that African-American and Mexican-American children tend to receive less favorable feedback from teachers than do white children, a circumstance that undermines their achievement motivation.

Recall from Chapter 8 that ethnic minority children often have unique language customs, knowledge, and skills that differ sharply from those valued at school. Teachers who are unaware of this fact may interpret the minority pupil's behavior as uncooperative when it is not. For this reason, it is vital that teachers understand the values and practices that culturally different children bring to the classroom. Then they can adjust learning experiences to take account of the child's background, and negative self-fulfilling prophecies can be avoided.

GROUPING PRACTICES

In many schools, students are ability grouped or tracked into classes in which children of similar achievement levels are taught together. The practice is designed to ease teachers' task of having to meet a wide range of academic needs. Yet teachers' treatment of different groups may be an especially powerful source of self-fulfilling prophecies.

■ GROUPING IN ELEMENTARY SCHOOL. In American elementary schools, children are often assigned to *homogeneous* groups or classes. In "low-ability" groups, pupils get more drill on basic facts and skills, less discussion, a slower learning pace, and less time on academic work. Gradually, they show a drop in self-esteem, are viewed by themselves and others as "not smart," and limit their friendship choices to children within their own group. Not surprisingly, homogeneous grouping widens the gap between high and low achievers and promotes segregated peer interaction (Dornbusch, Glasgow, & Lin, 1996; Fuligni, Eccles, & Barber, 1995).

Partly because of these findings, some schools have increased the *heterogeneity* of pupils taught together. In *multigrade classrooms*, pupils who otherwise would be assigned to different grades are placed in the same classroom. When academic performance differs between multigrade and single-grade classrooms, it favors the multigrade arrangement. Self-esteem and attitudes toward school are also more positive, perhaps because multigrade

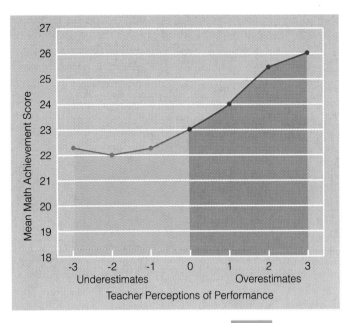

FIGURE 15.7

Teacher overestimates and underestimates of sixth graders' math talent, effort, and performance in relation to later math achievement. Overestimates of capacity led to substantial gains in achievement; underestimates led to a slight decline. These findings illustrate how believing in students' ability to succeed can inspire them to work harder and improve.

(Adapted from S. Madon, L. Jussim, & J. Eccles, 1997, "In search of the powerful self-fulfilling prophecy," *Journal of Personality and Social Psychology, 72,* p. 800. Copyright © by the American Psychological Association. Reprinted by permission of the publisher and author.)

classrooms decrease competition and increase harmony (Jensen & Green, 1993; Pratt, 1986). The opportunity multigrade grouping affords for peer tutoring (see page 613) may also contribute to its favorable outcomes.

Yet multigrade classrooms may not work in favor of low-achieving pupils if principals create them for convenience (for example, to deal with uneven enrollments) rather than for philosophical reasons. When multigrade and single-grade classrooms coexist in the same school, principals tend to place higher-ability and more independent pupils in the multigrade settings to ease the instructional demands on teachers (Burns & Mason, 1998). This produces an alternative form of homogeneous grouping!

Finally, recall from our discussion of Vygotsky's theory that more expert children can foster learning in less expert children, as long as participants resolve conflicts, share responsibility, and consider one another's ideas (see Chapter 6, page 265). In many classrooms, however, heterogeneous groups yield poorer-quality interaction (less accurate explanations and answers) than do homogeneous groups composed of above-average pupils (Fuchs et al., 1998; Webb, Nemer, & Chizhik, 1998). For collaboration between heterogeneous peers to succeed, children need extensive training and guidance.

When teachers provide this assistance, heterogeneous classes are desirable into middle or junior high school. They do not stifle the more able students, and they have cognitive and social benefits for poorly performing youngsters (Oakes, Gamoran, & Page, 1992).

■ **GROUPING IN HIGH SCHOOL.** By high school, some homogeneous grouping is unavoidable because certain aspects of instruction must dovetail with the young person's future educational and career plans. In the United States, high school students are counseled into college preparatory, vocational, or general education tracks. Unfortunately, this sorting tends to perpetuate educational inequalities of earlier years.

Low-income minority students are assigned in large numbers to noncollege tracks. One study found that a good student from an economically disadvantaged family had only half as much chance of ending up in an academically oriented program as did a student of equal ability from a middle-SES background (Vanfossen, Jones, & Spade, 1987). When high-ability students end up in low tracks, they "sink" to the achievement level of their trackmates. Furthermore, teachers of noncollege-track classes tend to view the parental role in education as passive. They are less likely to communicate with parents about what they can do to support their child's learning. Indeed, these parents are often unaware of their child's track placement (Dornbusch & Glasgow, 1997).

High school students are separated into academic and vocational tracks in virtually all industrialized nations. But the American system differs from those of China, Japan, and Western Europe in important respects. In most of those countries, students take a national examination to determine their placement in high school. The outcome usually fixes future possibilities for the young person. In the United States, educational decisions are more fluid. Students who are not assigned to a college preparatory track or who do poorly in high school can still get a college education. But by the adolescent years, SES differences in quality of education and academic achievement have already sorted American students more drastically than in other countries. In the end, many economically disadvantaged and minority young people do not benefit from this more open system. Compared to other developed nations, the United States has a higher percentage of high school dropouts and adolescents with very limited academic skills.

TEACHING PUPILS WITH SPECIAL NEEDS

So far, we have seen that effective teachers flexibly adjust their teaching strategies to accommodate pupils with a wide range of characteristics. These adjustments, however, are especially challenging when children have learning difficulties. Over the past 3 decades, extra steps have been taken to create appropriate learning environments for these pupils.

mainstreaming Placement of pupils with learning difficulties in regular classrooms for part of the school day.

■ **CHILDREN WITH LEARNING DIFFICULTIES.** The Individuals with Disabilities Education Act (Public Law 101–475), first passed in 1975 and revised in 1990, mandates that schools place children who require special supports for learning in the "least restrictive" environments that meet their educational needs. The law led to a rapid increase in **main-**

streaming, or placement of pupils with learning difficulties in regular classrooms for part of the school day, a practice designed to better prepare them for participation in society. Largely due to parental pressures, in some schools, mainstreaming has been extended to **full inclusion**—placement in regular classrooms full time (Siegel, 1996).

Some mainstreamed pupils are **mildly mentally retarded**—children whose IQs fall between 55 and 70 and who also show problems in adaptive behavior, or skills of everyday living (American Psychiatric Association, 1994). But the largest number have **learning disabilities.** Learning-disabled pupils, who constitute 5 to 10 percent of school-age children, have difficulties with one or more aspects of learning, usually with reading. As a result, their achievement is considerably behind what would be expected on the basis of their IQ. Their problems cannot be traced to any obvious physical or emotional difficulty or to environmental disadvantage. Instead, faulty brain functioning is believed to be responsible (Bender, 1996; Polloway et al., 1997). In most instances, the cause is unknown.

The pupil on the left, who has a learning disability, has been fully included in a regular classroom. Because his teacher takes special steps to encourage peer acceptance, individualizes instruction, minimizes comparisons with classmates, and promotes cooperative learning, this boy looks forward to school and is doing well.

(Will Hart)

■ **HOW EFFECTIVE ARE MAINSTREAMING AND FULL INCLUSION?** Does placement of these pupils in regular classes accomplish its two goals—providing more appropriate academic experiences and integrated participation in classroom life? At present, the evidence is not positive on either of these points.

Achievement differences between mainstreamed pupils and those in self-contained classrooms are not great (Buysse & Bailey, 1993; MacMillan, Keogh, & Jones, 1986). Furthermore, children with disabilities in regular classrooms are often rejected by peers. Those who are mentally retarded are overwhelmed by the social skills of their classmates; they cannot interact quickly or adeptly in a conversation or game. And the processing deficits of some children with learning disabilities also lead to problems in social awareness and responsiveness (Gresham & MacMillan, 1997; Vaughn, Elbaum, & Schumm, 1996).

Does this mean that children with special needs cannot be served in regular classrooms? This extreme conclusion is not warranted. When high-quality support services are available, full inclusion can help many pupils with mild disabilities. Otherwise, children may do best when they receive instruction in a resource room for part of the day and in the regular classroom for the remainder. In the resource room, a special education teacher works with pupils on an individual and small-group basis. Then, depending on their abilities, children are mainstreamed for different subjects and amounts of time. This flexible approach helps ensure that the unique academic needs of each child will be served (Hocutt, 1996; Keogh, 1988).

Once children enter the regular classroom, special steps must be taken to promote peer acceptance. Cooperative learning and peer-tutoring experiences in which mainstreamed children and their classmates work together lead to friendly interaction and improved social acceptance (Scruggs & Mastropieri, 1994; Siegel, 1996). Teachers can also prepare children for the arrival of a pupil with special needs and enlist parents' assistance in modeling and encouraging positive attitudes—a process best begun in the preschool years, before children have become less accepting of peers with disabilities (Okagaki et al., 1998). Under these conditions, mainstreaming and full inclusion can foster gains in tolerance, emotional sensitivity, and prosocial behavior among regular classmates.

PARENT–SCHOOL PARTNERSHIPS

Regardless of students' abilities, parent involvement in education—keeping tabs on the child's progress, communicating often with teachers, and making sure that the child is enrolled in challenging, well-taught classes—is crucial for optimum learning. Parents who are in frequent contact with the school send a message to their child about the value of education, model constructive solutions to academic problems, and (as children get

full inclusion Placement of pupils with learning difficulties in regular classrooms for the entire school day.

mild mental retardation Children whose IQs fall between 55 and 70 and who also show problems in adaptive behavior.

learning disabilities Specific learning disorders (for, example, in reading, writing, or math computation) that result in poor school achievement, despite an average or above-average IQ.

older) promote wise educational decisions. Involved parents can also prevent school personnel from placing a bright student not working up to potential in unstimulating learning situations (Grolnick & Slowiaczek, 1994). Although many parents reduce their school involvement as their children get older, it is just as important in secondary school as it is during preschool and elementary school.

Schools can increase parent involvement in the following ways:

- fostering personal relationships between parents and teachers;

- showing parents how to support their child's education at home;

- building bridges between minority home cultures and the culture of the school;

- developing assignments that give parents a meaningful role to play, such as having students find out about their parents' experiences while growing up; and

- including parents in basic planning and governance to ensure that they are invested in school goals (Eccles & Harold, 1993).

Community characteristics affect the ease with which schools attain these goals. In ethnic minority neighborhoods, value conflicts and misunderstandings between parents and school personnel are common. (See Chapter 2, page 53, for an example.) To have any chance of home–school harmony, schools must find ways to integrate minority belief systems into educational practices (Greenfield & Suzuki, 1998). Parents in poverty-stricken, inner-city areas are often more preoccupied with protecting their children from danger than in developing their talents. And since these parents face many daily stresses that reduce the time and energy they have for school involvement, they are particularly hard for schools to reach. Yet schools could relieve some of this stress by forging stronger home–school links. There are parents who are highly involved in their child's education in every minority group and neighborhood (Eccles & Harold, 1996).

ASK YOURSELF . . .

◆ Ray is convinced that his 5-year-old son, Tripper, would do better in school if only Tripper's kindergarten teacher would provide more teacher-directed lessons and worksheets and reduce the time devoted to learning-center activities. Is Ray correct? Explain.

◆ Tanisha is finishing sixth grade. She could either continue in her current school through eighth grade or switch to a much larger junior high school. What would you suggest she do, and why?

◆ Sandy, a parent of a third grader, wonders whether she should support her school board's decision to teach first, second, and third graders together, in multigrade classrooms. How would you advise Sandy, and why?

◆ CONNECTIONS
How are teachers' optimistic and pessimistic views of pupils' academic competence, which create self-fulfilling prophecies, likely to affect children's attributions for success and failure in achievement situations? (See Chapter 11, pages 453–455.)

BRIEF REVIEW

Schools are powerful forces in children's development. Small class size in the early grades fosters academic achievement. In secondary school, a student body size of 500 to 700 promotes extracurricular participation and achievement. Although older school-age pupils in traditional classrooms are slightly advantaged in achievement, the approach undermines younger children's motivation and learning. Children in open classrooms are more critical thinkers, tolerant of individual differences, and positive about school. New philosophical directions based on Vygotsky's sociocultural theory are inspiring educational reforms that stress communication and collaboration as vital for learning. Many schools have begun to collaborate with community agencies in a full-service approach. School transitions create new adjustment problems. Supportive ties to peers and teachers ease entry into kindergarten. The earlier school transition takes place in adolescence, the more likely it is to depress psychological well-being, especially when it coincides with other life stresses.

Teachers who are effective classroom managers and who provide cognitively stimulating activities enhance children's involvement and academic performance. Educational self-fulfilling prophecies are likely to occur when teachers emphasize competition and comparisons between pupils and have difficulty controlling the class. Disruptive children, withdrawn children, and low-SES, ethnic minority children are more likely to be targets of biased teacher expectations, and children achieving poorly are more affected by them. Placement in low-ability groups is linked to poor self-esteem and achievement. Self-esteem, school attitudes, and academic performance tend to be higher in multigrade than single-grade classrooms. Low-income, ethnic minority high school students are assigned in large numbers to noncollege tracks, reducing their educational and life chances.

To be effective, mainstreaming and full inclusion must be carefully tailored to meet the academic and social needs of children with learning difficulties. Parent involvement in education is crucial for children to learn at their best.

How Well Educated Are American Young People?

ur discussion has focused largely on what teachers can do to support the education of children and adolescents. Yet we have also seen, in this and earlier chapters, that many factors—both within and outside schools—affect children's learning. Societal values, school resources, quality of teaching, and parent involvement all play important roles. The combined impact of these multiple influences becomes strikingly apparent when schooling is examined in cross-national perspective.

CROSS-NATIONAL RESEARCH ON ACADEMIC ACHIEVEMENT

American students fare unevenly when their achievement is compared with students in other industrialized nations. In previous international studies of mathematics and science achievement, young people from Hong Kong, Japan, Korea, and Taiwan have consistently been among the top performers, whereas Americans have scored no better than at the mean and often below it (International Education Association, 1988; Lapointe, Askew, & Mead, 1992: Lapointe, Mead, & Askew, 1992).

The most recent assessment, comparing nations at three levels of schooling—fourth grade, eighth grade, and the final year of high school—revealed a sharp decline in performance with increasing grade. In math, fourth graders in the United States were comparable to those in many other countries; in science, they were near the top. U.S. eighth graders sustained the science advantage but scored below the international average in math. By twelfth grade, U.S. math and science knowledge was near the bottom in relation to 21 countries participating in high school testing (see Figure 15.8). When seniors taking advanced math and physics were considered, again U.S. performance was among the lowest. The director of the National Science Foundation concluded, "[American] students appear to disengage from learning critical mathematics and science content as they progress through the school system" (U.S. Department of Education, 1998, p. 7).

Why do American young people fall behind in academic accomplishment? According to the international study, math instruction in the United States is not as challenging and focused as it is in other countries—findings consistent with in-depth research on learning environments in top-performing Asian nations. In a comparison of elementary school children in Japan, Taiwan, and the United States, large differences in math achievement were present in kindergarten and became greater with increasing grade. Although less extreme gaps occurred in reading, by high school both Asian groups scored better in this area as well (Stevenson, 1992; Stevenson & Lee, 1990).

A common assumption is that Asian pupils are high achievers because they are "smarter," but this is not true. Except for the influence of language on early counting skills (see page 308), they do not start school with cognitive advantages over their American peers (Geary, 1996). Instead, as the Cultural Influences box on page 638 explains, a variety of social forces combine to foster a stronger commitment to learning in many Asian families and schools.

An increasing number of jobs are demanding high levels of literacy and technical knowledge. School reforms are currently under way, aimed at helping American young people master the language, math, and science skills necessary to meet work-force needs. Perhaps as a result of these efforts, the achievement of U.S. elementary and secondary school students has improved over the past decade in math and science, in

FIGURE 15.8

Performance of students in the final year of high school from 21 countries on the math general knowledge test in the most recent international study of mathematics and science achievement. The United States fell well below the international average, ranking among far less wealthy and technologically advanced nations.

(Adapted from Mullis, 1998.)

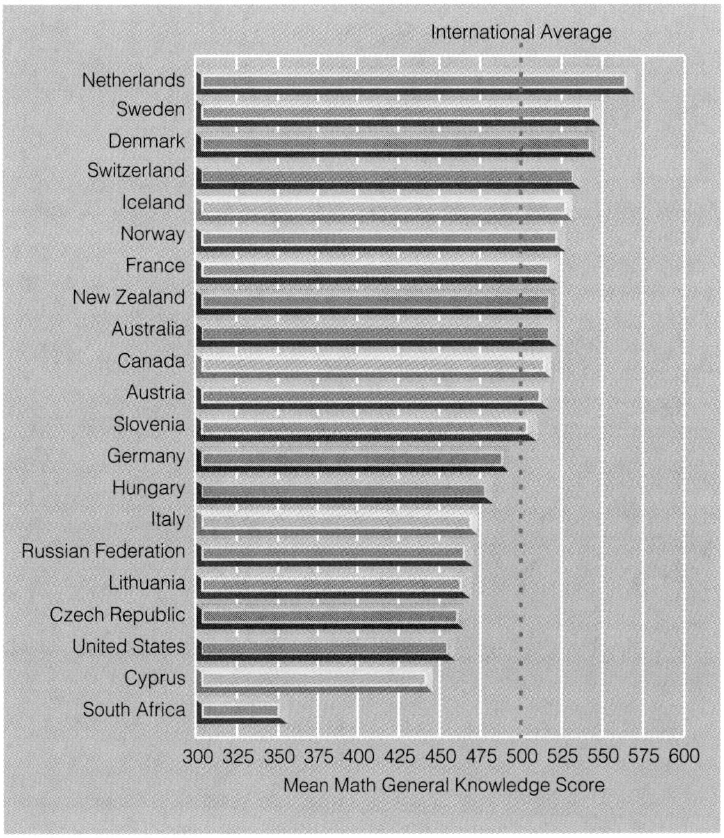

Education in Japan, Taiwan, and the United States

WHY DO ASIAN children perform so well academically? Research examining societal, school, and family conditions in Japan, Taiwan, and the United States provides some answers.

CULTURAL VALUING OF ACADEMIC ACHIEVEMENT. In Japan and Taiwan, natural resources are limited. Progress in science and technology is essential for economic well-being. Since a well-educated work force is necessary to meet this goal, children's mastery of academic skills is vital. In the United States, attitudes toward academic achievement are far less unified. Many Americans believe that it is more important to encourage children to feel good about themselves and to explore various areas of knowledge than to perform well in school.

EMPHASIS ON EFFORT. Japanese and Taiwanese parents and teachers believe that all children have the potential to master challenging academic tasks if they work hard enough. In contrast, many more of their American counterparts regard native ability as the key to academic success (Stevenson, 1992). These differences in attitude may contribute to the fact that American parents are less inclined to encourage activities at home that might enhance school performance. Japanese and Taiwanese children spend more free time studying, reading, and playing academic-related games than do children in the United States (Stevenson & Lee, 1990). In high school, Asian students continue to devote more time to academic pursuits, whereas American students spend more time working and socializing—factors related to both cross-cultural and individual differences in achievement (Fuligni & Stevenson, 1995).

INVOLVEMENT OF PARENTS IN EDUCATION. Asian parents devote many hours to helping their children with homework. American parents spend very little and, at least while their children are in elementary school, do not regard homework as especially important. Overall, American parents are far more satisfied with the quality of their children's education, hold lower standards for their children's academic performance, and are less concerned about how well their youngsters are doing in school (Stevenson, Chen, & Lee, 1993; Stevenson & Lee, 1990).

HIGH-QUALITY EDUCATION FOR ALL. Unlike American teachers, Japanese and Taiwanese teachers do not make early educational decisions on the basis of achievement. There are no separate ability groups in elementary school. Instead, all pupils receive the same nationally mandated, high-quality instruction. Academic lessons are particularly well organized and presented in ways that capture children's attention and involve them actively. Topics in mathematics are treated in greater depth, and there is less repetition of material taught the previous year.

MORE TIME DEVOTED TO INSTRUCTION. In Japan and Taiwan, the school year is over 50 days longer than in the United States. When one American elementary school experimented by adding 30 days to its school year, extended-year pupils scored higher in reading, general-knowledge, and (especially) math achievement than did pupils in similar-quality schools with a traditional calendar (Frazier & Morrison, 1998).

Furthermore, on a day-to-day basis, Japanese and Taiwanese teachers devote much more time to academic

Japanese children achieve considerably better than their American counterparts for a variety of reasons. A longer school day permits frequent alternation of academic instruction with pleasurable activity. This approach probably makes learning easier and more enjoyable.
(Eiji Miyazawa/Black Star)

pursuits, especially mathematics. In one comparison of elementary school academic lessons, the teacher was the leader of the children's activity 90 percent of the time in Taiwan, 74 percent in Japan, but only 46 percent in the United States. Most often, American children worked on their own at their desks, which often resulted in loss of focus on the purpose of the activity. In contrast, Japanese and Taiwanese teachers alternated between short seatwork periods and group discussion of problems, thereby embedding independent work into the larger lesson and keeping children involved. Furthermore, Asian schools are not regimented places, as many Americans believe. An 8-hour school day permits extra recesses and a longer lunch period, with plenty of time for play, social interaction, field trips, and extracurricular activities (Stevenson, 1992, 1994).

COMMUNICATION BETWEEN TEACHERS AND PARENTS. Japanese and Taiwanese teachers get to know their pupils especially well. They teach the same children for 2 or 3 years and make visits to the home once or twice a year. Continuous communication between teachers and parents takes place with the aid of small notebooks that children carry back and forth every day and in which messages about assignments, academic performance, and behavior are written. No such formalized system of frequent teacher–parent communication exists in the United States (Stevenson & Lee, 1990).

Do Japanese and Taiwanese children pay a price for the pressure placed on them to succeed? By high school, academic work often displaces other experiences, since Asian adolescents must pass a highly competitive entrance exam to gain admission to college. Yet Asian parenting practices that encourage academic competence do not undermine children's social development (Huntsinger, Jose, & Larson, 1998). In fact, the highest performing Asian students are very well adjusted (Crystal et al., 1994). Awareness of the ingredients of Asian success has prompted Americans to rethink current educational practices.

reading and writing less so (Campbell, Voelkl, & Donahue, 1997). Effective educational change, however, must take into account the life backgrounds and future goals of students. Simply toughening academic standards is likely to further discourage many low-SES, poorly achieving young people, who can only fall farther behind under these conditions (Parrish, 1991). As we will see next, besides strengthening academic instruction, special efforts are needed in vocational education to help non-college-bound youths prepare for productive work roles.

MAKING THE TRANSITION FROM SCHOOL TO WORK

Approximately 25 percent of American adolescents graduate from high school without plans to go to college. Although they have a much better chance of finding employment than do those who drop out, non-college-bound youths have fewer work opportunities than they did several decades ago. More than one-fourth of high school graduates younger than age 20 who do not continue their education are unemployed (U.S. Bureau of the Census, 1998). When they do find work, most are limited to low-paid, unskilled jobs. In addition, they have few alternatives to turn to for vocational counseling and job placement as they make the transition from school to work (Bailey, 1993).

American employers prefer to hire young adults, regarding the recent high school graduate as poorly prepared for a demanding, skilled occupation. Indeed, there is some truth to this conclusion. During high school, almost half of American adolescents are employed—a greater percentage than in any other developed country. But most of these are middle-SES students in pursuit of spending money rather than vocational exploration and training. Low-income teenagers who need to contribute to family income find it harder to get jobs (Children's Defense Fund, 1999).

Furthermore, the jobs adolescents hold are limited to low-level, repetitive tasks that provide little contact with adult supervisors and do not prepare them for well-paid careers. A heavy commitment to such jobs is actually harmful. High school students who work more than 15 hours a week have poorer school attendance, lower grades, and less time for extracurricular activities. They also report more drug and alcohol use and feel more distant from their parents. And perhaps because of the menial nature of their jobs, employed teenagers tend to become cynical about work life. Many admit to having stolen from their employers (Barling, Rogers, & Kelloway, 1995; Steinberg & Dornbusch, 1991; Steinberg, Fegley, & Dornbusch, 1993).

When work experiences are specially designed to meet educational and vocational goals and involve responsibility and challenge, outcomes are very different. Work–study programs are related to positive work and school attitudes, improved achievement, and lower dropout rates among teenagers whose low-income backgrounds and weak academic skills make them especially vulnerable to unemployment (Owens, 1982; Steinberg, 1984). Yet high-quality vocational preparation for American adolescents who do not go to college is scarce. Unlike European nations, the United States has no widespread training system to prepare its youths for skilled business and industrial occupations and manual trades (Marshall, 1997). The federal government does support some job-training programs, but most are too short to make a difference in the lives of poorly skilled adolescents, who need intensive training and academic remediation before they are ready to enter the job market. And at present, these programs serve only a small minority of young people who need assistance (Children's Defense Fund, 1999).

Inspired by successful programs in Europe, youth apprenticeship strategies that coordinate on-the-job training with classroom instruction are being considered as an important dimension of educational reform in the United States. Bringing together the worlds of schooling and work offers many benefits. These include helping non-college-bound adolescents establish productive lives right after graduation; motivating at-risk youths, who learn more effectively when basic skills are linked to everyday experiences; and contributing to the nation's economic growth (Hamilton, 1993; Safyer, Leahy, & Colan, 1995).

Nevertheless, implementing an apprenticeship system poses major challenges. Among these are overcoming the reluctance of employers to assume part of the responsibility for youth vocational training; creating institutional structures that ensure cooperation between schools and businesses; and finding ways to prevent underprivileged youths from

ASK YOURSELF . . .

◆ Explain how education in Japan and Taiwan illustrates findings presented earlier in this chapter on aspects of schooling that promote high achievement.

◆CONNECTIONS
Do Chinese child-rearing beliefs and practices complement the experiences Taiwanese children typically encounter in school? Explain. (See Chapter 14, page 569.)

being concentrated in the lowest-skilled apprenticeship placements, a circumstance that would perpetuate current social inequalities (Hamilton, 1994). Pilot apprenticeship projects are currently under way, in an effort to solve these problems and build bridges between learning and working in the United States. Young people well prepared for an economically and personally satisfying vocation are much more likely to become productive citizens, devoted family members, and contented adults. The support of schools, communities, and society as a whole can contribute greatly to a positive outcome.

SUMMARY

THE IMPORTANCE OF PEER RELATIONS

Discuss evidence indicating that both parental and peer relationships are vital for children's development.

◆ Research on nonhuman primates suggests that parent and peer relations complement one another. The parent–child bond provides children with the security to enter the world of peers. Peer interaction, in turn, permits children to expand the social skills acquired within the family. Studies of **peer-only rearing** reveal that peer relations can, to some extent, fill in for the early parent–child bond. However, peer-only-reared monkeys do not develop as well as their counterparts with typical parental and peer upbringing.

DEVELOPMENT OF PEER SOCIABILITY

Trace the development of peer sociability from infancy into adolescence.

◆ Peer sociability begins in infancy with isolated social acts that are gradually replaced by coordinated exchanges in the second year of life. During the preschool years, interactive play with peers increases. According to Parten, it begins with **nonsocial activity,** shifts to **parallel play,** and then becomes **associative** and **cooperative play.** However, preschoolers do not follow this straightforward developmental sequence. Solitary play and parallel play remain common throughout early childhood. Sociodramatic play becomes especially frequent and enhances cognitive, emotional, and social skills.

◆ During middle childhood, peer interaction is more sensitively tuned to others' perspectives and increasingly governed by prosocial norms, and play emphasizes rule-oriented games. Also, **rough-and-tumble play** becomes more common. In our evolutionary past, this friendly chasing and play-fighting may have been important for the development of fighting skill and dominance relations. Adolescents show greater skill at working on tasks cooperatively.

INFLUENCES ON PEER SOCIABILITY

How do parental encouragement, play materials, age mix of children, and cultural values influence peer sociability?

◆ Parents influence early peer relations by arranging informal peer play activities; offering advice, guidance, and examples of how to act toward others; and using a style of interaction while playing with their child that emphasizes cooperation and exchange of positive affect.

◆ Situational factors affect peer sociability. When toys and space are in short supply, negative interactions increase. Cooperative play occurs more often when preschoolers play with open-ended, relatively unstructured materials. Although same-age peers engage in more intense and harmonious exchanges, mixed-age interaction has benefits. It provides older children with practice in prosocial behavior and younger children with opportunities to learn from their older companions. In early adolescence, mixed-age interaction increases and becomes more satisfying.

◆ In collectivist societies, large-group imitative play involving acting out of highly scripted activities is common. When caregivers value the cognitive and educational benefits of make-believe and stress individuality and self-expression, sociodramatic play occurs more often.

PEER ACCEPTANCE

Describe major categories of peer acceptance, the relationship of physical appearance and social behavior to likability, and ways to help rejected children.

◆ **Sociometric techniques** distinguish four types of peer acceptance: (1) **popular children,** who are liked by many agemates; (2) **rejected children,** who are actively disliked; (3) **controversial children,** who are both liked and disliked; and (4) **neglected children,** who are seldom chosen, either positively or negatively. Rejected children often experience lasting adjustment difficulties.

◆ Physically attractive children are better accepted by peers. Over time, attractive and unattractive children may respond in kind to the way they are treated, sustaining peer opinion.

◆ The most powerful determinant of peer acceptance is social behavior. Popular children communicate with agemates in sensitive, friendly, and cooperative ways. At least two subtypes of peer rejection exist. **Rejected-aggressive** children are hostile, hyperactive, inattentive, and impulsive, whereas **rejected-withdrawn** children are passive and socially awkward. Controversial children display a blend of positive and negative social behaviors. Although neglected children often choose to play by themselves, they are usually socially competent and well adjusted.

◆ Interventions that lead to gains in rejected children's peer acceptance include coaching in social skills; intensive academic tutoring; and social-cognitive interventions, such as training in perspective taking and social problem solving. Teaching rejected children to attribute peer difficulties to internal, changeable causes helps motivate them to improve their peer relations.

PEER GROUPS

Describe peer group formation in middle childhood and adolescence, including factors that influence group norms and social structures.

◆ By the end of middle childhood, **peer groups** with unique norms and social structures of leaders and followers emerge. Late childhood and early adolescent peer groups are organized around **cliques,** small groups of good friends. As interest in dating increases, boys' and girls' cliques come together, providing a supportive context for interacting with the other sex.

◆ Adolescents also form **crowds**—larger, more loosely organized groups that provide an identity within the larger social structure of the school. Many peer group norms are extensions of ones acquired at home. Once teenagers join a group, its norms influence their beliefs and behavior further.

◆ Group social structures sometimes consist of **dominance hierarchies,** which serve the adaptive function of limiting aggression among group members. In many instances, leadership is not based on dominance but on managerial skills and talents that support important normative activities of the group.

PEER RELATIONS AND SOCIALIZATION

What techniques do peers use to socialize one another?

◆ Peers serve as socialization agents through reinforcement, modeling, and direct pressures to conform to social behaviors. Peer conformity is strongest during early adolescence. However, peers seldom demand total conformity, and most peer pressures do not conflict with important adult values.

TELEVISION

Cite factors that affect how much time children devote to TV viewing, and describe age-related changes in television literacy.

◆ Children spend more time watching TV than in any other waking activity. Low-SES, ethnic minority children and children from large families tend to be heavier viewers. Excessive TV watching is linked to family and peer difficulties.

◆ Cognitive development and experience in watching TV gradually lead to gains in **television literacy.** Not until age 7 do children fully grasp the unreality of TV fiction. Understanding of cinematic forms and memory for information important to plot comprehension increase sharply from middle childhood to adolescence.

Discuss the influence of television on children's development, including aggression; ethnic and gender stereotypes; consumerism; prosocial behavior; and academic learning and imagination.

◆ Televised violence promotes aggressive behavior, tolerance of aggression in others, and a violent and dangerous view of the world. TV also conveys stereotypes that affect children's beliefs about ethnicity and gender. Children are easily manipulated by TV commercials. Not until age 8 or 9 do they understand the selling purpose of the ads.

◆ Television can foster prosocial behavior as long as it is free of violent content. Programs such as "Sesame Street" promote academic learning. TV fare with disconnected bits of information or with violent content and product-related shows with toys as main characters are detrimental to children's imagination.

COMPUTERS

Discuss children's classroom and home-based computer use, noting benefits and concerns.

◆ Computers can have rich cognitive and social benefits. In classrooms, pupils often use computers collaboratively. Computer-assisted instruction (CAI) leads to gains in academic skills, and word processing results in longer, higher-quality written prose. Programming promotes a wide variety of higher cognitive processes. Learning activities that use the Internet can broaden children's understanding of other people and places.

◆ Since computers appear most often in the homes of economically well-off children, particularly boys, they may be widening SES and gender gaps in cognitive performance. Children's extensive use of home computers for videogame play fosters attentional and spatial skills. However, violent videogames, like violent TV, increase aggression and desensitize children to violence. Heavy Internet use at home undermines social involvement and psychological well-being.

SCHOOLING

Discuss the influence of class and student body size and teachers' educational philosophies on academic and social development.

◆ Schools powerfully influence many aspects of development. Smaller classes in the early elementary grades leads to gains in academic achievement. In small high schools, adolescents are more actively involved in extracurricular activities and develop a sense of social obligation that carries over to academic achievement.

◆ Teachers' educational philosophies play a major role in children's learning experiences. Older school-age pupils in **traditional classrooms** are advantaged in academic achievement. However, whole-class, teacher-directed instruction disrupts young children's learning and confidence in their abilities. Pupils in **open classrooms** tend to be critical thinkers who respect individual differences and have more positive attitudes toward school.

◆ New philosophical approaches based on Vygotsky's sociocultural theory emphasize the importance of rich, socially communicative environments and teaching adapted to each child's zone of proximal development. **Full-service schools** collaborate with community agencies to provide children and adolescents at risk for poor achievement with the health and social services they need to benefit fully from education.

Cite factors that affect adjustment to school transitions in early childhood and adolescence.

◆ Experience in preschool and supportive ties to peers and teachers predict favorable kindergarten adjustment. Overtly aggressive children and peer-avoidant children, who have difficulty forming positive relationships, often adapt poorly to kindergarten.

◆ School transitions in adolescence can also be stressful. With each school change, academic standards tighten, course grades decline, and young people typically enter a less personal environment. Girls experience more adjustment difficulties after the elementary-to-junior-high transition, since other life changes (puberty and the beginning of dating) tend to occur at the same time. Poorly achieving and poverty-stricken young people show an especially sharp drop in school performance that can lead to failure and dropping out.

Discuss the role of teacher–pupil interaction and grouping practices in academic achievement.

◆ Patterns of teacher–pupil interaction affect children's academic progress. Teachers who are effective classroom managers have pupils who achieve especially well. Instruction that encourages higher-level thinking promotes pupil interest and involvement in classroom activities.

◆ **Educational self-fulfilling prophecies** are most likely to occur when teachers emphasize competition and public evaluation and fear losing control of the class. Disruptive pupils; withdrawn pupils; and low-SES and ethnic minority pupils are especially vulnerable to negative self-fulfilling prophecies. Teachers' biased expectations have a greater impact on poorly achieving than high-achieving children.

◆ Ability grouping in elementary school is linked to poorer quality instruction and a drop in self-esteem and achievement for children in low-ability groups. Multigrade classrooms promote self-esteem and positive school attitudes. However, teachers must provide extensive training and assistance for collaboration between heterogeneous peers to succeed.

◆ By high school. separate educational tracks that dovetail with adolescents' future plans are necessary. Unfortunately, high school tracking in the United States usually extends the educational inequalities of earlier years.

Under what conditions is placement of mildly mentally retarded and learning disabled children in regular classrooms successful, and how can schools increase parent involvement in education?

◆ Pupils with **mild mental retardation** and **learning disabilities** are often placed in regular classrooms, usually through **mainstreaming** but also through **full inclusion.** The success of regular classroom placement depends on tailoring learning experiences to children's needs and promoting positive peer relations.

◆ Schools can increase parent involvement by fostering relationships between parents and teachers, building bridges between minority home cultures and the culture of the school, and involving parents in school governance. Reaching out to ethnic minority parents and parents in poverty-stricken, inner-city areas is especially important.

HOW WELL EDUCATED ARE AMERICAN YOUNG PEOPLE?

Why does the United States fall behind Asian nations in academic achievement, and what prevents American non-college-bound youths from making an effective school-to-work transition?

◆ In cross-national comparisons of math and science achievement, students in Asian nations are consistently among the top performers, whereas Americans score no better than at the mean and often below it. A strong cultural commitment to learning, which pervades homes and schools, is responsible for the academic success of Japanese and Taiwanese pupils.

◆ Besides strengthening academic standards, the United States needs to help its non-college-bound high school graduates make an effective transition from school to work. Unlike their European counterparts, American adolescents have no widespread vocational training system to assist them in preparing for challenging, well-paid careers in business, industry, and manual trades.

IMPORTANT TERMS AND CONCEPTS

associative play (p. 598)
clique (p. 609)
controversial children (p. 604)
cooperative play (p. 598)
crowd (p. 610)
dominance hierarchy (p. 611)
educational self-fulfilling prophecy (p. 632)
full inclusion (p. 635)
full-service schools (p. 629)

learning disabilities (p. 635)
mainstreaming (p. 634)
mild mental retardation (p. 635)
neglected children (p. 604)
nonsocial activity (p. 598)
open classroom (p. 627)
parallel play (p. 598)
peer group (p. 609)
peer victimization (p. 606)

peer-only rearing (p. 598)
popular children (p. 604)
rejected children (p. 604)
rejected-aggressive children (p. 606)
rejected-withdrawn children (p. 606)
rough-and-tumble play (p. 601)
sociometric techniques (p. 604)
television literacy (p. 617)
traditional classroom (p. 627)

A

AB search error   The error made by 8- to 12-month-olds after an object is moved from hiding place A to hiding place B. Infants in Piaget's Substage 4 search for it only in the first hiding place (A).

accommodation   That part of adaptation in which an individual adjusts old schemes and creates new ones to produce a better fit with the environment. Distinguished from *assimilation.*

achievement motivation   The tendency to persist at challenging tasks.

adaptation   In Piaget's theory, the process of building schemes through direct interaction with the environment. Consists of two complementary activities: *assimilation* and *accommodation.*

adolescent initiation ceremony   A ritual, or rite of passage, announcing to the community that a young person is ready to make the transition from childhood into adolescence or full adulthood.

affordances   The action possibilities a situation offers an organism with certain motor capabilities. Discovery of affordances is believed to guide perceptual development.

age of viability   The age at which the fetus can first survive if born early. Occurs sometime between 22 and 26 weeks.

allele   Each of two or more forms of a gene located at the same place on the chromosomes.

amnion   The inner membrane that forms a protective covering around the prenatal organism and encloses it in amniotic fluid, which helps keep temperature constant and provides a cushion against jolts caused by the mother's movement.

analogical problem solving   Extracting a solution strategy from one problem-solving context and applying it in other contexts with similar goals but different features.

androgens   Hormones produced chiefly by the testes, and in smaller quantities by the adrenal glands, that influence the pubertal growth spurt, the appearance of body hair, and male sex characteristics.

androgyny   A type of gender identity in which the person scores high on both masculine and feminine personality characteristics.

animistic thinking   The belief that inanimate objects have lifelike qualities, such as thoughts, wishes, feelings, and intentions.

anorexia nervosa   An eating disorder in which individuals (usually females) starve themselves because of a compulsive fear of getting fat.

Apgar Scale   A rating system used to assess the newborn baby's physical condition immediately after birth.

applied behavior analysis   Procedures that combine conditioning and modeling to eliminate undesirable behaviors and increase socially acceptable responses.

assimilation   That part of adaptation in which an individual interprets the external world in terms of current schemes. Distinguished from *accommodation.*

associative play   A form of true social participation in which children engage in separate activities but interact by exchanging toys and commenting on one another's behavior. Distinguished from *nonsocial activity, parallel play,* and *cooperative play.*

attachment   The strong affectional tie that humans feel toward special people in their lives.

Attachment Q-Sort   An efficient method for assessing the quality of the attachment bond, in which a parent or an expert informant sorts a set of 90 descriptors of attachment-related behaviors on the basis of how well they characterize the child. A score permits children to be assigned to securely or insecurely attached groups.

attention-deficit hyperactivity disorder   A childhood disorder involving inattention, impulsivity, and excessive motor activity. Often leads to academic failure and social problems.

attribution retraining   An approach to intervention that uses adult feedback to modify the attributions of learned-helpless children, thereby encouraging them to believe they can overcome failure if only they exert more effort.

attributions   Common, everyday explanations for the causes of behavior.

authentic assessment   An approach that measures intellectual progress by examining students' real performance in school over time.

authoritarian style   A parenting style that is demanding but low in responsiveness to children's rights and needs. Conformity and obedience are valued over open communication. Distinguished from *authoritative, permissive,* and *uninvolved styles.*

authoritative style   A parenting style that is demanding and responsive. A rational, democratic approach in which both parents' and children's rights are respected. Distinguished from *authoritarian, permissive,* and *uninvolved styles.*

autobiographical memory   Representations of special, one-time events that are long lasting because they are imbued with personal meaning.

automatization   The extent to which cognitive processes are well learned, or automatic, and therefore require little or no attentional resources.

autonomous morality   Piaget's second stage of moral development, in which children view rules as flexible, socially agreed-on principles that can be revised to suit the will of the majority.

autonomy   A sense of oneself as a separate, self-governing individual. An important developmental task of adolescence that is closely related to the quest for identity.

autosomes   The 22 matching chromosome pairs in each human cell.

autostimulation theory   The theory that REM sleep provides stimulation necessary for central nervous system development in young infants.

avoidant attachment   The quality of insecure attachment characterizing infants who are usually not distressed by parental separation and who avoid the parent when she returns. Distinguished from *secure, resistant,* and *dissorganized/disoriented attachment.*

B

babbling   Repetition of consonant–vowel combinations in long strings, beginning around 4 months of age.

basic emotions   Emotions that can be directly inferred from facial expressions, such as happiness, interest, surprise, fear, anger, sadness, and disgust.

basic-skills approach   An approach to beginning reading instruction that emphasizes training in phonics—the basic rules for translating written symbols into sounds—and simplified reading materials. Distinguished from *whole-language approach.*

behavioral genetics   A field of study devoted to uncovering the hereditary and environmental origins of individual differences in human traits and abilities.

behaviorism   An approach that views directly observable events—stimuli and responses—as the appropriate focus of study and the development of behavior as taking place through classical and operant conditioning.

belief–desire theory of mind   The theory of mind that emerges around age 3 to 4 in which both beliefs and desires determine behavior and that closely resembles the everyday psychology of adults.

biased sampling   Failure to select participants who are representative of the population of interest in a study.

bicultural identity   The identity constructed by adolescents who explore and adopt values from both their subculture and the dominant culture.

binocular depth cues   Depth cues that rely on each eye receiving a slightly different view of the visual field; the brain blends the two images, creating three-dimensionality.

blended, or reconstituted, family   A family structure resulting from cohabitation or remarriage that includes parent, stepparent, and children.

body image   Conception of and attitude toward one's physical appearance.

brain plasticity   The ability of other parts of the brain to take over functions of damaged regions.

breech position   A position of the baby in the uterus that would cause the buttocks or feet to be delivered first.

Broca's area   A language structure located in the frontal lobe of the cerebral cortex that controls language production.

bulimia   An eating disorder in which individuals (mainly females) engage in binge eating followed by deliberate vomiting, purging with laxatives, and strict dieting.

C

canalization   The tendency of heredity to restrict the development of some characteristics to just one or a few outcomes.

cardinality   A principle specifying that the last number in a counting sequence indicates the quantity of items in the set.

carrier   A heterozygous individual who can pass a recessive trait to his or her offspring.

catch-up growth   Physical growth that returns to its genetically determined path after being delayed by environmental factors.

categorical self   Early classification of the self according to salient ways people differ, such as age, sex, physical characteristics, and goodness and badness.

categorical speech perception   The tendency to perceive as identical a range of sounds that belong to the same phonemic class as identical.

central conceptual structures   In Case's neo-Piagetian theory, networks of concepts and relations that permit children to think about a wide range of situations in more advanced ways. Formation of new central conceptual structures marks the transition to a new Piagetian stage.

centration   The tendency to focus on one aspect of a situation and neglect other important features.

cephalocaudal trend   An organized pattern of physical growth and motor control that proceeds from head to tail.

cerebellum   A brain structure that aids in balance and control of body movements.

cerebral cortex   The largest structure of the human brain; accounts for the highly developed intelligence of the human species.

child development   A field of study devoted to understanding all aspects of human growth and change from conception through adolescence.

child-directed speech (CDS)   The form of language adults use to speak to infants and toddlers that consists of short sentences with high-pitched, exaggerated expression, clear pronunciation, and distinct pauses between speech segments.

childhood social indicators   Periodic measures of children's health, living conditions, achievement, and psychological well-being that lend insight into their overall status in a community, state, or nation.

chorion The outer membrane that forms a protective covering around the prenatal organism. It sends out tiny hairlike villi, from which the placenta begins to emerge.

chromosomes Rodlike structures in the cell nucleus that store and transmit genetic information.

chronosystem In ecological systems theory, temporal changes in children's environments, which produce new conditions that affect development. These changes can be imposed externally or arise from within the organism, since children select, modify, and create many of their own settings and experiences.

circular reaction In Piaget's theory, a means of building schemes in which infants try to repeat a chance event caused by their own motor activity.

classical conditioning A form of learning that involves associating a neutral stimulus with a stimulus that leads to a reflexive response.

clinical interview A method in which the researcher uses flexible, open-ended questions to probe for the participant's point of view.

clinical, or case study, method A method in which the researcher attempts to understand the unique individual child by combining interview data, observations, test scores, and sometimes psychophysiological assessments.

clique A small group of about five to seven members who are good friends.

codominance A pattern of inheritance in which both alleles, in a heterozygous combination, are expressed.

cognitive inhibition The ability to control internal and external distracting stimuli, preventing them from capturing attention and cluttering working memory with irrelevant information.

cognitive maps Mental representations of large-scale spaces.

cognitive self-regulation The process of continuously monitoring progress toward a goal, checking outcomes, and redirecting unsuccessful efforts.

cognitive-developmental theory An approach introduced by Piaget that views the child as actively constructing knowledge and cognitive development as taking place in stages.

cohort effects The effects of cultural-historical change on the accuracy of findings: Children born in one period of time are influenced by particular cultural and historical conditions.

collectivist societies Societies in which people define themselves as part of a group and stress group over individual goals. Distinguished from *individualistic societies*.

community-of-learners model A Vygotsky-inspired educational approach in which collaboration is a school-wide value; classrooms become learning communities in which adults and children jointly work on complex, real-world problems, drawing on many sources of expertise within and outside the school.

compliance Voluntary obedience to requests and commands.

componential analysis A research procedure aimed at clarifying the cognitive processes responsible for intelligence test scores by correlating them with laboratory measures designed to assess the speed and effectiveness of information processing.

comprehension In language development, the words and word combinations that children understand. Distinguished from *production.*

concordance rate The percentage of instances in which both twins show a trait when it is present in one twin.

concrete operational stage Piaget's third stage, during which thought is logical, flexible, and organized in its application to concrete information. However, the capacity for abstract thinking is not yet present. Spans the years from 7 to 11.

conditioned response (CR) In classical conditioning, an originally reflexive response that is produced by a conditioned stimulus (CS).

conditioned stimulus (CS) In classical conditioning, a neutral stimulus that, through pairing with an unconditioned stimulus (UCS), leads to a new, conditioned response (CR).

connectionism An approach that tries to explain development in terms of artificial neural networks, which are programmed into computers, set up to learn, and presented with tasks that children encounter. If the system's pattern of responses resembles that of children, then researchers conclude that the artificial network is a good model of how children learn.

conservation The understanding that certain physical characteristics of objects remain the same, even when their outward appearance changes.

construction The process of moral development in which children actively attend to and interrelate multiple aspects of situations in which social conflicts arise and derive new moral understandings.

constructivist approach An approach to cognitive development in which children discover virtually all knowledge about the world through their own activity. Consistent with Piaget's cognitive-developmental theory. Distinguished from *nativist approach.*

contexts Unique combinations of personal and environmental circumstances that can result in markedly different paths of development.

continuous development Development as a cumulative process of adding more of the same types of skills that were there to begin with. Distinguished from *discontinuous development.*

contrast sensitivity Ability to detect contrast—differences in light levels between adjacent spatial regions.

control deficiency The inability to execute a mental strategy effectively. Distinguished from *production* and *utilization deficiencies.*

controversial children Children who get a large number of positive and negative votes on sociometric measures of peer acceptance. Distinguished from *popular, neglected,* and *rejected children.*

conventional level Kohlberg's second level of moral development, in which moral understanding is based on conforming to social rules to ensure positive human relationships and societal order.

convergent thinking   The generation of a single correct answer to a problem. Type of cognition emphasized on intelligence tests. Distinguished from *divergent thinking*.

cooing   Pleasant vowel-like noises made by infants beginning around 2 months of age.

cooperative learning   A learning environment structured into groups of peers who work together toward a common goal. Distinguished from *nonsocial activity, parallel play,* and *associative play*.

cooperative play   A form of true social participation in which children's actions are directed toward a common goal. Distinguished from *nonsocial activity, parallel play,* and *associative play*.

coregulation   A transitional form of supervision in which parents exercise general oversight while permitting children to be in charge of moment-by-moment decision making.

corpus callosum   The large bundle of fibers that connects the two hemispheres of the brain.

correlation coefficient   A number, ranging from +1.00 to −1.00, that describes the strength and direction of the relationship between two variables. The size of the number shows the strength of the relationship. The sign of the number (+ or −) refers to the direction of the relationship.

correlational design   A research design in which the investigator gathers information without altering participants' experiences and examines relationships between variables. Does not permit inferences about cause and effect.

creativity   The ability to produce work that is original (that others have not thought of before) and that is appropriate (sensible or useful in some way).

cross-sectional design   A research design in which groups of participants of different ages are studied at the same point in time. Distinguished from *longitudinal design*.

crossing over   Exchange of genes between chromosomes next to each other during meiosis.

crowd   A large, loosely organized peer group in which membership is based on reputation and stereotype.

crystallized intelligence   In Cattell's theory, a form of intelligence that depends on culturally loaded, fact-oriented information. Distinguished from *fluid intelligence*.

D

debriefing   Providing a full account and justification of research activities to participants in a study in which deception was used.

deferred imitation   The ability to remember and copy the behavior of models who are not immediately present.

delay of gratification   Waiting for a more appropriate time and place to engage in a tempting act or obtain a desired object.

deoxyribonucleic acid (DNA)   Long, double-stranded molecules that make up chromosomes.

dependent variable   The variable the researcher expects to be influenced by the independent variable in an experiment. Distinguished from *independent variable*.

deprivation dwarfism   A growth disorder observed between 2 and 15 years of age. Characterized by substantially below-average stature, weight that is usually appropriate for height, immature skeletal age, and decreased GH secretion. Caused by severe emotional deprivation.

developmental psychology   A branch of psychology devoted to understanding all changes that human beings experience throughout the life span.

developmentally appropriate practice   A set of standards devised by the National Association for the Education of Young Children that specifies program characteristics that meet the developmental and individual needs of young children of varying ages, based on current research and the consensus of experts.

differentiation theory   The view that perceptual development involves the detection of increasingly fine-grained, invariant features in the environment.

difficult child   A child whose temperament is such that he or she is irregular in daily routines, is slow to accept new experiences, and tends to react negatively and intensely. Distinguished from *easy child* and *slow-to-warm-up child*.

discontinuous development   Development as taking place in stages, in which new and different ways of interpreting and responding to the world emerge at particular time periods. Distinguished from *continuous development*.

dishabituation   Increase in responsiveness after stimulation changes.

disorganized/disoriented attachment   The quality of insecure attachment characterizing infants who respond in a confused, contradictory fashion when reunited with the parent. Distinguished from *secure, avoidant,* and *resistant attachment*.

distance curve   A growth curve that plots the average height and weight of a sample of children at each age. Shows typical yearly progress toward mature body size.

distributive justice   Beliefs about how to divide resources fairly.

divergent thinking   The generation of multiple and unusual possibilities when faced with a task or problem. Associated with creativity. Distinguished from *convergent thinking*.

divorce mediation   A series of meetings between divorcing adults and a trained professional, who tries to help them settle disputes. Aimed at avoiding legal battles that intensify family conflict.

dizygotic twins   See *fraternal twins*.

domain-general changes   Similar transformations across all types of knowledge, resulting in the perfection of general reasoning abilities. Distinguished from *domain-specific changes*.

domain-specific changes   Distinct transformations within each type of knowledge, resulting in the perfection of separate, specialized abilities. Distinguished from *domain-general changes*.

dominance hierarchy   A stable ordering of group members that predicts who will win when conflict arises between group members.

dominant cerebral hemisphere   The hemisphere of the brain responsible for skilled motor action. The left hemisphere is dominant in right-handed individuals. In left-handed individuals, the right hemisphere may be dominant, or motor and language skills may be shared between the hemispheres.

dominant-recessive inheritance   A pattern of inheritance in which, under heterozygous conditions, the influence of only one allele is apparent.

dynamic testing   An approach to testing consistent with Vygotsky's concept of the zone of proximal development, in which purposeful teaching is introduced into the testing situation to see what the child can do with social support.

dynamic systems perspective   A view that regards the child's mind, body, and physical and social worlds as a dynamic, integrated system. A change in any part of the system leads the child to reorganize his or her behavior so that the system operates in a more complex and effective way.

dynamic systems theory of motor development   A theory that views new motor skills as reorganizations of previously mastered skills that lead to more effective ways of exploring and controlling the environment. Motor development is jointly influenced by central nervous system maturation, movement possibilities of the body, environmental supports for the skill, and the task the child has in mind.

E

easy child   A child whose temperament is such that he or she quickly establishes regular routines in infancy, is generally cheerful, and adapts easily to new experiences. Distinguished from *difficult child* and *slow-to-warm-up child.*

ecological systems theory   Bronfenbrenner's approach, which views the child as developing within a complex system of relationships affected by multiple levels of the environment, from immediate settings of family and school to broad cultural values and programs.

educational self-fulfilling prophecy   The idea that pupils may adopt teachers' positive or negative attitudes toward them and start to live up to these views.

effective strategy use   Consistent use of a mental strategy that leads to improvement in performance. Distinguished from *production, control,* and *utilization deficiencies.*

egocentrism   The inability to distinguish the symbolic viewpoints of others from one's own.

elaboration   The memory strategy of creating a relationship between two or more pieces of information that are not members of the same category.

embryo   The prenatal organism from 2 to 8 weeks after conception, during which time the foundations of all body structures and internal organs are laid down.

emergent literacy   Young children's active efforts to construct literacy knowledge through informal experiences.

emotion   An expression of readiness to establish, maintain, or change one's relation to the environment on a matter of personal importance.

emotional display rules   Rules that specify when, where, and how it is culturally appropriate to express emotions.

emotional self-regulation   Strategies for adjusting our emotional state to a comfortable level of intensity so we can accomplish our goals.

empathy   The ability to understand another's emotional state and feel with that person, or respond emotionally in a similar way.

entity view of ability   The view that ability is a fixed characteristic and cannot be changed. Distinguished from *incremental view of ability.*

environmental cumulative deficit hypothesis   A view that attributes the age-related decline in IQ among poverty-stricken ethnic minority children to the compounding effects of underprivileged rearing conditions.

epiphyses   Growth centers in the bones where new cartilage cells are produced and gradually harden.

episodic memory   Memory for personally experienced events.

equilibration   In Piaget's theory, back-and-forth movement between cognitive equilibrium and disequilibrium throughout development, which leads to more effective schemes.

estrogens   Hormones produced chiefly by the ovaries that cause the breasts, uterus, and vagina to mature and the body to take on feminine proportions during puberty.

ethnography   A method by which the researcher attempts to understand the unique values and social processes of a culture or a distinct social group by living with its members and taking field notes for a period of months or years.

ethological theory of attachment   A theory formulated by Bowlby, which views the infant's emotional tie to the familiar caregiver as an evolved response that promotes survival.

ethology   An approach concerned with the adaptive, or survival, value of behavior and its evolutionary history.

event sampling   An observational procedure in which the researcher records all instances of a particular behavior during a specified time period.

exosystem   In ecological systems theory, social settings that do not contain children but that affect their experiences in immediate settings. Examples are parents' workplace and health and welfare services in the community.

expansions   Adult responses that elaborate on a child's utterance, increasing its complexity.

experimental design   A research design in which the investigator randomly assigns participants to two or more treatment conditions. Permits inferences about cause and effect.

expressive style   A style of early language learning in which toddlers use language mainly to talk about the feelings and needs of themselves and other people. Distinguished from *referential style.*

expressive traits   Feminine-stereotyped personality traits that reflect warmth, caring, and sensitivity. Distinguished from *instrumental traits.*

extended-family household   A household in which parent and child live with one or more adult relatives.

extinction   In classical conditioning, decline of the conditioned response (CR), as a result of presenting the conditioned stimulus (CS) enough times without the unconditioned stimulus (UCS).

F

factor analysis   A complicated statistical procedure that combines scores from many separate test items into a few factors, which substitute for the separate scores. Used to identify mental abilities that contribute to performance on intelligence tests.

fast-mapping   Connecting a new word with an underlying concept after only a brief encounter.

fetal alcohol effects (FAE)   The condition of children who display some but not all of the defects of fetal alcohol syndrome. Usually their mothers drank alcohol in smaller quantities during pregnancy.

fetal alcohol syndrome (FAS)   A set of defects that results when pregnant women consume large amounts of alcohol during most or all of pregnancy. Includes mental retardation; impaired motor coordination, attention, memory, and language; overactivity; slow physical growth; and facial abnormalities.

fetus   The prenatal organism from the beginning of the third month to the end of pregnancy, during which time completion of body structures and dramatic growth in size take place.

field experiment   A research design in which participants are randomly assigned to treatment conditions in natural settings.

fluid intelligence   In Cattell's theory, a form of intelligence that requires very little specific knowledge but involves the ability to see complex relationships and solve problems. Distinguished from *crystallized intelligence.*

fontanels   Six soft spots that separate the bones of the skull at birth.

formal operational stage   Piaget's final stage, in which adolescents develop the capacity for abstract, scientific thinking, begins around age 11.

fraternal, or dizygotic, twins   Twins that result from the release and fertilization of two ova. They are genetically no more alike than ordinary siblings. Distinguished from *identical, or monozygotic, twins.*

full inclusion   Placement of pupils with learning difficulties in regular classrooms for the entire school day.

full-service schools   Schools that collaborate with community agencies to provide children and adolescents at risk for poor achievement with the health and social services they need to benefit fully from education.

functionalist approach   A perspective emphasizing that the broad function of emotions is to prompt action in the ser- vice of personal goals and that emotions are central forces in all aspects of human activity.

fuzzy trace theory   A theory that proposes two types of encoding, one that automatically reconstructs information into a fuzzy version called a *gist,* which is especially useful for reasoning; and a second, verbatim version that is adapted for answering questions about specifics.

G

gametes   Human sperm and ova, which contain half as many chromosomes as a regular body cell.

gender consistency   Kohlberg's final stage of gender understanding, in which children master gender constancy.

gender constancy   The understanding that sex remains the same even if clothing, hairstyle, and play activities change.

gender identity   The perception of oneself as relatively masculine or feminine in characteristics.

gender intensification   Development of more traditional gender identities in early adolescence.

gender labeling   Kohlberg's first stage of gender understanding, in which preschoolers can label the sex of themselves and others correctly.

gender roles   The reflection of gender stereotypes in everyday behavior.

gender schema theory   An information-processing approach to gender typing that combines social learning and cognitive-developmental features to explain how social pressures and cognitions work together to affect stereotyping, gender-role identity, and gender-role adoption.

gender stability   Kohlberg's second stage of gender understanding, in which preschoolers have a partial understanding of the permanence of sex; they grasp its stability over time.

gender stereotypes   Widely held beliefs about characteristics deemed appropriate for males and females.

gender typing   The process of developing gender-linked beliefs, gender roles, and a gender-role identity.

gender-stereotype flexibility   Belief that both genders can display a gender-stereotyped personality trait or activity.

gender   In this book, characterization of differences between males and females in which judgments are being made about either biological or environmental influences.

gene   A segment of a DNA molecule that contains instructions for production of various proteins that contribute to growth and functioning of the body.

general factor, or "g"   In Spearman's theory of intelligence, a common factor representing abstract reasoning power that underlies a wide variety of test items.

general growth curve   Curve that represents changes in overall body size—rapid growth during infancy, slower gains in early and middle childhood, and rapid growth once more during adolescence.

generalized other A blend of what we imagine important people in our lives think of us; contributes to a self-concept comprising personality traits.

genetic counseling Counseling that helps couples assess the likelihood of giving birth to a baby with a hereditary disorder and choose the best course of action in view of risks and family goals.

genetic imprinting A pattern of inheritance in which alleles are imprinted, or chemically marked, in such a way that one pair member is activated, regardless of its makeup.

genetic-environmental correlation The idea that heredity influences the environments to which individuals are exposed.

genotype The genetic makeup of an individual.

gist A fuzzy representation of information that preserves essential content without details, is less likely to be forgotten than a verbatim version, and requires less mental effort to use.

glial cells Cells responsible for myelinization of neural fibers.

goodness-of-fit model Thomas and Chess's model, which states that an effective match, or "good fit," between child-rearing practices and a child's temperament leads to favorable development and psychological adjustment. When a "poor fit" exists, the outcome is distorted development and maladjustment.

grammar The component of language concerned with *syntax*, the rules by which words are arranged into sentences, and *morphology*, the use of grammatical markers that indicate number, tense, case, person, gender, active or passive voice, and other meanings.

grammatical morphemes Small markers that change the meaning of sentences, as in "John's dog" and "he *is* eating."

growth hormone (GH) A pituitary hormone that affects the development of all body tissues except the central nervous system and the genitals.

guided participation A concept that accounts for children's diverse opportunities to learn through involvement with others. Calls attention to both adult and child contributions to a cooperative dialogue, without conveying a particular model of communication.

H

habituation A gradual reduction in the strength of a response due to repetitive stimulation.

heritability estimate A statistic that measures the extent to which individual differences in complex traits in a specific population are due to genetic factors.

heteronomous morality Piaget's first stage of moral development, in which children view rules as handed down by authorities, as having a permanent existence, as unchangeable, and as requiring strict obedience.

heterozygous Having two different alleles at the same place on a pair of chromosomes. Distinguished from *homozygous*.

hierarchical classification The organization of objects into classes and subclasses on the basis of similarities and differences between the groups.

Home Observation for Measurement of the Environment (HOME) A checklist for gathering information about the quality of children's home lives through observation and parental interviews. Infancy, preschool, and middle childhood versions exist.

homozygous Having two identical alleles at the same place on a pair of chromosomes. Distinguished from *heterozygous*.

horizontal décalage Development within a Piagetian stage. Gradual mastery of logical concepts during the concrete operational stage is an example.

hostile aggression Aggression intended to harm another person. Distinguished from *instrumental aggression*.

human development An interdisciplinary field of study devoted to understanding all changes that human beings experience throughout the lifespan.

hypothalamus A structure located at the base of the brain that initiates and regulates pituitary secretions.

hypothesis A prediction about behavior drawn from a theory.

hypothetico-deductive reasoning A formal operational problem-solving strategy in which adolescents begin with a general theory of all possible factors that could affect an outcome in a problem and deduce specific hypotheses, which they test in an orderly fashion.

I

I-self A sense of self as subject, or agent, who is separate from but attends to and acts on objects and other people. Distinguished from *me-self*.

identical, or monozygotic, twins Twins that result when a zygote that has started to duplicate separates into two clusters of cells that develop into two individuals with the same genetic makeup. Distinguished from *fraternal*, or *dizygotic, twins*.

identity A well-organized conception of the self made up of values, beliefs, and goals to which the individual is solidly committed.

identity achievement The identity status of individuals who have explored and committed themselves to self-chosen values and goals. Distinguished from *moratorium, identity foreclosure*, and *identity diffusion*.

identity diffusion The identity status of individuals who do not have firm commitments to values and goals and are not actively trying to reach them. Distinguished from *identity achievement, moratorium*, and *identity foreclosure*.

identity foreclosure The identity status of individuals who have accepted ready-made values and goals that authority figures have chosen for them. Distinguished from *identity achievement, moratorium*, and *identity diffusion*.

illocutionary intent What a speaker means to say, regardless of whether the form of the utterance is perfectly consistent with it.

imaginary audience Adolescents' belief that they are the focus of everyone else's attention and concern.

imitation Learning by copying the behavior of another person. Also called modeling or observational learning. Also called *modeling* or *observational learning.*

incremental view of ability The view that ability can be improved through trying hard. Distinguished from *entity view of ability.*

independent variable The variable manipulated by the researcher in an experiment by randomly assigning participants to treatment conditions. Distinguished from *dependent variable.*

individualistic societies Societies in which people think of themselves as separate entities and are largely concerned with their own personal needs. Distinguished from *collectivist societies.*

induction A type of discipline in which the effects of the child's misbehavior on others are communicated to the child.

infant mortality The number of deaths in the first year of life per 1,000 live births.

infantile amnesia The inability of older children and adults to remember experiences that happened before age 3.

information processing An approach that views the human mind as a symbol-manipulating system through which information flows and that regards cognitive development as a continuous process.

informed consent The right of research participants, including children, to have explained to them, in language they can understand, all aspects of a study that may affect their willingness to participate.

inhibited, or shy, child A child whose temperament is such that he or she reacts negatively to and withdraws from novel stimuli. Distinguished from *uninhibited, or sociable, child.*

inner self Awareness of the self's private thoughts and imaginings.

instrumental aggression Aggression aimed at obtaining an object, privilege, or space with no deliberate intent to harm another person. Distinguished from *hostile aggression.*

instrumental traits Masculine-stereotyped personality traits that reflect competence, rationality, and assertiveness. Distinguished from *expressive traits.*

intelligence quotient (IQ) A score that permits an individual's performance on an intelligence test to be compared to the typical performance of same-age individuals.

intentional, or goal-directed, behavior A sequence of actions in which schemes are deliberately combined to solve a problem.

interactional synchrony A sensitively tuned "emotional dance," in which the caregiver responds to infant signals in a well-timed, appropriate fashion and both partners match emotional states, especially the positive ones.

intermodal perception Perception that combines information from more than one modality, or sensory system.

internal working model A set of expectations derived from early caregiving experiences concerning the availability of attachment figures, their likelihood of providing support during times of stress, and the self's interaction with those figures that affect all future close relationships.

internalization The process of adopting societal standards for right action as one's own.

intersubjectivity A process whereby two participants who begin a task with different understandings arrive at a shared understanding.

invariant features Features that remain stable in a constantly changing perceptual world.

investment theory of creativity Sternberg and Lubart's theory, in which investment in novel projects depends on the availability of diverse intellectual, personality, motivational, and environmental resources, each of which must be present at some minimum level.

invisible displacement task A type of object-hiding task in which the object is moved from one place to another while out of sight.

J

joint custody A child custody arrangement following divorce in which the court grants both parents equal say in important decisions about the child's upbringing.

K

kinetic depth cues Depth cues created by movements of the body or of objects in the environment.

kinship studies Studies comparing the characteristics of family members to determine the importance of heredity in complex human characteristics.

kwashiorkor A disease usually appearing between 1 and 3 years of age that is caused by a diet low in protein. Symptoms include an enlarged belly, swollen feet, hair loss, skin rash, and irritable, listless behavior.

L

laboratory experiment An experiment conducted in the laboratory, permitting the maximum possible control over treatment conditions.

language acquisition device (LAD) In Chomsky's theory, a biologically based, innate module for picking up language that permits children, as soon as they have acquired sufficient vocabulary, to combine words into grammatically consistent, novel utterances and to understand the meaning of sentences they hear.

language-making capacity (LMC) According to Slobin's theory, a built-in set of cognitive procedures for analyzing language that supports the discovery of grammatical regularities.

lanugo A white, downy hair that covers the entire body of the fetus, helping the vernix stick to the skin.

lateralization Specialization of functions of the two hemispheres of the cortex.

learned helplessness Attributions that credit success to external factors, such as luck, and failure to low ability. Leads to low expectancies of success and anxious loss of control in the face of challenging tasks. Distinguished from *mastery-oriented attributions.*

learning disabilities Specific learning disorders (for, example, in reading, writing, or math computation) that result in poor school achievement, despite an average or above-average IQ.

Level I–Level II theory Jensen's controversial theory, which states that ethnic and social-class differences in IQ are due to genetic differences in higher-order, abstract forms of intelligence (Level II) rather than basic memory skills (Level I).

levels-of-processing model A model of mental functioning in which retention of information depends on the depth to which it is processed. Attentional resources determine processing capacity.

lexical contrast theory A theory that assumes two principles govern semantic development: conventionality, children's natural desire to acquire the words and word meanings of their language community; and contrast, children's discovery of meanings by contrasting new words with ones they know and assigning them to gaps in their vocabulary.

logical necessity A basic property of propositional thought, which specifies that the validity of conclusions drawn from premises rests on the rules of logic, not on real-world confirmation. A grasp of logical necessity permits individuals to reason from premises that contradict reality or their own beliefs.

long-term memory The part of the mental system that contains our permanent knowledge base.

longitudinal design A research design in which one group of participants is studied repeatedly at different ages. Distinguished from *cross-sectional design.*

longitudinal-sequential design A research design with both longitudinal and cross-sectional components in which groups of participants born in different years are followed over time.

M

macrosystem In ecological systems theory, the values, laws, customs, and resources of a culture that influence experiences and interactions at inner levels of the environment.

mainstreaming Placement of pupils with learning difficulties in regular classrooms for part of the school day.

make-believe play A type of play in which children pretend, acting out everyday and imaginary activities.

marasmus A disease usually appearing in the first year of life that is caused by a diet low in all essential nutrients. Leads to a wasted condition of the body.

mastery-oriented attributions Attributions that credit success to high ability and failure to insufficient effort. Leads to high expectancies of success and a willingness to approach challenging tasks. Distinguished from *learned helplessness.*

matching A procedure in which participants are measured ahead of time on the factor in question, enabling researchers to assign participants with similar characteristics in equal numbers to each treatment condition in an experiment. Ensures that groups will be equivalent on factors likely to distort the results.

matters of personal choice Concerns that do not violate rights or harm others, are not socially regulated, and therefore are up to the individual. Distinguished from *moral imperatives* and *social conventions.*

maturation A genetically determined, naturally unfolding course of growth.

me-self A reflective observer who treats the self as an object of knowledge and evaluation. Distinguished from *I-self.*

meiosis The process of cell division through which gametes are formed and in which the number of chromosomes in each cell is halved.

menarche First menstruation.

mental representation An internal image of an absent object or a past event.

mental strategies Learned procedures that operate on and transform information, thereby increasing the efficiency and flexibility of thinking and that chances that information will be retained.

mesosystem In ecological systems theory, connections between children's immediate settings.

metacognition Awareness and understanding of various aspects of thought.

metalinguistic awareness The ability to think about language as a system.

microgenetic design A research design in which change is tracked from the time it begins until it stabilizes, as participants master an everyday or novel task.

microsystem In ecological systems theory, the activities and interaction patterns in the child's immediate surroundings.

mild mental retardation Children whose IQs fall between 55 and 70 and who also show problems in adaptive behavior.

mitosis The process of cell duplication, in which each new cell receives an exact copy of the original chromosomes.

model of strategy choice Siegler's evolutionary theory of cognitive development, which states that variation and selection characterize children's mental strategies, yielding adaptive problem-solving techniques and an overlapping-waves pattern of development.

modifier genes Genes that can enhance or dilute the effects of alleles controlling particular traits.

modular view of the mind A domain-specific, nativist view that regards the mind as a collection of separate modules—genetically prewired, independent, special purpose neural systems, each of which triggers new understandings with exposure to stimulation.

monozygotic twins See *identical twins.*

moral dilemma A conflict situation presented to research participants, who are asked to decide both what the main actor should do and why. Used to assess the development of moral reasoning.

moral imperatives Standards that protect people's rights and welfare. Distinguished from *social conventions* and *matters of personal choice.*

moral self-regulation The ability to monitor one's own conduct, constantly adjusting it as circumstances present opportunities to violate inner standards.

moratorium The identity status of individuals who are exploring alternatives in an effort to find values and goals to guide their life. Distinguished from *identity achievement, identity foreclosure,* and *identity diffusion.*

mutation A sudden but permanent change in a segment of DNA.

myelinization A process in which neural fibers are coated with an insulating fatty sheath (called myelin) that improves the efficiency of message transfer.

N

nativist approach An approach to cognitive development in which children are born with substantial innate knowledge, which guides their interpretations of reality and gets cognitive development off to a speedy, efficient start. Distinguished from *constructivist approach.*

natural experiment A research design in which the investigator studies already existing treatments in natural settings by carefully selecting groups of participants with similar characteristics.

natural, or prepared, childbirth An approach designed to reduce pain and medical intervention and to make childbirth a rewarding experience for parents.

naturalistic observation A method in which the researcher goes into the natural environment to observe the behavior of interest. Distinguished from *structured observation.*

nature–nurture controversy Disagreement among theorists about whether genetic or environmental factors are more important determinants of development and behavior.

neglected children Children who are seldom chosen, either positively or negatively, on sociometric measures of peer acceptance. Distinguished from *popular, rejected,* and *controversial children.*

neo-Piagetian theory A theory that reinterprets Piaget's stages within an information-processing framework.

Neonatal Behavioral Assessment Scale (NBAS) A test developed to assess the behavioral status of the infant during the newborn period.

neurons Nerve cells that store and transmit information in the brain.

niche-picking A type of genetic–environmental correlation in which individuals actively choose environments that complement their heredity.

noble savage Rousseau's view of the child as naturally endowed with a sense of right and wrong and with an innate plan for orderly, healthy growth.

non-rapid-eye-movement (NREM) sleep A "regular" sleep state in which the body is quiet and heart rate, breathing, and brain wave activity are slow and regular. Distinguished from *rapid-eye-movement (REM) sleep.*

nonorganic failure to thrive A growth disorder usually present by 18 months of age that is caused by lack of affection and stimulation.

nonshared environmental influences Environmental influences that make children living in the same family different from one another. Distinguished from *shared environmental influences.*

nonsocial activity Unoccupied, onlooker behavior and solitary play. Distinguished from *parallel play, associative play,* and *cooperative play.*

normative approach An approach in which age-related averages are computed to represent the typical child's development.

nuclear family unit The part of the family that consists of parents and their children.

O

obesity A greater-than-20-percent increase over average body weight, based on the child's age, sex, and physical build.

object permanence The understanding that objects continue to exist when they are out of sight.

observer bias The tendency of observers who are aware of the purposes of a study to see and record what is expected rather than participants' actual behaviors.

observer influence The tendency of participants to react to the presence of an observer and behave in unnatural ways.

open classroom A classroom based on the educational philosophy that children are active agents in their own development and learn at different rates. Teachers share decision making with pupils. Pupils are evaluated in relation to their own prior development. Distinguished from *traditional classroom.*

operant conditioning A form of learning in which a spontaneous behavior is followed by a stimulus that changes the probability that the behavior will occur again.

operations   In Piaget's theory, mental representations of actions that obey logical rules.

optical flow   Movements in the visual field signaling that the body is in motion, leading to postural adjustments so the body remains upright.

oral rehydration therapy (ORT)   A treatment for diarrhea, in which sick children are given a glucose, salt, and water solution that quickly replaces fluids the body loses.

ordinality   A principle specifying order (more-than and less-than) relationships between quantities.

organization   In Piaget's theory, the internal rearrangement and linking together of schemes so they form a strongly interconnected cognitive system. In information processing, the memory strategy of grouping information into meaningful chunks.

overextension   An early vocabulary error in which a word is applied too broadly, to a wider collection of objects and events than is appropriate. Distinguished from *underextension*.

overregularization   Application of regular grammatical rules to words that are exceptions.

overt aggression   A form of hostile aggression that harms others through physical injury or the threat of such injury—for example, hitting, kicking, or threatening to beat up a peer.

P

parallel play   A form of limited social participation in which the child plays near other children with similar materials but does not try to influence their behavior. Distinguished from *nonsocial activity, associative play,* and *cooperative play.*

peer group   Peers who form a social unit by generating unique values and standards of behavior and a social structure of leaders and followers.

peer victimization   A destructive form of peer interaction in which certain children become frequent targets of verbal and physical attacks or other forms of abuse.

peer-only rearing   A type of study in which nonhuman primates are reared together from birth without adults.

perception bound   Being easily distracted by the concrete, perceptual appearance of objects.

permissive style   A parenting style that is responsive but undemanding. An overly tolerant approach to child rearing. Distinguished from *authoritative, authoritarian,* and *uninvolved styles.*

person perception   The way individuals size up the attributes of people with whom they are familiar in everyday life.

personal fable   Adolescents' belief that they are special and unique. Leads them to conclude that others cannot possibly understand their thoughts and feelings. May promote a sense of invulnerability to danger.

perspective taking   The capacity to imagine what other people may be thinking and feeling.

phenotype   The individual's physical and behavioral characteristics, which are determined by both genetic and environmental factors.

phoneme   The smallest sound unit with distinctive features that can signal a difference in meaning.

phonological store   A special part of working memory that permits us to retain speech-based information. Supports early vocabulary development.

phonology   The component of language concerned with the rules governing the structure and sequencing of speech sounds.

physical causality   The causal action one object exerts on another through contact.

pictorial depth cues   Depth cues such as those that artists use to make a painting look three-dimensional, including receding lines, texture changes, and overlapping objects.

pincer grasp   The well-coordinated grasp emerging at the end of the first year, in which thumb and forefinger are used opposably.

pituitary gland   A gland located near the base of the brain that releases hormones affecting physical growth.

placenta   The organ that separates the mother's bloodstream from the embryo's or fetus's bloodstream but permits exchange of nutrients and waste products.

planning   Thinking out a sequence of acts ahead of time and allocating attention accordingly to reach a goal.

pleiotropism   The influence of a single gene on more than one characteristic.

polygenic inheritance   A pattern of inheritance involving many genes that applies to characteristics that vary continuously among people.

popular children   Children who get many positive votes on sociometric measures of peer acceptance. Distinguished from *rejected, controversial,* and *neglected children.*

postconventional level   Kohlberg's highest level of moral development, in which individuals define morality in terms of abstract principles and values that apply to all situations and societies.

practical intelligence   Abilities apparent in the real world, not in testing situations, that involve "knowing how" rather than "knowing that."

practice effects   Changes in participants' natural responses as a result of repeated testing.

pragmatics   The component of language concerned with how to engage in effective and appropriate communication with others.

preconventional level   Kohlberg's first level of moral development, in which moral understanding is based on rewards, punishment, and the power of authority figures.

preformationism   Medieval view of the child as a miniature adult.

prenatal diagnostic methods   Medical procedures that permit detection of developmental problems before birth.

preoperational stage Piaget's second stage, in which rapid development of representation takes place. However, thought is not yet logical. Spans the years from 2 to 7.

prereaching The poorly coordinated, primitive reaching movements of newborn babies.

preterm Infants born several weeks or more before their due date.

primary mental abilities In Thurstone's theory of intelligence, seven distinct mental abilities identified through factor analysis (verbal meaning, perceptual speed, reasoning, number, rote memory, word fluency, and spatial visualization).

primary sexual characteristics Physical features that involve the reproductive organs (ovaries, uterus, and vagina in females; penis, scrotum, and testes in males).

principle of mutual exclusivity The assumption by children in the early stages of vocabulary growth that words refer to entirely separate (nonoverlapping) categories.

private speech Self-directed speech that children use to plan and guide their own behavior.

production In language development, the words and word combinations that children use. Distinguished from *comprehension*.

production deficiency The failure to produce a mental strategy when it could be helpful. Distinguished from *control* and *utilization deficiencies*.

programmed cell death Death of many surrounding neurons during the peak period of development in any brain area to make room for growth of neural fibers that form synaptic connections.

Project Head Start A federal program that provides low-income children with a year or two of preschool, along with nutritional and medical services, and that encourages parent involvement in children's development.

propositional thought A type of formal operational reasoning in which adolescents evaluate the logic of verbal statements without referring to real-world circumstances.

prosocial, or altruistic, behavior Actions that benefit another person without any expected reward for the self.

protection from harm The right of research participants to be protected from physical or psychological harm.

protodeclarative A preverbal gesture through which infants make an assertion about an object by touching it, holding it up, or pointing to it.

protoimperative A preverbal gesture in which infants point, reach, and make sounds to get another person to do something.

proximodistal trend An organized pattern of physical growth and motor control that proceeds from the center of the body outward.

psychoanalytic perspective An approach to personality development introduced by Sigmund Freud that assumes children move through a series of stages in which they confront conflicts between biological drives and social expectations. The way these conflicts are resolved determines psychological adjustment.

psychometric approach A product-oriented approach to cognitive development that focuses on the construction of tests to assess mental abilities.

psychophysiological methods Methods that measure the relationship between physiological processes and behavior. Among the most common are measures of autonomic nervous system activity (such as heart rate and respiration) and measures of brain functioning (such as the electroencephalogram [EEG], event-related potentials [ERPs], and functional magnetic resonance imaging [fMRI]).

psychosexual theory Freud's theory, which emphasizes that how parents manage their child's sexual and aggressive drives during the first few years is crucial for healthy personality development.

psychosocial theory Erikson's theory, which expands Freud's theory by emphasizing that the ego is a positive force in development, ensuring that individuals acquire attitudes and skills that help them become active, contributing members of their society. Recognizes the lifespan nature of development and the impact of culture.

puberty Biological changes during adolescence that lead to an adult-sized body and sexual maturity.

public policy Laws and government programs designed to improve current conditions.

punishment In operant conditioning, removing a desirable stimulus or presenting an unpleasant one to decrease the occurrence of a response.

 R

random assignment An evenhanded procedure for assigning participants to treatment groups, such as drawing numbers out of a hat or flipping a coin. Increases the chances that participants' characteristics will be equally distributed across treatment conditions in an experiment.

range of reaction Each person's unique, genetically determined response to a range of environmental conditions.

rapid-eye-movement (REM) sleep An "irregular" sleep state in which brain wave activity is similar to that of the waking state; eyes dart beneath the lids; heart rate, blood pressure, and breathing are uneven; and slight body movements occur. Distinguished from *non-rapid-eye-movement (NREM) sleep*.

realism A view of rules as external features of reality rather than cooperative principles that can be modified at will. Characterizes Piaget's heteronomous stage.

recall A type of memory that involves generating a mental image of an absent stimulus. Distinguished from *recognition*.

recasts Adult responses that restructure a child's incorrect speech into appropriate form.

reciprocal teaching A method of teaching based on Vygotsky's theory in which a teacher and two to four pupils form a collaborative learning group. Dialogues occur that create a zone of proximal development in which reading comprehension improves.

reciprocity A standard of fairness in which individuals express the same concern for the welfare of others as they do for themselves.

recognition A type of memory that involves noticing whether a stimulus is identical or similar to one previously experienced. Distinguished from *recall*.

reconstruction A type of memory in which complex, meaningful material is reinterpreted in terms of existing knowledge.

recursive thought The self-embedded form of perspective taking that involves thinking about what another person is thinking.

referential communication skills The ability to produce clear verbal messages and to recognize when the meaning of others' messages is unclear.

referential style A style of early language learning in which toddlers use language mainly to label objects. Distinguished from *expressive style*.

reflex An inborn, automatic response to a particular form of stimulation.

rehearsal The memory strategy of repeating information.

reinforcer In operant conditioning, a stimulus that increases the occurrence of a response.

rejected children Children who are actively disliked and get many negative votes on sociometric measures of peer acceptance. Distinguished from *popular, controversial,* and *neglected children*.

rejected-aggressive children A subgroup of rejected children who engage in high rates of conflict, hostility, and hyperactive, inattentive, and impulsive behavior. Distinguished from *rejected-withdrawn children*.

rejected-withdrawn children A subgroup of rejected children who are passive and socially awkward. Distinguished from *rejected-aggressive children*.

relational aggression A form of hostile aggression that damages another's peer relationships, as in social exclusion or rumor spreading.

reliability The consistency, or repeatability, of measures of behavior.

remembered self Life-story narrative constructed from conversations with adults about the past that leads to an autobiographical memory.

resiliency The ability to adapt effectively in the face of adverse life circumstances.

resistant attachment The quality of insecure attachment characterizing infants who remain close to the parent before departure and display angry, resistive behavior when she returns. Distinguished from *secure, avoidant,* and *disorganized-disoriented attachment*.

reticular formation A structure in the brain stem that maintains alertness and consciousness.

reversibility The ability to mentally go through a series of steps and then reverse direction, returning to the starting point. In Piaget's theory, part of every logical operation.

Rh factor A protein that, when present in the fetus's blood but not in the mother's, can cause the mother to build up antibodies if the fetus's blood enters the mother's bloodstream. If these antibodies return to the fetus's system, they destroy red blood cells, reducing the oxygen supply to organs and tissues.

risks-versus-benefits ratio A comparison of the costs of a research study to participants in terms of inconvenience and possible psychological or physical injury against its value for advancing knowledge and improving conditions of life. Used in assessing the ethics of research.

rough-and-tumble play A form of peer interaction involving friendly chasing and play-fighting that, in our evolutionary past, may have been important for the development of fighting skill.

 S

scaffolding A changing quality of support over a teaching session in which adults adjust the assistance they provide to fit the child's current level of performance. Direct instruction is offered when a task is new; less help is provided as competence increases.

scheme In Piaget's theory, a specific structure, or organized way of making sense of experience, that changes with age.

scripts General representations of what occurs and when it occurs in a particular situation. A basic means through which children organize and interpret familiar everyday experiences.

secondary sexual characteristics Features visible on the outside of the body that serve as signs of sexual maturity but do not involve the reproductive organs (for example, breast development in females, appearance of underarm and pubic hair in both sexes).

secular trends in physical growth Changes in body size and rate of growth from one generation to the next.

secure attachment The quality of attachment characterizing infants who are distressed by parental separation and easily comforted by the parent when she returns. Distinguished from *resistant, avoidant,* and *disorganized-disoriented attachment*.

secure base The use of the familiar caregiver as a base from which the infant confidently explores the environment and to which the infant returns for emotional support.

selective attrition Selective loss of participants during an investigation, resulting in a biased sample.

self-care children Children who regularly look after themselves during after-school hours.

self-concept The set of attributes, abilities, attitudes, and values that an individual believes defines who he or she is.

self-conscious emotions Emotions that involve injury to or enhancement of the sense of self. Examples are shame, embarrassment, guilt, envy, and pride.

self-control Inhibiting an impulse to engage in behavior that violates a moral standard.

self-esteem The aspect of self-concept that involves judgments about one's own worth and the feelings associated with those judgments.

self-recognition Perception of the self as a separate being, distinct from other people and objects.

semantic bootstrapping Relying on the semantic properties of words to figure out basic grammatical regularities.

semantic memory The vast, intricately organized knowledge system in long-term memory.

semantics The component of language concerned with understanding the meaning of words and word combinations.

sensitive caregiving Caregiving involving prompt, consistent, and appropriate responding to infant signals.

sensitive period A time that is optimal for certain capacities to emerge and in which the individual is especially responsive to environmental influences.

sensorimotor stage Piaget's first stage, during which infants "think" with their eyes, ears, hands, and other sensorimotor equipment. Spans the first 2 years of life.

sensory register The first part of the mental system, where sights and sounds are represented directly but held only briefly.

separation anxiety An infant's distressed reaction to the departure of the familiar caregiver.

serial position effect In memory tasks involving lists of items, the tendency to remember those at the beginning and the end better than those in the middle. Over time, items at the end decay, whereas those at the beginning continue to be retained.

seriation The ability to arrange items along a quantitative dimension, such as length or weight.

sex chromosomes The twenty-third pair of chromosomes, which determines the sex of the child. In females, this pair is called XX; in males, it is called XY.

sex-related In this book, characterization of differences between males and females in which no inferences are being made about the source of the difference.

shading A conversational strategy in which a change of topic is initiated gradually by modifying the focus of discussion.

shape constancy Perception of an object's shape as stable, despite changes in the shape of its retinal image.

shared environmental influences Environmental influences that pervade the general atmosphere of the home and affect all children living in it to the same extent.

short-term memory See *working, or short-term, memory.*

size constancy Perception of an object's size as stable, despite changes in the size of its retinal image.

skeletal age An estimate of physical maturity based on development of the bones of the body.

skipped-generation family A family structure in which children live with grandparents but apart from parents.

slow-to-warm-up child A child whose temperament is such that he or she is inactive, shows mild, low-key reactions to environmental stimuli, is negative in mood, and adjusts slowly to new experiences. Distinguished from *easy child* and *difficult child.*

small for date Infants whose birth weight is below normal when length of pregnancy is taken into account. May be full term or preterm.

social cognition Thinking about the self, other people, and social relationships.

social comparisons Judgments of one's own abilities, behavior, appearance, and other characteristics in relation to those of others.

social conventions Customs determined solely by consensus, such as table manners, dress styles, and rituals of social interaction. Distinguished from *moral imperatives* and *matters of personal choice.*

social learning theory An approach that emphasizes the role of modeling, or observational learning, in the development of behavior.

social policy Any planned set of actions directed at solving a social problem or attaining a social goal.

social problem solving Resolving social conflicts in ways that are both acceptable to others and beneficial to the self. Involves encoding and interpreting social cues, clarifying a social goal, generating and evaluating strategies, and enacting a response.

social referencing Relying on another person's emotional reaction to appraise an uncertain situation.

social smile The smile evoked by the stimulus of the human face. First appears between 6 and 10 weeks.

social systems perspective A view of the family as a complex set of interacting relationships influenced by the larger social context.

sociobiology A field that assumes many morally relevant prosocial behaviors are rooted in our genetic heritage and have evolved because of their survival value.

sociocultural theory Vygotsky's theory, in which children acquire the ways of thinking and behaving that make up a community's culture through cooperative dialogues with more knowledgeable members of that society.

sociodramatic play The make-believe play with others that is under way by age 2½.

socioeconomic status (SES) A measure of a family's social position and economic well-being that combines three interrelated, but not completely overlapping, variables: (1) years of education and (2) the prestige of and skill required by one's job, both of which measure social status; and (3) income, which measures economic status.

sociometric techniques Self-report measures that ask peers to evaluate one another's likability.

Sociomoral Reflection Measure–Short Form (SRM–SF) A questionnaire for assessing moral understanding in which individuals rate the importance of moral values addressed by brief questions and explain their ratings. Does not require research participants to read and think about lengthy moral dilemmas.

specific factor, or "s" In Spearman's theory of intelligence, a mental ability factor that is unique to a particular task.

specimen record An observational procedure in which the researcher records a description of the participant's entire stream of behavior for a specified time period.

speech registers Language adaptations to social expectations.

spermarche First ejaculation of seminal fluid.

stability versus change Disagreement among theorists about whether stable individual differences emerge early and persist due to heredity and early experience, or whether change is possible and likely if new experiences support it.

stage A qualitative change in thinking, feeling, and behaving that characterizes a particular time period of development.

Stanford-Binet Intelligence Scale An individually administered intelligence test that is the modern descendent of Alfred Binet's first successful test for children. Measures general intelligence and four factors: verbal reasoning, quantitative reasoning, abstract/visual (spatial) reasoning, and short-term memory.

states rather than transformations The tendency to treat the initial and final states in a problem as completely unrelated.

states of arousal Different degrees of sleep and wakefulness.

store model Model of mental functioning that views information as being held in three parts of the system for processing: the sensory register, short-term memory, and long-term memory.

Strange Situation A procedure involving short separations from and reunions with the parent that assesses the quality of the attachment bond.

stranger anxiety The infant's expression of fear in response to unfamiliar adults. Appears in many babies after 7 months of age.

structured interview A method in which the researcher asks each participant the same questions in the same way.

structured observation A method in which the researcher sets up a situation that evokes the behavior of interest and observes it in a laboratory. Distinguished from *naturalistic observation*.

sudden infant death syndrome (SIDS) The unexpected death, usually during the night, of an infant under 1 year of age that remains unexplained after thorough investigation.

sympathy Feelings of concern or sorrow for another's plight.

synapses The gap between neurons, across which chemical messages are sent.

synaptic pruning Loss of connective fibers by seldom-stimulated neurons, thereby returning them to an uncommitted state so they can support the development of future skills.

syntactic bootstrapping Observing how words are used syntactically, in the structure of sentences, to deduce their meanings.

T

tabula rasa Locke's view of the child as a blank slate whose character is shaped by experience.

telegraphic speech Children's two-word utterances that, like a telegram, leave out smaller and less important words.

television literacy The task of learning television's specialized symbolic code of conveying information.

temperament Stable individual differences in quality and intensity of emotional reaction, activity level, attention, and emotional self-regulation.

teratogen Any environmental agent that causes damage during the prenatal period.

theory An orderly, integrated set of statements that describes, explains, and predicts behavior.

theory of mind A coherent understanding of people as mental beings, which children revise as they encounter new evidence. Includes knowledge of mental activity and awareness that people can have different perceptions, thoughts, and feelings about the same event.

theory of multiple intelligences Gardner's theory, which identifies eight independent intelligences on the basis of distinct sets of processing operations applied in culturally meaningful activities (linguistic, logico-mathematical, musical, spatial, bodily-kinesthetic, naturalist, interpersonal, intrapersonal).

three-stratum theory of intelligence Carroll's theory, which represents the structure of intelligence as a pyramid, with "g" at the top; eight broad, biologically based abilities at the second stratum; and narrower manifestations of these abilities at the lowest stratum that result from experience with particular tasks. The most comprehensive classification of mental abilities to be confirmed by factor-analytic research.

thyroxine A hormone released by the thyroid gland that is necessary for central nervous system development and body growth.

time out A form of mild punishment in which children are removed from the immediate setting until they are ready to act appropriately.

time sampling An observational procedure in which the researcher records whether or not certain behaviors occur during a sample of short time intervals.

traditional classroom A classroom based on the educational philosophy that children are passive learners who acquire information presented by teachers. Pupils are evaluated on the basis of how well they keep pace with a uniform set of standards for all pupils in their grade. Distinguished from *open classroom*.

transductive reasoning Reasoning from particular to particular, instead of from general to particular or particular to general.

transitive inference The ability to seriate—or arrange items along a quantitative dimension—mentally.

triarchic theory of intelligence Sternberg's theory, which states that information processing skills, prior experience with tasks, and contextual (or cultural) factors interact to determine intelligent behavior.

turnabout A conversational strategy in which the speaker not only comments on what has just been said but also adds a request to get the partner to respond again.

U

ulnar grasp The clumsy grasp of the young infant, in which the fingers close against the palm.

umbilical cord The long cord connecting the prenatal organism to the placenta that delivers nutrients and removes waste products.

unconditioned response UCR) In classical conditioning, a reflexive response that is produced by an unconditioned stimulus (UCS).

unconditioned stimulus (UCS) In classical conditioning, a stimulus that leads to a reflexive response.

underextension An early vocabulary error in which a word is applied too narrowly, to a smaller number of objects or events than is appropriate. Distinguished from *overextension*.

uninhibited, or sociable, child A child whose temperament is such that he or she displays positive emotion to and approaches novel stimuli. Distinguished from *inhibited, or shy, child*.

uninvolved style A parenting style that is both undemanding and unresponsive. Reflects minimal commitment to child rearing. Distinguished from *authoritative, authoritarian,* and *permissive styles*.

utilization deficiency The failure of performance to improve after consistently using a mental strategy. Distinguished from *control* and *production deficiencies*.

V

validity The extent to which methods in a research study accurately measure what the investigator set out to measure.

velocity curve A growth curve that plots the average amount of growth at each yearly interval for a sample of children. Clarifies the timing of growth spurts.

vernix A white, cheeselike substance covering the fetus that prevents the skin from chapping due to constant exposure to the amniotic fluid.

violation-of-expectation method A method for studying physical reasoning in which researchers habituate babies to a physical event and then determine whether they dishabituate to (look longer at) a possible event (a variation of the first event that conforms to physical laws) or an impossible event (a variation that violates physical laws). Dishabituation to the impossible event suggests surprise at a deviation from expected object actions and, therefore, an understanding of that aspect of physical reality.

visual acuity Fineness of visual discrimination.

visual cliff An apparatus used to study depth perception in infants. Consists of a glass-covered table and a central platform, from which babies are encouraged to crawl. Patterns placed beneath the glass create the appearance of a shallow and deep side.

W

washout effect The loss of IQ and achievement gains resulting from early intervention within a few years after the program ends.

Wechsler Intelligence Scale for Children–III (WISC–III) An individually administered intelligence test that includes both a measure of general intelligence and a variety of verbal and performance scores.

Wernicke's area A language structure located in the temporal lobe of the cortex that is responsible for interpreting language.

whole-language approach An approach to beginning reading instruction that parallels children's natural language learning and keeps reading materials whole and meaningful. Distinguished from *basic-skills approach*.

working, or short-term, memory The conscious part of the mental system, where we actively "work" on a limited amount of information to ensure that it will be retained.

X

X-linked inheritance A pattern of inheritance in which a recessive gene is carried on the X chromosome. Males are more likely to be affected.

Z

zone of proximal development In Vygotsky's theory, a range of tasks that the child cannot yet handle alone but can do with the help of more skilled partners.

zygote The union of sperm and ovum at conception.

A

AARON, R., & POWELL, G. (1982). Feedback practices as a function of teacher and pupil race during reading groups instruction. *Journal of Negro Education, 51,* 50–59.

ABBOTT, K., LEE, P. P., & FLAVELL, J. H. (1998). *Young children's understanding of intention.* Unpublished manuscript.

ABBOTT, S. (1992). Holding on and pushing away: Comparative perspectives on an eastern Kentucky child-rearing practice. *Ethos, 20,* 33–65.

ABBOTTS, B., & OSBORN, L. M. (1993). Immunization status and reasons for immunization delay among children using public health immunization clinics. *American Journal of Diseases of Children, 147,* 965–968.

ABELMAN, R. (1985). Styles of parental disciplinary practices as a mediator of children's learning from prosocial television portrayals. *Child Study Journal, 15,* 131–145.

ABOOD, D. A., & CHANDLER, S. B. (1997). Race and the role of weight, weight change, and body dissatisfaction in eating disorders. *American Journal of Health Behavior, 21,* 21–25.

ABRAMOVITCH, R., FREEDMAN, J. L., HENRY, K., & VAN BRUNSCHOT, M. (1995). Children's capacity to agree to psychological research: Knowledge of risks and benefits and voluntariness. *Ethics & Behavior, 5,* 25–48.

ABRAMOVITCH, R., FREEDMAN, J. L., THODEN, K., & NIKOLICH, C. (1991). Children's capacity to consent to participation in psychological research: Some empirical findings. *Child Development, 62,* 1100–1109.

ACHENBACH, T. M., & HOWELL, C. (1993). Are American children's problems getting worse? A 13-year comparison. *Journal of the American Academy of Child and Adolescent Psychiatry, 32,* 1145–1154.

ACHENBACH, T. M., PHARES, V., HOWELL, C. T., RAUH, V. A., & NURCOMBE, B. (1990). Seven-year outcome of the Vermont intervention program for low-birthweight infants. *Child Development, 61,* 1672–1681.

ACHENBACH, T. M., & WEISZ, J. R. (1975). A longitudinal study of developmental synchrony between conceptual identity, seriation, and transitivity of color, number, and length. *Child Development, 46,* 840–848.

ACKER, M. M., & O'LEARY, S. G. (1996). Inconsistency of mothers' feedback and toddlers' misbehavior and negative affect. *Journal of Abnormal Child Psychology, 24,* 703–714.

ACKERMAN, B. P. (1978). Children's understanding of speech acts in unconventional frames. *Child Development, 49,* 311–318.

ACKERMAN, B. P. (1993). Children's understanding of the speaker's meaning in referential communication. *Journal of Experimental Child Psychology, 55,* 56–86.

ACKERMAN, S. H., KELLER, S. E., SCHLEIFER, S. J., SHINDLEDECKER, R. D., CAMERINO, M., HOFER, M. A., WEINER, H., & STEIN, M. (1988). Premature maternal separation and lymphocyte function. *Brain and Behavior Immunology, 2,* 161–165.

ACREDOLO, L. P., & GOODWYN, S. W. (1990). Sign language in babies: The significance of symbolic gesturing for understanding language development. In R. Vasta (Ed.), *Annals of child development* (Vol. 7, pp. 1–42). Greenwich, CT: JAI Press.

ADAMS, L. B. (1997). An overview of adolescent eating behavior: Barriers to implementing dietary guidelines. In M. S. Jacobson, J. M. Rees, N. H. Golden, & C. E. Irwin (Eds.), *Adolescent nutritional disorders: Prevention and treatment* (pp. 36–48). New York: New York Academy of Sciences.

ADAMS, M. J., TREIMAN, R., & PRESSLEY, M. (1998). Reading, writing, and literacy. In I. E. Sigel & K. A. Renninger (Eds.), *Handbook of child psychology: Vol. 4. Cognition, perception, and language* (5th ed., pp. 275–355). New York: Wiley.

ADLER, P. A., & ADLER, P. (1995). Dynamics of inclusion and exclusion in preadolescent cliques. *Social Psychology Quarterly, 58,* 145–162.

ADOLPH, K. E. (1997). Learning in the development of infant locomotion. *Monographs of the Society for Research in Child Development, 62* (3, Serial No. 251).

ADOLPH, K. E., EPPLER, M. A., & GIBSON, E. J. (1993). Crawling versus walking infants' perception of affordances for locomotion over sloping surfaces. *Child Development, 64,* 1158–1174.

ADOLPH, K. E., VEREIJKEN, B., & DENNY, M. A. (1998). Learning to crawl. *Child Development, 69,* 1299–1312.

AHAJA, K. K., EMERSON, G., SEATON, A., MAMISO, J., & SIMONS, E. G. (1997). Widow's attempt to use her dead husband's sperm. *British Medical Journal, 314,* 143.

AHLSTEN, G., CNATTINGIUS, S., & LINDMARK, G. (1993). Cessation of smoking during pregnancy improves fetal growth and reduces infant morbidity in the neonatal period: A population-based prospective study. *Acta Paediatrica, 82,* 177–181.

AHMED, A., & RUFFMAN, T. (1998). Why do infants make A not B errors in a search task, yet show memory for the location of hidden objects in a nonsearch task? *Developmental Psychology, 34,* 441–453.

AINSWORTH, M. D. S., BLEHAR, M., WATERS, E., & WALL, S. (1978). *Patterns of attachment.* Hillsdale, NJ: Erlbaum.

AKHTAR, N., & TOMASELLO, M. (1996). Two-year-olds learn words for absent objects and actions. *British Journal of Developmental Psychology, 14,* 79–93.

ALAN GUTTMACHER INSTITUTE. (1994). *Sex and America's teenagers.* New York: Author.

ALAN GUTTMACHER INSTITUTE. (1998). *Facts in brief—teen sex and pregnancy.* New York: Author.

ALBERT, R. S. (1994). The achievement of eminence: A longitudinal study of exceptionally gifted boys and their families. In R. F. Subotnik & K. D. Arnold (Eds.), *Beyond Terman: Contemporary studies of giftedness and talent* (pp. 282–315). Norwood, NJ: Ablex.

ALDWIN, C. (1994). *Stress, coping, and development.* New York: Guilford Press.

ALES, K. L., DRUZIN, M. L., & SANTINI, D. L. (1990). Impact of advanced maternal age on the outcome of pregnancy. *Surgery, Gynecology & Obstetrics, 171,* 209–216.

ALESSANDRI, S. M., BENDERSKY, M., & LEWIS, M. (1998). Cognitive functioning in 8- to 18-month-old drug-exposed infants. *Developmental Psychology, 34,* 565–573.

ALESSANDRI, S. M., SULLIVAN, M. W., & LEWIS, M. (1990). Violation of expectancy and frustration in early infancy. *Developmental Psychology, 26,* 738–744.

ALEXANDER, G. M., & HINES, M. (1994). Gender labels and play styles: Their relative contribution to children's selection of playmates. *Child Development, 65,* 869–879.

ALEXANDER, J. M., CARR, M., & SCHWANENFLUGEL, P. J. (1995). Development of metacognition in gifted children: Directions for future research. *Developmental Review, 15,* 1–37.

ALEXANDER, J. M., LUCAS, M. J., RAMIN, S. M., MCINTIRE, D. D., & LEVENO, K. J. (1998). The course of labor with and without epidural analgesia. *American Journal of Obstetrics and Gynecology, 178,* 516–520.

ALEXANDER, J. M., & SCHWANENFLUGEL, P. J. (1996). Development of metacognitive concepts about thinking in gifted and nongifted children: Recent research. *Learning and Individual Differences, 8,* 305–325.

ALFIERI, T., RUBLE, D. N., & HIGGINS, E. T. (1996). Gender stereotypes during adolescence: Developmental changes and the transition to junior high school. *Developmental Psychology, 32,* 1129–1137.

ALIBALI, M. W. (1999). How children change their minds: Strategy change can be gradual or abrupt. *Developmental Psychology, 35,* 127–145.

ALIBALI, M. W., & GOLDIN-MEADOW, S. (1993). Gesture—speech mismatch and mechanisms of learning: What the hands reveal about a child's state of mind. *Cognitive Psychology, 25,* 468–523.

ALLAN, K., & COLTRANE, S. (1996). Gender displaying television commercials: A comparative study of television commercials in the 1950s and 1980s. *Sex Roles, 35,* 185–203.

ALLEN, J. P., HAUSER, S. T., BELL, K. L., & O'CONNOR, T. G. (1994). Longitudinal assessment of autonomy and relatedness in adolescent–family interactions as predictors of adolescent ego development and self-esteem. *Child Development, 65,* 179–194.

ALLEN, J. P., PHILLIBER, S., HERRLING, S., & KUPERMINC, G. P. (1997). Preventing teen pregnancy and academic failure: Experimental evaluation of a developmentally based approach. *Child Development, 64,* 729–742.

ALPERT-GILLIS, L. J., & CONNELL, J. P. (1989). Gender and sex-role influences on children's self-esteem. *Journal of Personality, 57,* 97–114.

ALSAKER, F. D. (1995). Timing of puberty and reactions to pubertal changes. In M. Rutter (Ed.), *Psychosocial disturbances in young people* (pp. 37–82). New York: Cambridge University Press.

ALWITT, L. F., ANDERSON, D. R., LORCH, E. P., & LEVIN, S. R. (1980). Preschool children's visual attention to attributes of television. *Human Communication Research, 7,* 52–67.

AMABILE, T. M. (1982). Children's artistic creativity: Detrimental effects of competition in a field setting. *Personality and Social Psychology Bulletin, 8,* 573–578.

AMABILE, T. M. (1983). *The social psychology of creativity.* New York: Springer-Verlag.

AMATO, P. R., LOOMIS, L. S., & BOOTH, A. (1995). Parental divorce, marital conflict, and offspring well-being during early adulthood. *Social Forces, 73,* 895–915.

AMERICAN ACADEMY OF FAMILY PHYSICIANS. (1997). Decline in SIDS rates. *American Family Physician, 55,* 358–359.

AMERICAN PSYCHIATRIC ASSOCIATION. (1994). *Diagnostic and statistical manual of mental disorders* (4th ed.). Washington, DC: Author.

AMERICAN PSYCHOLOGICAL ASSOCIATION. (1992). Ethical principles of psychologists and code of conduct. *American Psychologist, 44,* 1597–1611.

AMES, C. (1992). Classrooms: Goals, structures, and student motivation. *Journal of Educational Psychology, 84,* 261–271.

ANDERMAN, E. M., & MIDGLEY, C. (1997). Changes in achievement goal orientations, perceived academic competence, and grades across the transition to middle-level schools. *Contemporary Educational Psychology, 22,* 269–298.

ANDERSON, D. A. (1994). Lesbian and gay adolescents: Social and developmental considerations. *High School Journal, 77,* 13–19.

ANDERSON, D. R., COLLINS, P. A., SCHMITT, K. L., & JACOBVITZ, R. S. (1996). Stressful life events and television viewing. *Communication Research, 23,* 243–260.

ANDERSON, D. R., & SMITH, R. (1984). Young children's TV viewing: The problem of cognitive continuity. In F. J. Morrison, C. Lord, & D. P. Keating (Eds.), *Applied developmental psychology* (Vol. 1, pp. 115–163). Orlando, FL: Academic Press.

ANDERSON, E. (1992). *Speaking with style: The sociolinguistic skills of children.* London: Routledge.

ANDERSON, G. C. (1991). Current knowledge about skin-to-skin (kangaroo) care for preterm infants. *Journal of Perinatology, 11,* 216–226.

ANDERSON, H. R., & COOK, D. G. (1997). Passive smoking and sudden infant death syndrome: A review of the epidemiological evidence. *Thoraz, 52,* 1003–1009.

ANDERSSON, B-E. (1989). Effects of public day care—A longitudinal study. *Child Development, 60,* 857–866.

ANDERSSON, B-E. (1992). Effects of day-care on cognitive and socioemotional competence of thirteen-year-old Swedish schoolchildren. *Child Development, 63,* 20–36.

ANGLIN, J. M. (1993). Vocabulary development: A morphological analysis. *Monographs of the Society for Research in Child Development, 58* (10, Serial No. 238).

ANTELL, S. E., & KEATING, D. P. (1983). Perception of numerical invariance in neonates. *Child Development, 54,* 695–701.

ANTILL, J. K., COTTON, S., RUSSELL, G., & GOODNOW, J. J. (1996). Measures of children's sextyping in middle childhood: II. *Australian Journal of Psychology, 48,* 35–44.

ANTONARAKIS, S. E. (1992). The meiotic stage of nondisjunction in trisomy 21: Determination by using DNA polymorphisms. *American Journal of Human Genetics, 50,* 544–550.

APGAR, V. (1953). A proposal for a new method of evaluation in the newborn infant. *Current Research in Anesthesia and Analgesia, 32,* 260–267.

ARCHER, J. (1992). Childhood gender roles: Social content and organization. In H. McGurk (Ed.), *Childhood social development* (pp. 31–62). Hillsdale, NJ: Erlbaum.

ARCHER, J. (1994). Testosterone and aggression: A theoretical review. *Journal of Offender Rehabilitation, 21,* 3–39.

ARCHER, S. L. (1982). The lower age boundaries of identity development. *Child Development, 53,* 1551–1556.

ARCHER, S. L. (1989a). Gender differences in identity development: Issues of process, domain, and timing. *Journal of Adolescence, 2,* 117–138.

ARCHER, S. L. (1989b). The status of identity: Reflections on the need for intervention. *Journal of Adolescence, 12,* 345–359.

ARCHER, S. L., & WATERMAN, A. S. (1990). Varieties of identity diffusions and foreclosures: An exploration of subcategories of the identity statuses. *Journal of Adolescent Research, 5,* 96–111.

ARCHER, S. L., & WATERMAN, A. S. (1994). Adolescent identity development: Contextual perspectives. In C. B. Fisher & R. M. Lerner (Eds.), *Applied develop-*

mental psychology (pp. 76–100). New York: McGraw-Hill.

ARCUS, D., & KAGAN, J. (1995). Temperament and craniofacial variation in the first two years. *Child Development, 66,* 1529–1540.

ARIÈS, P. (1962). *Centuries of childhood.* New York: Random House.

ARNOLD, D. H., LONIGAN, C. J., WHITEHURST, G. J., & EPSTEIN, J. N. (1994). Accelerating language development through picture book reading: Replication and extension to a videotape training format. *Journal of Educational Psychology, 86,* 235–243.

ARNOLD, K. D. (1994). The Illinois Valedictorian Project: Early adult careers of academically talented male and female high school students. In R. F. Subotnik & K. D. Arnold (Eds.), *Beyond Terman: Contemporary longitudinal studies of giftedness and talent* (pp. 24–51). Norwood NJ: Ablex.

ARONSON, M., HAGBERG, B., & GILLBERG, C. (1997). Attention deficits and autistic spectrum problems in children exposed to alcohol during gestation: A follow-up study. *Developmental Medicine & Child Neurology, 39,* 583–587.

ARSENIO, W., & FLEISS, K. (1996). Typical and behaviourally disruptive children's understanding of the emotional consequences of socio-moral events. *British Journal of Developmental Psychology, 14,* 173–186.

ARSENIO, W., & KRAMER, R. (1992). Victimizers and their victims: Children's conceptions of the mixed emotional consequences of moral transgressions. *Child Development, 63,* 915–927.

ARSENIO, W., & LOVER, A. (1995). Children's conceptions of sociomoral affect: Happy victimizers, mixed emotions, and other expectancies. In M. Killen & D. Hart (Eds.), *Morality in everyday life* (pp. 87–128). Cambridge: Cambridge University Press.

ARTERBERRY, M. E. (1993). Development of spatial temporal integration in infancy. *Infant Behavior and Development, 16,* 343–364.

ARTERBERRY, M. E., CRATON, L. G., & YONAS, A. (1993). Infants' sensitivity to motion-carried information for depth and object properties. In C. E. Granrud (Ed.), *Visual perception and cognition in infancy* (pp. 215–234). Hillsdale, NJ: Erlbaum.

ARTERBERRY, M. E., YONAS, A., & BENSEN, A. S. (1989). Self-produced locomotion and the development of responsiveness to linear perspective and texture

gradients. *Developmental Psychology, 25,* 976–982.

ARTMAN, L., & CAHAN, S. (1993). Schooling and the development of transitive inference. *Developmental Psychology, 29,* 753–759.

ASENDORPF, J. B., WARKENTIN, V., & BAUDONNIERE, P. (1996). Self-awareness and other-awareness II: Mirror self-recognition, social contingency awareness, and synchronic imitation. *Developmental Psychology, 32,* 313–321.

ASHER, S. R., & ROSE, A. J. (1997). Promoting children's social-emotional adjustment with peers. In P. Salovey & D. J. Sluyter (Eds.), *Emotional development and emotional intelligence* (pp. 193–195). New York: Basic Books.

ASHMEAD, D. H., McCARTY, M. E., LUCAS, L. S., & BELVEDERE, M. C. (1993). Visual guidance in infants' reaching toward suddenly displaced targets. *Child Development, 64,* 1111–1127.

ASHMEAD, D. H., & PERLMUTTER, M. (1980). Infant memory in everyday life. In M. Perlmutter (Ed.), *New directions for child development* (Vol. 10, pp. 1–16). San Francisco: Jossey-Bass.

ASLIN, R. N. (1987). Visual and auditory development in infancy. In J. D. Osofsky (Ed.), *Handbook of infant development* (2nd ed., pp. 5–97). New York: Wiley.

ASLIN, R. N. (1993). Perception of visual direction in human infants. In C. E. Granrud (Ed.), *Visual perception and cognition in infancy* (pp. 91–119). Hillsdale, NJ: Erlbaum.

ASLIN, R. N., JUSCZYK, P. W., & PISONI, D. B. (1998). Speech and auditory processing during infancy: Constraints on and precursors to language. In D. Kuhn & R. S. Siegler (Eds.), *Handbook of child psychology: Vol. 2. Cognition, perception, and language* (5th ed., pp. 147–198). New York: Wiley.

ASTINGTON, J. W. (1991). Intention in the child's theory of mind. In C. Moore & D. Frye (Eds.), *Children's theories of mind* (pp. 157–172). Hillsdale, NJ: Erlbaum.

ASTINGTON, J. W. (1993). *The child's discovery of the mind.* Cambridge: Cambridge University Press.

ASTINGTON, J. W. (1995). Commentary: Talking it over with my brain. In J. H. Flavell, F. L. Green, & E. R. Flavell, Young children's knowledge about thinking. *Monographs of the Society for Research in Child Development, 60* (1, Serial No. 243).

ASTINGTON, J. W., & JENKINS, J. M. (1995). Theory of mind development and social understanding. *Cognition & Emotion, 9,* 151–165.

ASTLEY, S. J., CLARREN, S. K., LITTLE, R. E., SAMPSON, P. D., & DALING, J. R. (1992). Analysis of facial shape in children gestationally exposed to marijuana, alcohol, and/or cocaine. *Pediatrics, 89,* 67–77.

ATKINSON, R. C., & SHIFFRIN, R. M. (1968). Human memory: A proposed system and its control processes. In K. W. Spence & J. T. Spence (Eds.), *Advances in the psychology of learning and motivation* (Vol. 2, pp. 90–195). New York: Academic Press.

ATKINSON-KING, K. (1973). Children's acquisition of phonological stress contrasts. *UCLA Working Papers in Phonetics, 25.*

ATTIE, I., & BROOKS-GUNN, J. (1996). The development of eating regulation across the life span. In D. Cicchetti & D. J. Cohen (Eds.), *Developmental psychology: Vol. 2. Risk, disorder, and adaptation* (pp. 332–368). New York: Wiley.

AU, K. H. (1997). A sociocultural model of reading instruction: The Kamehameha Elementary Education Program. In S. A. Stahl & D. A. Hayes (Eds.), *Instructional models in reading* (pp. 181–202). Mahwah, NJ: Erlbaum.

AU, T. K. (1994). Developing an intuitive understanding of substance kinds. *Cognitive Psychology, 27,* 71–111.

AU, T. K., DAPRETTO, M., & SONG, Y-K. (1994). Input vs. constraints: Early word acquisition in Korean and English. *Journal of Memory and Language, 33,* 567–582.

AU, T. K., SIDLE, A. L., & ROLLINS, K. B. (1993). Developing an intuitive understanding of conservation and contamination: Invisible particles as a plausible mechanism. *Developmental Psychology, 29,* 286–299.

AZMITIA, M. (1988). Peer interaction and problem solving: When are two heads better than one? *Child Development, 59,* 87–96.

AZMITIA, M., & HESSER, J. (1993). Why siblings are important agents of cognitive development: A comparison of siblings and peers. *Child Development, 64,* 430–444.

B

BADDELEY, A. D. (1992). Working memory. *Science, 255,* 556–559.

BADDELEY, A. D. (1994). The magic number seven: Still magic after all these years? *Psychological Review, 101,* 353–356.

BADER, A. P. (1995). Engrossment revisited: Fathers are still falling in love with their newborn ba-

bies. In J. L. Shapiro, M. J. Diamond, & M. Greenberg (Eds.), *Becoming a father* (pp. 224–233). New York: Springer.

BAENNINGER, M., & NEWCOMBE, N. (1995). Environmental input to the development of sex-related differences in spatial and mathematical ability. *Learning and Individual Differences, 7,* 363–379.

BAER, J. (1991). *Creativity and divergent thinking: A task-specific approach.* Hillsdale, NJ: Erlbaum.

BAGWELL, C. L., NEWCOMB, A. F., & BUKOWSKI, W. M. (1998). Preadolescent friendship and peer rejection as predictors of adult adjustment. *Child Development, 69,* 140–153.

BAHRICK, L. E. (1983). Infants' perception of substance and temporal synchrony in multimodal events. *Infant Behavior and Development, 6,* 429–451.

BAHRICK, L. E. (1988). Intermodal learning in infancy: Learning on the basis of two kinds of invariant relations in audible and visible events. *Child Development, 59,* 197–209.

BAHRICK, L. E. (1992). Infants' perceptual differentiation of amodal and modality-specific audio-visual relations. *Journal of Experimental Child Psychology, 53,* 180–199.

BAHRICK, L. E., MOSS, L., & FADIL, C. (1996). Development of visual self-recognition in infancy. *Ecological Psychology, 8,* 189–208.

BAI, D. L., & BERTENTHAL, B. I. (1992). Locomotor status and the development of spatial search skills. *Child Development, 63,* 215–226.

BAILEY, J. M., BOBROW, D., WOLFE, M., & MIKACH, S. (1995). Sexual orientation of adult sons of gay fathers. *Developmental Psychology, 31,* 124–129.

BAILEY, J. M., & PILLARD, R. C. (1991). A genetic study of male sexual orientation. *Archives of General Psychiatry, 43,* 808–812.

BAILEY, J. M., PILLARD, R. C., NEALE, M. C., & AGYEI, Y. (1993). Heritable factors influence sexual orientation in women. *Archives of General Psychiatry, 50,* 217–223.

BAILEY, R. C. (1990). Growth of African pygmies in early childhood. *New England Journal of Medicine, 323,* 1146.

BAILEY, T. (1993). Can youth apprenticeship thrive in the United States? *Educational Researcher, 22* (3), 4–10.

BAILLARGEON, R. (1987). Object permanence in 3.5- and 4.5-month-old infants. *Developmental Psychology, 23,* 655–664.

BAILLARGEON, R. (1994a). How do infants learn about the physical world? *Current Directions in*

Psychological Science, 3, 133–140.

BAILLARGEON, R. (1994b). Physical reasoning in infancy. In M. S. Gazzaniga (Ed.), *The cognitive neurosciences* (pp. 181–204). Cambridge, MA: MIT Press.

BAILLARGEON, R. (1995). A model of physical reasoning in infancy. In C. K. Rovee-Collier & L. P. Lipsitt (Eds.), *Advances in infancy research* (Vol. 9, pp. 305–371). Norwood, NJ: Ablex.

BAILLARGEON, R. (1998). Infants' understanding of the physical world. In M. Sabourin, F. I. M. Craik, & M. Robert (Eds.), *Advances in psychological science: Vol. 2. Biological and cognitive aspects* (pp. 503–529). London: Psychology Press.

BAILLARGEON, R., & DEVOS, J. (1991). Object permanence in young infants: Further evidence. *Child Development, 62,* 1227–1246.

BAILLARGEON, R., GRABER, M., DEVOS, J., & BLACK, J. (1990). Why do young infants fail to search for hidden objects? *Cognition, 36,* 255–284.

BAILLARGEON, R., NEEDHAM, A., & DEVOS, J. (1992). The development of young infants' intuitions about support. *Early Development and Parenting, 1,* 68–78.

BAKEMAN, R., ADAMSON, L. B., KONNER, M., & BARR, R. G. (1990). !Kung infancy: The social context of object exploration. *Child Development, 61,* 794–809.

BAKER-WARD, L., GORDON, B. N., ORNSTEIN, P. A., LARUS, D. M., & CLUBB, P. A. (1993). Young children's long-term retention of a pediatric examination. *Child Development, 64,* 1519–1533.

BAKER-WARD, L., ORNSTEIN, P. A., & HOLDEN, D. J. (1984). The expression of memorization in early childhood. *Journal of Experimental Child Psychology, 37,* 555–575.

BALDWIN, A., BALDWIN, C., & COLE, R. E. (1990). Stress-resistant families and stress-resistant children. In J. E. Rolf, A. S. Masten, D. Cicchetti, K. N. Wechterlein, & S. Weintraub (Eds.), *Risk and protective factors in the development of psychopathology* (pp. 257–280). New York: Cambridge University Press.

BALDWIN, D. V., & SKINNER, M. L. (1989). Structural model for antisocial behavior: Generalization to single-mother families. *Developmental Psychology, 25,* 45–50.

BALDWIN, J. M. (1895). *Mental development in the child and the race: Methods and processes.* New York: Macmillan.

BALDWIN, J. M. (1897). *Social and ethnic interpretations in mental development: A study in*

social psychology. New York: Macmillan.

BALLARD, B. D., GIPSON, M. T., GUTTENBERG, W., & RAMSEY, K. (1980). Palatability of food as a factor influencing obese and normal-weight children's eating habits. *Behavior Research and Therapy, 18,* 598–600.

BANDURA, A. (1977). *Social learning theory.* Englewood Cliffs, NJ: Prentice-Hall.

BANDURA, A. (1986). *Social foundations of thought and action: A social cognitive theory.* Englewood Cliffs, NJ: Prentice-Hall.

BANDURA, A. (1989). Social cognitive theory. In R. Vasta (Ed.), *Annals of child development* (Vol. 6, pp. 1–60). Greenwich, CT: JAI Press.

BANDURA, A. (1991). Social cognitive theory of moral thought and action. In W. M. Kurtines & J. L. Gewirtz (Eds.), *Handbook of moral behavior and development* (Vol. 1, pp. 45–103). Hillsdale, NJ: Erlbaum.

BANDURA, A. (1992). Perceived self-efficacy in cognitive development and functioning. *Educational Psychologist, 28,* 117–148.

BANDURA, A. (1997). *Self-efficacy: The exercise of control.* New York: Freeman.

BANISH, M. T. (1997). *Neuropsychology: The neural bases of mental function.* Boston: Houghton Mifflin.

BANISH, M. T. (1998). Integration of information between the cerebral hemispheres. *Current Directions in Psychological Science, 7,* 32–37.

BANISH, M. T., & HELLER, W. (1998). Evolving perspectives on lateralization of function. *Current Directions in Psychological Science, 7,* 1–2.

BANKS, M. S. (1980). The development of visual accommodation during early infancy. *Child Development, 51,* 646–666.

BANKS, M. S., & BENNETT, P. J. (1988). Optical and photoreceptor immaturities limit the spatial and chromatic vision of human neonates. *Journal of the Optical Society of America, 5,* 2059–2079.

BANKS, M. S., & GINSBURG, A. P. (1985). Early visual preferences: A review and new theoretical treatment. In H. W. Reese (Ed.), *Advances in child development and behavior* (Vol. 19, pp. 207–246). New York: Academic Press.

BANKS, M. S., & SALAPATEK, P. (1983). Infant visual perception. In M. M. Haith & J. J. Campos (Eds.), *Handbook of child psychology: Vol. 2. Infancy and developmental psychobiology* (4th ed., pp. 436–571). New York: Wiley.

BANKS, M. S., & SHANNON, E. (1993). Spatial and chromatic

visual efficiency in human neonates. In C. Granrud (Ed.), *Visual perception and cognition in infancy* (pp. 1–46). Hillsdale, NJ: Erlbaum.

BARDWELL, J. R., COCHRAN, S. W., & WALKER, S. (1986). Relationship of parental education, race, and gender to sex role stereotyping in five-year-old kindergartners. *Sex Roles, 15,* 275–281.

BARENBOIM, C. (1981). The development of person perception in childhood and adolescence: From behavioral comparisons to psychological constructs to psychological comparisons. *Child Development, 52,* 129–144.

BARKER, D. J. P. (1994). *Mothers, babies, and disease in later life.* London: British Medical Journal Publishing.

BARKER, D. J. P., GLUCKMAN, P. D., GODFREY, K. M., HARDING, J. E., OWENS, J. A., & ROBINSON, J. S. (1993). Fetal nutrition and cardiovascular disease in adult life. *Lancet, 341,* 938–941.

BARKER, R. G., & GUMP, P. V. (1964). *Big school, small school: High school size and student behavior.* Stanford, CA: Stanford University Press.

BARKLEY, R. A. (1997a). *ADHD and the nature of self-control.* New York: Guilford.

BARKLEY, R. A. (1997b). Behavioral inhibition, sustained attention, and executive functions: Constructing a unifying theory of ADHD. *Psychological Bulletin, 121,* 65–94.

BARLING, J., ROGERS, K., & KELLOWAY, K. (1995). Some effects of teenagers' part-time employment: The quantity and quality of work make the differences. *Journal of Organizational Behavior, 16,* 143–154.

BARNAS, M. V., & CUMMINGS, E. M. (1994). Caregiver stability and toddlers' attachment-related behavior toward caregivers in day care. *Infant Behavior and Development, 17,* 141–147.

BARNAT, S. B., KLEIN, P. J., & MELTZOFF, A. N. (1996). Deferred imitation across changes in context and object: Memory and generalization in 14-month-old infants. *Infant Behavior and Development, 19,* 241–251.

BARNES, K. E. (1971). Preschool play norms: A replication. *Developmental Psychology, 5,* 99–103.

BARNES-JOSIAH, D., & AUGUSTIN, A. (1995). Secular trend in the age at menarche in Haiti. *American Journal of Human Biology, 7,* 357–362.

BARNETT, D., MANLY, J., & CICCHETTI, D. (1993). Defining child maltreatment: The interface between policy and research. In D. Cicchetti & S. Toth (Eds.), *Child abuse, child devel-*opment, and social policy* (pp. 7–73). Norwood, NJ: Ablex.

BARNETT, W. S. (1993). Benefit-cost analysis of preschool education: Findings from a 25-year follow-up. *American Journal of Orthopsychiatry, 63,* 500–508.

BARON-COHEN, S. (1991). Do people with autism understand what causes emotion? *Child Development, 62,* 385–395.

BARON-COHEN, S. (1993). From attention–goal psychology to belief–desire psychology: The development of a theory of mind and its dysfunction. In S. Baron-Cohen, H. Tager-Flusberg, & D. Cohen (Eds.), *Understanding other minds: Perspectives from autism* (pp. 59–82). Oxford, England: Oxford University Press.

BARON-COHEN, S., BALDWIN, D. A., & CROWSON, M. (1997). Do children with autism use the speaker's direction of gaze strategy to crack the code of language? *Child Development, 68,* 48–57.

BARR, H. M., STREISSGUTH, A. P., DARBY, B. L., & SAMPSON, P. D. (1990). Prenatal exposure to alcohol, caffeine, tobacco, and aspirin: Effects on fine and gross motor performance in 4-year-old children. *Developmental Psychology, 26,* 339–348.

BARR, R., DOWDEN, A., & HAYNE, H. (1996). Developmental changes in deferred imitation by 6- to 24-month-old infants. *Infant Behavior and Development, 19,* 159–170.

BARR, R. G., CHEN, S., HOPKINS, B., & WESTRA, T. (1996). Crying patterns in preterm infants. *Developmental Medicine and Child Neurology, 38,* 345–355.

BARR, R. G., KONNER, M., BAKEMAN, R., & ADAMSON, L. (1991). Crying in !Kung San infants: A test of the cultural specificity hypothesis. *Developmental Medicine and Child Neurology, 33,* 601–610.

BARRATT, M. S., ROACH, M. A., & LEAVITT, L. A. (1996). The impact of low-risk prematurity on maternal behaviour and toddler outcomes. *International Journal of Behavioral Development, 19,* 581–602.

BARRETT, K. C., & CAMPOS, J. J. (1987). Perspectives on emotional development II: A functionalist approach to emotions. In J. D. Osofsky (Ed.), *Handbook of infant development* (2nd ed., pp. 555–578). New York: Wiley.

BARRON, F. (1988). Putting creativity to work. In R. J. Sternberg (Ed.), *The nature of creativity: Contemporary psychological perspectives* (pp. 76–98). New York: Cambridge University Press.

BARTH, J. M., & PARKE, R. D. (1993). Parent–child relation-ship influences on children's transition to school. *Merrill-Palmer Quarterly, 39,* 173–195.

BARTLETT, F. C. (1932). *Remembering.* Cambridge: Cambridge University Press.

BARTON, M. E., & STROSBERG, R. (1997). Conversational patterns of two-year-old twins in mother–twin–twin triads. *Journal of Child Language, 24,* 257–269.

BARTON, M. E., & TOMASELLO, M. (1991). Joint attention and conversation in mother–infant-sibling triads. *Child Development, 62,* 517–529.

BARTON, S. J., HARRIGAN, R., & TSE, A. M. (1995). Prenatal cocaine exposure: Implications for practice, policy development, and needs for future research. *Journal of Perinatology, 15,* 10–22.

BARTSCH, K., & WELLMAN, H. M. (1995). *Children talk about the mind.* New York: Oxford University Press.

BASHIR, L. M. (1997). Female genital mutilation—balancing intolerance of the practice with tolerance of culture. *Journal of Women's Health, 6,* 11–14.

BASINGER, K. S., GIBBS, J. C., & FULLER, D. (1995). Context and the measurement of moral judgment. *International Journal of Behavioral Development, 18,* 537–556.

BASTIAN, H. (1993). Personal beliefs and alternative childbirth choices: A survey of 552 women who planned to give birth at home. *Birth, 20,* 186–192.

BATES, E. (1995). *Modularity, domain specificity, and the development of language.* Unpublished manuscript, University of California, San Diego.

BATES, E., & MACWHINNEY, B. (1987). Competition, variation, and language learning. In B. MacWhinney (Ed.), *Mechanisms of language acquisition* (pp. 157–193). Hillsdale, NJ: Erlbaum.

BATES, E., MARCHMAN, V., THAL, D., FENSON, L., DALE, P., REZNICK, J. S., REILLY, J., & HARTUNG, J. (1994). Developmental and stylistic variation in the composition of early vocabulary. *Journal of Child Language, 21,* 85–123.

BATES, J. E., WACHS, T. D., & EMDE, R. N. (1994). Toward practical uses for biological concepts. In J. E. Bates & T. D. Wachs (Eds.), *Temperament: Individual differences at the interface of biology and behavior* (pp. 275–306). Washington, DC: American Psychological Association.

BAUER, P. J. (1996). What do infants recall of their lives? Memory for specific events by one-to two-year-olds. *American Psychologist, 51,* 29–41.

BAUER, P. J. (1997). Development of memory in early childhood. In N. Cowan (Ed.), *The development of memory in childhood* (pp. 83–111). Hove, UK: Psychology Press.

BAUMEISTER, R. F., SMART, L., & BODEN, J. M. (1996). Relation of threatened egotism to violence and aggression: The dark side of high self-esteem. *Psychological Review, 103,* 5–33.

BAUMRIND, D. (1967). Child care practices anteceding three patterns of preschool behavior. *Genetic Psychology Monographs, 75,* 43–88.

BAUMRIND, D. (1971). Current patterns of parental authority. *Developmental Psychology Monograph, 4* (1, Pt. 2).

BAUMRIND, D. (1983). Rejoinder to Lewis's reinterpretation of parental firm control effects: Are authoritative families really harmonious? *Psychological Bulletin, 94,* 132–142.

BAUMRIND, D. (1991). The influence of parenting style on adolescent competence and substance use. *Journal of Early Adolescence, 11,* 56–95.

BAUMRIND, D. (1995). Commentary on sexual orientation: Research and social policy implications. *Developmental Psychology, 31,* 130–136.

BAUMRIND, D., & BLACK, A. E. (1967). Socialization practices associated with dimensions of competence in preschool boys and girls. *Child Development, 38,* 291–327.

BAUMWELL, L., TAMIS-LEMONDA, C. S., & BORNSTEIN, M. H. (1997). Maternal verbal sensitivity and child language comprehension. *Infant Behavior and Development, 20,* 247–258.

BAYLEY, N. (1969). *Bayley Scales of Infant Development.* New York: Psychological Corporation.

BAYLEY, N. (1993). *Bayley Scales of Infant Development* (2nd ed.). New York: Psychological Corporation.

BEAL, C. R. (1990). The development of text evaluation and revision skills. *Child Development, 61,* 247–258.

BEARISON, D. J. (1998). Pediatric psychology and children's medical problems. In I. G. Sigel & K. A. Renninger (Eds.), *Handbook of child psychology: Vol. 4. Child psychology in practice* (5th ed., pp. 635–711). New York: Wiley.

BEATTY, W. W. (1992). Gonadal hormones and sex differences in nonreproductive behaviors. In A. A. Gerall, H. Moltz, & I. L. Ward (Eds.), *Handbook of behavioral neurobiology: Vol. 11. Sexual differentiation* (pp. 85–128). New York: Plenum.

BEAUCHAMP, G. K., COWART, B. J., MENNELLA, J. A., & MARSH, R. R. (1994). Infant salt taste: Developmental, methodological, and contextual factors. *Developmental Psychobiology, 27,* 353–365.

BECK, M. (1994, January 17). How far should we push Mother Nature? *Newsweek,* pp. 54–57.

BECKER, J. (1990). Processes in the acquisition of pragmatic competence. In G. Conti-Ramsden & C. Snow (Eds.), *Children's language* (Vol. 7, pp. 7–24). Hillsdale, NJ: Erlbaum.

BECKWITH, L., & SIGMAN, M. D. (1995). Preventive interventions in infancy. *Child and Adolescent Psychiatric Clinics of North America, 4,* 683–700.

BEERE, C. A. (1990). *Gender roles: A handbook of tests and measures.* New York: Greenwood Press.

BEGLEY, S. (1995, February 13). Surprising new lessons from the controversial science of race. *Newsweek,* pp. 67–68.

BEHREND, D. A. (1988). Overextensions in early language comprehension: Evidence from a signal detection approach. *Journal of Child Language, 15,* 63–75.

BEHREND, D. A., ROSENGREN, K. S., & PERLMUTTER, M. (1992). The relation between private speech and parental interactive style. In R. M. Diaz & L. E. Berk (Eds.), *Private speech: From social interaction to self-regulation* (pp. 85–100). Hillsdale, NJ: Erlbaum.

BEHRMAN, R. D., KLIEGMAN, R. M., & ARVIN, A. M. (Eds.). (1996). *Nelson textbook of pediatrics* (15th ed.). Philadelphia: Saunders.

BEILIN, H. (1978). Inducing conservation through training. In G. Steiner (Ed.), *Psychology of the twentieth century* (Vol. 7, pp. 260–289). Munich: Kindler.

BEILIN, H. (1992). Piaget's enduring contribution to developmental psychology. *Developmental Psychology, 28,* 191–204.

BELL, A., WEINBERG, M., & HAMMERSMITH, S. (1981). *Sexual preference: Its development in men and women.* Bloomington: Indiana University Press.

BELL, M. A., & FOX, N. A. (1992). The relations between frontal brain electrical activity and cognitive development during infancy. *Child Development, 63,* 1142–1163.

BELL, M. A., & FOX, N. A. (1994). Brain development over the first year of life: Relations between EEG frequency and coherence and cognitive and affective behaviors. In G. Dawson & K. W. Fischer (Eds.), *Human behavior and the developing brain* (pp. 314–345). New York: Guilford.

BELL, M. A., & FOX, N. A. (1996). Crawling experience is related to changes in cortical organization during infancy: Evidence from EEG coherence. *Developmental Psychobiology, 29,* 551–561.

BELL, R. J., PALMA, S. M., & LUMLEY, J. M. (1995). The effect of vigorous exercise during pregnancy on birth-weight. *Australian and New Zealand Journal of Obstetrics and Gynaecology, 35,* 46–51.

BELL, S. M., & AINSWORTH, M. D. S. (1972). Infant crying and maternal responsiveness. *Child Development, 43,* 1171–1190.

BELL-DOLAN, D. J., FOSTER, S. L., & SIKORA, D. M. (1989). Effects of sociometric testing on children's behavior and loneliness in school. *Developmental Psychology, 25,* 306–311.

BELLAMY, C. (1998). *The state of the world's children 1998.* New York: Oxford University Press (in cooperation with UNICEF).

BELLE, D. (1997). A qualitative look at children's experiences in the after-school hours. *Merrill-Palmer Quarterly, 43,* 478–496.

BELLINGER, D., LEVITON, A., WATERNAUX, C., NEEDLEMAN, H., & RABINOWITZ, M. (1987). Longitudinal analysis of prenatal and postnatal lead exposure and early cognitive development. *New England Journal of Medicine, 316,* 1037–1043.

BELLUGI, U., BIHRLE, A., NEVILLE, H., JERNIGAN, T., & DOHERTY, S. (1992). Language, cognition, and brain organization in a neurodevelopmental disorder. In M. Gunnar & C. Nelson (Eds.), *Developmental behavioral neuroscience* (pp. 201–232). Hillsdale, NJ: Erlbaum.

BELLUGI, U., & WANG, P. P. (1999). Williams syndrome: From cognition to brain to gene. In *Encyclopaedia of Neuroscience.* Amsterdam: Elsevier Science.

BELMONT, L., & MAROLLA, F. A. (1973). Birth order, family size, and intelligence. *Science, 182,* 1096–1101.

BELSKY, J. (1989). Infant-parent attachment and day care: In defense of the Strange Situation. In J. Lande, S. Scarr, & N. Gunzenhauser (Eds.), *Caring for children: Challenge to America* (pp. 23–48). Hillsdale, NJ: Erlbaum.

BELSKY, J. (1992). Consequences of child care for children's development: A deconstructionist view. In A. Booth (Ed.), *Child care in the 1990s: Trends and consequences* (pp. 83–85). Hillsdale, NJ: Erlbaum.

BELSKY, J. (1993). Etiology of child maltreatment: A developmental ecological analysis. *Psychological Bulletin, 114,* 413–434.

BELSKY, J. (1996). Parent, infant, and social-contextual antecedents of father–son attachment security. *Developmental Psychology, 32,* 905–913.

BELSKY, J., CAMPBELL, S. B., COHN, J. F., & MOORE, G. (1996). Instability of infant–parent attachment security. *Developmental Psychology, 32,* 921–924.

BELSKY, J., & CASSIDY, J. (1994). Attachment: Theory and evidence. In M. Rutter & D. Hay (Eds.), *Development through life* (pp. 373–402). Oxford, England: Blackwell.

BELSKY, J., FISH, M., & ISABELLA, R. A. (1991). Continuity and discontinuity in infant negative and positive emotionality: Family antecedents and attachment consequences. *Developmental Psychology, 27,* 421–431.

BEM, S. L. (1974). The measurement of psychological androgyny. *Journal of Consulting and Clinical Psychology, 42,* 155–162.

BEM, S. L. (1977). On the utility of alternative procedures for assessing psychological androgyny. *Journal of Consulting and Clinical Psychology, 45,* 196–205.

BEM, S. L. (1981). Gender schema theory: A cognitive account of sex typing. *Psychological Review, 88,* 354–364.

BEM, S. L. (1983). Gender schema theory and its implications for child development: Raising gender aschematic children in a gender-schematic society. *Signs: Journal of Women in Culture and Society, 8,* 598–616.

BEM, S. L. (1989). Genital knowledge and gender constancy in preschool children. *Child Development, 60,* 649–662.

BEM, S. L. (1993). *The lenses of gender: Transforming the debate on sexual inequality.* New Haven, CT: Yale University Press.

BEM, S. L. (1998). *An unconventional family.* New Haven, CT: Yale University Press.

BENBOW, C. P., & ARJIMAND, O. (1990). Predictors of high academic achievement in mathematics and science by mathematically talented students: A longitudinal study. *Journal of Educational Psychology, 82,* 430–441.

BENBOW, C. P., & STANLEY, J. C. (1983). Sex differences in mathematical reasoning: More facts. *Science, 222,* 1029–1031.

BENCH, R. J., COLLYER, Y., MENTZ, L., & WILSON, I. (1976). Studies in infant behavioural audiometry: I. Neonates. *Audiology, 15,* 85–105.

BENDER, S. L., WORD, C. O., DICLEMENTE, R. J., CRITTENDEN, M. R., PERSAUD, N. A., & PONTON, L. (1995). The developmental implications of prenatal and/or postnatal crack cocaine exposure in preschool children: A preliminary report. *Developmental and Behavioral Pediatrics, 16,* 418–424.

BENDER, W. N. (1996). Learning disabilities. In P. J. McLaughlin & P. Wehman (Eds.), *Mental retardation and developmental disabilities* (2nd ed., pp. 259–279). Austin TX: PRO-ED.

BENDERSKY, M., & LEWIS, M. (1994). Environmental risk, biological risk, and developmental outcome. *Developmental Psychology, 30,* 484–494.

BENEDICT, R. (1934). *Patterns of culture.* Boston: Houghton Mifflin.

BENENSON, J. F. (1993). Greater preference among females than males for dyadic interaction in early childhood. *Child Development, 64,* 544–555.

BENENSON, J. F., APOSTOLERIS, N. H., & PARNASS, J. (1997). Age and sex differences in dyadic and group interaction. *Developmental Psychology, 33,* 538–543.

BENENSON, J. F., APOSTOLERIS, N., & PARNASS, J. (1998). The organization of children's same-sex peer relationships. In W. M. Bukowski & A. H. Cillessen (Eds.), *New directions for child development* (No. 80, pp. 55–82). San Francisco: Jossey-Bass.

BENNETTO, L., PENNINGTON, B. F., & ROGERS, S. J. (1996). Intact and impaired memory functions in autism. *Child Development, 67,* 1816–1835.

BENOIT, D., & PARKER, K. C. H. (1994). Stability and transmission of attachment across three generations. *Child Development, 65,* 1444–1456.

BERENBAUM, S. A., & HINES, M. (1992). Early androgens are related to childhood sex-typed toy preferences. *Psychological Science, 3,* 203–206.

BERENBAUM, S. A., & SNYDER, E. (1995). Early hormonal influences on childhood sex-typed activity and playmate preferences: Implications for the development of sexual orientation. *Developmental Psychology, 31,* 31–42.

BERK, L. E. (1985). Relationship of caregiver education to child-oriented attitudes, job satisfaction, and behaviors toward children. *Child Care Quarterly, 14,* 103–129.

BERK, L. E. (1992a). Children's private speech: An overview of theory and the status of research. In R. M. Diaz & L. E. Berk (Eds.), *Private speech: From social interaction to self-regulation* (pp. 17–53). Hillsdale, NJ: Erlbaum.

BERK, L. E. (1992b). The extracurriculum. In P. W. Jackson (Ed.), *Handbook of research on curriculum* (pp. 1002–1043). New York: Macmillan.

BERK, L. E. (1994a). Vygotsky's theory: The importance of make-believe play. *Young Children, 50,* 30–39.

BERK, L. E. (1994b). Why children talk to themselves. *Scientific American, 271* (5), 78–83.

BERK, L. E. (1999). Development. In J. Halonen & S. Davis (Eds.), *The many faces of psychological research in the twenty-first century.* Washington, DC: American Psychological Association.

BERK, L. E., & LANDAU, S. (1993). Private speech of learning disabled and normally achieving children in classroom academic and laboratory contexts. *Child Development, 64,* 556–571.

BERK, L. E., & LANDAU, S. (1997, April). Private speech in the face of academic challenge: The failure of impulsive children to get their act together. In L. E. Berk & J. R. Jamieson (Chairs), *Private speech and self-regulation in children with and without special needs.* Symposium conducted at the biennial meeting of the Society for Research in Child Development, Washington, DC.

BERK, L. E., & SPUHL, S. T. (1995). Maternal interaction, private speech, and task performance in preschool children. *Early Childhood Research Quarterly, 10,* 145–169.

BERKEY, C. S., WANG, X., DOCKERY, D. W., & FERRIS, B. G., JR. (1994). Adolescent height growth of U.S. children. *Annals of Human Biology, 21,* 435–442.

BERKOWITZ, M. W., & GIBBS, J. C. (1983). Measuring the developmental features of moral discussion. *Merrill-Palmer Quarterly, 29,* 399–410.

BERMAN, P. (1980). Are women more responsive than men to the young? A review of developmental and situational variables. *Psychological Bulletin, 88,* 668–695.

BERMEJO, V. (1996). Cardinality development and counting. *Developmental Psychology, 32,* 263–268.

BERNDT, T. J. (1988). The nature and significance of children's friendships. In R. Vasta (Ed.), *Annals of child development* (Vol. 5, pp. 155–186). Greenwich, CT: JAI Press.

BERNDT, T. J., CHEUNG, P. C., LAU, S., HAU, K-T., & LEW, W. J. F. (1993). Perceptions of parenting in mainland China, Taiwan, and Hong Kong: Sex differences and societal differences. *Developmental Psychology, 29,* 156–164.

BERNDT, T. J., & KEEFE, K. (1995). Friends' influence on adolescents' adjustment to school. *Child Development, 66,* 1312–1329.

BERNIER, J. C., & SIEGEL, D. H. (1994). Attention-deficit hyperactivity disorder: A family ecological systems perspective. *Families in Society, 75,* 142–150.

BERRUETA-CLEMENT, J. R., SCHWEINHART, L. J., BARNETT, W. S.,

EPSTEIN, A. S., & WEIKART, D. P. (1984). Changed lives: The effects of the Perry Preschool Program on youths through age 19. *Monographs of the High/Scope Research Foundation, 8.*

BERSOFF, D. M., & MILLER, J. G. (1993). Culture, context, and the development of moral accountability judgments. *Developmental Psychology, 29,* 664–676.

BERTENTHAL, B. I. (1993). Infants' perception of biomechanical motions: Instrinsic image and knowledge-based constraints. In C. Granrud (Ed.), *Visual perception and cognition in infancy* (pp. 175–214). Hillsdale, NJ: Erlbaum.

BERTENTHAL, B. I. (1996). Origins and early development of perception, action, and representation. *Annual Review of Psychology, 47,* 431–459.

BERTENTHAL, B. I., & CAMPOS, J. J. (1987). New directions in the study of early experience. *Child Development, 58,* 560–567.

BERTENTHAL, B. I., CAMPOS, J. J., & BARRETT, K. (1984). Self-produced locomotion: An organizer of emotional, cognitive, and social development in infancy. In R. Emde & R. Harmon (Eds.), *Continuities and discontinuities in development* (pp. 174–210). New York: Plenum.

BERTENTHAL, B. I., & CLIFTON, R. K. (1998). Perception and action. In D. Kuhn & R. S. Siegler (Eds.), *Handbook of child psychology: Vol. 2. Cognition, perception, and language* (pp. 51–102). New York: Wiley.

BERTENTHAL, B. I., PROFFITT, D. R., KRAMER, S. J., & SPETNER, N. B. (1987). Infants' encoding of kinetic displays varying in relative coherence. *Developmental Psychology, 23,* 171–178.

BERTENTHAL, B. I., PROFFITT, D. R., SPETNER, N. B., & THOMAS, M. A. (1985). The development of infant sensitivity to biomechanical motions. *Child Development, 56,* 531–543.

BERTENTHAL, B. I., ROSE, J. L., & BAI, D. L. (1997). Perception–action coupling in the development of visual control of posture. *Journal of Experimental Psychology: Human Perception and Performance, 23,* 1631–1643.

BERZONSKY, M. D. (1993). A constructivist view of identity development: People as post-positivist self-theorists. In J. Kroger (Ed.), *Discussions on ego identity* (pp. 169–203). Hillsdale, NJ: Erlbaum.

BEST, D. L. (1993). Inducing children to generate mnemonic organizational strategies: An examination of long-term re-

tention and materials. *Developmental Psychology, 29,* 324–336.

BEST, D. L., & ORNSTEIN, P. A. (1986). Children's generation and communication of mnemonic organizational strategies. *Developmental Psychology, 22,* 845–853.

BEST, D. L., WILLIAMS, J. E., CLOUD, J. M., DAVIS, S. W., ROBERTSON, L. S., EDWARDS, J. R., GILES, H., & FOWLES, J. (1977). Development of sex-trait stereotypes among young children in the United States, England, and Ireland. *Child Development, 48,* 1375–1384.

BETZ, C. (1994). Beyond time-out: Tips from a teacher. *Young Children, 49* (3), 10–14.

BEUNEN, G., & MALINA, R. M. (1996). Growth and biological maturation: Relevance to athletic performance. In O. Bar-Or (Ed.), *The child and adolescent athlete* (pp. 2–24). Oxford: Blackwell Science.

BEYER, S. (1995). Maternal employment and children's academic achievement: Parenting styles as mediating variable. *Developmental Review, 15,* 212–253.

BEYTH-MAROM, R., AUSTIN, L., FISCHHOFF, B., PALMGREN, C., & JACOBS-QUADREL, M. (1993). Perceived consequences of risky behaviors: Adults and adolescents. *Developmental Psychology, 29,* 549–563.

BEYTH-MAROM, R., & FISCHHOFF, B. (1997). Adolescents' decisions about risks: A cognitive perspective. In J. Schulenberg, J. L. Maggs, & K. Hurrelmann (Eds.), *Health risks and developmental transitions during adolescence* (pp. 110–135). New York: Cambridge University Press.

BHATT, R. S., ROVEE-COLLIER, C. K. & WEINER, S. (1994). Developmental changes in the interface between perception and memory retrieval. *Developmental Psychology, 30,* 151–162.

BIALYSTOK, E. (1986). Factors in the growth of linguistic awareness. *Child Development, 57,* 498–510.

BIALYSTOK, E. (1997). Effects of bilingualism and biliteracy on children's emerging concepts of print. *Developmental Psychology, 33,* 429–440.

BIANCHI, B. D., & BAKEMAN, R. (1978). Sex-typed affiliation preferences observed in preschoolers: Traditional and open school differences. *Child Development, 49,* 910–912.

BICKERTON, D. (1981). *Roots of language.* Ann Arbor, MI: Karoma.

BICKERTON, D. (1990). *Language & species.* Chicago: University of Chicago Press.

BIELINSKI, J., & DAVISON, M. L. (1998). Gender differences by item difficulty interactions in multiple-choice mathematics

items. *American Educational Research Journal, 35,* 455–476.

BIERMAN, K. L., MILLER, C. L., & STABB, S. D. (1987). Improving the social behavior and peer acceptance of rejected boys: Effects of social skill training with instructions and prohibitions. *Journal of Consulting and Clinical Psychology, 55,* 194–200.

BIERNAT, M. (1991a). A multi-component, developmental analysis of sex-typing. *Sex Roles, 24,* 567–586.

BIERNAT, M. (1991b). Gender stereotypes and the relationship between masculinity and femininity: A developmental analysis. *Journal of Personality and Social Psychology, 61,* 351–365.

BIGELOW, A. (1992). Locomotion and search behavior in blind infants. *Infant Behavior and Development, 15,* 179–189.

BIGELOW, B. J. (1977). Children's friendship expectations: A cognitive-developmental study. *Child Development, 48,* 246–253.

BIGLER, R. S. (1995). The role of classification skill in moderating environmental influences on children's gender stereotyping: A study of the functional use of gender in the classroom. *Child Development, 66,* 1072–1087.

BIGLER, R. S., JONES, L. C., & LOBLINER, D. B. (1997). Social categorization and the formation of intergroup attitudes in children. *Child Development, 68,* 530–543.

BIGNER, J. J., & JACOBSEN, R. B. (1989). Parenting behaviors of homosexual and heterosexual fathers. *Journal of Homosexuality, 18,* 173–186.

BIGLER, R. S., & LIBEN, L. S. (1992). Cognitive mechanisms in children's gender stereotyping: Theoretical and educational implications of a cognitive-based intervention. *Child Development, 63,* 1351–1363.

BIGLER, R. S., & LIBEN, L. S. (1993). A cognitive-developmental approach to racial stereotyping and reconstructive memory in Euro-American children. *Child Development, 64,* 1507–1518.

BIJELJAC-BABIC, R., BERTONCINI, J., & MEHLER, J. (1993). How do 4-day-old infants categorize multisyllable utterances? *Developmental Psychology, 29,* 711–721.

BIRCH, E. E. (1993). Stereopsis in infants and its developmental relation to visual acuity. In K. Simons (Ed.), *Early visual development: Normal and abnormal* (pp. 224–236). New York: Oxford University Press.

BIRCH, L. L., & FISHER, J. A. (1995). Appetite and eating behavior in children. *Pediatric Clinics of North America, 42,* 931–953.

BIRCH, L. L., JOHNSON, S. L., ANDRESEN, G., PETERS, J. C., & SCHULTE, M. C. (1991). The variability of young children's energy intake. *New England Journal of Medicine, 324,* 232–235.

BIRCH, L. L., ZIMMERMAN, S., & HIND, H. (1980). The influence of social-affective context on preschool children's food preferences. *Child Development, 51,* 856–861.

BIRCH, S. H., & LADD, G. W. (1997). The teacher–child relationship and children's early school adjustment. *Journal of School Psychology, 35,* 61–79.

BIRCH, S. H., & LADD, G. W. (1998). Children's interpersonal behaviors and the teacher–child relationship. *Developmental Psychology, 34,* 934–946.

BIRENBAUM-CARMELI, D. (1995). Maternal smoking during pregnancy: Social, medical, and legal perspectives on the conception of a human being. *Health Care for Women International, 16,* 57–73.

BIRINGEN, Z., EMDE, R. N., CAMPOS, J. J., & APPELBAUM, M. I. (1995). Affective reorganization in the infant, the mother, and the dyad: The role of upright locomotion and its timing. *Child Development, 66,* 499–514.

BIRMAHER, B., RYAN, N., WILLIAMSON, D., BRENT, D., & KAUFMAN, J. (1996). Childhood and adolescent depression: A review of the past 10 years. Part II. *Journal of the American Academy of Child and Adolescent Psychiatry, 35,* 1575–1583.

BISCHOFSHAUSEN, S. (1985). Developmental differences in schema dependency for temporally ordered story events. *Journal of Psycholinguistic Research, 14,* 543–556.

BIVENS, J. A., & BERK, L. E. (1990). A longitudinal study of the development of elementary school children's private speech. *Merrill-Palmer Quarterly, 36,* 443–463.

BJORKLUND, D. F. (1995). *Children's thinking: Developmental function and individual differences* (2nd ed.). Pacific Grove, CA: Brooks/Cole.

BJORKLUND, D. F. (1997). In search of a metatheory for cognitive development (or, Piaget is dead and I don't feel so good myself). *Child Development, 68,* 144–148.

BJORKLUND, D. F., & COYLE, T. R. (1995). Utilization deficiencies in the development of memory strategies. In F. E. Weinert & W. Schneider (Eds.), *Research on memory development: State of the art and future directions* (pp. 161–180). Hillsdale, NJ: Erlbaum.

BJORKLUND, D. F., & DOUGLAS, R. N. (1997). The development of memory strategies. In N. Cowan (Ed.), *The development of memory in childhood* (pp. 83–111). Hove, UK: Psychology Press.

BJORKLUND, D. F., & HARNISHFEGER, K. K. (1990). The resources construct in cognitive development: Diverse sources of evidence and a theory of inefficient inhibition. *Developmental Review, 1,* 48–71.

BJORKLUND, D. F., & HARNISHFEGER, K. K. (1995). The evolution of inhibition mechanisms and their role in human cognition and behavior. In M. L. Howe & R. Pasnak (Eds.), *Emerging themes in cognitive development: Vol. 1. Foundations* (pp. 141–173). New York: Springer-Verlag.

BJORKLUND, D. F., & JACOBS, J. W. (1985). Associative and categorical processes in children's memory: The role of automaticity in the development of organization in free recall. *Journal of Experimental Child Psychology, 39,* 599–617.

BJORKLUND, D. F., MILLER, P. H., COYLE, T. R., & SLAWINSKI, J. L. (1997). Instructing children to use memory strategies: Evidence of utilization deficiencies in memory training studies. *Developmental Review, 17,* 411–441.

BJORKLUND, D. F., SCHNEIDER, W., CASSEL, W. S., & ASHLEY, E. (1994). Training and extension of a memory strategy: Evidence for utilization deficiencies in high- and low-IQ children. *Child Development, 65,* 951–965.

BLACK, B., & LOGAN, A. (1995). Links between communication patterns in mother–child, father–child, and child–peer interactions and children's social status. *Child Development, 66,* 255–271.

BLACK, M. M., HUTCHESON, J. J., DUBOWITZ, H., & BERENSON-HOWARD, J. (1994). Parenting style and developmental status among children with nonorganic failure to thrive. *Journal of Pediatric Psychology, 19,* 689–707.

BLAKE, I. K. (1994). Language development and socialization in young African-American children. In P. M. Greenfield & R. R. Cocking (Eds.), *Cross-cultural roots of minority child development* (pp. 167–195). Hillsdale, NJ: Erlbaum.

BLAKE, J. (1989). *Family size and achievement.* Berkeley: University of California Press.

BLAKE, J., & BOYSSON-BARDIES, B. DE (1992). Patterns in babbling: A cross-linguistic study. *Journal of Child Language, 19,* 51–74.

BLANCHARD, B., & BOGAERT, A. F. (1996). Homosexuality in men and number of older brothers. *American Journal of Psychiatry, 153,* 27–31.

BLANCHARD, M., & MAIN, M. (1979). Avoidance of the attachment figure and social-emotional adjustment in day-care infants. *Developmental Psychology, 15,* 445–446.

BLANCHARD, R., ZUCKER, K. J., BRADLEY, S. J., & HUME, C. S. (1995). Birth order and sibling sex ratio in homosexual male adolescents and probably prehomosexual feminine boys. *Developmental Psychology, 31,* 22–30.

BLASI, A. (1994a). Bridging moral cognition and moral action: A critical review of the literature. In B. Puka (Ed.), *Fundamental research in moral development: A compendium* (Vol. 2, pp. 123–167). New York: Garland.

BLASI, A. (1994b). Moral identity: Its role in moral functioning (pp. 168–179). In B. Puka (Ed.), *Fundamental research in moral development: A compendium* (Vol. 2, pp. 123–167). New York: Garland.

BLASS, E. M., GANCHROW, J. R., & STEINER, J. E. (1984). Classical conditioning in newborn humans 2–48 hours of age. *Infant Behavior and Development, 7,* 223–235.

BLATCHFORD, P., & MORTIMORE, P. (1994). The issue of class size for young children in schools: What can we learn from research? *Oxford Review of Education, 20,* 411–428.

BLATT, M., & KOHLBERG, L. (1975). The effects of classroom moral discussion upon children's level of moral judgment. *Journal of Moral Education, 4,* 129–161.

BLEWITT, P. (1994). Understanding categorical hierarchies: The earliest levels of skill. *Child Development, 65,* 1279–1298.

BLOCK, J. H. (1978). Another look at sex differentiation in the socialization behaviors of mothers and fathers. In J. Sherman & F. L. Denmark (Eds.), *Psychology of women: Future directions for research* (pp. 29–87). New York: Psychological Dimensions.

BLOCK, J. H. (1983). Differential premises arising from differential socialization of the sexes: Some conjectures. *Child Development, 54,* 1335–1354.

BLOCK, J. H., BLOCK, J., & HARRINGTON, D. (1975). *Sex role typing and instrumental behavior: A developmental study.* Paper presented at the annual meeting of the Society for Research in Child Development, Denver.

BLOCK, S. S., MOORE, B. D., & SCHARRE, J. E. (1997). Visual anomalies in young children exposed to cocaine. *Optometry and Visual Sciences, 74,* 28–36.

BLOOM, L. (1970). *Language development: Form and function in emerging grammars.* Cambridge, MA: MIT Press.

BLOOM, L. (1990). Developments in expression: Affect and speech. In N. Stein & T. Trabasso (Eds.), *Psychological and biological approaches to emotion* (pp. 215–245). Hillsdale, NJ: Erlbaum.

BLOOM, L. (1991). *Language development from two to three.* New York: Cambridge University Press.

BLOOM, L. (1993). *The transition from infancy to language: Acquiring the power of expression.* Cambridge: Cambridge University Press.

BLOOM, L. (1998). Language acquisition in its developmental context. In D. Kuhn & R. S. Siegler (Eds.), *Handbook of child psychology: Vol. 2. Cognition, perception, and language* (5th ed., pp. 309–370). New York: Wiley.

BLOOM, L., LAHEY, M., LIFTEN, K., & FIESS, K. (1980). Complex sentences: Acquisition of syntactic connections and the semantic relations they encode. *Journal of Child Language, 7,* 235–256.

BLOTNER, R., & BEARISON, D. J. (1984). Developmental consistencies in socio-moral knowledge: Justice reasoning and altruistic behavior. *Merrill-Palmer Quarterly, 30,* 349–367.

BLUM, N. J., & CAREY, W. B. (1996). Sleep problems among infants and young children. *Pediatrics in Review, 17,* 87–93.

BLUMBERG, M. S., & LUCAS, D. E. (1996). A developmental and component analysis of active sleep. *Developmental Psychobiology, 29,* 1–22.

BLUMSTEIN, S. E. (1995). *The neurobiology of language.* San Diego: Academic Press.

BLYTH, D. A., SIMMONS, R. G., & ZAKIN, D. F. (1985). Satisfaction with body image for early adolescent females: The impact of pubertal timing within different school environments. *Journal of Youth and Adolescence, 14,* 207–225.

BODMER, W., & McKIE, R. (1997). *The book of man: The Human Genome Project and the quest to discover our genetic heritage.* New York: Oxford University Press.

BODROVA, E. & LEONG, D. J. (1996). *Tools of the mind: The Vygotskian approach to early childhood education.* Englewood Cliffs, NJ: Merrill.

BOHANNON, J. N., III, & BONVILLIAN, J. D. (1997). Theoretical approaches to language acquisition. In J. Berko Gleason (Ed.), *The development of language* (4th ed., pp. 259–316). Boston: Allyn and Bacon.

BOHANNON, J. N., III, & STANOWICZ, L. (1988). The issue of negative evidence: Adult responses to children's language errors. *Developmental Psychology, 24,* 684–689.

BOHANNON, J. N., III, & SYMONS, V. (1988, April). *Conversational conditions of children's imitation.* Paper presented at the biennial Conference on Human Development, Charleston, SC.

BOHMAN, M., & SIGVARDSSON, S. (1990). Outcome in adoption: Lessons from longitudinal studies. In D. M. Bordzkinsky & M. D. Schechter (Eds.), *The psychology of adoption* (pp. 93–106). New York: Oxford University Press.

BOIVIN, M., & HYMEL, S. (1997). Peer experiences and social self-perceptions: A sequential model. *Developmental Psychology, 33,* 135–145.

BOLDIZAR, J. P. (1991). Assessing sex typing and androgyny in children: The children's sex role inventory. *Developmental Psychology, 27,* 505–515.

BOLDIZAR, J. P., PERRY, D. G., & PERRY, L. C. (1989). Outcome values and aggression. *Child Development, 60,* 571–579.

BONVILLIAN, J., NELSON, K. E., & CHARROW, V. (1976). Language and language-related skills in deaf and hearing children. *Sign Language Studies, 12,* 211–250.

BORGHESE, I. F., MINARD, K. L., & THOMAN, E. B. (1995). Sleep rhythmicity in premature infants: Implications for developmental status. *Sleep, 18,* 523–530.

BORKE, H. (1975). Piaget's mountains revisited: Changes in the egocentric landscape. *Developmental Psychology, 11,* 240–243.

BORKOWSKI, J. G., & MUTHUKRISNA, N. (1995). Learning environments and skill generalization: How contexts facilitate regulatory processes and efficacy beliefs. In F. Weinert & W. Schneider (Eds.), *Memory performances and competence: Issues in growth and development* (pp. 283–300). Hillsdale, NJ: Erlbaum.

BORNHOLT, L. J., GOODNOW, J. J., & COONEY, G. H. (1994). Influences of gender stereotypes on adolescents' perceptions of their own achievement. *American Educational Research Journal, 31,* 675–692.

BORNSTEIN, M. H. (1989). Sensitive periods in development: Structural characteristics and causal interpretations. *Psychological Bulletin, 105,* 179–197.

BORNSTEIN, M. H., KESSEN, W., & WEISKOPF, S. (1976). The categories of hue in infancy. *Science, 191,* 201–202.

BORNSTEIN, M. H., & LAMB, M. E. (1992). *Development in infancy: An introduction* (3rd ed.). New York: McGraw-Hill.

BORNSTEIN, M. H., TAL, J., RAHN, C., GALPERÍN, C. Z., PÀCHEUX, M., LAMOUR, M., TODA, S., AZUMA, H., OGINO, M., & TAMIS-LEMONDA, C. S. (1992a). Functional analysis of the contents of maternal speech to infants of 5 and 13 months in four cultures: Argentina, France, Japan, and the United States. *Developmental Psychology, 28,* 593–603.

BORNSTEIN, M. H., VIBBERT, M., TAL, J., & O'DONNELL, K. (1992b). Toddler language and play in the second year: Stability, covariation, and influences of parenting. *First Language, 12,* 323–338.

BORST, C. G. (1995). *Catching babies: The professionalization of childbirth, 1870–1920.* Cambridge, MA: Harvard University Press.

BORSTELMANN, L. J. (1983). Children before psychology: Ideas about children from antiquity to the late 1800s. In W. Kessen (Ed.), *Handbook of child psychology: Vol. 1. History, theory, and methods* (4th ed., pp. 1–40). New York: Wiley.

BOSTOCK, C. (1994). Does the expansion of grandparent visitation rights promote the best interests of the child?: A survey of grandparent visitation laws in fifty states. *Columbia Journal of Law and Social Problems, 27,* 319–373.

BOUCHARD, C. (1994). *The genetics of obesity.* Boca Raton, FL: CRC Press.

BOUCHARD, T. J., JR. (1997). IQ similarity in twins reared apart: Findings and responses to critics. In R. J. Sternberg & E. L. Grigorenko (Eds.), *Intelligence, heredity, and environment* (pp. 126–160). New York: Cambridge University Press.

BOUCHARD, T. J., JR., LYKKEN, D. T., MCGUE, M., SEGAL, N. L., & TELLEGEN, A. (1990). Sources of human psychological differences: The Minnesota Study of Twins Reared Apart. *Science, 250,* 223–228.

BOUCHARD, T. J., JR., & MCGUE, M. (1981). Familial studies of intelligence: A review. *Science, 212,* 1055–1058.

BOUKYDIS, C. F. Z., & BURGESS, R. L. (1982). Adult physiological response to infant cries: Effects of temperament of infant, parental status and gender. *Child Development, 53,* 1291–1298.

BOULTON, M. J. (1996). A comparison of 8- and 11-year-old girls' and boys' participation in specific types of rough-and-tumble play and aggressive fighting: Implications for functional hypotheses. *Aggressive Behavior, 22,* 271–287.

BOULTON, M. J., & SMITH, P. K. (1994). Bully/victim problems in middle-school children: Stability, self-perceived competence, peer perceptions and peer acceptance. *British Journal of Developmental Psychology, 12,* 315–329.

BOULTON, M. J., & UNDERWOOD, K. (1992). Bully/victim problems among middle school children. *British Journal of Educational Psychology, 62,* 73–87.

BOWERMAN, M. (1973). *Early syntactic development: A cross-linguistic study with special reference to Finnish.* Cambridge: Cambridge University Press.

BOWLBY, J. (1969). *Attachment and loss: Vol. 1. Attachment.* New York: Basic Books.

BOWLBY, J. (1980). *Attachment and loss: Vol. 3. Loss.* New York: Basic Books.

BOWMAN, M. C., & SAUNDERS, D. M. (1994). Community attitudes to maternal age and pregnancy after assisted reproductive technology: Too old at 50 years? *Human Reproduction, 9,* 167–171.

BOYER, K., & DIAMOND, A. (1992). Development of memory for temporal order in infants and young children. In A. Diamond (Ed.), *Development and neural bases of higher cognitive function* (pp. 267–317). New York: New York Academy of Sciences.

BOYES, M. C., & ALLEN, S. G. (1993). Styles of parent–child interaction and moral reasoning in adolescence. *Merrill-Palmer Quarterly, 39,* 551–570.

BOYES, M. C., & CHANDLER, M. (1992). Cognitive development, epistemic doubt, and identity formation in adolescence. *Journal of Youth and Adolescence, 21,* 277–304.

BOYSSON-BARDIES, B. DE, & VIHMAN, M. M. (1991). Adaptation to language: Evidence from babbling and first words in four languages. *Language, 67,* 297–319.

BRABECK, M. (1983). Moral judgment: Theory and research on differences between males and females. *Developmental Review, 3,* 274–291.

BRACKBILL, Y., MCMANUS, K., & WOODWARD, L. (1985). *Medication in maternity: Infant exposure and maternal information.* Ann Arbor: University of Michigan Press.

BRADDICK, O. (1993). Orientation and motion-selective mechanisms in infants. In K. Simons (Ed.), *Early visual development: Normal and abnormal* (pp. 163–177). New York: Oxford University Press.

BRADLEY, R. H., & CALDWELL, B. M. (1976). The relation of infants' home environments to mental test performance at fifty-four months: A follow-up study. *Child Development, 47,* 1172–1174.

BRADLEY, R. H., & CALDWELL, B. M. (1979). Home Observation for Measurement of the Environment: A revision of the preschool scale. *American Journal of Mental Deficiency, 84,* 235–244.

BRADLEY, R. H., & CALDWELL, B. M. (1981). The HOME Inventory: A validation of the preschool scale for black children. *Child Development, 52,* 708–710.

BRADLEY, R. H., & CALDWELL, B. M. (1982). The consistency of the home environment and its relation to child development. *International Journal of Behavioral Development, 5,* 445–465.

BRADLEY, R. H., CALDWELL, B. M., & ROCK, S. L. (1988). Home environment and school performance: A ten-year follow-up and examination of three models of environmental action. *Child Development, 59,* 852–867.

BRADLEY, R. H., CALDWELL, B. M., ROCK, S. L., HAMRICK, H. M., & HARRIS, P. (1988). Home Observation for Measurement of the Environment: Development of a home inventory for use with families having children 6 to 10 years old. *Contemporary Educational Psychology, 13,* 58–71.

BRADLEY, R. H., CALDWELL, B. M., ROCK, S. L., RAMEY, C. T., BARNARD, K. E., GRAY, C., HAMMOND, M. A., MITCHELL, S., GOTTFRIED, A., SIEGEL, L., & JOHNSON, D. L. (1989). Home environment and cognitive development in the first 3 years of life: A collaborative study involving six sites and three ethnic groups in North America. *Developmental Psychology, 25,* 217–235.

BRADLEY, R. H., WHITESIDE, L., MUNDFROM, D. J., CASEY, P. H., KELLEHER, K. J., & POPE, S. K. (1994). Contribution of early intervention and early caregiving experiences to resilience in low-birthweight, premature children living in poverty. *Journal of Clinical Child Psychology, 23,* 425–434.

BRAET, C., MERVIELDE, I., & VANDEREYCKEN, W. (1997). Psychological aspects of childhood obesity: A controlled study in a clinical and nonclinical sample. *Journal of Pediatric Psychology, 22,* 59–71.

BRAINE, L. G., POMERANTZ, E., LORBER, D., & KRANTZ, D. H. (1991). Conflicts with authority: Children's feelings, actions, and justifications. *Developmental Psychology, 27,* 829–840.

BRAINE, L. G., SCHAUBLE, L., KUGELMASS, S., & WINTER, A. (1993). Representation of depth by children: Spatial strategies and lateral biases. *Developmental Psychology, 29,* 466–479.

BRAINE, M. D. S. (1976). Children's first word combinations. *Monographs of the Society for Research in Child Development, 41* (1, Serial No. 164).

BRAINE, M. D. S. (1992). What sort of innate structure is needed to "bootstrap" into syntax? *Cognition, 45,* 77–100.

BRAINE, M. D. S. (1994). Is nativism sufficient? *Journal of Child Language, 21,* 1–23.

BRAINERD, C. J., & GORDON, L. L. (1994). Development of verbatim and gist memory for numbers. *Developmental Psychology, 30,* 163–177.

BRAINERD, C. J., & REYNA, V. F. (1990). Gist is the grist: Fuzzy-trace theory and the new intuitionism. *Developmental Review, 10,* 3–47.

BRAINERD, C. J., & REYNA, V. F. (1993). Memory independence and memory interference in cognitive development. *Psychological Review, 100,* 42–67.

BRAINERD, C. J., & REYNA, V. F. (1995). Learning rate, learning opportunities, and the development of forgetting. *Developmental Psychology, 31,* 251–262.

BRAND, J. E., & GREENBERG, B. S. (1994). Commercials in the classroom: The impact of Channel One advertising. *Journal of Advertising Research, 34,* 18–27.

BRAUNGART, J. M., FULKER, D. W., & PLOMIN, R. (1992). Genetic mediation of the home environment during infancy: A sibling adoption study of the HOME. *Developmental Psychology, 28,* 1048–1055.

BRAUNGART, J. M., PLOMIN, R., DEFRIES, J. C., & FULKER, D. W. (1992). Genetic influence on tester-rated infant temperament as assessed by Bayley's Infant Behavior Record: Nonadoptive and adoptive siblings and twins. *Developmental Psychology, 28,* 40–47.

BRAVERMAN, P. K., & STRASBURGER, V. C. (1994). Sexually transmitted diseases. *Clinical Pediatrics, 33,* 26–37.

BRAY, J. H., & BERGER, S. H. (1993). Developmental issues in Step-families Research Project: Family relationships and parent–child interactions. *Journal of Family Psychology, 7,* 7–17.

BRAZELTON, T. B., KOSLOWSKI, B., & TRONICK, E. Z. (1976). Neonatal behavior among urban Zambians and Americans. *Journal of the American Academy of Child Psychiatry, 15,* 97–107.

BRAZELTON, T. B., & NUGENT, J. K. (1995). *Neonatal Behavioral Assessment Scale.* London: Mac Keith Press.

BRAZELTON, T. B., NUGENT, J. K., & LESTER, B. M. (1987). Neonatal Behavioral Assessment Scale. In J. D. Osofsky (Ed.), *Handbook of infant development* (2nd ed., pp. 780–817). New York: Wiley.

BREAD FOR THE WORLD INSTITUTE. (1994). *Hunger 1994.* Silver Spring, MD: Author.

BREDEKAMP, S., & COPPLE, C. (Eds.). (1997). *Developmentally appropriate practice in early childhood programs* (rev. ed.). Washington, DC: National Association for the Education of Young Children.

BRENES, M. E., EISENBERG, N., & HELMSTADTER, G. C. (1985). Sex role development of preschoolers from two-parent and one-parent families. *Merrill-Palmer Quarterly, 31,* 33–46.

BRENNAN, W. M., AMES, E. W., & MOORE, R. W. (1966). Age differences in infants' attention to patterns of different complexities. *Science, 151,* 354–356.

BRENNER, D., & HINSDALE, G. (1978). Body build stereotypes and self-identification in three age groups of females. *Adolescence, 13,* 551–562.

BRENNER, E., & SALOVEY, P. (1997). Emotion regulation during childhood: Developmental, interpersonal, and individual considerations. In P. Salovey & D. Sluyter (Eds.), *Emotional literacy and emotional development* (pp. 168–192). New York: Basic Books.

BRETHERTON, I. (1992). The origins of attachment theory: John Bowlby and Mary Ainsworth. *Developmental Psychology, 28,* 759–775.

BRETHERTON, I., FRITZ, J., ZAHN-WAXLER, C., & RIDGEWAY, D. (1986). Learning to talk about emotions: A functionalist perspective. *Child Development, 57,* 529–548.

BREWAEYS, A., PONJAERT, I., VAN HALL, E. V., & GOLOMBOK, S. (1997). Donor insemination: Child development and family functioning in lesbian mother families. *Human Reproduction, 12,* 1349–1359.

BRIEN, M. J., & WILLIS, R. J. (1997). Costs and consequences for the fathers. In R. A. Maynard (Ed.), *Kids having kids* (pp. 95–144). Washington, DC: Urban Institute.

BRIGGS, F., & HAWKINS, R. (1996). *Keeping ourselves safe: Who benefits?* Wellington, New Zealand: New Zealand Council for Educational Research.

BRIGGS, F., & HAWKINS, R. (1999). The importance of parent involvement in child protection curricula. In L. E. Berk (Ed.), *Landscapes of development* (pp. 321–335). Belmont, CA: Wadsworth.

BRITO, G. N. O., LINS, M. F. C., PAUMGARTEN, F. J. R., & BRITO, L. S. O. (1992). Hand preference in 4- to 7-year-old children: An analysis with the Edinburgh Inventory in Brazil. *Developmental Neuropsychology, 8,* 59–68.

BROBERG, A., LAMB, M. E., & HWANG, P. (1990). Inhibition: Its stability and correlates in 16- to 40-month-old children. *Child Development, 61,* 1153–1163.

BROBERG, A. G., WESSELS, H., LAMB, M. E., & HWANG, C. P. (1997). Effects of day care on the development of cognitive abilities in 8-year-olds: A longitudinal study. *Developmental Psychology, 33,* 62–69.

BRODY, G. H., & FLOR, D. L. (1998). Maternal resources, parenting practices, and child competence in rural, single-parent African American families. *Child Development, 69,* 803–816.

BRODY, G. H., GRAZIANO, W. G., & MUSSER, L. M. (1983). Familiarity and children's behavior in same-age and mixed-age peer groups. *Developmental Psychology, 19,* 568–576.

BRODY, G. H., STONEMAN, Z., & FLOR, D. (1995). Linking family processes and academic competence among rural African American youths. *Journal of Marriage and the Family, 57,* 567–570.

BRODY, G. H., STONEMAN, Z., & FLOR, D. (1996). Parental religiosity, family processes, and youth competence in rural, two-parent African American families. *Developmental Psychology, 32,* 696–706.

BRODY, G. H., STONEMAN, Z., & McCOY, J. K. (1992). Associations of maternal and paternal direct and differential behavior with sibling relationships: Contemporaneous and longitudinal analyses. *Child Development, 63,* 82–92.

BRODY, G. H., STONEMAN, Z., & McCOY, J. K. (1994). Forecasting sibling relationships in early adolescence from child temperaments and family processes in middle childhood. *Child Development, 65,* 771–784.

BRODY, G. H., STONEMAN, Z., McCOY, J. K., & FOREHAND, R. (1992). Contemporaneous and longitudinal associations of sibling conflict with family relationship assessments and family discussions about sibling problems. *Child Development, 63,* 391–400.

BRODY, N. (1987). Jensen, Gottfredson, and the black–white difference in intelligence test scores. *Behavioral and Brain Sciences, 10,* 507–508.

BRODY, N. (1992). *Intelligence* (2nd ed.). San Diego: Academic Press.

BRONFENBRENNER, U. (1979). *The ecology of human development: Experiments by nature and design.* Cambridge, MA: Harvard University Press.

BRONFENBRENNER, U. (1989). Ecological systems theory. In R. Vasta (Ed.), *Annals of child development* (Vol. 6, pp. 187–251). Greenwich, CT: JAI Press.

BRONFENBRENNER, U. (1993). The ecology of cognitive development: Research models and fugitive findings. In R. H. Wozniak & K. W. Fischer (Eds.), *Development in context* (pp. 3–44). Hillsdale, NJ: Erlbaum.

BRONFENBRENNER, U. (1995). The bioecological model from a life course perspective: Reflections of a participant observer. In P. Moen, G. H. Elder, Jr., & K. Lüscher (Eds.), *Examining lives in context* (pp. 599–618). Washington, DC: American Psychological Association.

BRONFENBRENNER, U., & CECI, S. J. (1994). Nature–nurture reconceptualized in developmental perspective: A bioecological model. *Psychological Review, 101,* 568–586.

BRONFENBRENNER, U., & MORRIS, P. A. (1998). The ecology of developmental processes. In R. M. Lerner (Ed.), *Handbook of child psychology: Vol. 1. Theoretical models of human development* (5th ed., pp. 535–584). New York: Wiley.

BRONFENBRENNER, U., & NEVILLE, P. R. (1995). America's children and families: An international perspective. In S. L. Kagan & B. Weissbourd (Eds.), *Putting families first* (pp. 3–27). San Francisco: Jossey-Bass.

BRONSON, G. W. (1991). Infant differences in rate of visual encoding. *Child Development, 62,* 44–54.

BROOKS, P. J., & TOMASELLO, M. (1999). Young children learn to produce passives with nonce words. *Developmental Psychology, 35,* 29–44.

BROOKS-GUNN, J. (1986). The relationship of maternal beliefs about sex typing to maternal and young children's behavior. *Sex Roles, 14,* 21–35.

BROOKS-GUNN, J. (1988a). Antecedents and consequences of variations in girls' maturational timing. *Journal of Adolescent Health Care, 9,* 365–373.

BROOKS-GUNN, J. (1988b). The impact of puberty and sexual activity upon the health and education of adolescent girls and boys. *Peabody Journal of Education, 64,* 88–113.

BROOKS-GUNN, J., & CHASE-LANSDALE, P. L. (1995). Adolescent parenthood. In M. H. Bornstein (Ed.), *Handbook of parenting: Vol. 3. Status and social conditions of parenting* (pp. 113–149). Mahwah, NJ: Erlbaum.

BROOKS-GUNN, J., McCARTON, C. M., CASEY, P. H., McCORMICK, M. C., BAUER, C. R., BERNBAUM, J. C., TYSON, J., SWANSON, M., BENNETT, F. C., SCOTT, D. T., TONASCIA, J., & MEINERT, C. L. (1994). Early intervention in low-birth-weight premature infants. *Journal of the American Medical Association, 272,* 1257–1262.

BROOKS-GUNN, J., & RUBLE, D. N. (1980). Menarche: The interaction of physiology, cultural, and social factors. In A. J. Dan, E. A. Graham, & C. P. Beecher (Eds.), *The menstrual cycle: A synthesis of interdisciplinary research* (pp. 141–159). New York: Springer-Verlag.

BROOKS-GUNN, J., & RUBLE, D. N. (1983). The experience of menarche from a developmental perspective. In J. Brooks-Gunn & A. C. Peterson (Eds.), *Girls at puberty* (pp. 155–177). New York: Plenum.

BROOKS-GUNN, J., & WARREN, M. P. (1989). Biological and social contributions to negative affect in young adolescent girls. *Child Development, 60,* 40–55.

BROOKS-GUNN, J., WARREN, M. P., SAMELSON, M., & FOX, R. (1986). Physical similarity of and disclosure of menarcheal status to friends: Effects of grade and pubertal status. *Journal of Early Adolescence, 6,* 3–14.

BROPHY, J. E. (1983). Research on the self-fulfilling prophecy and teacher expectations. *Journal of Educational Psychology, 75,* 631–661.

BROWN, A. L. (1997). Transforming schools into communities of thinking and learning about serious matters. *American Psychologist, 52,* 399–413.

BROWN, A. L., & CAMPIONE, J. C. (1972). Recognition memory for perceptually similar pictures in preschool children. *Journal of Experimental Psychology, 95,* 55–62.

BROWN, A. L., & CAMPIONE, J. C. (1994). Guided discovery in a community of learners. In K. McGilly (Ed.), *Classroom lessons: Integrating cognitive theory and classroom practice* (pp. 229–270). Cambridge, MA: MIT Press.

BROWN, A. L., & FERRARA, R. A. (1985). Diagnosing zones of proximal development. In J. Wertsch (Ed.), *Culture, communication, and cognition* (pp. 273–305). New York: Cambridge University Press.

BROWN, A. L., SMILEY, S. S., DAY, J. D., TOWNSEND, M., & LAWTON, S. Q. C. (1977). Intrusion of a thematic idea in children's recall of prose. *Child Development, 48,* 1454–1466.

BROWN, A. L., SMILEY, S. S., & LAWTON, S. Q. C. (1978). The effects of experience on the selection of suitable retrieval cues for studying texts. *Child Development, 49,* 829–835.

BROWN, A. M. (1990). Development of visual sensitivity to light and color vision in human infants: A critical review. *Vision Research, 30,* 1159–1188.

BROWN, B. (1990). Peer groups. In S. Feldman & G. Elliott (Eds.), *At the threshold: The developing adolescent* (pp. 171–196). Cambridge, UK: Cambridge University Press.

BROWN, B. B., CLASEN, D., & EICHER, S. (1986). Perceptions of peer pressure, peer conformity dispositions, and self-reported behavior among adolescents. *Developmental Psychology, 22,* 521–530.

BROWN, B. B., LOHR, M. J., & MC-CLENAHAN, E. L. (1986). Early adolescents' perceptions of peer pressure. *Journal of Early Adolescence, 6,* 139–154.

BROWN, D. (1991). *Human universals.* New York: McGraw-Hill.

BROWN, J. R., DONELAN-McCALL, N., & DUNN, J. (1996). Why talk about mental states? The significance of children's conversations with friends, siblings and mothers. *Child Development, 67,* 836–849.

BROWN, J. R., & DUNN, J. (1992). Talk with your mother or your sibling? Developmental changes in early family conversations about feelings. *Child Development, 63,* 336–349.

BROWN, R. (1973). *A first language: The early stages.* Cambridge, MA: Harvard University Press.

BROWN, R., & HANLON, C. (1970). Derivational complexity and order of acquisition in child speech. In J. R. Hayes (Ed.), *Cognition and the development of language* (pp. 11–53). New York: Wiley.

BROWNELL, C. A., & CARRIGER, M. S. (1990). Changes in cooperation and self-other differentiation during the second year. *Child Development, 61,* 1164–1174.

BRUCK, M., CECI, S. J., FRANCOEUR, E., & RENICK, A. (1995). Anatomically detailed dolls do not facilitate preschoolers' reports of a pediatric examination involving genital touching. *Journal of Experimental Psychology: Applied, 1,* 95–109.

BRUCK, M., CECI, S. J., & HEMBROOKE, H. (1998). Reliability and credibility of young children's reports. *American Psychologist, 53,* 136–151.

BRUERD, B., & JONES, C. (1996). Preventing baby bottle tooth decay: Eight-year results. *Public Health Reports, 111,* 63–65.

BRUNER, J. S. (1983). The acquisition of pragmatic commitments. In R. M. Golinkoff (Ed.), *The transition from prelinguistic to linguistic communication* (pp. 27–42). Hillsdale, NJ: Erlbaum.

BRYAN, Y. E., & NEWMAN, J. D. (1988). Influence of infant cry structure on the heart rate of the listener. In J. D. Newman (Ed.), *The physiological control of mammalian vocalization* (pp. 413–432). New York: Plenum.

BRYK, A. S., LEE, V. E., & HOLLAND, P. B. (1993). *Catholic schools and the common good.* Cambridge, MA: Harvard University Press.

BUCHANAN, A. (1996). *Cycles of child maltreatment.* Chichester, UK: Wiley.

BUCHANAN, C. M., ECCLES, J. S., & BECKER, J. B. (1992). Are adolescents the victims of raging hormones? Evidence for activational effects of hormones on moods and behavior at adolescence. *Psychological Bulletin, 111,* 62–107.

BUCHANAN, C. M., MACCOBY, E. E., & DORNBUSCH, S. M. (1996). *Adolescents after divorce.* Cambridge, MA: Harvard University Press.

BUDWIG, N. (1995). *A developmental-functionalist approach to child language.* Mahwah, NJ: Erlbaum.

BUEKENS, P., KOTELCHUCK, M., BLONDEL, B., KRISTENSEN, F. B., CHEN, J-H., & MASUY-STROOBANT, G. (1993). A comparison of prenatal care use in the United States and Europe. *American Journal of Public Health, 83,* 31–36.

BUGENTAL, D. B., BLUE, J., CORTEZ, V., FLECK, K., & RODRIQUEZ, A. (1992). Influences of a witnessed affect of information processing in children. *Child Development, 63,* 774–786.

BUGENTAL, D. B., BLUE, J., & CRUZ-COSA, M. (1989). Perceived control over caregiving outcomes: Implications for child abuse. *Developmental Psychology, 25,* 532–539.

BUHRMESTER, D. (1996). Need fulfillment, interpersonal competence, and the developmental contexts of early adolescent friendship. In W. M. Bukowski, A. F. Newcomb, & W. W. Hartup (Eds.), *The company they keep: Friendship during childhood and adolescence* (pp. 158–185). New York: Cambridge University Press.

BUHRMESTER, D., & CARBERY, J. (1992, March). *Daily patterns of self-disclosure and adolescent adjustment.* Paper presented at the biennial meeting of the Society for Research on Adolescence, Washington, DC.

BUHRMESTER, D., & FURMAN, W. (1990). Perceptions of sibling relationships during middle childhood and adolescence. *Child Development, 61,* 1387–1398.

BUHRMESTER, D., & PRAGER, K. (1995). Patterns and functions of self-disclosure during childhood and adolescence. In K. J. Rotenberg (Ed.), *Disclosure processes in children and adolescents* (pp. 10–56). New York: Cambridge University Press.

BULLOCK, M., & LUTKENHAUS, P. (1990). Who am I? The development of self-understanding in toddlers. *Merrill-Palmer Quarterly, 36,* 217–238.

BURCHINAL, M. R., ROBERTS, J. E., NABORS, L. A., & BRYANT, D. M. (1996). Quality of center child care and infant cognitive and language development. *Child Development, 67,* 606–620.

BURHANS, K. K., & DWECK, C. S. (1995). Helplessness in early childhood: The role of contingent worth. *Child Development, 66,* 1719–1738.

BURKETT, G., YASIN, S. Y., PALOW, D., LaVOIE, L., & MARTINEZ, M. (1994). Patterns of cocaine binging: Effect on pregnancy. *American Journal of Obstetrics and Gynecology, 171,* 372–379.

BURKHARDT, S. A., & ROTATORI, A. F. (1995). *Treatment and prevention of childhood sexual abuse.* Washington, DC: Taylor & Francis.

BURNS, R. B., & MASON, D. A. (1998). Class formation and composition in elementary schools. *American Educational Research Journal, 35,* 739–772.

BURNS, S. M., & BRAINERD, C. J. (1979). Effects of constructive and dramatic play on perspective taking in very young children. *Developmental Psychology, 15,* 512–521.

BURR, D. C., MORRONE, C., & FIORENTINI, A. (1996). Spatial and temporal properties of infant colour vision. In F. Vital-Durand, J. Atkinson, & O. J. Braddick (Eds.), *Infant vision* (pp. 63–77). Oxford, UK: Oxford University Press.

BURTON, B. K. (1992). Limb anomalies associated with chorionic villus sampling. *Obstetrics and Gynecology, 79* (Pt. 1), 726–730.

BURTON, L. M. (1992). Black grandparents rearing children of drug-addicted parents: Stressors, outcomes, and social service needs. *Gerontologist, 32,* 744–751.

BURTS, D. C., HART, C. H., CHARLESWORTH, R., FLEEGE, P. O., MOSLEY, J., & THOMASSON, R. H. (1992). Observed activities and stress behaviors of children in developmentally appropriate and inappropriate kindergarten classrooms. *Early Childhood Research Quarterly, 7,* 297–318.

BUSHNELL, E. W. (1985). The decline of visually guided reaching during infancy. *Infant Behavior and Development, 8,* 139–155.

BUSHNELL, E. W., & BOUDREAU, J. P. (1993). Motor development and the mind: The potential role of motor abilities as a determinant of aspects of perceptual development. *Child Development, 64,* 1005–1021.

BUSINK, R. (1997). Reading and phonological awareness: What we have learned and how we can use it. *Reading Research and Instruction, 36,* 199–215.

BUSSEY, K. (1992). Lying and truthfulness: Children's definitions, standards, and evaluative reactions. *Child Development, 63,* 129–137.

BUSSEY, K., & BANDURA, A. (1984). Influence of gender constancy and social power on sex-linked modeling. *Journal of Personality and Social Psychology, 47,* 1292–1302.

BUSSEY, K., & BANDURA, A. (1992). Self-regulatory mechanisms governing gender development. *Child Development, 63,* 1236–1250.

BUTLER, G. E., MCKIE, M., & RATCLIFFE, S. G. (1990). The cyclical nature of prepubertal growth. *Annals of Human Biology, 17,* 177–198.

BUTLER, R. (1998). Age trends in the use of social and temporal comparison for self-evaluation: Examination of a novel developmental hypothesis. *Child Development, 69,* 1054–1073.

BUTLER, R. (1999). Information seeking and achievement motivation in middle childhood and adolescence: The role of conceptions of ability. *Developmental Psychology, 35,* 146–163.

BUTLER, R., & RUZANY, N. (1993). Age and socialization effects on the development of social comparison motives and normative ability assessment in kibbutz and urban children. *Child Development, 64,* 532–543.

BUYSSE, U., & BAILEY, D. B. (1993). Behavioral and developmental outcomes in young children with disabilities in integrated and segregated settings: A review of comparative studies. *Journal of Special Education, 26,* 434–461.

BYBEE, J., & SLOBIN, D. (1982). Rules and schemes in the development and use of the English past tense. *Language, 58,* 265–289.

BYRNE, B. M., & SHAVELSON, R. J. (1996). On the structure of social self-concept for pre-, early, and late adolescents: A test of the Shavelson, Hubner, & Stanton (1976) model. *Journal of Personality and Social Psychology, 70,* 599–613.

BYRNE, D. F. (1973). The development of role taking in adolescence. Dissertation *Abstracts International, 34,* 56478. (University Microfilms No. 74–11, 314).

BYRNES, J. P., & TAKAHIRA, S. (1993). Explaining gender differences on SAT-math items. *Developmental Psychology, 29,* 805–810.

C

CADOFF, J. (1995). Can we prevent SIDS? *Parents, 70*(3), 30–31, 35.

CAIN, K. M., & DWECK, C. S. (1995). The relation between motivational patterns and achievement cognitions through the elementary school years. *Merrill-Palmer Quarterly, 41,* 25–52.

CAINE, N. (1986). Behavior during puberty and adolescence. In G. Mitchell & J. Erwin (Eds.), *Comparative primate biology: Vol. 2A. Behavior, conservation, and ecology* (pp. 327–361). New York: Alan R. Liss.

CAIRNS, E. (1996). *Children and political violence.* Cambridge: Blackwell.

CAIRNS, R. B. (1992). The making of a developmental science: The contributions and intellectual heritage of James Mark Baldwin. *Developmental Psychology, 28,* 17–24.

CAIRNS, R. B. (1998). The making of developmental psychology. In R. M. Lerner (Ed.), *Handbook of child psychology: Vol. 1. Theoretical models of human development* (5th ed., pp. 25–105). New York: Wiley.

CAIRNS, R. B., LEUNG, M. C., BUCHANAN, L., & CAIRNS, B. D. (1995). Friendships and social networks in childhood and adolescence: Fluidity, reliability, and interrelations. *Child Development, 66,* 1330–1345.

CALDERA, Y. M., HUSTON, A. C., & O'BRIEN, M. (1989). Social interactions and play patterns of parents and toddlers with feminine, masculine, and neutral toys. *Child Development, 60,* 70–76.

CALDWELL, B. M., & BRADLEY, R. H. (1994). Environmental issues in developmental follow-up research. In S. L. Friedman & H. C. Haywood (Eds.), *Developmental follow-up* (pp. 235–256). San Diego: Academic Press.

CALDWELL, C. H., & ANTONUCCI, T. C. (1997). Childbearing during adolescence: Mental health risks and opportunities. In J. Schulenberg, J. L. Maggs, & K. Hurrelmann (Eds.), *Health risks and developmental transitions during adolescence* (pp. 220–245). New York: Cambridge University Press.

CALISO, J., & MILNER, J. (1992). Childhood history of abuse and child abuse screening. *Child Abuse and Neglect, 16,* 647–659.

CALKINS, S. D., FOX, N. A., & MARSHALL, T. R. (1996). Behavioral and physiological antecedents of inhibited and uninhibited behavior. *Child Development, 67,* 523–540.

CALLANAN, M. A. (1991). Parent-child collaboration in young children's understanding of category hierarchies. In S. A. Gelman & J. P. Byrnes (Eds.), *Perspectives on language and thought: Interrelations in development* (pp. 440–484). Cambridge: Cambridge University Press.

CAMARA, K. A., & RESNICK, G. (1988). Interparental conflict and cooperation: Factors moderating children's post-divorce adjustment. In E. M. Hetherington & J. D. Arasteh (Ed.), *Impact of divorce, single parenting, and stepparenting on children* (pp. 169–195). Hillsdale, NJ: Erlbaum.

CAMARATA, S., & LEONARD, L. B. (1986). Young children pronounce object words more accurately than action words. *Journal of Child Language, 13,* 51–65.

CAMPBELL, F. A., & RAMEY, C. T. (1991). The Carolina Abecedarian Project. In M. Burchinal (Chair), *Early experience and children's competencies: New findings from four longitudinal studies.* Symposium presented at the biennial meeting of the Society for Research in Child Development, Seattle, WA.

CAMPBELL, F. A., & RAMEY, C. T. (1994). Effects of early intervention on intellectual and academic achievement: A follow-up study of children from low-income families. *Child Development, 65,* 684–698.

CAMPBELL, F. A., & RAMEY, C. T. (1995). Cognitive and school outcomes for high-risk African-American students at middle adolescence: Positive effects of early intervention. *American Educational Research Journal, 32,* 743–772.

CAMPBELL, J. R., VOELKL, K. E., & DONAHUE, P. L. (1997). *NAEP 1996 trends in academic progress.* Washington, DC: U.S. Government Printing Office.

CAMPBELL, P. F., & SCHWARTZ, S. S. (1986). Microcomputers in the preschool: Children, parents, and teachers. In P. Campbell & G. Fein (Eds.), *Young children and microcomputers* (pp. 45–60). Englewood Cliffs, NJ: Prentice-Hall.

CAMPBELL, R., & SAIS, E. (1995). Accelerated metalinguistic (phonological) awareness in bilingual children. *British Journal of Developmental Psychology, 13,* 61–68.

CAMPBELL, S. B., COHN, J. F., & MEYERS, T. (1995). Depression in first-time mothers: Mother–infant interaction and depression chronicity. *Developmental Psychology, 31,* 349–357.

CAMPIONE, J. C., & BROWN, A. L. (1987). Linking dynamic assessment with school achievement. In C. S. Lidz (Ed.), *Dynamic as-*

sessment: An interactional approach to evaluation of learning potential (pp. 173–195). New York: Guilford.

CAMPOS, J. J., & BERTENTHAL, B. I. (1989). Locomotion and psychological development. In F. Morrison, K. Lord, & D. Keating (Eds.), *Applied developmental psychology* (Vol. 3, pp. 229–258). New York: Academic Press.

CAMPOS, J. J., CAPLOVITZ, K. B., LAMB, M. E., GOLDSMITH, H. H., & STENBERG, C. (1983). Socioemotional development. In M. M. Haith & J. J. Campos (Eds.), *Handbook of child psychology: Vol. 3. Infancy and developmental psychobiology* (pp. 783–915). New York: Wiley.

CAMPOS, J. J., KERMOIAN, R., & ZUMBAHLEN, M. R. (1992). Socioemotional transformation in the family system following infant crawling onset. In N. Eisenberg & R. A. Fabes (Eds.), *New directions for child development* (No. 55, pp. 25–40). San Francisco: Jossey-Bass.

CAMPOS, J. J., MUMME, D., DERMOIAN, R., & CAMPOS, R. (1994). A functionalist perspective on the nature of emotion. In N. Fox (Ed.), The development of emotion regulation: Biological and behavioral considerations. *Monographs of the Society for Research in Child Development, 59*(2/3, Serial No. 240).

CAMPOS, R., RAFFAELLI, M., UDE, W., GRECO, M., RUFF, A., ROLF, J., ANTUNES, C. M., HALSEY, N., GRECO, D., & STREET YOUTH STUDY GROUP. (1994). Social networks and daily activities of street youth in Belo Horitzonte, Brazil. *Child Development, 65,* 319–330.

CAMPOS, R. G. (1989). Soothing pain-elicited distress in infants with swaddling and pacifiers. *Child Development, 60,* 781–792.

CAMRAS, L. A. (1992). Expressive development and basic emotions. *Cognition and Emotion, 6,* 267–283.

CAMRAS, L. A., OSTER, H., CAMPOS, J. J., MIYAKE, K., & BRADSHAW, D. (1992). Japanese and American infants' responses to arm restraint. *Developmental Psychology, 28,* 578–583.

CAMRAS, L. A., & SACHS, V. B. (1991). Social referencing and caretaker expressive behavior in a day care setting. *Infant Behavior and Development, 14,* 27–36.

CANDY-GIBBS, S., SHARP, K., & PETRUN, C. (1985). The effects of age, object, and cultural/religious background on children's concepts of death. *Omega, 154,* 329–345.

CANICK, J. A., & SALLER, D. N., JR. (1993). Maternal serum screening for aneuploidy and open fetal defects. *Obstetrics and*

Gynecology Clinics of North America, 20, 443–454.

CANOBI, K. H., REEVE, R. A., & PATTISON, P. E. (1998). The role of conceptual understanding in children's addition problem solving. *Developmental Psychology, 34,* 882–891.

CANTOR, J., & HARRISON, K. (1997). Ratings and advisories for television programming. In Center for Communication and Social Policy (Ed.), *National television violence study* (Vol. 2). Newbury Park, CA: Sage.

CAPALDI, D. M., & PATTERSON, G. R. (1991). Relation of parental transitions to boys' adjustment problems: I. A linear hypothesis. II. Mothers at risk for transitions and unskilled parenting. *Developmental Psychology, 27,* 489–504.

CAPELLI, C. A., NAKAGAWA, N., & MADDEN, C. M. (1990). How children understand sarcasm: The role of context and intonation. *Child Development, 61,* 1824–1841.

CAPLAN, M., VESPO, J., PEDERSEN, J., & HAY, D. F. (1991). Conflict and its resolution in small groups of one- and two-year-olds. *Child Development, 62,* 1513–1524.

CAPLAN, N., CHOY, M. H., & WHITMORE, J. K. (1991). *Children of the boat people: A study of educational success.* Ann Arbor: University of Michigan Press.

CARDON, L. R., FULKER, D. W., DEFRIES, J. C., & PLOMIN, R. (1992). Continuity and change in general cognitive ability from 1 to 7 years of age. *Developmental Psychology, 28,* 64–73.

CAREY, S., & SPELKE, E. (1994). Domain-specific knowledge and conceptual change. In L. A. Hirschfeld & S. A. Gelman (Eds.), *Mapping the mind* (pp. 169–200). New York: Cambridge University Press.

CARPENDALE, J. I., & CHANDLER, M. J. (1996). On the distinction between false belief understanding and subscribing to an interpretive theory of mind. *Child Development, 67,* 1686–1706.

CARPENTER, C. J. (1983). Activity structure and play: Implications for socialization. In M. Liss (Ed.), *Social and cognitive skills: Sex roles and children's play* (pp. 117–145). New York: Academic Press.

CARPENTER, C. J., HUSTON, A. C., & HOLT, W. (1986). Modification of preschool sex-typed behaviors by participation in adult-structured activities. *Sex Roles, 14,* 603–615.

CARPENTER, M., NAGELL, K., & TOMASELLO, M. (1998). Social cognition, joint attention, and communicative competence. *Monographs of the Society for Research in Child Development, 63*(4, Serial No. 255).

CARR, J. (1995). *Down syndrome: Children growing up.* Cambridge: Cambridge University Press.

CARR, M., & SCHNEIDER, W. (1991). Long-term maintenance of organizational strategies in kindergarten children. *Contemporary Educational Psychology, 16,* 61–75.

CARR, S., DABBS, J., & CARR, T. (1975). Mother–infant attachment: The importance of the mother's visual field. *Child Development, 46,* 331–338.

CARRAHER, T., SCHLIEMANN, A. D., & CARRAHER, D. W. (1988). Mathematical concepts in everyday life. In G. B. Saxe & M. Gearhart (Eds.), *New directions for child development* (Vol. 41, pp. 71–87). San Francisco: Jossey-Bass.

CARROLL, J. B. (1993). *Human cognitive abilities: A survey of factor-analytic studies.* New York: Cambridge University Press.

CARROLL, J. B. (1997). The three-stratum theory of cognitive abilities. In D. P. Flanagan, J. L. Genshaft, & P. Harrison (Eds.), *Contemporary intellectual assessment* (pp. 122–130). New York: Guilford.

CARRUTH, B. R., GOLDBERG, D. L., & SKINNER, J. D. (1991). Do parents and peers mediate the influence of television advertising on food-related purchases? *Journal of Adolescent Research, 6,* 253–271.

CARTER, D. B., & LEVY, G. D. (1991). Gender schemas and the salience of gender: Individual differences in nonreversal discrimination learning. *Sex Roles, 25,* 555–567.

CASAER, P. (1993). Old and new facts about perinatal brain development. *Journal of Child Psychology and Psychiatry, 34,* 101–109.

CASE, R. (1992). *The mind's staircase.* Hillsdale, NJ: Erlbaum.

CASE, R. (1996). Introduction: Reconceptualizing the nature of children's conceptual structures and their development in middle childhood. In R. Case & Y. Okamoto (Eds.), The role of central conceptual structures in the development of children's thought. *Monographs of the Society for Research in Child Development, 61*(1–2, Serial No. 246), pp. 1–26.

CASE, R. (1998). The development of central conceptual structures. In D. Kuhn & R. Siegler (Eds.), *Handbook of child psychology: Vol. 2. Cognition, perception, and language* (5th ed., pp. 745–800). New York: Wiley.

CASE, R., GRIFFIN, S., McKEOUGH, A., & OKAMOTO, Y. (1992). Parallels in the development of children's social, numerical, and spatial thought. In R. Case (Ed.), *The mind's staircase* (pp. 269–284). Hillsdale, NJ: Erlbaum.

CASE, R., & OKAMOTO, Y. (Eds.). (1996). The role of central conceptual structures in the development of children's thought. *Monographs of the Society for Research in Child Development, 61*(1–2, Serial No. 246).

CASELLI, M. C., BATES, E., CASADIO, P., FENSON, J., FENSON, L., SANDERL, L., & WEIR, J. (1995). A cross-linguistic study of early lexical development. *Cognitive Development, 10,* 159–199.

CASEY, M. B., NUTTALL, R. L., & PEZARIS, E. (1997). Mediators of gender differences in mathematics college entrance test scores: A comparison of spatial skills with internalized beliefs and anxieties. *Developmental Psychology, 33,* 669–680.

CASEY, M. B., NUTTALL, R., PEZARIS, E., & BENBOW, C. P. (1995). The influence of spatial ability on gender differences in mathematics college entrance test scores across diverse samples. *Developmental Psychology, 31,* 697–705.

CASPI, A. (1998). Personality development across the life course. In N. Eisenberg (Ed.), *Handbook of child psychology: Vol. 3. Social, emotional, and personality development* (5th ed., pp. 311–388). New York: Wiley.

CASPI, A., ELDER, G. H., JR., & BEM, D. J. (1987). Moving against the world: Life-course patterns of explosive children. *Developmental Psychology, 23,* 308–313.

CASPI, A., ELDER, G. H., JR., & BEM, D. J. (1988). Moving away from the world: Life-course patterns of shy children. *Developmental Psychology, 24,* 824–831.

CASPI, A., LYNAM, D., MOFFITT, T. E., & SILVA, P. A. (1993). Unraveling girls' delinquency: Biological, dispositional, and contextual contributions to adolescent misbehavior. *Developmental Psychology, 29,* 19–30.

CASPI, A., & SILVA, P. A. (1995). Temperamental qualities at age three predict personality traits in young adulthood: Longitudinal evidence from a birth cohort. *Child Development, 66,* 486–498.

CASSIDY, J., & BERLIN, L. J. (1994). The insecure/ambivalent pattern of attachment: Theory and research. *Child Development, 65,* 971–991.

CASSIDY, J., PARKE, R. D., BUTKOVSKY, L., & BRAUNGART, J. M. (1992). Family–peer connections: The roles of emotional expressiveness within the family and children's understanding of emotions. *Child Development, 63,* 603–618.

CASSIDY, S. B. (1995). Uniparental disomy and genomic imprinting as causes of human genetic disease. *Environmental and Molecular Mutagenesis, 25,* 13–20.

CATHERWOOD, D., CRASSINI, B., & FREIBERG, K. (1989). Infant response to stimuli of similar hue and dissimilar shape: Tracing the origins of the categorization of objects by hue. *Child Development, 60,* 752–762.

CATSAMBIS, S. (1994). The path to math: Gender and racial-ethnic differences in mathematics participation from middle school to high school. *Sociology of Education, 67,* 199–215.

CATTELL, J. M. (1890). Mental tests and measurements. *Mind, 15,* 373–381.

CATTELL, R. B. (1971). *Abilities: Their structure, growth and action.* Boston: Houghton Mifflin.

CATTELL, R. B. (1987). *Intelligence: Its structure, growth and action.* Amsterdam: North-Holland.

CAUCE, A. M. (1987). School and peer competence in early adolescence: A test of domain-specific self-perceived competence. *Developmental Psychology, 23,* 287–291.

CAVALLI-SFORZA, L. L., MENOZZI, P., & PIAZZA, A. (1994). *The history and geography of human genes.* Princeton, NJ: Princeton University Press.

CECI, S. J. (1990). *On intelligence . . . More or less.* Englewood Cliffs, NJ: Prentice-Hall.

CECI, S. J. (1991). How much does schooling influence general intelligence and its cognitive components? A reassessment of the evidence. *Developmental Psychology, 27,* 703–722.

CECI, S. J., & BRUCK, M. (1993). Suggestibility of the child witness: A historical review and synthesis. *Psychological Bulletin, 113,* 403–439.

CECI, S. J., & BRUCK, M. (1998). Children's testimony: Applied and basic issues. In I. Sigel & K. A. Renninger (Eds.), *Handbook of child psychology: Vol. 4. Child psychology in practice* (5th ed., pp. 713–774). New York: Wiley.

CECI, S. J., LEICHTMAN, M. D., & BRUCK, M. (1994). The suggestibility of children's eyewitness reports: Methodological issues. In F. Weinert & W. Schneider (Eds.), *Memory development: State of the art and future directions* (pp. 323–347). Hillsdale, NJ: Erlbaum.

CECI, S. J., & LIKER, J. (1986). Academic and nonacademic intelligence: An experimental separation. In R. J. Sternberg & R. K. Wagner (Eds.), *Practical intelligence: Nature and origins of competence in the everyday world* (pp. 119–142). New York: Cambridge University Press.

CECI, S. J., & ROAZZI, A. (1994). The effects of context on cognition: Postcards from Brazil. In R. J. Sternberg (Ed.), *Mind in context* (pp. 74–101). New York: Cambridge University Press.

CECI, S. J., ROSENBLUM, T. B., & KUMPF, M. (1998). The shrinking gap between high- and low-scoring groups: Current trends and possible causes. In U. Neisser (Ed.), *The rising curve* (pp. 287–302). Washington, DC: American Psychological Association.

CECI, S. J., & WILLIAMS, W. M. (1997). Schooling, intelligence, and income. *American Psychologist, 52,* 1051–1058.

CENTER FOR COMMUNICATION AND SOCIAL POLICY. (ED.). (1998). *National television violence study* (Vol. 2). Newbury Park, CA: Sage.

CENTRAL INTELLIGENCE AGENCY. (1998). *The world fact book.* Washington, DC: U.S. Government Printing Office.

CERNOCH, J. M., & PORTER, R. H. (1985). Recognition of maternal axillary odors by infants. *Child Development, 56,* 1593–1598.

CERVANTES, C. A., & CALLANAN, M. A. (1998). Labels and explanations in mother–child emotion talk: Age and gender differentiation. *Developmental Psychology, 34,* 88–98.

CHALL, J. S. (1983). *Stages of reading development.* New York: McGraw-Hill.

CHALMERS, J. B., & TOWNSEND, M. A. R. (1990). The effects of training in social perspective taking on socially maladjusted girls. *Child Development, 61,* 178–190.

CHAN, R. W., RABOY, B., & PATTERSON, C. J. (1998). Psychosocial adjustment among children conceived via donor insemination by lesbian and heterosexual mothers. *Child Development, 69,* 443–457.

CHANDLER, M. J. (1973). Egocentrism and antisocial behavior: The assessment and training of social perspective-taking skills. *Developmental Psychology, 9,* 326–332.

CHANDLER, M. J., & CARPENDALE, J. I. (1998). Inching toward a mature theory of mind. In M. Ferrari & R. J. Sternberg (Eds.), *Self-awareness: Its nature and development* (pp. 148–190). New York: Guilford.

CHANDRA, R. K. (1991). Interactions between early nutrition and the immune system. In *Ciba Foundation Symposium* (No. 156, pp. 77–92). Chichester, England: Wiley.

CHANEY, C. (1992). Language development, metalinguistic skills, and print awareness in 3-year-old children. *Applied Psycholinguistics, 13,* 485–514.

CHAO, R. K. (1994). Beyond parental control and authoritarian parenting style: Understanding Chinese parenting through the cultural notion of training. *Child Development, 65,* 1111–1119.

CHAPMAN, K. L., LEONARD, L. B., & MERVIS, C. B. (1986). The effect of feedback on young children's inappropriate word usage. *Journal of Child Language, 13,* 101–117.

CHAPMAN, M., & LINDENBERGER, U. (1988). Functions, operations, and décalage in the development of transitivity. *Developmental Psychology, 24,* 542–551.

CHAPMAN, M., ZAHN-WAXLER, C., IANNOTTI, R., & COOPERMAN, G. (1987). Empathy and responsibility in the motivation of children's helping. *Developmental Psychology, 23,* 140–145.

CHARMAN, T., SWETTENHAM, J., BARON-COHEN, S., COX, A., BAIRD, G., & DREW, A. (1997). Infants with autism: An investigation of empathy, pretend play, joint attention, and imitation. *Developmental Psychology, 33,* 781–789.

CHASE, C., TEELE, D. W., KLEIN, J. O., & ROSNER, B. A. (1995). Behavioral sequelae of otitis media for infants at one year of age and their mothers. In D. J., Lim, C. D. Bluestone, J. O. Klein, J. D. Nelson, & P. L. Ogra (Eds.), *Recent advances in otitis media.* Ontario: Decker.

CHASE-LANSDALE, P. L., BROOKS-GUNN, J., & ZAMSKY, E. S. (1994). Young African-American multigenerational families in poverty: Quality of mothering and grandmothering. *Child Development, 65,* 373–393.

CHASE-LANSDALE, P. L., CHERLIN, A. J., & KIERNAIN, K. E. (1995). The long-term effects of parental divorce on the mental health of young children. *Child Development, 66,* 1614–1634.

CHASE-LANSDALE, P. L., GORDON, R., BROOKS-GUNN, J., & KLEBANOV, P. K. (1997). Neighborhood and family influences on the intellectual and behavioral competence of preschool and early school-age children. In J. Brooks-Gunn, G. Duncan, & J. L. Aber (Eds.), *Neighborhood poverty: Context and consequences for development* (pp. 79–118). New York: Russell Sage Foundation.

CHASE-LANSDALE, P. L., & VINOVSKIS, M. A. (1995). *Escape from poverty: What makes a difference for children?* New York: Cambridge University Press.

CHASSIN, L., CURRAN, P. J., HUSSONG, A. M., & COLDER, C. R. (1996). The relation of parent alcoholism to adolescent substance use: A longitudinal follow-up

study. *Journal of Abnormal Psychology, 105,* 70–80.

CHATKUPT, S., MINTZ, M., EPSTEIN, L. G., BHANSALI, D., & KOENIGSBERGER, M. R. (1989). Neuroimaging studies in children with human immunodeficiency virus type 1 infection. *Annals of Neurology, 26,* 453.

CHEN, C., & STEVENSON, H. W. (1995). Motivation and mathematics achievement: A comparative study of Asian-American, Caucasian-American, and East Asian high school students. *Child Development, 66,* 1215–1234.

CHEN, X., HASTINGS, P. D., RUBIN, K. H., CHEN, H., CEN, G., & STEWART, S. L. (1998). Child-rearing attitudes and behavioral inhibition in Chinese and Canadian toddlers: A cross-cultural study. *Developmental Psychology, 34,* 677–686.

CHEN, X., RUBIN, K. H., & LI, D. (1997). Relation between academic achievement and social adjustment: Evidence from Chinese children. *Developmental Psychology, 33,* 518–525.

CHEN, X., RUBIN, K. H., & LI, Z. (1995). Social functioning and adjustment in Chinese children: A longitudinal study. *Developmental Psychology, 31,* 531–539.

CHEN, Y-C., YU, M-L., ROGAN, W., GLADEN, B., & HSU, C-C. (1994). A 6-year follow-up of behavior and activity disorders in the Taiwan Yu-cheng children. *American Journal of Public Health, 84,* 415–421.

CHEN, Y-J., & HSU, C-C. (1994). Effects of prenatal exposure to PCBs on the neurological function of children: A neuropsychological and neurophysiological study. *Developmental Medicine & Child Neurology, 36,* 312–320.

CHEN, Z., SANCHEZ, R. P., & CAMPBELL, T. (1997). From beyond to within their grasp: The rudiments of analogical problem solving in 10- to 13-month-olds. *Developmental Psychology, 33,* 790–801.

CHERLIN, A. J., & FURSTENBERG, F. F., JR. (1986). *The new American grandparent.* New York: Basic Books.

CHERLIN, A. J., FURSTENBERG, F. F., JR., CHASE-LANSDALE, P. L., KIERNAN, K. E., ROBINS, P. K., MORRISON, D. R., & TEITLER, J. O. (1991). Longitudinal studies of effects of divorce on children in Great Britain and the United States. *Science, 252,* 1386–1389.

CHERLIN, A. J., KIERNAN, K. E., & CHASE-LANSDALE, P. L. (1995). Parental divorce in childhood and demographic outcomes in young adulthood. *Demography, 32,* 299–318.

CHERNY, S. S. (1994). Home environmental influences on general cognitive ability. In J. C. DeFries, R. Plomin, & D. W. Fulker (Eds.), *Nature and nurture during middle childhood* (pp. 262–280). Cambridge, MA: Blackwell.

CHESS, S., & THOMAS, A. (1984). *Origins and evolution of behavior disorders.* New York: Brunner/Mazel.

CHI, M. T. H. (1978). Knowledge structures and memory development. In R. S. Siegler (Ed.), *Children's thinking: What develops?* (pp. 73–96). Hillsdale, NJ: Erlbaum.

CHILD, A. H. (1997). Marfan syndrome—Current medical and genetic knowledge: How to treat and when. *Journal of Cardiac Surgery, 12*(2, Suppl.), 131–135.

CHILDREN'S DEFENSE FUND. (1998). *The state of America's children: Yearbook 1998.* Washington, DC: Author.

CHILDREN'S DEFENSE FUND. (1999). *The state of America's children: Yearbook 1999.* Washington, DC: Author.

CHILDS, C. P., & GREENFIELD, P. M. (1982). Informal modes of learning and teaching: The case of Zinacanteco weaving. In N. Warren (Ed.), *Advances in cross-cultural psychology* (Vol. 2, pp. 269–316). London: Academic Press.

CHISHOLM, J. S. (1989). Biology, culture, and the development of temperament: A Navajo example. In J. K. Nugent, B. M. Lester, & T. B. Brazelton (Eds.), *Biology, culture, and development* (Vol. 1, pp. 341–364). Norwood, NJ: Ablex.

CHIU, L-H. (1992–1993). Self-esteem in American and Chinese (Taiwanese) children. *Current Psychology: Research and Reviews, 11,* 309–313.

CHOI, S. (1991). Early acquisition of epistemic meaning in Korean: A study of sentence-ending suffixes in the spontaneous speech of three children. *First Language, 11,* 93–120.

CHOMSKY, N. (1957). *Syntactic structures.* The Hague: Mouton.

CHOMSKY, N. (1959). Review of B. F. Skinner's *Verbal Behavior. Language, 35,* 26–129.

CHOMSKY, N. (1976). *Reflections on language.* London: Temple Smith.

CHOMSKY, N. (1981). *Lectures on government and binding.* Dordrecht, Holland: Foris.

CHOMSKY, N. (1988). *Language and problems of knowledge.* Cambridge, MA: MIT Press.

CHUGANI, H. T. (1994). Development of regional brain glucose metabolism in relation to behavior and plasticity. In G. Dawson & K. W. Fischer (Eds.),

Human behavior and the developing brain (pp. 153–175). New York: Guilford.

CICCHETTI, D., & ABER, J. L. (1986). Early precursors of later depression: An organizational perspective. In L. P. Lipsitt & C. Rovee-Collier (Eds.), *Advances in infancy research* (Vol. 4, pp. 87–137). Norwood, NJ: Ablex.

CICCHETTI, D., & GARMEZY, N. (1993). Prospects and promises in the study of resilience. *Development and Psychopathology, 5,* 497–502.

CICCHETTI, D., & TOTH, S. L. (1998a). The development of depression in children and adolescents. *American Psychologist, 53,* 221–241.

CICCHETTI, D., & TOTH, S. L. (1998b). Perspectives on research and practice in developmental psychopathology. In I. E. Sigel & K. A. Renninger (Eds.), *Handbook of child psychology: Vol. 4. Child psychology in practice* (5th ed., pp. 479–582). New York: Wiley.

CLANCY, P. (1985). Acquisition of Japanese. In D. I. Slobin (Ed.), *The crosslinguistic study of language acquisition: Vol. 1. The data* (pp. 323–524). Hillsdale, NJ: Erlbaum.

CLANCY, P. (1989). Form and function in the acquisition of Korean wh- questions. *Journal of Child Language, 16,* 323–347.

CLARK, D. C., & MOKROS, H. B. (1993). Depression and suicidal behavior. In P. H. Tolan & B. J. Cohler (Eds.), *Handbook of clinical research and practice with adolescents* (pp. 333–358). New York: Wiley.

CLARK, E. V. (1973). Nonlinguistic strategies and the acquisition of word meanings. *Cognition, 2,* 161–182.

CLARK, E. V. (1983). Meanings and concepts. In P. H. Mussen (Ed.), *Handbook of child psychology: Vol. 3. Cognitive development* (pp. 787–840). New York: Wiley.

CLARK, E. V. (1990). On the pragmatics of contrast. *Journal of Child Language, 17,* 417–431.

CLARK, E. V. (1993). *The lexicon in acquisition.* Cambridge: Cambridge University Press.

CLARK, E. V. (1995). The lexicon and syntax. In J. L. Miller & P. D. Eimas (Eds.), *Speech, language, and communication* (pp. 303–337). San Diego: Academic Press.

CLARK, R., HYDE, J. S., ESSEX, M. J., & KLEIN, M. H. (1997). Length of maternity leave and quality of mother–infant interaction. *Child Development, 68,* 364–383.

CLARKE-STEWART, K. A. (1978). Recasting the Lone Stranger. In J. Glick & K. A. Clarke-Stewart (Eds.), *The development of social understanding* (pp. 109–176). New York: Gardner Press.

CLARKE-STEWART, K. A. (1992). Consequences of child care for children's development. In A. Booth (Ed.), *Child care in the 1990s: Trends and consequences* (pp. 63–83). Hillsdale, NJ: Erlbaum.

CLARKE-STEWART, K. A., & HAYWARD, C. (1996). Advantages of father custody and contact for the psychological well-being of school-age children. *Journal of Applied Developmental Psychology, 17,* 239–270.

CLAUDE, D., & FIRESTONE, P. (1995). The development of ADHD boys: A 12-year follow-up. *Canadian Journal of Behavioural Science, 27,* 226–249.

CLAUSEN, J. A. (1975). The social meaning of differential physical and sexual maturation. In S. E. Dragastin & G. H. Elder (Eds.), *Adolescence in the life cycle: Psychological change and the social context* (pp. 25–47). New York: Halsted.

CLEMENTS, D. H. (1990). Metacomponential development in a Logo programming environment. *Journal of Educational Psychology, 82,* 141–149.

CLEMENTS, D. H. (1995). Teaching creativity with computers. *Educational Psychology Review, 7,* 141–161.

CLEMENTS, D. H., & NASTASI, B. K. (1992). Computers and early childhood education. In M. Gettinger, S. N. Elliott, & T. R. Kratochwill (Eds.), *Advances in school psychology: Preschool and early childhood treatment directions* (pp. 187–246). Hillsdale, NJ: Erlbaum.

CLEMENTS, D. H., NASTASI, B. K., & SWAMINATHAN, S. (1993). Young children and computers: Crossroads and directions from research. *Young Children, 48* (2), 56–64.

CLIFTON, R. K., PERRIS, E., & BULLINGER, A. (1991). Infants' perception of auditory space. *Developmental Psychology, 27,* 161–171.

CLIFTON, R. K., ROCHAT, P., ROBIN, D. J., & BERTHIER, N. E. (1994). Multimodal perception in the control of infant reaching. *Journal of Experimental Psychology: Human Perception and Performance, 20,* 876–886.

CLINTON, H. R. (1996). *It takes a village: And other lessons children teach us.* New York: Simon & Schuster.

CLOPTON, N. A., & SORELL, G. T. (1993). Gender differences in moral reasoning: Stable or situational? *Psychology of Women Quarterly, 17,* 85–101.

COAKLEY, J. (1990). *Sport and society: Issues and controversies* (4th ed.). St. Louis: Mosby.

COCHRAN, M. (1993). Personal networks in the ecology of human development. In M. Cochran, M. Larner, D. Riley, L. Gunnarsson, & C. R. Henderson, Jr. (Eds.), *Extending families: The social networks of parents and their children* (pp. 1–33). New York: Cambridge University Press.

COCKING, R. R., & GREENFIELD, P. M. (1996). Introduction. In P. M. Greenfield & R. Cocking (Eds.), *Interacting with video* (pp. 3–7). Norwood, NJ: Ablex.

COE, C. L., LUBACH, G. R., SCHNEIDER, M. L., DIERSCHKE, D. J., & ERSHLER, W. B. (1992). Early rearing conditions alter immune responses in the developing infant primate. *Pediatrics, 90,* 505–509.

COHEN, F. L. (1993). HIV infection and AIDS: An overview. In F. L. Cohen & J. D. Durham (Eds.), *Women, children, and HIV/AIDS* (pp. 3–30). New York: Springer.

COHEN, K. M., & SAVIN-WILLIAMS, R. C. (1996). Developmental perspectives on coming out to self and others. In W. R. Savin, K. M. Cohen, & R. C. Savin-Williams (Eds.), *The lives of lesbians, gays, and bisexuals: Children to adults* (pp. 113–151). Ft. Worth, TX: Harcourt Brace.

COHEN, S., & WILLIAMSON, G. M. (1991). Stress and infectious disease in humans. *Psychological Bulletin, 109,* 5–24.

COHN, D. A., COWAN, P. A., COWAN, C. P., & PEARSON, J. (1992). Mothers' and fathers' working models of childhood attachment relationships, parenting styles, and child behavior. *Development and Psychopathology, 4,* 417–432.

COIE, J. D., & DODGE, K. A. (1998). Aggression and antisocial behavior. In N. Eisenberg (Ed.), *Handbook of child psychology: Vol. 3. Social, emotional, and personality development* (5th ed., pp. 779–862). New York: Wiley.

COIE, J. D., DODGE, K. A., & COPPOTELLI, H. (1982). Dimensions and types of social status: A cross-age perspective. *Developmental Psychology, 18,* 557–570.

COIE, J. D., & KREHBIEL, G. (1984). Effects of academic tutoring on the social status of low-achieving, socially rejected children. *Child Development, 55,* 1465–1478.

COLBY, A., & KOHLBERG, L. (1987). *The measurement of moral judgment: Theoretical foundations and research validation* (Vol. 1). Cambridge: Cambridge University Press.

COLBY, A., KOHLBERG, L., GIBBS, J. C., & LIEBERMAN, M. (1983). A longitudinal study of moral judgment. *Monographs of the Society for Research in Child Development, 48* (1–2, Serial No. 200).

COLE, M. (1990). Cognitive development and formal schooling: The evidence from cross-cultural research. In L. C. Moll (Ed.), *Vygotsky and education* (pp. 89–110). New York: Cambridge University Press.

COLE, P. M., & TAMANG, B. L. (1998). Nepali children's ideas about emotional displays in hypothetical challenges. *Developmental Psychology, 34,* 640–646.

COLEY, R. L. (1998). Children's socialization experiences and functioning in single-mother households: The importance of fathers and other men. *Child Development, 69,* 219–230.

COLEY, R. L., & CHASE-LANSDALE, P. L. (1998). Adolescent pregnancy and parenthood: Recent evidence and future directions. *American Psychologist, 53,* 152–166.

COLLAER, M. L., & HINES, M. (1995). Human behavioral sex differences: A role for gonadal hormones during early development? *Psychological Bulletin, 118,* 55–107.

COLLINS, W. A. (1983). Children's processing of television content: Implications for prevention of negative effects. *Prevention in Human Services, 2,* 53–66.

COLLINS, W. A. (1997). Relationships and development during adolescence: Interpersonal adaptation to individual change. *Personal Relationships, 4,* 1–14.

COLLINS, W. A., HARRIS, M. L., & SUSMAN, A. (1996). Parenting during middle childhood. In M. H. Bornstein (Ed.), *Handbook of parenting: Vol. 1. Children and parenting* (pp. 65–90). Mahwah, NJ: Erlbaum.

COLLINS, W. A., LAURSEN, B., MORTENSEN, N., LUEBKER, C., & FERREIRA, M. (1997). Conflict processes and transitions in parent and peer relationships: Implications for autonomy and regulation. *Journal of Adolescent Research, 12,* 178–198.

COLLINS, W. A., WELLMAN, H., KENISTON, A. H., & WESTBY, S. D. (1978). Age-related aspects of comprehension and inference from a televised dramatic narrative. *Child Development, 49,* 389–399.

COLLIS, B. A., KNEZEK, G. A., LAI, K-W., MIYASHITA, K. T., PELGRUM, W. J., PLOMP, T., & SAKAMOTO, T. (1996). *Children and computers in school.* Mahwah, NJ: Erlbaum.

COLOMBO, J. (1993). *Infant cognition: Predicting later intellectual functioning.* Newbury Park, CA: Sage.

COLOMBO, J. (1995). On the neural mechanisms underlying developmental and individual differences in visual fixation in infancy. *Developmental Review, 15,* 97–135.

COLTRANE, S. (1990). Birth timing and the division of labor in dual-earner families. *Journal of Family Issues, 11,* 157–181.

COLTRANE, S. (1996). *Family man.* New York: Oxford University Press.

COMPAS, B., PHARES, V., & LEDOUX, N. (1989). Stress and coping: Preventive interventions for children and adolescents. In L. Bond & B. Compas (Eds.), *Primary prevention in the schools* (pp. 319–340). London: Sage.

COMSTOCK, G. A. (1993). The medium and society: The role of television in American life. In G. L. Berry & J. K. Asamen (Eds.), *Children and television* (pp. 117–131). Newbury Park, CA: Sage.

COMSTOCK, G. A., & PAIK, H. (1994). The effects of television violence on antisocial behavior: A meta-analysis. *Communication Research, 21,* 269–277.

CONDRY, J. C., & ROSS, D. F. (1985). Sex and aggression: The influence of gender label on the perception of aggression in children. *Child Development, 56,* 225–233.

CONGER, K. J., CONGER, R. D., & SCARAMELLA, L. V. (1997). Parents, siblings, psychological control, and adolescent adjustment. *Journal of Adolescent Research, 12,* 113–138.

CONGER, R. D., CONGER, K. J., ELDER, G. H., JR., LORENZ, F. O., SIMONS, R. L., & WHITBECK, L. B. (1992). A family process model of economic hardship and adjustment of early adolescent boys. *Child Development, 63,* 527–541.

CONGER, R. D., PATTERSON, G. R., & GE, X. (1995). It takes two to replicate: A mediational model for the impact of parents' stress on adolescent adjustment. *Child Development, 66,* 80–97.

CONNER, D. B., KNIGHT, D. K., & CROSS, D. R. (1997). Mothers' and fathers' scaffolding of their 2-year-olds during problem-solving and literacy interactions. *British Journal of Developmental Psychology, 15,* 323–338.

CONNOLLY, J. A., & DOYLE, A. B. (1984). Relations of social fantasy play to social competence in preschoolers. *Developmental Psychology, 20,* 797–806.

CONSTANZO, P. R., & WOODY, E. Z. (1979). Externality as a function of obesity in children: Pervasive style or eating-specific attribute? *Journal of Personality and Social Psychology, 37,* 2286–2296.

COOK, R., GOLOMBOK, S., BISH, A., & MURRAY, C. (1995). Disclosure of donor insemination: Parental attitudes. *American Orthopsychiatric Association, 65,* 549–559.

COOKE, R. A. (1982). The ethics and regulation of research involving children. In B. B. Wolman (Ed.), *Handbook of developmental psychology* (pp. 149–172). Englewood Cliffs, NJ: Prentice-Hall.

COON, H., FULKER, D. W., DEFRIES, J. C., & PLOMIN, R. (1990). Home environment and cognitive ability of 7-year-old children in the Colorado Adoption Project: Genetic and environmental etiologies. *Developmental Psychology, 26,* 459–468.

COONTZ, S. (1997). *The way we really are: Coming to terms with America's changing families.* New York: Basic Books.

COOPER, C. R. (1998). *The weaving of maturity: Cultural perspectives on adolescent development.* New York: Oxford University Press.

COOPER, H. M. (1979). Pygmalion grows up: A model for teacher expectation communication and performance. *Review of Educational Research, 49,* 389–410.

COOPER, M. L., & ORCUTT, H. K. (1997). Drinking and sexual experience on first dates among adolescents. *Journal of Abnormal Psychology, 106,* 191–202.

COOPER, P., & MURRAY, L. (1997). Prediction, detection, and treatment of postnatal depression. *Archives of Diseases of Children, 77,* 97–99.

COOPER, R. P., & ASLIN, R. N. (1994). Developmental differences in infant attention to the spectral properties of infant-directed speech. *Child Development, 65,* 1663–1677.

COPLAN, R. J., RUBIN, K. H., FOX, N. A., CALKINS, S. D., & STEWART, S. L. (1994). Being alone, playing alone, and acting alone: Distinguishing among reticence and passive and active solitude in young children. *Child Development, 65,* 129–137.

COPPER, R. L., GOLDENBERG, R. L., CREASY, R. K., DuBARD, M. B., DAVIS, R. O., ENTMAN, S. S., IAMS, J. D., & CLIVER, S. P. (1993). A multicenter study of preterm birth weight and gestational age-specific neonatal mortality. *American Journal of Obstetrics and Gynecology, 168,* 78–84.

CORAH, N. L., ANTHONY, E. J., PAINTER, P., STERN, J. A., & THURSTON, D. L. (1965). Effects of perinatal anoxia after seven years. *Psychological Monographs, 79* (3, No. 596).

CORRIGAN, R. (1987). A developmental sequence of actor-object pretend play in young children. *Merrill-Palmer Quarterly, 33,* 87–106.

CORWIN, M. J., LESTER, B. M., SEPKOSKI, C., PEUCKER, M., KAYNE, H., & GOLUB, H. L. (1995). Newborn acoustic cry characteristics of infants subsequently dying of sudden infant death syndrome. *Pediatrics, 96,* 73–77.

COSDEN, M., PEERSON, S., & ELLIOTT, K. (1997). Effects of prenatal drug exposure on birth outcomes and early child development. *Journal of Drug Issues, 27,* 525–539.

COST, QUALITY, AND OUTCOMES STUDY TEAM. (1995). Cost, quality, and child outcomes in child care centers: Key findings and recommendations. *Young Children, 50*(4), 40–44.

COSTABILE, A., SMITH, P. K., MATHESON, L., ASTON, J., HUNTER, T., & BOULTON, M. (1991). Cross-national comparison of how children distinguish serious and playful fighting. *Developmental Psychology, 27,* 881–887.

COSTELLO, E. J., & ANGOLD, A. (1995). Developmental epidemiology. In D. Cicchetti & D. Cohen (Eds.), *Developmental psychopathology: Vol. 1. Theory and method* (pp. 23–56). New York: Wiley.

COTTON, P. (1990). Sudden infant death syndrome: Another hypothesis offered but doubts remain. *Journal of the American Medical Association, 263,* 2865, 2869.

COTTON, P. (1994). Smoking cigarettes may do developing fetus more harm than ingesting cocaine, some experts say. *Journal of the American Medical Association, 271,* 576–577.

COULTON, C. J., KORBIN, J. E., SU, M., & CHOW, J. (1995). Community level factors and child maltreatment rates. *Child Development, 66,* 1262–1276.

COURAGE, M. L., & ADAMS, R. J. (1990). Visual acuity assessment from birth to three years using the acuity card procedures: Cross-sectional and longitudinal samples. *Optometry and Vision Science, 67,* 713–718.

COWAN, C. P., & COWAN, P. A. (1995). Interventions to ease the transition to parenthood: Why they are needed and what they can do. *Family Relations, 44,* 412–423.

COWAN, C. P., & COWAN, P. A. (1997). Working with couples during stressful transitions. In S. Dreman (Ed.), *The family on the threshold of the 21st century* (pp. 17–47). Mahwah, NJ: Erlbaum.

COWAN, P. A., POWELL, D., & COWAN, C. P. (1998). Parenting interventions: A family systems perspective. In I. E. Sigel & K. A. Renninger (Eds.), *Handbook of child psychology: Vol. 4. Child psychology in practice* (5th ed., pp. 3–72). New York: Wiley.

COX, M. (1993). *Children's drawings of the human figure.* Hillsdale, NJ: Erlbaum.

COX, M., & LITTLETON, K. (1995). Children's use of converging obliques in their perspective drawings. *Educational Psychology, 15,* 127–139.

COX, M. J., OWEN, M. T., HENDERSON, V. K., & MARGAND, N. A. (1992). Prediction of infant–father and infant–mother attachment. *Developmental Psychology, 28,* 474–483.

COYLE, T. R., & BJORKLUND, D. F. (1997). Age differences in, and consequences of, multiple- and variable-strategy use on a multitrial sort-recall task. *Developmental Psychology, 33,* 372–380.

CRAIK, F. I. M., & LOCKHART, R. S. (1972). Levels of processing: A framework for memory research. *Journal of Verbal Learning and Verbal Behavior, 11,* 671–684.

CRAIN, R. M. (1996). The influence of age, race, and gender on child and adolescent multidimensional self-concept. In B. A. Bracken (Ed.), *Handbook of self-concept: Developmental, social, and clinical considerations* (pp. 395–420). New York: Wiley.

CRAIN-THORESON, C., & DALE, P. S. (1992). Do early talkers become early readers? Linguistic precocity, preschool language, and emergent literacy. *Developmental Psychology, 28,* 421–429.

CRATTY, B. J. (1986). *Perceptual and motor development in infants and children* (3rd ed.). Englewood Cliffs, NJ: Prentice-Hall.

CRAWFORD, J. (1995). *Bilingual education: History, politics, theory, and practice.* Los Angeles: Bilingual Education Services.

CRAWFORD, J. (1997). *Best evidence: Research foundations of the Bilingual Education Act.* Washington, DC: National Clearinghouse for Bilingual Education.

CREASEY, G. L., JARVIS, P. A., & BERK, L. E. (1998). Play and social competence. In O. N. Saracho & B. Spodek (Eds.), *Multiple perspectives on play in early childhood education* (pp. 116–143). Albany: State University of New York Press.

CREATSAS, G. K., VEKEMANS, M., HOREJSI, J., UZEL, R., LAURITZEN, C., & OSLER, M. (1995). Adolescent sexuality in Europe: A multicentric study. *Adolescent and Pediatric Gynecology, 8,* 59–63.

CRICK, N. R. (1996). The role of overt aggression, relational aggression, and prosocial behavior in the prediction of children's future social adjustment. *Child Development, 67,* 2317–2327.

CRICK, N. R. (1997). Engagement in gender normative versus nonnormative forms of aggression:

Links to social-psychological adjustment. *Developmental Psychology, 33,* 610–617.

CRICK, N. R., CASAS, J. F., & MOSHER, M. (1997). Relational and overt aggression in preschool. *Developmental Psychology, 33,* 579–588.

CRICK, N. R., & DODGE, K. A. (1994). A review and reformulation of social information-processing mechanisms in children's social adjustment. *Psychological Bulletin, 115,* 74–101.

CRICK, N. R., & GROTPETER, J. K. (1995). Relational aggression, gender, and social-psychological adjustment. *Child Development, 66,* 710–722.

CRICK, N. R., & GROTPETER, J. K. (1996). Children's treatment by peers: Victims of relational and overt aggression. *Development and Psychopathology, 8,* 367–380.

CRICK, N. R., & LADD, G. W. (1993). Children's perceptions of their peer experiences: Attributions, loneliness, social anxiety, and social avoidance. *Developmental Psychology, 29,* 244–254.

CROCKETT, L. J. (1990). Sex role and sex-typing in adolescence. In R. M. Lerner, A. C. Petersen, & J. Brooks-Gunn (Eds.), *The encyclopedia of adolescence* (Vol. 2, pp. 1007–1017). New York: Garland.

CROUTER, A. C., MANKE, B. A., & MCHALE, S. M. (1995). The family context of gender intensification in early adolescence. *Child Development, 66,* 317–329.

CROWE, H. P., & ZESKIND, P. S. (1992). Psychophysiological and perceptual responses to infant cries varying in pitch: Comparison of adults with low and high scores on the child abuse potential inventory. *Child Abuse & Neglect, 16,* 19–29.

CRYSTAL, D. S., CHEN, C., FULIGNI, A. J., STEVENSON, H. W., HSU, C-C., KO, H-J., KITAMURA, S., & KIMURA, S. (1994). Psychological maladjustment and academic achievement: A cross-cultural study of Japanese, Chinese, and American high school students. *Child Development, 65,* 738–753.

CSIKSZENTMIHALYI, M. (1988). Motivation and creativity: Toward a synthesis of structural and energistic approaches to cognition. *New Ideas in Psychology, 6,* 159–176.

CSIKSZENTMIHALYI, M., & LARSON, R. (1984). *Being adolescent: Conflict and growth in the teenage years.* New York: Basic Books.

CUDDY-CASEY, M., & ORVASCHEL, H. (1997). Children's understanding of death in relation to child suicidality and homicidality.

Clinical Psychology Review, 17, 33–45.

CULBERTSON, F. M. (1997). Depression and gender: An international review. *American Psychologist, 52,* 25–51.

CUMMINGS, E. M., & CICCHETTI, D. (1990). Towards a transactional model of relations between attachment and depression. In M. Greenberg, D. Cicchetti, & E. M. Cummings (Eds.), *Attachment in the preschool years: Theory, research, and intervention* (pp. 339–372). Chicago: University of Chicago Press.

CUMMINGS, E. M., & DAVIES, P. T. (1994a). *Children and marital conflict.* New York: Guilford.

CUMMINGS, E. M., & DAVIES, P. T. (1994b). Maternal depression and child development. *Journal of Child Psychology and Psychiatry, 35,* 73–112.

CUMMINGS, E. M., IANNOTTI, R. J., & ZAHN-WAXLER, C. (1985). Influence of conflict between adults on the emotions and aggression of young children. *Developmental Psychology, 21,* 495–507.

CUMMINGS, E. M., & ZAHN-WAXLER, C. (1992). Emotions and the socialization of aggression: Adults' angry behavior and children's arousal and aggression. In A. Fraczek & H. Zumkley (Eds.), *Socialization and aggression* (pp. 61–84). New York: Springer-Verlag.

CUNNINGHAM, A. E., & STANOVICH, K. E. (1990). Early spelling acquisition: Writing beats the computer. *Journal of Educational Psychology, 82,* 159–162.

CURRIE, J., & THOMAS, D. (1995). Does Head Start make a difference? *American Economic Review, 85,* 341–364.

CURRIE, J., & THOMAS, D. (1997). Can Head Start lead to long term gains in cognition after all? *SRCD Newsletter, 40*(2), 3–5.

CURTISS, S. (1977). *Genie: A psycholinguisitc study of a modern-day "wild child."* New York: Academic Press.

CURTISS, S. (1989). The independence and task-specificity of language. In M. H. Bornstein & J. S. Bruner (Eds.), *Interaction in human development* (pp. 105–137). Hillsdale, NJ: Erlbaum.

D

DAHL, R. E., SCHER, M. S., WILLIAMSON, D. E., ROBLES, N., & DAY, N. (1995). A longitudinal study of prenatal marijuana use. Effects on sleep and arousal at age 3 years. *Archives of Pediatric and Adolescent Medicine, 149,* 145–150.

DALY, M., & WILSON, M. (1988). *Homicide.* New York: Aldine de Gruyter.

DAMON, W. (1977). *The social world of the child.* San Francisco: Jossey-Bass.

DAMON, W. (1988). *The moral child.* New York: Free Press.

DAMON, W. (1990). Self-concept, adolescent. In R. M. Lerner, A. C. Petersen, & J. Brooks-Gunn (Eds.), *The encyclopedia of adolescence* (Vol. 2, pp. 67–91). New York: Garland.

DAMON, W. (1995). *Greater expectations: Overcoming the culture of indulgence in America's homes and schools.* New York: Free Press.

DAMON, W., & HART, D. (1988). *Self-understanding in childhood and adolescence.* New York: Cambridge University Press.

DANFORTH, J. S., BARKLEY, R. A., & STOKES, T. F. (1990). Observations of parent–child interactions with hyperactive children: Research and clinical applications. *Clinical Psychology Review, 11,* 703–727.

DANIELS, K., & LEWIS, G. M. (1996). Openness of information in the use of donor gametes: Developments in New Zealand. *Journal of Reproductive and Infant Psychology, 14,* 57–68.

DANNEMILLER, J. L. (1989). A test of color constancy in 9- and 20-week-old human infants following simulated illuminant changes. *Developmental Psychology, 25,* 171–184.

DANNEMILLER, J. L., & STEPHENS, B. R. (1988). A critical test of infant pattern preference models. *Child Development, 59,* 210–216.

DARLING-HAMMOND, L., ANCESS, J., & FALK, B. (1995). *Authentic assessment: Studies of schools and students at work.* New York: Teachers College Press.

DARWIN, C. (1877). Biographical sketch of an infant. *Mind, 2,* 285–294.

DARWIN, C. (1936). *On the origin of species by means of natural selection.* New York: Modern Library. (Original work published 1859)

DAS GUPTA, P., & BRYANT, P. E. (1989). Young children's causal inferences. *Child Development, 60,* 1138–1146.

DATTEL, B. J. (1997). Antiretroviral therapy during pregnancy. Beyond AZT (ZDV). *Obstetrics and Gynecology Clinics of North America, 24,* 645–657.

DAVENPORT, E. C., JR., DAVISON, M. L., KUANG, H., DING, S., KIM, S., & KWAK, N. (1998). High school mathematics course-taking by gender and ethnicity. *American Educational Research Journal, 35,* 497–514.

DAVIDSON, E., LEVINE, M., MALVERN, J., NIEBYL, J., & TOBIN, M. (1993). A rebirth of obstet-

rical care. *Medical World News, 34*(5), 42–47.

DAVIDSON, P., & YOUNISS, J. (1991). Which comes first, morality or identity? In W. M. Kurtines & J. L. Gewirtz (Eds.), *Handbook of moral behavior and development* (Vol. 1, pp. 105–121). Hillsdale, NJ: Erlbaum.

DAVIDSON, R. J. (1994). Asymmetric brain function, affective style, and psychopathology: The role of early experience and plasticity. *Development and Psychopathology, 6,* 741–758.

DAVIES, P. T., & CUMMINGS, M. T. (1994). Marital conflict and child adjustment: An emotional security hypothesis. *Psychological Bulletin, 116,* 387–411.

DAVIS, D. L., GOTTLIEB, M. B., & STAMPNITZKY, J. R. (1998). Reduced ratio of male to female births in several industrial countries. *Journal of the American Medical Association, 279,* 1018–1023.

DAVIS, J. N., & DALY, M. (1997). Evolutionary theory and the human family. *Quarterly Review of Biology, 72,* 407–435.

DAVYDOV, V. (1990). *Types of generalization in instruction: Logical and psychological problems in the structuring of school curricula* (Soviet Studies in Mathematics Education, Vol. 2). Reston, VA: National Council of Teachers of Mathematics.

DAWSON, G., MELTZOFF, A. N., OSTERLING, J., & RINALDI, J. (1998). Neuropsychological correlates of early symptoms of autism. *Child Development, 69,* 1276–1285.

DAY, S. (1993). Why genes have a gender. *New Scientist, 138* (1874), 34–38.

DE LISI, R., & GALLAGHER, A. M. (1991). Understanding gender stability and constancy in Argentinean children. *Merrill-Palmer Quarterly, 37,* 483–502.

DE VILLIERS, J. G., & DE VILLIERS, P. A. (1973). A cross-sectional study of the acquisition of grammatical morphemes in child speech. *Journal of Psycholinguistic Research, 2,* 267–278.

DE VILLIERS, P. A., & DE VILLIERS, J. G. (1992). Language development. In M. H. Bornstein & M. E. Lamb (Eds.), *Developmental psychology: An advanced textbook* (3rd ed., pp. 337–418). Hillsdale, NJ: Erlbaum.

DE WINTER, M., BALLEDUZ, M., & DE MARE, J. (1997). A critical evaluation of Dutch preventive child health care. *Child: Care, Health and Development, 23,* 437–446.

DE WOLFF, M. S., & VAN IJZENDOORN, M. H. (1997). Sensitivity and attachment: A meta-analysis on parental antecedents of infant attachment.

Child Development, 68, 571–591.

DEAN, R. S., & ANDERSON, J. L. (1997). Lateralization of cerebral function. In A. M. Horton, Jr., D. Wedding, & J. Webster (Eds.), *The neuropsychology handbook: Vol. 1. Foundations and assessment* (2nd ed., pp. 139–168). New York: Springer.

DEARY, I. J. (1995). Auditory inspection time and intelligence: What is the direction of causation? *Developmental Psychology, 31,* 237–250.

DEARY, I. J., & STOUGH, C. (1996). Intelligence and inspection time: Achievements, prospects, and problems. *American Psychologist, 51,* 599–608.

DEATER-DECKARD, K., & DODGE, K. A. (1997). Externalizing behavior problems and discipline revisited: Nonlinear effects and variation by culture, context, and gender. *Psychological Inquiry, 8,* 161–175.

DEATER-DECKARD, K., DODGE, K. A., BATES, J. E., & PETTIT, G. S. (1996). Physical discipline among African American and European American mothers: Links to children's externalizing behaviors. *Developmental Psychology, 32,* 1065–1072.

DEATER-DECKARD, K., SCARR, S., MCCARTNEY, K., & EISENBERG, M. (1994). Paternal separation anxiety: Relationships with parenting stress, child-rearing attitudes, and maternal anxieties. *Psychological Science, 5,* 341–346.

DEAUX, K. (1993). Commentary: Sorry, wrong number—A reply to Gentile's call. *Psychological Science, 4,* 125–126.

DEAUX, K., & LEWIS, L. L. (1984). Structure of gender stereotypes: Interrelationships among components and gender label. *Journal of Personality and Social Psychology, 46,* 991–1004.

DEBERRY, K. M., SCARR, S., & WEINBERG, R. (1996). Family racial socialization and ecological competence: Longitudinal assessments of African-American transracial adoptees. *Child Development, 67,* 2375–2399.

DECASPER, A. J., & SPENCE, M. J. (1986). Prenatal maternal speech influences newborns' perception of speech sounds. *Infant Behavior and Development, 9,* 133–150.

DEGROOT, A. D. (1951). War and the intelligence of youth. *Journal of Abnormal and Social Psychology, 46,* 596–597.

DEKOVIĆ, M., & GERRIS, J. R. M. (1994). Developmental analysis of social cognitive and behavioral differences between popular and rejected children. *Journal of Applied Developmental Psychology, 15,* 367–386.

DEKOVIĆ, M., & JANSSENS, J. M. A. M. (1992). Parents' child-rearing style and child's sociometric status. *Developmental Psychology, 28,* 925–932.

DEKOVIĆ, M., & MEEUS, W. (1997). Peer relations in adolescence: Effects of parenting and adolescents' self-concept. *Journal of Adolescence, 20,* 163–176.

DEKOVIĆ, M., NOOM, M. J., & MEEUS, W. (1997). Expectations regarding development during adolescence: Parent and adolescent perceptions. *Journal of Youth and Adolescence, 26,* 253–271.

DELANEY-BLACK, V., COVINGTON, C., OSTREA, E., JR., ROMERO, A., BAKER, D., TAGLE, M., & NORDSTROM-KLEE, B. (1996). Prenatal cocaine and neonatal outcome: Evaluation of dose-response relationship. *Pediatrics, 98,* 735–740.

DELGADO-GAITAN, C. (1992). School matters in the Mexican-American home: Socializing children to education. *American Educational Research Journal, 29,* 495–515.

DELGADO-GAITAN, C. (1994). Socializing young children in Mexican-American families: An intergenerational perspective. In P. M. Greenfield & R. R. Cocking (Eds.), *Cross-cultural roots of minority child development* (pp. 55–86). Hillsdale, NJ: Erlbaum.

DELOACHE, J. S. (1987). Rapid change in symbolic functioning of very young children. *Science, 238,* 1556–1557.

DELOACHE, J. S. (1991). Symbolic functioning in very young children: Understanding of pictures and models. *Child Development, 62,* 736–752.

DELOACHE, J. S. (1995). Early symbolic understanding and use. In D. Medin (Ed.), *The psychology of learning and motivation* (Vol. 33, pp. 65–114). New York: Academic Press.

DELOACHE, J. S., MILLER, K. F., & ROSENGREN, K. S. (1997). The credible shrinking room: Very young children's performance with symbolic and nonsymbolic relations. *Psychological Science, 8,* 308–313.

DELOACHE, J. S., & TODD, C. M. (1988). Young children's use of spatial categorization as a mnemonic strategy. *Journal of Experimental Child Psychology, 46,* 1–20.

DEMARIE-DREBLOW, D. (1991). Relation between knowledge and memory: A reminder that correlation does not imply causality. *Child Development, 62,* 484–498.

DEMARIE-DREBLOW, D., & MILLER, P. H. (1988). The development of children's strategies for selective attention: Evidence for a transitional period. *Child Development, 59,* 1504–1513.

DEMO, D. H., & ACOCK, A. C. (1996). Family structure, family process, and adolescent well-being. *Journal of Research on Adolescence, 6,* 457–488.

DEMPSTER, F. N. (1993). Resistance to interference: Developmental changes in a basic processing mechanism. In M. L. Howe & R. Pasnak (Eds.), *Emerging themes in cognitive development: Vol. 1. Foundations* (pp. 3–27). New York: Springer-Verlag.

DEMPSTER, F. N. (1995). Interference and inhibition in cognition: An historical perspective. In F. N. Dempster & C. J. Brainerd (Eds.), *Interference and inhibition in cognition* (pp. 3–26). San Diego: Academic Press.

DEMUTH, K. (1996). The prosodic structure of early words. In J. Morgan & K. Demuth (Eds.), *From signal to syntax* (pp. 171–184). Mahwah, NJ: Erlbaum.

DENCKLA, M. B. (1996). Biological correlates of learning and attention: What is relevant to learning disability and attention-deficit hyperactivity disorder? *Developmental and Behavioral Pediatrics, 17,* 114–119.

DENHAM, S. A., RENWICK, S. M., & HOLT, R. W. (1991). Working and playing together: Prediction of preschool social-emotional competence from mother-child interaction. *Child Development, 62,* 242–249.

DENHAM, S. A., ZOLLER, D., & COUCHOUD, E. (1994). Socialization of preschoolers' emotion understanding. *Developmental Psychology, 30,* 928–936.

DENNIS, W. (1960). Causes of retardation among institutionalized children: Iran. *Journal of Genetic Psychology, 96,* 47–59.

DENNIS, W. (1973). *Children of the Creche.* New York: Appleton-Century-Crofts.

DENNIS, W., & NAJARIAN, P. (1957). Infant development under environmental handicap. *Psychological Monographs, 71,* 1–13.

DEROM, C., THIERY, E., VLIETINCK, R., LOOS, R., & DEROM, R. (1996). Handedness in twins according to zygosity and chorion type: A preliminary report. *Behavior Genetics, 26,* 407–408.

DEROSIER, M. E., CILLESSEN, A. H. N., COIE, J. D., & DODGE, K. A. (1994). Group social context and children's aggressive behavior. *Child Development, 65,* 1068–1079.

DEUTSCH, W., & PECHMANN, T. (1982). Social interaction and the development of definite descriptions. *Cognition, 11,* 159–184.

DEVLIN, B., FIENBERG, S. E., RESNICK, D. P., & ROEDER, K. (1995). Galton redux: Intelligence, race and society: A review of "The Bell Curve: Intelligence and Class Structure in American Life." *American Statistician, 90,* 1483–1488.

DEVRIES, M. W. (1984). Temperament and infant mortality among the Masai of East Africa. *American Journal of Psychiatry, 141,* 1189–1194.

DEWSBURY, D. A. (1992). Comparative psychology and ethology: A reassessment. *American Psychologist, 47,* 208–215.

DIAMOND, A. (1991). Neuropsychological insights into the meaning of object concept development. In S. Carey & R. Gelman (Eds.), *The epigenesis of mind: Essays on biology and knowledge* (pp. 67–110). Hillsdale, NJ: Erlbaum.

DIAMOND, A. CRUTTENDEN, L, & NEIDERMAN, D. (1994). AB with multiple wells: 1. Why are multiple wells sometimes easier than two wells? 2. Memory or memory + inhibition. *Developmental Psychology, 30,* 192–205.

DIAMOND, A., PREVOR, M. B., CALLENDER, G., & DRUIN, D. P. (1997). Prefrontal cortex cognitive deficits in children treated early and continuously for PKU. *Monographs of the Society for Research in Child Development, 62*(4, Serial No. 252).

DIAMOND, M., JOHNSON, R., YOUNG, D., & SINGH, S. (1983). Age-related morphologic differences in the rat cerebral cortex and hippocampus: Male–female; right–left. *Experimental Neurology, 81,* 1–13.

DIAS, M. G., & HARRIS, P. L. (1990). The influence of imagination on reasoning by young children. *British Journal of Developmental Psychology, 8,* 305–318.

DIAZ, R. M., & BERK, L. E. (1995). A Vygotskian critique of self-instructional training. *Development and Psychopathology, 7,* 369–392.

DICK-READ, G. (1959). *Childbirth without fear.* New York: Harper & Brothers.

DICKINSON, D. K. (1984). First impressions: Children's knowledge of words gained from a single exposure. *Applied Psycholinguistics, 5,* 359–373.

DICLEMENTE, R. J. (1993). Preventing HIV/AIDS among adolescents. *Journal of the American Medical Association, 270,* 760–762.

DIEKSTRA, R. F. W., KIENHORST, C. W. M., & DE WILDE, E. J. (1995). Suicide and suicidal behaviour among adolescents. In M. Rutter & D. J. Smith (Eds.), *Psychosocial disorders in young people* (pp. 686–761). Chichester, England: Wiley.

DIENER, M. L., GOLDSTEIN, L. H., & MANGELSDORF, S. C. (1995). The role of prenatal expectations in parents' reports of infant temperament. *Merrill-Palmer Quarterly, 41,* 172–190.

DIETZ, W. H., JR., BANDINI, L. G., & GORTMAKER, S. (1990). Epidemiologic and metabolic risk factors for childhood obesity. *Klinische Pädiatrie, 202,* 69–72.

DILALLA, L. F., KAGAN, J., & REZNICK, J. S. (1994). Genetic etiology of behavioral inhibition among 2-year-old children. *Infant Behavior and Development, 17,* 405–412.

DILDY, G. A., JACKSON, G. M., FOWERS, G. K., OSHIRO, B. T., VARNER, M. W., & CLARK, S. L. (1996). Very advanced maternal age. Pregnancy after age 45. *American Journal of Obstetrics and Gynecology, 175,* 668–674

DILLON, P. A., & EMERY, R. E. (1996). Divorce mediation and resolution of child custody disputes: Long-term effects. *American Journal of Orthopsychiatry, 66,* 131–140.

DIMATTEO, M. R., & KAHN, K. L. (1997). Psychosocial aspects of childbirth. In S. J. Gallant, G. P. Keita, & R. Royak-Schaler (Eds.), *Health care for women: Psychological, social, and behavioral influences* (pp. 175–186). Washington, DC: American Psychological Association.

DIPIETRO, J. A., HODGSON, D. M., COSTIGAN, K. A., & HILTON, S. C. (1996a). Fetal neurobehavioral development. *Child Development, 67,* 2553–2567.

DIPIETRO, J. A., HODGSON, D. M., COSTIGAN, K. A., & JOHNSON, T. R. B. (1996b). Fetal antecedents of infant temperament. *Child Development, 67,* 2568–2583.

DIRKS, J. (1982). The effect of a commercial game on children's Block Design scores on the WISC-R test. *Intelligence, 6,* 109–123.

DISHION, T. J., ANDREWS, D. W., & CROSBY, L. (1995). Antisocial boys and their friends in early adolescence: Relationship characteristics, quality, and interactional processes. *Child Development, 66,* 139–151.

DISHION, T. J., PATTERSON, G. R., & GRIESLER, P. C. (1994). Peer adaptations in the development of antisocial behavior: A confluence model. In L. R. Huesmann (Ed.), *Current perspectives on aggressive behavior* (pp. 61–95). New York: Plenum.

DIXON, R. A., & LERNER, R. M. (1999). History and systems in developmental psychology. In M. H. Bornstein & M. E. Lamb (Eds.), *Developmental psychology: An advanced textbook* (4th ed., pp. 3–46). Mahwah, NJ: Erlbaum.

DLUGOSZ, L., & BRACKEN, M. B. (1992). Reproductive effects of caffeine: A review and theoretical analysis. *Epidemiological Review, 14,* 83–100.

DODD, B. J. (1972). Effects of social and vocal stimulation on infant babbling. *Developmental Psychology, 7,* 80–83.

DODGE, K. A. (1985). A social information processing model of social competence in children. In M. Perlmutter (Ed.), *Minnesota Symposia on Child Psychology* (Vol. 18, pp. 77–125). Hillsdale, NJ: Erlbaum.

DODGE, K. A., BATES, J. E., & PETTIT, G. S. (1990). Mechanisms in the cycle of violence. *Science, 250,* 1678–1683.

DODGE, K. A., MCCLASKEY, C. L., & FELDMAN E. (1985). A situational approach to the assessment of social competence in children. *Journal of Consulting and Clinical Psychology, 53,* 344–353.

DODGE, K. A., PETTIT, G. S., & BATES, J. E. (1994). Socialization mediators of the relation between socioeconomic status and child conduct problems. *Child Development, 65,* 649–665.

DODGE, K. A., PETTIT, G. S., MCCLASKEY, C. L., & BROWN, M. M. (1986). Social competence in children. *Monographs of the Society for Research in Child Development, 51* (2, Serial No. 213).

DODGE, K. A., & PRICE, J. M. (1994). On the relation between social information processing and socially competent behavior in early school-aged children. *Child Development, 65,* 1385–1397.

DODGE, K. A., & SOMBERG, D. R. (1987). Hostile attributional biases among aggressive boys are exacerbated under conditions of threats to the self. *Child Development, 58,* 213–224.

DODWELL, P. C., HUMPHREY, G. K., & MUIR, D. W. (1987). Shape and pattern perception. In P. Salapatek & L. Cohen (Eds.), *Handbook of infant perception* (Vol. 2, pp. 1–77). Orlando, FL: Academic Press.

DOLLAGHAN, C. (1985). Child meets word: "Fast mapping" in preschool children. *Journal of Speech and Hearing Research, 28,* 449–454.

DONDI, M., SIMION, F., & CALTRAN, G. (1999). Can newborns discriminate between their own cry and the cry of another newborn infant? *Developmental Psychology, 35,* 418–426.

DONNERSTEIN, E., SLABY, R. G., & ERON, L. D. (1994). The mass media and youth aggression. In L. D. Eron, J. H. Gentry, & P. Schlegel (Eds.), *Reason to hope:*

A psychosocial perspective on violence and youth (pp. 219–250). Washington, DC: American Psychological Association.

DONOVAN, P. (1998). While nationwide birthrate is stable, black women achieve a record low and teenagers' rates decline. *Family Planning Perspectives, 30,* 151–152.

DORNBUSCH, S. M., & GLASGOW, K. L. (1997). The structural context of family–school relations. In A. Booth & J. F. Dunn (Eds.), *Family–school links: How do they affect educational outcomes?* (pp. 35–55). Mahwah, NJ: Erlbaum.

DORNBUSCH, S. M., GLASGOW, K. L., & LIN, I-C. (1996). The social structure of schooling. *Annual Review of Psychology, 47,* 401–427.

DORRIS, M. (1989). *The broken cord.* New York: Harper & Row.

DOUGHERTY, T. M., & HAITH, M. M. (1997). Infant expectations and reaction time as predictors of childhood speed of processing and IQ. *Developmental Psychology, 33,* 146–155.

DOWNEY, G., & WALKER, E. (1989). Social cognition and adjustment in children at risk for psychopathology. *Developmental Psychology, 25,* 835–845.

DOWNS, A. C., & FULLER, M. J. (1991). Recollections of spermarche: An exploratory investigation. *Current Psychology: Research and Reviews, 10,* 93–102.

DOWNS, A. C., & LANGLOIS, J. H. (1988). Sex typing: Construct and measurement issues. *Sex Roles, 18,* 87–100.

DOYLE, A. B., & ABOUD, F. E. (1995). A longitudinal study of white children's racial prejudice as a social-cognitive development. *Merrill-Palmer Quarterly, 41,* 209–228.

DOYLE, C. (1994). *Child sexual abuse.* London: Chapman & Hall.

DRABMAN, R. S., CORDUA, G. D., HAMMER, D., JARVIE, G. J., & HORTON, W. (1979). Developmental trends in eating rates of normal and overweight preschool children. *Child Development, 50,* 211–216.

DRAPER, P., & CASHDAN, E. (1988). Technological change and child behavior among the !Kung. *Ethnology, 27,* 339–365.

DROEGE, K. L., & STIPEK, D. J. (1993). Children's use of dispositions to predict classmates' behavior. *Developmental Psychology, 29,* 646–654.

DROTAR, D., PALLOTTA, J., & ECKERLE, D. (1994). A prospective study of family environments of children hospitalized for nonorganic failure-to-thrive. *Developmental and Behavioral Pediatrics, 15,* 78–85.

DRYFOOS, J. G. (1990). *Adolescents at risk: Prevalence and prevention.* New York: Oxford University Press.

DRYFOOS, J. G. (1996). Full-service schools. *Educational Leadership, 53*(7), 18–23.

DUBOIS, D. L., & HIRSCH, B. J. (1990). School and neighborhood friendship patterns of black and whites in early adolescence. *Child Development, 61,* 524–536.

DUBOW, E. F., & MILLER, L. S. (1996). Television violence viewing and aggressive behavior. In T. M. MacBeth (Eds.), *Tuning in to young viewers* (pp. 117–147). Thousand Oaks, CA: Sage.

DUBOW, E. F., TISAK, J., CAUSEY, D., HRYSHKO, A., & REID, G. (1991). A two-year longitudinal study of stressful life events, social support, and social problem-solving skills: Contributions to children's behavioral and academic adjustment. *Child Development, 62,* 583–599.

DUCHAN, J. (1989). Evaluating adults' talk to children: Assessing adult attunement. *Seminars in Speech and Language, 10,* 17–27.

DUNCAN, G. J., BROOKS-GUNN, J., & KLEBANOV, P. K. (1994). Economic deprivation and early childhood development. *Child Development, 65,* 296–318.

DUNCAN, R. M., & PRATT, M. W. (1997). Microgenetic change in the quantity and quality of preschoolers' private speech. *International Journal of Behavioral Development, 20,* 367–383.

DUNHAM, P., & DUNHAM, F. (1996). The semantically reciprocating robot: Adult influences on children's early conversational skills. *Social Development, 5,* 261–274.

DUNHAM, P., DUNHAM, F., TRAN, S., & AKHTAR, N. (1991). The nonreciprocating robot: Effects on verbal discourse, social play, and social referencing at two years of age. *Child Development, 62,* 1489–1502.

DUNHAM, P. J., & DUNHAM, F. (1992). Lexical development during middle infancy: A mutually driven infant–caregiver process. *Developmental Psychology, 28,* 414–420.

DUNIZ, M., SCHEER, P. J., TROJOVSKY, A., KASCHNITZ, W., KVAS, E., & MACARI, S. (1996). *European Child & Adolescent Psychiatry, 5,* 93–100.

DUNN, J. (1989). Siblings and the development of social understanding in early childhood. In P. G. Zukow (Ed.), *Sibling interaction across cultures* (pp. 106–116). New York: Springer-Verlag.

DUNN, J. (1992). Sisters and brothers: Current issues in developmental research. In F. Boer & J. Dunn (Eds.), *Children's sibling relationships* (pp. 1–17). Hillsdale, NJ: Erlbaum.

DUNN, J. (1994). Temperament, siblings, and the development of relationships. In W. B. Carey & S. C. McDevitt (Eds.), *Prevention and early intervention* (pp. 50–58). New York: Brunner/Mazel.

DUNN, J. (1996). Sibling relationships and perceived self-competence: Patterns of stability between childhood and early adolescence. In A. J. Sameroff & M. M. Haith (Eds.), *The five to seven year shift* (pp. 253–270). Chicago: University of Chicago Press.

DUNN, J., BROWN, J. R., & MAGUIRE, M. (1995). The development of children's moral sensibility: Individual differences and emotion understanding. *Developmental Psychology, 31,* 649–659.

DUNN, J., BROWN, J., SLOMKOWSKI, C. T., & YOUNGBLADE, L. (1991). Young children's understanding of other people's feelings and beliefs: Individual differences and their antecedents. *Child Development, 62,* 1352–1366.

DUNN, J., & KENDRICK, C. (1982). *Siblings: Love, envy and understanding.* Cambridge, MA: Harvard University Press.

DUNN, J., & PLOMIN, R. (1990). *Separate lives: Why siblings are so different.* New York: Basic Books.

DUNN, J., SLOMKOWSKI, C., & BEARDSALL, L. (1994). Sibling relationships from the preschool period through middle childhood and early adolescence. *Developmental Psychology, 30,* 315–324.

DUNN, J., SLOMKOWSKI, C., BEARDSALL, L., & RENDE, R. (1994). Adjustment in middle childhood and early adolescence: Links with earlier and contemporary sibling relationships. *Journal of Child Psychology and Psychiatry, 35,* 491–504.

DUNN, J. T. (1993). Iodine supplementation and the prevention of cretinism. *Annals of the New York Academy of Sciences, 678,* 158–168.

DURBIN, D. L., DARLING, N., STEINBERG, L., & BROWN, B. B. (1993). Parenting style and peer group membership among European-American adolescents. *Journal of Research on Adolescence, 3,* 87–100.

DWECK, C. S. (1991). Self-theories and goals: Their role in motivation, personality and development. In R. Dienstbier (Ed.), *Nebraska Symposia on Motivation* (Vol. 36, pp. 199–235). Lincoln: University of Nebraska Press.

DYE-WHITE, E. (1986). Environmental hazards in the work setting: Their effect on women of child-bearing age. *American Association of Occupational Health and Nursing Journal, 34,* 76–78.

DYKENS, E. M., HODAPP, R. M., & EVANS, D. W. (1994). Profiles and development of adaptive behavior in children with Down syndrome. *American Journal on Mental Retardation, 98,* 580–587.

E

EAGLY, A. H. (1995). The science and politics of comparing women and men. *American Psychologist, 50,* 145–158.

EAST, P. L., & FELICE, M. E. (1996). *Adolescent pregnancy and parenting: Findings from a racially diverse sample.* Mahwah, NJ: Erlbaum.

EAST, P. L., & ROOK, K. S. (1992). Compensatory patterns of support among children's peer relationships: A test using school friends, nonschool friends, and siblings. *Developmental Psychology, 28,* 168–172.

EBBECK, M., & EBBECK, F. (1999). Child-care policy in Australia. In L. E. Berk (Ed.), *Landscapes of development* (pp. 181–191). Belmont, CA: Wadsworth.

EBELING, K. S., & GELMAN, S. A. (1994). Children's use of context in interpreting "big" and "little." *Child Development, 65,* 1178–1192.

EBERHART-PHILLIPS, J. E., FREDERICK, P. D., & BARON, R. C. (1993). Measles in pregnancy: A descriptive study of 58 cases. *Obstetrics and Gynecology, 82,* 797–801.

ECCLES, J. S. (1994). Understanding women's educational and occupational choices: Applying the Eccles et al. model of achievement-related choices. *Psychology of Women Quarterly, 18,* 585–609.

ECCLES, J. S., EARLY, D., FRASIER, K., BELANSKY, E., & McCARTHY, K. (1997). The relation of connection, regulation, and support for autonomy to adolescents' functioning. *Journal of Adolescent Research, 12,* 263–286.

ECCLES, J. S., & HAROLD, R. D. (1991). Gender differences in sport involvement: Applying the Eccles' expectancy-value model. *Journal of Applied Sport Psychology, 3,* 7–35.

ECCLES, J. S., & HAROLD, R. D. (1993). Parent–school involvement during the early adoles- cent years. *Teachers College Record, 94,* 568–587.

ECCLES, J. S., & HAROLD, R. D. (1996). Family involvement in children's and adolescents' schooling. In A. Booth & J. F. Dunn (Eds.), *Family-school links: How do they affect educational outcomes?* (pp. 3–34). Mahwah, NJ: Erlbaum.

ECCLES, J. S., JACOBS, J. E., & HAROLD, R. D. (1990). Gender-role stereotypes, expectancy effects, and parents' role in the socialization of gender differences in self-perceptions and skill acquisition. *Journal of Social Issues, 46,* 183–201.

ECCLES, J. S., LORD, S., & BUCHANAN, C. M. (1996). School transitions in early adolescence: What are we doing to our young people? In J. A. Graber, J. Brooks-Gunn, & A. C. Petersen (Eds.), *Transitions through adolescence* (pp. 251–284). Mahwah, NJ: Erlbaum.

ECCLES, J., WIGFIELD, A., HAROLD, R. D., & BLUMFELD, P. (1993a). Age and gender differences in children's self-and task perceptions during elementary school. *Child Development, 64,* 830–847.

ECCLES, J. S., MIDGLEY, C. WIGFIELD, A., BUCHANAN, C. M., REUMAN, D., FLANAGAN, C., & MAC IVER, D. (1993b). Development during adolescence: The impact of stage-environment fit on young adolescents' experiences in schools and in families. *American Psychologist, 48,* 90–101.

ECCLES, J. S., WIGFIELD, A., MIDGLEY, C., REUMAN, D., MAC IVER, D., & FELDLAUFER, H. (1993c). Negative effects of traditional middle schools on students' motivation. *Elementary School Journal, 93,* 553–574.

ECCLES, J. S., WIGFIELD, A., & SCHIEFELE, U. (1998). Motivation to succeed. In N. Eisenberg (Ed.), *Handbook of child psychology: Vol. 3. Social, emotional, and personality development* (5th ed., pp. 1017–1095). New York: Wiley.

ECKENRODE, J., LAIRD, M., & DORIS, J. (1993). School performance and disciplinary problems among abused and neglected children. *Developmental Psychology, 29,* 53–62.

ECKERMAN, C. O., DAVIS, C. C., & DIDOW, S. M. (1989). Toddlers' emerging ways of achieving social coordination with a peer. *Child Development, 60,* 440–453.

ECKERMAN, C. O., & DIDOW, S. M. (1996). Nonverbal imitation and toddlers' mastery of verbal means of achieving coordinated interaction. *Developmental Psychology, 32,* 141–152.

EDER, D., & PARKER, S. (1987). The cultural production and reproduction of gender: The effect of extracurricular activities on peer-group culture. *Sociology of Education, 60,* 200–213.

EDER, R. A. (1989). The emergent personologist: The structure and content of 3½-, 5½-, and 7½-year-olds' concepts of themselves and other persons. *Child Development, 60,* 1218–1228.

EDER, R. A. (1990). Uncovering young children's psychological selves: Individual and developmental differences. *Child Development, 61,* 849–863.

EDWARDS, C. A. (1994). Leadership in groups of school-age girls. *Developmental Psychology, 30,* 920–927.

EDWARDS, C. P. (1978). Social experiences and moral judgment in Kenyan young adults. *Journal of Genetic Psychology, 133,* 19–30.

EDWARDS, W. J. (1996). A sociological analysis of an invisible minority group: Male adolescent homosexuals. *Youth & Society, 27,* 334–353.

EGELAND, B., & HIESTER, M. (1995). The long-term consequences of infant day-care and mother–infant attachment. *Child Development, 66,* 474–485.

EGELAND, B., JACOBVITZ, D., & SROUFE, L. A. (1988). Breaking the cycle of abuse. *Child Development, 59,* 1080–1088.

EGELAND, B., KALKOSKE, M., GOTTESMAN, N., & ERICKSON, M. F. (1990). Preschool behavior problems: Stability and factors accounting for change. *Journal of Child Psychology and Psychiatry, 31,* 891–909.

EHRHARDT, A. A. (1975). Prenatal hormone exposure and psychosexual differentiation. In E. J. Sachar (Ed.), *Topics in psychoendocrinology* (pp. 67–82). New York: Grune & Stratton.

EHRHARDT, A. A., & BAKER, S. W. (1974). Fetal androgens, human central nervous system differentiation, and behavior sex differences. In R. C. Friedman, R. M. Richart, & R. L. VandeWiele (Eds.), *Sex differences in behavior* (pp. 33–51). New York: Wiley.

EIBEN, B., HAMMANS, W., HANSEN, S., TRAWICKI, W., OSTHELDER, B., STELZER, A., JASPERS, K-D., & GOEBEL, R. (1997). On the complication risk of early amniocentesis versus standard amniocentesis. *Fetal Diagnosis and Therapy, 12,* 140–144.

EIBL-EIBESFELDT, I. (1989). *Human ethology.* Hawthorne, NY: Aldine.

EIDEN, R. D., & REIFMAN, A. (1996). Effects of Brazelton demonstrations on later parenting: A meta-analysis. *Journal of Pediatric Psychology, 21,* 857–868.

EILERS, R. E., & OLLER, D. K. (1994). Infant vocalizations and the early diagnosis of severe hearing impairment. *Journal of Pediatrics, 124,* 199–203.

EISENBERG, N. (1982). The development of reasoning regarding prosocial behavior. In N. Eisenberg (Ed.), *The development of prosocial behavior* (pp. 219–249). New York: Academic Press.

EISENBERG, N. (1986). *Altruistic emotion, cognition, and behavior.* Hillsdale, NJ: Erlbaum.

EISENBERG, N. (1998). Introduction. In N. Eisenberg (Ed.), *Handbook of child psychology: Vol. 3. Social, emotional, and personality development* (pp. 1–24). New York: Wiley.

EISENBERG, N., CARLO, G., MURPHY, B., & VAN COURT, P. (1995a). Prosocial development in late adolescence: A longitudinal study. *Child Development, 66,* 1179–1197.

EISENBERG, N., & FABES, R. A. (1994). Emotion regulation and the development of social competence. In M. Clark (Ed.), *Review of personality and social psychology* (pp. 119–150). Newbury Park, CA: Sage.

EISENBERG, N., & FABES, R. A. (1998). Prosocial development. In N. Eisenberg (Ed.), *Handbook of child psychology: Vol. 3. Social, emotional, and personality development* (5th ed., pp. 701–778). New York: Wiley.

EISENBERG, N., FABES, R. A., CARLO, G., SPEER, A. L., SWITZER, G., KARBON, M., & TROYER, D. (1993). The relations of empathy-related emotions and maternal practices to children's comforting behavior. *Journal of Experimental Child Psychology, 55,* 131–150.

EISENBERG, N., FABES, R., CARLO, G., TROYER, D., SPEER, A., KARBON, M., & SWITZER, G. (1992). The relations of maternal practices and characteristics to children's vicarious emotional responsiveness. *Child Development, 63,* 583–602.

EISENBERG, N., FABES, R., MURPHY, B., KARBON, M., SMITH, M., & MASZK, P. (1996). The relations of children's dispositional empathy-related responding to their emotionality, regulation, and social functioning. *Developmental Psychology, 32,* 195–209.

EISENBERG, N., FABES, R. A., MURPHY, B., MASZK, P., SMITH, M., & KARBON, M. (1995b). The role of emotionality and regulation in children's social functioning: A longitudinal study. *Child Development, 66,* 1360–1384.

EISENBERG, N., FABES, R. A., SHEPARD, S. A., MURPHY, B. C., GUTHRIE, I. K., JONES, S., FRIEDMAN, J., POULIN, R., & MASZK, P. (1997a). Contemporaneous and longitudinal prediction of children's social functioning from regulation and emotionality.

Child Development, 68, 642–664.

EISENBERG, N., FABES, R. A., SHEPARD, S. A., MURPHY, B. C., JONES, S., & GUTHRIE, I. K. (1998). Contemporaneous and longitudinal prediction of children's sympathy from dispositional regulation and emotionality. *Developmental Psychology, 34,* 910–924.

EISENBERG, N., GUTHRIE, I. K., FABES, R. A., REISER, M., MURPHY, B. C., HOLGREN, R., MASZK, P., & LOSOYA, S. (1997b). The relations of regulation and emotionality to resiliency and competent social functioning in elementary school children. *Child Development, 58,* 295–311.

EISENBERG, N., & LENNON, R. (1983). Sex differences in empathy and related capacities. *Psychological Bulletin, 94,* 100–131.

EISENBERG, N., LOSOYA, S., & GUTHRIE, I. K. (1997). Social cognition and prosocial development. In S. Hala (Ed.), *The development of social cognition* (pp. 329–363). Hove, UK: Psychology Press.

EISENBERG, N., & MCNALLY, S. (1993). Socialization and mothers' and adolescents' empathy-related characteristics. *Journal of Research on Adolescence, 3,* 171–191.

EISENBERG, N., MILLER, P. A., SHELL, R., MCNALLEY, S., & SHEA, C. (1991). Prosocial development in adolescence: A longitudinal study. *Developmental Psychology, 27,* 849–857.

EISENBERG, N., MURPHY, B. C., & SHEPARD, S. (1997). The development of empathic accuracy. In W. Ickes (Ed.), *Empathic accuracy* (pp. 73–116). New York: Guilford.

EISENBERG, N., SHELL, R., PASTERNACK, J., LENNON, R., BELLER, R., & MATHY, R. M. (1987). Prosocial development in middle childhood: A longitudinal study. *Developmental Psychology, 23,* 712–718.

EKMAN, P., & FRIESEN, W. (1972). Constants across culture in the face of emotion. *Journal of Personality and Social Psychology, 17,* 124–129.

EL-SHEIKH, M., CUMMINGS, E. M., & REITER, S. (1996). Preschoolers' responses to ongoing interadult conflict: The role of prior exposure to resolved versus unresolved arguments. *Journal of Abnormal Child Psychology, 24,* 665–679.

ELARDO, R., BRADLEY, R. H., & CALDWELL, B. M. (1975). The relation of infants' home environments to mental test performance from six to thirty-six months: A longitudinal analysis. *Child Development, 46,* 71–76.

ELARDO, R., BRADLEY, R. H., & CALDWELL, B. M. (1977). A longitudinal study of the relation of infants' home environments to language development at age 3. *Child Development, 48,* 595–603.

ELDER, G. H., JR. (1974). *Children of the Great Depression.* Chicago: University of Chicago Press.

ELDER, G. H., JR., & CASPI, A. (1988). Human development and social change: An emerging perspective on the life course. In N. Bolger, A. Caspi, G. Downey, & M. Moorehouse (Eds.), *Persons in context: Developmental processes* (pp. 77–113). Cambridge: Cambridge University Press.

ELDER, G. H., JR., CASPI, A., & VAN NGUYEN, T. (1986). Resourceful and vulnerable children: Family influences in hard times. In R. K. Silbereisen, K. Eysferth, & G. Rodinger (Eds.), *Development as action in context: Problem behavior and normal youth development* (pp. 167–186). New York: Springer-Verlag.

ELDER, G. H., JR., & CLIPP, E. (1988). Wartime losses and social bonding: Influences across 40 years in men's lives. *Psychiatry, 51,* 177–198.

ELDER, G. H., JR., & HAREVEN, T. K. (1993). Rising above life's disadvantage: From the Great Depression to war. In G. H. Elder, Jr., J. Modell, & R. D. Parke (Eds.), *Children in time and place* (pp. 47–72). Cambridge, England: Cambridge University Press.

ELDER, G. H., JR., LIKER, J. K., & CROSS, C. E. (1984). Parent–child behavior in the Great Depression: Life course and intergenerational influences. In P. B. Baltes & O. G. Brim (Eds.), *Lifespan development and behavior* (Vol. 6, pp. 109–158). New York: Academic Press.

ELDER, G. H., JR., VAN NGUYEN, T., & CASPI, A. (1985). Linking family hardship to children's lives. *Child Development, 56,* 361–375.

ELIAS, C. L., & BERK, L. E. (1999, April). *Self-regulation in young children: Is there a role for sociodramatic play?* Paper presented at the biennial meeting of the Society for Research in Child Development, Albuquerque, NM.

ELIAS, G., & BROERSE, J. (1996). Developmental changes in the incidence and likelihood of simultaneous talk during the first two years: A question of function. *Journal of Child Language, 23,* 201–217.

ELIAS, M. J., GARA, M., UBRIACO, M., ROTHMAN, P. A., CLABBY, J. F., & SCHUYLER, T. (1986). Impact of preventive social prob-

lem solving intervention on children's coping with middle-school stressors. *American Journal of Community Psychology, 14,* 259–276.

ELICKER, J., ENGLUND, M., & SROUFE, L. A. (1992). Predicting peer competence and peer relationships in childhood from early parent–child relationships. In R. D. Parke & G. W. Ladd (Eds.), *Family–peer relationships: Modes of linkage* (pp. 77–106). Hillsdale, NJ: Erlbaum.

ELKIND, D. (1994). *A sympathetic understanding of the child: Birth to sixteen* (3rd ed.). Boston: Allyn and Bacon.

ELKIND, D., & BOWEN, R. (1979). Imaginary audience behavior in children and adolescence. *Developmental Psychology, 15,* 33–44.

ELLIOTT, D. S. (1994). Serious violent offenders: Onset, developmental course, and termination. *Criminology, 32,* 1–21.

ELLIOTT, D. S., WILSON, W. J., HUIZINGA, D., SAMPSON, R. J., ELLIOTT, A., & RANKIN, B. (1996). The effects of neighborhood disadvantage on adolescent development. *Journal of Research in Crime and Delinquency, 33,* 389–426.

ELLIOTT, E. S., & DWECK, C. S. (1988). Goals: An approach to motivation and achievement. *Journal of Personality and Social Psychology, 54,* 5–12.

ELLIS, S., & GAUVAIN, M. (1992). Social and cultural influences on children's collaborative interactions. In L. T. Winegar & J. Valsiner (Eds.), *Children's development within social context* (Vol. 2, pp. 155–180). Hillsdale, NJ: Erlbaum.

ELLIS, S., KLAHR, D., & SIEGLER, R. S. (1994, April). *The birth, life, and sometimes death of good ideas in collaborative problem-solving.* Paper presented at the meeting of the American Educational Research Association, New Orleans.

ELLIS, S., ROGOFF, B., & CROMER, C. (1981). Age segregation in children's social interactions. *Developmental Psychology, 17,* 399–407.

ELLSWORTH, C. P., MUIR, D. W., & HAINS, S. M. J. (1993). Social competence and person-object differentiation: An analysis of the still-face effect. *Developmental Psychology, 29,* 63–73.

ELMAN, J. (1993). Incremental learning, or the importance of starting small. *Cognition, 49,* 71–99.

ELMAN, J. L., BATES, E. A., JOHNSON, M. H., KARMILOFF-SMITH, A., PARISI, D., & PLUNKETT, K. (1996). *Rethinking innateness: A connectionist perspective on development.* Cambridge, MA: MIT Press.

ELSEN, H. (1994). Phonological constraints and overextensions. *First Language, 14,* 305–315.

ELY, R. (1997). Language and literacy in the school years. In J. Berko Gleason (Ed.), *The development of language* (4th ed., pp. 398–439). Boston: Allyn and Bacon.

ELY, R., & MCCABE, A. (1994). The language play of kindergarten children. *First Language, 14,* 19–35.

EMDE, R. N. (1992). Individual meaning and increasing complexity: Contributions of Sigmund Freud and René Spitz to developmental psychology. *Developmental Psychology, 28,* 347–359.

EMDE, R. N., BIORINGEN, Z., CLYMAN, R. B., & OPPENHEIM, D. (1991). The moral self of infancy: Affective core and procedural knowledge. *Developmental Review, 11,* 251–270.

EMDE, R. N., & BUCHSBAUM, H. K. (1990). "Didn't you hear my mommy?" Autonomy with connectedness in moral self-emergence. In D. Cicchetti & M. Beeghly (Eds.), *Development of the self through transition* (pp. 35–60). Chicago: University of Chicago Press.

EMDE, R. N., & OPPENHEIM, D. (1995). Shame, guilt, and the Oedipal drama: Developmental considerations concerning morality and the referencing of critical others. In J. P. Tangney & K. W. Fischer (Eds.), *Self-conscious emotions: The psychology of shame, guilt, embarrassment, and pride* (pp. 413–436). New York: Guilford.

EMDE, R. N., PLOMIN, R., ROBINSON, J., CORLEY, R., DEFRIES, J., FULKER, D. W., REZNICK, J. S., CAMPOS, J., KAGAN, J., & ZAHN-WAXLER, C. (1992). Temperament, emotion, and cognition at fourteen months: The MacArthur Longitudinal Twin Study. *Child Development, 63,* 1437–1455.

EMERY, R. E. (1988). *Marriage, divorce, and children's adjustment.* Newbury Park, CA: Sage.

EMERY, R. E., & LAUMANN-BILLINGS, L. (1998). An overview of the nature, causes, and consequences of abusive family relationships: Toward differentiating maltreatment and violence. *American Psychologist, 53,* 121–135.

EMERY, R. E., MATHEWS, S. G., & KITZMANN, K. M. (1994). Child custody mediation and litigation: Parents' satisfaction and functioning a year after settlement. *Journal of Consulting and Clinical Psychology, 62,* 124–129.

EMLEN, S. T. (1995). An evolutionary theory of the family. *Proceedings of the National Academy of Sciences, 92,* 8092–8099.

EMMERICH, W. (1981). Non-monotonic developmental trends in social cognition: The case of gender constancy. In S. Strauss (Ed.), *U-shaped behavioral growth* (pp. 249–269). New York: Academic Press.

EMORY, E. K., SCHLACKMAN, L. J., & FIANO, K. (1996). Drug–hormone interactions on neurobehavioral responses in human neonates. *Infant Behavior and Development, 19,* 213–220.

EMORY, E. K., & TOOMEY, K. A. (1988). Environmental stimulation and human fetal responsibility in late pregnancy. In W. P. Smotherman & S. R. Robinson (Eds.), *Behavior of the fetus* (pp. 141–161). Caldwell, NJ: Telford.

ENGLIERT, C. S., & PALINCSAR, A. S. (1991). Reconsidering instructional research in literacy from a sociocultural perspective. *Learning Disabilities Research and Practice, 6,* 225–229.

ENRIGHT, R. D., BJERSTEDT, A., EN-RIGHT, W. F., LEVY, W. M., JR., LAPSLEY, D. K., BUSS, R. R., HAR-WELL, M., & ZINDLER, M. (1984). Distributive justice development: Cross-cultural, contextual, and longitudinal evaluations. *Child Development, 55,* 1737–1751.

ENRIGHT, R. D., FRANKLIN, C. C., & MANHEIM, L. A. (1980). Children's distributive justice reasoning: A standardized and objective scale. *Developmental Psychology, 16,* 193–202.

ENRIGHT, R. D., LAPSLEY, D. K., & SHUKLA, D. (1979). Adolescent egocentrism in early and late adolescence. *Adolescence, 14,* 687–695.

ENRIGHT, R. D., & SUTTERFIELD, S. J. (1980). An ecological validation of social cognitive development. *Child Development, 51,* 156–161.

EPSTEIN, H. T. (1980). EEG developmental stages. *Developmental Psychobiology, 13,* 629–631.

EPSTEIN, L. H., MCCURLEY, J., WING, R. R., & VALOSKI, A. (1990). Five-year follow-up of family-based treatments for childhood obesity. *Journal of Consulting and Clinical Psychology, 58,* 661–664.

EPSTEIN, L. H., MCKENZIE, S. J., VALOSKI, A., KLEIN, K. R., & WING, R. R. (1994). Effects of mastery criteria and contingent reinforcement for family-based child weight control. *Addictive Behaviors, 19,* 135–145.

EPSTEIN, L. H., SAELENS, B. E., MYERS, M. D., & VITO, D. (1997). Effects of decreasing sedentary behaviors on activity choice in obese children. *Health Psychology, 16,* 107–113.

EPSTEIN, L. H., SAELENS, B. E., & O'BRIEN, J. G. (1995). Effects of reinforcing increases in active versus decreases in sedentary behavior for obese children. *International Journal of Behavioral Medicine, 2,* 41–50.

ERDLEY, C. A., CAIN, K. M., LOOMIS, C. C., DUMAS-HINES, F., & DWECK, C. S. (1997). Relations among children's social goals, implicit personality theories, and responses to social failure. *Developmental Psychology, 33,* 263–272.

EREL, O., & BURMAN, B. (1995). Interrelatedness of marital relations and parent–child relations: A meta-analytic review. *Psychological Bulletin, 118,* 108–132.

ERIKSON, E. H. (1950). *Childhood and society.* New York: Norton.

ERIKSON, E. H. (1968). *Identity, youth, and crisis.* New York: Norton.

ERVIN-TRIPP, S. (1991). Play in language development. In B. Scales, M. Almy, A. Nicolopoulou, & S. Ervin-Tripp (Eds.), *Play and the social context of development in early care and education* (pp. 84–97). New York: Teachers College Press.

ESKENAZI, B. (1993). Caffeine during pregnancy: Grounds for concern? *Journal of the American Medical Association, 270,* 2973–2974.

ESSA, E. L., & MURRAY, C. I. (1994). Young children's understanding and experience with death. *Young Children, 49*(4), 74–81.

ETAUGH, C., & LISS, M. B. (1992). Home, school, and playroom: Training grounds for adult gender roles. *Sex Roles, 26,* 129–147.

EVELETH, P. B., & TANNER, J. M. (1990). *Worldwide variation in human growth* (2nd ed.). Cambridge: Cambridge University Press.

F

FABES, R. A., EISENBERG, N., & EISENBUD, L. (1993). Behavioral and physiological correlates of children's reactions to others' distress. *Developmental Psychology, 29,* 655–663.

FABES, R. A., EISENBERG, N., KAR-BON, M., TROYER, D., & SWITZER, G. (1994). The relations of children's emotion regulation to their vicarious emotional responses and comforting behavior. *Child Development, 65,* 1678–1693.

FABES, R. A., EISENBERG, N., NYMAN, M., & MICHEALIEU, Q. (1991). Young children's appraisals of others' spontaneous emotional reactions. *Developmental Psychology, 27,* 858–866.

FABRICIUS, W. V., & WELLMAN, H. M. (1993). Two roads diverged: Young children's ability to judge distance. *Child Development, 64,* 399–414.

FACCHINETTI, F., BATTAGLIA, C., BENATTI, R., BORELLA, P., & GENAZZANI, A. R. (1992). Oral magnesium supplementation improves fetal circulation. *Magnesium Research, 3,* 179–181.

FAGAN, J. F., III. (1973). Infant's delayed recognition memory and forgetting. *Journal of Experimental Child Psychology, 16,* 424–450.

FAGAN, J. F., III, & DETTERMAN, D. K. (1992). The Fagan Test of Infant Intelligence: A technical summary. *Journal of Applied Developmental Psychology, 13,* 173–193.

FAGAN, J. F., III, & SINGER, L. T. (1979). The role of simple feature differences in infants' recognition of faces. *Infant Behavior and Development, 2,* 39–45.

FAGAN, J. F., III, & SINGER, L. T. (1983). Infant recognition memory as a measure of intelligence. In L. P. Lipsitt (Ed.), *Advances in infancy research* (Vol. 2, pp. 31–78). Norwood, NJ: Ablex.

FAGARD, J., & PEZÉ, A. (1997). Age changes in interlimb coupling and the development of bimanual coordit Intelligence: A technical summary. *Journal of Applied Developmental Psychology, 13,* 173–193.

FAGOT, B. I. (1974). Sex differences in toddlers' behavior and parental reaction. *Developmental Psychology, 10,* 554–558.

FAGOT, B. I. (1977). Consequences of moderate cross-gender behavior in preschool children. *Child Development, 48,* 902–907.

FAGOT, B. I. (1978). The influence of sex of child on parental reactions to toddler children. *Child Development, 49,* 459–465.

FAGOT, B. I. (1985a). Beyond the reinforcement principle: Another step toward understanding sex role development. *Developmental Psychology, 21,* 1097–1104.

FAGOT, B. I. (1985b). Changes in thinking about early sex role development. *Developmental Review, 5,* 83–98.

FAGOT, B. I., & HAGAN, R. I. (1991). Observations of parent reactions to sex-stereotyped behaviors: Age and sex effects. *Child Development, 62,* 617–628.

FAGOT, B. I., & LEINBACH, M. D. (1989). The young child's

gender schema: Environmental input, internal organization. *Child Development, 60,* 663–672.

FAGOT, B. I., LEINBACH, M. D., & HAGAN, R. I. (1986). Gender labeling and the adoption of sex-typed behaviors. *Developmental Psychology, 22,* 440–443.

FAGOT, B. I., LEINBACH, M. D., & O'BOYLE, C. (1992). Gender labeling, gender stereotyping, and parenting behaviors. *Developmental Psychology, 28,* 225–230.

FAGOT, B. I., & PATTERSON, G. R. (1969). An in vivo analysis of reinforcing contingencies for sex-role behaviors in the pre-school child. *Developmental Psychology, 1,* 563–568.

FAGOT, B. I., PEARS, K. C., CAPALDI, D. M., CROSBY, L., & LEE, C. S. (1998). Becoming an adolescent father: Precursors and parenting. *Developmental Psychology, 34,* 1209–1219.

FAHRMEIER, E. D. (1978). The development of concrete operations among the Hausa. *Journal of Cross-Cultural Psychology, 9,* 23–44.

FAIRBURN, C. G., & BEGLIN, S. J. (1990). Studies of the epidemiology of bulimia nervosa. *American Journal of Psychiatry, 147,* 401–408.

FALBO, T. (1992). Social norms and the one-child family: Clinical and policy implications. In F. Boer & J. Dunn (Eds.), *Children's sibling relationships* (pp. 71–82). Hillsdale, NJ: Erlbaum.

FALBO, T., & POLIT, D. (1986). A quantitative review of the only-child literature: Research evidence and theory development. *Psychological Bulletin, 100,* 176–189.

FALBO, T., & POSTON, D. L., JR. (1993). The academic, personality, and physical outcomes of only children in China. *Child Development, 64,* 18–35.

FALBO, T., POSTON, D. L., JR., TRISCARI, R. S., & ZHANG, X. (1997). Self-enhancing illusions among Chinese schoolchildren. *Journal of Cross-Cultural Psychology, 28,* 172–191.

FALLER, K. C. (1990). *Understanding child sexual maltreatment.* Newbury Park, CA: Sage.

FANTZ, R. L. (1961). The origin of form perception. *Scientific American, 204,* 66–72.

FARKAS, S., & JOHNSON, J. (1997). *Kids these days: What Americans really think about the next generation.* New York: Public Agenda.

FARRAR, M. J. (1990). Discourse and the acquisition of grammatical morphemes. *Journal of Child Language, 17,* 607–624.

FARRAR, M. J., & GOODMAN, G. S. (1992). Developmental changes in event memory. *Child Development, 63,* 173–187.

FARRINGTON, D. P. (1987). Epidemiology. In H. C. Quay (Ed.), *Handbook of juvenile delinquency* (pp. 33–61). New York: Wiley.

FARVER, J. M. (1993). Cultural differences in scaffolding pretend play: A comparison of American and Mexican mother–child and sibling–child pairs. In K. MacDonald (Ed.), *Parent–child play* (pp. 349–366). Albany, NY: SUNY Press.

FARVER, J. M., & BRANSTETTER, W. H. (1994). Preschoolers' prosocial responses to their peers' distress. *Developmental Psychology, 30,* 334–341.

FARVER, J. M., & WIMBARTI, S. (1995a). Indonesian toddlers' social play with their mothers and older siblings. *Child Development, 66,* 1493–1503.

FARVER, J. M., & WIMBARTI, S. (1995b). Paternal participation in toddlers' pretend play. *Social Development, 4,* 19–31.

FARVER, J. M., KIM, Y. K., & LEE, Y. (1995). Cultural differences in Korean- and Anglo-American preschoolers' social interaction and play behaviors. *Child Development, 66,* 1088–1099.

FEAGANS, L. V., KIPP, E., & BLOOD, I. (1994). The effects of otitis media on the attention skills of day-care-attending toddlers. *Developmental Psychology, 30,* 701–708.

FEAGANS, L. V., & PROCTOR, A. (1994). The effects of mild illness in infancy on later development: The sample case of the effects of otitis media (middle ear effusion). In C. B. Fisher & R. M. Lerner (Eds.), *Applied developmental psychology* (pp. 139–173). New York: McGraw-Hill.

FEAGANS, L. V., SANYAL, M., HENDERSON, F., COLLIER, A., & APPELBAUM, M. I. (1987). The relationship of middle ear disease in early childhood to later narrative and attention skills. *Journal of Pediatric Psychology, 12,* 581–594.

FEATHERMAN, D. (1980). Schooling and occupational careers: Constancy and change in worldly success. In O. Brim, Jr., & J. Kagan (Eds.), *Constancy and change in human development* (pp. 675–738). Cambridge, MA: Harvard University Press.

FEE, E. J. (1997). The prosodic framework for language learning. *Topics in Language Disorders, 17,* 53–62.

FEIN, G. G., GARIBOLDI, A., & BONI, R. (1993). The adjustment of infants and toddlers to group care: The first six months. *Early Childhood Research Quarterly, 8,* 1–14.

FEINGOLD, A. (1988). Cognitive gender differences are disappearing. *American Psychologist, 43,* 95–103.

FEINGOLD, A. (1993). Cognitive gender differences: A developmental perspective. *Sex Roles, 29,* 91–112.

FEINGOLD, A. (1994). Gender differences in personality: A meta-analysis. *Psychological Bulletin, 116,* 429–456.

FEIRING, C., & TASKA, L. S. (1996). Family self-concept: Ideas on its meaning. In B. Bracken (Ed.), *Handbook of self-concept* (pp. 317–373). New York: Wiley.

FELDHUSEN, J. F. (1986). A conception of giftedness. In R. J. Sternberg & J. E. Davidson (Eds.), *Conceptions of giftedness* (pp. 112–127). New York: Cambridge University Press.

FELDMAN, D. H., & GOLDSMITH, L. T. (1991). *Nature's gambit.* New York: Teachers College Press.

FELNER, R. D., & ADAN, A. M. (1988). The School Transitional Environment Project: An ecological intervention and evaluation. In R. H. Price, E. L. Cowan, R. P. Lorion, & J. Ramos-McKay (Eds.), *14 ounces of prevention: A casebook for practitioners* (pp. 111–122). Washington, DC: American Psychological Association.

FENSON, L., DALE, P. S., REZNICK, J. S., BATES, E., THAL, D. J., & PETHICK, S. J. (1994). Variability in early communicative development. *Monographs of the Society for Research in Child Development, 59* (5, Serial No. 242).

FERGUSSON, D. M., HORWOOD, L. J., & LYNSKEY, M. T. (1993). Maternal smoking before and after pregnancy: Effects on behavioral outcomes in middle childhood. *Pediatrics, 92,* 815–822.

FERGUSSON, D. M., HORWOOD, L. J., & SHANNON, F. T. (1987). Breastfeeding and subsequent social adjustment in six- to eight-year-old children. *Journal of Child Psychology and Psychiatry, 28,* 378–386.

FERNALD, A., & MORIKAWA, H. (1993). Common themes and cultural variations in Japanese and American mothers' speech to infants. *Child Development, 64,* 637–656.

FERNALD, A., TAESCHNER, T., DUNN, J., PAPOUSEK, M., BOYSSON-BARDIES, B., & FUKUI, I. (1989). A cross-language study of prosodic modifications in mothers' and fathers' speech to preverbal infants. *Journal of Child Language, 16,* 477–502.

FESHBACH, N. D., & FESHBACH, S. (1982). Empathy training and the regulation of aggression: Potentialities and limitation. *Academic Psychology Bulletin, 4,* 399–413.

FEUERSTEIN, R. (1979). *Dynamic assessment of retarded performers: The learning potential assessment device: Theory, instruments, and techniques.* Baltimore: University Park Press.

FEUERSTEIN, R. (1980). *Instrumental enrichment.* Baltimore: University Park Press.

FICHTER, M. M., & QUADFLIEG, N. (1996). Course and two-year outcome in anorexic and bulimic adolescents. *Journal of Youth and Adolescence, 25,* 545–562.

FIELD, T. M. (1998). Massage therapy effects. *American Psychologist, 53,* 1270–1281.

FIELD, T. M. (1994). The effects of mother's physical and emotional unavailability on emotion regulation. In N. A. Fox (Ed.), The development of emotion regulation: Biological and behavioral considerations. *Monographs of the Society for Research in Child Development, 59* (2–3, Serial No. 240).

FIELD, T. M., SCHANBERG, S. M., SCAFIDI, F., BAUER, C. R., VEGA-LAHR, N., GARCIA, R., NYSTROM, J., & KUHN, C. M. (1986). Effects of tactile/kinesthetic stimulation on preterm neonates. *Pediatrics, 77,* 654–658.

FIELD, T. M., WOODSON, R., GREENBERG, R., & COHEN, D. (1982). Discrimination and imitation of facial expressions by neonates. *Science, 218,* 179–181.

FIGUEROA-COLON, R., FRANKLIN, F. A., LEE, J. Y., ALDRIDGE, R., & ALEXANDER, L. (1997). Prevalence of obesity with increased blood pressure in elementary school-aged children. *Southern Medical Journal, 90,* 806–813.

FILIPOVIC, Z. (1994). *Zlata's diary: A child's life in Sarajevo.* New York: Penguin.

FINE, G. A. (1980). The natural history of preadolescent male friendship groups. In H. C. Foot, A. J. Chapman, & J. R. Smith (Eds.), *Friendship and social relations in children* (pp. 293–320). Chichester, England: Wiley.

FINEGAN, J. K., NICCOLS, G. A., & SITARENIOS, G. (1992). Relations between prenatal testosterone levels and cognitive abilities at 4 years. *Developmental Psychology, 28,* 1075–1089.

FISCHER, K. W., & BIDELL, T. R. (1998). Dynamic development of psychological structures in action and thought. In R. M. Lerner (Ed.), *Handbook of child psychology: Vol. 1. Theoretical models of human development* (5th ed., pp. 467–561). New York: Wiley.

FISCHER, K. W., & FARRAR, M. J. (1987). Generalizations about generalizations: How a theory of skill development explains both generality and specificity.

International Journal of Psychology, 22, 643–677.

FISCHER, K. W., & HENCKE, R. W. (1996). Infants' construction of actions in context: Piaget's contribution to research on early development. *Psychological Science, 7,* 204–210.

FISCHER, K. W., & PIPP, S. L. (1984). Processes of cognitive development: Optimal level and skill acquisition. In R. J. Sternberg (Ed.), *Mechanisms of cognitive development* (pp. 45–80). New York: Freeman.

FISCHER, K. W., & ROSE, S. P. (1994). Dynamic development of coordination of components in brain and behavior: A framework for theory. In G. Dawson & K. W. Fischer (Eds.), *Human behavior and the developing brain* (pp. 3–66). New York: Guilford.

FISCHER, K. W., & ROSE, S. P. (1995, Fall). Concurrent cycles in the dynamic development of brain and behavior. *SRCD Newsletter,* pp. 3–4, 15–16.

FISCHMAN, M. G., MOORE, J. B., & STEELE, K. H. (1992). Children's one-hand catching as a function of age, gender, and ball location. *Research Quarterly for Exercise and Sport, 63,* 349–355.

FISHER, C. B. (1993, Winter). Integrating science and ethics in research with high-risk children and youth. *Social Policy Report of the Society for Research in Child Development, 4*(4).

FISHER, C. B., HALL, D. G., RAKOWITZ, S., & GLEITMAN, L. (1994). When it is better to receive than to give: Syntactic and conceptual constraints on vocabulary growth. *Lingua, 92,* 333–375.

FISHER, J. A., & BIRCH, L. L. (1995). 3–5 year-old children's fat preferences and fat consumption are related to parental adiposity. *Journal of the American Dietetic Association, 95,* 759–764.

FISHER-THOMPSON, D. (1993). Adult toy purchase for children: Factors affecting sex-typed toy selection. *Journal of Applied Developmental Psychology, 14,* 385–406.

FITCH, M., HUSTON, A. C., & WRIGHT, J. C. (1993). From television forms to genre schemata: Children's perceptions of television reality. In G. L. Berry & J. K. Asamen (Eds.), *Children and television* (pp. 38–52). Newbury Park, CA: Sage.

FITZGERALD, J. (1987). Research on revision in writing. *Review of Educational Research, 57,* 481–506.

FIVUSH, R. (1984). Learning about school: The development of kindergartners' school scripts. *Child Development, 55,* 1697–1709.

FIVUSH, R. (1989). Exploring sex differences in the emotional content of mother—child conversations about the past. *Sex Roles, 20,* 675–691.

FIVUSH, R. (1995). Language, narrative, and autobiography. *Consciousness and Cognition, 4,* 100–103.

FIVUSH, R., & HAMOND, N. R. (1990). Autobiographical memory across the preschool years: Toward reconceptualizing childhood amnesia. In R. Fivush & J. A. Hudson (Eds.), *Knowing and remembering in young children* (pp. 223–248). New York: Cambridge University Press.

FIVUSH, R., HADEN, C., & ADAM, S. (1995). Structure and coherence of preschoolers' personal narratives over time: Implications for childhood amnesia. *Journal of Experimental Child Psychology, 60,* 32–56.

FIVUSH, R., KUEBLI, J., & CLUBB, P. A. (1992). The structure of events and event representations: A developmental analysis. *Child Development, 63,* 188–201.

FIVUSH, R., & REESE, E. (1992). The social construction of autobiographical memory. In M. A. Conway, D. C. Rubin, H. Spinler, & W. A. Wagenaar (Eds.), *Theoretical perspectives on autobiographical memory* (pp. 115–132). Ultrecht, Netherlands: Kluwer.

FLAKE, A., RONCAROLO, M., PUCK, J. M., ALMEIDAPORADA, G., EVINS, M. I., JOHNSON, M. P., ABELLA, E. M., HARRISON, D. D., & ZANJANI, E. D. (1996). Treatment of X-linked severe combined immunodeficiency by in utero transplantation of paternal bone marrow. *New England Journal of Medicine, 335,* 1806–1810.

FLANAGAN, C. A., & ECCLES, J. S. (1993). Changes in parents' work status and adolescents' adjustment at school. *Child Development, 64,* 246–257.

FLANNERY, K. A., & LIEDERMAN, J. (1995). Is there really a syndrome involving the co-occurrence of neurodevelopmental disorder, talent, nonright handedness and immune disorder among children? *Cortex, 31,* 503–515.

FLAVELL, J. H. (1985). *Cognitive development* (2nd ed.). Englewood Cliffs, NJ: Prentice-Hall.

FLAVELL, J. H. (1992). Cognitive development: Past, present, and future. *Developmental Psychology, 28,* 998–1005.

FLAVELL, J. H. (1993). The development of children's understanding of false belief and the appearance–reality distinction. *International Journal of Psychology, 28,* 595–604.

FLAVELL, J. H., BOTKIN, P. T., FRY, C. L., JR., WRIGHT, J. W., & JARVIS, P. E. (1968). *The development of role-taking and communication skills in children.* New York: Wiley.

FLAVELL, J. H., FLAVELL, E. R., GREEN, F. L., & KORFMACHER, J. E. (1990). Do young children think of television images as pictures or real objects? *Journal of Broadcasting and Electronic Media, 34,* 399–419.

FLAVELL, J. H., GREEN, F. L., & FLAVELL, E. R. (1987). Development of knowledge about the appearance–reality distinction. *Monographs of the Society for Research in Child Development, 51* (1, Serial No. 212).

FLAVELL, J. H., GREEN, F. L., & FLAVELL, E. R. (1989). Young children's ability to differentiate appearance–reality and level 2 perspectives in the tactile modality. *Child Development, 60,* 201–213.

FLAVELL, J. H., GREEN, F. L., & FLAVELL, E. R. (1993). Children's understanding of the stream of consciousness. *Child Development, 64,* 387–398.

FLAVELL, J. H., GREEN, F. L., & FLAVELL, E. R. (1995). Young children's knowledge about thinking. *Monographs of the Society for Research in Child Development, 60* (1, Serial No. 243).

FLAVELL, J. H., GREEN, F. L., FLAVELL, E. R., & GROSSMAN, J. B. (1997). The development of children's knowledge about inner speech. *Child Development, 68,* 39–47.

FLAVELL, J. H., & MILLER, P. H. (1998). Social cognition. In D. Kuhn & R. S. Siegler (Eds.), *Handbook of child psychology: Vol. 2. Cognition, perception, and language* (4th ed., pp. 851–898). New York: Wiley.

FLEMING, P. J., BLAIR, P. S., BACON, C., BENSLEY, D., SMITH, I., TAYLOR, E., BERRY, J., GOLDING, J., & TRIPP, J. (1996). Environment of infants during sleep and risk of the sudden infant death syndrome: Results of 1993–5 case control study for confidential inquiry into stillbirths and deaths in infancy. *British Medical Journal, 313,* 191–195.

FLETCHER, A. C., DARLING, N. E., STEINBERG, L., & DORNBUSCH, S. M. (1995). The company they keep: Relation of adolescents' adjustment and behavior to their friends' perceptions of authoritative parenting in the social network. *Developmental Psychology, 31,* 300–310.

FLETCHER, J. M., LANDRY, S. H., BOHAN, T. P., DAVIDSON, K. C., BROOKSHIRE, B. L., LACHAR, D., DRAMER, L. A., & FRANCIS, D. J. (1997). Effects of intraventricular hemorrhage and hydro-cephalus on the long-term neurobehavioral development of preterm very-low-birthweight infants. *Developmental Medicine & Child Neurology, 39,* 596–606.

FLETCHER-FLINN, C. M., & GRAVATT, B. (1995). The efficacy of computer-assisted instruction (CAI): A meta-analysis. *Journal of Educational Computing Research, 12,* 219–242.

FLOCCIA, C., CHRISTOPHE, A., & BERTONCINI, J. (1997). High-amplitude sucking and newborns: The quest for underlying mechanisms. *Journal of Experimental Child Psychology, 64,* 175–198.

FLORIAN, V., & KRAVETZ, S. (1985). Children's concepts of death: A cross-cultural comparison among Muslims, Druze, Christians, and Jews in Israel. *Journal of Cross-Cultural Psychology, 16,* 174–179.

FLORSHEIM, P., TOLAN, P., & GORMAN-SMITH, D. (1998). Family relationships, parenting practices, the availability of male family members, and the behavior of inner-city boys in single-mother and two-parent families. *Child Development, 69,* 1437–1447.

FLYNN, J. R. (1996). What environmental factors affect intelligence: The relevance of IQ gains over time. In D. K. Detterman (Ed.), *The environment. Current topics in human intelligence* (Vol. 5, pp. 17–29). Norwood, NJ: Ablex.

FLYNN, J. R. (1999). Searching for justice: The discovery of IQ gains over time. *American Psychologist, 54,* 5–20.

FOGEL, A. (1993). *Developing through relationships. Origins of communication, self and culture.* New York: Harvester Wheatsheaf.

FOGEL, A., MELSON, G. F., TODA, S., & MISTRY, T. (1987). Young children's responses to unfamiliar infants. *International Journal of Behavioral Development, 10,* 1071–1077.

FOGEL, A., TODA, S., & KAWAI, M. (1988). Mother–infant face-to-face interaction in Japan and the United States: A laboratory comparison using 3-month-old infants. *Developmental Psychology, 24,* 398–406.

FOLTZ, C., OVERTON, W. F., & RICCO, R. B. (1995). Proof construction: Adolescent development from inductive to deductive problem-solving strategies. *Journal of Experimental Child Psychology, 59,* 179–195.

FONZI, A., SCHNEIDER, B. H., TANI, F., & TOMADA, G. (1997). Predicting children's friendship status from their dyadic interaction in structured situations of potential conflict. *Child Development, 68,* 496–506.

FORD, C., & BEACH, F. (1951). *Patterns of sexual behavior.* New York: Harper & Row.

FOREHAND, R., WIERSON, M., THOMAS, A. M., FAUBER, R., ARMISTEAD, L., KEMPTON, T., & LONG, N. (1991). A short-term longitudinal examination of young adolescent functioning following divorce: The role of family factors. *Journal of Abnormal Child Psychology, 19,* 97–111.

FORMAN, E. A., & MCPHAIL, J. (1993). Vygotskian perspective on children's collaborative problem-solving activities. In E. A. Forman, N. Minick, & C. A. Stone (Eds.), *Contexts for learning* (pp. 323–347). New York: Cambridge University Press.

FORMAN, E. A., MINICK, N., & STONE, C. A. (Eds.). (1993). *Contexts for learning.* New York: Oxford University Press.

FORTIER, I., MARCOUX, S., & BEAULAC-BAILLARGEON, L. (1993). Relation of caffeine intake during pregnancy to intrauterine growth retardation and preterm birth. *American Journal of Epidemiology, 137,* 931–940.

FORTIER, I., MARCOUX, S., & BRISSON, J. (1994). Passive smoking during pregnancy and the risk of delivering a small-for-gestational-age infant. *American Journal of Epidemiology, 139,* 294–301.

FOX, N. A., BELL, M. A., & JONES, N. A. (1992). Individual differences in response to stress and cerebral asymmetry. *Developmental Neuropsychology, 8,* 161–184.

FOX, N. A., CALKINS, S. D., & BELL, M. A. (1994). Neural plasticity and development in the first two years of life: Evidence from cognitive and socioemotional domains of research. *Development and Psychopathology, 6,* 677–696.

FOX, N. A., & DAVIDSON, R. J. (1986). Taste-elicited changes in facial signs of emotion and the asymmetry of brain electrical activity in newborn infants. *Neuropsychologia, 24,* 417–422.

FOX, N. A., & FITZGERALD, H. E. (1990). Autonomic function in infancy. *Merrill-Palmer Quarterly, 36,* 27–51.

FOX, N. A., KIMMERLY, N. L., & SCHAFER, W. D. (1991). Attachment to mother/attachment to father: A meta-analysis. *Child Development, 62,* 210–225.

FRACASSO, M. P., & BUSCH-ROSSNAGEL, N. A. (1992). Parents and children of Hispanic origin. In M. E. Procidano & C. B. Fisher (Eds.), *Contemporary families: A handbook for school professionals* (pp. 93–98). New York: Teachers College Press.

FRAIBERG, S. (1977). *Insights from the blind: Comparative studies of blind and sighted infants.* New York: Basic Books.

FRANCIS, P. L., & MCCROY, G. (1983). *Bimodal recognition of human stimulus configurations.* Paper presented at the biennial meeting of the Society for Research in Child Development, Detroit.

FRANK, S. J., PIRSCH, L. A., & WRIGHT, V. C. (1990). Late adolescents' perceptions of their relationships with their parents: Relationships among deidealization, autonomy, relatedness, and insecurity and implications for adolescent adjustment and ego identity status. *Journal of Youth and Adolescence, 19,* 571–588.

FRANKEL, K. A., & BATES, J. E. (1990). Mother-toddler problem solving: Antecedents in attachment, home behavior, and temperament. *Child Development, 61,* 810–819.

FRAZIER, J. A., & MORRISON, F. J. (1998). The influence of extended-year schooling on growth of achievement and perceived competence in early elementary school. *Child Development, 69,* 495–517.

FREDERICKS, M., & MILLER, S. I. (1997). Some brief notes on the "unfinished business" of qualitative inquiry. *Quality & Quantity, 31,* 1–13.

FREEDMAN, D. G., & FREEDMAN, N. (1969). Behavioral differences between Chinese-American and European-American newborns. *Nature, 224,* 1227.

FREEMAN, D. (1983). *Margaret Mead and Samoa: The making and unmaking of an anthropological myth.* Cambridge, MA: Harvard University Press.

FREUD, A., & DANN, S. (1951). An experiment in group upbringing. *Psychoanalytic Study of the Child, 6,* 127–168.

FREUD, S. (1961). Some psychological consequences of the anatomical distinction between the sexes. In J. Strachey (Ed.), *Standard edition of the complete psychological works of Sigmund Freud* (Vol. 19, pp. 248–258). London: Hogarth Press. (Original work published 1925)

FREUD, S. (1974). *The ego and the id.* London: Hogarth. (Original work published 1923)

FREY, K. S., & RUBLE, D. N. (1992). Gender constancy and the "cost" of sex-typed behavior: A test of the conflict hypothesis. *Developmental Psychology, 28,* 714–721.

FRIED, M. N., & FRIED, M. H. (1980). *Transitions: Four rituals in eight cultures.* New York: Norton.

FRIED, P. A. (1993). Prenatal exposure to tobacco and marijuana: Effects during pregnancy, infancy, and early childhood. *Clinical Obstetrics and Gynecology, 36,* 319–337.

FRIED, P. A., & MAKIN, J. E. (1987). Neonatal behavioral correlates of prenatal exposure to marijuana, cigarettes, and alcohol in a low risk population. *Neurobehavioral Toxicology and Teratology, 9,* 1–7.

FRIED, P. A., & WATKINSON, B. (1990). 36- and 48-month neurobehavioral follow-up of children prenatally exposed to marijuana, cigarettes, and alcohol. *Journal of Developmental and Behavioral Pediatrics, 11,* 49–58.

FRIEDERICI, A. D., & WESSELS, J. M. I. (1993). Phonotactic knowledge and its use in infant speech perception. *Perception and Psychophysics, 54,* 287–295.

FRIEDMAN, H. S., TUCKER, J. S., SCHWARTZ, J. R., WINGARD, D. L., & CRIQUI, M. H. (1995). Psychosocial and behavioral predictors of longevity: The aging and death of the "Termites." *American Psychologist, 50,* 69–78.

FRIEDMAN, J. M. (1996). *The effects of drugs on the fetus and nursing infant: A handbook for health care professionals.* Baltimore: Johns Hopkins University Press.

FRIEDMAN, S. L., & SCHOLNICK, E. K. (1997). An evolving "blueprint" for planning: Psychological requirements, task characteristics, and social–cultural influences. In S. L. Friedman & E. K. Scholnick (Eds.), *The developmental psychology of planning: Why, how, and when do we plan?* (pp. 3–22). Mahwah, NJ: Erlbaum.

FRIEDRICH-COFER, L. K., TUCKER, C. J., NORRIS-BAKER, C., FARNSWORTH, J. B., FISHER, D. P., HANNINGTON, C. M., & HOXIE, K. (1978). *Perceptions by adolescents of television heroines.* Paper presented at the annual meeting of the Southwestern Psychological Association, New Orleans.

FRODI, A. (1985). When empathy fails: Aversive infant crying and child abuse. In B. M. Lester & C. F. Z. Boukydis (Eds.), *Infant crying: Theoretical and research perspectives* (pp. 263–277). New York: Plenum.

FROOM, J., & CULPEPPER, L. (1991). Otitis media in day-care children: A report from the International Primary Care Network. *Journal of Family Practice, 32,* 289–294.

FROST, J. J., & FORREST, J. D. (1995). Understanding the impact of effective teenage pregnancy prevention programs. *Family Planning Perspectives, 27,* 188–195.

FRY, A. F., & HALE, S. (1996). Processing speed, working memory, and fluid intelligence: Evidence for a developmental cascade. *Psychological Science, 7,* 237–241.

FUCHS, I., EISENBERG, N., HERTZ-LAZAROWITZ, R., & SHARABANY, R. (1986). Kibbutz, Israeli city, and American children's moral reasoning about prosocial moral conflicts. *Merrill-Palmer Quarterly, 32,* 37–50.

FUCHS, L. S., FUCHS, D., HAMLETT, C. L., & KARNS, K. (1998). High-achieving students' interactions and performance on complex mathematical tasks as a function of homogeneous and heterogeneous pairings. *American Educational Research Journal, 35,* 227–267.

FUHRMAN, T., & HOLMBECK, G. N. (1995). A contextual-moderator analysis of emotional autonomy and adjustment in adolescence. *Child Development, 66,* 793–811.

FUJINAGA, T., KASUGA, T., UCHIDA, N., & SAIGA, H. (1990). Long-term follow-up study of children developmentally retarded by early environmental deprivation. *Genetic, Social and General Psychology Monographs, 116,* 37–104.

FULIGNI, A. J. (1997). The academic achievement of adolescents from immigrant families: The roles of family background, attitudes, and behavior. *Child Development, 68,* 351–363.

FULIGNI, A. J., & ECCLES, J. S. (1993). Perceived parent–child relationships and early adolescents' orientation toward peers. *Developmental Psychology, 29,* 622–632.

FULIGNI, A. J., ECCLES, J. S., & BARBER, B. L. (1995). The long-term effects of seventh-grade ability grouping in mathematics. *Journal of Early Adolescence, 15,* 58–89.

FULIGNI, A. J., & STEVENSON, H. W. (1995). Time use and mathematics achievement among American, Chinese, and Japanese high school students. *Child Development, 66,* 830–842.

FURMAN, E. (1990). Plant a potato—Learn about life (and death). *Young Children, 46*(1), 15–20.

FURMAN, W., & BUHRMESTER, D. (1992). Age and sex differences in perceptions of networks of personal relationships. *Child Development, 63,* 103–115.

FURSTENBERG, F. F., JR., BROOKS-GUNN, J., & MORGAN, S. P. (1987). *Adolescent mothers and their children in later life.* Cambridge: Cambridge University Press.

FURSTENBERG, F. F., JR., & CHERLIN, A. J. (1991). *Divided families.* Cambridge, MA: Harvard University Press.

FURSTENBERG, F. F., JR., & HARRIS, K. M. (1993). When and why fathers matter: Impact of father involvement on children of adolescent mothers. In R. I. Lerman & T. J. Ooms (Eds.), *Young unwed fathers* (pp. 117–138). Philadelphia: Temple University Press.

FURSTENBERG, F. F., JR., HUGHES, M. E., & BROOKS-GUNN, J. (1992). The next generation: Children of teenage mothers grow up. In M. K. Rosenheim & M. F. Testa (Eds.), *Early parenthood* (pp. 113–135). New Brunswick, NJ: Rutgers University Press.

FURUNO, S., O'REILLY, K., INATSUKA, T., HOSAKA, C., ALLMAN, T., & ZEISLOFT-FALBEY, B. (1987). *Hawaii Early Learning Profile.* Palo Alto, CA: VORT Corporation.

FUSON, K. C. (1990). Issues in place-value and multidigit addition and subtraction learning and teaching. *Journal of Research in Mathematics Education, 21,* 273–280.

FUSON, K. C. (1992). Research on learning and teaching addition and subtraction of whole numbers. In G. Leinhardt, R. T. Putnam, & R. A. Hattrup (Eds.), *The analysis of arithmetic for mathematics teaching* (pp. 53–187). Hillsdale, NJ: Erlbaum.

FUSON, K. C., & KWON, Y. (1992). Korean children's understanding of multidigit addition and subtraction. *Child Development, 63,* 491–506.

G

GADDIS, A., & BROOKS-GUNN, J. (1985). The male experience of pubertal change. *Journal of Youth and Adolescence, 14,* 61–69.

GAENSBAUER, T. J. (1980). Anaclitic depression in a three-and-one-half month-old child. *American Journal of Psychiatry, 137,* 841–842.

GAGNON, A., & MORASSE, I. (1995, March). *Self-esteem and intergroup discrimination in second-grade schoolchildren.* Paper presented at the biennial meeting of the Society for Research in Child Development, Indianapolis.

GALAMBOS, N. L., ALMEIDA, D. M., & PETERSEN, A. C. (1990). Masculinity, femininity, and sex role attitudes in early adolescence: Exploring gender intensification. *Child Development, 61,* 1904–1914.

GALAMBOS, N. L., & MAGGS, J. L. (1991). Children in self-care: Figures, facts, and fiction. In J. V. Lerner & N. L. Galambos (Eds.), *Employed mothers and their children* (pp. 131–157). New York: Garland.

GALIN, D., JOHNSTONE, J., NAKELL, L., & HERRON, J. (1979). Development of the capacity for tactile information transfer between hemispheres in normal children. *Science, 204,* 1330–1332.

GALINSKY, E., HOWES, C., KONTOS, S., & SHINN, M. (1994). *The study of children in family child care and relative care: Highlights of findings.* New York: Families and Work Institute.

GALLER, J. R., RAMSEY, C. F., MORLEY, D. S., ARCHER, E., & SALT, P. (1990). The long-term effects of early kwashiorkor compared with marasmus. IV. Performance on the National High School Entrance Examination. *Pediatric Research, 28,* 235–239.

GALLER, J. R., RAMSEY, F., & SOLIMANO, G. (1985a). A follow-up study of the effects of early malnutrition on subsequent development: I. Physical growth and sexual maturation during adolescence. *Pediatric Research, 19,* 518–523.

GALLER, J. R., RAMSEY, F., & SOLIMANO, G. (1985b). A follow-up study of the effects of early malnutrition on subsequent development: II. Fine motor skills in adolescence. *Pediatric Research, 19,* 524–527.

GALLER, J. R., RAMSEY, F., SOLIMANO, G., KUCHARSKI, L. T., & HARRISON, R. (1984). The influence of early malnutrition on subsequent behavioral development: IV. Soft neurological signs. *Pediatric Research, 18,* 826–832.

GALLISTEL, C. R., & GELMAN, R. (1992). Preverbal and verbal counting and computation. *Cognition, 44,* 43–74.

GALOTTI, K. M., KOZBERG, S. F., & FARMER, M. C. (1991). Gender and developmental differences in adolescents' conceptions of moral reasoning. *Journal of Youth and Adolescence, 20,* 13–30.

GALPER, A., WIGFIELD, A., & SEEFELDT, C. (1997). Head Start parents' beliefs about their children's abilities, task values, and performances on different activities. *Child Development, 68,* 897–907.

GALTON, F. (1883). *Inquiries into human faculty and its development.* London: Macmillan.

GANDOUR, M. J. (1989). Activity level as a dimension of temperament in toddlers: Its relevance for the organismic specificity hypothesis. *Child Development, 60,* 1092–1098.

GANNON, S., & KORN, S. J. (1983). Temperament, cultural variation, and behavior disorder in preschool children. *Child Psychiatry and Human Development, 13,* 203–212.

GANONG, L. H., & COLEMAN, M. (1994). *Remarried family relationships.* Thousand Oaks, CA: Sage.

GARBARINO, J. (1997). The role of economic deprivation in the social context of child maltreatment. In M. E. Helfer, R. S. Kempe, & R. D. Krugman (Eds.), *The battered child* (5th ed., 49–60). Chicago: University of Chicago Press.

GARBARINO, J., & KOSTELNY, K. (1993). Neighborhood and community influences on parenting. In T. Luster & L. Okagaki (1993). *Parenting: An ecological perspective* (pp. 203–226). Hillsdale, NJ: Erlbaum.

GARBER, J., BRAAFLADT, N., & WEISS, B. (1995). Affect regulation in depressed and nondepressed children and young adolescents. *Developmental and Psychopathology, 7,* 93–115.

GARBER, J., QUIGGLE, N., PANAK, W., & DODGE, K. (1991). Aggression and depression in children: Comorbidity, specificity, and social cognitive processing. In D. Cicchetti & S. L. Toth (Eds.), *Rochester Symposium on Developmental Psychopathology: Vol. 2. Internalizing and externalizing expressions of dysfunction* (pp. 225–264). Hillsdale, NJ: Erlbaum.

GARCÍA-COLL, C., & MAGNUSON, K. (1997). The psychological experience of immigration: A developmental perspective. In A. Booth, A. C. Crouter, & N. Landale (Eds.), *Immigration and the family* (pp. 91–131). Mahwah, NJ: Erlbaum.

GARDNER, H. (1980). *Artful scribbles: The significance of children's drawings.* New York: Basic Books.

GARDNER, H. (1983). *Frames of mind.* New York: Basic Books.

GARDNER, H. (1993). *Multiple intelligences: The theory in practice.* New York: Basic Books.

GARDNER, H. (1997). *Extraordinary minds.* New York: Basic Books.

GARDNER, H., HATCH, T., & TORFF, B. (1997). A third perspective: The symbol systems approach. In R. J. Sternberg & E. L. Grigoenko (Eds.), *Intelligence, heredity, and environment* (pp. 243–268). New York: Cambridge University Press.

GARDNER, H. E. (1998a). Are there additional intelligences? The case of the naturalist, spiritual, and existential intelligences. In J. Kane (Ed.), *Educational information and transformation.* Upper Saddle River, NJ: Prentice-Hall.

GARDNER, H. E. (1998b). Extraordinary cognitive achievements (ECA): A symbol systems approach. In W. Damon & R. M. Lerner (Eds.), *Handbook of child psychology: Vol. 1. Theoretical models of human development* (5th ed., pp. 415–466). New York: Wiley.

GARDNER, M. J., SNEE, M. P., HALL, A. J., POWELL, C. A., DOWNES, S., & TERRELL, J. D. (1990). Leukemia cases linked to fathers' radiation dose. *Nature, 343,* 423–429.

GARDNER, R. A., & GARDNER, B. T. (1969). Teaching sign language to a chimpanzee. *Science, 165,* 664–672.

GARFINKEL, I., & MCLANAHAN, S. (1995). The effects of child support reform on child well-being. In P. L. Chase-Lansdale & J. Brooks-Gunn (Eds.), *Escape from poverty: What makes a difference for children?* (pp. 211–238). New York: Cambridge University Press.

GARLAND, A. F., & ZIGLER, E. (1993). Adolescent suicide prevention: Current research and social policy implications. *American Psychologist, 48,* 169–182.

GARMEZY, N. (1993). Children in poverty: Resilience despite risk. *Psychiatry, 56,* 127–136.

GARMON, L. C., BASINGER, K. S., GREGG, V. R., & GIBBS, J. C. (1996). Gender differences in stage and expression of moral judgment. *Merrill-Palmer Quarterly, 42,* 418–437.

GARNER, P. W. (1996). The relations of emotional role taking, affective/moral attributions, and emotional display rule knowledge to low-income school-age children's social competence. *Journal of Applied Developmental Psychology, 17,* 19–36.

GARNER, P. W., JONES, D. C., & MINER, J. L. (1994). Social competence among low-income preschoolers: Emotion socialization practices and social cognitive correlates. *Child Development, 65,* 622–637.

GARRETT, P., NG'ANDU, N., & FERRON, J. (1994). Poverty experiences of young children and the quality of their home environments. *Child Development, 65,* 331–345.

GARVEY, C. (1974). Requests and responses in children's speech. *Journal of Child Language, 2,* 41–60.

GARVEY, C. (1990). *Play.* Cambridge, MA: Harvard University Press.

GASH, H., & MORGAN, M. (1993). School-based modifications of children's gender-related beliefs. *Journal of Applied Developmental Psychology, 14,* 277–287.

GASKINS, S. (1994). Symbolic play in a Mayan village. *Merrill-Palmer Quarterly, 40,* 344–359.

GATHERCOLE, S. E. (1995). Is non-word repetition a test of phonological memory or long-term knowledge? It all depends on the nonwords. *Memory and Cognition, 23,* 83–94.

GATHERCOLE, S. E., HITCH, G. J., SERVICE, E., & MARTIN, A. J. (1997). Phonological short-term memory and new word learning in children. *Developmental Psychology, 33,* 966–979.

GAUB, M., & CARLSON, C. L. (1997). Gender differences in ADHD: A meta-analysis and critical review. *Journal of the American Academy of Child and Adolescent Psychiatry, 36,* 1036–1045.

GAUVAIN, M., & ROGOFF, B. (1989). Collaborative problem solving and children's planning skills. *Developmental Psychology, 25,* 139–151.

GE, X., CONGER, R. D., & ELDER, G. H., JR. (1996). Coming of age too early: Pubertal influences on girls' vulnerability to psychological distress. *Child Development, 67,* 3386–3400.

GEARY, D. C. (1994). *Children's mathematical development.* Washington, DC: American Psychological Association.

GEARY, D. C. (1996). International differences in mathematics achievement: Their nature, causes, and consequences. *Current Directions in Psychological Science, 5,* 133–137.

GEARY, D. C., BOW-THOMAS, C. C., LIU, F., & SIEGLER, R. S. (1996). Development of arithmetical competencies in Chinese and American children: Influence of age, language, and schooling. *Child Development, 67,* 2022–2044.

GEARY, D. C., & BURLINGHAM-DUBREE, M. (1989). External validation of the strategy choice model for addition. *Journal of Experimental Child Psychology, 47,* 175–192.

GELLATLY, A. R. H. (1987). Acquisition of a concept of logical necessity. *Human Development, 30,* 32–47.

GELMAN, R. (1972). Logical capacity of very young children: Number invariance rules. *Child Development, 43,* 75–90.

GELMAN, R., & SHATZ, M. (1978). Appropriate speech adjustments: The operation of conversational constraints on talk to two-year-olds. In M. Lewis & L. A. Rosenblum (Eds.), *Interaction, conversation, and the development of language* (pp. 27–61). New York: Wiley.

GELMAN, S. A., & COLEY, J. D. (1990). The importance of knowing a dodo is a bird: Categories and inferences in 2-year-old children. *Developmental Psychology, 26,* 796–804.

GELMAN, S. A., COLEY, J. D., ROSENGREN, K. S., HARTMAN, E., & PAPPAS, A. (1998). Beyond labeling: The role of maternal input in the acquisition of richly structured categories. *Monographs of the Society for Research in Child Development, 63*(1, Serial No. 253).

GELMAN, S. A., & WELLMAN, H. M. (1991). Insides and essences: Early understandings of the non-obvious. *Cognition, 38,* 213–244.

GENESEE, F., NICOLADIS, E., & PARADIS, J. (1995). Language differentiation in early bilingual development. *Journal of Child Language, 22,* 611–631.

GENTNER, D., & RATTERMANN, M. J. (1991). Language and the career of similarity. In S. A. Gelman & J. P. Byrnes (Eds.), *Perspectives on language and thought: Interrelations in development* (pp. 225–277). Cambridge: Cambridge University Press.

GEORGE, C., KAPLAN, N., & MAIN, M. (1985). *The Adult Attachment Interview.* Unpublished manuscript, University of California at Berkeley.

GEORGE, T. P., & HARTMANN, D. P. (1996). Friendship networks of unpopular, average, and popular children. *Child Development, 67,* 2301–2316.

GERBNER, G., & SIGNORIELLI, N. (1990). *Violence profile, 1967 through 1988–1989. Enduring patterns.* Unpublished manuscript, Annenberg School of Communication, University of Pennsylvania, Philadelphia.

GERSHOFF-STOWE, L., & SMITH, L. B. (1997). A curvilinear trend in naming errors as a function of early vocabulary growth. *Cognitive Psychology, 34,* 37–71.

GERSHOFF-STOWE, L., THAL, D. J., SMITH, L. B., & NAMY, L. L. (1997). Categorization and its developmental relation to early language. *Child Development, 68,* 843–859.

GERVAI, J., TURNER, P. J., & HINDE, R. A. (1995). Gender-related behaviour, attitudes, and personality in parents of young children in England and Hungary. *International Journal of Behavioral Development, 18,* 105–126.

GESELL, A. (1933). Maturation and patterning of behavior. In C. Murchison (Ed.), *A handbook of child psychology.* Worcester, MA: Clark University Press.

GETCHELL, N., & ROBERTON, M. A. (1989). Whole body stiffness as a function of developmental level in children's hopping. *Developmental Psychology, 25,* 920–928.

GETTINGER, M., DOLL, B., & SALMON, D. (1994). Effects of social problem solving, goal setting, and parent training on children's peer relations. *Journal of Applied Developmental Psychology, 15,* 141–163.

GETZELS, J., & CSIKSZENTMIHALYI, M. (1976). *The creative vision: A longitudinal study of problem-finding in art.* New York: Wiley.

GEWIRTZ, J. L., & BOYD, E. F. (1977). Does maternal responding imply reduced infant crying? A critique of the 1972 Bell and Ainsworth report. *Child Development, 48,* 1200–1207.

GHIM, H. R. (1990). Evidence for perceptual organization in infants: Perception of subjective contours by young infants. *Infant Behavior and Development, 13,* 221–248.

GIBBS, J. C. (1991). Toward an integration of Kohlberg's and Hoffman's theories of morality. In W. M. Kurtines & J. L. Gewirtz (Eds.), *Handbook of moral behavior and development* (Vol. 1, pp. 183–222). Hillsdale, NJ: Erlbaum.

GIBBS, J. C. (1993). Moral-cognitive interventions. In A. P. Goldstein & C. R. Huff (Eds.), *The gang intervention handbook* (pp. 159–185). Champaign, IL: Research Press.

GIBBS, J. C. (1995). The cognitive developmental perspective. In W. M. Kurtines & J. L. Gewirtz (Eds.), *Moral development: An introduction* (pp. 27–48). Boston: Allyn and Bacon.

GIBBS, J. C., BASINGER, K. S., & FULLER, D. (1992). *Moral maturity: Measuring the development of sociomoral reflection.* Hillsdale, NJ: Erlbaum.

GIBBS, J. C., CLARK, P. M., JOSEPH, J. A., GREEN, J. L., GOODRICK, T. S., & MAKOWSKI, D. G. (1986). Relations between moral judgment, moral courage, and field independence. *Child Development, 57,* 185–193.

GIBBS, J. C., POTTER, G. B., & GOLDSTEIN, A. P. (1995). *The EQUIP program: Teaching youth to think and act responsibly through a peer-helping approach.* Champaign, IL: Research Press.

GIBBS, J. C., & SCHNELL, S. V. (1985). Moral development "versus" socialization. *American Psychologist, 40,* 1071–1080.

GIBSON, E. J. (1970). The development of perception as an adaptive process. *American Scientist, 58,* 98–107.

GIBSON, E. J. (1988). Exploratory behavior in the development of perceiving, acting, and the acquiring of knowledge. *Annual Review of Psychology, 39,* 1–41.

GIBSON, E. J., & WALK, R. D. (1960). The "visual cliff." *Scientific American, 202,* 64–71.

GIBSON, J. J. (1979). *The ecological approach to visual perception.* Boston: Houghton Mifflin.

GIEDD, J. N., SNELL, J. W., LANGE, N., RAJAPAKSE, J. C., CASEY, B. J., KOZUCH, P. L., & VAITUZIS, A. C. (1996). Quantitative magnetic resonance imaging of human brain development: Ages 4–18. *Cerebral Cortex, 6,* 551–560.

GILFILLAN, M. C., CURTIS, L., LISTON, W. A., PULLEN, I., WHYTE, D. A., & BROCK, D. J. H. (1992). Prenatal screening for cystic fibrosis. *Lancet, 340,* 214–216.

GILLIGAN, C. F. (1982). *In a different voice.* Cambridge, MA: Harvard University Press.

GILLMORE, M. R., HAWKINS, J. D., DAY, L. E., & CATALANO, R. F. (1997). Friendship and deviance: New evidence on an old controversy. *Journal of Early Adolescence, 16,* 80–95.

GINDIS, B. (1995). The social/cultural implication of disability: Vygotsky's paradigm for special education. *Educational Psychologist, 30,* 77–81.

GINSBURG, H. P. (1997). *Entering the child's mind: The clinical interview in psychological research and practice.* New York: Cambridge University Press.

GINSBURG, H. P., KLEIN, A., & STARKEY, P. (1998). The development of children's mathematical thinking: Connecting research with practice. In I. E. Sigel & K. A. Renninger (Eds.), *Handbook of child psychology: Vol. 4. Cognition, perception, and language* (5th ed., pp. 401–476). New York: Wiley.

GINSBURG, H. P., & OPPER, S. (1988). *Piaget's theory of intellectual development* (3rd ed.). Englewood Cliffs, NJ: Prentice-Hall.

GIUSTI, R. M., IWAMOTO, K., & HATCH, E. E. (1995). Diethyl-stilbestrol revisited: A review of the long-term health effects. *Annals of Internal Medicine, 122,* 778–788.

GLADWELL, M. (1998, February 2). The Pima paradox. *The New Yorker,* pp. 44–57.

GLASSMAN, B. S. (Ed.). (1996). *The new view almanac.* Woodbridge, CT: Blackbirch Press.

GLEITMAN, L., GLEITMAN, H., LANDAU, B., & WANNER, E. (1988). Where learning begins: Initial representations for language learning. In F. Newmeyer (Ed.), *Language: Psychological and biological aspects* (Vol. 3, pp. 150–193). Cambridge: Cambridge University Press.

GLEITMAN, L. R. (1990). The structural sources of verb meanings. *Language Acquisition, 1,* 3–55.

GLICK, J. (1975). Cognitive development in cross-cultural perspective. In F. Horowitz (Ed.), *Review of child development research* (Vol. 4, pp. 595–654). Chicago: University of Chicago Press.

GLICK, P. C. (1997). Demographic pictures of African American families. In H. P. McAdoo (Ed.), *Black families* (3rd ed., pp. 118–138). Thousand Oaks, CA: Sage.

GLOSTEN, B. (1998). Controversies in obstetric anesthesia. *Anesthesia and Analgesia, 428*(Suppl.), 32–38.

GLOVER, J. A. (1977). Risky shift and creativity. *Social Behavior and Personality, 5,* 317–320.

GNEPP, J. (1983). Children's social sensitivity: Inferring emotions from conflicting cues. *Developmental Psychology, 19,* 805–814.

GODUKA, I. N., POOLE, D. A., & AOTAKI-PHENICE, L. (1992). A comparative study of black South African children from three different contexts. *Child Development, 63,* 509–525.

GOELMAN, H. (1986). The language environments of family day care. In S. Kilmer (Ed.), *Advances in early education and day care* (Vol. 4, pp. 153–179). Greenwich, CT: JAI Press.

GOLDBERG, W. A., & EASTERBROOKS, M. A. (1988). Maternal employment when children are toddlers and kindergartners. In A. E. Gottfried & A. W. Gottfried (Eds.), *Maternal employment and children's development: Longitudinal research.* New York: Plenum.

GOLDBERG-GLEN, R., SANDS, R. G., COLE, R. D., & CRISTOFALO, C. (1998). Multigenerational patterns and internal structures in families in which grandparents raise grandchildren. *Families in Society, 79,* 477–489.

GOLDFIELD, B. A. (1987). The contributions of child and caregiver to referential and expressive language. *Applied Psycholinguistics, 8,* 267–280.

GOLDIN-MEADOW, S., ALIBALI, M. W., & CHURCH, R. B. (1993). Transitions in concept acquisition: Using the hand to read the mind. *Psychological Review, 100,* 279–297.

GOLDIN-MEADOW, S., BUTCHER, C., MYLANDER, C., & DODGE, M. (1994). Nouns and verbs in a self-styled gesture system: What's in a name? *Cognitive Psychology, 27,* 259–319.

GOLDIN-MEADOW, S., MYLANDER, C., & BUTCHER, C. (1995). The resilience of combinatorial structure at the word level: Morphology in self-styled gesture systems. *Cognition, 56,* 88–96.

GOLDSMITH, H. H., BUSS, K. A., & LEMERY, K. S. (1997). Toddler and childhood temperament: Expanded content, stronger genetic evidence, new evidence for the importance of the environment. *Developmental Psychology, 33,* 891–905.

GOLDSMITH, L., & FELDMAN, D. (1989). Wang Yani: Gifts well given. In W-C. Ho (Ed.), *Yani: The brush of innocence* (pp. 51–64). New York: Hudson Hills Press.

GOLDSTEIN, J. H. (1994). Sex differences in toy play and use of video games. In J. H. Goldstein (Ed.), *Toys, play, and child development* (pp. 110–129). New York: Cambridge University Press.

GOLEMAN, D. (1980, February). 1,528 little geniuses and how they grew. *Psychology Today, 13* (9), 28–53.

GOLINKOFF, R. M., HIRSH-PASEK, K., BAILEY, L. M., & WENGER, N. R. (1992). Young children and adults use lexical principles to learn new nouns. *Developmental Psychology, 28,* 99–108.

GOLOMB, C. (1992). *The child's creation of a pictorial world.* Berkeley: University of California Press.

GOLOMB, C., & GALASSO, L. (1995). Make believe and reality: Explorations of the imaginary realm. *Developmental Psychology, 31,* 800–810.

GOLOMBOK, S., COOK, R., BISH, A., & MURRAY, C. (1995). Families created by the new reproductive technologies: Quality of parenting and social and emotional development of the children. *Child Development, 66,* 285–298.

GOLOMBOK, S., & TASKER, F. L. (1996). Do parents influence the sexual orientation of their children? Findings from a longitudinal study of lesbian families. *Developmental Psychology, 32,* 3–11.

GOLUB, M. S. (1996). Labor analgesia and infant brain development. *Pharmacology Biochemistry and Behavior, 55,* 619–628.

GOMEZ-SCHWARTZ, B., HOROWITZ, J. M., & CARDARELLI, A. P. (1990). *Child sexual abuse: Initial effects.* Newbury Park, CA: Sage.

GÖNCÜ, A. (1993). Development of intersubjectivity in the dyadic play of preschoolers. *Early Childhood Research Quarterly, 8,* 99–116.

GONZALES, N. A., CAUCE, A. M., FRIEDMAN, R. J., & MASON, C. A. (1996). Family, peer, and neighborhood influences on academic achievement among African-American adolescents: One-year prospective effects. *American Journal of Community Psychology, 24,* 365–387.

GOOD, T. L., & BROPHY, J. E. (1996). *Looking in classrooms* (7th ed.). New York: Addison-Wesley.

GOODALL, J. (1990). *Through a window: My thirty years with the chimpanzees of Gombe.* Boston: Houghton Mifflin.

GOODENOUGH, F. L. (1931). *Anger in young children.* Minneapolis: University of Minnesota Press.

GOODFELLOW, P. N., & LOVELL, B. R. (1993). SRY and sex determination in mammals. *Annual Review of Genetics, 27,* 71–92.

GOODMAN, S. H., BROGAN, D., LYNCH, M. E., & FIELDING, B. (1993). Social and emotional competence in children of depressed mothers. *Child Development, 64,* 516–531.

GOODMAN, S. H., GRAVITT, G. W., JR., & KASLOW, N. J. (1995). Social problem solving: A moderator of the relation between negative life stress and depression symptoms in children. *Journal of Abnormal Child Psychology, 23,* 473–485.

GOODMAN, G. S., HIRSCHMAN, J. E., HEPPS, D., & RUDY, L. (1991). Children's memory for stressful events. *Merrill-Palmer Quarterly, 37,* 109–158.

GOODMAN, G. S., & TOBEY, A. E. (1994). Memory development within the context of child sexual abuse investigations. In C. B. Fisher & R. M. Lerner (Eds.), *Applied developmental psychology* (pp. 46–75). New York: McGraw-Hill.

GOODNOW, J. J. (1992). Analyzing agreement between generations: Do parents' ideas have consequences for children's ideas? In I. E. Sigel, A. McGillicuddy-DeLisi, & J. J. Goodnow (Eds.), *Parental belief systems* (pp. 293–317). Hillsdale, NJ: Erlbaum.

GOOSSENS, F. A., & VAN IJZENDOORN, M. H. (1990). Quality of infants' attachments to professional caregivers: Relation to infant–parent attachment and day-care characteristics. *Child Development, 61,* 832–837.

GOPNIK, A., & CHOI, S. (1990). Do linguistic differences lead to cognitive differences? A cross-linguistic study of semantic and cognitive development. *First Language, 11,* 199–215.

GOPNIK, A., & CHOI, S. (1995). Names, relational words, and cognitive development in English and Korean speakers: Nouns are not always learned before verbs. In A. Gopnik & S. Choi (Eds.), *Beyond names for things: Children's acquisition of verbs* (pp. 63–80). Hillsdale, NJ: Erlbaum.

GOPNIK, A., & MELTZOFF, A. N. (1986). Relations between semantic and cognitive development in the one-word stage: The specificity hypothesis. *Child Development, 57,* 1040–1053.

GOPNIK, A., & MELTZOFF, A. N. (1987a). The development of categorization in the second year and its relation to other cognitive and linguistic developments. *Child Development, 58,* 1523–1531.

GOPNIK, A., & MELTZOFF, A. N. (1987b). Language and thought in the young child: Early semantic developments and their relationships to object permanence, means-ends understanding, and categorization. In K. Nelson & A. Van Kleeck (Eds.), *Children's language* (Vol. 6, pp. 191–212). Hillsdale, NJ: Erlbaum.

GOPNIK, A., & WELLMAN, H. M. (1994). The 'theory' theory. In L. A. Hirschfeld & S. A. Gelman (Eds.), *Mapping the mind: Domain specificity in cognition and culture* (pp. 257–293). Cambridge: Cambridge University Press.

GORDON, P., & CHAFETZ, J. (1990). Verb-based versus class-based accounts of actionality effects in children's comprehension of passives. *Cognition, 36,* 227–254.

GORSKI, P. A., & VANDENBERG, K. A. (1996). *Atypical infant development* (2nd ed.). Austin, TX: Pro-Ed.

GORTMAKER, S. L., DIETZ, W. H., & CHEUNG, L. W. Y. (1990). Inactivity, diet, and the fattening of America. *Journal of the American Dietetic Association, 90,* 1247–1252.

GORTMAKER, S. L., MUST, A., PERRIN, J. M., SOBOL, A. M., & DIETZ, W. H., JR. (1993). Social and economic consequences of overweight in adolescence and young adulthood. *New England Journal of Medicine, 329,* 1008–1012.

GOSWAMI, U. (1995). Transitive relational mappings in three- and four-year-olds: The analogy of Goldilocks and the Three Bears. *Child Development, 66,* 877–892.

GOSWAMI, U. (1996). Analogical reasoning and cognitive development. In H. Reese (Ed.), *Advances in child development and behavior* (Vol. 26, pp. 91–138). New York: Academic Press.

GOSWAMI, U., & BROWN, A. (1989). Melting chocolate and melting snowmen: Analogical reasoning and causal relations. *Cognition, 35,* 69–95.

GOTTESMAN, I. I. (1963). Genetic aspects of intelligent behavior. In N. R. Ellis (Ed.), *Handbook of mental deficiency* (pp. 253–296). New York: McGraw-Hill.

GOTTESMAN, I. I. (1991). *Schizophrenia genetics: The origins of madness.* New York: Freeman.

GOTTESMAN, I. I., CAREY, G., & HANSON, D. R. (1983). Pearls and perils in epigenetic psychopathology. In S. B. Guze, E. J. Earls, & J. E. Barrett (Eds.), *Childhood psychopathology and development* (pp. 287–300). New York: Raven Press.

GOTTFREDSON, L. S. (1996). Gott-fredson's theory of circumspection and compromise. In D. Brown & L. Brooks (Eds.), *Career choice and development* (3rd ed.). San Francisco: Jossey-Bass.

GOTTFRIED, A. E. (1991). Maternal employment in the family setting: Developmental and environmental issues. In J. V. Lerner & N. L. Galambos (Eds.), *Employed mothers and their children* (pp. 63–84). New York: Garland.

GOTTLIEB, G. (1996). Developmental psychobiological theory. In R. B. Cairns, G. H. Elder, Jr., & E. J. Costello (Eds.), *Developmental science: Cambridge studies in social and emotional development* (pp. 63–77). New York: Cambridge University Press.

GOTTMAN, J. M., KATZ, L. F., & HOOVEN, C. (1996). *Meta-emotion: How families communicate emotionally.* Mahwah, NJ: Erlbaum.

GOUBET, N., & CLIFTON, R. K. (1998). Object and event representation in 6½-month-old infants. *Development Psychology, 34,* 63–76.

GOULD, J. L., & KEETON, W. T. (1996). *Biological science* (6th ed.). New York: Norton.

GOY, R. W., & GOLDFOOT, D. A. (1974). Experiential and hormonal factors influencing development of sexual behavior in the male rhesus monkey. In R. O. Schmitt & F. G. Worden (Eds.), *The neurosciences* (pp. 571–581). Cambridge, MA: MIT Press.

GRABER, J. A., BROOKS-GUNN, J., PAIKOFF, R. L. & WARREN, M. P. (1994). Prediction of eating problems: An 8-year study of adolescent girls. *Developmental Psychology, 30,* 823–834.

GRABER, J. A., PETERSEN, A. C., & BROOKS-GUNN, J. (1996). Pubertal processes: Methods, measures, and models. In J. A. Graber, J. Brooks-Gunn, & A. C. Petersen (Eds.), *Transitions through adolescence* (pp. 23–53). Mahwah, NJ: Erlbaum.

GRAHAM, S., DOUBLEDAY, C., & GUARINO, P. A. (1984). The development of relations between perceived controllability and the emotions of pity, anger, and guilt. *Child Development, 55,* 561–565.

GRALINSKI, J. H., & KOPP, C. B. (1993). Everyday rules for behavior: Mothers' requests to young children. *Developmental Psychology, 29,* 573–584.

GRANOT, M., SPITZER, A., AROIAN, K. J., RAVID, C., TAMIR, B., & NOAM, R. (1996). Pregnancy and delivery practices and beliefs of Ethiopian immigrant women in Israel. *Western Journal of Nursing Research, 18,* 299–313.

GRANT, J. (1998). *Raising baby by the book: The education of American mothers.* New Haven, CT: Yale University Press.

GRANT, J. P. (1994). *The state of the world's children 1994.* New York: Oxford University Press for UNICEF.

GRANT, J. P. (1995). *The state of the world's children 1995.* New York: Oxford University Press for UNICEF.

GRANTHAM-McGREGOR, S., POWELL, C., WALKER, S., CHANG, S., & FLETCHER, P. (1994). The long-term follow-up of severely malnourished children who participated in an intervention program. *Child Development, 65,* 428–439.

GRATTAN, M. P., DE VOS, E., LEVY, J., & McCLINTOCK, M. K. (1992). Asymmetric action in the human newborn: Sex differences in patterns of organization. *Child Development, 63,* 273–289.

GRAVEL, J. S., & WALLACE, I. F. (1992). Listening and language at 4 years of age: Effects of early otitis media. *Journal of Speech and Hearing Research, 35,* 588–595.

GRAVES, S. B. (1993). Television, the portrayal of African Americans, and the development of children's attitudes. In G. L. Berry & J. K. Asamen (Eds.), *Children and television* (pp. 179–190). Newbury Park, CA: Sage.

GRAY, C. E. (1966). A measurement of creativity in Western civilization. *American Anthropologist, 68,* 1384–1417.

GRAY, J. (1997). *Mars and Venus on a date.* New York: Harper-Collins.

GRAY, P., & FELDMAN, J. (1997). Patterns of age mixing and gender mixing among children and adolescents at an ungraded democratic school. *Merrill-Palmer Quarterly, 43,* 67–86.

GREEN, J., COUPLAND, V., & KITZINGER, J. (1990). Expectations, experiences, and psychological outcomes of childbirth: A prospective study of 825 women. *Birth, 17,* 15–24.

GREEN, R. (1987). *The "sissy boy" syndrome and the development of homosexuality.* New Haven, CT: Yale University Press.

GREENBERGER, E., & GOLDBERG, W. A. (1989). Work, parenting, and the socialization of children. *Developmental Psychology, 25,* 22–35.

GREENBERGER, E., O'NEIL, R., & NAGEL, S. K. (1994). Linking workplace and homeplace: Relations between the nature of adults' work and their parenting behaviors. *Developmental Psychology, 30,* 990–1002.

GREENDORFER, S. L., LEWKO, J. H., & ROSENGREN, K. S. (1996). Family and gender-based socialization of children and adolescents. In F. L. Smoll & R. E. Smith (Eds.), *Children and youth in sport: A biopsychological perspective* (pp. 89–111). Dubuque, IA: Brown & Benchmark.

GREENFIELD, P. (1992, June). *Notes and references for developmental psychology.* Conference on Making Basic Texts in Psychology More Culture-Inclusive and Culture-Sensitive, Western Washington University, Bellingham, WA.

GREENFIELD, P. M. (1994). Independence and interdependence as developmental scripts: Implications for theory, research, and practice. In P. M. Greenfield & R. R. Cocking (Eds.), *Cross-cultural roots of minority child development* (pp. 1–37). Hillsdale, NJ: Erlbaum.

GREENFIELD, P. M. (1997). You can't take it with you: Why ability assessments don't cross cultures. *American Psychologist, 52,* 1115–1124.

GREENFIELD, P. M., deWINSTANLEY, P., KILPATRICK, H., & KAYE, D. (1994). Action video games and informal education: Effects on strategies for dividing visual attention. *Journal of Applied Developmental Psychology, 15,* 105–123.

GREENFIELD, P. M., & SUZUKI, L. (1998). Culture and human development: Implications for parenting education, pediatrics, and mental health. In I. E. Sigel & K. A. Renninger (Eds.), *Handbook of child psychology: Vol. 4. Child psychology in practice* (5th ed., pp. 1059–1109). New York: Wiley.

GREENFIELD, P. M., YUT, E., CHUNG, M., LAND, D., KREIDER, H., PANTOJA, M., & HORSLEY, K. (1990). The program-length commercial: A study of the effects of television/toy tie-ins on imaginative play. *Psychology and Marketing, 7,* 237–255.

GREENO, J. G. (1989). A perspective on thinking. *American Psychologist, 44,* 134–141.

GREENOUGH, W. T., & BLACK, J. E. (1992). Induction of brain structure by experience: Substrates for cognitive development. In M. R. Gunnar & C. A. Nelson (Eds.), *Minnesota Symposia on Child Psychology* (pp. 155–200). Hillsdale, NJ: Erlbaum.

GREENOUGH, W. T., BLACK, J. E., & WALLACE, C. S. (1987). Experience and brain development. *Child Development, 58,* 539–559.

GREENOUGH, W. T., WALLACE, C. S., ALCANTARA, A. A., ANDERSON, B. J., HAWRYLAK, N., SIREVAAG, A. M., WEILER, I. J., & WITHERS, G. S. (1993). Development of the brain: Experience affects the structure of neurons, glia, and blood vessels. In N. J. Anastasiow & S. Harel (Eds.), *At-risk infants: Interventions, families, and research* (pp. 173–185). Baltimore: Paul H. Brookes.

GREGG, V., GIBBS, J. C., & BASINGER, K. S. (1994). Patterns of developmental delay in moral judgment by male and female delinquents. *Merrill-Palmer Quarterly, 40,* 538–553.

GREGG, V., GIBBS, J. C., & FULLER, D. (1994). Patterns of developmental delay in moral judgment by male and female delinquents. *Merrill-Palmer Quarterly, 40,* 538–553.

GREIF, E. B. (1979). *Sex differences in parent–child conversations: Who interrupts who?* Paper presented at the annual meeting of the Society for Research in Child Development, Boston.

GRESHAM, F. M., & MACMILLAN, D. L. (1997). Social competence and affective characteristics of students with mild disabilities. *Review of Educational Research, 67,* 377–415.

GRIBBLE, P. A., COWEN, E. L., WYMAN, P. A., WORK, W. C., WANNON, M., & RAOOF, A. (1993). Parent and child views of parent–child relationship qualities and resilient outcomes among urban children. *Journal of Child Psychology and Psychiatry, 34,* 507–519.

GRIGORENKO, E. L., & STERNBERG, R. J. (1998). Dynamic testing. *Psychological Bulletin, 124,* 75–111.

GRISSO, T. (1992). Minors' assent to behavioral research without parental consent. In B. Stanley & J. E. Sieber (Eds.), *Social research on children and adolescents: Ethical issues* (pp. 109–139). Newbury Park, CA: Sage.

GROFF, J. Y., MULLEN, P. D., MONGOVEN, M., & BURAU, K. (1997). Prenatal weight gain patterns and infant birthweight associated with maternal smoking. *Birth, 24,* 234–239.

GROLNICK, W. S., BRIDGES, L. J., & CONNELL, J. P. (1996). Emotion regulation in two-year-olds: Strategies and emotional expression in four contexts. *Child Development, 67,* 928–941.

GROLNICK, W. S., & SLOWIACZEK, M. L. (1994). Parents' involvement in children's schooling: A multidimensional conceptualization and motivational model. *Child Development, 65,* 237–252.

GRONAU, R. C., & WAAS, G. A. (1997). Delay of gratification

and cue utilization: An examination of children's social information processing. *Merrill-Palmer Quarterly, 43,* 305–322.

GROOME, L. J., SWIBER, M. J., ATTERBURY, J. L., BENTZ, L. S., & HOLLAND, S. B. (1997). Similarities and differences in behavioral state organization during sleep periods in the perinatal infant before and after birth. *Child Development, 68,* 1–11.

GROSSMANN, K., GROSSMANN, K. E., SPANGLER, G., SUESS, G., & UNZNER, L. (1985). Maternal sensitivity and newborns' orientation responses as related to quality of attachment in Northern Germany. In I. Bretherton & E. Waters (Eds.), Growing points of attachment theory and research. *Monographs of the Society for Research in Child Development, 50* (1–2, Serial No. 209).

GROTEVANT, H. D. (1978). Sibling constellations and sex-typing of interests in adolescence. *Child Development, 49,* 540–542.

GROTEVANT, H. D., & COOPER, C. R. (1985). Patterns of interaction in family relationships and the development of identity exploration in adolescence. *Child Development, 56,* 415–428.

GROTEVANT, H. D., & COOPER, C. R. (1988). The role of family experience in career exploration during adolescence. In P. Baltes, D. Featherman, & R. Lerner (Eds.), *Life-span development and behavior* (Vol. 8, pp. 231–258). Hillsdale, NJ: Erlbaum.

GROTEVANT, H. D., & COOPER, C. R. (1998). Individuality and connectedness in adolescent development: Review and prospects for research on identity, relationships, and context. In E. Skoe & A. von der Lippe (Eds.), *Personality development in adolescence* (pp. 3–37). London: Routledge & Kegan Paul.

GROTPETER, J. K., & CRICK, N. R. (1996). Relational aggression, overt aggression, and friendship. *Child Development, 67,* 2328–2338.

GRUSEC, J. E. (1988). *Social development: History, theory, and research.* New York: Springer-Verlag.

GRUSEC, J. E., & GOODNOW, J. J. (1994). Impact of parental discipline methods on the child's internalization of values: A reconceptualization of current points of view. *Developmental Psychology, 30,* 4–19.

GRUSEC, J. E., KUCZYNSKI, L., RUSHTON, J., & SIMUTIS, Z. (1979). Learning resistance to temp-

tation through observation. *Developmental Psychology, 15,* 233–240.

GRYCH, J. H., & FINCHAM, F. D. (1997). Children's adaptation to divorce: From description to explanation. In S. A. Wolchik & I. N. Sandler (Eds.), *Handbook of children's coping: Linking theory to intervention* (pp. 159–193). New York: Plenum.

GUERRA, N. G., ATTAR, B., & WEISSBERG, R. P. (1997). Prevention of aggression and violence among inner-city youths. In D. M. Stoff, J. Breiling, & J. D. Maser (Eds.), *Handbook of antisocial behavior* (pp. 375–383). New York: Wiley.

GUERRA, N. G., & SLABY, R. G. (1990). Cognitive mediators of aggression in adolescent offenders: 2. Intervention. *Developmental Psychology, 26,* 269–277.

GUIDUBALDI, J., & CLEMINSHAW, H. K. (1985). Divorce, family health and child adjustment. *Family Relations, 34,* 35–41.

GUILFORD, J. P. (1985). The structure-of-intellect model. In B. B. Wolman (Ed.), *Handbook of intelligence* (pp. 225–266). New York: Wiley.

GULLONE, E., & KING, N. J. (1997). Three-year follow-up of normal fear in children and adolescents aged 7 to 18 years. *British Journal of Developmental Psychology, 15,* 97–111.

GUNNAR, M. R. (1998). Quality of early care and buffering of neuroendocrine stress reactions: Potential effects on the developing human brain. *Preventive Medicine, 27,* 208–211.

GUNNAR, M. R., & NELSON, C. A. (1994). Event-related potentials in year-old infants: Relations with emotionality and cortisol. *Child Development, 65,* 80–94.

GURUCHARRI, C., & SELMAN, F. L. (1982). The development of interpersonal understanding during childhood, preadolescence, and adolescence: A longitudinal follow-up study. *Child Development, 53,* 924–927.

GUSTAFSON, G. E., GREEN, J. A., & CLELAND, J. W. (1994). Robustness of individual identity in the cries of human infants. *Developmental Psychobiology, 27,* 1–9.

GUSTAFSON, G. E., & HARRIS, K. L. (1990). Women's responses to young infants' cries. *Developmental Psychology, 26,* 144–152.

GUTTENTAG, R. (1997). Memory development and processing resources. In N. Cowan (Ed.), *The development of memory in childhood* (pp. 247–274). Hove, UK: Psychology Press.

H

HACK, M., WRIGHT, L. L., SHANKARAN, S., & TYSON, J. E. (1995). Very low birth weight outcomes of the National Institute of Child Health and Human Development Neonatal Network, November 1989 to October 1990. *American Journal of Obstetrics and Gynecology, 172,* 457–464.

HACK, M. B., TAYLOR, H. G., KLEIN, N., EIBEN, R., SCHATSCHNEIDER, C., & MERCURI-MINICH, N. (1994). School-age outcomes in children with birth weights under 750 g. *New England Journal of Medicine, 331,* 753–759.

HACKEL, L. S., & RUBLE, D. N. (1992). Changes in the marital relationship after the first baby is born: Predicting the impact of expectancy disconfirmation. *Journal of Personality and Social Psychology, 62,* 944–957.

HADEN, C. A., HAINE, R. A., & FIVUSH, R. (1997). Developing narrative structure in parent–child reminiscing across the preschool years. *Developmental Psychology, 33,* 295–307.

HADWIN, J., & PERNER, J. (1991). Pleased and surprised: Children's cognitive theory of emotion. *British Journal of Developmental Psychology, 9,* 215–234.

HAGEKULL, B., BOHLIN, G., & RYDELL, A. (1997). Maternal sensitivity, infant temperament, and the development of early feeding problems. *Infant Mental Health Journal, 18,* 92–106.

HAGERMAN, R. J. (1996). Biomedical advances in developmental psychology. *Developmental Psychology, 32,* 416–424.

HAIER, R. J., NUECHTERLEIN, K. H., HAZLETT, E., WU, J. C., PAEK, J., BROWNING, H. L., & BUCHSBAUM, M. S. (1988). Cortical glucose metabolic rate correlates of abstract reasoning and attention studied with positron emission tomography. *Intelligence, 12,* 199–217.

HAIER, R. J., SIEGEL, B., TANG, C., ABEL, L., & BUCHSBAUM, M. S. (1992). Intelligence and changes in regional cerebral glucose metabolic rate following learning. *Intelligence, 16,* 415–426.

HAIGHT, W. L., & MILLER, P. J. (1993). *Pretending at home: Early development in a sociocultural context.* Albany, NY: SUNY Press.

HAINLINE, L. (1993). Conjugate eye movements of infants. In K. Simons (Ed.), *Early visual development: Normal and abnormal* (pp. 47–55). New York: Oxford University Press.

HAITH, M. M. (1997). The development of future thinking as

essential for the emergence of skill in planning. In S. L. Friedman & E. K. Scholnick (Eds.), *The developmental psychology of planning: Why, how, and when do we plan?* (pp. 25–42). Mahwah, NJ: Erlbaum.

HAITH, M. M., & BENSON, J. B. (1998). Infant cognition. In D. Kuhn & R. S. Siegler (Eds.), *Handbook of child psychology: Vol. 2. Cognition, perception, and language* (5th ed., pp. 199–254). New York: Wiley.

HAKUTA, K., FERDMAN, B. M., & DIAZ, R. M. (1987). Bilingualism and cognitive development: Three perspectives. In S. Rosenberg (Ed.), *Advances in applied psycholinguistics: Vol. 2. Reading, writing, and language learning* (pp. 284–319). New York: Cambridge University Press.

HALFORD, G. S. (1992). Analogical reasoning and conceptual complexity in cognitive development. *Human Development, 35,* 193–217.

HALFORD, G. S. (1993). *Children's understanding: The development of mental models.* Hillsdale, NJ: Erlbaum.

HALL, D. G. (1996). Preschoolers' default assumptions about word meaning: Proper names designate unique individuals. *Developmental Psychology, 32,* 177–186.

HALL, G. S. (1904). *Adolescence* (Vols. 1–2). New York: Appleton-Century-Crofts.

HALL, J. A. (1978). Gender effects in decoding nonverbal cues. *Psychological Bulletin, 85,* 845–857.

HALL, J. A., & HALBERSTADT, A. G. (1980). Masculinity and femininity in children: Development of the Children's Attributes Questionnaire. *Developmental Psychology, 16,* 270–280.

HALL, J. A., & HALBERSTADT, A. G. (1981). Sex roles and nonverbal communication skills. *Sex Roles, 7,* 273–287.

HALLIDAY, J. L., WATSON, L. F., LUMLEY, J., DANKS, D. M., & SHEFFIELD, L. S. (1995). New estimates of Down syndrome risks at chorionic villus sampling, amniocentesis, and live birth in women of advanced maternal age from a uniquely defined population. *Prenatal Diagnosis, 15,* 455–465.

HALPERN, C. T., UDRY, J. R., & SUCHINDRAN, C. (1997). Testosterone predicts initiation of coitus in adolescent females. *Psychosomatic Medicine, 59,* 161–171.

HALPERN, D. F. (1992). *Sex differences in cognitive abilities* (2nd ed.). Hillsdale, NJ: Erlbaum.

HALPERN, D. F. (1997). Sex differences in intelligence. *American Psychologist, 52,* 1091–1102.

HALPERN, L. F., MacLEAN, W. E., & BAUMEISTER, A. A. (1995). Infant sleep–wake characteristics: Relation to neurological status and the prediction of developmental outcome. *Developmental Review, 15,* 255–291.

HAMELIN, K., & RAMACHANDRAN, C. (1993, June). Kangaroo care. *Canadian Nurse, 89* (6), 15–17.

HAMER, D. H., HU, S., MAGNUSON, V. L., HU, N., & PATTATUCCI, A. M. L. (1993). A linkage between DNA markers on the X chromosome and male sexual orientation. *Science, 261,* 321–327.

HAMILTON, S. F. (1993). Prospects for an American-style youth apprenticeship system. *Educational Researcher, 22*(3), 11–16.

HAMILTON, S. F. (1994). Social roles for youths: Interventions in unemployment. In A. C. Petersen & J. T. Mortimer (Eds.), *Youth employment and society* (pp. 248–269). New York: Cambridge University Press.

HAMMERSLEY, M. (1992). *What's wrong with ethnography?* New York: Routledge.

HAN, J. J., LEICHTMAN, M. D., & WANG, Q. (1998). Autobiographical memory in Korean, Chinese, and American children. *Developmental Psychology, 34,* 701–713.

HANDLER, A. S., MASON, E. D., ROSENBERG, D. L., & DAVIS, F. G. (1994). The relationship between exposure during pregnancy to cigarette smoking and cocaine use and placenta previa. *American Journal of Obstetrics and Gynecology, 170,* 884–889.

HANNA, E., & MELTZOFF, A. N. (1993). Peer imitation by toddlers in laboratory, home, and day-care contexts: Implications for social learning and memory. *Developmental Psychology, 29,* 701–710.

HAPPÉ, F. G. E. (1995). The role of age and verbal ability in the theory of mind task performance of subjects with autism. *Child Development, 66,* 843–855.

HARE, J. (1994). Concerns and issues faced by families headed by a lesbian couple. *Families in Society, 43,* 27–35.

HARE, J., & RICHARDS, L. (1993). Children raised by lesbian couples: Does context of birth affect father and partner involvement? *Family Relations, 42,* 249–255.

HARLEY, B., & WANG, W. (1997). The critical period hypothesis: Where are we now? In A. M. B. de Groot & J. F. Kroll (Eds.), *Tutorials in bilingualism* (pp. 19–51). Mahwah, NJ: Erlbaum.

HARLOW, H. F. (1969). Age-mate or peer affectional system. In D. S. Lehrman, R. A. Hinde, & E. Shaw (Eds.), *Advances in the study of behavior* (Vol. 2,

pp. 333–383). New York: Academic Press.

HARLOW, H. F., & ZIMMERMAN, R. (1959). Affectional responses in the infant monkey. *Science, 130,* 421–432.

HÄRNQVIST, K. (1968). Changes in intelligence from 13 to 18. *Scandinavian Journal of Psychology, 9,* 50–82.

HAROLD, G. T., & CONGER, R. D. (1997). Marital conflict and adolescent distress: The role of adolescent awareness. *Child Development, 68,* 333–350.

HARRINGTON, R., RUTTER, M., & FOMBONNE, E. (1996). Developmental pathways in depression: Multiple meanings, antecedents, and endpoints. *Development and Psychopathology, 8,* 601–616.

HARRIS, G. (1993). Introducing the infant's first solid food. *British Food Journal, 95*(9), 7–10.

HARRIS, G. (1997). Development of taste perception and appetite regulation. In G. Bremner, A. Slater, & G. Butterworth (Eds.), *Infant development: Recent advances* (pp. 9–30). East Sussex, England: Erlbaum.

HARRIS, G., & BOOTH, D. A. (1987). Infants' preference for salt in food: Its dependence upon recent dietary experience. *Journal of Reproductive and Infant Psychology, 5,* 97–104.

HARRIS, I. B. (1996). *Children in jeopardy.* New Haven, CT: Yale University Press.

HARRIS, N. G. S., BELLUGI, U., BATES, E., JONES, W., & ROSSEN, M. (1997). Contrasting profiles of language development in children with Williams syndrome. *Developmental Neuropsychology, 13,* 345–370.

HARRIS, R. I. (1978). Impulse control in deaf children: Research and clinical issues. In L. S. Liben (Ed.), *Deaf children: Developmental perspectives* (pp. 137–156). New York: Academic Press.

HARRIS, R. T. (1991, March–April). Anorexia nervosa and bulimia nervosa in female adolescents. *Nutrition Today, 26* (2), 30–34.

HARRIS, S., KASARI, C., & SIGMAN, M. (1996). Joint attention and language gains in children with Down syndrome. *American Journal of Mental Retardation, 100,* 608–618.

HARRIS, S., MUSSEN, P. H., & RUTHERFORD, E. (1976). Some cognitive, behavioral, and personality correlates of maturity of moral judgment. *Journal of Genetic Psychology, 128,* 123–135.

HARRISON, A. O., WILSON, M. N., PINE, C. J., CHAN, S. Q., & BURIEL, R. (1994). Family ecologies of ethnic minority children. In G. Handel & G. G. Whitchurch (Eds.), *The psychosocial interior*

of the family (pp. 187–210). New York: Aldine De Gruyter.

HARRIST, A. W., PETTIT, G. S., DODGE, K. A., & BATES, J. E. (1994). Dyadic synchrony in mother–child interaction—Relation with children's subsequent kindergarten adjustment. *Family Relations, 43,* 417–424.

HARRIST, A. W., ZAIA, A. F., BATES, J. E., DODGE, K. A., & PETTIT, G. S. (1997). Subtypes of social withdrawal in early childhood: Sociometric status and social–cognitive differences across four years. *Child Development, 68,* 278–294.

HART, B. (1991). Input frequency and children's first words. *First Language, 11,* 289–300.

HART, B., & RISLEY, T. R. (1995). *Meaningful differences in the everyday experience of young American children.* Baltimore: Paul H. Brookes.

HART, B. I., & THOMPSON, J. M. (1996). Gender role characteristics and depressive symptomatology among adolescents. *Journal of Early Adolescence, 16,* 407–426.

HART, C. H., BURTS, D. C., DURLAND, M. A., CHARLESWORTH, R., DeWOLF, M., & FLEEGE, P. O. (1998). Stress behaviors and activity type participation of preschoolers in more and less developmentally appropriate classrooms: SES and sex differences. *Journal of Research in Childhood Education, 13,* 176–196.

HART, D., & FEGLEY, S. (1995). Prosocial behavior and caring in adolescence: Relations to self-understanding and social judgment. *Child Development, 66,* 1346–1359.

HART, J., GUNNAR, M., & CICCHETTI, D. (1995). Salivary cortisol in maltreated children: Evidence of relations between neuroendocrine activity and social competence. *Development and Psychopathology, 7,* 11–26.

HARTER, S. (1982). The perceived competence scale for children. *Child Development, 53,* 87–97.

HARTER, S. (1986). Processes underlying the construction, maintenance, and enhancement of self-concept in children. In S. Suhls & A. Greenwald (Eds.), *Psychological perspectives of the self* (Vol. 3, pp. 136–182). Hillsdale, NJ: Erlbaum.

HARTER, S. (1990). Issues in the assessment of the self-concept of children and adolescents. In A. LaGreca (Ed.), *Through the eyes of a child* (pp. 292–325). Boston: Allyn and Bacon.

HARTER, S. (1996). Developmental changes in self-understanding across the 5 to 7 shift. In A. J. Sameroff & M. M. Haith (Eds.), *The five to seven year shift*

(pp. 207–236). Chicago: University of Chicago Press.

HARTER, S. (1998). The development of self-representations. In N. Eisenberg (Ed.), *Handbook of child psychology: Vol. 3. Social, emotional, and personality development* (5th ed., pp. 553–618). New York: Wiley.

HARTER, S., & MONSOUR, A. (1992). Developmental analysis of conflict caused by opposing attributes in the adolescent self-portrait. *Developmental Psychology, 28,* 251–260.

HARTER, S., & WHITESELL, N. (1989). Developmental changes in children's understanding of simple, multiple, and blended emotion concepts. In C. Saarni & P. Harris (Eds.), *Children's understanding of emotion* (pp. 81–116). Cambridge: Cambridge University Press.

HARTER, S., MAROLD, D. B., WHITESELL, N. R., & COBBS, G. (1996). A model of the effects of parent and peer support on adolescent false self-behavior. *Child Development, 67,* 360–374.

HARTER, S., WATERS, P., & WHITESELL, N. R. (1998). Relational self-worth: Differences in perceived worth as a person across interpersonal contexts among adolescents. *Child Development, 69,* 756–766.

HARTSHORN, K., & ROVEE-COLLIER, C. (1997). Infant learning and long-term memory at 6 months: A confirming analysis. *Developmental Psychobiology, 30,* 71–85.

HARTUP, W. W. (1974). Aggression in childhood: Developmental perspectives. *American Psychologist, 29,* 336–341.

HARTUP, W. W. (1983). Peer relations. In E. M. Hetherington (Ed.), *Handbook of child psychology: Vol. 4. Socialization, personality, and social development* (4th ed., pp. 103–196). New York: Wiley.

HARTUP, W. W. (1996). The company they keep: Friendships and their developmental significance. *Child Development, 67,* 1–13.

HARTUP, W. W., & MOORE, S. G. (1990). Early peer relations: Developmental significance and prognostic implications. *Early Childhood Research Quarterly, 5,* 1–17.

HASELAGER, J. T., HARTUP, W. W., VAN LIESHOUT, C. F. M., & RIKSEN-WALRAVEN, J. M. A. (1998). Similarities between friends and nonfriends in middle childhood. *Child Development, 69,* 1198–1208.

HASHIMOTO, K., NOGUCHI, M., & NAKATSUJI, N. (1992). Mouse offspring derived from fetal ovaries or reaggregates which were cultured and transplanted into adult females. *Development: Growth & Differentiation, 34*, 233–238.

HASSELHORN, M. (1992). Task dependency and the role of category typicality and metamemory in the development of an organizational strategy. *Child Development, 63*, 202–214.

HATANO, G. (1994). Introduction: Conceptual change—Japanese perspectives. *Human Development, 37*, 189–197.

HATCH, M. C., SHU, X-O., MCLEAN, D. E., LEVIN, B., BEGG, M., REUSS, L., & SUSSER, M. (1993). Maternal exercise during pregnancy, physical fitness, and fetal growth. *American Journal of Epidemiology, 137*, 1105–1114.

HATCHER, P. J., HULME, C., & ELLIS, A. W. (1994). Ameliorating early reading failure by integrating the teaching of reading and phonological skills: The phonological linkage hypothesis. *Child Development, 65*, 41–57.

HATTON, D. D., BAILEY, D. B., JR., BURCHINAL, M. R., & FERRELL, K. A. (1997). Developmental growth curves of preschool children with vision impairments. *Child Development, 68*, 788–806.

HAUSER, S. T., POWERS, S. I., & NOAM, G. G. (1991). *Adolescents and their families: Paths of ego development.* New York: Free Press.

HAUSFATHER, A., TOHARIA, A., LAROCHE, C., & ENGELSMANN, F. (1997). Effects of age of entry, day-care quality, and family characteristics on preschool behavior. *Journal of Child Psychology and Psychiatry, 38*, 441–448.

HAUTH, J. C., GOLDENBERG, R. L., PARKER, C. R., CUTTER, G. R., & CLIVER, S. P. (1995). Low-dose aspirin—Lack of association with an increase in abruptio placentae or perinatal mortality. *Obstetrics and Gynecology, 85*, 1055–1058.

HAWKE, S., & KNOX, D. (1978). The one-child family: A new lifestyle. *The Family Coordinator, 27*, 215–219.

HAWKINS, A. J., CHRISTIANSEN, S. L., SARGENT, K. P., & HILLS, E. J. (1993). Rethinking fathers' involvement in child care: A developmental perspective. *Journal of Family Issues, 14*, 531–549.

HAWKINS, D. J., & LAM, T. (1987). Teacher practices, social development, and delinquency. In J. D. Burchard & S. N. Burchard (Eds.), *Prevention of delinquent behavior* (pp. 241–274). Newbury Park, CA: Sage.

HAWKINS, J. N. (1994). Issues of motivation in Asian education. In H. F. O'Neil, Jr., & M.

Drillings (Eds.), *Motivation: Theory and research* (pp. 101–115). Hillsdale, NJ: Erlbaum.

HAWORTH, K., & STROSNIDER, K. (1997, March 14). Controversy grows over cloning research as scientists report new breakthroughs. *Chronicle of Higher Education*, p. A14.

HAY, D. F. (1984). Social conflict in early childhood. In G. Whitehurst (Ed.), *Annals of child development* (Vol. 1, pp. 1–44). Greenwich, CT: JAI Press.

HAY, D. F., CAPLAN, M., CASTLE, J., & STIMSON, C. A. (1991). Does sharing become increasingly "rational" in the second year of life? *Developmental Psychology, 27*, 987–993.

HAYDEN-THOMSON, L., RUBIN, K. H., & HYMEL, S. (1987). Sex preferences in sociometric choices. *Developmental Psychology, 23*, 558–562.

HAYGHE, H. V. (1990, March). Family members in the work force. *Monthly Labor Review, 113*, 14–19.

HAYNE, H., & ROVEE-COLLIER, C. K. (1995). The organization of reactivated memory in infancy. *Child Development, 66*, 893–906.

HAYNE, H., ROVEE-COLLIER, C. K., & PERRIS, E. E. (1987). Categorization and memory retrieval by three-month-olds. *Child Development, 58*, 750–767.

HAYNES, S. N. (1991). Clinical applications of psychophysiological assessment: An introduction and overview. *Psychological Assessment, 3*, 307–308.

HAYSLIP, B., JR. (1994). Stability of intelligence. In R. J. Sternberg (ED.), *Encyclopedia of human intelligence* (Vol. 2, pp. 1019–1026). New York: Macmillan.

HEAROLD, S. (1986). A synthesis of 1,043 effects of television on social behavior. In G. Comstock (Ed.), *Public communications and behavior* (Vol. 1, pp. 65–133). New York: Academic Press.

HEATH, S. B. (1982). Questioning at home and at school: A comparative study. In G. Spindler (Ed.), *Doing the ethnography of schooling: Educational anthropology in action* (pp. 102–127). New York: Holt.

HEATH, S. B. (1989). Oral and literate traditions among black Americans living in poverty. *American Psychologist, 44*, 367–373.

HEATH, S. B. (1990). The children of Trackton's children: Spoken and written language and social change. In J. Stigler, G. Herdt, & R. A. Shweder (Eds.), *Cultural psychology: Essays on comparative human development* (pp. 496–519). New York: Cambridge University Press.

HECKMAN, J. J. (1995). Lessons from The Bell Curve. *Journal of Political Economy, 193*, 1091–1120.

HEDGES, L. V., & NOWELL, A. (1995). Sex differences in mental test scores: Variability and numbers of high-scoring individuals. *Science, 269*, 41–45.

HEFFERNAN, K. (1994). Sexual orientation as a factor in risk for binge eating and bulimia nervosa: A review. *International Journal of Eating Disorders, 16*, 335–348.

HEFFNER, R. W., & KELLEY, M. L. (1994). Nonorganic failure to thrive: Developmental outcomes and psychosocial assessment and intervention issues. *Research in Developmental Disabilities, 15*, 247–268.

HEINE, S. J., & LEHMAN, D. R. (1995). Cultural variation in unrealistic optimism: Does the West feel more invulnerable than the East? *Journal of Personality and Social Psychology, 68*, 595–607.

HEINL, T. (1983). *The baby massage book.* London: Coventure.

HEINONEN, O. P., SLONE, D., & SHAPIRO, S. (1977). *Birth defects and drugs in pregnancy.* Littleton, MA: PSG Publishing.

HELBURN, S. W. (Ed.). (1995). *Cost, quality and child outcomes in child care centers.* Denver: University of Colorado.

HELD, R. (1993). What can rates of development tell us about underlying mechanisms? In C. E. Granrud (Ed.), *Visual perception and cognition in infancy* (pp. 75–89). Hillsdale, NJ: Erlbaum.

HELWIG, C. C. (1995). Adolescents' and young adults' conceptions of civil liberties: Freedom of speech and religion. *Child Development, 66*, 152–166.

HENDRICK, J., & STANGE, T. (1991). Do actions speak louder than words? An effect of the functional use of language on dominant sex role behavior in boys and girls. *Early Childhood Research Quarterly, 6*, 565–576.

HENDRIX, L., & JOHNSON, G. D. (1985). Instrumental and expressive socialization: A false dichotomy. *Sex Roles, 13*, 581–595.

HENNESSY, K. D., RABIDEAU, G. J., & CICCHETTI, D. (1994). Responses of physically abused and nonabused children to different forms of interadult anger. *Child Development, 65*, 815–828.

HENRY, B., MOFFITT, T. E., CASPI, A., LANGLEY, J., & SILVA, P. A. (1994). On the "remembrance of things past": A longitudinal evaluation of the retrospective method. *Psychological Assessment, 6*, 92–101.

HEPPER, P. G. (1997). Fetal habituation: Another Pandora's box?

Developmental Medicine and Child Neurology, 39, 274–278.

HERDT, G., & BOXER, A. M. (1993). *Children of horizons: How gay and lesbian teens are leading a new way out of the closet.* Boston: Beacon Press.

HERDT, G. H., & DAVIDSON, J. (1988). The Sambia "Turnim-Man": Sociocultural and clinical aspects of gender formation in male pseudohermaphrodites with 5-alpha-reductase deficiency in Papua, New Guinea. *Archives of Sexual Behavior, 17*, 33–56.

HERMAN, M. R., DORNBUSCH, S. M., HERRON, M. C., & HERTING, J. R. (1997). The influence of family regulation, connection, and psychological autonomy on six measures of adolescent functioning. *Journal of Adolescent Research, 12*, 34–67.

HERNANDEZ, D. J. (1994, Spring). Children's changing access to resources: A historical perspective. *Social Policy Report of the Society for Research in Child Development, 8* (1).

HERNANDEZ, F. D., & CARTER, A. S. (1996). Infant response to mothers and fathers in the still-face paradigm. *Infant Behavior and Development, 19*, 502.

HERRNSTEIN, R. J., & MURRAY, C. (1994). *The bell curve: Intelligence and class structure in American life.* New York: Free Press.

HETHERINGTON, E. M. (1989). Coping with family transitions: Winners, losers and survivors. *Child Development, 60*, 1–14.

HETHERINGTON, E. M. (1991). The role of individual differences and family relationships in children's coping with divorce and remarriage. In P. A. Cowan & M. Hetherington (Eds.), *Family transitions* (pp. 165–194). Hillsdale, NJ: Erlbaum.

HETHERINGTON, E. M. (1993). An overview of the Virginia Longitudinal Study of Divorce and Remarriage: A focus on early adolescence. *Journal of Family Psychology, 7*, 39–56.

HETHERINGTON, E. M. (1997). Teenaged childbearing and divorce. In S. Luthar, J. A. Burack, D. Cicchetti, & J. Weisz (Eds.), *Developmental psychopathology: Perspectives on adjustment, risk, and disorders* (pp. 350–373). Cambridge, United Kingdom: Cambridge University Press.

HETHERINGTON, E. M. (1999). Social capital and the development of youth from nondivorced, divorced, and remarried families. In A. Collins (Ed.), *Minnesota Symposia on Child Psychology* (Vol. 29). Hillsdale, NJ: Erlbaum.

HETHERINGTON, E. M., BRIDGES, M., & INSABELLA, G. M. (1998). What matters? What does not? Five perspectives on the association between marital transitions and children's adjustment. *American Psychologist, 53,* 167–184.

HETHERINGTON, E. M., & HENDERSON, S. H. (1997). Fathers in stepfamilies. In M. E. Lamb (Ed.), *The role of the father in child development* (pp. 212–226). New York: Wiley.

HETHERINGTON, E. M., & JODL, K. M. (1994). Stepfamilies as settings for child development. In A. Booth & J. Dunn (Eds.), *Stepfamilies: Who benefits? Who does not?* (pp. 55–79). Hillsdale, NJ: Erlbaum.

HETHERINGTON, E. M., & STANLEY-HAGAN, M. M. (1997). The effects of divorce on fathers and their children. In M. E. Lamb (Ed.), *The role of the father in child development* (pp. 191–211). New York: Wiley.

HETHERINGTON, P. (1995, March). *The changing American family and the well-being of children.* Master lecture presented at the biennial meeting of the Society for Research in Child Development, Indianapolis.

HETHERINGTON, S. E. (1990). A controlled study of the effect of prepared childbirth classes on obstetric outcomes. *Birth, 17,* 86–90.

HEWLETT, B. S. (1992). Husband–wife reciprocity and the father–infant relationship among Aka pygmies. In B. S. Hewlett (Ed.), *Father–child relations: Cultural and biosocial contexts* (pp. 153–176). New York: Aldine De Gruyter.

HEWLETT, S. A., & WEST, C. (1998). *The war against parents: What we can do for America's beleaguered moms and dads.* Boston: Houghton Mifflin.

HEYMAN, G. D., & DWECK, C. S. (1992). Achievement goals and intrinsic motivation: Their relation and their role in adaptive motivation. *Motivation and Emotion, 16,* 231–247.

HEYMAN, G. D., & DWECK, C. S. (1998). Children's thinking about traits: Implications for judgments of the self and others. *Child Development, 69,* 391–403.

HEYMAN, G. D., DWECK, C. S., & CAIN, K. M. (1992). Young children's vulnerability to self-blame and helplessness: Relationship to beliefs about goodness. *Child Development, 63,* 401–415.

HEYNS, B. (1978). *Summer learning and the effects of schooling.* San Diego: Academic Press.

HICKEY, T. L., & PEDUZZI, J. D. (1987). Structure and development of the visual system. In P. Salapatek & L. Cohen (Eds.), *Handbook of infant perception: Vol. 1. From sensation to perception* (pp. 1–42). New York: Academic Press.

HIER, D. B., & CROWLEY, W. F. (1982). Spatial ability in androgen-deficient men. *New England Journal of Medicine, 302,* 1202–1205.

HIGLEY, J. D., HOPKINS, W. D., THOMPSON, W. W., BYRNE, E. A., HIRSCH, R. M., & SUOMI, S. J. (1992). Peers as primary attachment sources in yearling rhesus monkeys (*Macaca mulatta*). *Developmental Psychology, 28,* 1163–1171.

HILL, H. M., SORIANO, F. I., CHEN, S. A., & LAFROMBOISE, T. D. (1994). Sociocultural factors in the etiology and prevention of violence among ethnic minority youth. In L. D. Eron, J. H. Gentry, & P. Schlegel (Eds.), *Reason to hope* (pp. 59–97). Washington, DC: American Psychological Association.

HILL, J., & HOLMBECK, G. N. (1986). Attachment and autonomy during adolescence. In G. Whitehurst (Ed.), *Annals of child development* (Vol. 3, pp. 145–189). Greenwich, CT: JAI Press.

HILL, P. M., & HUMPHREY, P. (1982). *Human growth and development throughout life: A nursing perspective.* New York: Delmar.

HIMES, J. H., STORY, M., CZAPLINSKI, K., & DAHLBERG-LUBY, E. (1992). Indications of early obesity in low-income Hmong children. *American Journal of Diseases of Children, 146,* 67–69.

HINDE, R. A. (1989). Ethological and relationships approaches. In R. Vasta (Ed.), *Annals of child development* (Vol. 6, pp. 251–285). Greenwich, CT: JAI Press.

HINDE, R. A., STEVENSON-HINDE, J., & TAMPLIN, A. (1985). Characteristics of 3- to 4-year-olds assessed at home and their interactions in preschool. *Developmental Psychology, 21,* 130–140.

HINES, M. (1982). Prenatal gonadal hormones and sex differences in human behavior. *Psychological Bulletin, 92,* 56–80.

HINES, M., & GREEN, R. (1991). Human hormonal and neural correlates of sex-typed behaviors. *Review of Psychiatry, 10,* 536–555.

HINES, M., & KAUFMAN, F. R. (1994). Androgen and the development of human sex-typical behavior: Rough-and-tumble play and sex of preferred playmates in children with congenital adrenal hyperplasia (CAH). *Child Development, 65,* 1042–1053.

HIRSCHFELD, L. A. (1995). Do children have a theory of race? *Cognition, 54,* 209–252.

HIRSH-PASEK, K., KEMLER NELSON, D. G., JUSCZYK, P. W., CASSIDY, K. W., DRUSS, B., & KENNEDY, L. (1987). Clauses are perceptual units for young infants. *Cognition, 26,* 269–286.

HOBART, C., & BROWN, D. (1988). Effects of prior marriage children on adjustment in remarriages: A Canadian study. *Journal of Comparative Family Studies, 19,* 381–396.

HOBSON, R. P. (1993). *Autism and the development of mind.* London: Erlbaum.

HOCHSCHILD, A. R. (1997). *The time bind: When work becomes home and home becomes work.* New York: Metropolitan Books.

HOCUTT, A. M. (1996). Effectiveness of special education: Is placement a critical factor? *Future of Children, 6,* 77–102.

HODAPP, R. M. (1996). Down syndrome: Developmental, psychiatric, and management issues. *Child and Adolescent Psychiatric Clinics of North America, 5,* 881–894.

HODGES, E. V. E., BOIVIN, M., VITARO, F., & BUKOWSKI, W. M. (1999). The power of friendship: Protection against an escalating cycle of peer victimization. *Developmental Psychology, 35,* 94–101.

HODGES, J., & TIZARD, B. (1989). Social and family relationships of ex-institutional adolescents. *Journal of Child Psychology and Psychiatry, 30,* 77–97.

HODGES, R. M., & FRENCH, L. A. (1988). The effect of class and collection labels on cardinality, class-inclusion, and number conservation tasks. *Child Development, 59,* 1387–1396.

HOFF-GINSBURG, E. (1994). Influences of mother and child on maternal talkativeness. *Discourse Processes, 18,* 105–117.

HOFFERTH, S. L. (1995). Who enrolls in Head Start? A demographic analysis of Head Start—eligible children. *Early Childhood Research Quarterly, 9,* 243–268.

HOFFMAN, L. W. (1989). Effects of maternal employment in the two-parent family. *American Psychologist, 44,* 283–292.

HOFFMAN, L. W. (1991). The influence of the family environment on personality: Accounting for sibling differences. *Psychological Bulletin, 110,* 187–203.

HOFFMAN, L. W. (1994). Commentary on Plomin, R. (1994). A proof and a disproof questioned. *Social Development, 3,* 60–63.

HOFFMAN, M. L. (1980). Moral development in adolescence. In J. Adelson (Ed.), *Handbook of adolescent psychology* (pp. 295–343). New York: Wiley.

HOFFMAN, M. L. (1981). Is altruism part of human nature? *Journal of Personality and Social Psychology, 40,* 121–137.

HOFFMAN, M. L. (1983). Affective and cognitive processes in moral internalization. In E. T. Higgins, D. N. Ruble, & W. W. Hartup (Eds.), *Social cognition and social development: A sociocultural perspective* (pp. 236–274). Cambridge: Cambridge University Press.

HOFFMAN, M. L. (1984). Interaction of affect and cognition in empathy. In C. E. Izard, J. Kagan, & R. B. Zajonc (Eds.), *Emotions, cognition, and behavior* (pp. 103–131). Cambridge: Cambridge University Press.

HOFFMAN, M. L. (1988). Moral development. In M. H. Bornstein & M. E. Lamb (Eds.), *Developmental psychology: An advanced textbook* (2nd ed., pp. 497–548). Hillsdale, NJ: Erlbaum.

HOFFMAN, M. L. (1991a). Commentary on: Toward an integration of Kohlberg's and Hoffman's moral development theories. *Human Development, 34,* 105–110.

HOFFMAN, M. L. (1991b). Empathy, cognition, and social action. In W. M. Kurtines & J. L. Gewirtz (Eds.), *Handbook of moral behavior and development* (Vol. 1, pp. 275–303). Hillsdale, NJ: Erlbaum.

HOFFMAN, S., & HATCH, M. C. (1996). Stress, social support and pregnancy outcome: A reassessment based on research. *Paediatric and Perinatal Epidemiology, 10,* 380–405.

HOFFNER, C., & BADZINSKI, D. M. (1989). Children's integration of facial and situational cues to emotion. *Child Development, 60,* 411–422.

HOFSTADTER, M., & REZNICK, J. S. (1996). Response modality affects human infant delayed-response performance. *Child Development, 67,* 646–658.

HOFSTEN, C. VON. (1984). Developmental changes in the organization of prereaching movements. *Developmental Psychology, 20,* 378–388.

HOFSTEN, C. VON. (1989). Motor development as the development of systems: Comments on the special section. *Developmental Psychology, 25,* 950–953.

HOFSTEN, C. VON, & SPELKE, E. S. (1985). Object perception and object-directed reaching in infancy. *Journal of Experimental Psychology: General, 114,* 198–212.

HOKODA, A., & FINCHAM, F. D. (1995). Origins of children's helpless and mastery achievement patterns in the family. *Journal of Educational Psychology, 87,* 375–385.

HOLDEN, G. W. (1983). Avoiding conflict: Mothers as tacticians in the supermarket. *Child Development, 54,* 233–240.

HOLDEN, G. W., COLEMAN, S. M., & SCHMIDT, K. L. (1995). Why 3-year-old children get spanked: Determinants as reported by college-educated mothers. *Merrill-Palmer Quarterly, 41,* 431–452.

HOLDEN, G. W., GEFFNER, R., & JOURILES, E. N. (Eds.). (1998). *Children exposed to marital violence.* Washington, DC: American Psychological Association.

HOLDEN, G. W., & WEST, M. J. (1989). Proximate regulation by mothers: A demonstration of how differing styles affect young children's behavior. *Child Development, 60,* 64–69.

HOLMBECK, G. N. (1996). A model of family relational transformations during the transition to adolescence: Parent–adolescent conflict and adaptation. In J. A. Graber, J. Brooks-Gunn, & A. C. Petersen (Eds.), *Transitions through adolescence* (pp. 167–199). Mahwah, NJ: Erlbaum.

HOLMBECK, G. N., & HILL, J. P. (1991). Conflictive engagement, positive affect, and menarche in families with seventh-grade girls. *Child Development, 62,* 1030–1048.

HOLMBECK, G. N., WATERS, K. A., & BROOKMAN, R. R. (1990). Psychosocial correlates of sexually transmitted diseases and sexual activity in black adolescent females. *Journal of Adolescent Research, 5,* 431–448.

HOLMES, W. C., & SLAP, G. B. (1998). Sexual abuse of boys: Definition, prevalence, correlates, sequelae, and management. *Journal of the American Medical Association, 280,* 1855–1862.

HOLTZMAN, W. H. (1997). Community psychology and full-service schools in different cultures. *American Psychologist, 52,* 381–389.

HONZIK, M. P., MACFARLANE, J. W., & ALLEN, L. (1948). The stability of mental test performance between two and eighteen years. *Journal of Experimental Education, 17,* 309–329.

HOOD, B. M., MURRAY, L., KING, F., HOOPER, R., ATKINSON, J., & BRADDICK, O. (1996). Habituation changes in early infancy: Longitudinal measures from birth to 6 months. *Journal of Reproductive and Infant Psychology, 14,* 177–185.

HOOK, E. B. (1982). Epidemiology of Down syndrome. In S. M. Pueschel & J. E. Rynders (Eds.), *Down syndrome: Advances in biomedicine and the behavioral sciences* (pp. 21–43). Cambridge, MA: Ware Press.

HOPKINS, B., & BUTTERWORTH, G. (1997). Dynamical systems approaches to the development of action. In G. Bremner, A. Slater, & G. Butterworth (Eds.), *Infant development: Recent advances* (pp. 75–100). East Sussex, England: Psychology Press.

HOPKINS, B., & WESTRA, T. (1988). Maternal handling and motor development: An intracultural study. *Genetic, Social and General Psychology Monographs, 14,* 377–420.

HORGAN, D. (1978). The development of the full passive. *Journal of Child Language, 5,* 65–80.

HORN, J. L. (1994). Theory of fluid and crystallized intelligence. In R. J. Sternberg (Ed.), *Encyclopedia of intelligence* (pp. 443–451). New York: Macmillan.

HORN, J. M. (1983). The Texas Adoption Project: Adopted children and their intellectual resemblance to biological and adoptive parents. *Child Development, 54,* 268–275.

HORNER, T. M. (1980). Two methods of studying stranger reactivity in infants: A review. *Journal of Child Psychology and Psychiatry, 21,* 203–219.

HOROWITZ, F. D. (1987). *Exploring developmental theories: Toward a structural/behavioral model of development.* Hillsdale, NJ: Erlbaum.

HOROWITZ, F. D. (1992). John B. Watson's legacy: Learning and environment. *Developmental Psychology, 28,* 360–367.

HORT, B. E., LEINBACH, M. D., & FAGOT, B. I. (1991). Is there coherence among the cognitive components of gender acquisition? *Sex Roles, 24,* 195–207.

HORTON, R. (1995, July 13). Is homosexuality inherited? *New York Review of Books,* pp. 36–41.

HOTZ, V. J., McELROY, S. W., & SANDERS, S. G. (1997). The costs and consequences of teenage childbearing for mothers. In R. A. Maynard (Ed.), *Kids having kids* (pp. 55–94). Washington, DC: Urban Institute.

HOWE, D., KAHN, P. H., JR., & FRIEDMAN, B. (1996). Along the Rio Negro: Brazilian children's environmental views and values. *Developmental Psychology, 32,* 979–987.

HOWE, M. L., & COURAGE, M. L. (1993). On resolving the enigma of infantile amnesia. *Psychological Bulletin, 113,* 305–326.

HOWE, M. L., & COURAGE, M. L. (1997). The emergence and early development of autobiographical memory. *Psychological Review, 104,* 499–523.

HOWES, C. (1988a). Peer interaction of young children. *Monographs of the Society for Research in Child Development, 53* (1, Serial No. 217).

HOWES, C. (1988b). Relations between early child care and schooling. *Developmental Psychology, 24,* 53–57.

HOWES, C. (1990). Can the age of entry into child care and the quality of child care predict adjustment in kindergarten? *Developmental Psychology, 26,* 292–303.

HOWES, C. (1992). *The collaborative construction of pretend.* Albany, NY: SUNY Press.

HOWES, C., & FARVER, J. (1987). Social pretend play in 2-year-olds: Effects of age of partner. *Early Childhood Research Quarterly, 2,* 305–314.

HOWES, C., & HAMILTON, C. E. (1993). The changing experience of child care: Changes in teachers and in teacher–child relationships and children's social competence with peers. *Early Childhood Research Quarterly, 8,* 15–32.

HOWES, C., & MATHESON, C. C. (1992). Sequences in the development of competent play with peers: Social and social pretend play. *Developmental Psychology, 28,* 961–974.

HOWES, C., PHILLIPS, D. A., & WHITEBOOK, M. (1992). Thresholds of quality: Implications for the social development of children in center-based child care. *Child Development, 63,* 449–460.

HUBBARD, F. O. A., & VAN IJZENDOORN, M. H. (1991). Maternal unresponsiveness and infant crying across the first 9 months: A naturalistic longitudinal study. *Infant Behavior and Development, 14,* 299–312.

HUBEL, D. H., & WIESEL, T. N. (1970). The period of susceptibility to the physiological effects of unilateral eye closure in kittens. *Journal of Physiology, 206,* 419–436.

HUDSON, J. A., & FIVUSH, R. (1991). As time goes by: Sixth graders remember a kindergarten experience. *Applied Cognitive Psychology, 5,* 347–360.

HUDSON, J. A., FIVUSH, R., & KUEBLI, J. (1992). Scripts and episodes: The development of event memory. *Applied Cognitive Psychology, 6,* 483–505.

HUDSON, J. A., & NELSON, K. (1983). Effects of script structure on children's story recall. *Developmental Psychology, 19,* 625–635.

HUDSON, J. A., SOSA, B. B., & SHAPIRO, L. R. (1997). Scripts and plans: The development of preschool children's event knowledge and event planning. In S. L. Friedman & E. K. Scholnick (Eds.), *The developmental psychology of planning: Why, how, and when do we plan?* (pp. 77–102). Mahwah, NJ: Erlbaum.

HUDSPETH, W. J., & PRIBRAM, K. H. (1992). Psychophysiological indices of cerebral maturation. *International Journal of Psychophysiology, 12,* 19–29.

HUESMANN, L. R. (1986). Psychological processes promoting the relation between exposure to media violence and aggressive behavior by the viewer. *Journal of Social Issues, 42,* 125–139.

HUESMANN, L. R., ERON, L. D., LEFKOWITZ, M. M., & WALDER, L. O. (1984). Stability of aggression over time and generations. *Developmental Psychology, 20,* 1120–1134.

HUGHES, C., & DUNN, J. (1998). Understanding mind and emotion: Longitudinal associations with mental-state talk between young friends. *Developmental Psychology, 34,* 1026–1037.

HUGHES, F. P. (1998). Play in special populations. In O. N. Saracho & B. Spodek (Eds.), *Multiple perspectives on play in early childhood education* (pp. 171–193). Albany: State University of New York Press.

HUGHES, J. N., CAVELL, T. A., & GROSSMAN, P. B. (1997). A positive view of self: Risk or protection for aggressive children? *Development and Psychopathology, 9,* 75–94.

HUGHES, M., & MACLEOD, H. (1986). Part II: Using LOGO with very young children. In R. Lawler, B. D. Boulay, M. Hughes, & H. Macleod (Eds.), *Cognition and computers: Studies in learning* (pp. 179–219). Chichester, England: Ellis Horwood.

HUMAN GENOME PROGRAM. (1998). *Count of mapped genes by chromosome.* Washington, DC: U.S. Department of Energy, Office of Biological and Environmental Research.

HUMPHREY, T. (1978). Function of the nervous system during prenatal life. In U. Stave (Ed.), *Perinatal physiology* (pp. 651–683). New York: Plenum.

HUMPHREYS, A. P., & SMITH, P. K. (1987). Rough and tumble, friendship, and dominance in schoolchildren: Evidence for continuity and change with age. *Child Development, 58,* 201–212.

HUMPHREYS, L. G. (1989). Intelligence: Three kinds of instability and their consequences for policy. In R. L. Linn (Ed.), *Intelligence* (pp. 193–216). Urbana: University of Illinois Press.

HUNT, E., STREISSGUTH, A. P., KERR, B., & OLSON, H. C. (1995). Mothers' alcohol consumption during pregnancy: Effects on spatial-visual reasoning in 14-year-old children. *Psychological Science, 6,* 339–342.

HUNTER, J. E., & HUNTER, R. F. (1984). Validity and utility of alternative predictors of job performance. *Psychological Bulletin, 96,* 72–98.

HUNTINGTON, L., HANS, S. L., & ZESKIND, P. S. (1990). The relations among cry characteristics, demographic variables, and developmental test scores in infants prenatally exposed to methadone. *Infant Behavior and Development, 13,* 533–538.

HUNTSINGER, C. S., JOSE, P. E., & LARSON, S. L. (1998). Do parent practices to encourage academic competence influence the social adjustment of young European American and Chinese American children? *Developmental Psychology, 34,* 747–756.

HURA, S. L., & ECHOLS, C. H. (1996). The role of stress and articulatory difficulty in children's early productions. *Developmental Psychology, 32,* 165–176.

HUSTON, A. C. (1983). Sex-typing. In E. M. Hetherington (Ed.), *Handbook of child psychology: Vol. 4. Socialization, personality, and social development* (4th ed., pp. 387–467). New York: Wiley.

HUSTON, A. C. (Ed.). (1991). *Children in poverty: Child development and public policy.* Cambridge, England: Cambridge University Press.

HUSTON, A. C. (1994, Summer). Children in poverty: Designing research to affect policy. *Social Policy Report of the Society for Research in Child Development, 8* (2).

HUSTON, A. C., & ALVAREZ, M. M. (1990). The socialization context of gender role development in early adolescence. In R. Montemayor, G. R. Adams, & T. P. Gullotta (Eds.), *From childhood to adolescence: A transitional period?* (pp. 156–179). Newbury Park, CA: Sage.

HUSTON, A. C., DONNERSTEIN, E., FAIRCHILD, H., FESHBACH, N. D., KATZ, P. A., MURRAY, J. P., RUBINSTEIN, E. A., WILCOX, B. L., & ZUCKERMAN, D. (1992). *Big world, small screen: The role of television in American society.* Lincoln: University of Nebraska Press.

HUSTON, A. C., & WRIGHT, J. C. (1998). Mass media and children's development. In I. E. Sigel & K. A. Renninger (Eds.), *Handbook of child psychology: Vol. 4. Child psychology in practice* (5th ed., pp. 999–1058). New York: Wiley.

HUSTON, T. L., & VANGELISTI, A. L. (1995). How parenthood affects marriage. In M. A. Fitzpatrick & Anita L. Vangelisti (Eds.), *Explaining family interactions* (pp. 147–176). Thousand Oaks, CA: Sage.

HUSTON-STEIN, A. C., FOX, S., GREER, D., WATKINS, B. A., & WHITAKER, J. (1981). The effects of TV action and violence on chil-

dren's social behavior. *Journal of Genetic Psychology, 138,* 183–191.

HUTTENLOCHER, J., HAIGHT, W., BRYK, A., SELTZER, M., & LYONS, T. (1991). Early vocabulary growth: Relation to language input and gender. *Developmental Psychology, 27,* 236–248.

HUTTENLOCHER, P. R. (1994). Synaptogenesis in human cerebral cortex. In G. Dawson & K. W. Fischer (Eds.), *Human behavior and the developing brain* (pp. 137–152). New York: Guilford.

HYDE, J. S. (1995). Women and maternity leave: Empirical data and public policy. *Psychology of Women Quarterly, 19,* 299–313.

HYDE, J. S., FENEMA, E., & LAMON, S. J. (1990). Gender differences in mathematics performance: A meta-analysis. *Psychological Bulletin, 107,* 139–155.

HYDE, J. S., KLEIN, M. H., ESSEX, M. J., & CLARK, R. (1995). Maternity leave and women's mental health. *Psychology of Women Quarterly, 19,* 257–285.

HYDE, J. S., & LINN, M. C. (1988). Gender differences in verbal ability: A meta-analysis. *Psychological Bulletin, 104,* 53–69.

HYDE, J. S., & PLANT, E. A. (1995). Magnitude of psychological gender differences: Another side to the story. *American Psychologist, 50,* 159–161.

HYND, G. W., HORN, K. L., VOELLER, K. K., & MARSHALL, R. M. (1991). Neurobiological basis of attention-deficit hyperactivity disorder (ADHD). *School Psychology Review, 20,* 174–186.

IMPERATO-MCGINLEY, J., PETERSON, R. E., GAUTIER, T., & STURLA, E. (1979). Steroid 5 alpha-reductase deficiency in man: An inherited form of male pseudohermaphroditism. *Science, 186,* 1213–1243.

INCIARDI, J. A., SURRATT, H. L., & SAUM, C. A. (1997). *Cocaine-exposed infants: Social, legal, and public health issues.* Thousand Oaks, CA: Sage.

INFANTE-RIVARD, C., FERNÁNDEZ, A., GAUTHIER, R., & RIVARD, G. E. (1993). Fetal loss associated with caffeine intake before and during pregnancy. *Journal of the American Medical Association, 270,* 2940–2943.

INGRAM, D. (1986). Phonological development: Production. In P. Fletcher & M. Garman (Eds.), *Language acquisition* (2nd ed., pp. 223–239). Cambridge: Cambridge University Press.

INHELDER, B., & PIAGET, J. (1958). *The growth of logical thinking from childhood to adolescence: An essay on the construction of*

formal operational structures. New York: Basic Books. (Original work published 1955)

INOFF-GERMAIN, G., ARNOLD, G. S., NOTTELMAN, E. D., SUSMAN, E. J., CUTLER, G. B., JR., & CROUSOS, G. P. (1988). Relations between hormone levels and observational measures of aggressive behavior of young adolescents in family interactions. *Developmental Psychology, 24,* 129–139.

INTERNATIONAL EDUCATION ASSOCIATION. (1988). *Science achievement in seventeen countries: A preliminary report.* Oxford: Pergamon Press.

INTONS-PETERSON, M. J. (1988). *Gender concepts of Swedish and American youth.* Hillsdale, NJ: Erlbaum.

IRGENS, L. M., MARKESTAD, T. BASTE, V., SCHREUDER, P., SKJAERVEN, R., & OYEN, N. (1995). Sleeping position and sudden infant death syndrome in Norway 1967–1991. *Archives of Disease in Childhood, 72,* 478–482.

IRVINE, J. J. (1986). Teacher–student interactions: Effects of student race, sex, and grade level. *Journal of Educational Psychology, 78,* 14–21.

IRWIN, A. R., & GROSS, A. M. (1995). Cognitive tempo, violent video games, and aggressive behavior in young boys. *Journal of Family Violence, 10,* 337–350.

ISABELLA, R. A. (1993). Origins of attachment: Maternal interactive behavior across the first year. *Child Development, 64,* 605–621.

ISABELLA, R. A., & BELSKY, J. (1991). Interactional synchrony and the origins of infant–mother attachment: A replication study. *Child Development, 62,* 373–384.

ISABELLA, R. A., BELSKY, J., & VON EYE, A. (1989). Origins of infant–mother attachment: An examination of interactional synchrony during the infant's first year. *Developmental Psychology, 25,* 12–21.

IVERSON, J. M., CAPIRCI, O., & CASELLI, M. C. (1994). From communication to language in two modalities. *Cognitive Development, 9,* 23–43.

IZARD, C. E. (1979). *The maximally discriminative facial movement scoring system.* Unpublished manuscript, University of Delaware.

IZARD, C. E. (1991). *The psychology of emotions.* New York: Plenum.

IZARD, C. E., FANTAUZZO, C. A., CASTLE, J. M., HAYNES, O. M., RAYIAS, M. F., & PUTNAM, P. H. (1995). The ontogeny and significance of infants' facial expressions in the first 9 months of life. *Developmental Psychology, 31,* 997–1013.

IZARD, C. E., HEMBREE, E. A., & HUEBNER, R. R. (1987). Infants' emotion expressions to acute pain. *Developmental Psychology, 23,* 105–113.

IZARD, C. E., & MALATESTA, C. Z. (1987). Perspectives on emotional development I: Differential emotions theory of early emotional development. In J. D. Osofsky (Ed.), *Handbook of infant development* (2nd ed., pp. 494–554). New York: Wiley.

IZARD, C. E., PORGES, S. W., SIMONS, R. F., HAYNES, O. M., HYDE, C., PARISI, M., & COHEN, B. (1991). Infant cardiac activity: Developmental changes and relations with attachment. *Developmental Psychology, 27,* 432–439.

JACKLIN, C. N., & MACCOBY, E. E. (1978). Social behavior at thirty-three months in same-sex and mixed-sex dyads. *Child Development, 49,* 557–569.

JACKSON, P. W. (1968). *Life in classrooms.* New York: Holt, Rinehart & Winston.

JACOBS, J. E. (1991). Influence of gender stereotypes on parent and child mathematics attitudes. *Journal of Educational Psychology, 83,* 518–527.

JACOBS, J. E., & ECCLES, J. S. (1992). The influence of parent stereotypes on parent and child ability beliefs in three domains. *Journal of Personality and Social Psychology, 63,* 932–944.

JACOBS, J. E., & WEISZ, V. (1994). Gender stereotypes: Implications for gifted education. *Roeper Review, 16,* 152–155.

JACOBSON, J. L., JACOBSON, S. W., FEIN, G., SCHWARTZ, P. M., & DOWLER, J. (1984). Prenatal exposure to an environmental toxin: A test of the multiple effects model. *Developmental Psychology, 20,* 523–532.

JACOBSON, J. L., JACOBSON, S. W., & HUMPHREY, H. E. B. (1990). Effects of in utero exposure to polychlorinated biphenyls on cognitive functioning in young children. *Journal of Pediatrics, 116,* 38–45.

JACOBSON, J. L., JACOBSON, S. W., PADGETT, R. J., BRUMITT, G. A., & BILLINGS, R. L. (1992). Effects of prenatal PCB exposure on cognitive processing efficiency and sustained attention. *Developmental Psychology, 28,* 297–306.

JACOBSON, S. W., FEIN, G. G., JACOBSON, J. L., SCHWARTZ, P. M., & DOWLER, J. (1985). The effect of intrauterine PCB exposure on visual recognition memory. *Child Development, 56,* 853–860.

JADACK, R. A., HYDE, J. S., MOORE, C. F., & KELLER, M. L. (1995). Moral reasoning about sexually transmitted diseases. *Child Development, 66*, 167–177.

JAMES, W. (1963). *Psychology*. New York: Fawcett. (Original work published 1890)

JAMESON, S. (1993). Zinc status in pregnancy: The effect of zinc therapy on perinatal mortality, prematurity, and placental ablation. *Annals of the New York Academy of Sciences, 678*, 178–192.

JAMIESON, J. R (1994). Teaching as transaction: Vygotskian perspectives on deafness and mother–child interaction. *Exceptional Children, 60*, 434–449.

JAMIESON, J. R. (1995a). Interactions between mothers and children who are deaf. *Journal of Early Intervention, 19*, 108–117.

JAMIESON, J. R. (1995b). Visible thought: Deaf children's use of signed and spoken private speech. *Sign Language Studies, 86*, 63–80.

JAMIN, J. R. (1994). Language and socialization of the child in African families living in France. In P. M. Greenfield & R. R. Cocking (Eds.), *Cross-cultural roots of minority child development* (pp. 147–166). Hillsdale, NJ: Erlbaum.

JANSSENS, J. M. A. M., & DEKOVIĆ, M. (1997). Child rearing, prosocial moral reasoning, and prosocial behaviour. *International Journal of Behavioral Development, 20*, 509–527.

JARROLD, C., BADDELEY, A. D., & HEWES, A. K. (1998). Verbal and nonverbal abilities in the Williams syndrome phenotype: Evidence for diverging developmental trajectories. *Journal of Child Psychology and Psychiatry, 39*, 511–523.

JARROLD, C., CARRUTHERS, P., SMITH, P. K., & BOUCHER, J. (1994). Pretend play: Is it metarepresentational? *Mind & Language, 9*, 445–468.

JENCKS, C. (1972). *Inequality: A reassessment of the effect of family and schooling in America*. New York: Basic Books.

JENDREK, M. P. (1994). Grandparents who parent their grandchildren: Circumstances and decisions. *Gerontologist, 34*, 206–216.

JENKINS, J. M., & ASTINGTON, J. W. (1996). Cognitive factors and family structure associated with theory of mind development in young children. *Developmental Psychology, 32*, 70–78.

JENKINS, M. R., & CULBERTSON, J. L. (1996). Prenatal exposure to alcohol. In R. L. Adams, O. A. Parsons, J. L. Culbertson, & S. J. Nixon (Eds.), *Neuropsychology for clinical practice: Etiology, assessment, and treatment of common neurological disorders* (pp. 409–452). Washington, DC: American Psychological Association.

JENSEN, A. R. (1969). How much can we boost IQ and scholastic achievement? *Harvard Educational Review, 39*, 1–123.

JENSEN, A. R. (1974). Cumulative deficit: A testable hypothesis. *Developmental Psychology, 10*, 996–1019.

JENSEN, A. R. (1980). *Bias in mental testing*. New York: Free Press.

JENSEN, A. R. (1985). The nature of the black-white difference on various psychometric tests: Spearman's hypothesis. *Behavioral and Brain Sciences, 8*, 193–219.

JENSEN, A. R. (1988). Speed of information processing and population differences. In S. H. Irvine & J. W. Berry (Eds.), *Human abilities in cultural context* (pp. 105–145). New York: Cambridge University Press.

JENSEN, A. R. (1997). The puzzle of nongenetic variance. In R. J. Sternberg & E. L. Grigorenko (Eds.), *Intelligence, heredity, and environment* (pp. 42–88). New York: Cambridge University Press.

JENSEN, A. R. (1998). *The g factor: The science of mental ability*. New York: Praeger.

JENSEN, A. R., & FIGUEROA, R. A. (1975). Forward and backward digit-span interaction with race and IQ: Predictions from Jensen's theory. *Journal of Educational Psychology, 67*, 882–893.

JENSEN, A. R., & REYNOLDS, C. R. (1982). Race, social class and ability patterns on the WISC-R. *Personality and Individual Differences, 3*, 423–438.

JENSEN, A. R., & WHANG, P. A. (1994). Speed of accessing arithmetic facts in long-term memory: A comparison of Chinese-American and Anglo-American children. *Contemporary Educational Psychology, 19*, 1–12.

JENSEN, M. K., & GREEN, V. P. (1993). The effects of multi-age grouping on young children and teacher preparation. *Early Child Development and Care, 91*, 25–31.

JESSOR, R. (1996). Ethnographic methods in contemporary perspective. In R. Jessor, A. Colby, & R. A. Shweder (Eds.), *Ethnography and human development* (pp. 3–14). Chicago: University of Chicago Press.

JIAO, S., JI, G., & JING, Q. (1996). Cognitive development of Chinese urban only children and children with siblings. *Child Development, 67*, 387–395.

JOHNSON, C., & CONNORS, M. E. (1987). *The etiology and treatment of bulimia nervosa: A biopsychosocial perspective*. New York: Basic Books.

JOHNSON, J. E., & HOOPER, F. E. (1982). Piagetian structuralism and learning: Two decades of educational application. *Contemporary Educational Psychology, 7*, 217–237.

JOHNSON, J. S., & NEWPORT, E. L. (1989). Critical period effects in second language learning: The influence of maturational state on the acquisition of English as a second language. *Cognitive Psychology, 21*, 60–99.

JOHNSON, K. E., SCOTT, P., & MERVIS, C. B. (1997). Development of children's understanding of basic-subordinate inclusion relations. *Developmental Psychology, 33*, 745–763.

JOHNSON, M. H. (1995). The inhibition of automatic saccades in early infancy. *Developmental Psychobiology, 28*, 281–291.

JOHNSON, M. H. (1998). The neural basis of cognitive development. In D. Kuhn & R. S. Siegler (Ed.), *Handbook of child psychology: Vol. 2. Cognition, perception, and language* (5th ed., pp. 1–49). New York: Wiley.

JOHNSON, M. H., POSNER, M. I., & ROTHBART, M. K. (1991). Components of visual orienting in early infancy: Contingency learning, anticipatory looking, and disengaging. *Journal of Cognitive Neuroscience, 4*, 335–344.

JOHNSON, S. L., & BIRCH, L. L. (1994). Parents' and children's adiposity and eating style. *Pediatrics, 94*, 653–661.

JOHNSON, S. P. (1996). Habituation patterns and object perception in young infants. *Journal of Reproductive and Infant Psychology, 14*, 207–218.

JOHNSON, S. P. (1997). Young infants' perception of object unity: Implications for development of attentional and cognitive skills. *Current Directions in Psychological Science, 6*, 5–11.

JOHNSON, S. P., & ASLIN, R. N. (1995). Perception of object unity in 2-month-old infants. *Developmental Psychology, 31*, 739–745.

JOHNSON, S. P., & ASLIN, R. N. (1996). Perception of object unity in young infants: The roles of motion, depth, and orientation. *Cognitive Development, 11*, 161–180.

JOHN-STEINER, V., & MAHN, H. (1996). Sociocultural approaches to learning and development: A Vygotskian framework. *Educational Psychologist, 3*, 191–206.

JOHNSTON, J. R., KLINE, M., & TSCHANN, J. M. (1989). Ongoing postdivorce conflict: Effects on children of joint custody and frequent access. *American Journal of Orthopsychiatry, 59*, 576–592.

JOHNSTON, J. R., & SLOBIN, D. I. (1979). The development of locative expressions in English, Italian, Serbo-Croatian, and Turkish. *Journal of Child Language, 16*, 531–547.

JONES, C. P., & ADAMSON, L. B. (1987). Language use in mother–child–sibling interactions. *Child Development, 58*, 356–366.

JONES, G. P., & DEMBO, M. H. (1989). Age and sex role differences in intimate friendships during childhood and adolescence. *Merrill-Palmer Quarterly, 35*, 445–462.

JONES, K. L. (1997). *Smith's recognizable patterns of human malformation* (5th ed.). Philadelphia: Saunders.

JONES, M. C. (1965). Psychological correlates of somatic development. *Child Development, 36*, 899–911.

JONES, M. C., & BAYLEY, N. (1950). Physical maturing among boys as related to behavior. *Journal of Educational Psychology, 41*, 129–148.

JONES, M. C., & MUSSEN, P. H. (1958). Self-conceptions, motivations, and interpersonal attitudes of early- and late-maturing girls. *Child Development, 29*, 491–501.

JONES, M. G., & GERIG, T. M. (1994). Silent sixth-grade students: Characteristics, achievement, and teacher expectations. *Elementary School Journal, 95*, 169–182.

JONES, N. A., FIELD, T., FOX, N. A., LUNDY, B., & DAVALOS, M. (1997). EEG activation in 1-month-old infants of depressed mothers. *Development and Psychopathology, 9*, 491–505.

JONES, S. S., & RAAG, T. (1989). Smile production in older infants: The importance of a social recipient for the facial signal. *Child Development, 60*, 811–818.

JORDAN, B. (1993). *Birth in four cultures*. Prospect Heights, IL: Waveland.

JORGENSEN, M., & KEIDING, N. (1991). Estimation of spermarche from longitudinal spermaturia data. *Biometrics, 47*, 177–193.

JOSEPH, R. M. (1998). Intention and knowledge in preschoolers' conception of pretend. *Child Development, 69*, 966–980.

JOSSELSON, R. (1994). The theory of identity development and the question of intervention. In S. L. Archer (Ed.), *Interventions for adolescent identity development* (pp. 12–25). Thousand Oaks, CA: Sage.

JOUEN, F., & LEPECQ, J-C. (1989). Sensitivity to optical flow in neonates. *Psychologie Française, 34,* 13–18.

JOURILES, E. N., MURPHY, C. M., FARRIS, A. M., SMITH, D. A., RICHTERS, J. E., & WATERS, E. (1991). Marital adjustment, parental disagreements about child rearing, and behavior problems in boys: Increasing the specificity of the marital assessment. *Child Development, 62,* 1424–1433.

JOVANOVIC, J., & KING, S. S. (1998). Boys and girls in the performance-based science classroom: Who's doing the performing? *American Educational Research Journal, 35,* 477–496.

JOYNER, M. H., & KURTZ-COSTES, B. (1997). Metamemory development. In W. Schneider & F. E. Weinert (Eds.), *Memory performance and competencies: Issues in growth and development* (pp. 275–300). Hillsdale, NJ: Erlbaum.

JUSCZYK, P. W. (1995). Language acquisition: Speech sounds and phonological development. In J. L. Miller & P. D. Eimas (Eds.), *Handbook of perception and cognition: Vol. 11. Speech, language, and communication* (pp. 263–301). Orlando, FL: Academic Press.

JUSCZYK, P. W. (1997). Finding and remembering words: Some beginnings by English-learning infants. *Current Directions in Psychological Science, 6,* 170–174.

JUSCZYK, P. W., & ASLIN, R. N. (1995). Infants' detection of the sound patterns of words in fluent speech. *Cognitive Psychology, 29,* 1–23.

JUSCZYK, P. W., CHARLES-LUCE, J., & LUCE, P. A. (1994). Infants' sensitivity to high frequency vs. low-frequency phonetic sequences in the native language. *Journal of Memory and Language, 33,* 630–645.

JUSCZYK, P. W., CUTLER, A., & REDANZ, N. (1993). Preference for the predominant stress patterns of English words. *Child Development, 64,* 675–687.

JUSCZYK, P. W., & HOHNE, E. A. (1997). Infants' memory for spoken words. *Science, 277,* 1984–1986.

JUSTICE, E. M. (1986). Developmental changes in judgments of relative strategy effectiveness. *British Journal of Developmental Psychology, 4,* 75–81.

JUSTICE, E. M., BAKER-WARD, L., GUPTA, S., & JANNINGS, L. R. (1997). Means to the goal of remembering: Developmental changes in awareness of strategy use–performance relations. *Journal of Experimental Child Psychology, 65,* 293–314.

KAGAN, J. (1989). *Unstable ideas: Temperament, cognition, and self.* Cambridge, MA: Cambridge University Press.

KAGAN, J. (1992). Behavior, biology, and the meanings of temperamental constructs. *Pediatrics, 90,* 510–513.

KAGAN, J. (1994). *Galen's prophecy.* New York: Basic Books.

KAGAN, J. (1998a). Biology and the child. In N. Eisenberg (Ed.), *Handbook of child psychology: Vol. 3. Social, emotional, and personality development* (5th ed., pp. 177–236). New York: Wiley.

KAGAN, J. (1998b). *Three seductive ideas.* Cambridge, MA: Harvard University Press.

KAGAN, J., ARCUS, D., SNIDMAN, N., FENG, W. Y., HENDLER, J., & GREENE, S. (1994). Reactivity in infants: A cross-national comparison. *Developmental Psychology, 30,* 342–345.

KAGAN, J., KEARSLEY, R. B., & ZELAZO, P. R. (1978). *Infancy: Its place in human development.* Cambridge, MA: Harvard University Press.

KAGAN, J., & SNIDMAN, N. (1991). Temperamental factors in human development. *American Psychologist, 46,* 856–862.

KAHN, A., GROSWASSER, J., SOTTIAUX, M., KELMANSON, I., REBUFFAT, E., FRANCO, P., DRAMAIZ, M., & WAYENBERG, J. L. (1994). Prenatal exposure to cigarettes in infants with obstructive sleep apneas. *Pediatrics, 93,* 778–783.

KAHN, P. H., JR. (1992). Children's obligatory and discretionary moral judgments. *Child Development, 63,* 416–430.

KAHN, P. H., JR. (1997a). Bayous and jungle rivers: Cross-cultural perspectives on children's environmental moral reasoning. In H. D. Saltzstein (ED.), *New Directions for Child Development* (No. 76, pp. 23–36). San Francisco: Jossey-Bass.

KAHN, P. H., JR. (1997b). Children's moral and ecological reasoning about the Prince William Sound oil spill. *Developmental Psychology, 33,* 1091–1096.

KAHN, P. H., JR., & FRIEDMAN, B. (1995). Environmental views and values of children in an inner-city black community. *Child Development, 66,* 1403–1417.

KAIL, R. (1988). Developmental functions for speeds of cognitive processes. *Journal of Experimental Child Psychology, 45,* 339–364.

KAIL, R. (1991). Processing time declines exponentially during

childhood and adolescence. *Developmental Psychology, 27,* 259–266.

KAIL, R. (1993). The role of a global mechanism in developmental change in speed of processing. In M. L. Howe & R. Pasnak (Eds.), *Emerging themes in cognitive development: Vol. 1. Foundations.* New York: Springer-Verlag.

KAIL, R. (1997). Processing time, imagery, and spatial memory. *Journal of Experimental Child Psychology, 64,* 67–78.

KAIL, R., & PARK, Y. (1992). Global developmental change in processing time. *Merrill-Palmer Quarterly, 38,* 525–541.

KAIL, R., & PARK, Y. (1994). Processing time, articulation time, and memory span. *Journal of Experimental Child Psychology, 57,* 281–291.

KAIL, R., & SALTHOUSE, T. A. (1994). Processing speed as a mental capacity. *Acta Psychologica, 86,* 199–225.

KAITZ, M., MEIROV, H., LANDMAN, I., & EIDELMAN, A. I. (1993a). Infant recognition by tactile cues. *Infant Behavior and Development, 16,* 333–341.

KAITZ, M., SHIRI, S., DANZIGER, S., HERSHKO, Z., & EIDELMAN, A. I. (1993b). Fathers can also recognize their newborns by touch. *Infant Behavior and Development, 17,* 205–207.

KALB, C. (1997, May 5). How old is too old? *Newsweek,* p. 64.

KALER, S. R., & KOPP, C. B. (1990). Compliance and comprehension in very young toddlers. *Child Development, 61,* 1997–2003.

KALLÓS, D., & BROMAN, I. T. (1997). Swedish child care and early childhood education in transition. *Early Education & Development, 8,* 265–284.

KAMERMAN, S. B. (1993). International perspectives on child care policies and programs. *Pediatrics, 91,* 248–252.

KANDALL, S. R., GAINES, J., HABEL, L., DAVIDSON, G., & JESSOP, D. (1993). Relationship of maternal substance abuse to subsequent sudden infant death syndrome in offspring. *Journal of Pediatrics, 123,* 120–126.

KANNER, A. D., FELDMAN, S. S., WEINBERGER, D. A., & FORD, M. E. (1987). Uplifts, hassles, and adaptational outcomes in early adolescents. *Journal of Early Adolescence, 7,* 371–394.

KAO, G., & TIENDA, M. (1995). Optimism and achievement: The educational performance of immigrant youth. *Social Science Quarterly, 76,* 1–19.

KAPLAN, P. S., ZARLENGO-STROUSE, P., KIRK, L. S., & ANGEL, C. L. (1997). Selective and nonselective associations between speech segments and faces in

human infants. *Developmental Psychology, 33,* 990–999.

KARADSHEH, R. (1991, March). *This room is a junkyard! Children's comprehension of metaphorical language.* Paper presented at the biennial meeting of the Society for Research in Child Development, Seattle, WA.

KARMILOFF-SMITH, A. (1992a). *Beyond modularity: A developmental perspective on cognitive science.* Cambridge, MA: MIT Press.

KARMILOFF-SMITH, A. (1992b). Nature, nurture, and PDP: Preposterous developmental postulates? *Connection Science, 4,* 253–269.

KARMILOFF-SMITH, A. (1997). Crucial differences between developmental cognitive neuroscience and adult neuropsychology. *Developmental Neuropsychology, 13,* 513–524.

KARMILOFF-SMITH, A., GRANT, J., BERTHOUD, I., DAVIES, M., HOWLIN, P., & UDWIN, O. (1997). Language and Williams syndrome: How intact is "intact"? *Child Development, 68,* 246–262.

KARMILOFF-SMITH, A., GRANT, J., SIMS, K., JONES, M., & CUCKLE, P. (1996). Rethinking metalinguistic awareness: Representing and accessing knowledge about what counts as a word. *Cognition, 58,* 197–219.

KARMILOFF-SMITH, A., TYLER, L. K., VOICE, K., SIMS, K., UDWIN, O., HOWLIN, P., & DAVIES, M. (1998). Linguistic dissociations in Williams syndrome: Evaluating receptive syntax in on-line and off-line tasks. *Neuropsychologia, K-ABC). In B. B. Wolman (Ed.), Handbook of intelligence* (pp. 663–698). New York: Wiley.

KATCHADOURIAN, H. (1977). *The biology of adolescence.* San Francisco: Freeman.

KATCHADOURIAN, H. (1990). Sexuality. In S. S. Feldman & G. R. Elliott (Eds.), *At the threshold: The developing adolescent* (pp. 330–351). Cambridge, MA: Harvard University Press.

KAUFMAN, A. S., KAMPHAUS, R. W., & KAUFMAN, N. L. (1985). New directions in intelligence testing: The Kaufman Assessment Battery for Children (K-ABC). In B. B. Wolman (Ed.), *Handbook of intelligence* (pp. 663–698). New York: Wiley.

KAVANAUGH, R. D., & ENGEL, S. (1998). The development of pretense and narrative in early childhood. In O. N. Saracho & B. Spodek (Eds.), *Multiple perspectives on play in early childhood education* (pp. 80–99). Albany: State University of New York Press.

KAVANAUGH, R. D., & HARRIS, P. L. (1994). Imagining the outcome of pretend transformations: Assessing the competence of normal children and children with autism. *Developmental Psychology, 30,* 847–854.

KAWASAKI, C., NUGENT, J. K., MIYASHITA, H., MIYAHARA, H., & BRAZELTON, T. B. (1994). The cultural organization of infants' sleep. *Children's Environments, 11,* 135–141.

KAYE, K., & MARCUS, J. (1981). Infant imitation: The sensory-motor agenda. *Developmental Psychology, 17,* 258–265.

KAZDIN, A. E. (1993). Treatment of conduct disorder: Progress and directions in psychotherapy research. *Development and Psychopathology, 5,* 276–310.

KEARINS, J. M. (1981). Visual spatial memory in Australian aboriginal children of desert regions. *Cognitive Psychology, 13,* 434–460.

KEATING, D. (1979). Adolescent thinking. In J. Adelson (Ed.), *Handbook of adolescent psychology* (pp. 211–246). New York: Wiley.

KEATING, D. (1990). Adolescent thinking. In S. S. Feldman & G. R. Elliott (Eds.), *At the threshold* (pp. 54–89). Cambridge, MA: Harvard University Press.

KEATING, D., & CLARK, L. V. (1980). Development of physical and social reasoning in adolescence. *Developmental Psychology, 16,* 23–30.

KEATS, D. M., & FANG, F-X. (1992). The effect of modification of the cultural content of stimulus materials on social perspective taking ability in Chinese and Australian children. In S. Iwawaki, & Y. Kashina (Eds.), *Innovations in cross-cultural psychology* (pp. 319–327). Amsterdam: Swets & Zeitlinger.

KEENEY, T. J., CANIZZO, S. R., & FLAVELL, J. H. (1967). Spontaneous and induced verbal rehearsal in a recall task. *Child Development, 38,* 953–966.

KEIL, F. C. (1986). Conceptual domains and the acquisition of metaphor. *Cognitive Development, 1,* 72–96.

KEIL, F. C. (1989). *Concepts, kinds, and cognitive development.* Cambridge, MA: MIT Press.

KEINAN, G. (1997). Social support, stress, and personality: Do all women benefit from husband's presence during childbirth? In G. R. Pierce, B. Lakey, I. G. Sarason, & B. R. Sarason (Eds.), *Sourcebook of social support and personality* (pp. 409–427). New York: Plenum.

KELLER, M., & WOOD, P. (1989). Development of friendship reasoning: A study of interindividual differences and intraindividual change. *Developmental Psychology, 25,* 820–826.

KELLEY, M. L., POWER, T. G., & WIMBUSH, D. D. (1992). Determinants of disciplinary practices in low-income black mothers. *Child Development, 63,* 573–582.

KELLMAN, P. J. (1993). Kinematic foundations of infant visual perception. In C. E. Granrud (Ed.), *Visual perception and cognition in infancy* (pp. 121–173). Hillsdale, NJ: Erlbaum.

KELLMAN, P. J. (1996). The origins of object perception. In W. Epstein & S. Rogers (Eds.), *Handbook of perception and cognition* (pp. 3–48). New York: Academic Press.

KEMP, J. S., & THACH, B. T. (1993). A sleep position-dependent mechanism for infant death on sheepskins. *American Journal of Diseases of Children, 147,* 642–646.

KEMPE, C. H., SILVERMAN, B. F., STEELE, P. W., DROEGEMUELLER, P. W., & SILVER, H. K. (1962). The battered-child syndrome. *Journal of the American Medical Association, 181,* 17–24.

KENDALL-TACKETT, K. A., WILLIAMS, L. M., & FINKELHOR, D. (1993). Impact of sexual abuse on children: A review and synthesis of recent empirical studies. *Psychological Bulletin, 113,* 164–180.

KENNELL, J., KLAUS, M., MCGRATH, S., ROBERTSON, S., & HINKLEY, C. (1991). Continuous emotional support during labor in a U.S. hospital. *Journal of the American Medical Association, 265,* 2197–2201.

KEOGH, B. K. (1988). Improving services for problem learners. *Journal of Learning Disabilities, 21,* 6–11.

KERNS, K. A., & BERENBAUM, S. A. (1991). Sex differences in spatial ability in children. *Behavior Genetics, 21,* 383–396.

KERR, B. A. (1983). Raising the career aspirations of gifted girls. *Vocational Guidance Quarterly, 32,* 37–43.

KERR, M., LAMBERT, W. W., STATTIN, H., & KLACKENBERG-LARSSON, I. (1994). Stability of inhibition in a Swedish longitudinal sample. *Child Development, 65,* 138–146.

KESSEN, W. (1967). Sucking and looking: Two organized congenital patterns of behavior in the human newborn. In H. W. Stevenson, E. H. Hess, & H. L. Rheingold (Eds.), *Early behavior: Comparative and developmental approaches* (pp. 147–179). New York: Wiley.

KESSLER, R., MCGONAGLE, K., ZHAO, S., NELSON, C., HUGHES, M., ESHLEMAN, S., WITTCHEN, H., & KENDLER, K. (1994). Lifetime and 12-month prevalence of DSM-III-R psychiatric disorders in the United States: Results from the national comorbidity survey. *Archives of General Psychiatry, 51,* 8–19.

KILLEN, M. (1991). Social and moral development in early childhood. In W. M. Kurtines & J. L. Gewirtz (Eds.), *Handbook of moral behavior and development: Vol. 2. Research* (pp. 115–138). Hillsdale, NJ: Erlbaum.

KILLEN, M., & NUCCI, L. P. (1995). Morality, autonomy, and social conflict. In M. Killen & D. Hart (Eds.), *Morality in everyday life: Developmental perspectives* (pp. 52–86). Cambridge: Cambridge University Press.

KIM, J. M. (1998). Korean children's concepts of adult and peer authority and moral reasoning. *Developmental Psychology, 34,* 947–955.

KIM, J. M., & TURIEL, E. (1996). Korean children's concepts of adult and peer authority. *Social Development, 5,* 310–329.

KIM, K., & SPELKE, E. S., (1992). Infants' sensitivity to effects of gravity on visible object motion. *Journal of Experimental Psychology: Human Perception and Performance, 18,* 385–393.

KINDER, M. (1996). Contextualizing video game violence: From Teenage Mutant Ninja Turtles to Mortal Kombat 2. In P. M. Greenfield & R. R. Cocking (Eds.), *Interacting with video* (pp. 25–37). Norwood, NJ: Ablex.

KINDERMANN, T. (1998). Children's development within peer groups: Using composite social maps to identify peer networks and to study their influences. In W. M. Bukowski & A. H. Cillessen (Eds.), *New directions for child development* (No. 80, pp. 55–82). San Francisco: Jossey-Bass.

KING, C. A. (1997). Suicidal behavior in adolescence. In R. W. Maris, M. M. Silverman, & S. S. Canetto (Eds.), *Review of suicidology, 1997* (pp. 61–95). New York: Guilford.

KING, T. (1997). Epidural anesthesia in labor: Benefits versus risks. *Journal of Nurse Midwifery, 42,* 377–388.

KINSMAN, C. A., & BERK, L. E. (1979). Joining the block and housekeeping areas: Changes in play and social behavior. *Young Children, 35* (1), 66–75.

KINZIE, J. D., SACK, W., ANGELL, R., CLARKE, G., & BEN, R. (1989). A three-year follow-up of Cambodian young people traumatized as children. *Journal of the American Academy of Child and Adolescent Psychiatry, 28,* 501–504.

KIRBY, D., SHORT, L., COLLINS, J., RUGG, D., KOLBE, L., HOWARD, M., MILLER, B., SONENSTEIN, F., & ZABIN, L. S. (1994). School-based programs to reduce sexual behaviors: A review of effectiveness. *Public Health Reports, 109* (3), 339–360.

KISILEVSKY, B. S., HAINS, S. M. J., LEE, K., MUIR, D. W., FU, G., ZHAO, Z. Y., & YANG, R. L. (1998). The still-face effect in Chinese and Canadian 3- to 6-month-old infants. *Developmental Psychology, 34,* 629–639.

KISILEVSKY, B. S., & LOW, J. A. (1998). Human fetal behavior: 100 years of study. *Developmental Review, 18,* 1–29.

KITCHENER, K. S., LYNCH, C. L., FISCHER, K. W., & WOOD, P. K. (1993). Developmental range of reflective judgment: The effect of contexual support and practice on developmental stage. *Developmental Psychology, 29,* 893–906.

KLAHR, D. (1992). Information-processing approaches to cognitive development. In M. H. Bornstein & M. E. Lamb (Eds.), *Developmental psychology: An advanced textbook* (3rd ed., pp. 273–335). Hillsdale, NJ: Erlbaum.

KLAHR, D., & MACWHINNEY, B. (1998). Information processing. In D. Kuhn & R. S. Siegler (Eds.), *Information processing. In D. Kuhn & R. S. Siegler (Eds.), *Handbook of child psychology: Vol. 2. Cognition, perception, and language* (5th ed., pp. 631–678). New York: Wiley.

KLEBANOV, P. K., BROOKS-GUNN, J., MCCARTON, C., & MCCORMICK, M. C. (1998). The contribution of neighborhood and family income to developmental test scores over the first three years of life. *Child Development, 69,* 1420–1436.

KLIEWER, W., FEARNOW, M. D., & MILLER, P. A. (1996). Coping socialization in middle childhood: Tests of maternal and paternal influences. *Child Development, 67,* 2339–2357.

KLIMES-DOUGAN, B., & KISTNER, J. (1990). Physically abused preschoolers' responses to peers' distress. *Developmental Psychology, 26,* 599–602.

KLINEBERG, O. (1963). Negro–white differences in intelligence test performance: A new look at an old problem. *American Psychologist, 18,* 198–203.

KNOBLOCH, H., & PASAMANICK, B. (Eds.). (1974). *Gesell and Amatruda's Developmental Diagnosis.* Hagerstown, MD: Harper & Row.

KNOERS, N., VAN DEN OUWELAND, A., DREESEN, J., VERDIJK, M., MONNENS, L. S., & VAN OOST, B. A. (1993). Nephrogenic diabetes insipidus: Identification of the genetic defect. *Pediatric Nephrology, 7,* 685–688.

KOBAYASHI, Y. (1994). Conceptual acquisition and change through social interaction. *Human Development, 37,* 233–241.

KOCHANSKA, G. (1991). Socialization and temperament in the development of guilt and conscience. *Child Development, 62,* 1379–1392.

KOCHANSKA, G. (1992). Children's interpersonal influence with mothers and peers. *Developmental Psychology, 28,* 491–499.

KOCHANSKA, G. (1993). Toward a synthesis of parental socialization and child temperament in early development of conscience. *Child Development, 64,* 325–347.

KOCHANSKA, G. (1995). Children's temperament, mothers' discipline, and security of attachment: Multiple pathways to emerging internalization. *Child Development, 66,* 597–615.

KOCHANSKA, G. (1997a) Multiple pathways to conscience for children with different temperaments: From toddlerhood to age 5. *Developmental Psychology, 33,* 228–240.

KOCHANSKA, G. (1997b) Mutually responsive orientation between mothers and their young children: Implications for early socialization. *Child Development, 68,* 94–112.

KOCHANSKA, G. (1998). Mother–child relationship, child fearfulness, and emerging attachment: A short-term longitudinal study. *Developmental Psychology, 34,* 480–490.

KOCHANSKA, G., & AKSAN, N. (1995). Mother–child mutually positive affect, the quality of child compliance to requests and prohibitions, and maternal control as correlates of early internalization. *Child Development, 66,* 597–615.

KOCHANSKA, G., AKSAN, N., & KOENIG, A. L. (1995). A longitudinal study of the roots of preschoolers' conscience: Committed compliance and emerging internalization. *Child Development, 66,* 1752–1769.

KOCHANSKA, G., CASEY, R. J., & FUKUMOTO, A. (1995). Toddlers' sensitivity to standard violations. *Child Development, 66,* 643–656.

KOCHANSKA, G., DEVET, K., GOLDMAN, M., MURRAY, K., & PUTNAM, S. P. (1994). Maternal reports of conscience development and temperament in young children. *Child Development, 65,* 852–868.

KOCHANSKA, G., KUCZYNSKI, L., & RADKE-YARROW, M. (1989). Correspondence between mothers' self-reported and observed child-rearing practices. *Child Development, 60,* 56–63.

KOCHANSKA, G., MURRAY, K., & COY, K. C. (1997). Inhibitory control as a contributor to conscience in childhood: From toddler to early school age. *Child Development, 68,* 263–277.

KOCHANSKA, G., & RADKE-YARROW, M. (1992). Inhibition in toddlerhood and the dynamics of the child's interaction with an unfamiliar peer at age five. *Child Development, 63,* 325–335.

KOESTNER, R., FRANZ, C., & WEINBERGER, J. (1990). The family origins of empathic concern: A 26-year longitudinal study. *Journal of Personality and Social Psychology, 58,* 709–717.

KOHLBERG, L. (1966). A cognitive-developmental analysis of children's sex-role concepts and attitudes. In E. E. Maccoby (Ed.), *The development of sex differences* (pp. 82–173). Stanford, CA: Stanford University Press.

KOHLBERG, L. (1969). Stage and sequence: The cognitive-developmental approach to socialization. In D. A. Goslin (Ed.), *Handbook of socialization theory and research* (pp. 347–480). Chicago: Rand McNally.

KOHLBERG, L. (1976). Moral stages and moralization: The cognitive-developmental approach. In T. Lickona (Ed.), *Moral development and behavior: Theory, research, and social issues* (pp. 31–53). New York: Holt.

KOHLBERG, L. (1984). *Essays on moral development. Vol. 2: The psychology of moral development.* San Francisco: Harper & Row.

KOHLBERG, L., LEVINE, C., & HEWER, A. (1983). *Moral stages: A current formulation and a response to critics.* Basel: Karger.

KOHUT, A. (1994). *The role of technology in American life.* Los Angeles: Times Mirror Center for the People and the Press.

KOJIMA, H. (1986). Childrearing concepts as a belief-value system of the society and the individual. In H. Stevenson, H. Azuma, & K. Hakuta (Eds.), *Child development and education in Japan* (pp. 39–54). New York: Freeman.

KOLSTAD, V., & AGUIAR, A. (1995, March). *Means-end sequences in young infants.* Paper presented at the biennial meeting of the Society for Research in Child Development, Indianapolis.

KOLVIN, I., & TROWELL, J. (1996). Child sexual abuse. In I. Rosen (Ed.), *Sexual deviation* (3rd ed., pp. 337–360). Oxford, England: Oxford University Press.

KOPP, C. B. (1987). The growth of self-regulation: Caregivers and children. In N. Eisenberg (Ed.), *Contemporary topics in developmental psychology* (pp. 34–55). New York: Wiley.

KOPP, C. B. (1994). Infant assessment. In C. B. Fisher & R. M. Lerner (Eds.), *Applied developmental psychology* (pp. 265–293). New York: McGraw-Hill.

KORENMAN, S., MILLER, J., & SJAASTAD, J. (1995). Long-term poverty and child development in the United States: Results from the NLSY. *Children and Youth Services Review, 17,* 127–155.

KORNER, A. F. (1996). Reliable individual differences in preterm infants' excitation management. *Child Development, 67,* 1793–1805.

KOTOVSKY, L., & BAILLARGEON, R. (1998). The development of calibration-based reasoning about collision events in young infants. *Cognition, 67,* 311–351.

KOVACS, M. (1996). Presentation and course of major depressive disorder during childhood and later years of the lifespan. *Journal of the American Academy of Child and Adolescent Psychiatry, 35,* 705–715.

KOVACS, M., AKISKAL, H., GATSONIS, C., & PARRONE, P. (1994). Childhood-onset dysthymic disorder: Clinical features and prospective naturalistic outcome. *Archives of General Psychiatry, 51,* 365–374.

KOZULIN, A. (1990). *Vygotsky's psychology: A biography of ideas.* Cambridge, MA: Harvard University Press.

KRAFFT, K., & BERK, L. E. (1998). Private speech in two preschools: Significance of open-ended activities and make-believe play for verbal self-regulation. *Early Childhood Research Quarterly, 13,* 637–658.

KRAMER, L., & GOTTMAN, J. M. (1992). Becoming a sibling: "With a little help from my friends." *Developmental Psychology, 28,* 685–699.

KRAMER, L. R. (1991). The social construction of ability perceptions: An ethnographic study of gifted adolescent girls. *Journal of Early Adolescence, 11,* 340–362.

KRANZLER, J. H. (1997). Educational and policy issues related to the use and interpretation of intelligence tests in the schools. *School Psychology Review, 26,* 150–162.

KRASCUM, R. M., & ANDREWS, S. (1998). The effects of theories on children's acquisition of family-resemblance categories. *Child Development, 69,* 333–346.

KRAUT, R., MUKHOPADHYAY, T., SZCZYPULA, J., KIESLER, S., & SCHERLIS, W. (1998a). Communication and information: Alternative uses of the Internet in households. In *Proceedings of the CHI 98* (pp. 368–383). New York: ACM.

KRAUT, R., PATTERSON, M., LUNDMARK, V., KIESLER, S., MUKOPADHYAY, T., & SCHERLIS, W. (1998b). Internet paradox: A social technology that reduces social involvement and psychological well-being? *American Psychologist, 53,* 1017–1031.

KREBS, D., & GILLMORE, J. (1982). The relationship among the first stages of cognitive development, role-taking abilities, and moral development. *Child Development, 53,* 877–886.

KREUTZER, M. A., LEONARD, C., & FLAVELL, J. H. (1975). An interview study of children's knowledge about memory. *Monographs of the Society for Research in Child Development, 40* (1, Serial No. 159).

KREVANS, J., & GIBBS, J. C. (1996). Parents' use of inductive discipline: Relations to children's empathy and prosocial behavior. *Child Development, 67,* 3263–3277.

KROGER, J. (1995). The differentiation of "firm" and "developmental" foreclosure identity statuses: A longitudinal study. *Journal of Adolescent Research, 10,* 317–337.

KRUGER, A. C. (1993). Peer collaboration: Conflict, cooperation, or both? *Social Development, 2,* 165–182.

KRUMHANSL, C. L., & JUSCZYK, P. W. (1990). Infants' perception of phrase structure in music. *Psychological Science, 1,* 70–73.

KUCZAJ, S. A., II. (1986). Thoughts on the intentional basis of early object word extension: Evidence from comprehension and production. In S. A. Kuczaj, II, & M. D. Barrett (Eds.), *The development of word meaning* (pp. 99–120). New York: Springer-Verlag.

KUCZYNSKI, L. (1984). Socialization goals and mother–child interaction: Strategies for long-term and short-term compliance. *Developmental Psychology, 20,* 1061–1073.

KUCZYNSKI, L., & HILDEBRANDT, N. (1997). Models of conformity and resistance in socialization theory. In J. E. Grusec & L. Kuczynski (Eds.), *Parenting and children's internalization of values* (pp. 227–256). New York: Wiley.

KUCZYNSKI, L., & KOCHANSKA, G. (1990). Development of children's noncompliance strategies from toddlerhood to age 5. *Developmental Psychology, 26,* 398–408.

KUCZYNSKI, L., & KOCHANSKA, G. (1995). Function and content of maternal demands: Developmental significance of early demands for competent action. *Child Development, 66,* 616–628.

KUEBLI, J., BUTLER, S., & FIVUSH, R. (1995). Mother–child talk about past emotions: relations of maternal language and child gender over time. *Cognition & Emotion, 9,* 265–283.

KUEBLI, J., & FIVUSH, R. (1992). Gender differences in parent-child conversations about past emotions. *Sex Roles, 27,* 683–698.

KUHL, P. K., WILLIAMS, K. A., LACERDA, F., STEVENS, K. N., & LINDBLOM, B. (1992). Linguistic experience alters phonetic perception in infants by 6 months of age. *Science, 255,* 606–608.

KUHN, D. (1989). Children and adults as intuitive scientists. *Psychological Review, 96,* 674–689.

KUHN, D. (1992). Cognitive development. In M. H. Bornstein & M. E. Lamb (Eds.), *Developmental psychology: An advanced textbook* (3rd ed., pp. 211–272). Hillsdale, NJ: Erlbaum.

KUHN, D. (1993). Connecting scientific and informal reasoning. *Merrill-Palmer Quarterly, 39,* 74–103.

KUHN, D. (1995). Microgenetic study of change: What has it told us? *Psychological Science, 6,* 133–139.

KUHN, D., AMSEL, E., & O'LOUGHLIN, M. (1988). *The development of scientific thinking* skills. Orlando, FL: Academic Press.

KUHN, D., GARCIA-MILA, M., ZOHAR, A., & ANDERSEN, C. (1995). Strategies of knowledge acquisition. *Monographs of the Society for Research in Child Development, 60* (245, Serial No. 4).

KUHN, D., HO, V., & ADAMS, C. (1979). Formal reasoning among pre- and late adolescents. *Child Development, 50,* 1128–1135.

KUHN, D., NASH, S. C., & BRUCKEN, L. (1978). Sex role concepts of two- and three-year-olds. *Child Development, 49,* 445–451.

KUHN, L., & STEIN, Z. (1997). Infant survival, HIV infection, and feeding alternatives in less-developed countries. *American Journal of Public Health, 87,* 926–931.

KUNZINGER, E. L., III. (1985). A short-term longitudinal study of memorial development during early grade school. *Developmental Psychology, 21,* 642–646.

KUPERSMIDT, J. B., DEROSIER, M. E., & PATTERSON, C. P. (1995). Similarity as the basis for children's friendships: The roles of sociometric status, aggressive and withdrawn behavior, academic achievement, and demographic characteristics. *Journal of Social & Personal Relationships, 12,* 439–452.

KUPERSMIDT, J. B., GRIESLER, P. C., DE ROSIER, M. E., PATTERSON, C. J., & DAVIS, P. W. (1995). Childhood aggression and peer relations in the context of family and neighborhood factors. *Child Development, 66,* 360–375.

KURDEK, L. A., & FINE, M. A. (1994). Family acceptance and family control as predictors of adjustment in young adolescents: Linear, curvilinear, or interactive effects? *Child Development, 65,* 1137–1146.

L

LABARRE, W. (1954). *The human animal.* Chicago: University of Chicago Press.

LACKEY, P. N. (1989). Adults' attitudes about assignments of household chores to male and female children. *Sex Roles, 20,* 271–281.

LADD, G. W. (1990). Having friends, keeping friends, making friends, and being liked by peers in the classroom: Predictors of children's early school adjustment? *Child Development, 61,* 1081–1100.

LADD, G. W., & CAIRNS, E. (1996). Children: Ethnic and political violence. *Child Development, 67,* 14–18.

LADD, G. W., KOCHENDERFER, B. J., & COLEMAN, C. C. (1996). Friendship quality as a predictor of young children's early school adjustment. *Child Development, 67,* 1103–1118.

LADD, G. W., KOCHENDERFER, B. J., & COLEMAN, C. C. (1997). Classroom peer acceptance, friendship, and victimization: Distinct relational systems that contribute uniquely to children's school adjustment? *Child Development, 68,* 1181–1197.

LADD, G. W., & LADD, B. K. (1998). Parenting behaviors and parent-child relationships: Correlates of peer victimization in kindergarten? *Developmental Psychology, 34,* 1450–1458.

LADD, G. W., LESIEUR, K., & PROFILET, S. M. (1993). Direct parental influences on young children's peer relations. In S. Duck (Ed.), *Learning about relationships* (Vol. 2, pp. 152–183). London: Sage.

LADD, G. W., & PRICE, J. M. (1987). Predicting children's social and school adjustment following the transition from preschool to kindergarten. *Child Development, 58,* 1168–1189.

LAGATTUTA, K. H., WELLMAN, H. M., & FLAVELL, J. H. (1997). Preschoolers' understanding of the link between thinking and feeling: Cognitive cuing and

emotional change. *Child Development, 68,* 1081–1104.

LAGERCRANTZ, H., & SLOTKIN, T. A. (1986). The "stress" of being born. *Scientific American, 254,* 100–107.

LAHEY, B. B., & LOEBER, R. (1997). Attention-deficit/hyperactivity disorder, oppositional defiant disorder, conduct disorder, and adult antisocial behavior: A life span perspective. In D. M. Stoff, J. Breiling, & J. D. Maser (Eds.), *Handbook of antisocial behavior* (pp. 51–59). New York: Wiley.

LAIRD, R. D., PETTIT, G. S., MIZE, J., & LINDSEY, E. (1994). Mother–child conversations about peers: Contributions to competence. *Family Relations, 43,* 425–432.

LAMAZE, F. (1958). *Painless childbirth.* London: Burke.

LAMB, M. E. (1987). *The father's role: Cross-cultural perspectives.* Hillsdale, NJ: Erlbaum.

LAMB, M. E. (1997). The development of father–infant relationships. In M. E. Lamb (Ed.), *The role of the father in child development* (3rd ed., pp. 104–120). New York: Wiley.

LAMB, M. E. (1998). Nonparental child care: Context, quality, correlates, and consequences. In I. E. Sigel & K. A. Renninger (Eds.), *Handbook of child psychology: Vol. 4. Child psychology in practice* (5th ed., pp. 73–133). New York: Wiley.

LAMB, M. E., & OPPENHEIM, D. (1989). Fatherhood and father–child relationships: Five years of research. In S. H. Cath, A. Gurwitt, & L. Gunsberg (Eds.), *Fathers and their families* (pp. 11–26). Hillsdale, NJ: Erlbaum.

LAMB, M. E., STERNBERG, K. J., & PRODROMIDIS, M. (1992). Nonmaternal care and the security of infant–mother attachment: A reanalysis of the data. *Infant Behavior and Development, 15,* 71–83.

LAMB, M. E., THOMPSON, R. A., GARDNER, W., CHARNOV, E. L., & CONNELL, J. P. (1985). *Infant–mother attachment: The origins and developmental significance of individual differences in Strange Situation behavior.* Hillsdale, NJ: Erlbaum.

LAMBORN, S. D., MOUNTS, N. S., STEINBERG, L., & DORNBUSCH, S. M. (1991). Patterns of competence and adjustment among adolescents from authoritative, authoritarian, indulgent, and neglectful families. *Child Development, 62,* 1049–1065.

LAMBORN, S. D., & STEINBERG, L. (1993). Emotional autonomy redux: Revisiting Ryan and Lynch. *Child Development, 64,* 483–499.

LAMPL, M. (1993). Evidence of altatory growth in infancy. *American Journal of Human Biology, 5,* 641–652.

LAMPL, M., VELDHUIS, J. D., & JOHNSON, M. L. (1992). Saltation and stasis: A model of human growth. *Science, 258,* 801–803.

LANCASTER, J. B., & WHITTEN, P. (1980). Family matters. *The Sciences, 20,* 10–15.

LANDAU, R. (1982). Infant crying and fussing. *Journal of Cross-Cultural Psychology, 13,* 427–443.

LANDAU, S., LORCH, E. P., & MILICH, R. (1992). Visual attention to and comprehension of television in attention-deficit hyperactivity disordered and normal boys. *Child Development, 63,* 928–937.

LANDER, E. S. (1996). The new genomics: Global views of biology. *Science, 274,* 536–539.

LANDER, J., BRADY-FRYER, B., METCALFE, J. B., NAZARALI, S., & MUTTITT, S. (1997). Comparison of ring block, dorsal penile nerve block, and topical anesthesia for neonatal circumcision. *Journal of the Amercian Medical Association, 279,* 1170–1171.

LANDESMAN, S., & RAMEY, C. (1989). Developmental psychology and mental retardation: Integrating scientific principles with treatment practices. *American Psychologist, 44,* 409–415.

LANDRY, S. H., GARNER, P. W., SWANK, P. R., & BALDWIN, C. D. (1996). Effects of maternal scaffolding during joint toy play with preterm and full-term infants. *Merrill-Palmer Quarterly, 42,* 177–199.

LANDRY, S. H., & WHITNEY, J. A. (1996). The impact of prenatal cocaine exposure: Studies of the developing infant. *Seminars in Perinatology, 20,* 99–106.

LANE, D. M., & PEARSON, D. A. (1982). The development of selective attention. *Merrill-Palmer Quarterly, 28,* 317–337.

LANGE, G., & CARROLL, D. E. (1997, April). *Relationships between mother–child interaction styles and children's laboratory memory for narrative and non-narrative materials.* Paper presented at the biennial meeting of the Society for Research in Child Development, Washington, DC.

LANGE, G., & PIERCE, S. H. (1992). Memory-strategy learning and maintenance in preschool children. *Developmental Psychology, 28,* 453–462.

LANGLOIS, J. H., & DOWNS, A. C. (1979). Peer relations as a function of physical attractiveness: The eye of the beholder or behavioral reality? *Child Development, 50,* 409–418.

LANGLOIS, J. H., & DOWNS, A. C. (1980). Mothers, fathers, and peers as socialization agents of sex-typed play behaviors in young children. *Child Development, 51*, 1237–1247.

LANGLOIS, J. H., & STEPHAN, C. W. (1981). Beauty and the beast: The role of physical attractiveness in peer relationships and social behavior. In S. S. Brehm, S. M. Kassin, & S. X. Gibbons (Eds.), *Developmental social psychology: Theory and research* (pp. 152–168). New York: Oxford University Press.

LANGLOIS, J. H., RITTER, J. M., CASEY, R. J., & SAWIN, D. B. (1995). Infant attractiveness predicts maternal behaviors and attitudes. *Developmental Psychology, 31*, 464–472.

LANGLOIS, J. H., RITTER, J. M., ROGGMAN, L. A., & VAUGHN, L. S. (1991). Facial diversity and infant preferences for attractive faces. *Developmental Psychology, 27*, 79–84.

LANGLOIS, J. H., ROGGMAN, L. A., & RIESER-DANNER, L. A. (1990). Infants' differential social responses to attractive and unattractive faces. *Developmental Psychology, 26*, 153–159.

LANGLOIS, J. H., & STYCZYNSKI, L. E. (1979). The effects of physical attractiveness on the behavioral attributions and peer preferences of acquainted children. *International Journal of Behavioral Development, 2*, 325–342.

LAPOINTE, A. E., ASKEW, J. M., & MEAD, N. A. (1992). *Learning mathematics.* Princeton, NJ: Educational Testing Service.

LAPOINTE, A. E., MEAD, N. A., & ASKEW, J. M. (1992). *Learning science.* Princeton, NJ: Educational Testing Service.

LAPSLEY, D. K. (1993). Toward an integrated theory of adolescent ego development: The "new look" at adolescent egocentrism. *American Journal of Orthopsychiatry, 63*, 562–571.

LAPSLEY, D. K., JACKSON, S., RICE, K., & SHADID, G. (1988). Self-monitoring and the "new look" at the imaginary audience and personal fable: An ego-developmental analysis. *Journal of Adolescent Research, 3*, 17–31.

LAPSLEY, D. K., MILSTEAD, M., QUINTANA, S., FLANNERY, D., & BUSS, R. (1986). Adolescent egocentrism and formal operations: Tests of a theoretical assumption. *Developmental Psychology, 22*, 800–807.

LARSON, D. E. (1996). *Mayo Clinic family health book.* New York: Morrow.

LARSON, R., & HAM, M. (1993). Stress and "storm and stress" in early adolescence: The relationship of negative events with dysphoric affect. *Developmental Psychology, 29*, 130–140.

LARSON, R., & LAMPMAN-PETRAITIS, C. (1989). Daily emotional states as reported by children and adolescents. *Child Development, 60*, 1250–1260.

LARSON, R. W., RICHARDS, M. H., MONETA, G., HOLMBECK, G., & DUCKETT, E. (1996). Changes in adolescents' daily interactions with their families from ages 10 to 18: Disengagement and transformation. *Developmental Psychology, 32*, 744–754.

LARZELERE, R. E., SCHNEIDER, W. N., LARSON, D. B., & PIKE, P. L. (1996). The effects of discipline responses in delaying toddler midbehavior recurrences. *Child & Family Behavior Therapy, 18*, 35–57.

LAUCHT, M., ESSER, G., & SCHMIDT, M. H. (1997). Developmental outcome of infants born with biological and psychosocial risks. *Journal of Child Psychology and Psychiatry, 38*, 843–853.

LAUDENSLAGER, M. L., & REITE, M. R. (1984). Loss and separations: Immunological consequences and health implications. In P. Shaver (Ed.), *Review of personality and social psychology* (Vol. 5, pp. 285–311). Beverly Hills, CA: Sage.

LAUPA, M. (1991). Children's reasoning about three authority attributes: Adult status, knowledge, and social position. *Developmental Psychology, 27*, 321–329.

LAUPA, M. (1995). "Who's in charge?" Preschool children's concepts of authority. *Early Childhood Research Quarterly, 9*, 1–7.

LAURSEN, B., HARTUP, W. W., & KOPLAS, A. L. (1996). Toward understanding peer conflict. *Merrill-Palmer Quarterly, 42*, 76–102.

LAZAR, A., & TORNEY-PURTA, J. (1991). The development of the subconcepts of death in young children: A short-term longitudinal study. *Child Development, 62*, 1321–1333.

LAZAR, I., & DARLINGTON, R. (1982). Lasting effects of early education: A report from the Consortium for Longitudinal Studies. *Monographs of the Society for Research in Child Development, 47* (2–3, Serial No. 195).

LAZARUS, R. (1991). *Emotion and adaptation.* New York: Oxford University Press.

LEMARE, L. J., & RUBIN, K. H. (1987). Perspective taking and peer interaction: Structural and developmental analyses. *Child Development, 58*, 306–315.

LEPORE, P. C., & WARREN, J. R. (1997). A comparison of single-sex and coeducational Catholic secondary schooling: Evidence from the National Educational Longitudinal Study of 1988. *American Educational Research Journal, 34*, 485–511.

LEVAY, S. (1993). *The sexual brain.* Cambridge, MA: MIT Press.

LEVINE, R. A., DIXON, S., LEVINE, S., RICHMAN, A., LEIDERMAN, P. H., KEEFER, C. H., & BRAZELTON, T. B. (1994). *Child care and culture: Lessons from Africa.* New York: Cambridge University Press.

LEAHY, R. L., & EITER, M. (1980). Moral judgment and the development of real and ideal androgynous self-image derived from adult temperament. *Child Development, 56*, 1314–1325.

LEAPER, C. (1994). Exploring the correlates and consequences of gender segregation: Social relationships in childhood, adolescence, and adulthood. In C. Leaper (Ed.), *New directions for child development* (No. 65, pp. 67–86). San Francisco: Jossey-Bass.

LEAPER, C., ANDERSON, K. J., & SANDERS, P. (1998). Moderators of gender effects on parents' talk to their children: A meta-analysis. *Developmental Psychology, 34*, 3–27.

LEE, C. L., & BATES, J. E. (1985). Mother–child interaction at age two years and perceived difficult temperament. *Child Development, 56*, 1314–1325.

LEE, K., CAMERON, C., XU, F., FU, G., & BOARD, J. (1997). Chinese and Canadian children's evaluations of lying and truth telling: Similarities and differences in the context of pro- and anti-social behaviors. *Child Development, 68*, 924–934.

LEE, S. H., EWERT, D. P., FREDERICK, P. D., & MASCOLA, L. (1992). Resurgence of congenital rubella syndrome in the 1990s. *Journal of the American Medical Association, 267*, 2616–2620.

LEE, V. E., BROOKS-GUNN, J., & SCHNUR, E. (1988). Does Head Start work? A 1-year follow-up comparison of disadvantaged children attending Head Start, no preschool, and other preschool programs. *Developmental Psychology, 24*, 210–222.

LEE, V. E., BROOKS-GUNN, J., SCHNUR, E., & LIAW, F. (1990). Are Head Start effects sustained? A longitudinal follow-up comparison of disadvantaged children attending Head Start, no preschool, and other preschool programs. *Child Development, 61*, 495–507.

LEE, V. E., & LOEB, S. (1995). Where do Head Start attendees end up? One reason preschool effects fade out. *Educational Evaluation & Policy Analysis, 17*, 62–82.

LEE, V. E., & SMITH, J. B. (1995). Effects of high school restructuring and size on early gains in achievement and engagement. *Sociology of Education, 68*, 241–270.

LEEKAM, S. (1993). Children's understanding of mind. In M. Bennett (Ed.), *The development of social cognition* (pp. 26–61). New York: Guilford.

LEEMAN, L. W., GIBBS, J. C., & FULLER, D. (1993). Evaluation of a multi-component group treatment program for juvenile delinquents. *Aggressive Behavior, 19*, 281–292.

LEFKOWITZ, M. M., ERON, L. D., WALDER, L. O., & HUESMANN, L. R. (1972). Television violence and child aggression: A follow-up study. In G. A. Comstock & E. A. Rubinstein (Eds.), *Television and social behavior* (Vol. 3, pp. 35–135). Washington, DC: U.S. Government Printing Office.

LEHMAN, D. R., & NISBETT, R. E. (1990). A longitudinal study of the effects of undergraduate training on reasoning. *Developmental Psychology, 26*, 952–960.

LEHNERT, K. L., OVERHOLSER, J. C., & SPIRITO, A. (1994). Internalized and externalized anger in adolescent suicide attempters. *Journal of Adolescent Research, 9*, 105–119.

LEICHTMAN, M. D., & CECI, S. J. (1995). The effect of stereotypes and suggestions on preschoolers' reports. *Developmental Psychology, 31*, 568–578.

LEMERY, K. S., GOLDSMITH, H. H., KLINNERT, M. D., & MRAZEK, D. A. (1999). Developmental models of infant and childhood temperament. *Developmental Psychology, 35*, 189–204.

LEMPERT, H. (1990). Acquisition of passives: The role of patient animacy, salience, and lexical accessibility. *Journal of Child Language, 17*, 677–696.

LENNEBERG, E. H. (1967). *Biological foundations of language.* New York: Wiley.

LEONARD, M. F., RHYMES, J. P., & SOLNIT, A. J. (1986). Failure to thrive in infants: A family problem. *American Journal of Diseases of Children, 111*, 600–612.

LERMAN, R. I. (1993). A national profile of young unwed fathers. In R. I. Lerman & T. J. Ooms (Eds.), *Young unwed fathers* (pp. 27–51). Philadelphia: Temple University Press.

LERNER, J. V., & ABRAMS, A. (1994). Developmental correlates of maternal employment influences on children. In C. B. Fisher & R. M. Lerner (Eds.), *Applied developmental psychology* (pp. 174–206). New York: McGraw-Hill.

LERNER, R. M., OSTROM, C. W., & FREEL, M. A. (1997). *Preventing health-compromising behaviors among youth and promoting their positive development: A de-*

velopmental contextual perspective (pp. 522–546). New York: Cambridge University Press.

LERNER, R. M., & SCHROEDER, C. (1971). Physique identification, preference, and aversion in kindergarten children. *Developmental Psychology, 5*, 538.

LESTER, B. M. (1985). Introduction: There's more to crying than meets the ear. In B. M. Lester & C. F. Z. Boukydis (Eds.), *Infant crying* (pp. 1–27). New York: Plenum.

LESTER, B. M. (1987). Developmental outcome prediction from acoustic cry analysis in term and preterm infants. *Pediatrics, 80*, 529–534.

LESTER, B. M., & DREHER, M. (1989). Effects of marijuana use during pregnancy on newborn cry. *Child Development, 60*, 765–771.

LESTER, B. M., KOTELCHUCK, M., SPELKE, E., SELLERS, M. J., & KLEIN, R. E. (1974). Separation protest in Guatemalan infants: Cross-cultural and cognitive findings. *Developmental Psychology, 10*, 79–85.

LEUNG, M-C. (1996). Social networks and self-enhancement in Chinese children: A comparison of self reports and peer reports of group membership. *Social Development, 5*, 146–157.

LEVESQUE, R. J. R. (1996). International children's rights: Can they make a difference in American family policy? *American Psychologist, 51*, 1251–1256.

LEVIN, S. R., PETROS, T. V., & PETRELLA, F. W. (1982). Preschoolers' awareness of television advertising. *Child Development, 53*, 933–937.

LEVINE, L. E. (1983). Mine: Self-definition in 2-year-old boys. *Developmental Psychology, 19*, 544–549.

LEVINE, L. J. (1995). Young children's understanding of the causes of anger and sadness. *Child Development, 66*, 697–709.

LEVITT, A. G., & UTMANN, J. G. A. (1992). From babbling towards the sound systems of English and French: A longitudinal two-case study. *Journal of Child Language, 19*, 19–49.

LEVY, G. D., TAYLOR, M. G., & GELMAN, S. A. (1995). Traditional and evaluative aspects of flexibility in gender roles, social conventions, moral rules, and physical laws. *Child Development, 66*, 515–531.

LEVY, Y. (1996). Modularity of language reconsidered. *Brain and Language, 55*, 240–263.

LEVY-SHIFF, R. (1994). Individual and contextual correlates of marital change across the transition to parenthood. *Developmental Psychology, 30*, 591–601.

LEVY-SHIFF, R., & ISRAELASHVILI, R. (1988). Antecedents of fathering: Some further exploration. *Developmental Psychology, 24*, 434–440.

LEW, A. R., & BUTTERWORTH, G. (1997). The development of hand–mouth coordination in 2- to 5-month-old infants: Similarities with reaching and grasping. *Infant Behavior and Development, 20*, 59–69.

LEWIS, C., FREEMAN, N. H., KYRIADIDOU, C., MARIDAKIKASSOTAKI, K., & BERRIDGE, D. M. (1996). Social influences on false belief access—specific sibling influences or general apprenticeship? *Child Development, 67*, 2930–2947.

LEWIS, C. C. (1981). The effects of parental firm control: A reinterpretation of findings. *Psychological Bulletin, 90*, 547–563.

LEWIS, M. (1992). *Shame: The exposed self.* New York: Free Press.

LEWIS, M. (1994). Myself and me. In S. T. Parker, R. W. Mitchell, & M. L. Boccia (Eds.), *Self-awareness in animals and humans: Developmental perspectives* (pp. 20–34). New York: Cambridge University Press.

LEWIS, M. (1995). Cognition-emotion feedback and the self-organization of developmental paths. *Human Development, 38*, 71–102.

LEWIS, M. (1997). *Altering fate: Why the past does not predict the future.* New York: Guilford.

LEWIS, M., ALESSANDRI, S. M., & SULLIVAN, M. W. (1992). Differences in shame and pride as a function of children's gender and task difficulty. *Child Development, 63*, 630–638.

LEWIS, M., & BROOKS-GUNN, J. (1979). *Social cognition and the acquisition of self.* New York: Plenum.

LEWIS, M., RAMSAY, D. S., & KAWAKAMI, K. (1993). Differences between Japanese infants and Caucasian American infants in behavioral and cortisol response to inoculation. *Child Development, 64*, 1722–1731.

LEWIS, M., SULLIVAN, M. W., & RAMSAY, D. S. (1992). Individual differences in anger and sad expressions during extinction: Antecedents and consequences. *Infant Behavior and Development, 15*, 443–452.

LEWIS, M., SULLIVAN, M. W., STANGER, C., & WEISS, M. (1989). Self development and self-conscious emotions. *Child Development, 60*, 146–156.

LEWIS, M., SULLIVAN, M. W., & VASEN, A. (1987). Making faces: Age and emotion differences in the posing of emotional expressions. *Developmental Psychology, 23*, 690–697.

LEWONTIN, R. C. (1976). Race and intelligence. In N. J. Block & G. Dworkin (Eds.), *The IQ controversy* (pp. 78–92). New York: Pantheon Books.

LIAU, A. K., BARRIGA, A. Q., & GIBBS, J. C. (1998). Relations between self-serving cognitive distortion and overt vs. covert antisocial behavior in adolescents. *Aggressive Behavior, 24*, 335–346.

LIAW, F., & BROOKS-GUNN, J. (1993). Patterns of low-birth-weight children's cognitive development. *Developmental Psychology, 29*, 1024–1035.

LIBEN, L. S., & DOWNS, R. M. (1989). Understanding maps as symbols: The development of map concepts in children. In H. W. Reese (Ed.), *Advances in child development and behavior* (Vol. 22, pp. 146–202). San Diego: Academic Press.

LIBEN, L. S., & SIGNORELLA, M. L. (1993). Gender-schematic processing in children: The role of initial interpretations of stimuli. *Developmental Psychology, 29*, 141–149.

LIBEN, L. S., & YEKEL, C. A. (1996). Preschoolers' understanding of plan and oblique maps: The role of geometric and representational correspondence. *Child Development, 67*, 2780–2796.

LICKONA, T. (1976). Research on Piaget's theory of moral development. In T. Lickona (Ed.), *Moral development and behavior* (pp. 219–240). New York: Holt, Rinehart & Winston.

LIDZ, C. S. (1991). *Practitioner's guide to dynamic assessment.* New York: Guilford.

LIDZ, C. S. (1997). Dynamic assessment: Psychoeducational assessment with cultural sensitivity. *Journal of Social Distress and the Homeless, 6*, 95–111.

LIFSCHITZ, M., BERMAN, D., GALILI, A., & GILAD, D. (1977). Bereaved children: The effects of mother's perception and social system organization on their short-range adjustment. *Journal of Child Psychiatry, 16*, 272–284.

LIGHT, P., & PERRETT-CLERMONT, A. (1989). Social context effects in learning and testing. In A. R. H. Gellatly, D. Rogers, & J. Sloboda (Eds.), *Cognition and social worlds* (pp. 99–112). Oxford: Clarendon Press.

LILLARD, A. S. (1998). Playing with a theory of mind. In O. N. Saracho & B. Spodek (Eds.), *Multiple perspectives on play in early childhood education* (pp. 11–33). Albany: State University of New York Press.

LIMBER, S. P., & WILCOX, B. L. (1996). Application of the U. N. Convention on the Rights of the Child to the United States. *American Psychologist, 51*, 1246–1250.

LINN, F. L., & BAKER, E. L. (1996). Can performance-based student assessments be psychometrically sound? In J. B. Baron & D. P. Wolf (Eds.), *Performance-based student assessment: Challenges and possibilities, 95th yearbook of the National Society for the Study of Education, Part I* (pp. 84–103). Chicago: University of Chicago Press.

LINN, M. C., & HYDE, J. S. (1989). Gender, mathematics, and science. *Educational Researcher, 18*, 17–27.

LINN, M. C., & PETERSEN, A. C. (1985). Emergence and characterization of sex differences in spatial ability: A meta-analysis. *Child Development, 56*, 1479–1498.

LIPSITT, L. P. (1990). Learning and memory in infants. *Merrill-Palmer Quarterly, 36*, 53–66.

LISS, M. B., REINHARDT, L. C., & FREDRIKSEN, S. (1983). TV heroes: The impact of rhetoric and deeds. *Journal of Applied Developmental Psychology, 4*, 175–187.

LISSENS, W., & SERMON, K. (1997). Preimplantation genetic diagnosis—Current status and new developments. *Human Reproduction, 12*, 1756–1761.

LITOVSKY, R. Y., & ASHMEAD, D. H. (1997). Development of binaural and spatial hearing in infants and children. In R. H. Gilkey & T. R. Anderson (Eds.), *Binaural and spatial hearing in real and virtual environments* (pp. 571–592). Mahwah, NJ: Erlbaum.

LITOWITZ, B. (1977). Learning to make definitions. *Journal of Child Language, 8*, 165–175.

LIVESLEY, W. J., & BROMLEY, D. B. (1973). *Person perception in childhood and adolescence.* New York: Wiley.

LIVSON, N., & PESHKIN, H. (1980). Perspectives on adolescence from longitudinal research. In J. Adelson (Ed.), *Handbook of adolescent psychology* (pp. 47–98). New York: Wiley.

LLOYD, B., & SMITH, C. (1985). The social representation of gender and young children's play. *British Journal of Developmental Psychology, 3*, 65–73.

LLOYD, P., BOADA, H., & FORNS, H. (1992). New directions in referential communication research. *British Journal of Developmental Psychology, 10*, 385–403.

LOBEL, T. E., & MENASHRI, J. (1993). Relations of conceptions of gender-role transgressions and gender constancy to gender-typed toy preferences. *Developmental Psychology, 29*, 150–155.

LOCHMAN, J. E., COIE, J. D., UNDERWOOD, M. K., & TERRY, R. (1993). Effectiveness of a social relations intervention program for aggressive and nonaggressive, rejected children. *Journal of Consulting and Clinical Psychology, 61,* 1053–1058.

LOCKE, J. (1892). Some thoughts concerning education. In R. H. Quick (Ed.), *Locke on education* (pp. 1–236). Cambridge: Cambridge University Press. (Original work published 1690)

LOCKHART, R. S., & CRAIK, F. I. M. (1990). Levels of processing: A retrospective commentary on a framework for memory research. *Canadian Journal of Psychology, 44,* 87–112.

LOCKHEED, M. E. (1986). Reshaping the social order: The case of gender segregation. *Sex Roles, 14,* 617–628.

LOCKHEED, M. E., & HARRIS, A. M. (1984). Cross-sex collaborative learning in elementary classrooms. *American Educational Research Journal, 21,* 275–294.

LOEBER, R., & SCHMALING, K. B. (1985). Empirical evidence for overt and covert patterns of antisocial conduct problems: A meta-analysis. *Journal of Abnormal Child Psychology, 11,* 1–14.

LOEBER, R., & STOUTHAMER-LOEBER, M. (1998). Development of juvenile aggression and violence: Some common misconceptions and controversies. *American Psychologist, 53,* 242–259.

LOEHLIN, J. C. (1992). *Genes and environment in personality development.* Newbury Park, CA: Sage.

LOEHLIN, J. C., HORN, J. M., & WILLERMAN, L. (1997). Heredity, environment, and IQ in the Texas Adoption Project. In R. J. Sternberg & E. L. Grigorenko (Eds.), *Intelligence, heredity, and environment* (pp. 105–125). New York: Cambridge University Press.

LOEHLIN, J. C., WILLERMAN, L., & HORN, J. M. (1988). Human behavior genetics. *Annual Review of Psychology, 38,* 101–133.

LOMBARDI, J. (1993). Looking at the child care landscape. *Pediatrics, 91,* 179–188.

LONIGAN, C. J., & WHITEHURST, G. J. (1998). Relative efficacy of parent and teacher involvement in a shared-reading intervention for preschool children from low-income backgrounds. *Early Childhood Research Quarterly, 13,* 263–290.

LORENZ, K. Z. (1943). Die angeborenen Formen möglicher Erfahrung. *Zeitschrift für Tierpsychologie, 5,* 235–409.

LORENZ, K. Z. (1952). *King Solomon's ring.* New York: Crowell.

LOSEY, K. M. (1995). Mexican-American students and classroom interaction: An overview and critique. *Review of Educational Research, 65,* 283–318.

LOZOFF, B. (1989). Nutrition and behavior. *American Psychologist, 44,* 231–236.

LOZOFF, B., ASKEW, G. L., & WOLF, A. W. (1996). Cosleeping and early childhood sleep problems: Effects of ethnicity and socioeconomic status. *Developmental and Behavioral Pediatrics, 17,* 9–15.

LOZOFF, B., KLEIN, N. K., NELSON, E. C., McCLISH, D. K., MANUEL, M., & CHACON, M. E. (1998). Behavior of infants with iron-deficiency anemia. *Child Development, 69,* 24–36.

LOZOFF, B., WOLF, A., LATZ, S., & PALUDETTO, R. (1995, March). *Cosleeping in Japan, Italy, and the U.S.: Autonomy versus interpersonal relatedness.* Paper presented at the biennial meeting of the Society for Research in Child Development, Indianapolis.

LUBART, T. I. (1994). Creativity. In R. J. Sternberg (Ed.), *Thinking and problem solving* (pp. 289–332). San Diego: Academic Press.

LUBART, T. I., & STERNBERG, R. J. (1995). An investment approach to creativity: Theory and data. In S. M. Smith, T. B. Ward, & R. A. Finke (Eds.), *The creative cognition approach* (pp. 271–302). Cambridge, MA: MIT Press.

LUBINSKI, D., & BENBOW, C. P. (1994). The study of mathematically precocious youth: The first three decades of a planned 50-year study of intellectual talent. In R. F. Subotnik & K. D. Arnold (Eds.), *Beyond Terman: Contemporary longitudinal studies of giftedness and talent* (pp. 255–281). Norwood, NJ: Ablex.

LUCARIELLO, J., (1988). Together wherever we go: The ethnographic child and the developmentalist. *Child Development, 69,* 355–358.

LUCARIELLO, J., KYRATZIS, A., & NELSON, K. (1992). Taxonomic knowledge: What kind and when? *Child Development, 63,* 978–998.

LUCARIELLO, J., & MINDOLOVICH, C. (1995). The development of complex metarepresentations reasoning: The case of situational irony. *Cognitive Development, 10,* 551–576.

LUDEMANN, P. M. (1991). Generalized discrimination of positive facial expressions by seven- and ten-month-old infants. *Child Development, 62,* 55–67.

LUECKE-ALEKSA, D., ANDERSON, D. R., COLLINS, P. A., & SCHMITT, K. L. (1995). Gender constancy and television viewing. *Developmental Psychology, 31,* 773–780.

LUEPTOW, L. B., GAROVICH, L., & LUEPTOW, M. B. (1997). The

persistence of gender stereotypes in the face of changing seucariello, J., & Nelson, K. (1985). Slot-filler categories as memory organizers for young children. *Developmental Psychology, 21,* 272–282.

LUKER, K. (1996). *Dubious conceptions: The politics of teenage pregnancy.* Cambridge, MA: Harvard University Press.

LUMMIS, M., & STEVENSON, H. W. (1990). Gender differences in beliefs about achievement: A cross-cultural study. *Developmental Psychology, 26,* 254–263.

LURIA, A. R. (1976). *Cognitive development: Its cultural and social foundations.* Cambridge, MA: Harvard University Press.

LUSTER, T., & DUBOW, E. (1992). Home environment and maternal intelligence as predictors of verbal intelligence: A comparison of preschool and school-age children. *Merrill-Palmer Quarterly, 38,* 151–175.

LUSTER, T., & McADOO, H. (1996). Family and child influences on educational attainment: A secondary analysis of the High/Scope Perry Preschool data. *Developmental Psychology, 32,* 26–39.

LUSTER, T., RHOADES, K., & HAAS, B. (1989). The relation between parental values and parenting behavior. Journal of Marriage and the Family, 51, 139–147.

LUTHAR, S. S., & CUSHING, G. (1997). Substance use and personal adjustment among disadvantaged teenagers: A six-month prospective study. *Journal of Youth and Adolescence, 26,* 353–372.

LUTHAR, S. S., CUSHING, T. J., & McMAHON, T. J. (1997). Interdisciplinary interface: Developmental principles brought to substance abuse research. In S. S. Luthar, J. A. Burack, D. Cicchetti, & J. R. Weisz, *Developmental psychopathology* (pp. 437–456). Cambridge: Cambridge University Press.

LUTHAR, S. S., & ZIGLER, E. (1991). Vulnerability and competence: A review of research on resilience in childhood. *American Journal of Orthopsychiatry, 6,* 6–22.

LUTZ, S. E., & RUBLE, D. N. (1995). Children and gender prejudice: Context, motivation, and the development of gender conception. In R. Vasta (Ed.), *Annals of child development* (Vol. 10, pp. 131–166). London: Jessica Kingsley.

LYON, T. D., & FLAVELL, J. H. (1994). Young children's understanding of "remember" and "forget." *Child Development, 65,* 1357–1371.

LYONS-RUTH, K., & BLOCK, D. (1996). The disturbed caregiv-

ing system: Relations among childhood trauma, maternal caregiving, and infant affect and attachment. *Infant Mental Health Journal, 17,* 257–275.

LYONS-RUTH, K., CONNELL, D. B., GRUNEBAUM, H. U., & BOTEIN, S. (1990). Infants at social risk: Maternal depression and family support services as mediators of infant development and security of attachment. *Child Development, 61,* 85–98.

LYOO, K., NOAM, G. G., LEE, C. K., LEE, H. K., KENNEDY, B. P., & RENSHAW, P. F. (1996). The corpus callosum and lateral ventricles in children with attention-deficit hyperactivity disorder: A brain magnetic resonance imaging study. *Biological Psychiatry, 40,* 1060–1063.

LYTTON, H., & ROMNEY, D. M. (1991). Parents' sex-related differential socialization of boys and girls: A meta-analysis. *Psychological Bulletin, 109,* 267–296.

MACCOBY, E. E. (1984). Socialization and developmental change. *Child Development, 55,* 317–328.

MACCOBY, E. E. (1988). Gender as a social category. *Developmental Psychology, 24,* 755–765.

MACCOBY, E. E. (1990a). Gender and relationships. *American Psychologist, 45,* 513–520.

MACCOBY, E. E. (1990b). The role of gender identity and gender constancy in sex-differentiated development. In D. Schrader (Ed.), *New directions for child development* (No. 47, pp. 5–20). San Francisco: Jossey-Bass.

MACCOBY, E. E., & JACKLIN, C. N. (1987). Gender segregation in childhood. In E. H. Reese (Ed.), *Advances in child development and behavior* (Vol. 20, pp. 239–287). New York: Academic Press.

MACCOBY, E. E., & MARTIN, J. A. (1983). Socialization in the context of the family. In E. M. Hetherington (Ed.), *Handbook of Child Psychology: Vol. 4. Socialization, personality, and social development* (pp. 1–101). New York: Wiley.

MACFARLANE, J. (1971). From infancy to adulthood. In M. C. Jones, N. Bayley, J. W. Macfarlane, & M. P. Honzik (Eds.), *The course of human development* (pp. 406–410). Waltham, MA: Xerox College Publishing.

MACKEY, M. C. (1995). Women's evaluation of their childbirth performance. *Maternal—Child Nursing Journal, 23,* 57–72.

MacKinnon, C. E. (1989). An observational investigation of sibling interactions in married and divorced families. *Developmental Psychology, 25,* 36–44.

MacKinnon-Lewis, C., Starnes, R., Volling, B., & Johnson, S. (1997). Perceptions of parenting as predictors of boys' sibling and peer relations. *Developmental Psychology, 33,* 1024–1031.

MacMillan, D. L., Keogh, B. K., & Jones, R. L. (1986). Special educational research on mildly handicapped learners. In M. C. Wittrock (Ed.), *Handbook of research on teaching* (3rd ed., pp. 686–724). New York: Macmillan.

Macrides, R., Bartke, A., & Dalterio, S. (1975). Strange females increase plasma testosterone levels in male mice. *Science, 189,* 1104–1105.

Madon, S., Jussim, L., & Eccles, J. (1997). In search of the powerful self-fulfilling prophecy. *Journal of Personality and Social Psychology, 72,* 791–809.

Maggs, J. L., Schulenberg, J., & Hurrelmann, K. (1997). Developmental transitions during adolescence: Health promotion implications. In J. Schulenberg, J. L. Maggs, & K. Hurrelmann (Eds.), *Health risks and developmental transitions during adolescence* (pp. 522–546). New York: Cambridge University Press.

Magnusson, D., & Stattin, H. (1998). Person-context interaction theories. In R. M. Lerner (Ed.), *Handbook of child psychology: Vol. 1. Theoretical models of human development* (5th ed., pp. 685–759). New York: Wiley.

Magura, S., & Laudet, A. B. (1996). Parental substance abuse and child maltreatment: Review and implications for intervention. *Children and Youth Services Review, 18,* 193–220.

Mahoney, J. L., & Cairns, R. B. (1997). Do extracurricular activities protect against early school dropout? *Developmental Psychology, 33,* 241–253.

Main, M., & Cassidy, J. (1988). Categories of response to reunion with the parent at age 6: Predictable from infant attachment classifications and stable over a 1-month period. *Developmental Psychology, 24,* 415–426.

Main, M., & Goldwyn, R. (1994). *Interview-based adult attachment classifications: Related to infant–mother and infant–father attachment.* Unpublished manuscript, University of California, Berkeley.

Main, M., & Solomon, J. (1990). Procedures for identifying infants as disorganized/disoriented during the Ainsworth Strange Situation. In M. Greenberg, D. Cicchetti, & M. Cummings (Eds.), *Attachment in the preschool years: Theory, research, and intervention* (pp. 121–160). Chicago: University of Chicago Press.

Makin, J. W., Fried, P. A., & Watkinson, B. (1991). A comparison of active and passive smoking during pregnancy: Long-term effects. *Neurotoxicology and Teratology, 13,* 5–12.

Makin, J. W., & Porter, R. H. (1989). Attractiveness of lactating females' breast odors to neonates. *Child Development, 60,* 803–810.

Malatesta, C. Z., & Haviland, J. M. (1982). Learning display rules: The socialization of emotion expression in infancy. *Child Development, 53,* 991–1003.

Malatesta, C. Z., Grigoryev, P., Lamb, C., Albin, M., & Culver, C. (1986). Emotion socialization and expressive development in preterm and full-term infants. *Child Development, 57,* 316–330.

Malatesta-Magai, C. Z., Izard, C. E., & Camras, L. A. (1991). Conceptualizing early infant affect: Emotions as fact, fiction or artifact? In K. Strongman (Ed.), *International review of studies on emotion* (pp. 1–36). New York: Wiley.

Malina, R. M. (1975). *Growth and development: The first twenty years in man.* Minneapolis: Burgess Publishing.

Malina, R. M. (1990). Physical growth and performance during the transition years (9–16). In R. Montemayor, G. R. Adams, & T. P. Gullotta (Eds.), *From childhood to adolescence: A transitional period?* (pp. 41–62). Newbury Park, CA: Sage.

Malina, R. M., & Bouchard, C. (1991). *Growth, maturation, and physical activity.* Champaign, IL: Human Kinetics.

Malloy, M. H., & Hoffman, H. J. (1995). Prematurity, sudden infant death syndrome, and age of death. *Pediatrics, 96,* 464–471.

Maloney, M., & Kranz, R. (1991). *Straight talk about eating disorders.* New York: Facts on File.

Mandler, J. M. (1984). *Stories, scripts, and scenes: Aspects of schema theory.* Hillsdale, NJ: Erlbaum.

Mandler, J. M. (1992a). The foundations of conceptual thought in infancy. *Cognitive Development, 7,* 273–285.

Mandler, J. M. (1992b). How to build a baby: II. Conceptual primitives. *Psychological Review, 99,* 587–604.

Mandler, J. M. (1998). Representation. In D. Kuhn & R. S. Siegler (Eds.), *Handbook of child psychology: Vol. 2. Cognition, perception, and language* (5th ed., pp. 255–308). New York: Wiley.

Mandler, J. M., Bauer, P. J., & McDonough, L. (1991). Separating the sheep from the goats: Differentiating global categories. *Cognitive Psychology, 23,* 263–298.

Mandler, J. M., & McDonough, L. (1993). Concept formation in infancy. *Cognitive Development, 8,* 291–318.

Mandler, J. M., & McDonough, L. (1996). Drinking and driving don't mix: Inductive generalization in infancy. *Cognition, 59,* 307–335.

Mandler, J. M., & McDonough, L. (1998). On developing a knowledge base in infancy. *Developmental Psychology, 34,* 1274–1288.

Mandler, J. M., & Robinson, C. A. (1978). Developmental changes in picture recognition. *Journal of Experimental Child Psychology, 26,* 122–136.

Mange, E. J., & Mange, A. P. (1994). *Basic human genetics.* Sunderland, MA: Sinauer Associates.

Mangelsdorf, S. C., Gunnar, M., Kestenbaum, R., Lang, S., & Andreas, D. (1990). Infant proneness-to-distress temperament, maternal personality, and mother–infant attachment: Associations and goodness of fit. *Child Development, 61,* 830–831.

Mant, C. M., & Perner, J. (1988). The child's understanding of commitment. *Developmental Psychology, 24,* 343–351.

Maqsud, M. (1977). The influence of social heterogeneity and sentimental credibility on moral judgments of Nigerian Muslim adolescents. *Journal of Cross-Cultural Psychology, 8,* 113–122.

Maratsos, M. (1998). The acquisition of grammar. In D. Kuhn & R. S. Siegler (Eds.), *Handbook of child psychology: Vol. 2. Cognition, perception and language* (5th ed., pp. 421–466). New York: Wiley.

Maratsos, M. P. (1983). Some current issues in the study of the acquisition of grammar. In P. H. Mussen (Ed.), *Handbook of child psychology* (Vol. 3, pp. 707–786). New York: Wiley.

Maratsos, M. P., & Chalkley, M. A. (1980). The internal

language of children's syntax: The ontogenesis and representation of syntactic categories. In K. Nelson (Ed.), *Children's language* (Vol. 2, pp. 127–214). New York: Gardner Press.

Marcia, J. E. (1980). Identity in adolescence. In J. Adelson (Ed.), *Handbook of adolescent psychology* (pp. 159–187). New York: Wiley.

Marcia, J. E., Waterman, A. S., Matteson, D. R., Archer, S. L., & Orlofsky, J. L. (1993). *Ego identity: A handbook for psychosocial research.* New York: Springer-Verlag.

Marcus, G. F. (1993). Negative evidence in language acquisition. *Cognition, 46,* 53–85.

Marcus, G. F. (1995). Children's overregularization of English plurals: A quantitative analysis. *Journal of Child Language, 22,* 447–459.

Marcus, G. F., Pinker, S., Ullman, M., Hollander, M., Rosen, T. J., & Xu, F. (1992). Overregularization in language acquisition. *Monographs of the Society for Research in Child Development, 57* (4, Serial No. 228).

Marcus, J., Maccoby, E. E., Jacklin, C. N., & Doering, C. H. (1985). Individual differences in mood in early childhood: Their relation to gender and neonatal sex steroids. *Developmental Psychobiology, 18,* 327–340.

Mareschal, D., Plunkett, K., & Harris, P. (1995). Developing object permanence: A connectionist model. In J. D. Moore & J. F. Lehman (Eds.), *Proceedings of the seventeenth annual conference of the Cognitive Science Society* (pp. 170–175). Mahwah, NJ: Erlbaum.

Marini, Z., & Case, R. (1989). Parallels in the development of preschoolers' knowledge about their physical and social worlds. *Merrill-Palmer Quarterly, 35,* 63–87.

Marini, Z., & Case, R. (1994). The development of abstract reasoning about the physical and social world. *Child Development, 65,* 147–159.

Markman, E. M. (1989). *Categorization and naming in children.* Cambridge, MA: MIT Press.

Markman, E. M. (1992). Constraints on word learning: Speculations about their nature, origins, and domain specificity. In M. R. Gunnar & M. P. Maratsos (Eds.), *Minnesota Symposia on Child Psychology* (Vol. 25, pp. 59–101). Hillsdale, NJ: Erlbaum.

Markovits, H., & Bouffard-Bouchard, T. (1992). The

belief-bias effect in reasoning: The development and activation of competence. *British Journal of Developmental Psychology, 10,* 269–284.

MARKOVITS, H., & VACHON, R. (1989). Reasoning with contrary-to-fact propositions. *Journal of Experimental Child Psychology, 47,* 398–412.

MARKOVITS, H., & VACHON, R. (1990). Conditional reasoning, representation, and level of abstraction. *Developmental Psychology, 26,* 942–951.

MARKSTROM-ADAMS, C., & ADAMS, G. R. (1995). Gender, ethnic group, and grade differences in psychosocial functioning during middle adolescence? *Journal of Youth and Adolescence, 24,* 397–417.

MARKUS, H. R., & KITAYAMA, S. (1991). Culture and the self: Implications for cognition, emotion, and motivation. *Psychological Review, 98,* 224–253.

MARKUS, H. R., MULLALLY, P. R., & KITAYAMA, S. (1997). Selfways: Diversity in modes of cultural participation. In U. Neisser & D. Jopling (Eds.), *The conceptual self in context* (pp. 13–61). New York: Cambridge University Press.

MARLIER, L., & SCHAAL, B. (1997). La perception de la familiarité olfactive chez le nouveau-né: Influence différentielle du mode d'alimentation? [The perception of olfactory familiarity in the neonate: Differential influence of the mode of feeding?] *Enfance, 1,* 47–61.

MARLIER, L., SCHAAL, B., & SOUSSIGNAN, R. (1998a). Bottle-fed neonates prefer an odor experienced in utero to an odor experienced postnatally in the feeding context. *Developmental Psychobiology, 33,* 133–145.

MARLIER, L., SCHAAL, B., & SOUSSIGNAN, R. (1998b). Neonatal responsiveness to the odor of amniotic and lacteal fluids: A test of perinatal chemosensory continuity. *Child Development, 69,* 611–623.

MARSH, D. T., SERAFICA, F. C., & BARENBOIM, C. (1981). Interrelationships among perspective taking, interpersonal problem solving, and interpersonal functioning. *Journal of Genetic Psychology, 138,* 37–48.

MARSH, H. W. (1990). The structure of academic self-concept: The Marsh/Shavelson model. *Journal of Educational Psychology, 82,* 623–636.

MARSH, H. W., BARNES, J., CAIRNS, L., & TIDMAN, M. (1984). Self-description questionnaire: Age and sex effects in the structure and level of self-concept for preadolescent children. *Journal*

of Educational Psychology, 76, 940–956.

MARSH, H. W., CRAVEN, R. G., & DEBUS, R. (1991). Self-concepts of young children 5 to 8 years of age: Measurement and multidimensional structure. *Journal of Educational Psychology, 83,* 377–392.

MARSH, H. W., CRAVEN, R., & DEBUS, R. (1998). Structure, stability, and development of young children's self-concepts: A multicohort-multioccasion study. *Child Development, 69,* 1030–1053.

MARSH, H. W., SMITH, I. D., & BARNES, J. (1985). Multidimensional self-concepts: Relations with sex and academic achievement. *Journal of Educational Psychology, 77,* 581–596.

MARSHALL, E. (1996). The genome program's conscience. *Science, 274,* 488–491.

MARSHALL, R. (1997). School-to-work processes in the United States. In R. Takanishi & D. A. Hamburg (Eds.), *Preparing adolescents for the twenty-first century: Challenges facing Europe and the United States* (pp. 195–226). New York: Cambridge University Press.

MARTIN, C. L. (1989). Children's use of gender-related information in making social judgments. *Developmental Psychology, 25,* 80–88.

MARTIN, C. L. (1993). New directions of investigating children's gender knowledge. *Developmental Review, 13,* 184–204.

MARTIN, C. L. (1995). Stereotypes about children with traditional and nontraditional gender roles. *Sex Roles, 33,* 727–751.

MARTIN, C. L., EISENBUD, L., & ROSE, H. (1995). Children's gender-based reasoning about toys. *Child Development, 66,* 1453–1471.

MARTIN, C. L., & HALVERSON, C. F., JR. (1981). A schematic processing model of sex typing and stereotyping in children. *Child Development, 52,* 1119–1134.

MARTIN, C. L., & HALVERSON, C. F., JR. (1983). The effects of sex-typing schemas on young children's memory. *Child Development, 54,* 563–574.

MARTIN, C. L., & HALVERSON, C. F., JR. (1987). The role of cognition in sex role acquisition. In D. B. Carter (Ed.), *Current conceptions of sex roles and sex typing: Theory and research* (pp. 123–137). New York: Praeger.

MARTIN, C. L., & LITTLE, J. K. (1990). The relation of gender understanding to children's sex-typed preferences and gender stereotypes. *Child Development, 61,* 1427–1439.

MARTIN, J. A. (1981). A longitudinal study of the consequences of early mother-infant interaction: A microanalytic approach. *Monographs of the Society for Research in Child Development, 46* (3, Serial No. 190).

MARTIN, J. C., BARR, H. M., MARTIN, D. C., & STREISSGUTH, A. P. (1996). Neonatal exposure to cocaine. *Neurotoxicology and Teratology, 18,* 617–625.

MARTIN, R. M. (1975). Effects of familiar and complex stimuli on infant attention. *Developmental Psychology, 11,* 178–185.

MARTIN, R. P., OLEJNIK, S., & GADDIS, L. (1994). Is temperament an important contributor to schooling outcomes in elementary school? Modeling effects of temperament and scholastic ability on academic achievement. In W. B. Carey & S. C. McDevitt (Eds.), *Prevention and early intervention* (pp. 59–68). New York: Brunner/Mazel.

MARTLEW, M., & CONNOLLY, K. J. (1996). Human figure drawings by schooled and unschooled children in Papua New Guinea. *Child Development, 67,* 2743–2762.

MARTORELL, R. (1980). Interrelationships between diet, infectious disease, and nutritional status. In L. S. Greene & F. E. Johnston (Eds.), *Social and biological predictors of nutritional status, physical growth, and neurological development* (pp. 81–106). New York: Academic Press.

MARZOLF, D. P., & DELOACHE, J. S. (1994). Transfer in young children's understanding of spatial representations. *Child Development, 65,* 1–15.

MASATAKA, N. (1992). Motherese in a signed language. *Infant Behavior and Development, 15,* 453–460.

MASCOLO, M. F., & FISCHER, K. W. (1995). Developmental transformations in appraisals for pride, shame, and guilt. In J. P. Tangney & K. W. Fischer (Eds.), *Self-conscious emotions* (pp. 114–139). New York: Guilford.

MASON, C. A., CAUCE, A. M., GONZALES, N., & HIRAGA, Y. (1996). Neither too sweet nor too sour: Problem peers, maternal control, and problem behavior in African American adolescents. *Child Development, 67,* 2115–2130.

MASON, M. G., & GIBBS, J. C. (1993a). Role-taking opportunities and the transition to advanced moral judgment. *Moral Education Forum, 18,* 1–12.

MASON, M. G., & GIBBS, J. C. (1993b). Social perspective taking and moral judgment among college students. *Jour-*

nal of Adolescent Research, 8, 109–123.

MASSEY, C. M., & GELMAN, R. (1988). Preschoolers' ability to decide whether a photographed unfamiliar object can move itself. *Developmental Psychology, 24,* 307–317.

MASTEN, A. S., & COATSWORTH, J. D. (1998). The development of competence in favorable and unfavorable environments: Lessons from research on successful children. *American Psychologist, 53,* 205–220.

MASTEN, A., COATSWORTH, J. D., NEEMANN, J., GEST, S. D., TELLEGEN, A., & GARMEZY, N. (1995). The structure and coherence of competence from childhood through adolescence. *Child Development, 66,* 1635–1659.

MASTEN, A. S., HUBBARD, J. J., GEST, S. D., TELLEGEN, A., GARMEZY, N., & RAMIREZ, M. (1999). Competence in the context of adversity: Pathways to resilience and maladaptation from childhood to late adolescence. *Development and Psychopathology, 11,* 143–169.

MASUR, E. F. (1995). Infants' early verbal imitation and their later lexical development. *Merrill-Palmer Quarterly, 41,* 286–306.

MASUR, E. F., MCINTYRE, C. W., & FLAVELL, J. H. (1973). Developmental changes in apportionment of study time among items in a multi-trial free recall task. *Journal of Experimental Child Psychology, 15,* 237–246.

MATAS, L., AREND, R., & SROUFE, L. A. (1978). Continuity of adaptation in the second year: The relationship between quality of attachment and later competence. *Child Development, 49,* 547–556.

MATHENY, A. P., JR. (1989). Temperament and cognition: Relations between temperament and mental test scores. In G. A. Kohnstamm, J. E. Bates, & M. K. Rothbart (Eds.), *Temperament in childhood* (pp. 263–282). New York: Wiley.

MATSUMOTO, D. (1990). Cultural similarities and differences in display rules. *Motivation and Emotion, 14,* 195–214.

MATTSON, S. N., & RILEY, E. P. (1995). Prenatal exposure to alcohol: What the images reveal. *Alcohol Health and World Research, 19,* 273–278.

MATTSON, S. N., RILEY, E. P., DELIS, D. C., & JONES, K. L. (1998). Neuropsychological comparison of alcohol-exposed children with or without physical features of fetal alcohol syndrome. *Neuropsychology, 12,* 146–153.

MATUTE-BIANCHI, M. E. (1986). Ethnic identities and patterns of school success and failure among Mexican-descent and Japanese-American students in a California high school: An ethnographic analysis. *American Journal of Education, 95,* 233–255.

MAYBERRY, R. I. (1994). The importance of childhood to language acquisition: Evidence from American Sign Language. In J. C. Goodman & H. C. Nusbaum (Eds.), *The development of speech perception: The transition from speech sounds to spoken words* (pp. 57–90). Cambridge, MA: MIT Press.

MAYES, L. C., & BORNSTEIN, M. H. (1997). Attention regulation in infants born at risk: Prematurity and prenatal cocaine exposure. In J. A. Burack & J. T. Enns (Eds.), *Attention, development, and psychopathology* (pp. 97–122). New York: Guilford.

MAYES, L. C., BORNSTEIN, M. H., CHAWARSKA, K., & HAYNES, O. M. (1996). Impaired regulation of arousal in 3-month-old infants exposed prenatally to cocaine and other drugs. *Development and Psychopathology, 8,* 29–42.

MAYES, L. C., & ZIGLER, E. (1992). An observational study of the affective concomitants of mastery in infants. *Journal of Child Psychology and Psychiatry, 33,* 659–667.

MAYNARD, R., & MCGINNIS, E. (1993). Policies to meet the need for high quality child care. In A. Booth (Ed.), *Child care for the '90s* (pp. 189–208). Hillsdale, NJ: Erlbaum.

MAYS, V. M., BULLOCK, M., ROSENZWEIG, M. R., & WESSELLS, M. (1998). Ethnic conflict: Global challenges and psychological conflict. *American Psychologist, 53,* 737–742.

MAZUR, E. (1993). Developmental differences in children's understanding of marriage, divorce, and remarriage. *Journal of Applied Developmental Psychology, 14,* 191–212.

MAZZOCCO, M. M. M., NORD, A. M., VAN DOORNINCK, W., GREEN, C. L., KOVAR, C. G., & PENNINGTON, B. F. (1994). Cognitive development among children with early-treated phenylketonuria. *Developmental Neuropsychology, 10,* 133–151.

MCADOO, H. P. (1993). Ethnic families: Strengths that are found in diversity. In H. P. McAdoo (Ed.), *Family ethnicity* (pp. 3–14). Newbury Park, CA: Sage.

MCANARNEY, E. R., KREIPE, R. E., ORR, D. P., & COMERCI, G. D. (1992). *Textbook of adolescent development.* Philadelphia: Saunders.

MCBRIDE, J. (1997). Foods to be fortified with folic acid. *Agricultural Research, 45,* 16–17.

MCCABE, A. (1997). Developmental and cross-cultural aspects of children's narration. In M. Bamberg (Ed.), *Narrative development: Six approaches* (pp. 137–174). Mahwah, NJ: Erlbaum.

MCCABE, A. E. (1998). *Chameleon readers: Teaching children to appreciate all kinds of good stories.* New York: McGraw-Hill.

MCCABE, A. E., & PETERSON, C. (1988). A comparison of adults' versus children's spontaneous use of *because* and *so. Journal of Genetic Psychology, 149,* 257–268.

MCCABE, A., & PETERSON, C. (1991). Getting the story: A longitudinal study of parental styles in eliciting narratives and developing narrative skill. In A. McCabe & C. Peterson (Eds.), *Developing narrative structure* (pp. 217–253). Hillsdale, NJ: Erlbaum.

MCCALL, R. B. (1977). Childhood IQs as predictors of adult educational and occupational status. *Science, 197,* 482–483.

MCCALL, R. B. (1993). Developmental functions for general mental performance. In D. K. Detterman (Ed.), *Current topics in human intelligence* (Vol. 3, pp. 3–29). Norwood, NJ: Ablex.

MCCALL, R. B., APPELBAUM, M. I., & HOGARTY, P. S. (1973). Developmental changes in mental performance. *Monographs of the Society for Research in Child Development, 38* (3, Serial No. 150).

MCCALL, R. B., & CARRIGER, M. S. (1993). A meta-analysis of infant habituation and recognition memory performance as predictors of later IQ. *Child Development, 64,* 57–79.

MCCARTON, C. M., BROOKS-GUNN, J., WALLACE, I. F., BAUER, C. R., BENNETT, F. C., BERNBAUM, J. C., BROYLES, R. S., CASEY, P. H., MCCORMICK, M. C., SCOTT, D. T., TYSON, J., TONASCIA, J., & MEINERT, C. L. (1997). Results at age 8 years of early intervention for low-birth-weight premature infants: The infant health and development program. *Journal of the American Medical Association, 277,* 126–132.

MCCLELLAND, J. L. (1989). Parallel distributed processing: Implications for cognition and development. In R. G. M. Morris (Ed.), *Parallel distributed processing: Implications for psychology and neurobiology* (pp. 9–45). Oxford, UK: Clarendon Press.

MCCLELLAND, J. L. (1995). A connectionist perspective on knowledge and development. In T. J. Simon & G. S. Halford (Eds.), *Developing cognitive competence: New approaches to process modeling* (pp. 157–204). Hillsdale, NJ: Erlbaum.

MCCONAGHY, M. J. (1979). Gender permanence and the genital basis of gender: Stages in the development of constancy of gender identity. *Child Development, 50,* 1223–1226.

MCCONAGHY, N., & SILOVE, D. (1992). Do sex-linked behaviors in children influence relationships with their parents? *Archives of Sexual Behavior, 21,* 469–479.

MCCORMICK, C. M., & MAURER, D. M. (1988). Unimanual hand preferences in 6-month-olds: Consistency and relation to familial-handedness. *Infant Behavior and Development, 11,* 21–29.

MCCUNE, L. (1993). The development of play as the development of consciousness. In M. H. Bornstein & A. O'Reilly (Eds.), *New directions for child development* (No. 59, pp. 67–79). San Francisco: Jossey-Bass.

MCCUNE, L. (1995). A normative study of representational play at the transition to language. *Developmental Psychology, 31,* 198–206.

MCGEE, G. (1997). Legislating gestation. *Human Reproduction, 12,* 407–408.

MCGEE, L. M., & RICHGELS, D. J. (1996). *Literacy's beginnings: Supporting young readers and writers.* Boston: Allyn and Bacon.

MCGILLICUDDY-DE LISI, A. V., WATKINS, C., & VINCHUR, A. J. (1994). The effect of relationship on children's distributive justice reasoning. *Child Development, 65,* 1694–1700.

MCGILLY, K., & SIEGLER, R. S. (1990). The influence of encoding and strategic knowledge on children's choices among serial recall strategies. *Developmental Psychology, 26,* 931–941.

MCGROARTY, M. (1992, March). The societal context of bilingual education. *Educational Researcher, 21* (2), 7–9.

MCGUE, M., BOUCHARD, T. J., JR., IACONO, W. G., & LYKKEN, D. T. (1993). Behavioral genetics of cognitive ability: A lifespan perspective. In R. Plomin & G. E. McClearn (Eds.), *Nature, nurture, and psychology* (pp. 59–76). Washington, DC: American Psychological Association.

MCGUFFIN, P., & SARGEANT, M. P. (1991). Major affective disorder. In P. McGuffin & R. Murray (Eds.), *The new genetics of mental illness* (pp. 165–181).

London: Butterworth-Heinemann.

MCGUINNESS, D., & PRIBRAM, K. H. (1980). The neuropsychology of attention: Emotional and motivational controls. In M. C. Wittcock (Ed.), *The brain and psychology* (pp. 95–139). New York: Academic Press.

MCHALE, S. M., BARTKO, W. T., CROUTER, A. C., & PERRY-JENKINS, M. (1990). Children's housework and psychosocial functioning: The mediating effects of parents' sex-role behaviors and attitudes. *Child Development, 61,* 68–81.

MCHALE, S. M., CROUTER, A. C., MCGUIRE, S. A., & UPDEGRAFF, K. A. (1995). Congruence between mothers' and fathers' differential treatment of siblings: Links with family relations and children's well-being. *Child Development, 66,* 116–128.

MCKENNA, J. J. (1996). Sudden infant death syndrome in cross-cultural perspective: Is infant–parent cosleeping protective? *Annual Review of Anthropology, 25,* 201–216.

MCKENNA, J. J., MOSKO, S., RICHARD, C., DRUMMOND, S., HUNT, L., CETEL, M. B., & ARPAIA, J. (1994). Experimental studies of infant-parent cosleeping: Mutual physiological and behavioral influences and their relevance to SIDS (sudden infant death syndrome). *Early Human Development, 38,* 187–201.

MCKENRY, P. C., & PRICE, S. J. (1995). Divorce: A comparative perspective. In B. B. Ingoldsby & S. Smith (Eds.), *Families in multicultural perspective* (pp. 187–212). New York: Guilford.

MCKUSICK, V. A. (1995). *Mendelian inheritance in man: Catalogs of autosomal dominant, autosomal recessive, and X-linked phenotypes* (10th ed.). Baltimore: Johns Hopkins University Press.

MCLANAHAN, S., & SANDEFUR, G. (1994). *Growing up with a single parent.* Cambridge, MA: Harvard University Press.

MCLEAN, D. F., TIMAJCHY, K. H., WINGO, P. A., & FLOYD, R. L. (1993). Psychosocial measurement: Implications of the study of preterm delivery in black women. *American Journal of Preventive Medicine, 9,* 39–81.

MCLEOD, J. D., & SHANAHAN, M. J. (1996). Trajectories of poverty and children's mental health. *Journal of Health and Social Behavior, 37,* 207–220.

MCLOYD, V. C. (1998a). Children in poverty: Development, public policy, and practice. In I. Sigel & A. Renninger (Eds.), *Handbook of child psychology:*

Vol. 4. Child psychology in practice (5th ed., pp. 135–208). New York: Wiley.

McLoyd, V. C. (1998b). Socioeconomic disadvantage and child development. *American Psychologist, 53,* 185–204.

McLoyd, V. C., Jayaratne, T. E., Ceballo, R., & Borquez, J. (1994). Unemployment and work interruption among African American single mothers: Effects on parenting and adolescent socioemotional functioning. *Child Development, 65,* 562–589.

McLoyd, V. C., Warren, D., & Thomas, E. A. C. (1984). Anticipatory and fantastic role enactment in preschool triads. *Developmental Psychology, 20,* 807–814.

McMahon, C. A., Ungerer, J. A., Beaurepaire, J., Tennant, C., & Saunders, D. (1995). Psychosocial outcomes for parents and children after in vitro fertilization: A review. *Journal of Reproductive and Infant Psychology, 13,* 1–6.

McManus, I. C., Sik, G., Cole, D. R., Mellon, A. F., Wong, J., & Kloss, J. (1988). The development of handedness in children. *British Journal of Developmental Psychology, 6,* 257–273.

McMurphy, M. P., Cesqueira, M. T., Connor, S. L., & Connor, W. E. (1991). Changes in lipid and lipoprotein levels and body weight in Tarahumara Indians after consumption of an affluent diet. *New England Journal of Medicine, 325,* 1704–1708.

McNamee, S., & Peterson, J. (1986). Young children's distributive justice reasoning, behavior, and role taking: Their consistency and relationship. *Journal of Genetic Psychology, 146,* 399–404.

McNeill, D. (1992). *Hand and mind.* Chicago: University of Chicago Press.

MCR Vitamin Study Research Group. (1991). Prevention of neural tube defects: Results of the Medical Research Council Vitamin Study. *Lancet, 338,* 131–137.

Mead, G. H. (1934). *Mind, self, and society.* Chicago: University of Chicago Press.

Mead, M. (1928). *Coming of age in Samoa.* Ann Arbor, MI: Morrow.

Mead, M. (1963). *Sex and temperament in three primitive societies.* New York: Morrow. (Original work published 1935)

Mead, M., & Newton, N. (1967). Cultural patterning of perinatal behavior. In S. Richardson & A. Guttmacher (Eds.), *Childbearing: Its social and psychological*

aspects (pp. 142–244). Baltimore: Williams & Wilkins.

Meadow-Orlans, K. P., & Steinberg, A. G. (1993). Effects of infant hearing loss and maternal support on mother–infant interactions at 18 months. *Journal of Applied Developmental Psychology, 14,* 407–426.

Mebert, C. J. (1991). Dimensions of subjectivity in parents' ratings of infant temperament. *Child Development, 62,* 352–361.

Mehler, J., Dupoux, E., Nazzi, T., & Dehaene-Lambertz, G. (1996). Coping with linguistic diversity: The infant's point of view. In J. L. Morgan & K. Demuth (Eds.), *Signal to syntax* (pp. 101–116). Mahwah, NJ: Erlbaum.

Mehlmadrona, L., & Madrona, M. M. (1997). Physician- and midwife-attended home births—Effects of breech, twin, and post-dates outcome data on mortality rates. *Journal of Nurse-Midwifery, 42,* 91–98.

Meilman, P. W. (1979). Cross-sectional age changes in ego identity status during adolescence. *Developmental Psychology, 15,* 230–231.

Meisels, S. J., Dichtelmiller, M., & Liaw, F. R. (1993). A multidimensional analysis of early childhood intervention programs. In C. H. Zeanah (Ed.), *Handbook of infant mental health* (pp. 361–385). New York: Guilford.

Melnikow, J., & Alemagno, S. (1993). Adequacy of prenatal care among inner-city women. *Journal of Family Practice, 37,* 575–582.

Melson, G. F., & Fogel, A. (1988, January). Learning to care. *Psychology Today, 22* (1), 39–45.

Meltzoff, A. N. (1990). Towards a developmental cognitive science. *Annals of the New York Academy of Sciences, 608,* 1–37.

Meltzoff, A. N. (1994). What infant memory tells us about infantile amnesia: Long-term recall and deferred imitation. *Journal of Experimental Child Psychology, 59,* 497–515.

Meltzoff, A. N. (1995). Understanding the intentions of others: Re-enactment of intended acts by 18-month-old children. *Developmental Psychology, 31,* 838–850.

Meltzoff, A. N. (1996). The human infant as an imitative generalist: A 20-year progress report on infant imitation with implications for comparative psychology. In C. M. Heyes & B. G. Galef, Jr. (Eds.), *Social learning in animals: The roots of culture* (pp. 347–370). San Diego: Academic Press.

Meltzoff, A. N., & Borton, R. W. (1979). Intermodal matching by human neonates. *Nature, 282,* 403–404.

Meltzoff, A. N., & Gopnik, A. (1993). The role of imitation in understanding persons and developing a theory of mind. In S. Baron-Cohen & H. Tager-Flusberg (Eds.), *Understanding other minds* (pp. 335–366). Oxford: Oxford University Press.

Meltzoff, A. N., & Kuhl, P. K. (1994). Faces and speech: Intermodal processing of biologically relevant signals in infants and adults. In D. J. Lewkowicz & R. Lickliter (Eds.), *The development of intersensory perception: Comparative perspectives* (pp. 335–369). Hillsdale, NJ: Erlbaum.

Meltzoff, A. N., & Moore, M. K. (1977). Imitation of facial and manual gestures by human neonates. *Science, 198,* 75–78.

Meltzoff, A. N., & Moore, M. K. (1994). Imitation, memory, and the representation of persons. *Infant Behavior and Development, 17,* 83–99.

Mendelson, B. K., White, D. R., & Mendelson, M. J. (1996). Self-esteem and body esteem: Effects of gender, age, and weight. *Journal of Applied Developmental Psychology, 17,* 321–346.

Menyuk, P., Liebergott, J. W., & Schultz, M. C. (1995). *Early language development in full-term and premature infants.* Hillsdale, NJ: Erlbaum.

Meredith, N. V. (1978). *Human body growth in the first ten years of life.* Columbia, SC: State Printing.

Merriman, J., Rovee-Collier, C., & Wilk, A. (1997). Exemplar spacing and infants' memory for category information. *Infant Behavior and Development, 20,* 223–236.

Mervis, C. B. (1987). Child-basic object categories and early lexical development. In U. Neisser (Ed.), *Concepts and conceptual development: Ecological and intellectual factors in categorization* (pp. 201–233). Cambridge: Cambridge University Press.

Mervis, C. B., Golinkoff, R. M., & Bertrand, J. (1994). Two-year-olds readily learn multiple labels for the same basic-level category. *Child Development, 65,* 1163–1177.

Mervis, C., Morris, C. A., Bertrand, J., & Robinson, B. F. (1998). Williams syndrome: Findings from an integrated program of research. In H. Tager-Flusberg (Ed.), *Neurodevelopmental disorders: Contribution to a new framework from the cognitive neurosciences.* Cambridge, MA: MIT Press.

Meyer-Bahlburg, H. F. L., Ehrhardt, A. A., Rosen, L. R., Gruen, R. S., Veridiano, N. P., Vann, F. H., & Neuwalder, H. F. (1995). Prenatal estrogens and the development of homosexual orientation. *Developmental Psychology, 31,* 12–21.

Meyers, C., Adam, R., Dungan, J., & Prenger, V. (1997). Aneuploidy in twin gestations: When is maternal age advanced? *Obstetrics and Gynecology, 89,* 248–251.

Miceli, P. J., Whitman, T. L., Borkowski, J. G., Braungart-Riekder, J., & Mitchell, D. W. (1998). Individual differences in infant information processing: The role of temperamental and maternal factors. *Infant Behavior and Development, 21,* 119–136.

Michael, R. T., Gagnon, J. H., Laumann, E. O., & Kolata, G. (1994). *Sex in America.* Boston: Little, Brown.

Michel, C. (1989). Radiation embryology. *Experientia, 45,* 69–77.

Micheli, R. (1985, June). Water babies. *Parents, 60* (6), 8–13.

Milberger, S., Biederman, J., Faraone, S. V., Guite, J., & Tsuang, M. T. (1997). Pregnancy, delivery and infancy complications and attention deficit hyperactivity disorder: Issues of gene—environment interaction. *Biological Psychiatry, 41,* 65–75.

Miles, C. (1935). Sex in social psychology. In C. Murchison (Ed.), *Handbook of social psychology* (pp. 699–704). Worcester, MA: Clark University Press.

Milgram, N. A., & Palti, G. (1993). Psychosocial characteristics of resilient children. *Journal of Research in Personality, 27,* 207–221.

Miller, J. G. (1994). Cultural diversity in the morality of caring: Individually oriented versus duty-based interpersonal moral codes. *Cross-cultural Research: The Journal of Comparative Social Science, 28,* 3–39.

Miller, J. G. (1997). Culture and self: Uncovering the cultural grounding of psychological theory. In J. G. Snodgrass & R. L. Thompson (Eds.), *Annals of the New York Academy of Sciences* (Vol. 18, pp. 217–231). New York: New York Academy of Sciences.

Miller, J. G., & Bersoff, D. M. (1995). Development in the context of everyday family relationships: Culture, interpersonal morality, and adaptation. In M. Killen & D. Hart (Eds.), *Morality in everyday life: Developmental perspectives* (pp. 259–282). Cambridge: Cambridge University Press.

MILLER, J. G., & LUTHAR, S. (1989). Issues of interpersonal responsibility and accountability: A comparison of Indians' and Americans' moral judgments. *Social Cognition, 7,* 237–261.

MILLER, J. M., BOUDREAUX, M. C., & REGAN, F. A. (1995). A case-control study of cocaine use in pregnancy. *American Journal of Obstetrics and Gynecology, 172,* 180–185.

MILLER, K. F., & BAILLARGEON, R. (1990). Length and distance: Do preschoolers think that occlusion brings things together? *Developmental Psychology, 26,* 103–114.

MILLER, L. T., & VERNON, P. A. (1992). The general factor in short-term memory, intelligence, and reaction time. *Intelligence, 16,* 5–29.

MILLER, L. T., & VERNON, P. A. (1997). Developmental changes in speed of information processing in young children. *Developmental Psychology, 33,* 549–554.

MILLER, N. B., COWAN, P. A., COWAN, C. P., HETHERINGTON, E. M., & CLINGEMPEEL, W. G. (1993). Externalizing in preschoolers and early adolescents: A cross-study replication of a family model. *Developmental Psychology, 29,* 3–16.

MILLER, P. A., EISENBERG, N., FABES, R., SHELL, R., & GULAR, S. (1989). Mothers' emotional arousal as a moderator in the socialization of children's empathy. In N. Eisenberg (Ed.), *New directions for child development* (No. 44, pp. 65–83). San Francisco: Jossey-Bass.

MILLER, P. A., EISENBERG, N., FABES, R. A., & SHELL, R. (1996). Relations of moral reasoning and vicarious emotion to young children's prosocial behavior toward peers and adults. *Developmental Psychology, 32,* 210–219.

MILLER, P. H. (1993). *Theories of developmental psychology* (3rd ed.). New York: Freeman.

MILLER, P. H., & BIGI, L. (1979). The development of children's understanding of attention. *Merrill-Palmer Quarterly, 25,* 235–250.

MILLER, P. H., HAYNES, V. F., DE-MARIE-DREBLOW, D., & WOODY-RAMSEY, J. (1986). Children's strategies for gathering information in three tasks. *Child Development, 57,* 1429–1439.

MILLER, P. H., KESSEL, F. S., & FLAVELL, J. H. (1970). Thinking about people thinking about people thinking about . . . : A study of social cognitive development. *Child Development, 41,* 613–623.

MILLER, P. H., SEIER, W. L., PROBERT, J. S., & ALOISE, P. A. (1991). Age differences in the capacity demands of a strategy among spontaneously strategic children. *Journal of Experimental Child Psychology, 52,* 149–165.

MILLER, P. H., & ZALENSKI, R. (1982). Preschoolers' knowledge about attention. *Developmental Psychology, 18,* 871–875.

MILLER, P. H., WOODY-RAMSEY, J., & ALOISE, P. A. (1991). The role of strategy effortfulness in strategy effectiveness. *Developmental Psychology, 27,* 738–745.

MILLER, P. J., FUNG, H., & MINTZ, J. (1996). Self-construction through narrative practices: A Chinese and American comparison of early socialization. *Ethos, 24,* 1–44.

MILLER, P. J., & SPERRY, L. L. (1987). The socialization of anger and aggression. *Merrill-Palmer Quarterly, 33,* 1–31.

MILLER, P. J., WILEY, A. R., FUNG, H., & LIANG, C-H. (1997). Personal storytelling as a medium of socialization in Chinese and American families. *Child Development, 68,* 557–568.

MILLER, S. A. (1998). *Developmental research methods* (2nd ed.). Englewood Cliffs, NJ: Prentice-Hall.

MILLER, S. A., & DAVIS, T. L. (1992). Beliefs about children: A comparative study of mothers, teachers, peers, and self. *Child Development, 63,* 1251–1265.

MILLER-JONES, D. (1989). Culture and testing. *American Psychologist, 44,* 360–366.

MILLS, D. L., COFFEY-CORINA, S. A., & NEVILLE, H. J. (1993). Language acquisition and cerebral specialization in 20-month-old infants. *Journal of Cognitive Neuroscience, 5,* 317–334.

MILLS, D. L., COFFEY-CORINA, S. A., & NEVILLE, H. J. (1994). Variability in cerebral organization during primary language acquisition. In G. Dawson & K. W. Fischer (Eds.), *Human behavior and the developing brain* (pp. 427–455). New York: Guilford.

MILLS, D. L., COFFEY-CORINA, S., & NEVILLE, H. J. (1997). Language comprehension and cerebral specialization from 13 to 20 months. *Developmental Neuropsychology, 13,* 397–445.

MILLS, R., & GRUSEC, J. E. (1989). Cognitive, affective, and behavioral consequences of praising altruism. *Merrill-Palmer Quarterly, 35,* 299–326.

MINKLER, M., FULLER-THOMSON, E., MILLER, D., & DRIVE, D. (1997). Depression in grandparents raising grandchildren: Results of a national longitudinal study. *Archives of Family Medicine, 6,* 445–452.

MISCHEL, H. N., & LIEBERT, R. M. (1966). Effects of discrepancies between observed and imposed reward criteria on their acquisition and transmission. *Journal of Personality and Social Psychology, 3,* 45–53.

MISCHEL, H. N., & MISCHEL, W. (1983). The development of children's knowledge of self-control strategies. *Child Development, 54,* 603–619.

MISCHEL, W. (1996). From good intentions to willpower. In P. M. Gollwitzer & J. A. Bargh (Eds.), *The psychology of action* (pp. 197–218). New York: Guilford.

MISCHEL, W., & BAKER, N. (1975). Cognitive appraisals and transformations in delay behavior. *Journal of Personality and Social Psychology, 31,* 254–261.

MISCHEL, W., SHODA, Y., & PEAKE, P. K. (1988). The nature of adolescent competencies predicted by preschool delay of gratification. *Journal of Personality and Social Psychology, 54,* 687–696.

MISTRY, J. (1997). The development of remembering in cultural context. In N. Cowan (Ed.), *The development of memory in childhood* (pp. 343–368). Hove, UK: Psychology Press.

MIYAKE, K., CHEN, S., & CAMPOS, J. J. (1985). Infant temperament, mother's mode of interaction, and attachment in Japan: An interim report. In I. Bretherton & E. Waters (Eds.), Growing points of attachment theory and research. *Monographs of the Society for Research in Child Development, 50* (1–2, Serial No. 209).

MIZE, J., & LADD, G. W. (1988). Predicting preschoolers' peer behavior and status from their interpersonal strategies: A comparison of verbal and enactive responses to hypothetical social dilemmas. *Developmental Psychology, 24,* 782–788.

MIZE, J., & LADD, G. W. (1990). A cognitive-social learning approach to social skill training with low-status preschool children. *Developmental Psychology, 26,* 388–397.

MIZE, J., & PETTIT, G. S. (1997). Mothers' social coaching, mother–child relationship style, and children's peer competence: Is the medium the message? *Child Development, 68,* 312–332.

MOELY, B. E. (1977). Organizational factors in the development of memory. In R. V. Kail & J. W. Hagen (Eds.), *Perspectives on the development of memory and cognition* (pp. 203–236). Hillsdale, NJ: Erlbaum.

MOERK, E. L. (1992). *A first language taught and learned.* Baltimore: Paul H. Brookes.

MOFFITT, T. E. (1990). Juvenile delinquency and attention deficit disorder: Boys' developmental trajectories from age 3 to age 15. *Child Development, 61,* 893–910.

MOFFITT, T. E., CASPI, A., DICKSON, N., SILVA, P., & STANTON, W. (1996). Childhood-onset versus adolescent-onset antisocial conduct problems in males: Natural history from ages 3 to 18 years. *Development and Psychopathology, 8,* 399–424.

MOFFITT, T. E., LYNAM, D. R., & SILVA, P. A. (1994). Neuropsychological tests predicting persistent male delinquency. *Criminology, 32,* 277–300.

MOHANTY, A. K., & PERREGAUX, C. (1997). Language acquisition and bilingualism. In J. W. Berry, P. R. Dasen, & T. S. Saraswathi (Eds.), *Handbook of cross-cultural psychology: Vol. 2. Basic processes and human development* (2nd ed., pp. 217–254). Boston: Allyn and Bacon.

MOLL, I. (1994). Reclaiming the natural line in Vygotsky's theory of cognitive development. *Human Development, 37,* 333–342.

MONDIMORE, F. M. (1996). *A natural history of homosexuality.* Baltimore: Johns Hopkins University Press.

MONEY, J. (1985). Pediatric sexology and hermaphroditism. *Journal of Sex and Marital Therapy, 11,* 139–156.

MONEY, J. (1993). Specific neurocognitional impairments associated with Turner (45,X) and Klinefelter (47,XXY) syndromes: A review. *Social Biology, 40,* 147–151.

MONEY, J., & EHRHARDT, A. A. (1972). *Man and woman, boy and girl.* Baltimore: Johns Hopkins University Press.

MONROE, S., GOLDMAN, P., & SMITH, V. E. (1988). *Brothers: Black and poor—A true story of courage and survival.* New York: Morrow.

MONTEMAYOR, R., & EISEN, M. (1977). The development of self-conceptions from childhood to adolescence. *Developmental Psychology, 13,* 314–319.

MOON, C., COOPER, R. P., & FIFER, W. P. (1993). Two-day-old infants prefer their native language. *Infant Behavior and Development, 16,* 495–500.

MOON, S. M., & FELDHUSEN, J. F. (1994). The Program for Academic and Creative Enrichment (PACE): A follow-up study ten years later. In R. F. Subotnik & K. D. Arnold (Eds.), *Beyond Terman: Contemporary longitudinal studies of giftedness and talent* (pp. 375–400). Norwood, NJ: Ablex.

MOORE, D. S., SPENCE, M. J., & KATZ, G. S. (1997). Six-month-olds' categorization of natural infant-directed utterances. *Developmental Psychology, 33*, 980–989.

MOORE, E. G. J. (1986). Family socialization and the IQ test performance of traditionally and transracially adopted black children. *Developmental Psychology, 22*, 317–326.

MOORE, G. A., COHN, J. F., & CAMPBELL, S. B. (1997). Mothers' affective behavior with infant siblings: Stability and change. *Developmental Psychology, 33*, 856–860.

MOORE, K. A., MILLER, B. C., SUGLAND, B. W., MORRISON, D. R., GLEI, D. A., & BLUMENTHAL, C. (1998). *Beginning too soon: Adolescent sexual behavior, pregnancy and parenthood.* Washington, DC: U.S. Government Printing Office.

MOORE, K. A., MORRISON, D. R., & GREENE, A. D. (1997). Effects on the children born to adolescent mothers. In R. A. Maynard (Ed.), *Kids having kids* (pp. 145–180). Washington, DC: Urban Institute.

MOORE, K. A., MYERS, D. E., MORRISON, D. R., NORD, C. W., BROWN, B., & EDMONSTON, B. (1993). Age at first childbirth and later poverty. *Journal of Research on Adolescence, 3*, 393–422.

MOORE, K. L., & PERSAUD, T. V. N. (1998). Before we are born (5th ed.). Philadelphia: Saunders.

MOORE, K. L., PERSAUD, T. V. N., & SHIOTA, K. (1994). *Color atlas of clinical embryology.* Philadelphia: Saunders.

MOORE, M. T. (1985). The relationship between the originality of essays and variables in the problem-discovery process: A study of creative and noncreative middle school students. *Research in the Teaching of English, 19*, 84–95.

MOOREHOUSE, M. J. (1991). Linking maternal employment patterns to mother–child activities and children's school competence. *Developmental Psychology, 27*, 295–303.

MORAN, G. F., & VINOVSKIS, M. A. (1986). The great care of godly parents: Early childhood in Puritan New England. In A. B. Smuts & J. W. Hagen (Eds.), History and research in child development. *Monographs of the Society for Research in Child Development, 50* (4–5, Serial No. 211), pp. 24–37.

MORELLI, G., ROGOFF, B., OPPENHEIM, D., & GOLDSMITH, D. (1992). Cultural variation in infants' sleeping arrangements: Questions of independence. *Developmental Psychology, 28*, 604–613.

MORFORD, J. P., & GOLDIN-MEADOW, S. (1997). From here and now to there and then: The development of displaced reference in homesign and English. *Child Development, 68*, 420–435.

MORGAN, J. L., BONAMA, K. M., & TRAVIS, L. L. (1995). Negative evidence on negative evidence. *Developmental Psychology, 31*, 180–197.

MORGAN, J. L., & SAFFRAN, J. R. (1995). Emerging integration of sequential and suprasegmental information in preverbal speech segmentation. *Child Development, 66*, 911–936.

MORGANE, P. J., AUSTIN-LAFRANCE, R., BRONZINO, J., TONKISS, J., DIAZ-CINTRA, S., CINTRA, L., KEMPER, T., & GALLER, J. R. (1993). Prenatal malnutrition and development of the brain. *Neuroscience and Biobehavioral Reviews, 17*, 91–128.

MORONEY, J. T., & ALLEN, M. H. (1994). Cocaine and alcohol use in pregnancy. In O. Devinsky, F. Feldmann, & B. Hainline (Eds.), *Neurological complications of pregnancy* (pp. 231–242). New York: Raven Press.

MORRIS, A. K., & SLOUTSKY, V. M. (1998). Understanding of logical necessity: Developmental antecedents and cognitive consequences. *Child Development, 69*, 721–741.

MORRISON, F. J., SMITH, L., & DOW-EHRENSBERGER, M. (1995). Education and cognitive development: A natural experiment. *Developmental Psychology, 31*, 789–799.

MORRONGIELLO, B. A. (1986). Infants' perception of multiple-group auditory patterns. *Infant Behavior and Development, 9*, 307–319.

MORTON, J. (1993). Mechanisms in infant face processing. In B. de Boysson-Bardies, S. de Schonen, P. Jusczyk, P. McNeilage, & J. Morton (Eds.), *Developmental neurocognition: Speech and face processing in the first year of life* (pp. 93–102). London: Kluwer.

MORTON, J., & JOHNSON, M. H. (1991). CONSPEC and CONLERN: A two-process theory of infant face recognition. *Psychological Review, 98*, 164–181.

MOSHMAN, D. (1998). Identity as a theory of oneself. *Genetic Epistemologist, 26*(3), 1–9.

MOSHMAN, D. (1999). *Adolescent psychological development: Rationality, morality, and identity.* Mahwah, NJ: Erlbaum.

MOSHMAN, D., & FRANKS, B. A. (1986). Development of the concept of inferential validity. *Child Development, 57*, 153–165.

MOSS, M., COLOMBO, J., MITCHELL, D. W., & HOROWITZ, F. D. (1988). Neonatal behavioral organization and visual processing at three months. *Child Development, 59*, 1211–1220.

MOSTELLER, F. (1995). The Tennessee Study of Class Size in the Early School Grades. *Future of Children, 5*(2), 113–127.

MOUNTS, N. S., & STEINBERG, L. (1995). An ecological analysis of peer influence on adolescent grade point average and drug use. *Developmental Psychology, 31*, 915–922.

MULLEN, M. K. (1994). Earliest recollections of childhood: A demographic analysis. *Cognition, 52*, 55–79.

MULLIS, I. V. S. (1998). *Mathematics and science achievement in the final year of secondary school.* Chestnut Hill, MA: Boston College.

MUNAKATA, Y., MCCLELLAND, J. L., JOHNSON, M. H., & SIEGLER, R. S. (1997). Rethinking infant knowledge: Toward an adaptive process account of successes and failures in object permanence tasks. *Psychological Review, 104*, 686–713.

MUNRO, G., & ADAMS, G. R. (1977). Ego identity formation in college students and working youth. *Developmental Psychology, 13*, 523–524.

MURETT-WAGSTAFF, S., & MOORE, S. G. (1989). The Hmong in America: Infant behavior and rearing practices. In J. K. Nugent, B. M. Lester, & T. B. Brazelton (Eds.), *Biology, culture, and development* (Vol. 1, pp. 319–339). Norwood, NJ: Ablex.

MURPHY-BERMAN, V., & WEISZ, V. (1996). U. N. Convention on the Rights of the Child: Current challenges. *American Psychologist, 51*, 1231–1233.

MURRAY, A. D. (1985). Aversiveness is in the mind of the beholder. In B. M. Lester & C. F. Z. Boukydis (Eds.), *Infant crying* (pp. 217–239). New York: Plenum.

MURRAY, A. D., JOHNSON, J., & PETERS, J. (1990). Fine-tuning of utterance length to preverbal infants: Effects on later language development. *Journal of Child Language, 17*, 511–525.

MURRAY, L., & COOPER, P. J. (1997). Postpartum depression and child development. *Psychological Medicine, 27*, 253–260.

MUSSEN, P., & EISENBERG-BERG, N. (1977). *Roots of caring, sharing, and helping.* San Francisco: Freeman.

N

NACHTIGALL, R. D. (1993). Secrecy: An unresolved issue in the practice of donor insemination. *American Journal of Obstetrics and Gynecology, 168*, 1846–1851.

NACHTIGALL, R. D., PITCHER, L., TSCHANN, J. M., BECKER, G., & QUIROGA, S. S. (1997). Stigma, disclosure, and family functioning among parents of children conceived through donor insemination. *Fertility and Sterility, 68*, 83–89.

NAIGLES, L. G., & GELMAN, S. A. (1995). Overextensions in comprehension and production revisited: Preferential-looking in a study of dog, cat, and cow. *Journal of Child Language, 22*, 19–46.

NAMY, L. L., & WAXMAN, S. R. (1998). Words and gestures: Infants' interpretations of different forms of symbolic reference. *Child Development, 69*, 295–308.

NÁNEZ, J., SR. (1987). Perception of impending collision in 3- to 6-week-old infants. *Infant Behavior and Development, 11*, 447–463.

NÁNEZ, J., SR., & YONAS, A. (1994). Effects of luminance and texture motion on infant defensive reactions to optical collision. *Infant Behavior and Development, 17*, 165–174.

NARVAEZ, D., & REST, J. (1995). The four components of acting morally. In W. M. Kurtines & J. L. Gewirtz (Eds.), *Moral development: An introduction* (pp. 385–400). Boston: Allyn and Bacon.

NASTASI, B. K., & CLEMENTS, D. H. (1992). Social-cognitive behaviors and higher-order thinking in educational computer environments. *Learning and Instruction, 2*, 215–238.

NASTASI, B. K., & CLEMENTS, D. H. (1994). Effectance motivation, perceived scholastic competence, and higher-order thinking in two cooperative computer environments. *Journal of Educational Computing Research, 10*, 249–275.

NATIONAL ASSOCIATION FOR THE EDUCATION OF YOUNG CHILDREN. (1998). *Accreditation criteria and procedures of the National Academy of Early Childhood Programs* (2nd ed.). Washington, DC: Author.

NATIONAL CENTER FOR HEALTH STATISTICS. (1998). *Advance Report of Final Natality Statistics* (Vol. 45). Washington, DC: U.S. Government Printing Office.

NATIONAL FEDERATION OF STATE HIGH SCHOOL ASSOCIATIONS. (1997). *High school athletic participation survey.* Kansas City, MO: Author.

NATIONAL INSTITUTE FOR CHILD HEALTH AND DEVELOPMENT, EARLY CHILD CARE RESEARCH NETWORK. (1996). Characteristics of infant care: Factors contributing to positive caregiving.

Early Childhood Research Quarterly, 11, 269–306.

NATIONAL INSTITUTE FOR CHILD HEALTH AND DEVELOPMENT, EARLY CHILD CARE RESEARCH NETWORK. (1997). The effects of infant child care on infant–mother attachment security: Results of the NICHD Study of Early Child Care. *Child Development, 68,* 860–879.

NATIONAL INSTITUTE FOR CHILD HEALTH AND DEVELOPMENT, EARLY CHILD CARE RESEARCH NETWORK. (1998). Early child care and self-control, compliance, and problem behavior at twenty-four and thirty-six months. *Child Development, 69,* 1145–1170.

NEISSER, U., BOODOO, G., BOUCHARD, T. J., JR., BOYKIN, A. W., BRODY, N., CECI, S. J., HALPERN, D. F., LOEHLIN, J. C., PERLOFF, R., STERNBERG, R. J., & URBINA, S. (1996). Intelligence: Knowns and unknowns. *American Psychologist, 51,* 77–101.

NELSON, C. A. (1995). The ontogeny of human memory: A cognitive neuroscience perspective. *Developmental Psychology, 31,* 723–738.

NELSON, K. (1973). Structure and strategy in learning to talk. *Monographs of the Society for Research in Child Development, 38* (1–2, Serial No. 149).

NELSON, K. (1976). Some attributes of adjectives used by young children. *Cognition, 4,* 13–30.

NELSON, K. (1981). Individual differences in language development: Implications for development and language. *Developmental Psychology, 17,* 170–187.

NELSON, K. (1993). The psychological and social origins of autobiographical memory. *Psychological Science, 1,* 1–8.

NELSON, W. E. (Ed.). (1996). *Nelson textbook of pediatrics.* Philadelphia: Saunders.

NELSON-LE GALL, S. A. (1985). Motive-outcome matching and outcome foreseeability: Effects on attribution of intentionality and moral judgments. *Developmental Psychology, 21,* 332–337.

NEPPL, T. K., & MURRAY, A. D. (1997). Social dominance and play patterns among preschoolers: Gender comparisons. *Sex Roles, 36,* 381–393.

NESSE, R. M. (1990). Evolutionary explanations of emotions. *Human Nature, 1,* 261–289.

NETLEY, C. T. (1986). Summary overview of behavioural development in individuals with neonatally identified X and Y aneuploidy. *Birth Defects, 22,* 293–306.

NEUBAUER, A. C., & BUCIK, V. (1996). The mental speed–IQ

relationship: Unitary or modular? *Intelligence, 22,* 23–48.

NEUMÄRKER, K. (1997). Mortality and sudden death in anorexia nervosa. *International Journal of Eating Disorders, 21,* 205–212.

NEVILLE, H. J. (1991). Neurobiology of cognitive and language processing: Effects on early experience. In K. R. Gibson, & A. C. Petersen (Eds.), *Brain maturation and cognitive development: Comparative and cross-cultural perspectives* (pp. 355–380). New York: Aldine De Gruyter.

NEVILLE, H. J., COFFEY, S. A., HOLCOMB, P. J., & TALLAL, P. (1993). The neurobiology of sensory and language processing in language-impaired children. *Journal of Cognitive Neuroscience, 5,* 235–253.

NEWBORG, J., STOCK, J. R., & WNEK, L. (1984). *Batelle Developmental Inventory.* Allen, TX: LINC Associates.

NEWCOMB, A. F., & BAGWELL, C. (1995). Children's friendship relations: A meta-analytic review. *Psychological Bulletin, 117,* 306–347.

NEWCOMB, A. F., BUKOWSKI, W. M., & PATTEE, L. (1993). Children's peer relations: A meta-analytic review of popular, rejected, neglected, controversial, and average sociometric status. *Psychological Bulletin, 113,* 99–128.

NEWCOMB, M. D., & BENTLER, P. M. (1989). Substance use and abuse among children and teenagers. *American Psychologist, 44,* 242–248.

NEWCOMBE, N. (1982). Development of spatial cognition and cognitive development. In R. Cohen (Ed.), *Children's conceptions of spatial relationships* (pp. 65–81). San Francisco: Jossey-Bass.

NEWCOMBE, N., & DUBAS, J. S. (1992). A longitudinal study of predictors of spatial ability in adolescent females. *Child Development, 63,* 37–46.

NEWCOMBE, N., & FOX, N. A. (1994). Infantile amnesia: Through a glass darkly. *Child Development, 65,* 31–40.

NEWCOMBE, N., & HUTTENLOCHER, J. (1992). Children's early ability to solve perspective-taking problems. *Developmental Psychology, 28,* 635–643.

NEWCOMBE, P. A., & BOYLE, G. J. (1995). High school students' sports personalities: Variations across participation level, gender, type of sport, and success. *International Journal of Sports Psychology, 26,* 277–294.

NEWMAN, B. S., & MUZZONIGRO, P. G. (1993). The effects of traditional family values on the coming out

process of gay male adolescents. *Adolescence, 28,* 213–226.

NEWMAN, L. S. (1990). Intentional and unintentional memory in young children: Remembering vs. playing. *Journal of Experimental Child Psychology, 50,* 243–258.

NEWMANN, F. M. (1996). *Authentic achievement: Restructuring schools for intellectual quality.* San Francisco: Jossey-Bass.

NEWMANN, F. M., MARKS, H., & GAMORAN, A. (1996). Authentic pedagogy and student performance. *American Journal of Education, 104,* 280–312.

NEWNHAM, J. P., EVANS, S. F., MICHAEL, C. A., STANLEY, F. J., & LANDAU, L. I. (1993). Effects of frequent ultrasound during pregnancy: A randomized controlled trial. *Lancet, 342,* 887–890.

NEWPORT, E. L. (1991). Contrasting conceptions of the critical period for language. In S. Carey & R. Gelman (Eds.), *The epigenesis of mind: Essays on biology and cognition* (pp. 111–130). Hillsdale, NJ: Erlbaum.

NEWSON, J., & NEWSON, E. (1975). Intersubjectivity and the transmission of culture: On the social origins of symbolic functioning. *Bulletin of the British Psychological Society, 28,* 437–446.

NICHOLLS, A. L., & KENNEDY, J. M. (1992). Drawing development: From similarity of features to direction. *Child Development, 63,* 227–241.

NICHOLLS, J. G. (1978). The development of concepts of effort and ability, perception of academic attainment, and the understanding that difficult tasks require more ability. *Child Development, 49,* 800–814.

NICHOLS, R. C. (1978). Heredity and environment: Major findings from twin studies of ability, personality, and interests. *Home, 29,* 158–173.

NICOLOPOULOU, A. (1993). Play, cognitive development, and the social world: Piaget, Vygotsky, and beyond. *Human Development, 36,* 1–23.

NIDORF, J. F. (1985). Mental health and refugee youths: A model for diagnostic training. In T. C. Owen (Ed.), *Southeast Asian mental health: Treatment, prevention, services, training, and research* (pp. 391–427). Washington, DC: National Institute of Mental Health.

NILSSON, L., & HAMBERGER, L. (1990). *A child is born.* New York: Delacorte.

NIPPOLD, M. A., TAYLOR, C. L., & BAKER, J. M. (1996). Idiom understanding in Australian youth: A cross-cultural comparison. *Journal of Speech and Hearing Research, 39,* 442–447.

NISBETT, R. (1995). Race, IQ, and scientism. In S. Fraser (Ed.), *The bell curve wars: Race, intelligence and the future of America* (pp. 36–57). New York: Basic Books.

NODDINGS, N. (1992). Gender and the curriculum. In P. W. Jackson (Ed.), *Handbook of research on curriculum* (pp. 659–684). New York: Macmillan.

NOLEN-HOEKSEMA, S., & GIRGUS, J. S. (1994). The emergence of gender differences in depression in adolescence. *Psychological Bulletin, 115,* 424–443.

NOTTELMANN, E. D. (1987). Competence and self-esteem during transition from childhood to adolescence. *Developmental Psychology, 23,* 441–450.

NOTTELMANN, E. D., INOFF-GERMAIN, G., SUSMAN, E. J., & CHROUSOS, G. P. (1990). Hormones and behavior at puberty. In J. Bancroft & J. M. Reinisch (Eds.), *Adolescence and puberty* (pp. 88–123). New York: Oxford University Press.

NOURSE, C. B., & BUTLER, K. M. (1998). Perinatal transmission of HIV and diagnosis of HIV infection in infants: A review. *Irish Journal of Medical Science, 167,* 28–32.

NOVAK, G. P., SOLANTO, M., & ABIKOFF, H. (1995). Spatial orienting and focused attention in attention deficit hyperactivity disorder. *Journal of Psychophysiology, 32,* 546–559.

NOVY, M. J., McGREGOR, J. A., & IAMS, J. D. (1995). New perspectives on the prevention of extreme prematurity. *Clinical Obstetrics and Gynecology, 38,* 790–808.

NOWAKOWSKI, R. S. (1987). Basic concepts of CNS development. *Child Development, 58,* 568–595.

NUCCI, L. P. (1996). Morality and the personal sphere of action. In E. Reed, E. Turiel, & T. Brown (Eds.), *Values and knowledge* (pp. 41–60). Hillsdale, NJ: Erlbaum.

NUCCI, L. P., CAMINO, C., & SAPIRO, C. M. (1996). Social class effects on Northeastern Brazilian children's conceptions of areas of personal choice and social regulation. *Child Development, 67,* 1223–1242.

NUCCI, L. P., & SMETANA, J. G. (1996). Mother's concepts of young children's areas of personal freedom. *Child Development, 67,* 1870–1886.

NUCCI, L. P., & WEBER, E. (1995). Social interactions in the home and the development of young children's conceptions of the personal. *Child Development, 66,* 1438–1452.

NUCCI, L., & TURIEL, E. (1978). Social interactions and the

development of social concepts in preschool children. *Child Development, 49,* 400–407.

NUCKOLLS, K. B., CASSEL, J., & KAPLAN, B. H. (1972). Psychosocial assets, life crisis, and the prognosis of pregnancy. *American Journal of Epidemiology, 95,* 431–441.

NURMI, J., POOLE, M. E., & KALAKOSKI, V. (1996). Age differences in adolescent identity exploration and commitment in urban and rural environments. *Journal of Adolescence, 19,* 443–452.

O'BRIEN, M., & HUSTON, A. C. (1985). Development of sex-typed play behavior in toddlers. *Developmental Psychology, 21,* 866–871.

O'CALLAGHAN, M. J., BURN, Y. R., MOHAY, H. A., ROGERS, Y., & TUDEHOPE, D. I. (1993). The prevalence and origins of left hand preference in high risk infants, and its implications for intellectual, motor, and behavioral performance at four and six years. *Cortex, 29,* 617–627.

O'CONNOR, B. P. (1995). Identity development and perceived parental behavior as sources of adolescent egocentrism. *Journal of Youth and Adolescence, 24,* 205–227.

O'CONNOR, C. (1997). Dispositions toward (collective) struggle and educational resilience in the inner city: A case analysis of six African-American high school students. *American Educational Research Journal, 34,* 593–629.

O'MAHONEY, J. F. (1989). Development of thinking about things and people: Social and nonsocial cognition during adolescence. *Journal of Genetic Psychology, 150,* 217–224.

O'MALLEY, P. M., JOHNSTON, L. D., & BACHMAN, J. G. (1995). Adolescent substance use: Epidemiology and implications for public policy. *Pediatric Clinics of North America, 42* (2), 241–260.

O'NEIL, R., WELSH, M., PARKE, R. D., WANG, S., & STRAND, C. (1997). A longitudinal assessment of the academic correlates of early peer acceptance and rejection. *Journal of Clinical Child Psychology, 26,* 290–303.

O'REILLY, A. W. (1995). Using representations: Comprehension and production of actions with imagined objects. *Child Development, 66,* 999–1010.

O'REILLY, A. W., & BORNSTEIN, M. H. (1993). Caregiver–child interaction in play. In M. H.

Bornstein & A. W. O'Reilly (Eds.), *New directions for child development* (No. 59, pp. 55–66). San Francisco: Jossey-Bass.

OAKES, J., GAMORAN, A., & PAGE, R. N. (1992). Curriculum differentiation: Opportunities, outcomes, and meanings. In P. W. Jackson (Ed.), *Handbook of research on curriculum* (pp. 570–608). New York: Macmillan.

OAKES, L. M. (1994). Development of infants' use of continuity cues in their perception of causality. *Developmental Psychology, 30,* 869–879.

OAKES, L. M., & COHEN, L. B. (1995). Infant causal perception. In C. K. Rovee-Collier & L. P. Lipsitt (Eds.), *Advances in infancy research* (Vol. 9, pp. 1–54). Norwood, NJ: Ablex.

OAKES, L. M., COPPAGE, D. J., & DINGEL, A. (1997). By land or by sea: The role of perceptual similarity in infants' categorization of animals. *Developmental Psychology, 33,* 396–407.

OAKLAND, T., & PARMELEE, R. (1985). Mental measurement of minority-group children. In B. B. Wolman (Ed.), *Handbook of intelligence* (pp. 699–736). New York: Wiley.

OATES, R. K., PEACOCK, A., & FORREST, D. (1985). Long-term effects of nonorganic failure to thrive. *Pediatrics, 75,* 36–40.

OBERG, C. N. (1988, Spring). Children and the uninsured. *Social Policy Report* (Society for Research in Child Development), *3* (No. 1).

OCHS, E. (1988). *Culture and language development: Language acquisition and language socialization in a Samoan village.* Cambridge: Cambridge University Press.

OCHSE, R. (1990). *Before the gates of excellence: The determinants of creative genius.* New York: Cambridge University Press.

OETTINGEN, G. (1985). The influence of kindergarten teachers on sex differences in behavior. *International Journal of Behavioral Development, 8,* 3–13.

OGBU, J. U. (1997). Understanding the school performance of urban blacks: Some essential background knowledge. In H. J. Walberg, O. Reyes, & R. P. Weissberg (Eds.), *Children and youth: Interdisciplinary perspectives* (pp. 190–222). Thousand Oaks, CA: Sage.

OKAGAKI, L., & FRENSCH, P. A. (1996). Effects of video game playing on measures of spatial performance: Gender effects in late adolescence. In P. M. Greenfield & R. R. Cocking

(Eds.), *Interacting with video* (pp. 115–140). Norwood, NJ: Ablex.

OKAGAKI, L., DIAMOND, K. E., KONTOS, S. J., & HESTENES, L. L. (1998). Correlates of young children's interactions with classmates with disabilities. *Early Childhood Research Quarterly, 13,* 67–86.

OKAGAKI, L., & STERNBERG, R. J. (1993). Parental beliefs and children's school performance. *Child Development, 64,* 36–56.

OLLENDICK, T. H., YANG, B., KING, N. J., DONG, Q., & AKANDE, A. (1996). Fears in American, Australian, Chinese, and Nigerian children and adolescents: A cross-cultural study. *Journal of Child Psychology and Psychiatry, 37,* 213–220.

OLLER, D. K., & EILERS, R. E. (1988). The role of audition in infant babbling. *Child Development, 59,* 441–449.

OLLER, D. K., EILERS, R. E., URBANO, R., & COBO-LEWIS, A. B. (1997). Development of precursors to speech in infants exposed to two languages. *Journal of Child Language, 24,* 407–425.

OLSEN, O. (1997). Meta-analysis of the safety of home birth. *Birth—Issues in Perinatal Care, 24,* 4–13.

OLWEUS, D. (1978). *Aggression in the schools: Bullies and whipping boys.* Washington, DC: Hemisphere.

OLWEUS, D. (1980). Familial and temperamental determinants of aggressive behavior in adolescent boys: A causal analysis. *Developmental Psychology, 16,* 644–666.

OLWEUS, D. (1984). Aggressors and their victims: Bullying at school. In N. Frude & H. Gault (Eds.), *Disruptive behaviors in schools* (pp. 57–76). New York: Wiley.

OLWEUS, D. (1993). *Bullying at school.* Oxford: Blackwell.

OLWEUS, D. (1995). Bullying or peer abuse at school: Facts and intervention. *Current Directions in Psychological Science, 4,* 196–200.

OLWEUS, D., MATTISON, A., SCHALLING, D., & LOW, H. (1988). Circulating testosterone levels and aggression in adolescent males: A causal analysis. *Psychosomatic Medicine, 50,* 261–272.

OMER, H., & EVERLY, G. S. (1988). Psychological factors in preterm labor: Critical review and theoretical synthesis. *American Journal of Psychiatry, 145,* 1507–1513.

OOSTERWEGEL, A., & OPPENHEIMER, L. (1993). *The self-system: Developmental changes between and within self-concepts.* Hillsdale, NJ: Erlbaum.

ORNSTEIN, P. A. (1995, August 22). Personal communication.

ORNSTEIN, P. A., NAUS, M. J., & LIBERTY, C. (1975). Rehearsal and organizational processes in children's memory. *Child Development, 46,* 818–830.

ORNSTEIN, P. A., SHAPIRO, L. R., CLUBB, P. A., & FOLLMER, A. (1997). The influence of prior knowledge on children's memory for salient medical experiences. In N. Stein, P. A. Ornstein, C. J. Brainerd, & B. Tversky (Eds.), *Memory for everyday and emotional events* (pp. 83–112). Hillsdale, NJ: Erlbaum.

OSHER, T. W., & TELESFORD, M. (1996). Involving families to improve research. In K. Hoagwood, P. S. Jensen, & C. B. Fisher (Eds.), *Ethical issues in mental health research with children and adolescents* (pp. 29–39). Mahwah, NJ: Erlbaum.

OSHERSON, D. N., & MARKMAN, E. M. (1975). Language and the ability to evaluate contradictions and tautologies. *Cognition, 2,* 213–226.

OSTREA, E. M., JR., OSTREA, A. R., & SIMPSON, P. M. (1997). Mortality within the first 2 years in infants exposed to cocaine, opiate, or cannabinoid during gestation. *Pediatrics, 100,* 79–83.

OWEN, M. T., & COX, M. J. (1997). Marital conflict and the development of infant–parent attachment relationships. *Journal of Family Psychology, 11,* 152–164.

OWEN, M. T., EASTERBROOKS, M. A., CHASE-LANSDALE, L., & GOLDBERG, W. A. (1984). The relation between maternal employment status and the stability of attachments to mother and father. *Child Development, 55,* 1894–1901.

OWENS, R. (1996). *Language development: An introduction* (4th ed.). New York: Merrill.

OWENS, T. (1982). Experience-based career education: Summary and implications of research and evaluation findings. *Child and Youth Services Journal, 4,* 77–91.

PADGHAM, J. J., & BLYTH, D. A. (1990). Dating during adolescence. In R. M. Lerner, A. C. Peterson, & J. Brooks-Gunn (Eds.), *The encyclopedia of adolescence* (Vol. 1, pp. 196–198). New York: Garland.

PADILLA, M. L., & LANDRETH, G. L. (1989). Latchkey children: A review of the literature. *Child Welfare, 68,* 445–454.

PALINCSAR, A. S. (1992, April). *Beyond reciprocal teaching: A retrospective and prospective view.* Raymond B. Cattell Early Career Award Address at the annual meeting of the American Educational Research Association, San Francisco.

PALINCSAR, A. S., BROWN, A. L., & CAMPIONE, J. C. (1993). First-grade dialogues for knowledge-acquisition and use. In E. A. Forman, N. Minick, & C. A. Stone (Eds.), *Contexts for learning* (pp. 43–57). New York: Oxford University Press.

PALINCSAR, A. S., & KLENK, L. (1992). Fostering literacy learning in supportive contexts. *Journal of Learning Disabilities, 25,* 211–225.

PALMLUND, I. (1996). Exposure to a xenoestrogen before birth: The diethylstilbestrol experience. *Journal of Psychosomoatic Obstetrics and Gynaecology, 17,* 71–84.

PAN, H. W. (1994). Children's play in Taiwan. In J. L. Roopnarine, J. E. Johnson, & F. H. Hooper (Eds.), *Children's play in diverse cultures* (pp. 31–50). Albany, NY: SUNY Press.

PAPINI, D. R. (1994). Family interventions. In S. L. Archer (Ed.), *Interventions for adolescent identity development* (pp. 47–61). Thousand Oaks, CA: Sage.

PAPOUSEK, M., & PAPOUSEK, H. (1996). Infantile persistent crying, state regulation, and interaction with parents: A systems view. In M. H. Bornstein & J. L. Genevro (Eds.), *Child development and behavioral pediatrics* (pp. 11–33). Mahwah, NJ: Erlbaum.

PARIKH, B. (1980). Development of moral judgment and its relation to family environmental factors in Indian and American families. *Child Development, 51,* 1030–1039.

PARIS, S. G., LAWTON, T. A., TURNER, J. C., & ROTH, J. L. (1991). A developmental perspective on standardized achievement testing. *Educational Researcher, 20* (5), 12–20.

PARK, S-Y., BELSKY, J., PUTNAM, S., & CRNIC, K. (1997). Infant emotionality, parenting, and 3-year inhibition: Exploring stability and lawful discontinuity in a male sample. *Developmental Psychology, 33,* 218–227.

PARKE, R. (1996). *Fatherhood.* Cambridge, MA: Cambridge University Press.

PARKE, R. D. (1994). Progress, paradigms and unresolved problems: A commentary on recent advances in our understanding of children's emotions. *Merrill-Palmer Quarterly, 40,* 157–169.

PARKE, R. D., & BURIEL, R. (1998). Socialization in the family: Eth-nic and ecological perspectives. In N. Eisenberg (Ed.), *Handbook of child psychology: Vol. 3. Social, emotional, and personality development* (5th ed., pp. 463–552). New York: Wiley.

PARKE, R. D., BURKS, V. M., CARSON, J. L., NEVILLE, B., & BOYUM, L. A. (1994). Family–peer relationships: A tripartite model. In R. D. Parke & S. G. Kellam (Eds.), *Exploring family relationships with other social contexts* (pp. 115–145). Hillsdale, NJ: Erlbaum.

PARKE, R. D., & KELLAM, S. G. (Eds.) (1994). *Exploring family relationships with other social contexts.* Hillsdale, NJ: Erlbaum.

PARKE, R. D., & TINSLEY, B. R. (1981). The father's role in infancy: Determinants of involvement in caregiving and play. In M. E. Lamb (Ed.), *The role of the father in child development* (pp. 429–458). New York: Wiley.

PARKER, J. G., & ASHER, S. R. (1987). Peer relations and later personal adjustment: Are low-accepted children at risk? *Psychological Bulletin, 102,* 357–389.

PARKER, J. G., & ASHER, S. R. (1993). Friendship and friendship quality in middle childhood: Links with peer group acceptance and feelings of loneliness and social dissatisfaction. *Developmental Psychology, 29,* 611–621.

PARKER, J. G., RUBIN, K. H., PRICE, J., & DEROSIER, M. E. (1995). Peer relationships, child development, and adjustment: A developmental psychopathology perspective. In D. Cicchetti & D. Cohen (Eds.), *Developmental psychopathology: Vol. 2. Risk, disorder, and adaptation* (pp. 96–161). New York: Wiley.

PARKHURST, J. T., & ASHER, S. R. (1992). Peer rejection in middle school: Subgroup differences in behavior, loneliness, and interpersonal concerns. *Developmental Psychology, 28,* 231–241.

PARKS, W. (1996). Human immunodeficiency virus. In R. D. Behrman, R. M. Kliegman, & A. M. Arvin (Eds.), *Nelson textbook of pediatrics* (15th ed., pp. 916–919). Philadelphia: Saunders.

PARRISH, L. H. (1991). Community resources and dropout prevention. In L. L. West (Ed.), *Effective strategies for dropout prevention of at-risk youth* (pp. 217–232). Gaithersburg, MD: Aspen.

PARSONS, J. E., ADLER, T. F., & KACZALA, C. M. (1982). Socialization of achievement attitudes and beliefs: Parental influences. *Child Development, 53,* 310–321.

PARTEN, M. (1932). Social participation among preschool chil-dren. *Journal of Abnormal and Social Psychology, 27,* 243–269.

PASSMAN, R. H. (1987). Attachments to inanimate objects: Are children who have security blankets insecure? *Journal of Consulting and Clinical Psychology, 55,* 825–830.

PATTERSON, C. J. (1995). Sexual orientation and human development: An overview. *Developmental Psychology, 31,* 3–11.

PATTERSON, C. J. (1996). Lesbian and gay parenthood. In M. H. Bornstein (Ed.), *Handbook of parenting* (Vol. 3, pp. 255–274). Mahwah, NJ: Erlbaum.

PATTERSON, G. R. (1982). *Coercive family processes.* Eugene, OR: Castilia Press.

PATTERSON, G. R. (1995). Coercion—A basis for early age of onset for arrest. In J. McCord (Ed.), *Coercion and punishment in long-term perspective* (pp. 81–105). New York: Cambridge University Press.

PATTERSON, G. R. (1997). Performance models for parenting: A social interactional perspective. In J. E. Grusec & L. Kuczynski (Eds.), *Parenting and children's internalization of values* (pp. 193–226). New York: Wiley.

PATTERSON, G. R., DEBARYSHE, B. D., & RAMSEY, E. (1989). A developmental perspective on antisocial behavior. *American Psychologist, 44,* 329–335.

PATTERSON, G. R., & FLEISHMAN, M. J. (1979). Maintenance of treatment effects: Some considerations concerning family systems and follow-up data. *Behavior Therapy, 10,* 168–185.

PATTERSON, G. R., LITTMAN, R. A., & BRICKER, W. (1967). Assertive behavior in children: A step toward a theory of aggression. *Monographs of the Society for Research in Child Development, 35* (5, Serial No. 113).

PATTERSON, G. R., REID, J. B., & DISHION, T. J. (1992). *Antisocial boys.* Eugene, OR: Castalia.

PATTESON, D. M., & BARNARD, K. E. (1990). Parenting of low birth weight infants: A review of issues and interventions. *Infant Mental Health Journal, 11,* 37–56.

PAYNE, R. J. (1998). *Getting beyond race: The changing American culture.* Boulder, CO: Westview.

PEARSON, J. L., HUNTER, A. G., ENSMINGER, M. E., & KELLAM, S. G. (1990). Black grandmothers in multigenerational households: Diversity in family structure and parenting involvement in the Woodlawn community. *Child Development, 61,* 434–442.

PECKHAM, C. S., & LOGAN, S. (1993). Screening for toxoplasmosis during pregnancy. *Archives of Disease in Childhood, 68,* 3–5.

PEDERSON, D. R., GLEASON, K. E., MORAN, G., & BENTO, S. (1998). Maternal attachment representations, maternal sensitivity, and the infant-mother attachment relationship. *Developmental Psychology, 34,* 925–933.

PEDERSON, D. R., & MORAN, G. (1995). A categorical description of infant–mother relationships in the home and its relation to Q-sort measures of infant–mother interaction. In E. Waters, B. E. Vaughn, G. Posada, & K. Kondo-Ikemura (Eds.), Caregiving, cultural, and cognitive perspectives on secure-base behavior and working models: New growing points of attachment theory and research. *Monographs of the Society for Research in Child Development, 60* (2–3, Serial No. 244).

PEDERSON, D. R., & MORAN, G. (1996). Expressions of the attachment relationship outside of the Strange Situation. *Child Development, 67,* 915–927.

PEDLOW, R., SANSON, A., PRIOR, M., & OBERKLAID, F. (1993). Stability of maternally reported temperament from infancy to 8 years. *Developmental Psychology, 29,* 998–1007.

PELHAM, W. E., JR., & HOZA, B. (1996). Intensive treatment: A summer treatment program for children with ADHD. In E. D. Hibbs & P. S. Jensen (Eds.), *Psychosocial treatments for child and adolescent disorders: Empirically based strategies for clinical practice* (pp. 311–340). Washington, DC: American Psychological Association.

PELLEGRINI, A. D. (1995). A longitudinal study of boys' rough-and-tumble play and dominance during early adolescence. *Journal of Applied Developmental Psychology, 16,* 77–93.

PELLEGRINI, A. D., & SMITH, P. K. (1998). Physical activity play: The nature and function of a neglected aspect of play. *Child Development, 69,* 577–598.

PENNER, S. G. (1987). Parental responses to grammatical and ungrammatical utterances. *Child Development, 58,* 376–384.

PENNINGTON, B. F., BENDER, B., PUCK, M., SALBENBLATT, J., & ROBINSON, A. (1982). Learning disabilities in children with sex chromosome anomalies. *Child Development, 53,* 1182–1192.

PEOPLES, C. E., FAGAN, J. F., III, & DROTAR, D. (1995). The influence of race on 3-year-old children's performance on the Stanford-Binet: Fourth Edition. *Intelligence, 21,* 69–82.

PERES, Y., & PASTERNACK, R. (1991). To what extent can the school reduce the gaps between children raised by divorced and intact families? *Journal of Divorce and Remarriage, 15,* 143–158.

PERFETTI, C. A. (1988). Verbal efficiency in reading ability. In M. Daneman, G. E. MacKinnon, & T. G. Waller (Eds.), *Reading research: Advances in theory and practice* (Vol. 6, pp. 109–143). San Diego: Academic Press.

PERLETH, C., & HELLER, K. A. (1994). The Munich Longitudinal Study of Giftedness. In R. F. Subotnik & K. D. Arnold (Eds.), *Beyond Terman: Contemporary studies of giftedness and talent* (pp. 77–114). Norwood, NJ: Ablex.

PERLMUTTER, M. (1984). Continuities and discontinuities in early human memory: Paradigms, processes, and performances. In R. V. Kail, Jr., & N. R. Spear (Eds.), *Comparative perspectives on the development of memory* (pp. 253–287). Hillsdale, NJ: Erlbaum.

PERNER, J. (1988). Higher-order beliefs and intentions in children's understanding of social interaction. In J. W. Astington, P. L. Harris, & D. R. Olson (Eds.), *Developing theories of mind* (pp. 271–294). New York: Cambridge University Press.

PERNER, J. (1991). *Understanding the representational mind.* Cambridge, MA: MIT Press.

PERRY, D. G., PERRY, L. C., & RASMUSSEN, P. (1986). Cognitive social learning mediators of aggression. *Child Development, 57,* 700–711.

PERRY, D. G., PERRY, L. C., & WEISS, R. J. (1989). Sex differences in the consequences that children anticipate for aggression. *Developmental Psychology, 25,* 171–184.

PERRY, D. G., WILLIARD, J. C., & PERRY, L. C. (1990). Peers' perceptions of the consequences that victimized children provide aggressors. *Child Development, 61,* 1310–1325.

PESHKIN, A. (1978). *Growing up American: Schooling and the survival of the community.* Chicago: University of Chicago Press.

PESHKIN, A. (1997). *Places of memory: Whiteman's schools and native American communities.* Mahwah, NJ: Erlbaum.

PETERSON, C. C., PETERSON, J. L., & SEETO, D. (1983). Developmental changes in ideas about lying. *Child Development, 54,* 1529–1535.

PETERSON, L. (1982). An alternative perspective to norm-based explanations of modeling and children's generosity: A reply to Lipscomb, Larrieu, McAllister, and Bregman. *Merrill-Palmer Quarterly, 28,* 283–290.

PETITTO, L. A., & MARENTETTE, P. F. (1991). Babbling in the manual mode: Evidence for the ontogeny of language. *Science, 251,* 1493–1496.

PETRILL, S. A., SAUDINO, K., CHERNEY, S. S., EMDE, R. N., FULKER, D. W., HEWITT, J. K., & PLOMIN, R. (1998). Exploring the genetic and environmental etiology of high general cognitive ability in fourteen- to thirty-six-month-old twins. *Child Development, 69,* 68–74.

PETTIT, G. S., BAKSHI, A., DODGE, K. A., & COIE, J. D. (1990). The emergence of social dominance in young boys' play groups: Developmental differences and behavioral correlates. *Developmental Psychology, 26,* 1017–1025.

PETTIT, G. S., BATES, J. E., & DODGE, K. A. (1997). Supportive parenting, ecological context, and children's adjustment: A seven-year longitudinal study. *Child Development, 68,* 908–923.

PETTIT, G. S., CLAWSON, M. A., DODGE, K. A., & BATES, J. E. (1996). Stability and change in peer-rejected status: The role of child behavior, parenting, and family ecology. *Merrill-Palmer Quarterly, 42,* 267–294.

PHELPS, K. E., & WOOLLEY, J. D. (1994). The form and function of young children's magical beliefs. *Developmental Psychology, 30,* 385–394.

PHILLIPS, C. A., ROLLS, S., ROUSE, A., & GRIFFITHS, M. D. (1995). Home video game playing in schoolchildren—A study of incidence and patterns of play. *Journal of Adolescence, 18,* 687–691.

PHILLIPS, D. A. (1987). Socialization of perceived academic competence among highly competent children. *Child Development, 58,* 1308–1320.

PHILLIPS, D. A., HOWES, C., & WHITEBOOK, M. (1992). The social policy context of child care: Effects on quality. *American Journal of Community Psychology, 20,* 25–51.

PHILLIPS, D. A., VORAN, M., KISKER, E., HOWES, C., & WHITEBOOK, M. (1994). Child care for children in poverty: Opportunity or inequity? *Child Development, 65,* 472–492.

PHILLIPS, K., & FULKER, D. W. (1989). Quantitative genetic analysis of longitudinal trends in adoption designs with application to IQ in the Colorado Adoption Project. *Behavior Genetics, 19,* 621–658.

PHILLIPS, M. (1997). What makes schools effective? A comparison of the relationships of communitarian climate and academic climate to mathematics achievement and attendance during middle school. *American Educa-*
tional Research Journal, 34, 633–662.

PHILLIPS, O. P., & ELIAS, S. (1993). Prenatal genetic counseling issues in women of advanced reproductive age. *Journal of Women's Health, 2,* 1–5.

PHINNEY, J. S. (1989). Stages of ethnic identity development in minority group adolescents. *Journal of Early Adolescence, 9,* 34–49.

PHINNEY, J. S. (1993). A three stage model of ethnic identity development in adolescents. In M. E. Bernal & G. P. Knight (Eds.), *Ethnic identity: Formation and transmission among Hispanic and other minorities* (pp. 61–80). Albany, NY: State University of New York.

PHINNEY, J. S., & CHAVIRA, V. (1995). Parental ethnic socialization and adolescent outcomes in ethnic minority families. *Journal of Research on Adolescence, 5,* 31–53.

PHINNEY, J. S., & KOHATSU, E. L. (1997). Ethnic and racial identity development and mental health. In J. Schulenberg, J. L. Maggs, & K. Hurrelmann (Eds.), *Health risks and developmental transitions during adolescence* (pp. 420–443). Cambridge: Cambridge University Press.

PIAGET, J. (1926). *The language and thought of the child.* New York: Harcourt, Brace & World. (Original work published 1923)

PIAGET, J. (1928). *Judgment and reasoning in the child.* New York: Harcourt, Brace & World. (Original work published 1926)

PIAGET, J. (1929). *The child's conception of physical causality.* New York: Harcourt, Brace & World. (Original work published 1926)

PIAGET, J. (1930). *The child's conception of the world.* New York: Harcourt, Brace & World. (Original work published 1926)

PIAGET, J. (1950). *The psychology of intelligence.* New York: International Universities Press.

PIAGET, J. (1951). *Play, dreams, and imitation in childhood.* New York: Norton. (Original work published 1945)

PIAGET, J. (1952a). Jean Piaget (autobiographical sketch). In E. G. Boring, H. S. Langfeld, H. Werner, & R. M. Yerkes (Eds.), *A history of psychology in autobiography* (pp. 237–256). Worcester, MA: Clark University Press.

PIAGET, J. (1952b). *The origins of intelligence in children.* New York: International Universities Press. (Original work published 1936)

PIAGET, J. (1965). *The moral judgment of the child.* New York: Free Press. (Original work published 1932)

PIAGET, J. (1967). *Six psychological studies.* New York: Vintage.

PIAGET, J. (1971). *Biology and knowledge.* Chicago: University of Chicago Press.

PIAGET, J. (1985). *The equilibration of cognitive structures: The central problem of intellectual development.* Chicago: University of Chicago Press.

PIAGET, J., & INHELDER, B. (1956). *The child's conception of space.* London: Routledge & Kegan Paul. (Original work published 1948)

PIAGET, J., & INHELDER, B. (1969). *The psychology of the child.* London: Routledge & Kegan Paul. (Original work published 1967)

PIAGET, J., INHELDER, B., & SZEMINSKA, A. (1960). *The child's conception of geometry.* New York: Basic Books. (Original work published 1948)

PIANTA, R. C., EGELAND, B., & ERICKSON, M. F. (1989). The antecedents of maltreatment: Results of the Mother-Child Interaction Research Project. In D. Cicchetti & V. Carlson (Eds.), *Child maltreatment* (pp. 203–253). New York: Cambridge University Press.

PIANTA, R. C., SROUFE, L. A., & EGELAND, B. (1989). Continuity and discontinuity in maternal sensitivity at 6, 24, and 42 months in a high-risk sample. *Child Development, 60,* 481–487.

PIATT, B. (1993). *Only English? Law and language policy in the United States.* Albuquerque: University of New Mexico Press.

PICK, A. D., & FRANKEL, G. W. (1974). A developmental study of strategies of visual selectivity. *Child Development, 45,* 1162–1165.

PICK, H. L., JR. (1989). Motor development: The control of action. *Developmental Psychology, 25,* 867–870.

PICKENS, J., FIELD, T., NAWROCKI, T. I., MARTINEZ, A., SOUTULLO, D., & GONZALEZ, J. (1994). Full-term and preterm infants' perception of face–voice synchrony. *Infant Behavior and Development, 17,* 447–455.

PICKERING, L. K., GRANOFF, D. M., ERICKSON, J. R., MASON, M. L., & CORDLE, C. T. (1998). Modulation of the immune system by human milk and infant formula containing nucleotides. *Pediatrics, 101,* 242–249.

PIERCE, J. W., & WARDLE, J. (1997). Cause and effect beliefs and self-esteem of overweight children. *Journal of Child Psychology and Psychiatry, 38,* 645–650.

PIERCE, W. D., & EPLING, W. F. (1995). *Behavior analysis and learning.* Englewood Cliffs, NJ: Prentice-Hall.

PIKE, K. M., & RODIN, J. (1991). Mothers, daughters, and disordered eating. *Journal of Abnormal Psychology, 100*, 198–204.

PILLEMER, D. B., & WHITE, S. H. (1989). Childhood events recalled by children and adults. In H. W. Reese (Ed.), *Advances in child development and behavior* (Vol. 21, pp. 297–340). New York: Academic Press.

PILLOW, B. H. (1991). Understanding of biased social cognition. *Developmental Psychology, 27*, 539–551.

PILLOW, B. H. (1995). Two trends in the development of conceptual perspective taking. An elaboration of the passive–active hypothesis. *International Journal of Behavioral Development, 18*, 649–676.

PINE, J. M. (1995). Variation in vocabulary development as a function of birth order. *Child Development, 66*, 272–281.

PINKER, S. (1981). On the acquisition of grammatical morphemes. *Journal of Child Language, 8*, 477–484.

PINKER, S. (1994). *The language instinct: How the mind creates language.* New York: William Morrow.

PINKER, S., LEBEAUX, D. S., & FROST, L. A. (1987). Productivity and constraints in the acquisition of the passive. *Cognition, 26*, 195–267.

PINSON-MILLBURN, N. M., FABIAN, E. S., SCHLOSSBERG, N. K., & PYLE, M. (1996). Grandparents raising grandchildren. *Journal of Counseling & Development, 74*, 548–554.

PINTO, J., & DAVIS, P. V. (1991, April). *The categorical perception of human gait in 3- and 5-month-old infants.* Paper presented at the biennial meeting of the Society for Research in Child Development, Seattle, WA.

PIPES, P. L. (1996). *Nutrition in infancy and childhood* (6th ed.). St. Louis: Mosby.

PIPP, S., EASTERBROOKS, M. A., & BROWN, S. R. (1993). Attachment status and complexity of infants' self- and other-knowledge when tested with mother and father. *Social Development, 2*, 1–14.

PIPP, S., & HAITH, M. M. (1984). Infant visual responses to pattern: Which metric predicts best? *Journal of Experimental Child Psychology, 38*, 373–379.

PLOMIN, R. (1994a). The Emanuel Miller Memorial Lecture 1993: Genetic research and identification of environmental influences. *Journal of Child Psychology and Psychiatry, 35*, 817–834.

PLOMIN, R. (1994b). Genetics and children's experiences in the family. *Journal of Child Psychology and Psychiatry, 36*, 33–68.

PLOMIN, R. (1994c). *Genetics and experience: The interplay be-

tween nature and nurture.* Thousand Oaks, CA: Sage.

PLOMIN, R. (1994d). Nature, nurture, and social development. *Social Development, 3*, 37–53.

PLOMIN, R., CHIPUER, H. M., & LOEHLIN, J. C. (1990). Behavior genetics and personality. In L. A. Pervin (Ed.), *Handbook of personality theory and research* (pp. 225–243). New York: Guilford.

PLOMIN, R., & DEFRIES, J. C. (1983). The Colorado Adoption Project. *Child Development, 54*, 276–289.

PLOMIN, R., DEFRIES, J. C., MCCLEARN, G. E., & RUTTER, M. (Eds.). (1997). *Behavioral genetics.* New York: Freeman.

PLOMIN, R., EMDE, R. N., BRAUNGART, J. M., CAMPOS, J., KAGAN, J., REZNICK, J. S., ROBINSON, J., ZAHN-WAXLER, C., & DEFRIES, J. C. (1993). Genetic change and continuity from fourteen to twenty months: The MacArthur Longitudinal Twin Study. *Child Development, 64*, 1354–1376.

PLOMIN, R., REISS, D., HETHERINGTON, E. M., & HOWE, G. W. (1994). Nature and nurture: Genetic contributions to measures of the family environment. *Developmental Psychology, 30*, 32–43.

PLOMIN, R., & RUTTER, M. (1998). Child development, molecular genetics, and what to do with genes once they are found. *Child Development, 69*, 1223–1242.

PLUCKER, J. A., CALLAHAN, C. M., & TOMCHIN, E. M. (1996). Wherefore art thou, multiple intelligences? Alternative assessments for identifying talent in ethnically diverse and low income students. *Gifted Child Quarterly, 40*, 81–92.

PLUMERT, J. M. (1994). Flexibility in children's use of spatial and categorical organizational strategies in recall. *Developmental Psychology, 30*, 738–747.

PLUMERT, J. M., PICK, H. L., JR., MARKS, R. A., KINTSCH, A. S., & WEGESIN, D. (1994). Locating objects and communicating about locations: Organizational differences in children's searching and direction-giving. *Developmental Psychology, 30*, 443–453.

PLUNKETT, K. (1993). Lexical segmentation and vocabulary growth in early language acquisition. *Journal of Child Language, 20*, 43–60.

PLUNKETT, K., KARMILOFF-SMITH, A., BATES, E., ELMAN, J. L., & JOHNSON, M. H. (1997). Connectionism and developmental psychology. *Journal of Child Psychology and Psychiatry, 38*, 53–80.

PLUNKETT, K., & MARCHMAN, V. A. (1993). From rote learning to system building: Acquiring verb

morphology in children and connectionist nets. *Cognition, 48*, 21–69.

PLUNKETT, K., & MARCHMAN, V. A. (1996). Learning from a connectionist model of the acquisition of the English past tense. *Cognition, 61*, 299–308.

PLUNKETT, K., SINHA, C., MØLLER, M. F., & STRANDSBY, O. (1992). Symbol grounding of the emergence of symbols? Vocabulary growth in children and a connectionist net. *Connection Science, 4*, 293–312.

PODROUZEK, W., & FURROW, D. (1988). Preschoolers' use of eye contact while speaking: The influence of sex, age, and conversational partner. *Journal of Psycholinguistic Research, 17*, 89–93.

POLANSKY, N. A., GAUDIN, J. M., AMMONS, P. W., & DAVIS, K. B. (1985). The psychological ecology of the neglectful mother. *Child Abuse & Neglect, 9*, 265–275.

POLIT, D. F., QUINT, J. C., & RICCIO, J. A. (1988). *The challenge of serving teenage mothers: Lessons from Project Redirection.* New York: Manpower Demonstration Research Corporation.

POLKA, L., & WERKER, J. F. (1994). Developmental changes in perception of non-native vowel contrasts. *Journal of Experimental Psychology: Human Perception and Performance, 20*, 421–435.

POLLACK, S., CICCHETTI, D., KLORMAN, R., & BRUMAGHIM, J. (1997). Cognitive brain event-related potentials and emotion processing in maltreated children. *Child Development, 68*, 773–787.

POLLITT, E., GORMAN, K. S., ENGLE, P. L., MARTORELL, R., & RIVERA, J. (1993). Early supplementary feeding and cognition. *Monographs of the Society for Research in Child Development, 58* (7, Serial No. 235).

POLLOCK, L. (1987). *A lasting relationship: Parents and children over three centuries.* Hanover, NH: University Press of New England.

POLLOWAY, E. A., PATTON, J. R., SMITH, T. E. C., & BUCK, G. H. (1997). Mental retardation and learning disabilities: Conceptual and applied issues. *Journal of Learning Disabilities, 30*, 297–308.

POMERANTZ, E. M., & RUBLE, D. N. (1998a). The multidimensional nature of control: Implications for the development of sex differences in self-evaluation. In J. Heckhausen & C. S. Dweck (Eds.), *Motivation and self-regulation across the life span* (pp. 159–184). New York: Cambridge University Press.

POMERANTZ, E. M., & RUBLE, D. N. (1998b). The role of maternal

control in the development of sex differences in child self-evaluative factions. *Child Development, 69*, 458–478.

POMERANTZ, E. M., RUBLE, D. N., FREY, K. S., & GREULICH, F. (1995). Meeting goals and confronting conflict: Children's changing perceptions of social comparison. *Child Development, 66*, 723–738.

POMERLEAU, A., BOLDUC, D., MALCUIT, G., & COSSETTE, L. (1990). Pink or blue: Environmental gender stereotypes in the first two years of life. *Sex Roles, 22*, 359–367.

POPKIN, B. M. (1994). The nutrition transition in low-income countries: An emerging crisis. *Nutrition Review, 52*, 285–298.

POPKIN, B. M., & DOAK, C. M. (1998). The obesity epidemic is a worldwide phenomenon. *Nutrition Reviews, 56*, 106–114.

POPKIN, B. M., RICHARDS, M. K., & MONTIERO, C. A. (1996). Stunting is associated with overweight in children of four nations that are undergoing the nutrition transition. *Journal of Nutrition, 126*, 3009–3016.

PORGES, S. W. (1991). Autonomic regulation and attention. In B. A. Campbell, H. Hayne, & R. Richardson (Eds.), *Attention and information processing in infants and adults* (pp. 201–223). Hillsdale, NJ: Erlbaum.

PORTER, R. H., MAKIN, J. W., DAVIS, L. B., & CHRISTENSEN, K. M. (1992). An assessment of the salient olfactory environment of formula-fed infants. *Physiology & Behavior, 50*, 907–911.

POSADA, G., GAO, Y., WU, F., POSADA, R., TASCON, M., SCHÖELMERICH, A., SAGI, A., KONDO-IKEMURA, K., HAALAND, W., & SYNNEVAAG, B. (1995). The secure-base phenomenon across cultures: Children's behavior, mothers' preferences, and experts' concepts. In E. Waters, B. E. Vaughn, G. Posada, & K. Kondo-Ikemura (Eds.), Caregiving, cultural, and cognitive perspectives on secure-base behavior and working models: New growing points of attachment theory and research. *Monographs of the Society for Research in Child Development, 60* (2–3, Serial No. 244).

POSNER, J. K., & VANDELL, D. L. (1994). Low-income children's after-school care: Are there beneficial effects of after-school programs? *Child Development, 64*, 440–456.

POSNER, M. I., ROTHBART, M. K., GERARDI, G., & THOMAS-THRAPP, L. (1997). Functions of orienting in early infancy. In P. Lange, M. Balaban, & R. F. Simmons (Eds.), *The study of attention:*

Cognitive perspectives from psychophysiology, reflexology, and neuroscience (pp. 327–345). Hillsdale, NJ: Erlbaum.

POST, G. B., & KEMPER, H. C. G. (1993). Nutrient intake and biological maturation during adolescence: The Amsterdam growth and health longitudinal study. *European Journal of Clinical Nutrition, 47,* 400–408.

POULIN-DUBOIS, D., & HÉROUX, G. (1994). Movement and children's attributions of life properties. *International Journal of Behavioral Development, 17,* 329–347.

POULIN-DUBOIS, D., SERBIN, L. A., KENYON, B., & DERBYSHIRE, A. (1994). Infants' intermodal knowledge about gender. *Developmental Psychology, 30,* 436–442.

POWELL, B., & STEELMAN, L. C. (1993). The educational benefits of being spaced out: Sibship density and educational progress. *American Sociological Review, 58,* 367–381.

POWERS, S. I., HAUSER, S. T., & KILNER, L. A. (1989). Adolescent mental health. *American Psychologist, 44,* 200–208.

POWLISHTA, K. K., SERBIN, L. A., & MOLLER, L. C. (1993). The stability of individual differences in gender typing: Implications for understanding gender segregation. *Sex Roles, 29,* 723–737.

POWLISHTA, K. K., SERBIN, L. A., DOYLE, A., & WHITE, D. R. (1994). Gender, ethnic, and body type biases: The generality of prejudice in childhood. *Developmental Psychology, 30,* 526–536.

POWLS, A., BOTTING, N., COOKE, R. W. I., & MARLOW, N. (1996). Handedness in very-low-birthweight (VLBW) children at 12 years of age: Relation to perinatal and outcome variables. *Developmental Medicine and Child Neurology, 38,* 594–602.

PRATT, D. (1986). On the merits of multiage classrooms: Their work life. *Research in Rural Education, 3,* 111–116.

PRATT, M. W., GREEN, D., & MACVICAR, J. (1992). The mathematical parent: Parental scaffolding, parenting style, and learning outcomes in long-division mathematics homework. *Journal of Applied Developmental Psychology, 24,* 832–839.

PRECHTL, H. F. R. (1958). Problems of behavioral studies in the newborn infant. In D. S. Lehrmann, R. A. Hinde, & E. Shaw (Eds.), *Advances in the study of behavior* (Vol. 1, pp. 75–98). New York: Academic Press.

PRECHTL, H. F. R., & BEINTEMA, D. (1965). *The neurological examination of the full-term newborn infant.* London: William Heinemann Medical Books.

PREISLER, G. M. (1991). Early patterns of interaction between blind infants and their sighted mothers. *Child: Care, Health and Development, 17,* 65–90.

PREISLER, G. M. (1993). A descriptive study of blind children in nurseries with sighted children. *Child: Care, Health and Development, 19,* 295–315.

PREMACK, A. J. (1976). *Why chimps can read.* New York: Harper & Row.

PRESSLEY, M. (1992). How not to study strategy discovery. *American Psychologist, 47,* 1240–1241.

PRESSLEY, M. (1994). State-of-the-science primary-grades reading instruction or whole language? *Educational Psychologist, 29,* 211–215.

PRESSLEY, M. (1995a). *Advanced educational psychology for educators, researchers, and policymakers.* New York: HarperCollins.

PRESSLEY, M. (1995b). More about the development of self-regulation: Complex, long-term, and thoroughly social. *Educational Psychologist, 30,* 207–212.

PRESSLEY, M., & EL-DINARY, P. B. (Eds.). (1993). Strategies instruction [Special issue]. *Elementary School Journal, 94* (2).

PRESTON, R. C. (1962). Reading achievement of German and American children. *School and Society, 90,* 350–354.

PREVIC, F. H. (1991). A general theory concerning the prenatal origins of cerebral lateralization. *Psychological Review, 98,* 299–334.

PREYER, W. (1888). *The mind of the child* (2 vols.). New York: Appleton. (Original work published 1882)

PRIOR, M., SMART, D., SANSON, A., & OBERKLAID, F. (1993). Sex differences in psychological adjustment from infancy to 8 years. *Journal of the American Academy of Child and Adolescent Psychiatry, 32,* 291–304.

PROFFITT, D. R., & BERTENTHAL, B. I. (1990). Converging operations revisited: Assessing what infants perceive using discrimination measures. *Perception & Psychophysics, 47,* 1–11.

PROOS, L. A. (1993). Anthropometry in adolescence–secular trends, adoption, ethnic and environmental differences. *Hormone Research, 39,* 18–24.

PROVINS, K. A. (1997). Handedness and speech: A critical reappraisal of the role of genetic and environmental factors in the cerebral lateralization of function. *Psychological Review, 104,* 554–571.

PROVISIONAL COMMITTEE ON PEDIATRIC AIDS, AMERICAN ACADEMY OF PEDIATRICS. (1995). Perinatal human immunodeficiency virus testing. *Pediatrics, 95,* 303–307.

PULKKINEN, L. (1982). Self-control and continuity from childhood to late adolescence. In P. B. Baltes & O. G. Brim, Jr. (Eds.), *Life-span development and behavior* (Vol. 4, pp. 63–105). New York: Academic Press.

PURCELL-GATES, V. (1996). Stories, coupons, and the TV Guide: Relationships between home literacy experiences and emergent literacy knowledge. *Reading Research Quarterly, 31,* 406–428.

PYERITZ, R. E. (1998). Sex: What we make of it. *Journal of the American Medical Association, 279,* 269.

Q

QAZI, Q. H., SHEIKH, T. M., FIKRIG, S., & MENIKOFF, H. (1988). Lack of evidence for craniofacial dysmorphism in perinatal human immunodeficiency virus infection. *Journal of Pediatrics, 112,* 7–11.

QUINN, P. C., & EIMAS, P. D. (1996). Perceptual organization and categorization in young infants. In C. Rovee-Collier & L. P. Lipsitt (Eds.), *Advances in infancy research* (Vol. 10, pp. 1–36). Norwood, NJ: Ablex.

QUINN, T. M., & ADZICK, N. S. (1997). Fetal surgery. *Obstetrics and Gynecology Clinics of North America, 24,* 143–157.

QUINT, J. C., BOX, J. M., & POLIT, D. F. (1997, July). *New chance: Final report on a comprehensive program for disadvantaged young mothers and their children.* New York: Manpower Demonstration Research Corporation.

QUINTERO, R. A., PUDER, K. S., & COTTON, D. B. (1993). Embryoscopy and fetoscopy. *Obstetrics and Gynecology Clinics of North America, 20,* 563–581.

R

RABINER, D. L., KEANE, S. P., & MACKINNON-LEWIS, C. (1993). Children's beliefs about familiar and unfamiliar peers in relation to their sociometric status. *Developmental Psychology, 29,* 236–243.

RADIN, N. (1994). Primary caregiving fathers in intact families. In A. E. Gottfried & A. W. Gottfried (Eds.), *Redefining families: Implications for children's development* (pp. 11–54). New York: Plenum.

RADZISZEWSKA, B., & ROGOFF, B. (1988). Influence of adult and peer collaboration on the development of children's planning skills. *Developmental Psychology, 24,* 840–848.

RÄIHÄ, N. C. R., & AXELSSON, I. E. (1995). Protein nutrition during infancy. *Pediatric Clinics of North America, 42,* 745–763.

RAIJAMKERS, M. E. J., KOTEN, S. V., & MOLENAAR, P. C. M. (1996). On the validity of simulating stagewise development by means of PDP networks: families: Implications for children's development (pp. 11–54). New York: Plenum.

RAIJAMKERS, M. E. J., KOTEN, S. V., & MOLENAAR, P. C. M. (1996). On the validity of simulating stagewise development by means of PDP networks for children of poverty. *Intelligence, 14,* 1–9.

RAIKES, H. (1998). Investing in child care subsidy: What are we buying? *Social Policy Report of the Society for Research in Child Development, 12*(2).

RAKISON, D. H., & BUTTERWORTH, G. E. (1998). Infants' use of object parts in early categorization. *Developmental Psychology, 34,* 49–62.

RAMEY, C. T., & RAMEY, S. L. (1998). Early intervention and early experience. *American Psychologist, 53,* 109–120.

RAMIREZ, J. D., YUEN, S. D., RAMEY, D. R., & PASTA, D. (1991). *Longitudinal study of structured English immersion strategy, early exit and late-exit transitional bilingual education programs for language minority: Final report* (Vols. 1 & 2). San Mateo, CA: Aguirre International.

RAMPHAL, C. (1962). *A study of three current problems in education.* Unpublished doctoral dissertation, University of Natal, India.

RAMSAY, D. S. (1985). Fluctuations in unimanual hand preference in infants following the onset of duplicated babbling. *Developmental Psychology, 21,* 318–324.

RAMSAY, D. S., & MCCUNE, L. (1984). *Fluctuations in bimanual handedness in the second year of life.* Unpublished manuscript, Rutgers University.

RAMSAY, M., GISEL, E. G., & BOUTRY, M. (1993). Non-organic failure to thrive: Growth failure secondary to feeling-skills disorder. *Developmental Medicine and Child Neurology, 35,* 285–297.

RAMSEY, P. G. (1991). Young children's awareness and understanding of social class differences. *Journal of Genetic Psychology, 152,* 71–82.

RAMSEY, P. G. (1995, September). Growing up with the contradictions of race and class. *Young Children, 50*(6), 18–22.

RAND, Y., & KANIEL, S. (1987). Group administration of the LPAD. In C. S. Lidz (Ed.), *Dynamic assessment: An interactional approach to evaluating learning potential* (pp. 196–214). New York: Guilford.

RAPPORT, M. D., & KELLY, K. L. (1993). Psychostimulant effects on learning and cognitive function in children with attention deficit hyperactivity disorder: Findings and implications. In J. L. Matson (Ed.), *Hyperactivity in children: A handbook* (pp. 97–136). Boston: Allyn and Bacon.

RAST, M., & MELTZOFF, A. N. (1995). Memory and representation in young children with Down syndrome: Exploring deferred imitation and object permanence. *Development and Psychopathology, 7*, 393–407.

RATCLIFFE, S. G., PAN, H., & MCKIE, M. (1992). Growth during puberty in the XYY boy. *Annals of Human Biology, 19*, 579–587.

RATNER, N. B. (1997). Atypical language development. In J. Berko Gleason (Ed.), *The development of language* (4th ed., pp. 1–39). Boston: Allyn and Bacon.

RAVUSSIN, E., VALENCIA, M. E., ESPARZA, J., BENNETT, P. H., & SCHULZ, L. O. (1994). Effects of a traditional lifestyle on obesity in Pima Indians. *Diabetes Care, 17*, 1067–1074.

RAYNER, K., & POLLATSEK, A. (1989). *The psychology of reading.* Englewood Cliffs, NJ: Prentice-Hall.

RAZ, S., SHAH, F., & SANDER, C. J. (1996). Differential effects of perinatal hypoxic risk on early developmental outcome: A twin study. *Neuropsychology, 10*, 429–436.

READ, C. R. (1991). Achievement and career choices: Comparisons of males and females. *Roeper Review, 13*, 188–193.

REES, M. (1993). Menarche when and why? *Lancet, 342*, 1375–1376.

REESE, E., HADEN, C. A., & FIVUSH, R. (1993). Mother–child conversations about the past: Relationships of style and memory over time. *Cognitive Development, 8*, 403–430.

REESE, E., HADEN, C. A., & FIVUSH, R. (1996). Mothers, fathers, daughters and sons: Gender differences in autobiographical reminiscing. *Research on Language and Social Interaction, 29*(1), 27–56.

REESE, H. W. (1977). Imagery and associative memory. In R. V.

Kail & J. W. Hagen (Eds.), *Perspectives on the development of memory and cognition* (pp. 113–116). Hillsdale, NJ: Erlbaum.

REINISCH, J. M. (1981). Prenatal exposure to synthetic progestins increases potential for aggression in humans. *Science, 211*, 1171–1173.

REIS, M. (1992). Making connections from urban schools. *Education and Urban Society, 24*, 477–488.

REISER, J., YONAS, A., & WIKNER, K. (1976). Radial localization of odors by human neonates. *Child Development, 47*, 856–859.

REISMAN, J. E. (1987). Touch, motion, and proprioception. In P. Salapatek & L. Cohen (Eds.), *Handbook of infant perception: Vol. 1. From sensation to perception* (pp. 265–303). Orlando, FL: Academic Press.

REMEZ, L. (1997). Planned home birth can be as safe as hospital delivery for women with low-risk pregnancies. *Family Planning Perspectives, 29*, 141–143.

RENNINGER, K. A. (1998). Developmental psychology and instruction: Issues from and for practice. In I. Sigel & K. A. Renninger (Eds.), *Handbook of child psychology: Vol. 4. Child psychology and practice* (pp. 211–274). New York: Wiley.

RENZETTI, C. M., & CURRAN, D. J. (1998). *Living sociology.* Boston: Allyn and Bacon.

RENZULLI, J. (1986). The three-ring conception of giftedness: A developmental model for creative productivity. In R. Sternberg & J. Davidson (Eds.), *Conceptions of giftedness* (pp. 51–92). New York: Cambridge University Press.

REPACHOLI, B. M. (1998). Infants' use of attentional cues to identify the referent of another person's emotional expression. *Developmental Psychology, 34*, 1017–1025.

REPACHOLI, B. M., & GOPNIK, A. (1997). Early reasoning about desires: Evidence from 14- and 18-month-olds. *Developmental Psychology, 33*, 12–21.

REPKE, J. T. (1992). Drug supplementation in pregnancy. *Current Opinion in Obstetrics and Gynecology, 4*, 802–806.

RESNICK, L. B. (1989). Developing mathematical knowledge. *American Psychologist, 44*, 162–169.

REST, J. R. (1979). *Development in judging moral issues.* Minneapolis: University of Minnesota Press.

REST, J. R. (1986). *Moral development: Advances in research and theory.* New York: Praeger.

REST, J. R., & NARVAEZ, D. (1991). The college experience and moral development. In W. M.

Kurtines & J. L. Gewirtz (Eds.), *Handbook of moral behavior and development* (Vol. 2, pp. 229–245). Hillsdale, NJ: Erlbaum.

REVELLE, G. L., KARABENICK, J. D., & WELLMAN, H. M. (1981). *Comprehension monitoring in preschool children.* Paper presented at the biennial meeting of the Society for Research in Child Development, Boston.

REYNA, V. F., & BRAINERD, C. J. (1992). A fuzzy-trace theory of reasoning and remembering: Paradoxes, patterns, and parallelism. In A. Healy, S. Kosslyn, & R. Shiffrin (Eds.), *From learning processes to cognitive processes* (Vol. 2, pp. 235–259). Hillsdale, NJ: Erlbaum.

REYNA, V. F., & KIERNAN, B. (1994). Development of gist versus verbatim memory in sentence recognition: Effects of lexical familiarity, semantic content, encoding instructions, and retention interval. *Developmental Psychology, 30*, 178–191.

REYNOLDS, A. J., & TEMPLE, J. M. (1981). *Comprehension monitoring in preschool children.* Paper presented at the biennial meeting of the Society for Research in Child Development, Boston.

REYNOLDS, A. J., & TEMPLE, J. A. (1998). Extended early childhood intervention and school achievement: Age thirteen findings from the Chicago Longitudinal Study. *Child Development, 69*, 231–246.

REYNOLDS, C. R., & KAISER, S. M. (1990). Test bias in psychological assessment. In T. B. Gutkin & C. R. Reynolds (Eds.), *The handbook of school psychology* (pp. 487–525). New York: Wiley.

REZNICK, J. S., GIBBONS, J. L., JOHNSON, M. O., & MCDONOUGH, P. M. (1989). Behavioral inhibition in a normative sample. In J. S. Reznick (Ed.), *Perspectives on behavioral inhibition* (pp. 25–49). Chicago: University of Chicago Press.

REZNICK, J. S., & GOLDFIELD, B. A. (1992). Rapid change in lexical development in comprehension and production. *Developmental Psychology, 28*, 406–413.

RHOLES, W. S., NEWMAN, L. S., & RUBLE, D. N. (1990). Understanding self and others: Developmental and motivational aspects of perceiving persons in terms of invariant dispositions. In E. Higgins & R. Sorrentino (Eds.), *Handbook of motivation and cognition: Foundations of social behavior* (Vol. 2, pp. 369–407). New York: Guilford.

RICARD, M., & KAMBERK-KILICCI, M. (1995). Children's empathic responses to emotional complexity. *International Journal of*

Behavioral Development, 18, 211–225.

RICCIARDELLI, L. A. (1992). Bilingualism and cognitive development: Relation to threshold theory. *Journal of Psycholinguistic Research, 21*, 301–316.

RICCIO, C. A., HYND, G. W., COHEN, M. J., & GONZALEZ, J. J. (1993). Neurological basis of attention deficit hyperactivity disorder. *Exceptional Children, 60*, 118–124.

RICCO, R. B. (1989). Operational thought and the acquisition of taxonomic relations involving figurative dissimilarity. *Developmental Psychology, 25*, 996–1003.

RICE, C., KOINIS, D., SULLIVAN, K., & TAGER-FLUSBERG, H. (1997). When 3-year-olds pass the appearance–reality test. *Developmental Psychology, 33*, 54–61.

RICE, J. K. (1994). Reconsidering research on divorce, family life cycle, and the meaning of family. *Psychology of Women Quarterly, 18*, 558–584.

RICE, M. L., HUSTON, A. C., & WRIGHT, J. C. (1982). The forms of television: Effects on children's attention, comprehension, and social behavior. In D. Pearl, L. Bouthilet, & J. Lazar (Eds.), *Television and behavior: Ten years of scientific progress and implications for the eighties* (Vol. 2, pp. 24–38). Washington, DC: U.S. Government Printing Office.

RICE, M. L., HUSTON, A. C., & WRIGHT, J. C. (1986). Replays as repetitions: Young children's interpretation of television forms. *Journal of Applied Developmental Psychology, 7*, 61–76.

RICE, M. L., HUSTON, A. C., TRUGLIO, R., & WRIGHT, J. (1990). Words from "Sesame Street": Learning vocabulary while viewing. *Developmental Psychology, 26*, 421–428.

RICE, M. L., & WOODSMALL, L. (1988). Lessons from television: Children's word learning when viewing. *Child Development, 59*, 420–429.

RICHARDS, D. D., & SIEGLER, R. S. (1986). Children's understandings of the attributes of life. *Journal of Experimental Child Psychology, 42*, 1–22.

RICHARDS, M. H., & DUCKETT, E. (1994). The relationship of maternal employment to early adolescent daily experience with and without parents. *Child Development, 65*, 225–236.

RICHARDS-COLOCINO, N., MCKENZIE, P., & NEWTON, R. R. (1996). Project Success: Comprehensive intervention services for middle school high-risk youth. *Journal of Adolescent Research, 11*, 130–163.

RICHARDSON, G. A., HAMEL, S. C., GOLDSCHMIDT, L., & DAY, N. L. (1996). The effects of prenatal cocaine use on neonatal neurobehavioral status. *Neurotoxicology and Teratology, 18,* 519–528.

RICHMAN, A. L., MILLER, P. M., & LEVINE, R. A. (1992). Cultural and educational variations in maternal responsiveness. *Developmental Psychology, 28,* 614–621.

RICKEL, A. U., & BECKER, E. (1997). *Keeping children from harm's way.* Washington, DC: American Psychological Association.

RIDDERINKHOF, K. R., & MOLEN, M. W. VAN DER (1997). Mental resources, processing speed, and inhibitory control: A developmental perspective. *Biological Psychology, 45,* 241–261.

RIJSDIJK, F. V., & BOOMSMA, D. I. (1997). Genetic mediation of the correlation between peripheral nerve conduction velocity and IQ. *Behavior Genetics, 27,* 87–98.

RITTS, V., PATTERSON, M. L., & TUBBS, M. E. (1992). Expectations, impressions, and judgments of physically attractive students: A review. *Review of Educational Research, 62,* 413–426.

ROAZZI, A., & BRYANT, P. (1997). Explicitness and conservation: Social class differences. *International Journal of Behavioral Development, 21,* 51–70.

ROBERT, M. (1989). Reduction of demand characteristics in the measurement of certainty during modeled conservation. *Journal of Experimental Child Psychology, 47,* 451–466.

ROBERTON, M. A. (1984). Changing motor patterns during childhood. In J. R. Thomas (Ed.), *Motor development during childhood and adolescence* (pp. 48–90). Minneapolis: Burgess Publishing.

ROBERTS, J. E., BURCHINAL, M. R., & CAMPBELL, F. (1994). Otitis media in early childhood and patterns of intellectual development and later academic performance. *Journal of Pediatric Psychology, 19,* 347–367.

ROBERTS, R. J., JR., & AMAN, C. J. (1993). Developmental differences in giving directions: Spatial frames of reference and mental rotation. *Child Development, 64,* 1258–1270.

ROBINSON, B. E., & CANADAY, H. (1978). Sex-role behaviors and personality traits of male day care teachers. *Sex Roles, 4,* 853–865.

ROBINSON, T. N., KILLEN, J. D., LITT, I. F., HAMMER, L. D., WILSON, D. M., HAYDEL, K. F., HAYWARD, C., & TAYLOR, C. B. (1996). Ethnicity and body dissatisfaction: Are Hispanic and Asian girls at in-

creased risk for eating disorders? *Journal of Adolescent Health, 19,* 384–393.

ROCHAT, P. (1992). Self-sitting and reaching in 5- to 8-month-old infants: The impact of posture and its development on early eye–hand coordination. *Journal of Motor Behavior, 24,* 210–220.

ROCHAT, P., & GOUBET, N. (1995). Development of sitting and reaching in 5- to 6-month-old infants. *Infant Behavior and Development, 18,* 53–68.

ROCHE, A. F. (1979). Secular trends in stature, weight, and maturation. In A. F. Roche (Ed.), *Secular trends in human growth, maturation, and development. Monographs of the Society for Research in Child Development, 44* (3–4, Serial No. 179).

RODRIGUEZ, M. L., MISCHEL, W., & SHODA, Y. (1989). Cognitive and personality variables in the delay of gratification of older children at risk. *Journal of Personality and Social Psychology, 57,* 358–367.

ROE, K. V., ROE, A., DRIVAS, A., & BRONSTEIN, R. (1990). A curvilinear relationship between maternal vocal stimulation and three-month-olds' cognitive processing: A cross-cultural phenomenon. *Infant Mental Health Journal, 11,* 175–189.

ROFFWARG, H. P., MUZIO, J. N., & DEMENT, W. C. (1966). Ontogenetic development of the human sleep-dream cycle. *Science, 152,* 604–619.

ROGERS, L., RESNICK, M. D., MITCHELL, J. E., & BLUM, R. W. (1997). The relationship between socioeconomic status and eating disordered behaviors in a community sample of adolescent girls. *International Journal of Eating Disorders, 22,* 15–23.

ROGGMAN, L. A., LANGLOIS, J. H., HUBBS-TAIT, L., & RIESER-DANNER, L. A. (1994). Infant day-care, attachment, and the "file drawer problem." *Child Development, 65,* 1429–1443.

ROGOFF, B. (1990). *Apprenticeship in thinking.* New York: Oxford University Press.

ROGOFF, B. (1994). Developing understanding of the idea of community learners. *Mind, Culture, and Activity, 1,* 209–229.

ROGOFF, B. (1998). Cognition as a collaborative process. In D. Kuhn & R. S. Siegler (Eds.), *Handbook of child psychology: Vol. 2. Cognition, perception, and language* (5th ed., pp. 679–744). New York: Wiley.

ROGOFF, B., & CHAVAJAY, P. (1995). What's become of research on the cultural basis of cognitive development? *American Psychologist, 50,* 859–877.

ROGOFF, B., & MISTRY, J. (1985). Memory development in cul-

tural context. In M. Pressley & C. Brainerd (Eds.), *Cognitive learning and memory in children* (pp. 117–142). New York: Springer-Verlag.

ROGOFF, B., MISTRY, J., GÖNCÜ, A., & MOSIER, C. (1993). Guided participation in cultural activity by toddlers and caregivers. *Monographs of the Society for Research in Child Development, 58* (8, Serial No. 236).

ROGOFF, B., & WADDELL, K. J. (1982). Memory for information organized in a scene by children from two cultures. *Child Development, 53,* 1224–1228.

ROGOW, S. (1988). *Helping the visually impaired child with developmental problems: Effective practice in home, school, and community.* New York: Teachers College Press.

ROHNER, R. P., & ROHNER, E. C. (1981). Parental acceptance-rejection and parental control: Cross-cultural codes. *Ethnology, 20,* 245–260.

ROLAND, A. (1988). *In search of self in India and Japan: Toward a cross-cultural psychology.* Princeton, NJ: Princeton University Press.

ROMANS, S. M., ROELTGEN, D. P., KUSHNER, H., & ROSS, J. L. (1997). Executive function in girls with Turner's syndrome. *Developmental Neuropsychology, 13,* 23–40.

ROME-FLANDERS, T., & CRONK, C. (1995). A longitudinal study of infant vocalizations during mother–infant games. *Journal of Child Language, 22,* 259–274.

ROOPNARINE, J. L., HOSSAIN, Z., GILL, P., & BROPHY, H. (1994). Play in the East Indian context. In J. L. Roopnarine, J. E. Johnson, & F. H. Hooper (Eds.), *Children's play in diverse cultures* (pp. 9–30). Albany, NY: SUNY Press.

ROOPNARINE, J. L., LASKER, J., SACKS, M., & STORES, M. (1998). The cultural contexts of children's play. In O. N. Saracho & B. Spodek (Eds.), *Multiple perspectives on play in early childhood education* (pp. 194–219). Albany, NY: State University of New York Press.

ROOPNARINE, J. L., TALUKDER, E., JAIN, D., JOSHI, P., & SRIVASTAVE, P. (1990). Characteristics of holding, patterns of play, and social behaviors between parents and infants in New Delhi, India. *Developmental Psychology, 26,* 667–673.

ROSA, R. W. (1993). Retinoid embryopathy in humans. In G. Koren (Ed.), *Retinoids in clinical practice* (pp. 77–109). New York: Marcel Dekker.

ROSE, A. J., & ASHER, S. R. (1999). Children's goals and strategies

in response to conflicts within a friendship. *Developmental Psychology, 35,* 69–79.

ROSE, J. L., & BERTENTHAL, B. I. (1995). A longitudinal study of the visual control of posture in infancy. In B. G. Bardy, R. J. Bootsma, & Y. Guiard (Eds.), *Studies in perception and action* (pp. 251–253). Mahwah, NJ: Erlbaum.

ROSE, R. J. (1995). Genes and human behavior. *Annual Review of Psychology, 46,* 625–654.

ROSE, R. M., HOLADAY, J. W., & BERNSTEIN, I. S. (1976). Plasma testosterone, dominance rank and aggressive behavior in male rhesus monkeys. *Nature, 231,* 366–368.

ROSE, S. A. (1988). Shape recognition in infancy: Visual integration of sequential information. *Child Development, 59,* 1161–1176.

ROSE, S. A., & FELDMAN, J. F. (1995). Prediction of IQ and specific cognitive abilities at 11 years from infancy measures. *Developmental Psychology, 31,* 685–696.

ROSE, S. A., & FELDMAN, J. F. (1997). Memory and speed: Their role in the relation of infant information processing to later IQ. *Child Development, 68,* 610–620.

ROSE, S. A., JANKOWSKI, J. J., & SENIOR, G. J. (1997). Infants' recognition of contour-deleted figures. *Journal of Experimental Psychology: Human Perception and Performance, 23,* 1206–1216.

ROSEN, A. B., & ROZIN, P. (1993). Now you see it, now you don't: The preschool child's conception of invisible particles in the context of dissolving. *Developmental Psychology, 29,* 300–311.

ROSEN, K. S., & ROTHBAUM, F. (1993). Quality of parental caregiving and security of attachment. *Developmental Psychology, 29,* 358–367.

ROSEN, W. D., ADAMSON, L. B., & BAKEMAN, R. (1992). An experimental investigation of infant social referencing: Mothers' messages and gender differences. *Developmental Psychology, 28,* 1172–1178.

ROSENBERG, D. R., SWEENEY, J. A., GILLEN, J. S., KIM, J., VARANELLI, M. J., O'HEARN, K. M., & ERB, P. A. (1997). Magnetic resonance imaging of children without sedation preparation with simulation. *Journal of the American Academy of Child and Adolescent Psychiatry, 36,* 853–859.

ROSENBERG, M. (1979). *Conceiving the self.* New York: Basic Books.

ROSENGREN, K. S., & HICKLING, A. K. (1994). Seeing is believing: Children's explanations of commonplace, magical, and extraordinary transformations. *Child Development, 65,* 1605–1626.

ROSENSHINE, B., & MEISTER, C. (1994). Reciprocal teaching: A review of nineteen experimental studies. *Review of Educational Research, 64,* 479–530.

ROSENSTEIN, D., & OSTER, H. (1988). Differential facial responses to four basic tastes in newborns. *Child Development, 59,* 1555–1568.

ROSENTHAL, J. A. (1992). *Special-needs adoption: A study of intact families.* New York: Praeger.

ROSS, H. S., CONANT, C., CHEYNE, J. A., & ALEVIZOS, E. (1992). Relationships and alliances in the social interactions of kibbutz toddlers. *Social Development, 1,* 1–17.

ROSS, R. P., CAMPBELL, T., HUSTON-STEIN, A., & WRIGHT, J. C. (1984). Nutritional misinformation of children: A developmental and experimental analysis of the effects of televised food commercials. *Journal of Applied Developmental Psychology, 1,* 329–347.

ROTENBERG, K. J., SIMOURD, L., & MOORE, D. (1989). Children's use of a verbal–nonverbal consistency principle to infer truth and lying. *Child Development, 60,* 309–322.

ROTHBART, M. K., & BATES, J. E. (1998). Temperament. In N. Eisenberg (Ed.), *Handbook of child psychology: Vol. 3. Social, emotional, and personality development* (5th ed., pp. 105–176). New York: Wiley.

ROTHBART, M. K., DERRYBERRY, D., & POSNER, M. I. (1994). A psychobiological approach to the development of temperament. In J. E. Bates & T. D. Wachs (Eds.), *Temperament: Individual differences at the interface of biology and behavior* (pp. 83–116). Washington, DC: American Psychological Association.

ROTHBART, M. K., & MAURO, J. A. (1990). Questionnaire approaches to the study of infant temperament. In J. W. Fagen & J. Colombo (Eds.), *Individual differences in infancy: Reliability, stability and prediction* (pp. 411–429). Hillsdale, NJ: Erlbaum.

ROTHBART, M. K., & ROTHBART, M. (1976). Birth-order, sex of child and maternal help giving. *Sex Roles, 2,* 39–46.

ROTHERAM-BORUS, M. J., & FERNANDEZ, I. (1995). Sexual orientation and developmental challenges experienced by gay and lesbian youths. *Suicide & Life-Threatening Behavior, 25,* 26–34.

ROTHMAN, K. J., MOORE, L. L., SINGER, M. R., NGUYEN, U.S.,

MANNENO, S. & MILUNSKY, A. (1995). Teratogenicity of high vitamin A intake. *New England Journal of Medicine, 333,* 1369–1373.

ROUSSEAU, J. J. (1955). *Emile.* New York: Dutton. (Original work published 1762)

ROVEE-COLLIER, C. (1996). Shifting the focus from what to why. *Infant Behavior and Development, 19,* 385–400.

ROVEE-COLLIER, C. K. (1987). Learning and memory. In J. D. Osofsky (Ed.), *Handbook of infant development* (2nd ed., pp. 98–148). New York: Wiley.

ROVEE-COLLIER, C. K., & HAYNE, H. (1987). Reactivation of infant memory: Implications for cognitive development. In H. W. Reese (Ed.), *Advances in child development and behavior* (Vol. 20, pp. 185–238). New York: Academic Press.

ROVEE-COLLIER, C. K., & SHYI, G. (1992). A functional and cognitive analysis of infant long-term retention. In C. J. Brainerd, M. L. Howe, & V. Reyna (Eds.), *Development of long-term retention* (pp. 3–55). New York: Springer-Verlag.

ROVET, J., NETLEY, C., KEENAN, M., BAILEY, J., & STEWART, D. (1996). The psychoeducational profile of boys with Klinefelter syndrome. *Journal of Learning Disabilities, 29,* 180–196.

ROWE, D. C. (1994). *The limits of family influence: Genes, experience, and behavior.* New York: Guilford.

ROYAL COLLEGE OF OBSTETRICIANS AND GYNECOLOGISTS. (1997, October). *Report of the panel to review fetal pain.* London: Author.

ROYCE, J. M., DARLINGTON, R. B., & MURRAY, H. W. (1983). Pooled analyses: Findings across studies. In Consortium for Longitudinal Studies (Ed.), *As the twig is bent: Lasting effects of preschool programs* (pp. 411–459). Hillsdale, NJ: Erlbaum.

RUBIN, J. Z., PROVENZANO, F. J., & LURIA, Z. (1974). The eye of the beholder: Parents' views on sex of newborns. *American Journal of Orthopsychiatry, 44,* 512–519.

RUBIN, K. H., BUKOWSKI, W., & PARKER, J. G. (1998). Peer interactions, relationships, and groups. In N. Eisenberg (Ed.), *Handbook of child psychology: Vol. 3. Social, emotional, and personality development* (5th ed., pp. 619–700). New York: Wiley.

RUBIN, K. H., & COPLAN, R. J. (1998). Social and nonsocial play in childhood: An individual differences perspective. In O. N. Saracho & B. Spodek (Eds.), *Multiple perspectives on

play in early childhood education* (pp. 144–170). Albany, NY: State University of New York Press.

RUBIN, K. H., COPLAN, R. J., FOX, N. A., & CALKINS, S. (1995). Emotionality, emotion regulation, and preschoolers' social adaptation. *Development and Psychopathology, 7,* 49–62.

RUBIN, K. H., FEIN, G. G., & VANDENBERG, B. (1983). Play. In E. M. Hetherington (Ed.), *Handbook of child psychology: Vol. 4. Socialization, personality, and social development* (4th ed., pp. 693–744). New York: Wiley.

RUBIN, K. H., HASTINGS, P. D., STEWART, S. L., HENDERSON, H. A., & CHEN, X. (1997). The consistency and concomitants of inhibition: Some of the children, all of the time. *Child Development, 68,* 467–483.

RUBIN, K. H., MAIONI, T. L., & HORNUNG, M. (1976). Free play behaviors in middle- and lower-class preschoolers: Parten and Piaget revisited. *Child Development, 47,* 414–419.

RUBIN, K. H., STEWART, S. L., & COPLAN, R. J. (1995). Social withdrawal in childhood: Conceptual and empirical perspectives. In T. H. Ollendick & R. J. Prinz (Eds.), *Advances in clinical child psychology* (Vol. 17, pp. 157–196). New York: Plenum.

RUBIN, K. H., WATSON, K. S., & JAMBOR, T. W. (1978). Free-play behaviors in preschool and kindergarten children. *Child Development, 49,* 534–536.

RUBLE, D. N., & DWECK, C. S. (1995). Self-conceptions, person conceptions, and their development. In N. Eisenberg (Ed.), *Social development* (pp. 109–139). Thousand Oaks, CA: Sage.

RUBLE, D. N., & FLETT, G. L. (1988). Conflicting goals in self-evaluative information-seeking: Developmental and ability level analyses. *Child Development, 59,* 97–106.

RUBLE, D. N., & FREY, K. S. (1991). Changing patterns of comparative behavior as skills are acquired: A functional model of self-evaluation. In J. Suls & T. A. Wills, (Eds.), *Social comparison: Contemporary theory and research* (pp. 70–112). Hillsdale, NJ: Erlbaum.

RUBLE, D. N., & MARTIN, C. L. (1998). Gender development. In N. Eisenberg (Ed.), *Handbook of child psychology: Vol. 3. Social, emotional, and personality development* (5th ed., pp. 933–1016). New York: Wiley.

RUFF, H. A., & LAWSON, K. R. (1990). Development of sustained, focused attention in young children during free play.

Developmental Psychology, 26, 85–93.

RUFF, H. A., LAWSON, K. R., PARRINELLO, R., & WEISSBERG, R. (1990). Long-term stability of individual differences in sustained attention in the early years. *Child Development, 61,* 60–75.

RUFF, H. A., SALTARELLI, L. M., CAPOZZOLI, M., & DUBINER, K. (1992). The differentiation of activity in infants' exploration of objects. *Developmental Psychology, 28,* 851–861.

RUFFMAN, T., PERNER, J., NAITO, M., PARKIN, L., & CLEMENTS, W. A. (1998). Older (but not younger) siblings facilitate false belief understanding. *Developmental Psychology, 34,* 161–174.

RUFFMAN, T., PERNER, J., OLSON, D. R., & DOHERTY, M. (1993). Reflecting on scientific thinking: Children's understanding of the hypothesis–evidence relation. *Child Development, 64,* 1617–1636.

RUMBAUGH, D. M. (1977). *Language learning by a chimpanzee: The Lana project.* New York: Academic Press.

RUNCO, M. A. (1992a). Children's divergent thinking and creative ideation. *Developmental Review, 12,* 233–264.

RUNCO, M. A. (1992b). The evaluative, valuative, and divergent thinking of children. *Journal of Creative Behavior, 25,* 311–319.

RUNCO, M. A. (1993). Divergent thinking, creativity, and giftedness. *Gifted Child Quarterly, 37,* 16–22.

RUNCO, M. A., & OKUDA, S. M. (1988). Problem, discovery, divergent thinking, and the creative process. *Journal of Youth and Adolescence, 17,* 211–220.

RUSSELL, J. A. (1990). The preschooler's understanding of the causes and consequences of emotion. *Child Development, 61,* 1872–1881.

RUTTER, M. (1985). Resilience in the face of adversity: Protective factors and resistance to psychiatric disorder. *British Journal of Psychiatry, 147,* 598–611.

RUTTER, M. (1987). Psychosocial resilience and protective mechanisms. *American Journal of Orthopsychiatry, 57,* 316–331.

RUTTER, M. (1996). Maternal deprivation. In M. H. Bornstein (Ed.), *Handbook of parenting: Vol. 4. Applied and practical parenting* (pp. 3–31). Mahwah, NJ: Erlbaum.

RUTTER, M., & THE ENGLISH AND ROMANIAN ADOPTEES STUDY TEAM. (1998). Developmental catch-up, and deficit, following adoption after severe global early privation. *Journal of Child

Psychology and Psychiatry, 39, 465–476.

RYYNÄNEN, M., KIRKINEN, P., MANNERMAA, A, & SAARIKOSKI, S. (1995). Carrier diagnosis of the fragile X syndrome—A challenge in antenatal clinics. American Journal of Obstetrics and Gynecology, 172, 1236–1239.

S

SAARNI, C. (1993). Socialization of emotion. In M. Lewis & J. M. Haviland (Eds.), Handbook of emotions (pp. 435–446). New York: Guilford.

SAARNI, C. (1995). Socialization of emotion. In M. Lewis & J. M. Haviland (Eds.), Handbook of emotions (pp. 435–446). New York: Guilford Press.

SAARNI, C. (1997). Emotional competence and self-regulation in childhood. In P. Salovey & D. J. Sluyter (Eds.), Emotional development and emotional intelligence (pp. 35–66). New York: Basic Books.

SAARNI, C., MUMME, D. L., & CAMPOS, J. J. (1998). Emotional development: Action, communication, and understanding. In N. Eisenberg (Ed.), Handbook of child psychology: Vol. 3. Social, emotional, and personality development (5th ed., pp. 237–309). New York: Wiley.

SACKS, C. H., & MERGENDOLLER, J. R. (1997). The relationship between teachers' theoretical orientation toward reading and student outcomes in kindergarten children with different initial reading abilities. American Educational Research Journal, 34, 721–739.

SADEH, A. (1997). Sleep and melatonin in infants: A preliminary study. Sleep, 20, 185–191.

SADLER, T. W. (1995). Langman's medical embryology (7th ed.). Baltimore: Williams & Wilkins.

SAFYER, A. W., LEAHY, B. H., & COLAN, N. B. (1995). The impact of work on adolescent development. Families and Society, 76, 38–45.

SAHNI, R., SCHULZE, K. F., STEFANSKI, M., MYERS, M. M., & FIFER, W. P. (1995). Methodological issues in coding sleep states in immature infants. Developmental Psychobiology, 28, 85–101.

SALAPATEK, P. (1975). Pattern perception in early infancy. In L. B. Cohen & P. Salapatek (Eds.), Infant perception: From sensation to cognition (pp. 133–248). New York: Academic Press.

SALIDIS, J., & JOHNSON, J. S. (1997). The production of minimal words: A longitudinal case study of phonological development. Language Acquisition, 6, 1–36.

SAMENOW, S. E. (1984). Inside the criminal mind. New York: Random House.

SAMEROFF, A. J. (1994). Developmental systems and family functioning. In R. D. Parke & S. G. Kellam (Eds.), Exploring family relationships with other social contexts (pp. 199–214). Hillsdale, NJ: Erlbaum.

SAMEROFF, A. J., SEIFER, R., BALDWIN, A., & BALDWIN, C. (1993). Stability of intelligence from preschool to adolescence: The influence of social and family risk factors. Child Development, 64, 80–97.

SAMPSON, R. J., & LAUB, J. H. (1993). Crime in the making: Pathways and turning points through life. Cambridge, MA: Harvard University Press.

SAMSON, L. F. (1988). Perinatal viral infections and neonates. Journal of Perinatal Neonatal Nursing, 1, 56–65.

SAMUELS, N., & SAMUELS, M. (1996). The new well pregnancy book. New York: Summitt.

SANDERS, O. (1997). Keeping ourselves safe. Public lecture, Illinois State University, Normal, IL.

SANDMAN, C. A., WADHWA, P., HETRICK, W., PORTO, M., & PEEKE, H. V. S. (1997). Human fetal heart rate dishabituation between thirty and thirty-two weeks gestation. Child Development, 68, 1031–1040.

SANDQVIST, K. (1992). Sweden's sex-role scheme and commitment to gender equality. In S. Lewis, D. N. Izraeli, & H. Hottsmans (Eds.), Dual-earner families: International perspectives. London: Sage.

SANSAVINI, A., BERTONCINI, J., & GIOVANELLI, G. (1997). Newborns discriminate the rhythm of multisyllabic stressed words. Developmental Psychology, 33, 3–11.

SANSON, A. V., PEDLOW, R., CANN, W., PRIOR, M., & OBERKLAID, F. (1996). Shyness ratings: Stability and correlates in early childhood. International Journal of Behavioural Development, 19, 705–724.

SARASON, I. G. (1980). Test anxiety: Theory, research, and applications. Hillsdale, NJ: Erlbaum.

SAUDINO, K., & EATON, W. O. (1991). Infant temperament and genetics: An objective twin study. Child Development, 62, 1167–1174.

SAVAGE-RUMBAUGH, E. S., MURPHY, J., SEVCIK, R. A., BRAKKE, K. E., WILLIAMS, S. L., & RUMBAUGH, D. M. (1993). Language comprehension in ape and child. Monographs of the Society for Research in Child Development, 58 (3–4, Serial No. 233).

SAVIN-WILLIAMS, R. C. (1980). Dominance hierarchies in groups of middle to late adolescent males. Journal of Youth and Adolescence, 9, 75–85.

SAVIN-WILLIAMS, R. C., & BERNDT, T. J. (1990). Friendship and peer relations. In S. S. Feldman & G. R. Elliott (Eds.), At the threshold: The developing adolescent (pp. 277–307). Cambridge, MA: Harvard University Press.

SAXE, G. B. (1985). Effects of schooling on arithmetical understandings: Studies with Oksapmin children in Papua New Guinea. Journal of Educational Psychology, 77, 503–513.

SAXE, G. B. (1988, August–September). Candy selling and math learning. Educational Researcher, 17 (6), 14–21.

SAYWITZ, K. J. (1989). Children's conceptions of the legal system: "Court is a place to play basketball." In M. P. Toglia (Eds.), Perspectives on children's testimony (pp. 131–157). New York: Springer-Verlag.

SAYWITZ, K. J., & NATHANSON, R. (1993). Children's testimony and their perceptions of stress in and out of the courtroom. Child Abuse & Neglect, 17, 613–622.

SCARR, S. (1985). Constructing psychology: Making facts and fables for our times. American Psychologist, 40, 499–512.

SCARR, S. (1996). Individuality and community: The contrasting role of the state in family life in the United States and Sweden. Scandinavian Journal of Psychology, 37, 93–102.

SCARR, S. (1997). Behavior-genetic and socialization theories of intelligence: Truce and reconciliation. In R. J. Sternberg & E. L. Grigorenko (Eds.), Intelligence, heredity, and environment (pp. 3–41). New York: Cambridge University Press.

SCARR, S. (1998). American child care today. American Psychologist, 53, 95–108.

SCARR, S., & MCCARTNEY, K. (1983). How people make their own environments: A theory of genotype environment effects. Child Development, 54, 424–435.

SCARR, S., PHILLIPS, D. A., & MCCARTNEY, K. (1990). Facts, fantasies, and the future of child care in America. Psychological Science, 1, 26–35.

SCARR, S., PHILLIPS, D., MCCARTNEY, K., & ABBOTT-SHIM, M. (1993). Quality of child care as an aspect of family and child care policy in the United States. Pediatrics, 91, 182–188.

SCARR, S., & WEINBERG, R. A. (1976). IQ test performance of black children adopted by white families. American Psychologist, 31, 726–739.

SCARR, S., & WEINBERG, R. A. (1983). The Minnesota Adoption Studies: Genetic differences and malleability. Child Development, 54, 260–267.

SCHACHAR, R., TANNOCK, R., MARRIOTT, M., & LOGAN, G. (1995). Deficient inhibitory control in attention deficit hyperactivity disorder. Journal of Abnormal Child Psychology, 23, 411–437.

SCHACHTER, F. F., & STONE, R. K. (1985). Difficult sibling, easy sibling: Temperament and the within-family environment. Child Development, 56, 1335–1344.

SCHAFER, G., & PLUNKETT, K. (1998). Rapid word learning by fifteen-month-olds under tightly controlled conditions. Child Development, 69, 309–320.

SCHAFFER, J., & KRAL, R. (1988). Adoptive families. In C. S. Chilman, E. W. Nunnally, & F. M. Cox (Eds.), Variant family forms (pp. 165–184). Newbury Park, CA: Sage.

SCHANBERG, S., & FIELD, T. M. (1987). Sensory deprivation stress and supplemental stimulation in the rat pup and preterm human neonate. Child Development, 58, 1431–1447.

SCHAUBLE, L. (1996). The development of scientific reasoning in knowledge-rich contexts. Developmental Psychology, 32, 102–119.

SCHIAVI, R. C., THEILGAARD, A., OWEN, D., & WHITE, D. (1984). Sex chromosome anomalies, hormones, and aggressivity. Archives of General Psychiatry, 41, 93–99.

SCHIEFFELIN, B. B., & OCHS, E. (1987). Language socialization across cultures. New York: Cambridge University Press.

SCHIFTER, T., HOFFMAN, J. M., HATTEN, H. P., & HANSON, M. W. (1994). Neuroimaging in infantile autism. Journal of Child Neurology, 9, 155–161.

SCHLEGEL, A. (1995). A cross-cultural approach to adolescence. Ethos, 23, 5–32.

SCHLEGEL, A., & BARRY, H., III. (1980). The evolutionary significance of adolescent initiation ceremonies. American Ethnologist, 7, 696–715.

SCHLEGEL, A., & BARRY, H., III. (1991). Adolescence: An anthropological inquiry. New York: Free Press.

SCHNEIDER, W. (1986). The role of conceptual knowledge and metamemory in the development of organizational processes in memory. Journal of Experimental Child Psychology, 42, 218–236.

SCHNEIDER, W. (1993). Domain-specific knowledge and memory performance in children.

Educational Psychology Review, 5, 257–274.

SCHNEIDER, W., & BJORKLUND, D. F. (1992). Expertise, aptitude, and strategic remembering. *Child Development, 63,* 461–473.

SCHNEIDER, W., & BJORKLUND, D. F. (1998). Memory. In D. Kuhn & R. S. Siegler (Eds.), *Handbook of child psychology: Vol. 2. Cognition, perception, and language* (5th ed., pp. 467–521). New York: Wiley.

SCHNEIDER, W., & PRESSLEY, M. (1997). *Memory development between two and twenty* (2nd ed.). Mahwah, NJ: Erlbaum.

SCHNUR, E., BROOKS-GUNN, J., & SHIPMAN, V. C. (1992). Who attends programs serving poor children? The case of Head Start attendees and nonattendees. *Journal of Applied Developmental Psychology, 13,* 405–421.

SCHOLL, T. O., HEIDIGER, M. L., & BELSKY, D. (1996). Prenatal care and maternal health during adolescent pregnancy: A review and meta-analysis. *Journal of Adolescent Health, 15,* 444–456.

SCHOLNICK, E. K. (1995, Fall). Knowing and constructing plans. *SRCD Newsletter,* pp. 1–2, 17.

SCHONFELD, D. J., & SMILANSKY, S. (1989). A cross-cultural comparison of Israeli and American children's death concepts. *Death Studies, 13,* 593–604.

SCHOTHORST, P. F., & VAN ENGELAND, H. (1996). Long-term behavioral sequelae of prematurity. *Journal of the American Academy of Child and Adolescent Psychiatry, 35,* 175–183.

SCHROEDER, K. A., BLOOD, L. L., & MALUSO, D. (1993). Gender differences and similarities between male and female undergraduate students regarding expectations for career and family roles. *College Student Journal, 27,* 237–249.

SCHULER, G. D., BOGUSKI, M. S., STEWARD, E. A., STEIN, L. D., GYAPAY, G., RICE, K., & WHITE, R. E. (1996). A gene map of the human genome. *Science, 274,* 540–546.

SCHUNK, D. H. (1983). Ability versus effort attributional feedback: Differential effects on self-efficacy and achievement. *Journal of Educational Psychology, 75,* 848–856.

SCHUNK, D. H., & ZIMMERMAN, B. J. (Eds.). (1994). *Self-regulation of learning and performance.* Englewood Cliffs, NJ: Erlbaum.

SCHUSTER, B., RUBLE, D. N., & WEINERT, F. E. (1998). Causal inferences and the positivity bias in children: The role of the covariation principle. *Child Development, 69,* 1577–1596.

SCHWANENFLUGEL, P. J., FABRICIUS, W. V., & NOYES, C. R. (1996). Developing organization of mental verbs: Evidence for the development of a constructivist theory of mind in middle childhood. *Cognitive Development, 11,* 265–294.

SCRIBNER, S. (1986). Thinking in action: Some characteristics of practical thought. In R. J. Sternberg & R. K. Wagner (Eds.), *Practical intelligence: Nature and origins of competence in the everyday world* (pp. 13–30). New York: Cambridge University Press.

SCRUGGS, T. E., & MASTROPIERI, M. A. (1994). Successful mainstreaming in elementary science classes: A qualitative study of three reputational cases. *American Educational Research Journal, 31,* 785–811.

SEARS, R. R., MACCOBY, E. E., & LEVIN, H. (1957). *Patterns of child rearing.* New York: Harper & Row.

SEBALD, H. (1986). Adolescents' shifting orientation toward parents and peers: A curvilinear trend over recent decades. *Journal of Marriage and the Family, 48,* 5–13.

SEGAL, B. M., & STEWART, J. C. (1996). Substance use and abuse in adolescence: An overview. *Child Psychiatry and Human Development, 26,* 193–210.

SEGAL, L. B., OSTER, H., COHEN, M., CASPI, B., MYERS, M., & BROWN, D. (1995). Smiling and fussing in seven-month-old preterm and full-term black infants in the still-face situation. *Child Development, 66,* 1829–1843.

SEIDMAN, E., ALLEN, L., ABER, J. L., MITCHELL, C., & FEINMAN, J. (1994). The impact of school transitions in early adolescence on the self-system and perceived social context of poor urban youth. *Child Development, 65,* 507–522.

SEIDMAN, E., & FRENCH, S. E. (1997). Normative school transitions among urban adolescents: When, where, and how to intervene. In H. J. Walberg, O. Reyes, & R. P. Weissberg (Eds.), *Children and youth: Interdisciplinary perspectives* (pp. 166–189). Thousand Oaks, CA: Sage.

SEIFER, R., & SCHILLER, M. (1995). The role of parenting sensitivity, infant temperament, and dyadic interaction in attachment theory and assessment. In E. Waters, B. E. Vaughn, G. Posada, & K. Kondo-Ikemura (Eds.), Caregiving, cultural, and cognitive perspectives on secure-base behavior and working models: New growing points of attachment theory and research. *Monographs of the Society for Research in Child Development, 60* (2–3, Serial No. 244).

SEIFER, R., SCHILLER, M., SAMEROFF, A. J., RESNICK, S., & RIORDAN, K. (1996). Attachment, maternal sensitivity, and infant temperament during the first year of life. *Developmental Psychology, 32,* 12–25.

SEITZ, V., & APFEL, N. H. (1993). Adolescent mothers and repeated childbearing: Effects of a school-based intervention program. *American Journal of Orthopsychiatry, 63,* 572–581.

SEITZ, V., & APFEL, N. H. (1994). Effects of a school for pregnant students on the incidence of low-birthweight deliveries. *Child Development, 65,* 666–676.

SEITZ, V., APFEL, N. H., & ROSENBAUM, L. K. (1991). Effects of an intervention program for pregnant adolescents: Educational outcomes at two years postpartum. *American Journal of Community Psychology, 6,* 911–930.

SELIGMAN, M. E. P. (1975). *Helplessness: On depression, development, and death.* San Francisco: Freeman.

SELIGMANN, J. (1994, May 4). The pressure to lose. *Newsweek,* pp. 60–61.

SELMAN, R. L. (1976). Social-cognitive understanding: A guide to educational and clinical practice. In T. Lickona (Ed.), *Moral development and behavior: Theory, research, and social issues* (pp. 299–316). New York: Holt, Rinehart & Winston.

SELMAN, R. L. (1980). *The growth of interpersonal understanding.* New York: Academic Press.

SELMAN, R. L. (1981). The child as a friendship philosopher. In S. R. Asher & J. M. Gottman (Eds.), *The development of friendships* (pp. 242–272). New York: Cambridge University Press.

SELMAN, R. L., & BYRNE, D. F. (1974). A structural-developmental analysis of levels of role taking in middle childhood. *Child Development, 45,* 803–806.

SERBIN, L. A., CONNOR, J. M., & CITRON, C. C. (1978). Environmental control of independent and dependent behaviors in preschool girls and boys: A model for early independence training. *Sex Roles, 4,* 867–875.

SERBIN, L. A., CONNOR, J. M., & ILER, I. (1979). Sex-stereotyped and nonstereotyped introductions of new toys in the preschool classroom: An observational study of teacher behavior and its effects. *Psychology of Women Quarterly, 4,* 261–265.

SERBIN, L. A., POWLISHTA, K. K., & GULKO, J. (1993). The development of sex typing in middle childhood. *Monographs of the Society for Research in Child Development, 58* (2, Serial No. 232).

SERBIN, L. A., TONICK, I. J., & STERNGLANZ, S. H. (1977). Shaping cooperative cross-sex play. *Child Development, 48,* 924–929.

SERDULA, M. K., IVERY, D., COATES, R. J., FREEDMAN, D. S., WILLIAMSON, D. F., & BYERS, T. (1993). Do obese children become obese adults? A review of the literature. *Preventive Medicine, 22,* 167–177.

SEVER, J. L. (1983). Maternal infections. In C. C. Brown (Ed.), *Childhood learning disabilities and prenatal risk* (pp. 31–38). New York: Johnson & Johnson.

SHAGLE, S. C., & BARBER, B. K. (1993). Effects of family, marital, and parent–child conflict on adolescent self-derogation and suicidal ideation. *Journal of Marriage and the Family, 55,* 964–974.

SHAHAR, S. (1990). *Childhood in the Middle Ages.* London: Routledge & Kegan Paul.

SHAINESS, N. (1961). A re-evaluation of some aspects of femininity through a study of menstruation: A preliminary report. *Comparative Psychiatry, 2,* 20–26.

SHALALA, D. E. (1993). Giving pediatric immunizations the priority they deserve. *Journal of the American Medical Association, 269,* 1844–1845.

SHEDLER, J., & BLOCK, J. (1990). Adolescent drug use and psychological health: A longitudinal inquiry. *American Psychologist, 45,* 612–630.

SHEINGOLD, K. (1973). Developmental differences in intake and storage of visual information. *Journal of Experimental Child Psychology, 16,* 1–11.

SHELEY, J. F., & WRIGHT, J. D. (1995). *In the line of fire.* New York: Aldine De Gruyter.

SHEPARDSON, D. P., & PIZZINI, E. L. (1992). Gender bias in female elementary teachers' perceptions of the scientific ability of students. *Science Education, 76,* 147–153.

SHERIF, M., HARVEY, O. J., WHITE, B. J., HOOD, W. R., & SHERIF, C. W. (1961). *The Robbers Cave experiment: Intergroup conflict and cooperation.* Norman: University of Oklahoma Press.

SHERMAN, D. K., IACONO, W. G., & McGUE, M. K. (1997). Attention-deficit hyperactivity disorder dimensions: A twin study of inattention and impulsivity–hyperactivity. *Journal of the American Academy of Child and*

Adolescent Psychiatry, 36, 745–753.

SHERMAN, M., & KEY, C. B. (1932). The intelligence of isolated mountain children. *Child Development, 3,* 279–290.

SHIELDS, P. J., & ROVEE-COLLIER, C. K. (1992). Long-term memory for context-specific category information at six months. *Child Development, 63,* 245–259.

SHILLER, V., IZARD, C. E., & HEMBREE, E. A. (1986). Patterns of emotion expression during separation in the Strange Situation. *Developmental Psychology, 22,* 378–382.

SHILOH, S. (1996). Genetic counseling: A developing area of interest for psychologists. *Professional Psychology: Research and Practice, 27,* 475–486.

SHINN, M. W. (1900). *The biography of a baby.* Boston: Houghton Mifflin.

SHODA, Y., MISCHEL, W., & PEAKE, P. K. (1990). Predicting adolescent cognitive and self-regulatory competencies from preschool delay of gratification: Identifying diagnostic conditions. *Developmental Psychology, 26,* 978–986.

SHULMAN, S., ELICKER, J., & SROUFE, A. (1994). Stages of friendship growth in preadolescence as related to attachment history. *Journal of Social and Personal Relationships, 11,* 341–361.

SHURE, M. B. (1997). Interpersonal cognitive problem solving: Primary prevention of early high-risk behaviors in the preschool and primary years. In G. W. Albee & T. P. Gullotta (Eds.), *Primary prevention works* (pp. 167–188). Thousand Oaks, CA: Sage.

SHURTLEFF, D. B., & LEMIRE, R. J. (1995). Epidemiology, etiologic factors, and prenatal diagnosis of open spinal dysraphism. *Neurosurgery Clinics of North America, 6,* 183–193.

SHWEDER, R. A. (1996). True ethnography: The lore, the law, and the lure. In R. Jessor, A. Colby, & R. A. Shweder (Eds.), *Ethnography and human development* (pp. 15–52). Chicago: University of Chicago Press.

SHWEDER, R. A., GOODNOW, J., HATANO, G., LEVINE, R. A., MARKUS, H., & MILLER, P. (1998). The cultural psychology of development: One mind, many mentalities. In W. Damon & R. M. Lerner (Eds.), *Handbook of child psychology: Vol. 1. Theoretical models of human development* (5th ed., pp. 865–937). New York: Wiley.

SHWEDER, R. A., & HAIDT, J. (1993). The future of moral psychology: Truth, intuition, and the pluralistic way. *Psychological Science, 6,* 360–365.

SHWEDER, R. A., MAHAPATRA, M., & MILLER, J. G. (1990). Culture and moral development. In J. Stigler, R. A. Shweder, & G. Herdt (Eds.), *Cultural psychology: Essays on comparative human development* (pp. 130–204). New York: Cambridge University Press.

SIEGEL, A. W. (1981). The externalization of cognitive maps by children and adults: In search of ways to ask better questions. In L. S. Liben, A. H. Patterson, & N. Newcombe (Eds.), *Spatial representation and behavior across the life span* (pp. 167–194). New York: Academic Press.

SIEGEL, B. (1996, Spring). Is the emperor wearing clothes? Social policy and the empirical support for full inclusion of children with disabilities in the preschool and early elementary school grades. *Social Policy Report of the Society for Research in Child Development, 10*(2–3), 2–17.

SIEGLER, R. S. (1981). Developmental sequences within and between concepts. *Monographs of the Society for Research in Child Development, 46*(2, Serial No. 189).

SIEGLER, R. S. (1988). Individual differences in strategy choices: Good students, not-so-good students, and perfectionists. *Child Development, 59,* 833–851.

SIEGLER, R. S. (1992). The other Alfred Binet. *Developmental Psychology, 28,* 179–190.

SIEGLER, R. S. (1995a). Children's thinking: How does change occur? In W. Schneider & F. E. Weinert (Eds.), *Memory performance and competencies: Issues in growth and development* (pp. 405–430). Hillsdale, NJ: Erlbaum.

SIEGLER, R. S. (1995b). How does change occur? A microgenetic study of number conservation. *Cognitive Psychology, 28,* 225–273.

SIEGLER, R. S. (1996). *Emerging minds: The process of change in children's thinking.* New York: Oxford University Press.

SIEGLER, R. S. (1998). *Children's thinking* (3rd ed.). Upper Saddle River, NJ: Prentice-Hall.

SIEGLER, R. S., & CROWLEY, K. (1991). The microgenetic method: A direct means for studying cognitive development. *American Psychologist, 46,* 606–620.

SIEGLER, R. S., & CROWLEY, K. (1992). Microgenetic methods revisited. *American Psychologist, 47,* 1241–1243.

SIEGLER, R. S., & ELLIS, S. (1996). Piaget on childhood. *Psychological Science, 7,* 211–215.

SIEGLER, R. S., & JENKINS, E. (1989). *How children discover new strategies.* Hillsdale, NJ: Erlbaum.

SIEGLER, R. S., & MUNAKATA, Y. (1993, Winter). Beyond the immaculate transition: Advances in the understanding of change. *Newsletter of the Society for Research in Child Development.*

SIEGLER, R. S., & RICHARDS, D. D. (1980). *College students' prototypes of children's intelligence.* Paper presented at the annual meeting of the American Psychological Association, New York.

SIEGLER, R. S., & ROBINSON, M. (1982). The development of numerical understandings. In H. W. Reese & L. P. Lipsitt (Eds.), *Advances in child development and behavior* (Vol. 16, pp. 241–312). New York: Academic Press.

SIGMAN, M. (1995). Nutrition and child development: More food for thought. *Current Directions in Psychological Science, 4,* 52–55.

SIGMAN, M., COHEN, S. E., & BECKWITH, L. (1997). Why does infant attention predict adolescent intelligence? *Infant Behavior and Development, 20,* 133–140.

SIGMAN, M., & KASARI, C. (1995). Joint attention across contexts in normal and autistic children. In C. Moore & P. J. Dunham (Eds.), *Joint attention: Its origins and role in development* (pp. 189–203). Hillsdale, NJ: Erlbaum.

SIGMAN, M. D., KASARI, C., KWON, J. H., & YIRMIYA, N. (1992). Responses to the negative emotions of others by autistic, mentally retarded, and normal children. *Child Development, 63,* 786–807.

SIGNORELLA, M. L., BIGLER, R. S., & LIBEN, L. S. (1993). Developmental differences in children's gender schemata about others: A meta-analytic review. *Developmental Review, 13,* 147–183.

SIGNORELLA, M. L., & JAMISON, W. (1986). Masculinity, femininity, androgyny, and cognitive performance: A meta-analysis. *Psychological Bulletin, 100,* 207–228.

SIGNORIELLI, N. (1993). Television, the portrayal of women, and children's attitudes. In G. L. Berry & J. K. Asamen (Eds.), *Children and television: Images in a changing sociocultural world* (pp. 229–242). Newbury Park, CA: Sage.

SILVERMAN, W. K., LA GRECA, A. M., & WASSERSTEIN, S. (1995). What do children worry about? Worries and their relation to anxiety. *Child Development, 66,* 671–686.

SIMMONS, R. G., BLACK, A., & ZHOU, Y. (1991). African-American versus white children and the transition to junior high school. *American Journal of Education, 99,* 481–520.

SIMMONS, R. G., & BLYTH, D. A. (1987). Moving into adolescence. New York: Aldine De Gruyter.

SIMON, R., ALTSTEIN, H., & MELLI, M. S. (1994). *The case for transracial adoption.* Washington, DC: American University Press.

SIMONS, R. L., & CHAO, W. (1996). Conduct problems. In R. L. Simons & Associates (Eds.), *Understanding differences between divorced and intact families* (pp. 125–143). Thousand Oaks, CA: Sage.

SIMONS, R. L., & JOHNSON, C. (1996). Mother's parenting. In R. L. Simons & Associates (Eds.), *Understanding differences between divorced and intact families* (pp. 45–63). Thousand Oaks, CA: Sage.

SIMONS, R. L., LORENZ, F. O., WU, C-I., & CONGER, R. D. (1993). Social network and marital support as mediators and moderators of the impact of stress and depression on parental behavior. *Developmental Psychology, 29,* 368–381.

SIMONS, R. L., WHITBECK, L. B., CONGER, R. D., & CHYI-IN, W. (1991). Intergenerational transmission of harsh parenting. *Developmental Psychology, 27,* 159–171.

SIMONS, R. L., WU, C., CONGER, R. D., & LORENZ, F. O. (1994). Two routes to delinquency: Differences between early and late starters in the impact of parenting and deviant peers. *Criminology, 32,* 247–274.

SIMONTON, D. K. (1988). *Scientific genius: A psychology of science.* New York: Cambridge University Press.

SIMPSON, S. A., & HARDING, A. E. (1993). Predictive testing for Huntington's disease after the gene. *Journal of Medical Genetics, 30,* 1036–1038.

SINGER, D. G., & SINGER, J. L. (1990). *The house of make-believe.* Cambridge, MA: Harvard University Press.

SITSKOORN, M. M., & SMITSMAN, A. W. (1995). Infants' perception of dynamic relations between objects: Passing through or support? *Developmental Psychology, 31,* 437–447.

SIVARD, R. L. (1996). *World military and social expenditures* (16th ed.). Leesburg, VA: WMSE.

SKINNER, B. F. (1957). *Verbal behavior.* New York: Appleton-Century-Crofts.

SKINNER, E. A. (1995). *Perceived control, motivation, and coping.* Thousand Oaks, CA: Sage.

SKINNER, E. A., ZIMMER-GEMBECK, M. J., & CONNELL, J. P. (1998).

Individual differences and the development of perceived control. *Monographs of the Society for Research in Child Development, 63*(2–3, Serial No. 254).

SKODAK, M., & SKEELS, H. M. (1949). A follow-up study of one hundred adopted children. *Journal of Genetic Psychology, 75,* 85–125.

SKOUTERIS, H., McKENZIE, B. E., & DAY, R. H. (1992). Integration of sequential information for shape perception by infants: A developmental study. *Child development, 63,* 1164–1176.

SLABY, R. G., & FREY, K. S. (1975). Development of gender constancy and selective attention to same-sex models. *Child Development, 46,* 849–856.

SLABY, R. G., ROEDELL, W. C., AREZZO, D., & HENDRIX, K. (1995). *Early violence prevention.* Washington, DC: National Association for the Education of Young Children.

SLATER, A. M. (1996). The organization of visual perception in early infancy. In F. Vital-Durand, J. Atkinson, & O. J. Braddick (Eds.), *Infant vision* (pp. 309–325). Oxford, England: Oxford University Press.

SLATER, A. M. (1997). Visual perception and its organisation in early infancy. In G. Bremner, A. Slater, & G. Butterworth (Eds.), *Infant development: Recent advances* (pp. 31–53). Hove, England: Taylor & Francis.

SLATER, A. M., BROWN, E., MATTOCK, A., & BORNSTEIN, M. H. (1996). Continuity and change in habituation in the first 4 months from birth. *Journal of Reproductive and Infant Psychology, 14,* 187–194.

SLATER, A. M., MATTOCK, A., & BROWN, E. (1990). Size constancy at birth: Newborn infants' responses to retinal and real size. *Journal of Experimental Child Psychology, 49,* 314–322.

SLOBIN, D. I. (1982). Universal and particular in the acquisition of language. In L. R. Gleitman & H. E. Wanner (Eds.), *Language acquisition: The state of the art* (pp. 128–170). Cambridge: Cambridge University Press.

SLOBIN, D. I. (1985). Crosslinguistic evidence for the language-making capacity. In D. I. Slobin (Ed.), *The crosslinguistic study of language acquisition: Vol. 2. Theoretical issues* (pp. 1157–1256). Hillsdale, NJ: Erlbaum.

SMETANA, J. G. (1981). Preschool children's conceptions of moral and social rules. *Child Development, 52,* 1333–1336.

SMETANA, J. G. (1985). Preschool children's conceptions of transgressions: Effects of varying moral and conventional domain-related attributes. *De-*

velopmental Psychology, 21, 18–29.

SMETANA, J. G. (1995). Morality in context: Abstractions, ambiguities, and applications. In R. Vasta (Ed.), *Annals of child development* (Vol. 10, 83–130). London: Jessica Kingsley.

SMETANA, J. G., & ASQUITH, P. (1994). Adolescents' and parents' conceptions of parental authority and adolescent autonomy. *Child Development, 65,* 1147–1162.

SMETANA, J. G., & BRAEGES, J. L. (1990). The development of toddlers' moral and conventional judgments. *Merrill-Palmer Quarterly, 36,* 329–346.

SMILEY, P. A., & DWECK, C. S. (1994). Individual differences in achievement goals among young children. *Child Development, 65,* 1723–1743.

SMITH, B. A., & BLASS, E. M. (1996). Taste-mediated calming in premature, preterm, and full-term human infants. *Developmental Psychology, 32,* 1084–1089.

SMITH, C. L., & TAGER-FLUSBERG, H. (1982). Metalinguistic awareness and language development. *Journal of Experimental Child Psychology, 34,* 449–468.

SMITH, H. (1992). The detrimental health effects of ionizing radiation. *Nuclear Medicine Communications, 13,* 4–10.

SMITH, J., & PRIOR, M. (1995). Temperament and stress resilience in school-age children: A within-families study. *Journal of the American Academy of Child and Adolescent Psychiatry, 34,* 168–179.

SMITH, J., & RUSSELL, G. (1984). Why do males and females differ? Children's beliefs about sex differences. *Sex Roles, 11,* 1111–1119.

SMITH, K. E., LANDRY, S. H., SWANK, P. R., BALDWIN, C. D., DENSON, S. E., & WILDIN, S. (1996). The relation of medical risk and maternal stimulation with preterm infants' development of cognitive, language and daily living skills. *Journal of Child Psychology and Psychiatry, 37,* 855–864.

SMITH, M. C. (1978). Cognizing the behavior stream: The recognition of intentional action. *Child Development, 49,* 736–743.

SMITH, P. K., & CONNOLLY, K. J. (1980). *The ecology of preschool behaviour.* Cambridge: Cambridge University Press.

SMITH, P. K., & HUNTER, T. (1992). Children's perceptions of play-fighting, playchasing and real fighting: A cross-national study. *Social Development, 1,* 211–229.

SMITH, S. (Ed.). (1995). Two-generation programs for families in poverty: A new intervention

strategy. *Advances in applied developmental psychology* (Vol. 9). Norwood, NJ: Ablex.

SMYTH, R. (1995). Conceptual perspective-taking and children's interpretation of pronouns in reported speech. *Journal of Child Language, 22,* 171–187.

SNAREY, J. R. (1995). In a communitarian voice: The sociological expansion of Kohlbergian theory, research, and practice. In W. M. Kurtines & J. L. Gewirtz (Eds.), *Moral development: An introduction* (pp. 109–134). Boston: Allyn and Bacon.

SNAREY, J. R., REIMER, J., & KOHLBERG, L. (1985). The development of social-moral reasoning among kibbutz adolescents: A longitudinal cross-cultural study. *Developmental Psychology, 20,* 3–17.

SNIDMAN, N., KAGAN, J., RIORDAN, L., & SHANNON, D. C. (1995). Cardiac function and behavioral reactivity. *Psychophysiology, 32,* 199–207.

SO, L. K. H., & DODD, B. J. (1995). The acquisition of phonology by Cantonese-speaking children. *Journal of Child Language, 22,* 473–495.

SOCIETY FOR RESEARCH IN CHILD DEVELOPMENT. (1993). Ethical standards for research with children. In *Directory of Members* (pp. 337–339). Ann Arbor, MI: Author.

SODIAN, B., TAYLOR, C., HARRIS, P. L., & PERNER, J. (1991). Early deception and the child's theory of mind: False trails and genuine markers. *Child Development, 62,* 468–483.

SOKEN, N. H., & PICK, A. D. (1992). Intermodal perception of happy and angry expressive behaviors by seven-month-old infants. *Child Development, 63,* 787–795.

SOLOMON, J. C., & MARX, J. (1995). "To grandmother's house we go": Health and school adjustment of children raised solely by grandparents. *Gerontologist, 35,* 386–394.

SOMMERS-FLANAGAN, R., SOMMERS-FLANAGAN, J., & DAVIS, B. (1993). What's happening on music television? A gender-role content analysis. *Sex Roles, 28,* 745–753.

SOMMERVILLE, J. (1982). *The rise and fall of childhood.* Beverly Hills, CA: Sage.

SONENSTEIN, F. L., PLECK, J. H., & KU, L. C. (1991). Levels of sexual activity among adolescent males in the United States. *Family Planning Perspectives, 23,* 162–167.

SONNENSCHEIN, S. (1986a). Development of referential communication: Deciding that a message is uninformative. *Developmental Psychology, 22,* 164–168.

SONNENSCHEIN, S. (1986b). Development of referential commu-

nication skills: How familiarity with a listener affects a speaker's production of redundant messages. *Developmental Psychology, 22,* 549–552.

SONNENSCHEIN, S. (1988). The development of referential communication: Speaking to different listeners. *Child Development, 59,* 694–702.

SONTAG, C. W., BAKER, C. T., & NELSON, V. L. (1958). Mental growth and personality development: A longitudinal study. *Monographs of the Society for Research in Child Development, 23* (2, Serial No. 68).

SOPHIAN, C. (1988). Early developments in children's understanding of number: Inferences about numerosity and one-to-one correspondence. *Child Development, 59,* 1397–1414.

SOPHIAN, C. (1995). Representation and reasoning in early numerical development: Counting, conservation, and comparisons between sets. *Child Development, 66,* 559–577.

SORCE, J., EMDE, R., CAMPOS, J., & KLINNERT, M. (1985). Maternal emotional signaling: Its effect on the visual cliff behavior of 1-year-olds. *Developmental Psychology, 21,* 195–200.

SOSA, R., KENNELL, J., KLAUS, M., ROBERTSON, S., & URRUTIA, J. (1980). The effect of a supportive companion on perinatal problems, length of labor, and mother–infant interaction. *New England Journal of Medicine, 303,* 597–600.

SOSTEK, A. M., SMITH, Y. F., KATZ, K. S., & GRANT, E. G. (1987). Developmental outcome of preterm infants with intraventricular hemorrhage at one and two years of age. *Child Development, 58,* 779–786.

SOUTHERN, W. T., JONES, E. D., & STANLEY, J. C. (1994). Acceleration and enrichment: The context and development of program options. In K. A. Heller, F. J., Jonks, & H. A. Passow (Eds.), *International handbook of research and development of giftedness and talent* (pp. 387–409). Oxford: Pergamon Press.

SPÄTLING, L., & SPÄTLING, G. (1988). Magnesium supplementation in pregnancy: A double-blind study. *British Journal of Obstetrics and Gynecology, 95,* 120–125.

SPEARMAN, C. (1927). *The abilities of man: Their nature and measurement.* New York: Macmillan.

SPEECE, M. W., & BRENT, S. B. (1992). The acquisition of a mature understanding of three components of the concept of death. *Death Studies, 16,* 211–229.

SPEECE, M. W., & BRENT, S. B. (1996). The development of children's understanding of death. In C. A. Corr & D. M. Corr (Eds.), *Handbook of childhood death and bereavement* (pp. 29–50). New York: Springer.

SPEER, J. R., & FLAVELL, J. H. (1979). Young children's knowledge of the relative difficulty of recognition and recall memory tasks. *Developmental Psychology, 15*, 214–217.

SPEICHER, B. (1994). Family patterns of moral judgment during adolescence and early adulthood. *Developmental Psychology, 30*, 624–632.

SPELKE, E. S. (1987). The development of intermodal perception. In P. Salapatek & L. Cohen (Eds.), *Handbook of infant perception: Vol. 2. From perception to cognition* (pp. 233–273). Orlando, FL: Academic Press.

SPELKE, E. S. (1994). Initial knowledge: Six suggestions. *Cognition, 50*, 431–445.

SPELKE, E. S., BREINLINGER, K., MACOMBER, J., & JACOBSON, K. (1992). Origins of knowledge. *Psychological Review, 99*, 605–632.

SPELKE, E. S., GUTHEIL, G., & VAN DE WALLE, G. (1995). The development of object perception. In S. M. Kosslyn & D. N. Osherson (Eds.), *Visual cognition* (pp. 297–330). Cambridge, MA: MIT Press.

SPELKE, E. S., & HERMER, L. (1996). Early cognitive development: Objects and space. In R. Gelman & T. K. Au (Eds.), *Perceptual and cognitive development* (pp. 71–114). San Diego: Academic Press.

SPELKE, E. S., HOFSTEN, C. VON, & KESTENBAUM, R. (1989). Object perception in infancy: Interaction of spatial and kinetic information for object boundaries. *Developmental Psychology, 25*, 185–196.

SPELKE, E. S., & NEWPORT, E. L. (1998). Nativism, empiricism, and the development of knowledge. In R. M. Lerner (Ed.), *Handbook of child psychology: Vol. 1. Theoretical models of human development* (5th ed., pp. 199–254). New York: Wiley.

SPELTZ, M. L., ENDRIGA, M. C., FISHER, P. A., & MASON, C. A. (1997). Early predictors of attachment in infants with cleft lip and/or palate. *Child Development, 68*, 12–25.

SPENCE, J. T., HELMREICH, R., & STAPP, J. (1975). Ratings of self and peers on sex role attributes and their relation to self-esteem and conceptions of masculinity and femininity. *Journal of Personality and Social Psychology, 32*, 29–39.

SPENCE, M. J., & DECASPER, A. J. (1987). Prenatal experience with low-frequency maternal voice sounds influences neonatal perception of maternal voice samples. *Infant Behavior and Development, 10*, 133–142.

SPENCER, P. E., BODNER-JOHNSON, B. A., & GUTFREUND, M. K. (1992). Interacting with infants with a hearing loss: What can we learn from mothers who are deaf? *Journal of Early Intervention, 16*, 64–78.

SPENCER, P. E., & LEDERBERG, A. (1997) Different modes, different models: Communication and language of young deaf children and their mothers. In L. B. Adamson & Romski (Eds.), *Communication and language acquisition: Discoveries from atypical development* (pp. 203–230). Baltimore, MD: Paul Brookes.

SPENCER, P. E., & MEADOW-ORLANS, K. P. (1996). Play, language, and maternal responsiveness: A longitudinal study of deaf and hearing infants. *Child Development, 67*, 3176–3191.

SPINDLER, G. D. (1970). The education of adolescents: An anthropological perspective. In D. Ellis (Ed.), *Adolescents: Readings in behavior and development* (pp. 152–161). Hinsdale, IL: Dryden.

SPINETTA, J., & RIGLER, D. (1972). The child-abusing parent: A psychological review. *Psychological Bulletin, 77*, 296–304.

SPITZ, R. A. (1946). Anaclitic depression. *Psychoanalytic Study of the Child, 2*, 313–342.

SPIVACK, G., & SHURE, M. B. (1974). *Social adjustment of young children: A cognitive approach to solving real-life problems.* San Francisco: Jossey-Bass.

SPOCK, B., & PARKER, S. J. (1998). *Dr. Spock's baby and child care* (7th ed.). New York: Pocket.

SROUFE, L. A. (1979). The ontogenesis of emotion. In J. D. Osofsky (Ed.), *Handbook of infant development* (pp. 462–516). New York: Wiley.

SROUFE, L. A. (1985). Attachment classification from the perspective of infant–caregiver relationships and infant temperament. *Child Development, 56*, 1–14.

SROUFE, L. A. (1988). A developmental perspective on day care. *Early Childhood Research Quarterly, 3*, 293–292.

SROUFE, L. A., EGELAND, B., & KREUTZER, T. (1990). The fate of early experience following developmental change: Longitudinal approaches to individual adaptation. *Child Development, 61*, 1363–1373.

SROUFE, L. A., & WATERS, E. (1976). The ontogenesis of smiling and laughter: A perspective on the organization of development in infancy. *Psychological Review, 83*, 173–189.

SROUFE, L. A., & WUNSCH, J. P. (1972). The development of laughter in the first year of life. *Child Development, 43*, 1324–1344.

ST JAMES-ROBERTS, I., & HALIL, T. (1991). Infant crying patterns in the first year: Normal community and clinical findings. *Journal of Child Psychology and Psychiatry, 32*, 951–968.

ST. PETERS, M., FITCH, M., HUSTON, A. C., WRIGHT, J. C., & EAKINS, D. J. (1991). Television and families: What do young children watch with their parents? *Child Development, 62*, 1409–1423.

STACK, D. M., & MUIR, D. W. (1992). Adult tactile stimulation during face-to-face interactions modulates five-month-olds' affect and attention. *Child Development, 63*, 1509–1525.

STAHL, S. A. (1992). Saying the "p" word: Nine guidelines for effective phonics instruction. *The Reading Teacher, 45*, 618–625.

STAHL, S. A., MCKENNA, M. C., & PAGNUCCO, J. R. (1994). The effects of whole-language instruction: An update and reappraisal. *Educational Psychologist, 29*, 175–185.

STANKOV, L., HORN, J. L., ROY, T. (1980). On the relationship between Gf/Gc theory and Jensen's Level I/Level II theory. *Journal of Educational Psychology, 72*, 796–809.

STAPLES, R., & JOHNSON, L. B. (1993). *Black families at the crossroads.* San Francisco: Jossey-Bass.

STARK, L. J., ALLEN, K. D., HURST, M., NASH, D. A., RIGNEY, B., & STOKES, T. F. (1989). Distraction: Its utilization and efficacy with children undergoing dental treatment. *Journal of Applied Behavior Analysis, 22*, 297–307.

STATTIN, H., & MAGNUSSON, D. (1990). *Pubertal maturation in female development.* Hillsdale, NJ: Erlbaum.

STAUB, E. (1996). Cultural-societal roots of violence. *American Psychologist, 51*, 117–132.

STECHLER, G., & HALTON, A. (1982). Prenatal influences on human development. In B. B. Wolman (Ed.), *Handbook of developmental psychology* (pp. 175–189). Englewood Cliffs, NJ: Prentice-Hall.

STEELE, C. D., WAPNER, R. J., SMITH, J. B., HAYNES, M. K., & JACKSON, L. G. (1996). Prenatal diagnosis using fetal cells isolated from maternal blood: A review. *Clinical Obstetrics and Gynecology, 39*, 801–813.

STEIN, J. H., & REISER, L. W. (1994). A study of white middle-class adolescent boys' responses to "semenarche" (the first ejaculation). *Journal of Youth and Adolescence, 23*, 373–384.

STEIN, Z., SUSSER, M., SAENGER, G., & MAROLLA, F. (1975). *Famine and human development: The Dutch hunger winter of 1944–1945.* New York: Oxford University Press.

STEINBERG, L. D. (1984). The varieties and effects of work during adolescence. In M. Lamb, A. Brown, & B. Rogoff (Eds.), *Advances in developmental psychology* (Vol. 3, pp. 1–37). Hillsdale, NJ: Erlbaum.

STEINBERG, L. D. (1986). Latchkey children and susceptibility to peer pressure: An ecological analysis. *Developmental Psychology, 22*, 433–439.

STEINBERG, L. D. (1987). The impact of puberty on family relations: Effects of pubertal status and pubertal timing. *Developmental Psychology, 23*, 451–460.

STEINBERG, L. D. (1990). Interdependence in the family: Autonomy, conflict, and harmony in the parent–adolescent relationship. In S. S. Feldman & G. R. Elliott (Eds.), *At the threshold: The developing adolescent* (pp. 255–276). Cambridge, MA: Harvard University Press.

STEINBERG, L. D. (1999). *Adolescence* (5th ed.). New York: McGraw-Hill.

STEINBERG, L.D., DARLING, N. E., & FLETCHER, A. C. (1995). Authoritative parenting and adolescent development: An ecological journey. In P. Moen, G. H. Elder, & K. Luscher (Eds.), *Examining lives in context* (pp. 423–466). Washington, DC: American Psychological Association.

STEINBERG, L. D., & DORNBUSCH, S. M. (1991). Negative correlates of part-time employment during adolescence: Replication and elaboration. *Developmental Psychology, 27*, 304–313.

STEINBERG, L. D., FEGLEY, S., & DORNBUSCH, S. (1993). Negative impact of part-time work on adolescent adjustment: Evidence from a longitudinal study. *Developmental Psychology, 29*, 171–180.

STEINBERG, L. D., FLETCHER, A., & DARLING, N. (1994). Parental monitoring and peer influences on adolescent substance use. *Pediatrics, 93*, 1060–1064.

STEINBERG, L. D., LAMBORN, S. D., DARLING, N., MOUNTS, N. S., & DORNBUSCH, S. M. (1994). Over-time changes in adjustment and competence among adolescents from authoritative, authoritarian, indulgent, and neglectful families. *Child Development, 65,* 754–770.

STEINBERG, L. D., & SILVERBERG, S. (1986). The vicissitudes of autonomy in early adolescence. *Child Development, 57,* 841–851.

STEINER, J. E. (1979). Human facial expression in response to taste and smell stimulation. In H. W. Reese & L. P. Lipsitt (Eds.), *Advances in child development and behavior* (Vol. 13, pp. 257–295). New York: Academic Press.

STENBERG, C., & CAMPOS, J. (1990). The development of anger expressions in infancy. In N. Stein, B. Leventhal, & T. Trabasso (Eds.), *Psychological and biological approaches to emotion* (pp. 247–282). Hillsdale, NJ: Erlbaum.

STENBERG, C., CAMPOS, J., & EMDE, R. (1983). The facial expression of anger in seven-month-old infants. *Child Development, 54,* 178–184.

STERN, M., & KARRAKER, K. H. (1989). Sex stereotyping of infants: A review of gender labeling studies. *Sex Roles, 20,* 501–522.

STERNBERG, K. J., LAMB, M. E., GREENBAUM, C., CICCHETTI, D., DAWUD, S., CORTES, R. M., KRISPIN, O., & LOREY, F. (1993). Effects of domestic violence on children's behavior problems and depression. *Developmental Psychology, 29,* 44–52.

STERNBERG, R. J. (1982, April). Who's intelligent? *Psychology Today, 16*(4), 30–39.

STERNBERG, R. J. (1985). *Beyond IQ: A triarchic theory of human intelligence.* New York: Cambridge University Press.

STERNBERG, R. J. (1986). A triarchic theory of intellectual giftedness. In R. Sternberg & J. Davidson (Eds.), *Conceptions of giftedness* (pp. 223–243). New York: Cambridge University Press.

STERNBERG, R. J. (1988). A triarchic view of intelligence in cross-cultural perspective. In S. H. Irvine & J. W. Berry (Eds.), *Human abilities in cultural context* (pp. 60–85). New York: Cambridge University Press.

STERNBERG, R. J. (1989). Intelligence, wisdom, and creativity: Their natures and interrelationships. In R. L. Linn (Ed.), *Intelligence: Measurement, theory, and public policy* (pp. 119–146). Urbana: University of Illinois Press.

STERNBERG, R. J. (1997). *Successful intelligence.,* New York: Plume.

STERNBERG, R. J., & DETTERMAN, D. K. (1986). *What is intelligence?* Norwood, NJ: Ablex.

STERNBERG, R. J., & GRIGORENKO, E. L. (1993). Thinking styles and the gifted. *Roeper Review, 16,* 122–130.

STERNBERG, R. J., & LUBART, T. I. (1991a). Creating creative minds. *Phi Delta Kappan, 72*(8), 608–614.

STERNBERG, R. J., & LUBART, T. I. (1991b). An investment theory of creativity and its development. *Human Development, 34,* 1–31.

STERNBERG, R. J., & LUBART, T. I. (1995). *Defying the crowd.* New York: Basic Books.

STERNBERG, R. J., & LUBART, T. I. (1996). Investing in creativity. *American Psychologist, 51,* 677–688.

STERNBERG, R. J., WAGNER, R. K., WILLIAMS, W. M., & HORVATH, J. A. (1995). Testing common sense. *American Psychologist, 50,* 912–927.

STEVENS, J. H. (1984). Black grandmothers' and black adolescent mothers' knowledge about parenting. *Developmental Psychology, 20,* 1017–1025.

STEVENS-SIMON, C., KELLY, L., SINGER, D., & COX, A. (1996). Why pregnant adolescents say they did not use contraceptives prior to conception. *Journal of Adolescent Health, 19,* 48–53.

STEVENSON, H. W. (1992, December). Learning from Asian schools. *Scientific American, 267*(6), 32–38.

STEVENSON, H. W. (1994). Extracurricular programs in East Asian schools. *Teachers College Record, 95,* 389–407.

STEVENSON, H. W., CHEN, C., & LEE, S-Y. (1993). Mathematics achievement of Chinese, Japanese, and American children: Ten years later. *Science, 259,* 53–58.

STEVENSON, H. W., & LEE, S-Y. (1990). Contexts of achievement: A study of American, Chinese, and Japanese children. *Monographs of the Society for Research in Child Development, 55*(1–2, Serial No. 221).

STEVENSON, M. R., & BLACK, K. N. (1995). *How divorce affects offspring: A research approach.* Dubuque, IA: Brown & Benchmark.

STEVENSON, R., & POLLITT, C. (1987). The acquisition of temporal terms. *Journal of Child Language, 14,* 533–545.

STEWARD, M. S., & STEWARD, D. S. (1996). Interviewing young children about body touching and handling. *Monographs of the Society for Research in Child Development, 61*(4–5, Serial No. 248).

STEWART, D. A. (1982). *Children with sex chromosome aneuploidy: Follow-up studies.* New York: Alan R. Liss.

STEWART, S. L., & RUBIN, K. H. (1995). The social problem-solving skills of anxious-withdrawn children. *Development and Psychopathology, 7,* 323–336.

STICE, E., & BARRERA, M., JR. (1995). A longitudinal examination of the reciprocal relations between perceived parenting and adolescents' substance use and externalizing behaviors. *Developmental Psychology, 31,* 322–334.

STIFTER, C. A., COULEHAN, C. M., & FISH, M. (1993). Linking employment to attachment: The mediating effects of maternal separation anxiety and interactive behavior. *Child Development, 64,* 1451–1460.

STILES, J. (1998). The effects of early focal brain injury on lateralization of cognitive function. *Current Directions in Psychological Science, 7,* 21–26.

STILES, J., BATES, E. A., THAL, D., TRAUNER, D., & REILLY, J. (1999). Linguistic, cognitive and affective development in children with pre- and perinatal focal brain injury: A ten-year overview from the San Diego Longitudinal Project. In C. Rovee-Collier (Ed.), *Advances in infancy research* (Vol. 13). Norwood, NJ: Ablex.

STIPEK, D. (1995). The development of pride and shame in toddlers. In J. P. Tangney & K. W. Fischer (Eds.), *Self-conscious emotions* (pp. 237–252). New York: Guilford.

STIPEK, D. J., & BYLER, P. (1997). Early childhood education teachers: Do they practice what they preach? *Early Childhood Research Quarterly, 12,* 305–326.

STIPEK, D. J., FEILER, R., DANIELS, D., & MILBURN, S. (1995). Effects of different instructional approaches on young children's achievement and motivation. *Child Development, 66,* 209–223.

STIPEK, D. J., GRALINSKI, J. H., & KOPP, C. B. (1990). Self-concept development in the toddler years. *Developmental Psychology, 26,* 972–977.

STIPEK, D. J., & MACIVER, D. (1989). Developmental change in children's assessment of intellectual competence. *Child Development, 60,* 531–538.

STIPEK, D. J., RECCHIA, S., & MCCLINTIC, S. (1992). Self-evaluation in young children. *Monographs of the Society for Research in Child Development, 57*(1, Serial No. 226).

STOCH, M. B., SMYTHE, P. M., MOODIE, A. D., & BRADSHAW, D. (1982). Psychosocial outcome and CT findings after growth undernourishment during infancy: A 20-year developmental study. *Developmental Medicine and Child Neurology, 24,* 419–436.

STOCKER, C. M., & DUNN, J. (1994). Sibling relationships in childhood and adolescence. In J. C. DeFries, R. Plomin, & D. W. Fulker (Eds.), *Nature and nurture in middle childhood* (pp. 214–232). Cambridge, MA: Blackwell.

STOCKER, C. M., & MCHALE, S. M. (1992). The nature and family correlates of preadolescents' perceptions of their sibling relationships. *Journal of Social and Personal Relationships, 9,* 179–195.

STOCKMAN, I. J., & VAUGHN-COOKE, F. (1992). Lexical elaboration in children's locative action expressions. *Child Development, 63,* 1104–1125.

STODOLSKY, S. S. (1988). *The subject matters.* Chicago: University of Chicago Press.

STOEL-GAMMON, C., & MENN, L. (1997). Phonological development: Learning sounds and sound patterns. In J. Berko Gleason (Ed.), *The development of language* (4th ed., pp. 69–121). Boston: Allyn and Bacon.

STOEL-GAMMON, C., & OTOMO, K. (1986). Babbling development of hearing-impaired and normally hearing subjects. *Journal of Speech and Hearing Disorders, 51,* 33–41.

STONE, L. (1977). *The family, sex, and marriage in England, 1500–1800.* New York: Harper & Row.

STONEMAN, Z., BRODY, G. H., & MACKINNON, C. E. (1986). Same-sex and cross-sex siblings: Activity choices, roles, behavior, and gender stereotypes. *Sex Roles, 15,* 495–511.

STORMSHAK, E. A., BELLANTI, C. J., BIERMAN, K. L., & CONDUCT PROBLEMS PREVENTION RESEARCH GROUP. (1996). The quality of sibling relationships and the development of social competence and behavioral control in aggressive children. *Developmental Psychology, 32,* 79–89.

STRAIN, P. S. (1977). An experimental analysis of peer social initiation on the behavior of withdrawn preschool children: Some training and generalization effects. *Journal of Abnormal Child Psychology, 5,* 445–455.

STRASSBERG, Z. (1995). Social information processing in compliance situations by mothers of behavior-problem boys. *Child Development, 66,* 376–389.

STRASSBERG, Z., DODGE, K., PETTIT, G. S., & BATES, J. E. (1994). Spanking in the home and children's subsequent aggression toward kindergarten peers. *Development and Psychopathology, 6,* 445–461.

STRAUSS, M. S., & CURTIS, L. E. (1984). Development of numerical concepts in infancy. In C. Sophian (Ed.), *Origins of cognitive skills: The Eighteenth Annual Carnegie Symposium on Cognition* (pp. 131–155). Hillsdale, NJ: Erlbaum.

STRAUSS, S. (1998). Cognitive development and science education: Toward a middle level model. In I. E. Sigel & K. Renninger (Eds.), *Handbook of child psychology: Vol. 4. Child psychology in practice* (5th ed., pp. 357–399). New York: Wiley.

STREISSGUTH, A. P. (1997). *Fetal alcohol syndrome.* Baltimore: Paul H. Brookes.

STREISSGUTH, A. P., BARR, H. M., SAMPSON, P. D., & BOOKSTEIN, F. L. (1994). Prenatal alcohol and offspring development: The first fourteen years. *Drug & Alcohol Dependence, 36,* 89–99.

STREISSGUTH, A. P., BARR, H. M., SAMPSON, P. D., DARBY, B. L., & MARTIN, D. C. (1989). IQ at age 4 in relation to maternal alcohol use and smoking during pregnancy. *Developmental Psychology, 25,* 3–11.

STREISSGUTH, A. P., BOOKSTEIN, F. L., & BARR, H. M. (1996). A dose-response study of the enduring effects of prenatal alcohol exposure: Birth to 14 years. In H-L. Spohr & H-C. Steinhausen (Eds.), *Alcohol, pregnancy and the developing child* (pp. 141–168). New York: Cambridge University Press.

STREISSGUTH, A. P., TREDER, R., BARR, H. M., SHEPARD, T., BLEYER, W. A., SAMPSON, P. D., & MARTIN, D. (1987). Aspirin and acetaminophen use by pregnant women and subsequent child IQ and attention decrements. *Teratology, 35,* 211–219.

STRICKLAND, C. J. (1997). Suicide among American Indian, Alaskan Native, and Canadian Aboriginal youth: Advancing the research agenda. *International Journal of Mental Health, 25,* 11–32.

STROBER, M., McCRACKEN, J., & HANNA, G. (1990). Affective disorders. In R. M. Lerner, A. C. Petersen, & J. Brooks-Gunn (Eds.), *The encyclopedia of adolescence* (Vol. 1, pp. 18–25). New York: Garland.

STRUTT, G. F., ANDERSON, D. R., & WELL, A. D. (1975). A developmental study of the effects of irrelevant information on speeded classification. *Journal of Experimental Child Psychology, 20,* 127–135.

STUNKARD, A. J., & SØRENSON, T. I. A. (1993). Obesity and

socioeconomic status—A complex relation. *New England Journal of Medicine, 329,* 1036–1037.

STUNKARD, A. J., SØRENSON, T. I. A., HANIS, C., TEASDALE, T. W., CHAKRABORTY, R., SCHULL, W. J., & SCHULSINGER, F. (1986). An adoption study of human obesity. *New England Journal of Medicine, 314,* 193–198.

SUAREZ-OROZCO, M. M. (1989). *Central American refugees and U.S. high schools: A psychosocial study of motivation and achievement.* Stanford, CA: Stanford University Press.

SUBBOTSKY, E. V. (1994). Early rationality and magical thinking in preschoolers: Space and time. *British Journal of Developmental Psychology, 12,* 97–108.

SUBRAHMANYAM, K., & GREENFIELD, P. M. (1996). Effect of video game practice on spatial skills in girls and boys. In P. M. Greenfield & R. R. Cocking (Eds.), *Interacting with video* (pp. 95–114). Norwood, NJ: Ablex.

SULLIVAN, H. S. (1953). *The interpersonal theory of psychiatry.* New York: Norton.

SULLIVAN, M. L. (1993). Culture and class as determinants of out-of-wedlock childbearing and poverty during late adolescence. *Journal of Research on Adolescence, 3,* 295–316.

SULLIVAN, S. A., & BIRCH, L. L. (1990). Pass the sugar, pass the salt: Experience dictates preference. *Developmental Psychology, 26,* 546–551.

SULLIVAN, S. A., & BIRCH, L. L. (1994). Infant dietary experience and acceptance of solid foods. *Pediatrics, 93,* 271–277.

SULZBY, E. (1985). Children's emergent reading of favorite books: A developmental study. *Reading Research Quarterly, 20,* 458–481.

SUOMI, S. J., & HARLOW, H. F. (1978). Early experience and social development in rhesus monkeys. In M. E. Lamb (Ed.) *Social and personality development* (pp. 252–271). New York: Holt, Rinehart & Winston.

SUPER, C. M. (1981). Behavioral development in infancy. In R. H. Monroe, R. L. Monroe, & B. B. Whiting (Eds.), *Handbook of cross-cultural human development* (pp. 181–270). New York: Garland.

SUPER, C. M., & HARKNESS, S. (1982). The infant's niche in rural Kenya and metropolitan America. In L. L. Adler (Ed.), *Cross-cultural research at issue* (pp. 247–255). New York: Academic Press.

SUREAU, C. (1997). Trials and tribulations of surrogacy: From surrogacy to parenthood. *Human Reproduction, 12,* 410–411.

SUZUKI, L. A., & VALENCIA, R. R. (1997). Race–ethnicity and measured intelligence. *American Psychologist, 52,* 1103–1114.

SWANSON, H. L. (1990). Influence of metacognitive knowledge and aptitude on problem solving. *Journal of Educational Psychology, 82,* 306–314.

SWAYZE, V. W., JOHNSON, V. P., HANSON, J. W., PIVEN, J., SATO, Y., GIEDD, J. N., MOSNIK, D., & ANDREASEN, N. C. (1997). Magnetic resonance imaging of brain anomalies in fetal alcohol syndrome. *Pediatrics, 99,* 232–240.

SZEPKOUSKI, G. M., GAUVAIN, M., & CARBERRY, M. (1994). The development of planning skills in children with and without mental retardation. *Journal of Applied Developmental Psychology, 15,* 187–206.

SZINOVACZ, M. E. (1998). Grandparents today: A demographic profile. *Gerontologist, 38,* 37–52.

T

TADDIO, A., KATZ, J., ILERSICH, A. L., & KOREN, G. (1997). Effect of neonatal circumcision on pain response during subsequent routine vaccination. *Lancet, 349,* 599–603.

TAGER-FLUSBERG, H. (1997). Putting words together: Morphology and syntax in the preschool years. In J. Berko Gleason (Ed.), *The development of language* (4th ed., pp. 159–209). Boston: Allyn and Bacon.

TAGER-FLUSBERG, H., & SULLIVAN, K. (1994). Predicting and explaining behavior: A comparison of autistic, mentally retarded, and normal children. *Journal of Child Psychology and Psychiatry, 35,* 1059–1079.

TAKAHASHI, K. (1990). Are the key assumptions of the "Strange Situation" procedure universal? A view from Japanese research. *Human Development, 33,* 23–30.

TAMIS-LeMONDA, C. S., & BORNSTEIN, M. H. (1989). Habituation and maternal encouragement of attention in infancy as predictors of toddler language, play and representational competence. *Child Development, 60,* 738–751.

TAMIS-LeMONDA, C. S., & BORNSTEIN, M. H. (1994). Specificity in mother–toddler language–play relations across the second year. *Developmental Psychology, 30,* 283–292.

TANNER, J. M. (1990). *Foetus into man* (2nd ed.). Cambridge, MA: Harvard University Press.

TANNER, J. M., & WHITEHOUSE, R. H. (1975). Revised standards

for triceps and subscapular skinfolds in British children. *Archives of Disease in Childhood, 50,* 142–145.

TANNER, J. M., WHITEHOUSE, R. H., CAMERON, N., MARSHALL, W. A., HEALEY, M. J. R., & GOLDSTEIN, H. (1983). *Assessment of skeletal maturity and prediction of adult height* (TW2 Method), (2nd. ed.). London: Academic Press.

TARDIF, T. (1996). Nouns are not always learned before verbs: Evidence from Mandarin speakers' early vocabularies. *Developmental Psychology, 32,* 492–504.

TASKER, F. L., & RICHARDS, M. P. M. (1994). Adolescents' attitudes toward marriage and marital prospects after parental divorce: A review. *Journal of Adolescent Research, 9,* 340–362.

TASSABEHJI, M. K., METCALFE, K., FERGUSSON, W. D., CARETTE, M. J. A., DORE, J. F., DONNAI, D., READ, A. P., PROSCHEL, C., GUTOWSKI, N. J., MAO, X., & SHEER, D. (1996). LIM-kinase detected in Williams syndrome. *Nature Genetics, 13,* 272–273.

TAUBER, M. A. (1979). Parental socialization techniques and sex differences in children's play. *Child Development, 50,* 225–234.

TAYLOR, J. A., & SANDERSON, M. (1995). A reexamination of the risk factors for the sudden infant death syndrome. *Journal of Pediatrics, 126,* 887–891.

TAYLOR, M. (1996). The development of children's beliefs about the social and biological aspects of gender differences. *Child Development, 67,* 1555–1571.

TAYLOR, M., & CARLSON, S. M. (1997). The relation between individual differences in fantasy and theory of mind. *Child Development, 68,* 436–455.

TAYLOR, M., CARTWRIGHT, B. S., & BOWDEN, T. (1991). Perspective taking and theory of mind: Do children predict interpretive diversity as a function of differences in observers' knowledge? *Child Development, 62,* 1334–1351.

TAYLOR, M., CARTWRIGHT, B. S., & CARLSON, S. M. (1993). A developmental investigation of children's imaginary companions. *Developmental Psychology, 29,* 276–285.

TAYLOR, M., ESBENSEN, B. M., & BENNETT, R. T. (1994). Children's understanding of knowledge acquisition: The tendency for children to report that they have always known what they have just learned. *Child Development, 65,* 1581–1604.

TAYLOR, M. C., & HALL, J. A. (1982). Psychological androgyny: Theories, methods, and conclusions. *Psychological Bulletin, 92,* 347–366.

TAYLOR, R. D., & ROBERTS, D. (1995). Kinship support and maternal and adolescent well-being in economically disadvantaged African-American families. *Child Development, 66,* 1585–1597.

TEBBUTT, J., SWANSTON, H., OATES, R. K., & O'TOOLE, B. I. (1997). Five years after child sexual abuse: Persisting dysfunction and problems of prediction. *Journal of the American Academy of Child and Adolescent Psychiatry, 36,* 330–339.

TEDDER, J. L. (1991). Using the Brazelton Neonatal Assessment Scale to facilitate the parent-infant relationship in a primary care setting. *Nurse Practitioner, 16,* 27–36.

TEELE, D. W., KLEIN, J. O., CHASE, C., MENYUK, P., ROSNER, B. A., & THE GREATER BOSTON OTITIS MEDIA STUDY GROUP. (1990). Otitis media in infancy and intellectual ability, school achievement, speech, and language at age 7 years. *Journal of Infectious Diseases, 162,* 685–694.

TEMPLE, C. M., & CARNEY, R. A. (1995). Patterns of spatial functioning in Turner's syndrome. *Cortex, 31,* 109–118.

TENNES, K., EMDE, R., KISLEY, A., & METCALF, D. (1972). The stimulus barrier in early infancy: An exploration of some formulations of John Benjamin. In R. Holt and E. Peterfreund (Eds.), *Psychoanalysis and contemporary science* (Vol. 1, pp. 206–234). New York: Macmillan.

TERMAN, L., & ODEN, M. H. (1959). *Genetic studies of genius: Vol. 4. The gifted group at midlife.* Stanford, CA: Stanford University Press.

TERRACE, H. S., PETITTO, L. A., SANDERS, R. J., & BEVER, T. G. (1980). On the grammatical capacity of apes. In K. E. Nelson (Ed.), *Children's language* (Vol. 2, pp. 371–495). New York: Cambridge University Press.

TETI, D. M., GELFAND, D. M., MESSINGER, D. S., & ISABELLA, R. (1995). Maternal depression and the quality of early attachment: An examination of infants, preschoolers, and their mothers. *Developmental Psychology, 31,* 364–376.

TETI, D. M., & MCGOURTY, S. (1996). Using mothers versus trained observers in assessing children's secure base behavior: Theoretical and methodological considerations. *Child Development, 67,* 597–605.

TETI, D. M., SAKEN, J. W., KUCERA, E., & CORNS, K. M. (1996). And baby makes four: Predictors of attachment security among preschool-age firstborns during the transition to siblinghood. *Child Development, 67,* 579–596.

THAKWRAY, D. E., SMITH, M. C., BODFISH, J. W., & MEYERS, A. W. (1993). A comparison of behavioral and cognitive-behavioral interventions for bulimia nervosa. *Journal of Consulting and Clinical Psychology, 61,* 639–645.

THAPAR, A., GOTTESMAN, I. I., OWEN, M. J., O'DONOVAN, M. C., & MCGUFFIN, P. (1994). The genetics of mental retardation. *British Journal of Psychiatry, 164,* 747–758.

THARP, R. G. (1989). Psychocultural variables and constants: Effects on teaching and learning in schools. *American Psychologist, 44,* 349–359.

THARP, R. G. (1993). Institutional and social context of educational practice and reform. In E. A. Forman, N. Minick, & C. A. Stone (Eds.), *Contexts for learning* (pp. 269–282). New York: Oxford University Press.

THARP, R. G. (1994). Intergroup differences among Native Americans in socialization and child cognition: An ethnogenetic analysis. In P. M. Greenfield & R. Cocking (Eds.), *Cross-cultural roots of minority child development* (pp. 87–105). Hillsdale, NJ: Erlbaum.

THARP, R. G., & GALLIMORE, R. (1988). *Rousing minds to life: Teaching, learning, and schooling in social context.* New York: Cambridge University Press.

THATCHER, R. W. (1991). Maturation of human frontal lobes: Physiological evidence for staging. *Developmental Neuropsychology, 7,* 397–419.

THATCHER, R. W. (1994). Cyclic cortical reorganization: Origins of human cognitive development. G. Dawson & K. W. Fischer (Eds.), *Human behavior and the developing brain* (pp. 232–266). New York: Guilford.

THATCHER, R. W., LYON, G. R., RUMSEY, J., & KRASNEGOR, J. (1996). *Developmental neuroimaging.* San Diego, CA: Academic Press.

THELEN, E. (1983). Learning to walk is still an "old" problem: A reply to Zelazo. *Journal of Motor Behavior, 15,* 139–161.

THELEN, E. (1989). The (re)discovery of motor development: Learning new things from an old field. *Developmental Psychology, 25,* 946–949.

THELEN, E. (1994). Three-month-old infants can learn task-specific patterns of interlimb coordination. *Psychological Science, 5,* 280–285.

THELEN, E. (1995). Motor development: A new synthesis. *American Psychologist, 50,* 79–95.

THELEN, E., & ADOLPH, K. E. (1992). Arnold Gesell: The paradox of nature and nurture. *Developmental Psychology, 28,* 368–380.

THELEN, E., CORBETTA, D., & SPENCER, J. P. (1996). Development of reaching during the first year: Role of movement speed. *Journal of Experimental Psychology: Human Perception and Performance, 22,* 1059–1076.

THELEN, E., CORBETTA, D., KAMM, K., SPENCER, J. P., SCHNEIDER, K., & ZERNICKE, R. F. (1993). The transition to reaching: Mapping intention and intrinsic dynamics. *Child Development, 64,* 1058–1098.

THELEN, E., FISHER, D. M., & RIDLEY-JOHNSON, R. (1984). The relationship between physical growth and a newborn reflex. *Infant Behavior and Development, 7,* 479–493.

THELEN, E., & SMITH, L. B. (1994). *A dynamic systems approach to the development of cognition and action.* Cambridge, MA: MIT Press.

THELEN, E., & SMITH, L. B. (1998). Dynamic systems theories. In R. M. Lerner (Ed.), *Handbook of child psychology: Vol. 1. Theoretical models of human development* (5th ed., pp. 563–634). New York: Wiley.

THOMAN, E. B., & DAVIS, D. H., & DENENBERG, V. H. (1987). The sleeping and waking states of infants: Correlations acorss the time and person. *Physiology & Behavior, 41,* 531–537.

THOMAN, E. B., & INGERSOLL, E. W. (1993). Learning in premature infants. *Developmental Psychology, 29,* 692–700.

THOMAN, E. B., & WHITNEY, M. P. (1990). Behavioral states in infants: Individual differences and individual analyses. In J. Colombo & J. W. Fagen (Eds.), *Individual differences in infancy: Reliability, stability, and prediction* (pp. 113–135). Hillsdale, NJ: Erlbaum.

THOMAS, A., & CHESS, S. (1977). *Temperament and development.* New York: Brunner/Mazel.

THOMAS, A., CHESS, S., & BIRCH, H. G. (1968). *Temperament and behavior disorders in children.* New York: New York University Press.

THOMAS, N. G., & BERK, L. E. (1981). Effects of school environments on the development of young children's creativity. *Child Development, 52,* 1152–1162.

THOMPSON, J. G., & MYERS, N. A. (1985). Inferences and recall at ages four and seven. *Child Development, 56,* 1134–1144.

THOMPSON, L. A., DETTERMAN, D. K., & PLOMIN, R. (1991). Associations between cognitive abilities and scholastic achievement: Genetic overlap but environmental differences. *Psychological Science, 2,* 158–165.

THOMPSON, R. A. (1990a). On emotion and self-regulation. In R. A. Thompson (Ed.), *Nebraska Symposium on Motivation* (Vol. 36, pp. 383–483). Lincoln: University of Nebraska Press.

THOMPSON, R. A. (1990b). Vulnerability in research: A developmental perspective on research risk. *Child Development, 61,* 1–16.

THOMPSON, R. A. (1992). Developmental changes in research risk and benefit: A changing calculus of concerns. In B. Stanley & J. E. Sieber (Eds.), *Social research on children and adolescents: Ethical issues* (pp. 31–64). Newbury Park, CA: Sage.

THOMPSON, R. A. (1994). Emotion regulation: A theme in search of definition. In N. A. Fox (Ed.), *The development of emotion regulation: Biological and behavioral considerations. Monographs of the Society for Research in Child Development, 59* (2–3, Serial No. 240).

THOMPSON, R. A. (1997). Sensitivity and security: New questions to ponder. *Child Development, 68,* 595–597.

THOMPSON, R. A. (1998). Early sociopersonality development. In N. Eisenberg (Ed.), *Handbook of child psychology: Vol. 3. Social, emotional, and personality development* (5th ed., pp. 25–104). New York: Wiley.

THOMPSON, R. A., LAMB, M., & ESTES, D. (1982). Stability of infant–mother attachment and its relationship to changing life circumstances in an unselected middle-class sample. *Child Development, 53,* 144–148.

THOMPSON, R. A., & LEGER, D. W. (1999). From squalls to calls: The cry as a developing socioemotional signal. In B. Lester, J. Newman, & F. Pedersen, (Eds.), *Biological and social aspects of infant crying.* New York: Plenum.

THOMPSON, R. A., & LIMBER, S. (1991). "Social anxiety" in infancy: Stranger wariness and separation distress. In H. Leitenberg (Ed.), *Handbook of social and evaluation anxiety* (pp. 85–137). New York: Plenum.

THOMPSON, R. J., GUSTAFSON, K. E., OEHLER, J. M., CATLETT, A. T., BRAZY, J. E., & GOLDSTEIN, R. F. (1997). Developmental outcome of very low birth weight infants at four years of age as a function of biological risk and psychosocial risk. *Developmental and Behavioral Pediatrics, 18,* 91–96.

THORNDIKE, R. L., HAGEN, E. P., & SATTLER, J. M. (1986). *The Stanford-Binet Intelligence Scale: Fourth edition. Guide for administering and scoring.* Chicago: Riverside Publishing.

THORNE, B. (1993). *Gender play: Girls and boys in school.* New Brunswick, NJ: Rutgers University Press.

THORNTON, M., & TAYLOR, R. (1988). Black American perceptions of black Africans. *Ethnic and Racial Studies, 11,* 139–150.

THURSTONE, L. L. (1938). *Primary mental abilities.* Chicago: University of Chicago Press.

TIETJEN, A., & WALKER, L. (1985). Moral reasoning and leadership among men in a Papua, New Guinea village. *Developmental Psychology, 21,* 982–992.

TISAK, M. S. (1995). Domains of social reasoning and beyond. In R. Vasta (Ed.), *Annals of child development* (Vol. 11, pp. 95–130). London: Jessica Kingsley.

TIZARD, B., & HODGES, J. (1978). The effect of early institutional rearing on the development of eight-year-old children. *Journal of Child Psychology and Psychiatry, 19,* 99–118.

TIZARD, B., & REES, J. (1975). The effect of early institutional rearing on the behaviour problems and affectional relationships of four-year-old children. *Journal of Child Psychology and Psychiatry, 16,* 61–73.

TOLAROVA, M. (1986). Cleft lip and palate and isolated cleft palate in Czechoslovakia. *Advances in Bioscience, 61,* 251–268.

TOLSON, T. F. J., & WILSON, M. N. (1990). The impact of two- and three-generational black family structure on perceived family climate. *Child Development, 61,* 416–428.

TOMADA, G., & SCHNEIDER, B. H. (1997). Relational aggression, gender, and peer acceptance: Invariance across culture, stability over time, and concordance among informants. *Developmental Psychology, 33,* 601–609.

TOMASELLO, M. (1992). The social bases of language acquisition. *Social Development, 1,* 68–87.

TOMASELLO, M. (1995). Language is not an instinct. *Cognitive Development, 10,* 131–156.

TOMASELLO, M. (1999). Understanding intentions and learning words in the second year of life. In M. Bowerman & S. Levinson (Eds.), *Language acquisition and conceptual development.* Cambridge: Cambridge University Press.

TOMASELLO, M., & AKHTAR, N. (1995). Two-year-olds use prag-

matic cues to differentiate reference to objects and actions. *Cognitive Development, 10,* 201–224.

TOMASELLO, M., AKHTAR, N., DODSON, K., & REKAU, L. (1997). Differential productivity in young children's use of nouns and verbs. *Journal of Child Language, 24,* 373–387.

TOMASELLO, M., & BARTON, M. (1994). Learning words in nonostensive contexts. *Developmental Psychology, 30,* 639–650.

TOMASELLO, M., & BROOKS, P. (1999). Early syntactic development. In M. Barrett (Ed.), *The development of language.* London: UCL Press.

TOMASELLO, M., CALL, J., & GLUCKMAN, A. (1997). Comprehension of novel communicative signs by apes and human children. *Child Development, 68,* 1067–1080.

TOMASELLO, M., & CAMAIONI, L. (1997). A comparison of the gestural communication of apes and human infants. *Human Development, 40,* 7–24.

TOMASELLO, M., MANNLE, S., & KRUGER, A. C. (1986). Linguistic environment of 1- to 2-year-old twins. *Developmental Psychology, 22,* 169–176.

TONER, I. J., & SMITH, R. A. (1977). Age and overt verbalization in delay maintenance behavior in children. *Journal of Experimental Child Psychology, 24,* 123–128.

TONER, M. A., & MUNRO, D. (1996). Peer-social attributions and self-efficacy of peer-rejected preadolescents. *Merrill-Palmer Quarterly, 42,* 339–357.

TONG, S., CADDY, D., & SHORT, R. V. (1997). Use of dizygotic to monozygotic twinning ratio as a measure of fertility. *Lancet, 349,* 843–845.

TORRANCE, E. P. (1980). *The Torrance Tests of Creative Thinking.* New York: Scholastic Testing Service.

TORRANCE, E. P. (1988). The nature of creativity as manifest in its testing. In R. J. Sternberg (Ed.), *The nature of creativity: Contemporary psychological perspectives* (pp. 43–75). New York: Cambridge University Press.

TOTH, S. L., & CICCHETTI, D. (1996). Patterns of relatedness, depressive symptomatology, and perceived competence in maltreated children. *Journal of Consulting and Clinical Psychology, 64,* 32–41.

TOUWEN, B. C. L. (1978). Variability and stereotype in normal and deviant development. In J. Apley (Ed.), *Care of the handicapped child* (pp. 99–110). Philadelphia: Lippincott.

TOUWEN, B. C. L. (1984). Primitive reflexes—Conceptual or semantic problem? In H. F. R. Prechtl (Ed.), *Continuity of neural functions from prenatal to postnatal life* (Clinics in Developmental Medicine, No. 94, pp. 115–125). Philadelphia: Lippincott.

TOWER, R. B., SINGER, D. G., SINGER, J. L., & BIGGS, A. (1979). Differential effects of television programming on preschoolers' cognition, imagination, and social play. *American Journal of Orthopsychiatry, 49,* 265–281.

TRAUSE, M. A. (1977). Stranger responses: Effects of familiarity, stranger's approach, and sex of infant. *Child Development, 48,* 1657–1661.

TREMBLAY, R. E., SCHAAL, B., BOULERICE, B., ARSENEAULT, L., SOUSSIGNAN, R., & PERUSSE, D. (1997). Male physical aggression, social dominance, and testosterone levels at puberty: A developmental perspective. In A. Raine & P. A. Brennan (Eds.), *Biosocial bases of violence. NATO ASI Series: Series A: Life sciences* (Vol. 292, pp. 271–291). New York: Plenum.

TRENT, K., & HARLAN, S. L. (1994). Teenage mothers in nuclear and extended households. *Journal of Family Issues, 15,* 309–337.

TREVETHAN, S. D., & WALKER, L. J. (1989). Hypothetical versus real-life moral reasoning among psychopathic and delinquent youth. *Development and Psychopathology, 1,* 91–103.

TRIANDIS, H. C. (1995). *Individualism and collectivism.* Boulder, CO: Westview Press.

TRIANDIS, H. C. (1998, May). *Cross-cultural versus cultural psychology: A synthesis?* Colloquium presented at Illinois Wesleyan University, Bloomington, IL.

TRICKETT, P. K., ABER, J. L., CARLSON, V., & CICCHETTI, D. (1991). Relationship of socioeconomic status to the etiology and developmental sequelae of physical child abuse. *Developmental Psychology, 27,* 148–158.

TRIVERS, R. L. (1971). The evolution of reciprocal altruism. *Quarterly Review of Biology, 46,* 35–57.

TRONICK, E. Z. (1989). Emotions and emotional communication in infants. *American Psychologist, 44,* 115–123.

TRONICK, E. Z., & COHN, J. F. (1989). Infant–mother face-to-face interaction: Age and gender differences in coordination and the occurrence of miscoordination. *Child Development, 60,* 85–92.

TRONICK, E., MORELLI, G., & IVEY, P. (1992). The Efe forager infant and toddler's pattern of social relationships: Multiple and simultaneous. *Developmental Psychology, 28,* 568–577.

TRONICK, E. Z., THOMAS, R. B., & DALTABUIT, M. (1994). The Quechua manta pouch: A caretaking practice for buffering the Peruvian infant against the multiple stressors of high altitude. *Child Development, 65,* 1005–1013.

TRÖSTER, H., & BRAMBRING, M. (1992). Early social-emotional development in blind infants. *Child: Care, Health and Development, 18,* 207–227.

TRÖSTER, H., & BRAMBRING, M. (1993). Early motor development in blind infants. *Journal of Applied Developmental Psychology, 14,* 83–106.

TUDGE, J. R. H. (1992). Processes and consequences of peer collaboration: A Vygotskian analysis. *Child Development, 63,* 1364–1379.

TUDGE, J. R. H., & WINTERHOFF, P. A. (1993). Vygotsky, Piaget, and Bandura: Perspectives on the relations between the social world and cognitive development. *Human Development, 36,* 61–81.

TULVISTE, P. (1991). *Cultural-historical development of verbal thinking: A psychological study.* Commack, NY: Nova Science Publishers.

TUNMER, W. E., & NESDALE, A. R. (1982). The effects of digraphs and pseudo-words on phonemic segmentation in young children. *Journal of Applied Psycholinguistics, 3,* 299–311.

TURIEL, E. (1998). The development of morality. In N. Eisenberg (Ed.), *Handbook of child psychology: Vol. 3. Social, emotional, and personality development* (Vol. 3, pp. 863–932). New York: Wiley.

TURIEL, E., SMETANA, J. G., & KILLEN, M. (1991). Social contexts in social cognitive development. In W. M. Kurtines & J. L. Gewirtz (Eds.), *Handbook of moral behavior and development* (Vol. 2, pp. 307–332). Hillsdale, NJ: Erlbaum.

TURK, J. (1995). Fragile X syndrome. *Archives of Diseases of Children, 72,* 3–5.

TURKHEIMER, E., & GOTTESMAN, I. I. (1991). Individual differences and the canalization of human behavior. *Developmental Psychology, 27,* 18–22.

TURNER, P. J., & GERVAI, J. (1995). A multidimensional study of gender typing in preschool children and their parents: Personality, attitudes, preferences, behavior, and cultural differences. *Devel-*

opmental Psychology, 31, 759–772.

TURNER, P. J., GERVAI, J. & HINDE, R. A. (1993). Gender typing in young children: Preferences, behaviour and cultural differences. *British Journal of Developmental Psychology, 11,* 323–342.

TUSS, P., ZIMMER, J., & HO, H-Z. (1995). Causal attributions of underachieving fourth-grade students in China, Japan, and the United States. *Journal of Cross-Cultural Psychology, 26,* 408–425.

TYC, V. L., FAIRCLOUGH, D., FLETCHER, B., & LEIGH, L. (1995). Children's distress during magnetic resonance imaging procedures. *Children's Health Care, 24,* 5–19.

TZURIEL, D., & FEUERSTEIN, R. (1992). Dynamic group testing for prescriptive teaching: Differential effects of treatment. In H. C. Haywood & D. Tzuriel (Eds.), *Interactive testing* (pp. 187–206). New York: Springer-Verlag.

U

U.S. BUREAU OF THE CENSUS. (1997). *Who's minding our preschoolers?* (Current Population Reports, P70-62). Washington, DC: U.S. Government Printing Office.

U.S. BUREAU OF THE CENSUS. (1998). *Statistical abstract of the United States* (118th ed.). Washington, DC: U.S. Government Printing Office.

U.S. CENTERS FOR DISEASE CONTROL. (1998). *Sexually transmitted disease surveillance,* 1997. Atlanta: Author.

U.S. DEPARTMENT OF EDUCATION. (1998). *Pursuing excellence: A study of U.S. twelfth-grade mathematics and science achievement in international context.* Washington, DC: U.S. Government Printing Office.

U.S. DEPARTMENT OF HEALTH AND HUMAN SERVICES. (1997). Update: Prevalence of overweight among children, adolescents, and adults—United States, 1988–94. *Morbidity and Mortality Weekly Report, 46,* 199–202.

U.S. DEPARTMENT OF HEALTH AND HUMAN SERVICES. (1998a). *National survey results on drug use from The Monitoring the Future Study, 1975–1997: Vol. 1. Secondary school students.* Washington, DC: U.S. Government Printing Office.

U.S. DEPARTMENT OF HEALTH AND HUMAN SERVICES. (1998b). *Vital statistics of the United States,* 1995. Washington, DC: U.S. Government Printing Office.

U.S. DEPARTMENT OF HEALTH AND HUMAN SERVICES. (1998c, August 14). Youth risk behavior surveillance—United States, 1997. *Morbidity and Mortality Weekly Report, 47* (No. SS-3).

U.S. DEPARTMENT OF HEALTH AND HUMAN SERVICES. (1999). *Health United States 1997–1998 and injury chartbook.* Washington, DC: U.S. Bureau of the Census.

U.S. DEPARTMENT OF JUSTICE. (1998). *Crime in the United States.* Washington, DC: U.S. Government Printing Office.

U.S. DEPARTMENT OF LABOR, BUREAU OF LABOR STATISTICS. (1999, February). Consumer price index. *Monthly Labor Review, 121*(2).

UDRY, J. R. (1990). Hormonal and social determinants of adolescent sexual initiation. In J. Bancroft & J. M. Reinisch (Eds.), *Adolescence and puberty* (pp. 70–87). New York: Oxford University Press.

UHARI, M., KONTIOKARI, T., & NIEMELÄ, M. (1998). A novel use of xylitol sugar in preventing acute otitis media. *Pediatrics, 102,* 879–884.

ULLIAN, D. Z. (1976). The development of conceptions of masculinity and femininity. In B. Lloyd & J. Archer (Eds.), *Exploring sex differences* (pp. 25–47). London: Academic Press.

UNDERWOOD, M. K., COIE, J. D., & HERBSMAN, C. R. (1992). Display rules for anger and aggression in school-age children. *Child Development, 63,* 366–380.

UNGER, R. K., & CRAWFORD, M. (1993). Sex and gender—The troubled relationship between terms and concepts. *Psychological Science, 4,* 122–124.

UNGER, R., KREEGER, L., & CHRISTOFFEL, K. K. (1990). Childhood obesity: Medical and familial correlates and age of onset. *Clinical Pediatrics, 29,* 368–372.

UPDEGRAFF, K. A., MCHALE, S. M., & CROUTER, A. C. (1996). Gender roles in marriage: What do they mean for girls' and boys' school achievement? *Journal of Youth and Adolescence, 25,* 73–88.

URBERG, K. A. (1979, March). *The development of androgynous sex-role concepts in young children.* Paper presented at the biennial meeting of the Society for Research in Child Development, San Francisco.

URBERG, K. A., DEGIRMENCIOGLUE, S. M., TOLSON, J. M., & HALLIDAY-SCHER, K. (1995). The structure of adolescent peer networks. *Developmental Psychology, 31,* 540–547.

URIBE, F. M. T., LEVINE, R. A., & LEVINE, S. E. (1994). Maternal behavior in a Mexican community: The changing environments of children. In P. M. Greenfield & R. R. Cocking (Eds.), *Cross-cultural roots of minority child development* (pp. 41–54). Hillsdale, NJ: Erlbaum.

USMIANI, S., & DANILUK, J. (1997). Mothers and their adolescent daughters: Relationship between self-esteem, gender role identity, and body image. *Journal of Youth and Adolescence, 26,* 45–60.

UTTAL, D. H., MARZOLF, D. P., PIERROUTSAKOS, S. L., SMITH, C. M., TROSETH, G. L., SCUDDER, K. V., & DELOACHE, J. S. (1998). Seeing through symbols: The development of children's understanding of symbol relations. In O. N. Saracho & B. Spodek (Eds.), *Multiple perspectives on play in early childhood education* (pp. 59–79). Albany: State University of New York Press.

UTTAL, D. H., & WELLMAN, H. M. (1989). Young children's representation of spatial information acquired from maps. *Developmental Psychology, 25,* 128–138.

UŽGIRIS, I. C., & HUNT, J. McV. (1975). *Assessment in infancy: Ordinal scales of psychological development.* Urbana: University of Illinois Press.

V

VAIDYANATHAN, R. (1988). Development of forms and functions of interrogatives in children: A language study of Tamil. *Journal of Child Language, 15,* 533–549.

VAIDYANATHAN, R. (1991). Development of forms and functions of negation in the early stages of language acquisition: A study of Tamil. *Journal of Child Language, 18,* 51–66.

VALDÉS, G. (1998). The world outside and inside schools: Language and immigrant children. *Educational Researher, 27*(6), 4–18.

VALDEZ, R., ATHENS, M. A., THOMPSON, G. H., BRADSHAW, G. H., & STERN, M. P. (1994). Birthweight and adult health outcomes in a biethnic population in the U.S.A. *Diabetologia, 37,* 624.

VALIAN, V. V. (1986). Syntactic categories in the speech of young children. *Developmental Psychology, 22,* 562–579.

VALIAN, V. V. (1991). Syntactic subjects in the early speech of American and Italian children. *Cognition, 40,* 21–81.

VALIAN, V. V. (1996). *Parental replies: Linguistic status and didactic role.* Cambridge, MA: MIT Press.

VAN BALEN, F. (1996). Child rearing following in vitro fertilization. *Journal of Child Psychology and Psychiatry, 37,* 687–693.

VAN DEN BOOM, D. C. (1995). Do first-year intervention effects endure? Follow-up during toddlerhood of a sample of Dutch irritable infants. *Child Development, 66,* 1798–1816.

VAN DEN BOOM, D. C., & HOEKSMA, J. B. (1994). The effect of infant irritability on mother–infant interaction: A growth-curve analysis. *Developmental Psychology, 30,* 581–590.

VAN DER VOORT, T. H., & VALKENBURG, P. M. (1994). Television's impact on fantasy play: A review of research. *Developmental Review, 14,* 227–251.

VAN DYKE, D. C., LANG, D. J., HEIDE, F., VAN DUYNE, S., & SOUCEK, M. J. (Eds.). (1990). *Clinical perspectives in the management of Down syndrome.* New York: Springer-Verlag.

VAN GEERT, P. (1997). Que será será: Determinism and nonlinear dynamic model building in development. In A. Fogel, M. C. D. P. Lyra, & J. Valsiner (Eds.), *Dynamics and indeterminism in developmental and social processes* (pp. 13–38). Mahwah, NJ: Erlbaum.

VAN IJZENDOORN, M. H. (1995a). Adult attachment representations, parental responsiveness, and infant attachment: A meta-analysis on the predictive validity of the Adult Attachment Interview. *Psychological Bulletin, 117,* 387–403.

VAN IJZENDOORN, M. H. (1995b). Of the way we are: On temperament, attachment, and the transmission gap: A rejoinder to Fox (1995). *Psychological Bulletin, 117,* 411–415.

VAN IJZENDOORN, M. H., & BAKERMANS-KRANENBURG, M. J. (1996). Adult Attachment Interview classifications in mothers, fathers, adolescents, and clinical groups: A meta-analytic search for normative data. *Journal of Consulting and Clinical Psychology, 64.*

VAN IJZENDOORN, M. H., & DE WOLFF, M. S. (1997). In search of the absent father—Meta-analyses of infant-father attachment: A rejoinder to our discussants. *Child Development, 68,* 604–609.

VAN IJZENDOORN, M. H., GOLDBERG, S., KROONENBERG, P. M., & FRENKEL, O. J. (1992). The relative effects of maternal and child problems on the quality of attachment: A meta-analysis of attachment in clinical samples.

Child Development, 63, 840–858.

VAN IJZENDOORN, M. H., & KROONENBERG, P. M. (1988). Cross-cultural patterns of attachment: A meta-analysis of the Strange Situation. *Child Development, 59,* 147–156.

VANDELL, D. L. (1996). *Social behavior and interaction in 6- to 12-month-olds.* Unpublished manuscript, University of Texas at Dallas.

VANDELL, D. L., & CORASANITI, M. A. (1988). The relation between third-graders' after school care and social, academic, and emotional functioning. *Child Development, 59,* 868–875.

VANDELL, D. L., & HEMBREE, S. E. (1994). Peer social status and friendship: Independent contributors to children's social and academic adjustment. *Merrill-Palmer Quarterly, 40,* 461–477.

VANDELL, D. L., & MUELLER, E. C. (1995). Peer play and friendships during the first two years. In H. C. Foot, A. J. Chapman, & J. R. Smith (Eds.), *Friendship and social relations in children* (pp. 181–208). New Brunswick, NJ: Transaction.

VANDELL, D. L., & WILSON, K. S. (1987). Infants' interactions with mother, sibling, and peer: Contrasts and relations between interaction systems. Child Development, 58, 176–186.

VANDELL, D. L., WILSON, K. S., & BUCHANAN, N. R. (1980). Peer interaction in the first year of life: An examination of its structure, content, and sensitivity to toys. *Child Development, 51,* 481–488.

VANFOSSEN, B., JONES, J., & SPADE, J. (1987). Curriculum tracking and status maintenance. *Sociology of Education, 60,* 104–122.

VARTANIAN, L. R. (1997). Separation–individuation, social support, and adolescent egocentrism: An exploratory study. *Journal of Early Adolescence, 17,* 245–270.

VARTANIAN, L. R., & POWLISHTA, K. K. (1996). A longitudinal examination of the social-cognitive foundations of adolescent egocentrism. *Journal of Early Adolescence, 16,* 157–178.

VASUDEV, J., & HUMMEL, R. C. (1987). Moral stage sequence and principled reasoning in an Indian sample. *Human Development, 30,* 105–118.

VAUGHN, B. E., BRADLEY, C. F., JOFFE, L. S., SEIFER, R., & BARGLOW, P. (1987). Maternal characteristics measured prenatally are predictive of ratings of temperamental "difficulty" on the Carey Infant Temperament Questionnaire. *Developmental Psychology, 23,* 152–161.

VAUGHN, B. E., EGELAND, B., SROUFE, L. A., & WATERS, E. (1979). Individual differences in infant-mother attachment at twelve and eighteen months: Stability and change in families under stress. *Child Development, 50,* 971–975.

VAUGHN, B. E., KOPP, C. B., & KRAKOW, J. B. (1984). The emergence and consolidation of self-control from eighteen to thirty months of age: Normative trends and individual differences. *Child Development, 55,* 990–1004.

VAUGHN, B. E., STEVENSON-HINDE, J., WATERS, E., KOTSAFTIS, A., LEFEVER, G. B., SHOULDICE, A., TRUDEL, M., & BELSKY, J. (1992). Attachment security and temperament in infancy and early childhood: Some conceptual clarifications. *Developmental Psychology, 28,* 463–473.

VAUGHN, S., ELBAUM, B. E., & SCHUMM, J. S. (1996). The effects of inclusion on the social functioning of students with learning disabilities. *Journal of Learning Disabilities, 29,* 598–608.

VENTURA, S. J. (1989). Trends and variations in first births to older women in the United States, 1970–86. *Vital and Health Statistics* (Series 21). Hyattsville, MD: U.S. Department of Health and Human Services.

VENTURA, S. J., MARTIN, J. A., CURTIN, S. C., & MATHEWS, T. J. (1997). *Report of final natality statistics, 1995. Monthly Vital Statistics Report, 45*(11, Suppl. 2). Hyattsville, MD: National Center for Health Statistics.

VERGNAUD, G. (1996). Education, the best portion of Piaget's heritage. *Swiss Journal of Psychology, 55,* 112–118.

VERHULST, F. C., ALTHAUS, M., & VERSLUIS-DEN BIEMAN, H. J. M. (1990). Problem behavior in international adoptees: I. An epidemiological study. *Journal of the American Academy of Child and Adolescent Psychiatry, 29,* 94–103.

VERHULST, F. C., & VERSLUIS-DEN BIEMAN, H. J. M. (1995). Developmental course of problem behaviors in adolescent adoptees. *Journal of the American Academy of Child and Adolescent Psychiatry, 34,* 151–159.

VERNON, P. A. (1981). Level I and Level II: A review. *Educational Psychologist, 16,* 45–64.

VERNON, P. A. (1987). Level I and Level II revisited. In S. Modgil & C. Modgil (Eds.), *Arthur Jensen: Consensus and contro-* versy (pp. 17–24). New York: Falmer Press.

VERNON, P. A. (1993). Intelligence and neural efficiency. In D. K. Detterman (Ed.), *Current topics in human intelligence* (Vol. 3, pp. 171–187). Norwood, NJ: Ablex.

VERNON, P. A., & MORI, M. (1992). Intelligence, reaction times, and peripheral nerve conduction velocity. *Intelligence, 8,* 273–288.

VERNON-FEAGANS, L., MANLOVE, E. E., & VOLLING, B. L. (1996). Otitis media and the social behavior of day-care-attending children. *Child Development, 67,* 1528–1539.

VIBBERT, S., & BORNSTEIN, M. H. (1989). Specific associations between domains of mother–child interaction and toddler referential language and pretend play. *Infant Behavior and Development, 12,* 163–184.

VIHMAN, M. M. (1996). *Phonological development.* London: Blackwell.

VINDEN, P. G. (1996). Junín Quechua children's understanding of mind. *Child Development, 67,* 1707–1716.

VISHER, J. S. (1994). Stepfamilies: A work in progress. *American Journal of Family Therapy, 22,* 337–344.

VITALARI, N. P., VENKATESH, A., & GRONHAUG, K. (1985). Computing in the home: Shifts in the time allocation patterns of households. *Communications of the ACM, 28,* 512–522.

VOGEL, D. A., LAKE, M. A., EVANS, S., & KARRAKER, H. (1991). Children's and adults' sex-stereotyped perceptions of infants. *Sex Roles, 24,* 605–616.

VOGEL, G. (1997). Cocaine wreaks subtle damage on developing brains. (1996). Education, the best portion of Piaget's heritage. *Swiss Journal of Psychology, 55,* 112–118.

VOHR, B. R., & GARCÍA-COLL, C. T. (1988). Follow-up studies of high-risk low-birth-weight infants: Changing trends. In H. E. Fitzgerald, B. M. Lester, & M. W. Yogman (Eds.), *Theory and research in behavioral pediatrics* (pp. 1–65). New York: Plenum.

VOLLING, B. L., & ELINS, J. L. (1998). Family relationships and children's emotional adjustment as correlates of maternal and paternal differential treatment: A replication with toddler and preschool siblings. *Child Development, 69,* 1640–1656.

VOLTERRA, V., CAPIRCI, O., PEZZINI, G., SABBADINI, L., & VICARI, S. (1996). Linguistic abilities in Italian children with Williams syndrome. *Cortex, 32,* 663–677.

VORHEES, C. V. (1986). Principles of behavioral teratology. In E. P. Riley & C. V. Vorhees (Eds.), *Handbook of behavioral teratology* (pp. 23–48). New York: Plenum.

VORHEES, C. V., & MOLLNOW, E. (1987). Behavioral teratogenesis: Long-term influences on behavior from early exposure to environmental agents. In J. D. Osofsky (Ed.), *Handbook of infant development* (2nd ed., pp. 913–971). New York: Wiley.

VOYER, D., VOYER, S., & BRYDEN, M. P. (1995). Magnitude of sex differences in spatial abilities: A meta-analysis and consideration of critical variables. *Psychological Bulletin, 117,* 250–270.

VUCHINICH, S., HETHERINGTON, E. M., VUCHINICH, R. A., & CLINGEMPEEL, W. G. (1991). Parent–child interaction and gender differences in early adolescents' adaptation to stepfamilies. *Developmental Psychology, 27,* 618–626.

VURPILLOT, E. (1968). The development of scanning strategies and their relation to visual differentiation. *Journal of Experimental Child Psychology, 6,* 632–650.

VYGOTSKY, L. S. (1978). *Mind in society: The development of higher mental processes.* Cambridge, MA: Harvard University Press. (Original works published 1930, 1933, and 1935)

VYGOTSKY, L. S. (1986). *Thought and language* (A. Kozulin, Trans.). Cambridge, MA: MIT Press. (Original work published 1934)

VYGOTSKY, L. S. (1987). Thinking and speech. In R. W. Rieber, A. S. Carton (Eds.), & N. Minick (Trans.), *The collected works of L. S. Vygotsky: Vol. 1. Problems of general psychology* (pp. 37–285). New York: Plenum. (Original work published 1934)

VYGOTSKY, L. S. (1993). The fundamentals of defectology. In R. W. Rieber & A. S. Carton (Eds.), *The collected works of L. S. Vygotsky* (Vol. 2). New York: Plenum. (Original work published 1925)

W

WACHS, T. D. (1975). Relation of infants' performance on Piaget scales between twelve and twenty-four months and their Stanford-Binet performance at thirty-one months. *Child Development, 46,* 929–935.

WACHS, T. D. (1993). Environment and the development of disadvantaged children. In R. J. Karp (Ed.), *Malnourished children in* the United States caught in the cycle of poverty (pp. 13–30). New York: Springer.

WACHS, T. D. (1995). Relation of mild-to-moderate malnutrition to human development: Correlational studies. *Journal of Nutrition, 125,* 2245S–2254S.

WADDINGTON, C. H. (1957). *The strategy of the genes.* London: Allen and Unwin.

WAGNER, B. M., & PHILLIPS, D. A. (1992). Beyond beliefs: Parent and child behaviors and children's perceived academic competence. *Child Development, 63,* 1380–1391.

WAGNER, M. E., SCHUBERT, H. J. P., & SCHUBERT, D. S. P. (1985). Family size effects: A review. *Journal of Genetic Psychology, 146,* 65–78.

WAGNER, M. E., SCHUBERT, H. J. P., & SCHUBERT, D. S. P. (1993). Sex-of-sibling effects: Part 1. Gender role, intelligence, achievement, and creativity. In Hayne W. Reese (Ed.), *Advances in child development and behavior* (Vol. 24, pp. 181–214). San Diego: Academic Press.

WAGNER, R. K. (1994). Context counts: The case of cognitive ability testing for job selection. In R. J. Sternberg & R. K. Wagner (Eds.), *The mind in context* (pp. 133–151). New York: Cambridge University Press.

WAGNER, R. K. (1997). Intelligence, training, and employment. *American Psychologist, 52,* 1059–1069.

WAHLSTEN, D. (1994). The intelligence of heritability. *Canadian Psychology, 35,* 244–259.

WAINRYB, C. (1997). The mismeasure of diversity: Reflections on the study of cross-cultural differences. In H. D. Saltzstein (Ed.), *New directions for child development* (No. 76, pp. 51–65). San Francisco: Jossey-Bass.

WALBERG, H. J. (1986). Synthesis of research on teaching. In M. C. Wittrock (Ed.), *Handbook of research on teaching* (3rd ed., pp. 214–229). New York: Macmillan.

WALDMAN, I. D. (1997). Unresolved questions and future directions in behavior-genetic studies of intelligence. In R. J. Sternberg & E. L. Grigorenko (Eds.), *Intelligence, heredity, and environment* (pp. 552–570). New York: Cambridge University Press.

WALDMAN, I. D., WEINBERG, R. A., & SCARR, S. (1994). Racial-group differences in IQ in the Minnesota Transracial Adoption Study: A reply to Levin and Lynn. *Intelligence, 19,* 29–44.

WALES, R. (1990). Children's pictures. In R. Grieve & M. Hughes (Eds.), *Understanding children* (pp. 140–155). Oxford, England: Blackwell.

WALKER, D., GREENWOOD, C., HART, B., & CARTA, J. (1994). Prediction of school outcomes based on early language production and socioeconomic factors. *Child Development, 65,* 606–621.

WALKER, L. J. (1980). Cognitive and perspective-taking prerequisites for moral development. *Child Development, 51,* 131–139.

WALKER, L. J. (1989). A longitudinal study of moral reasoning. *Child Development, 60,* 157–166.

WALKER, L. J. (1995). Sexism in Kohlberg's moral psychology? In W. M. Kurtines & J. L. Gewirtz (Eds.), *Moral development: An introduction* (pp. 83–107). Boston: Allyn and Bacon.

WALKER, L. J., & HENNIG, K. H. (1997). Moral development in the broader context of personality. In S. Hala (Ed.), *The development of social cognition* (pp. 297–327). Hove, UK: Psychology Press.

WALKER, L. J., & MORAN, T. J. (1991). Moral reasoning in a communist Chinese society. *Journal of Moral Education, 20,* 139–155.

WALKER, L. J., PITTS, R. C., HENNIG, K. H., & MATSUBA, M. K. (1995). Reasoning about morality and real-life moral problems. In M. Killen & D. Hart (Eds.), *Morality in everyday life* (pp. 37–407). New York: Cambridge University Press.

WALKER, L. J., & RICHARDS, B. S. (1979). Stimulating transitions in moral reasoning as a function of stage of cognitive development. *Developmental Psychology, 15,* 95–103.

WALKER, L. J., & TAYLOR, J. H. (1991a). Family interactions and the development of moral reasoning. *Child Development, 62,* 264–283.

WALKER, L. J., & TAYLOR, J. H. (1991b). Stage transitions in moral reasoning: A longitudinal study of developmental processes. *Developmental Psychology, 27,* 330–337.

WALKER-ANDREWS, A. S. (1997). Infants' perception of expressive behaviors: Differentiation of multimodal information. *Psychological Bulletin, 121,* 437–456.

WALKER-ANDREWS, A. S., & GROLNICK, W. (1983). Discrimination of vocal expressions by young infants. *Infant Behavior and Development, 6,* 491–498.

WALLERSTEIN, J. S., CORBIN, S. B., & LEWIS, J. M. (1988). Children of divorce: A ten-year study. In E. M. Hetherington & J. Arasteh (Eds.), *Impact of divorce, single parenting, and stepparenting on children* (pp. 198–214). Hillsdale, NJ: Erlbaum.

WALLERSTEIN, J. S., & KELLY, J. B. (1980). *Surviving the break-up: How children and parents cope with divorce.* New York: Basic Books.

WALTON, G. E., & BOWER, T. G. R. (1993). Amodal representations of speech in infants. *Infant Behavior and Development, 16,* 233–243.

WANSKA, S. K., & BEDROSIAN, J. L. (1985). Conversational structure and topic performance in mother–child interaction. *Journal of Speech and Hearing Research, 28,* 579–584.

WAPNER, R. J. (1997). Chorionic villus sampling. *Obstetrics and Gynecology Clinics of North America, 24,* 83–110.

WARD, L. M. (1995). Talking about sex: Common themes about sexuality in the prime-time television programs children and adolescents view most. *Journal of Youth and Adolescence, 24,* 595–616.

WARD, S., WACKMAN, D., & WARTELLA, E. (1977). *How children learn to buy: The development of consumer information-processing skills.* Beverly Hills, CA: Sage.

WARK, G. R., & KREBS, D. L. (1996). Gender and dilemma differences in real-life moral judgment. *Developmental Psychology, 32,* 220–230.

WARREN, A. R., & TATE, C. S. (1992). Egocentrism in children's telephone conversations. In R. M. Diaz & L. E. Berk (Eds.), *Private speech: From social interaction to self-regulation* (pp. 245–264). Hillsdale, NJ: Erlbaum.

WARREN, D. H. (1994). Blindness and children: An individual difference approach. New York: Cambridge University Press.

WARTNER, U. G., GROSSMANN, K., FREMMER-BOMBIK, E., & SUESS, G. (1994). Attachment patterns at age six in south Germany: Predictability from infancy and implications for preschool behavior. *Child Development, 65,* 1014–1027.

WATERMAN, A. S. (1989). Curricula interventions for identity change: Substantive and ethical considerations. *Journal of Adolescence, 12,* 389–400.

WATERS, E., VAUGHN, B. E., POSADA, G., & KONDO-IKEMURA K. (Eds.). (1995). Caregiving, cultural, and cognitive perspectives on secure-base behavior and working models: New growing points of attachment theory and research. *Monographs of the Society for Research in Child Development, 60* (2–3, Serial No. 244).

WATERS, M. C. (1994). Ethnic and racial identities of second-generation black immigrants in New York City. *International Migration Review, 28,* 795–820.

WATKINS, W. E., & POLLITT, E. (1998). Iron deficiency and cognition among school-age children. In S. G. McGregor (Ed.), *Recent advances in research on the effects of health and nutrition on children's development and school achievement in the Third World.* Washington, DC: Pan American Health Organization.

WATSON, D. J. (1989). Defining and describing whole language. *Elementary School Journal, 90,* 129–141.

WATSON, J. B., & RAYNOR, R. (1920). Conditioned emotional reactions. *Journal of Experimental Psychology, 3,* 1–14.

WATSON, M. (1990). Aspects of self development as reflected in children's role playing. In D. Cicchetti & M. Beeghly (Eds.), *The self in transition: Infancy to childhood* (pp. 281–307). Chicago: University of Chicago Press.

WAXMAN, S. R., & HATCH, T. (1992). Beyond the basics: Preschool children label objects flexibly at multiple hierarchical levels. *Journal of Child Language, 19,* 153–166.

WAXMAN, S. R., & MARKOW, D. B. (1998). Object properties and object kind: Twenty-one-month-old infants' extension of novel adjectives. *Child Development, 69,* 1313–1329.

WAXMAN, S. R., & SENGHAS, A. (1992). Relations among word meanings in early lexical development. *Developmental Psychology, 28,* 862–873.

WEBB, N. M., NEMER, K. M., & CHIZHIK, A. W. (1998). Equity issues in collaborative group assessment: Group composition and performance. *American Educational Research Journal, 35,* 607–651.

WEBER-FOX, C. M., & NEVILLE, H. J. (1992). Maturational constraints on cerebral specialization for language processing: ERP and behavioral evidence in bilingual speakers. *Society for Neuroscience Abstracts, 18.*

WECHSLER, D. (1989). *Manual for the Wechsler Preschool and Primary Scale of Intelligence–Revised.* New York: The Psychological Corporation.

WECHSLER, D. (1991). *Manual for the Wechsler Intelligence Test for Children–III.* New York: The Psychological Corporation.

WEHREN, A., DE LISI, R., & ARNOLD, M. (1981). The development of noun definition. *Journal of Child Language, 8,* 165–175.

WEINBERG, M. K., & TRONICK, E. Z. (1994). Beyond the face: An empirical study of infant affective configurations of facial, vocal, gestural, and regulatory behaviors. *Child Development, 65,* 1503–1515.

WEINBERG, M. K., & TRONICK, E. Z. (1996). Infant affective reactions to the resumption of maternal interaction after the still face. *Child Development, 67,* 905–914.

WEINBERG, R. A., SCARR, S., & WALDMAN, I. D. (1992). The Minnesota Transracial Adoption Study: A follow-up of IQ test performance at adolescence. *Intelligence, 16,* 117–135.

WEINRAUB, M., CLEMENS, L. P., SOCKLOFF, A., ETHRIDGE, T., GRACELY, E., & MYERS, B. (1984). The development of sex role stereotypes in the third year: Relationships to gender labeling, gender identity, sex-typed toy preference, and family characteristics. *Child Development, 55,* 1493–1503.

WEINSTEIN, R. S., MARSHALL, H. H., SHARP, L., & BOTKIN, M. (1987). Pygmalion and the student: Age and classroom differences in children's awareness of teacher expectations. Child Development, 58, 1079–1093.

WEISBERG, R. W. (1993). *Creativity: Beyond the myth of genius.* New York: Freeman.

WEISFIELD, G. E. (1986). Teaching about sex differences in human behavior and the biological approach in general. *Politics and the Life Sciences, 5,* 36–43.

WEISFIELD, G. E. (1990). Sociobiological patterns of Arab culture. *Ethology and Sociobiology, 11,* 23–49.

WEISFIELD, G. E. (1997). Puberty rites as clues to the nature of human adolescence. *Cross-Cultural Research, 31,* 27–54.

WEISNER, T. S. (1996). Why ethnography should be the most important method in the study of human development. In R. Jessor, A. Colby, & R. A. Shweder (Eds.), *Ethnography and human development* (pp. 15–52). Chicago: University of Chicago Press.

WEISNER, T. S., & WILSON-MITCHELL, J. E. (1990). Nonconventional family life-styles and sex typing in six-year-olds. *Child Development, 61,* 1915–1933.

WEISZ, J. R., CHAIYASIT, W., WEISS, B., EASTMAN, K. L., & JACKSON, E. W. (1995). A multimethod study of problem behavior among Thai and American children in school: Teacher reports versus direct observations. *Child Development, 66,* 402–415.

WELLMAN, H. M. (1990). *The child's theory of mind.* Cambridge, MA: MIT Press.

WELLMAN, H. M., & BANERJEE, M. (1991). Mind and emotion: Children's understanding of the emotional consequences of beliefs and desires. *British Journal of Developmental Psychology, 9,* 191–214.

WELLMAN, H. M., & BARTSCH, K. (1988). Young children's reasoning about beliefs. *Cognition, 30,* 239–277.

WELLMAN, H. M., & GELMAN, S. A. (1992). Cognitive development: Foundational theories of core domains. *Annual Review of Psychology, 43,* 337–375.

WELLMAN, H. M., & HICKLING, A. K. (1994). The mind's "I": Children's conception of the mind as an active agent. *Child Development, 65,* 1564–1580.

WELLMAN, H. M., SOMERVILLE, S. C., & HAAKE, R. J. (1979). Development of search procedures in real-life spatial environments. *Developmental Psychology, 15,* 530–542.

WENTWORTH, N., & HAITH, M. M. (1992). Event-specific expectations of 2- and 3-month-old infants. *Developmental Psychology, 28,* 842–850.

WENTWORTH, N., & HAITH, M. M. (1998). Infants' acquisition of spatiotemporal expectations. *Developmental Psychology, 24,* 247–257.

WENTZEL, K. R., & ASHER, S. R. (1995). The academic lives of neglected, rejected, popular, and controversial children. *Child Development, 66,* 754–763.

WERKER, J. F., PEGG, J. E., & MCLEOD, P. (1994). A cross-language investigation of infant preference for infant-directed communication. *Infant Behavior and Development, 17,* 323–333.

WERNER, E. E. (1989). Children of the Garden Island. *Scientific American, 260* (4), 106–111.

WERNER, E. E. (1993). Risk, resilience, and recovery: Perspectives from the Kauai Longitudinal Study. *Development and Psychopathology, 5,* 503–515.

WERNER, E. E., & SMITH, R. S. (1982). *Vulnerable but invincible.* New York: McGraw-Hill.

WERNER, E. E., & SMITH, R. S. (1992). *Overcoming the odds: High risk children from birth to adulthood.* Ithaca, NY: Cornell University Press.

WERTHEIM, E. H., PAXTON, S. J., SCHUTZ, H. K., & MUIR, S. L. (1997). Why do adolescent girls watch their weight? An interview study examining sociocultural pressures to be thin.

Journal of Psychosomatic Research, 42, 345–355.

WERTSCH, J. V., & TULVISTE, P. (1992). L. S. Vygotsky and contemporary developmental psychology. *Developmental Psychology, 28,* 548–557.

WHEELER, M. D. (1991). Physical changes of puberty. *Endocrinology and Metabolism Clinics of North America, 20,* 1–14.

WHITE, B. (1990). *The first three years of life.* New York: Prentice-Hall.

WHITE, B., & HELD, R. (1966). Plasticity of sensorimotor development in the human infant. In J. F. Rosenblith & W. Allinsmith (Eds.), *The causes of behavior* (pp. 60–70). Boston: Allyn and Bacon.

WHITE, J. L., MOFFITT, T. E., CASPI, A., BARTUSCH, D. J., NEEDLES, D. J., & STOUTHAMER-LOEBER, M. (1996). Measuring impulsivity and examining its relationship to delinquency. *Journal of Abnormal Psychology, 103,* 192–205.

WHITE, K. R., TAYLOR, M. J., & MOSS, V. D. (1992). Does research support claims about the benefits of involving parents in early intervention programs? *Review of Educational Research, 62,* 91–125.

WHITE, R. W. (1959). Motivation reconsidered: The concept of competence. *Psychological Review, 66,* 297–333.

WHITE, S. H. (1992). G. Stanley Hall: From philosophy to developmental psychology. *Developmental Psychology, 28,* 25–34.

WHITEHURST, G. J., ARNOLD, D. S., EPSTEIN, J. N., ANGELL, A. L., SMITH, M., & FISCHEL, J. E. (1994). A picture book reading intervention in day care and home for children from low-income families. *Developmental Psychology, 30,* 679–689.

WHITEHURST, G. J., EPSTEIN, J. N., ANGELL, A. C., PAYNE, A. C., CRONE, D. A., & FISCHEL, J. E. (1994). Outcomes of an emergent literacy intervention in Head Start. *Journal of Educational Psychology, 86,* 542–555.

WHITEHURST, G. J., FISCHEL, J. E., CAULFIELD, M. B., DEBARYSHE, B. D., & VALDEZ-MENCHACA, M. C. (1989). Assessment and treatment of early expressive language delay. In P. R. Zelazo & R. Barr (Eds.), *Challenges to developmental paradigms: Implications for assessment and treatment* (pp. 113–135). Hillsdale, NJ: Erlbaum.

WHITEHURST, G. J., & VASTA, R. (1975). Is language acquired through imitation? *Journal of Psycholinguistic Research, 4,* 37–59.

WHITING, B., & EDWARDS, C. P. (1988a). *Children of different worlds.* Cambridge, MA: Harvard University Press.

WHITING, B., & EDWARDS, C. P. (1988b). A cross-cultural analysis of sex differences in the behavior of children aged 3 through 11. In G. Handel (Ed.), *Childhood socialization* (pp. 281–297). New York: Aldine De Gruyter.

WHITINGTON, V., & WARD, C. (1998). Intersubjectivity in caregiver–child communication. In L. E. Berk (Ed.), *Landscapes of development* (pp. 109–120). Belmont, CA: Wadsworth.

WHITLEY, B. E. (1983). Sex role orientation and self-esteem: A critical meta-analytic review. *Journal of Personality and Social Psychology, 44,* 765–778.

WHITNEY, M. P., & THOMAN, E. B. (1994). Sleep in premature and full-term infants from 24-hour home recordings. *Infant Behavior and Development, 17,* 223–234.

WICHSTRØM, L. (1999). The emergence of gender difference in depressed mood during adolescence: The role of intensified gender socialization. *Developmental Psychology, 35,* 232–245.

WIGFIELD, A., & ECCLES, J. S. (1994). Children's competence beliefs, achievement values, and general self-esteem change across elementary and middle school. *Journal of Early Adolescence, 14,* 107–138.

WIGFIELD, A., ECCLES, J. S., YOON, K. S., HAROLD, R. D., ARBRETON, A. J., FREEDMAN-DOAN, C., & BLUMENFELD, P. C. (1997). Changes in children's competence beliefs and subjective task values across the elementary school years: A three-year study. *Journal of Educational Psychology, 89,* 451–469.

WIGGINS, G. P. (1993). *Assessing student performance.* San Francisco: Jossey-Bass.

WIGGINS, G. P. (1998). Letter. *Educational Researcher, 22* (6), 20–22.

WILCOX, A. J., WEINBERG, C. R., & BAIRD, D. D. (1995). Timing of sexual intercourse in relation to ovulation: Effects on the probability of conception, survival of the pregnancy, and sex of the baby. *New England Journal of Medicine, 333,* 1517–1519.

WILLE, D. E. (1991). Relation of preterm birth with quality of infant–mother attachment at one year. *Infant Behavior and Development, 14,* 227–240.

WILLER, B., HOFFERTH, S. L., KISKER, E. E., DIVINE-HAWKINS, P., FARQUHAR, E., & GLANTZ, F. B. (1991). *The demand and supply of child care in 1990: Joint find-*

ings from the National Child Care Survey 1990 and A Profile of Child Care Settings. Washington, DC: National Association for the Education of Young Children.

WILLERMAN, L. (1979). Effects of families on intellectual development. *American Psychologist, 34,* 923–929.

WILLIAMS, E., & RADIN, N. (1993). Paternal involvement, maternal employment, and adolescents' academic achievement: An 11-year follow-up. *American Journal of Orthopsychiatry, 63,* 306–312.

WILLIAMS, E., RADIN, N., & ALLEGRO, T. (1992). Sex-role attitudes of adolescents reared primarily by their fathers: An 11-year follow-up. *Merrill-Palmer Quarterly, 38,* 457–476.

WILLIAMS, G. C. (1997). Review of *Adaptation,* edited by Michael R. Rose and George V. Lauder. *Copeia, No. 3,* 645–647.

WILLIAMS, J. E., & BEST, D. L. (1990). *Measuring sex stereotypes: A multination study.* Newbury Park, CA: Sage.

WILLIAMS, T. M. (1986). *The impact of television: A natural experiment in three communities.* Orlando, FL: Academic Press.

WILLIAMS, T. M., & COX, R. (1995, March). *Informative versus other children's TV programs: Portrayals of ethnic diversity, gender, and aggression.* Paper presented at the biennial meeting of the Society for Research in Child Development, Indianapolis.

WILLIAMSON, M. L. (1997). Circumcision anesthesia: A study of nursing implications for dorsal penile nerve block. *Pediatric Nursing, 23,* 59–63.

WILLS, T. A., McNAMARA, G., VACCARO, D., & HIRKY, A. E. (1996). Escalated substance use: A longitudinal grouping analysis from early to middle adolescence. *Journal of Abnormal Psychology, 105,* 166–180.

WILSON, E. O. (1975). *Sociobiology: The new synthesis.* Cambridge, MA: Harvard University Press.

WILSON, M. N., GREENE-BATES, C., McKIM, L., SIMMONS, T. A., CURRY-EL, J., & HINTON, I. D. (1995). African American family life: The dynamics of interactions, relationships, and roles. In M. N. Wilson (Ed.), *African American family life: Its structural and ecological aspects* (pp. 5–21). San Francisco: Jossey-Bass.

WILSON, R., & CAIRNS, E. (1988). Sex-role attributes, perceived competence, and the development of depression in adolescence. *Journal of Child Psychology and Psychiatry, 29,* 635–650.

WINDLE, M. A. (1994). A study of friendship characteristics and problem behaviors among middle adolescents. *Child Development, 65,* 1764–1777.

WINDSCHITL, M. (1998). The WWW and classroom research: What path should we take? *Educational Researcher, 27*(1), 28–33.

WINER, G., CRAIG, R. K., & WEINBAUM, E. (1992). Adults' failure on misleading weight-conservation tests: A developmental analysis. *Developmental Psychology, 28,* 109–120.

WINN, S., ROKER, D., & COLEMAN, J. (1995). Knowledge about puberty and sexual development in 11–16 year-olds: Implications for health and sex education in schools. *Educational Studies, 21,* 187–201.

WINNER, E. (1986, August). Where pelicans kiss seals. *Psychology Today, 20* (8), 25–35.

WINNER, E. (1988). *The point of words: Children's understanding of metaphor and irony.* Cambridge, MA: Harvard University Press.

WINNER, E. (1996). *Gifted children: Myths and realities.* New York: Basic Books.

WINTRE, M. G., & VALLANCE, D. D. (1994). A developmental sequence in the comprehension of emotions: Intensity, multiple emotions, and valence. *Developmental Psychology, 30,* 509–514.

WITHERELL, C. S., & EDWARDS, C. P. (1991). Moral versus social-conventional reasoning: A narrative and culture critique. *Journal of Moral Education, 20,* 293–304.

WOLF, A., & LOZOFF, B. (1989). Object attachment, thumbsucking, and the passage to sleep. *Journal of the American Academy of Child and Adolescent Psychiatry, 28,* 287–292.

WOLFER, L. T., & MOEN, P. (1996). Staying in school: Maternal employment and the timing of black and white daughters' school exit. *Journal of Family Issues, 17,* 540–560.

WOLFF, P. H. (1966). The causes, controls and organization of behavior in the neonate. *Psychological Issues, 5* (1, Serial No. 17).

WOLPE, J., & PLAUD, J. J. (1997). Pavlov's contributions to behavior therapy: The obvious and not so obvious. *American Psychologist, 52,* 966–972.

WOOD, D. J. (1989). Social interaction as tutoring. In M. H. Bornstein & J. S. Bruner (Eds.), *Interaction in human development.* Hillsdale, NJ: Erlbaum.

WOODWARD, A. L., & MARKMAN, E. M. (1998). Early word learning. In D. Kuhn & R. S. Siegler (Eds.), *Handbook of child psychology: Vol. 2. Cognition, perception, and language* (5th ed., pp. 371–420). New York: Wiley.

WOODWARD, A. L., MARKMAN, E. M., & FITZSIMMONS, C. M. (1994). Rapid word learning in 13- and 18-month-olds. *Developmental Psychology, 30,* 553–566.

WOODWORTH, R. S. (1996). You're not alone. . . .You're one in a million. *Child Welfare, 65,* 619–635.

WOODY-RAMSEY, J., & MILLER, P. H. (1988). The facilitation of selective attention in preschoolers. *Child Development, 59,* 1497–1503.

WOOLLEY, J. D. (1997). Thinking about fantasy: Are children fundamentally different thinkers and believers from adults? *Child Development, 68,* 991–1011.

WOOLLEY, J. D., & WELLMAN, H. M. (1990). Young children's understanding of realities, nonrealities, and appearances. *Child Development, 61,* 946–961.

WOOLLEY, J. D., & WELLMAN, H. M. (1992). Children's conception of dreams. *Cognitive Development, 7,* 365–380.

WRIGHT, J. C., & HUSTON, A. C. (1995, June). *Effects of educational TV viewing of lower income preschoolers on academic skills, school readiness, and school adjustment one to three years later.* Report to Children's Television Workshop, Center for Research on the Influences of Television on Children, University of Kansas, Lawrence.

WRIGHT, J. C., HUSTON, A. C., REITZ, A. L., & PIEMYAT, S. (1994). Young children's perceptions of television reality: Determinants and developmental differences. *Developmental Psychology, 30,* 229–239.

WROBLEWSKI, R., & HUSTON, A. C. (1987). Televised occupational stereotypes and their effects on early adolescents: Are they changing? *Journal of Early Adolescence, 7,* 283–298.

WYMAN, P. A., COWEN, E. L., WORK, W. C., RAOOF, A., GRIBBLE, P. A., PARKER, G. R., & WANNON, M. (1992). Interviews with children who experienced major life stress: Family and child attributes that predict resilient outcomes. *Journal of the American Academy of Child and Adolescent Psychiatry, 31,* 904–910.

WYNN, K. (1992). Addition and subtraction by human infants. *Nature, 358,* 749–750.

Y

YAMADA, J. E. (1990). *Laura—A case for the modularity of language.* Cambridge, MA: MIT Press.

YANG, B., OLLENDICK, T. H., DONG, Q., XIA, Y., & LIN, L. (1995). Only children and children with siblings in the People's Republic of China: Levels of fear, anxiety, and depression. *Child Development, 66,* 1301–1311.

YARROW, M. R., CAMPBELL, J. D., & BURTON, R. V. (1970). Recollections of childhood: A study of the retrospective method. *Monographs of the Society for Research in Child Development, 35* (5, Serial No. 138).

YARROW, M. R., SCOTT, P. M., & WAXLER, C. Z. (1973). Learning concern for others. *Developmental Psychology, 8,* 240–260.

YAZIGI, R. A., ODEM, R. R., & POLAKOSKI, K. L. (1991). Demonstration of specific binding of cocaine to human spermatozoa. *Journal of the American Medical Association, 266,* 1956–1959.

YEATES, K. O., SCHULTZ, L. H., & SELMAN, R. L. (1991). The development of interpersonal negotiation strategies in thought and action: A social-cognitive link to behavioral adjustment and social status. *Merrill-Palmer Quarterly, 37,* 369–405.

YIRMIYA, N., & SHULMAN, C. (1996). Seriation, conservation, and theory of mind abilities in individuals with autism, individuals with mental retardation, and normally developing children. *Child Development, 67,* 2045–2059.

YIRMIYA, N., SOLOMONICA-LEVI, D., & SHULMAN, C. (1996). The ability to manipulate behavior and to understand manipulation of beliefs: A comparison of individuals with autism, mental retardation, and normal development. *Developmental Psychology, 32,* 62–69.

YOGMAN, M. W. (1981). Development of the father–infant relationship. In H. Fitzgerald, B. Lester, & M. W. Yogman (Eds.), *Theory and research in behavioral pediatrics* (Vol. 1, pp. 221–279). New York: Plenum.

YONAS, A., GRANRUD, E. C., ARTERBERRY, M. E., & HANSON, B. L. (1986). Infants' distance perception from linear perspective and texture gradients. *Infant Behavior and Development, 9,* 247–256.

YONAS, A., & HARTMAN, B. (1993). Perceiving the affordance of contact in four- and five-month-old infants. *Child Development, 64,* 298–308.

YOUNG, D. (1997). Epidurals under scrutiny in the United States. *Birth, 24,* 139–140.

YOUNG, K. T. (1990). American conceptions of infant development from 1955 to 1984: What the experts are telling parents. *Child Development, 61,* 17–28.

YOUNGBLADE, L. M., & DUNN, J. (1995). Individual differences in young children's pretend play with mother and sibling: Links to relationships and understanding of other people's feelings and beliefs. *Child Development, 66,* 1472–1492.

YOUNGER, B. A. (1985). The segregation of items into categories by ten-month-old infants. *Child Development, 56,* 1574–1583.

YOUNGER, B. A. (1993). Understanding category members as "the same sort of thing": Explicit categorization in ten-month infants. *Child Development, 64,* 309–320.

YU, Y., & NELSON, K. (1993). Slot-filler and conventional category organization in young Korean children. *International Journal of Behavioral Development, 16,* 1–14.

YUILL, N., & PEARSON, A. (1998). The development of bases for trait attribution: Children's understanding of traits as causal mechanisms based on desire. *Developmental Psychology, 34,* 574–586.

YUILL, N., & PERNER, J. (1988). Intentionality and knowledge in children's judgments of actor's responsibility and recipient's emotional reaction. *Developmental Psychology, 24,* 358–365.

Z

ZABIN, L. S., & HAYWARD, S. C. (1993). *Adolescent sexual behavior and childbearing.* Newbury Park, CA: Sage.

ZABIN, L. S., STARK, H. A., & EMERSON, M. R. (1991). Reasons for delay in contraceptive clinic utilization: Adolescent clinic and non-clinic populations compared. *Journal of Adolescent Health, 12,* 225–232.

ZAHAVI, S., & ASHER, S. R. (1978). The effect of verbal instructions on preschool children's aggressive behavior. *Journal of School Psychology, 16,* 146–153.

ZAHN-WAXLER, C. (1991). The case for empathy: A developmental review. *Psychological Inquiry, 2,* 155–158.

ZAHN-WAXLER, C., COLE, P. M., & BARRETT, K. C. (1991). Guilt and empathy: Sex differences and implications for the development of depression. In J. Garber & K. A. Dodge (Eds.), *The development of emotion regulation and dysregulation* (pp. 243–272). Cambridge: Cambridge University Press.

ZAHN-WAXLER, C., IANNOTTI, R. J., CUMMINGS, E. M., & DENHAM, S. (1990). Antecedents of problem behaviors in children of depressed mothers. *Development and Psychopathology, 2,* 271–291.

ZAHN-WAXLER, C., KOCHANSKA, G., KRUPNICK, J., & MCKNEW, D. (1990). Patterns of guilt in children of depressed and well mothers. *Developmental Psychology, 26,* 51–59.

ZAHN-WAXLER, C., RADKE-YARROW, M., & KING, R. M. (1979). Child-rearing and children's prosocial initiations toward victims of distress. *Child Development, 50,* 319–330.

ZAHN-WAXLER, C., RADKE-YARROW, M., WAGNER, E., & CHAPMAN, M. (1992). Development of concern for others. *Developmental Psychology, 28,* 126–136.

ZAHN-WAXLER, C., & RADKE-YARROW, M. (1990). The origins of empathic concern. *Motivation and Emotion, 14,* 107–130.

ZAHN-WAXLER, C., & ROBINSON, J. (1995). Empathy and guilt: Early origins of feelings of responsibility. In J. P. Tangney & K. W. Fischer (Eds.), *Self-conscious emotions* (pp. 143–173). New York: Guilford.

ZAHN-WAXLER, C., ROBINSON, J. L., & EMDE, R. N. (1992). The development of empathy in twins. *Developmental Psychology, 28,* 1038–1047.

ZAJONC, R. B. (1976). Family configuration and intelligence. *Science, 192,* 227–236.

ZAJONC, R. B., & MULLALLY, P. R. (1997). Birth order: Reconciling conflicting effects. *American Psychologist, 52,* 685–699.

ZAMETKIN, A. J. (1995). Attention-deficit disorder: Born to be hyperactive? *Journal of the American Medical Association, 273,* 1871–1874.

ZELAZO, N. A., ZELAZO, P. R., COHEN, K. M., & ZELAZO, P. D. (1993). Specificity of practice effects on elementary neuromotor patterns. *Developmental Psychology, 29,* 686–691.

ZELAZO, P. R. (1983). The development of walking: New findings on old assumptions. *Journal of Motor Behavior, 2,* 99–137.

ZELAZO, P. R., ZELAZO, N. A., & KOLB, S. (1972). "Walking" in the newborn. *Science, 176,* 314–315.

ZEMAN, J., & GARBER, J. (1996). Display rules for anger, sadness, and pain: It depends on who is watching. *Child Development, 67,* 957–973.

ZESKIND, P. S., & BARR, R. G. (1997). Acoustic characteristics of naturally occurring cries of infants with "colic." *Child Development, 68,* 394–403.

ZESKIND, P. S., & RAMEY, C. T. (1978). Fetal malnutrition: An experimental study of its consequences on infant development in two caregiving environments. *Child Development, 49,* 1155–1162.

ZESKIND, P. S., & RAMEY, C. T. (1981). Preventing intellectual and interactional sequelae of fetal malnutrition: A longitudinal, transactional, and synergistic approach to development. *Child Development, 52,* 213–218.

ZHANG, J., CAI, W., & LEE, D. J. (1992). Occupational hazards and pregnancy outcomes. *American Journal of Industrial Medicine, 21,* 397–408.

ZIGLER, E. F., & FINN-STEVENSON, M. (1999). Applied developmental psychology. IN M. H. BORNSTEIN & M. E. LAMB (EDS.), *Developmental psychology: An advanced textbook* (4th ed., pp. 555–598). Mahwah, NJ: Erlbaum.

ZIGLER, E. F., & GILMAN, E. (1993). Day care in America: What is needed? *Pediatrics, 91,* 175–178.

ZIGLER, E. F., & HALL, N. W. (1989). Physical child abuse in America: Past, present, and future. In D. Cicchetti & V. Carlson (Eds.), *Child maltreatment* (pp. 203–253). New York: Cambridge University Press.

ZIGLER, E. F., & SEITZ, V. (1982). Social policy and intelligence. In R. J. Sternberg (Ed.), *Handbook of human intelligence* (pp. 586–641). Cambridge: Cambridge University Press.

ZIGLER, E., & STYFCO, S. J. (1994). Head Start: Criticisms in a constructive context. *American Psychologist, 49,* 127–132.

ZILL, N., DAVIES, E., & DALY, M. (1994). *Viewing of Sesame Street by preschool children in the United States and its relationship to school readiness.* Rockville, MD: Westat.

ZILLMAN, D., BRYANT, J., & HUSTON, A. C. (1994). *Media, family, and children.* Hillsdale, NJ: Erlbaum.

ZIMMERMAN, B. J., & RISEMBERG, R. (1997). Self-regulatory dimensions of academic learning and motivation. In G. D. Phye (Ed.), *Handbook of academic learning: Construction of knowledge* (pp. 105–125). San Diego: Academic Press.

ZIMMERMAN, M. A., & ARUNKUMAR, R. (1994). Resiliency research: Implications for schools and policy. *Social Policy Report of the Society for Research in Child Development, 8* (4).

ZIMMERMAN, M. A., COPELAND, L. A., SHOPE, J. T., & DIELMAN, T. E. (1997). A longitudinal study of self-esteem: Implications for adolescent development. *Journal of Youth and Adolescence, 26,* 117–141.

ZUCKER, K. J., BRADLEY, S. J., OLIVER, G., BLAKE, J., FLEMING, S., & HOOD, J. (1996). Psychosexual development of women with congenital adrenal hyperplasia. *Hormones and Behavior, 30,* 300–318.

A

Abbott, S., 132, 462
Abbotts, B., 199
Abelman, R., 620
Aber, J. L., 140
Abikoff, H., 288
Abood, D. A., 209
Aboud, F. E., 463
Abramovitch, R., 67
Abrams, A., 585
Achenbach, T. M., 15, 115, 249
Acker, M. M., 486, 486n
Ackerman, B. P., 386, 388
Acock, A. C., 577
Acredolo, L. P., 369
Adam, S., 297
Adams, C., 256
Adams, G. R., 457, 461
Adams, L. B., 194
Adams, M. J., 305
Adams, R. J., 154
Adamson, L. B., 387, 408
Adan, A. M., 631
Adler, P., 611, 612
Adler, P. A., 611, 612
Adler, T. F., 454
Adolph, K. E., 14, 146, 166
Adzick, N. S., 85
Ahaja, K. K., 84
Ahlsten, G., 99
Ahmed, A., 228
Ainsworth, M. D. S., 135, 423, 423n, 424, 426
Akhtar, N., 378
Aksan, N., 483, 506
Alan Guttmacher Institute, 212, 214, 215n
Albert, R. S., 353
Aldwin, C., 406
Alemagno, S., 116
Ales, K. L., 105
Alessandri, S. M., 99, 399, 402, 403, 404
Alexander, B., 530
Alexander, J. M., 111, 321
Alfieri, T., 62, 63n
Alibali, M. W., 282, 283
Allan, K., 619
Allegro, T., 536
Allen, J. P., 216, 567
Allen, L., 327, 328
Allen, M. H., 99
Allen, S. G., 497
Almeida, D. M., 541
Aloise, P. A., 285
Alpert-Gillis, L. J., 538
Alsaker, F. D., 207
Althaus, M., 575
Altstein, H., 576
Alvarez, M. M., 541

Alwitt, L. F., 618
Amabile, T. M., 349, 350, 351, 353
Aman, C. J., 251
Amato, P. R., 580
American Academy of Family Physicians, 140
American Psychiatric Association, 288, 635
American Psychological Association, 65, 66n
Ames, C., 456, 456n
Ames, E. W., 159
Amsel, E., 309n
Ancess, J., 342
Anderman, E. M., 630
Anderson, D. A., 213
Anderson, D. R., 284, 285n, 617
Anderson, E., 388
Anderson, E. S., 618
Anderson, G. C., 115
Anderson, H. R., 140
Anderson, J. L., 189
Anderson, K. J., 374, 533
Andersson, B-E., 434
Andrews, J. A., 247, 514
Andrews, S., 247, 247n
Anglin, J. M., 372
Angold, A., 202
Antell, S. E., 306
Antill, J. K., 526
Antonarakis, S. E., 82
Aotaki-Phenice, L., 572
Apgar, V., 108, 108n
Appelbaum, M. I., 328
Archer, J., 526
Archer, S. L., 457, 458, 460, 551
Arcus, D., 417
Arend, R., 431
Ariès, P., 11
Arnold, D. H., 386
Arnold, K. D., 386, 534
Aronson, M., 100
Arsenio, W., 410, 501
Arterberry, M. E., 157, 158, 161
Artman, L., 252
Arunkumar, R., 10
Asendorpf, J. B., 442
Asher, S. R., 469, 473, 515, 604, 606, 608
Ashmead, D. H., 148, 153, 292
Askew, J. M., 132, 637
Aslin, R. N., 154, 164, 367
Asquith, P., 503
Astington, J. W., 301, 444, 462
Astley, S. J., 101
Atkinson, R. C., 23, 272
Atkinson-King, K., 371
Attar, B., 517
Attie, I., 210
Au, K. H., 628
Au, T. K., 245, 375
Augustin, A., 185
Axelsson, I. E., 193n
Azmitia, M., 266, 574

B

Bachman, J. G., 615
Baddeley, A. D., 274, 365
Bader, A. P., 430
Badzinski, D. M., 410
Baenninger, M., 547
Baer, J., 352
Bagwell, C. L., 470, 604
Bahrick, L. E., 166, 441
Bai, D. L., 152, 153n, 159
Bailey, D. B., 635
Bailey, J. M., 81, 212, 576
Bailey, R. C., 192
Bailey, T., 639
Baillargeon, R., 227, 228, 228n, 229, 229n, 232, 251
Baird, D. D., 89
Bakeman, R., 28, 408, 536
Baker, C. T., 328
Baker, E. L., 342
Baker, J. M., 377
Baker-Ward, L., 287, 299
Baldwin, A., 570
Baldwin, C., 570
Baldwin, D. A., 446
Baldwin, J. M., 14, 16
Ballard, B. D., 197
Balleduz, M., 199
Bandini, L. G., 195
Bandura, A., 20, 484, 485, 487, 508, 527, 540
Banerjee, M., 443
Banish, M. T., 188, 190
Banks, M. S., 154, 159, 159n, 161
Barber, B. K., 459
Barber, B. L., 633
Bardwell, J. R., 526
Barenboim, C., 463, 466
Barker, D. J. P., 104, 196
Barker, R. G., 627
Barkley, R. A., 27, 288, 289, 509
Barling, J., 639
Barnard, K. E., 113
Barnas, M. V., 433
Barnat, S. B., 230
Barnes, J., 451
Barnes, K. E., 599n
Barnes-Josiah, D., 185
Barnett, D., 589
Barnett, W. S., 346
Baron, R. C., 102
Baron-Cohen, S., 446
Barr, H. M., 98, 99
Barr, R., 136, 230
Barratt, M. S., 113
Barrera, M. E., 565
Barrera, M., Jr., 565
Barrett, K. C., 158, 398, 399
Barriga, A. Q., 514
Barron, F., 349, 352

Barry, H., III., 203, 204, 205, 206
Barth, R. P., 602
Bartke, A., 531
Bartlett, F. C., 292
Barton, M. E., 378, 387, 387n
Barton, S. J., 98
Bartsch, K., 443
Bashir, L. M., 205n
Basinger, K. S., 492, 499, 514
Bastian, H., 110
Bates, E., 279n, 364, 366, 374, 375, 384
Bates, J. E., 262, 412, 415, 416, 418, 420, 512, 515, 560, 568
Baudonniere, P., 442
Bauer, C. R., 295
Bauer, P. J., 246, 292
Baumeister, A. A., 134
Baumeister, R. F., 134, 514
Baumrind, D., 563, 564, 565
Baumwell, L., 369
Bayley, N., 145n, 149n, 206, 325
Beach, F., 210
Beal, C. R., 302
Beardsall, L., 62
Bearison, D. J., 208, 504
Beatty, W. W., 529, 530
Beauchamp, G. K., 151
Beck, M., 85
Becker, E., 36
Becker, J., 389
Becker, J. B., 205
Beckwith, L., 114, 142
Bedrosian, J. L., 386
Beere, C. A., 524
Begley, S., 338
Behrend, D. A., 260, 262, 376
Behrman, R. E., 79n
Beilin, H., 21, 222, 240, 248
Beintema, D., 129n
Bell, A., 212
Bell, K. L., 159
Bell, M. A., 159, 191, 228, 417
Bell, R. J., 103
Bell, S. M., 135
Bell-Dolan, D. J., 66
Bellamy, C., 34, 35n, 116, 194, 198, 199, 572
Belle, D., 587
Bellinger, D., 101
Bellugi, U., 365
Belmont, L., 345n
Belmont, M. J., 345, 345n
Belsky, D., 104, 215
Belsky, J., 420, 425, 426, 427, 430, 431, 433, 589, 592n
Bem, D. J., 59
Bem, S. L., 538, 539, 539n, 541, 552
Benbow, C. P., 534, 545n, 546
Bench, R. J., 153
Bender, B. G., 99
Bender, W. N., 635
Bendersky, M., 168
Benedict, R., 210, 404

C

Capelli, C. A., 377
Capirci, O., 369
Caplan, M., 344, 442
Carberry, M., 286, 286n
Carbery, J., 471
Cardarelli, A. P., 590, 591
Cardon, L. R., 328
Carey, G., 120n
Carey, S., 234
Carey, W. B., 131
Carlson, C. L., 288
Carlson, S. M., 237, 444
Carney, R. A., 82, 547
Carpendale, J. I., 300, 301, 466
Carpenter, C. J., 549
Carpenter, M., 369
Carr, M., 82, 289, 321, 409
Carraher, D. W., 266
Carraher, T., 266
Carriger, M. S., 142, 442
Carroll, J. B., 318, 319, 319n
Carruth, B. R., 197
Carter, D. B., 399, 543
Cartwright, B. S., 237, 466, 466n, 466n
Casaer, P., 92, 187
Casas, J. F., 511
Case, R., 22, 258, 276, 277, 278, 278n
Caselli, M. C., 369, 375
Casey, M. B., 323, 547
Casey, R. J., 479
Cashdan, E., 28
Caspi, A., 59, 61, 206, 207, 416, 417, 419, 420
Cassel, J., 105
Cassidy, J., 410, 425, 427, 431
Cassidy, S. B., 80
Catherwood, D., 156
Catsambis, S., 547
Cattell, J. M., 317
Cattell, R. B., 318, 319, 322
Cauce, A. M., 449
Cavalli-Sforza, L. L., 338
Cavell, T. A., 452
Ceci, S. J., 120, 253, 253n, 298, 299, 329, 330, 332, 338, 339
Center for Communication and Social Policy, 618, 619n
Central Intelligence Agency, 35n, 117n
Cernoch, J. M., 152
Cervantes, C. A., 410, 532
Chafetz, J., 383
Chalkley, M. A., 379, 384
Chalmers, J. B., 467
Chan, S. Q., 576
Chandler, M. J., 300, 301, 458, 466, 467
Chandler, S. B., 209
Chandra, R. K., 104
Chaney, C., 389
Chao, R. K., 54, 569, 579
Chao, W., 579
Chapman, M., 249, 377, 483
Charman, T., 446
Charrow, V., 374
Chase, C., 155
Chase-Lansdale, P. L., 34, 36, 105, 214, 215, 217, 344, 571, 579, 580
Chassin, L., 615
Chatkupt, S., 102n
Chavajay, P., 26, 252, 290

Chavira, V., 461
Chen, C., 452, 638
Chen, S., 425
Chen, X., 52, 231, 331, 420, 575, 606
Chen, Y-C., 101
Chen, Y-J., 101
Chen, Z., 232n
Cherlin, A. J., 560, 579, 580, 581
Cherny, S. S., 344
Chess, S., 9, 412, 414, 415n, 420
Cheung, L. W. Y., 197
Chi, M. T. H., 294, 294n
Child, A. H., 79n
Children's Defense Fund, 29, 34, 35, 35n, 38, 105, 112, 116, 195, 198, 434, 435, 578, 586, 639
Childs, C. P., 26
Chipuer, H. M., 418n
Chisholm, J. S., 137
Chiu, L-H., 451
Chizhik, A. W., 634
Choi, S., 247, 375
Chomsky, N., 234, 358, 363, 364
Christoffel, K. K., 195
Christophe, A., 139
Chugani, H. T., 189
Cicchetti, D., 9, 10, 140, 400, 545n, 549, 552, 589, 592, 592n, 593
Clancy, P., 382, 383
Clark, D. C., 459
Clark, E. V., 375, 376, 378
Clark, L. V., 466
Clark, R., 117
Clarke-Stewart, K. A., 430, 433, 580
Clasen, D., 613
Claude, E., 288
Clausen, J. A., 206
Cleland, J. W., 134
Clements, D. H., 623, 624
Cleminshaw, H. K., 579
Clifton, R. K., 148, 150, 153, 228
Clinton, H. R., 15
Clopton, N. A., 499
Clubb, P. A., 295
Cnattingius, S., 99
Coakley, J., 180
Coatsworth, J. D., 10
Cochran, M., 562
Cochran, S. W., 526
Cocking, R. R., 624, 625
Coffey-Corina, S. A., 188, 363
Cohen, F. L., 102n
Cohen, K. M., 213
Cohen, L., 234
Cohen, L. B., 105, 229
Cohen, S. E., 142
Cohn, J. F., 399, 400, 429, 573
Coie, J. D., 331, 407, 509, 512, 604, 608
Colan, N. B., 639
Colby, A., 491, 492, 494, 494n
Cole, M., 256
Cole, P. M., 407
Cole, R. E., 570
Coleman, J., 212
Coleman, M., 577
Coleman, S. M., 485
Coleman, C. C., 607, 629
Coley, R. L., 34, 105, 214, 217, 246, 577
Collaer, M. L., 531, 546

Collins, J. A., 75n
Collins, W. A., 561, 566, 568, 618
Collis, B. A., 621
Colombo, J., 142, 325
Coltrane, S., 561, 584, 619
Compas, B., 406
Comstock, G. A., 617, 618
Condry, J., 551
Conger, K. J., 574
Conger, R. D., 206, 400, 560, 569, 574
Connell, J. P., 405, 455, 538
Conner, D. B., 262
Connolly, J. A., 237
Connolly, K. J., 239, 239n, 602
Connors, M. E., 210
Constanzo, P. R., 197
Cook, D. G., 140
Cook, R., 84, 140
Cooke, R. A., 68
Coon, H., 344
Cooney, G. H., 534
Coontz, S., 15
Cooper, C. R., 330, 460
Cooper, H. M., 633
Cooper, M. L., 211
Cooper, P., 400
Cooper, R. P., 154, 367
Coplan, R. J., 8, 417, 600
Coppage, D. J., 230
Copper, R. L., 113
Copple, C., 434, 435n, 586n
Coppotelli, H., 604
Corah, N. L., 112
Corasaniti, M. A., 587
Corbetta, D., 148
Corbin, S. B., 579
Corrigan, R., 236
Corwin, M. J., 140
Cosden, M., 98
Cost, Quality, and Outcomes Study Team, 34, 434n
Costabile, A., 601
Costello, E. J., 202
Cotton, D. B., 86n
Cotton, P., 99, 140
Couchoud, E., 410
Coulehan, C. M., 433
Coulton, C., 591
Coupland, V., 110
Courage, M. L., 154, 296
Cowan, C. P., 28, 561
Cowan, P. A., 28, 561
Cox, M., 238, 239
Cox, M. J., 428, 429, 430
Cox, R., 619
Coyle, T. R., 287, 290
Craig, K. D., 253
Craig, R. K., 253
Craik, F. I. M., 23, 274
Crain, R. L., 451
Crain-Thoreson, C., 305
Crassini, B., 156
Craton, L. G., 157
Cratty, B. J., 178n, 180
Craven, R., 449, 450
Crawford, J., 393
Creasey, G. L., 237
Creatsas, G. K., 211
Crick, N. R., 470, 473, 473n, 511, 545n, 550, 550n, 551, 606, 607
Crockett, L. J., 541
Cronk, C., 369

Cross, D. R., 262
Crouter, A. C., 536, 541, 548
Crowe, H. P., 134
Crowley, K., 63, 64
Crowley, W. F., 547
Crowson, M., 446
Cruttenden, L., 228
Cruzcosa, M., 589
Crystal, D. S., 452, 638
Csikszentmihalyi, M., 205, 351, 601
Cuddy-Casey, M., 245
Culbertson, F. M., 100, 550
Culpepper, L., 155
Cummings, E. M., 56, 57n, 400, 406, 433, 552
Cummings, M. T., 28
Cunningham, T. F., 624
Curran, D. J., 338
Curran, P. J., 338
Currie, J., 346, 347, 349
Curtis, L. E., 306
Curtiss, S., 363
Cushing, G., 615
Cushing, T. J., 615
Cutler, A., 367

D

Dahl, R. E., 99
Dale, P. S., 305
Daltabuit, M., 135
Dalterio, S., 531
Daly, M., 528, 558, 621
Damon, W., 15, 447, 448, 452, 468, 469, 486, 496, 503, 504, 504n
Danforth, J. S., 27
Daniels, K., 85
Daniluk, J., 207
Dann, S., 598
Dannemiller, J. L., 155, 162
Dapretto, M., 375
Darling, N. E., 451, 564, 615
Darling-Hammond, L., 342
Darlington, R. B., 346, 346n
Darwin, C., 13
Das Gupta, P., 246
Datell, B. J., 103
Davenport, G. G., 548
Davidson, E., 110
Davidson, P., 492
Davidson, R. J., 188
Davies, E., 621
Davies, P. T., 28, 400, 406
Davis, B., 620
Davis, C. C., 599
Davis, D. H., 133
Davis, D. L., 79
Davis, L. B., 48
Davis, L. G., 558
Davis, P. V., 162
Davis, T. L., 48
Davison, M. L., 545n, 547
Dawson, G., 446
Day, R. H., 161
Day, S., 80
De Lisi, R., 377, 539
de Mare, J., 199
de Villiers, J. G., 379, 381, 385
de Villiers, P. A., 379, 381, 385

Fletcher, A. C., 451, 564, 610, 614, 615
Fletcher, J. M., 112
Fletcher-Flinn, C. M., 624
Flor, D., 570
Florian, V., 245
Florsheim, P., 577
Flynn, J. R., 60
Fogel, A., 30, 419, 548
Foltz, C., 309
Fombonne, E., 550
Fonzi, A., 470
Ford, C., 210
Forehand, R., 574, 579
Forman, E. A., 265, 266, 628
Forrest, D., 199
Forrest, J. D., 216
Fortier, L., 98, 100
Foster, S. L., 66
Fox, N. A., 49, 159, 188, 191, 228, 296, 417, 427
Fracasso, M. P., 569
Fraiberg, S., 160
Francis, P. L., 230
Frank, S. J., 567
Frankel, G. W., 284
Frankel, K. A., 262
Franklin, C. C., 503
Franklin, F. A., 503
Franks, B. A., 256
Franz, C., 412
Frazier, M. M., 638
Frederick, P. D., 102
Fredericks, M., 55
Fredriksen, S., 620
Freedman, D. G., 137
Freedman, N., 137
Freel, M. A., 217
Freeman, D., 203
Freiberg, K., 156
French, L. A., 249
French, S. E., 631
Frensch, P. A., 547, 625
Freud, A., 598
Freud, S., 17, 481, 484
Frey, K. S., 450, 539, 540
Fried, M. H., 205
Fried, M. N., 205
Fried, P. A., 99, 100
Friederici, A. D., 367
Friedman, B., 506
Friedman, H. S., 399
Friedman, R. J., 97, 98, 99
Friedman, S. L., 286
Friedrich-Cofer, L., 620
Friesen, W., 401
Frodi, A., 136
Froom, J., 155
Frost, J. J., 216
Frost, L. A., 383
Fry, A. F., 275, 320
Fuchs, I., 497, 634
Fuhrman, T., 567
Fujinaga, T., 168
Fukumoto, A., 479
Fuligni, A. J., 344, 604, 614, 633, 638
Fulker, D. W., 334n, 344
Fuller, D., 492, 517
Fuller, M. J., 203
Fung, H., 442
Furman, E., 245
Furman, W., 60, 567, 574

Furrow, D., 386
Furstenberg, F. F., Jr., 215, 216, 217, 560, 581
Furuno, S., 178n
Fuson, K. C., 306, 307, 308

G

Gaddis, A., 203, 419
Gaddis, L., 419
Gaensbauer, T. J., 403
Gagnon, J. H., 464
Galambos, N. L., 541
Galambos, S. J., 587
Galasso, L., 247
Galin, D., 190
Galinsky, E., 434, 585
Gallagher, A. M., 539
Galler, J. R., 195
Gallimore, R., 629, 629n
Gallistel, C. R., 306
Galotti, K. M., 499
Galper, A., 347
Galton, F., 317
Gamoran, A., 342, 634
Ganchrow, J. R., 138
Gandour, M. J., 420
Gannon, S., 420
Ganong, L. H., 577
Gapenne, O., 152
Garbarino, J., 562, 590, 591
Garber, J., 407, 550
García-Coll, C. T., 112, 113, 461
Gardner, B. T., 360
Gardner, H., 50, 51, 238n, 322, 323, 323n, 324, 349, 353
Gardner, M. J., 81
Gardner, R. A., 360
Garfinkel, I., 581
Gariboldi, A., 433
Garland, A. F., 459
Garmezy, N., 10
Garmon, L. C., 499
Garner, P. W., 407, 410
Garovich, L., 523
Garrett, P., 569
Garvey, C., 237, 263, 386, 600
Gash, H., 536
Gaskins, S., 264
Gathercole, S. E., 377, 378
Gaub, M., 288
Gauvain, M., 251, 266, 286, 286n
Ge, X., 206, 400
Geary, D. C., 24, 306, 308, 321, 637
Gellatly, A. R. H., 256
Gelman, R., 243, 245, 246, 306
Gelman, S. A., 234, 243, 247, 376, 526
Genesee, F., 392
Gentner, D., 375
George, C., 429
George, T. P., 606
Gerbner, G., 622
Gerig, T. M., 633
Gerris, J. R. M., 606
Gershoff-Stowe, L., 247, 373
Gervai, J., 526, 532, 535, 536
Gesell, A., 14
Getchell, N., 177
Gettinger, M., 474

Getzels, J. W., 351
Gewirtz, J. L., 135
Ghim, H. R., 161, 161n
Gibbs, J. C., 481, 482, 488, 492, 494n, 497, 499, 500, 514, 517
Gibson, E. J., 157, 166
Gibson, J. J., 166
Giedd, J. N., 50
Gilfillan, M. C., 79n
Gillberg, C., 100
Gilligan, C. F., 498, 499
Gillmore, J., 466, 495
Gillmore, M. R., 610
Gilman, E., 586
Gindis, B., 263
Ginsburg, A. P., 159
Ginsburg, H. P., 48, 259, 306
Giovanelli, G., 153
Girgus, J. S., 550
Gisel, E. G., 199
Giusti, R. M., 101
Gladwell, M., 197
Glasgow, K. L., 633, 634
Glassman, B. S., 211
Gleitman, L., 378, 379
Glick, P. C., 271, 577
Glosten, B., 111
Glover, J. A., 352
Gluckman, P. D., 360, 362n
Gnepp, J., 410
Goduka, I. N., 572
Goelman, H., 386
Goldberg, D. L., 197
Goldberg, W. A., 583
Goldberg-Glen, R., 584
Goldfield, B. A., 236, 373, 373n, 374
Goldfoot, D. A., 598
Goldin-Meadow, S., 283, 361, 361n, 373
Goldsmith, H. H., 416
Goldsmith, L. T., 50, 51, 323, 353
Goldstein, A. P., 517
Goldstein, H., 179n
Goldstein, J. H., 625
Goldstein, L. H., 415
Goldwyn, R., 429n
Goleman, D., 330
Golinkoff, R. M., 378
Golomb, C., 238, 247
Golombok, S., 84, 576
Golub, H. L., 111
Gomez-Schwartz, B., 590, 591
Göncü, A., 236
Gonzales, N. A., 562
Good, T. L., 536, 632
Goodall, J., 480
Goodenough, F. L., 511
Goodfellow, P. N., 76
Goodman, G. S., 295, 299, 398
Goodman, S. H., 400, 474
Goodnow, J. J., 481, 485, 487, 534
Goodwyn, S. W., 369
Goossens, F. A., 427
Gopnik, A., 231, 236, 247, 299, 373, 375, 409, 443, 444
Gordon, P., 383
Gorman-Smith, D., 577
Gorski, P. A., 137
Gortmaker, S. L., 195, 197, 198
Goswami, U., 231, 245, 246n, 250

Gottesman, I. I., 120n, 121, 122
Gottfredson, L. S., 534
Gottfried, A. E., 584
Gottlieb, G., 79, 121
Gottlieb, M. B., 79
Gottman, J. M., 602, 603
Goubet, N., 149, 149n, 228
Gould, J. L., 75
Goy, R. W., 598
Graber, J. A., 201, 209
Graham, S., 404
Gralinski, H., 507, 507n
Gralinski, J. H., 442, 507n
Granot, M., 110
Grant, J., 15
Grant, J. P., 103, 194, 198, 572
Grantham-McGregor, S., 105
Grattan, M. P., 188
Gravatt, B., 624
Gravel, J. S., 155
Graves, S. B., 619, 620
Gravitt, G. W., Jr., 474
Gray, C. E., 352
Gray, J., 523
Gray, P., 603
Graziano, W. G., 603
Green, F. L., 247, 300, 300n, 301
Green, J., 110
Green, J. A., 134, 212
Green, R., 528
Green, V. P., 634
Greenberger, E., 568, 583
Greendorfer, S. L., 180
Greene, A. D., 215
Greenfield, P. M., 26, 147, 339, 340, 547, 621, 624, 625, 636
Greeno, J. G., 24, 311
Greenough, W. T., 187, 191
Gregg, V., 499, 514
Greif, E. B., 533
Gresham, F. M., 635
Gribble, P. A., 10
Grigorenko, E. L., 341, 352
Grisso, T., 67
Groff, J. Y., 99
Grolnick, W. S., 28, 154, 405, 636
Gronau, R. C., 509
Gronhaug, K., 625
Groome, L. J., 134
Gross, A. M., 625
Grossman, P. B., 452
Grossmann, K., 425
Grotevant, H. D., 330, 457, 458, 460, 537, 561
Grotpeter, J. K., 470, 511, 545n, 550, 550n, 551, 607
Grusec, J. E., 481, 484, 485
Grych, J. H., 580
Guarino, P. A., 404
Guerra, N. G., 517
Guidubaldi, J., 579
Guilford, J. P., 350
Gulko, J., 525, 525n, 526, 527, 529, 540
Gullone, E., 406
Gump, P. V., 627
Gunnar, M. R., 417, 593
Gurucharri, C., 465
Gustafson, G. E., 134
Gutfreund, M., 263
Gutheil, G., 164
Guthrie, I. K., 505
Guttentag, R., 275

H

Haake, R. J., 286
Haas, B., 568
Hack, M. B., 112
Hackel, L. S., 561
Haden, C. A., 297
Hadwin, J., 443
Hagan, R. I., 524, 532
Hagberg, B., 100
Hagekull, B., 199
Hagen, E. P., 324
Hagerman, R. J., 81
Haidt, J., 36
Haier, R. J., 320
Haight, W. L., 236, 263
Hainline, L., 154
Hains, S. M. J., 402, 402n
Haith, M. M., 167, 234, 286, 320
Hakuta, K., 392
Halberstadt, A. G., 541, 545n, 548
Hale, S., 275, 320
Halford, G. S., 249, 258, 276
Halil, T., 136n
Hall, D. G., 378
Hall, G. S., 14
Hall, J. A., 538, 541, 545n, 548
Hall, N. W., 592
Halliday, J. L., 82n
Halpern, C. T., 210
Halpern, D. F., 79, 545
Halpern, L. F., 134
Halton, A., 111
Halverson, C. F., Jr., 541, 542, 542n
Ham, M., 205
Hamberger, L., 91n, 93
Hamelin, K., 115
Hamer, D. H., 212
Hamilton, C. E., 599
Hamilton, S. F., 639, 640
Hammersley, M., 54
Hammersmith, S., 212
Han, J. J., 297
Handler, A. S., 98, 112
Hanlon, C., 385
Hanna, E., 230
Hanna, G., 550
Hans, S. L., 136
Hanson, D. R., 120n
Happé, F. G. E., 446
Harding, A. E., 79n
Hare, J., 576, 577
Harkness, S., 131
Harlan, S. L., 571
Harley, E. E., 363
Harlow, H. F., 421, 598
Härnqvist, K., 329
Harold, G. T., 560
Harold, R. D., 180, 525, 533, 636
Harrigan, R., 98
Harrington, D., 533
Harrington, R., 533, 550
Harris, A. M., 537
Harris, G., 151
Harris, I. B., 35n, 38
Harris, K. L., 134
Harris, K. M., 217
Harris, M. L., 566
Harris, N. G. S., 365
Harris, P., 279

Harris, P. L., 237, 238
Harris, R. I., 263
Harris, R. T., 210
Harris, S., 82, 496, 499
Harrison, A. O., 569, 570
Harrist, A. W., 602, 606
Hart, B., 344, 374, 386
Hart, B. I., 550
Hart, C. H., 628
Hart, D., 447, 500
Hart, J., 593
Harter, S., 404, 441, 445, 447, 448, 449, 451
Hartman, B., 148
Hartmann, D. P., 606
Hartshorn, K., 142
Hartup, W. W., 331, 470, 470n, 511, 598, 601
Haselager, J. T., 470
Hashimoto, K., 85
Hasselhorn, M., 301
Hatano, G., 266
Hatch, E. E., 101
Hatch, M. C., 103, 105
Hatch, T., 323, 378
Hatcher, P. J., 305
Hatton, D. D., 160
Hauser, S. T., 450, 460
Hausfather, A., 585
Hauth, J. C., 98
Haviland, J. M., 407
Hawke, S., 575n
Hawkins, A. J., 561
Hawkins, D. J., 515
Hawkins, J. N., 451
Hawkins, R., 591
Haworth, K., 85
Hay, D. F., 472, 480
Hayden-Thomson, L., 529
Hayghe, H. V., 36
Hayne, H., 139, 142, 230
Haynes, S. N., 50
Hayslip, B., Jr., 327
Hayward, C., 580
Hayward, S. C., 216
Healy, M. J. R., 179n
Hearold, S., 620
Heath, S. B., 339, 569
Heckman, J. J., 329
Hedges, L. V., 546
Heffernan, K., 210
Heffner, R. W., 199
Heidiger, M. L., 104, 215
Heine, S. J., 451
Heinl, T., 135n
Heinonen, O. P., 105
Helburn, S. W., 386, 434, 435, 585
Held, R., 149, 154
Heller, K. A., 188, 353
Heller, W., 188
Helmstadter, G. C., 536
Helwig, C. C., 503
Hembree, E. A., 403
Hembree, S. E., 403, 472
Henderson, S. H., 578
Hendrick, J., 535, 536n
Hendrix, K., 528
Hennessy, K. D., 552
Hennig, K. H., 495
Henry, K., 48
Hepper, P. G., 141
Herdt, G., 213, 531
Herman, M. R., 564

Hermer, L., 164
Hernandez, D. J., 38, 399
Héroux, G., 243
Herrnstein, R., 332
Hesser, J., 574
Hetherington, E. M., 577, 578, 579, 580, 581, 582
Hetherington, S. E., 110
Hewer, A., 492
Hewlett, B. S., 15, 431, 431n, 558
Heyman, G. D., 453, 454, 464
Heyns, B., 329
Hickey, T. L., 154
Hickling, A. K., 244, 301, 377
Hier, D. B., 547
Hiester, M., 433
Higgins, E. T., 62, 63n
Higley, J. D., 598
Hildebrandt, N., 487
Hill, H. M., 515
Hill, J. P., 206, 567
Hill, P. M., 182
Himes, J. H., 196
Hind, H., 194
Hinde, R. A., 24, 25, 419, 526, 535
Hines, M., 528, 530, 531, 546
Hinsdale, G., 197
Hirsch, B. J., 471
Hirsh-Pasek, K., 153, 367
Hirshfeld, L. A., 247
Ho, H. Z., 455
Ho, V., 256
Hobart, C., 582
Hobson, R. P., 446
Hocutt, A. M., 635
Hodapp, R. M., 81, 82
Hodges, E. V. E., 607
Hodges, J., 426
Hodges, R. M., 249
Hoeksma, J. B., 420
Hoff-Ginsberg, E., 374
Hofferth, S. L., 349
Hoffman, H. J., 140
Hoffman, L., 419
Hoffman, L. W., 120, 536, 583
Hoffman, M. L., 411, 480, 482, 483, 484
Hoffman, S., 105
Hoffner, C., 410
Hofstadter, M., 228
Hofsten, C. von, 146, 148, 164
Hogarty, P. S., 328
Hohne, E. A., 367
Hokoda, A., 454
Holaday, J. W., 531
Holden, G. W., 287, 485, 487, 592
Holland, P. B., 548
Holmbeck, G. N., 206, 212, 567
Holmes, L. B., 590, 591
Holt, R. W., 549, 564
Holt, W., 549
Holtzman, D., 629
Honzik, M. P., 327, 328
Hood, B. M., 141, 142
Hooper, F. E., 259
Hooven, C., 602
Hopkins, B., 146, 147, 148n
Horgan, D., 383
Horn, J. L., 319, 333
Horn, J. M., 119, 334n, 336
Horner, T. M., 403
Hornung, M., 599n

Horowitz, F. D., 19, 21
Horowitz, J. M., 590, 591
Hort, B. E., 526
Horton, W., 212
Horwood, L. J., 99, 194
Hotz, V. J., 215
Howe, D., 506
Howe, M. L., 296
Howes, C., 236, 434, 585, 586, 599, 600, 603
Hoza, B., 289
Hsu, C-C., 101
Hubbard, F. O. A., 135
Hubel, D. H., 190
Hudson, J. A., 292, 295
Hudspeth, W. J., 191
Huesmann, L. R., 512, 512n, 619, 619n
Hughes, C., 410
Hughes, J. N., 452
Hughes, F. P., 445, 446
Hughes, M., 597
Hughes, M. E., 215
Hulme, C., 305
Human Genome Program, 88
Hummel, R. C., 498
Humphrey, G. K., 159
Humphrey, H. E. B., 102
Humphrey, P., 182
Humphrey, T., 151
Humphreys, A. P., 601
Humphreys, L. G., 327
Hunt, E., 100
Hunt, J. McV., 326
Hunter, J. E., 330
Hunter, R. F., 330
Hunter, T., 601
Huntington, L., 136
Huntsinger, C. S., 569, 569n, 638
Hura, S. L., 370
Hurrelmann, K., 173, 217
Huston, A. C., 37, 38, 524, 527, 536, 541, 549, 617, 618, 620, 621, 622, 625
Huston, T. L., 561
Huston-Stein, A., 621
Huttenlocher, J., 242, 374
Huttenlocher, P. R., 186, 187
Hwang, C. P., 419
Hyde, J. S., 117, 544, 545, 545n, 547
Hymel, S., 529, 606
Hynd, G. W., 289

I

Iacono, W. G., 335n
Iams, J. D., 112
Iannotti, R. J., 552
Imperato-McGinley, J., 531
Inciardi, J. A., 99
Infante-Rivard, C., 98
Ingersoll, E. W., 139
Ingram, D., 370, 371n
Inhelder, B., 222, 240, 249, 251, 254, 255
Inoff-Germain, G., 551
Insabella, G. M., 578, 579, 580
International Education Association, 637

Intons-Peterson, M. J., 529
Irgens, L. M., 140
Irvine, J. J., 455
Irwin, A. R., 625
Isabella, R., 420, 426, 427
Israelashvili, R., 430
Iverson, J. M., 369
Ivey, P., 403
Iwamoto, K., 101
Izard, C. E., 49, 398, 401, 401n, 403

J

Jacklin, C. N., 529, 530
Jackson, P. W., 632
Jacobs, F. H., 533
Jacobs, J., 180, 525, 533
Jacobsen, R. B., 576
Jacobson, J. L., 102
Jacobson, S. W., 102
Jacobvitz, D., 593
Jadack, R. A., 499
Jambor, T. W., 599n, 600
James, W., 440
Jameson, S., 104
Jamieson, J. R., 263
Jamin, J. R., 374
Janssens, J. M. A. M., 505, 605
Jarrold, C., 237, 365
Jarvis, P. A., 237
Jencks, C., 332
Jendrek, M. P., 584
Jenkins, J. M., 100, 281, 444
Jensen, A. R., 120, 308, 318n, 328,
    329, 332, 333, 335, 338, 345
Jensen, M. K., 634
Jessor, R., 52
Ji, G., 575
Jiao, S., 575
Jing, Q., 575
Jodl, K. M., 581, 582
Jouen, F., 152
John-Steiner, V., 265
Johnson, C., 210, 580
Johnson, H. M., 154
Johnson, J., 15, 368
Johnson, J. E., 259
Johnson, J. S., 364n, 371
Johnson, L.B., 570
Johnson, M. H., 162, 187, 189,
    279n, 405
Johnson, M. L., 157
Johnson, S. L., 197
Johnson, S. P., 142, 164, 164n, 247
Johnston, J. R., 382, 581
Johnston, L. D., 615
Jones, C., 193n
Jones, C. P., 387
Jones, D. C., 410
Jones, G. P., 471
Jones, J., 634
Jones, K. L., 49, 87
Jones, M. C., 206
Jones, M. G., 633
Jones, N. A., 417
Jones, R. L., 635
Jones, S. S., 402
Jordan, B., 109
Jorgensen, M., 202
Jose, P. E., 569, 569n, 638

Joseph, J. A., 462
Josselson, R., 457
Jouen, F., 152
Jouriles, E. N., 560
Jovanovic, J., 548
Joyner, M. H., 302
Jusczyk, P. W., 153, 154, 367
Jussim, L., 633, 633n
Justice, E. M., 301, 302

K

Kaczala, C. M., 454
Kagan, J., 49, 416, 417, 419, 423n,
    427, 479
Kahn, K. L., 110
Kahn, P. H., Jr., 99, 110, 499, 502,
    506
Kail, R., 275, 275n, 276
Kaiser, S. M., 338
Kaitz, M., 151
Kalakoski, V., 460
Kalb, C., 85
Kaler, S. R., 506
Kallós, D., 529
Kamberk-Kilicci, M., 411
Kamerman, S. B., 29, 117, 587
Kamphaus, R. W., 328
Kandall, S. R., 98
Kaniel, S., 341
Kanner, A. D., 471
Kao, G., 344
Kaplan, B. H., 105
Kaplan, N., 429
Kaplan, P. S., 368
Karabenick, J. D., 388
Karadsheh, R., 376
Karmiloff-Smith, A., 234, 276,
    279n, 280, 364, 365, 389, 390
Karraker, K. H., 531
Kasari, C., 82, 444
Kaslow, N. J., 474
Katchadourian, H., 202, 216
Katz, G. S., 368
Katz, L. F., 602
Kaufman, A. S., 328
Kaufman, N. L., 328
Kavanaugh, R. D., 237, 238
Kawai, M., 419
Kawakami, K., 419
Kawasaki, C., 132
Kaye, K., 225
Kazdin, A. E., 517
Keane, S. P., 606
Kearins, J. M., 266
Kearsley, R. B., 423n
Keating, D. P., 256, 306, 466
Keats, D. M., 465
Keefe, K., 471, 472
Keeney, T. J., 287
Keeton, W. T., 75
Keiding, N., 202
Keil, F. C., 246, 376
Keinan, G., 110
Kellam, S. G., 559
Keller, M., 469
Kelley, M. L., 199, 570
Kellman, P. J., 158, 163, 164
Kelloway, K., 639
Kelly, J. B., 578

Kelly, K. L., 289
Kemp, J. S., 140
Kempe, C. H., 589
Kemper, H. C. G., 202
Kendall-Tackett, K. A., 590
Kendrick, C., 573
Kennedy, J. M., 238
Kennell, J. H., 110
Keogh, B. K., 635
Kermoian, R., 144
Kerns, K. A., 546
Kerr, B. A., 534
Kerr, M., 416
Kessel, F. S., 466, 467n
Kessen, W., 129, 156
Kessler, R., 549
Kestenbaum, R., 164
Kienhorst, C. W. M., 459
Kiernan, B., 293
Kiernan, K. E., 293, 579, 580
Killen, M., 487, 496, 501
Kilner, L. A., 450
Kim, J. M., 490
Kim, K., 229
Kimmerly, N. L., 427
Kinder, M., 625
Kindermann, T., 612, 613
King, C. A., 459
King, N. J., 406
King, R. M., 482
King, S. S., 548
King, T., 111
Kinsman, C. A., 537
Kinzie, J. D., 516
Kipp, E., 155
Kirby, D., 216
Kisilevsky, B. S., 94, 399
Kistner, J., 412
Kitayama, S., 442, 448
Kitchener, K. S., 191
Kitzinger, J., 110
Kitzmann, K. M., 580
Klahr, D., 23, 24, 248, 265, 272,
    274, 384
Klebanov, P. K., 344, 569
Klein, A., 306
Klein, P. J., 230
Klenk, L., 265
Kliewer, W., 406
Klimes-Dougan, B., 412
Kline, M., 581
Klineberg, O., 328
Knight, D. K., 262
Knight, G. J., 262
Knobloch, H., 129n, 130
Knoers, N., 79n
Knox, D., 575n
Kobayashi, Y., 265
Kochanska, G., 48, 416, 426, 427,
    479, 482, 483, 487, 506, 507,
    509, 602
Kochenderfer, B. J., 607, 629
Koestner, R., 412
Kohatsu, E. L., 461
Kohlberg, L., 491, 492, 493, 494,
    494n, 495, 496n, 497, 498, 499,
    500, 504, 505, 518, 539
Kohut, A., 625
Kojima, H., 419
Kolb, S., 130
Kolstad, V., 231
Kolvin, I., 590
Kontiokari, T., 155

Koplas, A. L., 470
Kopp, C. B., 325, 442, 506, 507,
    507n, 508
Korenman, S., 569
Korn, S. J., 420
Korner, A. F., 115
Koslowski, B., 137
Kostelny, K., 562, 591
Koten, S. V., 280
Kotovsky, L., 229
Kovacs, M., 549, 550
Kozberg, S. F., 499
Kozulin, A., 259
Krafft, K., 47, 263
Krakow, J. B., 507, 507n
Kramer, L., 603
Kramer, L. R., 534
Kramer, R., 410, 501
Kranz, R., 209
Kranzler, J. H., 320
Krascum, R. M., 247, 247n
Kraut, R., 624, 625
Kravetz, S., 245
Krebs, D., 466, 495
Krebs, D. L., 499
Kreeger, L., 195
Krehbiel, G., 608
Kreutzer, M. A., 300, 301
Kreutzer, T., 9, 169
Krevans, J., 482
Kroger, J., 458
Kroonenberg, P. M., 425n
Kruger, A. C., 387, 504
Krumhansl, C. L., 153
Ku, L. C., 211
Kuczaj, S. A., II., 372
Kuczynski, L., 485, 487, 506
Kuebli, J., 295, 532, 549
Kuhl, P. K., 143, 153, 367
Kuhn, D., 21, 63, 64, 256, 309,
    309n, 524
Kuhn, L., 194
Kunzinger, E. L., III., 288
Kupersmidt, J. B., 470, 515
Kurdek, L. A., 564, 565
Kurtz-Costes, B., 302
Kwon, Y., 308
Kyratzis, A., 295

L

La Greca, A. M., 406
LaBarre, W. 1954, 174
Lackey, P. N., 526
Ladd, G. W., 474, 516, 602, 606,
    607, 608, 629, 630
Ladd, B. K., 607
Lagattuta, K. H., 409
Lagercrantz, H., 108
Lahey, B. B., 289
Laird, M., 593, 602
Lam, T., 515
Lamaze, F., 109
Lamb, M. E., 403, 408, 425, 430,
    431, 432, 433, 585
Lamborn, S. D., 564, 565, 567
Lamon, S. J., 545n, 547
Lampl, M., 157, 175
Lampman-Petraitis, C., 205
Lancaster, J. B., 558

Landau, R., 135
Landau, S., 46, 47*n*, 260
Lander, E. S., 88, 151
Landesman, S., 340
Landreth, G. L., 587
Landry, S. H., 98, 115
Lane, D. M., 284
Lange, G., 289, 386
Langlois, J. H., 527, 536, 605
Lapointe, A. E., 637
Lapsley, D. K., 255, 256
Larson, D. E., 183
Larson, R., 205, 206, 568, 601
Larson, S. L., 569, 569*n*, 638
Larzelere, R. E., 486
Laub, J. H., 9, 513
Laucht, M., 117
Laudenslager, M. L., 399
Laudet, A. B., 590
Laupa, M., 490
Laursen, B., 470
Lawson, K. R., 284
Lawton, S. Q. C., 284
Lazar, A., 245
Lazar, I., 346
Lazarus, R., 398
Leahy, B. H., 639
Leaper, C., 374, 533, 537
Leavitt, L. A., 113
Lebeaux, D. S., 383
Ledoux, N., 406
Lee, C. L., 420
Lee, D. J., 81
Lee, J. Y., 490
Lee, S. H., 102
Lee, S-Y., 637, 638
Lee, V. E., 347, 548, 627
Leekam, S., 444
Leeman, L. W., 517
Lefkowitz, M. M., 512*n*, 619
Leger, D. W., 134
Lehman, D. R., 256, 451
Lehnert, K. L., 459
Leichtman, M. D., 297, 299
Leinbach, M. D., 511, 524, 526, 540
LeMare, L. J., 466
Lemery, K. S., 416
Lemire, R. J., 86*n*
Lempert, H., 383
Lenneberg, E. H., 188, 363
Lennon, R., 545*n*, 548
Leonard, C., 300, 301
Leonard, L. B., 371
Leonard, M. F., 199
Leong, D. J., 265
Lepecq, J-C., 152
LePore, P. C., 548
Lerman, R. I., 217
Lerner, J. V., 585
Lerner, R. M., 14, 197, 217
LeSieur, K., 602
Lester, B. M., 99, 111, 135*n*, 136, 137, 422
Leung, M-C., 610
LeVay, S., 212
Levesque, R. J. R., 39
Levin, H., 421
Levin, S. R., 620
Levine, C., 492
Levine, L. E., 442
Levine, L. J., 409
LeVine, R. A., 52, 427, 568

LeVine, S. E., 568
Levitt, A. G., 368
Levy, G. D., 526
Levy, Y., 366
Levy-Shiff, R., 430, 561
Lew, W. J. F., 151
Lewis, C., 445
Lewis, C. C., 565
Lewis, G. M., 85
Lewis, J. M., 579
Lewis, L. L., 523
Lewis, M., 30, 168, 398, 404, 407, 419, 431, 441, 442
Lewko, J. H., 180
Lewontin, R., 335
Li, Z., 420, 575, 606
Liau, A. K., 514
Liaw, F., 114
Liaw, F. R., 561
Liben, L. S., 23, 251, 463, 524, 527, 542, 543
Liberty, C., 288
Lickona, T., 489, 491, 495
Lidz, C. S., 341
Liebergott, J. W., 372
Lieberman, M., 494*n*
Liebert, R. M., 485
Liederman, J., 190
Lifschitz, M., 516
Light, P., 252, 253
Lillard, A. S., 237
Limber, S., 403
Limber, S. P., 39
Lin, I-C., 633
Lindenberger, U., 249
Lindmark, G., 99
Linn, F. L., 342
Linn, M. C., 544, 545, 546, 546*n*
Lipsitt, L. P., 139, 140
Liss, M. B., 532, 620
Lissens, W., 86*n*
Litovsky, R. W., 153
Litowitz, B., 377
Little, J. K., 540
Littleton, K., 238
Littman, R. A., 612
Livesley, W. J., 448
Livson, N., 208
Lloyd, B., 388, 537
Lobel, T. E., 540
Lochman, J. E., 608
Locke, J., 12
Lockhart, R. S., 23, 274
Lockheed, M. E., 537
Loeb, S., 347
Loeber, R., 289, 511, 513
Loehlin, J. C., 119, 123, 334, 336, 345, 418*n*
Logan, G., 605
Logan, S., 102*n*, 103
Lohr, M. J., 613, 613*n*
Lombardi, J., 585
Lonigan, C. J., 386
Loomis, L. S., 580
Lorch, E. P., 46, 47*n*
Lord, S., 630
Lorenz, K. Z., 25, 108
Losey, K. M., 455
Losoya, S., 505
Lovell, B. R., 76
Lover, A., 501
Low, J. A., 94
Lozoff, B., 104, 132, 195

Lubart, T. I., 349, 350, 351, 351*n*, 352, 353
Lubinski, D., 545*n*, 546
Lucariello, J., 295, 377
Lucas, D. E., 133
Ludemann, P. M., 163
Luecke-Aleksa, D., 540
Lueptow, L. B., 523
Lueptow, M. B., 523
Luker, K., 215
Lumley, J. M., 103
Lummis, M., 525
Luria, A. R., 257
Luria, Z., 532
Luster, T., 343, 344, 564, 568
Luthar, S., 498
Luthar, S. S., 10, 615
Lutkenhaus, P., 441
Lutz, S. E., 523
Lykken, D. T., 335*n*
Lynam, D. R., 513
Lynskey, M. T., 99
Lyon, T. D., 300
Lyons-Ruth, K., 427, 429
Lyoo, K., 50, 288
Lytton, H., 532, 535

M

Maccoby, E. E., 421, 529, 530, 537, 540, 565, 567, 582
Macfarlane, J. W., 208, 327, 328
Mackey, M. C., 110
MacKinnon, C. E., 537, 579
MacKinnon-Lewis, C., 573, 606
MacLean, W. E., 134
Macleod, H., 597
MacMillan, D. L., 635
Macrides, R., 531
MacWhinney, B., 23, 24, 384
Madden, C. M., 377
Madon, S., 633, 633*n*
Madrona, M. M., 111
Maggs, J. L., 173, 217, 587
Magnuson, K., 461
Magnusson, D., 63, 206, 207, 208
Maguire, M., 410
Magura, S., 590
Mahapatra, M., 503
Mahn, H., 265
Mahoney, J. L., 60, 627
Main, M., 424, 425, 429, 429*n*
Maioni, T. L., 599*n*
Makin, J. E., 99, 100
Makin, J. W., 152
Malatesta, C. Z., 403, 407, 549
Malatesta-Magai, C. Z., 401
Malina, R. M., 174*n*, 175*n*, 177, 178, 178*n*, 179, 180, 185, 192, 194
Malloy, M. H., 140
Maloney, M., 209
Maluso, D., 534
Mandler, J. M., 167, 230, 231, 231*n*, 234, 236, 246, 291, 293
Mange, A. P., 75*n*, 78, 79
Mange, E. J., 75*n*, 78, 79
Mangelsdorf, S. C., 415, 428
Manheim, L. A., 503
Manke, B. A., 541

Manlove, E. E., 155
Manly, J., 589
Mannle, S., 387
Mant, C. M., 490
Maqsud, M., 496
Maratsos, M. P., 364, 379, 380, 381, 384, 385
Marchman, V. A., 384
Marcia, J. E., 457
Marcus, G. F., 382, 385
Marcus, J., 225, 551
Marentette, P. F., 368
Mareschal, D., 279
Marini, Z., 258
Markman, E. M., 255, 373, 378
Markovits, H., 256
Marks, H., 342
Marks, R. A., 342
Markstrom-Adams, C., 461
Markus, H. R., 442, 448
Marlier, L., 152
Marolla, F., 345, 345*n*
Marsh, D. T., 466
Marsh, H. W., 449, 450, 451
Marshall, E., 89
Marshall, R., 639
Marshall, T. R., 417
Marshall, W. A., 179*n*
Martin, C. L., 23, 455, 523, 524, 525, 527, 536, 540, 541, 542, 542*n*
Martin, J. A., 56, 542, 565
Martin, J. C., 98
Martin, R. M., 142
Martin, R. P., 419
Martlew, M., 239, 239*n*
Martorell, R., 198
Marzolf, D. P., 240
Masataka, N., 367
Mascolo, M. F., 404
Mason, C. A., 614
Mason, D. A., 634
Mason, M. G., 497
Massey, C. M., 243
Masten, A. S., 10, 111, 331
Mastropieri, M. A., 635
Masur, E. F., 284, 374
Matas, L., 431
Matheny, A. P., Jr., 419
Matheson, C. C., 236, 599
Mathews, S. G., 580
Matsumoto, D., 407
Mattock, A., 163*n*
Mattson, S. N., 100
Matute-Bianche, M. E., 461
Maurer, D., 189
Mauro, J. A., 414, 415*n*
Mayberry, R. I., 363
Mayes, L. C., 99, 112, 144
Maynard, R., 586
Mays, V. M., 516
Mazur, E., 579
Mazzocco, M. M. M., 77
McAdoo, H. P., 564, 571
McAnarney, E. R., 185
McBride, J., 104
McCabe, A., 246, 297, 339, 377
McCall, R. B., 142, 328, 330, 345
McCartney, K., 122, 123, 418, 433
McCarton, C. M., 115
McClaskey, C. L., 606
McClelland, J. L., 279
McClenahan, E. L., 613, 613*n*

McClintic, S., 404, 449, 453
McConaghy, M. J., 212, 539
McCormick, S. E., 189
McCoy, J. K., 420, 574
McCracken, J., 550
McCune, L., 189, 236, 373
McElroy, S. W., 215
McGee, G., 85
McGee, L. M., 304n, 305
McGillicuddy-De Lisi, A. V., 504
McGilly, K., 288
McGinnis, E., 586
McGregor, J. A., 112
McGroarty, M., 393
McGue, M., 334, 334n, 335n
McGuffin, P., 120n
McGuinness, D., 190
McHale, S. M., 535, 536, 541, 548, 573, 574
McKenna, M. C., 131, 140
McKenry, P. C., 578n
McKenzie, B. E., 161
McKenzie, P., 615
McKie, M., 83n
McKie, R., 89
McKusick, V. A., 76n, 79n, 80
McLanahan, S., 580, 581
McLean, D. E., 105
McLeod, J. D., 562, 569
McLeod, P. J., 368
McLoyd, V. C., 37, 38, 349, 569, 602
McMahon, C. A., 84
McMahon, T. J., 615
McManus, I. C., 189
McManus, K., 111
McMurphy, M. P., 197
McNamee, S., 504
McNeill, D., 283
MCR Vitamin Study Research Group, 104, 104n
Mead, G. H., 448
Mead, M., 109, 528
Mead, N. A., 637
Meadow-Orlans, K. P., 263
Mebert, C. J., 415
Meeus, W., 206, 451
Mehler, J., 153, 367
Mehlmadrona, L., 111
Meilman, P. W., 457
Meisels, S. J., 561
Meister, C., 265
Melli, M. S., 576
Melnikow, J., 116
Melson, G. F., 548
Meltzoff, A. N., 143, 143n, 164, 166, 230, 232, 373, 444
Menashri, J., 540
Mendelson, B. K., 207
Mendelson, M. J., 207
Menozzi, P., 338
Menyuk, P., 372
Meredith, N. V., 184
Mergendoller, J. R., 305
Merriman, J., 274
Mervielde, I., 197
Mervis, C. B., 365, 378
Meyer-Bahlburg, H. F. L., 212
Meyers, C., 82n, 83
Meyers, T., 400
Miceli, P. J., 420
Michael, R. T., 210, 212
Michel, C., 101

Micheli, L. J., 130
Midgley, C., 630
Milberger, S., 289
Miles, C., 522
Milgram, N. A., 10
Milich, R., 46, 47n
Miller, J., 569
Miller, J. G., 498, 502, 503
Miller, J. M., 98
Miller, K. F., 251
Miller, L. S., 623
Miller, L. T., 276, 321
Miller, N. B., 18, 25, 235, 257, 592
Miller, P. A., 406, 412, 505
Miller, P. H., 285, 300, 443, 466, 467n
Miller, P. J., 236, 264, 406, 442, 443n
Miller, P. M., 568
Miller, S. A., 46, 48, 55
Miller, S. J., 285
Miller-Jones, D., 315
Mills, D. L., 188, 363
Mills, R., 484
Milner, J., 593
Minard, K. L., 130
Mindolovich, C., 377
Miner, J. L., 410
Minick, N., 628
Minkler, M., 584
Mintz, J., 442
Mintz, M., 442
Mischel, W., 485, 508, 509
Mistry, J., 290
Miyake, K., 425
Mize, J., 474, 602, 608
Moely, B. E., 289
Moen, P., 583
Moerk, E. L., 359
Moffitt, T. E., 513
Mohanty, A. K., 392
Mokros, H. R., 459
Molen, M. W. van der, 285
Molenaar, P. C. M., 280
Moll, I., 267
Mollnow, E., 98, 101
Mondimore, F. M., 213
Money, J., 82, 83n, 530, 531
Monsour, A., 447
Montemayor, R., 447
Montiero, C. A., 196, 196n
Moon, C., 154, 367
Moon, S. M., 353
Moore, B. D., 99
Moore, D., 462
Moore, D. S., 368
Moore, E., 337
Moore, G. A., 573
Moore, J. B., 180
Moore, K. A., 211, 215
Moore, K. L., 75, 83n, 86n, 87n, 90, 90n, 91n, 92, 93, 95n, 97n, 98
Moore, M. K., 143, 143n, 230
Moore, M. T., 351
Moore, R. W., 159
Moore, S. G., 137
Moorehouse, M. J., 584
Moran, G., 426, 427
Moran, G. F., 11
Moran, T. J., 495
Morelli, G., 132, 403
Morford, M., 361, 361n, 373
Morgan, J. L., 367, 385

Morgan, M., 536
Morgan, S. P., 216
Morgane, P. J., 104
Mori, L., 320
Morikawa, H., 374
Moroney, J. T., 99
Morrison, D. R., 215, 638
Morrone, C., 155
Morrongiello, B. A., 153
Mortimore, P., 626
Morton, J., 162, 163
Mosher, M., 511
Moshman, D., 256, 456, 457
Moss, L., 441
Moss, M., 131
Mosteller, F., 626
Mounts, N. S., 611
Mueller, E. C., 599, 603
Muir, D. W., 151, 159, 402, 402n
Mullally, P. R., 345, 442
Mullen, M. K., 297
Mullis, I. V. S., 637n
Mumme, D. L., 398, 403, 404, 409
Munakata, Y., 235
Munro, D., 608
Munro, G., 457, 608
Murett-Wagstaff, S., 137
Murphy-Berman, V., 39
Murray, A. D., 134, 368, 537
Murray, C., 332
Murray, C. I., 245
Murray, H. W., 346n
Murray, L., 400, 509
Mussen, P. H., 206, 485, 496, 499
Musser, L. M., 603
Muthukrisna, N., 456
Muzio, J. N., 133, 133n
Muzzonigro, P. G., 213

Nachtigall, R. D., 84
Nagell, K., 369
Naigles, L. G., 376
Najarian, P., 168
Nakagawa, N., 377
Nakatsuji, N., 85
Namy, L. L., 369
Nánez, J., Sr., 157
Narvaez, D., 497, 499
Nash, S. C., 524
Nastasi, B. K., 623, 624
Nathanson, R., 299
National Association for the Education of Young Children, 434, 435n, 586n
National Center for Health Statistics, 194
Naus, M. J., 288
Needham, A., 229, 229n
Neiderman, D., 228
Neisser, U., 330, 331
Nelson, C. A., 228, 417
Nelson, K., 50, 295, 296, 372, 372n, 374, 375
Nelson, M. A., 102n
Nelson, V. L., 328
Nelson-Le Gall, S. A., 490
Nemer, K. M., 634
Neppl, T. K., 537

Nesdale, A. R., 390
Nesse, R. M., 558
Netley, C. T., 82, 83n
Neubauer, A. C., 320
Neumärker, K., 209
Neville, H. J., 188, 363
Newborg, J., 178n
Newcomb, A. F., 470, 470n, 604, 606
Newcomb, M. D., 615
Newcombe, N., 242, 251, 296, 541, 547
Newcombe, P. A., 181
Newman, B. S., 213
Newman, J. D., 136
Newman, L. S., 237, 290, 463
Newmann, F. M., 342
Newnham, J. P., 86n
Newport, E. L., 234, 363, 364n
Newson, E., 261
Newson, J., 261
Newton, N., 109
Newton, R. R., 615
Ng'andu, N., 569
Niccols, G. A., 547
NICHD Early Child Care Research Network, 433
Nicholls, A. L., 238, 453
Nichols, R. C., 418n
Nicoladis, E., 392
Nicolopoulou, A., 237
Nidorf, J. F., 461
Niemelä, M., 155
Nilsson, L., 91n, 93
Nippold, M. A., 377
Nisbett, R., 332
Nisbett, R. E., 256
Noam, G. G., 460
Noddings, N., 536
Noguchi, M., 85
Nolen-Hoeksema, S., 550
Noom, M. J., 206
Nottelmann, E. D., 205, 450
Nourse, C. B., 103
Novak, G. P., 288
Novy, M. J., 112
Nowakowski, R. S., 93
Nowell, A., 546
Noyes, C. R., 300
Nucci, L. P., 490, 496, 501, 502, 503
Nuckolls, K. B., 105
Nugent, J. K., 111, 137
Nurmi, J., 460
Nuttall, R. L., 323, 547

Oakes, J., 634
Oakes, L. M., 229, 230, 234
Oakland, T., 338
Oates, R. K., 199
Oberg, C. N., 34
O'Boyle, C., 540
O'Brien, J. G., 198
O'Brien, M., 524
O'Callaghan, M. J., 190
Ochs, E., 369, 389
Ochse, R., 349
O'Connor, B. P., 457
O'Connor, C., 461

Redanz, N. J., 367
Rees, J., 426
Rees, M., 202
Reese, E., 297
Reese, H. W., 290
Reeve, R. A., 282, 307
Reid, J. B., 560
Reifman, A., 137
Reimer, J., 498
Reinhardt, L. C., 620
Reinisch, J. M., 531
Reis, S. M., 624
Reiser, J., 152
Reiser, L. W., 203
Reisman, J. E., 135n
Reite, M. R., 399
Reiter, S., 56, 57n
Remez, L., 111
Renninger, K. A., 613
Renwick, S. M., 564
Renzetti, C. M., 338
Renzulli, J., 349
Repacholi, B. M., 408, 409
Repke, J. T., 104
Resnick, G., 580
Resnick, L. B., 307
Rest, J. R., 493, 494, 495, 497, 499
Revelle, G. L., 388
Reyna, V. F., 293, 294
Reynolds, A. J., 347
Reynolds, C. R., 332, 338
Reznick, J. S., 236, 373, 373n, 416, 545n
Rhoades, K., 568
Rholes, W. S., 463
Rhymes, J. P., 199
Ricard, M., 411
Ricciardelli, L. A., 392
Riccio, C. A., 288
Ricco, R. B., 247, 309
Rice, C., 248
Rice, J. K., 577
Rice, K., 373
Rice, M. L., 617, 618, 621
Richards, B. S., 495
Richards, D. D., 243
Richards, L., 577
Richards, M. H., 584
Richards, M. K., 196, 196n
Richards-Colocino, N., 615
Richardson, G. A., 99, 137
Richgels, D. J., 304n, 305
Richman, A. L., 568
Rickel, A. U., 36
Ridderinkhof, K. R., 285
Ridley-Johnson, R., 130
Rieser-Danner, L. A., 605
Rigler, D., 589
Rijsdijk, F. V., 320
Riley, E. P., 100
Riley, W. T., 100
Risemberg, R., 302
Risley, T. R., 344, 374, 386
Ritts, V., 605
Roach, M. A., 113
Roazzi, A., 248, 253, 253n
Robert, M., 253
Roberton, M. A., 177, 178n, 180
Roberts, D., 571
Roberts, J. E., 155
Roberts, R. J., Jr., 251
Robinson, B. E., 535
Robinson, J., 487

Robinson, M., 248
Robinson, T. N., 209
Rochat, P., 149, 149n
Roche, A. F., 185
Rock, S. L., 344
Rodin, J., 209
Rodriguez, M. L., 508
Roe, K. V., 169
Roffwarg, H. P., 133, 133n
Rogers, K., 639
Rogers, L., 209
Rogers, S. J., 446
Roggman, L. A., 433, 605
Rogoff, B., 26, 27, 251, 252, 260, 261, 262, 266, 267, 286, 290, 602
Rogow, S., 160
Rohner, E. C., 568
Rohner, R. P., 568
Roker, D., 212
Roland, A., 407
Rollins, K. B., 245
Romans, S. M., 82
Rome-Flanders, T., 369
Romney, D. M., 532, 535
Rook, K. S., 574
Roopnarine, J. L., 237, 430, 603
Rosa, R. W., 104
Rose, A. J., 473
Rose, H., 542
Rose, J. L., 152, 153n
Rose, R. J., 81
Rose, R. M., 531
Rose, S. A., 142, 161, 162n, 418
Rose, S. P., 187, 191
Rosen, A. B., 245
Rosen, K. S., 427
Rosen, W. D., 408
Rosenberg, D. R., 50
Rosenberg, M., 448
Rosengren, K. S., 180, 240, 244, 260, 262
Rosenshine, B., 265
Rosenstein, D., 151
Rosenthal, J. A., 576
Ross, D. F., 551
Ross, H. S., 599
Ross, R. P., 620
Rotatori, A. F., 590
Rotenberg, K. J., 462
Rothbart, M. K., 405, 412, 414, 415, 415n, 416, 418, 533
Rothbaum, F., 427
Rotheram-Borus, M. J., 213
Rothman, K. J., 104
Rousseau, J. J., 12
Rovee-Collier, C. K., 138, 139, 140, 142, 230, 274
Rovet, J., 82
Rowe, D. C., 345
Roy, T., 333
Royal College of Obstetricians and Gynecologists, 94
Royce, J. M., 346n
Rozin, P., 245
Rubin, J. Z., 532
Rubin, K. H., 8, 331, 417, 420, 466, 470, 529, 575, 599n, 600, 600n, 604, 606, 608
Ruble, D. N., 23, 62, 63n, 203, 450, 453, 455, 463, 523, 527, 533, 533n, 536, 540, 561
Ruff, H. A., 151, 284, 416
Ruffman, T., 228, 256, 445

Rumbaugh, D. M., 360
Runco, M. A., 350, 351, 352
Russell, G., 526
Russell, J. A., 409
Rutherford, E., 496, 499
Rutter, M., 10, 89, 168, 169n, 426, 550
Ruzany, N., 455
Rydell, A., 199
Ryynänen, M., 80, 83

S

Saarni, C., 398, 403, 404, 406, 407, 409, 410, 545n, 548
Sacks, C. H., 305
Sadeh, A., 131
Sadler, T. W., 91
Saelens, B. E., 198
Saffran, J. R., 367
Safyer, A. W., 639
Sahni, R., 133
Sais, E., 392
Salapatek, P., 159n, 161n
Salidis, J., 371
Saller, D. N., Jr., 86n
Salmon, D., 474
Samenow, S. E., 514
Sameroff, A. J., 10, 344, 559
Sampson, R. J., 9, 513
Samson, L. F., 102n
Samuels, M., 101, 103, 110
Samuels, N., 101, 103, 110
Sanchez, R. P., 232n
Sandefur, G., 580
Sanders, O., 591
Sanders, P., 374, 533
Sanders, S. G., 215
Sanderson, M., 140
Sandman, C. A., 141
Sandqvist, K., 529, 529n
Sansavini, A., 153
Sanson, A., 416
Santini, D. L., 105
Sapiro, C. M., 502, 503
Sarason, I. G., 398
Sargeant, M. P., 120n
Sattler, J. M., 324
Saudino, K., 416
Saum, C. A., 99
Saunders, D. M., 85
Savage-Rumbaugh, E. S., 362
Savin-Williams, R. C., 213, 471, 612
Saxe, G. B., 26, 306, 307n
Saywitz, K. J., 299
Scaramella, L. V., 574
Scarr, S., 6, 36, 119, 120, 122, 123, 334n, 336, 337, 344, 345, 418n, 433, 576, 587
Schaal, B., 152
Schachar, R., 288
Schachter, F. F., 418
Schafer, W. D., 373, 427
Schaffer, H. R., 576
Scharre, J. E., 99
Schauble, L., 309
Schiavi, R. C., 83
Schiefele, U., 456, 456n
Schieffelin, B. B., 369, 389

Rumbaugh, D. M., 360
Schifter, T., 50
Schiller, M., 428
Schlegel, A., 203, 204, 205, 206
Schliemann, A. D., 266
Schmidt, K. L., 117, 485
Schmidt, M. H., 117
Schneider, B. H., 606
Schneider, W., 285, 290, 292, 294, 295, 301, 302
Schnell, J. V., 481
Schnur, E., 347
Scholl, T. O., 104, 215
Scholnick, E. K., 285, 286
Schonfeld, D. J., 245
Schothorst, P. F., 113
Schroeder, C., 197
Schroeder, K. A., 534
Schubert, D. S. P., 537, 572
Schubert, H. J. P., 537, 572
Schuler, G. D., 72
Schultz, L. H., 473
Schultz, M. C., 372
Schumm, J. S., 635
Schunk, D. H., 302, 456
Schuster, B., 453
Schwanenflugel, P. J., 300, 321
Schwartz, S. S., 623
Scott, D. T., 247
Scott, P. M., 57, 485
Scribner, S., 330
Scruggs, T. E., 635
Sears, R. R., 421
Sebald, H., 613
Seefeldt, C., 347
Seeto, D., 490
Segal, N. L., 399, 615
Seidman, E., 631
Seifer, R., 425, 427, 428
Seitz, V., 216, 340
Seligman, M. E. P., 140
Seligmann, J., 209
Selman, F. L., 465
Selman, R. L., 464, 465, 465n, 466, 468, 469, 473, 495, 496n, 504
Senghas, A., 378
Serafica, F. C., 466
Serbin, L. A., 525, 525n, 526, 527, 529, 536, 537, 540, 549
Serdula, M. K., 195
Sermon, K., 86n
Sever, J. L., 102n
Shagle, S. C., 459
Shahar, S., 11
Shainess, N., 203
Shalala, D. E., 199
Shanahan, M. J., 562, 569
Shannon, D. C., 194
Shapiro, S., 105
Sharp, K., 245
Shatz, M., 243
Shavelson, R. J., 449
Shedler, J., 614
Sheley, J. F., 515
Shepardson, D. P., 534
Sherif, M., 609
Sherman, A., 288, 329
Shields, P. J., 139
Shiffrin, R. M., 23, 272
Shiller, V., 403
Shiloh, S., 81, 83
Shinn, M. W., 13
Shipman, G., 347
Shoda, Y., 508, 509

Short, R. V., 75
Shukla, D., 255
Shulman, C., 431, 446
Shure, M. B., 474
Shurtleff, D. B., 86*n*
Shweder, R. A., 36, 52, 503
Shyi, G., 142
Sidle, A. L., 245
Siegel, A. W., 251
Siegel, B., 635
Siegel, D. H., 289
Siegler, R. S., 14, 24, 25, 63, 64,
    235, 243, 248, 257, 265, 272,
    279, 281, 281*n*, 282, 288, 305,
    307, 316, 316*n*, 495
Sigman, M., 82, 142, 195, 444, 446
Sigman, M. D., 114
Signiorelli, N., 620
Signorella, M. L., 23, 524, 527, 541,
    542
Signorielli, N., 622
Sigvardsson, S., 576, 576*n*
Sikora, D. M., 66
Silva, P. A., 416, 417, 419, 513
Silverberg, S. B., 567
Silverman, W. K., 406
Simmons, R. G., 207, 630, 631,
    631*n*
Simon, R., 324, 576
Simon, T., 316, 317
Simons, R. L., 513, 562, 579, 580,
    589
Simonton, D. K., 351
Simourd, L., 462
Simpson, P. M., 98
Simpson, S. A., 79*n*
Singer, D. G., 237, 621
Singer, J. L., 237, 621
Singer, L. T., 141, 141*n*, 332
Sitarenios, G., 547
Sitskoorn, M. M., 229
Sivard, R. L., 35*n*
Sjaastad, J., 569
Skeels, H., 336
Skinner, B. F., 358, 359
Skinner, E. A., 453, 455
Skinner, J. D., 197
Skodak, M., 336
Skouteris, H., 161
Slaby, R. G., 517, 539, 618, 619,
    622, 623*n*
Slater, A. M., 141, 163, 163*n*
Slobin, D., 366, 382, 384
Slomkowski, C., 62
Slone, D., 105
Slotkin, T. A., 108
Slowiaczek, M. L., 28, 636
Smetana, J. G., 490, 501, 503
Smilansky, S., 245
Smiley, P. A., 284, 453
Smiley, S. S., 284
Smith, B. A., 151
Smith, C. L., 390
Smith, H., 101
Smith, I. D., 451
Smith, J., 10, 526, 618
Smith, K. E., 115
Smith, L. B., 30, 146, 373
Smith, M. C., 462, 599*n*
Smith, P. K., 601, 602, 607
Smith, R. A., 508
Smith, R. S., 9, 10, 115, 117
Smith, S., 347

Smitsman, A. W., 229
Smyth, R., 384
Snarey, J., 497, 498
Snidman, N., 417
Snyder, L., 531
So, L. K. H., 371
Society for Research in Child De-
    velopment, 65, 66*n*
Sodian, B., 443, 444*n*
Soken, H. H., 166
Solanto, M., 288
Solimano, G., 195
Solnit, A. J., 199
Solomon, J., 424, 584
Solomonica-Levi, D., 446
Somberg, D. R., 514
Somerville, S. C., 286
Sommers-Flanagan, J., 620
Sommers-Flanagan, R., 620
Sommerville, J., 11
Sonenstein, F. L., 211
Song, Y-K., 375
Sonnenschein, S., 388, 389
Sontag, C. W., 328
Sophian, C., 248, 306
Sorce, J., 408
Sorell, G. T., 499
Sørenson, T. I. A., 195
Sosa, R., 110, 295
Sostek, A. M., 188
Soussignan, R., 152
Southern, W. T., 353
Spade, J., 634
Spätling, G., 104
Spätling, L., 104
Spearman, C., 317, 319
Speece, M. W., 245
Speer, J. R., 301
Speicher, B., 497
Spelke, E. S., 164, 166, 229, 234
Speltz, M. L., 428
Spence, M. J., 94, 154, 368, 538
Spencer, H. C., 263
Spencer, J., 148, 263
Sperry, L., 407
Spindler, G. D., 204
Spinetta, J., 589
Spirito, A., 459
Spitz, R., 426
Spivack, G., 474
Spock, B., 132
Spuhl, S. T., 260, 262
Sroufe, A., 431
Sroufe, L. A., 9, 169, 401, 402, 404,
    428, 431, 433, 593
St. James-Roberts, I., 136*n*
St. Peters, M., 47
Stack, D. M., 151
Stahl, S. A., 305
Stampnitzky, J. R., 79
Stange, T., 535, 536*n*
Stankov, L., 333
Stanley, J. C., 546
Stanley-Hagan, M. M., 577
Stanowicz, L., 385
Staples, R., 570
Stark, L. J., 21, 211
Starkey, P., 306
Stattin, H., 63, 206, 207, 208
Staub, E., 592
Stechler, G., 111
Steele, C. D., 85, 86*n*
Steele, K. H., 180

Steelman, L. C., 572
Stein, J. H., 203
Stein, Z., 104, 194
Steinberg, A. G., 263
Steinberg, L., 206, 451, 564, 567,
    568, 587, 611, 615, 639
Steiner, J. E., 138, 151, 152
Stenberg, C., 402, 403
Stephan, C. W., 605
Stephens, B. R., 162
Stern, M., 531
Sternberg, K. J., 433
Sternberg, R. J., 57, 58*n*, 316, 321,
    322, 324, 330, 338, 339, 349,
    350, 351*n*, 352, 353, 592
Stevens, J. H., 571
Stevens-Simon, C., 211
Stevenson, H. W., 452, 525, 604,
    637, 638
Stevenson, M. R., 581
Stevenson, R., 375
Stevenson-Hinde, J., 419
Steward, E. A., 299
Stewart, D. A., 82
Stewart, S. L., 417, 606
Stice, E., 565
Stifter, C. A., 433
Stiles, J., 188, 189
Stipek, D. J., 404, 442, 449, 450,
    453, 463, 627, 628
Stoch, M. B., 195
Stock, J. R., 178*n*
Stocker, C. M., 573, 574
Stockman, M. E., 375
Stodolsky, S. S., 632
Stoel-Gammon, C., 368, 370
Stokes, T. F., 27
Stone, C. A., 628
Stone, L., 11
Stone, R. K., 418
Stoneman, Z., 420, 537, 570, 574
Stormshak, E. A., 573
Stouthamer-Loeber, M., 513
Strain, P. S., 613
Strasburger, V. C., 211
Strassberg, Z., 485, 516
Strauss, M. S., 306
Strauss, S., 266
Streissguth, A. P., 98, 99, 100
Strickland, C. J., 459
Strober, M., 550
Strosberg, R., 387
Strosnider, K., 85
Strutt, G. F., 284, 285*n*
Stunkard, A. J., 192, 195
Styfco, S. J., 37, 349
Suarez-Orozco, M. M., 344
Subbotsky, E. V., 243
Subrahmanyam, K., 339, 547, 625
Suchindran, C., 210
Sullivan, H. S., 471
Sullivan, K., 446
Sullivan, M. L., 211
Sullivan, M. W., 398, 404, 407
Sullivan, S. A., 193*n*, 194
Sulzby, E., 304
Suomi, S., 598
Super, C. M., 131, 147
Sureau, C., 84
Surratt, H. L., 99
Susman, A., 566
Sutterfield, S. J., 496
Suzuki, L. A., 332, 335, 339, 353, 636

Swaminathan, S., 623, 624
Swanson, H. L., 321
Swayze, V. W., 100
Szeminska, A., 222, 251
Szepkouski, G. M., 286, 286*n*
Szinovacz, M. E., 584

T

Taddio, A., 151, 151*n*
Tager-Flusberg, H., 364, 382, 383,
    390, 446
Takahashi, K., 132, 425
Takahira, S., 547
Tamang, B. L., 407
Tamis-LeMonda, C. S., 56, 262, 369
Tanner, J. M., 175, 177, 179*n*, 180,
    182, 183, 184, 185, 190, 192,
    198, 200, 201, 202
Tardif, T., 375
Taska, L. S., 451
Tasker, F., 576, 579
Tassabehji, M. K., 365
Tate, C. S., 388, 388*n*
Tauber, M. A., 537
Taylor, C. L., 377
Taylor, J., 497
Taylor, J. A., 140
Taylor, J. H., 494, 497
Taylor, M., 237, 300, 444, 466,
    466*n*, 526, 526*n*
Taylor, M. C., 538
Taylor, M. G., 526
Taylor, R., 571
Tebbutt, J., 590
Tedder, J. L., 137
Teele, D. W., 155
Telesford, M., 67
Temple, C. M., 82, 347, 547
Temple, J. M., 347
Tennes, K., 134
Terman, L., 317, 330, 330*n*
Terrace, H. S., 360
Teti, D. M., 400, 425, 427, 428
Thach, B. T., 140
Thakwray, D. E., 210
Thapar, A., 81
Tharp, R. G., 340, 628, 629, 629*n*
Thatcher, R. W., 187, 191
Thelen, E., 14, 30, 130, 145, 146,
    147, 148
Thoman, E. B., 130, 131, 133, 139
Thomas, A., 9, 412, 414, 415*n*, 420
Thomas, D., 346, 347, 349, 353
Thomas, R. B., 135
Thompson, J. M., 550
Thompson, R. A., 67, 117, 134,
    293, 329, 401, 403, 405, 425,
    428, 431
Thorndike, R. L., 324
Thorne, B., 535, 541
Thornton, M., 571
Thurstone, L., 317, 319
Tienda, M., 344
Tietjen, A., 498
Tinsley, B. R., 430
Tisak, J., 501, 502
Tizard, B., 426
Tobey, A. E., 299
Toda, S., 419

Todd, C. M., 289
Tolan, P. H., 577
Tolarova, M., 104
Tolson, T. F. J., 571
Tomada, G., 606
Tomasello, M., 360, 361, 361*n*, 362, 362*n*, 364, 366, 368, 369, 378, 380, 380*n*, 383, 386, 387, 387*n*
Tomchin, E. M., 353
Toner, I. J., 508
Toner, M. A., 608
Tong, S., 75
Toomey, K. A., 108
Torff, B., 323
Torney-Purta, J., 245
Torrance, E. P., 350, 350*n*, 352
Toth, S. L., 9, 545*n*, 549, 592, 592*n*
Touwen, B. C. L., 129, 130
Tower, R. B., 621
Townsend, M. A. R., 467
Trause, M. A., 403
Travis, L. L., 385
Treiman, R., 305
Tremblay, R. E., 551
Trent, K., 571
Trevethan, S. D., 514
Triandis, H. C., 36, 52
Trickett, P. K., 590
Trivers, R. L., 480
Tronick, E. Z., 135, 137, 399, 401, 403, 427
Tröster, H., 160
Trowell, J., 590
Tschann, J. M., 581
Tse, A. M., 98
Tubbs, M. E., 605
Tudge, J. R. H., 265
Tulviste, P., 26, 27, 260, 266, 267
Tunmer, W. E., 390
Turiel, E., 481, 482, 490, 499, 501, 503
Turk, J., 80
Turkheimer, E., 122
Turner, P. J., 526, 532, 535, 536
Tuss, P., 455
Tyc, V. L., 50
Tzuriel, D., 341

U

Udry, J. R., 210
Uhari, M., 155
Ullian, D. Z., 540
Underwood, K., 607
Underwood, M. K., 407, 607
Unger, R., 195, 522
Updegraff, K. A., 536, 548
Urberg, K. A., 540, 610
Uribe, F. M. T., 568
U.S. Bureau of the Census, 34, 99, 392, 432, 459*n*, 526, 534, 534*n*, 577, 583, 584, 586*n*, 622, 639
U.S. Centers for Disease Control, 214
U.S. Department of Education, 637
U.S. Department of Health and Human Services, 34, 106*n*, 181,
195, 198, 211, 211*n*, 459, 588, 589, 590, 593, 614, 614*n*
U.S. Department of Justice, 511
U.S. Department of Labor, 559
Usmiani, S., 207
Uttal, D. H., 239, 251
Uz̆giris, I. C., 326

V

Vachon, R., 256
Vaidyanathan, R., 382, 383
Valdés, G., 52
Valdez, R., 196
Valencia, R. R., 332, 335, 353
Valian, V. V., 379, 381, 385
Valkenberg, P. M., 621
Vallance, D. D., 410
van Balen, F., 84
Van de Walle, G., 164
van den Boom, D. C., 420, 428
van der Voort, T. H., 621
Van Dyke, D. C., 82
van Engeland, H., 113
van Geert, P., 30
van IJzendoorn, M. H., 135, 425*n*, 426, 427, 428, 428*n*, 429, 430
Vandell, D. L., 472, 587, 599, 603
Vandenberg, B., 137, 600*n*
VandenBerg, K. A., 137
Vandereycken, W., 197
Vanfossen, B., 634
Vangelisti, A. L., 561
Vartanian, L. R., 255, 256
Vasen, A., 407
Vasta, R., 359
Vasudev, J., 498
Vaughn, B. E., 415, 425, 427, 507, 507*n*
Vaughn, S., 635
Veldhuis, J. D., 157
Venkatesh, A., 625
Ventura, S. J., 106*n*, 214
Vergnaud, G., 259
Verhulst, F. C., 575
Vernon, P. A., 276, 320, 321, 333
Vernon-Feagans, L., 155
Versluis-den Bieman, H. J. M., 575
Vibbert, M., 369
Vihman, M. M., 368, 370, 371
Vinchur, A. J., 504
Vinden, P. G., 444
Vinovskis, M. A., 11, 36
Visher, J. S., 583
Vitalari, N. P., 625
Voelkl, K. E., 35, 545, 545*n*, 548, 632, 639
Vogel, D. A., 98, 531
Vohr, B. R., 112, 113
Volling, B. L., 155, 573
Volterra, V., 365
von Eye, A., 426
Vorhees, C. V., 98, 101, 102*n*
Voyer, D., 546
Voyer, S., 546
Vuchinich, S., 581
Vurpillot, E., 286
Vygotsky, L. S., 26, 221, 261, 262, 263, 265, 507, 603, 634

W

Waas, G. A., 509
Wachs, T. D., 195, 326, 415
Wackman, D., 620
Waddell, S., 290
Waddington, C. H., 121
Wagner, B. M., 454
Wagner, M. E., 537, 572
Wagner, R. K., 330
Wahlsten, D., 121, 121*n*
Wainryb, C., 503
Walberg, H. J., 627
Walder, L. O., 512*n*
Waldman, I. D., 335, 337
Wales, R., 239
Walk, R. D., 157
Walker, D., 344
Walker, E., 473, 474
Walker, L., 466, 494, 495, 497, 498, 499, 514
Walker, S., 526
Walker-Andrews, A. S., 154, 408
Wallace, C. S., 191
Wallerstein, J. S., 578, 579
Walton, G. E., 166
Wang, P. P., 365
Wang, Q., 297, 363, 365
Wanska, S. K., 386
Wapner, R. J., 86*n*
Ward, C., 261
Ward, L. M., 210
Ward, S., 620
Wardle, J., 197
Wark, G. R., 499
Warkentin, V., 442
Warren, A. R., 388, 388*n*
Warren, J. R., 548
Warren, M. P., 160, 205
Wartella, E., 620
Wartner, U. G., 425
Wasserstein, S., 406
Waterman, A. S., 457, 458, 460
Waters, E., 402, 424
Waters, K. A., 212
Waters, M. C., 344
Watkins, C., 504
Watkins, W. E., 195
Watkinson, B., 99, 100
Watson, D. J., 305
Watson, J. B., 19
Watson, K. S., 599*n*, 600
Watson, M., 445
Waxler, C. Z., 57, 485
Waxman, S. R., 369, 378
Webb, N. M., 634
Weber-Fox, C. M., 363
Wechsler, D., 325
Wehren, A., 377
Weinbaum, E., 253
Weinberg, C. R., 89
Weinberg, M., 212
Weinberg, M. K., 401
Weinberg, R. A., 119, 334*n*, 336, 337, 345, 576
Weinberger, J., 412
Weiner, S., 230
Weinert, F. E., 453
Weinraub, M., 527
Weinstein, R. S., 632

Weisberg, P., 349, 351
Weisfield, G. E., 203, 204, 205, 205*n*
Weisner, T. S., 52, 535
Weiss, B., 550
Weiss, R. J., 551
Weissberg, R. P., 517
Weisz, J. R., 249, 420
Weisz, V., 39, 525
Well, A. D., 284, 285*n*
Wellman, H. M., 234, 247, 251, 286, 300, 301, 377, 388, 409, 443
Wentworth, N., 286
Wentzel, K. R., 606
Werker, J. F., 153, 367, 368
Werner, E. E., 9, 10, 115, 117
Wertheim, E. H., 207
Wertsch, J. V., 26, 27, 260, 267
Wessels, H., 367
Wessels, J. M. I., 367
West, M. J., 487
Westra, T., 147, 148*n*
Whang, P. A., 308
Wheeler, M. D., 176, 200
White, B., 149, 169
White, D. R., 207
White, J. L., 513
White, R. W., 453
White, S. H., 14, 347
Whitebook, M., 434, 585
Whitehouse, R. H., 177, 179*n*
Whitehurst, G. J., 359, 386
Whitesell, N., 404
Whiting, B., 511, 528, 529, 535
Whitington, V., 261
Whitley, B. E., 538
Whitney, J. A., 98
Whitney, M. P., 98, 130, 131
Whitten, P., 558
Wichstrøm, L., 545*n*, 550
Wiesel, T. N., 190
Wigfield, A., 347, 456, 456*n*, 630
Wigfield, R. E., 450
Wiggins, G. P., 342
Wikner, K., 152
Wilcox, A. J., 89
Wilcox, B. L., 39
Wilk, A., 274
Wille, D. E., 427
Willer, B., 586
Willerman, L., 119, 123, 334, 336, 336*n*, 345
Williams, B. C., 523
Williams, E., 536, 583, 585
Williams, L. M., 590
Williams, T. M., 617, 619
Williams, W. M., 329, 338, 558
Williamson, M. L., 151
Williard, J. C., 607
Willis, R. J., 215
Wills, T. A., 615
Wilson, E. O., 480
Wilson, K. S., 599
Wilson, M. N., 571
Wilson, R., 550
Wilson-Mitchell, J. E., 535
Wimbarti, S., 264, 603
Wimbush, D. D., 570
Windle, M. A., 470
Windschitl, M., 624
Winer, G., 253
Winn, S., 212
Winner, E., 51, 238, 323, 353, 376, 377, 534

XYY syndrome and, 82
Anxiety, 4. *See also* Fear; Stress
    authoritarian parenting and, 564
    child maltreatment victims, 592
    depression and, 550
    divorce and, 578
    family size and, 572
    friendships and, 472
    IQ scores and, 331
    make-believe play and, 237
    prenatal development and, 105
    rejected-withdrawn children, 606
    separation. *See* Separation anxiety
    sex-related differences in, 545
    sexual abuse victims, 590
    social problem solving and, 473
    stranger anxiety, 403
    "whipping boys" and, 607
Apes. *See* Monkeys and apes
Apgar Scale, 108
Aphasia, 362
Appalachians, cosleeping arrangements in infancy and childhood, 132
Appearance-reality distinction, 247–248
Appetite. *See* Eating habits; Nutrition
Applied behavior analysis, 21
    anorexia nervosa treatment, 209
Applied field of child development, 4. *See also* Public policies; Social policies and issues
Apprenticeship programs, 639–640
Approach-withdrawal, as temperament dimension, 414
Arithmetic. *See* Mathematics
Arms. *See* Limbs; Skeletal development
Arousal. *See* States of arousal
Artificial neural networks, for computer simulations of information processing, 278–280
    grammatical development and, 384
Artistic expression. *See also* Creativity; Drawing
    early childhood, 237–239
Asian Americanss
    anorexia nervosa among, 209
    extended-family households, 570
    identity development in adolescence, 461
    intelligence traits, valuing of, 339
    IQ scores of, 332
    teenage pregnancy among, 215
Asian Pacific Islanders. *See* Pacific Islanders
Asian societies. *See also specific countries or cultures*
    academic achievement among, 452, 637–638
    autobiographical memory among, 297
    body size, 184
    mathematics learning among, 307–308, 637–638
    newborn behavior and child-rearing practices, 137
    science learning among, 637–638
    sexual attitudes and behavior among, 210
Aspirin, prenatal development and maternal use of, 98
Assertiveness
    empathy and, 411
    parent-adolescent relationship and, 568–567
Assimilation
    cognitive-developmental theory, 223

neo-Piagetian theory, 277
Assisted discovery learning, 264
Associative play, 599–600
Asthma, and genetic imprinting, 80
Asynchronous process of physical development, 185
Athletics. *See also* Exercise; Extracurricular activities
    gender stereotyping in, 180–181
    gender typing and, 537
    gross motor development and, 177–178, 180–181
    maturational timing and, 206
    menarche and, 202
Atiya Piatiya (game in India), 603
Attachment, 421–435
    adoption and, 426
    avoidant attachment. *See* Avoidant attachment
    behaviorist theories of, 421–422
    Bowlby's theory of, 25, 422–423
    child care and, 432–435, 599
    child maltreatment and, 427–428
    continuity of caregiving and, 431–432
    cultural differences in, 425–426
    defined, 421
    depression and, 550
    disorganized/disoriented attachment. *See* Disorganized/disoriented attachment
    ethological theory of, 422–423, 430
    factors affecting, 426–429
    fathers and, 429–431
    home environment and, 428–429, 433
    homosexual parents and, 576–577
    infant characteristics and, 427–428
    internal working model of, 423, 429
    later development and, 430–432
    measurement of attachment security, 423–425
    moral development and, 483–484
    multiple attachments, 430
    objects of, 422
    opportunity for, 426
    phases of, 422–423
    postpartum depression and, 400
    psychoanalytic theories of, 421–422, 430
    quality of caregiving and, 426–429
    resistant attachment. *See* Resistant attachment
    secure attachment. *See* Secure attachment
    sibling relationship and, 573
    stability of, 425
    theories of, 421–423
    uninvolved parenting and, 565
Attachment-in-the-making phase, 422
Attachment Q-sort, 424–426
Attendance, school. *See* School attendance
Attention, 284–289, 310
    adaptability in, 284
    ADHD and, 288–289
    automization and, 274, 277
    cognitive inhibition and, 284–285
    drug use during pregnancy and, 98–99
    emotional self-regulation and, 404–405
    fetal alcohol syndrome and, 100
    habituation-dishabituation response and, 141–142

heart rate and, 49
IQ scores and, 320
joint attention. *See* Joint attention
low birth weight and, 112–113
malnutrition and, 195
metacognition and, 300–301
otitis media and, 155
planning and, 285–287
preterm infants, 115
private speech and, 260
reticular formation and, 190
selectivity in, 284–285
self-control and, 508
small-for-date infants, 113
smoking during pregnancy and, 99–100
strategies, 284–285
videogames and, 625
Attention-deficit hyperactivity disorder (ADHD), 286–287
    delinquent behavior and, 513
    origins of, 286–287
    symptoms of, 288
    treatment of, 289
Attention from parents. *See* Parent *entries*
Attention span, as temperament dimension, 414–415
Attribution retraining, 455–456
Attributions. *See also* Personality traits
    achievement-related attributions. *See* Achievement-related attributions
    defined, 452
    mastery-oriented attributions, 453–456
    person perception and, 462–464
    physical attractiveness and, 605
Atypical lateralization of brain, 189
Australia
    aboriginal groups. *See* Aboriginal groups
    body size, 184
    child-care facilities, 587
    family size, 572
    fears in childhood, 406
    identity development in, 460
    infant mortality rate, 117
    reproductive technology laws, 85
    SIDS public education programs, 140
    teenage pregnancy rate, 214–215
Austria
    family size, 572
    infant mortality rate, 117
Authentic assessment of intelligence, 342
Authoritarian parenting, 564–565
    family size and, 572
    peer pressure and, 614
    self-esteem and, 451
Authoritative parenting, 563–566. *See also* Responsive parenting
    adolescent development and, 568
    benefits of, 565–566
    divorce and, 580
    maternal employment and, 583
    middle childhood, 566
    peer group membership in adolescence and, 610
    peer pressure and, 614
    self-care children and, 587
    television viewing and, 620–621
Autism, 445–446
    fragile X syndrome and, 80–81
Autobiographical memory, 296–299
    infantile amnesia and, 296

narrative thinking and, 296–297
remembered self and, 442
Automization
    levels-of-processing model of information processing, 274
    memory and, 294
    neo-Piagetian theory, 277
Automobile accidents and depression, 550
Autonomic nervous system. *See* Nervous system
Autonomous morality, 489–491
Autonomy
    adolescence, 567–568
    anorexia nervosa and, 209
    authoritative parenting and, 564
    gender typing and, 533
    moral reasoning and, 503
    psychosocial stages of development, 19, 567
    school transitions and, 631–632
Autosomal diseases, 80–82
Autosomes, 76
Autostimulation theory, 133
Avoidant attachment, 424
    child care and, 433
    later development and, 431
    mother-infant relationship and, 427
    mother's internal working model and, 429

B

Babbling, in language development, 368, 599
Babinski reflex, 129
Baby and Child Care (Spock), 14, 132
Baby biographies, 13
Baby fat, 177
Baby(ies). *See* Childbirth; Infancy and toddlerhood; Newborns; Pregnancy; Prenatal *entries*
"Back to basics" movement, 627
Bacterial diseases. *See also* Infectious diseases
    breastfeeding and, 194
    prenatal development and, 102–103
Balance, 177
    cerebellum and, 190
    infancy, 152–153
    sex-related differences, 180
    visual impairment and, 160
Balance-scale problem, connectionist modeling of, 279–280
Baldwin's theory of development, 14–16
Ball skills, 177–178, 180
Bandura's social learning theory. *See* Social learning theory (Bandura)
Bantu, body size among, 184
Bar mitzvah, 204
Bases, in DNA, 72–73
Basic emotions, 401–406
Basic-skills approach to reading, 305
Basic trust, as psychosocial stage of development, 19
Bat mitzvah, 204
Batting skills. *See* Ball skills
Bayley Scales of Infant Development, 325
Bedouins, and parental response to crying, 135

styles of, 563–566. *See also specific style (e.g., Authoritative parenting; Permissive parenting)*
substance abuse and, 615
teenage parenthood, 215–217
temperament and, 414, 417, 420–421, 565
uninvolved style. *See* Uninvolved parenting
"whipping boys" and, 607
Child support, 578
divorce mediation and, 580
enforcement and public policy, 38
legal proceedings, 581
teenage parenthood, 217
Childbearing. *See* Conception; Pregnancy; Prenatal *entries*
Childbirth, 106–118. *See also* Birth *entries;* Newborns
age of. *See* Maternal age
approaches to, 109–111
cesarean delivery, 111–112
complications during. *See* Birth complications
home delivery, 109–111
instrument delivery, 111
medical interventions, 109, 111
medications during, 111
multiple births, 75. *See also* Twins
natural (prepared) childbirth, 109–110
paid leave, 37
positions for delivery, 110
stages of, 106–107
Childhood social indicators, 33–35
Children's Defense Fund, 38
Children's rights, 38–39
Chimpanzees. *See* Monkeys and apes
Chinese. *See also* Asian societies
achievement-related attributions among, 455
attachment style of infants, 426
child maltreatment among, 592
child-rearing practices among, 52–53, 569
fears in childhood, 406
growth stunting among, 196
inhibition, valuing of, 606
language development among, 375
maternity leave, 117
mathematical skills, 308
moral reasoning among, 490
national examinations, 634
one-child families, 574–575
peer group membership, 610
play in early childhood, 603
remembered self stories among, 442
self-concept among, 448
self-esteem among, 451
shyness, valuing of, 420, 606
temperament of infants, 419
Chinese Americans. *See also* Asian Americans
child-rearing practices among, 569–570
English grammar performance by, 363–364
Chomsky's theory of language development. *See* Nativist theory of language development
Chorion, 91
Chorionic villus sampling, 84, 86–87, 91
Christianity, and development of death concept, 245
Chromosomal abnormalities, 81–83, 365

Chromosomes, 72–73
autosomes, 76
crossing over, 73–75
mapping of, 88–89
sex chromosomes, 76
Chronic illnesses. *See specific illness (e.g., Diabetes)*
Chronosystem, in ecological systems theory, 29–30, 560
Cigarettes. *See* Smoking
Circular reactions, in sensorimotor stage of cognitive development, 224–226
Circulatory system. *See* Cardiovascular system
Circumcision, 151, 205
Class inclusion problems, 242–243, 247–249, 252–253
Classical conditioning, 19, 138–139
Classification, hierarchical, 241–242, 246–247
Classification abilities. *See* Categorization abilities
Classrooms. *See* Schools; Teacher *entries*
Clear-cut attachment phase, 422–423
Cleft palate
attachment security and, 428
stress during pregnancy and, 105
Clinical interviews
Kohlberg's use of, 491–492
Piaget's use of, 22, 47–48, 488–489
Clinical method of research, 36–37, 45, 50–52
identity status studies, 457–458
psychoanalytic theorists' use of, 18
reliability, 55
Cliques, 609–612
Cloning, 85
Coaching. *See* Athletics
Cocaine. *See also* Drug use and abuse
prenatal development and, 98–99
teenage use, 614
Codominance of inheritance, 77–78
Coercive parenting. *See* Authoritarian parenting
Cognition. *See* Cognitive development; Reasoning
abstract. *See* Abstract thinking
metacognition. *See* Metacognition
Cognitive development, 221–395. *See also* Intelligence *entries;* Language development; Learning; Mental retardation
adolescence, 254–257
AIDS and, 103
alcohol use during pregnancy and, 100
attachment and later development, 431
autonomy and, 567
behaviorist perspective, 222
bilingualism and, 392
brain growth spurts and, 191, 276
child care and, 433, 585
child maltreatment victims, 592–593
constructivist theory of, 222
creativity and, 351–352
cultural influences on, 252–253, 271
definition, 4–5
delinquent behavior and, 513
domain-general and domain-specific changes in. *See* Domain-general and domain-specific changes in cognitive development

drawing and, 237–239
dynamic systems perspective, 30, 258
early childhood, 235–248
early deprivation and, 168–169
early intervention programs, 346–349
emotional and social development and, 398, 402–403, 409–410
environmental pollution and, 101–102
ethological theory of, 25
fetal alcohol syndrome and, 100
gender identity and, 539
gender stereotyping and, 524
habituation-dishabituation response studies, 141–142
hearing loss and, 263
home environment and, 348
identity development and, 457–458
infancy and toddlerhood, 224–235
information processing theories. *See* Information processing theories
innate knowledge and, 222, 234
language development and, 255, 373, 375
lateralization of brain and, 189–190
lead exposure and, 101
low birth weight and, 112
make-believe play and, 237, 262, 264
medications during childbirth and, 111
microgenetic research, 63
middle childhood, 249–253
milestones in, 233, 250
modular view of mind, 234, 258
moral development and, 479–480, 495–496
motor development and, 144
nativistic theory of, 222, 234
neo-Piagetian perspective. *See* Neo-Piagetian perspective (Case)
newborns' states of arousal and, 131
nonorganic failure to thrive and, 199
nutrition during pregnancy and, 104
oxygen deprivation during childbirth and, 112
perceptual development and, 150, 232–234
perspective taking and, 465–466
phenylketonuria and, 76–77
Piaget's theory of. *See* Cognitive-developmental theory (Piaget)
play and, 600
preterm infants, 115
psychometric approach, 315. *See also* Intelligence tests
reproductive technologies and, 84
self-concept and, 447–448
self-control and, 508
sex chromosomal disorders and, 82
sex-related differences in, 544–548
small-for-date infants, 113
social-cognitive learning theory, 20
socially mediated process of, 26
sociocultural theory of. *See* Sociocultural theory of cognitive development (Vygotsky)
sociodramatic play and, 236–237, 600

television literacy and, 618
television viewing and, 621
temperament and, 419
touch and, 151
toxoplasmosis and, 102–103
uninvolved parenting and, 565
visual impairment and, 160
Cognitive-developmental theory (Piaget), 21–22, 32, 221–259
accommodation in, 223, 240
adaptation in, 21, 223, 257
assimilation in, 223
clinical interviews, 22, 47–48, 488–489
disequilibrium in, 223, 492, 496
educational principles based on, 258–259, 627
equilibration in, 223, 257
equilibrium in, 21, 223, 257
evaluation of, 257–258
gender identity, 539–540
gender typing and, 522
make-believe play and, 264
moral development and, 488–491, 496
neo-Piagetian perspective. *See* Neo-Piagetian perspective (Case)
organization in, 223, 257
peer relations and, 603
perspective taking stages and, 465–466
schemes in, 222–224, 236
stages of, 21–22, 222, 257–258. *See also specific stages (e.g., Formal operational stage of cognitive development; Sensorimotor stage of cognitive development)*
Cognitive inhibition, 284–285, 310
self-control and, 506
Cognitive maps, in concrete operational stage of cognitive development, 251
Cognitive psychology. *See* Information processing theories
Cognitive self-regulation, 301–302
Cohort effects, 60, 62
Coinage of words, in language development, 376
Colic, 136
Collectivist societies, 36
cooperative learning and, 266
emotional display rules and, 407
moral development and, 497–498
moral reasoning and, 503
perspective taking and, 465
play and peer relations in, 603
self-concept among, 448
College education. *See* Higher education
College-preparatory education, 634
Color vision, 165
infancy and toddlerhood, 154–156
X-linked inheritance, 78–79
Columbia, body size in, 184
Commitment
friendships and, 468–467
identity formation and, 456, 458
Communication. *See* Language development; Speech
Community influences, 562. *See also* Cultural influences
aggression, 515
child maltreatment, 591
identity development, 460
maternal employment, 585
parent-school involvement, 636

Community-of-learners model of education, 266
Compassion, 470. *See also* Empathy; Prosocial behavior
Compliance. *See also* Conformity
  maternal behavior and child's compliance with parental demands, 56
  self-control and, 506
  sex-related differences in, 545, 549
Componential analysis of intelligence, 320–321
Componential subtheory of intelligence (Sternberg), 321–322
Comprehension monitoring, 302
Comprehension versus production of language, 372
Computer-assisted instruction (CAI), 623–624
Computer simulations of information processing, 272, 278–280, 311
Computers, 597, 621–626
  home computers, 624–625
  programming, 624
  school classrooms, 621–624
  word processing, 624
Concealment, in research, 68
Conception, 88–90. *See also* Fertility; Pregnancy; Prenatal *entries*
  breastfeeding's effect on, 193–194
  maternal age. *See* Maternal age
  menarche and, 200–201
  paternal age and chromosomal abnormalities, 82
  sex-related differences in, 79–80
  spermarche and, 202
  zygote, 74–75
Concordance rates, 119–121
  autism, 446
  depression, 549
  obesity, 196
Concrete operational stage of cognitive development, 21–22, 222, 249–253
  classification in, 249
  conservation in, 249
  defined, 249
  evaluation of theory, 253
  limitations of, 251–252
  research on, 252–253
  seriation in, 249–250
  spatial reasoning in, 251
Conditioned response (CR), 138–139
Conditioned stimulus (CS), 138–139
Conditioning. *See also* Classical conditioning; Operant conditioning
  applied behavior analysis, 21
  social learning theory, 20
  taste preferences, 151
Condoms. *See* Contraception
Confirmation, religious, 204
Conflict, 472–474. *See also* Aggression; Social problem solving; Violence
  adolescence, 173
  adult conflict, effect on children, 56–57
  friendships and, 468–470
  marital. *See* Divorce
  parent-adolescent relationship, 204, 206, 503, 560–561, 567–568
  peer acceptance and, 606
  sibling relationships, 573–574
  temperament and, 419–420
Conformity. *See also* Compliance

adolescent peer pressure and, 613–614
authoritative parenting and, 564
social conventions, to, 487–488. *See also* Moral development
Confucianism and child-rearing practices, 569
Congenital adrenal hyperplasia (CAH), 530–531, 551
Connectionism, 276, 278–281, 311
  grammatical development theory, 384
Connectives, in grammatical development, 383
Conscience. *See* Moral *entries*; Superego
Consent to research, 66–67
Conservation
  concrete operational stage of cognitive development, 249
  defined, 240
  gender constancy and, 539
  neo-Piagetian theory and, 277
  preoperational stage of cognitive development, 240–241, 245–246, 248
Consortium for Longitudinal Studies, 346
Construction, in moral development, 488–489
  milestones in, 510
Constructive memory, 292–294
Constructive play, 600
Constructivist approach to cognitive development, 222
  reconstruction as memory strategy and, 292
Consumerism, and television, 620–621
Contexts for development, 8, 24, 258. *See also* Environmental influences; *specific influences (e.g., Cultural influences; Home environment)*
Contextual subtheory of intelligence (Sternberg), 321–322
Continuous course of development, 6–9
  behaviorism, 20
  information processing theories, 24
  Locke's theories, 12
  stance of major developmental theories, 32
Contraception, 572
  adolescents' use of, 211–212, 216
  sexually transmitted diseases and, 214
  teenage pregnancy rate and, 214
Contractions, in childbirth, 106–107
Contrast, in lexical contrast theory of semantic development, 378
Contrast sensitivity, 159
Control deficiencies, in mental strategies
  attentional strategies, 285
  memory strategies, 287
Control processes. *See* Mental strategies
Controversial children, as category of peer acceptance, 604, 606
Convention on the Rights of the Child, 38–39
Conventional level of moral development, 493, 500
Conventionality, in lexical contrast theory of semantic development, 378

Convergent thinking, 350–351
Conversation. *See* Pragmatic development; Speech
Cooing, in language development, 368
Cooley's anemia, 78
Cooperation. *See also* Compliance; Prosocial behavior
  attachment security and, 431
  child-rearing practices and, 560
  extended-family households and, 571
  friendships and, 470
  morality of, 489, 493
  peer relations and, 603
  self-recognition and, 442
  sociodramatic play and, 237
Cooperative learning, 265–266
  KEEP classrooms, 628–629
  mainstreaming of students with learning difficulties and, 635
  reciprocal teaching, 628
Cooperative play, 599–600, 629
Coordination of secondary circular reactions, in sensorimotor stage of cognitive development, 225–226
Coping strategies. *See also* Emotional self-regulation
  divorce of parents, response to, 579
  friendships and, 471–472
  gender-typed coping styles and depression, 550
  maturational timing and, 208
  self-control and, 508
  teenage substance abuse and, 615
Coregulation, in supervision of children, 566–567
Corporal punishment, 592–593
Corpus callosum, 190
  ADHD and, 288
Corpus luteum, 89
Correlation coefficients, 56
Correlational research, 55–56, 59
Correlational stability of IQ scores, 327
Cortex. *See* Cerebral cortex
Cortisol and temperamental style, 417
Cosleeping arrangements, 131–132
Counseling
  anorexia nervosa, 209
  blended families, 582–583
  bulimia, 210
  genetic counseling, 83–84, 89
  maternal depression, 400
  newborns, adjustments to, 561
  school services, 629
  sexual abuse victims, 591
  substance abuse, 615
  suicide, 459
Counting, in early childhood, 306
Course of development, 6–9. *See also* Continuous course of development; Discontinuous course of development
  Locke's theory of, 12
  Rousseau's theory of, 12
  stance of major developmental theories, 32
Court proceedings. *See* Legal proceedings
Covert aggression, 511
CR (conditioned response), 138–139
Crack, 99. *See also* Cocaine; Drug use and abuse
Crawling, 145–146. *See also* Motor development
  brain growth spurts and, 191

depth perception and, 156–159
EEG activity and, 159
emotional self-regulation and, 405
visual impairment and, 160
Creativity, 349–353. *See also* Drawing
  cognitive resources, 351–352
  computer programming and, 624
  corpus callosum and, 190
  defined, 349
  environmental resources, 351, 353
  investment theory of, 351–353
  make-believe play and, 237
  motivational resources, 351–353
  personality resources, 351–352
  psychometric approach to, 350
  television watching and, 621
Creoles, 361
Cri du chat (crying-of-the-cat) syndrome, 136
Criminality. *See also* Antisocial behavior; Child maltreatment; Delinquency; Violence
  aggression in childhood and, 512
  concordance rates, 119–120
  peer acceptance and, 604
  television viewing in childhood and, 619
Crisis intervention for child maltreatment, 593
Critical period (ethology), 25. *See also* Sensitive periods
Critical thinking
  identity development and, 457
  open classrooms and, 627
  teacher-pupil interaction and, 632
Cross-cultural research. *See also* Cultural influences
  academic achievement, 637–638
  attachment styles, 425–426, 429
  child-directed speech, 368
  environmental moral reasoning, 502
  folic acid and prenatal development, 104
  gender stereotyping of academic subjects, 525
  gender stereotyping of personality traits, 523–525
  gender typing, 528
  grammatical development, 384–385
  learning and verbal instruction, 266–267
  mathematical reasoning, 306
  moral development, 497–498
  moral-social-conventional distinction, 502–503
  motor development, 147
  multicultural, 26
  self-esteem, 452
  separation anxiety, 423
  sexual attitudes and behavior, 210
  sociocultural theory, 26–27
  speed of processing, 275–276
Cross-gender reasoning and behavior. *See also* Androgynous traits
  adolescence, 541
  middle childhood, 525–526
  modeling of, 536
  peer acceptance and, 536
  sibling relationships and, 537
Cross-sectional research, 60–62, 65
  friendship understanding, 469
  gender-stereotyping flexibility, 525
  identity formation, 457
  moral reasoning, 494–495
  prosocial reasoning, 505

Selman's stages of perspective taking, 465
Crossing over, of chromosomes, 73–75
Crowds, adolescent membership in, 610–611
Crying
    abnormal crying, 136
    adult responsiveness to infant cries, 134
    newborns, 131, 134–136
    SIDS and, 140
    soothing crying infants, 134–136
    temperament dimension, 414
Crying-of-the-cat syndrome, 136
Crystallized intelligence (Cattell), 318–319, 328
CS (conditioned stimulus), 138–139
Cuba, infant mortality rate, 117
Cults and identity development, 458
Cultural bias in intelligence tests, 319, 324, 333, 338–342
Cultural influences. See also Cross-cultural research; Ethnicity and race; specific entries (e.g., African societies; Native Americanss)
    abstract thinking, 256–257
    academic achievement, 53, 637–638
    adolescence, 202–205
    adolescent initiation ceremony, 203–205
    aggression, 515–516
    anorexia nervosa, 209
    attachment, 425–426
    child maltreatment, 592
    child-rearing practices, 15, 420, 569–570
    childbirth, 109
    cognitive development, 252–253, 271
    death concept, development of, 245
    drawing, development of, 239
    emotional display rules, 407
    emotional sensitivity, 548–549
    ethnographic research, 52–54
    fears in childhood, 406
    food preferences, 194
    gender stereotyping, 522–523, 529
    gender typing, 522, 528–529
    identity development, 460–461
    infant mortality, 116–117
    infant sleeping arrangements, 131–132
    intelligence, 339–340
    IQ scores, 329
    language development, 361, 374
    learned helplessness, 455
    learning, 266–267
    make-believe play, 264
    mathematical skills, 308
    memory strategies, 290–291
    moral development, 497–498, 502–503
    motor development, 147–148
    newborn behavior and child-rearing practices, 137
    parent-child relationship, 431, 529
    peer group membership, 610
    peer relations, 603–604
    play, 603–604
    psychosexual stages of development, 18
    psychosocial stages of development, 18
    pubertal changes, responses to, 203–205

pubertal development, 202–203
public policies, 36
self-concept, 448
self-conscious emotions, expression of, 404
self-esteem, 451
sexual activity, 210
sociocultural theory. See Sociocultural theory of cognitive development (Vygotsky)
stranger anxiety among infants and toddlers, 403
substance use and abuse, 614
temperament, 419
war, effect on children, 515–516
Custody of children, 580–582
    joint custody, 580–581
    remarriage and, 581–582
    sexual orientation of parent and, 576
    skipped-generation families, 584
Cystic fibrosis, 78, 88
Cytomegalovirus, and prenatal development, 102–103
Cytoplasm, 72
Czech Republic
    body size in, 184
    infant mortality rate, 117

D

Damon's sequence of distributive justice, 503–504
Darwin's theory of evolution, 12–13, 281
Dating and romantic relationships
    cliques and, 611
    friendships and, 471
    peer pressure and, 613
    school transitions and, 631
Day-care facilities. See Child care
Deafness. See Hearing loss
Death. See also Infant mortality; Suicide
    anorexia nervosa as cause of, 209
    child maltreatment as cause of, 593
    childhood understanding of and attitudes toward, 244–245
    concept of death, development of, 244–245
    diarrhea as cause of, 198
    genetic diseases and childhood deaths, 81
    obesity and, 195
    sex-related differences in child mortality, 79–80
    spirituality and, 245
    sudden infant death syndrome (SIDS), 140–141
Debriefing in research, 68
Decentration thinking, in cognitive-developmental theory, 249
Deception. See also Honesty
    research on children and, 68
    sexual abuse of children, 590
Deferred imitation, 227
    recall memory and, 292
    research on, 230
Deformities. See Birth defects; Chromosomal abnormalities; specific entries (e.g., Cleft palate)
Degrees, academic. See Educational attainment
Delay of gratification, 507–508

Delinquency
    blended families, adjustment to and, 582
    child maltreatment victims, 592
    concordance rates, 119–120
    depression and, 550
    divorce and, 579
    early-onset type, 513
    extended family households and, 571
    family size and, 572
    friendships and, 470
    Head Start programs and, 346, 349
    incidence of, 511
    IQ scores and, 331
    late-onset type, 513
    maturational timing and, 206–207
    paths of development, 513
    peer acceptance and, 604
    peer groups and, 610
    prevention and treatment, 517
    sex-related differences in, 511
    sexual abuse victims, 590
    sexual activity of adolescents and, 211
    uninvolved parenting and, 565
Demandingness, as dimension of child-rearing, 563
Denmark
    immunization rate, 199
    infant mortality rate, 117
    SIDS public education programs, 140
Dental development. See Teeth
Deoxyribonucleic acid (DNA), 72–73, 88–89
Dependency. See also Autonomy
    authoritarian parenting and, 564
    permissive parenting and, 564
    sex-related differences in, 545, 549
    "whipping boys" and, 607
Dependent variables, in experimental research design, 56
Depression. See also Suicide
    adolescence, 458–459, 549–550
    anorexia nervosa and, 290
    bulimia and, 210
    child maltreatment victims, 592
    concordance rates, 119–120
    factors related to, 549–550
    homosexuality in adolescence and, 213
    hormones and, 204–206
    incidence of, 549
    Internet usage and, 625
    IQ scores and, 331
    maternal depression. See Maternal depression
    obesity and, 197
    peer victimization and, 607
    postpartum depression, 400
    sex-related differences in, 545, 549–550
    sexual abuse victims, 590
    skipped-generation families and, 584
    substance abuse and, 615
    suicide and, 459
    symptoms of, in adolescence, 549
    uninvolved parenting and, 564–565
Deprivation. See also Malnutrition; Poverty; Sensitive periods; Socioeconomic influences
    early deprivation, 168–169
    environmental cumulative deficit hypothesis, 328
    language development and, 363

maternal deprivation and attachment, 426
nonorganic failure to thrive, 199, 399
oxygen deprivation. See Oxygen deprivation
sensory deprivation studies of animals, 190–191
Deprivation dwarfism, 199, 399
Depth perception, 156–159, 165
DES (diethylstilbestrol), 101
Despair. See also Depression
    psychosocial stage of development, 19
    suicide and, 459
Determinants of development, 8–9. See also Environmental influences; Genetic entries; Nature-nurture controversy
    stance of major developmental theories, 32
Development. See Child development; specific entries (e.g., Cognitive development; Physical development)
Developmental disability. See Mental retardation
Developmental psychology, 4
Developmental research designs, 58–64
Developmentally appropriate practices for child-care facilities, 434, 586
Diabetes
    genetic imprinting and, 80
    insipidus, 79
    obesity and, 195, 197
    prenatal malnutrition and, 104
Diarrhea, 198
Diet. See Eating habits; Malnutrition; Nutrition
Diethylstilbestrol (DES), 101
Differentiation theory of perceptual development, 166–167
Difficult child, as temperament type, 414–415
    child maltreatment risk factor, 589
    child-rearing practices and, 420
    delinquent behavior and, 513
    divorce of parents, response to, 579–580
    peer relations and, 605
Digestive system. See Gastrointestinal system
Dilation of cervix in childbirth, 106–107
Directions, in concrete operational stage of cognitive development, 251
Disability. See Learning disabilities; Mental retardation; Physical disabilities; specific disability (e.g., Hearing loss)
Disadvantaged. See Poverty; Socioeconomic influences
Discipline. See also Child-rearing practices; Punishment (disciplinary)
    aggression in children and, 512–514, 570
    cultural influences on, 570
    divorce's effect on, 578
    family size and, 572
    inductive, 482, 497, 549
    maternal depression and, 400
    middle childhood, 566
    moral development and, 481–482, 484–487

positive discipline, 487
socioeconomic influences on, 568
temperament and, 483
time out, 486, 515
withdrawal of privileges, 486, 515
Discontinuous course of development, 6–9
Rousseau's "noble savage," 12
stance of major developmental theories, 32
Discovery learning, 258
assisted discovery learning, 264
Discrimination. *See* Bias; Ethnicity and race; Socioeconomic status (SES)
Diseases. *See also* Health care; Immune system; Immunization; Infectious diseases; *specific diseases (e.g., Cancer; Diabetes)*
breastfeeding and, 193–194
dominant-recessive inheritance, 76–79
low birth weight and, 112
physical development and, 185
prenatal development and, 102–103
prenatal diagnosis. *See* Prenatal diagnosis
X-linked inheritance, 78–79
Disequilibrium, in cognitive-developmental theory, 223
moral development and, 492, 496
Dishabituation. *See* Habituation-dishabituation response
Disorganized/disoriented attachment, 424
mother-child relationship and, 427
mother's internal working model and, 429
Disposition. *See* Personality traits; Temperament
Distance comprehension, in concrete operational stage of cognitive development, 251
Distance curves, 174–175
Distractibility, as temperament dimension, 414–415
Distress. *See* Anxiety; Fear; Stress
Distributive justice, 503–504
Divergent thinking, 350–351
Divorce, 34, 577–581. *See also* Single-parent families
age of child and response to divorce, 578–579
child-rearing practices and, 580
custody arrangements. *See* Custody of children
family size and, 572
grandparent visitation rights, 581
immediate consequences of, 578–579
incidence of, 577–578, 583
interventions, 580–581
life span and, 399
long-term consequences of, 579–580
maternal employment and, 583
second marriages, 583
sex of child and response to divorce, 578–579
sexual activity of adolescents and, 211
teenage pregnancy and, 215
teenage substance abuse and, 615
temperament of child and response to, 578–580

Divorce mediation, 580
Dizygotic twins, 75. *See also* Twin studies; Twins
DNA, 72–73
DNA analysis, 88–89
Domain-general and domain-specific changes in cognitive development, 222, 257–258
connectionism, 280
neo-Piagetian theory, 278
Domains of development, 4–5. *See also specific domains (e.g., Cognitive development; Physical development)*
Domestic violence. *See* Child maltreatment; Spousal abuse
Domestic work
after-school chores for self-care children, 587
dual-earner families, 585
gender typing and, 533–535
Dominance hierarchy, 601, 611–612
Dominant cerebral hemisphere, 189
Dominant-recessive inheritance, 76–77
Dominican Republic, gender role changes in, 531
Donor insemination, 84–85
Donor ova, 85
Doubt, 19. *See also* Anxiety
Down syndrome, 81–82, 365
Drawing
cultural variations in development, 239
early childhood, 237–239
middle childhood, 251
realistic drawings, 238
representational shapes and forms, 238
scribbles, 238
Dress and grooming
adolescent peer pressure and, 613
suicide and, 459
Dribbling skills. *See* Ball skills
Drill-oriented instruction in mathematics, 307
Drinking. *See* Alcohol use and abuse
Drive-reduction theory (Hull), 20, 421
Dropping out of school
blended families, adjustment to and, 582
delinquent behavior and, 513
divorce and, 580
IQ scores, effect of, 329
peer acceptance and, 604
school transitions and, 631
semilingualism and, 393
student body size and, 627
work-study programs and, 639
Drug education programs, 615
Drug use and abuse. *See also* Medications
ADHD and, 289
adolescence, 614–615, 639
blended families, adjustment to and, 582
child maltreatment and parental drug use, 590
child maltreatment victims, 592
correlates and consequences of, 615
delinquent behavior and, 513
depression and, 550
employment during adolescence and, 639
experimentation, 614–615
friendships and, 470

homosexuality in adolescence and, 213
identity development and, 458
maturational timing and, 206–207
peer groups and, 610
permissive parenting and, 564
prenatal development and maternal drug use, 97–99
prevention strategies, 615
school treatment programs, 629
sexual abuse perpetrators and victims, 590
sexual activity of adolescents and, 211
sexually transmitted diseases and, 214
suicide and, 459
teenage pregnancy and, 214
uninvolved parenting and, 565
Druze, development of death concept among, 245
Dual-earner households. *See* Maternal employment
Duchenne muscular dystrophy, 79, 88
Dungeons and Dragons, 625
Dutch. *See* Netherlands
Dwarfism, deprivation, 199, 399
Dynamic systems perspective of development, 30–32, 258
emotional development and, 401
motor development and, 145–147, 178
Dynamic testing of intelligence, 340–342

E

E-mail, 624–625
Ear infections, 155
Early childhood, 5, 410–412
achievement-related attributions in, 453
aggression in, 509–511
artistic expression in, 237–239
body composition in, 177
body proportion in, 176
categorization abilities in, 246–247
child-rearing practices in, 563–565
cognitive development in, 235–248. *See also* Preoperational stage of cognitive development
death concept, development of, 244–245
drawing in, 237–239
eating habits in, 194
emergent literacy in, 304–305
emotional self-regulation in, 405–406
emotional understanding in, 409–410
empathy in, 411
fear in, 405
friendships in, 468
gender identity in, 539–540
gender stereotyping in, 523–524
gender typing in, 532
gross motor development in, 177–181
height in, 174–175
information processing in, 303
intentions, understanding of, 462

intervention programs, 346–349
language development in, 235–236
make-believe play in, 236–237, 247–248, 600
mathematical reasoning in, 306
memory in, 292, 295–296
memory strategies in, 287–291
mental representation in, 235–236
metacognition in, 300–301
moral development in, 481–482
moral reasoning in, 500–506
nutrition in, 194
parental relationships in. *See* Father-child relationship; Mother-child relationship; Parent-child relationship
peer relations in, 599–600
person perception in, 463
planning in, 286
play in, 468, 599–600
preschool. *See* Preschool and kindergarten
private speech in, 260, 262
reading in, 304–305
self-concept in, 445
self-conscious emotions in, 404
self-control in, 508
self-esteem in, 449–450
sibling relationship in, 573–574
social comparisons in, 450
television literacy in, 617–618
television watching in, 621
walking in, 177–178
weight in, 174–175
Early deprivation and enrichment, 168–169
Early intervention programs
cognitive development, 346–349
Down syndrome and, 82
educational enrichment for children living in poverty, 348
infancy and toddlerhood, 348
New Chance, 349
two-generation models, 347–349
Early learning centers, 169
Ears. *See also* Hearing
infections in, 155
otitis media, 155
prenatal development of, 93, 97
Easy child, as temperament type, 414–415
divorce of parents, response to, 579
Eating disorders, 209–210
Eating habits, 194. *See also* Feeding practices; Nutrition
anorexia nervosa and, 209
bulimia and, 209–210
obesity and, 197–198
Ecological systems theory (Bronfenbrenner), 27–30, 32
attachment and, 429
bidirectional influences, 27, 98, 559
chronosystem, 29–30, 560
exosystems, 29, 562
macrosystems, 29, 35
mesosystems, 28–29, 562
microsystems, 27–28
third-party influences, 28, 560
Economic influences. *See also* Poverty; Socioeconomic influences; Socioeconomic status (SES)
Great Depression of 1930s and, 61
public policies, 36–37
Ectoderm, formation of, 92

Employment. *See also* Unemployment; Vocational *entries*
  adolescence, 639
  delinquency and, 513
  depression and, 550
  flexible work hours, 561
  Head Start programs and, 346
  identity formation and, 457
  maternal employment. *See* Maternal employment
  never-married single-parent families and, 577
  parental leave, 37, 561, 585
  teenage pregnancy and, 215–216
  transition from school to work, 639–640
Endocrine system. *See* Hormones
Endoderm, formation of, 92
England. *See also* Great Britain
  childbirth practices, 109–110
  menarche, 184
  reproductive technology laws, 85
Enlightenment philosophies of childhood, 11–12
Enrichment programs. *See* Early intervention programs; Gifted children
Entity view of ability, 454–455
Environmental cumulative deficit hypothesis, 328
Environmental hazards. *See also* Radiation
  mutation of genes and, 81
  prenatal development and, 101–102
Environmental influences, 9. *See also* Nature-nurture controversy; *specific influences (e.g., Cultural influences; Families; Home environment)*
  ADHD, 289
  aggression, 551–552
  behavioral genetics, 118–123, 418
  canalization and, 121–122
  creativity, 351, 353
  depression, 549–550
  emotional disturbances, 120
  gender typing, 531–537
  grammatical development, 385
  intelligence, 119, 332, 335–337, 342–345
  IQ scores, 328–329
  moral development, 496–498
  multiple births, 75
  obesity, 196–197
  otitis media, 155
  pesticides, 79–80
  physical development, 184
  prenatal development, 95–106
  pubertal development, 202–203
  SIDS, 140
  spatial reasoning and skills, 547
  temperament, 418–419
Environmental moral reasoning, 502
Environmental pollutants. *See* Environmental hazards
Envy, 404. *See also* Jealousy
Enzymes and phenylketonuria, 76
Epilepsy, and oxygen deprivation during childbirth, 112
Epiphyses, 179, 182
Episodic memory, 295–296
Equal employment opportunity and maternal employment, 585
Equal pay and maternal employment, 585

Equality
  distributive justice reasoning, 504
  gender. *See* Gender equality
Equilibration, in cognitive-developmental theory, 223, 257
Equilibrium, in cognitive-developmental theory, 21, 223, 257
EQUIP (delinquency treatment program), 517
Erikson's psychosocial theory. *See* Psychosocial theory of development (Erikson)
ERPs. *See* Event-related potentials (ERPs)
Estrogens, 183–184, 212. *See also* Sex hormones
Ethics
  Human Genome Project, 89
  reproductive technologies and, 85
  research ethics, 43–44, 64–68
  universal ethical principle orientation in moral development, 494
"Ethic of care," in moral reasoning, 499
Ethiopia, body size in, 184
Ethnic bias. *See also* Ethnic stereotyping
  aggression and, 515
  bilingualism and, 392
  identity development and, 461
  intelligence tests, 324–325, 338–342
  person perception and, 463–464
Ethnic identity, 461
  extended-family households and, 571
  transracial adoptees, 576
Ethnic stereotyping. *See also* Ethnic bias
  television programming and, 619–620
  videogames and, 625
Ethnic violence, 515–516
Ethnicity and race. *See also* Cultural influences; *specific entries (e.g., African Americanss; Hispanics)*
  achievement-oriented attributions and, 455
  adoption and. *See* Transracial or transcultural adoption
  anorexia nervosa and, 290
  bias against. *See* Ethnic bias
  biological basis of, 338
  child-rearing practices and, 569–570
  delinquent behavior and, 511
  fraternal twinning and, 75
  friendships and, 470–471
  gender stereotyping and, 526
  identity and. *See* Ethnic identity
  IQ scores and, 331–333
  low birth weight and, 112
  obesity and, 196–197
  person perception and, 463–464
  physical development and, 184–185
  school tracking and, 634
  sexual activity of adolescents and, 211
  SIDS and, 140
  stereotyping of. *See* Ethnic stereotyping
  suicide and, 459
  teacher-pupil interaction and, 633
  teenage pregnancy and, 215

  television viewing and, 617, 619–620
  temperament and, 417
Ethnography, as research method, 45, 52–54
  reliability, 55
  remembered self study, 442
Ethology, 24–25, 32
  attachment theory and, 422–423, 430
  moral development theory and, 480
  parental response to crying and, 135
Europe. *See also specific countries or regions (e.g., Sweden; Western Europe)*
  body size in, 184
  childbirth practices in, 109
  "kangaroo baby care" for preterm infants, 115
  prenatal health care in, 117
  reproductive technology laws, 85
  secular gains in development, 184
Event-related potentials (ERPs), 50
  IQ scores and, 320
  language development studies, 363
Event sampling, in systematic observation research, 46
Evocative correlation, in genetic-environmental correlation, 122
Evolution, theories of
  body size and, 184
  Darwin, 12–13
  ethology, 24–25
  family system origins and, 558
  strategy-choice model of information processing and, 281–282
Exercise. *See also* Athletics
  anorexia nervosa and, 209
  obesity and, 197–198
  prenatal development and, 103
  pubertal development and, 202
  sex-related differences in, 181
Exosystems, in ecological systems theory, 29, 562
Expansions, in language development, 385–386
Experiential subtheory of intelligence (Sternberg), 321–322
Experimental research design, 56–58, 64
Exploratory mouthing, 151
Expressive style of language learning, 374
Expressive traits, in gender stereotyping, 523, 528
Expulsion from school, Teen Outreach program enrollees, 216
Extended-family households, 570
  African Americanss, 571, 577
  make-believe play and, 264
  teenage parenthood and, 216–217
Extinction, in classical conditioning, 138
Extracurricular activities. *See also* Athletics
  after-school programs, 587
  employment and, 639
  identity development and, 460
  school transitions and, 630–631
  student body size and, 627
Eye blink reflex, 129
Eyes. *See also* Vision
  postnatal development of, 154

  prenatal development of, 93, 97
  pupil dilation and temperamental style, 417
  REM sleep and oxygenation of, 133
Eyewitness testimony by children, 298–299

F

Face perception, 162–163
  emotional development and, 402, 408
Facial hair development, 183, 201
Factor analysis
  early analysts, 317–318
  intelligence test components, 317–320
  modern analysts, 318–320
  self-esteem, 449
FAE (fetal alcohol effects), 100–101
Fagan Test of Infant Intelligence, 325–326
Failure to thrive (nonorganic), 199, 399
Fairness. *See also* Justice; Prosocial behavior
  distributive justice and, 503–504
  moral development and, 488
  reciprocity as standard, 489
Faith. *See* Spirituality and religiosity
Fallopian tubes, 88–90. *See also* Reproductive system
False beliefs, children's recognition of, 443–446
Families, 557–595. *See also* Child-rearing practices; Grandparents; Home environment; Parent *entries*; Sibling relationship
  adaptation to change, 560–561, 566–568
  adoptive. *See* Adoption
  aggression in children and family dynamics, 512–514
  blended. *See* Blended families
  child care. *See* Child care
  child maltreatment and family dynamics, 589–591
  community and neighborhood influences on, 562
  computers in homes, 622, 624–625
  direct influences of, 559–560
  divorce. *See* Divorce
  evolutionary origins of, 557–558
  extended families. *See* Extended-family households
  functions of, 558–559
  homosexual families, 576–577
  indirect influences of, 560
  maternal employment. *See* Maternal employment
  never-married single-parent families, 577
  newborns, adjustments to, 561
  one-child families, 574–575
  reconstituted. *See* Blended families
  single-parent. *See* Single-parent families
  size of. *See* Family size
  skipped-generation families, 584
  social system perspective, 559–563, 589

societal influences on, 562
stepfamilies. *See* Blended families
substance abuse, family influences on, 615
television viewing and, 617, 619
transitions in, 571–588
types of family structures, 571–588
Family life education, for blended families, 582–583
Family planning. *See* Contraception
Family size, 572
gender typing and, 537
IQ scores and, 345
only children, 574–575
sexual activity of adolescents and, 211
television viewing and, 617
Family therapy. *See* Counseling
Family violence. *See* Child maltreatment; Spousal abuse
Fantasy play. *See* Make-believe play
FAS (fetal alcohol syndrome), 100–101
Fast-mapping, in vocabulary development, 373–374
Fat, body. *See also* Obesity
baby fat, 177
menarche and, 202
prenatal development, 94
Fat, dietary, 193. *See also* Nutrition
breastfeeding and, 193
Father. *See* Families; Parent *entries*
Father-adolescent relationship. *See also* Parent-adolescent relationship
incest. *See* Sexual abuse of children
pubertal changes, response to and, 203
Father-child relationship. *See also* Parent-child relationship
divorce and, 578–581
favoritism in, 574
gender stereotyping and, 535
homosexual fathers and, 576
incest. *See* Sexual abuse of children
maternal employment and, 584–585
remarriage and, 582
Sweden, 529
teenage parenthood and, 217
Father-headed households. *See* Single-parent families
Father-infant relationship. *See also* Parent-infant relationship
Aka of Central Africa, 431
attachment and, 429–431
cultural influences on, 431
newborns, 561
Father-stepmother families, 582
Fatness. *See* Fat *entries*; Obesity
Fear
conditioning of, 138
early childhood, 405
infancy and toddlerhood, 403
middle childhood, 406
rejected-withdrawn children, 606
self-care children, 587
sex-related differences in, 545
sexual abuse victims, 590
"whipping boys," 607
Fearful distress, as temperament dimension, 414
Feeding practices. *See also* Eating habits; Nutrition
attachment and, 421
bottle-feeding, 193–194
breastfeeding. *See* Breastfeeding

classical conditioning and, 138
obesity and, 197
Female vs. male development. *See* Gender *entries*; Sex-related differences
Feminine morality (Gilligan), 498–499
Femininity. *See* Gender *entries*
Fertility. *See also* Conception; Infertility
pubertal development and, 200–202
sexually transmitted diseases and, 214
Fertility drugs, 75
Fertilization, in vitro. *See* In vitro fertilization
Fetal alcohol effects (FAE), 100–101
Fetal Alcohol Syndrome (FAS), 100–101
Fetal medicine, 85–87
Fetoscopy, 86, 93
Fetus, period of prenatal development, 91, 93–103
Field experiments, 57, 59, 626
Fijians, moral development among, 479
Fine motor development
drawing and, 238
infancy and toddlerhood, 144–149
Finland
infant mortality rate, 117
menarche, 184
Firearms, and adolescent suicide, 459
Fitness. *See* Exercise; Health; Nutrition
Fluid intelligence (Cattell), 318–319, 338–339
fMRI (functional magnetic resonance imaging), 49–50, 288
Folic acid and prenatal nutrition, 104
Fontanels, 180, 182
Food. *See* Eating *entries*; Feeding practices; Malnutrition; Nutrition; Vitamins and minerals
Food supplement programs, 104, 195
Forceps, in childbirth, 111
Foreclosure, in identity development, 457–460
Formal operational stage of cognitive development, 21–22, 222, 254–257
cultural influences on, 256–257
egocentrism in, 255
hypothetico-deductive reasoning in, 254, 256
individual differences in, 256
propositional thought in, 254–256
research on, 256–257
Formulas (bottle-feeding), 193–194
Fragile X syndrome, 80–81
France
infant mortality rate, 117
reproductive technology laws, 85
teenage pregnancy rate, 214–215
Fraternal twins, 75. *See also* Twin studies; Twins
Freestanding birth centers, 109
Freud's psychosexual theory. *See* Psychosexual theory of development (Freud)
Friendships, 468–472. *See also* Peer relations
ability grouping in schools and, 633
aggression and, 514
attachment security and, 431

benefits of, 471–472
cliques, 609–610
interaction between friends, 469–471
levels of understanding of, 468–469
peer acceptance and, 606
peer victimization and, 607, 630
resemblance between friends, 470–471
school entry and, 629–630
sex-related differences in, 469–471
stability of, 469
understanding of, 468–469
Frontal lobes, 187, 190. *See also* Cerebral cortex
ADHD and brain activity, 288
autism and, 446
brain growth spurts and, 191
Broca's area, 362–364
cognitive inhibition and, 284–285
infantile amnesia and, 296
Full inclusion of students with learning difficulties, 635
Full-service schools, 629
Function words, in early vocabulary, 372
Functional brain-imaging techniques, 50
Functional magnetic resonance imaging (fMRI), 49–50
ADHD studies, 288
Functional play, 600
Functionalist approach to emotions, 398–401
Fuzzy-trace theory, 293–294

G

Games. *See also* Athletics; Play; Toys
cultural influences on, 603
gender stereotyping of, 523–524
language development and, 369
make-believe play and, 262
motor development and, 177–178
perspective taking games, 466
privileged-information game, 466
recursive thought and, 466
rule-oriented games, 600–601
videogames. *See* Videogames
Gametes, 73–76. *See also* Ova; Sperm
Gangs, and aggression, 515
Gardner's multiple intelligences theory, 322–324
educational principles based on, 353
Gastrointestinal system
breastfeeding and, 193
prenatal development of, 92–93
Gay men. *See* Homosexuality
Geese, imprinting studies, 422
Gender, defined, 522
Gender appropriate. *See* Gender stereotyping
Gender bias
person perception and, 463–464
sex-related differences in bias, 526
Gender consistency, in development of gender constancy, 539–540
Gender constancy, 539–540
Gender differences. *See* Sex-related differences
Gender equality
child-rearing practices and, 535

maternal employment and, 585
promoting, 552–554
sex-related differences in belief in, 526
Sweden, 528–529
Gender gap. *See* Sex-related differences
Gender identity, 538–544
adolescence, 541
cognitive-developmental theory of, 539–540
defined, 522
depression and, 550
early childhood, 539–540
emergence of, 539–540
friendships and, 471
gender schema theory of, 541–543
individual differences in, 541
middle childhood, 540–541
personality traits and, 538, 540
self-esteem and, 538
social learning theory of, 539–540
theories of, 539, 541–543
Gender intensification, 541
depression and, 550
Gender labeling, in development of gender constancy, 539–540
Gender-linked preferences. *See* Gender typing
Gender-role adoption. *See also* Gender stereotyping
defined, 522
gender constancy and, 540
gender stereotyping and, 527
identity development and, 460
milestones, 553
sex hormones and, 528–531
Gender-role identity. *See* Gender identity
Gender schema theory, 522, 541–543
Gender stability, in development of gender constancy, 539–540
Gender-stereotype flexibility, 525–527
gender constancy and, 540
maternal employment and, 584
Gender stereotyping, 522–527. *See also* Gender typing
academic subjects, 525
adolescence, 62–63, 524–526, 541
adolescent initiation ceremonies and, 536
cultural influences on, 522–523, 529
defined, 522
early childhood, 523–524
ethnic differences in stereotyping, 526
flexibility in. *See* Gender-stereotype flexibility
gender constancy and, 540
gender-role adoption and, 527
individual differences in stereotyping, 526
information processing principles and, 23–24
intelligence tests, 324–325
maternal employment and, 536, 583–584
middle childhood, 524–526
milestones, 553
parenthood and, 561
personality traits, 522–525
reducing, 543, 552–554
sex-related differences in math and science and, 548
sex-related differences in stereotyping, 526

socioeconomic differences in stereotyping, 526
sports and, 180–181
television viewing and, 617, 619–620
videogames and, 625
vocational development and, 534
Gender typing, 521–555. *See also* Gender identity; Gender stereotyping; Sex-related differences
adult perceptions and expectations and, 531–532
aggression and, 511
androgens and, 528–531
authoritative parenting and, 564
child-rearing practices and, 532–535, 564
cognitive-developmental theory of, 522
cultural influences on, 522, 528–529
defined, 522
depression and gender-typed coping styles, 550
early childhood, 532
environmental influences on, 531–537
factors affecting, 527–538
gender schema theory of, 522, 541–543
genetic influences on, 528–531
infancy and toddlerhood, 532
middle childhood, 532–533
milestones, 553
observational learning of, 536
peer relations and, 536–537
psychoanalytic theories of, 522
sibling relationships and, 537
social learning theory of, 522
teachers influencing, 535–536
television influencing, 536
theories of, 522
Gene mapping. *See* Genetic maps
Gene splicing, 89
General factor ("g"), in factor analysis of intelligence test components, 317–318
General growth curve, 185
Generalized other, in development of self-concept, 448
Generational differences, 62–63
Generativity, as psychosocial stage of development, 19
Genes, 72. *See also* Genetic *entries*
crossing over of, 73–75
dominant-recessive inheritance, 76–77
heterozygous, 76
homozygous, 76
Human Genome Project, 88–89
mapping. *See* Genetic maps
modifier genes, 77
mutation, 81
splicing, 89
Genetic code, 72–73
Genetic counseling, 83–84, 89
Genetic diagnosis, preimplantation, 86
Genetic disorders. *See* Chromosomal abnormalities
Genetic engineering, 86, 88–89
Genetic-environmental correlation, 122–123
HOME scores and, 344
Genetic imprinting, 80–81
Genetic maps, 86, 88–89
sexual orientation, 212

Genetics, 71–83. *See also* Chromosomal abnormalities; Chromosomes; Genes; Inheritance; Nature-nurture controversy
ADHD and, 288
behavioral genetics, 118–123, 418
depression and, 549
empathy development and, 412
family studies of. *See* Kinship studies; Twin studies
gender typing and, 528–531
hand preference and, 189
heritability estimates. *See* Heritability estimates
HOME scores and, 344
homosexuality and, 212
intelligence and, 119, 332–338
IQ scores and, 328–329
moral development and, 480–481
obesity and, 196
patterns of genetic inheritance, 76–81
physical development and, 192
pleiotropism, 77
pubertal development and, 202
shyness and, 417
sociability and, 417
temperament and, 416–418
Genital herpes, and prenatal development, 102–103
Genital stage of development (Freud), 17–18
Genitals. *See also* Reproductive system
abnormalities and cancer of, in DES daughters and sons, 101
ambiguous genitals, 531
circumcision, 205
congenital adrenal hyperplasia (CAH), 530–531
growth curve, 185
mutilation of female genitals, 205
prenatal development, 93, 97
pubertal development of, 200–202
Genotypes, 71–72, 75
German measles and prenatal development, 102
Germany
attachment style of infants, 425–426
family size, 572
infant mortality rate, 117
Gesell's schedule of child development, 14
Gestures
autism and, 446
chimpanzees, communication among, 360
preverbal, 369
sign language. *See* Sign language
speech-gesture mismatches, 283
GH. *See* Growth hormone (GH)
Gifted children
clinical method research study, 50–51
creativity and, 349
education of, 353, 534
multiple intelligences theory and, 323
sex-related differences in mathematical abilities, 546
Gilligan's theory of feminine morality, 498–499
Gists, in fuzzy-trace theory, 293–294
Glial cells, 93, 187
Goal-directed behavior, in sensorimotor stage of cognitive development, 225

Gonorrhea. *See* Sexually transmitted diseases (STDs)
"Good boy-good girl" orientation in moral development, 493, 500
Goodness-of-fit model of child-rearing, 420–421, 428, 483
Government policies. *See* Public policies
Grade structures of schools, 630–631
Grammatical development, 358, 379–385. *See also* Language development
complex grammatical forms, 382–383
connectionist modeling of mastery, 279, 384
early phase of, 380–382
environmental influences on, 385
first word combinations, 379–380
later development of, 383–384
metalinguistic awareness and, 390
milestones in, 391
morphology, 358
strategies for acquiring grammar, 384–385
syntax, 358
theories of, 384–385
universal grammar, 359–360, 364
Williams Syndrome and, 365
Grammatical morphemes, 381–382
Grandparents
extended-family households, 571
grandchildren raised by, 584
influence of, 560
visitation rights after divorce, 581
Grasp reflex, 149
Grasp skill development, 147–149
Great Britain. *See also* England
infant mortality rate, 117
secular gains in development, 185
SIDS public education programs, 140
teenage pregnancy rate, 214–215
Great Depression of 1930s, 61
Greater Expectations (Damon), 15
Greece, infant mortality rate, 117
Grooming. *See* Dress and grooming
Gross motor development, 177–181
infancy and toddlerhood, 144–146
sex-related differences in, 178–181
Group differences. *See* Ethnicity and race; Sex-related differences; Socioeconomic status (SES)
Groups. *See* Peer groups
Growth. *See* Body *entries*; Physical development
Growth centers, 179
Growth curves, 174–175, 185
Growth hormone (GH), 182–183, 192
deprivation dwarfism and, 199
Growth spurts
adolescence, 183–184
brain development, 190–191, 276
pubertal development and, 201
Growth stunting and obesity, 195–196
Guatemala
childbirth practices, 110
diarrhea among children, 198
malnutrition in rural villages, 195
Mayans. *See* Mayans
Guidance Study, 59, 61
Guided participation, 262
Guilt, 404
child maltreatment victims, 592
divorce of parents, response to, 579

moral development and, 480–484
perspective taking and, 467
psychosocial stage of development, 19
sexual abuse and, 590
Guns, and adolescent suicide, 459
Gusii of Kenya, mother-infant relationship and attachment, 427

H

Habituation-dishabituation response
categorization ability studies, 230–231
infant learning and, 141–142
intelligence predictions based on, 325
kinetic depth cues studies, 157
mathematical reasoning studies, 306–307
object perception studies, 163
object permanence studies, 227–228
object support studies, 229
perceptual development studies, 150
prenatal evidence of, 141
Hair
adolescence, facial and body hair growth, 183, 200–201
dominant-recessive inheritance, 76
Hall's theory of child development, 13–14
adolescence and, 173
Hand preference, 189–190
Handedness, 188–190
Handguns, and adolescent suicide, 459
Happiness. *See also* Emotional well-being
infancy and toddlerhood, 402
temperament dimension, 414
Harsh punishment. *See* Child maltreatment; Punishment (disciplinary)
Hausa of Nigeria, accomplishment of conservation tasks, 252
Hawaiians
creole English, 361
Kamehameha Elementary Education Program (KEEP), 628–629
Kauai study of birth complications, 115–117
language customs and IQ scores, 340
Head Start programs, 37, 346–347, 349
Health. *See also* Diseases; Immunization; Nutrition
adolescence, 208–217
emotions and, 399
family size and, 572
poverty and, 569
public health programs, 198–199
skipped-generation families and, 584
Health care, 4. *See also* Diseases; Medications; *specific procedures (e.g., Blood tests)*
anorexia nervosa, 209, 290
bulimia, 210
childbirth. *See* Childbirth

Immigrants. *See also specific culture (e.g., Asian Americanss)*
  educational endeavors, valuing of, 344
  intelligence traits, valuing of, 339
  language acquisition, 361, 363
Immune system
  emotions and, 399
  malnutrition and, 198
  prenatal development, 94–95
  prenatal nutrition and, 104
  stress and, 105
Immunization, 198–199
  rate of, among preschool children, 34
  rubella, 102
  uninsured children, 38
  United States in comparison to other nations, 35
Implantation of blastocyst, 90–92
Impoverishment. *See* Deprivation; Poverty
Imprinting, ethological, 25
  attachment and, 422
Imprinting, genetic, 80–81
Impulsivity. *See also* Emotional self-regulation; Self-control
  ADHD and, 288–289
  deaf child of hearing parents, 263
  maternal depression and, 400
  permissive parenting and, 564
  rejected-aggressive children, 606, 608
  substance abuse and, 615
In vitro fertilization, 84–85
  fraternal twinning and, 75
  preimplantation genetic diagnosis, 86
Inattention. *See* Attention
Incest. *See* Sexual abuse of children
Incremental view of ability, 454–455
Independence. *See* Autonomy; Dependency
Independent movement, and depth perception, 158–159
Independent variables, in experimental research design, 56
India
  emotional display rules, 407
  moral development in, 503
  moral reasoning in, 498
  play in early childhood, 603
Individual differences
  abstract thinking, 256
  divorce, child's response to, 578–580
  emotions. *See* Temperament
  empathy, 411–412
  gender identity, 541
  gender stereotyping, 526
  language development, 374
  learning, 259
  menarche, 202
  motor development, 145
  perspective taking, 465–466
  pubertal development, 202
  self-control, 508–509
  self-esteem, 449, 451
  sibling relationship, 573
  temperament. *See* Temperament
  voluntary reaching, 148
Individualistic societies, 36
  cooperative learning and, 266
  moral reasoning and, 503
  perspective taking and, 465
  self-concept among, 448
Individuals with Disabilities Education Act, 634

Indonesia
  make-believe play with infants and toddlers, 264
  mutilation of female genitals, 205
Inductive discipline, 482
  emotional sensitivity and, 549
  moral development and, 497
Indulgent parenting. *See* Permissive parenting
Industry, as psychosocial stage of development, 19
Infancy and toddlerhood, 5, 127–171. *See also* Newborns
  anger in, 401–403
  attachment in. *See* Attachment
  balance in, 152–153
  body composition in, 177
  body proportion in, 176
  categorization abilities in, 230–231
  cognitive development in, 224–235. *See also* Sensorimotor stage of cognitive development
  compliance in, 506
  cosleeping arrangements in, 131–132
  death in. *See* Infant mortality
  emotional expression in, 401–405
  emotional self-regulation in, 405
  empathic responses in, 411, 480
  fear in, 403
  fine motor development in, 144–149
  gender typing in, 532
  gross motor development in, 144–146, 177–178
  happiness in, 402
  hearing in, 153–154
  height in, 174–175
  intelligence tests in, 325–326
  intervention programs, 348
  language development, 366–370
  laughter in, 402
  learning capacities in, 137–144
  low birth weight. *See* Low birth weight
  make-believe play in, 227, 264, 599
  malnutrition in, 195
  memory in, 291–292
  motor development in, 144–150
  nutrition in, 193–194
  parental relationships in. *See* Father-infant relationship; Mother-infant relationship; Parent-infant relationship
  peer relations in, 599, 603
  perceptual development in, 150–167
  planning in, 285–286
  play in, 599
  preterm. *See* Preterm infants
  problem solving in, 231
  prosocial behavior in, 480
  recall memory in, 291–292
  recognition memory in, 291
  sadness in, 401–403
  self-conscious emotions in, 404
  self-control in, 506–507
  self-movement, 152–153
  sleep in, 131–132
  smiling in, 402
  vision in, 154–166
  visual acuity in, 154–156
  vocabulary in, 372–373
  weight in, 174–175
Infant-caregiver attachment. *See* Attachment

Infant mortality, 42, 115–117
  aspirin, maternal use of and, 98
  drug use during pregnancy and, 98
  home delivery and, 111
  pesticides and, 80
  Rh blood incompatibility and, 112
  sex-related differences in, 79, 180
  SIDS and, 140–141
  small-for-date infants, 113
  smoking during pregnancy and, 99
  United States compared to other nations, 116–117
Infant-parent relationship. *See* Attachment; Father-infant relationship; Mother-infant relationship; Parent-infant relationship
Infant Psychological Development Scale, 326
Infant-rearing practices. *See* Child-rearing practices
Infantile amnesia, 296
Infantile autism. *See* Autism
Infectious diseases, 198–199. *See also* Diseases; Immunization; *specific diseases (e.g., AIDS)*
  prenatal development and, 102–103
  pubertal development and, 202
  small-for-date infants, 113
Inferences. *See also* Person perception
  memory and, 293
  metacognition and, 300–301
  self-concept and, 448
  semantic development and, 378
  transitive, 249–250, 252
Inferiority. *See also* Self-esteem
  learned helplessness and, 454
  psychosocial stage of development, 19
Infertility. *See also* Reproductive technologies
  adoption and, 575
  fertility drugs, 75
Information processing theories, 23–24, 32, 271–313. *See also* Attention; Memory; Metacognition
  computer simulations of, 272, 278–280, 311
  connectionism. *See* Connectionism
  development theories of, 276–283
  educational principles based on, 303–310
  evaluation of, 310–311
    connectionism, 280–281
    neo-Piagetian theory, 278
    strategy-choice model, 282
  gender schema theory, 522, 541–543
  gender typing and, 522
  horizontal décalage and, 277–278
  implications for development, 274–276
  intelligence, 320–324
  levels-of-processing model, 274
  mechanisms of cognitive change, 310
  mental strategies. *See* Mental strategies
  milestones, 303
  neo-Piagetian perspective. *See* Neo-Piagetian perspective (Case)
  research on, 274
  sensory register in, 272–274
  social problem solving, 472–473
  store model of, 272–274

strategy-choice model. *See* Strategy-choice model of information processing (Siegler)
Informed consent of research participants, 66–67
Inhalants. *See also* Drug use and abuse
  teenage use, 614
Inheritance, 9. *See also* Genetic *entries*; Nature-nurture controversy
  codominance, 77–78
  concordance rates. *See* Concordance rates
  dominant-recessive, 76–77
  genetic imprinting, 80–81
  heritability estimates. *See* Heritability estimates
  multiple births, 75
  mutation of genes and, 81
  patterns of genetic inheritance, 76–81
  physical development and, 184
  polygenic, 81, 118
  teratogens and, 95
  X-linked inheritance, 78–80
Inhibited (shy) child, as temperament type, 416–417. *See also* Shyness
  peer relations and, 605
Inhibition
  ADHD and, 288
  Chinese, valuing of, 606
  cognitive, 284–285, 310
  emotional self-regulation and, 404–405
  self-control and, 506
  "whipping boys" and, 607
Initiation ceremonies in adolescence, 203–205
Initiative, as psychosocial stage of development, 19
Inner self, 443
Input layers, in artificial neural networks, 278–279
Insight process, and creativity, 351–352
Institutionalization, 168–169
  infant attachment and, 426
  motor development and, 147, 149
Instruction. *See* Education; Learning; Schools; Teacher *entries; specific subjects (e.g., Mathematics; Reading)*
Instrument delivery, 111
Instrumental aggression, 509, 511
Instrumental purpose orientation in moral development, 493
Instrumental traits, in gender stereotyping, 523, 528
Insurance. *See* Health insurance
Intellectual development. *See* Cognitive development
Intelligence, 315–355. *See also* Cognitive development
  ADHD and, 288
  alcohol use during pregnancy and, 100
  aspirin, maternal use of and, 98
  authentic assessment, 342
  brain growth spurts and, 191
  canalization, 121
  crystallized intelligence (Cattell), 318–319, 328
  cultural influences on, 329, 339–340
  definitions of, 316–324

early learning centers and, 169
environmental influences on,
    328–329, 332, 335–337,
    342–345
family size and, 572
fluid intelligence (Cattell),
    318–319, 338–339
genetic influences on, 328–329,
    332–338
habituation-dishabituation re-
    sponse and, 142, 325
heritability estimates, 119–120,
    418
hierarchical models of, 318
home environment and, 342–345
information processing theories
    of, 320–324
institutionalization and, 168–169
intervention programs, 120
kinship studies, 119
language customs and, 339–340
Level I-Level II theory of (Jensen),
    332–333, 335
low birth weight and, 112
malnutrition and, 195
maternal employment and, 584
measurement of. See Intelligence
    quotients (IQs); Intelligence
    tests
multiple intelligences theory
    (Gardner), 322–324, 353
NBAS "recovery curves" and, 137
object-permanence tasks as pre-
    dictor of, 326
poverty and, 569
practical intelligence, 330, 340
prenatal malnutrition and, 104
range of reaction and, 121
small-for-date infants, 113
smoking during pregnancy and,
    99
teenage parenthood and, 215
theories of, 317–324
three-stratum theory of (Carroll),
    319–320
triarchic theory of (Sternberg),
    321–322
two-factor theory of, 317–318
Intelligence quotients (IQs), 326–345
academic achievement and, 317,
    328–330
componential analyses of,
    320–321
computation and distribution of,
    326
correlational stability, 327
creativity and, 352
early intervention programs and,
    348
environmental cumulative deficit
    hypothesis and, 328
ethnic differences in, 331–332
gifted students, 349
Head Start programs and,
    346–347, 349
heritability estimates, 334–336,
    345
HOME scores and, 343–344
language customs and, 339–340
learning disabled students, 635
malnutrition and, 195
moral development and, 495
predicting later performance
    from, 326–331
prior exposure to test content
    and, 338–339
psychological adjustment and,
    330–331

schooling and, 329
socioeconomic differences in,
    328–329, 331–333
stability of, 327–328
temperament and, 419
transracial adoption and, 337
vocational attainment and perfor-
    mance and, 330
washout effect, 347
Intelligence tests, 315, 324–326
    Bayley Scales of Infant Develop-
        ment, 325
    computing scores, 326
    convergent thinking and, 350
    cultural bias in, 319, 324, 333,
        338–342
    developmental approach to con-
        struction, 317
    divergent thinking and, 350
    dynamic testing, 340–342
    factor analysis of components,
        317–320
    factors in, 324–325
    Fagan Test of Infant Intelligence,
        325–326
    gender bias in, 324–325
    general factor ("g"), 317–318
    group administered, 324
    individually administered, 324,
        341
    infant intelligence tests, 325–326
    Infant Psychological Development
        Scale, 326
    language customs and, 339–340
    Learning Potential Assessment
        Device, 341
    primary mental abilities, 317–318
    prior exposure to content,
        338–339
    Raven Progressive Matrices, 338
    reactions to testing conditions, 340
    reducing test bias, 340–342
    scores on. See Intelligence quo-
        tients (IQs)
    specific factor ("s"), 317–318
    Stanford-Binet Intelligence Scale,
        14, 316–317, 324–325
    subtests in, 324–325
    Wechsler Intelligence Scales, 325
Intensity of reaction, as tempera-
    ment dimension, 414
Intentional behavior, in sensorimo-
    tor stage of cognitive devel-
    opment, 225
Intentions, understanding of, 462
    aggression and, 514
    moral development and, 482
    moral reasoning and, 490
    rejected-aggressive children, 606
Interactional synchrony, in attach-
    ment, 426–427
Interactionist theories of language
    development, 364–366
Interactions. See Social interactions
    marital. See Marital relationship
    parent-child. See Father entries;
        Mother entries; Parent
        entries
    peer. See Peer entries
    sibling. See Sibling relationship
    teacher. See Teacher-parent
        interaction; Teacher-pupil
        interaction
Interdisciplinary nature of child
    development studies, 4
Intermodal perception, 164–166
Internal working model, in attach-
    ment theory, 423, 429

Internalization, and moral develop-
    ment, 481–483, 487, 497
milestones in, 510
Internalized values orientation, in
    prosocial reasoning, 505
Internet, 621, 624–625
Interpersonal behavior. See Families;
    Friendships; Marital
    relationship; Peer entries;
    Sibling relationship; Social
    interactions
Interpersonal intelligence (Gardner),
    323
Intersubjectivity, in sociocultural
    theory of cognitive develop-
    ment, 261–262
Intervention programs, 38. See also
    Early intervention programs;
    Public education programs
    ADHD, 289
    aggression, 515–517
    anorexia nervosa, 209
    athletic participation by girls, 181
    attachment security, 428–429
    attribution retraining, 455–456
    bulimia, 210
    child maltreatment, 593
    delinquency prevention and treat-
        ment, 517
    divorce, 580–581
    educational enrichment for chil-
        dren living in poverty, 348
    eyewitness testimony by children,
        299
    food supplement programs, 104,
        195
    gender-schematic thinking, 543
    immunization, 198–199
    intelligence and, 120
    malnutrition, 195
    maternal depression, 400
    moral reasoning training, 497
    newborns
        adjustments to, 561
        NBAS-based interventions, 137
        preterm infants, 114–115
    nonorganic failure to thrive, 199
    obesity, for, 198
    otitis media, 155
    peer acceptance, 608
    peer victimization, 607
    prenatal malnutrition, 104–105
    preterm infants, 114–115
    Project Head Start, 37, 346–347,
        349
    resiliency of children and, 10
    school transitions, 631–632
    sexual abuse victims, 591
    SIDS public education programs,
        140
    suicide, 459
    teenage pregnancy and parent-
        hood, 216–217
    teenage substance use and abuse,
        615
    visual impairment, 160
    war, effect on children, 516
Interview research methods, 45, 47–49
    temperament measurement, 415
Intestinal infections, 198
Intimacy. See also Peer relations
    friendships and, 469–471
    identity formation and, 457
    psychosocial stage of development,
        19
    sex-related differences in, 457
Intrapersonal intelligence (Gardner),
    323

Inuit, newborn behavior and child-
    rearing practices, 137
Invariant features, in differentiation
    theory, 166–167
Investment theory of creativity
    (Sternberg and Lubart),
    351–353
Invisible displacement task, in senso-
    rimotor stage of cognitive
    development, 227
Ionizing radiation. See Radiation
IQs. See Intelligence quotients (IQs)
Iran, motor development studies of
    institutionalized infants, 147
Ireland, infant mortality rate, 117
Iron, 193
    adolescence, 194
    deficiency in, 195
Irony, and language development,
    377
Irreversibility in thinking, 241,
    245–246
Irritable distress, as temperament di-
    mension, 414–416
    attachment and, 427–428
Isolation. See also Loneliness
    attachment security and, 431
    autism and, 446
    child maltreatment and family
        isolation, 29, 591
    homosexuality in adolescence
        and, 213
    otitis media and, 155
    psychosocial stage of develop-
        ment, 19
    suicide and, 459
Isolettes, for preterm infants, 114
Israel
    attachment style of infants, 426
    death concept, development of in
        childhood, 245
    infant mortality rate, 117
    parental response to crying, study
        of, 135
Israeli kibbutzim
    achievement-related attributions
        among, 455
    moral development among chil-
        dren, 497–498
    parental response to crying, study
        of, 135
    stranger anxiety among infants
        and toddlers, 403
    war, effect on children, 516
Italy
    infant mortality rate, 117
    menarche, 184
    reproductive technology laws, 85

J

Jamaican West Indians, motor devel-
    opment in infancy, 147–148
Japanese. See also Asian societies
    academic achievement among,
        452
    achievement-related attributions
        among, 455
    attachment style of infants,
        425–426
    child maltreatment among, 592
    cooperative learning among, 266
    cosleeping arrangements in in-
        fancy and childhood, 132
    emotional display rules, 407

family size, 572
infant mortality rate, 117
language development among, 374–375
mathematical skills, 308
mathematics and science achievement of students, 637–638
menarche, 202
motor development in infancy, 147
national examinations, 634
peer relations in adolescence, 604
secular gains in development, 184–185
self-concept among, 448
self-conscious emotions among, 404
self-esteem among, 451
temperament of infants, 419
Jarara of South America, childbirth practices, 109
Jealousy
friendships and, 470
sibling relationships and, 573–574
Jensen's Level I–Level II theory of intelligence, 332–333, 335
Jewish. See Judaism
Job training programs, 639–640. See also Vocational education
Jobs. See Employment; Vocational entries
Joint attention
autism and, 446
deaf child of hearing parents, 263
language development and, 368–369, 387
theory of mind and, 444
Joint custody of children, 581
Judaism
adolescent rites of passage, 204
death concept, development of and, 245
Jumping, 145, 177–178
sex-related differences, 180 in
Justice
distributive, 503–504
moral development and, 488–489
moral reasoning and, 498–499, 503
Juvenile delinquency. See Delinquency
Juveniles. See Adolescence

K

Kaluli of Papua New Guinea, language development among, 369, 389
Kamehameha Elementary Education Program (KEEP), 628–629
"Kangaroo baby care," for preterm infants, 115
Karyotype of chromosomes, 72
Kauai study on long-term consequences of birth complications, 115–117
KEEP (Kamehameha Elementary Education Program), 628–629
Kenya
Gusii, mother-infant relationship and attachment, 427
Kipsigis, motor development in infancy, 147
Nyansongo, gender typing among, 528

Kibbutzim. See Israeli Kibbutzim
Kindergartens. See Preschool and kindergarten; Schools
Kinetic depth cues, 157–158
Kinship studies, 119. See also Adoption studies; Twin studies
depression, 549
intelligence, 416–418
IQ scores, 333–337, 345
nonshared environmental influences in home environment, 345
temperament and personality, 416–418
Kipsigis of Kenya, motor development in infancy, 147
Klinefelter syndrome, 82–83
Knowledge, 310. See also Cognitive development; Education; Intelligence entries; Learning
cognitive capacity, of, 300–301
creativity and, 351–352
illocutionary, 386
memory and, 294–295
mental strategies, of, 302
metacognitive, 300–301. See also Metacognition
milestones in, 303
sociolinguistic knowledge, 358
Kohlberg's stages of gender constancy, 539–540
Kohlberg's theory of moral development, 491–496
challenges to, 498–500
research on, 494–495
stages of, 492–496, 500
Korean Americanss. See also Asian Americanss
English grammar performance, 363–364
play and peer relations in early childhood, 603–604
Koreans. See also Asian societies
language development among, 247, 375
mathematical skills, 308
mathematics and science achievement of students, 637
moral reasoning among, 490
Kpelle of Liberia, object sorting among, 271
!Kung of Botswana
adolescent initiation ceremony, 204–205
childbirth practices, 109
Kwashiorkor, 194–195

L

Labor. See Employment; Vocational entries
Labor, birthing. See Childbirth
Laboratory experiments, 56–57, 59
Language acquisition device (LAD), 359–360, 364
Language and Thought of the Child, The (Piaget), 221
Language customs and intelligence, 339–340
Language development, 357–395. See also Speech; specific components (e.g., Grammatical development; Semantic development)
aggression and, 511, 515

autism and, 446
behaviorist theories of, 359
bilingualism and, 392–393
brain areas for, 362–364
brain growth spurts and, 191
cerebral cortex and, 187–188
child-directed speech and, 367–368, 370
child-rearing practices and, 360, 368–369
cognitive development and, 255
components of language, 358
cooing and babbling, 368
cultural influences on, 361, 374
delays in, 374
delinquent behavior and, 513
Down syndrome and, 82
drug use during pregnancy and, 99
early childhood, 235–236
emotional self-regulation and, 405–406
empathy and, 411
expressive style of learning, 374
first words, 359, 370, 372
gestural communication and, 369
handedness and, 188
hearing loss and, 263, 364, 368
home environment and, 343–344
imitation and, 359, 374, 385, 389
individual differences in, 374
infants' hearing capacities and, 153–154
institutionalization and, 168
interactionist theories of, 364–366
intersubjectivity and, 262
joint attention and, 368–369
lateralization of brain and, 188–189, 363
low birth weight and, 112
make-believe play and, 237
mental retardation and, 365–366
metalinguistic awareness, 389–392
milestones in, 390–391
motor development and, 144
"naming explosion," 373
nativist theory of, 359–365
operant conditioning and, 359
otitis media and, 155
overextension in, 375–376
perceptual development and, 150
prelinguistic development, 366–370
preterm infants, 115
production versus comprehension, 372
referential style of learning, 374
reinforcement and, 359
self-control and, 507
self-development and, 442
sensitive period in, 363
sex-related differences in, 374, 545–546
sign language. See Sign language
telegraphic speech in, 379–380
theories of, 358–366
grammatical development, 384–385
semantic development, 377–378
theory of mind origins and, 444
turn-taking and, 369
two-word utterance phase, 379–380
underextension in, 375–376
visual impairment and, 160
Williams Syndrome and, 365

Language-making capacity (LMC), in grammatical development, 384–385
Languages
bilingualism. See Bilingualism
semilingualism, 393
universal grammar and, 359–360, 364
Lanugo, formation of, 93
Laotian Americanss, growth stunting among, 196
Latency stage of development (Freud), 17–18
Lateralization of brain, 187–190
atypical, 189
handedness and, 189–190
language development and, 363
temperamental style and, 417
Latin Americanss. See Hispanics; Mexican Americanss
Latvia, body size in, 184
Laughter in infancy and toddlerhood, 402
Laws. See Legal issues; Public policies
Lead poisoning, and prenatal development, 101
Learned drives, in drive-reduction theory, 20
attachment and, 421
Learned helplessness, 454–455
attribution retraining, 455–456
depression, 550
mathematical ability and, 547
rejected-withdrawn children and, 608
Learning. See also Cognitive development; specific forms (e.g., Imitation; Operant conditioning)
academic. See Education; Schools; Teacher entries; specific subjects (e.g., Mathematics; Reading)
achievement in. See Academic achievement
assisted discovery, 264
cooperative. See Cooperative learning
cultural influences on, 266–267
discovery learning, 258
early learning centers, 169
individual differences in, 259
infancy and toddlerhood, capacities in, 137–144
KEEP classrooms, learning activities and performance in, 628–629
observational. See Imitation; Modeling; Observational learning
peer collaboration, 264–266
readiness to learn, 258–259
sibling relationship and, 574
social learning theory. See Social learning theory (Bandura)
social referencing and, 408–409
speech-gesture mismatches and, 283
verbal instruction and, 267
Learning disabilities
attention-deficit hyperactivity disorder, 288–289
child maltreatment victims, 592
computer-assisted instruction and, 624
full inclusion of students, 635
mainstreaming of students, 634–635

oxygen deprivation during child-
	birth and, 112
private speech and, 260
sex-related differences in, 79, 545
Learning goals, and attributional
	style, 454–455
Learning Potential Assessment De-
	vice, 341
Left-handedness, 188–190
Legal issues. *See also* Ethics; Public
	policies
	Human Genome Project, 89
	reproductive technology, 84–85
Legal proceedings
	child maltreatment, 593
	child support, 581
	divorce mediation, 580
	eyewitness testimony by children,
		298–299
	juvenile justice system, 511
	sexual abuse, 591
Legs. *See* Limbs; Skeletal develop-
	ment
Lesbian women. *See* Homosexuality
Level I-Level II theory of intelligence
	(Jensen), 332–333, 335
Levels-of-processing model of infor-
	mation processing, 274
Lexical contrast theory of semantic
	development, 378
Liberia
	Kpelle, object sorting among, 271
	Mano, adolescent initiation cere-
		mony, 205
Licensing of child-care facilities, 586
Life span. *See also* Death; Infant
	mortality
	divorce and, 399
	Down syndrome and, 82
	emotions and, 399
	phenylketonuria and, 77
	sickle cell anemia and, 77
Light, fetal response to, 93
Limbic system, and autism, 446
Limbs. *See also* Skeletal development
	prenatal development of, 93, 97
Linguistic development. *See* Lan-
	guage development
Linguistic intelligence (Gardner),
	323
Liquor. *See* Alcohol use and abuse
Literacy. *See also* Language develop-
	ment; Reading; Writing
	emergent literacy, 304–305
	make-believe play and, 237
	map literacy, 251
	television literacy, 617–618
LMC (language-making capacity), in
	grammatical development,
	384–385
Locke's philosophy of child develop-
	ment, 12
Locomotion. *See* Crawling; Motor
	development; Running;
	Walking
Logical necessity, in propositional
	thought, 256
Logical reasoning
	early childhood, 248
	make-believe play and, 237
Logico-arithmetic operations, in
	concrete operational stage of
	cognitive development, 250
Logico-mathematical intelligence
	(Gardner), 323
LOGO (computer programming lan-
	guage), 624
Loneliness. *See also* Isolation

friendships and, 472
Internet usage and, 625
peer victimization and, 607
rejected-withdrawn children, 606
Long-term memory, 273–274,
	291–299. *See also* Memory
Longitudinal research, 58–60, 65
	adoptees' development, 575–576
	aggression, 331, 512, 619
	attachment and later development,
		431
	birth complications, long-term
		consequences of, 115–117
	child care, impact on develop-
		ment, 432–434
	Consortium for Longitudinal
		Studies, 346
	delinquency and adult criminal
		behavior, 513
	friendship understanding, 469
	identity formation, 457
	intelligence quotients, stability of,
		328
	language development and verbal
		interaction in home, 344
	mastery-oriented attributions
		and, 455
	moral reasoning, 494–495
	New York Longitudinal Study on
		temperament, 412–415
	play types, 599–600
	preschool intervention, 346
	prosocial reasoning, 505
	school transitions and self-esteem,
		630–631
	self-control, 508–509
	self-esteem, 449–450, 630–631
	Selman's stages of perspective tak-
		ing, 465
	shyness and sociability in infants
		and toddlers, 417
	sibling relationship, 573
	television viewing and aggression,
		619
	vocational attainment and IQ
		scores, 330
	vocational choice of women, 534
Longitudinal-sequential research,
	62–63, 65
Lorenz's study of imprinting, 25, 422
Love relationships. *See* Dating and
	romantic relationships; Mar-
	ital relationship
Low birth weight, 42, 112–115. *See
	also* Preterm infants
	aspirin, maternal use of and, 98
	caffeine, maternal use of and, 98
	drug use during pregnancy and,
		98–99
	environmental pollution and,
		101–102
	exercise during pregnancy and,
		103
	folic acid and, 104
	lead exposure during pregnancy
		and, 101
	neonatal mortality and, 116
	prenatal malnutrition and, 104
	rubella during pregnancy and, 102
	small-for-date infants, 113
	smoking during pregnancy and,
		99
	stress during pregnancy and, 105
	teenage pregnancies, 215–216
	United States in comparison to
		other nations, 35, 116
Low-income households. *See*
	Poverty; Socioeconomic

influences; Socioeconomic
	status (SES)
Loyalty, in friendships, 469
Lungs. *See* Respiratory system
Luxembourg, child maltreatment in,
	592
Lying. *See* Deception; Honesty
Lymph system, growth curve, 185

M

Macrosystems, in ecological systems
	theory, 29, 35
Magical thinking, 243–246
Magnesium
	adolescent deficiencies in, 194
	prenatal care and, 104
Mainstreaming (in schools), 634–635
Make-believe play
	advantages of, 237
	attachment security and, 431
	autism and, 446
	cognitive-developmental theory,
		264
	cultural influences on, 264,
		603–604
	early childhood, 236–237,
		247–248, 600
	emotional understanding and, 410
	hearing loss and, 263
	infancy and toddlerhood, 227,
		264, 599
	intentions, understanding of and,
		462
	peer relations in infancy, 599
	play materials and, 602
	preoperational stage of cognitive
		development, 236–237,
		247–248
	scripts (in memory development)
		and, 295
	sensorimotor stage of cognitive
		development, 227
	sociocultural theory of, 262–264
	television watching and, 621
	theory of mind origins and, 444
	time sampling study of preschool-
		ers, 46–47
Malaria
	prenatal development and, 102
	sickle cell allele and, 78
Male vs. female development. *See*
	Gender *entries;* Sex-related
	differences
Malnutrition, 194–196. *See also* Nu-
	trition
	anorexia nervosa and, 209
	brain development and, 37
	breastfeeding and, 193–194
	diseases and, 198
	growth stunting and, 195–196
	obesity and, 195–196
	prenatal malnutrition, 103–105
	pubertal development and, 202
	small-for-date infants, 113
Malocclusion, and breastfeeding, 193
Maltreatment. *See* Child maltreat-
	ment; Spousal abuse
Manipulation of objects, 147–149
	visual impairment and, 160
Mano of Liberia, adolescent initia-
	tion ceremony, 205
Map literacy, 251
Marasmus, 194–195
Marfan syndrome, 79

Marijuana. *See also* Drug use and
	abuse
	prenatal development and, 99
	teenage use, 614
Marital relationship. *See also* Di-
	vorce; Marriage
	abuse of spouse. *See* Spousal
		abuse
	ADHD and, 289
	aggression in children and, 512,
		551–552
	attachment and, 430
	child maltreatment and, 590
	child-rearing practices and, 28,
		560–561
	deprivation dwarfism and, 199
	newborns, adjustments to, 561
	parent-infant relationship and,
		430
	postpartum depression and, 400
	sexual abuse and, 590
Marriage. *See also* Marital relation-
	ship; Remarriage
	delinquency and, 513
	depression and, 550
	divorce. *See* Divorce
	teenage pregnancy and, 215
Masculinity. *See* Gender *entries*
Mastery-oriented attributions,
	453–456
Matching, in experimental research
	design, 57
Maternal age
	amniocentesis and, 84
	chorionic villus sampling and, 84
	Down syndrome and, 82
	first births, 105–106
	fraternal twinning and, 75
	genetic counseling and, 83
	prenatal development and, 105
Maternal blood analysis, 85–86
Maternal depression, 400
	attachment and, 427–428
	divorce and, 578
	postpartum depression, 400
Maternal deprivation and attach-
	ment, 426
Maternal employment, 583–585
	attachment and, 430, 432–435
	child care. *See* Child care
	child development and, 583–584
	family size and, 572
	gender stereotyping and, 536
	Great Depression of 1930s and, 61
	incidence of, 583
	peer relations in adolescence and,
		604
	rate of, 34
	support for employed mothers,
		585
	Sweden, 529
Maternal relationship. *See* Mother
	entries; Parent *entries*
Maternity leave, 37, 117, 561, 585
Mathematical reasoning, 306–307
	gender identity and, 541
	sex-related differences in, 545–548
Mathematics
	Asian students' skills, 307–308,
		637–638
	class size and achievement in, 626
	computer-assisted instruction
		and, 624
	cross-national research on
		achievement in, 637–639
	drill-oriented instruction, 307
	educational enrichment and
		achievement in, 348

extended school year and achievement in, 638

gender stereotyping and, 525, 534

information processing principles of, 306–307

logico-arithmetic operations, 250

logico-mathematical intelligence, 323

"number sense" basis for instruction, 307

sex-related differences in, 545–548

student body size and achievement in, 627

teacher-pupil interaction and achievement in, 632

Matters of personal choice, and moral reasoning, 501, 503

Maturation

brain. See Brain development

cognitive. See Cognitive development

concept of development, 12

emotional and social. See Emotional and social development

moral. See Moral development

motor skills. See Motor development

physical. See Physical development

sexual. See Sexual maturation

Maturational timing, 206–208

sexual activity and, 211

Maximally Discriminative Facial Movement (MAX) System for classifying emotions, 401

Mayans

childbirth practices, 109

cosleeping arrangements in infancy and childhood, 132

memory skills of, 290

Me-self, 440–441, 445–448. See also Self-concept

Means, in intelligence test scores, 326

Means-end action sequences, in sensorimotor stage of cognitive development, 225, 231

Measles, 198

immunizations, U.S. vs. other nations, 35

Media, 597. See also Computers; Public education programs; Television

suicide reports, 459

Mediation of divorce, 580

Medical care. See Health care; Medications

Medical insurance. See Health insurance

Medications. See also Anesthesia; Drug use and abuse

ADHD, 289

breastfeeding and, 194

childbirth, during, 109, 111

congenital adrenal hyperplasia (CAH), 530–531

prenatal development and maternal use of, 98–99

suicide prevention and treatment, 459

Medieval philosophy of childhood, 11

Meiosis (cell division), 73–75

chromosomal abnormalities and, 81–82

Melatonin, 131

Memory, 287–299

autism and, 446

autobiographical. See Autobiographical memory

constructive memory, 292–294

cultural influences on, 290–291

delinquent behavior and, 513

EEG measurements, 35

emotions and, 398

episodic memory, 295–296

everyday events and, 295–296

eyewitness testimony by children, 298–299

fetal alcohol syndrome and, 100

fuzzy-trace theory, 293–294

habituation-dishabituation response and, 141–142

infantile amnesia, 296

knowledge acquisition and, 294–295

levels-of-processing model of, 274

long-term memory, 273–274, 291–299

make-believe play and, 237

operant conditioning studies, 139, 142

phonological store, 377–378

recall ability. See Recall memory

recognition ability. See Recognition memory

reconstruction ability, 292–294

retrieval of information, 291–294

scripts in, 295–296

semantic development and, 377–378

semantic memory, 295–296

serial position effect, 274

short-term. See Working memory

store model of, 273–274

strategies. See Memory strategies

television literacy and, 618

working memory. See Working memory

Memory strategies, 273, 287–291

control deficiencies, 287

cultural influences on, 290–291

elaboration, 290, 292–293

metacognition and, 301–302

organization, 288–290, 292–293

production deficiencies, 287

rehearsal, 287–288

utilization deficiencies, 287–289

Menarche, 200–203

anorexia nervosa and, 209

reactions to, 203

secular trend, 184

twins, 192

Menopause, childbirth following, 85

Menstrual cycle, 89

anorexia nervosa and, 209

estrogens and, 183–184

menarche. See Menarche

Mental development. See Cognitive development; Intelligence entries

Mental health. See Adjustment problems; Counseling; Emotional disturbances; Emotional well-being; specific entries (e.g., Anxiety; Depression; Stress)

Mental inferences. See Inferences

Mental representation

brain growth spurts and, 191

drawing and, 238

infantile amnesia and, 296

interpretations and, 443–444

preoperational stage of cognitive development, 235–236

research on, 229–231

self-control and, 508

sensorimotor stage of cognitive development, 225–227, 229–231

sociodramatic play and, 236–237

Mental retardation

cri du chat (crying-of-the-cat) syndrome and, 136

Down syndrome and, 82

environmental pollution and, 101

fetal alcohol syndrome and, 100

fragile X syndrome and, 80

handedness and, 189–190

language development and, 365–366

mainstreaming of students, 634–635

phenylketonuria and, 76

Praeder-Willi syndrome, 80

Rh blood incompatibility and, 112

rubella during pregnancy and, 102

sex chromosome disorders and, 82

sex-related differences in, 79

thyroxine deficiency and, 183

Williams Syndrome and, 365

Mental rotations

concrete operational stage of cognitive development, 251

sex-related differences in ability, 546–547

Mental strategies, 272–275, 310

attention and, 284–285

control deficiencies, 285, 287

effective strategy use, 285

IQ scores and, 320–321

mathematics learning and, 307

memory strategies. See Memory strategies

metacognition and, 301

milestones in, 303

production deficiencies, 285, 287

utilization deficiencies, 285, 287–288

Mental testing movement, 14. See also Intelligence tests

Mercury and prenatal development, 101

Merit, in distributive justice reasoning, 504

Mesoderm, formation of, 92

Mesosystems, in ecological systems theory, 28–29, 562

Metacognition, 299–302, 310. See also Theory of mind

cognitive capacities, consciousness of, 300–301

cognitive self-regulation and, 301–302

computer programming and, 624

IQ scores and, 321

learned helplessness and, 454, 456

milestones in, 303

processing strategies, knowledge of, 301

scientific reasoning and, 309

self-control and, 508

social cognition and, 440

task variables, knowledge of, 301

Metalinguistic awareness, 389–392

bilingualism and, 391–392

milestones in, 391

Metaphors, in language development, 376–377

Methadone. See also Drug use and abuse

prenatal development and, 98

Methods of research. See Research methods

Mexican Americanss. See also Hispanics

academic achievement among, 53

achievement-related attributions among, 455

growth stunting among, 196

Head Start programs and IQ scores, 347

identity development in adolescence, 461

intelligence traits, valuing of, 339

teacher-pupil interaction and, 633

Mexico

make-believe play with infants and toddlers, 264

maternal education and child-rearing practices in, 568

Zinacanteco Indians. See Zinacanteco Indians

Microgenetic research, 63–65

motor development studies, 146–147

speech-gesture mismatches, 283

strategy-choice model studies, 281

Microsystems, in ecological systems theory, 27–28

Mid-twentieth century theories of development, 16–23

Middle childhood, 5

aggression in, 511–512

body composition in, 177

body proportion in, 176

child-rearing practices in, 566–567

cognitive development in, 249–253. See also Concrete operational stage of cognitive development

cross-gender reasoning and behavior in, 540–541

drawing in, 251

emotional self-regulation in, 406

emotional understanding in, 410

empathy in, 411

fear in, 406

friendships in, 468–469

gender identity in, 540–541

gender stereotyping in, 524–526

gender typing in, 532–533

gross motor development in, 177–180

height in, 174–175

hypothetico-deductive reasoning in, 256

information processing in, 303

intentions, understanding of, 462

mathematical reasoning in, 306–307

memory in, 292–293

memory strategies in, 287–291

metacognition in, 300–301

parental relationships in. See Father-child relationship; Mother-child relationship; Parent-child relationship

peer relations in, 600–601

person perception in, 463

planning in, 286

propositional thought in, 256

reading in, 305

self-concept in, 445–448

self-control in, 508

self-esteem in, 449–450

sibling relationships in, 574

social comparisons in, 450

television literacy in, 618

Middle East. See also specific countries

mutilation of female genitals, 205

sexual attitudes and behavior in, 210

"Middle-generation squeeze," 567

Middle-income households. See Socioeconomic influences; Socioeconomic status (SES)

Middle schools. *See* Schools
Midwives, 110–111
Mild mental retardation. *See also*
 Mental retardation
 mainstreaming of students,
 634–635
Milestones. *See also* Age
 cognitive development, 250
 infancy and toddlerhood, 233
 emotional and social development, 413
 social cognition, 475
 gender typing, 553
 information processing, 303
 language development, 390–391
 moral development, 510
 motor development, 145
 peer relations, 616
 perceptual development, 156
 prenatal development, 91
 pubertal development, 201
 social cognition, 475
 visual development, 165
 voluntary reaching, 149
Minerals. *See* Vitamins and minerals
Minimal parenting, 578. *See also* Uninvolved parenting
Minorities. *See* Ethnicity and race;
 *specific entries (e.g., African
 Americanss; Hispanics)*
Miscarriage
 caffeine, maternal use of and, 98
 diethylstilbestrol and, 101
 fetal medicine and, 85
 prenatal malnutrition and, 103
 radiation and, 81, 101
 sex-related differences in, 79
 smoking during pregnancy and, 99
 stress during pregnancy and, 105
Mistrust. *See also* Trust
 psychosocial stage of development,
 19
Mitosis (cell duplication), 72, 90, 92
Mixed-handedness, 190
Model of strategy choice. *See*
 Strategy-choice model of
 information processing
 (Siegler)
Modeling, 20. *See also* Imitation
 ADHD treatment programs, 289
 aggression, 485, 512–515
 applied behavior analysis, 21
 cross-gender reasoning and
 behavior, 536
 empathy development and, 412
 field experiment on effect of
 modeling by child-care
 provider, 57
 gender identity, 539
 language development and, 368,
 385–387, 389
 moral development and, 484–485
 peer acceptance intervention
 programs, 608
 peer relations and, 612–613, 616
Modified experimental research
 designs, 57–58
Modifier genes, 77
Modular view of mind, 234, 258
 multiple intelligences theory and,
 323
Molecular medicine, 89
Monkeys and apes
 attachment experiment, 421
 family groups among, 558
 language acquisition among,
 360–362

peer bonds among, 598
peer-only reared monkeys, 598
prosocial behavior among, 480
Monozygotic twins, 75. *See also* Twin
 studies; Twins
Mood quality, as temperament dimension, 414
Moodiness. *See also* Depression
 adolescence, 204–206
Moral construction, 488–489
 milestones in, 510
Moral development, 479–519. *See
 also* Aggression; Moral reasoning; Prosocial behavior;
 Self-control
 authoritative parenting and, 564
 autonomous morality, 489–491
 behavioral component, 479
 biological theories of, 479–481
 child-rearing practices and,
 481–482, 497, 564
 cognitive component, 479
 cognitive-developmental theory
 of, 488–491, 496
 cultural influences on, 497–498,
 502–503
 emotional component, 479
 environmental influences on,
 496–498
 extended-family households and,
 571
 Gilligan's theory of feminine
 morality, 498–499
 heteronomous morality, 489–491
 higher education and, 497
 Kohlberg's theory of. *See*
 Kohlberg's theory of moral
 development
 milestones in, 510
 modeling and, 484–485
 peer relations and, 496–497, 603
 psychoanalytic theories of, 479,
 481–484, 487–488
 punishment and, 485–487
 Rousseau's theory of, 12
 self-conscious emotions and, 404
 self-control and, 506–509
 sex-related differences in, 498–499
 sibling relationship and, 573
 social learning theories of,
 479–481, 484–488
 social understanding and,
 488–500
 societal norms and, 481–488
 Sociomoral Reflection Measure–
 Short Form (SRM-SF), 492
 temperament and, 419, 482–483
Moral dilemma research, 491–492
Moral imperatives, 501
Moral internalization, 481–483, 487,
 497
 milestones in, 510
Moral reasoning. *See also* Moral
 development
 age-related changes in, 494
 aggression and, 514
 authority, about, 490–491
 behavior and, 499–500
 cognitive prerequisites for, 495
 delinquent behavior and, 511
 distributive justice in, 503–504
 early childhood, 500–506
 environmental concerns and, 502
 gender identity and, 538
 hypothetical versus real-life
 dilemmas, 495
 identity development and, 457

intentions and, 490
 Kohlberg's stages of, 491–496
 personal choice and, 501, 503
 prosocial reasoning, 504–505
 social conventions and, 501–503
Moral rules, 489
 Kohlberg's stages of moral reason-
 ing and, 493
Moral self-regulation, 508–509
Morality of interpersonal coopera-
 tion, 493
Moratorium, in identity develop-
 ment, 457–460
Moro reflex, 128–129
Morphemes, grammatical, 381–382
Morphology. *See* Death; Infant mortality; Life span
Mortality. *See* Death; Infant mortality; Life span
Moslems, development of death
 concept, 245
Mother. *See* Families; Maternal
 entries; Parent *entries*
Mother-adolescent relationship.
 See Parent-adolescent
 relationship
 incest. *See* Sexual abuse of children
Mother-child relationship. *See also*
 Parent-child relationship
 divorce and, 578
 gender stereotyping and, 533, 535
 homosexual mothers and, 576
 incest. *See* Sexual abuse of children
 maternal depression and, 400
 maternal employment and,
 584–585
 remarriage and, 581–582
 teenage parenthood and, 215–217
 "whipping boys" and, 607
Mother-headed households. *See* Single-parent families
Mother-infant relationship. *See also*
 Parent-infant relationship
 attachment and, 426–427, 429. *See
 also* Attachment
 interactional synchrony in,
 426–427
 maternal depression and, 400
 newborns, 561
 teenage parenthood and, 215
Mother-stepfather families, 581–582
Motivation, 453
 child maltreatment victims, 592
 creativity and, 351–353
 Head Start programs and, 346
 motor development and, 146–147
 only children, 574
 prodigies, 51
 school transitions and, 630
 self-esteem inflation and, 451–452
 sex-related differences in, 545
 traditional classrooms and, 628
Motor development. *See also* Sensorimotor stage of cognitive
 development; *specific activities (e.g., Crawling; Drawing;
 Walking)*
 AIDS and, 103
 alcohol use during pregnancy and,
 100
 aspirin, maternal use of and, 98
 brain development and, 190
 brain growth spurts and, 191
 canalization, 121
 cerebellum and, 190
 cultural variations in, 147–148
 depth perception and, 156,
 158–159

Down syndrome and, 82
 drug use during pregnancy and,
 98–99
 dynamic systems perspective, 30,
 145–147, 178
 early deprivation and, 168–169
 emotional and social development
 and, 402–403
 fine. *See* Fine motor development
 gross. *See* Gross motor development
 infancy and toddlerhood, 144–150
 institutionalization and, 168
 low birth weight and, 112
 malnutrition and, 195
 microgenetic research studies,
 146–147
 milestones in, 145
 oxygen deprivation during childbirth and, 112
 perceptual development and, 150,
 166
 rate of, 144–146
 reflexes and, 129–130
 sequence of, 144–146
 visual impairment and, 160
 voluntary reaching in, 147–149
Motor vehicle accidents, and depression, 550
Movement. *See* Motor development
"Moving room" studies, 152–153
Multicultural research, 26. *See also*
 Cross-cultural research
Multiple births, 75. *See also* Twins
Multiple intelligences theory (Gardner), 322–324
 educational principles based on,
 353
Mumps and prenatal development,
 102
Muscle development, 177
 Apgar Scale, 108
 prenatal development, 92–93
 SIDS and, 140
 stepping reflex and, 130
Muscular dystrophy, Duchenne, 79
 genetic mapping, 88
Music, infants' response to, 153
Music television, 620
Musical intelligence (Gardner), 323
Mutation of genes, 81
Mutilation of female genitals, 205
Mutual exclusivity principle, in vo-
 cabulary development, 378
Myelinization, 187, 190
 brain growth spurts and, 191
 information processing and,
 275–276
 malnutrition and, 195

N

NAEYC (National Association for
 the Education of Young
 Children), 38, 434, 586
"Naming explosion," in language
 development, 373
Narratives
 autobiographical memory and,
 296–297, 442
 remembered self and, 442
National Association for the Education of Young Children
 (NAEYC), 38, 434, 586

National Television Violence Study, 618

Native Americanss. *See also specific tribes*
adolescent initiation ceremony, 204
alcohol abuse among, 100
extended-family households, 570
identity development in adolescence, 461
newborn behavior and child-rearing practices, 137
poverty among, 34
suicide rate among, 459
teenage pregnancy among, 215

Nativist theory of language development, 359–364
limitations of, 363–364
support for, 360–363

Nativistic theory of cognitive development, 222, 234

Natural childbirth, 109–110

Natural experiments, 57–59

Natural selection, Darwin's theory of, 12–13

Naturalist intelligence (Gardner), 323

Naturalistic observation research method, 45–46

Nature-nurture controversy, 8–9. *See also* Environmental influences; Genetic *entries*; Inheritance
adolescence and, 202–203
Baldwin's theory of, 16
behavioral genetics, 118–123, 418
behaviorist theories, 20
canalization, 121–122
concordance rates. *See* Concordance rates
genetic-environmental correlation, 122–123, 344
heritability estimates. *See* Heritability estimates
homosexuality, 212
intelligence, 328–329, 332–338
language development, 359
Locke's theory of, 12
motor development and, 147
perceptual development and, 150
range of reaction, 121
resilient children, 10
Rousseau's "noble savage," 12
sex-related differences in mathematical abilities, 547–548
stance of major developmental theories, 32
temperament in womb, 96

Navajo. *See also* Native Americanss
cooperative learning among, 266
language customs and IQ scores, 340

NBAS (Neonatal Behavioral Assessment Scale), 137

"Needs of others" orientation, in prosocial reasoning, 505

Negatives, in grammatical development, 382

Neglect of children, 564, 589. *See also* Child maltreatment

Neglected children, as category of peer acceptance, 604, 606

Neglectful parenting. *See* Uninvolved parenting

Neighborhood influences, 562. *See also* Community influences

Neo-Freudians. *See* Psychoanalytic theories; Psychosocial theory of development (Erikson)

Neo-Piagetian perspective (Case), 258, 276–278, 311

Neonatal Behavioral Assessment Scale (NBAS), 137

Neonatal mortality, 116. *See also* Infant mortality

Neonates. *See* Newborns

Nepal, Tamang of, emotional display rules among, 407

Nervous system. *See also* Brain *entries*
phenylketonuria and, 76
prenatal development of, 92–93, 97
prenatal malnutrition and, 104
psychophysiological research methods. *See* Psychophysiological research methods
REM sleep in newborns and development of, 133
SIDS and, 140

Netherlands
body size in, 184
childbirth practices in, 110
family size in, 572
immunization rate, 199
infant mortality rate, 117
maternity helpers in, 117
teenage pregnancy rate, 214–215

Neural tube, 92, 186
alcohol use during pregnancy and, 100
folic acid and, 104

Neurons, 186–187. *See also* Brain *entries*
prenatal development of, 92–93

Never-married single-parent families, 577

New Chance, early intervention program, 349

New Guinea. *See* Papua New Guinea

New York Longitudinal Study, 412–415

New Zealand
child abuse prevention program, 591
infant mortality rate, 117
reproductive technology laws, 85
sexual abuse education programs, 591
SIDS public education programs, 140

Newborns, 111–118, 127–144. *See also* Infancy and toddlerhood
adaptation to labor and delivery, 107–108
appearance of, 108
behavioral assessment of, 137
breastfeeding. *See* Breastfeeding
capacities of, 128–144
crying, 131, 134–136
death of. *See* Infant mortality
empathic responses, 411
face perception capacity, 162
family's adjustment to, 561
imitation capacity, 142–143
low birth weight. *See* Low birth weight
pattern perception, 159
physical assessment of, 108
preterm. *See* Preterm infants
reflex assessment of, 130, 137
reflexes of, 128–130
sensory capacities of, 151–154
sleep patterns, 130–134
"small for date," 113
states of arousal, 130–137

Niche-picking, 123
IQ scores and, 334

Nicotine. *See* Smoking

Nigeria, Hausa of, accomplishment of conservation tasks, 252

N'Jembe of Gabon, adolescent initiation ceremony, 204

"Noble savage" view of child development, 12

Non-prescription drugs. *See* Medications

Non-rapid-eye-movement (NREM) sleep, 132–134

Nonfunctionality, as component of death concept, 244–245

Nonorganic failure to thrive, 199, 399

Nonshared environmental influences of home environment, 343, 345, 418–419, 537

Nonsocial activity, 599–600

Normal curve, in intelligence test scores, 326

Normative approach to child study, 13–14

Norms, in intelligence test scores, 326

Norway
attachment style of infants, 426
body size in, 184
immunization rate, 199
infant mortality rate, 117
menarche in, 184
secular gains in development, 184–185

Nose
newborns' response to smell, 151–152
prenatal development of, 93

NREM sleep, 132–134

Nuclear family units, 570

Nucleus, of cells, 72

Numbers. *See* Mathematics

Nurse-midwives, 110–111

Nutrition. *See also* Eating habits; Malnutrition; Vitamins and minerals
ADHD and, 289
adolescence, 194
age-related needs, 193–194
breastfeeding and, 193–194
childhood, 194
infancy and toddlerhood, 193–194
maternal nutrition and fraternal twinning, 75
phenylketonuria and, 76
physical development and, 184–185, 193–198
prenatal development and, 103–105, 195
pubertal development and, 202
Special Supplemental Food Program for Women, Infants, and Children, 37, 104

Nyansongo of Kenya, gender typing among, 528

O

Oakland Growth Study, 61

Obesity, 195–198
causes of, 196–197
consequences of, 197–198
defined, 195
growth stunting and, 195–196
incidence of, 195

malnutrition and, 195–196
Praeder-Willi syndrome and, 80
treatment of, 198

Object-hiding tasks, in sensorimotor stage of cognitive development, 225, 228

Object manipulation, 147–149
visual impairment and, 160

Object motion, in sensorimotor stage of cognitive development, 229

Object perception, 163–165

Object permanence
connectionist modeling of, 279
intelligence predictions based on tasks of, 326
research on, 227–228
sensorimotor stage of cognitive development, 225–228
separation anxiety and, 422

Object-search behaviors, and brain growth spurts, 191

Object sorting, 231, 247
cultural influences on, 271

Object substance, in sensorimotor stage of cognitive development, 229

Object support, in sensorimotor stage of cognitive development, 229

Object unity, perception of, 164

Object words, in language development, 372, 375

Objects
attachment objects, 422
categorization. *See* Categorization abilities
conservation principle. *See* Conservation
seriation, 249–250

Observation research methods, 45
reliability, 54–55
temperament measurement, 415

Observational learning, 20, 267. *See also* Imitation; Modeling
gender typing and, 536

Observer bias, in systematic observation research, 47

Observer influence, in systematic observation research, 47

Occipital lobes, 187

Occupations. *See* Employment; Vocational *entries*

Odor, newborns' response to, 151–152

Oedipus conflict, 17, 481–482

Oksapmin of Papua New Guinea, counting strategies, 306–307

On-the-job training, 639–640

One-child families, 574–575

Only children, 574–575
IQ scores and, 345

Open classrooms, 627–628

Operant conditioning, 20, 138–141
categorization ability studies, 230
emotions and cognitions study, 398
language development and, 359
moral development and, 484
perceptual development studies, 150

Operations, in preoperational stage of cognitive development, 240, 248

Optical flow, 152–153

Optimism
emotional self-efficacy and, 406

"learning optimism" in early childhood, 453
Oral rehydration therapy (ORT), 198
Oral stage of development (Freud), 17–18
Ordinality, early childhood grasp of, 306
Organization
  cognitive-developmental theory, 223, 257
  memory strategy, 288–290
    constructive memory and, 292–293
  rejected-aggressive children, 608
Organs. *See also specific entries* (e.g., *Cardiovascular system; Respiratory system*)
  anorexia nervosa and, 209
  prenatal development of, 92–93
  prenatal malnutrition and, 104
Orphanages. *See* Institutionalization
ORT (oral rehydration therapy), 198
Otitis media, 155
Out-of-wedlock births, 577
  teenage pregnancy and, 214–215
Output layers, in artificial neural networks, 278–279
Ova, 73–74, 88–90
  aging of, 82
  donor ova, 85
Ovaries, 88–90. *See also* Reproductive system
Over-the-counter drugs. *See* Medications
Overactivity. *See* Hyperactivity
Overextension, in language development, 375–376
Overlapping-waves pattern, in strategy-choice model of information processing, 281–282
Overregularization, in grammatical development, 382
Overt aggression, 509, 511, 550–552, 601. *See also* Aggression
Overweight. *See* Obesity; Weight
Ovulation, 88–90. *See also* Menarche; Menstrual cycle
Ovum. *See* Ova
Oxygen deprivation
  alcohol use during pregnancy and, 100
  childbirth, during, 111–112
  eyes and, 133
  sickle cell anemia and, 77
  SIDS and, 140

P

Pacific Islanders. *See also* Hawaiians
  body size, 184
  child-rearing practices among, 569
  childbirth practices among, 109
  sexual attitudes and behavior, 210
Pain
  fetal response to, 94
  newborns' response to, 151
Pain-relievers, during childbirth, 111
Palate
  cleft. *See* Cleft palate
  prenatal development, 97
Palmar grasp reflex, 128–130, 149
Papua New Guinea
  gender typing reversals in, 528

Jimi Valley children, development of drawing among, 239
Kaluli, language development among, 369, 389
Oksapmin, counting strategies, 306–307
Sambia, gender role changes among, 531
Parallel distributed processing systems, 278–280
Parallel play, 599–600
  cultural influences on, 603
Parasitic diseases. *See also* Infectious diseases
  prenatal development and, 102–103
Parent-adolescent relationship, 567–568. *See also* Child-rearing practices; Families; Home environment
  anorexia nervosa and, 209
  bulimia and, 210
  conflict in, 204, 206, 503, 560–561, 567–568
  contraceptive use and, 212
  employment during adolescence and, 639
  identity development and, 458–460
  sexual attitudes and behavior and, 210
  sexual maturation and, 203
  substance abuse and, 615
Parent-child relationship. *See also* Child-rearing practices; Families; Father-child relationship; Home environment; Mother-child relationship
  academic achievement and, 635–636
  autobiographical memory and, 297
  cultural influences on, 431, 529
  divorce and, 578–579
  emotional self-regulation and, 405–406
  empathy development and, 412
  gender typing and, 532–535
  hearing loss and, 263
  intersubjectivity and, 261–262
  language development and, 386–387
  learned helplessness and, 456
  make-believe play and, 264
  middle childhood, 566–567
  only children, 574–575
  operant conditioning and, 139
  peer acceptance and, 608
  peer relations and, 598–599, 602
  punishment and, 485–486
  resiliency of children and, 10
  scaffolding and, 261–263
  sex-related differences in, 430
  sexual orientation and, 212–213
  visual impairment and, 160
Parent-infant relationship. *See also* Child-rearing practices; Families; Father-infant relationship; Home environment; Mother-infant relationship
  attachment, 426–429. *See also* Attachment
  cosleeping arrangements, 131–132
  interactional synchrony, 426–427
  marital relationship and, 430

medications during childbirth and, 111
Parent-school involvement, 635–636
Parent-teacher interaction. *See* Teacher-parent interaction
Parent training
  aggression and, 515–517
  school programs, 629
  teenage parenthood programs, 216
  teenage substance abuse and, 615
Parental leave, 37, 117, 561, 585
Parenthood. *See also* Child-rearing practices; Families; Father *entries*; Mother *entries*
  adoption and, 575
  postponement of, 572
  single parenting. *See* Single-parent families
  teenage parenting. *See* Teenage pregnancy and parenthood
  transition to, 561
Parents Anonymous, 593
Parents Without Partners, 580
Parietal lobes, 187
Part-time work and maternal employment, 584–585
Participant observation, in ethnography, 52
Passive correlation, in genetic-environmental correlation, 122
Passive voice, in language development, 383
Paternal age, and chromosomal abnormalities, 82
Paternal relationship. *See* Father *entries*
Paternity leave. *See* Parental leave
Pattern perception, 159–162, 165
  face perception, 162–163
Pavlov's theory of classical conditioning, 19, 138–139
PCBs and prenatal development, 101–102
PCP. *See also* Drug use and abuse
  teenage use, 614
Peddling, 177–178
Pedigree, in genetic counseling, 83
Peer acceptance, 604–608
  ADHD and, 288
  assessment of, 604
  attachment security and, 431
  cross-gender behavior and, 536
  defined, 604
  delinquent behavior and, 511, 513
  determinants of, 605–606, 608
  emotional self-regulation and, 406
  friendships and, 470
  gender identity and, 541
  homosexuality in adolescence and, 213
  intervention programs, 608
  IQ scores and, 331
  mainstreaming of students with learning difficulties and, 635
  maturational timing and, 206–207
  obesity and, 197
  only children, 575
  physical attractiveness and, 605
  school entry and, 629
  school transitions and, 631
  social behavior and, 606
  "whipping boys," 607
Peer collaboration, in learning, 264–266
Peer conformity, 613–614

Peer culture, and delinquency treatment, 517
Peer groups, 608–612
  adolescent initiation ceremony, 204
  defined, 609
  delinquent behavior and, 513
  formation of, 609
  homosexuality in adolescence and, 213
  leadership and, 612
  milestones in, 616
  norms of, 609–611
  self-concept and, 448
  social structures of, 609, 611–612
Peer-only rearing, 598
Peer pressure, 613–614
  milestones in, 616
Peer reinforcement, 612–613
  milestones in, 616
Peer relations, 597–616. *See also* Friendships; Peer groups; Play; Sociability
  ADHD and, 288–289
  adolescence, 601, 603–604
  after-school programs and, 587
  age mix of children and, 602–603
  aggression and, 512, 514–515, 601, 612
  attachment security and, 431, 599
  authoritarian parenting and, 564
  child maltreatment victims, 592
  comforting behavior toward peers, naturalistic observation research study, 45–46
  cultural influences on, 603–604
  development of, 598–601
  dominance hierarchy, 601, 611–612
  early childhood, 599–600
  emotional understanding and, 371
  ethnic identity and, 461
  gender typing and, 536–537
  importance of, 598
  infancy and toddlerhood, 599, 603
  influences on, 602–604
  intersubjectivity and, 261–262
  mainstreaming of students with learning difficulties and, 635
  maternal employment and, 583
  maturational timing and, 206–207
  middle childhood, 600–601
  milestones in, 616
  modeling and, 612–613, 616
  moral development and, 489, 496–497, 504, 603
  parent-child relationship and, 598–599
  parent encouragement of, 602
  play and, 600
  play materials and, 602
  reinforcement and, 612–613, 616
  same-sex preferences, 529—-530, 536–537
  school entry and, 629–630
  school transitions and, 631
  self-concept and, 448
  self-control and, 509
  self-esteem and, 449
  self-recognition and, 442
  sex-related differences in, 612
  sexual activity of adolescents and, 211
  sibling relationship and, 573
  socialization and, 612–615
  substance abuse and, 614–615
  suicide and, 459

television viewing and, 617, 619, 621

Peer tutoring. *See* Tutoring in schools

Peer victimization, 607
    school entry and, 630

Pendulum problem and abstract thinking, 254

Penis. *See also* Genitals; Reproductive system
    circumcision, 151
    pubertal development, 201–202

People's Republic of China. *See* Chinese

Perception-bound thinking, 241

Perceptual development, 150–167. *See also specific senses (e.g., Hearing; Touch; Vision)*
    canalization, 121
    cognitive development and, 232–234
    differentiation theory of, 166–167
    early deprivation and, 168–169
    habituation-dishabituation response studies, 141–142
    intermodal perception, 164–166
    milestones in, 156
    newborns, 151–154

Performance goals, and attributional style, 454–455

Periods of development, 5–6. *See also specific periods (e.g., Early childhood; Infancy and toddlerhood)*

Permanence
    death concept, component of, 244–245
    object permanence. *See* Object permanence

Permissive parenting, 564–565
    peer group membership in adolescence and, 610
    peer pressure and, 614
    self-esteem and, 451–452

Persistence
    achievement motivation and, 453
    attachment security and, 431
    authoritarian parenting and, 564
    creativity and, 352
    learned helplessness and, 454
    mastery-oriented attributions and, 454
    permissive parenting and, 564
    temperament dimension, 414–415
    Thai, valuing of, 420

Person perception, 462–464. *See also* Inferences
    ethnicity and social class, 463–464
    personality traits, 463

Personal choice, and moral reasoning, 501, 503

Personal fables
    abstract thinking and, 255
    suicide and, 459

Personal/social words, in early vocabulary, 372

Personal standards, in social-cognitive learning theory, 20

Personality development. *See* Emotional and social development; Self *entries*

Personality traits. *See also* Temperament; *specific traits (e.g., Aggression; Shyness)*
    anorexia nervosa and, 209
    bulimia and, 210
    canalization, 121
    creativity and, 351–352

expressive traits, 528
extreme personality styles, longitudinal study of, 58–59
friendships and, 468–467, 470–471
gender identity and, 538, 540
gender stereotyping of, 522–525
identity development and, 458
instrumental traits, 523, 528
person perception and, 463
resilient children, 10, 117
sex-related differences in, 545, 548–552
socioeconomic status and valuing of traits, 568

Perspective taking, 440, 464–467
    adolescence, 255–256
    aggression and, 514
    contraceptive use and, 211–212
    defined, 464
    empathy and, 411
    friendships and, 469, 471
    games, 466
    language development and, 384
    make-believe play and, 237
    moral development and, 492, 495–496, 499
    peer acceptance intervention programs, 608
    peer relations and, 601
    person perception and, 463–464
    recursive thought and, 466
    rejected-aggressive children, 606
    self-concept and, 448
    Selman's stages of, 464–466
    sibling relationship and, 573
    social interactions and, 466–467

Peru, Quechua of. *See* Quechua of Peru

Pesticides, 79–80

Pets, death of, explaining to children, 245

Phallic stage of development (Freud), 17–18, 481–482

Pharmaceuticals. *See* Medications

Phencyclidine (PCP), 614. *See also* Drug use and abuse

Phenotypes, 71–72

Phenylketonuria (PKU), 76–78

Philippines, Tagalog-speaking children, grammatical development among, 384

Phobias. *See* Fear

Phonemes, 367, 390–391

Phonics, 305

Phonological awareness, 391

Phonological development, 358, 370–372. *See also* Language development; Speech
    categorical speech perception, 367
    cooing and babbling, 368
    early phase of, 370
    later development of, 371–372
    milestones in, 390
    phonemes, 367, 390–391
    sex-related differences in, 545–546
    strategies, appearance of, 370–371

Phonological store, 377–378

Physical abuse of children, 588–589. *See also* Child maltreatment

Physical activities. *See* Athletics; Exercise; Extracurricular activities; Games; Motor development; Play

Physical attractiveness. *See* Body image and physical attractiveness

Physical causality, in sensorimotor stage of cognitive development, 225, 227–229

Physical deformities. *See* Birth defects; Chromosomal abnormalities; *specific entries (e.g., Cleft palate)*

Physical development, 173–219. *See also* Body *entries*; Growth *entries*; Motor development; Perceptual development; Skeletal *entries*; *specific entries (e.g., Brain development; Height; Weight)*
    adolescence. *See* Puberty; Sexual maturation
    asynchronies in, 185
    definition, 4
    Down syndrome and, 82
    emotional well-being and, 199
    environmental influences, 184
    factors affecting, 192–200
    fetal alcohol syndrome, 100
    genetic influences on, 184, 192
    hormonal influences on, 181–184, 192
    infectious diseases and, 198–199
    malnutrition and, 195
    medications during childbirth and, 111
    nutrition and, 193–198
    prenatal. *See* Prenatal development
    prenatal malnutrition and, 104
    radiation during pregnancy and, 101
    secular trends, 184–185
    sex-related differences in, 174–175
    SIDS and, 140

Physical disabilities
    adoptees, 575–576
    attachment and, 428

Physical education. *See* Exercise

Physical neglect of children, 589. *See also* Child maltreatment

Physical self-esteem, 449–451

Physical well-being. *See* Health

Physiological tests of temperament, 416–417

Piaget's cognitive-developmental theory. *See* Cognitive-developmental theory (Piaget)

Pictorial depth cues, 157–158

Pidgins, 361

Pima Indians, obesity among, 197

Pincer grasp, 148–149

Pituitary gland, 182–183, 199

PKU (phenylketonuria), 76–78

Placenta, 91–92, 107

Placenta abruptio, 112

Planning
    ADHD and, 288
    attention strategies and, 285–287
    play materials and, 602
    rejected-aggressive children, 608
    scripts (in memory development) and, 295
    suicide and, 459

Plasticity of brain, 188–189

Play. *See also* Games; Make-believe play; Peer relations; Toys
    associative play, 599–600
    attachment security and, 599
    child-care facilities, 585–586
    cognitive-developmental theory, 224

constructive play, 600
cooperative play, 599–600
cultural influences on, 603–604
developmental sequence, 599–601
early childhood, 468, 599–600
friendships in early childhood and, 468
functional play, 600
gender-role adoption and, 528–529
gender stereotyping of, 523–524
infancy and toddlerhood, 599
intersubjectivity and, 262
parallel play, 599–600
peer relations and, 599, 602
rough-and-tumble play, 601, 611
sex-related differences in play styles, 528–529
sibling relationship and, 573
sociodramatic. *See* Sociodramatic play
spatial reasoning and skills and, 547
television watching and, 621
uninvolved parenting and, 565
visual impairment and, 160

Play groups, 602

Pleiotropism, 77

Poisoning. *See* Environmental hazards

Political beliefs
    friendships and, 470
    identity development and, 460

Political violence, 515–516

Pollution. *See* Environmental hazards

Polychlorinated biphenyls (PCBs) and prenatal development, 101–102

Polygenic inheritance, 81, 118

Popular children, as category of peer acceptance, 604–606

Portugal, infant mortality rate, 117

Positive affect, as temperament dimension, 414

Positive discipline, 487

Postconventional level of moral development, 493–494, 500

Postpartum depression, 400

Poverty, 33–34. *See also* Socioeconomic influences; Socioeconomic status (SES)
    academic achievement and, 35
    aggression and, 515
    attachment and, 427
    birth complications, long-term consequences of and, 116
    breastfeeding and, 193
    child maltreatment and, 590–591, 593
    child-rearing practices and, 569
    early development and, 169
    educational attainment and, 35
    educational enrichment and, 348
    immunization and, 198–199
    infant mortality and, 116
    infectious diseases and, 198
    IQ scores and, 328
    low birth weight and, 112
    malnutrition and, 195
    never-married single-parent families and, 577
    obesity and, 196–197
    physical development and, 185
    prenatal malnutrition and, 105
    preterm infant intervention programs and, 115
    pubertal development and, 202

sexual abuse and, 590
sexual activity of adolescents and, 211
sexually transmitted diseases and, 214
SIDS and, 140
suicide and, 459
teenage pregnancy and, 34, 214–215
United States in comparison to other nations, 35
Practical intelligence, 330, 340
Practice effects, in longitudinal research, 60, 64
Praeder-Willi syndrome, 80
Pragmatic development, 358, 386–389. See also Language development
  acquisition of conversational skills, 386–387
  milestones in, 391
  referential communication skills, 388–389
  semantic development and, 378
  sociolinguistic knowledge, 358
  speech registers, 388–389
Preattachment phase, 422
Preconventional level of moral development, 492–493
Preformationism, 11
Pregnancy. See also Childbirth; Conception; Contraception; Prenatal entries
  abortion. See Abortion
  adolescents. See Teenage pregnancy and parenthood
  age of. See Maternal age
  alcohol use during, 100–101
  drug use during, 97–99
  exercise during, 103
  infectious diseases during, 102–103
  miscarriage. See Miscarriage
  nutrition during, 103–105
  radiation during, 101
  smoking during, 99–100
  stress during, 105
Preimplantation genetic diagnosis, 86
Prejudice. See Bias
Prelinguistic development, 366–370
Premarital sex, 210–212. See also Sexual attitudes and behavior
Premature infants. See Preterm infants
Prenatal development, 5, 88–106. See also Conception; Pregnancy
  age of viability, 93–94
  AIDS and, 102–103
  environmental influences on, 95–106
  habituation-dishabituation response, 141
  milestones in, 91
  nutrition and, 103–105, 195
  phases of, 90–95
  temperament of fetus, 96
  trimesters, 90–95
Prenatal diagnosis, 84–87, 89
  X-linked diseases, 78–79
Prenatal health care
  AIDS transmission, 103
  infant mortality and, 116–117
  teenage pregnancies, 215
Prenatal malnutrition, 103–105
  low birth weight and, 113
Preoperational stage of cognitive development, 21–22, 222, 235–248
  accommodation in, 240

animistic thinking in, 240, 243–244
appearance versus reality confusion in, 247–248
centration thinking in, 241
conservation in, 240–241, 245–246, 248
drawing and, 237–239
egocentrism in, 240, 242–243, 260, 464, 472
evaluation of theory, 248
hierarchical classification in, 241–242, 246–247
irreversible thinking in, 241, 245–246
language in, 235–236
limitations of, 240–242
magical thinking in, 243–244, 246
make-believe play in, 236–237, 247–248
mental representation in, 235–236
operations in, 240, 248
perception-bound thinking in, 241
research on, 242–248
spatial representation in, 237–239
spatial symbols in, 239–240
state-versus-transformation thinking in, 241
transductive reasoning in, 241, 245–246
Prepared childbirth, 109–110
Prereaching movements in infants, 148–149
Preschool and kindergarten, 346–349. See also Schools
  accreditation system, 38
  entry into kindergarten, 629–630
  gender typing, influences on, 537
  Head Start programs, 37, 346–347, 349
  traditional classrooms versus open classrooms, 627–628
Preschoolers. See Early childhood
Prescription drugs. See Medications
Pretending. See Make-believe play
Preterm infants, 112–115. See also Low birth weight
  caregiving for, 113–114
  child maltreatment and, 113, 589
  defined, 112–113
  drug use during pregnancy and, 98–99
  environmental pollution and, 101
  fetal medicine and, 85
  folic acid and, 104
  interventions for, 114–115
  lead exposure during pregnancy and, 101
  medical interventions, 114
  SIDS and, 140
  "small for date" versus preterm, 113
  smoking during pregnancy and, 99
  stress during pregnancy and, 105
  teenage pregnancies, 215
  twins, 113
  vitamin-mineral supplements to prevent, 104–105
Prevention programs. See Intervention programs
Preverbal gestures, 369
  autism and, 446
Pride, 399, 404
  adolescence, 450
  moral development and, 480

Primary circular reactions, in sensorimotor stage of cognitive development, 224–225
Primary drives, in drive-reduction theory, 20
  attachment and, 421
Primary mental abilities, in factor analysis of intelligence test components, 317–318
Primary sexual characteristics, 200
Principle of mutual exclusivity, in vocabulary development, 378
Principled level of moral development, 493–494
Privacy rights of research participants, 66
Private speech, 260, 262
  hearing loss and, 263
  metacognition and, 301
  self-control and, 507
Privileged-information game, 466
Privileges, withdrawal as disciplinary technique, 486, 515
Problem solving. See also Reasoning
  ADHD and, 288
  analogical, 231–232, 246, 249–250
  attachment security and, 431
  class inclusion problems, 242–243, 247–249, 252–253
  computer-assisted instruction and, 624
  computer programming and, 624
  creativity and, 351–352
  emotional self-regulation and, 406
  infancy and toddlerhood, 231–232
  intersubjectivity and, 262
  mixed-age groups and, 603
  pendulum problem, and abstract thinking, 254
  planning and, 286
  social. See Social problem solving
  three-mountains problem, 240–242
Problems, emotional. See Adjustment problems; Emotional disturbances; Stress
Processing capacity, 275, 310
Processing speed. See Speed of processing
Prodigies. See Gifted children
Production deficiencies, in mental strategies
  attentional strategies, 285
  memory strategies, 287
Production versus comprehension of language, 372
Programmed cell death, in brain development, 186
Programming (computers), 624
Project Head Start, 37, 346–347, 349
Pronoun reference, in language development, 383–384
Pronunciation. See Phonological development
Propositional thought, 254–256
Proprioception and voluntary reaching, 148
Proprioceptive stimulation, and postural changes, 152
Prosocial behavior. See also Empathy
  animals, 480
  controversial children, 606
  emotional display rules and, 407
  empathy and, 411–412, 480
  friendships and, 469–471

mainstreaming of students with learning difficulties and, 635
modeling of, 484–485
moral reasoning and, 499–500
peer relations and, 603
perspective taking and, 466–467
sex-related differences in, 548
television viewing and, 620–621
Prosocial reasoning, 504–505
Prostate. See Reproductive system
Protein, biochemical, 72
Protein, dietary, 193. See also Nutrition
  breastfeeding and, 193
  kwashiorkor and, 179
  phenylketonuria and, 76
Protodeclarative gestures, 369
Protoimperative gestures, 369
Proximal development, zone of. See Zone of proximal development, in sociocultural theory
Proximodistal trend, 145, 176
Psychoanalytic theories, 16–18, 32. See also specific theories (e.g., Psychosocial theory of development (Erikson))
  attachment and, 421–422, 430
  gender typing and, 522
  moral development, 479, 481–484, 487–488
  sibling rivalry and, 573
Psychological abuse of children, 589. See also Child maltreatment
Psychological development. See Emotional and social development; Moral development; Self entries; Social entries
Psychological disturbances. See Adjustment problems; Emotional disturbances
Psychological stress. See Stress
Psychological well-being. See Emotional well-being
Psychometric approach to cognitive development, 315, 350. See also Intelligence tests
Psychophysiological research methods, 45, 49–50. See also Electroencephalograms (EEGs)
  ADHD studies, 288
  fetal alcohol syndrome studies, 100
  perceptual development studies, 150
  reliability, 55
  temperament measurements, 415–417
Psychosexual theory of development (Freud), 17–18
  Erikson's expansion of. See Psychosocial theory of development (Erikson)
  gender typing and, 522
  moral development and, 481–483
Psychosocial theory of development (Erikson), 18–19
  identity versus identity diffusion, 456–457
  moral development and, 484
  overview of stages of, 19
Psychotherapy. See Counseling
Puberty, 173, 200–217. See also Adolescence; Sex hormones; Sexual maturation
  age of pubertal changes, 200–202

defined, 173
early vs. late maturation, 206–208
group differences in, 202
health issues in, 208–217
hormonal changes, 183–184, 200–202
individual differences in, 202
milestones in, 201
physical development in, 200–202
psychological impact of, 202–208
reactions to, 203–204
school transitions and, 631
secular trend, 184
Pubic hair development, 183–184, 200–201
Public education programs
AIDS education, 214
child maltreatment, 593
immunization, 198–199
sexual abuse of children, 591
SIDS, 140
Public health programs, 198–199
Public policies. *See also* Intervention programs; Social policies and issues
child care, 37–38, 434–435, 586–587
child development, generally, 35–38
cultural values and, 36
definition, 35
economic conditions and, 36–37
grandparent visitation rights, 581
Head Start programs, 37, 346–347, 349
immunization, 198–199
job training programs, 639
new policy developments, 38, 435
parental leave, 117, 585
preschool intervention programs, 346
research and, 37
special interest groups, 36
television programming, 621–623
Public television, 621
Puerto Ricans
difficult children, child-rearing practices, 420
self-concept among, 448
Pukapukans of Pacific Islands, child-birth practices, 109
Punishment, in operant conditioning, 20, 139
Punishment (disciplinary), 485–487
aggression and, 485, 512–516, 551, 570
child maltreatment and, 589
consistency of, 486
cooperation and, 560
corporal punishment, 592–593
difficult children and, 420
empathy development and, 412
Locke's theory of, 12
moral development and, 481–482, 484–487
principles of effective punishment, 486–487
Punishment/obedience orientation in moral development, 492–493
Pupil dilation and temperamental style, 417
Pupils. *See* Academic achievement; Schools; Teacher-pupil interaction
Purging, 209–210
Puritan philosophy of childhood, 11

Pyloric stenosis and stress during pregnancy, 105

Quality of mood, as temperament dimension, 414
Quechua of Peru
mental state vocabulary among, 444
swaddling of infants, 134–135
Questionnaires, as research method, 45, 48–49
temperament measurement, 415
Questions, in grammatical development, 382–383

Race. *See* Ethnicity and race
Radiation. *See also* X-rays
mutation of genes and, 81
prenatal development and, 101
Rage. *See* Anger
Random assignment, in experimental research design, 57
Range of reaction, 121
Rapid-eye-movement (REM) sleep, 131–134
Raven Progressive Matrices, 338
Reaching, voluntary. *See* Voluntary reaching
Reaction intensity, as temperament dimension, 414
Reaction range, 121
Reading
basic-skills approach, 305
class size and achievement in, 626
computer-assisted instruction and, 624
early childhood, 304–305
educational enrichment and achievement in, 348
extended school year and achievement in, 638
gender stereotyping in academic subject preferences, 525
information processing principles of, 304–305
KEEP classrooms and achievement in, 628
middle childhood, 305
phonics, 305
phonological awareness and, 391
sex-related differences in, 545–546
shared reading and language development, 386–387
student body size and achievement in, 627
television viewing and, 617, 621
whole-language approach, 305
word decoding and, 624
Realism, in moral development, 489
Reasoning
abstract. *See* Abstract thinking
ADHD and, 288
belief-desire reasoning, 443–444
computer-assisted instruction and, 624
cross-gender. *See* Cross-gender reasoning and behavior

distributive justice, 503–504
hypothetico-deductive reasoning, 254, 256
make-believe play and, 237
mathematical reasoning. *See* Mathematical reasoning
measuring. *See* Intelligence tests
moral. *See* Moral reasoning
propositional reasoning, 254–256
prosocial reasoning, 504–505
recursive thought, 466
scientific reasoning, 308–309
spatial. *See* Spatial reasoning and skills
transductive reasoning, 241, 245–246
Recall memory, 142, 273
eyewitness testimony by children, 298–299
language development and, 372
Recasts, in language development, 385
Recessive disorders, 76–79
Reciprocal relationships
ecological systems theory, 27–28
ethological theory of attachment, 423
recursive thought and, 466
Reciprocal teaching, 265, 293, 628–629
Reciprocity, in moral reasoning, 489
Recognition memory, 142, 291
language development and, 372
Reconstituted families. *See* Blended families
Reconstructed memory, 292–294
attachment internal working models and, 429
Recreational drugs. *See* Drug use and abuse
Recursive thought, 466
Referential communication skills, 388–389
Referential style of learning, in language development, 374
Reflective thought and brain growth spurts, 191
Reflexes
adaptive value of, 128–129
Apgar Scale, 108
assessment of newborns, 130, 137
classical conditioning and, 138
defined, 128
motor development and, 129–130
Neonatal Behavioral Assessment Scale (NBAS), 137
newborns' capacities, 128–130
SIDS and, 140
survival value of, 128–129
Reflexive schemes, in sensorimotor stage of cognitive development, 224–225
Reformation philosophy of childhood, 11
Rehearsal, as memory strategy, 287–288
Reinforcement
ADHD treatment programs, 289
aggression and, 515
authoritative parenting and, 566
friendships in early childhood and, 470
gender identity and, 539
language development and, 359, 368
obesity and, 197–198
operant conditioning, 20, 139

peer acceptance intervention programs, 608
peer reinforcement, 612–613, 616
social learning theory, 20
Rejected-aggressive children, 606
Rejected children, as category of peer acceptance, 604–608
interventions for, 607
peer victimization and, 607, 630
subtypes, 606
Rejected-withdrawn children, 606
Relational aggression, 509–511, 550–551, 601
Relationships. *See specific entries (e.g., Marital relationship; Parent-child relationship; Peer relations)*
Reliability of research method, 54–55
Religion. *See* Spirituality and religiosity
REM sleep, 131–134
Remarriage, 578. *See also* Blended families
repeated remarriages, 583
sexual abuse and, 590
Remembered self, 442
Representation, mental. *See* Mental representation
Reproduction. *See* Conception; Fertility; Pregnancy; Sexual maturation
Reproductive age, 73–75
Reproductive choices, 83–87, 572
genetic counseling, 83–84
prenatal diagnosis. *See* Prenatal diagnosis
in vitro fertilization. *See* In vitro fertilization
Reproductive system, 88–90. *See also* Genitals
DES and reproductive abnormalities, 101
pubertal development, 200–202
Reproductive technologies, 84–85. *See also* In vitro fertilization
homosexual families and, 576
never-married single-parent families and, 577
Research, 43–69. *See also* Research designs; Research methods; *specific topics or studies (e.g., Kinship studies; Twin studies)*
applications of, 4. *See also* Public policies; Social policies and issues
early studies of child development, 13–16
ethics, 64–68
ethics in, 43–44
hypotheses, 44
protection from harm, 66
public policies and, 37
rights of participants, 66–68
risks-versus-benefits ratio, 66
Research designs, 55–64. *See also specific designs (e.g., Correlational research; Longitudinal research)*
comparison, 59, 65
defined, 43
developmental research designs, 58–64
general research designs, 55–58
Research methods, 43–54. *See also specific methods (e.g., Clinical method of research;*

Psychophysiological research methods)
defined, 43
reliability, 54–55
validity, 55, 60
Research questions, 44
Research rights of participants, 66–68
Resilient children, 10
birth complications, long-term consequences, 116–117
Resistance to temptation. *See* Self-control
Resistant attachment, 424
later development and, 431
mother-child relationship and, 427
mother's internal working model and, 429
"whipping boys" and, 607
Resource rooms, in schools, 635
Respiratory distress syndrome, 112
Respiratory system
Apgar Scale, 108
asthma, 80
obesity and, 195
prenatal development of, 92–94
SIDS and, 140
Response, 19–20
conditioned, 138–139
habituation-dishabituation. *See* Habituation-dishabituation response
unconditioned, 138–139
Responsive parenting. *See also* Authoritative parenting
attachment and sensitive caregiving, 426–427, 430
homosexual fathers, 576
self-esteem and, 451
Responsiveness, as dimension of child-rearing, 563
Responsiveness threshold, as temperament dimension, 414
Retardation. *See* Mental retardation
Reticular formation, 190
Retrieval of information. *See* Memory
Reversibility in thinking, 249
Rh factor incompatibility, and prenatal development, 112
RhoGam, 112
Rhythmicity, as temperament dimension, 414
Riboflavin, deficiencies in adolescence, 194
Right-handedness, 188–190
Rights of children, 38–39
Risks-versus-benefits ratio, in research, 66–67
Rites of passage, 203–205
Rituals, in adolescent initiation ceremonies, 203–205
Robbers Cave experiment, 609, 612
Romantic relationships. *See* Dating and romantic relationships
Rooting reflex, 128–129
Rough-and-tumble play, 601, 611
Rousseau's philosophy of child development, 12, 173
Rubella, prenatal development and, 102
Rules
games and, 600–601
make-believe play and, 262–263
moral. *See* Moral rules
Running, 177–178
sex-related differences in, 180

Running away
divorce of parents and, 579
sexual abuse victims, 590
Russia, growth stunting in, 196

S

Sadness. *See also* Depression
infancy and toddlerhood, 401–403
peer victimization and, 607
Salt, newborns' response to, 151
Sambia of Papua New Guinea, gender role changes among, 531
Same-sex parent, identification with. *See* Identification with same-sex parent
Samoans
adolescence among, 202–203
language development among, 369
Sampling
biased sampling, in longitudinal research, 59–60
event sampling, in systematic observation research, 46
random assignment, in experimental research design, 57
time sampling, in systematic observation research, 46–47
Sarcasm, and language development, 377
SAT. *See* Scholastic Aptitude Test (SAT)
Scaffolding, in sociocultural theory of cognitive development, 261–263
emotional understanding and, 410
sibling relationship and, 574
Schemes
cognitive-developmental theory of, 222–224, 236
neo-Piagetian theory of, 277
Schizophrenia, concordance rates, 119–120
Scholastic achievement. *See* Academic achievement
Scholastic Aptitude Test (SAT)
self-control and scores on, 509
sex-related differences in scores, 546–547
School achievement. *See* Academic achievement
School-age children. *See* Middle childhood
School attendance. *See also* Dropping out of school
divorce and, 579
employment and, 639
full-service schools and, 629
peer acceptance and, 604
peer victimization and, 607, 630
suspension or expulsion, Teen Outreach program enrollees, 216
School transitions, 629–632
School years. *See* Middle childhood
Schools, 35, 597–598, 626–640. *See also* Education *entries*; Teacher *entries*; *specific subjects (e.g., Mathematics; Reading)*
ability grouping in, 633–634, 638
absenteeism. *See* School attendance
achievement in. *See* Academic achievement

after-school programs, 587
aggression and, 515
AIDS education, 214
"back to basics" movement, 627
bilingual education, 392–393
class size and learning, 626
community-of-learners model, 266
computers in classrooms, 621–624
concrete operational reasoning and, 252–253
contraceptive services, 216
corporal punishment, 592–593
dropping out. *See* Dropping out of school
drug education programs, 615
educational self-fulfilling prophecies, 632–633
entry into, 629–630
IQ scores and delayed entry, 329
extended school year, 638
friendships and school adjustments, 472
full inclusion of students with learning difficulties, 635
full-service schools, 629
gifted children. *See* Gifted children
grade structures of, 630–631
maturational timing and, 207
grouping practices in, 633–634
health services provided by, 629
heterogeneous classes, 633–634
homogeneous classes, 633
identity development and, 460
IQ scores, effect of schooling on, 329
KEEP classrooms, 628–629
kindergarten. *See* Preschool and kindergarten
mainstreaming of students with learning difficulties, 634–635
mastery-oriented learning and, 455–456
moral reasoning training, 497
multigrade classes, 633–634
open classrooms, 627–628
parent involvement in, 635–636
preschool. *See* Preschool and kindergarten
resource rooms for students with learning difficulties, 635
same-sex schools, 207, 548
sex education programs. *See* Sex education
social services provided by, 629
special needs students, 634–635
student body size and learning, 626–627
suicide prevention programs, 459
teenage parenthood programs, 216
tracking students, 634
traditional classrooms, 627–628
transitions in, 629–632
truancy. *See* School attendance
tutoring. *See* Tutoring in schools
work-study programs, 639–640
Science
cross-national research on achievement in, 637–639
gender stereotyping and, 534
sex-related differences in achievement in, 548
student body size and achievement in, 627
Scientific reasoning, 308–309

Scientific studies. *See* Research *entries*
Scotland. *See* Great Britain
Scripts, in memory development, 295–296
Scrotum, 201. *See also* Genitals
Second language. *See* Bilingualism
Secondary circular reactions, in sensorimotor stage of cognitive development, 225
Secondary drives, in drive-reduction theory, 20
attachment and, 421
Secondary schools. *See* Schools
Secondary sexual characteristics, 200
Secular trends in physical development, 184–185
Secure attachment, 424, 426–427
later development and, 431
mother-infant relationship and, 427
mother's internal working model and, 429
self-awareness and, 441
Secure base for attachment, 403, 408–409, 423
identity development and, 458–460
Segregation, and friendships, 471
Selective attrition, in longitudinal research, 60
Self-awareness, 440–442
categorical self, 442
emotions and, 399–401
empathy and, 411
inner self, 443
remembered self, 442
self-conscious emotions and, 404
self-control and, 506
self-recognition and, 441
Self-blame. *See* Guilt
Self-care children, 587
Self-concept, 445–448. *See also* Ethnic identity; Gender identity; Identity; Self-esteem
adolescence, 447
child maltreatment victims, 592
cognitive development and, 447–448
cultural influences on, 448
defined, 445
early childhood, 445
emotional self-efficacy and, 406
friendships and, 471
generalized other and, 448
infantile amnesia and, 296
middle childhood, 445–447
moral development and, 500
Self-confidence
adolescence, 450
anorexia nervosa and, 290
authoritative parenting and, 564
mathematical ability and, 547–548
maturational timing and, 206
school transitions and, 630
Self-conscious emotions, 404. *See also specific emotions (e.g., Guilt; Shame)*
Self-consciousness and abstract thinking, 255–256
Self-control, 506–509. *See also* Compliance; Emotional self-regulation; Self-regulation
aggression and, 515, 517
authoritative parenting and, 564
defined, 506
individual differences in, 508–509

infancy and toddlerhood, 506–507
milestones in, 510
permissive parenting and, 564
sexual abuse perpetrators, 590
strategies for, 508
Self-definition. *See* Self-concept
Self-development. *See also* Identity;
     Self-awareness; Self-concept;
     Self-esteem
   categorical and remembered
     selves, 442
   I-self and me-self, 440–441
   make-believe play and, 237
   milestones in, 475
   theory of mind and, 443–445
Self-disclosure in friendships,
     470–471
Self-efficacy, 20, 399
Self-esteem, 448–452
   ability grouping in schools and,
     633–634
   academic. *See* Academic self-
     esteem
   aggression and, 514
   attachment security and, 431
   authoritative parenting and, 564,
     566
   autonomy and, 567
   body image and physical attrac-
     tiveness and, 605
   changes in level of, 449–450
   child care and, 433
   child maltreatment victims, 592
   child-rearing practices and,
     451–452, 564, 566
   cultural influences on, 451
   defined, 448
   depression and, 550
   ethnic bias and, 464
   ethnic identity and, 461
   factor analysis of, 449
   gender identity and, 538
   global self-esteem, 449
   hierarchically structured, 449–450
   identity development and,
     457–458
   influences on, 451–452
   maternal employment and, 583
   multifaceted nature of, 449
   obesity and, 197
   only children, 574
   parent-adolescent relationship
     and, 567
   peer acceptance and, 604
   peer tutoring and, 613
   physical self-esteem, 449
   school transitions and, 630–631
   self-care children, 587
   sex-related differences in, 451
   sexual abuse victims, 590
   sibling relationship and, 574
   social problem solving and, 474
   social self-esteem, 449
   structure of, 449
   suicide and, 459
   "whipping boys," 607
Self-focusing
   abstract thinking and, 255–256
   recursive thought and, 466
   school transitions and, 631
Self-fulfilling prophecy, in teacher-
     pupil interaction, 632–633
Self-image. *See* Self-concept
Self-movement, in infancy, 152–153
Self-recognition, 441–442
Self-reflective perspective taking,
     255–256, 465

Self-regulation. *See also* Self-control
   cognitive self-regulation, 301–302
   computer programming and, 624
   delinquent behavior and, 513
   emotional. *See* Emotional self-
     regulation
   learned helplessness and, 454, 456
Self-reliance, 571. *See also* Autonomy
Self-report research methods, 45,
     47–49
   reliability, 55
   sociometric techniques, 604
Self-understanding. *See* Self-
     awareness; Self-concept
Self-worth. *See* Self-concept; Self-
     esteem
Selman's stages of perspective taking,
     464–466
Semantic bootstrapping, in gram-
     matical development, 384
Semantic complexity of grammatical
     morphemes, 381–382
Semantic development, 358,
     372–379. *See also* Language
     development
   adult feedback and, 377
   connectionist modeling of, 279
   early phase, 372–376
   later development, 376–377
   maternal behavior and, 56
   memory and, 377–378
   metacognition and, 300
   metalinguistic awareness and, 390
   milestones, 390
   phonological development and,
     370
   sex-related differences in, 545
   strategies for word learning, 378
   television watching and, 621
   theories of, 377–378
   Williams Syndrome and, 365
Semantic memory, 295–296
Semantic organization, and memory
     strategies, 289–290, 292
Semen, 89. *See also* Sperm
Semilingualism, 393
Sense of self. *See* Self *entries*
Senses. *See* Perceptual development;
     *specific senses (e.g., Hearing;
     Touch; Vision)*
Sensitive parenting. *See* Responsive
     parenting
Sensitive periods, 25
   brain development, 190–191
   infancy as, 168–169
   language development, 363
   prenatal development, 96–97
Sensitivity, emotional, sex-related
     differences in, 545, 548–549
Sensorimotor stage of cognitive de-
     velopment, 21–22, 222,
     224–235
   circular reactions in, 224–226
   evaluation of, 231–235
   research on, 227–231
   substages, 224–227
Sensory perception. *See* Perceptual
     development; *specific senses
     (e.g., Hearing; Touch; Vision)*
Sensory register, in information pro-
     cessing, 272–274
Separation. *See also* Autonomy
   adolescent initiation ceremonies,
     phase of, 204
   anger and sadness in infancy and,
     403
   marital. *See* Divorce

parent-adolescent conflict and,
     206
Separation anxiety
   attachment and, 422–425
   divorce and, 579
Sequential research designs, 62–63
Serial position effect, 274
Seriation, in concrete operational
     stage of cognitive develop-
     ment, 249–250
SES. *See* Socioeconomic status (SES)
"Sesame Street," 621
Sex. *See* Gender *entries;* Sexual atti-
     tudes and behavior
   differences in. *See* Sex-related dif-
     ferences
Sex cells, 73–75. *See also* Ova; Sperm
Sex chromosomes, 76
   abnormalities of, 82–83
   genetic imprinting and, 80–81
Sex education, 210, 216
   contraceptive use and, 212
   sexually transmitted diseases and,
     214
   teenage pregnancy rate and, 214
Sex hormones, 76, 101, 183–184. *See
     also specific hormones (e.g.,
     Androgens; Estrogens)*
   aggression and, 511, 551
   congenital adrenal hyperplasia
     (CAH) and, 530–531
   gender-role adoption and,
     528–531
   moodiness and, 204–206
   sexual orientation and, 212
Sex-related differences, 79, 544–552.
     See also Gender stereotyp-
     ing; Gender typing
   academic achievement, 545
   achievement-related attributions,
     455
   activity level, 545
   ADHD diagnosis, 288
   adjustment problems, 545
   adolescent initiation ceremony,
     204–205
   aggression, 511, 545, 607
   anxiety, 545
   autobiographical memory, 297
   blended families, adjustment to,
     581–582
   body composition, 177
   body proportions, 177
   cognitive development, 544–548
   communication styles, 535, 537
   compliance, 545, 549
   computer use, 624–625
   cross-gender behavior, 540–541
   defined, 522
   delinquency, 511
   dependency, 545, 549
   depression, 545, 549–550
   divorce of parents, response to,
     578–579
   economic hardship, effect of, 61
   emotional expression, 548
   emotional sensitivity, 545,
     548–549
   exercise, 181
   extreme personality styles, longi-
     tudinal study of, 59
   fear, 545
   friendships, 469–471
   gender identity development, 540
   gender stereotyping, 526
   gross motor development,
     178–181

identity development, 457
infant mortality, 180
intimacy development, 457
language development, 374,
     545–546
learning disabilities, 545
maternal employment, response
     to, 584
mathematical abilities, 545–548
maturational timing, reactions
     and responses to, 206–208
mental abilities, 544–548
milestones, 553
moral development, 498–499
motivation, 545
motor development, 180–181
muscle development, 177
newborn length and weight, 108
parent-child relationship, 430
peer relations, 612
peer victimization, 607
personality traits, 545, 548–552
physical attractiveness, valuing of,
     605
physical development, 174–175,
     200–202
play styles, 528–529
prosocial behavior, 548
reading ability, 545–546
rough-and-tumble play, 601
school transitions, adjustment to,
     630–631
self-esteem, 451
sexual abuse victims, 590–591
sexual activity, 211
sexual maturation, 200–202
shyness, 545
skeletal age, 179–180
spatial reasoning, 545–547
suicide rate, 459
television viewing, 617
vocational development, 534
writing ability, 545
Sex-role identity. *See* Gender
     identity
Sex stereotyping. *See* Gender
     stereotyping
Sex typing. *See* Gender typing
Sexual abuse of children, 588–591.
     See also Child maltreatment
   characteristics of abusers and
     victims, 590
   consequences of, 590
   incidence of, 590
   prevention and treatment, 591
Sexual attitudes and behavior. *See
     also* Sexual maturation
   adolescence, 210–214
   blended families, adjustment to
     and, 582
   cultural influences on, 210
   delinquent behavior and, 513
   divorce of parents and, 579–580
   education about. *See* Sex
     education
   maturational timing and, 207
   sexual abuse victims, 590
Sexual characteristics, primary and
     secondary, 200
Sexual identity of homosexual ado-
     lescents, 213
Sexual maturation, 183–184,
     200–202. *See also* Puberty
   depression and, 550
   self-esteem and, 451
Sexual orientation. *See* Homo-
     sexuality

Time sampling, in systematic observation research, 46–47
Timidity. *See* Anxiety; Fear; Shyness
Tiwi of Australia, adolescent initiation ceremony, 204
Tobacco. *See* Smoking
Tobago, infant mortality rate, 116
Toddlerhood. *See* Infancy and toddlerhood
Tonic neck reflex, 129–130
Tooth development. *See* Teeth
Touch
    intermodal perception, 164–166
    newborns' response to, 150–151
    prenatal response to, 93, 151
    preterm infants and, 114–115, 151
Toxins. *See* Environmental hazards
Toxoplasmosis, prenatal development and, 102–103
Toys. *See also* Games; Play
    child-care facilities, 585–586
    gender stereotyping of, 523–524, 542
    peer relations and, 602
Traditional classrooms, 627–628
Training. *See* Education; Intervention programs; Schools; Vocational education
Traits. *See also specific traits (e.g., Aggression; Shyness)*
    androgynous. *See* Androgynous traits
    carriers of. *See* Carriers, of inherited traits
    dominant-recessive, 76–77
    personality. *See* Personality traits
    polygenic, 118
Transductive reasoning, in preoperational stage of cognitive development, 241, 245–246
Transition period, in childbirth, 107
Transitions. *See also* Adjustment problems
    school to work, 639–640
    school transitions, 629–632
Transitive inference, in concrete operational stage of cognitive development, 249–250, 252
Transracial or transcultural adoption, 337, 575–576
    physical development of adoptees, 184–185
Treatment programs. *See* Counseling; Intervention programs
Trials, legal. *See* Legal proceedings
Triarchic theory of intelligence (Sternberg), 321–322
Tribal and village societies. *See also specific societies*
    abstract thinking among, 256–257
    adolescence among, 202–203
    adolescent rites of passage, 203–205
    childbirth practices, 109
    conservation tasks, delay in accomplishing, 252
    gender typing among, 528
    moral development among, 497–498
Tricycles, and motor development, 177–178
Trimesters, in prenatal development, 90–95
Trinidad, infant mortality rate, 116
Triple X syndrome, 82–83
Trisomy 21 (Down syndrome), 81–82

Trobriand Islanders of Melanesia, sexual attitudes and behavior among, 210
Truancy. *See* Dropping out of school; School attendance
Trust
    friendships and, 468–469, 471
    psychosocial stage of development, 19
    sexual abuse victims and, 590
Truthfulness. *See* Deception; Honesty
Tuberculosis
    breastfeeding and, 194
    prenatal development and, 102
Turnabout, in pragmatic development, 386
Turner syndrome, 82–83
Tutoring in schools, 613
    multigrade classes and, 634
    peer acceptance and, 608
    students with learning difficulties, 635
TV. *See* Television
Twentieth-century theories of development, 16–31
Twin studies. *See also* Kinship studies
    concordance rates, 119
    empathy development, 412
    heritability estimates, 119
    intelligence, 119
    IQ scores, 334–336, 345
    sexual orientation, 212
    temperament and personality, 416–418
Twins, 75
    ADHD among, 288
    hand preferences, 189
    menarche, 192
    obesity among, 196
    pragmatic development and, 387
    preterm infants, 113
    pubertal development, 202
Two-generation model of early intervention programs, 347–349

U

UCR (unconditioned response), 138–139
UCS (unconditioned stimulus), 138–139
Ulnar grasp, 148–149
Ultrasound, maternal, 84–86, 93
Umbilical cord, 92, 112
U.N. Convention on the Rights of the Child, 38–39
Unconditioned response (UCR), 138–139
Unconditioned stimulus (UCS), 138–139
Underarm hair development, 183–184, 200–201
Underextension, in language development, 375–376
Underweight babies. *See* Low birth weight
Undifferentiated perspective taking, 465, 504
Unemployment
    child maltreatment and, 29, 590
    delinquency and, 513
    education and, 639
    teenage pregnancy and, 215–216
    teenage substance abuse and, 615

Uninhibited (sociable) child, as temperament type, 416–417. *See also* Sociability
Uninvolved parenting, 564–565
    minimal parenting following divorce, 578
    peer group membership in adolescence and, 610
Universal ethical principle orientation in moral development, 494
Universal grammar, 359–360, 364
Universality, as component of death concept, 244–245
University education. *See* Higher education
Uterus. *See* Reproductive system
Utilization deficiencies, in mental strategies
    attentional strategies, 285
    memory strategies, 287–289
Utku Indians, moral development among, 479

V

V-Chip (Violence-Chip), 622–623
Vaccination. *See* Immunization
Vacuum extraction, in childbirth, 111
Vagina. *See* Genitals; Reproductive system
Validity of research method, 55, 60
Values. *See also* Bias; Cultural influences; Moral development; Spirituality and religiosity
    academic achievement, valuing of in Asian societies, 638
    child maltreatment and cultural values, 592
    extended-family households and, 571
    friendships and, 470–471
    inhibition, Chinese valuing of, 606
    peer group membership and, 610–611
    peer pressure and, 613
    public policies and, 36
    shyness, valuing of, 420, 606
Variables, in experimental research design, 56
Variations in development, 9. *See also* Individual differences; *specific group differences (e.g., Ethnicity and race; Sex-related differences)*
    autism, 445–446
    behavioral genetics, 118–123, 418
    body size, 184
    delinquency, 513
    hearing loss and cognitive development, 263
    language development and Williams Syndrome, 365
    peer victimization, 607, 630
    prodigies, 50–51
    resilient children, 10
    skipped-generation families, 584
    temperament in womb, 96
    visual impairments, 159–160
Velocity curves, 175
Verbal abilities. *See* Phonological development; Speech

Verbal-nonverbal consistency rule, in understanding of intentions, 462
Vernix, formation of, 93
Vestibular stimulation, and postural changes, 152
Victimization. *See* Abuse; Child maltreatment
Videogames, 625
    intelligence tests and, 339
    spatial reasoning and skills and, 547
Vietnamese
    body size, 184
    language development among, 374
Village societies. *See* Tribal and village societies
Violation-of-expectation method, 227–229
Violence. *See also* Aggression
    child maltreatment. *See* Child maltreatment
    cultural values and child maltreatment, 592–593
    delinquency and, 511
    television programming and, 618–619, 622–623
    videogames and, 625
    war, effect on children, 515–516
Viral diseases. *See also* Infectious diseases
    breastfeeding and, 194
    prenatal development and, 102–103
Vision. *See also* Eyes
    cerebral cortex and, 187
    color. *See* Color vision
    depth perception, 156–159, 165
    dominant-recessive inheritance, 76
    face perception. *See* Face perception
    impairment, effect on development, 159–160
    infancy and toddlerhood, 154–166
    intermodal perception, 164–166
    milestones in, 165
    newborns' capacities, 154
    object perception, 163–165
    optical flow, 152–153
    pattern perception, 159–162, 165
Visual acuity
    infancy and toddlerhood, 154–156, 165
    newborns' capacities, 154
Visual cliff studies, 157–158, 408
Visual impairment, effect on development, 159–160
Vitamins and minerals, 193. *See also* Nutrition; *specific entries (e.g., Calcium; Iron)*
    adolescence, deficiencies in, 194
    childbearing-age women, 104–105
    prenatal care and, 104–105
Vocabulary. *See* Semantic development
Vocational achievement
    identity formation and, 457
    IQ scores and, 330
    sex-related differences in, 534
Vocational development, 639–640. *See also* Employment; Maternal employment; Unemployment
    gender stereotypes and, 534
    identity development and, 460

maternal employment and, 583
sex-related differences in, 534
Vocational education, 634, 639–640
identity development and, 460
teenage parenthood and, 216
Voice changes in adolescence,
201–202
Voluntary reaching, 147–149
brain growth spurts and, 191
motor development and, 144
tonic neck reflex and, 129–130
visual impairment and, 160
Volunteers, in Teen Outreach program, 216
Vygotsky's sociocultural theory.
See Sociocultural theory
of cognitive development
(Vygotsky)

W

Walbiri of Australia, development of
drawing among, 239
Wales. *See* Great Britain
Walking, 144–147, 177–178. *See also*
Motor development
affordances and, 166–167
brain growth spurts and, 191
emotional self-regulation and, 405
stepping reflex and, 129–130
visual impairment and, 160
War, effect on children, 515–516
War Against Parents, The (Hewlett
and West), 15
Washout effect, 347
Watson's theory. *See* Behaviorism
Way We Really Are, The (Coontz), 15
Website-based learning activities, 624
Wechsler Intelligence Scales, 325
Weight, 173. *See also* Obesity
adolescence, 174–175, 183–184

anorexia nervosa and, 209
birth weight, 108. *See also* Low
birth weight
bulimia and, 210
deprivation dwarfism, 199
early childhood, 174–175
genetic influences on, 192
infancy and toddlerhood,
174–175
menarche and, 202
middle childhood, 174–175
variations in, worldwide, 184
Welfare programs. *See* Intervention
programs; Public policies
Well-being. *See* Emotional well-
being; Health
Wernicke's area of brain, 362–364
West Indians of Jamaica, motor development in infancy,
147–148
Western Europe. *See also specific
countries*
child-care facilities, 587
contraceptive services in schools,
216
immunization rate, 198
maternal employment, workplace
support for, 585
maternity leave, 117
menarche, 202
national examinations, 634
sexual activity of adolescents, 211
"Whipping boys," 607
Whites. *See* Caucasian Americanss
Whole-language approach to reading, 305
WIC (Special Supplemental Food
Program for Women, In-
fants, and Children), 37, 105
Williams Syndrome, 365
WISC-III (Wechsler Intelligence
Scale for Children-III), 325
Withdrawal of privileges, as disciplinary technique, 486, 515

Withdrawal reflex, 129
Wives. *See* Marital relationship;
Marriage
Women vs. men. *See* Gender *entries;*
Sex-related differences
Word processing in schools, 624
Work. *See* Employment; Vocational
entries
Work-study programs, 639–640. *See
also* Vocational education
Working memory, 287–291. *See also*
Memory
cognitive inhibition and, 284–285
levels-of-processing model of, 274
neo-Piagetian theory, 276–278
phonological store, 377–378
store model of, 273–274
Working mothers. *See* Maternal
employment
World War II, 61
prenatal malnutrition during,
103–104
radiation exposure during pregnancy, 101
World Wide Web, 624–625
WPPSI-R (Wechsler Preschool and
Primary Scale of Intelli-
gence-Revised), 325
Writing
emergent literacy, 304–305
sex-related differences in, 545
word processing and, 624

X

X-linked inheritance, 78–80, 212
X-rays. *See also* Radiation
genetic damage and, 81
skeletal age estimates by, 179
XO (Turner) syndrome, 82–83
XX chromosomes, 76

XXX syndrome, 82–83
XXY (Klinefelter) syndrome, 82–83
XY chromosomes, 76
Xylitol and otitis media, 155
XYY syndrome, 82–83

Y

Yolk sac, 90, 93
Youth. *See* Adolescence
Yurok Indians, breastfeeding among,
18

Z

Zaire. *See* Efe of Zaire
Zambia, newborn behavior and
child-rearing practices, 137
Zidovudine (ZDV), 103
Zinacanteco Indians
motor development in infancy,
147
social interaction and learning
among, 26–27
Zinc and prenatal health care, 104
Zone of proximal development, in
sociocultural theory,
261–263
dynamic testing of intelligence
and, 340
speech-gesture mismatches and,
283
teaching techniques and, 628
Zuni Indians, self-conscious emotions among, 404
Zygote, 74–75, 90–92, 97